TITLE 21—FOOD AND DRUGS

CHAPTER 1—ADULTERATED OR MISBRANDED FOODS OR DRUGS

SUBCHAPTER I—FEDERAL FOOD AND DRUGS ACT OF 1906

SUBCHAPTER I—FEDERAL FOOD AND DRUGS ACT OF 1906

§§ 1 to 5. Repealed. June 25, 1938, ch. 675, § 902(a), 52 Stat. 1059

Section 1, act June 30, 1906, ch. 3915, §1, 34 Stat. 768, made it unlawful to manufacture adulterated or misbranded foods or drugs in Territories or District of Columbia and provided penalty for violations. See sections 331 and 333 of this title.

Section 2, act June 30, 1906, ch. 3915, §2, 34 Stat. 768, prohibited introduction, shipment, delivery or sale of adulterated or misbranded foods or drugs in interstate or foreign commerce, provided penalty for violations and exempted exports conforming to specifications of foreign purchaser and not in conflict with laws of foreign country importing the same. See sections 331, 333 and 381 of this title.

Section 3, acts June 30, 1906, ch. 3915, §3, 34 Stat. 768; Mar. 4, 1913, ch. 141, §1, 37 Stat. 736, authorized Secretaries of the Treasury, Agriculture, and Commerce to make uniform rules and regulations for enforcement of food and drug laws, including collection and examination of specimens. See section 371 of this title.

Section 4, act June 30, 1906, ch. 3915, §12, 34 Stat. 772, provided that act or omission of officer, agent, and so forth, of corporation, shall be deemed act or omission of corporation.

Section 5, act June 30, 1906, ch. 3915, §12, 34 Stat. 772, defined "territory" and "person". See section 321 of this title and section 1 of Title 1, General Provisions.

EFFECTIVE DATE OF REPEAL

Section 902(a) of act June 25, 1938, ch. 675, 52 Stat. 1059, which repealed sections 1 to 5, 7 to 14, and 15 of this title, provided that the repeal of those sections should take effect upon the effective date of act June 25, 1938, which was to take effect twelve months after the date of its enactment. Act June 23, 1939, ch. 242, §2(b), 53 Stat. 854, provided that: "The provisions of such act of June 30, 1906, as amended, to the extent that they impose, or authorize the imposition of, any requirement imposed by section 403(k) of the Federal Food, Drug, and Cosmetic Act [section 343(k) of this title], shall remain in force until January 1, 1940."

§ 6. Transferred

CODIFICATION

Section, act Mar. 4, 1923, ch. 268, 42 Stat. 1500, was transferred to section 321a of this title.

§§ 7 to 14. Repealed. June 25, 1938, ch. 675, § 902(a), 52 Stat. 1059

Section 7, act June 30, 1906, ch. 3915, § 6, 34 Stat. 769, defined "drug" and "food". See section 321 of this title.

Section 8, act June 30, 1906, ch. 3915, § 7, 34 Stat. 769, deemed drugs to be adulterated when sold having a difference from recognized standards, except where there is an explanatory statement on or in container, and when sold below professed standard; confectioneries, when containing mineral substances, poisonous color or flavors, other deleterious ingredients, liquors or narcotics; food, when concerned with injurious mixtures, use of substitutes, abstraction of valuable constituents, concealment of damage or inferiority, deleterious ingredients, preservatives in shipment conditionally excepted, animal or vegetable substances unfit for food and products of animals diseased or having died otherwise than by slaughter. See sections 342 and 351 of this title.

Section 9, act June 30, 1906, ch. 3915, § 8, 34 Stat. 771, defined "misbranded" and provided for its application to drugs and food. See sections 343 and 352 of this title.

Section 10, acts June 30, 1906, ch. 3915, § 8, 34 Stat. 771; Aug. 23, 1912, ch. 352, 37 Stat. 416; Mar. 3, 1913, ch. 117, 37 Stat. 732; July 24, 1919, ch. 26, 41 Stat. 271; July 8, 1930, ch. 874, 46 Stat. 1019, deemed drugs to be misbranded when there is an imitation or use of name of other article, when there is removal and substitution of contents of package or failure to state on label quantity or proportion of narcotics therein, and when there is a false statement of curative or therapeutic effect; and food, when there is an imitation or use of name of other article, when there is a false label or brand removal and substitution of contents of package, or failure to state or label quantity or proportion of narcotics therein, when the packages are not marked with weight, with certain variations and exemptions permitted, when there are false or misleading statements on package or label as to ingredients or substances; and food, when mixtures or compounds under distinctive names, the articles are labeled, branded as compounds, imitations, or blends; construed the term "blend" and related to disclosure of trade formulas of proprietary foods, and canned food. See sections 321b, 341, 343 and 352 of this title.

Section 11, acts June 30, 1906, ch. 3915, § 4, 34 Stat. 769; Jan. 18, 1927, ch. 39, 44 Stat. 1003, provided for examination of specimens, notice of adulteration or misbranding, hearing, certification of violations to United States district attorney and notice of judgment.

Section 12, act June 30, 1906, ch. 3915, § 5, 34 Stat. 769, provided for prosecution by district attorneys for enforcement of penalties.

Section 13, act June 30, 1906, ch. 3915, § 9, 34 Stat. 771, provided for a seller's guaranty as protection to dealer. See section 333 of this title.

Section 14, act June 30, 1906, ch. 3915, § 10, 34 Stat. 771, provided for seizure of articles by libel for condemnation, at suit of and in name of United States, in United States district court where found, conforming to proceedings in admiralty, with right to trial by jury, destruction or sale of adulterated or misbranded articles, bond and payment of proceeds into Treasury of United States. See sections 332, 334 and 337 of this title.

EFFECTIVE DATE OF REPEAL

For effective date of repeal, see section 902(a) of act June 25, 1938, set out as a note under sections 1 to 5 of this title.

§ 14a. Transferred

CODIFICATION

Section, act June 30, 1906, ch. 3915, § 10A, as added June 22, 1934, ch. 712, 48 Stat. 1204, and amended, which related to examination of sea food on request of packer, marking of food with results, fees, and penalties, was successively renumbered section 702A and then 706 of the Federal Food, Drug, and Cosmetic Act by act July 12, 1943, ch. 221, title II, § 201, 57 Stat. 500, and by Pub. L. 102–571, title I, § 106(3), Oct. 29, 1992, 106 Stat. 4498, and was successively classified to section 372a and then 376 of this title.

§ 15. Repealed. June 25, 1938, ch. 675, § 902(a), 52 Stat. 1059

Section, act June 30, 1906, ch. 3915, § 11, 34 Stat. 772, provided for examination of samples of imports, refusal of admission and delivery to consignee, delivery to consignee pending examination and decision on bond and charges for storage and lien therefor. See section 381 of this title.

EFFECTIVE DATE OF REPEAL

For effective date of repeal, see section 902(a) of act June 25, 1938, set out as a note under sections 1 to 5 of this title.

SUBCHAPTER II—MISCELLANEOUS PROVISIONS

§ 16. Introduction into, or sale in, State or Territory or District of Columbia of dairy or food products falsely labeled or branded

No person or persons, company or corporation, shall introduce into any State or Territory of the United States or the District of Columbia from any other State or Territory of the United States or the District of Columbia, or sell in the District of Columbia or in any Territory any dairy or food products which shall be falsely labeled or branded as to the State or Territory in which they are made, produced, or grown, or cause or procure the same to be done by others.

(July 1, 1902, ch. 1357, § 1, 32 Stat. 632.)

§ 17. Penalty for sale or introduction of falsely labeled dairy or food products; venue

If any person or persons violate the provisions of section 16 of this title, either in person or through another, he shall be guilty of a misdemeanor and shall be punished by a fine of not less than $500 nor more than $2,000. The jurisdiction for the prosecution of said misdemeanor shall be within the district of the United States court in which it is committed.

(July 1, 1902, ch. 1357, § 2, 32 Stat. 632.)

§ 18. Suspension of importation of adulterated articles

Whenever the President is satisfied that there is good reason to believe that any importation is being made, or is about to be made, into the United States, from any foreign country, of any article used for human food or drink that is adulterated to an extent dangerous to the health or welfare of the people of the United States, or any of them, he may issue his proclamation suspending the importation of such articles from such country for such period of time as he may think necessary to prevent such importation; and during such period it shall be unlawful to import into the United States from the countries designated in the proclamation of the President any of the articles the importation of which is so suspended.

(Aug. 30, 1890, ch. 839, §4, 26 Stat. 415.)

§19. Repealed. May 29, 1928, ch. 901, §1(100), 45 Stat. 993

Section, act May 23, 1908, ch. 192, 35 Stat. 261, related to report to Congress of expenditures in enforcing food and drug laws.

§20. Apples in interstate commerce; standard grades

The standard grades for apples when packed in barrels which shall be shipped or delivered for shipment in interstate or foreign commerce, or which shall be sold or offered for sale within the District of Columbia or the Territories of the United States shall be as follows: Apples of one variety, which are well-grown specimens, hand picked, of good color for the variety, normal shape, practically free from insect and fungous injury, bruises, and other defects, except such as are necessarily caused in the operation of packing, or apples of one variety which are not more than 10 per centum below the foregoing specifications shall be "Standard grade minimum size two and one-half inches", if the minimum size of the apples is two and one-half inches in transverse diameter; "Standard grade minimum size two and one-fourth inches", if the minimum size of the apples is two and one-fourth inches in transverse diameter; or "Standard grade minimum size two inches", if the minimum size of the apples is two inches in transverse diameter.

(Aug. 3, 1912, ch. 273, §2, 37 Stat. 250.)

§21. Branding grades on barrels of apples

The barrels in which apples are packed in accordance with the provisions of sections 20 to 23 of this title may be branded in accordance with the provisions of section 20 of this title.

(Aug. 3, 1912, ch. 273, §3, 37 Stat. 251.)

§22. Barrels misbranded

Barrels packed with apples shall be deemed to be misbranded within the meaning of sections 20 to 23 of this title—

First. If the barrel bears any statement, design, or device indicating that the apples contained therein are "Standard" grade and the apples when packed do not conform to the requirements prescribed by section 20 of this title.

Second. If the barrel bears any statement, design, or device indicating that the apples contained therein are "Standard" grade and the barrel fails to bear also a statement of the name of the variety, the name of the locality where grown, and the name of the packer or the person by whose authority the apples were packed and the barrel marked.

(Aug. 3, 1912, ch. 273, §5, 37 Stat. 251.)

§23. Penalties

Any person, firm or corporation, or association who shall knowingly pack or cause to be packed apples in barrels or who shall knowingly sell or offer for sale such barrels in violation of the provisions of sections 20 to 23 of this title shall be liable to a penalty of $1 and costs for each such barrel so sold or offered for sale, to be recovered at the suit of the United States in any court of the United States having jurisdiction.

(Aug. 3, 1912, ch. 273, §6, 37 Stat. 251.)

CODIFICATION

Section is also set out as section 233 of Title 15, Commerce and Trade.

§24. Omitted

CODIFICATION

Section, act Mar. 4, 1915, ch. 144, 38 Stat. 1102, related to payment of the cost of inspection under a provision authorizing the investigation of the character of chemical and physical tests applied to American food products in foreign countries and the inspection of such products before shipment to such countries at the request of the shippers or owners. That provision was repeated in subsequent appropriation acts but was omitted from the appropriation act of July 12, 1943, ch. 221, 57 Stat. 494, and from all subsequent appropriation acts.

§25. Oleomargarine, butterine, or imitation butter or cheese transported into a State subject to its police powers

All articles known as oleomargarine, butterine, imitation, process, renovated, or adulterated butter, or imitation cheese, or any substance in the semblance of butter or cheese not the usual product of the dairy and not made exclusively of pure and unadulterated milk or cream, transported into any State or Territory or the District of Columbia, and remaining therein for use, consumption, sale, or storage therein, shall, upon the arrival within the limits of such State or Territory or the District of Columbia, be subject to the operation and effect of the laws of such State or Territory or the District of Columbia, enacted in the exercise of its police powers to the same extent and in the same manner as though such articles or substances had been produced in such State or Territory or the District of Columbia, and shall not be exempt therefrom by reason of being introduced therein in original packages or otherwise.

(May 9, 1902, ch. 784, §1, 32 Stat. 193.)

§26. Omitted

CODIFICATION

Section, which was from the appropriation acts of Jan. 18, 1927, ch. 39, 44 Stat. 984; May 16, 1928, ch. 572, 45 Stat. 548; Feb. 16, 1929, ch. 227, 45 Stat. 1198; May 27, 1930, ch. 341, 46 Stat. 424, and subsequent Department of Agriculture Appropriation Acts to and including act June 28, 1944, ch. 296, §4, 58 Stat. 461, and related to inspection of food and other products, is covered by section 2256 of Title 7, Agriculture.

CHAPTER 2—TEAS

§§41 to 50. Repealed. Pub. L. 104–128, §2, Apr. 9, 1996, 110 Stat. 1198

Section 41, acts Mar. 2, 1897, ch. 358, §1, 29 Stat. 604; May 16, 1908, ch. 170, 35 Stat. 163; May 31, 1920, ch. 217, 41 Stat. 712; 1940 Reorg. Plan No. IV, §12, eff. June 30, 1940, 5 F.R. 2421, 54 Stat. 1237; 1953 Reorg. Plan No. 1, §5, eff. Apr. 11, 1953, 18 F.R. 2053, 67 Stat. 631; May 24, 1962, Pub. L. 87–456, title III, §303(a), 76 Stat. 77; Aug. 23, 1988, Pub. L. 100–418, title I, §1214(*l*), 102 Stat. 1158, prohibited unlawful importation of substandard tea.

Section 42, acts Mar. 2, 1897, ch. 358, §2, 29 Stat. 605; May 31, 1920, ch. 217, 41 Stat. 712; 1940 Reorg. Plan No.

IV, § 12, eff. June 30, 1940, 5 F.R. 2421, 54 Stat. 1237; July 12, 1943, ch. 221, title II, 57 Stat. 500; 1953 Reorg. Plan No. 1, § 5, eff. Apr. 11, 1953, 18 F.R. 2053, 67 Stat. 631; Oct. 17, 1979, Pub. L. 96–88, title V, § 509(b), 93 Stat. 695, related to establishment and composition of board of experts in teas.

Section 43, acts Mar. 2, 1897, ch. 358, § 3, 29 Stat. 605; May 31, 1920, ch. 217, 41 Stat. 712; 1940 Reorg. Plan No. IV, § 12, eff. June 30, 1940, 5 F.R. 2421, 54 Stat. 1237; 1953 Reorg. Plan No. 1, § 5, eff. Apr. 11, 1953, 18 F.R. 2053, 67 Stat. 631; Oct. 17, 1979, Pub. L. 96–88, title V, § 509(b), 93 Stat. 695, authorized establishment of purity standards.

Section 44, acts Mar. 2, 1897, ch. 358, § 4, 29 Stat. 605; May 31, 1920, ch. 217, 41 Stat. 712; 1940 Reorg. Plan No. IV, § 12, eff. June 30, 1940, 5 F.R. 2421, 54 Stat. 1237; 1953 Reorg. Plan No. 1, § 5, eff. Apr. 11, 1953, 18 F.R. 2053, 67 Stat. 631; Oct. 17, 1979, Pub. L. 96–88, title V, § 509(b), 93 Stat. 695, related to bonds of importers, examination of imported teas, and importation at ports without examiners.

Section 45, act Mar. 2, 1897, ch. 358, § 5, 29 Stat. 605, related to delivery permits and reexamination and retention of substandard teas.

Section 46, acts Mar. 2, 1897, ch. 358, § 7, 29 Stat. 606; May 31, 1920, ch. 217, 41 Stat. 712, 713, related to examiners and examination according to usages of trade.

Section 46a, acts Mar. 2, 1897, ch. 358, § 13, formerly act July 1, 1941, ch. 269, title II, 55 Stat. 478; renumbered § 13 of act Mar. 2, 1897, and amended Aug. 10, 1993, Pub. L. 103–66, title IV, § 4401, 107 Stat. 378, related to deposit of fee prior to examination.

Section 47, acts Mar. 2, 1897, ch. 358, § 6, 29 Stat. 606; May 31, 1920, ch. 217, 41 Stat. 712, 713; 1940 Reorg. Plan No. IV, § 12, eff. June 30, 1940, 5 F.R. 2421, 54 Stat. 1237; 1953 Reorg. Plan No. 1, § 5, eff. Apr. 11, 1953, 18 F.R. 2053, 67 Stat. 631; Oct. 17, 1979, Pub. L. 96–88, title V, § 509(b), 93 Stat. 695, required referral of disputes to United States Board of Tea Appeals and authorized board to permit delivery or order destruction or exportation of substandard teas.

Section 48, acts Mar. 2, 1897, ch. 358, § 8, 29 Stat. 606; May 31, 1920, ch. 217, 41 Stat. 712, related to reexaminations, including findings by examiner and assistance of experts.

Section 49, acts Mar. 2, 1897, ch. 358, § 9, 29 Stat. 606; May 31, 1920, ch. 217, 41 Stat. 712, related to reimporting rejected teas and forfeitures for violation of provisions.

Section 50, acts Mar. 2, 1897, ch. 358, § 10, 29 Stat. 607; May 31, 1920, ch. 217, 41 Stat. 712; 1940 Reorg. Plan No. IV, § 12, eff. June 30, 1940, 5 F.R. 2421, 54 Stat. 1237; 1953 Reorg. Plan No. 1, § 5, eff. Apr. 11, 1953, 18 F.R. 2053, 67 Stat. 631; Oct. 17, 1979, Pub. L. 96–88, title V, § 509(b), 93 Stat. 695, authorized issuance of regulations.

Effective Date of Repeal

Section 3 of Pub. L. 104–128 provided that: "This Act [repealing this chapter] shall take effect on the date of enactment of this Act [Apr. 9, 1996]."

Short Title of Repeal

Section 1 of Pub. L. 104–128 provided that: "This Act [repealing this chapter] may be cited as the 'Federal Tea Tasters Repeal Act of 1996'."

Short Title

Act July 12, 1943, ch. 221, title II, 57 Stat. 499, provided in part that act Mar. 2, 1897, which was classified generally to this chapter, could be cited as the Tea Importation Act.

CHAPTER 3—FILLED MILK

Federal Food, Drug, and Cosmetic Act

By virtue of act June 25, 1938, ch. 675, § 902(c), 52 Stat. 1059 [section 392(b) of this title], nothing contained in section 301 et seq. of this title shall be construed as in any way affecting, modifying, repealing, or superseding the provisions of sections 61 to 64 of this title.

Bureau of Dairy Industry

General provisions, see sections 401 to 404 of Title 7, Agriculture.

§ 61. Definitions

Whenever used in this chapter—

(a) The term "person" includes an individual, partnership, corporation, or association;

(b) The term "interstate or foreign commerce" means commerce (1) between any State, Territory, or possession, or the District of Columbia, and any place outside thereof; (2) between points within the same State, Territory, or possession, or within the District of Columbia, but through any place outside thereof; or (3) within any Territory or possession, or within the District of Columbia; and

(c) The term "filled milk" means any milk, cream, or skimmed milk, whether or not condensed, evaporated, concentrated, powdered, dried, or desiccated, to which has been added, or which has been blended or compounded with, any fat or oil other than milk fat, so that the resulting product is in imitation or semblance of milk, cream, or skimmed milk, whether or not condensed, evaporated, concentrated, powdered, dried, or desiccated. This definition shall not include any distinctive proprietary food compound not readily mistaken in taste for milk or cream or for evaporated, condensed, or powdered milk, or cream where such compound (1) is prepared and designed for feeding infants and young children and customarily used on the order of a physician; (2) is packed in individual cans containing not more than sixteen and one-half ounces and bearing a label in bold type that the content is to be used only for said purpose; (3) is shipped in interstate or foreign commerce exclusively to physicians, wholesale and retail druggists, orphan asylums, child-welfare associations, hospitals, and similar institutions and generally disposed of by them.

(Mar. 4, 1923, ch. 262, § 1, 42 Stat. 1486.)

Short Title

Act July 12, 1943, ch. 221, title II, 57 Stat. 499, provided in part that act Mar. 4, 1923, which enacted this chapter, may be cited as the "Filled Milk Act".

§ 62. Manufacture, shipment, or delivery for shipment in interstate or foreign commerce prohibited

It is declared that filled milk, as defined in section 61 of this title, is an adulterated article of food, injurious to the public health, and its sale constitutes a fraud upon the public. It shall be unlawful for any person to manufacture within any Territory or possession, or within the District of Columbia, or to ship or deliver for shipment in interstate or foreign commerce, any filled milk.

(Mar. 4, 1923, ch. 262, § 2, 42 Stat. 1487.)

§ 63. Penalties; acts of agents deemed acts of principals

Any person violating any provision of this chapter shall upon conviction thereof be subject to a fine of not more than $1,000 or imprisonment of not more than one year, or both. When construing and enforcing the provisions of this chapter, the act, omission, or failure of any person acting for or employed by any individual, partnership, corporation, or association, within the scope of his employment or office, shall in every case be deemed the act, omission, or failure, of such individual, partnership, corporation, or association, as well as of such person.

(Mar. 4, 1923, ch. 262, § 3, 42 Stat. 1487.)

CODIFICATION

The original text of this section contained a further provision that no penalty should be enforced for any violation occurring within 30 days after act Mar. 4, 1923 became law and was omitted as temporary and obsolete.

§ 64. Regulations for enforcement

The Secretary of Health and Human Services is authorized and directed to make and enforce such regulations as may in his judgment be necessary to carry out the purposes of this chapter.

(Mar. 4, 1923, ch. 262, § 4, as added Aug. 27, 1935, ch. 743, 49 Stat. 885; 1940 Reorg. Plan No. IV, § 12, eff. June 30, 1940, 5 F.R. 2421, 54 Stat. 1237; 1953 Reorg. Plan No. 1, § 5, eff. Apr. 11, 1953, 18 F.R. 2053, 67 Stat. 631; Pub. L. 96–88, title V, § 509(b), Oct. 17, 1979, 93 Stat. 695.)

CHANGE OF NAME

"Secretary of Health and Human Services" substituted in text for "Secretary of Health, Education, and Welfare" pursuant to section 509(b) of Pub. L. 96–88, which is classified to section 3508(b) of Title 20, Education.

TRANSFER OF FUNCTIONS

For transfer of functions of Federal Security Administrator to Secretary of Health, Education, and Welfare [now Health and Human Services], and of Food and Drug Administration to Federal Security Agency, see notes set out under section 321 of this title.

CHAPTER 4—ANIMALS, MEATS, AND MEAT AND DAIRY PRODUCTS

SUBCHAPTER I—EXAMINATION OF ANIMALS, MEATS, AND MEAT AND DAIRY PRODUCTS

§§ 71 to 92. Transferred

CODIFICATION

Section 71, act Mar. 4, 1907, ch. 2907, 34 Stat. 1260, which related to inspection of meat and meat food products, examination of cattle before slaughtering, separate slaughtering of diseased animals and examination of carcasses, was transferred to section 603 of this title.

Section 72, act Mar. 4, 1907, ch. 2907, 34 Stat. 1260, which related to post mortem examination of carcasses, marking and labeling, destruction of condemned carcasses, and reinspection, was transferred to section 604 of this title.

Section 73, act Mar. 4, 1907, ch. 2907, 34 Stat. 1261, which related to examination of carcasses brought into slaughtering or packing establishments and of meat food products issued from and returned thereto, was transferred to section 605 of this title.

Section 74, act Mar. 4, 1907, ch. 2907, 34 Stat. 1261, which related to examination and inspection of meat food products, marks of inspection, destruction of condemned products, and products for export, was transferred to section 606 of this title and was subsequently repealed by Pub. L. 110–234, title XI, § 11016(b)(1)(B), May 22, 2008, 122 Stat. 1369, and Pub. L. 110–246, § 4(a), title XI, § 11016(b)(1)(B), June 18, 2008, 122 Stat. 1664, 2131.

Section 75, act Mar. 4, 1907, ch. 2907, 34 Stat. 1262, which related to labeling of receptacles and coverings of meat and meat food products inspected and passed, supervision by inspectors, prohibition of sales under false names, was transferred to section 607 of this title.

Section 76, act Mar. 4, 1907, ch. 2907, 34 Stat. 1262, which related to sanitary inspection and regulation of slaughtering and packing establishments, and rejection of meat or meat food products unfit for food, was transferred to section 608 of this title.

Section 77, act Mar. 4, 1907, ch. 2907, 34 Stat. 1262, which related to examination of cattle and food products thereof slaughtered and prepared during night time, was transferred to section 609 of this title.

Section 78, act Mar. 4, 1907, ch. 2907, 34 Stat. 1262, which related to prohibition of transportation of carcasses, meat, or meat food products not properly inspected and marked, was transferred to section 610 of this title.

Section 79, act Mar. 4, 1907, ch. 2907, 34 Stat. 1263, which related to forgery, alteration, and unauthorized use of marks, labels, and certificates, was transferred to section 611 of this title.

Section 80, act Mar. 4, 1907, ch. 2907, 34 Stat. 1263, which related to inspection of animals for export, was transferred to section 612 of this title and was subsequently repealed by Pub. L. 107–171, title X, § 10418(a)(19), May 13, 2002, 116 Stat. 508.

Section 81, act Mar. 4, 1907, ch. 2907, 34 Stat. 1263, which related to certificates of condition of animals for export, was transferred to section 613 of this title and was subsequently repealed by Pub. L. 107–171, title X, § 10418(a)(19), May 13, 2002, 116 Stat. 508.

Section 82, act Mar. 4, 1907, ch. 2907, 34 Stat. 1263, which related to clearance to vessels carrying cattle for export with proper certificate of inspection, was transferred to section 614 of this title and was subsequently repealed by Pub. L. 107–171, title X, § 10418(a)(19), May 13, 2002, 116 Stat. 508.

Section 83, act Mar. 4, 1907, ch. 2907, 34 Stat. 1263, which related to inspection of carcasses, the meat of which is intended for export, was transferred to section 615 of this title.

Section 84, act Mar. 4, 1907, ch. 2907, 34 Stat. 1263, which related to certificates of condition of carcasses, the meat of which is intended for export, was transferred to section 616 of this title.

Section 85, act Mar. 4, 1907, ch. 2907, 34 Stat. 1263, which related to clearance to vessels carrying meat for export with proper certificate of inspection, was transferred to section 617 of this title.

Section 86, act Mar. 4, 1907, ch. 2907, 34 Stat. 1263, which related to official certificates of inspection and delivery of copies thereof to different parties, was transferred to section 618 of this title.

Section 87, act Mar. 4, 1907, ch. 2907, 34 Stat. 1264, which related to prohibition of transportation or sale of meat or meat food products without complying with provisions of inspection law, was transferred to section 619 of this title.

Section 88, act Mar. 4, 1907, ch. 2907, 34 Stat. 1264, which related to offenses and penalties, was transferred to section 620 of this title.

Section 89, act Mar. 4, 1907, ch. 2907, 34 Stat. 1264, which related to appointment of inspectors, their duties, and rule making authority of the Secretary of Agriculture, was transferred to section 621 of this title.

Section 90, act Mar. 4, 1907, ch. 2907, 34 Stat. 1264, which related to penalties for bribery, was transferred to section 622 of this title.

Section 91, acts Mar. 4, 1907, ch. 2907, 34 Stat. 1265; June 29, 1938, ch. 810, 52 Stat. 1235, which related to definitions, exceptions to inspection requirements in case of farmers and retailers, and penalties for sale of meat and meat food products unfit for food, was transferred to section 623 of this title.

Section 92, act Mar. 4, 1907, ch. 2907, 34 Stat. 1265, which was a proviso following the first sentence of section 91 of this title, was restored to that section and has been transferred to section 623 of this title.

§ 93. Repealed. May 29, 1928, ch. 901, § 1(92), 45 Stat. 993

Section, act Mar. 4, 1907, ch. 2907, 34 Stat. 1265, related to statement in annual estimates as to persons employed, their compensation and expenses.

§§ 94 to 95. Transferred

CODIFICATION

Section 94, act June 30, 1914, ch. 131, 38 Stat. 420, which related to inspection of reindeer, was transferred to section 692 of this title.

Section 94a, act May 23, 1908, ch. 192, 35 Stat. 254, which related to inspection of dairy products for export, was transferred to section 693 of this title.

Section 95, acts June 30, 1906, ch. 3913, 34 Stat. 679; June 26, 1934, ch. 756, § 2, 48 Stat. 1225, which related to authorization of appropriations for expenses of inspection, was transferred to section 694 of this title.

§ 96. Repealed. Pub. L. 90–201, § 18, Dec. 15, 1967, 81 Stat. 600

Section, act July 24, 1919, ch. 26, 41 Stat. 241, provided for marking horse meat transported in interstate commerce. See section 619 of this title.

EFFECTIVE DATE OF REPEAL

Repeal effective Dec. 15, 1967, see section 20 of Pub. L. 90–201, set out as an Effective Date note under section 601 of this title.

§§ 97 to 97d. Omitted

CODIFICATION

Sections 97 to 97d, act July 30, 1947, ch. 356, title I, § 1, 61 Stat. 531, 532, set up a meat inspection fund and provided for payment for meat inspection service by the persons or organizations who were furnished such inspection on and after July 1, 1947. These provisions ceased to be effective on July 1, 1948, under section 98 of this title which requires the cost of such inspection to be borne by the United States. The unobligated balance in the meat inspection fund was carried to the general fund of the Treasury by act June 19, 1948, ch. 543, § 1, 62 Stat. 515.

§ 98. Transferred

CODIFICATION

Section, act June 5, 1948, ch. 423, 62 Stat. 344, which related to payment of cost of meat inspection, was transferred to section 695 of this title.

§ 99. Repealed. July 28, 1953, ch. 251, title I, § 101, 67 Stat. 208

Section, act Aug. 31, 1951, ch. 374, title I, § 101, 65 Stat. 229, related to reimbursement for excess expenses of meat inspection.

SUBCHAPTER II—IMPORTATION OF CATTLE AND QUARANTINE

§ 101. Suspension of importation of all animals

Whenever, in the opinion of the President, it shall be necessary for the protection of animals in the United States against infectious or contagious diseases, he may, by proclamation, suspend the importation of all or any class of animals for a limited time, and may change, modify, revoke, or renew such proclamation, as the public good may require; and during the time of such suspension the importation of any such animals shall be unlawful.

(Aug. 30, 1890, ch. 839, § 9, 26 Stat. 416.)

§§ 102 to 105. Repealed. Pub. L. 107–171, title X, § 10418(a)(6), May 13, 2002, 116 Stat. 507

Section 102, act Aug. 30, 1890, ch. 839, § 7, 26 Stat. 416, related to quarantine of imported animals.

Section 103, act Aug. 30, 1890, ch. 839, § 8, 26 Stat. 416, related to prohibition of importation of animals except at quarantine ports, slaughter of infected animals, appraisal, and payment.

Section 104, act Aug. 30, 1890, ch. 839, § 6, 26 Stat. 416; June 28, 1926, ch. 700, § 2, 44 Stat. 775; Feb. 28, 1931, ch. 348, 46 Stat. 1460; July 22, 1954, ch. 558, § 32, 68 Stat. 510; Jan. 28, 1956, ch. 12, § 1, 70 Stat. 5; Pub. L. 97–461, § 4, Jan. 12, 1983, 96 Stat. 2524; Pub. L. 103–182, title III, § 361(b), Dec. 8, 1993, 107 Stat. 2122; Pub. L. 103–465, title IV, § 431(h), Dec. 8, 1994, 108 Stat. 4969, related to importation of animals.

Section 105, act Aug. 30, 1890, ch. 839, § 10, 26 Stat. 417; Pub. L. 103–182, title III, § 361(c), Dec. 8, 1993, 107 Stat. 2122; Pub. L. 103–465, title IV, § 431(i), Dec. 8, 1994, 108 Stat. 4969, related to inspection of animals.

§§ 106, 107. Omitted

CODIFICATION

Sections, acts Aug. 10, 1917, ch. 52, § 9, 40 Stat. 275; Nov. 21, 1918, ch. 212, § 3, 40 Stat. 1048, related to slaugh-

ter of tick-infested cattle. Section 12 of act Aug. 10, 1917, provided that the act should cease to be in effect when the national emergency resulting from World War I had passed.

SUBCHAPTER III—PREVENTION OF INTRODUCTION AND SPREAD OF CONTAGION

§§ 111, 112. Repealed. Pub. L. 107–171, title X, § 10418(a)(7), (8), May 13, 2002, 116 Stat. 507, 508

Section 111, act Feb. 2, 1903, ch. 349, § 2, 32 Stat. 792; July 22, 1954, ch. 558, § 33, 68 Stat. 510; Jan. 28, 1956, ch. 12, § 2, 70 Stat. 5, related to regulations to prevent contagious diseases.

Section 112, act May 29, 1884, ch. 60, § 4, 23 Stat. 32; Feb. 2, 1903, ch. 349, § 1, 32 Stat. 791; Feb. 7, 1928, ch. 30, 45 Stat. 59, related to investigations as to pleuropneumonia and other diseases and regulations.

Short Title

Act Feb. 2, 1903, ch. 349, 32 Stat. 791, classified to former sections 112 and 120 to 122 of this title, is popularly known as the Cattle Contagious Diseases Act of 1903.

Act May 29, 1884, ch. 60, 23 Stat. 31, classified to former sections 112, 113 to 114a–1, 115, 116, 117 to 120, and 130 of this title and section 391 of Title 7, Agriculture, is popularly known as the Animal Industry Act.

§ 112a. Omitted

Codification

Section, act Feb. 7, 1928, ch. 30, 45 Stat. 59, amended acts May 29, 1884, ch. 60, 23 Stat. 31; Feb. 2, 1903, ch. 349, 32 Stat. 791; and Mar. 3, 1905, ch. 1496, 33 Stat. 1264, to include live poultry in their provisions, added "and/or live poultry" following "live stock" wherever the term "live stock" appeared, and extended the penalties, terms, and provisions of said acts to live poultry. For complete classification of such acts to the Code, see Short Title note set out under section 112 of this title and Tables.

§ 113. Repealed. Pub. L. 107–171, title X, § 10418(a)(7), (8), May 13, 2002, 116 Stat. 507, 508

Section, act May 29, 1884, ch. 60, § 5, 23 Stat. 32; Feb. 2, 1903, ch. 349, § 1, 32 Stat. 791; Feb. 7, 1928, ch. 30, 45 Stat. 59, related to measures to prevent exportation of diseased livestock and live poultry.

§ 113a. Establishment of research laboratories for foot-and-mouth disease and other animal diseases; research contracts; employment of technicians and scientists; appropriations

The Secretary of Agriculture is authorized to establish research laboratories, including the acquisition of necessary land, buildings, or facilities, and also the making of research contracts under the authority contained in section 427i(a) of title 7, for research and study, in the United States or elsewhere, of foot-and-mouth disease and other animal diseases which in the opinion of the Secretary constitute a threat to the livestock industry of the United States: *Provided*, That no live virus of foot-and-mouth disease may be introduced for any purpose into any part of the mainland of the United States (except coastal islands separated therefrom by water navigable for deep-water navigation and which shall not be connected with the mainland by any tunnel) unless the Secretary determines that it is necessary and in the public interest for the conduct of research and study in the United States (except at Brookhaven National Laboratory in Upton, New York) and issues a permit under such rules as the Secretary shall promulgate to protect animal health, except that the Secretary of Agriculture may transport said virus in the original package across the mainland under adequate safeguards, and except further, that in the event of outbreak of foot-and-mouth disease in this country, the Secretary of Agriculture may, at his discretion, permit said virus to be brought into the United States under adequate safeguards. To carry out the provisions of this section, the Secretary is authorized to employ technical experts or scientists: *Provided*, That the number so employed shall not exceed five and that the maximum compensation for each shall not exceed the highest rate of grade 18 of the General Schedule. There is authorized to be appropriated such sums as Congress may deem necessary; in addition, the Secretary is authorized to utilize in carrying out this section, funds otherwise available for the control or eradication of such diseases.

(May 29, 1884, ch. 60, § 12, as added Apr. 24, 1948, ch. 229, 62 Stat. 198; amended July 31, 1956, ch. 804, title I, § 119, 70 Stat. 742; Pub. L. 85–573, July 31, 1958, 72 Stat. 454; Pub. L. 87–793, § 1001(e), Oct. 11, 1962, 76 Stat. 864; Pub. L. 88–426, title III, § 305(1), Aug. 14, 1964, 78 Stat. 422; Pub. L. 101–624, title XVI, § 1618(b), Nov. 28, 1990, 104 Stat. 3733.)

Codification

Provisions that authorized the Secretary to employ technical experts and scientists "without regard to the Classification Act", meaning the Classification Act of 1923, were omitted as obsolete. Sections 1202 and 1204 of the Classification Act of 1949, 63 Stat. 972, 973, repealed the 1923 Act and all laws or parts of laws inconsistent with the 1949 Act. While section 1106(a) of the 1949 Act provided that references in other laws to the 1923 Act should be held and considered to mean the 1949 Act, it did not have the effect of continuing the exception contained in this section because of section 1106(b) which provided that the application of the 1949 Act to any position, officer, or employee shall not be affected by section 1106(a). The Classification Act of 1949 was repealed by Pub. L. 89–554, Sept. 6, 1966, § 8(a), 80 Stat. 632 (the first section of which revised and enacted Title 5, Government Organization and Employees, into law). Section 5102 of Title 5 contains the applicability provisions of the 1949 Act, and section 5103 of Title 5 authorizes the Office of Personnel Management to determine the applicability to specific positions and employees.

Amendments

1990—Pub. L. 101–624 substituted "United States (except" for "United States except" and "tunnel) unless the Secretary determines that it is necessary and in the public interest for the conduct of research and study in the United States (except at Brookhaven National Laboratory in Upton, New York) and issues a permit under such rules as the Secretary shall promulgate to protect animal health," for "tunnel, and".

1962—Pub. L. 87–793 substituted "shall not exceed the highest rate of grade 18 of the General Schedule" for "shall not exceed $19,000 per annum".

1958—Pub. L. 85–573 inserted in proviso clause of first sentence the exception clause respecting transportation of virus in original package across mainland under adequate safeguards.

Effective Date of 1962 Amendment

Amendment by Pub. L. 87–793 effective on first day of first pay period which begins on or after Oct. 11, 1962.

REPEALS

Act July 31, 1956, ch. 804, title I, §119, 70 Stat. 742, which increased the maximum compensation of technical experts or scientists, was repealed by Pub. L. 88–426, title III, §305(1), Aug. 14, 1964, 78 Stat. 422.

REFERENCES IN OTHER LAWS TO GS–16, 17, OR 18 PAY RATES

References in laws to the rates of pay for GS–16, 17, or 18, or to maximum rates of pay under the General Schedule, to be considered references to rates payable under specified sections of Title 5, Government Organization and Employees, see section 529 [title I, §101(c)(1)] of Pub. L. 101–509, set out in a note under section 5376 of Title 5.

LIVE VIRUS FOOT AND MOUTH DISEASE RESEARCH

Pub. L. 110–234, title VII, §7524, May 22, 2008, 122 Stat. 1273, and Pub. L. 110–246, §4(a), title VII, §7524, June 18, 2008, 122 Stat. 1664, 2034, provided that:

"(a) IN GENERAL.—The Secretary [of Agriculture] shall issue a permit required under section 12 of the Act of May 29, 1884 (21 U.S.C. 113a) to the Secretary of Homeland Security for work on the live virus of foot and mouth disease at any facility that is a successor to the Plum Island Animal Disease Center and charged with researching high-consequence biological threats involving zoonotic and foreign animal diseases (referred to in this section as the 'successor facility').

"(b) LIMITATION TO SINGLE FACILITY.—Not more than 1 facility shall be issued a permit under subsection (a).

"(c) LIMITATION ON VALIDITY.—The permit issued under this section shall be valid unless the Secretary determines that the study of live foot and mouth disease virus at the successor facility is not being carried out in accordance with the regulations promulgated by the Secretary pursuant to the Agricultural Bioterrorism Protection Act of 2002 (7 U.S.C. 8401 et seq.).

"(d) AUTHORITY.—The suspension, revocation, or other impairment of the permit issued under this section—

"(1) shall be made by the Secretary; and

"(2) is a nondelegable function."

[Pub. L. 110–234 and Pub. L. 110–246 enacted identical provisions. Pub. L. 110–234 was repealed by section 4(a) of Pub. L. 110–246, set out as a note under section 8701 of Title 7, Agriculture.]

§§ 114 to 114d–1. Repealed. Pub. L. 107–171, title X, § 10418(a)(8), (9), May 13, 2002, 116 Stat. 508

Section 114, act May 29, 1884, ch. 60, §3, 23 Stat. 32, related to regulations for suppression of diseases and cooperation of States and Territories.

Section 114a, act May 29, 1884, ch. 60, §11, as added Sept. 21, 1944, ch. 412, title I, §101(a), 58 Stat. 734; amended Oct. 30, 1951, ch. 637, §1, 65 Stat. 693; Aug. 8, 1953, ch. 381, 67 Stat. 493; Aug. 3, 1956, ch. 950, §2, 70 Stat. 1032; Pub. L. 87–518, §7, July 2, 1962, 76 Stat. 131; Pub. L. 101–624, title XXV, §2509(c)(2), Nov. 28, 1990, 104 Stat. 4071, related to control and eradication of diseases, cooperation of States and farmers' associations, purchase and destruction of diseased animals, and defined "State" for statutory purposes.

A prior section 11 of act May 29, 1884, required annual reports to Congress concerning the suppression of contagious diseases among domestic animals, and was classified to section 560 of former Title 5, prior to repeal by act May 29, 1928, ch. 901, §1, 45 Stat. 993.

Section 114a–1, act May 29, 1884, ch. 60, §13, as added Oct. 30, 1951, ch. 637, §2, 65 Stat. 693, related to interstate movement of domestic animals reacting to tests for brucellosis, immediate slaughter, and rules and regulations.

Section 114b, act Feb. 28, 1947, ch. 8, §1, 61 Stat. 7; Pub. L. 89–521, §1, July 27, 1966, 80 Stat. 330; Pub. L. 92–152, §1, Nov. 5, 1971, 85 Stat. 418; Pub. L. 94–231, §3, Mar. 15, 1976, 90 Stat. 216; Pub. L. 101–255, §1(1), Mar. 15, 1990, 104 Stat. 114; Pub. L. 101–624, title XXV, §2505, Nov. 28, 1990, 104 Stat. 4068, related to cooperation in animal disease control.

Section 114c, act Feb. 28, 1947, ch. 8, §2, 61 Stat. 7; Aug. 3, 1956, ch. 950, §3, 70 Stat. 1033; Pub. L. 92–152, §2, Nov. 5, 1971, 85 Stat. 419; Pub. L. 101–255, §1(2), Mar. 15, 1990, 104 Stat. 114, related to use of funds.

Section 114d, act Feb. 28, 1947, ch. 8, §3, as added Pub. L. 101–255, §1(3), Mar. 15, 1990, 104 Stat. 114, related to sale of sterile screwworms.

A prior section 114d, act Feb. 28, 1947, ch. 8, §3, 61 Stat. 8, related to reports by Secretary of Agriculture to Congress with respect to activities carried on under sections 114b and 114c of this title, prior to repeal by Pub. L. 86–533, §1(20), June 29, 1960, 74 Stat. 249.

Section 114d–1, act Feb. 28, 1947, ch. 8, §5, as added Pub. L. 89–521, §2, July 27, 1966, 80 Stat. 330; amended Pub. L. 101–255, §1(5), Mar. 15, 1990, 104 Stat. 114, related to cooperation with public and private entities.

SHORT TITLE

Section 6 of act Feb. 28, 1947, ch. 8, as added by Pub. L. 101–255, §1(6), Mar. 15, 1990, 104 Stat. 114, provided that the act Feb. 28, 1947, ch. 8, which enacted sections 114b to 114d–1 of this title and provisions set out as a note under former section 114b of this title, could be referred to as the "Animal Disease Control Cooperation Act of 1947".

§§ 114d–2 to 114d–6. Repealed. Pub. L. 92–152, § 3, Nov. 5, 1971, 85 Stat. 419

Section 114d–2, Pub. L. 90–388, §1, July 6, 1968, 82 Stat. 294, provided for cooperation with Central America in control and eradication of foot-and-mouth disease or rinderpest.

Section 114d–3, Pub. L. 90–388, §2, July 6, 1968, 82 Stat. 294, provided for uses of funds.

Section 114d–4, Pub. L. 90–388, §3, July 6, 1968, 82 Stat. 294, defined governments of Central America.

Section 114d–5, Pub. L. 90–388, §4, July 6, 1968, 82 Stat. 294, provided for cooperation with public and private organizations and individuals.

Section 114d–6, Pub. L. 90–388, §5, July 6, 1968, 82 Stat. 294, provided for authorization of appropriations.

§§ 114e to 114h. Repealed. Pub. L. 107–171, title X, § 10418(a)(10), (11), May 13, 2002, 116 Stat. 508

Section 114e, act June 16, 1948, ch. 477, §1, 62 Stat. 458, related to research and investigations into the control and eradication of cattle grubs.

Section 114f, act June 16, 1948, ch. 477, §2, 62 Stat. 458, defined the term "State" and authorized appropriations.

Section 114g, Pub. L. 87–209, §1, Sept. 6, 1961, 75 Stat. 481, related to hog cholera eradication program.

Section 114h, Pub. L. 87–209, §2, Sept. 6, 1961, 75 Stat. 481, related to advisory committee.

§ 114i. Pseudorabies eradication

(a) Findings

Congress finds that efforts to eradicate pseudorabies in United States swine populations by the Department of Agriculture in cooperation with State agencies and the pork industry have a high priority and should be continued until pseudorabies is completely eradicated in the United States.

(b) Establishment of program

The Secretary of Agriculture shall establish and carry out a program for the eradication of pseudorabies in United States swine populations.

(c) Use of funds for testing and control of pseudorabies

The Secretary shall ensure that not less than 65 percent of the funds appropriated for the program established under subsection (b) of this section shall be used for testing and screening of animals and for other purposes directly related to the eradication or control of pseudorabies. This requirement on the use of appropriated funds for this program shall not be implemented in a manner that would adversely affect any other animal or plant disease or pest eradication or control program.

(d) Authorization of appropriations

There are authorized to be appropriated for each of the fiscal years 1991 through 2007 such sums as may be necessary for the purpose of carrying out the program established under subsection (b) of this section.

(Pub. L. 101–624, title XXV, § 2506, Nov. 28, 1990, 104 Stat. 4068; Pub. L. 104–127, title IX, § 916, Apr. 4, 1996, 110 Stat. 1187; Pub. L. 107–171, title X, § 10505, May 13, 2002, 116 Stat. 511.)

AMENDMENTS

2002—Subsec. (d). Pub. L. 107–171 substituted "2007" for "2002".

1996—Subsec. (d). Pub. L. 104–127 substituted "2002" for "1995".

§§ 115 to 128. Repealed. Pub. L. 107–171, title X, § 10418(a)(7), (8), (12)–(14), May 13, 2002, 116 Stat. 507, 508

Section 115, act May 29, 1884, ch. 60, § 6, 23 Stat. 32; June 28, 1926, ch. 700, § 1, 44 Stat. 774; Feb. 7, 1928, ch. 30, 45 Stat. 59; Pub. L. 87–763, Oct. 9, 1962, 76 Stat. 762, prohibited transportation of diseased livestock and live poultry.

Section 116, act May 29, 1884, ch. 60, 23 Stat. 31; May 31, 1920, ch. 217, 41 Stat. 699, related to excepted shipment of certain cattle.

Section 117, act May 29, 1884, ch. 60, § 7, 23 Stat. 32; Feb. 7, 1928, ch. 30, 45 Stat. 59; Pub. L. 95–439, § 1, Oct. 10, 1978, 92 Stat. 1061; Pub. L. 97–461, § 5, Jan. 12, 1983, 96 Stat. 2524, related to penalties for transportation of diseased livestock or live poultry.

Section 118, act May 29, 1884, ch. 60, § 9, 23 Stat. 33; June 25, 1948, ch. 646, § 1, 62 Stat. 909, related to duty of United States attorneys.

Section 119, act May 29, 1884, ch. 60, § 2, 23 Stat. 31; Feb. 9, 1889, ch. 122, § 1, 25 Stat. 659; July 14, 1890, ch. 707, 26 Stat. 288; Feb. 7, 1928, ch. 30, 45 Stat. 59, related to appointment of agents to examine and report on methods of treatment of animals, and means for suppression of diseases.

Section 120, act May 29, 1884, ch. 60, §§ 4, 5, 23 Stat. 32; Feb. 2, 1903, ch. 349, § 1, 32 Stat. 791; Feb. 7, 1928, ch. 30, 45 Stat. 59, related to regulation of exportation and transportation of infected livestock and live poultry.

Section 121, act Feb. 2, 1903, ch. 349, § 1, 32 Stat. 791; Feb. 7, 1928, ch. 30, 45 Stat. 59, related to shipments from areas suspected to be infected and to control of animals and live poultry.

Section 122, act Feb. 2, 1903, ch. 349, § 3, 32 Stat. 792; Pub. L. 97–461, § 6, Jan. 12, 1983, 96 Stat. 2525, related to offenses and penalties.

Section 123, act Mar. 3, 1905, ch. 1496, § 1, 33 Stat. 1264; Feb. 7, 1928, ch. 30, 45 Stat. 59; Pub. L. 87–518, § 8(a), July 2, 1962, 76 Stat. 131; Pub. L. 95–439, § 2, Oct. 10, 1978, 92 Stat. 1061, related to quarantine.

Section 124, act Mar. 3, 1905, ch. 1496, § 2, 33 Stat. 1264; Feb. 7, 1928, ch. 30, 45 Stat. 59; Pub. L. 87–518, § 8(b), July 2, 1962, 76 Stat. 131, prohibited transportation or delivery therefor from quarantined State or Territory or portion thereof, of quarantined animals and live poultry.

Section 125, act Mar. 3, 1905, ch. 1496, § 3, 33 Stat. 1265; Feb. 7, 1928, ch. 30, 45 Stat. 59; Pub. L. 87–518, § 8(b), July 2, 1962, 76 Stat. 131; Pub. L. 95–439, § 3, Oct. 10, 1978, 92 Stat. 1061, related to regulations for inspection, disinfection, and certification, and delivery and shipment of quarantined animals and live poultry from State or Territory.

Section 126, act Mar. 3, 1905, ch. 1496, § 4, 33 Stat. 1265; Feb. 7, 1928, ch. 30, 45 Stat. 59; Pub. L. 87–518, § 8(b), July 2, 1962, 76 Stat. 131, related to moving quarantined animals and live poultry from State or Territory, under regulations.

Section 127, act Mar. 3, 1905, ch. 1496, § 6, 33 Stat. 1265; Pub. L. 97–461, § 7, Jan. 12, 1983, 96 Stat. 2525, related to penalties for transportation from quarantined State, Territory, etc.

Section 128, act June 30, 1914, ch. 131, 38 Stat. 419; Pub. L. 87–518, § 9, July 2, 1962, 76 Stat. 131, related to extension of quarantine law to carriers in interstate commerce.

SHORT TITLE

Act Mar. 3, 1905, ch. 1496, 33 Stat. 1264, which enacted sections 123 to 127 of this title, was popularly known as the "Cattle Contagious Diseases Act of 1905".

§ 129. Omitted

CODIFICATION

Section, Pub. L. 107–76, title I, Nov. 28, 2001, 115 Stat. 712, related to transfer of funds for emergency arrest of animal, poultry, or plant diseases or pests, and was from the Agriculture, Rural Development, Food and Drug Administration, and Related Agencies Appropriations Act, 2002. Similar provisions which are permanent are classified to sections 7772 and 8316 of Title 7, Agriculture.

PRIOR PROVISIONS

Provisions similar to those in this section were contained in the following prior appropriation acts:

Pub. L. 106–387, § 1(a) [title I], Oct. 28, 2000, 114 Stat. 1549, 1549A–9, repealed by Pub. L. 107–171, title X, § 10418(a)(15), May 13, 2002, 116 Stat. 508.

Pub. L. 106–78, title I, Oct. 22, 1999, 113 Stat. 1143.

Pub. L. 105–277, div. A, § 101(a) [title I], Oct. 21, 1998, 112 Stat. 2681, 2681–8.

Pub. L. 105–86, title I, Nov. 18, 1997, 111 Stat. 2086.

Pub. L. 104–180, title I, Aug. 6, 1996, 110 Stat. 1576.

Pub. L. 104–37, title I, Oct. 21, 1995, 109 Stat. 307.

Pub. L. 103–330, title I, Sept. 30, 1994, 108 Stat. 2443.

Pub. L. 103–111, title I, Oct. 21, 1993, 107 Stat. 1054.

Pub. L. 102–341, title I, Aug. 14, 1992, 106 Stat. 882.

Pub. L. 102–142, title I, Oct. 28, 1991, 105 Stat. 886.

Pub. L. 101–506, title I, Nov. 5, 1990, 104 Stat. 1323.

Pub. L. 101–161, title I, Nov. 21, 1989, 103 Stat. 959.

Pub. L. 100–460, title I, Oct. 1, 1988, 102 Stat. 2237.

Pub. L. 100–202, § 101(k) [title I], Dec. 22, 1987, 101 Stat. 1329–322, 1329–331.

Pub. L. 99–500, § 101(a) [title I], Oct. 18, 1986, 100 Stat. 1783, 1783–8, and Pub. L. 99–591, § 101(a) [title I], Oct. 30, 1986, 100 Stat. 3341, 3341–8.

Pub. L. 99–190, § 101(a) [H.R. 3037, title I], Dec. 19, 1985, 99 Stat. 1185; Pub. L. 100–202, § 106, Dec. 22, 1987, 101 Stat. 1329–433.

Pub. L. 97–370, title I, Dec. 18, 1982, 96 Stat. 1792.

Pub. L. 97–103, title I, Dec. 23, 1981, 95 Stat. 1472.

Pub. L. 96–528, title I, Dec. 15, 1980, 94 Stat. 3099.

Pub. L. 96–108, title I, Nov. 9, 1979, 93 Stat. 826.

Pub. L. 95–448, title I, Oct. 11, 1978, 92 Stat. 1076.

Pub. L. 95–97, title I, Aug. 12, 1977, 91 Stat. 813.

Pub. L. 94–351, title I, July 12, 1976, 90 Stat. 854.

Pub. L. 94–122, title I, Oct. 21, 1975, 89 Stat. 645.

Pub. L. 93–563, title I, Dec. 31, 1974, 88 Stat. 1824.

Pub. L. 93–135, title I, Oct. 24, 1973, 87 Stat. 472.

Pub. L. 92–399, title I, Aug. 22, 1972, 86 Stat. 594.

Pub. L. 92–73, title I, Aug. 10, 1971, 85 Stat. 185.

Pub. L. 91–566, title I, Dec. 22, 1970, 84 Stat. 1482.

Pub. L. 91–127, title I, Nov. 26, 1969, 83 Stat. 246.

Pub. L. 90–463, title I, Aug. 8, 1968, 82 Stat. 640.

Pub. L. 90–113, title I, Oct. 24, 1967, 81 Stat. 321.

Pub. L. 89–556, title I, Sept. 7, 1966, 80 Stat. 690.

Pub. L. 89–316, title I, Nov. 2, 1965, 79 Stat. 1166.
Pub. L. 88–573, title I, Sept. 2, 1964, 78 Stat. 863.
Pub. L. 88–250, title I, Dec. 30, 1963, 77 Stat. 821.
Pub. L. 87–879, title I, Oct. 24, 1962, 76 Stat. 1204.
Pub. L. 87–112, title I, July 26, 1961, 75 Stat. 228.
Pub. L. 86–532, title I, June 29, 1960, 74 Stat. 233.
Pub. L. 86–80, title I, July 8, 1959, 73 Stat. 168.
Pub. L. 85–459, title I, June 13, 1958, 72 Stat. 189.
Pub. L. 85–118, title I, Aug. 2, 1957, 71 Stat. 330.
June 4, 1956, ch. 355, title I, 70 Stat. 230.
May 23, 1955, ch. 43, title I, 69 Stat. 52.
June 29, 1954, ch. 409, title I, 68 Stat. 305.
July 28, 1953, ch. 251, title III, 67 Stat. 223.
July 5, 1952, ch. 574, title III, 66 Stat. 354.
Aug. 31, 1951, ch. 374, title II, 65 Stat. 243.
Sept. 6, 1950, ch. 896, Ch. VI, title I, 64 Stat. 661.
June 29, 1949, ch. 280, title I, 63 Stat. 332.
June 19, 1948, ch. 543, 62 Stat. 515.
July 30, 1947, ch. 356, title I, 61 Stat. 532.
June 22, 1946, ch. 445, 60 Stat. 278.
May 5, 1945, ch. 109, 59 Stat. 144.
June 28, 1944, ch. 296, 58 Stat. 434.
July 12, 1943, ch. 215, 57 Stat. 403.
July 22, 1942, ch. 516, 56 Stat. 676.
July 1, 1941, ch. 267, 55 Stat. 418.
June 25, 1940, ch. 421, 54 Stat. 542.
June 30, 1939, ch. 253, title I, 53 Stat. 951.
June 16, 1938, ch. 464, title I, 52 Stat. 722.
June 29, 1937, ch. 404, 50 Stat. 406.
June 4, 1936, ch. 489, 49 Stat. 1432.
May 17, 1935, ch. 131, title I, 49 Stat. 257.
Mar. 26, 1934, ch. 89, 48 Stat. 477.
Mar. 3, 1933, ch. 203, 47 Stat. 1442.
July 7, 1932, ch. 443, 47 Stat. 620.
Feb. 23, 1931, ch. 278, 46 Stat. 1252.
May 27, 1930, ch. 341, 46 Stat. 403.
Feb. 16, 1929, ch. 227, 45 Stat. 1198.
May 16, 1928, ch. 572, 45 Stat. 548.
Jan. 18, 1927, ch. 39, 44 Stat. 1005.
May 11, 1926, ch. 286, 44 Stat. 529.
Feb. 10, 1925, ch. 200, 43 Stat. 851.
Dec. 5, 1924, ch. 4, 43 Stat. 683.
June 5, 1924, ch. 266, 43 Stat. 458.
Apr. 2, 1924, ch. 81, 43 Stat. 40.
Feb. 26, 1923, ch. 119, 42 Stat. 1318.
May 11, 1922, ch. 185, 42 Stat. 536.
Mar. 4, 1917, ch. 179, 39 Stat. 1167.

§§ 129a to 131. Repealed. Pub. L. 107–171, title X, § 10418(a)(1), (8), (16), May 13, 2002, 116 Stat. 507, 508

Section 129a, Pub. L. 97–46, § 1, Sept. 25, 1981, 95 Stat. 953; Pub. L. 106–224, title IV, § 438(b), June 20, 2000, 114 Stat. 454, related to transfer of funds for emergency arrest of animal or poultry diseases. Section was formerly classified to section 147b of Title 7, Agriculture.

Section 130, act May 29, 1884, ch. 60, § 8, 23 Stat. 33; 1967 Reorg. Plan No. 3, § 402(430), eff. Aug. 11, 1967, 32 F.R. 11669, 81 Stat. 948; Pub. L. 93–198, title IV, § 401, Dec. 24, 1973, 87 Stat. 793, related to pleuropneumonia in District of Columbia and duties of Council of the District of Columbia.

Section 131, act May 26, 1910, ch. 256, 36 Stat. 440, related to fences along international boundary lines to keep out diseased animals.

Effective Date

Pub. L. 97–46, § 2, Sept. 25, 1981, 95 Stat. 953, provided that section 129a of this title was to become effective Sept. 25, 1981, prior to repeal by Pub. L. 107–171, title X, § 10418(a)(1), May 13, 2002, 116 Stat. 507.

§ 132. Transferred

Codification

Section, act May 23, 1908, ch. 192, 35 Stat. 254, which related to inspection of dairy products for export, was transferred to section 693 of this title.

§ 133. Repealed. July 13, 1949, ch. 307, 63 Stat. 410

Section, act July 24, 1946, ch. 592, 60 Stat. 633, related to establishment of a quarantine station on Swan Island.

§§ 134 to 135b. Repealed. Pub. L. 107–171, title X, § 10418(a)(17), (18), May 13, 2002, 116 Stat. 508

Section 134, Pub. L. 87–518, § 1, July 2, 1962, 76 Stat. 129, related to definitions for Pub. L. 87–518.

Section 134a, Pub. L. 87–518, § 2, July 2, 1962, 76 Stat. 129, related to seizure, quarantine, and disposal of livestock or poultry to guard against introduction or dissemination of communicable disease.

Section 134b, Pub. L. 87–518, § 3, July 2, 1962, 76 Stat. 130, related to regulations for clean and sanitary movement of animals.

Section 134c, Pub. L. 87–518, § 4, July 2, 1962, 76 Stat. 130, related to regulations for movement of animals affected or exposed to communicable disease.

Section 134d, Pub. L. 87–518, § 5, July 2, 1962, 76 Stat. 130, related to inspections, seizures, and issuance of warrants.

Section 134e, Pub. L. 87–518, § 6, July 2, 1962, 76 Stat. 131; Pub. L. 97–461, § 8, Jan. 12, 1983, 96 Stat. 2525, related to enforcement provisions.

Section 134f, Pub. L. 87–518, § 11, July 2, 1962, 76 Stat. 132, related to promulgation of regulations.

Section 134g, Pub. L. 87–518, § 12, July 2, 1962, 76 Stat. 132, related to authority in addition to other laws and repeal of inconsistent provisions.

Section 134h, Pub. L. 87–518, § 13, July 2, 1962, 76 Stat. 132, related to separability.

Section 135, Pub. L. 91–239, § 1, May 6, 1970, 84 Stat. 202; Pub. L. 103–465, title IV, § 431(j), Dec. 8, 1994, 108 Stat. 4969, related to the establishment of international animal quarantine station, acceptance of gifts, cooperation with breeders' organizations, and collection of fees.

Section 135a, Pub. L. 91–239, § 2, May 6, 1970, 84 Stat. 202; Pub. L. 97–461, § 9, Jan. 12, 1983, 96 Stat. 2525, related to smuggling penalties.

Section 135b, Pub. L. 91–239, § 3, May 6, 1970, 84 Stat. 202, related to authorization of appropriations.

§ 136. Additional inspection services

The Secretary of Agriculture, in carrying out regulations prohibiting or restricting the entry of materials that may harbor pests, or diseases, is authorized to enter into agreements with operators or owners of vessels or aircraft for the purpose of providing inspection services at points of entry in the United States in addition to the regular or on-call basis currently available in connection with such vessels or aircraft. Any such agreement shall provide for the payment by the operator or owner of an amount determined by the Secretary to be necessary to defray the costs of providing additional service pursuant to such agreement.

(Pub. L. 101–624, title XXV, § 2508, Nov. 28, 1990, 104 Stat. 4069.)

§ 136a. Collection of fees for inspection services

(a) Quarantine and inspection fees

(1) Fees authorized

The Secretary of Agriculture may prescribe and collect fees sufficient—

(A) to cover the cost of providing agricultural quarantine and inspection services in connection with the arrival at a port in the customs territory of the United States, or the preclearance or preinspection at a site outside the customs territory of the United States, of an international passenger, commercial vessel, commercial aircraft, commercial truck, or railroad car;

(B) to cover the cost of administering this subsection; and

(C) through fiscal year 2002, to maintain a reasonable balance in the Agricultural Quarantine Inspection User Fee Account established under paragraph (5).

(2) Limitation

In setting the fees under paragraph (1), the Secretary shall ensure that the amount of the fees is commensurate with the costs of agricultural quarantine and inspection services with respect to the class of persons or entities paying the fees. The costs of the services with respect to passengers as a class includes the costs of related inspections of the aircraft or other vehicle.

(3) Status of fees

Fees collected under this subsection by any person on behalf of the Secretary are held in trust for the United States and shall be remitted to the Secretary in such manner and at such times as the Secretary may prescribe.

(4) Late payment penalties

If a person subject to a fee under this subsection fails to pay the fee when due, the Secretary shall assess a late payment penalty, and the overdue fees shall accrue interest, as required by section 3717 of title 31.

(5) Agricultural quarantine inspection user fee account

(A) Establishment

There is established in the Treasury of the United States a fund, to be known as the "Agricultural Quarantine Inspection User Fee Account", which shall contain all of the fees collected under this subsection and late payment penalties and interest charges collected under paragraph (4) through fiscal year 2002.

(B) Use of account

For each of fiscal years 1996 through 2002, funds in the Agricultural Quarantine Inspection User Fee Account shall be available, in such amounts as are provided in advance in appropriations Acts, to cover the costs associated with the provision of agricultural quarantine and inspection services and the administration of this subsection. Amounts made available under this subparagraph shall be available until expended.

(C) Excess fees

Fees and other amounts collected under this subsection in any of fiscal years 1996 through 2002 in excess of $100,000,000 shall be available for the purposes specified in subparagraph (B) until expended, without further appropriation.

(6) Use of amounts collected after fiscal year 2002

After September 30, 2002, the unobligated balance in the Agricultural Quarantine Inspection User Fee Account and fees and other amounts collected under this subsection shall be credited to the Department of Agriculture accounts that incur the costs associated with the provision of agricultural quarantine and inspection services and the administration of this subsection. The fees and other amounts shall remain available to the Secretary until expended without fiscal year limitation.

(7) Staff years

The number of full-time equivalent positions in the Department of Agriculture attributable to the provision of agricultural quarantine and inspection services and the administration of this subsection shall not be counted toward the limitation on the total number of full-time equivalent positions in all agencies specified in section 5(b) of the Federal Workforce Restructuring Act of 1994 (Public Law 103–226; 5 U.S.C. 3101 note) or other limitation on the total number of full-time equivalent positions.

(b) Omitted

(c) Animal inspection and veterinary diagnostics

(1) Animal inspection

The Secretary may prescribe and collect fees to reimburse the Secretary for the cost of carrying out the provisions of the Federal Animal Quarantine Laws that relate to the importation, entry, and exportation of animals, articles, or means of conveyance.

(2) Veterinary diagnostics

The Secretary may prescribe and collect fees to recover the costs of carrying out the provisions of the Animal Health Protection Act [7 U.S.C. 8301 et seq.] that relate to veterinary diagnostics.

(3) Fees

All fees collected pursuant to this subsection and any late payment penalties or accrued interest collected pursuant to this subsection shall be credited to the accounts that incur the cost and shall remain available until expended without fiscal year limitation.

(4) Liability

Any person for whom an activity related to the importation, entry, or exportation of an animal, article, or means of conveyance or relating to veterinary diagnostics, is performed pursuant to the section, shall be liable for payment of fees assessed. Upon failure to pay such fees when due, the Secretary shall assess a late payment penalty, and such overdue fees shall accrue interest, as required by section 3717 of title 31. All fees, late payment penalties, and accrued interest collected shall be credited to such accounts that incur the costs and shall remain available until expended without fiscal year limitation.

(5) Leins[1]

(A) In general

The Secretary shall have a lien against the animal, article, means of conveyance, or facility for which services have been provided under this section for the fees, any late pay-

[1] So in original. Probably should be "Liens".

ment penalty, and any accrued interest assessed under this subsection.

(B) Other animals, etc.

In the case of any person who fails to make payment when due under this subsection, the Secretary shall have a lien against any animal, article, or means of conveyance thereafter imported, moved in interstate commerce, or attempted to be exported by the person after the date of such failure until the date on which such owner or operator make[2] full payment to the Secretary under this subsection.

(C) Sales of animals, etc.

(i) Authority

The Secretary may, if a person does not pay fees, late payment penalties, or accrued interest on such, after providing reasonable notice of default to such person, sell at public sale after reasonable public notice, or otherwise dispose of, any such animal, article, means of conveyance or facility on which the Secretary has a lien under this paragraph.

(ii) Excess proceeds

If the sale proceeds under clause (i) exceed the fees due, any late payment penalty assessed, any accrued interest on such, and the expenses associated with the sale, such excess shall be paid to the owner of the animal, article, means of conveyance, or facility if such owner submits an application for such excess together with proof of ownership not later than 6 months after the date of such sale. If no such application is made, such excess shall be credited to accounts that incur the costs associated with the fees collected and shall remain available until expended, without fiscal year limitation. The Secretary shall suspend performance of services to persons who have failed to pay fees, late payment penalty, or accrued interest under this section.

(d) Regulations

The Secretary may prescribe such regulations as the Secretary determines necessary to carry out the provisions of this section.

(e) Recovery of amounts owed

An action may be brought for the recovery of fees, late payment penalties, and accrued interest which have not been paid in accordance with this section against any person obligated for payment of such assessments under this section in any United States district court or other United States court for any territory or possession in any jurisdiction in which such person is found or resides or transacts business, and such court shall have jurisdiction to hear and decide such action.

(f) Definitions

(1) Animal quarantine laws

For purposes of this section, the term "animal quarantine laws" means—

(A) section 306 of the Tariff Act of 1930[3] (19 U.S.C. 1306);

(B) section 9 of the Act of August 30, 1890 (21 U.S.C. 101);

(C) the Animal Health Protection Act [7 U.S.C. 8301 et seq.]; or

(D) any other Act administered by the Secretary relating to plant or animal diseases or pests.

(2) Customs territory

For the purposes of subsection (a) of this section, the term "customs territory of the United States" means the 50 States, the District of Columbia, and Puerto Rico.

(3) Person

For the purposes of this section, the term "person" means an individual, corporation, partnership, trust, association, or any other public or private entity, or any officer, employee, or agent thereof.

(4) United States

For the purposes of subsection (b) of this section, the term "United States" means the several States of the United States, the District of Columbia, Guam, the Commonwealth of the Northern Mariana Islands, the Commonwealth of Puerto Rico, the Virgin Islands of the United States, and all other territories and possessions of the United States.

(5) Vessel

For the purposes of subsection (a) of this section, the term "vessel" does not include any ferry.

(Pub. L. 101–624, title XXV, § 2509, Nov. 28, 1990, 104 Stat. 4069; Pub. L. 101–508, title I, § 1203, Nov. 5, 1990, 104 Stat. 1388–11; Pub. L. 102–237, title X, § 1015, Dec. 13, 1991, 105 Stat. 1902; Pub. L. 104–127, title IX, § 917, Apr. 4, 1996, 110 Stat. 1187; Pub. L. 107–171, title X, § 10418(b)(5), May 13, 2002, 116 Stat. 509.)

REFERENCES IN TEXT

The Animal Health Protection Act, referred to in subsecs. (c)(2), (f)(1)(C), is subtitle E (§§ 10401–10418) of title X of Pub. L. 107–171, May 13, 2002, 116 Stat. 494, which is classified principally to chapter 109 (§ 8301 et seq.) of Title 7, Agriculture. For complete classification of this Act to the Code, see Short Title note set out under section 8301 of Title 7 and Tables.

Section 306 of the Tariff Act of 1930 (19 U.S.C. 1306), referred to in subsec. (f)(1)(A), was repealed by Pub. L. 107–171, title X, § 10418(a)(5), May 13, 2002, 116 Stat. 507.

CODIFICATION

Section is comprised of section 2509 of Pub. L. 101–624. Subsec. (b) and another subsec. (c)(2) of section 2509 of Pub. L. 101–624 amended section 7759(f) of Title 7, Agriculture, and section 114a of this title, respectively.

AMENDMENTS

2002—Subsec. (c)(2). Pub. L. 107–171, § 10418(b)(5)(A), added par. (2) relating to veterinary diagnostics.

Subsec. (f)(1)(B) to (O). Pub. L. 107–171, § 10418(b)(5)(B), added subpars. (B) to (D) and struck out former subpars. (B) to (O), which read as follows:

"(B) sections 6 through 10 of the Act of August 30, 1890 (26 Stat. 416, chapter 839; 21 U.S.C. 101–105);

"(C) section 2 of the Act of February 2, 1903 (32 Stat. 792, chapter 349; 21 U.S.C. 111);

[2] So in original. Probably should be "makes".

[3] See References in Text note below.

"(D) the Act of May 29, 1884 (23 Stat. 32, chapter 60; 21 U.S.C. 112 to 114a-1, 115, 117-119, and 130) (commonly known as the 'Animal Industry Act');

"(E) the Act of February 28, 1947 (61 Stat. 7, chapter 8; 21 U.S.C. 114b, 114c, and 114d-1);

"(F) the Act of June 16, 1948 (62 Stat. 458, chapter 477; 21 U.S.C. 114e and 114f);

"(G) Public Law 87-209 (21 U.S.C. 114g and 114h);

"(H) the Act of May 31, 1920 (41 Stat. 699, chapter 217; 21 U.S.C. 116);

"(I) the Act of February 2, 1903 (32 Stat. 791, chapter 349; 21 U.S.C. 112 and 120-122) (commonly known as the 'Cattle Contagious Diseases Act of 1903');

"(J) the Act of March 3, 1905 (33 Stat. 1264, chapter 1496; 21 U.S.C. 123-127) (commonly known as the 'Cattle Contagious Diseases Act of 1905');

"(K) the matter under the heading 'Bureau of Animal Industry' of the Act of June 30, 1914 (38 Stat. 419, chapter 131; 21 U.S.C. 128);

"(L) section 101 of Public Law 92-73 (21 U.S.C. 129);

"(M) the matter under the heading 'Miscellaneous' of the Act of May 26, 1910 (36 Stat. 440, chapter 256; 21 U.S.C. 131);

"(N) sections 1 through 6 and 11 through 13 of Public Law 87-518 (21 U.S.C. 134-134h); or

"(O) any other Act administered by the Secretary relating to plant or animal diseases or pests, other than the first section of Public Law 91-239 (21 U.S.C. 135)."

1996—Subsec. (a). Pub. L. 104-127 added subsec. (a) and struck out heading and text of former subsec. (a) which consisted of pars. (1) to (4) relating to quarantine, inspection, and transportation fees.

1991—Subsec. (a)(1). Pub. L. 102-237, §1015(1), designated existing provisions as subpar. (A), realigned margin, added heading, and added subpars. (B) to (D).

Subsec. (a)(3)(B)(ii). Pub. L. 102-237, §1015(2), added cl. (ii) and struck out former cl. (ii) which read as follows: "The Secretary of Treasury shall use the Account to provide reimbursements to any appropriations accounts that incur the costs associated with the services authorized in paragraph (1). Any such reimbursement shall be subject to appropriations under clause (v)."

Subsec. (a)(4). Pub. L. 102-237, §1015(3), substituted "Subject to the limits set forth in paragraph (1), the" for "The".

1990—Subsec. (a)(1). Pub. L. 101-508, §1203(1), substituted "an international passenger, commercial vessel, commercial aircraft, commercial truck, or railroad car," for "a commercial vessel, commercial aircraft, commercial truck, or railroad car,".

Subsec. (a)(3)(B)(ii). Pub. L. 101-508, §1203(2)(A), inserted at end "Any such reimbursement shall be subject to appropriations under clause (v)."

Subsec. (a)(3)(B)(v). Pub. L. 101-508, §1203(2)(B), added cl. (v).

EFFECTIVE DATE OF 1990 AMENDMENT

Amendment by Pub. L. 101-508 effective Nov. 29, 1990, see section 1301 of Pub. L. 101-508, set out as an Effective Date note under section 940d of Title 7, Agriculture.

REPORT ON AGRICULTURAL QUARANTINE INSPECTION FUND

Pub. L. 104-66, title I, §1012(c), Dec. 21, 1995, 109 Stat. 712, provided that: "The Secretary of Agriculture shall not be required to submit a report to the appropriate committees of Congress on the status of the Agricultural Quarantine Inspection fund more frequently than annually."

SUBCHAPTER IV—IMPORTATION OF MILK AND CREAM

FEDERAL FOOD, DRUG, AND COSMETIC ACT

By virtue of act June 25, 1938, ch. 675, §902(c), 52 Stat. 1059 [section 392(b) of this title], nothing contained in section 301 et seq. of this title shall be construed as in any way affecting, modifying, repealing, or superseding the provisions of this subchapter.

§141. Prohibition of importation without permit

On and after May 16, 1927, the importation into the United States of milk and cream is prohibited unless the person by whom such milk or cream is shipped or transported into the United States holds a valid permit from the Secretary of Health and Human Services.

(Feb. 15, 1927, ch. 155, §1, 44 Stat. 1101; 1940 Reorg. Plan No. IV, §12, eff. June 30, 1940, 5 F.R. 2421, 54 Stat. 1237; 1953 Reorg. Plan No. 1, §5, eff. Apr. 11, 1953, 18 F.R. 2053, 67 Stat. 631; Pub. L. 96-88, title V, §509(b), Oct. 17, 1979, 93 Stat. 695.)

CHANGE OF NAME

"Secretary of Health and Human Services" substituted in text for "Secretary of Health, Education, and Welfare" pursuant to section 509(b) of Pub. L. 96-88, which is classified to section 3508(b) of Title 20, Education.

SHORT TITLE

Act July 12, 1943, ch. 221, title II, 57 Stat. 499, provided in part that act Feb. 15, 1927, which is classified to this subchapter, may be cited as "Import Milk Act".

TRANSFER OF FUNCTIONS

For transfer of functions of Federal Security Administrator to Secretary of Health, Education, and Welfare [now Health and Human Services], and of Food and Drug Administration to Federal Security Agency, see notes set out under section 321 of this title.

§142. Milk or cream when unfit for importation

Milk or cream shall be considered unfit for importation (1) when all cows producing such milk or cream are not healthy and a physical examination of all such cows has not been made within one year previous to such milk being offered for importation; (2) when such milk or cream, if raw, is not produced from cows which have passed a tuberculin test applied by a duly authorized official veterinarian of the United States, or of the country in which such milk or cream is produced, within one year previous to the time of the importation, showing that such cows are free from tuberculosis; (3) when the sanitary conditions of the dairy farm or plant in which such milk or cream is produced or handled do not score at least fifty points out of one hundred points according to the methods for scoring as provided by the score cards used by the Bureau of Dairy Industry of the United States Department of Agriculture at the time such dairy farms or plants are scored; (4) in the case of raw milk if the number of bacteria per cubic centimeter exceeds three hundred thousand and in the case of raw cream seven hundred and fifty thousand, in the case of pasteurized milk if the number of bacteria per cubic centimeter exceeds one hundred thousand, and in the case of pasteurized cream five hundred thousand; (5) when the temperature of milk or cream at the time of importation exceeds fifty degrees Fahrenheit.

(Feb. 15, 1927, ch. 155, §2, 44 Stat. 1101.)

TRANSFER OF FUNCTIONS

Agricultural Research Service became the successor to functions of Bureau of Dairy Industry under Secretary of Agriculture's Memorandum 1320, Supplement 4, Nov. 2, 1953.

§ 143. Inspection; certified statement in lieu thereof; waiver of requirements of section 142; regulations; suspension and revocation of permits

The Secretary of Health and Human Services shall cause such inspections to be made as are necessary to insure that milk and cream are so produced and handled as to comply with the provisions of section 142 of this title, and in all cases when he finds that such milk and/or cream is produced and handled so as not to be unfit for importation under clauses 1, 2, and 3 of section 142 of this title, he shall issue to persons making application therefor permits to ship milk and/or cream into the United States: *Provided*, That in lieu of the inspections to be made by or under the direction of the Secretary he may, in his discretion, accept a duly certified statement signed by a duly accredited official of an authorized department of any foreign government and/or of any State of the United States or any municipality thereof that the provisions in clauses 1, 2, and 3 of section 142 of this title have been complied with. Such certificate of the accredited official of an authorized department of any foreign government shall be in the form prescribed by the Secretary, who is authorized and directed to prescribe such form as well as rules and regulations regulating the issuance of permits to import milk or cream into the United States.

The Secretary is authorized, in his discretion, to waive the requirement of clause 4 of section 142 of this title when issuing permits to operators of condenseries in which milk and/or cream is used when sterilization of the milk and/or cream is a necessary process: *Provided, however*, That no milk and/or cream shall be imported whose bacterial count per cubic centimeter in any event exceeds one million two hundred thousand: *Provided, further*, That such requirements shall not be waived unless the farm producing such milk to be imported is within a radius of fifteen miles of the condensery in which it is to be processed: *Provided further*, That if milk and/or cream imported when the requirements of clause 4 of section 142 of this title, have been so waived, is sold, used, or disposed of in its raw state or otherwise than as condensed milk by any person, the permit shall be revoked and the importer shall be subject to fine, imprisonment, or other penalty prescribed by this subchapter.

The Secretary is directed to waive the requirements of clauses 2 and 5 of section 142 of this title insofar as the same relate to milk when issuing permits to operators of, or to producers for delivery to, creameries and condensing plants in the United States within twenty miles of the point of production of the milk, and who import no raw milk except for pasteurization or condensing: *Provided*, That if milk imported when the requirements of clauses 2 and 5 of section 142 of this title have been so waived is sold, used, or disposed of in its raw state, or otherwise than as pasteurized, condensed, or evaporated milk by any person, the permit shall be revoked and the importer shall be subjected to fine, imprisonment, or other penalty prescribed by this subchapter.

The Secretary is authorized and directed to make and enforce such regulations as may in his judgment be necessary to carry out the purpose of this subchapter for the handling of milk and cream, for the inspection of milk, cream, cows, barns, and other facilities used in the production and handling of milk and/or cream and the handling, keeping, transporting, and importing of milk and/or cream: *Provided, however*, That unless and until the Secretary shall provide for inspections to ascertain that clauses 1, 2, and 3 of section 142 of this title have been complied with, the Secretary shall issue temporary permits to any applicants therefor to ship or transport milk and/or cream into the United States.

The Secretary is authorized to suspend or revoke any permit for the shipment of milk or cream into the United States when he shall find that the holder thereof has failed to comply with the provisions of or has violated this subchapter or any of the regulations made hereunder, or that the milk and/or cream brought or shipped by the holder of such permit into the United States is not produced and handled in conformity with, or that the quality thereof does not conform to, all of the provisions of section 142 of this title.

(Feb. 15, 1927, ch. 155, § 3, 44 Stat. 1102; 1940 Reorg. Plan No. IV, § 12, eff. June 30, 1940, 5 F.R. 2421, 54 Stat. 1237; 1953 Reorg. Plan No. 1, § 5, eff. Apr. 11, 1953, 18 F.R. 2053, 67 Stat. 631; Pub. L. 96–88, title V, § 509(b), Oct. 17, 1979, 93 Stat. 695.)

CHANGE OF NAME

"Secretary of Health and Human Services" substituted in text for "Secretary of Health, Education, and Welfare" pursuant to section 509(b) of Pub. L. 96–88, which is classified to section 3508(b) of Title 20, Education.

TRANSFER OF FUNCTIONS

For transfer of functions of Federal Security Administrator to Secretary of Health, Education, and Welfare [now Health and Human Services], and of Food and Drug Administration to Federal Security Agency, see notes set out under section 321 of this title.

§ 144. Unlawful receiving of imported milk or cream

It shall be unlawful for any person in the United States to receive milk or cream imported into the United States unless the importation is in accordance with the provisions of this subchapter.

(Feb. 15, 1927, ch. 155, § 4, 44 Stat. 1103.)

§ 145. Penalties

Any person who knowingly violates any provision of this subchapter shall, in addition to all other penalties prescribed by law, be punished by a fine of not less than $50 nor more than $2,000, or by imprisonment for not more than one year, or by both such fine and imprisonment.

(Feb. 15, 1927, ch. 155, § 5, 44 Stat. 1103.)

§ 146. Authorization of appropriations

There is authorized to be appropriated, out of any moneys in the Treasury not otherwise appropriated, the sum of $50,000 per annum, to enable the Secretary of Health and Human Services to carry out the provisions of this subchapter.

(Feb. 15, 1927, ch. 155, §6, 44 Stat. 1103; 1940 Reorg. Plan No. IV, §12, eff. June 30, 1940, 5 F.R. 2421, 54 Stat. 1237; 1953 Reorg. Plan No. 1, §5, eff. Apr. 11, 1953, 18 F.R. 2053, 67 Stat. 631; Pub. L. 96–88, title V, §509(b), Oct. 17, 1979, 93 Stat. 695.)

CHANGE OF NAME

"Secretary of Health and Human Services" substituted in text for "Secretary of Health, Education, and Welfare" pursuant to section 509(b) of Pub. L. 96–88, which is classified to section 3508(b) of Title 20, Education.

TRANSFER OF FUNCTIONS

For transfer of functions of Federal Security Administrator to Secretary of Health, Education, and Welfare [now Health and Human Services], and of Food and Drug Administration to Federal Security Agency, see Transfer of Functions notes set out under section 321 of this title.

§147. Repeal of inconsistent laws

Any laws or parts of laws inconsistent with this subchapter are repealed.

(Feb. 15, 1927, ch. 155, §7, 44 Stat. 1103.)

§148. Powers of State with respect to milk or cream lawfully imported

Nothing in this subchapter is intended nor shall be construed to affect the powers of any State, or any political subdivision thereof, to regulate the shipment of milk or cream into, or the handling, sale, or other disposition of milk or cream in, such State or political subdivision after the milk and/or cream shall have been lawfully imported under the provisions of this subchapter.

(Feb. 15, 1927, ch. 155, §8, 44 Stat. 1103.)

§149. Definitions

When used in this subchapter—

(a) The term "person" means an individual, partnership, association, or corporation.

(b) The term "United States" means the fifty States and the District of Columbia.

(Feb. 15, 1927, ch. 155, §9, 44 Stat. 1103; Pub. L. 86–70, §19, June 25, 1959, 73 Stat. 145; Pub. L. 86–624, §15, July 12, 1960, 74 Stat. 415.)

AMENDMENTS

1960—Subsec. (b). Pub. L. 86–624 substituted "means the fifty States and the District of Columbia" for "means continental United States, including Alaska".

1959—Subsec. (b). Pub. L. 86–70 inserted ", including Alaska" after "continental United States".

CHAPTER 5—VIRUSES, SERUMS, TOXINS, ANTITOXINS, AND ANALOGOUS PRODUCTS

Sec.

FEDERAL FOOD, DRUG, AND COSMETIC ACT

By virtue of act June 25, 1938, ch. 675, §902(c), 52 Stat. 1059 [section 392(b) of this title], nothing contained in section 301 et seq. of this title shall be construed as in any way affecting, modifying, repealing, or superseding the provisions of this chapter.

§151. Preparation and sale of worthless or harmful products for domestic animals prohibited; preparation to be in compliance with rules at licensed establishments

It shall be unlawful for any person, firm, or corporation to prepare, sell, barter, or exchange in the District of Columbia, or in the Territories, or in any place under the jurisdiction of the United States, or to ship or deliver for shipment in or from the United States, the District of Columbia, any territory of the United States, or any place under the jurisdiction of the United States, any worthless, contaminated, dangerous, or harmful virus, serum, toxin, or analogous product intended for use in the treatment of domestic animals, and no person, firm, or corporation shall prepare, sell, barter, exchange, or ship as aforesaid any virus, serum, toxin, or analogous product manufactured within the United States and intended for use in the treatment of domestic animals, unless and until the said virus, serum, toxin, or analogous product shall have been prepared, under and in compliance with regulations prescribed by the Secretary of Agriculture, at an establishment holding an unsuspended and unrevoked license issued by the Secretary of Agriculture as hereinafter authorized.

(Mar. 4, 1913, ch. 145, §1 (part), 37 Stat. 832; Pub. L. 99–198, title XVII, §1768(a), Dec. 23, 1985, 99 Stat. 1654.)

CODIFICATION

The sections of this chapter are comprised of the sentences of the eighth paragraph under the heading "Bureau of Animal Industry," in the Department of Agriculture Appropriation Act, 1914, as amended.

Another section 1768 of Pub. L. 99–198, cited as a credit to this section, amended section 136y of Title 7, Agriculture.

AMENDMENTS

1985—Pub. L. 99–198 substituted "in or from the United States, the District of Columbia, any territory of the United States, or any place under the jurisdiction of the United States" for "from one State or Territory or the District of Columbia to any other State or Territory or the District of Columbia".

EFFECTIVE DATE OF 1985 AMENDMENT

Section 1768(f) of Pub. L. 99–198 provided that:

"(1) Except as provided in paragraph (2), the amendments made by this section [enacting sections 154a and 159 of this title and amending this section and sections 154 and 157 of this title] shall become effective on the date of enactment of this Act [Dec. 23, 1985].

"(2)(A) Subject to subparagraphs (B) through (D), in the case of a person, firm, or corporation preparing, selling, bartering, exchanging, or shipping a virus, serum, toxin, or analogous product during the 12-month period ending on the date of enactment of this Act [Dec. 23, 1985] solely for intrastate commerce or for exportation, such product shall not after such date of enactment, as a result of its not having been licensed or produced in a licensed establishment, be considered in violation of the eighth paragraph of the matter under the heading 'BUREAU OF ANIMAL INDUSTRY' of the Act entitled 'An Act making appropriations for the Department of Agriculture for the fiscal year ending June thirtieth, nineteen hundred and fourteen', approved March 14, 1913 (as amended by this section) [this chapter], until the first day of the 49th month following the date of enactment of this Act.

"(B) The exemption granted by subparagraph (A) may be extended by the Secretary of Agriculture for a period up to 12 months in an individual case on a showing by a person, firm, or corporation of good cause and a good faith effort to comply with such eighth paragraph with due diligence.

"(C) The exemption granted by subparagraph (A) must be claimed by the person, firm, or corporation preparing such product by the first day of the 13th month following the date of enactment of this Act [Dec. 23, 1985], in the form and manner prescribed by the Secretary, unless the Secretary grants an extension of the time to claim such exemption in an individual case for good cause shown.

"(D) On the issuance by the Secretary of a license to such person, firm, or corporation for such product prior to the first day of the 49th month following the date of enactment of this Act [Dec. 23, 1985], or the end of an extension of the exemption granted by the Secretary, the exemption granted by subparagraph (A) shall terminate with respect to such product."

SHORT TITLE

Act Mar. 4, 1913, ch. 145, §1 [part], 37 Stat. 832, which is classified to this chapter, is popularly known as the "Virus-Serum-Toxin Act".

TRANSFER OF FUNCTIONS

For transfer of functions of the Secretary of Agriculture relating to agricultural import and entry inspection activities under this chapter to the Secretary of Homeland Security, and for treatment of related references, see sections 231, 551(d), 552(d), and 557 of Title 6, Domestic Security, and the Department of Homeland Security Reorganization Plan of November 25, 2002, as modified, set out as a note under section 542 of Title 6.

APPROPRIATIONS

An appropriation of $25,000 was made by act Mar. 4, 1913, for the purpose of carrying into effect these provisions. The appropriation for the fiscal year 1926 was by act Feb. 10, 1925, ch. 200, 43 Stat. 827.

§ 152. Importation regulated and prohibited

The importation into the United States of any virus, serum, toxin, or analogous product for use in the treatment of domestic animals, and the importation of any worthless, contaminated, dangerous, or harmful virus, serum, toxin, or analogous product for use in the treatment of domestic animals, is prohibited without (1) a permit from the Secretary of Agriculture, or (2) in the case of an article originating in Canada, such permit or, in lieu of such permit, such certification by Canada as may be prescribed by the Secretary of Agriculture.

(Mar. 4, 1913, ch. 145, §1 (part), 37 Stat. 832; Pub. L. 100–449, title III, §301(d), Sept. 28, 1988, 102 Stat. 1868.)

CODIFICATION

See note set out under section 151 of this title.

AMENDMENTS

1988—Pub. L. 100–449 amended section generally. Prior to amendment, section read as follows: "The importation into the United States, without a permit from the Secretary of Agriculture, of any virus, serum, toxin, or analogous product for use in the treatment of domestic animals, and the importation of any worthless, contaminated, dangerous, or harmful virus, serum, toxin, or analogous product for use in the treatment of domestic animals, are prohibited."

EFFECTIVE AND TERMINATION DATES OF 1988 AMENDMENT

Amendment by Pub. L. 100–449 effective on the date the United States-Canada Free-Trade Agreement enters into force (Jan. 1, 1989), and to cease to have effect on the date the Agreement ceases to be in force, see section 501(a), (c) of Pub. L. 100–449, set out in a note under section 2112 of Title 19, Customs Duties.

TRANSFER OF FUNCTIONS

For transfer of functions of the Secretary of Agriculture relating to agricultural import and entry inspection activities under this chapter to the Secretary of Homeland Security, and for treatment of related references, see sections 231, 551(d), 552(d), and 557 of Title 6, Domestic Security, and the Department of Homeland Security Reorganization Plan of November 25, 2002, as modified, set out as a note under section 542 of Title 6.

§ 153. Inspection of imports; denial of entry and destruction

The Secretary of Agriculture is authorized to cause the Bureau of Animal Industry to examine and inspect all viruses, serums, toxins, and analogous products, for use in the treatment of domestic animals, which are being imported or offered for importation into the United States, to determine whether such viruses, serums, toxins, and analogous products are worthless, contaminated, dangerous, or harmful, and if it shall appear that any such virus, serum, toxin, or analogous product, for use in the treatment of domestic animals, is worthless, contaminated, dangerous, or harmful, the same shall be denied entry and shall be destroyed or returned at the expense of the owner or importer.

(Mar. 4, 1913, ch. 145, §1 (part), 37 Stat. 832.)

CODIFICATION

See note set out under section 151 of this title.

TRANSFER OF FUNCTIONS

For transfer of functions of the Secretary of Agriculture relating to agricultural import and entry inspection activities under this chapter to the Secretary of Homeland Security, and for treatment of related references, see sections 231, 551(d), 552(d), and 557 of Title 6, Domestic Security, and the Department of Homeland Security Reorganization Plan of November 25, 2002, as modified, set out as a note under section 542 of Title 6.

§ 154. Regulations for preparation and sale; licenses

The Secretary of Agriculture is authorized to make and promulgate from time to time such rules and regulations as may be necessary to prevent the preparation, sale, barter, exchange, or shipment as aforesaid of any worthless, contaminated, dangerous, or harmful virus, serum, toxin, or analogous product for use in the treatment of domestic animals, or otherwise to carry out this chapter, and to issue, suspend, and revoke licenses for the maintenance of establishments for the preparation of viruses, serums, toxins, and analogous products, for use in the treatment of domestic animals, intended for sale, barter, exchange, or shipment as aforesaid.

(Mar. 4, 1913, ch. 145, §1 (part), 37 Stat. 832; Pub. L. 99–198, title XVII, §1768(b), Dec. 23, 1985, 99 Stat. 1654.)

CODIFICATION

See note set out under section 151 of this title.

Another section 1768 of Pub. L. 99–198, cited as a credit to this section, amended section 136y of Title 7, Agriculture.

AMENDMENTS

1985—Pub. L. 99–198 inserted "or otherwise to carry out this chapter," after "domestic animals,".

EFFECTIVE DATE OF 1985 AMENDMENT

Amendment by Pub. L. 99–198 effective Dec. 23, 1985, except as otherwise provided, see section 1768(f) of Pub. L. 99–198, set out as a note under section 151 of this title.

TRANSFER OF FUNCTIONS

For transfer of functions of the Secretary of Agriculture relating to agricultural import and entry inspection activities under this chapter to the Secretary of Homeland Security, and for treatment of related references, see sections 231, 551(d), 552(d), and 557 of Title 6, Domestic Security, and the Department of Homeland Security Reorganization Plan of November 25, 2002, as modified, set out as a note under section 542 of Title 6.

§ 154a. Special licenses for special circumstances; expedited procedure; conditions; exemptions; criteria

In order to meet an emergency condition, limited market or local situation, or other special circumstance (including production solely for intrastate use under a State-operated program), the Secretary may issue a special license under an expedited procedure on such conditions as are necessary to assure purity, safety, and a reasonable expectation of efficacy. The Secretary shall exempt by regulation from the requirement of preparation pursuant to an unsuspended and unrevoked license any virus, serum, toxin, or analogous product prepared by any person, firm, or corporation—

(1) solely for administration to animals of such person, firm, or corporation;

(2) solely for administration to animals under a veterinarian-client-patient relationship in the course of the State licensed professional practice of veterinary medicine by such person, firm, or corporation; or

(3) solely for distribution within the State of production pursuant to a license granted by such State under a program determined by the Secretary to meet criteria under which the State—

(A) may license virus, serum, toxin, and analogous products and establishments that produce such products;

(B) may review the purity, safety, potency, and efficacy of such products prior to licensure;

(C) may review product test results to assure compliance with applicable standards for purity, safety, and potency, prior to release to the market;

(D) may deal effectively with violations of State law regulating virus, serum, toxin, and analogous products; and

(E) exercises the authority referred to in subclauses (A) through (D) consistent with the intent of this chapter of prohibiting the preparation, sale, barter, exchange, or shipment of worthless, contaminated, dangerous, or harmful virus, serum, toxin, or analogous products.

(Mar. 4, 1913, ch. 145, §1 [part], as added Pub. L. 99–198, title XVII, §1768(c), Dec. 23, 1985, 99 Stat. 1654.)

CODIFICATION

See note set out under section 151 of this title.

Another section 1768 of Pub. L. 99–198, cited as a credit to this section, amended section 136y of Title 7, Agriculture.

EFFECTIVE DATE

Section effective Dec. 23, 1985, except as otherwise provided, see section 1768(f) of Pub. L. 99–198, set out as an Effective Date of 1985 Amendment note under section 151 of this title.

TRANSFER OF FUNCTIONS

For transfer of functions of the Secretary of Agriculture relating to agricultural import and entry inspection activities under this chapter to the Secretary of Homeland Security, and for treatment of related references, see sections 231, 551(d), 552(d), and 557 of Title 6, Domestic Security, and the Department of Homeland Security Reorganization Plan of November 25, 2002, as modified, set out as a note under section 542 of Title 6.

§ 155. Permits for importation

The Secretary of Agriculture is authorized to issue permits for the importation into the United States of viruses, serums, toxins, and analogous products, for use in the treatment of domestic animals, which are not worthless, contaminated, dangerous, or harmful.

(Mar. 4, 1913, ch. 145, §1 (part), 37 Stat. 833.)

CODIFICATION

See note set out under section 151 of this title.

TRANSFER OF FUNCTIONS

For transfer of functions of the Secretary of Agriculture relating to agricultural import and entry inspection activities under this chapter to the Secretary of Homeland Security, and for treatment of related references, see sections 231, 551(d), 552(d), and 557 of Title 6, Domestic Security, and the Department of Homeland Security Reorganization Plan of November 25, 2002, as modified, set out as a note under section 542 of Title 6.

§ 156. Licenses conditioned on permitting inspection; suspension of licenses

All licenses issued under authority of this chapter to establishments where such viruses, serums, toxins, or analogous products are prepared for sale, barter, exchange, or shipment as aforesaid, shall be issued on condition that the licensee shall permit the inspection of such establishments and of such products and their preparation; and the Secretary of Agriculture may suspend or revoke any permit or license issued under authority of said chapter, after opportunity for hearing has been granted the licensee or importer, when the Secretary of Agriculture is satisfied that such license or permit is being used to facilitate or effect the preparation, sale, barter, exchange, or shipment as aforesaid, or the importation into the United States of any worthless, contaminated, dangerous, or harmful virus, serum, toxin, or analogous product for use in the treatment of domestic animals.

(Mar. 4, 1913, ch. 145, §1 (part), 37 Stat. 833.)

REFERENCES IN TEXT

This chapter, referred to in text, was in the original "this Act", meaning act Mar. 4, 1913, ch. 145, 37 Stat. 828, which enacted this chapter, sections 155 and 393 of Title 7, Agriculture, section 316 of Title 15, Commerce and Trade, sections 501, 502, 512, 558, and 560 of Title 16, Conservation, and section 630 of former Title 31, Money and Finance, and amended section 83 of former Title 5, Executive Departments and Government Officers and Employees, and sections 518 and 673 of Title 16.

Section 316 of Title 15 was omitted from the Code as superseded by section 5701 et seq. of Title 5, Government Organization and Employees. Section 630 of former Title 31 was repealed by act Sept. 12, 1950, ch. 946, title III, §301(64), 64 Stat. 842. Section 83 of former Title 5 was repealed and reenacted as section 5946 of Title 5 by Pub. L. 89–554, Sept. 6, 1966, 80 Stat. 514. For complete classification of act Mar. 4, 1913, to the Code, see Tables.

CODIFICATION

See note set out under section 151 of this title.

TRANSFER OF FUNCTIONS

For transfer of functions of the Secretary of Agriculture relating to agricultural import and entry inspection activities under this chapter to the Secretary of Homeland Security, and for treatment of related references, see sections 231, 551(d), 552(d), and 557 of Title 6, Domestic Security, and the Department of Homeland Security Reorganization Plan of November 25, 2002, as modified, set out as a note under section 542 of Title 6.

§157. Inspection

Any officer, agent, or employee of the Department of Agriculture duly authorized by the Secretary of Agriculture for the purpose may, at any hour during the daytime or nighttime, enter and inspect any establishment where any virus, serum, toxin, or analogous product for use in the treatment of domestic animals is prepared for sale, barter, exchange, or shipment as aforesaid.

(Mar. 4, 1913, ch. 145, §1 (part), 37 Stat. 833; Pub. L. 99–198, title XVII, §1768(d), Dec. 23, 1985, 99 Stat. 1655.)

CODIFICATION

See note set out under section 151 of this title.

Another section 1768 of Pub. L. 99–198, cited as a credit to this section, amended section 136y of Title 7, Agriculture.

AMENDMENTS

1985—Pub. L. 99–198 struck out "licensed under this chapter" after "enter and inspect any establishment".

EFFECTIVE DATE OF 1985 AMENDMENT

Amendment by Pub. L. 99–198 effective Dec. 23, 1985, except as otherwise provided, see section 1768(f) of Pub. L. 99–198, set out as a note under section 151 of this title.

TRANSFER OF FUNCTIONS

For transfer of functions of the Secretary of Agriculture relating to agricultural import and entry inspection activities under this chapter to the Secretary of Homeland Security, and for treatment of related references, see sections 231, 551(d), 552(d), and 557 of Title 6, Domestic Security, and the Department of Homeland Security Reorganization Plan of November 25, 2002, as modified, set out as a note under section 542 of Title 6.

§158. Offenses; punishment

Any person, firm, or corporation who shall violate any of the provisions of this chapter shall be deemed guilty of a misdemeanor, and shall, upon conviction, be punished by a fine of not exceeding $1,000 or by imprisonment not exceeding one year, or by both such fine and imprisonment, in the discretion of the court.

(Mar. 4, 1913, ch. 145, §1 (part), 37 Stat. 833.)

REFERENCES IN TEXT

For explanation of "this chapter", referred to in text, see References in Text note set out under section 156 of this title.

CODIFICATION

See note set out under section 151 of this title.

§159. Enforcement; penalties applicable; Congressional findings

The procedures of sections 672, 673, and 674 of this title (relating to detentions, seizures and condemnations, and injunctions, respectively) shall apply to the enforcement of this chapter with respect to any product prepared, sold, bartered, exchanged, or shipped in violation of this chapter or a regulation promulgated under this chapter. The provisions (including penalties) of section 675 of this title shall apply to the performance of official duties under this chapter. Congress finds that (i) the products and activities that are regulated under this chapter are either in interstate or foreign commerce or substantially affect such commerce or the free flow thereof, and (ii) regulation of the products and activities as provided in this chapter is necessary to prevent and eliminate burdens on such commerce and to effectively regulate such commerce.

(Mar. 4, 1913, ch. 145, §1 (part), as added Pub. L. 99–198, title XVII, §1768(e), Dec. 23, 1985, 99 Stat. 1655.)

CODIFICATION

See note set out under section 151 of this title.

Another section 1768 of Pub. L. 99–198, cited as a credit to this section, amended section 136y of Title 7, Agriculture.

EFFECTIVE DATE

Section effective Dec. 23, 1985, except as otherwise provided, see section 1768(f) of Pub. L. 99–198, set out as an Effective Date of 1985 Amendment note under section 151 of this title.

CHAPTER 5A—BUREAU OF NARCOTICS

§§161 to 165. Omitted

CODIFICATION

Section 161, acts June 14, 1930, ch. 488, §1, 46 Stat. 585; Oct. 15, 1949, ch. 695, §6(a), 63 Stat. 881, established a Bureau of Narcotics in the Department of the Treasury and provided for appointment of a Commissioner of Narcotics for the Bureau with duty of making an annual report to Congress.

Section 162, acts June 14, 1930, ch. 488, § 2, 46 Stat. 585; June 26, 1930, ch. 623, § 1, 46 Stat. 819; Oct. 27, 1970, Pub. L. 91–513, title III, § 1101(a)(4), 84 Stat. 1291, provided for appointment and compensation of a deputy commissioner and other personnel for the Bureau of Narcotics, required the deputy to be an acting Commissioner during absence or disability of the Commissioner or a vacancy in the office, and authorized designation of a member of the Treasury Department as an acting Commissioner in event there is no Commissioner or deputy commissioner.

Section 163, act Mar. 3, 1927, ch. 348, § 4(a), 44 Stat. 1382, provided for transfer of control of narcotic drugs to the Secretary of the Treasury from the Commissioner of Internal Revenue and his assistants, agents, and inspectors.

Section 164, acts June 14, 1930, ch. 488, § 3, 46 Stat. 586; June 26, 1930, ch. 623, § 2, 46 Stat. 819; Ex. Ord. No. 6639, Mar. 10, 1934, abolished the Federal Narcotics Control Board and transferred powers of such Board to the Commissioner of Narcotics, authorized the Secretary of the Treasury to confer or impose his duties under section 163 of this title upon the Commissioner or other personnel of the Bureau of Narcotics, continued in effect orders, rules, and regulations in existence on July 1, 1930, until modified, superseded, or repealed by the Commissioner, with approval of the Secretary of the Treasury, and provided for determination before such Bureau of Narcotics of proceedings, investigations, and other matters pending on July 1, 1930 before Bureau of Prohibition or Federal Narcotics Control Board respecting narcotic drug law administration or enforcement. Bureau of Prohibition personnel, records, property, and unexpended balances of appropriations were previously transferred to Bureau of Narcotics as were powers of the Attorney General respecting the Bureau of Prohibition to the Commissioner of Internal Revenue.

Section 165, act June 14, 1930, ch. 488, § 5, 46 Stat. 587, provided for review of decisions of Commissioner of Narcotics by the Secretary of the Treasury.

Transfer of Functions

Functions of the Secretary of the Treasury administered through or respecting the Bureau of Narcotics and all functions of the Bureau, the Commissioner of Narcotics, and the officers, employees and agencies of the Bureau were transferred to the Attorney General and the Bureau and the office of Commissioner of Narcotics were abolished by Reorg. Plan No. 1 of 1968, eff. Apr. 8, 1968, 33 F.R. 5611, 82 Stat. 1367, set out in the Appendix to Title 5, Government Organization and Employees. All positions, personnel, property, records, and unexpended balances of appropriations, allocations, and other funds of the Bureau and the Treasury Department, in connection with functions transferred under this reorganization plan, were transferred to the Justice Department.

The Bureau of Narcotics and Dangerous Drugs, including the office of Director thereof, in the Department of Justice was abolished by Reorg. Plan No. 2 of 1973, eff. July 1, 1973, 38 F.R. 15932, 87 Stat. 1091, set out in the Appendix to Title 5, Government Organization and Employees. Reorg. Plan No. 2 of 1973 also created in the Department of Justice a single, comprehensive agency for the enforcement of drug laws to be known as the Drug Enforcement Administration, empowered the Attorney General to authorize the performance by officers, employees, and agencies of the Department of functions transferred to him, and directed the Attorney General to coordinate all drug law enforcement functions to assure maximum cooperation between the Drug Enforcement Administration, the Federal Bureau of Investigation, and the other units of the Department of Justice involved in drug law enforcement.

CHAPTER 6—NARCOTIC DRUGS

Executive Order No. 10302

Ex. Ord. No. 10302, Nov. 5, 1951, 16 F.R. 11257, formerly set out as a note preceding section 171, which established the Interdepartmental Committee on Narcotics, was revoked by Ex. Ord. No. 11529, Apr. 24, 1970, 35 F.R. 6697.

IMPORTATION OR EXPORTATION

§§ 171 to 174. Repealed. Pub. L. 91–513, title III, § 1101(a)(2), (4), Oct. 27, 1970, 84 Stat. 1291

Section 171, acts Feb. 9, 1909, ch. 100, § 1, 35 Stat. 614; Jan. 17, 1914, ch. 9, 38 Stat. 275; May 26, 1922, ch. 202, § 1, 42 Stat. 596; June 14, 1930, ch. 488, § 3, 46 Stat. 586; July 1, 1944, ch. 377, § 8, 58 Stat. 721; Mar. 8, 1946, ch. 81, § 7, 60 Stat. 39; Aug. 8, 1953, ch. 394, § 8, 67 Stat. 506, defined "narcotic drug", "United States", and "person". See section 801 et seq. of this title.

Section 172, acts Feb. 9, 1909, ch. 100, § 2(a), 35 Stat. 614; Jan. 17, 1914, ch. 9, 38 Stat. 275; June 7, 1924, ch. 352, 43 Stat. 657, established a Federal Narcotics Control Board. Act May 26, 1922, ch. 202, § 1, 42 Stat. 596, also classified to this section, was repealed by Pub. L. 89–554, § 8(a), Sept. 6, 1966, 80 Stat. 645.

Section 173, acts Feb. 9, 1909, ch. 100, § 2(b), (d), 35 Stat. 614; Jan. 17, 1914, ch. 9, 38 Stat. 275; May 26, 1922, ch. 202, § 1, 42 Stat. 596; June 7, 1924, ch. 352, 43 Stat. 657; June 14, 1930, ch. 488, § 3, 46 Stat. 586, prohibited importation of narcotic drugs. See section 801 et seq. of this title.

Section 173a, act June 14, 1930, ch. 488, § 6, 46 Stat. 587, provided for importation of additional amounts of coca leaves.

Section 174, acts Feb. 9, 1909, ch. 100, § 2(c), (f), 35 Stat. 614; Jan. 17, 1914, ch. 9, 38 Stat. 275; May 26, 1922, ch. 202, § 1, 42 Stat. 596; June 7, 1924, ch. 352, 43 Stat. 657; Nov. 2, 1951, ch. 666, §§ 1, 5(1), 65 Stat. 767; July 18, 1956, ch. 629, title I, § 105, 70 Stat. 570, set penalties for bringing narcotic drugs into the United States contrary to law. See chapter 13 of this title.

Effective Date of Repeal

Repeal effective on first day of seventh calendar month that begins after Oct. 27, 1970, see section 1105(a) of Pub. L. 91–513, set out as an Effective Date note under section 951 of this title.

Savings Provision

Section 1103 of Pub. L. 91–513 provided that:

"(a) Prosecutions for any violation of law occurring prior to the effective date of section 1101 [the first day of the seventh calendar month that begins after Oct. 26, 1970] shall not be affected by the repeals or amendments made by such section or section 1102 [repealing sections 171 to 174, 176 to 185, 188 to 188n, 191 to 193, 197, 198, 199, 501 to 517 of this title, sections 1401 to 1407, and 3616 of Title 18, Crimes and Criminal Procedure, sections 4701 to 4707, 4711 to 4716, 4721 to 4726, 4731 to 4736, 4741 to 4746, 4751 to 4757, 4761, 4762, 4771 to 4776, 7237, 7238, and 7491 of Title 26, Internal Revenue Code, sections 529a and 529g of former Title 31, Money and Finance, and section 1421m of Title 48, Territories and Insular Possessions, and amending sections 162 and 967 of this title, section 4251 of Title 18, section 1584 of Title 19, Customs Duties, sections 4901, 4905, 6808, 7012, 7103, 7236, 7607, 7609, 7641, 7651, and 7655 of Title 26, section 2901 of Title 28, Judiciary and Judicial Procedure, sections 529d, 529e, and 529f of former Title 31, section 304m of former Title 40, Public Buildings, Property, and Works, section 3411 of Title 42, The Public Health and Welfare, section 239a of Title 46, Shipping, and section 787 of former Title 49, Transportation], or abated by reason thereof.

"(b) Civil seizures or forfeitures and injunctive proceedings commenced prior to the effective date of section 1101 [the first day of the seventh calendar month that begins after Oct. 26, 1970] shall not be affected by the repeals or amendments made by such section or section 1102, or abated by reason thereof."

§175. Repealed. June 27, 1952, ch. 477, title IV, §403(a)(10), 66 Stat. 279

Section, acts Feb. 9, 1909, ch. 100, §2(e), 35 Stat. 614; Jan. 17, 1914, ch. 9, 38 Stat. 275; May 26, 1922, ch. 202, §1, 42 Stat. 596; June 7, 1924, ch. 352, 43 Stat. 657, related to deportation of convicted aliens. See section 1251 et seq. of Title 8, Aliens and Nationality.

§§176 to 185. Repealed. Pub. L. 91–513, title III, §1101(a)(2), (9), Oct. 27, 1970, 84 Stat. 1291, 1292

Section 176, acts Feb. 9, 1909, ch. 100, §2(g), 35 Stat. 614; Jan. 17, 1914, ch. 9, 38 Stat. 275; May 26, 1922, ch. 202 §1, 42 Stat. 596; June 7, 1924, ch. 352, 43 Stat. 657, covered liability of masters of vessels and persons in charge of railroad cars and other vehicles used to carry narcotic drugs.

Section 176a, act Feb. 9, 1909, ch. 100, §2(h), as added July 18, 1956, ch. 629, title I, §106, 70 Stat. 570, covered illegal importation of marihuana and set penalties for such illegal importation. See section 801 et seq. of this title.

Section 176b, act Feb. 9, 1909, ch. 100, §2(i), as added July 18, 1956, ch. 629, title I, §107, 70 Stat. 571, prohibited sale of heroin to juveniles and set penalties for such illegal sale. See section 801 et seq. of this title.

Section 177, acts Feb. 9, 1909, ch. 100, §2(a), 35 Stat. 614; Jan. 17, 1914, ch. 9, 38 Stat. 275; May 26, 1922, ch. 202, §1, 42 Stat. 596; June 7, 1924, ch. 352, 43 Stat. 657, vested administration of Narcotic Drugs Import and Export Act in Department of the Treasury.

Section 178, act Feb. 9, 1909, ch. 100, §4, as added Jan. 17, 1914, ch. 9, 38 Stat. 275, prohibited possession of smoking opium. See section 801 et seq. of this title.

Section 179, act Feb. 9, 1909, ch. 100, §4, as added Jan. 17, 1914, ch. 9, 38 Stat. 275, covered liability of masters of vessels and persons in charge of railroad cars or other vehicles for possession of smoking heroin. See section 801 et seq. of this title.

Section 180, act Feb. 9, 1909, ch. 100, §5, as added Jan. 17, 1914, ch. 9, 38 Stat. 275; amended May 26, 1922, ch. 202, §2, 42 Stat. 597; June 14, 1930, ch. 488, §3, 46 Stat. 586, prohibited admission of smoking opium even for transportation to another country or for transferal from one vessel to another.

Section 181, act Feb. 9, 1909, ch. 100, §3, as added Jan. 17, 1914, ch. 9, 38 Stat. 275, created a presumption of illegal importation based upon presence of smoking opium in United States.

Section 182, act Feb. 9, 1909, ch. 100, §6, as added Jan. 17, 1914, ch. 9, 348 Stat. 275; amended May 26, 1922, ch. 202, §2, 42 Stat. 597; June 14, 1930, ch. 488, §3, 46 Stat. 586; Apr. 22, 1960, Pub. L. 86–429, §15, 74 Stat. 66, forbade exportation of narcotic drugs. See section 801 et seq. of this title.

Section 183, act Feb. 9, 1909, ch. 100, §7, as added Jan. 17, 1914, ch. 9, 38 Stat. 277, set out penalties for illegal exportation of narcotic drugs.

Section 184, act Feb. 9, 1909, ch. 100, §8, as added Jan. 17, 1914, ch. 9, 38 Stat. 277; amended May 26, 1922, ch. 202, §3, 42 Stat. 598, provided for seizure and forfeiture of narcotic drugs found on vessels and not shown on manifest or landed from vessels without a permit.

Section 184a, acts July 11, 1941, ch. 289, §1, 55 Stat. 584; July 18, 1956, ch. 629, title I, §108, 70 Stat. 571, made illegal bringing on board a vessel of United States any narcotic drugs not constituting a part of the cargo.

Section 185, act Feb. 9, 1909, ch. 100, §9, as added May 26, 1922, ch. 202, §4, 42 Stat. 598, authorized the citation of act Feb. 9, 1909, ch. 100, as the "Narcotic Drugs Import and Export Act".

Effective Date of Repeal

Repeal effective on first day of seventh calendar month that begins after Oct. 26, 1970, see section 1105(a) of Pub. L. 91–513, set out as an Effective Date note under section 951 of this title.

Savings Provision

Prosecutions for any violation of law occurring, and civil seizures or forfeitures and injunctive proceedings commenced, prior to the effective date of repeal of these sections by section 1101 of Pub. L. 91–513 not to be affected or abated by reason thereof, see section 1103 of Pub. L. 91–513, set out as a note under sections 171 to 174 of this title.

MARIHUANA AND HEALTH REPORTING

§§186, 187. Transferred

Codification

Section 186, Pub. L. 91–296, title V, §501, June 30, 1970, 84 Stat. 352, which related to congressional findings as to marihuana use, the need for a better understanding of the health consequences, and the lack of information thereto, was transferred and set out as a note under section 242 of Title 42, The Public Health and Welfare.

Section 187, Pub. L. 91–296, title V, §502, June 30, 1970, 84 Stat. 352, which directed the Secretary of Health, Education and Welfare to report to Congress on the current information on the health consequence of marihuana use, with recommendations for legislative and administrative action and to submit a preliminary report no later than 90 days after June 30, 1970, was transferred and set out as a note under section 242 of Title 42.

DOMESTIC CONTROL OF PRODUCTION AND DISTRIBUTION OF THE OPIUM POPPY

§§188 to 188n. Repealed. Pub. L. 91–513, title III, §1101(a)(7), Oct. 27, 1970, 84 Stat. 1292

Sections, acts Dec. 11, 1942, ch. 720, 56 Stat. 1045; June 25, 1959, Pub. L. 86–70, §20, 73 Stat. 145; July 12, 1960, Pub. L. 86–624, §16, 74 Stat. 415, known as the "Opium Poppy Control Act of 1942", provided for the domestic control of production and distribution of the opium poppy. Sections 1 to 17 of said Act of Dec. 11, 1942, were classified, respectively, to sections 188, 188 notes, and 188a to 188n of this title.

Effective Date of Repeal

Repeal effective on first day of seventh calendar month that begins after Oct. 26, 1970, see section 1105(a) of Pub. L. 91–513, set out as an Effective Date note under section 951 of this title.

Savings Provision

Prosecutions for any violation of law occurring, and civil seizures or forfeitures and injunctive proceedings commenced, prior to the effective date of repeal of these sections by section 1101 of Pub. L. 91–513 not to be affected or abated by reason thereof, see section 1103 of Pub. L. 91–513, set out as a note under section 171 of this title.

IMPORTATION BY CHINESE SUBJECTS OR TRAFFICKING IN, IN CHINA, BY UNITED STATES CITIZENS

§§191 to 193. Repealed. Pub. L. 91–513, title III, §1101(a)(1), Oct. 27, 1970, 84 Stat. 1291

Sections, acts Feb. 23, 1887, ch. 210, 24 Stat. 409; June 25, 1948, ch. 646, §§5, 39, 62 Stat. 986, 992, prohibited importation of opium by Chinese subjects and the trafficking in, in China, of opium by United States citizens. Sections 1 to 3 of said Act of Feb. 23, 1887, were classified to sections 191 to 193, respectively, of this title.

Effective Date of Repeal

Repeal effective on first day of seventh calendar month that begins after Oct. 26, 1970, see section 1105(a) of Pub. L. 91–513, set out as an Effective Date note under section 951 of this title.

SAVINGS PROVISION

Prosecutions for any violation of law occurring, and civil seizures or forfeitures and injunctive proceedings commenced, prior to the effective date of repeal of these sections by section 1101 of Pub. L. 91–513 not to be affected or abated by reason thereof, see section 1103 of Pub. L. 91–513, set out as a Savings Provision note under section 171 of this title.

MISCELLANEOUS

§196. Repealed. July 1, 1944, ch. 373, title XIII, §1313, 58 Stat. 714

Section, act June 14, 1930, ch. 488, §4(b), (c), 46 Stat. 587; 1939 Reorg. Plan No. I, §§201, 205, eff. July 1, 1939, 4 F.R. 2728, 53 Stat. 1424, related to studies and investigations by Surgeon General of the Public Health Service. See section 242 of Title 42, The Public Health and Welfare.

RENUMBERING OF REPEALING ACT

Section 611 of act July 1, 1944, which repealed this section, was renumbered 711 by act Aug. 13, 1946, ch. 958, §5, 60 Stat. 1049, 713 by act Feb. 28, 1948, ch. 83, §9(b), 62 Stat. 47, 813 by act July 30, 1956, ch. 779, §3(b), 70 Stat. 720, 913 by Pub. L. 88–581, §4(b), Sept. 4, 1964, 78 Stat. 919, 1013 by Pub. L. 89–239, §3(b), Oct. 6, 1965, 79 Stat. 931, 1113 by Pub. L. 91–572, §6(b), Dec. 24, 1970, 84 Stat. 1506, 1213 by Pub. L. 92–294, §3(b), May 16, 1972, 86 Stat. 137, 1313 by Pub. L. 93–154, §2(b)(2), Nov. 16, 1973, 87 Stat. 604, and was repealed by Pub. L. 93–222, §7(b), Dec. 29, 1973, 87 Stat. 936.

§§197, 198. Repealed. Pub. L. 91–513, title III, §1101(a)(4), Oct. 27, 1970, 84 Stat. 1291

Section 197, act June 14, 1930, ch. 488, §7, 46 Stat. 587, directed Secretary of the Treasury to cooperate with Secretary of State in discharge of international obligations of United States concerning traffic in narcotic drugs.

Section 198, acts June 14, 1930, ch. 488, §8, 46 Stat. 587; July 18, 1956, ch. 629, title III, §302, 70 Stat. 575, directed Secretary of the Treasury to cooperate with the several States in suppression of abuse of narcotic drugs in their respective jurisdictions.

EFFECTIVE DATE OF REPEAL

Repeal effective on first day of seventh calendar month that begins after Oct. 26, 1970, see section 1105(a) of Pub. L. 91–513, set out as an Effective Date note under section 951 of this title.

SAVINGS PROVISION

Prosecutions for any violation of law occurring, and civil seizures or forfeitures and injunctive proceedings commenced, prior to the effective date of repeal of these sections by section 1101 of Pub. L. 91–513 not to be affected or abated by reason thereof, see section 1103 of Pub. L. 91–513, set out as a note under sections 171 to 174 of this title.

§§198a to 198c. Transferred

CODIFICATION

Section 198a, act Aug. 11, 1955, ch. 800, §1, 69 Stat. 684, as amended, which related to the authority of Secretary of the Treasury to issue subpenas, administer oaths and compel attendance of witnesses for purpose of any investigation, was transferred to section 967 of this title.

Section 198b, act Aug. 11, 1955, ch. 800, §2, 69 Stat. 685, which related to service of subpenas and proof of service, was transferred to section 968 of this title.

Section 198c, act Aug. 11, 1955, ch. 800, §3, 69 Stat. 685, which related to contempt proceedings, was transferred to section 969 of this title.

§199. Repealed. Pub. L. 91–513, title III, §1101(a)(5), Oct. 27, 1970, 84 Stat. 1292

Section, act July 3, 1930, ch. 829, 46 Stat. 850, authorized payment to persons giving information concerning violations of narcotics laws. See section 886(a) of this title.

EFFECTIVE DATE OF REPEAL

Repeal effective on first day of seventh calendar month that begins after Oct. 26, 1970, see section 1105(a) of Pub. L. 91–513, set out as an Effective Date note under section 951 of this title.

SAVINGS PROVISION

Prosecutions for any violation of law occurring, and civil seizures or forfeitures and injunctive proceedings commenced, prior to the effective date of repeal of this section by section 1101 of Pub. L. 91–513 not to be affected or abated by reason thereof, see section 1103 of Pub. L. 91–513, set out as a note under section 171 of this title.

§§200 to 200b. Repealed. Nov. 2, 1951, ch. 666, §5(2), 65 Stat. 769

Sections, acts Aug. 12, 1937, ch. 598, §§1–3, 50 Stat. 627; July 1, 1944, ch. 377, §9, 58 Stat. 721; Mar. 8, 1946, ch. 81, §8, 60 Stat. 39, related to punishment for offenses after first offense. See section 801 et seq. of this title.

SAVINGS PROVISION

Section 6 of act Nov. 2, 1951, provided that any rights or liabilities now existing under former sections 200 to 200b of this title should not be affected by their repeal.

CHAPTER 7—PRACTICE OF PHARMACY AND SALE OF POISONS IN CONSULAR DISTRICTS IN CHINA

Sec.

§201. Doing business without a license unlawful; employment of Chinese subjects

It shall be unlawful in the consular districts of the United States in China for any person whose permanent allegiance is due to the United States not licensed as a pharmacist within the meaning of this chapter to conduct or manage any pharmacy, drug or chemical store, apothecary shop, or other place of business for the retailing, compounding, or dispensing of any drugs, chemicals, or poisons, or for the compounding of physicians' prescriptions, or to keep exposed for sale at retail, any drugs, chemicals, or poisons, except as hereinafter provided, or, except as hereinafter provided, for any person whose permanent allegiance is due to the United States not licensed as a pharmacist within the meaning of this chapter to compound, dispense, or sell, at retail, any drug, chemical, poison, or pharmaceutical preparation upon the prescription of a physician, or otherwise, or to compound physicians' prescriptions, except as an aid to and under the proper supervision of a pharmacist licensed under this chapter. And it shall be unlawful for any person, firm, or corporation owing permanent allegiance to the United States owning partly or wholly or managing a pharmacy, drug store, or other place of business to cause or permit any person other than a licensed pharmacist to compound, dispense, or sell at retail any drug, medicine, or poison, except as an aid to and under the proper supervision of a licensed pharmacist. Where it is necessary for a person, firm, or corporation whose permanent allegiance is due to the United States and owning partly or wholly or managing a pharmacy, drug store, or other place of business to employ Chinese subjects to compound, dispense, or sell at retail any drug, medicine, or poison, such person, firm, or corporation, owner, part owner, or manager of a pharmacy, drug store, or other place of business may employ such Chinese subjects when their character, ability, and age of twenty-one years or over have been certified to by at least two recognized and reputable practitioners of medicine, or two pharmacists licensed under this chapter whose permanent allegiance is due to the United States.

(Mar. 3, 1915, ch. 74, §1, 38 Stat. 817.)

CODIFICATION

Section is comprised of part of section 1 of act Mar. 3, 1915. Remainder of such section 1 is classified to section 202 of this title.

§202. Certain classes of persons and corporations excepted; insecticides

Nothing in section 201 of this title shall be construed to interfere with any recognized and reputable practitioner of medicine, dentistry, or veterinary surgery in the compounding of his own prescriptions, or to prevent him from supplying to his patients such medicines as he may deem proper, except as hereinafter provided; nor with the exclusively wholesale business of any person, firm, or corporation whose permanent allegiance is due to the United States dealing and licensed as pharmacists, or having in their employ at least one person who is so licensed, except as hereinafter provided; nor with the sale by persons, firms, or corporations whose permanent allegiance is due to the United States other than pharmacists of poisonous substances sold exclusively for use in the arts, or as insecticides, when such substances are sold in unbroken packages bearing labels having plainly printed upon them the name of the contents, the word "Poison", when practicable the name of at least one suitable antidote, and the name and address of the vender.

(Mar. 3, 1915, ch. 74, §1, 38 Stat. 818.)

CODIFICATION

Section is comprised of part of section 1 of act Mar. 3, 1915. Remainder of such section 1 is classified to section 201 of this title.

§203. Application for license; requirements; qualifications for license

Every person whose permanent allegiance is due to the United States desiring to practice as a pharmacist in the consular districts in China shall file with the consul an application, duly verified under oath, setting forth the name and age of the applicant, the place or places at which he pursued and the time spent in the study of pharmacy, the experience which the applicant has had in compounding physicians' prescriptions under the direction of a licensed pharmacist, and the name and location of the school or college of pharmacy, if any, of which he is a graduate, and shall submit evidence sufficient to show to the satisfaction of said consul that he is of good moral character and not addicted to the use of alcoholic liquors or narcotic drugs so as to render him unfit to practice pharmacy. Applicants shall be not less than twenty-one years of age and shall have had at least four years' experience in the practice of pharmacy or shall have served three years under the instruction of a regularly licensed pharmacist, and any applicant who has been graduated from a school or college of pharmacy recognized by the proper board of his State, Territory, District of Columbia, or other possession of the United States as in good standing shall be entitled to practice upon presentation of his diploma.

(Mar. 3, 1915, ch. 74, §2, 38 Stat. 818.)

CODIFICATION

The words "now practicing as a pharmacist or," which preceded "desiring to practice" in the original text of this section, were omitted as obsolete.

§204. Issuance of license

If the applicant for license as a pharmacist has complied with the requirements of section 203 of this title, the consul shall issue to him a license which shall entitle him to practice pharmacy in the consular districts of the United States in China, subject to the provisions of this chapter.

(Mar. 3, 1915, ch. 74, §3, 38 Stat. 819.)

§205. Display of license in pharmacy

Every license to practice pharmacy shall be conspicuously displayed by the person to whom the same has been issued in the pharmacy, drug store, or place of business, if any, of which the said person is the owner or part owner or manager.

(Mar. 3, 1915, ch. 74, §5, 38 Stat. 819.)

§206. Revocation of license

The license of any person whose permanent allegiance is due to the United States to practice pharmacy in the consular districts of the United States in China may be revoked by the consul if such person be found to have obtained such license by fraud, or be addicted to the use of any narcotic or stimulant, or to be suffering from physical or mental disease, in such manner and to such extent as to render it expedient that in the interests of the public his license be canceled; or to be of an immoral character; or if such person be convicted in any court of competent jurisdiction of any offense involving moral turpitude. It shall be the duty of the consul to investigate any case in which it is discovered by him or made to appear to his satisfaction that any license issued under the provisions of this chapter is revocable and shall, after full hearing, if in his judgment the facts warrant it, revoke such license.

(Mar. 3, 1915, ch. 74, §4, 38 Stat. 819.)

§ 207. Restrictions on sales; written orders or prescriptions

It shall be unlawful for any person, firm, or corporation whose permanent allegiance is due to the United States, either personally or by servant or agent or as the servant or agent of any other person or of any firm or corporation, to sell, furnish, or give away any cocaine, salts of cocaine, or preparation containing cocaine or salts of cocaine, or morphine or preparation containing morphine or salts of morphine, or any opium or preparation containing opium, or any chloral hydrate or preparation containing chloral hydrate, except upon the original written order or prescription of a recognized and reputable practitioner of medicine, dentistry, or veterinary medicine, which order or prescription shall be dated and shall contain the name of the person for whom prescribed, or, if ordered by a practitioner of veterinary medicine, shall state the kind of animal for which ordered and shall be signed by the person giving the order or prescription. Such order or prescription shall be, for a period of three years, retained on file by the person, firm, or corporation who compounds or dispenses the article ordered or prescribed, and it shall not be compounded or dispensed after the first time except upon the written order of the original prescriber.

(Mar. 3, 1915, ch. 74, §6, 38 Stat. 819.)

CODIFICATION

Section is comprised of part of section 6 of act Mar. 3, 1915. Remainder of such section 6 is classified to section 208 of this title.

§ 208. Certain preparations and sales excepted

The provisions of section 207 of this title shall not apply to preparations containing not more than two grains of opium or not more than one-quarter grain of morphine, or not more than one-quarter grain of cocaine, or not more than two grains of chloral hydrate in the fluid ounce, or, of a solid preparation, in one avoirdupois ounce, nor shall they apply to preparations sold in good faith for diarrhea and cholera, each bottle or package of which is accompanied by specific directions for use and caution against habitual use, nor to liniments or ointments sold in good faith as such when plainly labeled "for external use only", nor to powder of ipecac and opium, commonly known as Dover's powder, when sold in quantities not exceeding twenty grains. The provisions of this section or section 207 of this title shall not be construed to permit the selling, furnishing, giving away, or prescribing for the use of any habitual users of the same any cocaine, salts of cocaine, or preparation containing cocaine or salts of cocaine, or morphine or salts of morphine, or preparations containing morphine or salts of morphine, or any opium or preparation containing opium, or any chloral hydrate or preparation containing chloral hydrate. But the preceding sentence shall not be construed to prevent any recognized or reputable practitioner of medicine whose permanent allegiance is due to the United States from furnishing in good faith for the use of any habitual user of narcotic drugs who is under his professional care such substances as he may deem necessary for their treatment, when such prescriptions are not given or substances furnished for the purpose of evading the provisions of this section. But the provisions of this section or section 207 of this title shall not apply to sales at wholesale between jobbers, manufacturers, and retail druggists, hospitals, and scientific or public institutions.

(Mar. 3, 1915, ch. 74, §6, 38 Stat. 819.)

CODIFICATION

Section is comprised of section 6 of act Mar. 3, 1915. Remainder of such section 6 is classified to section 207 of this title.

§ 209. Poisons; book entry of sale; labels

It shall be unlawful for any person, firm, or corporation whose permanent allegiance is due to the United States to sell or deliver to any other person any of the following-described substances, or any poisonous compound, combination, or preparation thereof, to wit: The compounds of and salts of antimony, arsenic, barium, chromium, copper, gold, lead, mercury, silver, and zinc, the caustic hydrates of sodium and potassium, solution or water of ammonia, methyl alcohol, paregoric, the concentrated mineral acids, oxalic and hydrocyanic acids and their salts, yellow phosphorus, Paris green, carbolic acid, the essential oils of almonds, pennyroyal, tansy, rue, and savin; croton oil, creosote, chloroform, cantharides, or aconite, belladonna, bitter almonds, colchicum, cotton root, cocculus indicus, conium, cannabis indica, digitalis, ergot, hyoscyamus, ignatia, lobelia, nux vomica, physostigma, phytolacca, strophanthus, stramonium, veratrum viride, or any of the poisonous alkaloids or alkaloidal salts derived from the foregoing, or any other poisonous alkaloids or their salts, or any other virulent poison, except in the manner following, and, moreover, if the applicant be less than eighteen years of age, except upon the written order of a person known or believed to be an adult.

It shall first be learned, by due inquiry, that the person to whom delivery is about to be made is aware of the poisonous character of the substance and that it is desired for a lawful purpose, and the box, bottle, or other package shall be plainly labeled with the name of the substance, the word "Poison", the name of at least one suitable antidote, when practicable, and the name and address of the person, firm, or corporation dispensing the substance. And before delivery be made of any of the foregoing substances, excepting solution or water of ammonia and sulphate of copper, there shall be recorded in a book kept for that purpose the name of the article, the quantity delivered, the purpose for which it is to be used, the date of delivery, the name and address of the person for whom it is procured, and the name of the individual personally dispensing the same; and said book shall be preserved by the owner thereof for at least three years after the date of the last entry therein. The foregoing provisions shall not apply to articles dispensed upon the order of persons believed by the dispenser to be recognized and reputable practitioners of medicine, dentistry, or veterinary surgery. When a physician writes upon his prescription a request that it be marked or labeled "Poison" the pharmacist shall, in the case of liquids, place the same in a colored glass, roughened bottle, of the kind commonly known in trade as a "poison bottle", and, in the case of dry substances, he shall place a poison label upon the container. The record of sale and delivery above mentioned shall not be required of manufacturers and wholesalers who shall sell any of the foregoing substances at wholesale to licensed pharmacists, but the box, bottle, or other package containing such substance, when sold at wholesale, shall be properly labeled with the name of the substance, the word "poison", and the name and address of the manufacturer or wholesaler. It shall not be necessary, in sales either at wholesale or at retail, to place a poison label upon, nor to record the delivery of, the sulphide of antimony, or the oxide or carbonate of zinc, or of colors ground in oil and intended for use as paints, or calomel; nor in the case of preparations containing any of the substances named in this section, when a single box, bottle, or other package, or when the bulk of one-half fluid ounce or the weight of one-half avoirdupois ounce does not contain more than an adult medicinal dose of such substance; nor in the case of liniments or ointments sold in good faith as such, when plainly labeled "For external use only"; nor, in the case of preparations put up and sold in the form of pills, tablets, or lozenges, containing any of the substances enumerated in this section and intended for internal use, when the dose recommended does not contain more than one-fourth of an adult medicinal dose of such substance.

For the purpose of this and of every other section of this chapter no box, bottle, or other package shall be regarded as having been labeled "Poison" unless the word "Poison" appears conspicuously thereon, printed in plain, uncondensed gothic letters in red ink.

(Mar. 3, 1915, ch. 74, § 7, 38 Stat. 820.)

§ 210. Pharmacist; unauthorized use of title

It shall be unlawful for any person whose permanent allegiance is due to the United States, not legally licensed as a pharmacist, to take, use, or exhibit the title of pharmacist, or licensed or registered pharmacist, or the title of druggist or apothecary, or any other title or description of like import.

(Mar. 3, 1915, ch. 74, § 10, 38 Stat. 821.)

§ 211. Preservation of originals of prescriptions compounded and copies thereof; inspection of prescriptions by consular officers; marking containers of drugs

Every person, firm, or corporation whose permanent allegiance is due to the United States owning, partly owning, or managing a drug store or pharmacy shall keep in his place of business a suitable book or file, in which shall be preserved for a period of not less than three years the original of every prescription compounded or dispensed at such store or pharmacy, or a copy of such prescription, except when the preservation of the original is required by section 207 or 208 of this title. Upon request the owner, part owner, or manager of such store shall furnish to the prescribing physician, or to the person for whom such prescription was compounded or dispensed, a true and correct copy thereof. Any prescription required by section 207 or 208 of this title, and any prescription for, or register of sales of, substances mentioned in such sections shall at all times be open to inspection by duly authorized consular officers in the consular districts of the United States in China. No person, firm, or corporation whose permanent allegiance is due to the United States shall, in a consular district, compound or dispense any drug or drugs or deliver the same to any other person without marking on the container thereof the name of the drug or drugs contained therein and directions for using the same.

(Mar. 3, 1915, ch. 74, § 9, 38 Stat. 821.)

§ 212. Offenses; punishment; duty to enforce provisions

Any person, firm, or corporation, whose permanent allegiance is due to the United States, violating any of the provisions of this chapter shall be deemed guilty of a misdemeanor and, upon conviction thereof, shall be punished by a fine of not less than $50 and not more than $100 or by imprisonment for not less than one month and not more than sixty days, or by both such fine and imprisonment, in the discretion of the court, and if the offense be continuing in its character, each week or part of a week during which it continues shall constitute a separate and distinct offense. And it shall be the duty of the consular and judicial officers of the United States in China to enforce the provisions of this chapter.

(Mar. 3, 1915, ch. 74, § 11, 38 Stat. 821.)

§ 213. Fraudulent representations to evade or defeat restrictions

No person, firm, or corporation whose permanent allegiance is due to the United States seeking to procure in the consular districts of the United States in China any substance the sale of which is regulated by the provisions of this chapter shall make any fraudulent representations so as to evade or defeat the restrictions herein imposed.

(Mar. 3, 1915, ch. 74, § 8, 38 Stat. 821.)

§ 214. Previous laws unaffected

Nothing in this chapter shall be construed as modifying or revoking any of the provisions of sections 191 to 193[1] of this title.

(Mar. 3, 1915, ch. 74, § 13, 38 Stat. 822.)

REFERENCES IN TEXT

Sections 191 to 193 of this title, referred to in text, were repealed by Pub. L. 91–513, title III, § 1101(a)(1), Oct. 27, 1970, 84 Stat. 1291. See section 801 et seq. of this title.

§ 215. "Consul" defined

The word "consul" as used in this chapter shall mean the consular officer in charge of the district concerned.

(Mar. 3, 1915, ch. 74, § 12, 38 Stat. 822.)

CHAPTER 8—NARCOTIC FARMS

§§ 221 to 237. Repealed. July 1, 1944, ch. 373, title XIII, § 1313, 58 Stat. 714

Section 221, act Jan. 19, 1929, ch. 82, § 1, 45 Stat. 1085, defined "habit-forming narcotic drug", "narcotic", and "addict". See section 201 of Title 42, The Public Health and Welfare.

Section 222, act Jan. 19, 1929, ch. 82, § 2, 45 Stat. 1085, provided for narcotic farms.

Section 222a, act June 23, 1935, ch. 725, § 1, 49 Stat. 1840, provided name for narcotic farm at Lexington, Ky.

Section 222b, act Mar. 28, 1938, ch. 55, § 1, 52 Stat. 134, provided name for narcotic farm at Fort Worth, Texas.

Section 223, act Jan. 19, 1929, ch. 82, § 3, 45 Stat. 1085; 1939 Reorg. Plan No. I, § 205(b), eff. July 1, 1939, 4 F.R. 2728, 53 Stat. 1425, provided for an annual estimate of expenses of maintenance of narcotic farms.

Section 224, act Jan. 19, 1929, ch. 82, § 4, 45 Stat. 1086, provided for construction of buildings for two of the narcotic farms.

Section 225, acts Jan. 19, 1929, ch. 82, § 5, 45 Stat. 1086; June 14, 1930, ch. 488, § 4(a), 46 Stat. 586; 1939 Reorg. Plan No. I, §§ 201, 205, eff. July 1, 1939, 4 F.R. 2728, 53 Stat. 1424, provided for control and management of narcotic farms.

Section 226, act Jan. 19, 1929, ch. 82, § 6, 45 Stat. 1086; 1939 Reorg. Plan No. I, §§ 201, 205, eff. July 1, 1939, 4 F.R. 2728, 53 Stat. 1424, 1425, provided for care and treatment of addicts.

Section 227, act Jan. 19, 1929, ch. 82, § 7, 45 Stat. 1086, provided for transfer to and from farms of addicts who are prisoners.

Section 228, act Jan. 19, 1929, ch. 82, § 8, 45 Stat. 1087, provided that it was the duty of prosecuting officers to report convicted persons believed to be addicts.

Section 229, act Jan. 19, 1929, ch. 82, § 9, 45 Stat. 1087; 1939 Reorg. Plan No. I, §§ 201, 205, eff. July 1, 1939, 4 F.R. 2728, 53 Stat. 1424, 1425, provided for employment of addicts.

Section 230, act Jan. 19, 1929, ch. 82, § 10, 45 Stat. 1087, provided for parole of inmates.

Section 231, act Jan. 19, 1929, ch. 82, § 11, 45 Stat. 1087; 1939 Reorg. Plan No. I, §§ 201, 205, eff. July 1, 1939, 4 F.R. 2728, 53 Stat. 1424, 1425, provided for discharge of addicts.

Section 232, act Jan. 19, 1929, ch. 82, § 12, 45 Stat. 1088; 1939 Reorg. Plan No. I, §§ 201, 205, eff. July 1, 1939, 4 F.R. 2728, 53 Stat. 1424, 1425, provided for admission of voluntary patients.

Section 233, act Jan. 19, 1929, ch. 82, § 13, 45 Stat. 1088; 1939 Reorg. Plan No. I, §§ 201, 205, eff. July 1, 1939, 4 F.R. 2728, 53 Stat. 1424, 1425, provided for furnishing of gratuities and transportation to discharged convicts.

Section 234, act. Jan. 19, 1929, ch. 82, § 14, 45 Stat. 1089; 1939 Reorg. Plan No. I, §§ 201, 205, eff. July 1, 1939, 4 F.R. 2728, 53 Stat. 1424, 1425, provided penalties for introduction of narcotic drugs into a narcotic farm.

Section 235, act Jan. 19, 1929, ch. 82, § 15, 45 Stat. 1089, provided penalties for escape of inmates.

Section 236, act Jan. 19, 1929, ch. 82, § 16, 45 Stat. 1089, provided penalties for procuring of escape by inmates.

Section 237, act Jan. 19, 1929, ch. 82, § 17, 45 Stat. 1089, provided for deportation of alien inmates who are entitled to a discharge from narcotic farms.

RENUMBERING OF REPEALING ACT

Section 611 of act July 1, 1944, which repealed this section, was renumbered § 711 by act Aug. 13, 1946, ch. 958, § 5, 60 Stat. 1049, § 713 by act Feb. 28, 1948, ch. 83, § 9(b), 62 Stat. 47, § 813 by act July 30, 1956, ch. 779, § 3(b), 70 Stat. 720, § 913 by Pub. L. 88–581, § 4(b), Sept. 4, 1964, 78 Stat. 919, § 1013 by Pub. L. 89–239, § 3(b), Oct. 6, 1965, 79 Stat. 931, § 1113 by Pub. L. 91–572, § 6(b), Dec. 24, 1970, 84 Stat. 1506, § 1213 by Pub. L. 92–294, § 3(b), May 16, 1972, 86 Stat. 137, § 1313 by Pub. L. 93–154, § 2(b)(2), Nov. 16, 1973, 87 Stat. 604, and was repealed by Pub. L. 93–222, § 7(b), Dec. 29, 1973, 87 Stat. 936.

CHAPTER 9—FEDERAL FOOD, DRUG, AND COSMETIC ACT

[1] See References in Text note below.

SUBCHAPTER I—SHORT TITLE

§ 301. Short title

This chapter may be cited as the Federal Food, Drug, and Cosmetic Act.

(June 25, 1938, ch. 675, § 1, 52 Stat. 1040.)

EFFECTIVE DATE; POSTPONEMENT IN CERTAIN CASES

Act June 23, 1939, ch. 242, §§ 1, 2, 53 Stat. 853, 854, provided that:

"[SEC. 1] (a) The effective date of the following provisions of the Federal Food, Drug, and Cosmetic Act is hereby postponed until January 1, 1940: Sections 402(c) [342(c) of this title]; 403(e)(1) [343(e)(1) of this title]; 403(g), (h), (i), (j), and (k) [343(g) to (k) of this title]; 501(a), (4) [351(a)(4) of this title]; 502(b), (d), (e), (f), (g), and (h) [352(b), (d) to (h) of this title]; 601(e) [361(e) of this title]; and 602(b) [362(b) of this title].

"(b) The Secretary of Agriculture shall promulgate regulations further postponing to July 1, 1940 the effective date of the provisions of sections 403(e)(1) [343(e)(1) of this title]; 403(g), (h), (i), (j), and (k) [343(g) to (k)]; 502(b), (d), (e), (f), (g), and (h) [352(b), (d) to (h) of this title]; and 602(b) [362(b) of this title] of such Act with respect to lithographed labeling which was manufactured prior to February 1, 1939, and to containers bearing labeling which, prior to February 1, 1939, was lithographed, etched, stamped, pressed, printed, fused or blown on or in such containers, where compliance with such provisions would be unduly burdensome by reason of causing the loss of valuable stocks of such labeling or containers, and where such postponement would not prevent the public interest being adequately served: Provided, That in no case shall such regulations apply to labeling which would not have complied with the requirements of the Food and Drugs Act of June 30, 1906, as amended.

"SEC. 2. (a) The provisions of section 8 [section 10 of this title], paragraph fifth, under the heading 'In the case of food:', of the Food and Drugs Act of June 30, 1906, as amended, and regulations promulgated thereunder, and all other provisions of such Act to the extent that they may relate to the enforcement of such section 8 [section 10 of this title] and of such regulations, shall remain in force until January 1, 1940.

"(b) The provisions of such Act of June 30, 1906, as amended, [sections 1 to 5, 7 to 15, and 372a of this title] to the extent that they impose, or authorize the imposition of, any requirement imposed by section 403(k) of the Federal Food, Drug, and Cosmetic Act [section 343(k) of this title], shall remain in force until January 1, 1940.

"(c) Notwithstanding the provisions of section 1 of this Act, such section shall not apply—

"(1) to the provisions of section 502(d) and (e) of the Federal Food, Drug, and Cosmetic Act [352(d), (e) of this title], insofar as such provisions relate to any substance named in section 8 [section 10 of this title], paragraph second, under the heading 'In the case of drugs:', of the Food and Drugs Act of June 30, 1906, as amended, or a derivative of any such substance; or

"(2) to the provisions of section 502(b), (d), (e), (f), (g), and (h) of the Federal Food, Drug, and Cosmetic Act [352(b), (d) to (h) of this title], insofar as such provisions relate to drugs to which section 505 [355 of this title] of such Act applies."

EFFECTIVE DATE

Section 902(a) of act June 25, 1938, provided that: "This Act [enacting this chapter and repealing sections 1 to 5 and 7 to 15 of this title], shall take effect twelve months after the date of its enactment [June 25, 1938]. The Federal Food and Drugs Act of June 30, 1906, as amended (U.S.C., 1934 ed., title 21, secs. 1–15), shall remain in force until such effective date, and, except as otherwise provided in this subsection, is hereby repealed effective upon such date: *Provided*, That the provisions of section 701 [section 371 of this title] shall become effective on the enactment of this Act, and thereafter the Secretary is authorized hereby to (1) conduct hearings and to promulgate regulations which shall become effective on or after the effective date of this Act as the Secretary shall direct, and (2) designate prior to the effective date of this Act food having common or usual names and exempt such food from the requirements of clause (2) of section 403(i) [section 343(i) of this title] for a reasonable time to permit the formulation, promulgation, and effective application of definitions and standards of identity therefor as provided by section 401 [section 341 of this title]: *Provided further*,

That sections 502(j), 505, and 601(a) [sections 352(j), 355, 361(a), respectively of this title], and all other provisions of this Act to the extent that they may relate to the enforcement of such sections, shall take effect on the date of the enactment of this Act, except that in the case of a cosmetic to which the proviso of section 601(a) [section 361(a) of this title], relates, such cosmetic shall not, prior to the ninetieth day after such date of enactment, be deemed adulterated by reason of the failure of its label to bear the legend prescribed in such proviso: *Provided further*, That the Act of March 4, 1923 (U.S.C., 1934 ed., title 21, sec. 6 [section 321a of this title]; 42 Stat. 1500, ch. 268), defining butter and providing a standard therefor; the Act of July 24, 1919 (U.S.C., 1934 ed., title 21, sec. 10 [section 321b of this title]; 41 Stat. 271, ch. 26], defining wrapped meats as in package form; and the amendment to the Food and Drugs Act, section 10A, approved August 27, 1935 (U.S.C. 1934 ed., Sup. III, title 21, sec. 14a [section 372a of this title]) shall remain in force and effect and be applicable to the provisions of this Act.''

SHORT TITLE OF 2008 AMENDMENT

Pub. L. 110–316, title I, §101(a), Aug. 14, 2008, 122 Stat. 3509, provided that: ''This title [enacting section 379j–13 of this title, amending sections 360b, 379j–11, and 379j–12 of this title, and enacting provisions set out as notes under sections 360b and 379j–11 of this title] may be cited as the 'Animal Drug User Fee Amendments of 2008'.''

Pub. L. 110–316, title II, §201(a), Aug. 14, 2008, 122 Stat. 3515, provided that: ''This title [enacting sections 379j–21 and 379j–22 of this title, amending sections 379k, 379*l*, and 379*o* of this title, and enacting provisions set out as notes under sections 379j–21 and 379j–22 of this title] may be cited as the 'Animal Generic Drug User Fee Act of 2008'.''

SHORT TITLE OF 2007 AMENDMENT

Pub. L. 110–85, §1, Sept. 27, 2007, 121 Stat. 823, provided that: ''This Act [enacting part I of subchapter VII of this chapter, chapter 26 of this title, sections 350f, 353b, 355–1, 355d, 355e, 360a, 360e–1, 360n, 360bbb–5, 360bbb–6, 379d–1, 379d–2, 379h–1, 379h–2, 379j–1, and 399a of this title, and section 247d–5a of Title 42, The Public Health and Welfare, amending sections 321, 331, 333, 334, 352, 355, 355a, 355c, 360, 360e, 360i, 360j, 360*l*, 360m, 360ee, 374, 379g, 379h, 379i, 379j, 379j–11, 379*l*, 381, and 393a of this title and sections 247d–3b, 262, 282, 283, 283a–2, 283a–3, 284m, 285g–10, 288–6, and 290b of Title 42, enacting provisions set out as notes under this section and sections 331, 350f, 352, 355, 355a, 355c, 360j, 379g, 379h, 379h–2, 379i, and 2110 of this title and section 282 of Title 42, and amending provisions set out as notes under section 284m of Title 42] may be cited as the 'Food and Drug Administration Amendments Act of 2007'.''

Pub. L. 110–85, title I, §101(a), Sept. 27, 2007, 121 Stat. 825, provided that: ''This title [enacting sections 379h–1 and 379h–2 of this title, amending sections 379g, 379h, and 379j–11 of this title, and enacting provisions set out as notes under sections 379g, 379h, and 379h–2 of this title] may be cited as the 'Prescription Drug User Fee Amendments of 2007'.''

Pub. L. 110–85, title II, §201(a), Sept. 27, 2007, 121 Stat. 842, provided that: ''This title [enacting section 379j–1 of this title, amending sections 333, 360, 360i, 360m, 374, 379i, and 379j of this title, and enacting provisions set out as notes under section 379i of this title] may be cited as the 'Medical Device User Fee Amendments of 2007'.''

Pub. L. 110–85, title III, §301, Sept. 27, 2007, 121 Stat. 859, provided that: ''This title [enacting section 360e–1 of this title, amending sections 360j, 360*l*, and 393a of this title and section 282 of Title 42, The Public Health and Welfare, enacting provisions set out as notes under section 360j of this title and section 282 of Title 42, and amending provisions set out as a note under section 284m of Title 42] may be cited as the 'Pediatric Medical Device Safety and Improvement Act of 2007'.''

Pub. L. 110–85, title IV, §401, Sept. 27, 2007, 121 Stat. 866, provided that: ''This title [enacting section 355d of this title, amending section 355c of this title, and enacting provisions set out as a note under section 355c of this title] may be cited as the 'Pediatric Research Equity Act of 2007'.''

Pub. L. 110–85, title V, §501, Sept. 27, 2007, 121 Stat. 876, provided that: ''This title [amending section 355a of this title and sections 284m, 285g–10, 288–6, and 290b of Title 42, The Public Health and Welfare, enacting provisions set out as a note under section 355a of this title, and amending provisions set out as a note under section 284m of Title 42] may be cited as the 'Best Pharmaceuticals for Children Act of 2007'.''

SHORT TITLE OF 2006 AMENDMENT

Pub. L. 109–462, §1, Dec. 22, 2006, 120 Stat. 3469, provided that: ''This Act [enacting sections 379aa and 379aa–1 of this title, amending sections 331, 343, 352, and 381 of this title, and enacting provisions set out as notes under sections 331, 343, 352, 379aa, and 381 of this title] may be cited as the 'Dietary Supplement and Nonprescription Drug Consumer Protection Act'.''

SHORT TITLE OF 2005 AMENDMENTS

Pub. L. 109–59, title VII, §7201, Aug. 10, 2005, 119 Stat. 1911, provided that: ''This subtitle [subtitle B (§§7201–7204) of title VII of Pub. L. 109–59, enacting section 350e of this title, amending sections 331, 342, and 373 of this title and section 5701 of Title 49, Transportation, omitting sections 5702 to 5714 of Title 49, and enacting provisions set out as a note under section 331 of this title] may be cited as the 'Sanitary Food Transportation Act of 2005'.''

Pub. L. 109–43, §1, Aug. 1, 2005, 119 Stat. 439, provided that: ''This Act [amending sections 352 and 379j of this title, enacting provisions set out as a note under section 352 of this title, and amending provisions set out as notes under sections 352 and 379i of this title] may be cited as the 'Medical Device User Fee Stabilization Act of 2005'.''

SHORT TITLE OF 2004 AMENDMENTS

Pub. L. 108–282, title I, §101, Aug. 2, 2004, 118 Stat. 891, provided that: ''This title [enacting sections 360ccc to 360ccc–2 of this title, amending sections 321, 331, 352, 353, 354, and 360b of this title, enacting provisions set out as notes under sections 360ccc and 393 of this title, and amending provisions set out as a note under section 360b of this title] may be cited as the 'Minor Use and Minor Species Animal Health Act of 2004'.''

Pub. L. 108–282, title II, §201, Aug. 2, 2004, 118 Stat. 905, provided that: ''This title [enacting section 374a of this title and section 242r of Title 42, The Public Health and Welfare, amending sections 321, 343, and 343–1 of this title, and enacting provisions set out as notes under sections 321 and 343 of this title and sections 243 and 300d–2 of Title 42] may be cited as the 'Food Allergen Labeling and Consumer Protection Act of 2004'.''

Pub. L. 108–214, §1, Apr. 1, 2004, 118 Stat. 572, provided that: ''This Act [amending sections 331, 352, 360, 360e, 374, 379i, and 379j of this title and provisions set out as notes under sections 352, 360*l*, and 379j of this title] may be cited as the 'Medical Devices Technical Corrections Act'.''

SHORT TITLE OF 2003 AMENDMENTS

Pub. L. 108–155, §1, Dec. 3, 2003, 117 Stat. 1936, provided that: ''This Act [enacting section 355c of this title, amending sections 355, 355a, and 355b of this title and sections 262 and 284m of Title 42, The Public Health and Welfare, enacting provisions set out as a note under section 355c of this title, and amending provisions set out as notes under section 355a of this title and section 284m of Title 42] may be cited as the 'Pediatric Research Equity Act of 2003'.''

Pub. L. 108–130, §1, Nov. 18, 2003, 117 Stat. 1361, provided that: ''This Act [enacting sections 379j–11 and 379j–12 of this title and provisions set out as notes under section 379j–11 of this title] may be cited as the 'Animal Drug User Fee Act of 2003'."

SHORT TITLE OF 2002 AMENDMENTS

Pub. L. 107–281, §1, Nov. 6, 2002, 116 Stat. 1992, provided that: "This Act [amending sections 360cc and 360ee of this title and enacting provisions set out as a note under section 360ee of this title] may be cited as the 'Rare Diseases Orphan Product Development Act of 2002'."

Pub. L. 107–250, §1(a), Oct. 26, 2002, 116 Stat. 1588, provided that: "This Act [enacting sections 379i and 379j of this title and section 289g–3 of Title 42, The Public Health and Welfare, amending sections 321, 331, 333, 335a, 352, 353, 360, 360c, 360e, 360m, and 374 of this title, and enacting provisions set out as notes under sections 352, 360e, 360j, 360l, 379i, and 379j of this title and section 289g–3 of Title 42] may be cited as the 'Medical Device User Fee and Modernization Act of 2002'."

Pub. L. 107–188, title V, §501, June 12, 2002, 116 Stat. 687, provided that: "This subtitle [subtitle A (§§501–509) of title V of Pub. L. 107–188, amending sections 356b, 379g, and 379h of this title and enacting provisions set out as notes under sections 356b and 379g of this title] may be cited as the 'Prescription Drug User Fee Amendments of 2002'."

Pub. L. 107–109, §1, Jan. 4, 2002, 115 Stat. 1408, provided that: "This Act [enacting sections 355b and 393a of this title and section 284m of Title 42, The Public Health and Welfare, amending sections 321, 355, 355a, and 379h of this title and sections 282, 284k, 284l, 285a–2, and 290b of Title 42, and enacting provisions set out as notes under sections 355 and 355a of this title and sections 284m and 289 of Title 42] may be cited as the 'Best Pharmaceuticals for Children Act'."

SHORT TITLE OF 2000 AMENDMENT

Pub. L. 106–387, §1(a) [title VII, §745(a)], Oct. 28, 2000, 114 Stat. 1549, 1549A–35, provided that: "This section [enacting section 384 of this title, amending sections 331, 333, and 381 of this title, and enacting provisions set out as a note under section 384 of this title] may be cited as the 'Medicine Equity and Drug Safety Act of 2000'."

Pub. L. 106–387, §1(a) [title VII, §746(a)], Oct. 28, 2000, 114 Stat. 1549, 1549A–40, provided that: "This section [amending section 381 of this title and enacting provisions set out as a note under section 381 of this title] may be cited as the 'Prescription Drug Import Fairness Act of 2000'."

SHORT TITLE OF 1998 AMENDMENT

Pub. L. 105–324, §1, Oct. 30, 1998, 112 Stat. 3035, provided that: "This Act [amending sections 321 and 346a of this title] may be cited as the 'Antimicrobial Regulation Technical Corrections Act of 1998'."

SHORT TITLE OF 1997 AMENDMENT

Pub. L. 105–115, §1(a), Nov. 21, 1997, 111 Stat. 2296, provided that: "This Act [enacting sections 343–3, 353a, 355a, 356 to 356c, 360m, 360aaa to 360aaa–6, 360bbb to 360bbb–2, 379k, 379l, 379o, 379r, 379s, 379v, 396, and 397 of this title and sections 247b–8 and 299a–3 of Title 42, The Public Health and Welfare, amending sections 321, 331, 334, 335a, 343, 348, 351 to 353, 355, 360, 360b to 360e, 360g, 360i, 360j, 360l, 360aa to 360cc, 360ee, 371, 374, 379a, 379g, 379h, 381 to 383, 393, and 802 of this title, section 45C of Title 26, Internal Revenue Code, section 156 of Title 35, Patents, section 8126 of Title 38, Veterans' Benefits, and sections 262, 263a, and 282 of Title 42, repealing sections 356 and 357 of this title, and enacting provisions set out as notes under sections 321, 348, 351, 352, 353a, 355 to 356b, 360i, 360l, 360aaa, 371, 379g, 379h, 379k, and 393 of this title and sections 247b–8 and 282 of Title 42] may be cited as the 'Food and Drug Administration Modernization Act of 1997'."

SHORT TITLE OF 1996 AMENDMENTS

Pub. L. 104–250, §1(a), Oct. 9, 1996, 110 Stat. 3151, provided that: "This Act [enacting section 354 of this title, amending sections 331, 353, and 360b of this title, and enacting provisions set out as notes under section 360b of this title] may be cited as the 'Animal Drug Availability Act of 1996'."

Pub. L. 104–170, title IV, §401(a), Aug. 3, 1996, 110 Stat. 1513, provided that: "This title [amending sections 321, 331, 333, 342, and 346a of this title] may be cited as the 'Food Quality Protection Act of 1996'."

[Another "Food Quality Protection Act of 1996", was enacted by Pub. L. 104–170, §1, 110 Stat. 1489, which is set out as a note under section 136 of Title 7, Agriculture.]

Pub. L. 104–134, title II, §2101(a), Apr. 26, 1996, 110 Stat. 1321–313, provided that: "This chapter [chapter 1A (§§2101–2105) of title II of Pub. L. 104–134, enacting section 382 of this title and amending sections 331 and 381 of this title and section 262 of Title 42, The Public Health and Welfare] may be cited as the 'FDA Export Reform and Enhancement Act of 1996'."

SHORT TITLE OF 1994 AMENDMENTS

Pub. L. 103–417, §1(a), Oct. 25, 1994, 108 Stat. 4325, provided that: "This Act [enacting sections 343–2 and 350b of this title and section 287c–11 of Title 42, The Public Health and Welfare, amending sections 321, 331, 342, 343, and 350 of this title and section 281 of Title 42, and enacting provisions set out as notes under sections 321 and 343 of this title] may be cited as the 'Dietary Supplement Health and Education Act of 1994'."

Pub. L. 103–396, §1, Oct. 22, 1994, 108 Stat. 4153, provided that: "This Act [amending sections 331, 343–1, 360b, and 371 of this title and enacting provisions set out as notes under section 360b of this title] may be cited as the 'Animal Medicinal Drug Use Clarification Act of 1994'."

SHORT TITLE OF 1993 AMENDMENT

Pub. L. 103–80, §1, Aug. 13, 1993, 107 Stat. 773, provided that: "This Act [amending sections 321, 331 to 333, 334, 335b, 341 to 343, 346a, 350a, 352, 355 to 358, 360b to 360e, 360i, 360cc, 360hh to 360ss, 361, 371, 372, 373, 374, 376, 379e, and 381 of this title and section 263b of Title 42, The Public Health and Welfare, and enacting provisions set out as a note under section 343 of this title] may be cited as the 'Nutrition Labeling and Education Act Amendments of 1993'."

SHORT TITLE OF 1992 AMENDMENTS

Pub. L. 102–571, title I, §101(a), Oct. 29, 1992, 106 Stat. 4491, provided that: "This title [enacting sections 379g and 379h of this title, transferring sections 372a, 376, and 379c of this title to sections 376, 379e and 379f, respectively, of this title, amending sections 321, 331, 342, 343, 346a, 351, 352, 360j, 361, 362, 453, 601, and 1033 of this title, enacting provisions set out as notes under section 379g of this title, and amending provisions set out as notes under sections 343 and 343–1 of this title] may be cited as the 'Prescription Drug User Fee Act of 1992'."

Pub. L. 102–571, title II, §201, Oct. 29, 1992, 106 Stat. 4500, provided that: "This title [enacting provisions set out as notes under sections 343 and 393 of this title and amending provisions set out as notes under sections 343 and 343–1 of this title] may be cited as the 'Dietary Supplement Act of 1992'."

Pub. L. 102–353, §1(a), Aug. 26, 1992, 106 Stat. 941, provided that: "This Act [amending sections 333, 353, and 381 of this title and enacting provisions set out as a note under section 353 of this title] may be cited as the 'Prescription Drug Amendments of 1992'."

Pub. L. 102–300, §1(a), June 16, 1992, 106 Stat. 238, provided that: "This Act [amending sections 321, 331, 334, 346a, 352, 353, 356, 357, 360c, 360d, 360g to 360i, 360l, 360mm, 371 to 372a, 376, and 381 of this title and section 262 of Title 42, The Public Health and Welfare and enacting and amending provisions set out as notes under section 360i of this title] may be cited as the 'Medical Device Amendments of 1992'."

Pub. L. 102–282, §1(a), May 13, 1992, 106 Stat. 149, provided that: "This Act [enacting sections 335a to 335c of this title, amending sections 321, 336, 337, and 355 of this title, and enacting provisions set out as notes under section 335a of this title] may be cited as the 'Generic Drug Enforcement Act of 1992'."

SHORT TITLE OF 1990 AMENDMENTS

Pub. L. 101–635, § 1(a), Nov. 28, 1990, 104 Stat. 4583, provided that: "This Act [enacting sections 379b to 379d and 394 of this title] may be cited as the 'Food and Drug Administration Revitalization Act'."

Pub. L. 101–629, § 1(a), Nov. 28, 1990, 104 Stat. 4511, provided that: "This Act [enacting sections 360*l* and 383 of this title, amending sections 321, 333, 351, 353, and 360c to 360j of this title and sections 263b to 263n of Title 42, The Public Health and Welfare, redesignating sections 263b to 263n of Title 42 as sections 360gg to 360ss of this title, repealing section 263b of Title 42, and enacting provisions set out as notes under sections 333, 360c, 360i, 360j, 360hh and 383 of this title] may be cited as the 'Safe Medical Devices Act of 1990'."

Pub. L. 101–535, § 1(a), Nov. 8, 1990, 104 Stat. 2353, provided that: "This Act [enacting section 343–1 of this title, amending sections 321, 337, 343, 345, and 371 of this title, and enacting provisions set out as notes under sections 343 and 343–1 of this title] may be cited as the 'Nutrition Labeling and Education Act of 1990'."

SHORT TITLE OF 1988 AMENDMENTS

Pub. L. 100–670, § 1(a), Nov. 16, 1988, 102 Stat. 3971, provided that: "This Act [amending sections 321, 353, and 360b of this title, section 2201 of Title 28, Judiciary and Judicial Procedure, and sections 156 and 271 of Title 35, Patents, and enacting provisions set out as notes under section 360b of this title] may be cited as the 'Generic Animal Drug and Patent Term Restoration Act'."

Pub. L. 100–607, title V, § 501, Nov. 4, 1988, 102 Stat. 3120, provided that: "This title [enacting section 393 of this title, amending sections 5315 and 5316 of Title 5, Government Organization and Employees, and enacting provisions set out as notes under section 393 of this title] may be cited as the 'Food and Drug Administration Act of 1988'."

Pub. L. 100–293, § 1(a), Apr. 22, 1988, 102 Stat. 95, provided that: "This Act [amending sections 331, 333, 353, and 381 of this title and enacting provisions set out as notes under section 353 of this title] may be cited as the 'Prescription Drug Marketing Act of 1987'."

Pub. L. 100–290, § 1, Apr. 18, 1988, 102 Stat. 90, provided that: "This Act [amending sections 360bb and 360ee of this title, enacting provisions set out as a note under section 360aa of this title, and amending provisions set out as a note under section 236 of Title 42, The Public Health and Welfare] may be cited as the 'Orphan Drug Amendments of 1988'."

SHORT TITLE OF 1986 AMENDMENT

Pub. L. 99–660, title I, § 101(a), Nov. 14, 1986, 100 Stat. 3743, provided that: "This title [enacting section 382 of this title, amending sections 241 and 262 of Title 42, The Public Health and Welfare, and enacting provisions set out as notes under section 333 of this title and section 262 of Title 42] may be cited as the 'Drug Export Amendments Act of 1986'."

SHORT TITLE OF 1985 AMENDMENT

Pub. L. 99–91, § 1, Aug. 15, 1985, 99 Stat. 387, provided that: "This Act [amending sections 360aa to 360cc, and 360ee of this title, and sections 295g–1 and 6022 of Title 42, The Public Health and Welfare, and enacting provisions set out as notes under section 360aa of this title and section 236 of Title 42] may be cited as the 'Orphan Drug Amendments of 1985'."

SHORT TITLE OF 1984 AMENDMENT

Pub. L. 98–417, § 1, Sept. 24, 1984, 98 Stat. 1585, provided: "That this Act [enacting section 156 of Title 35, Patents, amending sections 355 and 360cc of this title, sections 68b, 68c, and 70b of Title 15, Commerce and Trade, section 2201 of Title 28, Judiciary and Judicial Procedure, and sections 271 and 282 of Title 35, and enacting provisions set out as notes under section 355 of this title and section 68b of Title 15] may be cited as the 'Drug Price Competition and Patent Term Restoration Act of 1984'."

SHORT TITLE OF 1983 AMENDMENTS

Pub. L. 98–22, § 1, Apr. 22, 1983, 97 Stat. 173, provided: "That this Act [amending provisions set out as a note under section 348 of this title] may be cited as the 'Saccharin Study and Labeling Act Amendment of 1983'."

Pub. L. 97–414, § 1(a), Jan. 4, 1983, 96 Stat. 2049, provided that: "This Act [enacting part B of subchapter V of chapter 9 of this title, section 44H of Title 26, Internal Revenue Code, section 155 of Title 35, Patents, and sections 236, 255, and 298b–4 of Title 42, The Public Health and Welfare, amending sections 1274, 1472, 2055, 2060, 2064, 2068, and 2080 of Title 15, Commerce and Trade, section 904 of this title, sections 280C and 6096 of Title 26, and sections 209, 231, 242k, 242m, 243, 254c, 254j, 254m, 254*o*, 254p, 256, 294j, 295g–1, 295g–4, 295h, 295h–1a, 297–1, 300, 300a–1, 300a–3, 300b, 300e–1, 300m, 300n–5, 300q–2, 300u–5, 300w–3, 300x–1, 300x–4, 300y–11, 4577, and 4588 of Title 42, enacting provisions set out as notes under section 360aa of this title, section 44H of Title 26, and sections 241, 255, 287i, and 300x–1 of Title 42, and repealing provisions set out as a note under section 300t–11 of Title 42] may be cited as the 'Orphan Drug Act'."

SHORT TITLE OF 1981 AMENDMENT

Pub. L. 97–42, § 1, Aug. 14, 1981, 95 Stat. 946, provided: "That this Act [amending provisions set out as a note under section 348 of this title] may be cited as the 'Saccharin Study and Labeling Act Amendment of 1981'."

SHORT TITLE OF 1980 AMENDMENT

Pub. L. 96–359, § 1, Sept. 26, 1980, 94 Stat. 1190, provided: "That this Act [enacting section 350a of this title, amending sections 321, 331, 374, 830, 841 to 843, and 873 of this title, and enacting a provision set out as a note under section 350a of this title] may be cited as the 'Infant Formula Act of 1980'."

SHORT TITLE OF 1977 AMENDMENT

Pub. L. 95–203, § 1, Nov. 23, 1977, 91 Stat. 1451, provided that: "This Act [enacting section 343a of this title, amending sections 321 and 343 of this title, enacting provisions set out as notes under sections 343 and 348 of this title, and amending provisions set out as notes under sections 218 and 289*l*–1 of Title 42, The Public Health and Welfare] may be cited as the 'Saccharin Study and Labeling Act'."

SHORT TITLE OF 1976 AMENDMENT

Pub. L. 94–295, § 1(a), May 28, 1976, 90 Stat. 539, provided that: "This Act [enacting sections 360c to 360k, 379, and 379a of this title and section 3512 of Title 42, The Public Health and Welfare, and amending sections 321, 331, 334, 351, 352, 358, 360, 374, 379e, and 381 of this title and section 55 of Title 15, Commerce and Trade] may be cited as the 'Medical Device Amendments of 1976'."

SHORT TITLE OF 1972 AMENDMENT

Pub. L. 92–387, § 1, Aug. 16, 1972, 86 Stat. 559, provided that: "This Act [amending sections 331, 335, and 360 of this title and enacting provisions set out as notes under section 360 of this title] may be cited as the 'Drug Listing Act of 1972'."

SHORT TITLE OF 1968 AMENDMENTS

Pub. L. 90–602, § 1, Oct. 18, 1968, 82 Stat. 1173, provided that: "This Act [enacting provisions now comprising part C (§§ 360hh–360ss) of subchapter III of this chapter and provisions set out as notes under section 360hh of this title] may be cited as the 'Radiation Control for Health and Safety Act of 1968'."

Pub. L. 90–399, § 1, July 13, 1968, 82 Stat. 342, provided: "That this Act [enacting section 360b of this title, amending sections 321, 331, 342, 351, 352, 357, 381, and 392 of this title, and enacting provisions set out as a note under section 360b of this title] may be cited as the 'Animal Drug Amendments of 1968'."

SHORT TITLE OF 1965 AMENDMENT

Pub. L. 89–74, § 1, July 15, 1965, 79 Stat. 226, provided: "That this Act [amending sections 321, 331, 333, 334, 360, and 372 of this title and section 1114 of Title 18, Crimes and Criminal Procedure, and enacting provisions set out as notes under sections 321 and 352 of this title] may be cited as the 'Drug Abuse Control Amendments of 1965'."

SHORT TITLE OF 1962 AMENDMENT

Pub. L. 87–781, § 1, Oct. 10, 1962, 76 Stat. 780, provided in part that such Act [enacting sections 358 to 360 of this title, amending sections 321, 331, 332, 348, 351 to 353, 355, 357, 372, 374, 379e, and 381 of this title, and enacting provisions set out as notes under sections 321, 331, 332, 352, 355, 358, 360, and 374 of this title] may be cited as the 'Drug Amendments of 1962'."

SHORT TITLE OF 1960 AMENDMENT

Pub. L. 86–618, § 1, July 12, 1960, 74 Stat. 397, provided: "That this Act [amending sections 321, 331, 333, 342, 346, 351, 352, 361, 362, 371, and 379e of this title, repealing sections 354 and 364 of this title, and enacting notes set out under this section] may be cited as the 'Color Additive Amendments of 1960'."

SHORT TITLE OF 1958 AMENDMENT

Pub. L. 85–929, § 1, Sept. 6, 1958, 72 Stat. 1784, provided: "That this Act [amending sections 321, 331, 342, 346, 348 of this title and section 210 of Title 42, The Public Health and Welfare, and enacting provisions set out as notes under sections 321, 342, and 451 of this title] may be cited as the 'Food Additives Amendment of 1958'."

SEVERABILITY

Pub. L. 110–85, title XI, § 1105, Sept. 27, 2007, 121 Stat. 975, provided that: "If any provision of this Act [see Short Title of 2007 Amendment note above], an amendment made [by] this Act, or the application of such provision or amendment to any person or circumstance is held to be unconstitutional, the remainder of this Act, the amendments made by this Act, and the application of the provisions of such to any person or circumstances shall not be affected thereby."

HAZARDOUS SUBSTANCES

Federal Hazardous Substances Act as not modifying this chapter, see Pub. L. 86–613, § 18, July 12, 1960, 74 Stat. 380, set out as an Effect Upon Federal and State Laws note under section 1261 of Title 15, Commerce and Trade.

SUBCHAPTER II—DEFINITIONS

§ 321. Definitions; generally

For the purposes of this chapter—

(a)(1) The term "State", except as used in the last sentence of section 372(a) of this title, means any State or Territory of the United States, the District of Columbia, and the Commonwealth of Puerto Rico.

(2) The term "Territory" means any Territory or possession of the United States, including the District of Columbia, and excluding the Commonwealth of Puerto Rico and the Canal Zone.

(b) The term "interstate commerce" means (1) commerce between any State or Territory and any place outside thereof, and (2) commerce within the District of Columbia or within any other Territory not organized with a legislative body.

(c) The term "Department" means Department of Health and Human Services.

(d) The term "Secretary" means the Secretary of Health and Human Services.

(e) The term "person" includes individual, partnership, corporation, and association.

(f) The term "food" means (1) articles used for food or drink for man or other animals, (2) chewing gum, and (3) articles used for components of any such article.

(g)(1) The term "drug" means (A) articles recognized in the official United States Pharmacopoeia, official Homoeopathic Pharmacopoeia of the United States, or official National Formulary, or any supplement to any of them; and (B) articles intended for use in the diagnosis, cure, mitigation, treatment, or prevention of disease in man or other animals; and (C) articles (other than food) intended to affect the structure or any function of the body of man or other animals; and (D) articles intended for use as a component of any article specified in clause (A), (B), or (C). A food or dietary supplement for which a claim, subject to sections 343(r)(1)(B) and 343(r)(3) of this title or sections 343(r)(1)(B) and 343(r)(5)(D) of this title, is made in accordance with the requirements of section 343(r) of this title is not a drug solely because the label or the labeling contains such a claim. A food, dietary ingredient, or dietary supplement for which a truthful and not misleading statement is made in accordance with section 343(r)(6) of this title is not a drug under clause (C) solely because the label or the labeling contains such a statement.

(2) The term "counterfeit drug" means a drug which, or the container or labeling of which, without authorization, bears the trademark, trade name, or other identifying mark, imprint, or device, or any likeness thereof, of a drug manufacturer, processor, packer, or distributor other than the person or persons who in fact manufactured, processed, packed, or distributed such drug and which thereby falsely purports or is represented to be the product of, or to have been packed or distributed by, such other drug manufacturer, processor, packer, or distributor.

(h) The term "device" (except when used in paragraph (n) of this section and in sections 331(i), 343(f), 352(c), and 362(c) of this title) means an instrument, apparatus, implement, machine, contrivance, implant, in vitro reagent, or other similar or related article, including any component, part, or accessory, which is—

(1) recognized in the official National Formulary, or the United States Pharmacopeia, or any supplement to them,

(2) intended for use in the diagnosis of disease or other conditions, or in the cure, mitigation, treatment, or prevention of disease, in man or other animals, or

(3) intended to affect the structure or any function of the body of man or other animals, and

which does not achieve its primary intended purposes through chemical action within or on the body of man or other animals and which is not dependent upon being metabolized for the achievement of its primary intended purposes.

(i) The term "cosmetic" means (1) articles intended to be rubbed, poured, sprinkled, or sprayed on, introduced into, or otherwise applied to the human body or any part thereof for cleansing, beautifying, promoting attractiveness, or altering the appearance, and (2) articles intended for use as a component of any such articles; except that such term shall not include soap.

(j) The term "official compendium" means the official United States Pharmacopoeia, official Homoeopathic Pharmacopoeia of the United States, official National Formulary, or any supplement to any of them.

(k) The term "label" means a display of written, printed, or graphic matter upon the immediate container of any article; and a requirement made by or under authority of this chapter that any word, statement, or other information appear on the label shall not be considered to be complied with unless such word, statement, or other information also appears on the outside container or wrapper, if any there be, of the retail package of such article, or is easily legible through the outside container or wrapper.

(*l*) The term "immediate container" does not include package liners.

(m) The term "labeling" means all labels and other written, printed, or graphic matter (1) upon any article or any of its containers or wrappers, or (2) accompanying such article.

(n) If an article is alleged to be misbranded because the labeling or advertising is misleading, then in determining whether the labeling or advertising is misleading there shall be taken into account (among other things) not only representations made or suggested by statement, word, design, device, or any combination thereof, but also the extent to which the labeling or advertising fails to reveal facts material in the light of such representations or material with respect to consequences which may result from the use of the article to which the labeling or advertising relates under the conditions of use prescribed in the labeling or advertising thereof or under such conditions of use as are customary or usual.

(*o*) The representation of a drug, in its labeling, as an antiseptic shall be considered to be a representation that it is a germicide, except in the case of a drug purporting to be, or represented as, an antiseptic for inhibitory use as a wet dressing, ointment, dusting powder, or such other use as involves prolonged contact with the body.

(p) The term "new drug" means—

(1) Any drug (except a new animal drug or an animal feed bearing or containing a new animal drug) the composition of which is such that such drug is not generally recognized, among experts qualified by scientific training and experience to evaluate the safety and effectiveness of drugs, as safe and effective for use under the conditions prescribed, recommended, or suggested in the labeling thereof, except that such a drug not so recognized shall not be deemed to be a "new drug" if at any time prior to June 25, 1938, it was subject to the Food and Drugs Act of June 30, 1906, as amended, and if at such time its labeling contained the same representations concerning the conditions of its use; or

(2) Any drug (except a new animal drug or an animal feed bearing or containing a new animal drug) the composition of which is such that such drug, as a result of investigations to determine its safety and effectiveness for use under such conditions, has become so recognized, but which has not, otherwise than in such investigations, been used to a material extent or for a material time under such conditions.

(q)(1)(A) Except as provided in clause (B), the term "pesticide chemical" means any substance that is a pesticide within the meaning of the Federal Insecticide, Fungicide, and Rodenticide Act [7 U.S.C. 136 et seq.], including all active and inert ingredients of such pesticide. Notwithstanding any other provision of law, the term "pesticide" within such meaning includes ethylene oxide and propylene oxide when such substances are applied on food.

(B) In the case of the use, with respect to food, of a substance described in clause (A) to prevent, destroy, repel, or mitigate microorganisms (including bacteria, viruses, fungi, protozoa, algae, and slime), the following applies for purposes of clause (A):

(i) The definition in such clause for the term "pesticide chemical" does not include the substance if the substance is applied for such use on food, or the substance is included for such use in water that comes into contact with the food, in the preparing, packing, or holding of the food for commercial purposes. The substance is not excluded under this subclause from such definition if the substance is ethylene oxide or propylene oxide, and is applied for such use on food. The substance is not so excluded if the substance is applied for such use on a raw agricultural commodity, or the substance is included for such use in water that comes into contact with the commodity, as follows:

(I) The substance is applied in the field.

(II) The substance is applied at a treatment facility where raw agricultural commodities are the only food treated, and the treatment is in a manner that does not change the status of the food as a raw agricultural commodity (including treatment through washing, waxing, fumigating, and packing such commodities in such manner).

(III) The substance is applied during the transportation of such commodity between the field and such a treatment facility.

(ii) The definition in such clause for the term "pesticide chemical" does not include the substance if the substance is a food contact substance as defined in section 348(h)(6) of this title, and any of the following circumstances exist: The substance is included for such use in an object that has a food contact surface but is not intended to have an ongoing effect on any portion of the object; the substance is included for such use in an object that has a food contact surface and is intended to have an ongoing effect on a portion of the object but not on the food contact surface; or the substance is included for such use in or is applied for such use on food packaging (without regard to whether the substance is intended to have an ongoing effect on any portion of the packaging). The food contact substance is not excluded under this subclause from such definition if any of the following circumstances exist: The substance is applied for such use on a semipermanent or permanent food contact surface (other than being applied on food packaging); or the substance is included for such use in an object that has a semipermanent or permanent food contact surface (other than being included in food packaging) and the substance is intended to have an ongoing effect on the food contact surface.

With respect to the definition of the term "pesticide" that is applicable to the Federal Insecticide, Fungicide, and Rodenticide Act [7 U.S.C. 136 et seq.], this clause does not exclude any substance from such definition.

(2) The term "pesticide chemical residue" means a residue in or on raw agricultural commodity or processed food of—

(A) a pesticide chemical; or

(B) any other added substance that is present on or in the commodity or food primarily as a result of the metabolism or other degradation of a pesticide chemical.

(3) Notwithstanding subparagraphs (1) and (2), the Administrator may by regulation except a substance from the definition of "pesticide chemical" or "pesticide chemical residue" if—

(A) its occurrence as a residue on or in a raw agricultural commodity or processed food is attributable primarily to natural causes or to human activities not involving the use of any substances for a pesticidal purpose in the production, storage, processing, or transportation of any raw agricultural commodity or processed food; and

(B) the Administrator, after consultation with the Secretary, determines that the substance more appropriately should be regulated under one or more provisions of this chapter other than sections 342(a)(2)(B) and 346a of this title.

(r) The term "raw agricultural commodity" means any food in its raw or natural state, including all fruits that are washed, colored, or otherwise treated in their unpeeled natural form prior to marketing.

(s) The term "food additive" means any substance the intended use of which results or may reasonably be expected to result, directly or indirectly, in its becoming a component or otherwise affecting the characteristics of any food (including any substance intended for use in producing, manufacturing, packing, processing, preparing, treating, packaging, transporting, or holding food; and including any source of radiation intended for any such use), if such substance is not generally recognized, among experts qualified by scientific training and experience to evaluate its safety, as having been adequately shown through scientific procedures (or, in the case of a substance used in food prior to January 1, 1958, through either scientific procedures or experience based on common use in food) to be safe under the conditions of its intended use; except that such term does not include—

(1) a pesticide chemical residue in or on a raw agricultural commodity or processed food; or

(2) a pesticide chemical; or

(3) a color additive; or

(4) any substance used in accordance with a sanction or approval granted prior to September 6, 1958, pursuant to this chapter, the Poultry Products Inspection Act [21 U.S.C. 451 et seq.] or the Meat Inspection Act of March 4, 1907, as amended and extended [21 U.S.C. 601 et seq.];

(5) a new animal drug; or

(6) an ingredient described in paragraph (ff) in, or intended for use in, a dietary supplement.

(t)(1) The term "color additive" means a material which—

(A) is a dye, pigment, or other substance made by a process of synthesis or similar artifice, or extracted, isolated, or otherwise derived, with or without intermediate or final change of identity, from a vegetable, animal, mineral, or other source, and

(B) when added or applied to a food, drug, or cosmetic, or to the human body or any part thereof, is capable (alone or through reaction with other substance) of imparting color thereto;

except that such term does not include any material which the Secretary, by regulation, determines is used (or intended to be used) solely for a purpose or purposes other than coloring.

(2) The term "color" includes black, white, and intermediate grays.

(3) Nothing in subparagraph (1) of this paragraph shall be construed to apply to any pesticide chemical, soil or plant nutrient, or other agricultural chemical solely because of its effect in aiding, retarding, or otherwise affecting, directly or indirectly, the growth or other natural physiological processes of produce of the soil and thereby affecting its color, whether before or after harvest.

(u) The term "safe" as used in paragraph (s) of this section and in sections 348, 360b, 360ccc, and 379e of this title, has reference to the health of man or animal.

(v) The term "new animal drug" means any drug intended for use for animals other than man, including any drug intended for use in animal feed but not including such animal feed,—

(1) the composition of which is such that such drug is not generally recognized, among experts qualified by scientific training and experience to evaluate the safety and effectiveness of animal drugs, as safe and effective for use under the conditions prescribed, recommended, or suggested in the labeling thereof; except that such a drug not so recognized shall not be deemed to be a "new animal drug" if at any time prior to June 25, 1938, it was subject to the Food and Drug Act of June 30, 1906, as amended, and if at such time its labeling contained the same representations concerning the conditions of its use; or

(2) the composition of which is such that such drug, as a result of investigations to determine its safety and effectiveness for use under such conditions, has become so recog-

nized but which has not, otherwise than in such investigations, been used to a material extent or for a material time under such conditions.

Provided that any drug intended for minor use or use in a minor species that is not the subject of a final regulation published by the Secretary through notice and comment rulemaking finding that the criteria of paragraphs (1) and (2) have not been met (or that the exception to the criterion in paragraph (1) has been met) is a new animal drug.

(w) The term "animal feed", as used in paragraph (w)[1] of this section, in section 360b of this title, and in provisions of this chapter referring to such paragraph or section, means an article which is intended for use for food for animals other than man and which is intended for use as a substantial source of nutrients in the diet of the animal, and is not limited to a mixture intended to be the sole ration of the animal.

(x) The term "informal hearing" means a hearing which is not subject to section 554, 556, or 557 of title 5 and which provides for the following:

(1) The presiding officer in the hearing shall be designated by the Secretary from officers and employees of the Department who have not participated in any action of the Secretary which is the subject of the hearing and who are not directly responsible to an officer or employee of the Department who has participated in any such action.

(2) Each party to the hearing shall have the right at all times to be advised and accompanied by an attorney.

(3) Before the hearing, each party to the hearing shall be given reasonable notice of the matters to be considered at the hearing, including a comprehensive statement of the basis for the action taken or proposed by the Secretary which is the subject of the hearing and a general summary of the information which will be presented by the Secretary at the hearing in support of such action.

(4) At the hearing the parties to the hearing shall have the right to hear a full and complete statement of the action of the Secretary which is the subject of the hearing together with the information and reasons supporting such action, to conduct reasonable questioning, and to present any oral or written information relevant to such action.

(5) The presiding officer in such hearing shall prepare a written report of the hearing to which shall be attached all written material presented at the hearing. The participants in the hearing shall be given the opportunity to review and correct or supplement the presiding officer's report of the hearing.

(6) The Secretary may require the hearing to be transcribed. A party to the hearing shall have the right to have the hearing transcribed at his expense. Any transcription of a hearing shall be included in the presiding officer's report of the hearing.

(y) The term "saccharin" includes calcium saccharin, sodium saccharin, and ammonium saccharin.

[1] So in original. Probably should be paragraph "(v)".

(z) The term "infant formula" means a food which purports to be or is represented for special dietary use solely as a food for infants by reason of its simulation of human milk or its suitability as a complete or partial substitute for human milk.

(aa) The term "abbreviated drug application" means an application submitted under section 355(j) of this title for the approval of a drug that relies on the approved application of another drug with the same active ingredient to establish safety and efficacy, and—

(1) in the case of section 335a of this title, includes a supplement to such an application for a different or additional use of the drug but does not include a supplement to such an application for other than a different or additional use of the drug, and

(2) in the case of sections 335b and 335c of this title, includes any supplement to such an application.

(bb) The term "knowingly" or "knew" means that a person, with respect to information—

(1) has actual knowledge of the information, or

(2) acts in deliberate ignorance or reckless disregard of the truth or falsity of the information.

(cc) For purposes of section 335a of this title, the term "high managerial agent"—

(1) means—

(A) an officer or director of a corporation or an association,

(B) a partner of a partnership, or

(C) any employee or other agent of a corporation, association, or partnership,

having duties such that the conduct of such officer, director, partner, employee, or agent may fairly be assumed to represent the policy of the corporation, association, or partnership, and

(2) includes persons having management responsibility for—

(A) submissions to the Food and Drug Administration regarding the development or approval of any drug product,

(B) production, quality assurance, or quality control of any drug product, or

(C) research and development of any drug product.

(dd) For purposes of sections 335a and 335b of this title, the term "drug product" means a drug subject to regulation under section 355, 360b, or 382 of this title or under section 262 of title 42.

(ee) The term "Commissioner" means the Commissioner of Food and Drugs.

(ff) The term "dietary supplement"—

(1) means a product (other than tobacco) intended to supplement the diet that bears or contains one or more of the following dietary ingredients:

(A) a vitamin;

(B) a mineral;

(C) an herb or other botanical;

(D) an amino acid;

(E) a dietary substance for use by man to supplement the diet by increasing the total dietary intake; or

(F) a concentrate, metabolite, constituent, extract, or combination of any ingredient described in clause (A), (B), (C), (D), or (E);

(2) means a product that—

(A)(i) is intended for ingestion in a form described in section 350(c)(1)(B)(i) of this title; or

(ii) complies with section 350(c)(1)(B)(ii) of this title;

(B) is not represented for use as a conventional food or as a sole item of a meal or the diet; and

(C) is labeled as a dietary supplement; and

(3) does—

(A) include an article that is approved as a new drug under section 355 of this title or licensed as a biologic under section 262 of title 42 and was, prior to such approval, certification, or license, marketed as a dietary supplement or as a food unless the Secretary has issued a regulation, after notice and comment, finding that the article, when used as or in a dietary supplement under the conditions of use and dosages set forth in the labeling for such dietary supplement, is unlawful under section 342(f) of this title; and

(B) not include—

(i) an article that is approved as a new drug under section 355 of this title, certified as an antibiotic under section 357 of this title, or licensed as a biologic under section 262 of title 42, or

(ii) an article authorized for investigation as a new drug, antibiotic, or biological for which substantial clinical investigations have been instituted and for which the existence of such investigations has been made public,

which was not before such approval, certification, licensing, or authorization marketed as a dietary supplement or as a food unless the Secretary, in the Secretary's discretion, has issued a regulation, after notice and comment, finding that the article would be lawful under this chapter.

Except for purposes of paragraph (g) and section 350f of this title, a dietary supplement shall be deemed to be a food within the meaning of this chapter.

(gg) The term "processed food" means any food other than a raw agricultural commodity and includes any raw agricultural commodity that has been subject to processing, such as canning, cooking, freezing, dehydration, or milling.

(hh) The term "Administrator" means the Administrator of the United States Environmental Protection Agency.

(ii) The term "compounded positron emission tomography drug"—

(1) means a drug that—

(A) exhibits spontaneous disintegration of unstable nuclei by the emission of positrons and is used for the purpose of providing dual photon positron emission tomographic diagnostic images; and

(B) has been compounded by or on the order of a practitioner who is licensed by a State to compound or order compounding for a drug described in subparagraph (A), and is compounded in accordance with that State's law, for a patient or for research, teaching, or quality control; and

(2) includes any nonradioactive reagent, reagent kit, ingredient, nuclide generator, accelerator, target material, electronic synthesizer, or other apparatus or computer program to be used in the preparation of such a drug.

(jj) The term "antibiotic drug" means any drug (except drugs for use in animals other than humans) composed wholly or partly of any kind of penicillin, streptomycin, chlortetracycline, chloramphenicol, bacitracin, or any other drug intended for human use containing any quantity of any chemical substance which is produced by a micro-organism and which has the capacity to inhibit or destroy micro-organisms in dilute solution (including a chemically synthesized equivalent of any such substance) or any derivative thereof.

(kk) PRIORITY SUPPLEMENT.—The term "priority supplement" means a drug application referred to in section 101(4) of the Food and Drug Administration Modernization Act of 1997 (111 Stat. 2298).

(*ll*)(1) The term "single-use device" means a device that is intended for one use, or on a single patient during a single procedure.

(2)(A) The term "reprocessed", with respect to a single-use device, means an original device that has previously been used on a patient and has been subjected to additional processing and manufacturing for the purpose of an additional single use on a patient. The subsequent processing and manufacture of a reprocessed single-use device shall result in a device that is reprocessed within the meaning of this definition.

(B) A single-use device that meets the definition under clause (A) shall be considered a reprocessed device without regard to any description of the device used by the manufacturer of the device or other persons, including a description that uses the term "recycled" rather than the term "reprocessed".

(3) The term "original device" means a new, unused single-use device.

(mm)(1) The term "critical reprocessed single-use device" means a reprocessed single-use device that is intended to contact normally sterile tissue or body spaces during use.

(2) The term "semi-critical reprocessed single-use device" means a reprocessed single-use device that is intended to contact intact mucous membranes and not penetrate normally sterile areas of the body.

(nn) The term "major species" means cattle, horses, swine, chickens, turkeys, dogs, and cats, except that the Secretary may add species to this definition by regulation.

(*oo*) The term "minor species" means animals other than humans that are not major species.

(pp) The term "minor use" means the intended use of a drug in a major species for an indication that occurs infrequently and in only a small number of animals or in limited geographical areas and in only a small number of animals annually.

(qq) The term "major food allergen" means any of the following:

(1) Milk, egg, fish (e.g., bass, flounder, or cod), Crustacean shellfish (e.g., crab, lobster, or shrimp), tree nuts (e.g., almonds, pecans, or walnuts), wheat, peanuts, and soybeans.

(2) A food ingredient that contains protein derived from a food specified in paragraph (1), except the following:

(A) Any highly refined oil derived from a food specified in paragraph (1) and any ingredient derived from such highly refined oil.

(B) A food ingredient that is exempt under paragraph (6) or (7) of section 343(w) of this title.

(June 25, 1938, ch. 675, § 201, 52 Stat. 1040; July 22, 1954, ch. 559, § 1, 68 Stat. 511; Pub. L. 85–929, § 2, Sept. 6, 1958, 72 Stat. 1784; Pub. L. 86–618, title I, § 101, July 12, 1960, 74 Stat. 397; Pub. L. 87–781, title I, § 102(a), title III, § 307(a), Oct. 10, 1962, 76 Stat. 781, 796; Pub. L. 89–74, §§ 3(a), 9(b), July 15, 1965, 79 Stat. 227, 234; Pub. L. 90–399, § 102, July 13, 1968, 82 Stat. 351; Pub. L. 90–639, §§ 1, 4(a), Oct. 24, 1968, 82 Stat. 1361, 1362; Pub. L. 91–513, title II, § 701(a), (g), Oct. 27, 1970, 84 Stat. 1281, 1282; Pub. L. 92–516, § 3(3), Oct. 21, 1972, 86 Stat. 998; Pub. L. 94–278, title V, § 502(a)(2)(A), Apr. 22, 1976, 90 Stat. 411; Pub. L. 94–295, § 3(a)(1)(A), (2), May 28, 1976, 90 Stat. 575; Pub. L. 95–203, § 4(b)(3), Nov. 23, 1977, 91 Stat. 1453; Pub. L. 96–359, § 3, Sept. 26, 1980, 94 Stat. 1193; Pub. L. 100–670, title I, § 107(a)(1), Nov. 16, 1988, 102 Stat. 3984; Pub. L. 101–535, § 5(b), Nov. 8, 1990, 104 Stat. 2362; Pub. L. 101–629, § 16(b), Nov. 28, 1990, 104 Stat. 4526; Pub. L. 102–282, § 6, May 13, 1992, 106 Stat. 161; Pub. L. 102–300, § 6(a), (b), June 16, 1992, 106 Stat. 240; Pub. L. 102–571, title I, § 107(1), Oct. 29, 1992, 106 Stat. 4499; Pub. L. 103–80, §§ 3(b), (dd)(1), 4(b), Aug. 13, 1993, 107 Stat. 775, 779; Pub. L. 103–417, §§ 3(a), (b), 10(a), Oct. 25, 1994, 108 Stat. 4327, 4332; Pub. L. 104–170, title IV, § 402, Aug. 3, 1996, 110 Stat. 1513; Pub. L. 105–115, title I, §§ 121(a), 125(b)(2)(A), (e), Nov. 21, 1997, 111 Stat. 2320, 2325, 2327; Pub. L. 105–324, § 2(a), (c), Oct. 30, 1998, 112 Stat. 3035, 3037; Pub. L. 107–109, § 5(b)(1), Jan. 4, 2002, 115 Stat. 1413; Pub. L. 107–250, title III, § 302(d), Oct. 26, 2002, 116 Stat. 1619; Pub. L. 108–282, title I, § 102(b)(1), (5)(A), (B), title II, § 203(c)(1), Aug. 2, 2004, 118 Stat. 891, 902, 908; Pub. L. 110–85, title X, § 1005(c), Sept. 27, 2007, 121 Stat. 968.)

REFERENCES IN TEXT

The Food and Drugs Act of June 30, 1906, as amended, referred to in par. (p)(1), and the Food and Drug Act of June 30, 1906, as amended, referred to in par. (v)(1), is act June 30, 1906, ch. 3915, 34 Stat. 768, as amended, which was classified to subchapter I (§ 1 et seq.) of chapter 1 of this title, was repealed (except for section 14a which was transferred to section 372a of this title) by act June 25, 1938, ch. 675, § 902(a), 52 Stat. 1059, and is covered by this chapter.

The Federal Insecticide, Fungicide, and Rodenticide Act, referred to in par. (q)(1), is act June 25, 1947, ch. 125, as amended generally by Pub. L. 92–516, Oct. 21, 1972, 86 Stat. 973, which is classified generally to subchapter II (§ 136 et seq.) of chapter 6 of Title 7, Agriculture. For complete classification of this Act to the Code, see Short Title note set out under section 136 of Title 7 and Tables.

The Poultry Products Inspection Act, referred to in par. (s)(4), is Pub. L. 85–172, Aug. 28, 1957, 71 Stat. 441, as amended, which is classified generally to chapter 10 (§ 451 et seq.) of this title. For complete classification of this Act to the Code, see Short Title note set out under section 451 of this title and Tables.

The Meat Inspection Act of March 4, 1907, as amended and extended, referred to in par. (s)(4), is act Mar. 4, 1907, ch. 2907, titles I to IV, as added Dec. 15, 1967, Pub. L. 90–201, 81 Stat. 584, which are classified generally to subchapters I to IV (§ 601 et seq.) of chapter 12 of this title. For complete classification of this Act to the Code, see Short Title note set out under section 601 of this title and Tables.

Section 101(4) of the Food and Drug Administration Modernization Act of 1997, referred to in par. (kk), is section 101(4) of Pub. L. 105–115, which is set out as a note under section 379g of this title.

AMENDMENTS

2007—Par. (ff). Pub. L. 110–85 substituted "paragraph (g) and section 350f of this title" for "paragraph (g)" in concluding provisions.

2004—Par. (u). Pub. L. 108–282, § 102(b)(5)(A), substituted "360b, 360ccc" for "360b".

Par. (v). Pub. L. 108–282, § 102(b)(5)(B), inserted concluding provisions.

Pars. (nn) to (pp). Pub. L. 108–282, § 102(b)(1), added pars. (nn) to (pp).

Par. (qq). Pub. L. 108–282, § 203(c)(1), added par. (qq).

2002—Par. (kk). Pub. L. 107–109 added par. (kk).

Pars. (*ll*), (mm). Pub. L. 107–250 added pars. (*ll*) and (mm).

1998—Par. (q)(1). Pub. L. 105–324, § 2(a), added subpar. (1) and struck out former subpar. (1) which read as follows: "The term 'pesticide chemical' means any substance that is a pesticide within the meaning of the Federal Insecticide, Fungicide, and Rodenticide Act, including all active and inert ingredients of such pesticide."

Par. (q)(3). Pub. L. 105–324, § 2(c), substituted "subparagraphs (1) and (2)" for "paragraphs (1) and (2)" in introductory provisions.

1997—Par. (aa). Pub. L. 105–115, § 125(b)(2)(A), struck out "or 357" after "section 355(j)".

Par. (dd). Pub. L. 105–115, § 125(b)(2)(A), struck out "357," after "section 355,".

Par. (ff)(3)(A). Pub. L. 105–115, § 125(b)(2)(A), struck out ", certified as an antibiotic under section 357 of this title," before "or licensed as a biologic".

Par. (ii). Pub. L. 105–115, § 121(a), added par. (ii).

Par. (jj). Pub. L. 105–115, § 125(e), added par. (jj).

1996—Par. (q). Pub. L. 104–170, § 402(a), amended par. (q) generally. Prior to amendment, par. (q) read as follows: "The term 'pesticide chemical' means any substance which, alone, in chemical combination or in formulation with one or more other substances, is 'a pesticide' within the meaning of the Federal Insecticide, Fungicide, and Rodenticide Act as now in force or as hereafter amended, and which is used in the production, storage, or transportation of raw agricultural commodities."

Par. (s)(1), (2). Pub. L. 104–170, § 402(b), amended subpars. (1) and (2) generally. Prior to amendment, subpars. (1) and (2) read as follows:

"(1) a pesticide chemical in or on a raw agricultural commodity; or

"(2) a pesticide chemical to the extent that it is intended for use or is used in the production, storage, or transportation of any raw agricultural commodity; or".

Pars. (gg), (hh). Pub. L. 104–170, § 402(c), added pars. (gg) and (hh).

1994—Par. (g)(1). Pub. L. 103–417, § 10(a), amended last sentence generally. Prior to amendment, last sentence read as follows: "A food for which a claim, subject to sections 343(r)(1)(B) and 343(r)(3) of this title or sections 343(r)(1)(B) and 343(r)(5)(D) of this title, is made in accordance with the requirements of section 343(r) of this title is not a drug under clause (B) solely because the label or labeling contains such a claim."

Par. (s)(6). Pub. L. 103–417, § 3(b), added subpar. (6).

Par. (ff). Pub. L. 103–417, § 3(a), added par. (ff).

1993—Pars. (c), (d). Pub. L. 103–80, § 3(dd)(1), substituted "Health and Human Services" for "Agriculture".

Par. (h). Pub. L. 103–80, § 4(b), amended directory language of Pub. L. 102–300, § 6(a)(1). See 1992 amendment note below.

Pars. (v) to (ff). Pub. L. 103–80, § 3(b), redesignated pars. (w) to (ff) as (v) to (ee), respectively.

1992—Pars. (c), (d). Pub. L. 102–300, § 6(b)(1), which directed the substitution of "Health and Human Services" for "Health, Education, and Welfare", could not be executed because such words did not appear in the original statutory text. See 1993 Amendment note above and Transfer of Functions notes below.

Par. (h). Pub. L. 102–300, § 6(a)(1), as amended by Pub. L. 103–80, § 4(b), substituted "its primary" for "any of its principal" in two places in concluding provisions.

Par. (u). Pub. L. 102–571 substituted "379e" for "376".

Par. (y)(1). Pub. L. 102–300, § 6(b)(2), struck out "of Health, Education, and Welfare" after "employees of the Department".

Pars. (bb) to (ee). Pub. L. 102–282 added pars. (bb) to (ee).

Par. (ff). Pub. L. 102–300, § 6(a)(2), added par. (ff).

1990—Par. (g)(1). Pub. L. 101–629, § 16(b)(1), struck out "; but does not include devices or their components, parts, or accessories" after "clause (A), (B), or (C)".

Pub. L. 101–535 inserted at end "A food for which a claim, subject to sections 343(r)(1)(B) and 343(r)(3) of this title or sections 343(r)(1)(B) and 343(r)(5)(D) of this title, is made in accordance with the requirements of section 343(r) of this title is not a drug under clause (B) solely because the label or labeling contains such a claim."

Par. (h)(3). Pub. L. 101–629, § 16(b)(2), which directed the amendment of subpar. (3) by substituting "its primary" for "any of its principal", could not be executed because "any of its principal" did not appear in subpar. (3).

1988—Par. (w)(3). Pub. L. 100–670 struck out subpar. (3) which read as follows: "which drug is composed wholly or partly of any kind of penicillin, streptomycin, chlortetracycline, chloramphenicol, or bacitracin, or any derivative thereof, except when there is in effect a published order of the Secretary declaring such drug not to be a new animal drug on the grounds that (A) the requirement of certification of batches of such drug, as provided for in section 360b(n) of this title, is not necessary to insure that the objectives specified in paragraph (3) thereof are achieved and (B) that neither subparagraph (1) nor (2) of this paragraph (w) applies to such drug."

1980—Par. (aa). Pub. L. 96–359 added par. (aa).

1977—Par. (z). Pub. L. 95–203 added par. (z).

1976—Par. (h). Pub. L. 94–295, § 3(a)(1)(A), expanded definition of "device" to include implements, machines, implants, in vitro reagents, and other similar or related articles, added recognition in the National Formulary or the United States Pharmacopeia, or any supplement to the Formulary or Pharmacopeia, to the enumeration of conditions under which a device may qualify for inclusion under this chapter, and inserted requirements that a device be one which does not achieve any of its principal intended purposes through chemical action within or on the body of man or other animals and which is not dependent upon being metabolized for the achievement of any of its principal intended purposes.

Par. (n). Pub. L. 94–278 inserted "or advertising" after "labeling" wherever appearing.

Par. (y). Pub. L. 94–295, § 3(a)(2), added par. (y).

1972—Par. (q). Pub. L. 92–516 substituted reference to pesticide for reference to economic poison.

1970—Par. (a)(2). Pub. L. 91–513, § 701(g), struck out reference to sections 321, 331(i), 331(p), 331(q), 332, 333, 334, 337, 360, 360a, 372, 373, 374, and 375 of this title as they apply to depressant or stimulant drugs.

Par. (v). Pub. L. 91–513, § 701(a), struck out par. (v) which defined "depressant or stimulant drug".

1968—Par. (a)(2). Pub. L. 90–639, § 4(a), extended provisions to cover depressant and stimulant drugs, the containers thereof, and equipment used in manufacturing, compounding, or processing such drugs, to the Canal Zone.

Par. (p). Pub. L. 90–399, § 102(a), (b), inserted "(except a new animal drug or an animal feed bearing or containing a new animal drug)" after "Any drug" in subpars. (1) and (2), respectively.

Par. (s)(5). Pub. L. 90–399, § 102(c), added subpar. (5).

Par. (u). Pub. L. 90–399, § 102(d), inserted reference to section 360b of this title.

Par. (v)(3). Pub. L. 90–639, § 1, inserted reference to lysergic acid diethylamide.

Pars. (w), (x). Pub. L. 90–399, § 102(e), added pars. (w) and (x).

1965—Par. (g). Pub. L. 89–74, § 9(b), designated existing provisions as subpar. (1), redesignated cls. (1) to (4) thereof as (A) to (D), substituted "(A), (B), or (C)" for "(1), (2), or (3)" and added subpar. (2).

Par. (v). Pub. L. 89–74, § 3(a), added par. (v).

1962—Par. (a). Pub. L. 87–781, § 307(a), designated existing provisions as subpar. (2), inserted "Commonwealth of Puerto Rico and the", and added subpar. (1).

Par. (p)(1). Pub. L. 87–781, § 102(a)(1), inserted "and effectiveness" after "to evaluate the safety", and "and effective" after "as safe".

Par. (p)(2). Pub. L. 87–781, § 102(a)(2), inserted "and effectiveness" after "safety".

1960—Par. (s). Pub. L. 86–618, § 101(a), excluded color additives from definition of "food additive".

Par. (t). Pub. L. 86–618, § 101(c), added par. (t). Former par. (t) redesignated (u).

Par. (u). Pub. L. 86–618, § 101(b), redesignated par. (t) as (u) and inserted reference to section 376 of this title.

1958—Pars. (s), (t). Pub. L. 85–929 added pars. (s) and (t).

1954—Pars. (q), (r). Act July 22, 1954, added pars. (q) and (r).

EFFECTIVE DATE OF 2004 AMENDMENT

Pub. L. 108–282, title II, § 203(d), Aug. 2, 2004, 118 Stat. 908, provided that: "The amendments made by this section [amending this section and sections 343 and 343–1 of this title] shall apply to any food that is labeled on or after January 1, 2006."

EFFECTIVE DATE OF 1997 AMENDMENT

Section 501 of Pub. L. 105–115 provided that: "Except as otherwise provided in this Act [see Short Title of 1997 Amendment note set out under section 301 of this title], this Act and the amendments made by this Act, other than the provisions of and the amendments made by sections 111, 121, 125, and 307 [enacting section 355a of this title, amending this section and sections 331, 335a, 351, 352, 360, 360j, 360aa to 360cc, 360ee, 374, 379g, 381, and 382 of this title, section 45C of Title 26, Internal Revenue Code, section 156 of Title 35, Patents, and section 8126 of Title 38, Veterans' Benefits, repealing sections 356 and 357 of this title, and enacting provisions set out as notes under sections 351 and 355 of this title], shall take effect 90 days after the date of enactment of this Act [Nov. 21, 1997]."

EFFECTIVE DATE OF 1990 AMENDMENT

Amendment by Pub. L. 101–535 effective six months after the date of the promulgation of final regulations to implement section 343(r) of this title, or if such regulations are not promulgated, the date proposed regulations are to be considered as such final regulations (Nov. 8, 1992), with exception for persons marketing food the brand name of which contains a term defined by the Secretary under section 343(r)(2)(A)(i) of this title, see section 10(a) of Pub. L. 101–535, set out as a note under section 343 of this title.

EFFECTIVE DATE OF 1976 AMENDMENT

Amendment by Pub. L. 94–278 effective 180 days after Apr. 22, 1976, see section 502(c) of Pub. L. 94–278, set out as a note under section 334 of this title.

EFFECTIVE DATE OF 1972 AMENDMENT

Amendment by Pub. L. 92–516 effective at the close of Oct. 21, 1972, except if regulations are necessary for the implementation of any provision that becomes effective on Oct. 21, 1972, and continuation in effect of subchapter I of chapter 6 of Title 7, and regulations thereunder, relating to the control of economic poisons, as in existence prior to Oct. 21, 1972, until superseded by provisions of Pub. L. 92–516, and regulations thereunder, see section 4 of Pub. L. 92–516, set out as an Effective Date note under section 136 of Title 7, Agriculture.

EFFECTIVE DATE OF 1970 AMENDMENT

Amendment by Pub. L. 91–513 effective on first day of seventh calendar month that begins after Oct. 26, 1970, see section 704 of Pub. L. 91–513, set out as an Effective Date note under section 801 of this title.

EFFECTIVE DATE OF 1968 AMENDMENTS; TRANSITIONAL PROVISIONS

Section 6 of Pub. L. 90–639 provided that: "The amendments made by this Act [amending this section, sections 331, 333, 334, and 360a of this title, and provisions set out as a note under section 289a of Title 42, The Public Health and Welfare] shall apply only with respect to violations of the Federal Food, Drug, and Cosmetic Act [this chapter] committed after the date of the enactment of this Act [Oct. 24, 1968]."

Amendment by Pub. L. 90–399 effective on first day of thirteenth calendar month after July 13, 1968, except that in the case of a drug (other than one subject to section 360b(n) of this title) intended for use in animals other than man which, on Oct. 9, 1962, was commercially used or sold in the United States, was not a new drug as defined in par. (p) of this section then in force, and was not covered by an effective application under section 355 of this title, the words "effectiveness" and "effective" contained in par. (v) of this section not applicable to such drug when intended solely for use under conditions prescribed, recommended, or suggested in labeling with respect to such drug on that day, see section 108(a), (b)(3) of Pub. L. 90–399, as amended, set out as an Effective Date and Transitional Provisions note under section 360b of this title.

EFFECTIVE DATE OF 1965 AMENDMENT

Section 11 of Pub. L. 89–74 provided that: "The foregoing provisions of this Act [see Short Title of 1965 Amendment note set out under section 301 of this title] shall take effect on the first day of the seventh calendar month [Feb. 1, 1966] following the month in which this Act is enacted [July 15, 1965]; except that (1) the Secretary shall permit persons, owning or operating any establishment engaged in manufacturing, preparing, propagating, compounding, processing, wholesaling, jobbing, or distributing any depressant or stimulant drug, as referred to in the amendments made by section 4 of this Act to section 510 of the Federal Food, Drug, and Cosmetic Act [section 360 of this title], to register their name, places of business, and establishments, and other information prescribed by such amendments, with the Secretary prior to such effective date, and (2) sections 201(v) and 511(g) of the Federal Food, Drug, and Cosmetic Act, as added by this act [par. (v) of this section and par. (g) of section 360a of this title], and the provisions of sections 8 [amending section 372 of this title and section 1114 of Title 18, Crimes and Criminal Procedure] and 10 [set out as a note under this section] shall take effect upon the date of enactment of this Act [July 15, 1965]."

EFFECTIVE DATE OF 1962 AMENDMENT

Section 107 of Pub. L. 87–781 provided that:

"(a) Except as otherwise provided in this section, the amendments made by the foregoing sections of this part A [amending this section and sections 331, 332, 348, 351 to 353, 355, 357, 379e of this title, and enacting provisions set out as a note under section 355 of this title] shall take effect on the date of enactment of this Act [Oct. 10, 1962].

"(b) The amendments made by sections 101, 103, 105, and 106 of this part A [amending sections 331, 332, 351, 352, 355, and 357 of this title] shall, with respect to any drug, take effect on the first day of the seventh calendar month following the month in which this Act is enacted [Oct. 1962].

"(c)(1) As used in this subsection, the term 'enactment date' means the date of enactment of this Act; and the term 'basic Act' means the Federal Food, Drug, and Cosmetic Act [this chapter].

"(2) An application filed pursuant to section 505(b) of the basic Act [section 355(b) of this title] which was 'effective' within the meaning of that Act on the day immediately preceding the enactment date shall be deemed as of the enactment date, to be an application 'approved' by the Secretary within the meaning of the basic Act as amended by this Act.

"(3) In the case of any drug with respect to which an application filed under section 505(b) of the basic Act is deemed to be an approved application on the enactment date by virtue of paragraph (2) of this subsection—

"(A) the amendments made by this Act to section 201(p), and to subsections (b) and (d) of section 505, of the basic Act [par. (p) of this section, and subsecs. (b) and (d) of section 355 of this title], insofar as such amendments relate to the effectiveness of drugs, shall not, so long as approval of such application is not withdrawn or suspended pursuant to section 505(e) of that Act [section 355(e) of this title], apply to such drug when intended solely for use under conditions prescribed, recommended, or suggested in labeling covered by such approved application, but shall apply to any changed use, or conditions of use, prescribed, recommended, or suggested in its labeling, including such conditions of use as are the subject of an amendment or supplement to such application pending on, or filed after, the enactment date; and

"(B) clause (3) of the first sentence of section 505(e) of the basic Act, as amended by this Act [section 355(e) of this title], shall not apply to such drug when intended solely for use under conditions prescribed, recommended, or suggested in labeling covered by such approved application (except with respect to such use, or conditions of use, as are the subject of an amendment or supplement to such approved application, which amendment or supplement has been approved after the enactment date under section 505 of the basic Act as amended by this Act [section 355 of this title]) until whichever of the following first occurs: (i) the expiration of the two-year period beginning with the enactment date; (ii) the effective date of an order under section 505(e) of the basic Act [section 355(e) of this title], other than clause (3) of the first sentence of such section 505(e) [section 355(e) of this title], withdrawing or suspending the approval of such application.

"(4) In the case of any drug which, on the day immediately preceding the enactment date, (A) was commercially used or sold in the United States, (B) was not a new drug as defined by section 201(p) of the basic Act as then in force [par. (p) of this section], and (C) was not covered by an effective application under section 505 of that Act [section 355 of this title], the amendments to section 201(p) [par. (p) of this section] made by this Act shall not apply to such drug when intended solely for use under conditions prescribed, recommended, or suggested in labeling with respect to such drug on that day."

EFFECTIVE DATE OF 1960 AMENDMENT

Amendment by Pub. L. 86–618 effective July 12, 1960, subject to provisions of section 203 of Pub. L. 86–618, see section 202 of Pub. L. 86–618, set out as a note under section 379e of this title.

EFFECTIVE DATE OF 1958 AMENDMENT

Amendment by Pub. L. 85–929 effective Sept. 6, 1958, see section 6(a) of Pub. L. 85–929, set out as a note under section 342 of this title.

EFFECTIVE DATE OF 1954 AMENDMENT

For effective date of amendment by act July 22, 1954, see section 5 of that act, set out as a note under section 342 of this title.

CONSTRUCTION OF AMENDMENTS BY PUB. L. 102–282

Amendment by Pub. L. 102–282 not to preclude any other civil, criminal, or administrative remedy provided under Federal or State law, including any private right of action against any person for the same action subject to any action or civil penalty under an amendment made by Pub. L. 102–282, see section 7 of Pub. L. 102–282, set out as a note under section 335a of this title.

CONSTRUCTION OF AMENDMENTS BY PUB. L. 101–535

Amendments by Pub. L. 101–535 not to be construed to alter authority of Secretary of Health and Human Services and Secretary of Agriculture under the Federal Food, Drug, and Cosmetic Act (21 U.S.C. 301 et seq.), the Federal Meat Inspection Act (21 U.S.C. 601 et seq.), the Poultry Products Inspection Act (21 U.S.C. 451 et seq.), and the Egg Products Inspection Act (21 U.S.C. 1031 et seq.), see section 9 of Pub. L. 101–535, set out as a note under section 343 of this title.

SAVINGS PROVISION

Section 702 of Pub. L. 91–513, as amended by Pub. L. 93–481, §2, Oct. 26, 1974, 88 Stat. 1455, provided that:

"(a) Prosecutions for any violation of law occurring prior to the effective date [see Effective Date of 1970 Amendment note above] of section 701 [repealing section 360a of this title, and amending sections 321, 331, 333, 334, 360, 372, and 381 of this title, sections 1114 and 1952 of Title 18, Crimes and Criminal Procedure, and section 242 of Title 42, The Public Health and Welfare] shall not be affected by the repeals or amendments made by such section, or abated by reason thereof.

"(b) Civil seizures or forfeitures and injunctive proceedings commenced prior to the effective date of section 701 shall not be affected by the repeals or amendments made by such section, or abated by reason thereof.

"(c) All administrative proceedings pending before the Bureau of Narcotics and Dangerous Drugs [now the Drug Enforcement Administration] on the date of enactment of this Act [Oct. 27, 1970] shall be continued and brought to final determination in accord with laws and regulations in effect prior to such date of enactment. Where a drug is finally determined under such proceedings to be a depressant or stimulant drug, as defined in section 201(v) of the Federal Food, Drug, and Cosmetic Act [par. (v) of this section], such drug shall automatically be controlled under this title [subchapter I of chapter 13 of this title] by the Attorney General without further proceedings and listed in the appropriate schedule after he has obtained the recommendation of the Secretary. Any drug with respect to which such a final determination has been made prior to the date of enactment of this Act which is not listed in section 202 [section 812 of this title] within schedules I through V shall automatically be controlled under this title [subchapter I of chapter 13 of this title] by the Attorney General without further proceedings, and be listed in the appropriate schedule, after he has obtained the recommendations of the Secretary.

"(d) Notwithstanding subsection (a) of this section or section 1103 [of Pub. L. 91–513, set out as a note under sections 171 to 174 of this title], section 4202 of title 18, United States Code, shall apply to any individual convicted under any of the laws repealed by this title or title III [subchapter I or subchapter II of chapter 13 of this title] without regard to the terms of any sentence imposed on such individual under such law."

TRANSFER OF FUNCTIONS

Secretary and Department of Health, Education, and Welfare redesignated Secretary and Department of Health and Human Services by Pub. L. 96–88, title V, §509(b), Oct. 17, 1979, 93 Stat. 695, which is classified to section 3508(b) of Title 20, Education.

Functions of Secretary of Health, Education, and Welfare [now Health and Human Services] under Federal Food, Drug, and Cosmetic Act, to the extent such functions related to administration and enforcement of the Poison Prevention Packaging Act of 1970 (15 U.S.C. 1471 et seq.), transferred to Consumer Product Safety Commission by section 2079 of Title 15, Commerce and Trade.

Functions of Secretary of Health, Education, and Welfare [now Health and Human Services] under Drug Abuse Control Amendments of 1965 [see Short Title of 1965 Amendment note set out under section 301 of this title] transferred to Attorney General except function of regulating counterfeiting of those drugs which are not "depressant or stimulant" drugs, see section 2 of Reorg. Plan No. 1 of 1968, set out in the Appendix to Title 5, Government Organization and Employees.

Functions of Federal Security Administrator transferred to Secretary of Health, Education, and Welfare and all agencies of Federal Security Agency transferred to Department of Health, Education, and Welfare by section 5 of Reorg. Plan No. 1 of 1953, set out in the Appendix to Title 5, Government Organization and Employees. Federal Security Agency and office of Administrator abolished by section 8 of Reorg. Plan No. 1 of 1953.

Food and Drug Administration in Department of Agriculture and its functions, except those functions relating to administration of Insecticide Act of 1910 and Naval Stores Act, transferred to Federal Security Agency, to be administered under direction and supervision of Federal Security Administrator, by Reorg. Plan No. IV of 1940, set out in the Appendix to Title 5.

REGULATION OF TOBACCO

Section 422 of Pub. L. 105–115 provided that: "Nothing in this Act [see Short Title of 1997 Amendment note set out under section 301 of this title] or the amendments made by this Act shall be construed to affect the question of whether the Secretary of Health and Human Services has any authority to regulate any tobacco product, tobacco ingredient, or tobacco additive. Such authority, if any, shall be exercised under the Federal Food, Drug, and Cosmetic Act [21 U.S.C. 301 et seq.] as in effect on the day before the date of the enactment of this Act [Nov. 21, 1997]."

CONGRESSIONAL FINDINGS RELATING TO PUB. L. 103–417

Section 2 of Pub. L. 103–417 provided that: "Congress finds that—

"(1) improving the health status of United States citizens ranks at the top of the national priorities of the Federal Government;

"(2) the importance of nutrition and the benefits of dietary supplements to health promotion and disease prevention have been documented increasingly in scientific studies;

"(3)(A) there is a link between the ingestion of certain nutrients or dietary supplements and the prevention of chronic diseases such as cancer, heart disease, and osteoporosis; and

"(B) clinical research has shown that several chronic diseases can be prevented simply with a healthful diet, such as a diet that is low in fat, saturated fat, cholesterol, and sodium, with a high proportion of plant-based foods;

"(4) healthful diets may mitigate the need for expensive medical procedures, such as coronary bypass surgery or angioplasty;

"(5) preventive health measures, including education, good nutrition, and appropriate use of safe nutritional supplements will limit the incidence of chronic diseases, and reduce long-term health care expenditures;

"(6)(A) promotion of good health and healthy lifestyles improves and extends lives while reducing health care expenditures; and

"(B) reduction in health care expenditures is of paramount importance to the future of the country and the economic well-being of the country;

"(7) there is a growing need for emphasis on the dissemination of information linking nutrition and long-term good health;

"(8) consumers should be empowered to make choices about preventive health care programs based on data from scientific studies of health benefits related to particular dietary supplements;

"(9) national surveys have revealed that almost 50 percent of the 260,000,000 Americans regularly consume dietary supplements of vitamins, minerals, or herbs as a means of improving their nutrition;

"(10) studies indicate that consumers are placing increased reliance on the use of nontraditional health care providers to avoid the excessive costs of traditional medical services and to obtain more holistic consideration of their needs;

"(11) the United States will spend over $1,000,000,000,000 on health care in 1994, which is about 12 percent of the Gross National Product of the United States, and this amount and percentage will continue to increase unless significant efforts are undertaken to reverse the increase;

"(12)(A) the nutritional supplement industry is an integral part of the economy of the United States;

"(B) the industry consistently projects a positive trade balance; and

"(C) the estimated 600 dietary supplement manufacturers in the United States produce approximately 4,000 products, with total annual sales of such products alone reaching at least $4,000,000,000;

"(13) although the Federal Government should take swift action against products that are unsafe or adulterated, the Federal Government should not take any actions to impose unreasonable regulatory barriers limiting or slowing the flow of safe products and accurate information to consumers;

"(14) dietary supplements are safe within a broad range of intake, and safety problems with the supplements are relatively rare; and

"(15)(A) legislative action that protects the right of access of consumers to safe dietary supplements is necessary in order to promote wellness; and

"(B) a rational Federal framework must be established to supersede the current ad hoc, patchwork regulatory policy on dietary supplements."

DISSEMINATION OF INFORMATION REGARDING THE DANGERS OF DRUG ABUSE

Section 5 of Pub. L. 90–639 provided that: "It is the sense of the Congress that, because of the inadequate knowledge on the part of the people of the United States of the substantial adverse effects of misuse of depressant and stimulant drugs, and of other drugs liable to abuse, on the individual, his family, and the community, the highest priority should be given to Federal programs to disseminate information which may be used to educate the public, particularly young persons, regarding the dangers of drug abuse."

CONGRESSIONAL FINDINGS AND DECLARATION OF POLICY

Section 2 of Pub. L. 89–74 provided that: "The Congress hereby finds and declares that there is a widespread illicit traffic in depressant and stimulant drugs moving in or otherwise affecting interstate commerce; that the use of such drugs, when not under the supervision of a licensed practitioner, often endangers safety on the highways (without distinction of interstate and intrastate traffic thereon) and otherwise has become a threat to the public health and safety, making additional regulation of such drugs necessary regardless of the intrastate or interstate origin of such drugs; that in order to make regulation and protection of interstate commerce in such drugs effective, regulation of intrastate commerce is also necessary because, among other things, such drugs, when held for illicit sale, often do not bear labeling showing their place of origin and because in the form in which they are so held or in which they are consumed a determination of their place of origin is often extremely difficult or impossible; and that regulation of interstate commerce without the regulation of intrastate commerce in such drugs, as provided in this Act [see Short Title of 1965 Amendment note set out under section 301 of this title], would discriminate against and adversely affect interstate commerce in such drugs."

EFFECT OF DRUG ABUSE CONTROL AMENDMENTS OF 1965 ON STATE LAWS

Section 10 of Pub. L. 89–74 provided that:

"(a) Nothing in this Act [enacting section 360a of this title, amending sections 321, 331, 333, 334, 360, and 372 of this title and section 1114 of Title 18, Crimes and Criminal Procedure, and enacting provisions set out as notes under sections 321, 352, and 360a of this title] shall be construed as authorizing the manufacture, compounding, processing, possession, sale, delivery, or other disposal of any drug in any State in contravention of the laws of such State.

"(b) No provision of this Act nor any amendment made by it shall be construed as indicating an intent on the part of the Congress to occupy the field in which such provision or amendment operates to the exclusion of any State law on the same subject matter, unless there is a direct and positive conflict between such provision or amendment and such State law so that the two cannot be reconciled or consistently stand together.

"(c) No amendment made by this Act shall be construed to prevent the enforcement in the courts of any State of any statute of such State prescribing any criminal penalty for any act made criminal by any such amendment."

EFFECT OF DRUG AMENDMENTS OF 1962 ON STATE LAWS

Section 202 of Pub. L. 87–781 provided that: "Nothing in the amendments made by this Act [enacting sections 358 to 360, amending sections 321, 331, 332, 348, 351 to 353, 355, 357, 372, 374, 379e, and 381 of this title, and enacting provisions set out as notes under sections 321, 331, 332, 352, 355, 360, and 374 of this title] to the Federal Food, Drug, and Cosmetic Act [this chapter] shall be construed as invalidating any provision of State law which would be valid in the absence of such amendments unless there is a direct and positive conflict between such amendments and such provision of State law."

DEFINITIONS

Section 2 of Pub. L. 105–115 provided that: "In this Act [see Short Title of 1997 Amendment note set out under section 301 of this title], the terms 'drug', 'device', 'food', and 'dietary supplement' have the meaning given such terms in section 201 of the Federal Food, Drug, and Cosmetic Act (21 U.S.C. 321)."

§ 321a. "Butter" defined

For the purposes of the Food and Drug Act of June 30, 1906 (Thirty-fourth Statutes at Large, page 768) "butter" shall be understood to mean the food product usually known as butter, and which is made exclusively from milk or cream, or both, with or without common salt, and with or without additional coloring matter, and containing not less than 80 per centum by weight of milk fat, all tolerances having been allowed for.

(Mar. 4, 1923, ch. 268, 42 Stat. 1500.)

REFERENCES IN TEXT

The Food and Drug Act of June 30, 1906, referred to in text, is act June 30, 1906, ch. 3915, 34 Stat. 768, as amended, which was classified to subchapter I (§1 et seq.) of chapter 1 of this title, was repealed (except for section 14a which was transferred to section 376 of this title) by act June 25, 1938, ch. 675, §902(a), 52 Stat. 1059, and is covered by this chapter.

CODIFICATION

Section, which was not enacted as part of the Federal Food, Drug, and Cosmetic Act which comprises this chapter, was formerly classified to section 6 of this title. Section 902(a) of act June 25, 1938, set out as an Effective Date note under section 301 of this title, provided that this section should remain in force and effect and be applicable to the provisions of this chapter.

§ 321b. "Package" defined

The word "package" where it occurs the second and last time in the act entitled "An act to amend section 8 of an act entitled, 'An act for preventing the manufacture, sale, or transportation of adulterated or misbranded or poisonous deleterious foods, drugs, medicines, and liquors, and for regulating traffic therein, and for other purposes,'" approved March 3, 1913, shall include and shall be construed to include wrapped meats inclosed in papers or other materials as prepared by the manufacturers thereof for sale.

(July 24, 1919, ch. 26, 41 Stat. 271.)

REFERENCES IN TEXT

An act approved March 3, 1913, referred to in text, is act Mar. 3, 1913, ch. 117, 37 Stat. 732, which amended section 10 of this title. For complete classification of this Act to the Code, see Tables.

"An act for preventing the manufacture, sale, or transportation of adulterated or misbranded or poisonous deleterious foods, drugs, medicines, and liquors, and for regulating traffic therein, and for other purposes,", referred to in text, is act June 30, 1906, ch. 3915, 34 Stat. 768, which was classified to subchapter I (§1 et seq.) of chapter 1 of this title, was repealed (except for section 14a which was transferred to section 376 of this title) by act June 25, 1938, ch. 675, §902(a), 52 Stat. 1059, and is covered by this chapter.

CODIFICATION

Section, which was not enacted as part of the Federal Food, Drug, and Cosmetic Act which comprises this chapter, was formerly classified to the last sentence of paragraph third of section 10 of this title. Section 902(a) of act June 25, 1938, set out as an Effective Date note under section 301 of this title, provided that this section should remain in force and effect and be applicable to the provisions of this chapter.

§321c. Nonfat dry milk; "milk" defined

For the purposes of the Federal Food, Drug, and Cosmetic Act of June 26, 1938, (ch. 675, sec. 1, 52 Stat. 1040) [21 U.S.C. 301 et seq.] nonfat dry milk is the product resulting from the removal of fat and water from milk, and contains the lactose, milk proteins, and milk minerals in the same relative proportions as in the fresh milk from which made. It contains not over 5 per centum by weight of moisture. The fat content is not over 1½ per centum by weight unless otherwise indicated.

The term "milk", when used herein, means sweet milk of cows.

(Mar. 2, 1944, ch. 77, 58 Stat. 108; July 2, 1956, ch. 495, 70 Stat. 486.)

REFERENCES IN TEXT

The Federal Food, Drug, and Cosmetic Act of June 26, 1938 (ch. 675, sec. 1, 52 Stat. 1040), referred to in text, probably means act June 25, 1938, ch. 675, 52 Stat. 1040, as amended, which is classified generally to this chapter (§301 et seq.). For complete classification of this Act to the Code, see section 301 of this title and Tables.

CODIFICATION

Section was not enacted as a part of the Federal Food, Drug, and Cosmetic Act which comprises this chapter, but was made applicable thereto.

AMENDMENTS

1956—Act July 2, 1956, substituted "nonfat dry milk" for "nonfat dry milk solids or defatted milk solids".

§321d. Market names for catfish and ginseng

(a) Catfish labeling

(1) In general

Notwithstanding any other provision of law, for purposes of the Federal Food, Drug, and Cosmetic Act (21 U.S.C. 301 et seq.)—

(A) the term "catfish" may only be considered to be a common or usual name (or part thereof) for fish classified within the family Ictaluridae; and

(B) only labeling or advertising for fish classified within that family may include the term "catfish".

(2) Omitted

(b) Ginseng labeling

(1) In general

Notwithstanding any other provision of law, for purposes of the Federal Food, Drug, and Cosmetic Act (21 U.S.C. 301 et seq.)—

(A) the term "ginseng" may only be considered to be a common or usual name (or part thereof) for any herb or herbal ingredient derived from a plant classified within the genus Panax; and

(B) only labeling or advertising for herbs or herbal ingredients classified within that genus may include the term "ginseng".

(2) Omitted

(Pub. L. 107–171, title X, §10806, May 13, 2002, 116 Stat. 526.)

REFERENCES IN TEXT

The Federal Food, Drug, and Cosmetic Act, referred to in subsecs. (a)(1), (b)(1), is act June 25, 1938, ch. 675, 52 Stat. 1040, as amended, which is classified generally to this chapter. For complete classification of this Act to the Code, see section 301 of this title and Tables.

CODIFICATION

Section is comprised of section 10806 of Pub. L. 107–171. Subsecs. (a)(2) and (b)(2) of section 10806 of Pub. L. 107–171 amended section 343 of this title.

Section was enacted as part of the Farm Security and Rural Investment Act of 2002, and not as part of Federal Food, Drug, and Cosmetic Act which comprises this chapter.

SUBCHAPTER III—PROHIBITED ACTS AND PENALTIES

§331. Prohibited acts

The following acts and the causing thereof are prohibited:

(a) The introduction or delivery for introduction into interstate commerce of any food, drug, device, or cosmetic that is adulterated or misbranded.

(b) The adulteration or misbranding of any food, drug, device, or cosmetic in interstate commerce.

(c) The receipt in interstate commerce of any food, drug, device, or cosmetic that is adulterated or misbranded, and the delivery or proffered delivery thereof for pay or otherwise.

(d) The introduction or delivery for introduction into interstate commerce of any article in violation of section 344, 355, or 360bbb–3 of this title.

(e) The refusal to permit access to or copying of any record as required by section 350a, 350c,

350f(g), 350e, 354, 360bbb–3, 373, 374(a), 379aa, or 379aa–1 of this title; or the failure to establish or maintain any record, or make any report, required under section 350a, 350c(b), 350f, 350e, 354, 355(i) or (k), 360b(a)(4)(C), 360b(j), (*l*) or (m), 360ccc–1(i).,[1] 360e(f), 360i, 360bbb–3, 379aa, or 379aa–1 of this title, or the refusal to permit access to or verification or copying of any such required record.

(f) The refusal to permit entry or inspection as authorized by section 374 of this title.

(g) The manufacture within any Territory of any food, drug, device, or cosmetic that is adulterated or misbranded.

(h) The giving of a guaranty or undertaking referred to in section 333(c)(2) of this title, which guaranty or undertaking is false, except by a person who relied upon a guaranty or undertaking to the same effect signed by, and containing the name and address of, the person residing in the United States from whom he received in good faith the food, drug, device, or cosmetic; or the giving of a guaranty or undertaking referred to in section 333(c)(3) of this title, which guaranty or undertaking is false.

(i)(1) Forging, counterfeiting, simulating, or falsely representing, or without proper authority using any mark, stamp, tag, label, or other identification device authorized or required by regulations promulgated under the provisions of section 344 or 379e of this title.

(2) Making, selling, disposing of, or keeping in possession, control, or custody, or concealing any punch, die, plate, stone, or other thing designed to print, imprint, or reproduce the trademark, trade name, or other identifying mark, imprint, or device of another or any likeness of any of the foregoing upon any drug or container or labeling thereof so as to render such drug a counterfeit drug.

(3) The doing of any act which causes a drug to be a counterfeit drug, or the sale or dispensing, or the holding for sale or dispensing, of a counterfeit drug.

(j) The using by any person to his own advantage, or revealing, other than to the Secretary or officers or employees of the Department, or to the courts when relevant in any judicial proceeding under this chapter, any information acquired under authority of section 344, 348, 350a, 350c, 355, 360, 360b, 360c, 360d, 360e, 360f, 360h, 360i, 360j, 360ccc, 360ccc–1, 360ccc–2.,[1] 374, 379, or 379e of this title concerning any method or process which as a trade secret is entitled to protection; or the violating of section 346a(i)(2) of this title or any regulation issued under that section..[1] This paragraph does not authorize the withholding of information from either House of Congress or from, to the extent of matter within its jurisdiction, any committee or subcommittee of such committee or any joint committee of Congress or any subcommittee of such joint committee.

(k) The alteration, mutilation, destruction, obliteration, or removal of the whole or any part of the labeling of, or the doing of any other act with respect to, a food, drug, device, or cosmetic, if such act is done while such article is held for sale (whether or not the first sale) after shipment in interstate commerce and results in such article being adulterated or misbranded.

(*l*) Repealed. Pub. L. 105–115, title IV, § 421, Nov. 21, 1997, 111 Stat. 2380.

(m) The sale or offering for sale of colored oleomargarine or colored margarine, or the possession or serving of colored oleomargarine or colored margarine in violation of subsections (b) or (c) of section 347 of this title.

(n) The using, in labeling, advertising or other sales promotion of any reference to any report or analysis furnished in compliance with section 374 of this title.

(*o*) In the case of a prescription drug distributed or offered for sale in interstate commerce, the failure of the manufacturer, packer, or distributor thereof to maintain for transmittal, or to transmit, to any practitioner licensed by applicable State law to administer such drug who makes written request for information as to such drug, true and correct copies of all printed matter which is required to be included in any package in which that drug is distributed or sold, or such other printed matter as is approved by the Secretary. Nothing in this paragraph shall be construed to exempt any person from any labeling requirement imposed by or under other provisions of this chapter.

(p) The failure to register in accordance with section 360 of this title, the failure to provide any information required by section 360(j) or 360(k) of this title, or the failure to provide a notice required by section 360(j)(2) of this title.

(q)(1) The failure or refusal to (A) comply with any requirement prescribed under section 360h or 360j(g) of this title, (B) furnish any notification or other material or information required by or under section 360i or 360j(g) of this title, or (C) comply with a requirement under section 360*l* of this title.

(2) With respect to any device, the submission of any report that is required by or under this chapter that is false or misleading in any material respect.

(r) The movement of a device in violation of an order under section 334(g) of this title or the removal or alteration of any mark or label required by the order to identify the device as detained.

(s) The failure to provide the notice required by section 350a(c) or 350a(e) of this title, the failure to make the reports required by section 350a(f)(1)(B) of this title, the failure to retain the records required by section 350a(b)(4) of this title, or the failure to meet the requirements prescribed under section 350a(f)(3) of this title.

(t) The importation of a drug in violation of section 381(d)(1) of this title, the sale, purchase, or trade of a drug or drug sample or the offer to sell, purchase, or trade a drug or drug sample in violation of section 353(c) of this title, the sale, purchase, or trade of a coupon, the offer to sell, purchase, or trade such a coupon, or the counterfeiting of such a coupon in violation of section 353(c)(2) of this title, the distribution of a drug sample in violation of section 353(d) of this title or the failure to otherwise comply with the requirements of section 353(d) of this title, or the distribution of drugs in violation of section 353(e) of this title or the failure to otherwise comply with the requirements of section 353(e) of this title.

[1] So in original.

(u) The failure to comply with any requirements of the provisions of, or any regulations or orders of the Secretary, under section 360b(a)(4)(A), 360b(a)(4)(D), or 360b(a)(5) of this title.

(v) The introduction or delivery for introduction into interstate commerce of a dietary supplement that is unsafe under section 350b of this title.

(w) The making of a knowingly false statement in any statement, certificate of analysis, record, or report required or requested under section 381(d)(3) of this title; the failure to submit a certificate of analysis as required under such section; the failure to maintain records or to submit records or reports as required by such section; the release into interstate commerce of any article or portion thereof imported into the United States under such section or any finished product made from such article or portion, except for export in accordance with section 381(e) or 382 of this title, or with section 262(h) of title 42; or the failure to so export or to destroy such an article or portions thereof, or such a finished product.

(x) The falsification of a declaration of conformity submitted under section 360d(c) of this title or the failure or refusal to provide data or information requested by the Secretary under paragraph (3) of such section.

(y) In the case of a drug, device, or food—

(1) the submission of a report or recommendation by a person accredited under section 360m of this title that is false or misleading in any material respect;

(2) the disclosure by a person accredited under section 360m of this title of confidential commercial information or any trade secret without the express written consent of the person who submitted such information or secret to such person; or

(3) the receipt by a person accredited under section 360m of this title of a bribe in any form or the doing of any corrupt act by such person associated with a responsibility delegated to such person under this chapter.

(z) Omitted.

(aa) The importation of a prescription drug in violation of section 384 of this title, the falsification of any record required to be maintained or provided to the Secretary under such section, or any other violation of regulations under such section.

(bb) The transfer of an article of food in violation of an order under section 334(h) of this title, or the removal or alteration of any mark or label required by the order to identify the article as detained.

(cc) The importing or offering for import into the United States of an article of food by, with the assistance of, or at the direction of, a person debarred under section 335a(b)(3) of this title.

(dd) The failure to register in accordance with section 350d of this title.

(ee) The importing or offering for import into the United States of an article of food in violation of the requirements under section 381(m) of this title.

(ff) The importing or offering for import into the United States of a drug or device with respect to which there is a failure to comply with a request of the Secretary to submit to the Secretary a statement under section 381(*o*) of this title.

(gg) The knowing failure to comply with paragraph (7)(E) of section 374(g) of this title; the knowing inclusion by a person accredited under paragraph (2) of such section of false information in an inspection report under paragraph (7)(A) of such section; or the knowing failure of such a person to include material facts in such a report.

(hh) The failure by a shipper, carrier by motor vehicle or rail vehicle, receiver, or any other person engaged in the transportation of food to comply with the sanitary transportation practices prescribed by the Secretary under section 350e of this title.

(ii) The falsification of a report of a serious adverse event submitted to a responsible person (as defined under section 379aa or 379aa–1 of this title) or the falsification of a serious adverse event report (as defined under section 379aa or 379aa–1 of this title) submitted to the Secretary.

(jj)(1) The failure to submit the certification required by section 282(j)(5)(B) of title 42, or knowingly submitting a false certification under such section.

(2) The failure to submit clinical trial information required under subsection (j) of section 282 of title 42.

(3) The submission of clinical trial information under subsection (j) of section 282 of title 42 that is false or misleading in any particular under paragraph (5)(D) of such subsection (j).

(kk) The dissemination of a television advertisement without complying with section 353b of this title.

(*ll*) The introduction or delivery for introduction into interstate commerce of any food to which has been added a drug approved under section 355 of this title, a biological product licensed under section 262 of title 42, or a drug or a biological product for which substantial clinical investigations have been instituted and for which the existence of such investigations has been made public, unless—

(1) such drug or such biological product was marketed in food before any approval of the drug under section 355 of this title, before licensure of the biological product under such section 262 of title 42, and before any substantial clinical investigations involving the drug or the biological product have been instituted;

(2) the Secretary, in the Secretary's discretion, has issued a regulation, after notice and comment, approving the use of such drug or such biological product in the food;

(3) the use of the drug or the biological product in the food is to enhance the safety of the food to which the drug or the biological product is added or applied and not to have independent biological or therapeutic effects on humans, and the use is in conformity with—

(A) a regulation issued under section 348 of this title prescribing conditions of safe use in food;

(B) a regulation listing or affirming conditions under which the use of the drug or the biological product in food is generally recognized as safe;

(C) the conditions of use identified in a notification to the Secretary of a claim of exemption from the premarket approval requirements for food additives based on the notifier's determination that the use of the drug or the biological product in food is generally recognized as safe, provided that the Secretary has not questioned the general recognition of safety determination in a letter to the notifier;

(D) a food contact substance notification that is effective under section 348(h) of this title; or

(E) such drug or biological product had been marketed for smoking cessation prior to September 27, 2007; or

(4) the drug is a new animal drug whose use is not unsafe under section 360b of this title.

(mm) The failure to submit a report or provide a notification required under section 350f(d) of this title.

(nn) The falsification of a report or notification required under section 350f(d) of this title.

(June 25, 1938, ch. 675, § 301, 52 Stat. 1042; Dec. 22, 1941, ch. 613, § 1, 55 Stat. 851; July 6, 1945, ch. 281, § 1, 59 Stat. 463; Mar. 10, 1947, ch. 16, § 1, 61 Stat. 11; June 24, 1948, ch. 613, § 1, 62 Stat. 582; Mar. 16, 1950, ch. 61, § 3(b), 64 Stat. 20; Aug. 7, 1953, ch. 350, § 2, 67 Stat. 477; Pub. L. 85–929, § 5, Sept. 6, 1958, 72 Stat. 1788; Pub. L. 86–618, title I, §§ 104, 105(a), July 12, 1960, 74 Stat. 403; Pub. L. 87–781, title I, §§ 103(c), 104(e)(1), 106(c), 114(a), title III, § 304, Oct. 10, 1962, 76 Stat. 784, 785, 788, 791, 795; Pub. L. 89–74, §§ 5, 9(c), July 15, 1965, 79 Stat. 232, 235; Pub. L. 90–399, § 103, July 13, 1968, 82 Stat. 352; Pub. L. 90–639, § 2(b), Oct. 24, 1968, 82 Stat. 1361; Pub. L. 91–513, title II, § 701(a), Oct. 27, 1970, 84 Stat. 1281; Pub. L. 92–387, § 4(e), Aug. 16, 1972, 86 Stat. 562; Pub. L. 94–295, §§ 3(b), 4(b)(1), 7(b), May 28, 1976, 90 Stat. 576, 580, 582; Pub. L. 96–359, § 5, Sept. 26, 1980, 94 Stat. 1193; Pub. L. 99–570, title IV, § 4014(b)(2), Oct. 27, 1986, 100 Stat. 3207–120; Pub. L. 100–293, § 7(a), Apr. 22, 1988, 102 Stat. 99; Pub. L. 101–502, § 5(j), Nov. 3, 1990, 104 Stat. 1289; Pub. L. 101–508, title IV, § 4755(c)(2), Nov. 5, 1990, 104 Stat. 1388–210; Pub. L. 102–300, § 3(a)(1), June 16, 1992, 106 Stat. 238; Pub. L. 102–571, title I, § 107(2), (3), Oct. 29, 1992, 106 Stat. 4499; Pub. L. 103–80, § 3(c), Aug. 13, 1993, 107 Stat. 775; Pub. L. 103–396, § 2(b)(1), Oct. 22, 1994, 108 Stat. 4154; Pub. L. 103–417, § 10(b), Oct. 25, 1994, 108 Stat. 4332; Pub. L. 104–134, title II, § 2103, Apr. 26, 1996, 110 Stat. 1321–319; Pub. L. 104–170, title IV, § 403, Aug. 3, 1996, 110 Stat. 1514; Pub. L. 104–250, § 5(d), Oct. 9, 1996, 110 Stat. 3156; Pub. L. 105–115, title I, § 125(a)(2)(A), (C), (b)(2)(B), title II, §§ 204(b), 210(c), title IV, §§ 401(b), 421, Nov. 21, 1997, 111 Stat. 2325, 2336, 2345, 2364, 2380; Pub. L. 106–387, § 1(a) [title VII, § 745(d)(1)], Oct. 28, 2000, 114 Stat. 1549, 1549A–39; Pub. L. 107–188, title III, §§ 303(b), 304(d), 305(b), 306(c), 307(b), 321(b)(2), 322(b), June 12, 2002, 116 Stat. 664, 666, 668, 670, 672, 676, 677; Pub. L. 107–250, title II, § 201(d), Oct. 26, 2002, 116 Stat. 1609; Pub. L. 108–136, div. A, title XVI, § 1603(c), Nov. 24, 2003, 117 Stat. 1690; Pub. L. 108–173, title XI, § 1121(b)(1), Dec. 8, 2003, 117 Stat. 2469; Pub. L. 108–214, § 2(b)(2)(A), Apr. 1, 2004, 118 Stat. 575; Pub. L. 108–282, title I, § 102(b)(5)(C), (D), Aug. 2, 2004, 118 Stat. 902; Pub. L. 109–59, title VII, § 7202(d), (e), Aug. 10, 2005, 119 Stat. 1913; Pub. L. 109–462, §§ 2(c), 3(b), 4(a), Dec. 22, 2006, 120 Stat. 3472, 3475; Pub. L. 110–85, title VIII, § 801(b)(1), title IX, §§ 901(d)(1), 912(a), title X, § 1005(d), Sept. 27, 2007, 121 Stat. 920, 939, 951, 968.)

AMENDMENTS

2007—Par. (e). Pub. L. 110–85, § 1005(d)(1), substituted "350c, 350f(g)," for "350c," and "350c(b), 350f" for "350c(b)".

Par. (jj). Pub. L. 110–85, § 801(b)(1), added par. (jj).

Par. (kk). Pub. L. 110–85, § 901(d)(1), added par. (kk).

Par. (*ll*). Pub. L. 110–85, § 912(a), added par. (*ll*).

Pars. (mm), (nn). Pub. L. 110–85, § 1005(d)(2), added pars. (mm) and (nn).

2006—Par. (e). Pub. L. 109–462, § 3(b), substituted "374(a), 379aa, or 379aa–1" for "374(a), or 379aa" and "360bbb–3, 379aa, or 379aa–1" for "360bbb–3, or 379aa".

Pub. L. 109–462, § 2(c), substituted ", 374(a), or 379aa" for ", or 374(a)" and ", 360bbb–3, or 379aa" for ", or 360bbb–3".

Par. (ii). Pub. L. 109–462, § 4(a), added par. (ii).

2005—Par. (e). Pub. L. 109–59, § 7202(d), inserted "350e," before "354," in two places.

Par. (hh). Pub. L. 109–59, § 7202(e), added par. (hh).

2004—Par. (e). Pub. L. 108–282, § 102(b)(5)(C), which directed the substitution of "360b(a)(4)(C), 360b (j), (*l*) or (m), 360ccc–1(i)," for "360b(a)(4)(C), 360b(j), (*l*) or (m)" was executed by making the substitution for "360b(a)(4)(C), 360b(j), (*l*), or (m)", to reflect the probable intent of Congress.

Par. (j). Pub. L. 108–282, § 102(b)(5)(D), substituted "360j, 360ccc, 360ccc–1, 360ccc–2," for "360j".

Par. (gg). Pub. L. 108–214 amended par. (gg) generally. Prior to amendment, text read as follows: "The knowing failure of a person accredited under paragraph (2) of section 374(g) of this title to comply with paragraph (7)(E) of such section; the knowing inclusion by such a person of false information in an inspection report under paragraph (7)(A) of such section; or the knowing failure of such a person to include material facts in such a report."

2003—Par. (d). Pub. L. 108–136 substituted "section 344, 355, or 360bbb–3" for "section 344 or 355".

Par. (e). Pub. L. 108–136 inserted "360bbb–3," after "350c, 354," and substituted "360i, or 360bbb–3" for "or 360i".

Par. (aa). Pub. L. 108–173 substituted "prescription drug in violation of section 384" for "covered product in violation of section 384".

2002—Par. (e). Pub. L. 107–188, § 306(c)(1), substituted "by section 350a, 350c, 354, 373, or 374(a) of this title" for "by section 350a, 354, or 373 of this title" and "under section 350a, 350c(b)" for "under section 350a".

Par. (j). Pub. L. 107–188, § 306(c)(2), inserted "350c," after "350a,".

Par. (w). Pub. L. 107–188, § 322(b), amended par. (w) generally. Prior to amendment, par. (w) read as follows: "The making of a knowingly false statement in any record or report required or requested under subparagraph (A) or (B) of section 381(d)(3) of this title, the failure to submit or maintain records as required by sections 381(d)(3)(A) and 381(d)(3)(B) of this title, the release into interstate commerce of any article imported into the United States under section 381(d)(3) of this title or any finished product made from such article (except for export in accordance with section 381(e) or 382 of this title or section 262(h) of title 42), or the failure to export or destroy any component, part or accessory not incorporated into a drug, biological product or device that will be exported in accordance with section 381(e) or 382 of this title or section 262(h) of title 42."

Par. (bb). Pub. L. 107–188, § 303(b), added par. (bb).

Par. (cc). Pub. L. 107–188, § 304(d), added par. (cc).

Par. (dd). Pub. L. 107–188, § 305(b), added par. (dd).

Par. (ee). Pub. L. 107–188, § 307(b), added par. (ee).

Par. (ff). Pub. L. 107–188, § 321(b)(2), added par. (ff).

Par. (gg). Pub. L. 107–250 added par. (gg).

2000—Par. (aa). Pub. L. 106–387 added par. (aa).

1997—Par. (e). Pub. L. 105–115, § 125(b)(2)(B), struck out "357(d) or (g)," after "355(i) or (k),".

Par. (i)(1). Pub. L. 105–115, § 125(a)(2)(C), struck out ", 356, 357," before "or 379e of this title".

Par. (j). Pub. L. 105–115, §125(a)(2)(A), struck out "356, 357," before "360,".

Par. (l). Pub. L. 105–115, §421, struck out par. (l) which read as follows: "The using, on the labeling of any drug or device or in any advertising relating to such drug or device, of any representation or suggestion that approval of an application with respect to such drug or device is in effect under section 355, 360e, or 360j(g) of this title, as the case may be, or that such drug or device complies with the provisions of such section."

Par. (x). Pub. L. 105–115, §204(b), added par. (x).

Par. (y). Pub. L. 105–115, §210(c), added par. (y).

Par. (z). Pub. L. 105–115, §401(b), temporarily added par. (z) which related to dissemination of information in violation of section 360aaa of this title. See Effective and Termination Dates of 1997 Amendment note below.

1996—Par. (e). Pub. L. 104–250 inserted ", 354," before "or 373 of this title" and "354," before "355(i) or (k)".

Par. (j). Pub. L. 104–170 inserted before period at end of first sentence "; or the violating of section 346a(i)(2) of this title or any regulation issued under that section."

Pars. (u) to (w). Pub. L. 104–134 redesignated par. (u) relating to introduction into interstate commerce of unsafe dietary supplement as (v) and added par. (w).

1994—Par. (e). Pub. L. 103–396, §2(b)(1)(A), substituted "357(d) or (g), 360b(a)(4)(C)," for "357(d) or (g),".

Par. (u). Pub. L. 103–417 added par. (u) relating to introduction into interstate commerce of unsafe dietary supplement.

Pub. L. 103–396, §2(b)(1)(B), added par. (u) relating to failure to comply with regulations or orders of Secretary.

1993—Par. (j). Pub. L. 103–80, §3(c)(1), substituted "379, or 379e" for "379e, or 379".

Par. (s). Pub. L. 103–80, §3(c)(2), substituted "350a(e)" for "350a(d)".

1992—Pars. (i)(1), (j). Pub. L. 102–571 substituted "379e" for "376".

Par. (q)(1)(C). Pub. L. 102–300 added cl. (C).

1990—Par. (e). Pub. L. 101–502 substituted "or (k)" for "or (j)".

Par. (j). Pub. L. 101–508 inserted at end "This paragraph does not authorize the withholding of information from either House of Congress or from, to the extent of matter within its jurisdiction, any committee or subcommittee of such committee or any joint committee of Congress or any subcommittee of such joint committee."

1988—Par. (t). Pub. L. 100–293 added par. (t).

1986—Par. (s). Pub. L. 99–570 amended par. (s) generally. Prior to amendment, par. (s) read as follows: "The failure to provide the notice required by section 350a(b) or 350a(c), the failure to make the reports required by section 350a(d)(1)(B), or the failure to meet the requirements prescribed under section 350a(d)(2)."

1980—Par. (e). Pub. L. 96–359, §5(b), inserted reference to section 350a of this title in two places.

Par. (j). Pub. L. 96–359, §5(c), inserted reference to section 350a of this title.

Par. (s). Pub. L. 96–359, §5(a), added par. (s).

1976—Par. (e). Pub. L. 94–295, §3(b)(2), inserted references to sections 360e(f) and 360i of this title.

Par. (j). Pub. L. 94–295, §3(b)(3), inserted references to sections 360, 360c, 360d, 360e, 360f, 360h, 360i, 360j, and 379 of this title.

Par. (l). Pub. L. 94–295, §3(b)(4), substituted "drug or device" for "drug" wherever appearing, and inserted references to sections 360e and 360j(g) of this title.

Par. (p). Pub. L. 94–295, §4(b)(1), substituted "section 360(j) or 360(k) of this title," for "section 360(j) of this title,".

Par. (q). Pub. L. 94–295, §3(b)(1), added par. (q).

Par. (r). Pub. L. 94–295, §7(b), added par. (r).

1972—Par. (p). Pub. L. 92–387 added failure to provide information required by section 360(j) of this title, and failure to provide notice required by section 360(j)(2) of this title as prohibited acts.

1970—Par. (q). Pub. L. 91–513 struck out par. (q) which set out penalties for illegal manufacture, sale, disposition, possession and other traffic in stimulant and depressant drugs. See section 801 et seq. of this title.

1968—Par. (e). Pub. L. 90–399, §103(1), inserted reference to section 360b(j), (l), and (m) of this title.

Par. (j). Pub. L. 90–399, §103(2), inserted reference to section 360b of this title.

Par. (q). Pub. L. 90–639 divided cl. (3), which referred simply to possession in violation of section 360a(c) of this title, into subcls. (A) and (B) which refer, respectively, to possession in violation of section 360a(c)(1) of this title and possession in violation of section 360a(c)(2) of this title.

1965—Par. (i). Pub. L. 89–74, §9(c), designated existing provisions as subpar. (1) and added subpars. (2) and (3).

Par. (q). Pub. L. 89–74, §5, added par. (q).

1962—Par. (e). Pub. L. 87–781, §§103(c), 106(c), prohibited the failure to establish or maintain any record, or make any report, required under sections 355(i) or (j) and 507(d) or (g) of this title, or the refusal to permit access to, or verification or copying of, any such required record.

Par. (l). Pub. L. 87–781, §104(e)(1), inserted "approval of" before "an application", and substituted "in effect" for "effective".

Par. (o). Pub. L. 87–781, §114(a), added par. (o).

Par. (p). Pub. L. 87–781, §304, added par. (p).

1960—Par. (i). Pub. L. 86–618, §105(a), struck out references to sections 346(b), 354, and 364 of this title and inserted reference to section 376 of this title.

Par. (j). Pub. L. 86–618, §104, inserted reference to section 376 of this title.

1958—Par. (j). Pub. L. 85–929, inserted reference to section 348 of this title.

1953—Par. (n). Act Aug. 7, 1953, added par. (n).

1950—Par. (m). Act Mar. 16, 1950, added par. (m).

1948—Par. (k). Act June 24, 1948, inserted "(whether or not the first sale)" so as to make it clear that this subsection is not limited to the case where the act occurs while the article is held for the first sale after interstate shipment, and extended coverage of subsection to acts which result in adulteration.

1947—Par. (j). Act Mar. 10, 1947, inserted reference to sections 356 and 357 of this title.

1945—Par. (i). Act July 6, 1945, inserted reference to section 357 of this title.

1941—Par. (i). Act Dec. 22, 1941, inserted reference to section 356 of this title.

Effective Date of 2007 Amendment

Pub. L. 110–85, title IX, §909, Sept. 27, 2007, 121 Stat. 950, provided that:

"(a) Effective Date.—This subtitle [subtitle A (§§901–909) of title IX of Pub. L. 110–85, enacting sections 353b and 355–1 of this title, amending this section, sections 333, 352, and 355 of this title, and section 262 of Title 42, The Public Health and Welfare, and enacting provisions set out as notes under sections 352, 355, and 355a of this title] takes effect 180 days after the date of the enactment of this Act [Sept. 27, 2007].

"(b) Drugs Deemed to Have Risk Evaluation and Mitigation Strategies.—

"(1) In general.—A drug that was approved before the effective date of this Act [probably means "this subtitle", see above] is, in accordance with paragraph (2), deemed to have in effect an approved risk evaluation and mitigation strategy under section 505–1 of the Federal Food, Drug, and Cosmetic Act [21 U.S.C. 355–1] (as added by section 901) (referred to in this section as the 'Act') if there are in effect on the effective date of this Act elements to assure safe use—

"(A) required under section 314.520 or section 601.42 of title 21, Code of Federal Regulations; or

"(B) otherwise agreed to by the applicant and the Secretary for such drug.

"(2) Elements of strategy; enforcement.—The approved risk evaluation and mitigation strategy in effect for a drug under paragraph (1)—

"(A) is deemed to consist of the timetable required under section 505–1(d) and any additional elements under subsections (e) and (f) of such section in effect for such drug on the effective date of this Act; and

"(B) is subject to enforcement by the Secretary to the same extent as any other risk evaluation and mitigation strategy under section 505–1 of the Act, except that sections 303(f)(4) and 502(y) and (z) of the Act [21 U.S.C. 333(f)(4), 352(y), (z)] (as added by section 902) shall not apply to such strategy before the Secretary has completed review of, and acted on, the first assessment of such strategy under such section 505–1.

"(3) SUBMISSION.—Not later than 180 days after the effective date of this Act, the holder of an approved application for which a risk evaluation and mitigation strategy is deemed to be in effect under paragraph (1) shall submit to the Secretary a proposed risk evaluation and mitigation strategy. Such proposed strategy is subject to section 505–1 of the Act as if included in such application at the time of submission of the application to the Secretary."

EFFECTIVE DATE OF 2006 AMENDMENT

Amendment by section 2(c) of Pub. L. 109–462 effective 1 year after Dec. 22, 2006, see section 2(e)(1) of Pub. L. 109–462, set out as a note under section 352 of this title.

Amendment by section 3(b) of Pub. L. 109–462 effective 1 year after Dec. 22, 2006, see section 3(d)(1) of Pub. L. 109–462, set out as a note under section 343 of this title.

Pub. L. 109–462, §4(b), Dec. 22, 2006, 120 Stat. 3475, provided that: "The amendment made by this section [amending this section] shall take effect 1 year after the date of enactment of this Act [Dec. 22, 2006]."

EFFECTIVE DATE OF 2005 AMENDMENT

Pub. L. 109–59, title VII, §7204, Aug. 10, 2005, 119 Stat. 1914, provided that: "This subtitle [subtitle B (§§7201–7204) of title VII of Pub. L. 109–59, enacting section 350e of this title, amending this section, sections 342 and 373 of this title, and section 5701 of Title 49, Transportation, omitting sections 5702 to 5714 of Title 49, and enacting provisions set out as a note under section 301 of this title] takes effect on October 1, 2005."

EFFECTIVE DATE OF 2002 AMENDMENT

Pub. L. 107–188, title III, §321(c), June 12, 2002, 116 Stat. 676, provided that: "The amendments made by this section [amending this section and sections 360 and 381 of this title] take effect upon the expiration of the 180-day period beginning on the date of the enactment of this Act [June 12, 2002]."

Pub. L. 107–188, title III, §322(c), June 12, 2002, 116 Stat. 678, provided that: "The amendments made by this section [amending this section and section 381 of this title] take effect upon the expiration of the 90-day period beginning on the date of the enactment of this Act [June 12, 2002]."

EFFECTIVE AND TERMINATION DATES OF 1997 AMENDMENT

Amendment by sections 204, 210, and 421 of Pub. L. 105–115 effective 90 days after Nov. 21, 1997, except as otherwise provided, see section 501 of Pub. L. 105–115, set out as a note under section 321 of this title.

Amendment by section 401(b) of Pub. L. 105–115 effective 1 year after Nov. 21, 1997, or upon Secretary's issuance of final regulations pursuant to section 401(c) of Pub. L. 105–115, whichever is sooner, and ceases to be effective Sept. 30, 2006, see section 401(d), (e) of Pub. L. 105–115, set out as an Effective and Termination Dates note under former section 360aaa of this title.

EFFECTIVE DATE OF 1994 AMENDMENT

Amendment by Pub. L. 103–396 effective upon adoption of final regulations under section 2(c) of Pub. L. 103–396, set out as a Regulations note under section 360b of this title, see section 2(d) of Pub. L. 103–396, set out as a note under section 360b of this title.

EFFECTIVE DATE OF 1990 AMENDMENT

Section 4755(c)(2) of Pub. L. 101–508 provided that the amendment made by that section is effective as if included in subtitle D of title VI of the Omnibus Budget Reconciliation Act of 1989, Pub. L. 101–239, title VI, §§6601, 6602, Dec. 19, 1989, 103 Stat. 2285, see 42 U.S.C. 300aa–1 note, 300aa–10 note.

EFFECTIVE DATE OF 1988 AMENDMENT

Amendment by Pub. L. 100–293 effective upon expiration of 90 days after Apr. 22, 1988, see section 8(a) of Pub. L. 100–293, set out as a note under section 353 of this title.

EFFECTIVE DATE OF 1972 AMENDMENT

Amendment by Pub. L. 92–387 effective on first day of sixth month beginning after Aug. 16, 1972, see section 5 of Pub. L. 92–387, set out as a note under section 360 of this title.

EFFECTIVE DATE OF 1970 AMENDMENT

Amendment by Pub. L. 91–513 effective on first day of seventh calendar month that begins after Oct. 26, 1970, see section 704 of Pub. L. 91–513, set out as an Effective Date note under section 801 of this title.

EFFECTIVE DATE OF 1968 AMENDMENTS

Amendment by Pub. L. 90–399 effective on first day of thirteenth calendar month after July 13, 1968, see section 108(a) of Pub. L. 90–399, set out as an Effective Date and Transitional Provisions note under section 360b of this title.

Amendment by Pub. L. 90–639 applicable only with respect to violations of this chapter committed after Oct. 24, 1968, see section 6 of Pub. L. 90–639, set out as an Effective Date of 1968 Amendments; Transitional Provisions note under section 321 of this title.

EFFECTIVE DATE OF 1965 AMENDMENT

Amendment by Pub. L. 89–74 effective Feb. 1, 1966, see section 11 of Pub. L. 89–74, set out as a note under section 321 of this title.

EFFECTIVE DATE OF 1962 AMENDMENT

Amendment by sections 103(c) and 106(c) of Pub. L. 87–781 effective on first day of seventh calendar month following Oct. 1962, and amendment by section 104(e)(1) of Pub. L. 87–781 effective Oct. 10, 1962, see section 107 of Pub. L. 87–781, set out as a note under section 321 of this title.

Section 114(b) of Pub. L. 87–781 provided that: "This section [amending this section] shall take effect on the first day of the seventh calendar month following the month in which this Act is enacted [October 1962]."

EFFECTIVE DATE OF 1960 AMENDMENT

Amendment by Pub. L. 86–618 effective July 12, 1960, subject to provisions of section 203 of Pub. L. 86–618, see section 202 of Pub. L. 86–618, set out as a note under section 379e of this title.

EFFECTIVE DATE OF 1958 AMENDMENT

Amendment by Pub. L. 85–929 effective Sept. 6, 1958, see section 6(a) of Pub. L. 85–929, set out as a note under section 342 of this title.

EFFECTIVE DATE OF 1950 AMENDMENT

Amendment by act Mar. 16, 1950, effective July 1, 1950, see section 7 of that act, set out as an Effective Date note under section 347 of this title.

REGULATIONS

Secretary of Health and Human Services to promulgate regulations to implement amendments made by section 401 of Pub. L. 105–115 not later than 1 year after Nov. 21, 1997, see section 401(c) of Pub. L. 105–115, set out as a note under section 360aaa of this title.

SAVINGS PROVISION

Amendment by Pub. L. 91–513 not to affect or abate any prosecutions for violation of law or any civil seizures or forfeitures and injunctive proceedings commenced prior to the effective date of such amendment, and all administrative proceedings pending before the Bureau of Narcotics and Dangerous Drugs [now the Drug Enforcement Administration] on Oct. 27, 1970, to be continued and brought to final determination in accord with laws and regulations in effect prior to Oct. 27, 1970, see section 702 of Pub. L. 91–513, set out as a note under section 321 of this title.

CONSTRUCTION OF AMENDMENTS BY PUB. L. 107–188

Pub. L. 107–188, title III, §315, June 12, 2002, 116 Stat. 675, provided that: "Nothing in this title [enacting sections 350c, 350d, 398, 399, and 679c of this title, sections 3353, 3354, 8319, and 8320 of Title 7, Agriculture, and section 247b–20 of Title 42, The Public Health and Welfare, amending this section, sections 334, 335a, 342, 343, 360, 372, 374, and 381 of this title, and section 43 of Title 18, Crimes and Criminal Procedure, and enacting provisions set out as notes under this section and sections 341, 350c, 350d, and 381 of this title], or an amendment made by this title, shall be construed to alter the jurisdiction between the Secretaries of Agriculture and of Health and Human Services, under applicable statutes and regulations."

TRANSFER OF FUNCTIONS

For transfer of functions of Federal Security Administrator to Secretary of Health, Education, and Welfare [now Health and Human Services], and of Food and Drug Administration in the Department of Agriculture to Federal Security Agency, see notes set out under section 321 of this title.

§ 332. Injunction proceedings

(a) Jurisdiction of courts

The district courts of the United States and the United States courts of the Territories shall have jurisdiction, for cause shown[1] to restrain violations of section 331 of this title, except paragraphs (h), (i), and (j).

(b) Violation of injunction

In case of violation of an injunction or restraining order issued under this section, which also constitutes a violation of this chapter, trial shall be by the court, or, upon demand of the accused, by a jury.

(June 25, 1938, ch. 675, §302, 52 Stat. 1043; Pub. L. 87–781, title I, §103(d), title II, §201(c), Oct. 10, 1962, 76 Stat. 784, 793; Pub. L. 103–80, §3(d), Aug. 13, 1993, 107 Stat. 775.)

AMENDMENTS

1993—Subsec. (a). Pub. L. 103–80, §3(d)(1), struck out ", and subject to the provisions of section 17 (relating to notice to opposite party) of the Act entitled 'An Act to supplement existing laws against unlawful restraints and monopolies, and for other purposes', approved October 15, 1914, as amended (U.S.C., 1934 ed., title 28, sec. 381)," after "for cause shown".

Subsec. (b). Pub. L. 103–80, §3(d)(2), struck out at end "Such trial shall be conducted in accordance with the practice and procedure applicable in the case of proceedings subject to the provisions of section 22 of such Act of October 15, 1914, as amended (U.S.C., 1934 ed., title 28, sec. 387)."

1962—Subsec. (a). Pub. L. 87–781, §103(d), struck out "(e)," after "paragraphs".

Pub. L. 87–781, §201(c), struck out "(f)," after "paragraphs".

[1] So in original. Probably should be followed by a comma.

EFFECTIVE DATE OF 1962 AMENDMENT

Amendment by section 103(c) of Pub. L. 87–781 effective on first day of seventh calendar month following October 1962, see section 107 of Pub. L. 87–781, set out as a note under section 321 of this title.

Section 203 of title II of Pub. L. 87–781 provided that: "The amendments made by this title [amending this section and section 374 of this title and enacting provisions set out as notes under sections 321 and 374 of this title] shall take effect on the date of enactment of this Act [Oct. 10, 1962]."

§ 333. Penalties

(a) Violation of section 331 of this title; second violation; intent to defraud or mislead

(1) Any person who violates a provision of section 331 of this title shall be imprisoned for not more than one year or fined not more than $1,000, or both.

(2) Notwithstanding the provisions of paragraph (1) of this section,[1] if any person commits such a violation after a conviction of him under this section has become final, or commits such a violation with the intent to defraud or mislead, such person shall be imprisoned for not more than three years or fined not more than $10,000, or both.

(b) Prescription drug marketing violations

(1) Notwithstanding subsection (a) of this section, any person who violates section 331(t) of this title by—

(A) knowingly importing a drug in violation of section 381(d)(1) of this title,

(B) knowingly selling, purchasing, or trading a drug or drug sample or knowingly offering to sell, purchase, or trade a drug or drug sample, in violation of section 353(c)(1) of this title,

(C) knowingly selling, purchasing, or trading a coupon, knowingly offering to sell, purchase, or trade such a coupon, or knowingly counterfeiting such a coupon, in violation of section 353(c)(2) of this title, or

(D) knowingly distributing drugs in violation of section 353(e)(2)(A) of this title,

shall be imprisoned for not more than 10 years or fined not more than $250,000, or both.

(2) Any manufacturer or distributor who distributes drug samples by means other than the mail or common carrier whose representative, during the course of the representative's employment or association with that manufacturer or distributor, violated section 331(t) of this title because of a violation of section 353(c)(1) of this title or violated any State law prohibiting the sale, purchase, or trade of a drug sample subject to section 353(b) of this title or the offer to sell, purchase, or trade such a drug sample shall, upon conviction of the representative for such violation, be subject to the following civil penalties:

(A) A civil penalty of not more than $50,000 for each of the first two such violations resulting in a conviction of any representative of the manufacturer or distributor in any 10-year period.

(B) A civil penalty of not more than $1,000,000 for each violation resulting in a con-

[1] So in original. Words "of this section" probably should not appear.

viction of any representative after the second conviction in any 10-year period.

For the purposes of this paragraph, multiple convictions of one or more persons arising out of the same event or transaction, or a related series of events or transactions, shall be considered as one violation.

(3) Any manufacturer or distributor who violates section 331(t) of this title because of a failure to make a report required by section 353(d)(3)(E) of this title shall be subject to a civil penalty of not more than $100,000.

(4)(A) If a manufacturer or distributor or any representative of such manufacturer or distributor provides information leading to the institution of a criminal proceeding against, and conviction of, any representative of that manufacturer or distributor for a violation of section 331(t) of this title because of a sale, purchase, or trade or offer to purchase, sell, or trade a drug sample in violation of section 353(c)(1) of this title or for a violation of State law prohibiting the sale, purchase, or trade or offer to sell, purchase, or trade a drug sample, the conviction of such representative shall not be considered as a violation for purposes of paragraph (2).

(B) If, in an action brought under paragraph (2) against a manufacturer or distributor relating to the conviction of a representative of such manufacturer or distributor for the sale, purchase, or trade of a drug or the offer to sell, purchase, or trade a drug, it is shown, by clear and convincing evidence—

(i) that the manufacturer or distributor conducted, before the institution of a criminal proceeding against such representative for the violation which resulted in such conviction, an investigation of events or transactions which would have led to the reporting of information leading to the institution of a criminal proceeding against, and conviction of, such representative for such purchase, sale, or trade or offer to purchase, sell, or trade, or

(ii) that, except in the case of the conviction of a representative employed in a supervisory function, despite diligent implementation by the manufacturer or distributor of an independent audit and security system designed to detect such a violation, the manufacturer or distributor could not reasonably have been expected to have detected such violation,

the conviction of such representative shall not be considered as a conviction for purposes of paragraph (2).

(5) If a person provides information leading to the institution of a criminal proceeding against, and conviction of, a person for a violation of section 331(t) of this title because of the sale, purchase, or trade of a drug sample or the offer to sell, purchase, or trade a drug sample in violation of section 353(c)(1) of this title, such person shall be entitled to one-half of the criminal fine imposed and collected for such violation but not more than $125,000.

(6) Notwithstanding subsection (a) of this section, any person who is a manufacturer or importer of a prescription drug under section 384(b) of this title and knowingly fails to comply with a requirement of section 384(e) of this title that is applicable to such manufacturer or importer, respectively, shall be imprisoned for not more than 10 years or fined not more than $250,000, or both.

(c) Exceptions in certain cases of good faith, etc.

No person shall be subject to the penalties of subsection (a)(1) of this section, (1) for having received in interstate commerce any article and delivered it or proffered delivery of it, if such delivery or proffer was made in good faith, unless he refuses to furnish on request of an officer or employee duly designated by the Secretary the name and address of the person from whom he purchased or received such article and copies of all documents, if any there be, pertaining to the delivery of the article to him; or (2) for having violated section 331(a) or (d) of this title, if he establishes a guaranty or undertaking signed by, and containing the name and address of, the person residing in the United States from whom he received in good faith the article, to the effect, in case of an alleged violation of section 331(a) of this title, that such article is not adulterated or misbranded, within the meaning of this chapter designating this chapter or to the effect, in case of an alleged violation of section 331(d) of this title, that such article is not an article which may not, under the provisions of section 344 or 355 of this title, be introduced into interstate commerce; or (3) for having violated section 331(a) of this title, where the violation exists because the article is adulterated by reason of containing a color additive not from a batch certified in accordance with regulations promulgated by the Secretary under this chapter, if such person establishes a guaranty or undertaking signed by, and containing the name and address of, the manufacturer of the color additive, to the effect that such color additive was from a batch certified in accordance with the applicable regulations promulgated by the Secretary under this chapter; or (4) for having violated section 331(b), (c) or (k) of this title by failure to comply with section 352(f) of this title in respect to an article received in interstate commerce to which neither section 353(a) nor 353(b)(1) of this title is applicable, if the delivery or proffered delivery was made in good faith and the labeling at the time thereof contained the same directions for use and warning statements as were contained in the labeling at the time of such receipt of such article; or (5) for having violated section 331(i)(2) of this title if such person acted in good faith and had no reason to believe that use of the punch, die, plate, stone, or other thing involved would result in a drug being a counterfeit drug, or for having violated section 331(i)(3) of this title if the person doing the act or causing it to be done acted in good faith and had no reason to believe that the drug was a counterfeit drug.

(d) Exceptions involving misbranded food

No person shall be subject to the penalties of subsection (a)(1) of this section for a violation of section 331 of this title involving misbranded food if the violation exists solely because the food is misbranded under section 343(a)(2) of this title because of its advertising.

(e) Prohibited distribution of human growth hormone

(1) Except as provided in paragraph (2), whoever knowingly distributes, or possesses with intent to distribute, human growth hormone for any use in humans other than the treatment of a disease or other recognized medical condition, where such use has been authorized by the Secretary of Health and Human Services under section 355 of this title and pursuant to the order of a physician, is guilty of an offense punishable by not more than 5 years in prison, such fines as are authorized by title 18, or both.

(2) Whoever commits any offense set forth in paragraph (1) and such offense involves an individual under 18 years of age is punishable by not more than 10 years imprisonment, such fines as are authorized by title 18, or both.

(3) Any conviction for a violation of paragraphs (1) and (2) of this subsection shall be considered a felony violation of the Controlled Substances Act [21 U.S.C. 801 et seq.] for the purposes of forfeiture under section 413 of such Act [21 U.S.C. 853].

(4) As used in this subsection the term "human growth hormone" means somatrem, somatropin, or an analogue of either of them.

(5) The Drug Enforcement Administration is authorized to investigate offenses punishable by this subsection.

(f) Violations related to devices

(1)(A) Except as provided in subparagraph (B), any person who violates a requirement of this chapter which relates to devices shall be liable to the United States for a civil penalty in an amount not to exceed $15,000 for each such violation, and not to exceed $1,000,000 for all such violations adjudicated in a single proceeding. For purposes of the preceding sentence, a person accredited under paragraph (2) of section 374(g) of this title who is substantially not in compliance with the standards of accreditation under such section, or who poses a threat to public health or fails to act in a manner that is consistent with the purposes of such section, shall be considered to have violated a requirement of this chapter that relates to devices.

(B) Subparagraph (A) shall not apply—

(i) to any person who violates the requirements of section 360i(a) or 360j(f) of this title unless such violation constitutes (I) a significant or knowing departure from such requirements, or (II) a risk to public health,

(ii) to any person who commits minor violations of section 360i(e) or 360i(g) of this title (only with respect to correction reports) if such person demonstrates substantial compliance with such section, or

(iii) to violations of section 351(a)(2)(A) of this title which involve one or more devices which are not defective.

(2)(A) Any person who introduces into interstate commerce or delivers for introduction into interstate commerce an article of food that is adulterated within the meaning of section 342(a)(2)(B) of this title shall be subject to a civil money penalty of not more than $50,000 in the case of an individual and $250,000 in the case of any other person for such introduction or delivery, not to exceed $500,000 for all such violations adjudicated in a single proceeding.

(B) This paragraph shall not apply to any person who grew the article of food that is adulterated. If the Secretary assesses a civil penalty against any person under this paragraph, the Secretary may not use the criminal authorities under this section to sanction such person for the introduction or delivery for introduction into interstate commerce of the article of food that is adulterated. If the Secretary assesses a civil penalty against any person under this paragraph, the Secretary may not use the seizure authorities of section 334 of this title or the injunction authorities of section 332 of this title with respect to the article of food that is adulterated.

(C) In a hearing to assess a civil penalty under this paragraph, the presiding officer shall have the same authority with regard to compelling testimony or production of documents as a presiding officer has under section 346a(g)(2)(B) of this title. The third sentence of paragraph (5)(A) shall not apply to any investigation under this paragraph.

(3)(A) Any person who violates section 331(jj) of this title shall be subject to a civil monetary penalty of not more than $10,000 for all violations adjudicated in a single proceeding.

(B) If a violation of section 331(jj) of this title is not corrected within the 30-day period following notification under section 282(j)(5)(C)(ii)[2] of title 42, the person shall, in addition to any penalty under subparagraph (A), be subject to a civil monetary penalty of not more than $10,000 for each day of the violation after such period until the violation is corrected.

(4)(A) Any responsible person (as such term is used in section 355–1 of this title) that violates a requirement of section 355(*o*), 355(p), or 355–1 of this title shall be subject to a civil monetary penalty of—

(i) not more than $250,000 per violation, and not to exceed $1,000,000 for all such violations adjudicated in a single proceeding; or

(ii) in the case of a violation that continues after the Secretary provides written notice to the responsible person, the responsible person shall be subject to a civil monetary penalty of $250,000 for the first 30-day period (or any portion thereof) that the responsible person continues to be in violation, and such amount shall double for every 30-day period thereafter that the violation continues, not to exceed $1,000,000 for any 30-day period, and not to exceed $10,000,000 for all such violations adjudicated in a single proceeding.

(B) In determining the amount of a civil penalty under subparagraph (A)(ii), the Secretary shall take into consideration whether the responsible person is making efforts toward correcting the violation of the requirement of section 355(*o*), 355(p), or 355–1 of this title for which the responsible person is subject to such civil penalty.

(5)(A) A civil penalty under paragraph (1), (2), (3), or (4) shall be assessed by the Secretary by an order made on the record after opportunity for a hearing provided in accordance with this subparagraph and section 554 of title 5. Before

[2] See References in Text note below.

issuing such an order, the Secretary shall give written notice to the person to be assessed a civil penalty under such order of the Secretary's proposal to issue such order and provide such person an opportunity for a hearing on the order. In the course of any investigation, the Secretary may issue subpoenas requiring the attendance and testimony of witnesses and the production of evidence that relates to the matter under investigation.

(B) In determining the amount of a civil penalty, the Secretary shall take into account the nature, circumstances, extent, and gravity of the violation or violations and, with respect to the violator, ability to pay, effect on ability to continue to do business, any history of prior such violations, the degree of culpability, and such other matters as justice may require.

(C) The Secretary may compromise, modify, or remit, with or without conditions, any civil penalty which may be assessed under paragraph (1), (2), (3), or (4). The amount of such penalty, when finally determined, or the amount agreed upon in compromise, may be deducted from any sums owing by the United States to the person charged.

(6) Any person who requested, in accordance with paragraph (5)(A), a hearing respecting the assessment of a civil penalty and who is aggrieved by an order assessing a civil penalty may file a petition for judicial review of such order with the United States Court of Appeals for the District of Columbia Circuit or for any other circuit in which such person resides or transacts business. Such a petition may only be filed within the 60-day period beginning on the date the order making such assessment was issued.

(7) If any person fails to pay an assessment of a civil penalty—

(A) after the order making the assessment becomes final, and if such person does not file a petition for judicial review of the order in accordance with paragraph (6), or

(B) after a court in an action brought under paragraph (6) has entered a final judgment in favor of the Secretary,

the Attorney General shall recover the amount assessed (plus interest at currently prevailing rates from the date of the expiration of the 60-day period referred to in paragraph (6) or the date of such final judgment, as the case may be) in an action brought in any appropriate district court of the United States. In such an action, the validity, amount, and appropriateness of such penalty shall not be subject to review.

(g) Violations regarding direct-to-consumer advertising

(1) With respect to a person who is a holder of an approved application under section 355 of this title for a drug subject to section 353(b) of this title or under section 262 of title 42, any such person who disseminates or causes another party to disseminate a direct-to-consumer advertisement that is false or misleading shall be liable to the United States for a civil penalty in an amount not to exceed $250,000 for the first such violation in any 3-year period, and not to exceed $500,000 for each subsequent violation in any 3-year period. No other civil monetary penalties in this chapter (including the civil penalty in subsection (f)(4)) shall apply to a violation regarding direct-to-consumer advertising. For purposes of this paragraph: (A) Repeated dissemination of the same or similar advertisement prior to the receipt of the written notice referred to in paragraph (2) for such advertisements shall be considered one violation. (B) On and after the date of the receipt of such a notice, all violations under this paragraph occurring in a single day shall be considered one violation. With respect to advertisements that appear in magazines or other publications that are published less frequently than daily, each issue date (whether weekly or monthly) shall be treated as a single day for the purpose of calculating the number of violations under this paragraph.

(2) A civil penalty under paragraph (1) shall be assessed by the Secretary by an order made on the record after providing written notice to the person to be assessed a civil penalty and an opportunity for a hearing in accordance with this paragraph and section 554 of title 5. If upon receipt of the written notice, the person to be assessed a civil penalty objects and requests a hearing, then in the course of any investigation related to such hearing, the Secretary may issue subpoenas requiring the attendance and testimony of witnesses and the production of evidence that relates to the matter under investigation, including information pertaining to the factors described in paragraph (3).

(3) The Secretary, in determining the amount of the civil penalty under paragraph (1), shall take into account the nature, circumstances, extent, and gravity of the violation or violations, including the following factors:

(A) Whether the person submitted the advertisement or a similar advertisement for review under section 379h–1 of this title.

(B) Whether the person submitted the advertisement for review if required under section 353b of this title.

(C) Whether, after submission of the advertisement as described in subparagraph (A) or (B), the person disseminated or caused another party to disseminate the advertisement before the end of the 45-day comment period.

(D) Whether the person incorporated any comments made by the Secretary with regard to the advertisement into the advertisement prior to its dissemination.

(E) Whether the person ceased distribution of the advertisement upon receipt of the written notice referred to in paragraph (2) for such advertisement.

(F) Whether the person had the advertisement reviewed by qualified medical, regulatory, and legal reviewers prior to its dissemination.

(G) Whether the violations were material.

(H) Whether the person who created the advertisement or caused the advertisement to be created acted in good faith.

(I) Whether the person who created the advertisement or caused the advertisement to be created has been assessed a civil penalty under this provision within the previous 1-year period.

(J) The scope and extent of any voluntary, subsequent remedial action by the person.

(K) Such other matters, as justice may require.

(4)(A) Subject to subparagraph (B), no person shall be required to pay a civil penalty under paragraph (1) if the person submitted the advertisement to the Secretary and disseminated or caused another party to disseminate such advertisement after incorporating each comment received from the Secretary.

(B) The Secretary may retract or modify any prior comments the Secretary has provided to an advertisement submitted to the Secretary based on new information or changed circumstances, so long as the Secretary provides written notice to the person of the new views of the Secretary on the advertisement and provides a reasonable time for modification or correction of the advertisement prior to seeking any civil penalty under paragraph (1).

(5) The Secretary may compromise, modify, or remit, with or without conditions, any civil penalty which may be assessed under paragraph (1). The amount of such penalty, when finally determined, or the amount charged upon in compromise, may be deducted from any sums owed by the United States to the person charged.

(6) Any person who requested, in accordance with paragraph (2), a hearing with respect to the assessment of a civil penalty and who is aggrieved by an order assessing a civil penalty, may file a petition for de novo judicial review of such order with the United States Court of Appeals for the District of Columbia Circuit or for any other circuit in which such person resides or transacts business. Such a petition may only be filed within the 60-day period beginning on the date the order making such assessments was issued.

(7) If any person fails to pay an assessment of a civil penalty under paragraph (1)—

(A) after the order making the assessment becomes final, and if such person does not file a petition for judicial review of the order in accordance with paragraph (6), or

(B) after a court in an action brought under paragraph (6) has entered a final judgment in favor of the Secretary,

the Attorney General of the United States shall recover the amount assessed (plus interest at currently prevailing rates from the date of the expiration of the 60-day period referred to in paragraph (6) or the date of such final judgment, as the case may be) in an action brought in any appropriate district court of the United States. In such an action, the validity, amount, and appropriateness of such penalty shall not be subject to review.

(June 25, 1938, ch. 675, §303, 52 Stat. 1043; Oct. 26, 1951, ch. 578, §2, 65 Stat. 649; Pub. L. 86–618, title I, §105(b), July 12, 1960, 74 Stat. 403; Pub. L. 89–74, §§7, 9(d), July 15, 1965, 79 Stat. 233, 235; Pub. L. 90–639, §3, Oct. 24, 1968, 82 Stat. 1361; Pub. L. 91–513, title II, §701(b), Oct. 27, 1970, 84 Stat. 1281; Pub. L. 94–278, title V, §502(a)(2)(B), Apr. 22, 1976, 90 Stat. 411; Pub. L. 100–293, §7(b), Apr. 22, 1988, 102 Stat. 99; Pub. L. 100–690, title II, §2403, Nov. 18, 1988, 102 Stat. 4230; Pub. L. 101–629, §17(a), Nov. 28, 1990, 104 Stat. 4526; Pub. L. 101–647, title XIX, §1904, Nov. 29, 1990, 104 Stat. 4853; Pub. L. 102–353, §3, Aug. 26, 1992, 106 Stat. 941; Pub. L. 103–80, §3(e), Aug. 13, 1993, 107 Stat. 775; Pub. L. 103–322, title XXXIII, §330015, Sept. 13, 1994, 108 Stat. 2146; Pub. L. 104–170, title IV, §407, Aug. 3, 1996, 110 Stat. 1535; Pub. L. 106–387, §1(a) [title VII, §745(d)(2)], Oct. 28, 2000, 114 Stat. 1549, 1549A–40; Pub. L. 107–250, title II, §201(c), Oct. 26, 2002, 116 Stat. 1609; Pub. L. 108–173, title XI, §1121(b)(2), Dec. 8, 2003, 117 Stat. 2469; Pub. L. 110–85, title II, §226(b), title VIII, §801(b)(2), title IX, §§901(d)(4), 902(b), Sept. 27, 2007, 121 Stat. 854, 920, 940, 943.)

REFERENCES IN TEXT

The Controlled Substances Act, referred to in subsec. (e)(3), is title II of Pub. L. 91–513, Oct. 27, 1970, 84 Stat. 1242, as amended, which is classified principally to subchapter I (§801 et seq.) of chapter 13 of this title. For complete classification of this Act to the Code, see Short Title note set out under section 801 of this title and Tables.

Section 282(j)(5)(C)(ii) of title 42, referred to in subsec. (f)(3)(B), was in the original "section 402(j)(5)(C)(ii)", and was translated as meaning section 402(j)(5)(C)(ii) of the Public Health Service Act to reflect the probable intent of Congress because there is no subsec. (j) of section 402 of The Federal Food, Drug, and Cosmetic Act and section 402(j)(5)(C)(ii) of the Public Health Service Act relates to notification of noncompliance with clinical trial information requirements.

AMENDMENTS

2007—Subsec. (f). Pub. L. 110–85, §226(b)(1), redesignated subsec. (g) as (f).

Subsec. (f)(1)(B)(ii). Pub. L. 110–85, §226(b)(2), substituted "360i(g)" for "360i(f)".

Subsec. (f)(2)(C). Pub. L. 110–85, §801(b)(2)(C), substituted "paragraph (5)(A)" for "paragraph (3)(A)".

Subsec. (f)(3). Pub. L. 110–85, §801(b)(2)(B), added par. (3). Former par. (3) redesignated (5).

Subsec. (f)(4). Pub. L. 110–85, §902(b)(1), added par. (4). Pub. L. 110–85, §801(b)(2)(A), redesignated par. (4) as (6).

Subsec. (f)(5). Pub. L. 110–85, §801(b)(2)(A), redesignated par. (3) as (5). Former par. (5) redesignated (7).

Subsec. (f)(5)(A), (C). Pub. L. 110–85, §902(b)(2), substituted "paragraph (1), (2), (3), or (4)" for "paragraph (1), (2), or (3)".

Pub. L. 110–85, §801(b)(2)(D), substituted "paragraph (1), (2), or (3)" for "paragraph (1) or (2)".

Subsec. (f)(6). Pub. L. 110–85, §801(b)(2)(A), (E), redesignated par. (4) as (6) and substituted "paragraph (5)(A)" for "paragraph (3)(A)".

Subsec. (f)(7). Pub. L. 110–85, §801(b)(2)(A), (F), redesignated par. (5) as (7) and substituted "paragraph (6)" for "paragraph (4)" wherever appearing.

Subsec. (g). Pub. L. 110–85, §901(d)(4), added subsec. (g).

Pub. L. 110–85, §226(b)(1), redesignated subsec. (g) as (f).

2003—Subsec. (b)(6). Pub. L. 108–173, which directed amendment of subsec. (a)(6) by substituting "prescription drug under section 384(b)" for "covered product pursuant to section 384(a)", was executed by making the substitution in subsec. (b)(6), to reflect the probable intent of Congress.

2002—Subsec. (g)(1)(A). Pub. L. 107–250 inserted at end "For purposes of the preceding sentence, a person accredited under paragraph (2) of section 374(g) of this title who is substantially not in compliance with the standards of accreditation under such section, or who poses a threat to public health or fails to act in a manner that is consistent with the purposes of such section, shall be considered to have violated a requirement of this chapter that relates to devices."

2000—Subsec. (b)(6). Pub. L. 106–387 added par. (6).

1996—Subsec. (g)(2). Pub. L. 104–170, §407(1), (2), added par. (2). Former par. (2) redesignated (3).

Subsec. (g)(3). Pub. L. 104–170, §407(1), (3), redesignated par. (2) as (3) and substituted "paragraph (1) or

(2)" for "paragraph (1)" in subpars. (A) and (C). Former par. (3) redesignated (4).

Subsec. (g)(4). Pub. L. 104–170, §407(1), (4), redesignated par. (3) as (4) and substituted "paragraph (3)(A)" for "paragraph (2)(A)". Former par. (4) redesignated (5).

Subsec. (g)(5). Pub. L. 104–170, §407(1), (5), redesignated par. (4) as (5) and substituted "paragraph (4)" for "paragraph (3)" wherever appearing.

1994—Subsec. (e). Pub. L. 103–322 amended directory language of Pub. L. 101–647. See 1990 Amendment note below.

1993—Subsecs. (e) to (g). Pub. L. 103–80, which directed the amendment of this section by redesignating the second subsec. (e) and subsec. (f) as subsecs. (f) and (g), respectively, could only be executed by designating subsec. (f) as (g) because this section did not contain a second subsec. (e) subsequent to amendment of Pub. L. 101–647 by Pub. L. 103–322. See 1990 and 1994 amendment notes for subsec. (e) under this section.

1992—Subsec. (b)(1). Pub. L. 102–353, §3(a), amended par. (1) generally. Prior to amendment, par. (1) read as follows: "Notwithstanding subsection (a) of this section, any person who violates section 331(t) of this title because of an importation of a drug in violation of section 381(d)(1) of this title, because of a sale, purchase, or trade of a drug or drug sample or the offer to sell, purchase, or trade a drug or drug sample in violation of section 353(c) of this title, because of the sale, purchase, or trade of a coupon, the offer to sell, purchase, or trade such a coupon, or the counterfeiting of such a coupon in violation of section 353(c)(2) of this title, or the distribution of drugs in violation of section 353(e)(2)(A) of this title shall be imprisoned for not more than 10 years or fined not more than $250,000, or both."

Subsec. (b)(4)(A). Pub. L. 102–353, §3(b)(1), substituted "the institution of a criminal proceeding against, and conviction of," for "the arrest and conviction of".

Subsec. (b)(4)(B)(i). Pub. L. 102–353, §3(b)(1), (2), substituted "before the institution of a criminal proceeding against" for "before the arrest of" and "the institution of a criminal proceeding against, and conviction of," for "the arrest and conviction of".

Subsec. (b)(5). Pub. L. 102–353, §3(b)(3), substituted "the institution of a criminal proceeding against, and conviction of," for "the arrest and conviction of".

Subsec. (c). Pub. L. 102–353, §3(b)(4), substituted "subsection (a)(1) of this section" for "subsection (a) of this section".

Subsec. (d). Pub. L. 102–353, §3(b)(4), (5), substituted "subsection (a)(1) of this section" for "subsection (a) of this section" and struck out ", and no person shall be subject to the penalties of subsection (b) of this section for such a violation unless the violation is committed with the intent to defraud or mislead" after "advertising".

1990—Subsec. (e). Pub. L. 101–647, as amended by Pub. L. 103–322, amended subsec. (e) generally. Prior to amendment, subsec. (e) read as follows:

"(e)(1) Except as provided in paragraph (2), any person who distributes or possesses with the intent to distribute any anabolic steroid for any use in humans other than the treatment of disease pursuant to the order of a physician shall be imprisoned for not more than three years or fined under title 18, or both.

"(2) Any person who distributes or possesses with the intent to distribute to an individual under 18 years of age, any anabolic steroid for any use in humans other than the treatment of disease pursuant to the order of a physician shall be imprisoned for not more than six years or fined under title 18, or both."

Subsec. (f). Pub. L. 101–629 added subsec. (f).

1988—Subsecs. (a), (b). Pub. L. 100–293 designated existing subsecs. (a) and (b) as pars. (1) and (2) of subsec. (a), substituted "paragraph (1)" for "subsection (a)" in par. (2), and added subsec. (b).

Subsec. (e). Pub. L. 100–690 added subsec. (e).

1976—Subsec. (d). Pub. L. 94–278 added subsec. (d).

1970—Subsec. (a). Pub. L. 91–513 struck out reference to subsec. (b) and transferred to subsec. (b) provisions covering second offenses and offenses committed with intent to defraud or mislead.

Subsec. (b). Pub. L. 91–513 inserted provisions covering second offenses and offenses committed with intent to defraud or mislead formerly set out in subsec. (a) and struck out provisions covering violations involving depressant and stimulant drugs. See section 801 et seq. of this title.

1968—Subsecs. (a), (b). Pub. L. 90–639 made a general revision in the penalties prescribed for offenses involving depressant or stimulant drugs, set a fine of not to exceed $10,000 or imprisonment of not more than 5 years for offenses involving the unlawful manufacturing of, sale, or disposal of, or possession with intent to sell, a depressant or stimulant drug or involving counterfeit depressant or stimulant drugs, stiffened the penalties for unlawful sales or other disposals by persons over 18 to persons under 21, and set new penalties for possession of a depressant or stimulant drug for purposes other than sale or other disposal.

1965—Subsec. (a). Pub. L. 89–74, §7(a), inserted proviso limiting the penalties for depressant or stimulant drug violations to two years imprisonment or $5,000 fine or both for first offense and to two years imprisonment or $15,000 fine or both for subsequent offenses.

Subsec. (b). Pub. L. 89–74, §7(b), inserted parenthetical exception provision.

Subsec. (c)(5). Pub. L. 89–74, §9(d), added cl. (5).

1960—Subsec. (c)(3). Pub. L. 86–618 substituted "a color additive" for "a coal-tar color", "the color additive" for "the coal-tar color" and "such color additive was" for "such color was".

1951—Subsec. (c)(4). Act Oct. 26, 1951, added cl. (4).

Effective Date of 2007 Amendment

Amendment by sections 901(d)(4) and 902(b) of Pub. L. 110–85 effective 180 days after Sept. 27, 2007, see section 909 of Pub. L. 110–85, set out as a note under section 331 of this title.

Effective Date of 1994 Amendment

Section 330015 of Pub. L. 103–322 provided that the amendment made by that section is effective as of the date on which section 1904 of Pub. L. 101–647, which amended this section, took effect.

Effective Date of 1990 Amendment

Section 17(b) of Pub. L. 101–629 provided that:

"(b) Effective Date of Application to Device User Facilities.—

"(1) The Secretary of Health and Human Services shall conduct a study to determine whether there has been substantial compliance with the requirements of section 519(b) of the Federal Food, Drug, and Cosmetic Act [21 U.S.C. 360i(b)] by device user facilities (as defined in section 519(b)(5)(A) of such Act). The Secretary shall report the results of the study to the Congress after the expiration of 45 months after the date of the enactment of this Act [Nov. 28, 1990].

"(2)(A) If upon the expiration of 48 months after the date of the enactment of this Act [Nov. 28, 1990] the Secretary has not made the report required by paragraph (1), section 303(f) of the Federal Food, Drug, and Cosmetic Act [21 U.S.C. 333(f)], as added by the amendment made by subsection (a), shall take effect with respect to device user facilities (as defined in section 519(b)(5)(A) of such Act). [Secretary of Health and Human Services had not made the report required by par. (1) on the expiration of 48 months after Nov. 28, 1990.]

"(B) If in the report under paragraph (1) the Secretary reports that there has been substantial compliance with the requirements of such section 519(b) by a type of device user facility and if the Secretary does not make a determination under subparagraph (C) with respect to such type of facility, such section 303(f) shall not take effect with respect to such type of facility.

"(C) If the Secretary determines in the report under paragraph (1) that there is not substantial compliance with the requirements of such section 519(b) by a type of device user facility or if the Secretary makes such a determination after making the report under paragraph (1), such section 303(f) shall take effect with respect to such type of facility upon the effective date of the report."

EFFECTIVE DATE OF 1988 AMENDMENT

Amendment by Pub. L. 100–293 effective upon expiration of 90 days after Apr. 22, 1988, see section 8(a) of Pub. L. 100–293, set out as a note under section 353 of this title.

EFFECTIVE DATE OF 1976 AMENDMENT

Amendment by Pub. L. 94–278 effective 180 days after Apr. 22, 1976, see section 502(c) of Pub. L. 94–278, set out as a note under section 334 of this title.

EFFECTIVE DATE OF 1970 AMENDMENT

Amendment by Pub. L. 91–513 effective on first day of seventh calendar month that begins after Oct. 26, 1970, see section 704 of Pub. L. 91–513, set out as an Effective Date note under section 801 of this title.

EFFECTIVE DATE OF 1968 AMENDMENT

Amendment by Pub. L. 90–639 applicable only with respect to violations of this chapter committed after Oct. 24, 1968, see section 6 of Pub. L. 90–639, set out as an Effective Date of 1968 Amendments; Transitional Provisions note under section 321 of this title.

EFFECTIVE DATE OF 1965 AMENDMENT

Amendment by Pub. L. 89–74 effective Feb. 1, 1966, see section 11 of Pub. L. 89–74, set out as a note under section 321 of this title.

EFFECTIVE DATE OF 1960 AMENDMENT

Amendment by Pub. L. 86–618 effective July 12, 1960, subject to the provisions of section 203 of Pub. L. 86–618, see section 202 of Pub. L. 86–618, set out as a note under section 379e of this title.

EFFECTIVE DATE OF 1951 AMENDMENT

Section 3 of act Oct. 26, 1951, provided that: "The provisions of this Act [amending this section and section 353 of this title] shall take effect six months after the date of its enactment [Oct. 26, 1951]."

SAVINGS PROVISION

Amendment by Pub. L. 91–513 not to affect or abate any prosecutions for violation of law or any civil seizures or forfeitures and injunctive proceedings commenced prior to the effective date of such amendment, and all administrative proceedings pending before the Bureau of Narcotics and Dangerous Drugs [now the Drug Enforcement Administration] on Oct. 27, 1970, to be continued and brought to final determination in accord with laws and regulations in effect prior to Oct. 27, 1970, see section 702 of Pub. L. 91–513, set out as a note under section 321 of this title.

TRANSFER OF FUNCTIONS

For transfer of functions of Federal Security Administrator to Secretary of Health, Education, and Welfare [now Health and Human Services], and of Food and Drug Administration in the Department of Agriculture to Federal Security Agency, see notes set out under section 321 of this title.

ENFORCEMENT

Pub. L. 99–660, title I, § 103, Nov. 14, 1986, 100 Stat. 3751, provided that: "For the fines authorized to be imposed under section 303 of the Federal Food, Drug, and Cosmetic Act [21 U.S.C. 333], see section 3623 of title 18, United States Code, for the period ending October 31, 1986 [probably should be October 31, 1987], and sections 3559 and 3571 of such title for the period beginning November 1, 1986 [probably should be November 1, 1987]."

§ 333a. Repealed. Pub. L. 101–647, title XIX, § 1905, Nov. 29, 1990, 104 Stat. 4853

Section, Pub. L. 100–690, title II, § 2401, Nov. 18, 1988, 102 Stat. 4230, related to forfeiture and illegal trafficking in steroids or human growth hormones.

§ 334. Seizure

(a) Grounds and jurisdiction

(1) Any article of food, drug, or cosmetic that is adulterated or misbranded when introduced into or while in interstate commerce or while held for sale (whether or not the first sale) after shipment in interstate commerce, or which may not, under the provisions of section 331(*ll*), 344, or 355 of this title, be introduced into interstate commerce, shall be liable to be proceeded against while in interstate commerce, or at any time thereafter, on libel of information and condemned in any district court of the United States or United States court of a Territory within the jurisdiction of which the article is found. No libel for condemnation shall be instituted under this chapter, for any alleged misbranding if there is pending in any court a libel for condemnation proceeding under this chapter based upon the same alleged misbranding, and not more than one such proceeding shall be instituted if no such proceeding is so pending, except that such limitations shall not apply (A) when such misbranding has been the basis of a prior judgment in favor of the United States, in a criminal, injunction, or libel for condemnation proceeding under this chapter, or (B) when the Secretary has probable cause to believe from facts found, without hearing, by him or any officer or employee of the Department that the misbranded article is dangerous to health, or that the labeling of the misbranded article is fraudulent, or would be in a material respect misleading to the injury or damage of the purchaser or consumer. In any case where the number of libel for condemnation proceedings is limited as above provided the proceeding pending or instituted shall, on application of the claimant, seasonably made, be removed for trial to any district agreed upon by stipulation between the parties, or, in case of failure to so stipulate within a reasonable time, the claimant may apply to the court of the district in which the seizure has been made, and such court (after giving the United States attorney for such district reasonable notice and opportunity to be heard) shall by order, unless good cause to the contrary is shown, specify a district of reasonable proximity to the claimant's principal place of business, to which the case shall be removed for trial.

(2) The following shall be liable to be proceeded against at any time on libel of information and condemned in any district court of the United States or United States court of a Territory within the jurisdiction of which they are found: (A) Any drug that is a counterfeit drug, (B) Any container of a counterfeit drug, (C) Any punch, die, plate, stone, labeling, container, or other thing used or designed for use in making a counterfeit drug or drugs, and (D) Any adulterated or misbranded device.

(3)(A) Except as provided in subparagraph (B), no libel for condemnation may be instituted under paragraph (1) or (2) against any food which—

(i) is misbranded under section 343(a)(2) of this title because of its advertising, and

(ii) is being held for sale to the ultimate consumer in an establishment other than an establishment owned or operated by a manufacturer, packer, or distributor of the food.

(B) A libel for condemnation may be instituted under paragraph (1) or (2) against a food described in subparagraph (A) if—

(i)(I) the food's advertising which resulted in the food being misbranded under section 343(a)(2) of this title was disseminated in the establishment in which the food is being held for sale to the ultimate consumer,

(II) such advertising was disseminated by, or under the direction of, the owner or operator of such establishment, or

(III) all or part of the cost of such advertising was paid by such owner or operator; and

(ii) the owner or operator of such establishment used such advertising in the establishment to promote the sale of the food.

(b) Procedure; multiplicity of pending proceedings

The article, equipment, or other thing proceeded against shall be liable to seizure by process pursuant to the libel, and the procedure in cases under this section shall conform, as nearly as may be, to the procedure in admiralty; except that on demand of either party any issue of fact joined in any such case shall be tried by jury. When libel for condemnation proceedings under this section, involving the same claimant and the same issues of adulteration or misbranding, are pending in two or more jurisdictions, such pending proceedings, upon application of the claimant seasonably made to the court of one such jurisdiction, shall be consolidated for trial by order of such court, and tried in (1) any district selected by the claimant where one of such proceedings is pending; or (2) a district agreed upon by stipulation between the parties. If no order for consolidation is so made within a reasonable time, the claimant may apply to the court of one such jurisdiction and such court (after giving the United States attorney for such district reasonable notice and opportunity to be heard) shall by order, unless good cause to the contrary is shown, specify a district of reasonable proximity to the claimant's principal place of business, in which all such pending proceedings shall be consolidated for trial and tried. Such order of consolidation shall not apply so as to require the removal of any case the date for trial of which has been fixed. The court granting such order shall give prompt notification thereof to the other courts having jurisdiction of the cases covered thereby.

(c) Availability of samples of seized goods prior to trial

The court at any time after seizure up to a reasonable time before trial shall by order allow any party to a condemnation proceeding, his attorney or agent, to obtain a representative sample of the article seized and a true copy of the analysis, if any, on which the proceeding is based and the identifying marks or numbers, if any, of the packages from which the samples analyzed were obtained.

(d) Disposition of goods after decree of condemnation; claims for remission or mitigation of forfeitures

(1) Any food, drug, device, or cosmetic condemned under this section shall, after entry of the decree, be disposed of by destruction or sale as the court may, in accordance with the provisions of this section, direct and the proceeds thereof, if sold, less the legal costs and charges, shall be paid into the Treasury of the United States; but such article shall not be sold under such decree contrary to the provisions of this chapter or the laws of the jurisdiction in which sold. After entry of the decree and upon the payment of the costs of such proceedings and the execution of a good and sufficient bond conditioned that such article shall not be sold or disposed of contrary to the provisions of this chapter or the laws of any State or Territory in which sold, the court may by order direct that such article be delivered to the owner thereof to be destroyed or brought into compliance with the provisions of this chapter, under the supervision of an officer or employee duly designated by the Secretary, and the expenses of such supervision shall be paid by the person obtaining release of the article under bond. If the article was imported into the United States and the person seeking its release establishes (A) that the adulteration, misbranding, or violation did not occur after the article was imported, and (B) that he had no cause for believing that it was adulterated, misbranded, or in violation before it was released from customs custody, the court may permit the article to be delivered to the owner for exportation in lieu of destruction upon a showing by the owner that all of the conditions of section 381(e) of this title can and will be met. The provisions of this sentence shall not apply where condemnation is based upon violation of section 342(a)(1), (2), or (6), section 351(a)(3), section 352(j), or section 361(a) or (d) of this title. Where such exportation is made to the original foreign supplier, then subparagraphs (A) and (B) of section 381(e)(1) of this title and the preceding sentence shall not be applicable; and in all cases of exportation the bond shall be conditioned that the article shall not be sold or disposed of until the applicable conditions of section 381(e) of this title have been met. Any person seeking to export an imported article pursuant to any of the provisions of this subsection shall establish that the article was intended for export at the time the article entered commerce. Any article condemned by reason of its being an article which may not, under section 344 or 355 of this title, be introduced into interstate commerce, shall be disposed of by destruction.

(2) The provisions of paragraph (1) of this subsection shall, to the extent deemed appropriate by the court, apply to any equipment or other thing which is not otherwise within the scope of such paragraph and which is referred to in paragraph (2) of subsection (a) of this section.

(3) Whenever in any proceeding under this section, involving paragraph (2) of subsection (a) of this section, the condemnation of any equip-

ment or thing (other than a drug) is decreed, the court shall allow the claim of any claimant, to the extent of such claimant's interest, for remission or mitigation of such forfeiture if such claimant proves to the satisfaction of the court (i) that he has not committed or caused to be committed any prohibited act referred to in such paragraph (2) and has no interest in any drug referred to therein, (ii) that he has an interest in such equipment or other thing as owner or lienor or otherwise, acquired by him in good faith, and (iii) that he at no time had any knowledge or reason to believe that such equipment or other thing was being or would be used in, or to facilitate, the violation of laws of the United States relating to counterfeit drugs.

(e) Costs

When a decree of condemnation is entered against the article, court costs and fees, and storage and other proper expenses, shall be awarded against the person, if any, intervening as claimant of the article.

(f) Removal of case for trial

In the case of removal for trial of any case as provided by subsection (a) or (b) of this section—

(1) The clerk of the court from which removal is made shall promptly transmit to the court in which the case is to be tried all records in the case necessary in order that such court may exercise jurisdiction.

(2) The court to which such case was removed shall have the powers and be subject to the duties, for purposes of such case, which the court from which removal was made would have had, or to which such court would have been subject, if such case had not been removed.

(g) Administrative restraint; detention orders

(1) If during an inspection conducted under section 374 of this title of a facility or a vehicle, a device which the officer or employee making the inspection has reason to believe is adulterated or misbranded is found in such facility or vehicle, such officer or employee may order the device detained (in accordance with regulations prescribed by the Secretary) for a reasonable period which may not exceed twenty days unless the Secretary determines that a period of detention greater than twenty days is required to institute an action under subsection (a) of this section or section 332 of this title, in which case he may authorize a detention period of not to exceed thirty days. Regulations of the Secretary prescribed under this paragraph shall require that before a device may be ordered detained under this paragraph the Secretary or an officer or employee designated by the Secretary approve such order. A detention order under this paragraph may require the labeling or marking of a device during the period of its detention for the purpose of identifying the device as detained. Any person who would be entitled to claim a device if it were seized under subsection (a) of this section may appeal to the Secretary a detention of such device under this paragraph. Within five days of the date an appeal of a detention is filed with the Secretary, the Secretary shall after affording opportunity for an informal hearing by order confirm the detention or revoke it.

(2)(A) Except as authorized by subparagraph (B), a device subject to a detention order issued under paragraph (1) shall not be moved by any person from the place at which it is ordered detained until—

(i) released by the Secretary, or

(ii) the expiration of the detention period applicable to such order,

whichever occurs first.

(B) A device subject to a detention order under paragraph (1) may be moved—

(i) in accordance with regulations prescribed by the Secretary, and

(ii) if not in final form for shipment, at the discretion of the manufacturer of the device for the purpose of completing the work required to put it in such form.

(h) Administrative detention of foods

(1) Detention authority

(A) In general

An officer or qualified employee of the Food and Drug Administration may order the detention, in accordance with this subsection, of any article of food that is found during an inspection, examination, or investigation under this chapter conducted by such officer or qualified employee, if the officer or qualified employee has credible evidence or information indicating that such article presents a threat of serious adverse health consequences or death to humans or animals.

(B) Secretary's approval

An article of food may be ordered detained under subparagraph (A) only if the Secretary or an official designated by the Secretary approves the order. An official may not be so designated unless the official is the director of the district under this chapter in which the article involved is located, or is an official senior to such director.

(2) Period of detention

An article of food may be detained under paragraph (1) for a reasonable period, not to exceed 20 days, unless a greater period, not to exceed 30 days, is necessary, to enable the Secretary to institute an action under subsection (a) of this section or section 332 of this title. The Secretary shall by regulation provide for procedures for instituting such action on an expedited basis with respect to perishable foods.

(3) Security of detained article

An order under paragraph (1) with respect to an article of food may require that such article be labeled or marked as detained, and shall require that the article be removed to a secure facility, as appropriate. An article subject to such an order shall not be transferred by any person from the place at which the article is ordered detained, or from the place to which the article is so removed, as the case may be, until released by the Secretary or until the expiration of the detention period applicable under such order, whichever occurs first. This subsection may not be construed as authorizing the delivery of the article pursuant to the execution of a bond while the article is subject to the order, and section 381(b) of this title does not authorize the delivery of the article pursuant to the execution of a bond while the article is subject to the order.

(4) Appeal of detention order

(A) In general

With respect to an article of food ordered detained under paragraph (1), any person who would be entitled to be a claimant for such article if the article were seized under subsection (a) of this section may appeal the order to the Secretary. Within five days after such an appeal is filed, the Secretary, after providing opportunity for an informal hearing, shall confirm or terminate the order involved, and such confirmation by the Secretary shall be considered a final agency action for purposes of section 702 of title 5. If during such five-day period the Secretary fails to provide such an opportunity, or to confirm or terminate such order, the order is deemed to be terminated.

(B) Effect of instituting court action

The process under subparagraph (A) for the appeal of an order under paragraph (1) terminates if the Secretary institutes an action under subsection (a) of this section or section 332 of this title regarding the article of food involved.

(June 25, 1938, ch. 675, §304, 52 Stat. 1044; June 24, 1948, ch. 613, §2, 62 Stat. 582; Aug. 7, 1953, ch. 350, §3, 67 Stat. 477; Pub. L. 85–250, Aug. 31, 1957, 71 Stat. 567; Pub. L. 89–74, §6, July 15, 1965, 79 Stat. 232; Pub. L. 90–639, §4(b), Oct. 24, 1968, 82 Stat. 1362; Pub. L. 91–513, title II, §701(c), (d), Oct. 27, 1970, 84 Stat. 1281, 1282; Pub. L. 94–278, title V, §502(a)(2)(C), Apr. 22, 1976, 90 Stat. 411; Pub. L. 94–295, §§3(c), 7(a), May 28, 1976, 90 Stat. 576, 582; Pub. L. 102–300, §6(c), June 16, 1992, 106 Stat. 240; Pub. L. 103–80, §3(f), Aug. 13, 1993, 107 Stat. 775; Pub. L. 105–115, title IV, §418, Nov. 21, 1997, 111 Stat. 2379; Pub. L. 107–188, title III, §303(a), June 12, 2002, 116 Stat. 663; Pub. L. 110–85, title IX, §912(b)(1), Sept. 27, 2007, 121 Stat. 952.)

AMENDMENTS

2007—Subsec. (a)(1). Pub. L. 110–85 substituted "section 331(*ll*), 344, or 355" for "section 344 or 355".

2002—Subsec. (h). Pub. L. 107–188 added subsec. (h).

1997—Subsec. (d)(1). Pub. L. 105–115 substituted "subparagraphs (A) and (B) of section 381(e)(1) of this title" for "paragraphs (1) and (2) of section 381(e) of this title" and inserted "Any person seeking to export an imported article pursuant to any of the provisions of this subsection shall establish that the article was intended for export at the time the article entered commerce." before "Any article condemned by reason".

1993—Subsec. (a)(1). Pub. L. 103–80, §3(f)(1), substituted "found. No libel" for "found: *Provided, however*, That no libel".

Subsec. (d)(1). Pub. L. 103–80, §3(f)(2), substituted "sold. After entry" for "sold: *Provided*, That after entry", "met. The provisions of this sentence" for "met: *Provided, however*, That the provisions of this sentence", "title. Where such exportation" for "title: *And provided further*, That where such exportation", and "the preceding sentence shall not be applicable" for "the foregoing proviso shall not be applicable".

1992—Subsec. (d)(1). Pub. L. 102–300 substituted "381(e)" for "381(d)" in three places and "paragraphs" for "clauses" before "(1) and (2) of section 381(e)".

1976—Subsec. (a)(1). Pub. L. 94–295, §3(c)(1), struck out "device," after "Any article of food, drug,".

Subsec. (a)(2). Pub. L. 94–295, §3(c)(2), (3), added cl. (D) covering adulterated or misbranded devices.

Subsec. (a)(3). Pub. L. 94–278 added par. (3).

Subsec. (g). Pub. L. 94–295, §7(a), added subsec. (g).

1970—Subsec. (a)(2). Pub. L. 91–513, §701(c), struck out cls. (A) and (D) which dealt with depressant or stimulant drugs, struck out reference to depressant or stimulant drugs in cl. (C), and redesignated cls. (B), (C), and (E) as cls. (A), (B), and (C), respectively.

Subsec. (d)(3)(iii). Pub. L. 91–513, §701(d), struck out reference to depressant or stimulant drugs.

1968—Subsec. (a). Pub. L. 90–639 inserted references to the United States courts of Territories.

1965—Subsec. (a). Pub. L. 89–74, §6(a), designated existing provisions as par. (1), redesignated cls. (1) and (2) of proviso as (A) and (B), and added par. (2).

Subsec. (b). Pub. L. 89–74, §6(b)(1), inserted "equipment, or other thing proceeded against" after "article" in first sentence.

Subsec. (d). Pub. L. 89–74, §6(b)(2), designated existing provisions as par. (1), redesignated cls. (1) and (2) of the second sentence thereof as (A) and (B), and added pars. (2) and (3).

1957—Subsec. (d). Pub. L. 85–250 permitted, under certain circumstances, reexportation of articles condemned at places other than original port of entry.

1953—Subsec. (c). Act Aug. 7, 1953, provided that a true copy of the analysis in any case shall be furnished the owner.

1948—Subsec. (a). Act June 24, 1948, inserted "or while held for sale (whether or not the first sale) after shipment in interstate commerce" to make this subsection coextensive with section 331(k) of this title.

EFFECTIVE DATE OF 1997 AMENDMENT

Amendment by Pub. L. 105–115 effective 90 days after Nov. 21, 1997, except as otherwise provided, see section 501 of Pub. L. 105–115, set out as a note under section 321 of this title.

EFFECTIVE DATE OF 1976 AMENDMENT

Section 502(c) of Pub. L. 94–278 provided that: "The amendments made by subsection (a) [amending this section and sections 321, 333, and 343 of this title] shall take effect 180 days after the date of the enactment of this Act [Apr. 22, 1976]."

EFFECTIVE DATE OF 1970 AMENDMENT

Amendment by Pub. L. 91–513 effective on first day of seventh calendar month that begins after Oct. 26, 1970, see section 704 of Pub. L. 91–513, set out as an Effective Date note under section 801 of this title.

EFFECTIVE DATE OF 1968 AMENDMENT

Amendment by Pub. L. 90–639 applicable only with respect to violations of this chapter committed after Oct. 24, 1968, see section 6 of Pub. L. 90–639, set out as an Effective Date of 1968 Amendments; Transitional Provisions note under section 321 of this title.

EFFECTIVE DATE OF 1965 AMENDMENT

Amendment by Pub. L. 89–74 effective Feb. 1, 1966, see section 11 of Pub. L. 89–74, set out as a note under section 321 of this title.

SAVINGS PROVISION

Amendment by Pub. L. 91–513 not to affect or abate any prosecutions for any violation of law or any civil seizures or forfeitures and injunctive proceedings commenced prior to the effective date of such amendment, and all administrative proceedings pending before the Bureau of Narcotics and Dangerous Drugs [now the Drug Enforcement Administration] on Oct. 27, 1970, to be continued and brought to final determination in accord with laws and regulations in effect prior to Oct. 27, 1970, see section 702 of Pub. L. 91–513, set out as a note under section 321 of this title.

TRANSFER OF FUNCTIONS

For transfer of functions of Federal Security Administrator to Secretary of Health, Education, and Welfare [now Health and Human Services], and of Food and Drug Administration in the Department of Agriculture to Federal Security Agency, see notes set out under section 321 of this title.

§335. Hearing before report of criminal violation

Before any violation of this chapter is reported by the Secretary to any United States attorney for institution of a criminal proceeding, the person against whom such proceeding is contemplated shall be given appropriate notice and an opportunity to present his views, either orally or in writing, with regard to such contemplated proceeding.

(June 25, 1938, ch. 675, §305, 52 Stat. 1045.)

TRANSFER OF FUNCTIONS

For transfer of functions of Federal Security Administrator to Secretary of Health, Education, and Welfare [now Health and Human Services], and of Food and Drug Administration in the Department of Agriculture to Federal Security Agency, see notes set out under section 321 of this title.

§335a. Debarment, temporary denial of approval, and suspension

(a) Mandatory debarment; certain drug applications

(1) Corporations, partnerships, and associations

If the Secretary finds that a person other than an individual has been convicted, after May 13, 1992, of a felony under Federal law for conduct relating to the development or approval, including the process for development or approval, of any abbreviated drug application, the Secretary shall debar such person from submitting, or assisting in the submission of, any such application.

(2) Individuals

If the Secretary finds that an individual has been convicted of a felony under Federal law for conduct—

(A) relating to the development or approval, including the process for development or approval, of any drug product, or

(B) otherwise relating to the regulation of any drug product under this chapter,

the Secretary shall debar such individual from providing services in any capacity to a person that has an approved or pending drug product application.

(b) Permissive debarment; certain drug applications; food imports

(1) In general

The Secretary, on the Secretary's own initiative or in response to a petition, may, in accordance with paragraph (2), debar—

(A) a person other than an individual from submitting or assisting in the submission of any abbreviated drug application,

(B) an individual from providing services in any capacity to a person that has an approved or pending drug product application, or

(C) a person from importing an article of food or offering such an article for import into the United States.

(2) Persons subject to permissive debarment; certain drug applications

The following persons are subject to debarment under subparagraph (A) or (B) of paragraph (1):

(A) Corporations, partnerships, and associations

Any person other than an individual that the Secretary finds has been convicted—

(i) for conduct that—

(I) relates to the development or approval, including the process for the development or approval, of any abbreviated drug application; and

(II) is a felony under Federal law (if the person was convicted before May 13, 1992), a misdemeanor under Federal law, or a felony under State law, or

(ii) of a conspiracy to commit, or aiding or abetting, a criminal offense described in clause (i) or a felony described in subsection (a)(1) of this section,

if the Secretary finds that the type of conduct which served as the basis for such conviction undermines the process for the regulation of drugs.

(B) Individuals

(i) Any individual whom the Secretary finds has been convicted of—

(I) a misdemeanor under Federal law or a felony under State law for conduct relating to the development or approval, including the process for development or approval, of any drug product or otherwise relating to the regulation of drug products under this chapter, or

(II) a conspiracy to commit, or aiding or abetting, such criminal offense or a felony described in subsection (a)(2) of this section,

if the Secretary finds that the type of conduct which served as the basis for such conviction undermines the process for the regulation of drugs.

(ii) Any individual whom the Secretary finds has been convicted of—

(I) a felony which is not described in subsection (a)(2) of this section or clause (i) of this subparagraph and which involves bribery, payment of illegal gratuities, fraud, perjury, false statement, racketeering, blackmail, extortion, falsification or destruction of records, or interference with, obstruction of an investigation into, or prosecution of, any criminal offense, or

(II) a conspiracy to commit, or aiding or abetting, such felony,

if the Secretary finds, on the basis of the conviction of such individual and other information, that such individual has demonstrated a pattern of conduct sufficient to find that there is reason to believe that such individual may violate requirements under this chapter relating to drug products.

(iii) Any individual whom the Secretary finds materially participated in acts that were the basis for a conviction for an offense described in subsection (a) of this section or in clause (i) or (ii) for which a conviction was obtained, if the Secretary finds, on the basis of such participation and other information, that such individual has demonstrated a pattern of conduct sufficient to find that there is reason to believe that such individual may violate requirements under this chapter relating to drug products.

(iv) Any high managerial agent whom the Secretary finds—

(I) worked for, or worked as a consultant for, the same person as another individual during the period in which such other individual took actions for which a felony conviction was obtained and which resulted in the debarment under subsection (a)(2) of this section, or clause (i), of such other individual,

(II) had actual knowledge of the actions described in subclause (I) of such other individual, or took action to avoid such actual knowledge, or failed to take action for the purpose of avoiding such actual knowledge,

(III) knew that the actions described in subclause (I) were violative of law, and

(IV) did not report such actions, or did not cause such actions to be reported, to an officer, employee, or agent of the Department or to an appropriate law enforcement officer, or failed to take other appropriate action that would have ensured that the process for the regulation of drugs was not undermined, within a reasonable time after such agent first knew of such actions,

if the Secretary finds that the type of conduct which served as the basis for such other individual's conviction undermines the process for the regulation of drugs.

(3) Persons subject to permissive debarment; food importation

A person is subject to debarment under paragraph (1)(C) if—

(A) the person has been convicted of a felony for conduct relating to the importation into the United States of any food; or

(B) the person has engaged in a pattern of importing or offering for import adulterated food that presents a threat of serious adverse health consequences or death to humans or animals.

(4) Stay of certain orders

An order of the Secretary under clause (iii) or (iv) of paragraph (2)(B) shall not take effect until 30 days after the order has been issued.

(c) Debarment period and considerations

(1) Effect of debarment

The Secretary—

(A) shall not accept or review (other than in connection with an audit under this section) any abbreviated drug application submitted by or with the assistance of a person debarred under subsection (a)(1) or (b)(2)(A) of this section during the period such person is debarred,

(B) shall, during the period of a debarment under subsection (a)(2) or (b)(2)(B) of this section, debar an individual from providing services in any capacity to a person that has an approved or pending drug product application and shall not accept or review (other than in connection with an audit under this section) an abbreviated drug application from such individual, and

(C) shall, if the Secretary makes the finding described in paragraph (6) or (7) of section 335b(a) of this title, assess a civil penalty in accordance with section 335b of this title.

(2) Debarment periods

(A) In general

The Secretary shall debar a person under subsection (a) or (b) of this section for the following periods:

(i) The period of debarment of a person (other than an individual) under subsection (a)(1) of this section shall not be less than 1 year or more than 10 years, but if an act leading to a subsequent debarment under subsection (a) of this section occurs within 10 years after such person has been debarred under subsection (a)(1) of this section, the period of debarment shall be permanent.

(ii) The debarment of an individual under subsection (a)(2) of this section shall be permanent.

(iii) The period of debarment of any person under paragraph (2) or (3) of subsection (b) of this section shall not be more than 5 years.

The Secretary may determine whether debarment periods shall run concurrently or consecutively in the case of a person debarred for multiple offenses.

(B) Notification

Upon a conviction for an offense described in subsection (a) or (b) of this section or upon execution of an agreement with the United States to plead guilty to such an offense, the person involved may notify the Secretary that the person acquiesces to debarment and such person's debarment shall commence upon such notification.

(3) Considerations

In determining the appropriateness and the period of a debarment of a person under subsection (b) of this section and any period of debarment beyond the minimum specified in subparagraph (A)(i) of paragraph (2), the Secretary shall consider where applicable—

(A) the nature and seriousness of any offense involved,

(B) the nature and extent of management participation in any offense involved, whether corporate policies and practices encouraged the offense, including whether inadequate institutional controls contributed to the offense,

(C) the nature and extent of voluntary steps to mitigate the impact on the public of any offense involved, including the recall or the discontinuation of the distribution of suspect drugs, full cooperation with any investigations (including the extent of disclosure to appropriate authorities of all wrongdoing), the relinquishing of profits on drug approvals fraudulently obtained, and any other actions taken to substantially limit potential or actual adverse effects on the public health,

(D) whether the extent to which changes in ownership, management, or operations have corrected the causes of any offense involved and provide reasonable assurances that the offense will not occur in the future,

(E) whether the person to be debarred is able to present adequate evidence that current production of drugs subject to abbreviated drug applications and all pending abbreviated drug applications are free of fraud or material false statements, and

(F) prior convictions under this chapter or under other Acts involving matters within the jurisdiction of the Food and Drug Administration.

(d) Termination of debarment

(1) Application

Any person that is debarred under subsection (a) of this section (other than a person permanently debarred) or any person that is debarred under subsection (b) of this section may apply to the Secretary for termination of the debarment under this subsection. Any information submitted to the Secretary under this paragraph does not constitute an amendment or supplement to pending or approved abbreviated drug applications.

(2) Deadline

The Secretary shall grant or deny any application respecting a debarment which is submitted under paragraph (1) within 180 days of the date the application is submitted.

(3) Action by the Secretary

(A) Corporations

(i) Conviction reversal

If the conviction which served as the basis for the debarment of a person under subsection (a)(1) of this section or paragraph (2)(A) or (3) of subsection (b) of this section is reversed, the Secretary shall withdraw the order of debarment.

(ii) Application

Upon application submitted under paragraph (1), the Secretary shall terminate the debarment of a person if the Secretary finds that—

(I) changes in ownership, management, or operations have fully corrected the causes of the offense involved and provide reasonable assurances that the offense will not occur in the future, and

(II) in applicable cases, sufficient audits, conducted by the Food and Drug Administration or by independent experts acceptable to the Food and Drug Administration, demonstrate that pending applications and the development of drugs being tested before the submission of an application are free of fraud or material false statements.

In the case of persons debarred under subsection (a)(1) of this section, such termination shall take effect no earlier than the expiration of one year from the date of the debarment.

(B) Individuals

(i) Conviction reversal

If the conviction which served as the basis for the debarment of an individual under subsection (a)(2) of this section or clause (i), (ii), (iii), or (iv) of subsection (b)(2)(B) or subsection (b)(3) of this section is reversed, the Secretary shall withdraw the order of debarment.

(ii) Application

Upon application submitted under paragraph (1), the Secretary shall terminate the debarment of an individual who has been debarred under subsection (b)(2)(B) or subsection (b)(3) of this section if such termination serves the interests of justice and adequately protects the integrity of the drug approval process or the food importation process, as the case may be.

(4) Special termination

(A) Application

Any person that is debarred under subsection (a)(1) of this section (other than a person permanently debarred under subsection (c)(2)(A)(i) of this section) or any individual who is debarred under subsection (a)(2) of this section may apply to the Secretary for special termination of debarment under this subsection. Any information submitted to the Secretary under this subparagraph does not constitute an amendment or supplement to pending or approved abbreviated drug applications.

(B) Corporations

Upon an application submitted under subparagraph (A), the Secretary may take the action described in subparagraph (D) if the Secretary, after an informal hearing, finds that—

(i) the person making the application under subparagraph (A) has demonstrated that the felony conviction which was the basis for such person's debarment involved the commission of an offense which was not authorized, requested, commanded, performed, or recklessly tolerated by the board of directors or by a high managerial agent acting on behalf of the person within the scope of the board's or agent's office or employment,

(ii) all individuals who were involved in the commission of the offense or who knew or should have known of the offense have been removed from employment involving the development or approval of any drug subject to sections[1] 355 of this title,

(iii) the person fully cooperated with all investigations and promptly disclosed all

[1] So in original. Probably should be "section".

wrongdoing to the appropriate authorities, and

(iv) the person acted to mitigate any impact on the public of any offense involved, including the recall, or the discontinuation of the distribution, of any drug with respect to which the Secretary requested a recall or discontinuation of distribution due to concerns about the safety or efficacy of the drug.

(C) Individuals

Upon an application submitted under subparagraph (A), the Secretary may take the action described in subparagraph (D) if the Secretary, after an informal hearing, finds that such individual has provided substantial assistance in the investigations or prosecutions of offenses which are described in subsection (a) or (b) of this section or which relate to any matter under the jurisdiction of the Food and Drug Administration.

(D) Secretarial action

The action referred to in subparagraphs (B) and (C) is—

(i) in the case of a person other than an individual—

(I) terminating the debarment immediately, or

(II) limiting the period of debarment to less than one year, and

(ii) in the case of an individual, limiting the period of debarment to less than permanent but to no less than 1 year,

whichever best serves the interest of justice and protects the integrity of the drug approval process.

(e) Publication and list of debarred persons

The Secretary shall publish in the Federal Register the name of any person debarred under subsection (a) or (b) of this section, the effective date of the debarment, and the period of the debarment. The Secretary shall also maintain and make available to the public a list, updated no less often than quarterly, of such persons, of the effective dates and minimum periods of such debarments, and of the termination of debarments.

(f) Temporary denial of approval

(1) In general

The Secretary, on the Secretary's own initiative or in response to a petition, may, in accordance with paragraph (3), refuse by order, for the period prescribed by paragraph (2), to approve any abbreviated drug application submitted by any person—

(A) if such person is under an active Federal criminal investigation in connection with an action described in subparagraph (B),

(B) if the Secretary finds that such person—

(i) has bribed or attempted to bribe, has paid or attempted to pay an illegal gratuity, or has induced or attempted to induce another person to bribe or pay an illegal gratuity to any officer, employee, or agent of the Department of Health and Human Services or to any other Federal, State, or local official in connection with any abbreviated drug application, or has conspired to commit, or aided or abetted, such actions, or

(ii) has knowingly made or caused to be made a pattern or practice of false statements or misrepresentations with respect to material facts relating to any abbreviated drug application, or the production of any drug subject to an abbreviated drug application, to any officer, employee, or agent of the Department of Health and Human Services, or has conspired to commit, or aided or abetted, such actions, and

(C) if a significant question has been raised regarding—

(i) the integrity of the approval process with respect to such abbreviated drug application, or

(ii) the reliability of data in or concerning such person's abbreviated drug application.

Such an order may be modified or terminated at any time.

(2) Applicable period

(A) In general

Except as provided in subparagraph (B), a denial of approval of an application of a person under paragraph (1) shall be in effect for a period determined by the Secretary but not to exceed 18 months beginning on the date the Secretary finds that the conditions described in subparagraphs (A), (B), and (C) of paragraph (1) exist. The Secretary shall terminate such denial—

(i) if the investigation with respect to which the finding was made does not result in a criminal charge against such person, if criminal charges have been brought and the charges have been dismissed, or if a judgment of acquittal has been entered, or

(ii) if the Secretary determines that such finding was in error.

(B) Extension

If, at the end of the period described in subparagraph (A), the Secretary determines that a person has been criminally charged for an action described in subparagraph (B) of paragraph (1), the Secretary may extend the period of denial of approval of an application for a period not to exceed 18 months. The Secretary shall terminate such extension if the charges have been dismissed, if a judgment of acquittal has been entered, or if the Secretary determines that the finding described in subparagraph (A) was in error.

(3) Informal hearing

Within 10 days of the date an order is issued under paragraph (1), the Secretary shall provide such person with an opportunity for an informal hearing, to be held within such 10 days, on the decision of the Secretary to refuse approval of an abbreviated drug application. Within 60 days of the date on which such hearing is held, the Secretary shall notify the person given such hearing whether the Secretary's refusal of approval will be continued, terminated, or otherwise modified. Such notification shall be final agency action.

(g) Suspension authority

(1) In general

If—

(A) the Secretary finds—

(i) that a person has engaged in conduct described in subparagraph (B) of subsection (f)(1) of this section in connection with 2 or more drugs under abbreviated drug applications, or

(ii) that a person has engaged in flagrant and repeated, material violations of good manufacturing practice or good laboratory practice in connection with the development, manufacturing, or distribution of one or more drugs approved under an abbreviated drug application during a 2-year period, and—

(I) such violations may undermine the safety and efficacy of such drugs, and

(II) the causes of such violations have not been corrected within a reasonable period of time following notice of such violations by the Secretary, and

(B) such person is under an active investigation by a Federal authority in connection with a civil or criminal action involving conduct described in subparagraph (A),

the Secretary shall issue an order suspending the distribution of all drugs the development or approval of which was related to such conduct described in subparagraph (A) or suspending the distribution of all drugs approved under abbreviated drug applications of such person if the Secretary finds that such conduct may have affected the development or approval of a significant number of drugs which the Secretary is unable to identify. The Secretary shall exclude a drug from such order if the Secretary determines that such conduct was not likely to have influenced the safety or efficacy of such drug.

(2) Public health waiver

The Secretary shall, on the Secretary's own initiative or in response to a petition, waive the suspension under paragraph (1) (involving an action described in paragraph (1)(A)(i)) with respect to any drug if the Secretary finds that such waiver is necessary to protect the public health because sufficient quantities of the drug would not otherwise be available. The Secretary shall act on any petition seeking action under this paragraph within 180 days of the date the petition is submitted to the Secretary.

(h) Termination of suspension

The Secretary shall withdraw an order of suspension of the distribution of a drug under subsection (g) of this section if the person with respect to whom the order was issued demonstrates in a petition to the Secretary—

(1)(A) on the basis of an audit by the Food and Drug Administration or by experts acceptable to the Food and Drug Administration, or on the basis of other information, that the development, approval, manufacturing, and distribution of such drug is in substantial compliance with the applicable requirements of this chapter, and

(B) changes in ownership, management, or operations—

(i) fully remedy the patterns or practices with respect to which the order was issued, and

(ii) provide reasonable assurances that such actions will not occur in the future, or

(2) the initial determination was in error.

The Secretary shall act on a submission of a petition under this subsection within 180 days of the date of its submission and the Secretary may consider the petition concurrently with the suspension proceeding. Any information submitted to the Secretary under this subsection does not constitute an amendment or supplement to a pending or approved abbreviated drug application.

(i) Procedure

The Secretary may not take any action under subsection (a), (b), (c), (d)(3), (g), or (h) of this section with respect to any person unless the Secretary has issued an order for such action made on the record after opportunity for an agency hearing on disputed issues of material fact. In the course of any investigation or hearing under this subsection, the Secretary may administer oaths and affirmations, examine witnesses, receive evidence, and issue subpoenas requiring the attendance and testimony of witnesses and the production of evidence that relates to the matter under investigation.

(j) Judicial review

(1) In general

Except as provided in paragraph (2), any person that is the subject of an adverse decision under subsection (a), (b), (c), (d), (f), (g), or (h) of this section may obtain a review of such decision by the United States Court of Appeals for the District of Columbia or for the circuit in which the person resides, by filing in such court (within 60 days following the date the person is notified of the Secretary's decision) a petition requesting that the decision be modified or set aside.

(2) Exception

Any person that is the subject of an adverse decision under clause (iii) or (iv) of subsection (b)(2)(B) of this section may obtain a review of such decision by the United States District Court for the District of Columbia or a district court of the United States for the district in which the person resides, by filing in such court (within 30 days following the date the person is notified of the Secretary's decision) a complaint requesting that the decision be modified or set aside. In such an action, the court shall determine the matter de novo.

(k) Certification

Any application for approval of a drug product shall include—

(1) a certification that the applicant did not and will not use in any capacity the services of any person debarred under subsection (a) or (b) of this section, in connection with such application, and

(2) if such application is an abbreviated drug application, a list of all convictions, described in subsections (a) and (b) of this section which occurred within the previous 5 years, of the applicant and affiliated persons responsible for the development or submission of such application.

(*l*) Applicability

(1) Conviction

For purposes of this section, a person is considered to have been convicted of a criminal offense—

(A) when a judgment of conviction has been entered against the person by a Federal or State court, regardless of whether there is an appeal pending,

(B) when a plea of guilty or nolo contendere by the person has been accepted by a Federal or State court, or

(C) when the person has entered into participation in a first offender, deferred adjudication, or other similar arrangement or program where judgment of conviction has been withheld.

(2) Effective dates

Subsection (a) of this section, subparagraph (A) of subsection (b)(2) of this section, clauses (i) and (ii) of subsection (b)(2)(B) of this section, and subsection (b)(3)(A) of this section shall not apply to a conviction which occurred more than 5 years before the initiation of an agency action proposed to be taken under subsection (a) or (b) of this section. Clauses (iii) and (iv) of subsection (b)(2)(B) of this section, subsection (b)(3)(B) of this section, and subsections (f) and (g) of this section shall not apply to an act or action which occurred more than 5 years before the initiation of an agency action proposed to be taken under subsection (b), (f), or (g) of this section. Clause (iv) of subsection (b)(2)(B) of this section shall not apply to an action which occurred before June 1, 1992. Subsection (k) of this section shall not apply to applications submitted to the Secretary before June 1, 1992.

(m) Devices; mandatory debarment regarding third-party inspections and reviews

(1) In general

If the Secretary finds that a person has been convicted of a felony under section 331(gg) of this title, the Secretary shall debar such person from being accredited under section 360m(b) or 374(g)(2) of this title and from carrying out activities under an agreement described in section 383(b) of this title.

(2) Debarment period

The Secretary shall debar a person under paragraph (1) for the following periods:

(A) The period of debarment of a person (other than an individual) shall not be less than 1 year or more than 10 years, but if an act leading to a subsequent debarment under such paragraph occurs within 10 years after such person has been debarred under such paragraph, the period of debarment shall be permanent.

(B) The debarment of an individual shall be permanent.

(3) Termination of debarment; judicial review; other matters

Subsections (c)(3), (d), (e), (i), (j), and (*l*)(1) of this section apply with respect to a person (other than an individual) or an individual who is debarred under paragraph (1) to the same extent and in the same manner as such subsections apply with respect to a person who is debarred under subsection (a)(1) of this section, or an individual who is debarred under subsection (a)(2) of this section, respectively.

(June 25, 1938, ch. 675, § 306, as added Pub. L. 102–282, § 2, May 13, 1992, 106 Stat. 150; amended Pub. L. 105–115, title I, § 125(b)(2)(C), Nov. 21, 1997, 111 Stat. 2325; Pub. L. 107–188, title III, § 304(a)–(c), June 12, 2002, 116 Stat. 665, 666; Pub. L. 107–250, title II, § 203, Oct. 26, 2002, 116 Stat. 1610.)

PRIOR PROVISIONS

A prior section 306 of act June 25, 1938, was renumbered section 309 and is classified to section 336 of this title.

AMENDMENTS

2002—Subsec. (a). Pub. L. 107–188, § 304(b)(1), substituted "Mandatory debarment; certain drug applications" for "Mandatory debarment" in heading.

Subsec. (b). Pub. L. 107–188, § 304(b)(2)(A), substituted "Permissive debarment; certain drug applications; food imports" for "Permissive debarment" in heading.

Subsec. (b)(1)(C). Pub. L. 107–188, § 304(a)(1), added subpar. (C).

Subsec. (b)(2). Pub. L. 107–188, § 304(b)(2)(B), substituted "permissive debarment; certain drug applications" for "permissive debarment" in heading.

Pub. L. 107–188, § 304(a)(2)(A), inserted "subparagraph (A) or (B) of" before "paragraph (1)" in introductory provisions.

Subsec. (b)(3), (4). Pub. L. 107–188, § 304(a)(2)(B), (C), added par. (3) and redesignated former par. (3) as (4).

Subsec. (c)(2)(A)(iii). Pub. L. 107–188, § 304(b)(3), substituted "paragraph (2) or (3) of subsection (b)" for "subsection (b)(2)".

Subsec. (d)(3)(A)(i). Pub. L. 107–188, § 304(b)(4)(A), substituted "subsection (a)(1) of this section or paragraph (2)(A) or (3) of subsection (b)" for "subsection (a)(1) or (b)(2)(A)".

Subsec. (d)(3)(A)(ii)(II). Pub. L. 107–188, § 304(b)(4)(B), inserted "in applicable cases," before "sufficient audits".

Subsec. (d)(3)(B)(i). Pub. L. 107–188, § 304(b)(4)(C), inserted "or subsection (b)(3)" after "subsection (b)(2)(B)".

Subsec. (d)(3)(B)(ii). Pub. L. 107–188, § 304(b)(4)(C), (D), inserted "or subsection (b)(3)" after "subsection (b)(2)(B)" and "or the food importation process, as the case may be" before period.

Subsec. (*l*)(2). Pub. L. 107–188, § 304(c), in first sentence struck out "and" after "subsection (b)(2) of this section," and inserted ", and subsection (b)(3)(A) of this section" after "subsection (b)(2)(B) of this section" and in second sentence inserted ", subsection (b)(3)(B) of this section," after "subsection (b)(2)(B) of this section".

Subsec. (m). Pub. L. 107–250 added subsec. (m).

1997—Subsec. (d)(4)(B)(ii). Pub. L. 105–115 struck out "or 357" after "355".

CONSTRUCTION

Section 7 of Pub. L. 102–282 provided that: "No amendment made by this Act [enacting this section and sections 335b and 335c of this title and amending sections 321, 336, 337, and 355 of this title] shall preclude any other civil, criminal, or administrative remedy provided under Federal or State law, including any private right of action against any person for the same action subject to any action or civil penalty under an amendment made by this Act."

CONGRESSIONAL FINDINGS

Section 1(c) of Pub. L. 102–282 provided that: "The Congress finds that—

"(1) there is substantial evidence that significant corruption occurred in the Food and Drug Administration's process of approving drugs under abbreviated drug applications,

"(2) there is a need to establish procedures designed to restore and to ensure the integrity of the abbreviated drug application approval process and to protect the public health, and

"(3) there is a need to establish procedures to bar individuals who have been convicted of crimes pertaining to the regulation of drug products from working for companies that manufacture or distribute such products."

§ 335b. Civil penalties

(a) In general

Any person that the Secretary finds—

(1) knowingly made or caused to be made, to any officer, employee, or agent of the Department of Health and Human Services, a false statement or misrepresentation of a material fact in connection with an abbreviated drug application,

(2) bribed or attempted to bribe or paid or attempted to pay an illegal gratuity to any officer, employee, or agent of the Department of Health and Human Services in connection with an abbreviated drug application,

(3) destroyed, altered, removed, or secreted, or procured the destruction, alteration, removal, or secretion of, any material document or other material evidence which was the property of or in the possession of the Department of Health and Human Services for the purpose of interfering with that Department's discharge of its responsibilities in connection with an abbreviated drug application,

(4) knowingly failed to disclose, to an officer or employee of the Department of Health and Human Services, a material fact which such person had an obligation to disclose relating to any drug subject to an abbreviated drug application,

(5) knowingly obstructed an investigation of the Department of Health and Human Services into any drug subject to an abbreviated drug application,

(6) is a person that has an approved or pending drug product application and has knowingly—

(A) employed or retained as a consultant or contractor, or

(B) otherwise used in any capacity the services of,

a person who was debarred under section 335a of this title, or

(7) is an individual debarred under section 335a of this title and, during the period of debarment, provided services in any capacity to a person that had an approved or pending drug product application,

shall be liable to the United States for a civil penalty for each such violation in an amount not to exceed $250,000 in the case of an individual and $1,000,000 in the case of any other person.

(b) Procedure

(1) In general

(A) Action by the Secretary

A civil penalty under subsection (a) of this section shall be assessed by the Secretary on a person by an order made on the record after an opportunity for an agency hearing on disputed issues of material fact and the amount of the penalty. In the course of any investigation or hearing under this subparagraph, the Secretary may administer oaths and affirmations, examine witnesses, receive evidence, and issue subpoenas requiring the attendance and testimony of witnesses and the production of evidence that relates to the matter under investigation.

(B) Action by the Attorney General

In lieu of a proceeding under subparagraph (A), the Attorney General may, upon request of the Secretary, institute a civil action to recover a civil money penalty in the amount and for any of the acts set forth in subsection (a) of this section. Such an action may be instituted separately from or in connection with any other claim, civil or criminal, initiated by the Attorney General under this chapter.

(2) Amount

In determining the amount of a civil penalty under paragraph (1), the Secretary or the court shall take into account the nature, circumstances, extent, and gravity of the act subject to penalty, the person's ability to pay, the effect on the person's ability to continue to do business, any history of prior, similar acts, and such other matters as justice may require.

(3) Limitation on actions

No action may be initiated under this section—

(A) with respect to any act described in subsection (a) of this section that occurred before May 13, 1992, or

(B) more than 6 years after the date when facts material to the act are known or reasonably should have been known by the Secretary but in no event more than 10 years after the date the act took place.

(c) Judicial review

Any person that is the subject of an adverse decision under subsection (b)(1)(A) of this section may obtain a review of such decision by the United States Court of Appeals for the District of Columbia or for the circuit in which the person resides, by filing in such court (within 60 days following the date the person is notified of the Secretary's decision) a petition requesting that the decision be modified or set aside.

(d) Recovery of penalties

The Attorney General may recover any civil penalty (plus interest at the currently prevailing rates from the date the penalty became final) assessed under subsection (b)(1)(A) of this section in an action brought in the name of the United States. The amount of such penalty may be deducted, when the penalty has become final, from any sums then or later owing by the

United States to the person against whom the penalty has been assessed. In an action brought under this subsection, the validity, amount, and appropriateness of the penalty shall not be subject to judicial review.

(e) Informants

The Secretary may award to any individual (other than an officer or employee of the Federal Government or a person who materially participated in any conduct described in subsection (a) of this section) who provides information leading to the imposition of a civil penalty under this section an amount not to exceed—

(1) $250,000, or

(2) one-half of the penalty so imposed and collected,

whichever is less. The decision of the Secretary on such award shall not be reviewable.

(June 25, 1938, ch. 675, § 307, as added Pub. L. 102–282, § 3, May 13, 1992, 106 Stat. 159; amended Pub. L. 103–80, § 3(g), Aug. 13, 1993, 107 Stat. 776.)

PRIOR PROVISIONS

A prior section 307 of act June 25, 1938, was renumbered section 310 and is classified to section 337 of this title.

AMENDMENTS

1993—Subsec. (b)(3)(A). Pub. L. 103–80 made technical amendment to reference to May 13, 1992, to reflect correction of corresponding provision of original act.

CONSTRUCTION

This section not to preclude any other civil, criminal, or administrative remedy provided under Federal or State law, including any private right of action against any person for the same action subject to any action or civil penalty under an amendment made by Pub. L. 102–282, see section 7 of Pub. L. 102–282, set out as a note under section 335a of this title.

§ 335c. Authority to withdraw approval of abbreviated drug applications

(a) In general

The Secretary—

(1) shall withdraw approval of an abbreviated drug application if the Secretary finds that the approval was obtained, expedited, or otherwise facilitated through bribery, payment of an illegal gratuity, or fraud or material false statement, and

(2) may withdraw approval of an abbreviated drug application if the Secretary finds that the applicant has repeatedly demonstrated a lack of ability to produce the drug for which the application was submitted in accordance with the formulations or manufacturing practice set forth in the abbreviated drug application and has introduced, or attempted to introduce, such adulterated or misbranded drug into commerce.

(b) Procedure

The Secretary may not take any action under subsection (a) of this section with respect to any person unless the Secretary has issued an order for such action made on the record after opportunity for an agency hearing on disputed issues of material fact. In the course of any investigation or hearing under this subsection, the Secretary may administer oaths and affirmations, examine witnesses, receive evidence, and issue subpoenas requiring the attendance and testimony of witnesses and the production of evidence that relates to the matter under investigation.

(c) Applicability

Subsection (a) of this section shall apply with respect to offenses or acts regardless of when such offenses or acts occurred.

(d) Judicial review

Any person that is the subject of an adverse decision under subsection (a) of this section may obtain a review of such decision by the United States Court of Appeals for the District of Columbia or for the circuit in which the person resides, by filing in such court (within 60 days following the date the person is notified of the Secretary's decision) a petition requesting that the decision be modified or set aside.

(June 25, 1938, ch. 675, § 308, as added Pub. L. 102–282, § 4, May 13, 1992, 106 Stat. 160.)

CONSTRUCTION

This section not to preclude any other civil, criminal, or administrative remedy provided under Federal or State law, including any private right of action against any person for the same action subject to any action or civil penalty under an amendment made by Pub. L. 102–282, see section 7 of Pub. L. 102–282, set out as a note under section 335a of this title.

§ 336. Report of minor violations

Nothing in this chapter shall be construed as requiring the Secretary to report for prosecution, or for the institution of libel or injunction proceedings, minor violations of this chapter whenever he believes that the public interest will be adequately served by a suitable written notice or warning.

(June 25, 1938, ch. 675, § 309, formerly § 306, 52 Stat. 1045; renumbered § 309, Pub. L. 102–282, § 2, May 13, 1992, 106 Stat. 150.)

TRANSFER OF FUNCTIONS

For transfer of functions of Federal Security Administrator to Secretary of Health, Education, and Welfare [now Health and Human Services], and of Food and Drug Administration in the Department of Agriculture to Federal Security Agency, see notes set out under section 321 of this title.

§ 337. Proceedings in name of United States; provision as to subpoenas

(a) Except as provided in subsection (b) of this section, all such proceedings for the enforcement, or to restrain violations, of this chapter shall be by and in the name of the United States. Subpoenas for witnesses who are required to attend a court of the United States, in any district, may run into any other district in any proceeding under this section.

(b)(1) A State may bring in its own name and within its jurisdiction proceedings for the civil enforcement, or to restrain violations, of section 341, 343(b), 343(c), 343(d), 343(e), 343(f), 343(g), 343(h), 343(i), 343(k), 343(q), or 343(r) of this title if the food that is the subject of the proceedings is located in the State.

(2) No proceeding may be commenced by a State under paragraph (1)—

(A) before 30 days after the State has given notice to the Secretary that the State intends to bring such proceeding,

(B) before 90 days after the State has given notice to the Secretary of such intent if the Secretary has, within such 30 days, commenced an informal or formal enforcement action pertaining to the food which would be the subject of such proceeding, or

(C) if the Secretary is diligently prosecuting a proceeding in court pertaining to such food, has settled such proceeding, or has settled the informal or formal enforcement action pertaining to such food.

In any court proceeding described in subparagraph (C), a State may intervene as a matter of right.

(June 25, 1938, ch. 675, §310, formerly §307, 52 Stat. 1046; Sept. 3, 1954, ch. 1263, §37, 68 Stat. 1239; Pub. L. 101–535, §4, Nov. 8, 1990, 104 Stat. 2362; renumbered §310, Pub. L. 102–282, §2, May 13, 1992, 106 Stat. 150.)

AMENDMENTS

1990—Pub. L. 101–535 substituted "(a) Except as provided in subsection (b) of this section, all" for "All" and "any proceeding under this section" for "any such proceeding" and added subsec. (b).

1954—Act Sept. 3, 1954, struck out reference to section 654 of title 28.

EFFECTIVE DATE OF 1990 AMENDMENT

Amendment by Pub. L. 101–535 effective 24 months after Nov. 8, 1990, except that such amendment effective Dec. 31, 1993, with respect to dietary supplements of vitamins, minerals, herbs, or other similar nutritional substances, see section 10(a)(1)(C) of Pub. L. 101–535, set out as a note under section 343 of this title.

CONSTRUCTION OF AMENDMENTS BY PUB. L. 101–535

Amendments by Pub. L. 101–535 not to be construed to alter authority of Secretary of Health and Human Services and Secretary of Agriculture under the Federal Food, Drug, and Cosmetic Act (21 U.S.C. 301 et seq.), the Federal Meat Inspection Act (21 U.S.C. 601 et seq.), the Poultry Products Inspection Act (21 U.S.C. 451 et seq.), and the Egg Products Inspection Act (21 U.S.C. 1031 et seq.), see section 9 of Pub. L. 101–535, set out as a note under section 343 of this title.

SUBCHAPTER IV—FOOD

§ 341. Definitions and standards for food

Whenever in the judgment of the Secretary such action will promote honesty and fair dealing in the interest of consumers, he shall promulgate regulations fixing and establishing for any food, under its common or usual name so far as practicable, a reasonable definition and standard of identity, a reasonable standard of quality, or reasonable standards of fill of container. No definition and standard of identity and no standard of quality shall be established for fresh or dried fruits, fresh or dried vegetables, or butter, except that definitions and standards of identity may be established for avocadoes, cantaloupes, citrus fruits, and melons. In prescribing any standard of fill of container, the Secretary shall give due consideration to the natural shrinkage in storage and in transit of fresh natural food and to need for the necessary packing and protective material. In the prescribing of any standard of quality for any canned fruit or canned vegetable, consideration shall be given and due allowance made for the differing characteristics of the several varieties of such fruit or vegetable. In prescribing a definition and standard of identity for any food or class of food in which optional ingredients are permitted, the Secretary shall, for the purpose of promoting honesty and fair dealing in the interest of consumers, designate the optional ingredients which shall be named on the label. Any definition and standard of identity prescribed by the Secretary for avocadoes, cantaloupes, citrus fruits, or melons shall relate only to maturity and to the effects of freezing.

(June 25, 1938, ch. 675, §401, 52 Stat. 1046; Apr. 15, 1954, ch. 143, §1, 68 Stat. 54; Aug. 1, 1956, ch. 861, §1, 70 Stat. 919; Pub. L. 103–80, §3(h), Aug. 13, 1993, 107 Stat. 776.)

AMENDMENTS

1993—Pub. L. 103–80 substituted "or reasonable standards of fill of container. No definition" for "and/or reasonable standards of fill of container: *Provided*, That no definition".

1956—Act Aug. 1, 1956, designated provisions constituting subsec. (a) as entire section and repealed subsec. (b) which provided the procedure for establishment of regulations and is covered by section 371(e) of this title.

1954—Act Apr. 15, 1954, designated existing provisions as subsec. (a) and added subsec. (b).

SAVINGS PROVISION

Section 3 of act Aug. 1, 1956, provided that: "In any case in which, prior to the enactment of this Act [Aug. 1, 1956], a public hearing has been begun in accordance with section 401 of the Federal Food, Drug, and Cosmetic Act [341 of this title] upon a proposal to issue, amend, or repeal any regulation contemplated by such section, or has been begun in accordance with section 701(e) of such Act [section 371(e) of this title] upon a proposal to issue, amend, or repeal any regulation contemplated by section 403(j), 404(a), 406(a) or (b), 501(b), 502(d), 502(h), 504 or 604 of such Act [section 343(j), 344(a), 346(a) or (b), 351(b), 352(d), 352(h), 354, or 364 of this title], the provisions of such section 401 or 701(e), as the case may be, as in force immediately prior to the date of the enactment of this Act [Aug. 1, 1956], shall be applicable as though this Act [amending this section and section 371(e) of this title] had not been enacted."

TRANSFER OF FUNCTIONS

For transfer of functions of Federal Security Administrator to Secretary of Health, Education, and Welfare [now Health and Human Services], and of Food and Drug Administration in the Department of Agriculture to Federal Security Agency, see notes set out under section 321 of this title.

FOOD SAFETY AND SECURITY STRATEGY

Pub. L. 107–188, title III, §301, June 12, 2002, 116 Stat. 662, provided that:

"(a) IN GENERAL.—The President's Council on Food Safety (as established by Executive Order No. 13100 [set out below]) shall, in consultation with the Secretary of Transportation, the Secretary of the Treasury, other relevant Federal agencies, the food industry, consumer and producer groups, scientific organizations, and the States, develop a crisis communications and education strategy with respect to bioterrorist threats to the food supply. Such strategy shall address threat assessments; technologies and procedures for securing food processing and manufacturing facilities and modes of transportation; response and notification procedures; and risk communications to the public.

"(b) AUTHORIZATION OF APPROPRIATIONS.—For the purpose of implementing the strategy developed under subsection (a), there are authorized to be appropriated $750,000 for fiscal year 2002, and such sums as may be necessary for each subsequent fiscal year."

FOOD SAFETY COMMISSION

Pub. L. 107–171, title X, §10807, May 13, 2002, 116 Stat. 527, provided that:

"(a) ESTABLISHMENT.—

"(1) IN GENERAL.—There is established a commission to be known as the 'Food Safety Commission' (referred to in this section as the 'Commission').

"(2) MEMBERSHIP.—

"(A) COMPOSITION.—The Commission shall be composed of 15 members (including a Chairperson, appointed by the President[)].

"(B) ELIGIBILITY.—

"(i) IN GENERAL.—Members of the Commission—

"(I) shall have specialized training or significant experience in matters under the jurisdiction of the Commission; and

"(II) shall represent, at a minimum—

"(aa) consumers;

"(bb) food scientists;

"(cc) the food industry; and

"(dd) health professionals.

"(ii) FEDERAL EMPLOYEES.—Not more than 3 members of the Commission may be Federal employees.

"(C) DATE OF APPOINTMENTS.—The appointment of the members of the Commission shall be made as soon as practicable after the date on which funds authorized to be appropriated under subsection (e)(1) are made available.

"(D) VACANCIES.—A vacancy on the Commission—

"(i) shall not affect the powers of the Commission; and

"(ii) shall be filled—

"(I) not later than 60 days after the date on which the vacancy occurs; and

"(II) in the same manner as the original appointment was made.

"(3) MEETINGS.—

"(A) INITIAL MEETING.—The initial meeting of the Commission shall be conducted not later than 30 days after the date of appointment of the final member of the Commission.

"(B) OTHER MEETINGS.—The Commission shall meet at the call of the Chairperson.

"(4) QUORUM; STANDING RULES.—

"(A) QUORUM.—A majority of the members of the Commission shall constitute a quorum to conduct business.

"(B) STANDING RULES.—At the first meeting of the Commission, the Commission shall adopt standing rules of the Commission to guide the conduct of business and decisionmaking of the Commission.

"(b) DUTIES.—

"(1) RECOMMENDATIONS.—The Commission shall make specific recommendations to enhance the food safety system of the United States, including a description of how each recommendation would improve food safety.

"(2) COMPONENTS.—Recommendations made by the Commission under paragraph (1) shall address all food available commercially in the United States.

"(3) REPORT.—Not later than 1 year after the date on which the Commission first meets, the Commission shall submit to the President and Congress—

"(A) the findings, conclusions, and recommendations of the Commission, including a description of how each recommendation would improve food safety;

"(B) a summary of any other material used by the Commission in the preparation of the report under this paragraph; and

"(C) if requested by 1 or more members of the Commission, a statement of the minority views of the Commission.

"(c) POWERS OF THE COMMISSION.—

"(1) HEARINGS.—The Commission may, for the purpose of carrying out this section, hold such hearings, meet and act at such times and places, take such testimony, and receive such evidence as the Commission considers advisable.

"(2) INFORMATION FROM FEDERAL AGENCIES.—

"(A) IN GENERAL.—The Commission may secure directly, from any Federal agency, such information as the Commission considers necessary to carry out this section.

"(B) PROVISION OF INFORMATION.—

"(i) IN GENERAL.—Subject to subparagraph (C), on the request of the Commission, the head of a Federal agency described in subparagraph (A) may furnish information requested by the Commission to the Commission.

"(ii) ADMINISTRATION.—The furnishing of information by a Federal agency to the Commission shall not be considered a waiver of any exemption available to the agency under section 552 of title 5, United States Code.

"(C) INFORMATION TO BE KEPT CONFIDENTIAL.—

"(i) IN GENERAL.—For purposes of section 1905 of title 18, United States Code—

"(I) the Commission shall be considered an agency of the Federal Government; and

"(II) any individual employed by an individual, entity, or organization that is a party to a contract with the Commission under this section shall be considered an employee of the Commission.

"(ii) PROHIBITION ON DISCLOSURE.—Information obtained by the Commission, other than information that is available to the public, shall not be disclosed to any person in any manner except to an employee of the Commission as described in clause (i), for the purpose of receiving, reviewing, or processing the information.

"(d) COMMISSION PERSONNEL MATTERS.—

"(1) MEMBERS.—

"(A) COMPENSATION.—A member of the Commission shall serve without compensation for the services of the member on the Commission.

"(B) TRAVEL EXPENSES.—A member of the Commission shall be allowed travel expenses, including per diem in lieu of subsistence, at rates authorized for an employee of an agency under subchapter I of chapter 57 of title 5, United States Code, while away from the home or regular place of business of the member in the performance of the duties of the Commission.

"(2) STAFF.—

"(A) IN GENERAL.—The Chairperson of the Commission may, without regard to the civil service laws (including regulations), appoint and terminate the appointment of an executive director and such other additional personnel as are necessary to enable the Commission to perform the duties of the Commission.

"(B) CONFIRMATION OF EXECUTIVE DIRECTOR.—The employment of an executive director shall be subject to confirmation by the Commission.

"(C) COMPENSATION.—

"(i) IN GENERAL.—Except as provided in clause (ii), the Chairperson of the Commission may fix the compensation of the executive director and other personnel without regard to the provisions of chapter 51 and subchapter III of chapter 53 of title 5, United States Code, relating to classification of positions and General Schedule pay rates.

"(ii) MAXIMUM RATE OF PAY.—The rate of pay for the executive director and other personnel shall not exceed the rate payable for level II of the Executive Schedule under section 5316 of title 5, United States Code.

"(3) DETAIL OF FEDERAL GOVERNMENT EMPLOYEES.—

"(A) IN GENERAL.—An employee of the Federal Government may be detailed to the Commission, without reimbursement, for such period of time as is permitted by law.

"(B) CIVIL SERVICE STATUS.—The detail of the employee shall be without interruption or loss of civil service status or privilege.

"(4) PROCUREMENT OF TEMPORARY AND INTERMITTENT SERVICES.—The Chairperson of the Commission may procure temporary and intermittent services in accordance with section 3109(b) of title 5, United States Code, at rates for individuals that do not exceed the daily equivalent of the annual rate of basic pay prescribed for level II of the Executive Schedule under section 5316 of that title.

"(e) AUTHORIZATION OF APPROPRIATIONS.—

"(1) IN GENERAL.—There is authorized to be appropriated such sums as are necessary to carry out this section.

"(2) LIMITATION.—No payment may be made under subsection (d) except to the extent provided for in advance in an appropriations Act.

"(f) TERMINATION.—The Commission shall terminate on the date that is 60 days after the date on which the Commission submits the recommendations and report under subsection (b)(3)."

EX. ORD. NO. 13100. PRESIDENT'S COUNCIL ON FOOD SAFETY

Ex. Ord. No. 13100, Aug. 25, 1998, 63 F.R. 45661, as amended by Ex. Ord. No. 13286, §16, Feb. 28, 2003, 68 F.R. 10623, provided:

By the authority vested in me as President by the Constitution and the laws of the United States of America, and in order to improve the safety of the food supply through science-based regulation and well-coordinated inspection, enforcement, research, and education programs, it is hereby ordered as follows:

SECTION 1. *Establishment of President's Council on Food Safety.* (a) There is established the President's Council on Food Safety ("Council"). The Council shall comprise the Secretaries of Agriculture, Commerce, Health and Human Services, and Homeland Security, the Director of the Office of Management and Budget (OMB), the Administrator of the Environmental Protection Agency, the Assistant to the President for Science and Technology/Director of the Office of Science and Technology Policy, the Assistant to the President for Domestic Policy, and the Director of the National Partnership for Reinventing Government. The Council shall consult with other Federal agencies and State, local, and tribal government agencies, and consumer, producer, scientific, and industry groups, as appropriate.

(b) The Secretaries of Agriculture and of Health and Human Services and the Assistant to the President for Science and Technology/Director of the Office of Science and Technology Policy shall serve as Joint Chairs of the Council.

SEC. 2. *Purpose.* The purpose of the Council shall be to develop a comprehensive strategic plan for Federal food safety activities, taking into consideration the findings and recommendations of the National Academy of Sciences report "Ensuring Safe Food from Production to Consumption" and other input from the public on how to improve the effectiveness of the current food safety system. The Council shall make recommendations to the President on how to advance Federal efforts to implement a comprehensive science-based strategy to improve the safety of the food supply and to enhance coordination among Federal agencies, State, local, and tribal governments, and the private sector. The Council shall advise Federal agencies in setting priority areas for investment in food safety.

SEC. 3. *Specific Activities and Functions.* (a) The Council shall develop a comprehensive strategic Federal food safety plan that contains specific recommendations on needed changes, including measurable outcome goals. The principal goal of the plan should be the establishment of a seamless, science-based food safety system. The plan should address the steps necessary to achieve this goal, including the key public health, resource, and management issues regarding food safety. The planning process should consider both short-term and long-term issues including new and emerging threats and the special needs of vulnerable populations such as children and the elderly. In developing this plan, the Council shall consult with all interested parties, including State and local agencies, tribes, consumers, producers, industry, and academia.

(b) Consistent with the comprehensive strategic Federal food safety plan described in section 3(a) of this order, the Council shall advise agencies of priority areas for investment in food safety and ensure that Federal agencies annually develop coordinated food safety budgets for submission to the OMB that sustain and strengthen existing capacities, eliminate duplication, and ensure the most effective use of resources for improving food safety. The Council shall also ensure that Federal agencies annually develop a unified budget for submission to the OMB for the President's Food Safety Initiative and such other food safety issues as the Council determines appropriate.

(c) The Council shall ensure that the Joint Institute for Food Safety Research (JIFSR), in consultation with the National Science and Technology Council, establishes mechanisms to guide Federal research efforts toward the highest priority food safety needs. The JIFSR shall report to the Council on a regular basis on its efforts: (i) to develop a strategic plan for conducting food safety research activities consistent with the President's Food Safety Initiative and such other food safety activities as the JIFSR determines appropriate; and (ii) to coordinate efficiently, within the executive branch and with the private sector and academia, all Federal food safety research.

SEC. 4. *Cooperation.* All actions taken by the Council shall, as appropriate, promote partnerships and cooperation with States, tribes, and other public and private sector efforts wherever possible to improve the safety of the food supply.

SEC. 5. *General Provisions.* This order is intended only to improve the internal management of the executive branch and is not intended to, nor does it, create any right or benefit, substantive or procedural, enforceable at law by a party against the United States, its agencies, its officers or any person. Nothing in this order shall affect or alter the statutory responsibilities of any Federal agency charged with food safety responsibilities.

§ 342. Adulterated food

A food shall be deemed to be adulterated—

(a) Poisonous, insanitary, etc., ingredients

(1) If it bears or contains any poisonous or deleterious substance which may render it injurious to health; but in case the substance is not an added substance such food shall not be considered adulterated under this clause if the quantity of such substance in such food does not ordinarily render it injurious to health.[1] (2)(A) if it bears or contains any added poisonous or added deleterious substance (other than a substance that is a pesticide chemical residue in or on a raw agricultural commodity or processed food, a food additive, a color additive, or a new animal drug) that is unsafe within the meaning of section 346 of this title; or (B) if it bears or contains a pesticide chemical residue that is unsafe within the meaning of section 346a(a) of this title; or (C) if it is or if it bears or contains (i) any food additive that is unsafe within the meaning of section 348 of this title; or (ii) a new animal drug (or conversion product thereof) that is unsafe within the meaning of section 360b of this title; or (3) if it consists in whole or in part of any filthy, putrid, or decomposed substance, or if it is otherwise unfit for food; or (4) if it has

[1] So in original. The period probably should be "; or".

been prepared, packed, or held under insanitary conditions whereby it may have become contaminated with filth, or whereby it may have been rendered injurious to health; or (5) if it is, in whole or in part, the product of a diseased animal or of an animal which has died otherwise than by slaughter; or (6) if its container is composed, in whole or in part, of any poisonous or deleterious substance which may render the contents injurious to health; or (7) if it has been intentionally subjected to radiation, unless the use of the radiation was in conformity with a regulation or exemption in effect pursuant to section 348 of this title.

(b) Absence, substitution, or addition of constituents

(1) If any valuable constituent has been in whole or in part omitted or abstracted therefrom; or (2) if any substance has been substituted wholly or in part therefor; or (3) if damage or inferiority has been concealed in any manner; or (4) if any substance has been added thereto or mixed or packed therewith so as to increase its bulk or weight, or reduce its quality or strength, or make it appear better or of greater value than it is.

(c) Color additives

If it is, or it bears or contains, a color additive which is unsafe within the meaning of section 379e(a) of this title.

(d) Confectionery containing alcohol or nonnutritive substance

If it is confectionery, and—

(1) has partially or completely imbedded therein any nonnutritive object, except that this subparagraph shall not apply in the case of any nonnutritive object if, in the judgment of the Secretary as provided by regulations, such object is of practical functional value to the confectionery product and would not render the product injurious or hazardous to health;

(2) bears or contains any alcohol other than alcohol not in excess of one-half of 1 per centum by volume derived solely from the use of flavoring extracts, except that this clause shall not apply to confectionery which is introduced or delivered for introduction into, or received or held for sale in, interstate commerce if the sale of such confectionery is permitted under the laws of the State in which such confectionery is intended to be offered for sale;

(3) bears or contains any nonnutritive substance, except that this subparagraph shall not apply to a safe nonnutritive substance which is in or on confectionery by reason of its use for some practical functional purpose in the manufacture, packaging, or storage of such confectionery if the use of the substance does not promote deception of the consumer or otherwise result in adulteration or misbranding in violation of any provision of this chapter, except that the Secretary may, for the purpose of avoiding or resolving uncertainty as to the application of this subparagraph, issue regulations allowing or prohibiting the use of particular nonnutritive substances.

(e) Oleomargarine containing filthy, putrid, etc., matter

If it is oleomargarine or margarine or butter and any of the raw material used therein consisted in whole or in part of any filthy, putrid, or decomposed substance, or such oleomargarine or margarine or butter is otherwise unfit for food.

(f) Dietary supplement or ingredient: safety

(1) If it is a dietary supplement or contains a dietary ingredient that—

(A) presents a significant or unreasonable risk of illness or injury under—

(i) conditions of use recommended or suggested in labeling, or

(ii) if no conditions of use are suggested or recommended in the labeling, under ordinary conditions of use;

(B) is a new dietary ingredient for which there is inadequate information to provide reasonable assurance that such ingredient does not present a significant or unreasonable risk of illness or injury;

(C) the Secretary declares to pose an imminent hazard to public health or safety, except that the authority to make such declaration shall not be delegated and the Secretary shall promptly after such a declaration initiate a proceeding in accordance with sections 554 and 556 of title 5 to affirm or withdraw the declaration; or

(D) is or contains a dietary ingredient that renders it adulterated under paragraph (a)(1) under the conditions of use recommended or suggested in the labeling of such dietary supplement.

In any proceeding under this subparagraph, the United States shall bear the burden of proof on each element to show that a dietary supplement is adulterated. The court shall decide any issue under this paragraph on a de novo basis.

(2) Before the Secretary may report to a United States attorney a violation of paragraph[2] (1)(A) for a civil proceeding, the person against whom such proceeding would be initiated shall be given appropriate notice and the opportunity to present views, orally and in writing, at least 10 days before such notice, with regard to such proceeding.

(g) Dietary supplement: manufacturing practices

(1) If it is a dietary supplement and it has been prepared, packed, or held under conditions that do not meet current good manufacturing practice regulations, including regulations requiring, when necessary, expiration date labeling, issued by the Secretary under subparagraph (2).

(2) The Secretary may by regulation prescribe good manufacturing practices for dietary supplements. Such regulations shall be modeled after current good manufacturing practice regulations for food and may not impose standards for which there is no current and generally available analytical methodology. No standard of current good manufacturing practice may be imposed unless such standard is included in a regulation promulgated after notice and oppor-

[2] So in original. Probably should be "subparagraph".

tunity for comment in accordance with chapter 5 of title 5.

(h) Reoffer of food previously denied admission

If it is an article of food imported or offered for import into the United States and the article of food has previously been refused admission under section 381(a) of this title, unless the person reoffering the article affirmatively establishes, at the expense of the owner or consignee of the article, that the article complies with the applicable requirements of this chapter, as determined by the Secretary.

(i) Noncompliance with sanitary transportation practices

If it is transported or offered for transport by a shipper, carrier by motor vehicle or rail vehicle, receiver, or any other person engaged in the transportation of food under conditions that are not in compliance with regulations promulgated under section 350e of this title.

(June 25, 1938, ch. 675, §402, 52 Stat. 1046; Mar. 16, 1950, ch. 61, §3(d), 64 Stat. 21; July 22, 1954, ch. 559, §2, 68 Stat. 511; July 9, 1956, ch. 530, 70 Stat. 512; Pub. L. 85–929, §3(a), (b), Sept. 6, 1958, 72 Stat. 1784; Pub. L. 86–2, Mar. 17, 1959, 73 Stat. 3; Pub. L. 86–618, title I, §§102(a)(1), (2), 105(c), July 12, 1960, 74 Stat. 397, 398, 404; Pub. L. 89–477, June 29, 1966, 80 Stat. 231; Pub. L. 90–399, §104, July 13, 1968, 82 Stat. 352; Pub. L. 99–252, §10, Feb. 27, 1986, 100 Stat. 35; Pub. L. 102–571, title I, §107(4), Oct. 29, 1992, 106 Stat. 4499; Pub. L. 103–80, §3(i), Aug. 13, 1993, 107 Stat. 776; Pub. L. 103–417, §§4, 9, Oct. 25, 1994, 108 Stat. 4328, 4332; Pub. L. 104–170, title IV, §404, Aug. 3, 1996, 110 Stat. 1514; Pub. L. 107–188, title III, §309, June 12, 2002, 116 Stat. 673; Pub. L. 109–59, title VII, §7202(a), Aug. 10, 2005, 119 Stat. 1911.)

AMENDMENTS

2005—Par. (i). Pub. L. 109–59 added par. (i).

2002—Par. (h). Pub. L. 107–188 added par. (h).

1996—Par. (a). Pub. L. 104–170 added subpar. (2) and struck out former subpar. (2) which read as follows: "(2)(A) if it bears or contains any added poisonous or added deleterious substance (other than one which is (i) a pesticide chemical in or on a raw agricultural commodity; (ii) a food additive; (iii) a color additive; or (iv) a new animal drug) which is unsafe within the meaning of section 346 of this title, or (B) if it is a raw agricultural commodity and it bears or contains a pesticide chemical which is unsafe within the meaning of section 346a(a) of this title, or (C) if it is, or if it bears or contains, any food additive which is unsafe within the meaning of section 348 of this title: *Provided*, That where a pesticide chemical has been used in or on a raw agricultural commodity in conformity with an exemption granted or a tolerance prescribed under section 346a of this title and such raw agricultural commodity has been subjected to processing such as canning, cooking, freezing, dehydrating, or milling, the residue of such pesticide chemical remaining in or on such processed food shall, notwithstanding the provisions of sections 346 and 348 of this title, not be deemed unsafe if such residue in or on the raw agricultural commodity has been removed to the extent possible in good manufacturing practice and the concentration of such residue in the processed food when ready to eat is not greater than the tolerance prescribed for the raw agricultural commodity, or (D) if it is, or it bears or contains, a new animal drug (or conversion product thereof) which is unsafe within the meaning of section 360b of this title;". That part of Pub. L. 104–170 which directed the substitution of "or (3) if it consists" for "(3) if it consists" was executed by making the substitution for "(3) If it consists" to reflect the probable intent of Congress.

1994—Par. (f). Pub. L. 103–417, §4, added par. (f).

Par. (g). Pub. L. 103–417, §9, added par. (g).

1993—Par. (a). Pub. L. 103–80, §3(i)(1), substituted a period for "; or" at end of subpar. (1) and "If it" for "if it" at beginning of par. (3). That part of Pub. L. 103–80, §3(i)(1), which directed the substitution of a period for "; or" at end of subpar. (2) could not be executed because "; or" did not appear.

Par. (d)(1). Pub. L. 103–80, §3(i)(2), substituted ", except that this subparagraph" for ": *Provided*, That this clause".

Par. (d)(3). Pub. L. 103–80, §3(i)(3), substituted ", except that this subparagraph shall not apply" for ": *Provided*, That this clause shall not apply" and ", except that the Secretary may, for the purpose of avoiding or resolving uncertainty as to the application of this subparagraph" for ": *And provided further*, That the Secretary may, for the purpose of avoiding or resolving uncertainty as to the application of this clause".

1992—Par. (c). Pub. L. 102–571 substituted "379e(a)" for "376(a)".

1986—Par. (d)(2). Pub. L. 99–252 inserted provision that this clause not apply to confectionery introduced or delivered for introduction into or received or held for sale in, interstate commerce if the sale is permitted under the laws of the State in which the confectionery is intended to be offered for sale.

1968—Par. (a)(2). Pub. L. 90–399 added cls. (A)(iv) and (D).

1966—Par. (d). Pub. L. 89–477 permitted the imbedding of nonnutritive objects in confectionery foods if in the judgment of the Secretary of Health, Education, and Welfare, as provided by regulation, the imbedding of the object is of practical functional value to the confectionery product and would not render it injurious or hazardous to health, raised to one-half of 1 per centum by volume the upper limit for the allowable use of alcohol derived solely from the use of flavoring extracts, allowed the use of safe nonnutritive substances in and on confectionery foods by reason of their use for some practical and functional purpose in the manufacture, packaging, or storage of the confectionery foods if the use of the substances does not promote deception of the consumer or otherwise result in adulteration or misbranding, authorized the Secretary to issue regulations on the use of particular nonnutritive substances, and removed reference to nonnutritive masticatory substances added to chewing gum and harmless flavoring, harmless resinous glaze not in excess of four-tenths of 1 per centum, natural gum, authorized coloring, and pectin.

1960—Par. (a). Pub. L. 86–618, §102(a)(1), substituted "other than one which is (i) a pesticide chemical in or on a raw agricultural commodity; (ii) a food additive; or (iii) a color additive" for "(except a pesticide chemical in or on a raw agricultural commodity and except a food additive)" in cl. (2)(A).

Par. (c). Pub. L. 86–618, §102(a)(2), amended par. (c) generally, substituting provisions deeming a food adulterated if it is, or it bears or contains, a color additive which is unsafe within the meaning of section 376 of this title for provisions which related to food that bears or contains a coal-tar color other than one from a batch that has been certified in accordance with regulations as provided by section 346 of this title, and struck out provisos which related to the use of color on oranges.

Par. (d). Pub. L. 86–618, §105(c), substituted "authorized coloring" for "harmless coloring".

1959—Par. (c). Pub. L. 86–2 extended from Mar. 1, 1959, to May 1, 1959, the period during which subsection is inapplicable to oranges which have been colored with F.D. & C. Red 32, and inserted proviso requiring Secretary to establish regulations prescribing the conditions under which Citrus Red No. 2 may be safely used in coloring certain mature oranges, and providing for separately listing and for certification of batches of such color.

1958—Par. (a). Pub. L. 85–929, among other changes, inserted cl. (2)(C) relating to food additive unsafe within the meaning of section 348 of this title, and to pesticide chemical, and added cl. (7) relating to radiated food.

1956—Par. (c). Act July 9, 1956, inserted second proviso relating to coloring of oranges.

1954—Par. (a)(2). Act July 22, 1954, provided in the case of any raw agricultural commodity bearing or containing a pesticide chemical, that such commodity shall be deemed to be adulterated if such pesticide chemical is unsafe within the meaning of section 346a of this title.

1950—Par. (e). Act Mar. 16, 1950, added par. (e).

EFFECTIVE DATE OF 2005 AMENDMENT

Amendment by Pub. L. 109–59 effective Oct. 1, 2005, see section 7204 of Pub. L. 109–59, set out as a note under section 331 of this title.

EFFECTIVE DATE OF 1968 AMENDMENT

Amendment by Pub. L. 90–399 effective on first day of thirteenth calendar month after July 13, 1968, see section 108(a) of Pub. L. 90–399, set out as an Effective Date and Transitional Provisions note under section 360b of this title.

EFFECTIVE DATE OF 1960 AMENDMENT

Amendment by Pub. L. 86–618 effective July 12, 1960, subject to the provisions of section 203 of Pub. L. 86–618, see section 202 of Pub. L. 86–618, set out as a note under section 379e of this title.

EFFECTIVE DATE OF NEMATOCIDE, PLANT REGULATOR, DEFOLIANT, AND DESICCANT AMENDMENT OF 1959

Effective date of par. (a)(2) as in force prior to July 22, 1954, with respect to particular commercial use of a nematocide, plant regulator, defoliant, or desiccant in or on a raw agricultural commodity made before Jan. 1, 1958, see section 3(b) of Pub. L. 86–139, Aug. 7, 1959, 73 Stat. 288.

EFFECTIVE DATE OF 1958 AMENDMENT

Section 6 of Pub. L. 85–929, as amended by Pub. L. 87–19, §2, Apr. 7, 1961, 75 Stat. 42; Pub. L. 88–625, §2, Oct. 3, 1964, 78 Stat. 1002, provided that:

"(a) Except as provided in subsections (b) and (c) of this section, this Act [amending this section, sections 321, 331, 346, and 348 of this title, and section 210 of Title 42, The Public Health and Welfare, and enacting provisions set out as notes under sections 321 and 451 of this title] shall take effect on the date of its enactment [Sept. 6, 1958].

"(b) Except as provided in subsection (c) of this section, section 3 of this Act [amending this section and section 346 of this title] shall take effect on the one hundred and eightieth day after the date of enactment of this Act [Sept. 6, 1958].

"(c) With respect to any particular commercial use of a food additive, if such use was made of such additive before January 1, 1958, section 3 of this Act [amending this section and section 346 of this title] shall take effect—

"(1) Either (A) one year after the effective date established in subsection (b) of this section, or (B) at the end of such additional period (but not later than two years from such effective date established in subsection (b)) as the Secretary of Health, Education, and Welfare [now Health and Human Services] may prescribe on the basis of a finding that such extension involves no undue risk to the public health and that conditions exist which necessitate the prescribing of such an additional period, or

"(2) on the date on which an order with respect to such use under section 409 of the Federal Food, Drug, and Cosmetic Act [section 348 of this title] becomes effective,

whichever date first occurs. Whenever the Secretary has, pursuant to clause (1)(B) of this subsection, extended the effective date of section 3 of this Act [amending this section] to March 5, 1961, or has on that date a request for such extension pending before him, with respect to any such particular use of a food additive, he may, notwithstanding the parenthetical time limitation in that clause, further extend such effective date, not beyond June 30, 1964, under the authority of that clause (but subject to clause (2)) with respect to such use of the additive (or a more limited specified use or uses thereof) if, in addition to making the findings required by clause (1)(B), he finds (i) that bona fide action to determine the applicability of such section 409 [section 348 of this title] to such use or uses, or to develop the scientific data necessary for action under such section, was commenced by an interested person before March 6, 1960, and was thereafter pursued with reasonable diligence, and (ii) that in the Secretary's judgment such extension is consistent with the objective of carrying to completion in good faith, as soon as reasonably practicable, the scientific investigations necessary as a basis for action under such section 409 [section 348 of this title]: *Provided*, That if the Secretary has, pursuant to this sentence, granted an extension to June 30, 1964, he may, upon making the findings required by clause (1)(B) of this subsection and clauses (i) and (ii) of this sentence, further extend such effective date, but not beyond December 31, 1965. The Secretary may at any time terminate an extension so granted if he finds that it should not have been granted, or that by reason of a change in circumstances the basis for such extension no longer exists, or that there has been a failure to comply with a requirement for submission of progress reports or with other conditions attached to such extension."

EFFECTIVE DATE OF 1954 AMENDMENT

Section 5 of act July 22, 1954, provided that: "This Act [amending this section and section 321 of this title and enacting sections 346a and 346b of this title] shall take effect upon the date of its enactment [July 22, 1954], except that with respect to pesticide chemicals for which tolerances or exemptions have not been established under section 408 of the Federal Food, Drug, and Cosmetic Act [section 346a of this title], the amendment to section 402(a) of such Act [par. (a) of this section] made by section 2 of this Act shall not be effective—

"(1) for the period of one year following the date of the enactment of this Act [July 22, 1954]; or

"(2) for such additional period following such period of one year, but not extending beyond two years after the date of the enactment of this Act [July 22, 1954] as the Secretary of Health, Education, and Welfare [now Health and Human Services] may prescribe on the basis of a finding that conditions exist which necessitate the prescribing of such additional period."

EFFECTIVE DATE OF 1950 AMENDMENT

Amendment by act Mar. 16, 1950, effective July 1, 1950, see section 7 of act Mar. 16, 1950, set out as an Effective Date note under section 347 of this title.

EFFECTIVE DATE; POSTPONEMENT

Par. (c) effective Jan. 1, 1940, see act June 23, 1939, ch. 242, 53 Stat. 853, set out as an Effective Date; Postponement in Certain Cases note under section 301 of this title.

SHORT TITLE

Pub. L. 88–625, §1, Oct. 3, 1964, 78 Stat. 1002, provided: "That this Act [amending provisions set out as a note under this section and section 135 of Title 7, Agriculture] may be cited as the 'Food Additives Transitional Provisions Amendment of 1964'."

TRANSFER OF FUNCTIONS

For transfer of functions of Federal Security Administrator to Secretary of Health, Education, and Welfare [now Health and Human Services], and of Food and Drug Administration in the Department of Agriculture to Federal Security Agency, see notes set out under section 321 of this title.

DOMESTIC FISH OR FISH PRODUCT COMPLIANCE WITH FOOD SAFETY STANDARDS OR PROCEDURES DEEMED TO HAVE MET REQUIREMENTS FOR FEDERAL COMMODITY PURCHASE PROGRAMS

Pub. L. 104–180, title VII, §733, Aug. 6, 1996, 110 Stat. 1601, provided that: "Hereafter, notwithstanding any other provision of law, any domestic fish or fish product produced in compliance with food safety standards or procedures accepted by the Food and Drug Administration as satisfying the requirements of the 'Procedures for the Safe and Sanitary Processing and Importing of Fish and Fish Products' (published by the Food and Drug Administration as a final regulation in the Federal Register of December 18, 1995), shall be deemed to have met any inspection requirements of the Department of Agriculture or other Federal agency for any Federal commodity purchase program, including the program authorized under section 32 of the Act of August 24, 1935 (7 U.S.C. 612c) except that the Department of Agriculture or other Federal agency may utilize lot inspection to establish a reasonable degree of certainty that fish or fish products purchased under a Federal commodity purchase program, including the program authorized under section 32 of the Act of August 24, 1935 (7 U.S.C. 612c), meet Federal product specifications."

§ 343. Misbranded food

A food shall be deemed to be misbranded—

(a) False or misleading label

If (1) its labeling is false or misleading in any particular, or (2) in the case of a food to which section 350 of this title applies, its advertising is false or misleading in a material respect or its labeling is in violation of section 350(b)(2) of this title.

(b) Offer for sale under another name

If it is offered for sale under the name of another food.

(c) Imitation of another food

If it is an imitation of another food, unless its label bears, in type of uniform size and prominence, the word "imitation" and, immediately thereafter, the name of the food imitated.

(d) Misleading container

If its container is so made, formed, or filled as to be misleading.

(e) Package form

If in package form unless it bears a label containing (1) the name and place of business of the manufacturer, packer, or distributor; and (2) an accurate statement of the quantity of the contents in terms of weight, measure, or numerical count, except that under clause (2) of this paragraph reasonable variations shall be permitted, and exemptions as to small packages shall be established, by regulations prescribed by the Secretary.

(f) Prominence of information on label

If any word, statement, or other information required by or under authority of this chapter to appear on the label or labeling is not prominently placed thereon with such conspicuousness (as compared with other words, statements, designs, or devices, in the labeling) and in such terms as to render it likely to be read and understood by the ordinary individual under customary conditions of purchase and use.

(g) Representation as to definition and standard of identity

If it purports to be or is represented as a food for which a definition and standard of identity has been prescribed by regulations as provided by section 341 of this title, unless (1) it conforms to such definition and standard, and (2) its label bears the name of the food specified in the definition and standard, and, insofar as may be required by such regulations, the common names of optional ingredients (other than spices, flavoring, and coloring) present in such food.

(h) Representation as to standards of quality and fill of container

If it purports to be or is represented as—

(1) a food for which a standard of quality has been prescribed by regulations as provided by section 341 of this title, and its quality falls below such standard, unless its label bears, in such manner and form as such regulations specify, a statement that it falls below such standard;

(2) a food for which a standard or standards of fill of container have been prescribed by regulations as provided by section 341 of this title, and it falls below the standard of fill of container applicable thereto, unless its label bears, in such manner and form as such regulations specify, a statement that it falls below such standard; or

(3) a food that is pasteurized unless—

(A) such food has been subjected to a safe process or treatment that is prescribed as pasteurization for such food in a regulation promulgated under this chapter; or

(B)(i) such food has been subjected to a safe process or treatment that—

(I) is reasonably certain to achieve destruction or elimination in the food of the most resistant microorganisms of public health significance that are likely to occur in the food;

(II) is at least as protective of the public health as a process or treatment described in subparagraph (A);

(III) is effective for a period that is at least as long as the shelf life of the food when stored under normal and moderate abuse conditions; and

(IV) is the subject of a notification to the Secretary, including effectiveness data regarding the process or treatment; and

(ii) at least 120 days have passed after the date of receipt of such notification by the Secretary without the Secretary making a determination that the process or treatment involved has not been shown to meet the requirements of subclauses (I) through (III) of clause (i).

For purposes of paragraph (3), a determination by the Secretary that a process or treatment has not been shown to meet the requirements of subclauses (I) through (III) of subparagraph (B)(i) shall constitute final agency action under such subclauses.

(i) Label where no representation as to definition and standard of identity

Unless its label bears (1) the common or usual name of the food, if any there be, and (2) in case it is fabricated from two or more ingredients, the common or usual name of each such ingredient and if the food purports to be a beverage containing vegetable or fruit juice, a statement with appropriate prominence on the information panel of the total percentage of such fruit or vegetable juice contained in the food; except that spices, flavorings, and colors not required to be certified under section 379e(c) of this title[1] unless sold as spices, flavorings, or such colors, may be designated as spices, flavorings, and colorings without naming each. To the extent that compliance with the requirements of clause (2) of this paragraph is impracticable, or results in deception or unfair competition, exemptions shall be established by regulations promulgated by the Secretary.

(j) Representation for special dietary use

If it purports to be or is represented for special dietary uses, unless its label bears such information concerning its vitamin, mineral, and other dietary properties as the Secretary determines to be, and by regulations prescribes as, necessary in order fully to inform purchasers as to its value for such uses.

(k) Artificial flavoring, artificial coloring, or chemical preservatives

If it bears or contains any artificial flavoring, artificial coloring, or chemical preservative, unless it bears labeling stating that fact, except that to the extent that compliance with the requirements of this paragraph is impracticable, exemptions shall be established by regulations promulgated by the Secretary. The provisions of this paragraph and paragraphs (g) and (i) with respect to artificial coloring shall not apply in the case of butter, cheese, or ice cream. The provisions of this paragraph with respect to chemical preservatives shall not apply to a pesticide chemical when used in or on a raw agricultural commodity which is the produce of the soil.

(*l*) Pesticide chemicals on raw agricultural commodities

If it is a raw agricultural commodity which is the produce of the soil, bearing or containing a pesticide chemical applied after harvest, unless the shipping container of such commodity bears labeling which declares the presence of such chemical in or on such commodity and the common or usual name and the function of such chemical, except that no such declaration shall be required while such commodity, having been removed from the shipping container, is being held or displayed for sale at retail out of such container in accordance with the custom of the trade.

(m) Color additives

If it is a color additive, unless its packaging and labeling are in conformity with such packaging and labeling requirements, applicable to such color additive, as may be contained in regulations issued under section 379e of this title.

[1] So in original. Probably should be followed by a comma.

(n) Packaging or labeling of drugs in violation of regulations

If its packaging or labeling is in violation of an applicable regulation issued pursuant to section 1472 or 1473 of title 15.

(*o*) Repealed. Pub. L. 106–554, § 1(a)(1) [title V, § 517], Dec. 21, 2000, 114 Stat. 2763, 2763A–73

(p) Repealed. Pub. L. 104–124, § 1, Apr. 1, 1996, 110 Stat. 882

(q) Nutrition information

(1) Except as provided in subparagraphs (3), (4), and (5), if it is a food intended for human consumption and is offered for sale, unless its label or labeling bears nutrition information that provides—

(A)(i) the serving size which is an amount customarily consumed and which is expressed in a common household measure that is appropriate to the food, or

(ii) if the use of the food is not typically expressed in a serving size, the common household unit of measure that expresses the serving size of the food,

(B) the number of servings or other units of measure per container,

(C) the total number of calories—

(i) derived from any source, and

(ii) derived from the total fat,

in each serving size or other unit of measure of the food,

(D) the amount of the following nutrients: Total fat, saturated fat, cholesterol, sodium, total carbohydrates, complex carbohydrates, sugars, dietary fiber, and total protein contained in each serving size or other unit of measure,

(E) any vitamin, mineral, or other nutrient required to be placed on the label and labeling of food under this chapter before October 1, 1990, if the Secretary determines that such information will assist consumers in maintaining healthy dietary practices.

The Secretary may by regulation require any information required to be placed on the label or labeling by this subparagraph or subparagraph (2)(A) to be highlighted on the label or labeling by larger type, bold type, or contrasting color if the Secretary determines that such highlighting will assist consumers in maintaining healthy dietary practices.

(2)(A) If the Secretary determines that a nutrient other than a nutrient required by subparagraph (1)(C), (1)(D), or (1)(E) should be included in the label or labeling of food subject to subparagraph (1) for purposes of providing information regarding the nutritional value of such food that will assist consumers in maintaining healthy dietary practices, the Secretary may by regulation require that information relating to such additional nutrient be included in the label or labeling of such food.

(B) If the Secretary determines that the information relating to a nutrient required by subparagraph (1)(C), (1)(D), or (1)(E) or clause (A) of this subparagraph to be included in the label or labeling of food is not necessary to assist consumers in maintaining healthy dietary practices, the Secretary may by regulation remove information relating to such nutrient from such requirement.

(3) For food that is received in bulk containers at a retail establishment, the Secretary may, by regulation, provide that the nutrition information required by subparagraphs (1) and (2) be displayed at the location in the retail establishment at which the food is offered for sale.

(4)(A) The Secretary shall provide for furnishing the nutrition information required by subparagraphs (1) and (2) with respect to raw agricultural commodities and raw fish by issuing voluntary nutrition guidelines, as provided by clause (B) or by issuing regulations that are mandatory as provided by clause (D).

(B)(i) Upon the expiration of 12 months after November 8, 1990, the Secretary, after providing an opportunity for comment, shall issue guidelines for food retailers offering raw agricultural commodities or raw fish to provide nutrition information specified in subparagraphs (1) and (2). Such guidelines shall take into account the actions taken by food retailers during such 12-month period to provide to consumers nutrition information on raw agricultural commodities and raw fish. Such guidelines shall only apply—

(I) in the case of raw agricultural commodities, to the 20 varieties of vegetables most frequently consumed during a year and the 20 varieties of fruit most frequently consumed during a year, and

(II) to the 20 varieties of raw fish most frequently consumed during a year.

The vegetables, fruits, and raw fish to which such guidelines apply shall be determined by the Secretary by regulation and the Secretary may apply such guidelines regionally.

(ii) Upon the expiration of 12 months after November 8, 1990, the Secretary shall issue a final regulation defining the circumstances that constitute substantial compliance by food retailers with the guidelines issued under subclause (i). The regulation shall provide that there is not substantial compliance if a significant number of retailers have failed to comply with the guidelines. The size of the retailers and the portion of the market served by retailers in compliance with the guidelines shall be considered in determining whether the substantial-compliance standard has been met.

(C)(i) Upon the expiration of 30 months after November 8, 1990, the Secretary shall issue a report on actions taken by food retailers to provide consumers with nutrition information for raw agricultural commodities and raw fish under the guidelines issued under clause (A). Such report shall include a determination of whether there is substantial compliance with the guidelines.

(ii) If the Secretary finds that there is substantial compliance with the guidelines, the Secretary shall issue a report and make a determination of the type required in subclause (i) every two years.

(D)(i) If the Secretary determines that there is not substantial compliance with the guidelines issued under clause (A), the Secretary shall at the time such determination is made issue proposed regulations requiring that any person who offers raw agricultural commodities or raw fish to consumers provide, in a manner prescribed by regulations, the nutrition information required by subparagraphs (1) and (2). The Secretary shall issue final regulations imposing such requirements 6 months after issuing the proposed regulations. The final regulations shall become effective 6 months after the date of their promulgation.

(ii) Regulations issued under subclause (i) may require that the nutrition information required by subparagraphs (1) and (2) be provided for more than 20 varieties of vegetables, 20 varieties of fruit, and 20 varieties of fish most frequently consumed during a year if the Secretary finds that a larger number of such products are frequently consumed. Such regulations shall permit such information to be provided in a single location in each area in which raw agricultural commodities and raw fish are offered for sale. Such regulations may provide that information shall be expressed as an average or range per serving of the same type of raw agricultural commodity or raw fish. The Secretary shall develop and make available to the persons who offer such food to consumers the information required by subparagraphs (1) and (2).

(iii) Regulations issued under subclause (i) shall permit the required information to be provided in each area of an establishment in which raw agricultural commodities and raw fish are offered for sale. The regulations shall permit food retailers to display the required information by supplying copies of the information provided by the Secretary, by making the information available in brochure, notebook or leaflet form, or by posting a sign disclosing the information. Such regulations shall also permit presentation of the required information to be supplemented by a video, live demonstration, or other media which the Secretary approves.

(E) For purposes of this subparagraph, the term "fish" includes freshwater or marine fin fish, crustaceans, and mollusks, including shellfish, amphibians, and other forms of aquatic animal life.

(F) No person who offers raw agricultural commodities or raw fish to consumers may be prosecuted for minor violations of this subparagraph if there has been substantial compliance with the requirements of this paragraph.

(5)(A) Subparagraphs (1), (2), (3), and (4) shall not apply to food—

(i) which is served in restaurants or other establishments in which food is served for immediate human consumption or which is sold for sale or use in such establishments,

(ii) which is processed and prepared primarily in a retail establishment, which is ready for human consumption, which is of the type described in subclause (i), and which is offered for sale to consumers but not for immediate human consumption in such establishment and which is not offered for sale outside such establishment,

(iii) which is an infant formula subject to section 350a of this title,

(iv) which is a medical food as defined in section 360ee(b) of this title, or

(v) which is described in section 345(2) of this title.

(B) Subparagraphs (1) and (2) shall not apply to the label of a food if the Secretary determines by regulations that compliance with such subparagraphs is impracticable because the package of such food is too small to comply with the requirements of such subparagraphs and if the label of such food does not contain any nutrition information.

(C) If a food contains insignificant amounts, as determined by the Secretary, of all the nutrients required by subparagraphs (1) and (2) to be listed in the label or labeling of food, the requirements of such subparagraphs shall not apply to such food if the label, labeling, or advertising of such food does not make any claim with respect to the nutritional value of such food. If a food contains insignificant amounts, as determined by the Secretary, of more than one-half the nutrients required by subparagraphs (1) and (2) to be in the label or labeling of the food, the Secretary shall require the amounts of such nutrients to be stated in a simplified form prescribed by the Secretary.

(D) If a person offers food for sale and has annual gross sales made or business done in sales to consumers which is not more than $500,000 or has annual gross sales made or business done in sales of food to consumers which is not more than $50,000, the requirements of subparagraphs (1), (2), (3), and (4) shall not apply with respect to food sold by such person to consumers unless the label or labeling of food offered by such person provides nutrition information or makes a nutrition claim.

(E)(i) During the 12-month period for which an exemption from subparagraphs (1) and (2) is claimed pursuant to this subclause, the requirements of such subparagraphs shall not apply to any food product if—

(I) the labeling for such product does not provide nutrition information or make a claim subject to paragraph (r),

(II) the person who claims for such product an exemption from such subparagraphs employed fewer than an average of 100 full-time equivalent employees,

(III) such person provided the notice described in subclause (iii), and

(IV) in the case of a food product which was sold in the 12-month period preceding the period for which an exemption was claimed, fewer than 100,000 units of such product were sold in the United States during such preceding period, or in the case of a food product which was not sold in the 12-month period preceding the period for which such exemption is claimed, fewer than 100,000 units of such product are reasonably anticipated to be sold in the United States during the period for which such exemption is claimed.

(ii) During the 12-month period after the applicable date referred to in this sentence, the requirements of subparagraphs (1) and (2) shall not apply to any food product which was first introduced into interstate commerce before May 8, 1994, if the labeling for such product does not provide nutrition information or make a claim subject to paragraph (r), if such person provided the notice described in subclause (iii), and if—

(I) during the 12-month period preceding May 8, 1994, the person who claims for such product an exemption from such subparagraphs employed fewer than an average of 300 full-time equivalent employees and fewer than 600,000 units of such product were sold in the United States,

(II) during the 12-month period preceding May 8, 1995, the person who claims for such product an exemption from such subparagraphs employed fewer than an average of 300 full-time equivalent employees and fewer than 400,000 units of such product were sold in the United States, or

(III) during the 12-month period preceding May 8, 1996, the person who claims for such product an exemption from such subparagraphs employed fewer than an average of 200 full-time equivalent employees and fewer than 200,000 units of such product were sold in the United States.

(iii) The notice referred to in subclauses (i) and (ii) shall be given to the Secretary prior to the beginning of the period during which the exemption under subclause (i) or (ii) is to be in effect, shall state that the person claiming such exemption for a food product has complied with the applicable requirements of subclause (i) or (ii), and shall—

(I) state the average number of full-time equivalent employees such person employed during the 12 months preceding the date such person claims such exemption,

(II) state the approximate number of units the person claiming the exemption sold in the United States,

(III) if the exemption is claimed for a food product which was sold in the 12-month period preceding the period for which the exemption was claimed, state the approximate number of units of such product which were sold in the United States during such preceding period, and, if the exemption is claimed for a food product which was not sold in such preceding period, state the number of units of such product which such person reasonably anticipates will be sold in the United States during the period for which the exemption was claimed, and

(IV) contain such information as the Secretary may require to verify the information required by the preceding provisions of this subclause if the Secretary has questioned the validity of such information.

If a person is not an importer, has fewer than 10 full-time equivalent employees, and sells fewer than 10,000 units of any food product in any year, such person is not required to file a notice for such product under this subclause for such year.

(iv) In the case of a person who claimed an exemption under subclause (i) or (ii), if, during the period of such exemption, the number of full-time equivalent employees of such person exceeds the number in such subclause or if the number of food products sold in the United States exceeds the number in such subclause, such exemption shall extend to the expiration of 18 months after the date the number of full-time equivalent employees or food products sold exceeded the applicable number.

(v) For any food product first introduced into interstate commerce after May 8, 2002, the Secretary may by regulation lower the employee or units of food products requirement of subclause

(i) if the Secretary determines that the cost of compliance with such lower requirement will not place an undue burden on persons subject to such lower requirement.

(vi) For purposes of subclauses (i), (ii), (iii), (iv), and (v)—

(I) the term "unit" means the packaging or, if there is no packaging, the form in which a food product is offered for sale to consumers,

(II) the term "food product" means food in any sized package which is manufactured by a single manufacturer or which bears the same brand name, which bears the same statement of identity, and which has similar preparation methods, and

(III) the term "person" in the case of a corporation includes all domestic and foreign affiliates of the corporation.

(F) A dietary supplement product (including a food to which section 350 of this title applies) shall comply with the requirements of subparagraphs (1) and (2) in a manner which is appropriate for the product and which is specified in regulations of the Secretary which shall provide that—

(i) nutrition information shall first list those dietary ingredients that are present in the product in a significant amount and for which a recommendation for daily consumption has been established by the Secretary, except that a dietary ingredient shall not be required to be listed if it is not present in a significant amount, and shall list any other dietary ingredient present and identified as having no such recommendation;

(ii) the listing of dietary ingredients shall include the quantity of each such ingredient (or of a proprietary blend of such ingredients) per serving;

(iii) the listing of dietary ingredients may include the source of a dietary ingredient; and

(iv) the nutrition information shall immediately precede the ingredient information required under subclause (i), except that no ingredient identified pursuant to subclause (i) shall be required to be identified a second time.

(G) Subparagraphs (1), (2), (3), and (4) shall not apply to food which is sold by a food distributor if the food distributor principally sells food to restaurants or other establishments in which food is served for immediate human consumption and does not manufacture, process, or repackage the food it sells.

(r) Nutrition levels and health-related claims

(1) Except as provided in clauses (A) through (C) of subparagraph (5), if it is a food intended for human consumption which is offered for sale and for which a claim is made in the label or labeling of the food which expressly or by implication—

(A) characterizes the level of any nutrient which is of the type required by paragraph (q)(1) or (q)(2) to be in the label or labeling of the food unless the claim is made in accordance with subparagraph (2), or

(B) characterizes the relationship of any nutrient which is of the type required by paragraph (q)(1) or (q)(2) to be in the label or labeling of the food to a disease or a health-related condition unless the claim is made in accordance with subparagraph (3) or (5)(D).

A statement of the type required by paragraph (q) that appears as part of the nutrition information required or permitted by such paragraph is not a claim which is subject to this paragraph and a claim subject to clause (A) is not subject to clause (B).

(2)(A) Except as provided in subparagraphs (4)(A)(ii) and (4)(A)(iii) and clauses (A) through (C) of subparagraph (5), a claim described in subparagraph (1)(A)—

(i) may be made only if the characterization of the level made in the claim uses terms which are defined in regulations of the Secretary,

(ii) may not state the absence of a nutrient unless—

(I) the nutrient is usually present in the food or in a food which substitutes for the food as defined by the Secretary by regulation, or

(II) the Secretary by regulation permits such a statement on the basis of a finding that such a statement would assist consumers in maintaining healthy dietary practices and the statement discloses that the nutrient is not usually present in the food,

(iii) may not be made with respect to the level of cholesterol in the food if the food contains, as determined by the Secretary by regulation, fat or saturated fat in an amount which increases to persons in the general population the risk of disease or a health related condition which is diet related unless—

(I) the Secretary finds by regulation that the level of cholesterol is substantially less than the level usually present in the food or in a food which substitutes for the food and which has a significant market share, or the Secretary by regulation permits a statement regarding the absence of cholesterol on the basis of a finding that cholesterol is not usually present in the food and that such a statement would assist consumers in maintaining healthy dietary practices and the regulation requires that the statement disclose that cholesterol is not usually present in the food, and

(II) the label or labeling of the food discloses the level of such fat or saturated fat in immediate proximity to such claim and with appropriate prominence which shall be no less than one-half the size of the claim with respect to the level of cholesterol,

(iv) may not be made with respect to the level of saturated fat in the food if the food contains cholesterol unless the label or labeling of the food discloses the level of cholesterol in the food in immediate proximity to such claim and with appropriate prominence which shall be no less than one-half the size of the claim with respect to the level of saturated fat,

(v) may not state that a food is high in dietary fiber unless the food is low in total fat as defined by the Secretary or the label or labeling discloses the level of total fat in the food in immediate proximity to such statement and with appropriate prominence which shall be no less than one-half the size of the claim with respect to the level of dietary fiber, and

(vi) may not be made if the Secretary by regulation prohibits the claim because the claim is misleading in light of the level of another nutrient in the food.

(B) If a claim described in subparagraph (1)(A) is made with respect to a nutrient in a food and the Secretary makes a determination that the food contains a nutrient at a level that increases to persons in the general population the risk of a disease or health-related condition that is diet related, the label or labeling of such food shall contain, prominently and in immediate proximity to such claim, the following statement: "See nutrition information for _____ content." The blank shall identify the nutrient associated with the increased disease or health-related condition risk. In making the determination described in this clause, the Secretary shall take into account the significance of the food in the total daily diet.

(C) Subparagraph (2)(A) does not apply to a claim described in subparagraph (1)(A) and contained in the label or labeling of a food if such claim is contained in the brand name of such food and such brand name was in use on such food before October 25, 1989, unless the brand name contains a term defined by the Secretary under subparagraph (2)(A)(i). Such a claim is subject to paragraph (a).

(D) Subparagraph (2) does not apply to a claim described in subparagraph (1)(A) which uses the term "diet" and is contained in the label or labeling of a soft drink if (i) such claim is contained in the brand name of such soft drink, (ii) such brand name was in use on such soft drink before October 25, 1989, and (iii) the use of the term "diet" was in conformity with section 105.66 of title 21 of the Code of Federal Regulations. Such a claim is subject to paragraph (a).

(E) Subclauses (i) through (v) of subparagraph (2)(A) do not apply to a statement in the label or labeling of food which describes the percentage of vitamins and minerals in the food in relation to the amount of such vitamins and minerals recommended for daily consumption by the Secretary.

(F) Subclause (i) clause (A) does not apply to a statement in the labeling of a dietary supplement that characterizes the percentage level of a dietary ingredient for which the Secretary has not established a reference daily intake, daily recommended value, or other recommendation for daily consumption.

(G) A claim of the type described in subparagraph (1)(A) for a nutrient, for which the Secretary has not promulgated a regulation under clause (A)(i), shall be authorized and may be made with respect to a food if—

(i) a scientific body of the United States Government with official responsibility for public health protection or research directly relating to human nutrition (such as the National Institutes of Health or the Centers for Disease Control and Prevention) or the National Academy of Sciences or any of its subdivisions has published an authoritative statement, which is currently in effect, which identifies the nutrient level to which the claim refers;

(ii) a person has submitted to the Secretary, at least 120 days (during which the Secretary may notify any person who is making a claim as authorized by clause (C) that such person has not submitted all the information required by such clause) before the first introduction into interstate commerce of the food with a label containing the claim, (I) a notice of the claim, which shall include the exact words used in the claim and shall include a concise description of the basis upon which such person relied for determining that the requirements of subclause (i) have been satisfied, (II) a copy of the statement referred to in subclause (i) upon which such person relied in making the claim, and (III) a balanced representation of the scientific literature relating to the nutrient level to which the claim refers;

(iii) the claim and the food for which the claim is made are in compliance with clauses (A) and (B), and are otherwise in compliance with paragraph (a) and section 321(n) of this title; and

(iv) the claim is stated in a manner so that the claim is an accurate representation of the authoritative statement referred to in subclause (i) and so that the claim enables the public to comprehend the information provided in the claim and to understand the relative significance of such information in the context of a total daily diet.

For purposes of this clause, a statement shall be regarded as an authoritative statement of a scientific body described in subclause (i) only if the statement is published by the scientific body and shall not include a statement of an employee of the scientific body made in the individual capacity of the employee.

(H) A claim submitted under the requirements of clause (G) may be made until—

(i) such time as the Secretary issues a regulation—

(I) prohibiting or modifying the claim and the regulation has become effective, or

(II) finding that the requirements of clause (G) have not been met, including finding that the petitioner had not submitted all the information required by such clause; or

(ii) a district court of the United States in an enforcement proceeding under subchapter III of this chapter has determined that the requirements of clause (G) have not been met.

(3)(A) Except as provided in subparagraph (5), a claim described in subparagraph (1)(B) may only be made—

(i) if the claim meets the requirements of the regulations of the Secretary promulgated under clause (B), and

(ii) if the food for which the claim is made does not contain, as determined by the Secretary by regulation, any nutrient in an amount which increases to persons in the general population the risk of a disease or health-related condition which is diet related, taking into account the significance of the food in the total daily diet, except that the Secretary may by regulation permit such a claim based on a finding that such a claim would assist consumers in maintaining healthy dietary practices and based on a requirement that the label contain a disclosure of the type required by subparagraph (2)(B).

(B)(i) The Secretary shall promulgate regulations authorizing claims of the type described in subparagraph (1)(B) only if the Secretary determines, based on the totality of publicly available scientific evidence (including evidence from well-designed studies conducted in a manner which is consistent with generally recognized scientific procedures and principles), that there is significant scientific agreement, among experts qualified by scientific training and experience to evaluate such claims, that the claim is supported by such evidence.

(ii) A regulation described in subclause (i) shall describe—

(I) the relationship between a nutrient of the type required in the label or labeling of food by paragraph (q)(1) or (q)(2) and a disease or health-related condition, and

(II) the significance of each such nutrient in affecting such disease or health-related condition.

(iii) A regulation described in subclause (i) shall require such claim to be stated in a manner so that the claim is an accurate representation of the matters set out in subclause (ii) and so that the claim enables the public to comprehend the information provided in the claim and to understand the relative significance of such information in the context of a total daily diet.

(C) Notwithstanding the provisions of clauses (A)(i) and (B), a claim of the type described in subparagraph (1)(B) which is not authorized by the Secretary in a regulation promulgated in accordance with clause (B) shall be authorized and may be made with respect to a food if—

(i) a scientific body of the United States Government with official responsibility for public health protection or research directly relating to human nutrition (such as the National Institutes of Health or the Centers for Disease Control and Prevention) or the National Academy of Sciences or any of its subdivisions has published an authoritative statement, which is currently in effect, about the relationship between a nutrient and a disease or health-related condition to which the claim refers;

(ii) a person has submitted to the Secretary, at least 120 days (during which the Secretary may notify any person who is making a claim as authorized by clause (C) that such person has not submitted all the information required by such clause) before the first introduction into interstate commerce of the food with a label containing the claim, (I) a notice of the claim, which shall include the exact words used in the claim and shall include a concise description of the basis upon which such person relied for determining that the requirements of subclause (i) have been satisfied, (II) a copy of the statement referred to in subclause (i) upon which such person relied in making the claim, and (III) a balanced representation of the scientific literature relating to the relationship between a nutrient and a disease or health-related condition to which the claim refers;

(iii) the claim and the food for which the claim is made are in compliance with clause (A)(ii) and are otherwise in compliance with paragraph (a) and section 321(n) of this title; and

(iv) the claim is stated in a manner so that the claim is an accurate representation of the authoritative statement referred to in subclause (i) and so that the claim enables the public to comprehend the information provided in the claim and to understand the relative significance of such information in the context of a total daily diet.

For purposes of this clause, a statement shall be regarded as an authoritative statement of a scientific body described in subclause (i) only if the statement is published by the scientific body and shall not include a statement of an employee of the scientific body made in the individual capacity of the employee.

(D) A claim submitted under the requirements of clause (C) may be made until—

(i) such time as the Secretary issues a regulation under the standard in clause (B)(i)—

(I) prohibiting or modifying the claim and the regulation has become effective, or

(II) finding that the requirements of clause (C) have not been met, including finding that the petitioner has not submitted all the information required by such clause; or

(ii) a district court of the United States in an enforcement proceeding under subchapter III of this chapter has determined that the requirements of clause (C) have not been met.

(4)(A)(i) Any person may petition the Secretary to issue a regulation under subparagraph (2)(A)(i) or (3)(B) relating to a claim described in subparagraph (1)(A) or (1)(B). Not later than 100 days after the petition is received by the Secretary, the Secretary shall issue a final decision denying the petition or file the petition for further action by the Secretary. If the Secretary does not act within such 100 days, the petition shall be deemed to be denied unless an extension is mutually agreed upon by the Secretary and the petitioner. If the Secretary denies the petition or the petition is deemed to be denied, the petition shall not be made available to the public. If the Secretary files the petition, the Secretary shall deny the petition or issue a proposed regulation to take the action requested in the petition not later than 90 days after the date of such decision. If the Secretary does not act within such 90 days, the petition shall be deemed to be denied unless an extension is mutually agreed upon by the Secretary and the petitioner. If the Secretary issues a proposed regulation, the rulemaking shall be completed within 540 days of the date the petition is received by the Secretary. If the Secretary does not issue a regulation within such 540 days, the Secretary shall provide the Committee on Commerce of the House of Representatives and the Committee on Labor and Human Resources of the Senate the reasons action on the regulation did not occur within such 540 days.

(ii) Any person may petition the Secretary for permission to use in a claim described in subparagraph (1)(A) terms that are consistent with the terms defined by the Secretary under subparagraph (2)(A)(i). Within 90 days of the submission of such a petition, the Secretary shall issue a final decision denying the petition or granting such permission.

(iii) Any person may petition the Secretary for permission to use an implied claim described in subparagraph (1)(A) in a brand name. After publishing notice of an opportunity to comment on the petition in the Federal Register and making the petition available to the public, the Secretary shall grant the petition if the Secretary finds that such claim is not misleading and is consistent with terms defined by the Secretary under subparagraph (2)(A)(i). The Secretary shall grant or deny the petition within 100 days of the date it is submitted to the Secretary and the petition shall be considered granted if the Secretary does not act on it within such 100 days.

(B) A petition under clause (A)(i) respecting a claim described in subparagraph (1)(A) or (1)(B) shall include an explanation of the reasons why the claim meets the requirements of this paragraph and a summary of the scientific data which supports such reasons.

(C) If a petition for a regulation under subparagraph (3)(B) relies on a report from an authoritative scientific body of the United States, the Secretary shall consider such report and shall justify any decision rejecting the conclusions of such report.

(5)(A) This paragraph does not apply to infant formulas subject to section 350a(h) of this title and medical foods as defined in section 360ee(b) of this title.

(B) Subclauses (iii) through (v) of subparagraph (2)(A) and subparagraph (2)(B) do not apply to food which is served in restaurants or other establishments in which food is served for immediate human consumption or which is sold for sale or use in such establishments.

(C) A subparagraph (1)(A) claim made with respect to a food which claim is required by a standard of identity issued under section 341 of this title shall not be subject to subparagraph (2)(A)(i) or (2)(B).

(D) A subparagraph (1)(B) claim made with respect to a dietary supplement of vitamins, minerals, herbs, or other similar nutritional substances shall not be subject to subparagraph (3) but shall be subject to a procedure and standard, respecting the validity of such claim, established by regulation of the Secretary.

(6) For purposes of paragraph (r)(1)(B), a statement for a dietary supplement may be made if—

(A) the statement claims a benefit related to a classical nutrient deficiency disease and discloses the prevalence of such disease in the United States, describes the role of a nutrient or dietary ingredient intended to affect the structure or function in humans, characterizes the documented mechanism by which a nutrient or dietary ingredient acts to maintain such structure or function, or describes general well-being from consumption of a nutrient or dietary ingredient,

(B) the manufacturer of the dietary supplement has substantiation that such statement is truthful and not misleading, and

(C) the statement contains, prominently displayed and in boldface type, the following: "This statement has not been evaluated by the Food and Drug Administration. This product is not intended to diagnose, treat, cure, or prevent any disease.".

A statement under this subparagraph may not claim to diagnose, mitigate, treat, cure, or prevent a specific disease or class of diseases. If the manufacturer of a dietary supplement proposes to make a statement described in the first sentence of this subparagraph in the labeling of the dietary supplement, the manufacturer shall notify the Secretary no later than 30 days after the first marketing of the dietary supplement with such statement that such a statement is being made.

(7) The Secretary may make proposed regulations issued under this paragraph effective upon publication pending consideration of public comment and publication of a final regulation if the Secretary determines that such action is necessary—

(A) to enable the Secretary to review and act promptly on petitions the Secretary determines provide for information necessary to—

(i) enable consumers to develop and maintain healthy dietary practices;

(ii) enable consumers to be informed promptly and effectively of important new knowledge regarding nutritional and health benefits of food; or

(iii) ensure that scientifically sound nutritional and health information is provided to consumers as soon as possible; or

(B) to enable the Secretary to act promptly to ban or modify a claim under this paragraph.

Such proposed regulations shall be deemed final agency action for purposes of judicial review.

(s) Dietary supplements

If—

(1) it is a dietary supplement; and

(2)(A) the label or labeling of the supplement fails to list—

(i) the name of each ingredient of the supplement that is described in section 321(ff) of this title; and

(ii)(I) the quantity of each such ingredient; or

(II) with respect to a proprietary blend of such ingredients, the total quantity of all ingredients in the blend;

(B) the label or labeling of the dietary supplement fails to identify the product by using the term "dietary supplement", which term may be modified with the name of such an ingredient;

(C) the supplement contains an ingredient described in section 321(ff)(1)(C) of this title, and the label or labeling of the supplement fails to identify any part of the plant from which the ingredient is derived;

(D) the supplement—

(i) is covered by the specifications of an official compendium;

(ii) is represented as conforming to the specifications of an official compendium; and

(iii) fails to so conform; or

(E) the supplement—

(i) is not covered by the specifications of an official compendium; and

(ii)(I) fails to have the identity and strength that the supplement is represented to have; or

(II) fails to meet the quality (including tablet or capsule disintegration), purity, or compositional specifications, based on validated assay or other appropriate methods, that the supplement is represented to meet.

A dietary supplement shall not be deemed misbranded solely because its label or labeling contains directions or conditions of use or warnings.

(t) Catfish

If it purports to be or is represented as catfish, unless it is fish classified within the family Ictaluridae.

(u) Ginseng

If it purports to be or is represented as ginseng, unless it is an herb or herbal ingredient derived from a plant classified within the genus Panax.

(v) Failure to label; health threat

If—

(1) it fails to bear a label required by the Secretary under section 381(n)(1) of this title (relating to food refused admission into the United States);

(2) the Secretary finds that the food presents a threat of serious adverse health consequences or death to humans or animals; and

(3) upon or after notifying the owner or consignee involved that the label is required under section 381 of this title, the Secretary informs the owner or consignee that the food presents such a threat.

(w) Major food allergen labeling requirements

(1) If it is not a raw agricultural commodity and it is, or it contains an ingredient that bears or contains, a major food allergen, unless either—

(A) the word "Contains", followed by the name of the food source from which the major food allergen is derived, is printed immediately after or is adjacent to the list of ingredients (in a type size no smaller than the type size used in the list of ingredients) required under subsections (g) and (i) of this section; or

(B) the common or usual name of the major food allergen in the list of ingredients required under subsections (g) and (i) of this section is followed in parentheses by the name of the food source from which the major food allergen is derived, except that the name of the food source is not required when—

(i) the common or usual name of the ingredient uses the name of the food source from which the major food allergen is derived; or

(ii) the name of the food source from which the major food allergen is derived appears elsewhere in the ingredient list, unless the name of the food source that appears elsewhere in the ingredient list appears as part of the name of a food ingredient that is not a major food allergen under section 321(qq)(2)(A) or (B) of this title.

(2) As used in this subsection, the term "name of the food source from which the major food allergen is derived" means the name described in section 321(qq)(1) of this title; provided that in the case of a tree nut, fish, or Crustacean shellfish, the term "name of the food source from which the major food allergen is derived" means the name of the specific type of nut or species of fish or Crustacean shellfish.

(3) The information required under this subsection may appear in labeling in lieu of appearing on the label only if the Secretary finds that such other labeling is sufficient to protect the public health. A finding by the Secretary under this paragraph (including any change in an earlier finding under this paragraph) is effective upon publication in the Federal Register as a notice.

(4) Notwithstanding subsection (g), (i), or (k) of this section, or any other law, a flavoring, coloring, or incidental additive that is, or that bears or contains, a major food allergen shall be subject to the labeling requirements of this subsection.

(5) The Secretary may by regulation modify the requirements of subparagraph (A) or (B) of paragraph (1), or eliminate either the requirement of subparagraph (A) or the requirements of subparagraph (B) of paragraph (1), if the Secretary determines that the modification or elimination of the requirement of subparagraph (A) or the requirements of subparagraph (B) is necessary to protect the public health.

(6)(A) Any person may petition the Secretary to exempt a food ingredient described in section 321(qq)(2) of this title from the allergen labeling requirements of this subsection.

(B) The Secretary shall approve or deny such petition within 180 days of receipt of the petition or the petition shall be deemed denied, unless an extension of time is mutually agreed upon by the Secretary and the petitioner.

(C) The burden shall be on the petitioner to provide scientific evidence (including the analytical method used to produce the evidence) that demonstrates that such food ingredient, as derived by the method specified in the petition, does not cause an allergic response that poses a risk to human health.

(D) A determination regarding a petition under this paragraph shall constitute final agency action.

(E) The Secretary shall promptly post to a public site all petitions received under this paragraph within 14 days of receipt and the Secretary shall promptly post the Secretary's response to each.

(7)(A) A person need not file a petition under paragraph (6) to exempt a food ingredient described in section 321(qq)(2) of this title from the allergen labeling requirements of this subsection, if the person files with the Secretary a notification containing—

(i) scientific evidence (including the analytical method used) that demonstrates that the food ingredient (as derived by the method specified in the notification, where applicable) does not contain allergenic protein; or

(ii) a determination by the Secretary that the ingredient does not cause an allergic response that poses a risk to human health under a premarket approval or notification program under section 348 of this title.

(B) The food ingredient may be introduced or delivered for introduction into interstate commerce as a food ingredient that is not a major food allergen 90 days after the date of receipt of the notification by the Secretary, unless the Secretary determines within the 90-day period that the notification does not meet the requirements of this paragraph, or there is insufficient scientific evidence to determine that the food ingredient does not contain allergenic protein or does not cause an allergenic response that poses a risk to human health.

(C) The Secretary shall promptly post to a public site all notifications received under this subparagraph within 14 days of receipt and promptly post any objections thereto by the Secretary.

(x) Nonmajor food allergen labeling requirements

Notwithstanding subsection (g), (i), or (k) of this section, or any other law, a spice, flavoring, coloring, or incidental additive that is, or that bears or contains, a food allergen (other than a major food allergen), as determined by the Secretary by regulation, shall be disclosed in a manner specified by the Secretary by regulation.

(y) Dietary supplements

If it is a dietary supplement that is marketed in the United States, unless the label of such dietary supplement includes a domestic address or domestic phone number through which the responsible person (as described in section 379aa–1 of this title) may receive a report of a serious adverse event with such dietary supplement.

(June 25, 1938, ch. 675, § 403, 52 Stat. 1047; Pub. L. 86–537, § 1, June 29, 1960, 74 Stat. 251; Pub. L. 86–618, title I, § 102(a)(3), July 12, 1960, 74 Stat. 398; Pub. L. 91–601, § 6(c), formerly § 7(c), Dec. 30, 1970, 84 Stat. 1673, renumbered Pub. L. 97–35, title XII, § 1205(c), Aug. 13, 1981, 95 Stat. 716; Pub. L. 94–278, title V, § 502(a)(1), Apr. 22, 1976, 90 Stat. 411; Pub. L. 95–203, § 4(a)(1), (b)(1), Nov. 23, 1977, 91 Stat. 1452, 1453; Pub. L. 101–535, §§ 2(a), 3(a), 7, Nov. 8, 1990, 104 Stat. 2353, 2357, 2364; Pub. L. 102–108, § 2(a), (c), Aug. 17, 1991, 105 Stat. 549; Pub. L. 102–571, title I, § 107(5), (6), Oct. 29, 1992, 106 Stat. 4499; Pub. L. 103–80, §§ 2(b), 3(j), Aug. 13, 1993, 107 Stat. 773, 776; Pub. L. 103–417, §§ 6, 7(a)–(c), 10(c), Oct. 25, 1994, 108 Stat. 4329, 4330, 4332; Pub. L. 104–124, § 1, Apr. 1, 1996, 110 Stat. 882; Pub. L. 105–115, title III, §§ 301–305, Nov. 21, 1997, 111 Stat. 2350–2353; Pub. L. 106–554, § 1(a)(1) [title V, § 517], Dec. 21, 2000, 114 Stat. 2763, 2763A–73; Pub. L. 107–171, title X, §§ 10806(a)(2), (b)(2), 10808(b), May 13, 2002, 116 Stat. 526, 527, 530; Pub. L. 107–188, title III, § 308(b), June 12, 2002, 116 Stat. 672; Pub. L. 108–282, title II, § 203(a), Aug. 2, 2004, 118 Stat. 906; Pub. L. 109–462, § 3(c), Dec. 22, 2006, 120 Stat. 3475.)

AMENDMENTS

2006—Par. (y). Pub. L. 109–462 added par. (y).

2004—Pars. (w), (x). Pub. L. 108–282 added pars. (w) and (x).

2002—Par. (h). Pub. L. 107–171, § 10808(b), added subpar. (3) and concluding provisions.

Par. (t). Pub. L. 107–171, § 10806(a)(2), added par. (t).

Par. (u). Pub. L. 107–171, § 10806(b)(2), added par. (u).

Par. (v). Pub. L. 107–188 added par. (v).

2000—Par. (*o*). Pub. L. 106–554, which directed repeal of section 403(*o*) of the Food, Drug, and Cosmetic Act, was executed by repealing par. (*o*) of this section, which is section 403 of the Federal Food, Drug, and Cosmetic Act, to reflect the probable intent of Congress. Prior to repeal, par. (*o*) provided that a food containing saccharin was to be deemed misbranded unless a specified warning statement was placed in a conspicuous place on its label.

1997—Par. (r)(2)(B). Pub. L. 105–115, § 305, amended cl. (B) generally. Prior to amendment, cl. (B) read as follows: "If a claim described in subparagraph (1)(A) is made with respect to a nutrient in a food, the label or labeling of such food shall contain, prominently and in immediate proximity to such claim, the following statement: 'See ________ for nutrition information.'. In the statement—

"(i) the blank shall identify the panel on which the information described in the statement may be found, and

"(ii) if the Secretary determines that the food contains a nutrient at a level which increases to persons in the general population the risk of a disease or health-related condition which is diet related, taking into account the significance of the food in the total daily diet, the statement shall also identify such nutrient."

Par. (r)(2)(G), (H). Pub. L. 105–115, § 304, added cls. (G) and (H).

Par. (r)(3)(C), (D). Pub. L. 105–115, § 303, added cls. (C) and (D).

Par. (r)(4)(A)(i). Pub. L. 105–115, § 302, inserted after second sentence "If the Secretary does not act within such 100 days, the petition shall be deemed to be denied unless an extension is mutually agreed upon by the Secretary and the petitioner.", inserted "or the petition is deemed to be denied" after "If the Secretary denies the petition", and inserted at end "If the Secretary does not act within such 90 days, the petition shall be deemed to be denied unless an extension is mutually agreed upon by the Secretary and the petitioner. If the Secretary issues a proposed regulation, the rulemaking shall be completed within 540 days of the date the petition is received by the Secretary. If the Secretary does not issue a regulation within such 540 days, the Secretary shall provide the Committee on Commerce of the House of Representatives and the Committee on Labor and Human Resources of the Senate the reasons action on the regulation did not occur within such 540 days."

Par. (r)(7). Pub. L. 105–115, § 301, added subpar. (7).

1996—Par. (p). Pub. L. 104–124 struck out par. (p), which deemed products containing saccharin and offered for sale, but not for immediate consumption, by retail establishment, to be misbranded, unless notice of information required by subsec. (*o*) was provided by manufacturer and prominently displayed near product.

1994—Par. (q)(5)(F). Pub. L. 103–417, § 7(b), amended cl. (F) generally. Prior to amendment, cl. (F) read as follows: "If a food to which section 350 of this title applies (as defined in section 350(c) of this title) contains one or more of the nutrients required by subparagraph (1) or (2) to be in the label or labeling of the food, the label or labeling of such food shall comply with the requirements of subparagraphs (1) and (2) in a manner which is appropriate for such food and which is specified in regulations of the Secretary."

Par. (r)(2)(F). Pub. L. 103–417, § 7(c), added cl. (F).

Par. (r)(6). Pub. L. 103–417, § 6, added subpar. (6).

Par. (s). Pub. L. 103–417, § 10(c), inserted at end: "A dietary supplement shall not be deemed misbranded solely because its label or labeling contains directions or conditions of use or warnings."

Pub. L. 103–417, § 7(a), added par. (s).

1993—Par. (e). Pub. L. 103–80, § 3(j)(1), substituted "count, except that" for "count: *Provided*, That".

Par. (i). Pub. L. 103–80, § 3(j)(2), substituted "unless sold as spices, flavorings, or such colors" for ", other than those sold as such'' and ''naming each. To the extent'' for ''naming each: *Provided*, That, to the extent''.

Par. (k). Pub. L. 103–80, §3(j)(3), substituted '', except that'' for '': *Provided*, That''.

Par. (*l*). Pub. L. 103–80, §3(j)(4), substituted ''chemical, except that'' for ''chemical: *Provided, however*, That''.

Par. (q)(5)(E) to (G). Pub. L. 103–80, §2(b), added cl. (E) and redesignated former cls. (E) and (F) as (F) and (G), respectively.

Par. (r)(1)(B). Pub. L. 103–80, §3(j)(5), substituted ''(5)(D)'' for ''5(D)''.

Par. (r)(4)(B). Pub. L. 103–80, §3(j)(6), substituted ''paragraph'' for ''subsection''.

1992—Par. (i). Pub. L. 102–571, §107(5), substituted ''379e(c)'' for ''376(c)''.

Par. (m). Pub. L. 102–571, §107(6), substituted ''379e'' for ''376''.

1991—Par. (i). Pub. L. 102–108, §2(c), amended directory language of Pub. L. 101–535, §7(1), (3). See 1990 Amendment note below.

Par. (q)(4)(A). Pub. L. 102–108, §2(a), substituted ''(D)'' for ''(C)''.

1990—Par. (i). Pub. L. 101–535, §7, as amended by Pub. L. 102–108, §2(c), substituted ''Unless'' for ''If it is not subject to the provisions of paragraph (g) unless'', inserted ''and if the food purports to be a beverage containing vegetable or fruit juice, a statement with appropriate prominence on the information panel of the total percentage of such fruit or vegetable juice contained in the food'', and substituted ''colors not required to be certified under section 376(c) of this title'' for ''colorings'' the first time appearing.

Par. (q). Pub. L. 101–535, §2(a), added par. (q).

Par. (r). Pub. L. 101–535, §3(a), added par. (r).

1977—Par. (*o*). Pub. L. 95–203, §4(a)(1), added par. (*o*).

Par. (p). Pub. L. 95–203, §4(b)(1), added par. (p).

1976—Par. (a). Pub. L. 94–278 inserted ''(1)'' after ''If'' and inserted '', or (2) in the case of a food to which section 350 of this title applies, its advertising is false or misleading in a material respect or its labeling is in violation of section 350(b)(2) of this title'' after ''any particular''.

1970—Par. (n). Pub. L. 91–601 added par. (n).

1960—Par. (k). Pub. L. 86–537, §1(1), exempted pesticide chemicals when used in or on a raw agricultural commodity which is the produce of the soil.

Par. (*l*). Pub. L. 86–537, §1(2), added par. (*l*).

Par. (m). Pub. L. 86–618 added par. (m).

CHANGE OF NAME

Committee on Commerce of House of Representatives changed to Committee on Energy and Commerce of House of Representatives, and jurisdiction over matters relating to securities and exchanges and insurance generally transferred to Committee on Financial Services of House of Representatives by House Resolution No. 5, One Hundred Seventh Congress, Jan. 3, 2001.

Committee on Labor and Human Resources of Senate changed to Committee on Health, Education, Labor, and Pensions of Senate by Senate Resolution No. 20, One Hundred Sixth Congress, Jan. 19, 1999.

EFFECTIVE DATE OF 2006 AMENDMENT

Pub. L. 109–462, §3(d)(1), (2), Dec. 22, 2006, 120 Stat. 3475, provided that:

''(1) IN GENERAL.—Except as provided in paragraph (2), the amendments made by this section [enacting section 379aa–1 of this title and amending this section and section 331 of this title] shall take effect 1 year after the date of enactment of this Act [Dec. 22, 2006].

''(2) MISBRANDING.—Section 403(y) of the Federal Food, Drug, and Cosmetic Act [21 U.S.C. 343(y)] (as added by this section) shall apply to any dietary supplement labeled on or after the date that is 1 year after the date of enactment of this Act [Dec. 22, 2006].''

EFFECTIVE DATE OF 2004 AMENDMENT

Amendment by Pub. L. 108–282 applicable to any food that is labeled on or after Jan. 1, 2006, see section 203(d) of Pub. L. 108–282, set out as a note under section 321 of this title.

EFFECTIVE DATE OF 1997 AMENDMENT

Amendment by Pub. L. 105–115 effective 90 days after Nov. 21, 1997, except as otherwise provided, see section 501 of Pub. L. 105–115, set out as a note under section 321 of this title.

EFFECTIVE DATE OF 1994 AMENDMENT

Section 7(e) of Pub. L. 103–417 provided that: ''Dietary supplements—

''(1) may be labeled after the date of the enactment of this Act [Oct. 25, 1994] in accordance with the amendments made by this section [amending this section and section 350 of this title], and

''(2) shall be labeled after December 31, 1996, in accordance with such amendments.''

EFFECTIVE DATE OF 1990 AMENDMENT

Section 10(a) of Pub. L. 101–535, as amended by Pub. L. 102–571, title II, §202(a)(3), Oct. 29, 1992, 106 Stat. 4501, provided that:

''(1) Except as provided in paragraph (2)—

''(A) the amendments made by section 2 [amending this section] shall take effect 6 months after—

''(i) the date of the promulgation of all final regulations required to implement section 403(q) of the Federal Food, Drug, and Cosmetic Act [21 U.S.C. 343(q)], or

''(ii) if such regulations are not promulgated, the date proposed regulations are to be considered as such final regulations [Nov. 8, 1992, see 57 F.R. 56347],

except that section 403(q)(4) of such Act shall take effect as prescribed by such section,

''(B) the amendments made by section 3 [amending this section] shall take effect 6 months after—

''(i) the date of the promulgation of final regulations to implement section 403(r) of the Federal Food, Drug, and Cosmetic Act, or

''(ii) if such regulations are not promulgated, the date proposed regulations are to be considered as such final regulations [Nov. 8, 1992, see 57 F.R. 56347], except that any person marketing a food the brand name of which contains a term defined by the Secretary under section 403(r)(2)(A)(i) of the Federal Food, Drug, and Cosmetic Act shall be given an additional 6 months to comply with section 3,

''(C) the amendments made by section 4 [amending section 337 of this title] shall take effect 24 months after the date of the enactment of this Act [Nov. 8, 1990], except that such amendments shall take effect with respect to such dietary supplements [probably means dietary supplements of vitamins, minerals, herbs, or other similar nutritional substances, see section 202(a)(1) of Pub. L. 102–571, set out below] on December 31, 1993, and

''(D) the amendments made by section 5 [amending sections 321 and 345 of this title] shall take effect on the date the amendments made by section 3 take effect.

''(2) Section 403(q) of the Federal Food, Drug, and Cosmetic Act (as added by section 2) shall not apply with respect to food which was labeled before the effective date of the amendments made by section 2 and section 403(r) of the Federal Food, Drug, and Cosmetic Act (as added by section 3) shall not apply with respect to food which was labeled before the effective date of the amendments made by section 3.

''(3)(A) If the Secretary finds that a person who is subject to section 403(q)(4) of such Act is unable to comply with the requirements of such section upon the effective date of final regulations to implement section 403(q) of such Act or of proposed regulations to be considered as such final regulations because the Secretary has not made available to such person the information required by such section, the Secretary shall delay the application of such section to such person for such time as the Secretary may require to provide such information.

"(B) If the Secretary finds that compliance with section 403(q) or 403(r)(2) of such Act would cause an undue economic hardship, the Secretary may delay the application of such sections for no more than one year."

Section 10(c) of Pub. L. 101–535, as amended by Pub. L. 102–108, § 1, Aug. 17, 1991, 105 Stat. 549; Pub. L. 102–571, title I, § 107(17), Oct. 29, 1992, 106 Stat. 4500, provided that:

"(1) Except as provided in paragraphs (2) and (3), the amendments made by section 7 [amending this section] shall take effect one year after the date of the enactment of this Act [Nov. 8, 1990].

"(2)(A) If a food subject to section 403(g) of the Federal Food, Drug, and Cosmetic Act [21 U.S.C. 343(g)] or a food with one or more colors required to be certified under section 721(c) [of the Federal Food, Drug, and Cosmetic Act, 21 U.S.C. 379e(c)] bears a label which was printed before July 1, 1991, and which is attached to the food before May 8, 1993, such food shall not be subject to the amendments made by section 7(1) and section 7(3) [amending this section].

"(B) If a food described in subparagraph (A)—

"(i) bears a label which was printed after July 1, 1991, but before the date the proposed regulation described in clause (ii) takes effect as a final regulation and which was attached to the food before May 8, 1993, and

"(ii) meets the requirements of the proposed regulation of the Secretary of Health and Human Services published in 56 Fed. Reg. 28592–28636 (June 21, 1991) as it pertains to the amendments made by this Act [see Short Title of 1990 Amendment note set out under section 301 of this title],

such food shall not be subject to the amendments made by section 7(1) and section 7(3) [amending this section].

"(3) A food purported to be a beverage containing a vegetable or fruit juice which bears a label attached to the food before May 8, 1993, shall not be subject to the amendments made by section 7(2) [amending this section]."

EFFECTIVE DATE OF 1977 AMENDMENT

Section 4(a)(2) of Pub. L. 95–203 provided that: "The amendment made by paragraph (1) [amending this section] shall apply only with respect to food introduced or delivered for introduction in interstate commerce on and after the 90th day after the date of the enactment of this Act [Nov. 23, 1977]."

Section 4(b)(2) of Pub. L. 95–203 provided that: "The amendment made by paragraph (1) [amending this section] shall apply with respect to food which is sold in retail establishments on or after the 90th day after the effective date of the regulations of the Secretary of Health, Education, and Welfare [now Secretary of Health and Human Services] under paragraph (p)(4) of the Federal Food, Drug, and Cosmetic Act [21 U.S.C. 343(p)(4)]."

EFFECTIVE DATE OF 1976 AMENDMENT

Amendment by Pub. L. 94–278 effective 180 days after Apr. 22, 1976, see section 502(c) of Pub. L. 94–278, set out as a note under section 334 of this title.

EFFECTIVE DATE OF 1970 AMENDMENT

Amendment by Pub. L. 91–601 effective Dec. 30, 1970, and regulations establishing special packaging standards effective no sooner than 180 days or later than one year from date regulations are final, or an earlier date published in Federal Register, see section 8 of Pub. L. 91–601, set out as an Effective Date note under section 1471 of Title 15, Commerce and Trade.

EFFECTIVE DATE OF 1960 AMENDMENT

Amendment by Pub. L. 86–618 effective July 12, 1960, subject to the provisions of section 203 of Pub. L. 86–618, see section 202 of Pub. L. 86–618, set out as a note under section 379e of this title.

EFFECTIVE DATE; POSTPONEMENT

Subsecs. (e)(1) and (g) to (k) effective Jan. 1, 1940, and such subsections effective July 1, 1940, as provided by regulations for certain lithographed labeling and containers bearing certain labeling, see act June 23, 1939, ch. 242, 53 Stat. 853, set out as an Effective Date; Postponement in Certain Cases note under section 301 of this title.

CONSTRUCTION OF AMENDMENT BY PUB. L. 108–282

Pub. L. 108–282, title II, § 203(b), Aug. 2, 2004, 118 Stat. 908, provided that: "The amendments made by this section [amending this section and sections 321 and 343–1 of this title] that require a label or labeling for major food allergens do not alter the authority of the Secretary of Health and Human Services under the Federal Food, Drug, and Cosmetic Act (21 U.S.C. 301 et seq.) to require a label or labeling for other food allergens."

CONSTRUCTION OF AMENDMENT BY PUB. L. 107–188

Nothing in amendment by Pub. L. 107–188 to be construed to limit authority of Secretary of Health and Human Services or Secretary of the Treasury to require marking of articles of food imported or offered for import into the United States which are refused admission, see section 308(c) of Pub. L. 107–188, set out as a note under section 381 of this title.

CONSTRUCTION OF AMENDMENTS BY PUB. L. 101–535

Section 9 of Pub. L. 101–535 provided that: "The amendments made by this Act [enacting section 343–1 of this title and amending this section and sections 321, 337, 345, and 371 of this title] shall not be construed to alter the authority of the Secretary of Health and Human Services and the Secretary of Agriculture under the Federal Food, Drug, and Cosmetic Act [21 U.S.C. 301 et seq.], the Federal Meat Inspection Act [21 U.S.C. 601 et seq.], the Poultry Products Inspection Act [21 U.S.C. 451 et seq.], and the Egg Products Inspection Act [21 U.S.C. 1031 et seq.]."

FINDINGS

Pub. L. 108–282, title II, § 202, Aug. 2, 2004, 118 Stat. 905, provided that: "Congress finds that—

"(1) it is estimated that—

"(A) approximately 2 percent of adults and about 5 percent of infants and young children in the United States suffer from food allergies; and

"(B) each year, roughly 30,000 individuals require emergency room treatment and 150 individuals die because of allergic reactions to food;

"(2)(A) eight major foods or food groups—milk, eggs, fish, Crustacean shellfish, tree nuts, peanuts, wheat, and soybeans—account for 90 percent of food allergies;

"(B) at present, there is no cure for food allergies; and

"(C) a food allergic consumer must avoid the food to which the consumer is allergic;

"(3)(A) in a review of the foods of randomly selected manufacturers of baked goods, ice cream, and candy in Minnesota and Wisconsin in 1999, the Food and Drug Administration found that 25 percent of sampled foods failed to list peanuts or eggs as ingredients on the food labels; and

"(B) nationally, the number of recalls because of unlabeled allergens rose to 121 in 2000 from about 35 a decade earlier;

"(4) a recent study shows that many parents of children with a food allergy were unable to correctly identify in each of several food labels the ingredients derived from major food allergens;

"(5)(A) ingredients in foods must be listed by their 'common or usual name';

"(B) in some cases, the common or usual name of an ingredient may be unfamiliar to consumers, and many consumers may not realize the ingredient is derived from, or contains, a major food allergen; and

"(C) in other cases, the ingredients may be declared as a class, including spices, flavorings, and certain colorings, or are exempt from the ingredient labeling requirements, such as incidental additives; and

"(6)(A) celiac disease is an immune-mediated disease that causes damage to the gastrointestinal tract, central nervous system, and other organs;

"(B) the current recommended treatment is avoidance of glutens in foods that are associated with celiac disease; and

"(C) a multicenter, multiyear study estimated that the prevalence of celiac disease in the United States is 0.5 to 1 percent of the general population."

REGULATIONS

Section 2(b) of Pub. L. 101–535, as amended by Pub. L. 102–571, title II, § 202(a)(2)(A), (B), Oct. 29, 1992, 106 Stat. 4500, 4501, provided that:

"(1) The Secretary of Health and Human Services shall issue proposed regulations to implement section 403(q) of the Federal Food, Drug, and Cosmetic Act [21 U.S.C. 343(q)] within 12 months after the date of the enactment of this Act [Nov. 8, 1990], except that the Secretary shall issue, not later than June 15, 1993, proposed regulations that are applicable to dietary supplements of vitamins, minerals, herbs, or other similar nutritional substances to implement such section. Not later than 24 months after the date of the enactment of this Act, the Secretary shall issue final regulations to implement the requirements of such section, except that the Secretary shall issue, not later than December 31, 1993, such a final regulation applicable to dietary supplements of vitamins, minerals, herbs, or other similar nutritional substances..[sic] Such regulations shall—

"(A) require the required information to be conveyed to the public in a manner which enables the public to readily observe and comprehend such information and to understand its relative significance in the context of a total daily diet,

"(B) include regulations which establish standards, in accordance with paragraph (1)(A), to define serving size or other unit of measure for food,

"(C) permit the label or labeling of food to include nutrition information which is in addition to the information required by such section 403(q) and which is of the type described in subparagraph (1) or (2) of such section, and

"(D) permit the nutrition information on the label or labeling of a food to remain the same or permit the information to be stated as a range even though (i) there are minor variations in the nutritional value of the food which occur in the normal course of the production or processing of the food, or (ii) the food is comprised of an assortment of similar foods which have variations in nutritional value.

"(2) If the Secretary of Health and Human Services does not promulgate final regulations under paragraph (1) upon the expiration of 24 months after the date of the enactment of this Act, the proposed regulations issued in accordance with paragraph (1) shall be considered as the final regulations upon the expiration of such 24 months, except that the proposed regulations applicable to dietary supplements of vitamins, minerals, herbs, or other similar nutritional substances shall not be considered to be final regulations until December 31, 1993. There shall be promptly published in the Federal Register notice of new status of the proposed regulations [see 57 F.R. 56347].

"(3) If the Secretary of Health and Human Services does not promulgate final regulations under section 403(q)(4) of the Federal Food, Drug, and Cosmetic Act upon the expiration of 6 months after the date on which the Secretary makes a finding that there has been no substantial compliance with section 403(q)(4)(C) of such Act, the proposed regulations issued in accordance with such section shall be considered as the final regulations upon the expiration of such 6 months. There shall be promptly published in the Federal Register notice of new status of the proposed regulations."

[Section 202(a)(2)(C) of Pub. L. 102–571 provided that: "The amendments made by subparagraph (B) [amending sections 2(b) and 3(b) of Pub. L. 101–535, set out above and below] shall not be construed to modify the effective date of final regulations under sections 2(b) and 3(b) of the Nutrition Labeling and Education Act of 1990 [Pub. L. 101–535] (21 U.S.C. 343 note) with respect to foods that are not such dietary supplements."]

Section 3(b) of Pub. L. 101–535, as amended by Pub. L. 102–571, title II, § 202(a)(2)(A), (B), Oct. 29, 1992, 106 Stat. 4500, 4501, provided that:

"(1)(A) Within 12 months of the date of the enactment of this Act [Nov. 8, 1990], the Secretary of Health and Human Services shall issue proposed regulations to implement section 403(r) of the Federal Food, Drug, and Cosmetic Act [21 U.S.C. 343(r)], except that the Secretary shall issue, not later than June 15, 1993, proposed regulations that are applicable to dietary supplements of vitamins, minerals, herbs, or other similar nutritional substances to implement such section. Such regulations—

"(i) shall identify claims described in section 403(r)(1)(A) of such Act which comply with section 403(r)(2) of such Act,

"(ii) shall identify claims described in section 403(r)(1)(B) of such Act which comply with section 403(r)(3) of such Act,

"(iii) shall, in defining terms used to characterize the level of any nutrient in food under section 403(r)(2)(A)(i) of such Act, define—

"(I) free,

"(II) low,

"(III) light or lite,

"(IV) reduced,

"(V) less, and

"(VI) high,

unless the Secretary finds that the use of any such term would be misleading,

"(iv) shall permit statements describing the amount and percentage of nutrients in food which are not misleading and are consistent with the terms defined in section 403(r)(2)(A)(i) of such Act,

"(v) shall provide that if multiple claims subject to section 403(r)(1)(A) of such Act are made on a single panel of the food label or page of a labeling brochure, a single statement may be made to satisfy section 403(r)(2)(B) of such Act,

"(vi) shall determine whether claims respecting the following nutrients and diseases meet the requirements of section 403(r)(3) of such Act: Calcium and osteoporosis, dietary fiber and cancer, lipids and cardiovascular disease, lipids and cancer, sodium and hypertension, and dietary fiber and cardiovascular disease,

"(vii) shall not require a person who proposes to make a claim described in section 403(r)(1)(B) of such Act which is in compliance with such regulations to secure the approval of the Secretary before making such claim,

"(viii) may permit a claim described in section 403(r)(1)(A) of such Act to be made for butter,

"(ix) may, in defining terms under section 403(r)(2)(A)(i), include similar terms which are commonly understood to have the same meaning, and

"(x) shall establish, as required by section 403(r)(5)(D), the procedure and standard respecting the validity of claims made with respect to a dietary supplement of vitamins, minerals, herbs, or other similar nutritional substances and shall determine whether claims respecting the following nutrients and diseases meet the requirements of section 403(r)(5)(D) of such Act: folic acid and neural tube defects, antioxident [sic] vitamins and cancer, zinc and immune function in the elderly, and omega-3 fatty acids and heart disease.

"(B) Not later than 24 months after the date of the enactment of this Act, the Secretary shall issue final regulations to implement section 403(r) of the Federal Food, Drug, and Cosmetic Act, except that the Secretary shall issue, not later than December 31, 1993, such a final regulation applicable to dietary supplements of vitamins, minerals, herbs, or other similar nutritional substances..[sic]

"(2) If the Secretary does not promulgate final regulations under paragraph (1)(B) upon the expiration of 24 months after the date of the enactment of this Act, the proposed regulations issued in accordance with paragraph (1)(A) shall be considered as the final regulations upon the expiration of such 24 months, except that the proposed regulations applicable to dietary supplements of vitamins, minerals, herbs, or other similar nutritional substances shall not be considered to be final regulations until December 31, 1993. There shall be promptly published in the Federal Register notice of the new status of the proposed regulations [see 57 F.R. 56347]."

[For construction of amendment made by section 202(a)(2)(B) of Pub. L. 102–571 to section 3(b) of Pub. L. 101–535 set out above, see section 202(a)(2)(C) of Pub. L. 102–571 set out above following section 2(b) of Pub. L. 101–535.]

TRANSFER OF FUNCTIONS

For transfer of functions of Federal Security Administrator to Secretary of Health, Education, and Welfare [now Health and Human Services], and of Food and Drug Administration in the Department of Agriculture to Federal Security Agency, see notes set out under section 321 of this title.

RULEMAKING ON LABELING

Pub. L. 108–282, title II, § 206, Aug. 2, 2004, 118 Stat. 910, provided that: "Not later than 2 years after the date of enactment of this Act [Aug. 2, 2004], the Secretary of Health and Human Services, in consultation with appropriate experts and stakeholders, shall issue a proposed rule to define, and permit use of, the term 'gluten-free' on the labeling of foods. Not later than 4 years after the date of enactment of this Act, the Secretary shall issue a final rule to define, and permit use of, the term 'gluten-free' on the labeling of foods."

Pub. L. 107–171, title X, § 10809, May 13, 2002, 116 Stat. 531, provided that: "The Secretary of Health and Human Services (referred to in this section as the 'Secretary') shall publish a proposed rule and, with due consideration to public comment, a final rule to revise, as appropriate, the current regulation governing the labeling of foods that have been treated to reduce pest infestation or pathogens by treatment by irradiation using radioactive isotope, electronic beam, or x-ray. Pending promulgation of the final rule required by this subsection [probably should be "this section"], any person may petition the Secretary for approval of labeling, which is not false or misleading in any material respect, of a food which has been treated by irradiation using radioactive isotope, electronic beam, or x-ray. The Secretary shall approve or deny such a petition within 180 days of receipt of the petition, or the petition shall be deemed denied, except to the extent additional agency review is mutually agreed upon by the Secretary and the petitioner. Any denial of a petition under this subsection shall constitute final agency action subject to judicial review by the United States Court of Appeals for the District of Columbia Circuit. Any labeling approved through the foregoing petition process shall be subject to the provisions of the final rule referred to in the first sentence of the subparagraph on the effective date of such final rule."

COMMISSION ON DIETARY SUPPLEMENT LABELS

Section 12 of Pub. L. 103–417 provided that:

"(a) ESTABLISHMENT.—There shall be established as an independent agency within the executive branch a commission to be known as the Commission on Dietary Supplement Labels (hereafter in this section referred to as the 'Commission').

"(b) MEMBERSHIP.—

"(1) COMPOSITION.—The Commission shall be composed of 7 members who shall be appointed by the President.

"(2) EXPERTISE REQUIREMENT.—The members of the Commission shall consist of individuals with expertise and experience in dietary supplements and in the manufacture, regulation, distribution, and use of such supplements. At least three of the members of the Commission shall be qualified by scientific training and experience to evaluate the benefits to health of the use of dietary supplements and one of such three members shall have experience in pharmacognosy, medical botany, traditional herbal medicine, or other related sciences. Members and staff of the Commission shall be without bias on the issue of dietary supplements.

"(c) FUNCTIONS OF THE COMMISSION.—The Commission shall conduct a study on, and provide recommendations for, the regulation of label claims and statements for dietary supplements, including the use of literature in connection with the sale of dietary supplements and procedures for the evaluation of such claims. In making such recommendations, the Commission shall evaluate how best to provide truthful, scientifically valid, and not misleading information to consumers so that such consumers may make informed and appropriate health care choices for themselves and their families.

"(d) ADMINISTRATIVE POWERS OF THE COMMISSION.—

"(1) HEARINGS.—The Commission may hold hearings, sit and act at such times and places, take such testimony, and receive such evidence as the Commission considers advisable to carry out the purposes of this section.

"(2) INFORMATION FROM FEDERAL AGENCIES.—The Commission may secure directly from any Federal department or agency such information as the Commission considers necessary to carry out the provisions of this section.

"(3) AUTHORIZATION OF APPROPRIATIONS.—There are authorized to be appropriated such sums as may be necessary to carry out this section.

"(e) REPORTS AND RECOMMENDATIONS.—

"(1) FINAL REPORT REQUIRED.—Not later than 24 months after the date of enactment of this Act [Oct. 25, 1994], the Commission shall prepare and submit to the President and to the Congress a final report on the study required by this section.

"(2) RECOMMENDATIONS.—The report described in paragraph (1) shall contain such recommendations, including recommendations for legislation, as the Commission deems appropriate.

"(3) ACTION ON RECOMMENDATIONS.—Within 90 days of the issuance of the report under paragraph (1), the Secretary of Health and Human Services shall publish in the Federal Register a notice of any recommendation of Commission for changes in regulations of the Secretary for the regulation of dietary supplements and shall include in such notice a notice of proposed rulemaking on such changes together with an opportunity to present views on such changes. Such rulemaking shall be completed not later than 2 years after the date of the issuance of such report. If such rulemaking is not completed on or before the expiration of such 2 years, regulations of the Secretary published in 59 FR 395–426 on January 4, 1994, shall not be in effect."

EXTENSION OF COMPLIANCE DEADLINE FOR CERTAIN FOOD PRODUCTS PACKAGED PRIOR TO AUGUST 8, 1994

Pub. L. 103–261, May 26, 1994, 108 Stat. 705, provided: "That before August 8, 1994, sections 403(q) and 403(r)(2) of the Federal Food, Drug, and Cosmetic Act [21 U.S.C. 343(q), (r)(2)] and the provision of section 403(i) of such Act added by section 7(2) of the Nutrition Labeling and Education Act of 1990 [Pub. L. 101–535], shall not apply with respect to a food product which is contained in a package for which the label was printed before May 8, 1994 (or before August 8, 1994, in the case of a juice or milk food product if the person responsible for the labeling of such food product exercised due diligence in obtaining before such date labels which are in compliance with such sections 403(q) and 403(r)(2) and such provision of section 403(i)), if, before June 15, 1994, the person who introduces or delivers for introduction such food product into interstate commerce submits to the Secretary of Health and Human Services a certification that such person will comply with this section and will comply with such sections 403(q) and 403(r)(2) and such provision of section 403(i) after August 8, 1994.''

LIMITATIONS ON APPLICATION OF SMALL BUSINESS EXEMPTION

Section 2(a) of Pub. L. 103–80 provided that:

''(1) BEFORE MAY 8, 1995.—Before May 8, 1995, the exemption provided by section 403(q)(5)(D) of the Federal Food, Drug, and Cosmetic Act [21 U.S.C. 343(q)(5)(D)] shall be available in accordance with the regulations of the Secretary of Health and Human Services published at 21 C.F.R. 101.9(j)(1)(i)(1993).

''(2) AFTER MAY 8, 1995.—After May 8, 1995, the exemption provided by section 403(q)(5)(D) of the Federal Food, Drug, and Cosmetic Act shall only be available with respect to food when it is sold to consumers.''

PROHIBITION ON IMPLEMENTATION OF PUB. L. 101–535 WITH RESPECT TO DIETARY SUPPLEMENTS

Section 202(a)(1) of Pub. L. 102–571 provided that: ''Notwithstanding any other provision of law and except as provided in subsection (b) [set out as a note below] and in the amendment made by paragraph (2)(A) [amending provisions set out as notes above], the Secretary of Health and Human Services may not implement the Nutrition Labeling and Education Act of 1990 (Public Law 101–535; 104 Stat. 2353) [see Short Title of 1990 Amendments note set out under section 301 of this title], or any amendment made by such Act, earlier than December 15, 1993, with respect to dietary supplements of vitamins, minerals, herbs, or other similar nutritional substances.''

HEALTH CLAIMS MADE WITH RESPECT TO DIETARY SUPPLEMENTS

Section 202(b) of Pub. L. 102–571 provided that: ''Notwithstanding section 403(r)(5)(D) of the Federal Food, Drug, and Cosmetic Act (21 U.S.C. 343(r)(5)(D)) and subsection (a) [enacting provisions set out as notes above and amending provisions set out as notes above and under section 343–1 of this title], the Secretary of Health and Human Services may, earlier than December 15, 1993, approve claims made with respect to dietary supplements of vitamins, minerals, herbs, or other similar nutritional substances that are claims described in clauses (vi) and (x) of section 3(b)(1)(A) of the Nutrition Labeling and Education Act of 1990 [Pub. L. 101–535] (21 U.S.C. 343 note).''

UNITED STATES RECOMMENDED DAILY ALLOWANCES OF VITAMINS OR MINERALS

Section 203 of Pub. L. 102–571 provided that: ''Notwithstanding any other provision of Federal law, no regulations that require the use of, or are based upon, recommended daily allowances of vitamins or minerals may be promulgated before November 8, 1993 (other than regulations establishing the United States recommended daily allowances specified at section 101.9(c)(7)(iv) of title 21, Code of Federal Regulations, as in effect on October 6, 1992, or regulations under section 403(r)(1)(A) of the Federal Food, Drug, and Cosmetic Act (21 U.S.C. 343(r)(1)(A)) that are based on such recommended daily allowances).''

CONSUMER EDUCATION

Section 2(c) of Pub. L. 101–535 provided that: ''The Secretary of Health and Human Services shall carry out activities which educate consumers about—

''(1) the availability of nutrition information in the label or labeling of food, and

''(2) the importance of that information in maintaining healthy dietary practices.''

STUDIES CONCERNING CARCINOGENIC AND OTHER TOXIC SUBSTANCES IN FOOD AND IMPURITIES IN AND TOXICITY OF SACCHARIN

Section 2 of Pub. L. 95–203 directed Secretary of Health, Education, and Welfare to conduct a study concerning carcinogenic and other toxic substances in food and impurities in and toxicity of saccharin and make a report respecting the carcinogenic and other substances to Committee on Human Resources of the Senate within 12 months of Nov. 23, 1977, and a report respecting saccharin to such committee within 15 months of Nov. 23, 1977.

REPORT TO CONGRESSIONAL COMMITTEES RESPECTING ACTION TAKEN PURSUANT TO FORMER PAR. (*o*)(2)

Section 4(a)(3) of Pub. L. 95–203 provided that the Secretary was to report to specified congressional committees any action taken under former par. (*o*)(2) of this section.

STATE OR TERRITORIAL REQUIREMENTS

Section 2 of Pub. L. 86–537 provided that: ''Nothing in the amendments made by the first section of this Act [amending this section] shall affect any requirement of the laws of any State or Territory.''

§ 343–1. National uniform nutrition labeling

(a) Except as provided in subsection (b) of this section, no State or political subdivision of a State may directly or indirectly establish under any authority or continue in effect as to any food in interstate commerce—

(1) any requirement for a food which is the subject of a standard of identity established under section 341 of this title that is not identical to such standard of identity or that is not identical to the requirement of section 343(g) of this title, except that this paragraph does not apply to a standard of identity of a State or political subdivision of a State for maple syrup that is of the type required by sections 341 and 343(g) of this title,

(2) any requirement for the labeling of food of the type required by section 343(c), 343(e), 343(i)(2), 343(w), or 343(x) of this title that is not identical to the requirement of such section, except that this paragraph does not apply to a requirement of a State or political subdivision of a State that is of the type required by section 343(c) of this title and that is applicable to maple syrup,

(3) any requirement for the labeling of food of the type required by section 343(b), 343(d), 343(f), 343(h), 343(i)(1), or 343(k) of this title that is not identical to the requirement of such section, except that this paragraph does not apply to a requirement of a State or political subdivision of a State that is of the type required by section 343(h)(1) of this title and that is applicable to maple syrup,

(4) any requirement for nutrition labeling of food that is not identical to the requirement of section 343(q) of this title, except a requirement for nutrition labeling of food which is exempt under subclause (i) or (ii) of section 343(q)(5)(A) of this title, or

(5) any requirement respecting any claim of the type described in section 343(r)(1) of this title made in the label or labeling of food that is not identical to the requirement of section 343(r) of this title, except a requirement respecting a claim made in the label or labeling of food which is exempt under section 343(r)(5)(B) of this title.

Paragraph (3) shall take effect in accordance with section 6(b) of the Nutrition Labeling and Education Act of 1990.

(b) Upon petition of a State or a political subdivision of a State, the Secretary may exempt from subsection (a) of this section, under such conditions as may be prescribed by regulation, any State or local requirement that—

(1) would not cause any food to be in violation of any applicable requirement under Federal law,

(2) would not unduly burden interstate commerce, and

(3) is designed to address a particular need for information which need is not met by the requirements of the sections referred to in subsection (a) of this section.

(June 25, 1938, ch. 675, § 403A, as added Pub. L. 101–535, § 6(a), Nov. 8, 1990, 104 Stat. 2362; amended Pub. L. 102–108, § 2(b), Aug. 17, 1991, 105 Stat. 549; Pub. L. 103–396, § 3(a), Oct. 22, 1994, 108 Stat. 4154; Pub. L. 108–282, title II, § 203(c)(2), Aug. 2, 2004, 118 Stat. 908.)

REFERENCES IN TEXT

Section 6(b) of the Nutrition Labeling and Education Act of 1990 [Pub. L. 101–535], referred to in subsec. (a), is set out below.

AMENDMENTS

2004—Subsec. (a)(2). Pub. L. 108–282 substituted "343(i)(2), 343(w), or 343(x)" for "or 343(i)(2)".

1994—Subsec. (a)(1). Pub. L. 103–396, § 3(a)(1), inserted at end "except that this paragraph does not apply to a standard of identity of a State or political subdivision of a State for maple syrup that is of the type required by sections 341 and 343(g) of this title,".

Subsec. (a)(2). Pub. L. 103–396, § 3(a)(2), inserted at end "except that this paragraph does not apply to a requirement of a State or political subdivision of a State that is of the type required by section 343(c) of this title and that is applicable to maple syrup,".

Subsec. (a)(3). Pub. L. 103–396, § 3(a)(3), inserted at end "except that this paragraph does not apply to a requirement of a State or political subdivision of a State that is of the type required by section 343(h)(1) of this title and that is applicable to maple syrup,".

1991—Subsec. (a)(5). Pub. L. 102–108 substituted "section 343(r)(5)(B) of this title" for "clause (B) of such section".

EFFECTIVE DATE OF 2004 AMENDMENT

Amendment by Pub. L. 108–282 applicable to any food that is labeled on or after Jan. 1, 2006, see section 203(d) of Pub. L. 108–282, set out as a note under section 321 of this title.

EFFECTIVE DATE

Section 10(b) of Pub. L. 101–535, as amended by Pub. L. 102–571, title I, § 107(16), title II, § 202(a)(4), Oct. 29, 1992, 106 Stat. 4499, 4501, provided that:

"(1) IN GENERAL.—Except as provided in paragraph (2), the amendments made by section 6 [enacting this section] shall take effect—

"(A) with respect to a requirement of a State or political subdivision described in paragraph (1) of section 403A(a) of the Federal Food, Drug, and Cosmetic Act [subsec. (a)(1) of this section], on the date of the enactment of this Act [Nov. 8, 1990],

"(B) with respect to a requirement of a State or political subdivision described in paragraph (2) of section 403A(a) of the Federal Food, Drug, and Cosmetic Act, one year after the date of the enactment of this Act,

"(C) with respect to a requirement of a State or political subdivision described in paragraph (3) of section 403A(a) of the Federal Food, Drug, and Cosmetic Act, as prescribed by section 6(b) of the Nutrition Labeling and Education Act of 1990 [Pub. L. 101–535, set out below],

"(D) with respect to a requirement of a State or political subdivision described in paragraph (4) of section 403A(a) of the Federal Food, Drug, and Cosmetic Act, on the date regulations to implement section 403(q) of such Act [21 U.S.C. 343(q)] take effect, and

"(E) with respect to a requirement of a State or political subdivision described in paragraph (5) of section 403A(a) of the Federal Food, Drug, and Cosmetic Act, on the date regulations to implement section 403(r) of such Act take effect.

"(2) EXCEPTION.—If a State or political subdivision submits a petition under section 403A(b) of the Federal Food, Drug, and Cosmetic Act for a requirement described in section 403A(a) of such Act within 18 months of the date of the enactment of this Act, paragraphs (3) through (5) of such section 403A(a) shall not apply with respect to such State or political subdivision requirement until—

"(A) 24 months after the date of the enactment of this Act, or

"(B) action on the petition,

whichever occurs later.

"(3) REQUIREMENTS PERTAINING TO CERTAIN CLAIMS.—Notwithstanding subparagraphs (D) and (E) of paragraph (1) and except with respect to claims approved in accordance with section 202(b) of the Dietary Supplement Act of 1992 [Pub. L. 102–571, set out as a note under section 343 of this title], the requirements described in paragraphs (4) and (5) of section 403A(a) of the Federal Food, Drug, and Cosmetic Act (21 U.S.C. 343–1(a)(4) and (5)) that pertain to dietary supplements of vitamins, minerals, herbs, or other similar nutritional substances shall not take effect until the date final regulations take effect to implement subsection (q) or (r), as appropriate, of section 403 of such Act with respect to such dietary supplements."

Section 6(b) of Pub. L. 101–535 provided that:

"(1) For the purpose of implementing section 403A(a)(3) [21 U.S.C. 343–1(a)(3)], the Secretary of Health and Human Services shall enter into a contract with a public or nonprofit private entity to conduct a study of—

"(A) State and local laws which require the labeling of food that is of the type required by sections 403(b), 403(d), 403(f), 403(h), 403(i)(1), and 403(k) of the Federal Food, Drug, and Cosmetic Act [21 U.S.C. 343(b), (d), (f), (h), (i)(1), (k)], and

"(B) the sections of the Federal Food, Drug, and Cosmetic Act referred to in subparagraph (A) and the regulations issued by the Secretary to enforce such sections to determine whether such sections and regulations adequately implement the purposes of such sections.

"(2) The contract under paragraph (1) shall provide that the study required by such paragraph shall be completed within 6 months of the date of the enactment of this Act [Nov. 8, 1990].

"(3)(A) Within 9 months of the date of the enactment of this Act, the Secretary shall publish a proposed list of sections which are adequately being implemented by regulations as determined under paragraph (1)(B) and sections which are not adequately being implemented by regulations as so determined. After publication of the lists, the Secretary shall provide 60 days for comments on such lists.

"(B) Within 24 months of the date of the enactment of this Act, the Secretary shall publish a final list of sections which are adequately being implemented by regulations and a list of sections which are not adequately being implemented by regulations. With respect to a section which is found by the Secretary to be adequately implemented, no State or political subdivision of a State may establish or continue in effect as to any food in interstate commerce any requirement which is not identical to the requirement of such section.

"(C) Within 24 months of the date of the enactment of this Act, the Secretary shall publish proposed revisions to the regulations found to be inadequate under subparagraph (B) and within 30 months of such date shall issue final revisions. Upon the effective date of such final revisions, no State or political subdivision may establish or continue in effect any requirement which is not identical to the requirement of the section which had its regulations revised in accordance with this subparagraph.

"(D)(i) If the Secretary does not issue a final list in accordance with subparagraph (B), the proposed list issued under subparagraph (A) shall be considered the final list and States and political subdivisions shall be preempted with respect to sections found to be adequate in such proposed list in accordance with subparagraph (B).

"(ii) If the Secretary does not issue final revisions of regulations in accordance with subparagraph (C), the proposed revisions issued under such subparagraph shall be considered the final revisions and States and political subdivisions shall be preempted with respect to sections the regulations of which are revised by the proposed revisions.

"(E) Subsection (b) of section 403A of the Federal Food, Drug, and Cosmetic Act shall apply with respect to the prohibition prescribed by subparagraphs (B) and (C)."

CONSTRUCTION OF PUB. L. 101–535

Section 6(c) of Pub. L. 101–535 provided that:

"(1) The Nutrition Labeling and Education Act of 1990 [Pub. L. 101–535, see Short Title of 1990 Amendment note set out under section 301 of this title] shall not be construed to preempt any provision of State law, unless such provision is expressly preempted under section 403A of the Federal Food, Drug, and Cosmetic Act [this section].

"(2) The amendment made by subsection (a) [enacting this section] and the provisions of subsection (b) [set out as a note above] shall not be construed to apply to any requirement respecting a statement in the labeling of food that provides for a warning concerning the safety of the food or component of the food.

"(3) The amendment made by subsection (a), the provisions of subsection (b) and paragraphs (1) and (2) of this subsection shall not be construed to affect preemption, express or implied, of any such requirement of a State or political subdivision, which may arise under the Constitution, any provision of the Federal Food, Drug, and Cosmetic Act [this chapter] not amended by subsection (a), any other Federal law, or any Federal regulation, order, or other final agency action reviewable under chapter 7 of title 5, United States Code."

Amendments by Pub. L. 101–535 not to be construed to alter the authority of the Secretary of Health and Human Services and the Secretary of Agriculture under the Federal Food, Drug, and Cosmetic Act (21 U.S.C. 301 et seq.), the Federal Meat Inspection Act (21 U.S.C. 601 et seq.), the Poultry Products Inspection Act (21 U.S.C. 451 et seq.), and the Egg Products Inspection Act (21 U.S.C. 1031 et seq.), see section 9 of Pub. L. 101–535, set out as a note under section 343 of this title.

DELAYED APPLICABILITY OF CERTAIN PROVISIONS

Pub. L. 102–408, title III, §310, Oct. 13, 1992, 106 Stat. 2090, provided that: "Notwithstanding any other provision of law, section 403A(a)(1) of the Federal Food, Drug, and Cosmetic Act (21 U.S.C. 343–1(a)(1)) shall not apply with respect to any requirement of any State or political subdivision regarding maple syrup until September 1, 1994."

§343–2. Dietary supplement labeling exemptions

(a) In general

A publication, including an article, a chapter in a book, or an official abstract of a peer-reviewed scientific publication that appears in an article and was prepared by the author or the editors of the publication, which is reprinted in its entirety, shall not be defined as labeling when used in connection with the sale of a dietary supplement to consumers when it—

(1) is not false or misleading;

(2) does not promote a particular manufacturer or brand of a dietary supplement;

(3) is displayed or presented, or is displayed or presented with other such items on the same subject matter, so as to present a balanced view of the available scientific information on a dietary supplement;

(4) if displayed in an establishment, is physically separate from the dietary supplements; and

(5) does not have appended to it any information by sticker or any other method.

(b) Application

Subsection (a) of this section shall not apply to or restrict a retailer or wholesaler of dietary supplements in any way whatsoever in the sale of books or other publications as a part of the business of such retailer or wholesaler.

(c) Burden of proof

In any proceeding brought under subsection (a) of this section, the burden of proof shall be on the United States to establish that an article or other such matter is false or misleading.

(June 25, 1938, ch. 675, §403B, as added Pub. L. 103–417, §5, Oct. 25, 1994, 108 Stat. 4328.)

§343–3. Disclosure

(a) No provision of section 321(n), 343(a), or 348 of this title shall be construed to require on the label or labeling of a food a separate radiation disclosure statement that is more prominent than the declaration of ingredients required by section 343(i)(2) of this title.

(b) In this section, the term "radiation disclosure statement" means a written statement that discloses that a food has been intentionally subject to radiation.

(June 25, 1938, ch. 675, §403C, as added Pub. L. 105–115, title III, §306, Nov. 21, 1997, 111 Stat. 2353.)

EFFECTIVE DATE

Section effective 90 days after Nov. 21, 1997, except as otherwise provided, see section 501 of Pub. L. 105–115, set out as an Effective Date of 1997 Amendment note under section 321 of this title.

§343a. Repealed. Pub. L. 106–554, §1(a)(1) [title V, §517], Dec. 21, 2000, 114 Stat. 2763, 2763A–73

Section, Pub. L. 95–203, §4(c), (d), Nov. 23, 1977, 91 Stat. 1453, 1454, related to distribution of information on health risks of saccharin.

§344. Emergency permit control

(a) Conditions on manufacturing, processing, etc., as health measure

Whenever the Secretary finds after investigation that the distribution in interstate commerce of any class of food may, by reason of contamination with micro-organisms during the manufacture, processing, or packing thereof in any locality, be injurious to health, and that such injurious nature cannot be adequately determined after such articles have entered interstate commerce, he then, and in such case only, shall promulgate regulations providing for the issuance, to manufacturers, processors, or packers of such class of food in such locality, of permits to which shall be attached such conditions governing the manufacture, processing, or packing of such class of food, for such temporary period of time, as may be necessary to protect the public health; and after the effective date of such regulations, and during such temporary period, no person shall introduce or deliver for introduction into interstate commerce any such food manufactured, processed, or packed by any such manufacturer, processor, or packer unless such manufacturer, processor, or packer holds a permit issued by the Secretary as provided by such regulations.

(b) Violation of permit; suspension and reinstatement

The Secretary is authorized to suspend immediately upon notice any permit issued under authority of this section if it is found that any of the conditions of the permit have been violated. The holder of a permit so suspended shall be privileged at any time to apply for the reinstatement of such permit, and the Secretary shall, immediately after prompt hearing and an inspection of the establishment, reinstate such permit if it is found that adequate measures have been taken to comply with and maintain the conditions of the permit, as originally issued or as amended.

(c) Inspection of permit-holding establishments

Any officer or employee duly designated by the Secretary shall have access to any factory or establishment, the operator of which holds a permit from the Secretary, for the purpose of ascertaining whether or not the conditions of the permit are being complied with, and denial of access for such inspection shall be ground for suspension of the permit until such access is freely given by the operator.

(June 25, 1938, ch. 675, § 404, 52 Stat. 1048.)

TRANSFER OF FUNCTIONS

For transfer of functions of Federal Security Administrator to Secretary of Health, Education, and Welfare [now Health and Human Services], and of Food and Drug Administration in the Department of Agriculture to Federal Security Agency, see notes set out under section 321 of this title.

§ 345. Regulations making exemptions

The Secretary shall promulgate regulations exempting from any labeling requirement of this chapter (1) small open containers of fresh fruits and fresh vegetables and (2) food which is, in accordance with the practice of the trade, to be processed, labeled, or repacked in substantial quantities at establishments other than those where originally processed or packed, on condition that such food is not adulterated or misbranded under the provisions of this chapter upon removal from such processing, labeling, or repacking establishment. This section does not apply to the labeling requirements of sections 343(q) and 343(r) of this title.

(June 25, 1938, ch. 675, § 405, 52 Stat. 1049; Pub. L. 101–535, § 5(a), Nov. 8, 1990, 104 Stat. 2362.)

AMENDMENTS

1990—Pub. L. 101–535 inserted at end "This section does not apply to the labeling requirements of sections 343(q) and 343(r) of this title."

EFFECTIVE DATE OF 1990 AMENDMENT

Amendment by Pub. L. 101–535 effective six months after the date of the promulgation of final regulations to implement section 343(r) of this title, or if such regulations are not promulgated, the date proposed regulations are to be considered as such final regulations (Nov. 8, 1992), with exception for persons marketing food the brand name of which contains a term defined by the Secretary under section 343(r)(2)(A)(i) of this title, see section 10(a) of Pub. L. 101–535, set out as a note under section 343 of this title.

CONSTRUCTION OF AMENDMENTS BY PUB. L. 101–535

Amendments by Pub. L. 101–535 not to be construed to alter authority of Secretary of Health and Human Services and Secretary of Agriculture under the Federal Food, Drug, and Cosmetic Act (21 U.S.C. 301 et seq.), the Federal Meat Inspection Act (21 U.S.C. 601 et seq.), the Poultry Products Inspection Act (21 U.S.C. 451 et seq.), and the Egg Products Inspection Act (21 U.S.C. 1031 et seq.), see section 9 of Pub. L. 101–535, set out as a note under section 343 of this title.

TRANSFER OF FUNCTIONS

For transfer of functions of Federal Security Administrator to Secretary of Health, Education, and Welfare [now Health and Human Services], and of Food and Drug Administration in the Department of Agriculture to Federal Security Agency, see notes set out under section 321 of this title.

§ 346. Tolerances for poisonous or deleterious substances in food; regulations

Any poisonous or deleterious substance added to any food, except where such substance is required in the production thereof or cannot be avoided by good manufacturing practice shall be deemed to be unsafe for purposes of the application of clause (2)(A) of section 342(a) of this title; but when such substance is so required or cannot be so avoided, the Secretary shall promulgate regulations limiting the quantity therein or thereon to such extent as he finds necessary for the protection of public health, and any quantity exceeding the limits so fixed shall also be deemed to be unsafe for purposes of the application of clause (2)(A) of section 342(a) of this title. While such a regulation is in effect limiting the quantity of any such substance in the case of any food, such food shall not, by reason of bearing or containing any added amount of such substance, be considered to be adulterated within the meaning of clause (1) of section 342(a) of this title. In determining the quantity of such added substance to be tolerated in or on different articles of food the Secretary shall take into account the extent to which the use of such substance is required or cannot be avoided in the production of each such article, and the other ways in which the consumer may be affected by the same or other poisonous or deleterious substances.

(June 25, 1938, ch. 675, § 406, 52 Stat. 1049; Pub. L. 85–929, § 3(c), Sept. 6, 1958, 72 Stat. 1785; Pub. L. 86–618, title I, § 103(a)(1), July 12, 1960, 74 Stat. 398.)

AMENDMENTS

1960—Pub. L. 86–618 repealed subsec. (b) which required Secretary to promulgate regulations for listing of coal-tar colors.

1958—Subsec. (a). Pub. L. 85–929 substituted "clause (2)(A)" for "clause (2)" in first sentence.

EFFECTIVE DATE OF 1960 AMENDMENT

Amendment by Pub. L. 86–618 effective July 12, 1960, subject to the provisions of section 203 of Pub. L. 86–618, see section 202 of Pub. L. 86–618, set out as a note under section 379e of this title.

EFFECTIVE DATE OF NEMATOCIDE, PLANT REGULATOR, DEFOLIANT, AND DESICCANT AMENDMENT OF 1959

Effective date of subsec. (a) as in force prior to July 22, 1954, with respect to particular commercial use of a nematocide, plant regulator, defoliant, or desiccant in or on a raw agricultural commodity made before Jan. 1, 1958, see section 3(b) of Pub. L. 86–139, Aug. 7, 1959, 73 Stat. 288.

EFFECTIVE DATE OF 1958 AMENDMENT

For effective date of amendment by Pub. L. 85–929, see section 6(b), (c) of Pub. L. 85–929, set out as a note under section 342 of this title.

TRANSFER OF FUNCTIONS

Functions vested in Secretary of Health, Education, and Welfare [now Health and Human Services] in establishing tolerances for pesticide chemicals under this section together with authority to monitor compliance with tolerances and effectiveness of surveillance and enforcement and to provide technical assistance to States and conduct research under this chapter and section 201 et seq. of Title 42, The Public Health and Welfare, transferred to Administrator of Environmental Protection Agency by Reorg. Plan No. 3 of 1970, §2(a)(4), eff. Dec. 2, 1970, 35 F.R. 15623, 84 Stat. 2086, set out in the Appendix to Title 5, Government Organization and Employees.

For transfer of functions of Federal Security Administrator to Secretary of Health, Education, and Welfare [now Health and Human Services], and of Food and Drug Administration to Federal Security Agency, see notes set out under section 321 of this title.

§ 346a. Tolerances and exemptions for pesticide chemical residues

(a) Requirement for tolerance or exemption

(1) General rule

Except as provided in paragraph (2) or (3), any pesticide chemical residue in or on a food shall be deemed unsafe for the purpose of section 342(a)(2)(B) of this title unless—

(A) a tolerance for such pesticide chemical residue in or on such food is in effect under this section and the quantity of the residue is within the limits of the tolerance; or

(B) an exemption from the requirement of a tolerance is in effect under this section for the pesticide chemical residue.

For the purposes of this section, the term "food", when used as a noun without modification, shall mean a raw agricultural commodity or processed food.

(2) Processed food

Notwithstanding paragraph (1)—

(A) if a tolerance is in effect under this section for a pesticide chemical residue in or on a raw agricultural commodity, a pesticide chemical residue that is present in or on a processed food because the food is made from that raw agricultural commodity shall not be considered unsafe within the meaning of section 342(a)(2)(B) of this title despite the lack of a tolerance for the pesticide chemical residue in or on the processed food if the pesticide chemical has been used in or on the raw agricultural commodity in conformity with a tolerance under this section, such residue in or on the raw agricultural commodity has been removed to the extent possible in good manufacturing practice, and the concentration of the pesticide chemical residue in the processed food is not greater than the tolerance prescribed for the pesticide chemical residue in the raw agricultural commodity; or

(B) if an exemption for the requirement for a tolerance is in effect under this section for a pesticide chemical residue in or on a raw agricultural commodity, a pesticide chemical residue that is present in or on a processed food because the food is made from that raw agricultural commodity shall not be considered unsafe within the meaning of section 342(a)(2)(B) of this title.

(3) Residues of degradation products

If a pesticide chemical residue is present in or on a food because it is a metabolite or other degradation product of a precursor substance that itself is a pesticide chemical or pesticide chemical residue, such a residue shall not be considered to be unsafe within the meaning of section 342(a)(2)(B) of this title despite the lack of a tolerance or exemption from the need for a tolerance for such residue in or on such food if—

(A) the Administrator has not determined that the degradation product is likely to pose any potential health risk from dietary exposure that is of a different type than, or of a greater significance than, any risk posed by dietary exposure to the precursor substance;

(B) either—

(i) a tolerance is in effect under this section for residues of the precursor substance in or on the food, and the combined level of residues of the degradation product and the precursor substance in or on the food is at or below the stoichiometrically equivalent level that would be permitted by the tolerance if the residue consisted only of the precursor substance rather than the degradation product; or

(ii) an exemption from the need for a tolerance is in effect under this section for residues of the precursor substance in or on the food; and

(C) the tolerance or exemption for residues of the precursor substance does not state that it applies only to particular named substances and does not state that it does not apply to residues of the degradation product.

(4) Effect of tolerance or exemption

While a tolerance or exemption from the requirement for a tolerance is in effect under this section for a pesticide chemical residue with respect to any food, the food shall not by reason of bearing or containing any amount of such a residue be considered to be adulterated within the meaning of section 342(a)(1) of this title.

(b) Authority and standard for tolerance

(1) Authority

The Administrator may issue regulations establishing, modifying, or revoking a tolerance for a pesticide chemical residue in or on a food—

(A) in response to a petition filed under subsection (d) of this section; or

(B) on the Administrator's own initiative under subsection (e) of this section.

As used in this section, the term "modify" shall not mean expanding the tolerance to cover additional foods.

(2) Standard

(A) General rule

(i) Standard

The Administrator may establish or leave in effect a tolerance for a pesticide chemical residue in or on a food only if the Administrator determines that the tolerance is safe. The Administrator shall modify or revoke a tolerance if the Administrator determines it is not safe.

(ii) Determination of safety

As used in this section, the term "safe", with respect to a tolerance for a pesticide chemical residue, means that the Administrator has determined that there is a reasonable certainty that no harm will result from aggregate exposure to the pesticide chemical residue, including all anticipated dietary exposures and all other exposures for which there is reliable information.

(iii) Rule of construction

With respect to a tolerance, a pesticide chemical residue meeting the standard under clause (i) is not an eligible pesticide chemical residue for purposes of subparagraph (B).

(B) Tolerances for eligible pesticide chemical residues

(i) Definition

As used in this subparagraph, the term "eligible pesticide chemical residue" means a pesticide chemical residue as to which—

(I) the Administrator is not able to identify a level of exposure to the residue at which the residue will not cause or contribute to a known or anticipated harm to human health (referred to in this section as a "nonthreshold effect");

(II) the lifetime risk of experiencing the nonthreshold effect is appropriately assessed by quantitative risk assessment; and

(III) with regard to any known or anticipated harm to human health for which the Administrator is able to identify a level at which the residue will not cause such harm (referred to in this section as a "threshold effect"), the Administrator determines that the level of aggregate exposure is safe.

(ii) Determination of tolerance

Notwithstanding subparagraph (A)(i), a tolerance for an eligible pesticide chemical residue may be left in effect or modified under this subparagraph if—

(I) at least one of the conditions described in clause (iii) is met; and

(II) both of the conditions described in clause (iv) are met.

(iii) Conditions regarding use

For purposes of clause (ii), the conditions described in this clause with respect to a tolerance for an eligible pesticide chemical residue are the following:

(I) Use of the pesticide chemical that produces the residue protects consumers from adverse effects on health that would pose a greater risk than the dietary risk from the residue.

(II) Use of the pesticide chemical that produces the residue is necessary to avoid a significant disruption in domestic production of an adequate, wholesome, and economical food supply.

(iv) Conditions regarding risk

For purposes of clause (ii), the conditions described in this clause with respect to a tolerance for an eligible pesticide chemical residue are the following:

(I) The yearly risk associated with the nonthreshold effect from aggregate exposure to the residue does not exceed 10 times the yearly risk that would be allowed under subparagraph (A) for such effect.

(II) The tolerance is limited so as to ensure that the risk over a lifetime associated with the nonthreshold effect from aggregate exposure to the residue is not greater than twice the lifetime risk that would be allowed under subparagraph (A) for such effect.

(v) Review

Five years after the date on which the Administrator makes a determination to leave in effect or modify a tolerance under this subparagraph, and thereafter as the Administrator deems appropriate, the Administrator shall determine, after notice and opportunity for comment, whether it has been demonstrated to the Administrator that a condition described in clause (iii)(I) or clause (iii)(II) continues to exist with respect to the tolerance and that the yearly and lifetime risks from aggregate exposure to such residue continue to comply with the limits specified in clause (iv). If the Administrator determines by such date that such demonstration has not been made, the Administrator shall, not later than 180 days after the date of such determination, issue a regulation under subsection (e)(1) of this section to modify or revoke the tolerance.

(vi) Infants and children

Any tolerance under this subparagraph shall meet the requirements of subparagraph (C).

(C) Exposure of infants and children

In establishing, modifying, leaving in effect, or revoking a tolerance or exemption for a pesticide chemical residue, the Administrator—

(i) shall assess the risk of the pesticide chemical residue based on—

(I) available information about consumption patterns among infants and children that are likely to result in disproportionately high consumption of foods containing or bearing such residue among infants and children in comparison to the general population;

(II) available information concerning the special susceptibility of infants and children to the pesticide chemical residues, including neurological differences between infants and children and adults, and effects of in utero exposure to pesticide chemicals; and

(III) available information concerning the cumulative effects on infants and children of such residues and other substances that have a common mechanism of toxicity; and

(ii) shall—

(I) ensure that there is a reasonable certainty that no harm will result to infants and children from aggregate exposure to the pesticide chemical residue; and

(II) publish a specific determination regarding the safety of the pesticide chemical residue for infants and children.

The Secretary of Health and Human Services and the Secretary of Agriculture, in consultation with the Administrator, shall conduct surveys to document dietary exposure to pesticides among infants and children. In the case of threshold effects, for purposes of clause (ii)(I) an additional tenfold margin of safety for the pesticide chemical residue and other sources of exposure shall be applied for infants and children to take into account potential pre- and post-natal toxicity and completeness of the data with respect to exposure and toxicity to infants and children. Notwithstanding such requirement for an additional margin of safety, the Administrator may use a different margin of safety for the pesticide chemical residue only if, on the basis of reliable data, such margin will be safe for infants and children.

(D) Factors

In establishing, modifying, leaving in effect, or revoking a tolerance or exemption for a pesticide chemical residue, the Administrator shall consider, among other relevant factors—

(i) the validity, completeness, and reliability of the available data from studies of the pesticide chemical and pesticide chemical residue;

(ii) the nature of any toxic effect shown to be caused by the pesticide chemical or pesticide chemical residue in such studies;

(iii) available information concerning the relationship of the results of such studies to human risk;

(iv) available information concerning the dietary consumption patterns of consumers (and major identifiable subgroups of consumers);

(v) available information concerning the cumulative effects of such residues and other substances that have a common mechanism of toxicity;

(vi) available information concerning the aggregate exposure levels of consumers (and major identifiable subgroups of consumers) to the pesticide chemical residue and to other related substances, including dietary exposure under the tolerance and all other tolerances in effect for the pesticide chemical residue, and exposure from other non-occupational sources;

(vii) available information concerning the variability of the sensitivities of major identifiable subgroups of consumers;

(viii) such information as the Administrator may require on whether the pesticide chemical may have an effect in humans that is similar to an effect produced by a naturally occurring estrogen or other endocrine effects; and

(ix) safety factors which in the opinion of experts qualified by scientific training and experience to evaluate the safety of food additives are generally recognized as appropriate for the use of animal experimentation data.

(E) Data and information regarding anticipated and actual residue levels

(i) Authority

In establishing, modifying, leaving in effect, or revoking a tolerance for a pesticide chemical residue, the Administrator may consider available data and information on the anticipated residue levels of the pesticide chemical in or on food and the actual residue levels of the pesticide chemical that have been measured in food, including residue data collected by the Food and Drug Administration.

(ii) Requirement

If the Administrator relies on anticipated or actual residue levels in establishing, modifying, or leaving in effect a tolerance, the Administrator shall pursuant to subsection (f)(1) of this section require that data be provided five years after the date on which the tolerance is established, modified, or left in effect, and thereafter as the Administrator deems appropriate, demonstrating that such residue levels are not above the levels so relied on. If such data are not so provided, or if the data do not demonstrate that the residue levels are not above the levels so relied on, the Administrator shall, not later than 180 days after the date on which the data were required to be provided, issue a regulation under subsection (e)(1) of this section, or an order under subsection (f)(2) of this section, as appropriate, to modify or revoke the tolerance.

(F) Percent of food actually treated

In establishing, modifying, leaving in effect, or revoking a tolerance for a pesticide chemical residue, the Administrator may, when assessing chronic dietary risk, consider available data and information on the percent of food actually treated with the pesticide chemical (including aggregate pesticide use data collected by the Department of Agriculture) only if the Administrator—

(i) finds that the data are reliable and provide a valid basis to show what percentage of the food derived from such crop is likely to contain such pesticide chemical residue;

(ii) finds that the exposure estimate does not understate exposure for any significant subpopulation group;

(iii) finds that, if data are available on pesticide use and consumption of food in a particular area, the population in such area is not dietarily exposed to residues above those estimated by the Administrator; and

(iv) provides for the periodic reevaluation of the estimate of anticipated dietary exposure.

(3) Detection methods

(A) General rule

A tolerance for a pesticide chemical residue in or on a food shall not be established or modified by the Administrator unless the Administrator determines, after consultation with the Secretary, that there is a practical method for detecting and measuring the levels of the pesticide chemical residue in or on the food.

(B) Detection limit

A tolerance for a pesticide chemical residue in or on a food shall not be established at or modified to a level lower than the limit of detection of the method for detecting and measuring the pesticide chemical residue specified by the Administrator under subparagraph (A).

(4) International standards

In establishing a tolerance for a pesticide chemical residue in or on a food, the Administrator shall determine whether a maximum residue level for the pesticide chemical has been established by the Codex Alimentarius Commission. If a Codex maximum residue level has been established for the pesticide chemical and the Administrator does not propose to adopt the Codex level, the Administrator shall publish for public comment a notice explaining the reasons for departing from the Codex level.

(c) Authority and standard for exemptions

(1) Authority

The Administrator may issue a regulation establishing, modifying, or revoking an exemption from the requirement for a tolerance for a pesticide chemical residue in or on food—

(A) in response to a petition filed under subsection (d) of this section; or

(B) on the Administrator's initiative under subsection (e) of this section.

(2) Standard

(A) General rule

(i) Standard

The Administrator may establish or leave in effect an exemption from the requirement for a tolerance for a pesticide chemical residue in or on food only if the Administrator determines that the exemption is safe. The Administrator shall modify or revoke an exemption if the Administrator determines it is not safe.

(ii) Determination of safety

The term "safe", with respect to an exemption for a pesticide chemical residue, means that the Administrator has determined that there is a reasonable certainty that no harm will result from aggregate exposure to the pesticide chemical residue, including all anticipated dietary exposures and all other exposures for which there is reliable information.

(B) Factors

In making a determination under this paragraph, the Administrator shall take into account, among other relevant considerations, the considerations set forth in subparagraphs (C) and (D) of subsection (b)(2) of this section.

(3) Limitation

An exemption from the requirement for a tolerance for a pesticide chemical residue in or on food shall not be established or modified by the Administrator unless the Administrator determines, after consultation with the Secretary—

(A) that there is a practical method for detecting and measuring the levels of such pesticide chemical residue in or on food; or

(B) that there is no need for such a method, and states the reasons for such determination in issuing the regulation establishing or modifying the exemption.

(d) Petition for tolerance or exemption

(1) Petitions and petitioners

Any person may file with the Administrator a petition proposing the issuance of a regulation—

(A) establishing, modifying, or revoking a tolerance for a pesticide chemical residue in or on a food; or

(B) establishing, modifying, or revoking an exemption from the requirement of a tolerance for such a residue.

(2) Petition contents

(A) Establishment

A petition under paragraph (1) to establish a tolerance or exemption for a pesticide chemical residue shall be supported by such data and information as are specified in regulations issued by the Administrator, including—

(i)(I) an informative summary of the petition and of the data, information, and arguments submitted or cited in support of the petition; and

(II) a statement that the petitioner agrees that such summary or any information it contains may be published as a part of the notice of filing of the petition to be published under this subsection and as part of a proposed or final regulation issued under this section;

(ii) the name, chemical identity, and composition of the pesticide chemical residue and of the pesticide chemical that produces the residue;

(iii) data showing the recommended amount, frequency, method, and time of application of that pesticide chemical;

(iv) full reports of tests and investigations made with respect to the safety of the pesticide chemical, including full information as to the methods and controls used in conducting those tests and investigations;

(v) full reports of tests and investigations made with respect to the nature and amount of the pesticide chemical residue that is likely to remain in or on the food, including a description of the analytical methods used;

(vi) a practical method for detecting and measuring the levels of the pesticide chemical residue in or on the food, or for exemptions, a statement why such a method is not needed;

(vii) a proposed tolerance for the pesticide chemical residue, if a tolerance is proposed;

(viii) if the petition relates to a tolerance for a processed food, reports of investigations conducted using the processing method(s) used to produce that food;

(ix) such information as the Administrator may require to make the determination under subsection (b)(2)(C) of this section;

(x) such information as the Administrator may require on whether the pesticide chemical may have an effect in humans that is similar to an effect produced by a naturally occurring estrogen or other endocrine effects;

(xi) information regarding exposure to the pesticide chemical residue due to any tolerance or exemption already granted for such residue;

(xii) practical methods for removing any amount of the residue that would exceed any proposed tolerance; and

(xiii) such other data and information as the Administrator requires by regulation to support the petition.

If information or data required by this subparagraph is available to the Administrator, the person submitting the petition may cite the availability of the information or data in lieu of submitting it. The Administrator may require a petition to be accompanied by samples of the pesticide chemical with respect to which the petition is filed.

(B) Modification or revocation

The Administrator may by regulation establish the requirements for information and data to support a petition to modify or revoke a tolerance or to modify or revoke an exemption from the requirement for a tolerance.

(3) Notice

A notice of the filing of a petition that the Administrator determines has met the requirements of paragraph (2) shall be published by the Administrator within 30 days after such determination. The notice shall announce the availability of a description of the analytical methods available to the Administrator for the detection and measurement of the pesticide chemical residue with respect to which the petition is filed or shall set forth the petitioner's statement of why such a method is not needed. The notice shall include the summary required by paragraph (2)(A)(i)(I).

(4) Actions by the Administrator

(A) In general

The Administrator shall, after giving due consideration to a petition filed under paragraph (1) and any other information available to the Administrator—

(i) issue a final regulation (which may vary from that sought by the petition) establishing, modifying, or revoking a tolerance for the pesticide chemical residue or an exemption of the pesticide chemical residue from the requirement of a tolerance (which final regulation shall be issued without further notice and without further period for public comment);

(ii) issue a proposed regulation under subsection (e) of this section, and thereafter issue a final regulation under such subsection; or

(iii) issue an order denying the petition.

(B) Priorities

The Administrator shall give priority to petitions for the establishment or modification of a tolerance or exemption for a pesticide chemical residue that appears to pose a significantly lower risk to human health from dietary exposure than pesticide chemical residues that have tolerances in effect for the same or similar uses.

(C) Expedited review of certain petitions

(i) Date certain for review

If a person files a complete petition with the Administrator proposing the issuance of a regulation establishing a tolerance or exemption for a pesticide chemical residue that presents a lower risk to human health than a pesticide chemical residue for which a tolerance has been left in effect or modified under subsection (b)(2)(B) of this section, the Administrator shall complete action on such petition under this paragraph within 1 year.

(ii) Required determinations

If the Administrator issues a final regulation establishing a tolerance or exemption for a safer pesticide chemical residue under clause (i), the Administrator shall, not later than 180 days after the date on which the regulation is issued, determine whether a condition described in subclause (I) or (II) of subsection (b)(2)(B)(iii) of this section continues to exist with respect to a tolerance that has been left in effect or modified under subsection (b)(2)(B) of this section. If such condition does not continue to exist, the Administrator shall, not later than 180 days after the date on which the determination under the preceding sentence is made, issue a regulation under subsection (e)(1) of this section to modify or revoke the tolerance.

(e) Action on Administrator's own initiative

(1) General rule

The Administrator may issue a regulation—

(A) establishing, modifying, suspending under subsection (*l*)(3) of this section, or revoking a tolerance for a pesticide chemical or a pesticide chemical residue;

(B) establishing, modifying, suspending under subsection (*l*)(3) of this section, or revoking an exemption of a pesticide chemical residue from the requirement of a tolerance; or

(C) establishing general procedures and requirements to implement this section.

(2) Notice

Before issuing a final regulation under paragraph (1), the Administrator shall issue a notice of proposed rulemaking and provide a period of not less than 60 days for public comment on the proposed regulation, except that a shorter period for comment may be provided if the Administrator for good cause finds that it would be in the public interest to do so and states the reasons for the finding in the notice of proposed rulemaking.

(f) Special data requirements

(1) Requiring submission of additional data

If the Administrator determines that additional data or information are reasonably required to support the continuation of a tolerance or exemption that is in effect under this section for a pesticide chemical residue on a food, the Administrator shall—

(A) issue a notice requiring the person holding the pesticide registrations associated with such tolerance or exemption to submit the data or information under section 3(c)(2)(B) of the Federal Insecticide, Fungicide, and Rodenticide Act [7 U.S.C. 136a(c)(2)(B)];

(B) issue a rule requiring that testing be conducted on a substance or mixture under section 4 of the Toxic Substances Control Act [15 U.S.C. 2603]; or

(C) publish in the Federal Register, after first providing notice and an opportunity for comment of not less than 60 days' duration, an order—

(i) requiring the submission to the Administrator by one or more interested persons of a notice identifying the person or persons who will submit the required data and information;

(ii) describing the type of data and information required to be submitted to the Administrator and stating why the data and information could not be obtained under the authority of section 3(c)(2)(B) of the Federal Insecticide, Fungicide, and Rodenticide Act [7 U.S.C. 136a(c)(2)(B)] or section 4 of the Toxic Substances Control Act [15 U.S.C. 2603];

(iii) describing the reports of the Administrator required to be prepared during and after the collection of the data and information;

(iv) requiring the submission to the Administrator of the data, information, and reports referred to in clauses (ii) and (iii); and

(v) establishing dates by which the submissions described in clauses (i) and (iv) must be made.

The Administrator may under subparagraph (C) revise any such order to correct an error. The Administrator may under this paragraph require data or information pertaining to whether the pesticide chemical may have an effect in humans that is similar to an effect produced by a naturally occurring estrogen or other endocrine effects.

(2) Noncompliance

If a submission required by a notice issued in accordance with paragraph (1)(A), a rule issued under paragraph (1)(B), or an order issued under paragraph (1)(C) is not made by the time specified in such notice, rule, or order, the Administrator may by order published in the Federal Register modify or revoke the tolerance or exemption in question. In any review of such an order under subsection (g)(2) of this section, the only material issue shall be whether a submission required under paragraph (1) was not made by the time specified.

(g) Effective date, objections, hearings, and administrative review

(1) Effective date

A regulation or order issued under subsection (d)(4), (e)(1), or (f)(2) of this section shall take effect upon publication unless the regulation or order specifies otherwise. The Administrator may stay the effectiveness of the regulation or order if, after issuance of such regulation or order, objections are filed with respect to such regulation or order pursuant to paragraph (2).

(2) Further proceedings

(A) Objections

Within 60 days after a regulation or order is issued under subsection (d)(4), (e)(1)(A), (e)(1)(B), (f)(2), (n)(3), or (n)(5)(C) of this section, any person may file objections thereto with the Administrator, specifying with particularity the provisions of the regulation or order deemed objectionable and stating reasonable grounds therefor. If the regulation or order was issued in response to a petition under subsection (d)(1) of this section, a copy of each objection filed by a person other than the petitioner shall be served by the Administrator on the petitioner.

(B) Hearing

An objection may include a request for a public evidentiary hearing upon the objection. The Administrator shall, upon the initiative of the Administrator or upon the request of an interested person and after due notice, hold a public evidentiary hearing if and to the extent the Administrator determines that such a public hearing is necessary to receive factual evidence relevant to material issues of fact raised by the objections. The presiding officer in such a hearing may authorize a party to obtain discovery from other persons and may upon a showing of good cause made by a party issue a subpoena to compel testimony or production of documents from any person. The presiding officer shall be governed by the Federal Rules of Civil Procedure in making any order for the protection of the witness or the content of documents produced and shall order the payment of reasonable fees and expenses as a condition to requiring testimony of the witness. On contest, such a subpoena may be enforced by a Federal district court.

(C) Final decision

As soon as practicable after receiving the arguments of the parties, the Administrator shall issue an order stating the action taken upon each such objection and setting forth any revision to the regulation or prior order that the Administrator has found to be warranted. If a hearing was held under subparagraph (B), such order and any revision to the regulation or prior order shall, with respect to questions of fact at issue in the hearing, be based only on substantial evidence of record at such hearing, and shall set forth in detail the findings of facts and the conclusions of law or policy upon which the order or regulation is based.

(h) Judicial review

(1) Petition

In a case of actual controversy as to the validity of any regulation issued under subsection (e)(1)(C) of this section, or any order issued under subsection (f)(1)(C) or (g)(2)(C) of this section, or any regulation that is the subject of such an order, any person who will be adversely affected by such order or regulation may obtain judicial review by filing in the United States Court of Appeals for the circuit wherein that person resides or has its principal place of business, or in the United States Court of Appeals for the District of Columbia Circuit, within 60 days after publication of such order or regulation, a petition praying that the order or regulation be set aside in whole or in part.

(2) Record and jurisdiction

A copy of the petition under paragraph (1) shall be forthwith transmitted by the clerk of the court to the Administrator, or any officer designated by the Administrator for that purpose, and thereupon the Administrator shall file in the court the record of the proceedings on which the Administrator based the order or regulation, as provided in section 2112 of title 28. Upon the filing of such a petition, the court shall have exclusive jurisdiction to affirm or set aside the order or regulation complained of in whole or in part. As to orders issued following a public evidentiary hearing, the findings of the Administrator with respect to questions of fact shall be sustained only if supported by substantial evidence when considered on the record as a whole.

(3) Additional evidence

If a party applies to the court for leave to adduce additional evidence and shows to the satisfaction of the court that the additional evidence is material and that there were reasonable grounds for the failure to adduce the evidence in the proceeding before the Administrator, the court may order that the additional evidence (and evidence in rebuttal thereof) shall be taken before the Administrator in the manner and upon the terms and conditions the court deems proper. The Administrator may modify prior findings as to the facts by reason of the additional evidence so taken and may modify the order or regulation accordingly. The Administrator shall file with the court any such modified finding, order, or regulation.

(4) Final judgment; Supreme Court review

The judgment of the court affirming or setting aside, in whole or in part, any regulation or any order and any regulation which is the subject of such an order shall be final, subject to review by the Supreme Court of the United States as provided in section 1254 of title 28. The commencement of proceedings under this subsection shall not, unless specifically ordered by the court to the contrary, operate as a stay of a regulation or order.

(5) Application

Any issue as to which review is or was obtainable under this subsection shall not be the subject of judicial review under any other provision of law.

(i) Confidentiality and use of data

(1) General rule

Data and information that are or have been submitted to the Administrator under this section or section 348 of this title in support of a tolerance or an exemption from a tolerance shall be entitled to confidential treatment for reasons of business confidentiality and to exclusive use and data compensation to the same extent provided by sections 3 and 10 of the Federal Insecticide, Fungicide, and Rodenticide Act [7 U.S.C. 136a, 136h].

(2) Exceptions

(A) In general

Data and information that are entitled to confidential treatment under paragraph (1) may be disclosed, under such security requirements as the Administrator may provide by regulation, to—

(i) employees of the United States authorized by the Administrator to examine such data and information in the carrying out of their official duties under this chapter or other Federal statutes intended to protect the public health; or

(ii) contractors with the United States authorized by the Administrator to examine such data and information in the carrying out of contracts under this chapter or such statutes.

(B) Congress

This subsection does not authorize the withholding of data or information from either House of Congress or from, to the extent of matter within its jurisdiction, any committee or subcommittee of such committee or any joint committee of Congress or any subcommittee of such joint committee.

(3) Summaries

Notwithstanding any provision of this subsection or other law, the Administrator may publish the informative summary required by subsection (d)(2)(A)(i) of this section and may, in issuing a proposed or final regulation or order under this section, publish an informative summary of the data relating to the regulation or order.

(j) Status of previously issued regulations

(1) Regulations under section 346

Regulations affecting pesticide chemical residues in or on raw agricultural commodities promulgated, in accordance with section 371(e) of this title, under the authority of section 346(a)[1] of this title upon the basis of public hearings instituted before January 1, 1953, shall be deemed to be regulations issued under this section and shall be subject to modification or revocation under subsections (d) and (e) of this section, and shall be subject to review under subsection (q) of this section.

(2) Regulations under section 348

Regulations that established tolerances for substances that are pesticide chemical residues in or on processed food, or that otherwise stated the conditions under which such pesticide chemicals could be safely used, and that were issued under section 348 of this title on or before August 3, 1996, shall be deemed to be regulations issued under this section and shall be subject to modification or revocation under subsection (d) or (e) of this section, and shall be subject to review under subsection (q) of this section.

(3) Regulations under section 346a

Regulations that established tolerances or exemptions under this section that were issued on or before August 3, 1996, shall remain in effect unless modified or revoked under subsection (d) or (e) of this section, and shall be subject to review under subsection (q) of this section.

(4) Certain substances

With respect to a substance that is not included in the definition of the term "pesticide chemical" under section 321(q)(1) of this title but was so included on the day before October 30, 1998, the following applies as of October 30, 1998:

(A) Notwithstanding paragraph (2), any regulation applying to the use of the substance that was in effect on the day before October 30, 1998, and was on such day deemed in such paragraph to have been issued under this section, shall be considered to have been issued under section 348 of this title.

(B) Notwithstanding paragraph (3), any regulation applying to the use of the substance that was in effect on such day and was issued under this section (including any such regulation issued before August 3, 1996) is deemed to have been issued under section 348 of this title.

(k) Transitional provision

If, on the day before August 3, 1996, a substance that is a pesticide chemical was, with respect to a particular pesticidal use of the substance and any resulting pesticide chemical residue in or on a particular food—

(1) regarded by the Administrator or the Secretary as generally recognized as safe for use within the meaning of the provisions of subsection (a) of this section or section 321(s) of this title as then in effect; or

(2) regarded by the Secretary as a substance described by section 321(s)(4) of this title;

such a pesticide chemical residue shall be regarded as exempt from the requirement for a tolerance, as of August 3, 1996. The Administrator shall by regulation indicate which substances are described by this subsection. Any exemption under this subsection may be modified or revoked as if it had been issued under subsection (c) of this section.

(*l*) Harmonization with action under other laws

(1) Coordination with FIFRA

To the extent practicable and consistent with the review deadlines in subsection (q) of this section, in issuing a final rule under this subsection that suspends or revokes a tolerance or exemption for a pesticide chemical residue in or on food, the Administrator shall coordinate such action with any related necessary action under the Federal Insecticide, Fungicide, and Rodenticide Act [7 U.S.C. 136 et seq.].

(2) Revocation of tolerance or exemption following cancellation of associated registrations

If the Administrator, acting under the Federal Insecticide, Fungicide, and Rodenticide Act, cancels the registration of each pesticide that contains a particular pesticide chemical and that is labeled for use on a particular food, or requires that the registration of each such pesticide be modified to prohibit its use in connection with the production, storage, or transportation of such food, due in whole or in part to dietary risks to humans posed by residues of that pesticide chemical on that food, the Administrator shall revoke any tolerance or exemption that allows the presence of the pesticide chemical, or any pesticide chemical residue that results from its use, in or on that food. Subsection (e) of this section shall apply to actions taken under this paragraph. A revocation under this paragraph shall become effective not later than 180 days after—

(A) the date by which each such cancellation of a registration has become effective; or

(B) the date on which the use of the canceled pesticide becomes unlawful under the terms of the cancellation, whichever is later.

[1] See References in Text note below.

(3) Suspension of tolerance or exemption following suspension of associated registrations

(A) Suspension

If the Administrator, acting under the Federal Insecticide, Fungicide, and Rodenticide Act, suspends the use of each registered pesticide that contains a particular pesticide chemical and that is labeled for use on a particular food, due in whole or in part to dietary risks to humans posed by residues of that pesticide chemical on that food, the Administrator shall suspend any tolerance or exemption that allows the presence of the pesticide chemical, or any pesticide chemical residue that results from its use, in or on that food. Subsection (e) of this section shall apply to actions taken under this paragraph. A suspension under this paragraph shall become effective not later than 60 days after the date by which each such suspension of use has become effective.

(B) Effect of suspension

The suspension of a tolerance or exemption under subparagraph (A) shall be effective as long as the use of each associated registration of a pesticide is suspended under the Federal Insecticide, Fungicide, and Rodenticide Act. While a suspension of a tolerance or exemption is effective the tolerance or exemption shall not be considered to be in effect. If the suspension of use of the pesticide under that Act is terminated, leaving the registration of the pesticide for such use in effect under that Act, the Administrator shall rescind any associated suspension of tolerance or exemption.

(4) Tolerances for unavoidable residues

In connection with action taken under paragraph (2) or (3), or with respect to pesticides whose registrations were suspended or canceled prior to August 3, 1996, under the Federal Insecticide, Fungicide, and Rodenticide Act, if the Administrator determines that a residue of the canceled or suspended pesticide chemical will unavoidably persist in the environment and thereby be present in or on a food, the Administrator may establish a tolerance for the pesticide chemical residue. In establishing such a tolerance, the Administrator shall take into account both the factors set forth in subsection (b)(2) of this section and the unavoidability of the residue. Subsection (e) of this section shall apply to the establishment of such tolerance. The Administrator shall review any such tolerance periodically and modify it as necessary so that it allows no greater level of the pesticide chemical residue than is unavoidable.

(5) Pesticide residues resulting from lawful application of pesticide

Notwithstanding any other provision of this chapter, if a tolerance or exemption for a pesticide chemical residue in or on a food has been revoked, suspended, or modified under this section, an article of that food shall not be deemed unsafe solely because of the presence of such pesticide chemical residue in or on such food if it is shown to the satisfaction of the Secretary that—

(A) the residue is present as the result of an application or use of a pesticide at a time and in a manner that was lawful under the Federal Insecticide, Fungicide, and Rodenticide Act; and

(B) the residue does not exceed a level that was authorized at the time of that application or use to be present on the food under a tolerance, exemption, food additive regulation, or other sanction then in effect under this chapter;

unless, in the case of any tolerance or exemption revoked, suspended, or modified under this subsection or subsection (d) or (e) of this section, the Administrator has issued a determination that consumption of the legally treated food during the period of its likely availability in commerce will pose an unreasonable dietary risk.

(6) Tolerance for use of pesticides under an emergency exemption

If the Administrator grants an exemption under section 18 of the Federal Insecticide, Fungicide, and Rodenticide Act (7 U.S.C. 136p) for a pesticide chemical, the Administrator shall establish a tolerance or exemption from the requirement for a tolerance for the pesticide chemical residue. Such a tolerance or exemption from a tolerance shall have an expiration date. The Administrator may establish such a tolerance or exemption without providing notice or a period for comment on the tolerance or exemption. The Administrator shall promulgate regulations within 365 days after August 3, 1996, governing the establishment of tolerances and exemptions under this paragraph. Such regulations shall be consistent with the safety standard under subsections (b)(2) and (c)(2) of this section and with section 18 of the Federal Insecticide, Fungicide, and Rodenticide Act.

(m) Fees

(1) Amount

The Administrator shall by regulation require the payment of such fees as will in the aggregate, in the judgment of the Administrator, be sufficient over a reasonable term to provide, equip, and maintain an adequate service for the performance of the Administrator's functions under this section. Under the regulations, the performance of the Administrator's services or other functions under this section, including—

(A) the acceptance for filing of a petition submitted under subsection (d) of this section;

(B) establishing, modifying, leaving in effect, or revoking a tolerance or establishing, modifying, leaving in effect, or revoking an exemption from the requirement for a tolerance under this section;

(C) the acceptance for filing of objections under subsection (g) of this section; or

(D) the certification and filing in court of a transcript of the proceedings and the record under subsection (h) of this section;

may be conditioned upon the payment of such fees. The regulations may further provide for waiver or refund of fees in whole or in part when in the judgment of the Administrator such a waiver or refund is equitable and not contrary to the purposes of this subsection.

(2) Deposit

All fees collected under paragraph (1) shall be deposited in the Reregistration and Expedited Processing Fund created by section 4(k) of the Federal Insecticide, Fungicide, and Rodenticide Act [7 U.S.C. 136a–1(k)]. Such fees shall be available to the Administrator, without fiscal year limitation, for the performance of the Administrator's services or functions as specified in paragraph (1).

(3) Prohibition

During the period beginning on October 1, 2007, and ending on September 30, 2012, the Administrator shall not collect any tolerance fees under paragraph (1).

(n) National uniformity of tolerances

(1) "Qualifying pesticide chemical residue" defined

For purposes of this subsection, the term "qualifying pesticide chemical residue" means a pesticide chemical residue resulting from the use, in production, processing, or storage of a food, of a pesticide chemical that is an active ingredient and that—

(A) was first approved for such use in a registration of a pesticide issued under section 3(c)(5) of the Federal Insecticide, Fungicide, and Rodenticide Act [7 U.S.C. 136a(c)(5)] on or after April 25, 1985, on the basis of data determined by the Administrator to meet all applicable requirements for data prescribed by regulations in effect under that Act [7 U.S.C. 136 et seq.] on April 25, 1985; or

(B) was approved for such use in a reregistration eligibility determination issued under section 4(g) of that Act [7 U.S.C. 136a–1(g)] on or after August 3, 1996.

(2) "Qualifying Federal determination" defined

For purposes of this subsection, the term "qualifying Federal determination" means a tolerance or exemption from the requirement for a tolerance for a qualifying pesticide chemical residue that—

(A) is issued under this section after August 3, 1996, and determined by the Administrator to meet the standard under subsection (b)(2)(A) (in the case of a tolerance) or (c)(2) (in the case of an exemption) of this section; or

(B)(i) pursuant to subsection (j) of this section is remaining in effect or is deemed to have been issued under this section, or is regarded under subsection (k) of this section as exempt from the requirement for a tolerance; and

(ii) is determined by the Administrator to meet the standard under subsection (b)(2)(A) (in the case of a tolerance) or (c)(2) (in the case of an exemption) of this section.

(3) Limitation

The Administrator may make the determination described in paragraph (2)(B)(ii) only by issuing a rule in accordance with the procedure set forth in subsection (d) or (e) of this section and only if the Administrator issues a proposed rule and allows a period of not less than 30 days for comment on the proposed rule. Any such rule shall be reviewable in accordance with subsections (g) and (h) of this section.

(4) State authority

Except as provided in paragraphs (5), (6), and (8) no State or political subdivision may establish or enforce any regulatory limit on a qualifying pesticide chemical residue in or on any food if a qualifying Federal determination applies to the presence of such pesticide chemical residue in or on such food, unless such State regulatory limit is identical to such qualifying Federal determination. A State or political subdivision shall be deemed to establish or enforce a regulatory limit on a pesticide chemical residue in or on a food if it purports to prohibit or penalize the production, processing, shipping, or other handling of a food because it contains a pesticide residue (in excess of a prescribed limit).

(5) Petition procedure

(A) In general

Any State may petition the Administrator for authorization to establish in such State a regulatory limit on a qualifying pesticide chemical residue in or on any food that is not identical to the qualifying Federal determination applicable to such qualifying pesticide chemical residue.

(B) Petition requirements

Any petition under subparagraph (A) shall—

(i) satisfy any requirements prescribed, by rule, by the Administrator; and

(ii) be supported by scientific data about the pesticide chemical residue that is the subject of the petition or about chemically related pesticide chemical residues, data on the consumption within such State of food bearing the pesticide chemical residue, and data on exposure of humans within such State to the pesticide chemical residue.

(C) Authorization

The Administrator may, by order, grant the authorization described in subparagraph (A) if the Administrator determines that the proposed State regulatory limit—

(i) is justified by compelling local conditions; and

(ii) would not cause any food to be a violation of Federal law.

(D) Treatment

In lieu of any action authorized under subparagraph (C), the Administrator may treat a petition under this paragraph as a petition under subsection (d) of this section to modify or revoke a tolerance or an exemption. If the Administrator determines to treat a petition under this paragraph as a petition under subsection (d) of this section, the Administrator shall thereafter act on the petition pursuant to subsection (d) of this section.

(E) Review

Any order of the Administrator granting or denying the authorization described in subparagraph (A) shall be subject to review in the manner described in subsections (g) and (h) of this section.

(6) Urgent petition procedure

Any State petition to the Administrator pursuant to paragraph (5) that demonstrates that consumption of a food containing such pesticide residue level during the period of the food's likely availability in the State will pose a significant public health threat from acute exposure shall be considered an urgent petition. If an order by the Administrator to grant or deny the requested authorization in an urgent petition is not made within 30 days of receipt of the petition, the petitioning State may establish and enforce a temporary regulatory limit on a qualifying pesticide chemical residue in or on the food. The temporary regulatory limit shall be validated or terminated by the Administrator's final order on the petition.

(7) Residues from lawful application

No State or political subdivision may enforce any regulatory limit on the level of a pesticide chemical residue that may appear in or on any food if, at the time of the application of the pesticide that resulted in such residue, the sale of such food with such residue level was lawful under this section and under the law of such State, unless the State demonstrates that consumption of the food containing such pesticide residue level during the period of the food's likely availability in the State will pose an unreasonable dietary risk to the health of persons within such State.

(8) Savings

Nothing in this chapter preempts the authority of any State or political subdivision to require that a food containing a pesticide chemical residue bear or be the subject of a warning or other statement relating to the presence of the pesticide chemical residue in or on such food.

(*o*) Consumer right to know

Not later than 2 years after August 3, 1996, and annually thereafter, the Administrator shall, in consultation with the Secretary of Agriculture and the Secretary of Health and Human Services, publish in a format understandable to a lay person, and distribute to large retail grocers for public display (in a manner determined by the grocer), the following information, at a minimum:

(1) A discussion of the risks and benefits of pesticide chemical residues in or on food purchased by consumers.

(2) A listing of actions taken under subparagraph (B) of subsection (b)(2) of this section that may result in pesticide chemical residues in or on food that present a yearly or lifetime risk above the risk allowed under subparagraph (A) of such subsection, and the food on which the pesticide chemicals producing the residues are used.

(3) Recommendations to consumers for reducing dietary exposure to pesticide chemical residues in a manner consistent with maintaining a healthy diet, including a list of food that may reasonably substitute for food listed under paragraph (2).

Nothing in this subsection shall prevent retail grocers from providing additional information.

(p) Estrogenic substances screening program

(1) Development

Not later than 2 years after August 3, 1996, the Administrator shall in consultation with the Secretary of Health and Human Services develop a screening program, using appropriate validated test systems and other scientifically relevant information, to determine whether certain substances may have an effect in humans that is similar to an effect produced by a naturally occurring estrogen, or such other endocrine effect as the Administrator may designate.

(2) Implementation

Not later than 3 years after August 3, 1996, after obtaining public comment and review of the screening program described in paragraph (1) by the scientific advisory panel established under section 25(d) of the Federal Insecticide, Fungicide, and Rodenticide Act [7 U.S.C. 136w(d)] or the science advisory board established by section 4365[2] of title 42, the Administrator shall implement the program.

(3) Substances

In carrying out the screening program described in paragraph (1), the Administrator—

(A) shall provide for the testing of all pesticide chemicals; and

(B) may provide for the testing of any other substance that may have an effect that is cumulative to an effect of a pesticide chemical if the Administrator determines that a substantial population may be exposed to such substance.

(4) Exemption

Notwithstanding paragraph (3), the Administrator may, by order, exempt from the requirements of this section a biologic substance or other substance if the Administrator determines that the substance is anticipated not to produce any effect in humans similar to an effect produced by a naturally occurring estrogen.

(5) Collection of information

(A) In general

The Administrator shall issue an order to a registrant of a substance for which testing is required under this subsection, or to a person who manufactures or imports a substance for which testing is required under this subsection, to conduct testing in accordance with the screening program described in paragraph (1), and submit information obtained from the testing to the Administrator, within a reasonable time period that the Administrator determines is sufficient for the generation of the information.

[2] See References in Text note below.

(B) Procedures

To the extent practicable the Administrator shall minimize duplicative testing of the same substance for the same endocrine effect, develop, as appropriate, procedures for fair and equitable sharing of test costs, and develop, as necessary, procedures for handling of confidential business information.

(C) Failure of registrants to submit information

(i) Suspension

If a registrant of a substance referred to in paragraph (3)(A) fails to comply with an order under subparagraph (A) of this paragraph, the Administrator shall issue a notice of intent to suspend the sale or distribution of the substance by the registrant. Any suspension proposed under this paragraph shall become final at the end of the 30-day period beginning on the date that the registrant receives the notice of intent to suspend, unless during that period a person adversely affected by the notice requests a hearing or the Administrator determines that the registrant has complied fully with this paragraph.

(ii) Hearing

If a person requests a hearing under clause (i), the hearing shall be conducted in accordance with section 554 of title 5. The only matter for resolution at the hearing shall be whether the registrant has failed to comply with an order under subparagraph (A) of this paragraph. A decision by the Administrator after completion of a hearing shall be considered to be a final agency action.

(iii) Termination of suspensions

The Administrator shall terminate a suspension under this subparagraph issued with respect to a registrant if the Administrator determines that the registrant has complied fully with this paragraph.

(D) Noncompliance by other persons

Any person (other than a registrant) who fails to comply with an order under subparagraph (A) shall be liable for the same penalties and sanctions as are provided under section 16 of the Toxic Substances Control Act [15 U.S.C. 2615] in the case of a violation referred to in that section. Such penalties and sanctions shall be assessed and imposed in the same manner as provided in such section 16.

(6) Agency action

In the case of any substance that is found, as a result of testing and evaluation under this section, to have an endocrine effect on humans, the Administrator shall, as appropriate, take action under such statutory authority as is available to the Administrator, including consideration under other sections of this chapter, as is necessary to ensure the protection of public health.

(7) Report to Congress

Not later than 4 years after August 3, 1996, the Administrator shall prepare and submit to Congress a report containing—

(A) the findings of the Administrator resulting from the screening program described in paragraph (1);

(B) recommendations for further testing needed to evaluate the impact on human health of the substances tested under the screening program; and

(C) recommendations for any further actions (including any action described in paragraph (6)) that the Administrator determines are appropriate based on the findings.

(q) Schedule for review

(1) In general

The Administrator shall review tolerances and exemptions for pesticide chemical residues in effect on the day before August 3, 1996, as expeditiously as practicable, assuring that—

(A) 33 percent of such tolerances and exemptions are reviewed within 3 years of August 3, 1996;

(B) 66 percent of such tolerances and exemptions are reviewed within 6 years of August 3, 1996; and

(C) 100 percent of such tolerances and exemptions are reviewed within 10 years of August 3, 1996.

In conducting a review of a tolerance or exemption, the Administrator shall determine whether the tolerance or exemption meets the requirements of subsections[3] (b)(2) or (c)(2) of this section and shall, by the deadline for the review of the tolerance or exemption, issue a regulation under subsection (d)(4) or (e)(1) of this section to modify or revoke the tolerance or exemption if the tolerance or exemption does not meet such requirements.

(2) Priorities

In determining priorities for reviewing tolerances and exemptions under paragraph (1), the Administrator shall give priority to the review of the tolerances or exemptions that appear to pose the greatest risk to public health.

(3) Publication of schedule

Not later than 12 months after August 3, 1996, the Administrator shall publish a schedule for review of tolerances and exemptions established prior to August 3, 1996. The determination of priorities for the review of tolerances and exemptions pursuant to this subsection is not a rulemaking and shall not be subject to judicial review, except that failure to take final action pursuant to the schedule established by this paragraph shall be subject to judicial review.

(r) Temporary tolerance or exemption

The Administrator may, upon the request of any person who has obtained an experimental permit for a pesticide chemical under the Federal Insecticide, Fungicide, and Rodenticide Act [7 U.S.C. 136 et seq.] or upon the Administrator's

[3] So in original. Probably should be "subsection".

own initiative, establish a temporary tolerance or exemption for the pesticide chemical residue for the uses covered by the permit. Subsections (b)(2), (c)(2), (d), and (e) of this section shall apply to actions taken under this subsection.

(s) Savings clause

Nothing in this section shall be construed to amend or modify the provisions of the Toxic Substances Control Act [15 U.S.C. 2601 et seq.] or the Federal Insecticide, Fungicide, and Rodenticide Act [7 U.S.C. 136 et seq.].

(June 25, 1938, ch. 675, § 408, as added July 22, 1954, ch. 559, § 3, 68 Stat. 511; amended Pub. L. 85–791, § 20, Aug. 28, 1958, 72 Stat. 947; Pub. L. 91–515, title VI, § 601(d)(1), Oct. 30, 1970, 84 Stat. 1311; Pub. L. 92–157, title III, § 303(a), Nov. 18, 1971, 85 Stat. 464; Pub. L. 92–516, § 3(3), Oct. 21, 1972, 86 Stat. 998; Pub. L. 98–620, title IV, § 402(25)(A), Nov. 8, 1984, 98 Stat. 3359; Pub. L. 102–300, § 6(b)(1), June 16, 1992, 106 Stat. 240; Pub. L. 102–571, title I, § 107(7), Oct. 29, 1992, 106 Stat. 4499; Pub. L. 103–80, § 3(k), Aug. 13, 1993, 107 Stat. 776; Pub. L. 104–170, title IV, § 405, Aug. 3, 1996, 110 Stat. 1514; Pub. L. 105–324, § 2(b), Oct. 30, 1998, 112 Stat. 3036; Pub. L. 110–94, § 4(d)(2), Oct. 9, 2007, 121 Stat. 1002.)

REFERENCES IN TEXT

The Federal Rules of Civil Procedure, referred to in subsec. (g)(2)(B), are set out in the Appendix to Title 28, Judiciary and Judicial Procedure.

Section 346 of this title, referred to in subsec. (j)(1), originally consisted of subsecs. (a) and (b). Subsec. (a) was redesignated as the entire section 346 and subsec. (b) was repealed by Pub. L. 86–618, title I, § 103(a)(1), 74 Stat. 398.

The Federal Insecticide, Fungicide, and Rodenticide Act, referred to in subsecs. (*l*), (n)(1)(A), (r), and (s), is act June 25, 1947, ch. 125, as amended generally by Pub. L. 92–516, Oct. 21, 1972, 86 Stat. 973, which is classified generally to subchapter II (§ 136 et seq.) of chapter 6 of Title 7, Agriculture. For complete classification of this Act to the Code, see Short Title note set out under section 136 of Title 7 and Tables.

Section 4365 of title 42, referred to in subsec. (p)(2), was in the original "section 8 of the Environmental Research, Development, and Demonstration Act of 1978", and was translated as meaning section 8 of the Environmental Research, Development, and Demonstration Authorization Act of 1978, to reflect the probable intent of Congress.

The Toxic Substances Control Act, referred to in subsec. (s), is Pub. L. 94–469, Oct. 11, 1976, 90 Stat. 2003, as amended, which is classified generally to chapter 53 (§ 2601 et seq.) of Title 15, Commerce and Trade. For complete classification of this Act to the Code, see Short Title note set out under section 2601 of Title 15 and Tables.

CODIFICATION

August 3, 1996, referred to in subsecs. (k), (n)(1)(B), (2)(A), and (p)(1), (2), (7), was in the original references to the date of enactment of this subsection and the date of enactment of this section, which was translated as meaning the date of enactment of Pub. L. 104–170, which amended this section generally, to reflect the probable intent of Congress.

AMENDMENTS

2007—Subsec. (m)(3). Pub. L. 110–94 added par. (3).

1998—Subsec. (j)(4). Pub. L. 105–324 added par. (4).

1996—Pub. L. 104–170 amended section generally, substituting, in subsec. (a), provisions relating to requirement for tolerance or exemption for provisions relating to conditions for safety; in subsec. (b), provisions relating to authority and standard for tolerance for provisions relating to establishment of tolerances; in subsec. (c), provisions relating to authority and standard for exemptions for provisions relating to exemptions; in subsec. (d), provisions relating to petition for tolerance or exemption for provisions relating to regulations pursuant to petition, publication of notice, time for issuance, referral to advisory committees, effective date, and hearings; in subsec. (e), provisions relating to action on Administrator's own initiative for provisions relating to regulations pursuant to Administrator's proposals; in subsec. (f), provisions relating to special data requirements for provisions relating to data submitted as confidential; in subsec. (g), provisions relating to effective date, objections, hearings, and administrative review for provisions relating to advisory committees and their appointment, composition, compensation, and clerical assistance; in subsec. (h), provisions relating to judicial review for provisions relating to right of consultation; in subsec. (i), provisions relating to confidentiality and use of data for provisions relating to judicial review; in subsec. (j), provisions relating to status of previously issued regulations for provisions relating to temporary tolerances; in subsec. (k), provisions relating to transitions for provisions relating to regulations based on public hearings before January 1, 1953; in subsec. (*l*), provisions relating to harmonization with action under other laws for provisions relating to pesticides under Federal Insecticide, Fungicide, and Rodenticide Act, functions of Administrator of Environmental Protection Agency, certifications, hearings, time limitations, opinions, and regulations; in subsec. (m), provisions relating to fees for provisions relating to amendment of regulations; in subsec. (n), provisions relating to national uniformity of tolerances for provisions relating to guaranties; in subsec. (*o*), provisions relating to consumer right to know for provisions relating to payment of fees, services or functions conditioned on payment, and waiver or refund of fees; and adding subsecs. (p) to (s).

1993—Pub. L. 103–80, § 3(k)(6), substituted "Administrator" for "Secretary" wherever appearing except when followed by "of Agriculture".

Subsec. (a)(1). Pub. L. 103–80, § 3(k)(1), substituted "Administrator of the Environmental Protection Agency (hereinafter in this section referred to as the 'Administrator')" for "Secretary of Health and Human Services".

Subsec. (d)(5). Pub. L. 103–80, § 3(k)(2), substituted "section 556(c) of title 5" for "section 7(c) of the Administrative Procedure Act (5 U.S.C., sec. 1006(c))".

Subsec. (*l*). Pub. L. 103–80, § 3(k)(3), substituted "In the event" for "It the event" before "a hearing is requested".

Subsec. (n). Pub. L. 103–80, § 3(k)(4), made technical amendment to reference to section 333(c) of this title to reflect amendment of corresponding provision of original act.

Subsec. (*o*). Pub. L. 103–80, § 3(k)(5), which directed the substitution of "Administrator" for "Secretary of Health and Human Services" wherever appearing in the original text, was executed by making the substitution in the first sentence before "shall by regulation require", the only place "Secretary of Health and Human Services" appeared in the original text.

1992—Subsecs. (a), (d), (h), (i), (*l*), (m), (*o*). Pub. L. 102–300 substituted "Health and Human Services" for "Health, Education, and Welfare" wherever appearing in the original statutory text.

Subsec. (g). Pub. L. 102–571 substituted "379e" for "376".

1984—Subsec. (i)(5). Pub. L. 98–620 struck out provision that required the court to advance on the docket and expedite the disposition of all causes filed therein pursuant to this section.

1972—Subsecs. (d)(1), (e), (*l*). Pub. L. 92–516 substituted references to pesticide for references to economic poison wherever appearing therein.

1971—Subsec. (g). Pub. L. 92–157 struck out ", which the Secretary shall by rules and regulations prescribe," after "as compensation for their services a reasonable per diem" prior to amendment in 1970, by Pub. L. 91–515, which overlooked such language when amending subsec. (g) as provided in 1970 Amendment note.

1970—Subsec. (g). Pub. L. 91–515 substituted provisions authorizing members of an advisory committee to receive compensation and travel expenses in accordance with section 376(b)(5)(D) of this title, for provisions authorizing such members to receive as compensation a reasonable per diem for time actually spent on committee work, and necessary traveling and subsistence expenses while serving away from their places of residence.

1958—Subsec. (i)(2). Pub. L. 85–791, § 20(a), in first sentence, substituted "transmitted by the clerk of the court to the Secretary, or" for "served upon the Secretary, or upon", substituted "file in the court the record of the proceedings" for "certify and file in the court a transcript of the proceedings and the record", and inserted "as provided in section 2112 of title 28", and which, in second sentence, substituted "the filing of such petition" for "such filing".

Subsec. (i)(3). Pub. L. 85–791, § 20(b), in first sentence, substituted "transmitted by the clerk of the court to the Secretary of Agriculture, or" for "served upon the Secretary of Agriculture, or upon", substituted "file in the court the record of the proceedings" for "certify and file in the court a transcript of the proceedings and the record", and inserted "as provided in section 2112 of title 28", and, in second sentence, substituted "the filing of such petition" for "such filing".

EFFECTIVE DATE OF 2007 AMENDMENT

Amendment by Pub. L. 110–94 effective Oct. 1, 2007, see section 6 of Pub. L. 110–94, set out as a note under section 136a of Title 7, Agriculture.

EFFECTIVE DATE OF 1984 AMENDMENT

Amendment by Pub. L. 98–620 not applicable to cases pending on Nov. 8, 1984, see section 403 of Pub. L. 98–620, set out as an Effective Date note under section 1657 of Title 28, Judiciary and Judicial Procedure.

EFFECTIVE DATE OF 1972 AMENDMENT

Amendment by Pub. L. 92–516 effective at close of Oct. 21, 1972, except if regulations are necessary for implementation of any provision that becomes effective on Oct. 21, 1972, and continuation in effect of subchapter I of chapter 6 of Title 7, Agriculture, and regulations thereunder, relating to control of economic poisons, as in existence prior to Oct. 21, 1972, until superseded by provisions of Pub. L. 92–516 and regulations thereunder, see section 4 of Pub. L. 92–516, set out as an Effective Date note under section 136 of Title 7.

TOLERANCE FEES

Pub. L. 108–199, div. G, title V, § 501(d)(2), Jan. 23, 2004, 118 Stat. 422, provided that: "Notwithstanding section 408(m)(1) of the Federal Food, Drug, and Cosmetic Act (21 U.S.C. 346a(m)(1)), during the period beginning on October 1, 2003, and ending on September 30, 2008, the Administrator of the Environmental Protection Agency shall not collect any tolerance fees under that section."

DATA COLLECTION ACTIVITIES TO ASSURE HEALTH OF INFANTS AND CHILDREN

Section 301 of Pub. L. 104–170 provided that:

"(a) IN GENERAL.—The Secretary of Agriculture, in consultation with the Administrator of the Environmental Protection Agency and the Secretary of Health and Human Services, shall coordinate the development and implementation of survey procedures to ensure that adequate data on food consumption patterns of infants and children are collected.

"(b) PROCEDURES.—To the extent practicable, the procedures referred to in subsection (a) shall include the collection of data on food consumption patterns of a statistically valid sample of infants and children.

"(c) RESIDUE DATA COLLECTION.—The Secretary of Agriculture shall ensure that the residue data collection activities conducted by the Department of Agriculture in cooperation with the Environmental Protection Agency and the Department of Health and Human Services, provide for the improved data collection of pesticide residues, including guidelines for the use of comparable analytical and standardized reporting methods, and the increased sampling of foods most likely consumed by infants and children."

§ 346b. Authorization of appropriations

There are authorized to be appropriated, out of any moneys in the Treasury not otherwise appropriated, such sums as may be necessary for the purpose and administration of sections 321(q), (r), 342(a)(2), and 346a of this title.

(July 22, 1954, ch. 559, § 4, 68 Stat. 517.)

CODIFICATION

Section was not enacted as part of the Federal Food, Drug, and Cosmetic Act which comprises this chapter.

§ 347. Intrastate sales of colored oleomargarine

(a) Law governing

Colored oleomargarine or colored margarine which is sold in the same State or Territory in which it is produced shall be subject in the same manner and to the same extent to the provisions of this chapter as if it had been introduced in interstate commerce.

(b) Labeling and packaging requirements

No person shall sell, or offer for sale, colored oleomargarine or colored margarine unless—

(1) such oleomargarine or margarine is packaged,

(2) the net weight of the contents of any package sold in a retail establishment is one pound or less,

(3) there appears on the label of the package (A) the word "oleomargarine" or "margarine" in type or lettering at least as large as any other type or lettering on such label, and (B) a full and accurate statement of all the ingredients contained in such oleomargarine or margarine, and

(4) each part of the contents of the package is contained in a wrapper which bears the word "oleomargarine" or "margarine" in type or lettering not smaller than 20-point type.

The requirements of this subsection shall be in addition to and not in lieu of any of the other requirements of this chapter.

(c) Sales in public eating places

No person shall possess in a form ready for serving colored oleomargarine or colored margarine at a public eating place unless a notice that oleomargarine or margarine is served is displayed prominently and conspicuously in such place and in such manner as to render it likely to be read and understood by the ordinary individual being served in such eating place or is printed or is otherwise set forth on the menu in type or lettering not smaller than that normally used to designate the serving of other food items. No person shall serve colored oleomargarine or colored margarine at a public eating place, whether or not any charge is made therefor, unless (1) each separate serving bears or is accompanied by labeling identifying it as oleomargarine or margarine, or (2) each separate serving thereof is triangular in shape.

(d) Exemption from labeling requirements

Colored oleomargarine or colored margarine when served with meals at a public eating place shall at the time of such service be exempt from the labeling requirements of section 343 of this title (except paragraphs (a) and (f)) if it complies with the requirements of subsection (b) of this section.

(e) Color content of oleomargarine

For the purpose of this section colored oleomargarine or colored margarine is oleomargarine or margarine having a tint or shade containing more than one and six-tenths degrees of yellow, or of yellow and red collectively, but with an excess of yellow over red, measured in terms of Lovibond tintometer scale or its equivalent.

(June 25, 1938, ch. 675, § 407, as added Mar. 16, 1950, ch. 61, § 3(c), 64 Stat. 20.)

EFFECTIVE DATE

Section 7 of act Mar. 16, 1950, provided that: "This Act [enacting this section and sections 347a and 347b of this title and amending sections 331 and 342 of this title and sections 45 and 55 of Title 15, Commerce and Trade] shall become effective on July 1, 1950."

TRANSFER OF APPROPRIATIONS

Section 5 of act Mar. 16, 1950, provided that: "So much of the unexpended balances of appropriations, allocations, or other funds (including funds available for the fiscal year ending June 30, 1950) for the use of the Bureau of Internal Revenue of the Treasury Department in the exercise of functions under the Oleomargarine Tax Act (26 U.S.C., § 2300, subchapter A) [now section 4591 et seq. of Title 26, Internal Revenue Code], as the Director of the Bureau of the Budget [now Director of the Office of Management and Budget] may determine, shall be transferred to the Federal Security Agency (Food and Drug Administration) [now the Department of Health and Human Services] for use in the enforcement of this Act [see Effective Date note above]."

§ 347a. Congressional declaration of policy regarding oleomargarine sales

The Congress finds and declares that the sale, or the serving in public eating places, of colored oleomargarine or colored margarine without clear identification as such or which is otherwise adulterated or misbranded within the meaning of this chapter depresses the market in interstate commerce for butter and for oleomargarine or margarine clearly identified and neither adulterated nor misbranded, and constitutes a burden on interstate commerce in such articles. Such burden exists, irrespective of whether such oleomargarine or margarine originates from an interstate source or from the State in which it is sold.

(Mar. 16, 1950, ch. 61, § 3(a), 64 Stat. 20.)

CODIFICATION

Section was not enacted as part of the Federal Food, Drug, and Cosmetic Act which comprises this chapter.

EFFECTIVE DATE

Section effective July 1, 1950, see section 7 of act Mar. 16, 1950, set out as a note under section 347 of this title.

§ 347b. Contravention of State laws

Nothing in this Act shall be construed as authorizing the possession, sale, or serving of colored oleomargarine or colored margarine in any State or Territory in contravention of the laws of such State or Territory.

(Mar. 16, 1950, ch. 61, § 6, 64 Stat. 22.)

REFERENCES IN TEXT

This Act, referred to in text, is act Mar. 16, 1950, ch. 61, 64 Stat. 20, which is classified to sections 331, 342, 347 to 347b of this title, and sections 45 and 55 of Title 15, Commerce and Trade. For complete classification of this Act to the Code, see Tables.

CODIFICATION

Section was not enacted as part of the Federal Food, Drug, and Cosmetic Act which comprises this chapter.

EFFECTIVE DATE

Section effective July 1, 1950, see section 7 of act Mar. 16, 1950, set out as a note under section 347 of this title.

§ 348. Food additives

(a) Unsafe food additives; exception for conformity with exemption or regulation

A food additive shall, with respect to any particular use or intended use of such additives, be deemed to be unsafe for the purposes of the application of clause (2)(C) of section 342(a) of this title, unless—

(1) it and its use or intended use conform to the terms of an exemption which is in effect pursuant to subsection (j) of this section;

(2) there is in effect, and it and its use or intended use are in conformity with, a regulation issued under this section prescribing the conditions under which such additive may be safely used; or

(3) in the case of a food additive as defined in this chapter that is a food contact substance, there is—

(A) in effect, and such substance and the use of such substance are in conformity with, a regulation issued under this section prescribing the conditions under which such additive may be safely used; or

(B) a notification submitted under subsection (h) of this section that is effective.

While such a regulation relating to a food additive, or such a notification under subsection (h)(1) of this section relating to a food additive that is a food contact substance, is in effect, and has not been revoked pursuant to subsection (i) of this section, a food shall not, by reason of bearing or containing such a food additive in accordance with the regulation or notification, be considered adulterated under section 342(a)(1) of this title.

(b) Petition for regulation prescribing conditions of safe use; contents; description of production methods and controls; samples; notice of regulation

(1) Any person may, with respect to any intended use of a food additive, file with the Secretary a petition proposing the issuance of a regulation prescribing the conditions under which such additive may be safely used.

(2) Such petition shall, in addition to any explanatory or supporting data, contain—

(A) the name and all pertinent information concerning such food additive, including, where available, its chemical identity and composition;

(B) a statement of the conditions of the proposed use of such additive, including all directions, recommendations, and suggestions proposed for the use of such additive, and including specimens of its proposed labeling;

(C) all relevant data bearing on the physical or other technical effect such additive is intended to produce, and the quantity of such additive required to produce such effect;

(D) a description of practicable methods for determining the quantity of such additive in or on food, and any substance formed in or on food, because of its use; and

(E) full reports of investigations made with respect to the safety for use of such additive, including full information as to the methods and controls used in conducting such investigations.

(3) Upon request of the Secretary, the petitioner shall furnish (or, if the petitioner is not the manufacturer of such additive, the petitioner shall have the manufacturer of such additive furnish, without disclosure to the petitioner) a full description of the methods used in, and the facilities and controls used for, the production of such additive.

(4) Upon request of the Secretary, the petitioner shall furnish samples of the food additive involved, or articles used as components thereof, and of the food in or on which the additive is proposed to be used.

(5) Notice of the regulation proposed by the petitioner shall be published in general terms by the Secretary within thirty days after filing.

(c) Approval or denial of petition; time for issuance of order; evaluation of data; factors

(1) The Secretary shall—

(A) by order establish a regulation (whether or not in accord with that proposed by the petitioner) prescribing, with respect to one or more proposed uses of the food additive involved, the conditions under which such additive may be safely used (including, but not limited to, specifications as to the particular food or classes of food in or in which such additive may be used, the maximum quantity which may be used or permitted to remain in or on such food, the manner in which such additive may be added to or used in or on such food, and any directions or other labeling or packaging requirements for such additive deemed necessary by him to assure the safety of such use), and shall notify the petitioner of such order and the reasons for such action; or

(B) by order deny the petition, and shall notify the petitioner of such order and of the reasons for such action.

(2) The order required by paragraph (1)(A) or (B) of this subsection shall be issued within ninety days after the date of filing of the petition, except that the Secretary may (prior to such ninetieth day), by written notice to the petitioner, extend such ninety-day period to such time (not more than one hundred and eighty days after the date of filing of the petition) as the Secretary deems necessary to enable him to study and investigate the petition.

(3) No such regulation shall issue if a fair evaluation of the data before the Secretary—

(A) fails to establish that the proposed use of the food additive, under the conditions of use to be specified in the regulation, will be safe: *Provided*, That no additive shall be deemed to be safe if it is found to induce cancer when ingested by man or animal, or if it is found, after tests which are appropriate for the evaluation of the safety of food additives, to induce cancer in man or animal, except that this proviso shall not apply with respect to the use of a substance as an ingredient of feed for animals which are raised for food production, if the Secretary finds (i) that, under the conditions of use and feeding specified in proposed labeling and reasonably certain to be followed in practice, such additive will not adversely affect the animals for which such feed is intended, and (ii) that no residue of the additive will be found (by methods of examination prescribed or approved by the Secretary by regulations, which regulations shall not be subject to subsections (f) and (g) of this section) in any edible portion of such animal after slaughter or in any food yielded by or derived from the living animal; or

(B) shows that the proposed use of the additive would promote deception of the consumer in violation of this chapter or would otherwise result in adulteration or in misbranding of food within the meaning of this chapter.

(4) If, in the judgment of the Secretary, based upon a fair evaluation of the data before him, a tolerance limitation is required in order to assure that the proposed use of an additive will be safe, the Secretary—

(A) shall not fix such tolerance limitation at a level higher than he finds to be reasonably required to accomplish the physical or other technical effect for which such additive is intended; and

(B) shall not establish a regulation for such proposed use if he finds upon a fair evaluation of the data before him that such data do not establish that such use would accomplish the intended physical or other technical effect.

(5) In determining, for the purposes of this section, whether a proposed use of a food additive is safe, the Secretary shall consider among other relevant factors—

(A) the probable consumption of the additive and of any substance formed in or on food because of the use of the additive;

(B) the cumulative effect of such additive in the diet of man or animals, taking into account any chemically or pharmacologically related substance or substances in such diet; and

(C) safety factors which in the opinion of experts qualified by scientific training and experience to evaluate the safety of food additives are generally recognized as appropriate for the use of animal experimentation data.

(d) Regulation issued on Secretary's initiative

The Secretary may at any time, upon his own initiative, propose the issuance of a regulation prescribing, with respect to any particular use of a food additive, the conditions under which such additive may be safely used, and the reasons therefor. After the thirtieth day following publication of such a proposal, the Secretary may by order establish a regulation based upon the proposal.

(e) Publication and effective date of orders

Any order, including any regulation established by such order, issued under subsection (c) or (d) of this section, shall be published and shall be effective upon publication, but the Secretary may stay such effectiveness if, after issuance of such order, a hearing is sought with respect to such order pursuant to subsection (f) of this section.

(f) Objections and public hearing; basis and contents of order; statement

(1) Within thirty days after publication of an order made pursuant to subsection (c) or (d) of this section, any person adversely affected by such an order may file objections thereto with the Secretary, specifying with particularity the provisions of the order deemed objectionable, stating reasonable grounds therefor, and requesting a public hearing upon such objections. The Secretary shall, after due notice, as promptly as possible hold such public hearing for the purpose of receiving evidence relevant and material to the issues raised by such objections. As soon as practicable after completion of the hearing, the Secretary shall by order act upon such objections and make such order public.

(2) Such order shall be based upon a fair evaluation of the entire record at such hearing, and shall include a statement setting forth in detail the findings and conclusions upon which the order is based.

(3) The Secretary shall specify in the order the date on which it shall take effect, except that it shall not be made to take effect prior to the ninetieth day after its publication, unless the Secretary finds that emergency conditions exist necessitating an earlier effective date, in which event the Secretary shall specify in the order his findings as to such conditions.

(g) Judicial review

(1) In a case of actual controversy as to the validity of any order issued under subsection (f) of this section, including any order thereunder with respect to amendment or repeal of a regulation issued under this section, any person who will be adversely affected by such order may obtain judicial review by filing in the United States Court of Appeals for the circuit wherein such person resides or has his principal place of business, or in the United States Court of Appeals for the District of Columbia Circuit, within sixty days after the entry of such order, a petition praying that the order be set aside in whole or in part.

(2) A copy of such petition shall be forthwith transmitted by the clerk of the court to the Secretary, or any officer designated by him for that purpose, and thereupon the Secretary shall file in the court the record of the proceedings on which he based his order, as provided in section 2112 of title 28. Upon the filing of such petition the court shall have jurisdiction, which upon the filing of the record with it shall be exclusive, to affirm or set aside the order complained of in whole or in part. Until the filing of the record the Secretary may modify or set aside his order. The findings of the Secretary with respect to questions of fact shall be sustained if based upon a fair evaluation of the entire record at such hearing.

(3) The court, on such judicial review, shall not sustain the order of the Secretary if he failed to comply with any requirement imposed on him by subsection (f)(2) of this section.

(4) If application is made to the court for leave to adduce additional evidence, the court may order such additional evidence to be taken before the Secretary and to be adduced upon the hearing in such manner and upon such terms and conditions as to the court may seem proper, if such evidence is material and there were reasonable grounds for failure to adduce such evidence in the proceedings below. The Secretary may modify his findings as to the facts and order by reason of the additional evidence so taken, and shall file with the court such modified findings and order.

(5) The judgment of the court affirming or setting aside, in whole or in part, any order under this section shall be final, subject to review by the Supreme Court of the United States upon certiorari or certification as provided in section 1254 of title 28. The commencement of proceedings under this section shall not, unless specifically ordered by the court to the contrary, operate as a stay of an order.

(h) Notification relating to food contact substance

(1) Subject to such regulations as may be promulgated under paragraph (3), a manufacturer or supplier of a food contact substance may, at least 120 days prior to the introduction or delivery for introduction into interstate commerce of the food contact substance, notify the Secretary of the identity and intended use of the food contact substance, and of the determination of the manufacturer or supplier that the intended use of such food contact substance is safe under the standard described in subsection (c)(3)(A) of this section. The notification shall contain the information that forms the basis of the determination and all information required to be submitted by regulations promulgated by the Secretary.

(2)(A) A notification submitted under paragraph (1) shall become effective 120 days after the date of receipt by the Secretary and the food contact substance may be introduced or delivered for introduction into interstate commerce, unless the Secretary makes a determination within the 120-day period that, based on the data and information before the Secretary, such use of the food contact substance has not been shown to be safe under the standard described in subsection (c)(3)(A) of this section, and informs the manufacturer or supplier of such determination.

(B) A decision by the Secretary to object to a notification shall constitute final agency action subject to judicial review.

(C) In this paragraph, the term "food contact substance" means the substance that is the subject of a notification submitted under paragraph

(1), and does not include a similar or identical substance manufactured or prepared by a person other than the manufacturer identified in the notification.

(3)(A) The process in this subsection shall be utilized for authorizing the marketing of a food contact substance except where the Secretary determines that submission and review of a petition under subsection (b) of this section is necessary to provide adequate assurance of safety, or where the Secretary and any manufacturer or supplier agree that such manufacturer or supplier may submit a petition under subsection (b) of this section.

(B) The Secretary is authorized to promulgate regulations to identify the circumstances in which a petition shall be filed under subsection (b) of this section, and shall consider criteria such as the probable consumption of such food contact substance and potential toxicity of the food contact substance in determining the circumstances in which a petition shall be filed under subsection (b) of this section.

(4) The Secretary shall keep confidential any information provided in a notification under paragraph (1) for 120 days after receipt by the Secretary of the notification. After the expiration of such 120 days, the information shall be available to any interested party except for any matter in the notification that is a trade secret or confidential commercial information.

(5)(A)(i) Except as provided in clause (ii), the notification program established under this subsection shall not operate in any fiscal year unless—

(I) an appropriation equal to or exceeding the applicable amount under clause (iv) is made for such fiscal year for carrying out such program in such fiscal year; and

(II) the Secretary certifies that the amount appropriated for such fiscal year for the Center for Food Safety and Applied Nutrition of the Food and Drug Administration (exclusive of the appropriation referred to in subclause (I)) equals or exceeds the amount appropriated for the Center for fiscal year 1997, excluding any amount appropriated for new programs.

(ii) The Secretary shall, not later than April 1, 1999, begin accepting and reviewing notifications submitted under the notification program established under this subsection if—

(I) an appropriation equal to or exceeding the applicable amount under clause (iii) is made for the last six months of fiscal year 1999 for carrying out such program during such period; and

(II) the Secretary certifies that the amount appropriated for such period for the Center for Food Safety and Applied Nutrition of the Food and Drug Administration (exclusive of the appropriation referred to in subclause (I)) equals or exceeds an amount equivalent to one-half the amount appropriated for the Center for fiscal year 1997, excluding any amount appropriated for new programs.

(iii) For the last six months of fiscal year 1999, the applicable amount under this clause is $1,500,000, or the amount specified in the budget request of the President for the six-month period involved for carrying out the notification program in fiscal year 1999, whichever is less.

(iv) For fiscal year 2000 and subsequent fiscal years, the applicable amount under this clause is $3,000,000, or the amount specified in the budget request of the President for the fiscal year involved for carrying out the notification program under this subsection, whichever is less.

(B) For purposes of carrying out the notification program under this subsection, there are authorized to be appropriated such sums as may be necessary for each of the fiscal years 1999 through fiscal year 2003, except that such authorization of appropriations is not effective for a fiscal year for any amount that is less than the applicable amount under clause (iii) or (iv) of subparagraph (A), whichever is applicable.

(C) Not later than April 1 of fiscal year 1998 and February 1 of each subsequent fiscal year, the Secretary shall submit a report to the Committees on Appropriations of the House of Representatives and the Senate, the Committee on Commerce of the House of Representatives, and the Committee on Labor and Human Resources of the Senate that provides an estimate of the Secretary of the costs of carrying out the notification program established under this subsection for the next fiscal year.

(6) In this section, the term "food contact substance" means any substance intended for use as a component of materials used in manufacturing, packing, packaging, transporting, or holding food if such use is not intended to have any technical effect in such food.

(i) Amendment or repeal of regulations

The Secretary shall by regulation prescribe the procedure by which regulations under the foregoing provisions of this section may be amended or repealed, and such procedure shall conform to the procedure provided in this section for the promulgation of such regulations. The Secretary shall by regulation prescribe the procedure by which the Secretary may deem a notification under subsection (h) of this section to no longer be effective.

(j) Exemptions for investigational use

Without regard to subsections (b) to (i), inclusive, of this section, the Secretary shall by regulation provide for exempting from the requirements of this section any food additive, and any food bearing or containing such additive, intended solely for investigational use by qualified experts when in his opinion such exemption is consistent with the public health.

(June 25, 1938, ch. 675, §409, as added Pub. L. 85–929, §4, Sept. 6, 1958, 72 Stat. 1785; amended Pub. L. 86–546, §2, June 29, 1960, 74 Stat. 255; Pub. L. 87–781, title I, §104(f)(1), Oct. 10, 1962, 76 Stat. 785; Pub. L. 98–620, title IV, §402(25)(B), Nov. 8, 1984, 98 Stat. 3359; Pub. L. 105–115, title III, §309, Nov. 21, 1997, 111 Stat. 2354.)

AMENDMENTS

1997—Subsec. (a). Pub. L. 105–115, §309(a)(4), in closing provisions, substituted "While such a regulation relating to a food additive, or such a notification under subsection (h)(1) of this section relating to a food additive that is a food contact substance, is in effect, and has not been revoked pursuant to subsection (i) of this section, a food shall not, by reason of bearing or containing such a food additive in accordance with the regulation or notification, be considered adulterated under section 342(a)(1) of this title." for "While such a regulation relating to a food additive is in effect, a food shall not, by reason of bearing or containing such an additive in accordance with the regulation, be considered adulterated within the meaning of clause (1) of section 342(a) of this title."

Subsec. (a)(1). Pub. L. 105–115, §309(a)(1), substituted "subsection (j)" for "subsection (i)".

Subsec. (a)(3). Pub. L. 105–115, §309(a)(1)(B), (2), (3), added par. (3).

Subsec. (h). Pub. L. 105–115, §309(b)(2), added subsec. (h). Former subsec. (h) redesignated (i).

Subsec. (i). Pub. L. 105–115, §309(b)(1), (3), redesignated subsec. (h) as (i) and inserted at end "The Secretary shall by regulation prescribe the procedure by which the Secretary may deem a notification under subsection (h) of this section to no longer be effective."

Subsec. (j). Pub. L. 105–115, §309(b)(1), (4), redesignated subsec. (i) as (j) and substituted "subsections (b) to (i)" for "subsections (b) to (h)".

1984—Subsec. (g)(2). Pub. L. 98–620 struck out provision that required the court to advance on the docket and expedite the disposition of all causes filed therein pursuant to this section.

1962—Subsec. (c)(3)(A). Pub. L. 87–781 excepted proviso from applying to use of a substance as an ingredient of feed for animals raised for food production, if under conditions of use specified in proposed labeling, and which conditions are reasonably certain to be followed in practice, such additive will not adversely affect the animals and no residue will be found in any edible portion of such animal after slaughter, or in any food from the living animal.

1960—Subsec. (g)(2). Pub. L. 86–546 substituted "forthwith transmitted by the clerk of the court to the Secretary, or any officer" for "served upon the Secretary, or upon any officer", "shall file in the court the record of the proceedings on which he based his order, as provided in section 2112 of title 28" for "shall certify and file in the court a transcript of the proceedings and the record on which he based his order", and "Upon the filing of such petition the court shall have jurisdiction, which upon the filing of the record with it shall be exclusive," for "Upon such filing, the court shall have exclusive jurisdiction", and inserted sentence authorizing the Secretary to modify or set aside his order until the filing of the record.

CHANGE OF NAME

Committee on Commerce of House of Representatives changed to Committee on Energy and Commerce of House of Representatives, and jurisdiction over matters relating to securities and exchanges and insurance generally transferred to Committee on Financial Services of House of Representatives by House Resolution No. 5, One Hundred Seventh Congress, Jan. 3, 2001.

Committee on Labor and Human Resources of Senate changed to Committee on Health, Education, Labor, and Pensions of Senate by Senate Resolution No. 20, One Hundred Sixth Congress, Jan. 19, 1999.

EFFECTIVE DATE OF 1997 AMENDMENT

Amendment by Pub. L. 105–115 effective 90 days after Nov. 21, 1997, except as otherwise provided, see section 501 of Pub. L. 105–115, set out as a note under section 321 of this title.

EFFECTIVE DATE OF 1984 AMENDMENT

Amendment by Pub. L. 98–620 not applicable to cases pending on Nov. 8, 1984, see section 403 of Pub. L. 98–620, set out as an Effective Date note under section 1657 of Title 28, Judiciary and Judicial Procedure.

EFFECTIVE DATE OF 1962 AMENDMENT; EXCEPTIONS

Amendment by Pub. L. 87–781 effective Oct. 10, 1962, see section 107 of Pub. L. 87–781, set out as an Effective Date of 1962 Amendment note under section 321 of this title.

EFFECTIVE DATE

Section effective Sept. 6, 1958, see section 6(a) of Pub. L. 85–929, set out as an Effective Date of 1958 Amendment note under section 342 of this title.

GLASS AND CERAMIC WARE

Section 308 of Pub. L. 105–115 provided that:

"(a) IN GENERAL.—The Secretary may not implement any requirement which would ban, as an unapproved food additive, lead and cadmium based enamel in the lip and rim area of glass and ceramic ware before the expiration of one year after the date such requirement is published.

"(b) LEAD AND CADMIUM BASED ENAMEL.—Unless the Secretary determines, based on available data, that lead and cadmium based enamel on glass and ceramic ware—

"(1) which has less than 60 millimeters of decorating area below the external rim, and

"(2) which is not, by design, representation, or custom of usage intended for use by children,

is unsafe, the Secretary shall not take any action before January 1, 2003, to ban lead and cadmium based enamel on such glass and ceramic ware. Any action taken after January 1, 2003, to ban such enamel on such glass and ceramic ware as an unapproved food additive shall be taken by regulation and such regulation shall provide that such products shall not be removed from the market before 1 year after publication of the final regulation."

MORATORIUM ON AUTHORITY OF SECRETARY WITH RESPECT TO SACCHARIN

Pub. L. 95–203, §3, Nov. 23, 1977, 91 Stat. 1452, as amended by Pub. L. 96–88, title V, §509(b), Oct. 17, 1979, 93 Stat. 695; Pub. L. 96–273, June 17, 1980, 94 Stat. 536; Pub. L. 97–42, §2, Aug. 14, 1981, 95 Stat. 946; Pub. L. 98–22, §2, Apr. 22, 1983, 97 Stat. 173; Pub. L. 99–46, May 24, 1985, 99 Stat. 81; Pub. L. 100–71, title I, §101, July 11, 1987, 101 Stat. 431; Pub. L. 102–142, title VI, Oct. 28, 1991, 105 Stat. 910; Pub. L. 104–180, title VI, §602, Aug. 6, 1996, 110 Stat. 1594, provided that: "During the period ending May 1, 2002, the Secretary—

"(1) may not amend or revoke the interim food additive regulation of the Food and Drug Administration of the Department of Health and Human Services applicable to saccharin and published on March 15, 1977 (section 180.37 of part 180, subchapter B, chapter 1, title 21, Code of Federal Regulations (42 Fed. Reg. 14638)), or

"(2) may, except as provided in section 4 [enacting section 343a of this title, amending sections 321 and 343 of this title, and enacting provisions set out as notes under section 343 of this title] and the amendments made by such section, not take any other action under the Federal Food, Drug, and Cosmetic Act [this chapter] to prohibit or restrict the sale or distribution of saccharin, any food permitted by such interim food additive regulation to contain saccharin, or any drug or cosmetic containing saccharin,

solely on the basis of the carcinogenic or other toxic effect of saccharin as determined by any study made available to the Secretary before the date of the enactment of this Act [Nov. 23, 1977] which involved human studies or animal testing, or both."

For definition of "saccharin" as used in this note, see section 2(d) of Pub. L. 95–203.

§ 349. Bottled drinking water standards; publication in Federal Register

(a) Except as provided in subsection (b) of this section, whenever the Administrator of the Environmental Protection Agency prescribes interim or revised national primary drinking water regulations under section 1412 of the Public Health Service Act [42 U.S.C. 300g–1], the Secretary shall consult with the Administrator and within 180 days after the promulgation of such drinking water regulations either promulgate amendments to regulations under this chapter applicable to bottled drinking water or publish in the Federal Register his reasons for not making such amendments.

(b)(1) Not later than 180 days before the effective date of a national primary drinking water regulation promulgated by the Administrator of the Environmental Protection Agency for a contaminant under section 1412 of the Safe Drinking Water Act (42 U.S.C. 300g–1), the Secretary shall promulgate a standard of quality regulation under this subsection for that contaminant in bottled water or make a finding that such a regulation is not necessary to protect the public health because the contaminant is contained in water in public water systems (as defined under section 1401(4) of such Act (42 U.S.C. 300f(4))) but not in water used for bottled drinking water. The effective date for any such standard of quality regulation shall be the same as the effective date for such national primary drinking water regulation, except for any standard of quality of regulation promulgated by the Secretary before August 6, 1996, for which (as of August 6, 1996) an effective date had not been established. In the case of a standard of quality regulation to which such exception applies, the Secretary shall promulgate monitoring requirements for the contaminants covered by the regulation not later than 2 years after August 6, 1996.

(2) A regulation issued by the Secretary as provided in this subsection shall include any monitoring requirements that the Secretary determines appropriate for bottled water.

(3) A regulation issued by the Secretary as provided in this subsection shall require the following:

(A) In the case of contaminants for which a maximum contaminant level is established in a national primary drinking water regulation under section 1412 of the Safe Drinking Water Act (42 U.S.C. 300g–1), the regulation under this subsection shall establish a maximum contaminant level for the contaminant in bottled water which is no less stringent than the maximum contaminant level provided in the national primary drinking water regulation.

(B) In the case of contaminants for which a treatment technique is established in a national primary drinking water regulation under section 1412 of the Safe Drinking Water Act (42 U.S.C. 300g–1), the regulation under this subsection shall require that bottled water be subject to requirements no less protective of the public health than those applicable to water provided by public water systems using the treatment technique required by the national primary drinking water regulation.

(4)(A) If the Secretary does not promulgate a regulation under this subsection within the period described in paragraph (1), the national primary drinking water regulation referred to in paragraph (1) shall be considered, as of the date on which the Secretary is required to establish a regulation under paragraph (1), as the regulation applicable under this subsection to bottled water.

(B) In the case of a national primary drinking water regulation that pursuant to subparagraph (A) is considered to be a standard of quality regulation, the Secretary shall, not later than the applicable date referred to in such subparagraph, publish in the Federal Register a notice—

(i) specifying the contents of such regulation, including monitoring requirements; and

(ii) providing that for purposes of this paragraph the effective date for such regulation is the same as the effective date for the regulation for purposes of the Safe Drinking Water Act [42 U.S.C. 300f et seq.] (or, if the exception under paragraph (1) applies to the regulation, that the effective date for the regulation is not later than 2 years and 180 days after August 6, 1996).

(June 25, 1938, ch. 675, § 410, as added Pub. L. 93–523, § 4, Dec. 16, 1974, 88 Stat. 1694; amended Pub. L. 104–182, title III, § 305, Aug. 6, 1996, 110 Stat. 1684.)

REFERENCES IN TEXT

The Safe Drinking Water Act, referred to in subsec. (b)(4)(B)(ii), is title XIV of act July 1, 1944, as added Dec. 16, 1974, Pub. L. 93–523, § 2(a), 88 Stat. 1660, as amended, which is classified generally to subchapter XII (§ 300f et seq.) of chapter 6A of Title 42, The Public Health and Welfare. For complete classification of this Act to the Code, see Short Title note set out under section 201 of Title 42 and Tables.

AMENDMENTS

1996—Pub. L. 104–182 substituted "(a) Except as provided in subsection (b) of this section, whenever" for "Whenever" and added subsec. (b).

BOTTLED WATER STUDY

Section 114(b) of Pub. L. 104–182 provided that: "Not later than 18 months after the date of enactment of this Act [Aug. 6, 1996], the Administrator of the Food and Drug Administration, in consultation with the Administrator of the Environmental Protection Agency, shall publish for public notice and comment a draft study on the feasibility of appropriate methods, if any, of informing customers of the contents of bottled water. The Administrator of the Food and Drug Administration shall publish a final study not later than 30 months after the date of enactment of this Act."

§ 350. Vitamins and minerals

(a) Authority and limitations of Secretary; applicability

(1) Except as provided in paragraph (2)—

(A) the Secretary may not establish, under section 321(n), 341, or 343 of this title, maximum limits on the potency of any synthetic or natural vitamin or mineral within a food to which this section applies;

(B) the Secretary may not classify any natural or synthetic vitamin or mineral (or combination thereof) as a drug solely because it exceeds the level of potency which the Secretary determines is nutritionally rational or useful;

(C) the Secretary may not limit, under section 321(n), 341, or 343 of this title, the combination or number of any synthetic or natural—

(i) vitamin,

(ii) mineral, or

(iii) other ingredient of food,

within a food to which this section applies.

(2) Paragraph (1) shall not apply in the case of a vitamin, mineral, other ingredient of food, or

food, which is represented for use by individuals in the treatment or management of specific diseases or disorders, by children, or by pregnant or lactating women. For purposes of this subparagraph,[1] the term "children" means individuals who are under the age of twelve years.

(b) Labeling and advertising requirements for foods

(1) A food to which this section applies shall not be deemed under section 343 of this title to be misbranded solely because its label bears, in accordance with section 343(i)(2) of this title, all the ingredients in the food or its advertising contains references to ingredients in the food which are not vitamins or minerals.

(2) The labeling for any food to which this section applies may not list its ingredients which are not dietary supplement ingredients described in section 321(ff) of this title (i) except as a part of a list of all the ingredients of such food, and (ii) unless such ingredients are listed in accordance with applicable regulations under section 343 of this title. To the extent that compliance with clause (i) of this subparagraph is impracticable or results in deception or unfair competition, exemptions shall be established by regulations promulgated by the Secretary.

(c) Definitions

(1) For purposes of this section, the term "food to which this section applies" means a food for humans which is a food for special dietary use—

(A) which is or contains any natural or synthetic vitamin or mineral, and

(B) which—

(i) is intended for ingestion in tablet, capsule, powder, softgel, gelcap, or liquid form, or

(ii) if not intended for ingestion in such a form, is not represented as conventional food and is not represented for use as a sole item of a meal or of the diet.

(2) For purposes of paragraph (1)(B)(i), a food shall be considered as intended for ingestion in liquid form only if it is formulated in a fluid carrier and it is intended for ingestion in daily quantities measured in drops or similar small units of measure.

(3) For purposes of paragraph (1) and of section 343(j) of this title insofar as that section is applicable to food to which this section applies, the term "special dietary use" as applied to food used by man means a particular use for which a food purports or is represented to be used, including but not limited to the following:

(A) Supplying a special dietary need that exists by reason of a physical, physiological, pathological, or other condition, including but not limited to the condition of disease, convalescence, pregnancy, lactation, infancy, allergic hypersensitivity to food, underweight, overweight, or the need to control the intake of sodium.

(B) Supplying a vitamin, mineral, or other ingredient for use by man to supplement his diet by increasing the total dietary intake.

(C) Supplying a special dietary need by reason of being a food for use as the sole item of the diet.

[1] So in original. Probably should be "paragraph".

(June 25, 1938, ch. 675, § 411, as added Pub. L. 94–278, title V, § 501(a), Apr. 22, 1976, 90 Stat. 410; amended Pub. L. 103–417, §§ 3(c), 7(d), Oct. 25, 1994, 108 Stat. 4328, 4331.)

AMENDMENTS

1994—Subsec. (b)(2). Pub. L. 103–417, § 7(d), redesignated subpar. (A) as par. (2), substituted "dietary supplement ingredients described in section 321(ff) of this title" for "vitamins or minerals", and struck out former subpar. (B), which read as follows: "Notwithstanding the provisions of subparagraph (A), the labeling and advertising for any food to which this section applies may not give prominence to or emphasize ingredients which are not—

"(i) vitamins,

"(ii) minerals, or

"(iii) represented as a source of vitamins or minerals."

Subsec. (c)(1)(B)(i). Pub. L. 103–417, § 3(c)(1), inserted "powder, softgel, gelcap," after "capsule,".

Subsec. (c)(1)(B)(ii). Pub. L. 103–417, § 3(c)(2), struck out "does not simulate and" after "in such a form,".

EFFECTIVE DATE OF 1994 AMENDMENT

For provision that dietary supplements may be labeled after Oct. 25, 1994, in accordance with amendments made by section 7(d) of Pub. L. 103–417, and shall be so labeled after Dec. 31, 1996, see section 7(e) of Pub. L. 103–417, set out as a note under section 343 of this title.

AMENDMENT OF INCONSISTENT REGULATIONS BY SECRETARY

Section 501(b) of Pub. L. 94–278, as amended by Pub. L. 96–88, title V, § 509(b), Oct. 17, 1979, 93 Stat. 695, provided that: "The Secretary of Health and Human Services shall amend any regulation promulgated under the Federal Food, Drug, and Cosmetic Act [this chapter] which is inconsistent with section 411 of such Act [section 350 of this title] (as added by subsection (a)) and such amendments shall be promulgated in accordance with section 553 of title 5, United States Code."

§ 350a. Infant formulas

(a) Adulteration

An infant formula, including an infant formula powder, shall be deemed to be adulterated if—

(1) such infant formula does not provide nutrients as required by subsection (i) of this section,

(2) such infant formula does not meet the quality factor requirements prescribed by the Secretary under subsection (b)(1) of this section, or

(3) the processing of such infant formula is not in compliance with the good manufacturing practices and the quality control procedures prescribed by the Secretary under subsection (b)(2) of this section.

(b) Requirements for quality factors, good manufacturing practices, and retention of records

(1) The Secretary shall by regulation establish requirements for quality factors for infant formulas to the extent possible consistent with current scientific knowledge, including quality factor requirements for the nutrients required by subsection (i) of this section.

(2)(A) The Secretary shall by regulation establish good manufacturing practices for infant formulas, including quality control procedures that the Secretary determines are necessary to assure that an infant formula provides nutrients in accordance with this subsection and subsection (i) of this section and is manufactured in a manner designed to prevent adulteration of the infant formula.

(B) The good manufacturing practices and quality control procedures prescribed by the Secretary under subparagraph (A) shall include requirements for—

(i) the testing, in accordance with paragraph (3) and by the manufacturer of an infant formula or an agent of such manufacturer, of each batch of infant formula for each nutrient required by subsection (i) of this section before the distribution of such batch,

(ii) regularly scheduled testing, by the manufacturer of an infant formula or an agent of such manufacturer, of samples of infant formulas during the shelf life of such formulas to ensure that such formulas are in compliance with this section,

(iii) in-process controls including, where necessary, testing required by good manufacturing practices designed to prevent adulteration of each batch of infant formula, and

(iv) the conduct by the manufacturer of an infant formula or an agent of such manufacturer of regularly scheduled audits to determine that such manufacturer has complied with the regulations prescribed under subparagraph (A).

In prescribing requirements for audits under clause (iv), the Secretary shall provide that such audits be conducted by appropriately trained individuals who do not have any direct responsibility for the manufacture or production of infant formula.

(3)(A) At the final product stage, each batch of infant formula shall be tested for vitamin A, vitamin B1, vitamin C, and vitamin E to ensure that such infant formula is in compliance with the requirements of this subsection and subsection (i) of this section relating to such vitamins.

(B) Each nutrient premix used in the manufacture of an infant formula shall be tested for each relied upon nutrient required by subsection (i) of this section which is contained in such premix to ensure that such premix is in compliance with its specifications or certifications by a premix supplier.

(C) During the manufacturing process or at the final product stage and before distribution of an infant formula, an infant formula shall be tested for all nutrients required to be included in such formula by subsection (i) of this section for which testing has not been conducted pursuant to subparagraph (A) or (B). Testing under this subparagraph shall be conducted to—

(i) ensure that each batch of such infant formula is in compliance with the requirements of subsection (i) of this section relating to such nutrients, and

(ii) confirm that nutrients contained in any nutrient premix used in such infant formula are present in each batch of such infant formula in the proper concentration.

(D) If the Secretary adds a nutrient to the list of nutrients in the table in subsection (i) of this section, the Secretary shall by regulation require that the manufacturer of an infant formula test each batch of such formula for such new nutrient in accordance with subparagraph (A), (B), or (C).

(E) For purposes of this paragraph, the term "final product stage" means the point in the manufacturing process, before distribution of an infant formula, at which an infant formula is homogenous and is not subject to further degradation.

(4)(A) The Secretary shall by regulation establish requirements respecting the retention of records. Such requirements shall provide for—

(i) the retention of all records necessary to demonstrate compliance with the good manufacturing practices and quality control procedures prescribed by the Secretary under paragraph (2), including records containing the results of all testing required under paragraph (2)(B),

(ii) the retention of all certifications or guarantees of analysis by premix suppliers,

(iii) the retention by a premix supplier of all records necessary to confirm the accuracy of all premix certifications and guarantees of analysis,

(iv) the retention of—

(I) all records pertaining to the microbiological quality and purity of raw materials used in infant formula powder and in finished infant formula, and

(II) all records pertaining to food packaging materials which show that such materials do not cause an infant formula to be adulterated within the meaning of section 342(a)(2)(C) of this title,

(v) the retention of all records of the results of regularly scheduled audits conducted pursuant to the requirements prescribed by the Secretary under paragraph (2)(B)(iv), and

(vi) the retention of all complaints and the maintenance of files with respect to, and the review of, complaints concerning infant formulas which may reveal the possible existence of a hazard to health.

(B)(i) Records required under subparagraph (A) with respect to an infant formula shall be retained for at least one year after the expiration of the shelf life of such infant formula. Except as provided in clause (ii), such records shall be made available to the Secretary for review and duplication upon request of the Secretary.

(ii) A manufacturer need only provide written assurances to the Secretary that the regularly scheduled audits required by paragraph (2)(B)(iv) are being conducted by the manufacturer, and need not make available to the Secretary the actual written reports of such audits.

(c) Registration of persons distributing new infant formula

(1) No person shall introduce or deliver for introduction into interstate commerce any new infant formula unless—

(A) such person has, before introducing such new infant formula, or delivering such new infant formula for introduction, into interstate commerce, registered with the Secretary the name of such person, the place of business of such person, and all establishments at which such person intends to manufacture such new infant formula, and

(B) such person has at least 90 days before marketing such new infant formula, made the submission to the Secretary required by subsection (c)(1) of this section.

(2) For purposes of paragraph (1), the term "new infant formula" includes—

(A) an infant formula manufactured by a person which has not previously manufactured an infant formula, and

(B) an infant formula manufactured by a person which has previously manufactured infant formula and in which there is a major change, in processing or formulation, from a current or any previous formulation produced by such manufacturer.

For purposes of this paragraph, the term "major change" has the meaning given to such term in section 106.30(c)(2) of title 21, Code of Federal Regulations (as in effect on August 1, 1986), and guidelines issued thereunder.

(d) Submission of information about new infant formula required

(1) A person shall, with respect to any infant formula subject to subsection (c) of this section, make a submission to the Secretary which shall include—

(A) the quantitative formulation of the infant formula,

(B) a description of any reformulation of the formula or change in processing of the infant formula,

(C) assurances that the infant formula will not be marketed unless it meets the requirements of subsections (b)(1) and (i) of this section, as demonstrated by the testing required under subsection (b)(3) of this section, and

(D) assurances that the processing of the infant formula complies with subsection (b)(2) of this section.

(2) After the first production of an infant formula subject to subsection (c) of this section, and before the introduction into interstate commerce of such formula, the manufacturer of such formula shall submit to the Secretary, in such form as may be prescribed by the Secretary, a written verification which summarizes test results and records demonstrating that such formula complies with the requirements of subsections (b)(1), (b)(2)(A), (b)(2)(B)(i), (b)(2)(B)(iii), (b)(3)(A), (b)(3)(C), and (i) of this section.

(3) If the manufacturer of an infant formula for commercial or charitable distribution for human consumption determines that a change in the formulation of the formula or a change in the processing of the formula may affect whether the formula is adulterated under subsection (a) of this section, the manufacturer shall, before the first processing of such formula, make the submission to the Secretary required by paragraph (1).

(e) Additional notice requirements for manufacturer

(1) If the manufacturer of an infant formula has knowledge which reasonably supports the conclusion that an infant formula which has been processed by the manufacturer and which has left an establishment subject to the control of the manufacturer—

(A) may not provide the nutrients required by subsection (i) of this section, or

(B) may be otherwise adulterated or misbranded,

the manufacturer shall promptly notify the Secretary of such knowledge. If the Secretary determines that the infant formula presents a risk to human health, the manufacturer shall immediately take all actions necessary to recall shipments of such infant formula from all wholesale and retail establishments, consistent with recall regulations and guidelines issued by the Secretary.

(2) For purposes of paragraph (1), the term "knowledge" as applied to a manufacturer means (A) the actual knowledge that the manufacturer had, or (B) the knowledge which a reasonable person would have had under like circumstances or which would have been obtained upon the exercise of due care.

(f) Procedures applicable to recalls by manufacturer; regulatory oversight

(1) If a recall of infant formula is begun by a manufacturer, the recall shall be carried out in accordance with such requirements as the Secretary shall prescribe under paragraph (2) and—

(A) the Secretary shall, not later than the 15th day after the beginning of such recall and at least once every 15 days thereafter until the recall is terminated, review the actions taken under the recall to determine whether the recall meets the requirements prescribed under paragraph (2), and

(B) the manufacturer shall, not later than the 14th day after the beginning of such recall and at least once every 14 days thereafter until the recall is terminated, report to the Secretary the actions taken to implement the recall.

(2) The Secretary shall by regulation prescribe the scope and extent of recalls of infant formulas necessary and appropriate for the degree of risks to human health presented by the formula subject to the recall.

(3) The Secretary shall by regulation require each manufacturer of an infant formula who begins a recall of such formula because of a risk to human health to request each retail establishment at which such formula is sold or available for sale to post at the point of purchase of such formula a notice of such recall at such establishment for such time that the Secretary determines necessary to inform the public of such recall.

(g) Recordkeeping requirements for manufacturer; regulatory oversight and enforcement

(1) Each manufacturer of an infant formula shall make and retain such records respecting the distribution of the infant formula through any establishment owned or operated by such manufacturer as may be necessary to effect and monitor recalls of the formula. Such records shall be retained for at least one year after the expiration of the shelf life of the infant formula.

(2) To the extent that the Secretary determines that records are not being made or maintained in accordance with paragraph (1), the

Secretary may by regulation prescribe the records required to be made under paragraph (1) and requirements respecting the retention of such records under such paragraph. Such regulations shall take effect on such date as the Secretary prescribes but not sooner than the 180th day after the date such regulations are promulgated. Such regulations shall apply only with respect to distributions of infant formulas made after such effective date.

(h) Exemptions; regulatory oversight

(1) Any infant formula which is represented and labeled for use by an infant—

(A) who has an inborn error of metabolism or a low birth weight, or

(B) who otherwise has an unusual medical or dietary problem,

is exempt from the requirements of subsections (a), (b), and (c) of this section. The manufacturer of an infant formula exempt under this paragraph shall, in the case of the exempt formula, be required to provide the notice required by subsection (e)(1) of this section only with respect to adulteration or misbranding described in subsection (e)(1)(B) of this section and to comply with the regulations prescribed by the Secretary under paragraph (2).

(2) The Secretary may by regulation establish terms and conditions for the exemption of an infant formula from the requirements of subsections (a), (b), and (c) of this section. An exemption of an infant formula under paragraph (1) may be withdrawn by the Secretary if such formula is not in compliance with applicable terms and conditions prescribed under this paragraph.

(i) Nutrient requirements

(1) An infant formula shall contain nutrients in accordance with the table set out in this subsection or, if revised by the Secretary under paragraph (2), as so revised.

(2) The Secretary may by regulation—

(A) revise the list of nutrients in the table in this subsection, and

(B) revise the required level for any nutrient required by the table.

NUTRIENTS

Nutrient	Minimum[a]		Maximum[a]
Protein (gm)	1.8[b]	....	4.5.
Fat:			
gm	3.3	....	6.0.
percent cal	30.0	....	54.0.
Essential fatty acids (linoeate):			
percent cal	2.7	....	
mg	300.0	....	
Vitamins:			
A (IU)	250.0	(75 μg)[c]	750.0 (225 μg).[c]
D (IU)	40.0	....	100.0.
K (μg)	4.0	....	
E (IU)	0.7	(with 0.7 IU/gm linoleic acid).	
C (ascorbic acid) (mg).	8.0	....	
B_1 (thiamine) (μg)	40.0	....	
B_2 (riboflavin) (μg)	60.0	....	
B_6 (pyridoxine) (μg)	35.0	(with 15 μg/gm of protein in formula).	
B_{12} (μg)	0.15	....	
Niacin (μg)	250.0	....	
Folic acid (μg)	4.0	....	
Pantothenic acid (μg).	300.0	....	
Biotin (μg)	1.5[d]	....	
Choline (mg)	7.0[d]	....	
Inositol (mg)	4.0[d]	....	
Minerals:			
Calcium (mg)	50.0[e]	....	
Phosphorus (mg)	25.0[e]	....	
Magnesium (mg)	6.0	....	
Iron (mg)	0.15	....	
Iodine (μg)	5.0	....	
Zinc (mg)	0.5	....	
Copper (μg)	60.0	....	
Manganese (μg)	5.0	....	
Sodium (mg)	20.0	....	60.0.
Potassium (mg)	80.0	....	200.0.
Chloride (mg)	55.0	....	150.0.

[a] Stated per 100 kilocalories.
[b] The source of protein shall be at least nutritionally equivalent to casein.
[c] Retinol equivalents.
[d] Required to be included in this amount only in formulas which are not milk-based.
[e] Calcium to phosphorus ratio must be no less than 1.1 nor more than 2.0.

(June 25, 1938, ch. 675, § 412, as added Pub. L. 96–359, § 2, Sept. 26, 1980, 94 Stat. 1190; amended Pub. L. 99–570, title IV, § 4014(a), (b)(1), Oct. 27, 1986, 100 Stat. 3207–116, 3207–120; Pub. L. 103–80, § 3(*l*), Aug. 13, 1993, 107 Stat. 777.)

AMENDMENTS

1993—Subsec. (h)(1). Pub. L. 103–80 substituted "(e)(1)(B) of this section" for "(c)(1)(B) of this section," in concluding provisions.

1986—Subsecs. (a) to (d). Pub. L. 99–570, § 4014(a)(7), added subsecs. (a) to (d) and struck out former subsecs. (a) relating to adulteration and regulatory oversight, (b) relating to notice to the Secretary by a manufacturer and requirements and scope of that notice, (c) relating to additional notice requirements for the manufacturer, and (d) relating to procedures applicable to recalls by a manufacturer.

Subsecs. (e), (f). Pub. L. 99–570, § 4014(a)(1), (7), added subsecs. (e) and (f) and redesignated former subsecs. (e) and (f) as (g) and (h), respectively.

Subsec. (g). Pub. L. 99–570, § 4014(a)(1), (2), redesignated subsec. (e) as (g) and substituted "Such records shall be retained for at least one year after the expiration of the shelf life of the infant formula" for "No manufacturer shall be required under this subsection to retain any record respecting the distribution of an infant formula for a period of longer than 2 years from the date the record was made". Former subsec. (g) redesignated (i).

Subsec. (h). Pub. L. 99–570, § 4014(a)(1), redesignated subsec. (f) as (h).

Subsec. (h)(1). Pub. L. 99–570, § 4014(a)(3), (4), substituted "(a), (b), and (c)" for "(a) and (b)" and "(e)(1)" for "(c)(1)".

Pub. L. 99–570, § 4014(a)(5), which directed that "(d)(1)(B)" be substituted for "(e)(1)(B)" in second sentence could not be executed because "(e)(1)(B)" did not appear. See 1993 Amendment note above.

Subsec. (h)(2). Pub. L. 99–570, § 4014(a)(6), substituted "(a), (b), and (c)" for "(a) and (b)".

Subsec. (i). Pub. L. 99–570, § 4014(a)(1), (b)(1), redesignated subsec. (g) as (i), designated existing provisions as par. (1), substituted "paragraph (2)" for "subsection (a)(2) of this section", substituted a period for the colon after "as so revised", and added par. (2).

EFFECTIVE DATE OF 1980 AMENDMENT

Section 6 of Pub. L. 96–359 provided that: "Section 412 of the Federal Food, Drug, and Cosmetic Act (added by section 2) [this section] shall apply with respect to infant formulas manufactured on or after the 90th day after the date of the enactment of this Act [Sept. 26, 1980]."

§ 350b. New dietary ingredients

(a) In general

A dietary supplement which contains a new dietary ingredient shall be deemed adulterated under section 342(f) of this title unless it meets one of the following requirements:

(1) The dietary supplement contains only dietary ingredients which have been present in the food supply as an article used for food in a form in which the food has not been chemically altered.

(2) There is a history of use or other evidence of safety establishing that the dietary ingredient when used under the conditions recommended or suggested in the labeling of the dietary supplement will reasonably be expected to be safe and, at least 75 days before being introduced or delivered for introduction into interstate commerce, the manufacturer or distributor of the dietary ingredient or dietary supplement provides the Secretary with information, including any citation to published articles, which is the basis on which the manufacturer or distributor has concluded that a dietary supplement containing such dietary ingredient will reasonably be expected to be safe.

The Secretary shall keep confidential any information provided under paragraph (2) for 90 days following its receipt. After the expiration of such 90 days, the Secretary shall place such information on public display, except matters in the information which are trade secrets or otherwise confidential, commercial information.

(b) Petition

Any person may file with the Secretary a petition proposing the issuance of an order prescribing the conditions under which a new dietary ingredient under its intended conditions of use will reasonably be expected to be safe. The Secretary shall make a decision on such petition within 180 days of the date the petition is filed with the Secretary. For purposes of chapter 7 of title 5, the decision of the Secretary shall be considered final agency action.

(c) "New dietary ingredient" defined

For purposes of this section, the term "new dietary ingredient" means a dietary ingredient that was not marketed in the United States before October 15, 1994 and does not include any dietary ingredient which was marketed in the United States before October 15, 1994.

(June 25, 1938, ch. 675, § 413, as added Pub. L. 103–417, § 8, Oct. 25, 1994, 108 Stat. 4331.)

§ 350c. Maintenance and inspection of records

(a) Records inspection

If the Secretary has a reasonable belief that an article of food is adulterated and presents a threat of serious adverse health consequences or death to humans or animals, each person (excluding farms and restaurants) who manufactures, processes, packs, distributes, receives, holds, or imports such article shall, at the request of an officer or employee duly designated by the Secretary, permit such officer or employee, upon presentation of appropriate credentials and a written notice to such person, at reasonable times and within reasonable limits and in a reasonable manner, to have access to and copy all records relating to such article that are needed to assist the Secretary in determining whether the food is adulterated and presents a threat of serious adverse health consequences or death to humans or animals. The requirement under the preceding sentence applies to all records relating to the manufacture, processing, packing, distribution, receipt, holding, or importation of such article maintained by or on behalf of such person in any format (including paper and electronic formats) and at any location.

(b) Regulations concerning recordkeeping

The Secretary, in consultation and coordination, as appropriate, with other Federal departments and agencies with responsibilities for regulating food safety, may by regulation establish requirements regarding the establishment and maintenance, for not longer than two years, of records by persons (excluding farms and restaurants) who manufacture, process, pack, transport, distribute, receive, hold, or import food, which records are needed by the Secretary for inspection to allow the Secretary to identify the immediate previous sources and the immediate subsequent recipients of food, including its packaging, in order to address credible threats of serious adverse health consequences or death to humans or animals. The Secretary shall take into account the size of a business in promulgating regulations under this section.

(c) Protection of sensitive information

The Secretary shall take appropriate measures to ensure that there are in effect effective procedures to prevent the unauthorized disclosure of any trade secret or confidential information that is obtained by the Secretary pursuant to this section.

(d) Limitations

This section shall not be construed—

(1) to limit the authority of the Secretary to inspect records or to require establishment and maintenance of records under any other provision of this chapter;

(2) to authorize the Secretary to impose any requirements with respect to a food to the extent that it is within the exclusive jurisdiction of the Secretary of Agriculture pursuant to the Federal Meat Inspection Act (21 U.S.C. 601 et seq.), the Poultry Products Inspection Act (21 U.S.C. 451 et seq.), or the Egg Products Inspection Act (21 U.S.C. 1031 et seq.);

(3) to have any legal effect on section 552 of title 5 or section 1905 of title 18; or

(4) to extend to recipes for food, financial data, pricing data, personnel data, research data, or sales data (other than shipment data regarding sales).

(June 25, 1938, ch. 675, § 414, as added Pub. L. 107–188, title III, § 306(a), June 12, 2002, 116 Stat. 669.)

REFERENCES IN TEXT

The Federal Meat Inspection Act, referred to in subsec. (d)(2), is titles I to IV of act Mar. 4, 1907, ch. 2907, as added Pub. L. 90–201, Dec. 15, 1967, 81 Stat. 584, and amended, which are classified generally to subchapters I to IV (§ 601 et seq.) of chapter 12 of this title. For complete classification of this Act to the Code, see Short Title note set out under section 601 of this title and Tables.

The Poultry Products Inspection Act, referred to in subsec. (d)(2), is Pub. L. 85–172, Aug. 28, 1957, 71 Stat. 441, as amended, which is classified generally to chapter 10 (§ 451 et seq.) of this title. For complete classification of this Act to the Code, see Short Title note set out under section 451 of this title and Tables.

The Egg Products Inspection Act, referred to in subsec. (d)(2), is Pub. L. 91–597, Dec. 29, 1970, 84 Stat. 1620, as amended, which is classified generally to chapter 15 (§ 1031 et seq.) of this title. For complete classification of this Act to the Code, see Short Title note set out under section 1031 of this title and Tables.

EXPEDITED RULEMAKING

Pub. L. 107–188, title III, § 306(d), June 12, 2002, 116 Stat. 670, provided that: "Not later than 18 months after the date of the enactment of this Act [June 12, 2002], the Secretary shall promulgate proposed and final regulations establishing recordkeeping requirements under subsection 414(b) of the Federal Food, Drug, and Cosmetic Act [21 U.S.C. 350c(b)] (as added by subsection (a))."

§ 350d. Registration of food facilities

(a) Registration

(1) In general

The Secretary shall by regulation require that any facility engaged in manufacturing, processing, packing, or holding food for consumption in the United States be registered with the Secretary. To be registered—

(A) for a domestic facility, the owner, operator, or agent in charge of the facility shall submit a registration to the Secretary; and

(B) for a foreign facility, the owner, operator, or agent in charge of the facility shall submit a registration to the Secretary and shall include with the registration the name of the United States agent for the facility.

(2) Registration

An entity (referred to in this section as the "registrant") shall submit a registration under paragraph (1) to the Secretary containing information necessary to notify the Secretary of the name and address of each facility at which, and all trade names under which, the registrant conducts business and, when determined necessary by the Secretary through guidance, the general food category (as identified under section 170.3 of title 21, Code of Federal Regulations) of any food manufactured, processed, packed, or held at such facility. The registrant shall notify the Secretary in a timely manner of changes to such information.

(3) Procedure

Upon receipt of a completed registration described in paragraph (1), the Secretary shall notify the registrant of the receipt of such registration and assign a registration number to each registered facility.

(4) List

The Secretary shall compile and maintain an up-to-date list of facilities that are registered under this section. Such list and any registration documents submitted pursuant to this subsection shall not be subject to disclosure under section 552 of title 5. Information derived from such list or registration documents shall not be subject to disclosure under section 552 of title 5 to the extent that it discloses the identity or location of a specific registered person.

(b) Facility

For purposes of this section:

(1) The term "facility" includes any factory, warehouse, or establishment (including a factory, warehouse, or establishment of an importer) that manufactures, processes, packs, or holds food. Such term does not include farms; restaurants; other retail food establishments; nonprofit food establishments in which food is prepared for or served directly to the consumer; or fishing vessels (except such vessels engaged in processing as defined in section 123.3(k) of title 21, Code of Federal Regulations).

(2) The term "domestic facility" means a facility located in any of the States or Territories.

(3)(A) The term "foreign facility" means a facility that manufacturers, processes, packs, or holds food, but only if food from such facility is exported to the United States without further processing or packaging outside the United States.

(B) A food may not be considered to have undergone further processing or packaging for purposes of subparagraph (A) solely on the basis that labeling was added or that any similar activity of a de minimis nature was carried out with respect to the food.

(c) Rule of construction

Nothing in this section shall be construed to authorize the Secretary to require an application, review, or licensing process.

(June 25, 1938, ch. 675, § 415, as added Pub. L. 107–188, title III, § 305(a), June 12, 2002, 116 Stat. 667.)

REGULATIONS

Pub. L. 107–188, title III, § 305(e), June 12, 2002, 116 Stat. 669, provided that: "Not later than 18 months after the date of the enactment of this Act [June 12, 2002], the Secretary of Health and Human Services shall promulgate proposed and final regulations for the requirement of registration under section 415 of the Federal Food, Drug, and Cosmetic Act [21 U.S.C. 350d] (as added by subsection (a) of this section). Such requirement of registration takes effect—

"(1) upon the effective date of such final regulations; or

"(2) upon the expiration of such 18-month period if the final regulations have not been made effective as of the expiration of such period, subject to compliance with the final regulations when the final regulations are made effective."

ELECTRONIC FILING

Pub. L. 107–188, title III, § 305(d), June 12, 2002, 116 Stat. 668, provided that: "For the purpose of reducing paperwork and reporting burdens, the Secretary of Health and Human Services may provide for, and encourage the use of, electronic methods of submitting to the Secretary registrations required pursuant to this section [enacting this section, amending sections 331 and 381 of this title, and enacting provisions set out as a note under this section]. In providing for the electronic submission of such registrations, the Secretary shall ensure adequate authentication protocols are used to enable identification of the registrant and validation of the data as appropriate."

§ 350e. Sanitary transportation practices

(a) Definitions

In this section:

(1) Bulk vehicle

The term "bulk vehicle" includes a tank truck, hopper truck, rail tank car, hopper car, cargo tank, portable tank, freight container, or hopper bin, and any other vehicle in which food is shipped in bulk, with the food coming into direct contact with the vehicle.

(2) Transportation

The term "transportation" means any movement in commerce by motor vehicle or rail vehicle.

(b) Regulations

The Secretary shall by regulation require shippers, carriers by motor vehicle or rail vehicle, receivers, and other persons engaged in the transportation of food to use sanitary transportation practices prescribed by the Secretary to ensure that food is not transported under conditions that may render the food adulterated.

(c) Contents

The regulations under subsection (b) of this section shall—

(1) prescribe such practices as the Secretary determines to be appropriate relating to—

(A) sanitation;

(B) packaging, isolation, and other protective measures;

(C) limitations on the use of vehicles;

(D) information to be disclosed—

(i) to a carrier by a person arranging for the transport of food; and

(ii) to a manufacturer or other person that—

(I) arranges for the transportation of food by a carrier; or

(II) furnishes a tank vehicle or bulk vehicle for the transportation of food; and

(E) recordkeeping; and

(2) include—

(A) a list of nonfood products that the Secretary determines may, if shipped in a bulk vehicle, render adulterated food that is subsequently transported in the same vehicle; and

(B) a list of nonfood products that the Secretary determines may, if shipped in a motor vehicle or rail vehicle (other than a tank vehicle or bulk vehicle), render adulterated food that is simultaneously or subsequently transported in the same vehicle.

(d) Waivers

(1) In general

The Secretary may waive any requirement under this section, with respect to any class of persons, vehicles, food, or nonfood products, if the Secretary determines that the waiver—

(A) will not result in the transportation of food under conditions that would be unsafe for human or animal health; and

(B) will not be contrary to the public interest.

(2) Publication

The Secretary shall publish in the Federal Register any waiver and the reasons for the waiver.

(e) Preemption

(1) In general

A requirement of a State or political subdivision of a State that concerns the transportation of food is preempted if—

(A) complying with a requirement of the State or political subdivision and a requirement of this section, or a regulation prescribed under this section, is not possible; or

(B) the requirement of the State or political subdivision as applied or enforced is an obstacle to accomplishing and carrying out this section or a regulation prescribed under this section.

(2) Applicability

This subsection applies to transportation that occurs on or after the effective date of the regulations promulgated under subsection (b) of this section.

(f) Assistance of other agencies

The Secretary of Transportation, the Secretary of Agriculture, the Administrator of the Environmental Protection Agency, and the heads of other Federal agencies, as appropriate, shall provide assistance on request, to the extent resources are available, to the Secretary for the purposes of carrying out this section.

(June 25, 1938, ch. 675, § 416, as added Pub. L. 109–59, title VII, § 7202(b), Aug. 10, 2005, 119 Stat. 1911.)

EFFECTIVE DATE

Section effective Oct. 1, 2005, see section 7204 of Pub. L. 109–59, set out as an Effective Date of 2005 Amendment note under section 331 of this title.

§ 350f. Reportable food registry

(a) Definitions

In this section:

(1) Responsible party

The term "responsible party", with respect to an article of food, means a person that submits the registration under section 350d(a) of this title for a food facility that is required to register under section 350d(a) of this title, at which such article of food is manufactured, processed, packed, or held.

(2) Reportable food

The term "reportable food" means an article of food (other than infant formula) for which there is a reasonable probability that the use of, or exposure to, such article of food will cause serious adverse health consequences or death to humans or animals.

(b) Establishment

(1) In general

Not later than 1 year after September 27, 2007, the Secretary shall establish within the Food and Drug Administration a Reportable Food Registry to which instances of reportable food may be submitted by the Food and Drug Administration after receipt of reports under subsection (d), via an electronic portal, from—

(A) Federal, State, and local public health officials; or

(B) responsible parties.

(2) Review by Secretary

The Secretary shall promptly review and assess the information submitted under paragraph (1) for the purposes of identifying reportable food, submitting entries to the Reportable Food Registry, acting under subsection (c), and exercising other existing food safety authorities under this chapter to protect the public health.

(c) Issuance of an alert by the Secretary

(1) In general

The Secretary shall issue, or cause to be issued, an alert or a notification with respect to a reportable food using information from the Reportable Food Registry as the Secretary deems necessary to protect the public health.

(2) Effect

Paragraph (1) shall not affect the authority of the Secretary to issue an alert or a notification under any other provision of this chapter.

(d) Reporting and notification

(1) In general

Except as provided in paragraph (2), as soon as practicable, but in no case later than 24 hours after a responsible party determines that an article of food is a reportable food, the responsible party shall—

(A) submit a report to the Food and Drug Administration through the electronic portal established under subsection (b) that includes the data elements described in subsection (e) (except the elements described in paragraphs (8), (9), and (10) of such subsection); and

(B) investigate the cause of the adulteration if the adulteration of the article of food may have originated with the responsible party.

(2) No report required

A responsible party is not required to submit a report under paragraph (1) if—

(A) the adulteration originated with the responsible party;

(B) the responsible party detected the adulteration prior to any transfer to another person of such article of food; and

(C) the responsible party—

(i) corrected such adulteration; or

(ii) destroyed or caused the destruction of such article of food.

(3) Reports by public health officials

A Federal, State, or local public health official may submit a report about a reportable food to the Food and Drug Administration through the electronic portal established under subsection (b) that includes the data elements described in subsection (e) that the official is able to provide.

(4) Report number

The Secretary shall ensure that, upon submission of a report under paragraph (1) or (3), a unique number is issued through the electronic portal established under subsection (b) to the person submitting such report, by which the Secretary is able to link reports about the reportable food submitted and amended under this subsection and identify the supply chain for such reportable food.

(5) Review

The Secretary shall promptly review a report submitted under paragraph (1) or (3).

(6) Response to report submitted by a responsible party

After consultation with the responsible party that submitted a report under paragraph (1), the Secretary may require such responsible party to perform, as soon as practicable, but in no case later than a time specified by the Secretary, 1 or more of the following:

(A) Amend the report submitted by the responsible party under paragraph (1) to include the data element described in subsection (e)(9).

(B) Provide a notification—

(i) to the immediate previous source of the article of food, if the Secretary deems necessary;

(ii) to the immediate subsequent recipient of the article of food, if the Secretary deems necessary; and

(iii) that includes—

(I) the data elements described in subsection (e) that the Secretary deems necessary;

(II) the actions described under paragraph (7) that the recipient of the notification shall perform, as required by the Secretary; and

(III) any other information that the Secretary may require.

(7) Subsequent reports and notifications

Except as provided in paragraph (8), the Secretary may require a responsible party to perform, as soon as practicable, but in no case later than a time specified by the Secretary, after the responsible party receives a notification under subparagraph (C) or paragraph (6)(B), 1 or more of the following:

(A) Submit a report to the Food and Drug Administration through the electronic portal established under subsection (b) that includes those data elements described in subsection (e) and other information that the Secretary deems necessary.

(B) Investigate the cause of the adulteration if the adulteration of the article of food may have originated with the responsible party.

(C) Provide a notification—

(i) to the immediate previous source of the article of food, if the Secretary deems necessary;

(ii) to the immediate subsequent recipient of the article of food, if the Secretary deems necessary; and

(iii) that includes—

(I) the data elements described in subsection (e) that the Secretary deems necessary;

(II) the actions described under this paragraph that the recipient of the notification shall perform, as required by the Secretary; and

(III) any other information that the Secretary may require.

(8) Amended report

If a responsible party receives a notification under paragraph (6)(B) or paragraph (7)(C) with respect to an article of food after the responsible party has submitted a report to the Food and Drug Administration under paragraph (1) with respect to such article of food—

(A) the responsible party is not required to submit an additional report or make a notification under paragraph (7); and

(B) the responsible party shall amend the report submitted by the responsible party under paragraph (1) to include the data elements described in paragraph (9), and, with respect to both such notification and such report, paragraph (11) of subsection (e).

(e) Data elements

The data elements described in this subsection are the following:

(1) The registration numbers of the responsible party under section 350d(a)(3) of this title.

(2) The date on which an article of food was determined to be a reportable food.

(3) A description of the article of food including the quantity or amount.

(4) The extent and nature of the adulteration.

(5) If the adulteration of the article of food may have originated with the responsible party, the results of the investigation required under paragraph (1)(B) or (7)(B) of subsection (d), as applicable and when known.

(6) The disposition of the article of food, when known.

(7) Product information typically found on packaging including product codes, use-by dates, and names of manufacturers, packers, or distributors sufficient to identify the article of food.

(8) Contact information for the responsible party.

(9) The contact information for parties directly linked in the supply chain and notified under paragraph (6)(B) or (7)(C) of subsection (d), as applicable.

(10) The information required by the Secretary to be included in a notification provided by the responsible party involved under paragraph (6)(B) or (7)(C) of subsection (d) or required in a report under subsection (d)(7)(A).

(11) The unique number described in subsection (d)(4).

(f) Coordination of Federal, State, and local efforts

(1) Department of Agriculture

In implementing this section, the Secretary shall—

(A) share information and coordinate regulatory efforts with the Department of Agriculture; and

(B) if the Secretary receives a report submitted about a food within the jurisdiction of the Department of Agriculture, promptly provide such report to the Department of Agriculture.

(2) States and localities

In implementing this section, the Secretary shall work with the State and local public health officials to share information and coordinate regulatory efforts, in order to—

(A) help to ensure coverage of the safety of the food supply chain, including those food establishments regulated by the States and localities that are not required to register under section 350d of this title; and

(B) reduce duplicative regulatory efforts.

(g) Maintenance and inspection of records

The responsible party shall maintain records related to each report received, notification made, and report submitted to the Food and Drug Administration under this section for 2 years. A responsible party shall, at the request of the Secretary, permit inspection of such records as provided for section[1] 350c of this title.

(h) Request for information

Except as provided by section 350d(a)(4) of this title, section 552 of title 5 shall apply to any request for information regarding a record in the Reportable Food Registry.

(i) Safety report

A report or notification under subsection (d) shall be considered to be a safety report under section 379v of this title and may be accompanied by a statement, which shall be part of any report released for public disclosure, that denies that the report or the notification constitutes an admission that the product involved caused or contributed to a death, serious injury, or serious illness.

(j) Admission

A report or notification under this section shall not be considered an admission that the article of food involved is adulterated or caused or contributed to a death, serious injury, or serious illness.

(k) Homeland Security notification

If, after receiving a report under subsection (d), the Secretary believes such food may have been deliberately adulterated, the Secretary shall immediately notify the Secretary of Homeland Security. The Secretary shall make relevant information from the Reportable Food Registry available to the Secretary of Homeland Security.

(June 25, 1938, ch. 675, § 417, as added Pub. L. 110–85, title X, § 1005(b), Sept. 27, 2007, 121 Stat. 965.)

EFFECTIVE DATE

Pub. L. 110–85, title X, § 1005(e), Sept. 27, 2007, 121 Stat. 969, provided that: "The requirements of section 417(d) of the Federal Food, Drug, and Cosmetic Act [21 U.S.C.

[1] So in original. Probably should be "in section".

350f(d)], as added by subsection (a) [probably should be (b)], shall become effective 1 year after the date of the enactment of this Act [Sept. 27, 2007].''

FINDINGS

Pub. L. 110–85, title X, §1005(a), Sept. 27, 2007, 121 Stat. 964, provided that: "Congress makes the following findings:

"(1) In 1994, Congress passed the Dietary Supplement Health and Education Act of 1994 (Public Law 103–417) [see Short Title of 1994 Amendments note set out under section 301 of this title] to provide the Food and Drug Administration the legal framework which is intended to ensure that dietary supplements are safe and properly labeled foods.

"(2) In 2006, Congress passed the Dietary Supplement and Nonprescription Drug Consumer Protection Act (Public Law 109–462) [see Short Title of 2006 Amendment note set out under section 301 of this title] to establish a mandatory reporting system of serious adverse events for nonprescription drugs and dietary supplements sold and consumed in the United States.

"(3) The adverse event reporting system created under the Dietary Supplement and Nonprescription Drug Consumer Protection Act is intended to serve as an early warning system for potential public health issues associated with the use of these products.

"(4) A reliable mechanism to track patterns of adulteration in food would support efforts by the Food and Drug Administration to target limited inspection resources to protect the public health."

GUIDANCE

Pub. L. 110–85, title X, §1005(f), Sept. 27, 2007, 121 Stat. 969, provided that: "Not later than 9 months after the date of the enactment of this Act [Sept. 27, 2007], the Secretary [of Health and Human Services] shall issue a guidance to industry about submitting reports to the electronic portal established under section 417 of the Federal Food, Drug, and Cosmetic Act [21 U.S.C. 350f] (as added by this section) and providing notifications to other persons in the supply chain of an article of food under such section 417."

SUBCHAPTER V—DRUGS AND DEVICES

PART A—DRUGS AND DEVICES

§ 351. Adulterated drugs and devices

A drug or device shall be deemed to be adulterated—

(a) Poisonous, insanitary, etc., ingredients; adequate controls in manufacture

(1) If it consists in whole or in part of any filthy, putrid, or decomposed substance; or (2)(A) if it has been prepared, packed, or held under insanitary conditions whereby it may have been contaminated with filth, or whereby it may have been rendered injurious to health; or (B) if it is a drug and the methods used in, or the facilities or controls used for, its manufacture, processing, packing, or holding do not conform to or are not operated or administered in conformity with current good manufacturing practice to assure that such drug meets the requirements of this chapter as to safety and has the identity and strength, and meets the quality and purity characteristics, which it purports or is represented to possess; or (C) if it is a compounded positron emission tomography drug and the methods used in, or the facilities and controls used for, its compounding, processing, packing, or holding do not conform to or are not operated or administered in conformity with the positron emission tomography compounding standards and the official monographs of the United States Pharmacopoeia to assure that such drug meets the requirements of this chapter as to safety and has the identity and strength, and meets the quality and purity characteristics, that it purports or is represented to possess; or (3) if its container is composed, in whole or in part, of any poisonous or deleterious substance which may render the contents injurious to health; or (4) if (A) it bears or contains, for purposes of coloring only, a color additive which is unsafe within the meaning of section 379e(a) of this title, or (B) it is a color additive the intended use of which in or on drugs or devices is for purposes of coloring only and is unsafe within the meaning of section 379e(a) of this title; or (5) if it is a new animal drug which is unsafe within the meaning of section 360b of this title; or (6) if it is an animal feed bearing or containing a new animal drug, and such animal feed is unsafe within the meaning of section 360b of this title.

(b) Strength, quality, or purity differing from official compendium

If it purports to be or is represented as a drug the name of which is recognized in an official compendium, and its strength differs from, or its quality or purity falls below, the standard set forth in such compendium. Such determination as to strength, quality, or purity shall be made in accordance with the tests or methods of assay set forth in such compendium, except that whenever tests or methods of assay have not been prescribed in such compendium, or such tests or methods of assay as are prescribed are, in the judgment of the Secretary, insufficient for the making of such determination, the Secretary shall bring such fact to the attention of the appropriate body charged with the revision of such compendium, and if such body fails within a reasonable time to prescribe tests or methods of assay which, in the judgment of the Secretary, are sufficient for purposes of this paragraph, then the Secretary shall promulgate regulations prescribing appropriate tests or methods of assay in accordance with which such determination as to strength, quality, or purity shall be made. No drug defined in an official compendium shall be deemed to be adulterated under this paragraph because it differs from the standard of strength, quality, or purity therefor set forth in such compendium, if its difference in strength, quality, or purity from such standard is plainly stated on its label. Whenever a drug is recognized in both the United States Pharmacopoeia and the Homoeopathic Pharmacopoeia of the United States it shall be subject to the requirements of the United States Pharmacopoeia unless it is labeled and offered for sale as a homoeopathic drug, in which case it shall be subject to the provisions of the Homoeopathic Pharmacopoeia of the United States and not to those of the United States Pharmacopoeia.

(c) Misrepresentation of strength, etc., where drug is unrecognized in compendium

If it is not subject to the provisions of paragraph (b) of this section and its strength differs from, or its purity or quality falls below, that which it purports or is represented to possess.

(d) Mixture with or substitution of another substance

If it is a drug and any substance has been (1) mixed or packed therewith so as to reduce its quality or strength or (2) substituted wholly or in part therefor.

(e) Devices not in conformity with performance standards

(1) If it is, or purports to be or is represented as, a device which is subject to a performance standard established under section 360d of this title unless such device is in all respects in conformity with such standard.

(2) If it is declared to be, purports to be, or is represented as, a device that is in conformity with any standard recognized under section 360d(c) of this title unless such device is in all respects in conformity with such standard.

(f) Certain class III devices

(1) If it is a class III device—

(A)(i) which is required by a regulation promulgated under subsection (b) of section 360e of this title to have an approval under such section of an application for premarket approval and which is not exempt from section 360e of this title under section 360j(g) of this title, and

(ii)(I) for which an application for premarket approval or a notice of completion of a product development protocol was not filed with the Secretary within the ninety-day period beginning on the date of the promulgation of such regulation, or

(II) for which such an application was filed and approval of the application has been denied, suspended, or withdrawn, or such a notice was filed and has been declared not completed or the approval of the device under the protocol has been withdrawn;

(B)(i) which was classified under section 360c(f) of this title into class III, which under section 360e(a) of this title is required to have in effect an approved application for premarket approval, and which is not exempt from section 360e of this title under section 360j(g) of this title, and

(ii) which has an application which has been suspended or is otherwise not in effect; or

(C) which was classified under section 360j(*l*) of this title into class III, which under such section is required to have in effect an approved application under section 360e of this title, and which has an application which has been suspended or is otherwise not in effect.

(2)(A) In the case of a device classified under section 360c(f) of this title into class III and intended solely for investigational use, paragraph[1] (1)(B) shall not apply with respect to such device during the period ending on the ninetieth day after the date of the promulgation of the regulations prescribing the procedures and conditions required by section 360j(g)(2) of this title.

(B) In the case of a device subject to a regulation promulgated under subsection (b) of section 360e of this title, paragraph[1] (1) shall not apply with respect to such device during the period ending—

(i) on the last day of the thirtieth calendar month beginning after the month in which the classification of the device in class III became effective under section 360c of this title, or

(ii) on the ninetieth day after the date of the promulgation of such regulation,

whichever occurs later.

(g) Banned devices

If it is a banned device.

(h) Manufacture, packing, storage, or installation of device not in conformity with applicable requirements or conditions

If it is a device and the methods used in, or the facilities or controls used for, its manufacture, packing, storage, or installation are not in conformity with applicable requirements under section 360j(f)(1) of this title or an applicable condition prescribed by an order under section 360j(f)(2) of this title.

(i) Failure to comply with requirements under which device was exempted for investigational use

If it is a device for which an exemption has been granted under section 360j(g) of this title for investigational use and the person who was granted such exemption or any investigator who uses such device under such exemption fails to comply with a requirement prescribed by or under such section.

(June 25, 1938, ch. 675, §501, 52 Stat. 1049; Pub. L. 86–618, title I, §102(b)(1), July 12, 1960, 74 Stat. 398; Pub. L. 87–781, title I, §101, Oct. 10, 1962, 76 Stat. 780; Pub. L. 90–399, §101(a), July 13, 1968, 82 Stat. 343; Pub. L. 94–295, §§3(d), 9(b)(1), May 28, 1976, 90 Stat. 576, 583; Pub. L. 101–629, §9(b), Nov. 28, 1990, 104 Stat. 4521; Pub. L. 102–571, title I, §107(8), Oct. 29, 1992, 106 Stat. 4499; Pub. L. 105–115, title I, §121(b)(1), title II, §204(c), Nov. 21, 1997, 111 Stat. 2320, 2336.)

AMENDMENTS

1997—Par. (a)(2)(C). Pub. L. 105–115, §121(b)(1), inserted "; or (C) if it is a compounded positron emission tomography drug and the methods used in, or the facilities and controls used for, its compounding, processing, packing, or holding do not conform to or are not operated or administered in conformity with the positron emission tomography compounding standards and the official monographs of the United States Pharmacopoeia to assure that such drug meets the requirements of this chapter as to safety and has the identity and strength, and meets the quality and purity characteristics, that it purports or is represented to possess;" before "or (3)".

Par. (e). Pub. L. 105–115, §204(c), designated existing provisions as subpar. (1) and added subpar. (2).

1992—Par. (a)(4). Pub. L. 102–571 substituted "379e(a)" for "376(a)" in cls. (A) and (B).

1990—Par. (f)(1). Pub. L. 101–629, §9(b), which directed the amendment of subpars. (A) to (C) of par. (f), was executed by making the amendments in cls. (A) to (C) of subpar. (1) of par. (f) as follows to reflect the probable intent of Congress: in cl. (A)(ii)(II), substituted ", suspended, or withdrawn" for "or withdrawn"; in cl. (B)(ii), substituted "which has an application which has been suspended or is otherwise not in effect" for "which does not have such an application in effect"; and in cl. (C), substituted "which has an application which has been suspended or is otherwise not in effect" for "which does not have such an application in effect".

1976—Par. (a). Pub. L. 94–295, §9(b)(1), substituted "(3) if its" for "(3) if it is a drug and its" in cl. (3), sub-

[1] So in original. Probably should be "subparagraph".

stituted "(4) if (A) it bears or contains" for "(4) if (A) it is a drug which bears or contains" in cl. (4)(A), and substituted "drugs or devices" for "drugs" in cl. (4)(B).

Pars. (e) to (i). Pub. L. 94–295, § 3(d), added pars. (e) to (i).

1968—Par. (a). Pub. L. 90–399 added cls. (5) and (6).

1962—Par. (a). Pub. L. 87–781 designated existing provisions of cl. (2) as (A) and added (B).

1960—Par. (a). Pub. L. 86–618 substituted provisions in cl. (4) relating to unsafe color additives for provisions which related to a coal-tar color other than one from a batch that has been certified in accordance with regulations as provided by section 354 of this title.

EFFECTIVE AND TERMINATION DATES OF 1997 AMENDMENT

Section 121(b)(2) of Pub. L. 105–115 provided that: "Section 501(a)(2)(C) of the Federal Food, Drug, and Cosmetic Act (21 U.S.C. 351(a)(2)(C)) shall not apply 4 years after the date of enactment of this Act [Nov. 21, 1997] or 2 years after the date on which the Secretary of Health and Human Services establishes the requirements described in subsection (c)(1)(B) [section 121(c)(1)(B) of Pub. L. 105–115, set out as a note under section 355 of this title], whichever is later."

Amendment by Pub. L. 105–115 effective 90 days after Nov. 21, 1997, except as otherwise provided, see section 501 of Pub. L. 105–115, set out as an Effective Date of 1997 Amendment note under section 321 of this title.

EFFECTIVE DATE OF 1968 AMENDMENT

Amendment by Pub. L. 90–399 effective on first day of thirteenth calendar month after July 13, 1968, see section 108(a) of Pub. L. 90–399, set out as an Effective Date and Transitional Provisions note under section 360b of this title.

EFFECTIVE DATE OF 1962 AMENDMENT; EXCEPTIONS

Amendment by Pub. L. 87–781 effective on first day of seventh calendar month following October 1962, see section 107 of Pub. L. 87–781, set out as a note under section 321 of this title.

EFFECTIVE DATE OF 1960 AMENDMENT

Amendment by Pub. L. 86–618 effective July 12, 1960, subject to the provisions of section 203 of Pub. L. 86–618, see section 202 of Pub. L. 86–618, set out as a note under section 379e of this title.

EFFECTIVE DATE; POSTPONEMENT

Par. (a)(4) effective Jan. 1, 1940, see act June 23, 1939, ch. 242, 53 Stat. 853, set out as an Effective Date; Postponement in Certain Cases note under section 301 of this title.

TRANSFER OF FUNCTIONS

For transfer of functions of Federal Security Administrator to Secretary of Health, Education, and Welfare [now Health and Human Services], and of Food and Drug Administration in the Department of Agriculture to Federal Security Agency, see notes set out under section 321 of this title.

§ 352. Misbranded drugs and devices

A drug or device shall be deemed to be misbranded—

(a) False or misleading label

If its labeling is false or misleading in any particular. Health care economic information provided to a formulary committee, or other similar entity, in the course of the committee or the entity carrying out its responsibilities for the selection of drugs for managed care or other similar organizations, shall not be considered to be false or misleading under this paragraph if the health care economic information directly relates to an indication approved under section 355 of this title or under section 262(a) of title 42 for such drug and is based on competent and reliable scientific evidence. The requirements set forth in section 355(a) of this title or in section 262(a) of title 42 shall not apply to health care economic information provided to such a committee or entity in accordance with this paragraph. Information that is relevant to the substantiation of the health care economic information presented pursuant to this paragraph shall be made available to the Secretary upon request. In this paragraph, the term "health care economic information" means any analysis that identifies, measures, or compares the economic consequences, including the costs of the represented health outcomes, of the use of a drug to the use of another drug, to another health care intervention, or to no intervention.

(b) Package form; contents of label

If in package form unless it bears a label containing (1) the name and place of business of the manufacturer, packer, or distributor; and (2) an accurate statement of the quantity of the contents in terms of weight, measure, or numerical count: *Provided*, That under clause (2) of this paragraph reasonable variations shall be permitted, and exemptions as to small packages shall be established, by regulations prescribed by the Secretary.

(c) Prominence of information on label

If any word, statement, or other information required by or under authority of this chapter to appear on the label or labeling is not prominently placed thereon with such conspicuousness (as compared with other words, statements, designs, or devices, in the labeling) and in such terms as to render it likely to be read and understood by the ordinary individual under customary conditions of purchase and use.

(d) Repealed. Pub. L. 105–115, title I, § 126(b), Nov. 21, 1997, 111 Stat. 2327

(e) Designation of drugs or devices by established names

(1)(A) If it is a drug, unless its label bears, to the exclusion of any other nonproprietary name (except the applicable systematic chemical name or the chemical formula)—

(i) the established name (as defined in subparagraph (3)) of the drug, if there is such a name;

(ii) the established name and quantity or, if determined to be appropriate by the Secretary, the proportion of each active ingredient, including the quantity, kind, and proportion of any alcohol, and also including whether active or not the established name and quantity or if determined to be appropriate by the Secretary, the proportion of any bromides, ether, chloroform, acetanilide, acetophenetidin, amidopyrine, antipyrine, atropine, hyoscine, hyoscyamine, arsenic, digitalis, digitalis glucosides, mercury, ouabain, strophanthin, strychnine, thyroid, or any derivative or preparation of any such substances, contained therein, except that the requirement for stating the quantity of the active ingredients, other than the quantity of those specifically named in this subclause, shall not apply to nonprescription drugs not intended for human use; and

(iii) the established name of each inactive ingredient listed in alphabetical order on the outside container of the retail package and, if determined to be appropriate by the Secretary, on the immediate container, as prescribed in regulation promulgated by the Secretary, except that nothing in this subclause shall be deemed to require that any trade secret be divulged, and except that the requirements of this subclause with respect to alphabetical order shall apply only to nonprescription drugs that are not also cosmetics and that this subclause shall not apply to nonprescription drugs not intended for human use.

(B) For any prescription drug the established name of such drug or ingredient, as the case may be, on such label (and on any labeling on which a name for such drug or ingredient is used) shall be printed prominently and in type at least half as large as that used thereon for any proprietary name or designation for such drug or ingredient, except that to the extent that compliance with the requirements of subclause (ii) or (iii) of clause (A) or this clause is impracticable, exemptions shall be established by regulations promulgated by the Secretary.

(2) If it is a device and it has an established name, unless its label bears, to the exclusion of any other nonproprietary name, its established name (as defined in subparagraph (4)) prominently printed in type at least half as large as that used thereon for any proprietary name or designation for such device, except that to the extent compliance with the requirements of this subparagraph is impracticable, exemptions shall be established by regulations promulgated by the Secretary.

(3) As used in subparagraph (1), the term "established name", with respect to a drug or ingredient thereof, means (A) the applicable official name designated pursuant to section 358 of this title, or (B), if there is no such name and such drug, or such ingredient, is an article recognized in an official compendium, then the official title thereof in such compendium, or (C) if neither clause (A) nor clause (B) of this subparagraph applies, then the common or usual name, if any, of such drug or of such ingredient, except that where clause (B) of this subparagraph applies to an article recognized in the United States Pharmacopeia and in the Homoeopathic Pharmacopoeia under different official titles, the official title used in the United States Pharmacopeia shall apply unless it is labeled and offered for sale as a homoeopathic drug, in which case the official title used in the Homoeopathic Pharmacopoeia shall apply.

(4) As used in subparagraph (2), the term "established name" with respect to a device means (A) the applicable official name of the device designated pursuant to section 358 of this title, (B) if there is no such name and such device is an article recognized in an official compendium, then the official title thereof in such compendium, or (C) if neither clause (A) nor clause (B) of this subparagraph applies, then any common or usual name of such device.

(f) Directions for use and warnings on label

Unless its labeling bears (1) adequate directions for use; and (2) such adequate warnings against use in those pathological conditions or by children where its use may be dangerous to health, or against unsafe dosage or methods or duration of administration or application, in such manner and form, as are necessary for the protection of users, except that where any requirement of clause (1) of this paragraph, as applied to any drug or device, is not necessary for the protection of the public health, the Secretary shall promulgate regulations exempting such drug or device from such requirement. Required labeling for prescription devices intended for use in health care facilities or by a health care professional and required labeling for in vitro diagnostic devices intended for use by health care professionals or in blood establishments may be made available solely by electronic means, provided that the labeling complies with all applicable requirements of law, and that the manufacturer affords such users the opportunity to request the labeling in paper form, and after such request, promptly provides the requested information without additional cost.

(g) Representations as recognized drug; packing and labeling; inconsistent requirements for designation of drug

If it purports to be a drug the name of which is recognized in an official compendium, unless it is packaged and labeled as prescribed therein. The method of packing may be modified with the consent of the Secretary. Whenever a drug is recognized in both the United States Pharmacopoeia and the Homoeopathic Pharmacopoeia of the United States, it shall be subject to the requirements of the United States Pharmacopoeia with respect to packaging and labeling unless it is labeled and offered for sale as a homoeopathic drug, in which case it shall be subject to the provisions of the Homoeopathic Pharmacopoeia of the United States, and not those of the United States Pharmacopoeia, except that in the event of inconsistency between the requirements of this paragraph and those of paragraph (e) as to the name by which the drug or its ingredients shall be designated, the requirements of paragraph (e) shall prevail.

(h) Deteriorative drugs; packing and labeling

If it has been found by the Secretary to be a drug liable to deterioration, unless it is packaged in such form and manner, and its label bears a statement of such precautions, as the Secretary shall by regulations require as necessary for the protection of the public health. No such regulation shall be established for any drug recognized in an official compendium until the Secretary shall have informed the appropriate body charged with the revision of such compendium of the need for such packaging or labeling requirements and such body shall have failed within a reasonable time to prescribe such requirements.

(i) Drug; misleading container; imitation; offer for sale under another name

(1) If it is a drug and its container is so made, formed, or filled as to be misleading; or (2) if it

is an imitation of another drug; or (3) if it is offered for sale under the name of another drug.

(j) Health-endangering when used as prescribed

If it is dangerous to health when used in the dosage or manner, or with the frequency or duration prescribed, recommended, or suggested in the labeling thereof.

(k), (*l*) Repealed. Pub. L. 105–115, title I, § 125(a)(2)(B), (b)(2)(D), Nov. 21, 1997, 111 Stat. 2325

(m) Color additives; packing and labeling

If it is a color additive the intended use of which is for the purpose of coloring only, unless its packaging and labeling are in conformity with such packaging and labeling requirements applicable to such color additive, as may be contained in regulations issued under section 379e of this title.

(n) Prescription drug advertisements: established name; quantitative formula; side effects, contraindications, and effectiveness; prior approval; false advertising; labeling; construction of the Convention on Psychotropic Substances

In the case of any prescription drug distributed or offered for sale in any State, unless the manufacturer, packer, or distributor thereof includes in all advertisements and other descriptive printed matter issued or caused to be issued by the manufacturer, packer, or distributor with respect to that drug a true statement of (1) the established name as defined in paragraph (e) of this section, printed prominently and in type at least half as large as that used for any trade or brand name thereof, (2) the formula showing quantitatively each ingredient of such drug to the extent required for labels under paragraph (e) of this section, and (3) such other information in brief summary relating to side effects, contraindications, and effectiveness as shall be required in regulations which shall be issued by the Secretary in accordance with section 371(a) of this title, and in the case of published direct-to-consumer advertisements the following statement printed in conspicuous text: "You are encouraged to report negative side effects of prescription drugs to the FDA. Visit www.fda.gov/medwatch, or call 1-800-FDA-1088.", except that (A) except in extraordinary circumstances, no regulation issued under this paragraph shall require prior approval by the Secretary of the content of any advertisement, and (B) no advertisement of a prescription drug, published after the effective date of regulations issued under this paragraph applicable to advertisements of prescription drugs, shall with respect to the matters specified in this paragraph or covered by such regulations, be subject to the provisions of sections 52 to 57 of title 15. This paragraph (n) shall not be applicable to any printed matter which the Secretary determines to be labeling as defined in section 321(m) of this title. Nothing in the Convention on Psychotropic Substances, signed at Vienna, Austria, on February 21, 1971, shall be construed to prevent drug price communications to consumers. In the case of an advertisement for a drug subject to section 353(b)(1) of this title presented directly to consumers in television or radio format and stating the name of the drug and its conditions of use, the major statement relating to side effects and contraindications shall be presented in a clear, conspicuous, and neutral manner.

(*o*) Drugs or devices from nonregistered establishments

If it was manufactured, prepared, propagated, compounded, or processed in an establishment in any State not duly registered under section 360 of this title, if it was not included in a list required by section 360(j) of this title, if a notice or other information respecting it was not provided as required by such section or section 360(k) of this title, or if it does not bear such symbols from the uniform system for identification of devices prescribed under section 360(e) of this title as the Secretary by regulation requires.

(p) Packaging or labeling of drugs in violation of regulations

If it is a drug and its packaging or labeling is in violation of an applicable regulation issued pursuant to section 1472 or 1473 of title 15.

(q) Restricted devices using false or misleading advertising or used in violation of regulations

In the case of any restricted device distributed or offered for sale in any State, if (1) its advertising is false or misleading in any particular, or (2) it is sold, distributed, or used in violation of regulations prescribed under section 360j(e) of this title.

(r) Restricted devices not carrying requisite accompanying statements in advertisements and other descriptive printed matter

In the case of any restricted device distributed or offered for sale in any State, unless the manufacturer, packer, or distributor thereof includes in all advertisements and other descriptive printed matter issued or caused to be issued by the manufacturer, packer, or distributor with respect to that device (1) a true statement of the device's established name as defined in subsection (e) of this section, printed prominently and in type at least half as large as that used for any trade or brand name thereof, and (2) a brief statement of the intended uses of the device and relevant warnings, precautions, side effects, and contraindications and, in the case of specific devices made subject to a finding by the Secretary after notice and opportunity for comment that such action is necessary to protect the public health, a full description of the components of such device or the formula showing quantitatively each ingredient of such device to the extent required in regulations which shall be issued by the Secretary after an opportunity for a hearing. Except in extraordinary circumstances, no regulation issued under this paragraph shall require prior approval by the Secretary of the content of any advertisement and no advertisement of a restricted device, published after the effective date of this paragraph shall, with respect to the matters specified in this paragraph or covered by regulations issued hereunder, be subject to the provisions of sections 52 through 55 of title 15. This paragraph shall not be applicable to any printed matter which the Secretary determines to be labeling as defined in section 321(m) of this title.

(s) Devices subject to performance standards not bearing requisite labeling

If it is a device subject to a performance standard established under section 360d of this title, unless it bears such labeling as may be prescribed in such performance standard.

(t) Devices for which there has been a failure or refusal to give required notification or to furnish required material or information

If it is a device and there was a failure or refusal (1) to comply with any requirement prescribed under section 360h of this title respecting the device, (2) to furnish any material or information required by or under section 360i of this title respecting the device, or (3) to comply with a requirement under section 360*l* of this title.

(u) Identification of manufacturer

(1) Subject to paragraph (2), if it is a reprocessed single-use device, unless it, or an attachment thereto, prominently and conspicuously bears the name of the manufacturer of the reprocessed device, a generally recognized abbreviation of such name, or a unique and generally recognized symbol identifying such manufacturer.

(2) If the original device or an attachment thereto does not prominently and conspicuously bear the name of the manufacturer of the original device, a generally recognized abbreviation of such name, or a unique and generally recognized symbol identifying such manufacturer, a reprocessed device may satisfy the requirements of paragraph (1) through the use of a detachable label on the packaging that identifies the manufacturer and is intended to be affixed to the medical record of a patient.

(v) Reprocessed single-use devices

If it is a reprocessed single-use device, unless all labeling of the device prominently and conspicuously bears the statement "Reprocessed device for single use. Reprocessed by ____." The name of the manufacturer of the reprocessed device shall be placed in the space identifying the person responsible for reprocessing.

(w) New animal drugs

If it is a new animal drug—

(1) that is conditionally approved under section 360ccc of this title and its labeling does not conform with the approved application or section 360ccc(f) of this title, or that is not conditionally approved under section 360ccc of this title and its label bears the statement set forth in section 360ccc(f)(1)(A) of this title; or

(2) that is indexed under section 360ccc–1 of this title and its labeling does not conform with the index listing under section 360ccc–1(e) of this title or 360ccc–1(h) of this title, or that has not been indexed under section 360ccc–1 of this title and its label bears the statement set forth in section 360ccc–1(h) of this title.

(x) Nonprescription drugs

If it is a nonprescription drug (as defined in section 379aa of this title) that is marketed in the United States, unless the label of such drug includes a domestic address or domestic phone number through which the responsible person (as described in section 379aa of this title) may receive a report of a serious adverse event (as defined in section 379aa of this title) with such drug.

(y) Drugs subject to approved risk evaluation and mitigation strategy

If it is a drug subject to an approved risk evaluation and mitigation strategy pursuant to section 355(p) of this title and the responsible person (as such term is used in section 355–1 of this title) fails to comply with a requirement of such strategy provided for under subsection (d), (e), or (f) of section 355–1 of this title.

(z) Postmarket studies and clinical trials; new safety information in labeling

If it is a drug, and the responsible person (as such term is used in section 355(*o*) of this title) is in violation of a requirement established under paragraph (3) (relating to postmarket studies and clinical trials) or paragraph (4) (relating to labeling) of section 355(*o*) of this title with respect to such drug.

(June 25, 1938, ch. 675, §502, 52 Stat. 1050; June 23, 1939, ch. 242, §3, 53 Stat. 854; Dec. 22, 1941, ch. 613, §2, 55 Stat. 851; July 6, 1945, ch. 281, §2, 59 Stat. 463; Mar. 10, 1947, ch. 16, §2, 61 Stat. 11; July 13, 1949, ch. 305, §1, 63 Stat. 409; Aug. 5, 1953, ch. 334, §1, 67 Stat. 389; Pub. L. 86–618, title I, §102(b)(2), July 12, 1960, 74 Stat. 398; Pub. L. 87–781, title I, §§105(c), 112(a), (b), 131(a), title III, §305, Oct. 10, 1962, 76 Stat. 785, 790, 791, 795; Pub. L. 90–399, §105(a), July 13, 1968, 82 Stat. 352; Pub. L. 91–601, §6(d), formerly §7(d), Dec. 30, 1970, 84 Stat. 1673, renumbered Pub. L. 97–35, title XII, §1205(c), Aug. 13, 1981, 95 Stat. 716; Pub. L. 94–295, §§3(e), 4(b)(2), 5(a), 9(b)(2), May 28, 1976, 90 Stat. 577, 580, 583; Pub. L. 95–633, title I, §111, Nov. 10, 1978, 92 Stat. 3773; Pub. L. 102–300, §3(a)(2), June 16, 1992, 106 Stat. 239; Pub. L. 102–571, title I, §107(9), Oct. 29, 1992, 106 Stat. 4499; Pub. L. 103–80, §3(m), Aug. 13, 1993, 107 Stat. 777; Pub. L. 105–115, title I, §§114(a), 125(a)(2)(B), (b)(2)(D), 126(b), title IV, §412(c), Nov. 21, 1997, 111 Stat. 2312, 2325, 2327, 2375; Pub. L. 107–250, title II, §206, title III, §§301(a), 302(a)(1), Oct. 26, 2002, 116 Stat. 1613, 1616; Pub. L. 108–214, §2(b)(2)(B), Apr. 1, 2004, 118 Stat. 575; Pub. L. 108–282, title I, §102(b)(5)(E), Aug. 2, 2004, 118 Stat. 902; Pub. L. 109–43, §2(c)(1), Aug. 1, 2005, 119 Stat. 441; Pub. L. 109–462, §2(d), Dec. 22, 2006, 120 Stat. 3472; Pub. L. 110–85, title IX, §§901(d)(3)(A), (6), 902(a), 906(a), Sept. 27, 2007, 121 Stat. 940, 942, 943, 949.)

AMENDMENTS

2007—Par. (n). Pub. L. 110–85, §906(a), inserted "and in the case of published direct-to-consumer advertisements the following statement printed in conspicuous text: 'You are encouraged to report negative side effects of prescription drugs to the FDA. Visit www.fda.gov/medwatch, or call 1-800-FDA-1088.'," after "section 371(a) of this title,".

Pub. L. 110–85, §901(d)(6), substituted "section 371(a) of this title" for "the procedure specified in section 371(e) of this title".

Pub. L. 110–85, §901(d)(3)(A), inserted at end "In the case of an advertisement for a drug subject to section 353(b)(1) of this title presented directly to consumers in television or radio format and stating the name of the drug and its conditions of use, the major statement relating to side effects and contraindications shall be presented in a clear, conspicuous, and neutral manner."

Pars. (y), (z). Pub. L. 110–85, §902(a), added pars. (y) and (z).

2006—Par. (x). Pub. L. 109–462 added par. (x).

2005—Par. (u). Pub. L. 109–43 amended par. (u) generally. Prior to amendment, par. (u) read as follows: "If it is a device, unless it, or an attachment thereto, prominently and conspicuously bears the name of the manufacturer of the device, a generally recognized abbreviation of such name, or a unique and generally recognized symbol identifying such manufacturer, except that the Secretary may waive any requirement under this paragraph for the device if the Secretary determines that compliance with the requirement is not feasible for the device or would compromise the provision of reasonable assurance of the safety or effectiveness of the device."

2004—Par. (f). Pub. L. 108–214, in last sentence, inserted "or by a health care professional and required labeling for in vitro diagnostic devices intended for use by health care professionals or in blood establishments" after "in health care facilities", inserted comma after "means", substituted "requirements of law, and that the manufacturer affords such users the opportunity" for "requirements of law and, that the manufacturer affords health care facilities the opportunity", and struck out "the health care facility" after "promptly provides".

Par. (w). Pub. L. 108–282 added par. (w).

2002—Par. (f). Pub. L. 107–250, §206, inserted at end "Required labeling for prescription devices intended for use in health care facilities may be made available solely by electronic means provided that the labeling complies with all applicable requirements of law and, that the manufacturer affords health care facilities the opportunity to request the labeling in paper form, and after such request, promptly provides the health care facility the requested information without additional cost."

Par. (u). Pub. L. 107–250, §301(a), which directed amendment of section by adding par. (u) at end, was executed by adding par. (u) before par. (v) to reflect the probable intent of Congress.

Par. (v). Pub. L. 107–250, §302(a)(1), added par. (v).

1997—Par. (a). Pub. L. 105–115, §114(a), inserted at end "Health care economic information provided to a formulary committee, or other similar entity, in the course of the committee or the entity carrying out its responsibilities for the selection of drugs for managed care or other similar organizations, shall not be considered to be false or misleading under this paragraph if the health care economic information directly relates to an indication approved under section 355 of this title or under section 262(a) of title 42 for such drug and is based on competent and reliable scientific evidence. The requirements set forth in section 355(a) of this title or in section 262(a) of title 42 shall not apply to health care economic information provided to such a committee or entity in accordance with this paragraph. Information that is relevant to the substantiation of the health care economic information presented pursuant to this paragraph shall be made available to the Secretary upon request. In this paragraph, the term 'health care economic information' means any analysis that identifies, measures, or compares the economic consequences, including the costs of the represented health outcomes, of the use of a drug to the use of another drug, to another health care intervention, or to no intervention."

Par. (d). Pub. L. 105–115, §126(b), struck out par. (d) which read as follows: "If it is for use by man and contains any quantity of the narcotic or hypnotic substance alpha eucaine, barbituric acid, betaeucaine, bromal, cannabis, carbromal, chloral, coca, cocaine, codeine, heroin, marihuana, morphine, opium, paraldehyde, peyote, or sulphonmethane; or any chemical derivative of such substance, which derivative has been by the Secretary, after investigation, found to be, and by regulations designated as, habit forming; unless its label bears the name and quantity or proportion of such substance or derivative and in juxtaposition therewith the statement 'Warning—May be habit forming.'"

Par. (e)(1). Pub. L. 105–115, §412(c), amended subpar. (1) generally. Prior to amendment, subpar. (1) read as follows: "If it is a drug, unless (A) its label bears, to the exclusion of any other nonproprietary name (except the applicable systematic chemical name or the chemical formula), (i) the established name (as defined in subparagraph (3)) of the drug, if such there be, and (ii), in case it is fabricated from two or more ingredients, the established name and quantity of each active ingredient, including the quantity, kind, and proportion of any alcohol, and also including, whether active or not, the established name and quantity or proportion of any bromides, ether, chloroform, acetanilid, acetphenetidin, amidopyrine, antipyrine, atropine, hyoscine, hyoscyamine, arsenic, digitalis, digitalis glucosides, mercury ouabain strophanthin, strychnine, thyroid, or any derivative or preparation of any such substances, contained therein; *Provided*, That the requirement for stating the quantity of the active ingredients, other than the quantity of those specifically named in this paragraph, shall apply only to prescription drugs; and (B) for any prescription drug the established name of such drug or ingredient, as the case may be, on such label (and on any labeling on which a name for such drug or ingredient is used) is printed prominently and in type at least half as large as that used thereon for any proprietary name or designation for such drug or ingredient: *Provided*, That to the extent that compliance with the requirements of clause (A)(ii) or clause (B) of this subparagraph is impracticable, exemptions shall be established by regulations promulgated by the Secretary."

Par. (k). Pub. L. 105–115, §125(a)(2)(B), struck out par. (k) which read as follows: "If it is, or purports to be, or is represented as a drug composed wholly or partly of insulin, unless (1) it is from a batch with respect to which a certificate or release has been issued pursuant to section 356 of this title, and (2) such certificate or release is in effect with respect to such drug."

Par. (*l*). Pub. L. 105–115, §125(b)(2)(D), struck out par. (*l*) which read as follows: "If it is, or purports to be, or is represented as a drug (except a drug for use in animals other than man) composed wholly or partly of any kind of penicillin, streptomycin, chlortetracycline, chloramphenicol, bacitracin, or any other antibiotic drug, or any derivative thereof, unless (1) it is from a batch with respect to which a certificate or release has been issued pursuant to section 357 of this title, and (2) such certificate or release is in effect with respect to such drug: *Provided*, That this paragraph shall not apply to any drug or class of drugs exempted by regulations promulgated under section 357(c) or (d) of this title."

1993—Par. (e)(3). Pub. L. 103–80, §3(m)(1), substituted "of such ingredient, except that" for "of such ingredient: *Provided*, That".

Par. (f). Pub. L. 103–80, §3(m)(2), substituted "users, except that where" for "users: *Provided*, That where".

Par. (g). Pub. L. 103–80, §3(m)(3), substituted "prescribed therein. The method" for "prescribed therein: *Provided*, That the method" and "Pharmacopoeia, except that" for "Pharmacopoeia: *Provided further*, That,".

Par. (n). Pub. L. 103–80, §3(m)(4), substituted ", except that (A)" for ": *Provided*, That (A)".

1992—Par. (m). Pub. L. 102–571 substituted "379e" for "376".

Par. (t)(3). Pub. L. 102–300 added cl. (3).

1978—Par. (n). Pub. L. 95–633 inserted provision relating to the construction of the Convention on Psychotropic Substances.

1976—Par. (e). Pub. L. 94–295, §5(a), substituted "subparagraph (3)" for "subparagraph (2)" in subpar. (1), added subpar. (2), redesignated former subpar. (2) as (3) and in subpar. (3) as so redesignated substituted "subparagraph (1)" for "this paragraph (e)", and added subpar. (4).

Par. (j). Pub. L. 94–295, §3(e)(2), substituted "dosage or manner," for "dosage,".

Par. (m). Pub. L. 94–295, §9(b)(2), substituted "the intended use of which is for" for "the intended use of which in or on drugs is for".

Par. (*o*). Pub. L. 94–295, §4(b)(2), substituted "If it was manufactured" for "If it is a drug and was manufactured" and inserted ", if it was not included in a list required by section 360(j) of this title, if a notice or other information respecting it was not provided as required by such section or section 360(k) of this title, or if it does not bear such symbols from the uniform system for identification of devices prescribed under section 360(e) of this title as the Secretary by regulation requires".

Pars. (q) to (t). Pub. L. 94–295, §3(e)(1), added pars. (q) to (t).

1970—Par. (p). Pub. L. 91–601 added par. (p).

1968—Par. (*l*). Pub. L. 90–399 inserted "(except a drug for use in animals other than man)" after "represented as a drug".

1962—Par. (e). Pub. L. 87–781, §112(a), designated existing provisions as subpar. (1), substituted ", unless (A) its label bears, to the exclusion of any other nonproprietary name (except the applicable systematic chemical name or the chemical formula), (i) the established name (as defined in subparagraph (2) of this subsection) of the drug, if such there be, and (ii), in case it is fabricated from two or more ingredients, the established name and quantity" for "and is not designated solely by a name recognized in an official compendium unless its label bears (1) the common or usual name of the drug, if such there be; and (2), in case it is fabricated from two or more ingredients, the common or usual name", and "the established name" for "the name", provided that the requirement for stating the quantity of active ingredients, other than those specified in this par., applies only to prescription drugs, and that the established name of a drug on a label is to be printed prominently and in type at least half as large as used for any proprietary designation, and added subpar. (2) defining "established name".

Par. (g). Pub. L. 87–781, §112(b), provided that if there is an inconsistency between the provisions of this par. and those of par. (e), as to the name of a drug, the requirements of par. (e) should prevail.

Par. (*l*). Pub. L. 87–781, §105(c), substituted "bacitracin, or any other antibiotic drug" for "or bacitracin."

Par. (n). Pub. L. 87–781, §131(a), added par. (n).

Par. (*o*). Pub. L. 87–781, §305, added par. (*o*).

1960—Par. (m). Pub. L. 86–618 added par. (m).

1953—Par. (*l*). Act Aug. 5, 1953, substituted "chlortetracycline" for "aureomycin".

1949—Par. (*l*). Act July 13, 1949, inserted ", aureomycin, chloramphenicol, or bacitracin" after "streptomycin".

1947—Par. (*l*). Act Mar. 10, 1947, inserted "or streptomycin" after "penicillin".

1945—Par. (*l*). Act July 6, 1945, added par. (*l*).

1941—Par. (k). Act Dec. 22, 1941, added par. (k).

1939—Par. (d). Act June 29, 1939, substituted "name, and quality or proportion" for "name, quantity, and percentage".

EFFECTIVE DATE OF 2007 AMENDMENT

Amendment by Pub. L. 110–85 effective 180 days after Sept. 27, 2007, see section 909 of Pub. L. 110–85, set out as a note under section 331 of this title.

EFFECTIVE DATES OF 2006 AMENDMENT

Pub. L. 109–462, §2(e)(1), (2), Dec. 22, 2006, 120 Stat. 3472, provided that:

"(1) IN GENERAL.—Except as provided in paragraph (2), the amendments made by this section [enacting section 379aa of this title and amending this section and section 331 of this title] shall take effect 1 year after the date of enactment of this Act [Dec. 22, 2006].

"(2) MISBRANDING.—Section 502(x) of the Federal Food, Drug, and Cosmetic Act [21 U.S.C. 352(x)] (as added by this section) shall apply to any nonprescription drug (as defined in such section 502(x)) labeled on or after the date that is 1 year after the date of enactment of this Act [Dec. 22, 2006]."

EFFECTIVE DATE OF 2002 AMENDMENT

Pub. L. 107–250, title III, §301(b), Oct. 26, 2002, 116 Stat. 1616, as amended by Pub. L. 108–214, §2(c)(1), Apr. 1, 2004, 118 Stat. 575; Pub. L. 109–43, §2(d), Aug. 1, 2005, 119 Stat. 441, provided that: "Section 502(u) of the Federal Food, Drug, and Cosmetic Act [21 U.S.C. 352(u)] (as amended by section 2(c) of the Medical Device User Fee Stabilization Act of 2005 [Pub. L. 109–43])—

"(1) shall be effective—

"(A) with respect to devices described under paragraph (1) of such section, 12 months after the date of enactment of the Medical Device User Fee Stabilization Act of 2005 [Aug. 1, 2005], or the date on which the original device first bears the name of the manufacturer of the original device, a generally recognized abbreviation of such name, or a unique and generally recognized symbol identifying such manufacturer, whichever is later; and

"(B) with respect to devices described under paragraph (2) of such section 502(u), 12 months after such date of enactment; and

"(2) shall apply only to devices reprocessed and introduced or delivered for introduction in interstate commerce after such applicable effective date."

Pub. L. 107–250, title III, §302(a)(2), Oct. 26, 2002, 116 Stat. 1616, provided that: "The amendment made by paragraph (1) [amending this section] takes effect 15 months after the date of the enactment of this Act [Oct. 26, 2002], and only applies to devices introduced or delivered for introduction into interstate commerce after such effective date."

EFFECTIVE DATE OF 1997 AMENDMENT

Amendment by sections 114(a), 126(b), and 412(c) of Pub. L. 105–115 effective 90 days after Nov. 21, 1997, except as otherwise provided, see section 501 of Pub. L. 105–115, set out as a note under section 321 of this title.

EFFECTIVE DATE OF 1978 AMENDMENT

Amendment by Pub. L. 95–633 effective on date the Convention on Psychotropic Substances enters into force in the United States [July 15, 1980], see section 112 of Pub. L. 95–633, set out as an Effective Date note under section 801a of this title.

EFFECTIVE DATE OF 1970 AMENDMENT

Amendment by Pub. L. 91–601 effective Dec. 30, 1970, and regulations establishing special packaging standards effective no sooner than 180 days or later than one year from date regulations are final, or an earlier date published in Federal Register, see section 8 of Pub. L. 91–601, set out as an Effective Date note under section 1471 of Title 15, Commerce and Trade.

EFFECTIVE DATE OF 1968 AMENDMENT

Amendment by Pub. L. 90–399 effective on first day of thirteenth calendar month after July 13, 1968, see section 108(a) of Pub. L. 90–399, set out as an Effective Date and Transitional Provisions note under section 360b of this title.

EFFECTIVE DATE OF 1962 AMENDMENT

Section 112(c) of Pub. L. 87–781 provided that: "This section [amending this section] shall take effect on the first day of the seventh calendar month following the month in which this Act is enacted [October 1962]."

Section 131(b) of Pub. L. 87–781 provided that: "No drug which was being commercially distributed prior to the date of enactment of this Act [Oct. 10, 1962] shall be deemed to be misbranded under paragraph (n) of section 502 of the Federal Food, Drug, and Cosmetic Act

[21 U.S.C. 352(n)], as added by this section, until the earlier of the following dates: (1) the first day of the seventh month following the month in which this Act is enacted; or (2) the effective date of regulations first issued under clause (3) of such paragraph (n) in accordance with the procedure specified in section 701(e) of the Federal Food, Drug, and Cosmetic Act [21 U.S.C. 371(e)].''

Amendment by Pub. L. 87–781 effective on first day of seventh calendar month following October 1962, see section 107 of Pub. L. 87–781, set out as a note under section 321 of this title.

EFFECTIVE DATE OF 1960 AMENDMENT

Amendment by Pub. L. 86–618 effective July 12, 1960, subject to the provisions of section 203 of Pub. L. 86–618, see section 202 of Pub. L. 86–618, set out as a note under section 379e of this title.

EFFECTIVE DATE; POSTPONEMENT

Pars. (b) and (d) to (h) effective Jan. 1, 1940, and such paragraphs effective July 1, 1940, as provided by regulations for certain lithographed labeling and containers bearing certain labeling, see act June 23, 1939, ch. 242, 53 Stat. 853, set out as an Effective Date: Postponement in Certain Cases note under section 301 of this title.

REGULATIONS

Pub. L. 110–85, title IX, § 901(d)(3)(B), Sept. 27, 2007, 121 Stat. 940, provided that: ''Not later than 30 months after the date of the enactment of the Food and Drug Administration Amendments Act of 2007 [Sept. 27, 2007], the Secretary of Health and Human Services shall by regulation establish standards for determining whether a major statement relating to side effects and contraindications of a drug, described in section 502(n) of the Federal Food, Drug, and Cosmetic Act (21 U.S.C. 352(n)) (as amended by subparagraph (A)) is presented in the manner required under such section.''

TRANSFER OF FUNCTIONS

For transfer of functions of Federal Security Administrator to Secretary of Health, Education, and Welfare [now Health and Human Services], and of Food and Drug Administration in the Department of Agriculture to Federal Security Agency, see notes set out under section 321 of this title.

GUIDANCE; MISBRANDED DEVICES

Pub. L. 109–43, § 2(c)(2), Aug. 1, 2005, 119 Stat. 441, provided that: ''Not later than 180 days after the date of enactment of this Act [Aug. 1, 2005], the Secretary of Health and Human Services shall issue guidance to identify circumstances in which the name of the manufacturer of the original device, a generally recognized abbreviation of such name, or a unique and generally recognized symbol identifying such manufacturer, is not 'prominent and conspicuous', as used in section 502(u) of Federal Food, Drug, and Cosmetic Act [21 U.S.C. 352(u)] (as amended by paragraph (1)).''

STUDIES

Pub. L. 110–85, title IX, § 906(b), Sept. 27, 2007, 121 Stat. 950, provided that:

''(1) IN GENERAL.—In the case of direct-to-consumer television advertisements, the Secretary of Health and Human Services, in consultation with the Advisory Committee on Risk Communication under section 567 of the Federal Food, Drug, and Cosmetic Act [21 U.S.C. 360bbb–6] (as added by section 917), shall, not later than 6 months after the date of the enactment of this Act [Sept. 27, 2007], conduct a study to determine if the statement in section 502(n) of such Act [21 U.S.C. 352(n)] (as added by subsection (a)) required with respect to published direct-to-consumer advertisements is appropriate for inclusion in such television advertisements.

''(2) CONTENT.—As part of the study under paragraph (1), such Secretary shall consider whether the information in the statement described in paragraph (1) would detract from the presentation of risk information in a direct-to-consumer television advertisement. If such Secretary determines the inclusion of such statement is appropriate in direct-to-consumer television advertisements, such Secretary shall issue regulations requiring the implementation of such statement in direct-to-consumer television advertisements, including determining a reasonable length of time for displaying the statement in such advertisements. The Secretary shall report to the appropriate committees of Congress the findings of such study and any plans to issue regulations under this paragraph.''

Pub. L. 108–173, title I, § 107(f), Dec. 8, 2003, 117 Stat. 2171, directed the Secretary of Health and Human Services to undertake a study of how to make prescription pharmaceutical information, including drug labels and usage instructions, accessible to blind and visually-impaired individuals, and to submit a report to Congress not later than 18 months after Dec. 8, 2003.

Section 114(b) of Pub. L. 105–115 provided that: ''The Comptroller General of the United States shall conduct a study of the implementation of the provisions added by the amendment made by subsection (a) [amending this section]. Not later than 4 years and 6 months after the date of enactment of this Act [Nov. 21, 1997], the Comptroller General of the United States shall prepare and submit to Congress a report containing the findings of the study.''

COUNTERFEITING OF DRUGS; CONGRESSIONAL FINDINGS AND DECLARATION OF POLICY

Section 9(a) of Pub. L. 89–74, July 15, 1965, 79 Stat. 234, provided that: ''The Congress finds and declares that there is a substantial traffic in counterfeit drugs simulating the brand or other identifying mark or device of the manufacturer of the genuine article; that such traffic poses a serious hazard to the health of innocent consumers of such drugs because of the lack of proper qualifications, facilities, and manufacturing controls on the part of the counterfeiter, whose operations are clandestine; that, while such drugs are deemed misbranded within the meaning of section 502(i) of the Federal Food, Drug, and Cosmetic Act [21 U.S.C. 352(i)], the controls for the suppression of the traffic in such drugs are inadequate because of the difficulty of determining the place of interstate origin of such drugs and, if that place is discovered, the fact that the implements for counterfeiting are not subject to seizure, and that these factors require enactment of additional controls with respect to such drugs without regard to their interstate or intrastate origins.''

Provisions as effective Feb. 1, 1966, see section 11 of Pub. L. 89–74, set out as an Effective Date of 1965 Amendment note under section 321 of this title.

§ 353. Exemptions and consideration for certain drugs, devices, and biological products

(a) Regulations for goods to be processed, labeled, or repacked elsewhere

The Secretary is directed to promulgate regulations exempting from any labeling or packaging requirement of this chapter drugs and devices which are, in accordance with the practice of the trade, to be processed, labeled, or repacked in substantial quantities at establishments other than those where originally processed or packed, on condition that such drugs and devices are not adulterated or misbranded under the provisions of this chapter upon removal from such processing, labeling, or repacking establishment.

(b) Prescription by physician; exemption from labeling and prescription requirements; misbranded drugs; compliance with narcotic and marihuana laws

(1) A drug intended for use by man which—

(A) because of its toxicity or other potentiality for harmful effect, or the method of its use, or the collateral measures necessary to its use, is not safe for use except under the supervision of a practitioner licensed by law to administer such drug; or

(B) is limited by an approved application under section 355 of this title to use under the professional supervision of a practitioner licensed by law to administer such drug;

shall be dispensed only (i) upon a written prescription of a practitioner licensed by law to administer such drug, or (ii) upon an oral prescription of such practitioner which is reduced promptly to writing and filed by the pharmacist, or (iii) by refilling any such written or oral prescription if such refilling is authorized by the prescriber either in the original prescription or by oral order which is reduced promptly to writing and filed by the pharmacist. The act of dispensing a drug contrary to the provisions of this paragraph shall be deemed to be an act which results in the drug being misbranded while held for sale.

(2) Any drug dispensed by filling or refilling a written or oral prescription of a practitioner licensed by law to administer such drug shall be exempt from the requirements of section 352 of this title, except paragraphs (a), (i)(2) and (3), (k), and (*l*), and the packaging requirements of paragraphs (g), (h), and (p), if the drug bears a label containing the name and address of the dispenser, the serial number and date of the prescription or of its filling, the name of the prescriber, and, if stated in the prescription, the name of the patient, and the directions for use and cautionary statements, if any, contained in such prescription. This exemption shall not apply to any drug dispensed in the course of the conduct of a business of dispensing drugs pursuant to diagnosis by mail, or to a drug dispensed in violation of paragraph (1) of this subsection.

(3) The Secretary may by regulation remove drugs subject to section 355 of this title from the requirements of paragraph (1) of this subsection when such requirements are not necessary for the protection of the public health.

(4)(A) A drug that is subject to paragraph (1) shall be deemed to be misbranded if at any time prior to dispensing the label of the drug fails to bear, at a minimum, the symbol "Rx only".

(B) A drug to which paragraph (1) does not apply shall be deemed to be misbranded if at any time prior to dispensing the label of the drug bears the symbol described in subparagraph (A).

(5) Nothing in this subsection shall be construed to relieve any person from any requirement prescribed by or under authority of law with respect to drugs now included or which may hereafter be included within the classifications stated in sections 4721, 6001, and 6151 of title 26, or to marihuana as defined in section 4761 of title 26.

(c) Sales restrictions

(1) No person may sell, purchase, or trade or offer to sell, purchase, or trade any drug sample. For purposes of this paragraph and subsection (d) of this section, the term "drug sample" means a unit of a drug, subject to subsection (b) of this section, which is not intended to be sold and is intended to promote the sale of the drug. Nothing in this paragraph shall subject an officer or executive of a drug manufacturer or distributor to criminal liability solely because of a sale, purchase, trade, or offer to sell, purchase, or trade in violation of this paragraph by other employees of the manufacturer or distributor.

(2) No person may sell, purchase, or trade, offer to sell, purchase, or trade, or counterfeit any coupon. For purposes of this paragraph, the term "coupon" means a form which may be redeemed, at no cost or at a reduced cost, for a drug which is prescribed in accordance with subsection (b) of this section.

(3)(A) No person may sell, purchase, or trade, or offer to sell, purchase, or trade, any drug—

(i) which is subject to subsection (b) of this section, and

(ii)(I) which was purchased by a public or private hospital or other health care entity, or

(II) which was donated or supplied at a reduced price to a charitable organization described in section 501(c)(3) of title 26.

(B) Subparagraph (A) does not apply to—

(i) the purchase or other acquisition by a hospital or other health care entity which is a member of a group purchasing organization of a drug for its own use from the group purchasing organization or from other hospitals or health care entities which are members of such organization,

(ii) the sale, purchase, or trade of a drug or an offer to sell, purchase, or trade a drug by an organization described in subparagraph (A)(ii)(II) to a nonprofit affiliate of the organization to the extent otherwise permitted by law,

(iii) a sale, purchase, or trade of a drug or an offer to sell, purchase, or trade a drug among hospitals or other health care entities which are under common control,

(iv) a sale, purchase, or trade of a drug or an offer to sell, purchase, or trade a drug for emergency medical reasons, or

(v) a sale, purchase, or trade of a drug, an offer to sell, purchase, or trade a drug, or the dispensing of a drug pursuant to a prescription executed in accordance with subsection (b) of this section.

For purposes of this paragraph, the term "entity" does not include a wholesale distributor of drugs or a retail pharmacy licensed under State law and the term "emergency medical reasons" includes transfers of a drug between health care entities or from a health care entity to a retail pharmacy undertaken to alleviate temporary shortages of the drug arising from delays in or interruptions of regular distribution schedules.

(d) Distribution of drug samples

(1) Except as provided in paragraphs (2) and (3), no person may distribute any drug sample. For purposes of this subsection, the term "distribute" does not include the providing of a drug sample to a patient by a—

(A) practitioner licensed to prescribe such drug,

(B) health care professional acting at the direction and under the supervision of such a practitioner, or

(C) pharmacy of a hospital or of another health care entity that is acting at the direction of such a practitioner and that received such sample pursuant to paragraph (2) or (3).

(2)(A) The manufacturer or authorized distributor of record of a drug subject to subsection (b) of this section may, in accordance with this paragraph, distribute drug samples by mail or common carrier to practitioners licensed to prescribe such drugs or, at the request of a licensed practitioner, to pharmacies of hospitals or other health care entities. Such a distribution of drug samples may only be made—

(i) in response to a written request for drug samples made on a form which meets the requirements of subparagraph (B), and

(ii) under a system which requires the recipient of the drug sample to execute a written receipt for the drug sample upon its delivery and the return of the receipt to the manufacturer or authorized distributor of record.

(B) A written request for a drug sample required by subparagraph (A)(i) shall contain—

(i) the name, address, professional designation, and signature of the practitioner making the request,

(ii) the identity of the drug sample requested and the quantity requested,

(iii) the name of the manufacturer of the drug sample requested, and

(iv) the date of the request.

(C) Each drug manufacturer or authorized distributor of record which makes distributions by mail or common carrier under this paragraph shall maintain, for a period of 3 years, the request forms submitted for such distributions and the receipts submitted for such distributions and shall maintain a record of distributions of drug samples which identifies the drugs distributed and the recipients of the distributions. Forms, receipts, and records required to be maintained under this subparagraph shall be made available by the drug manufacturer or authorized distributor of record to Federal and State officials engaged in the regulation of drugs and in the enforcement of laws applicable to drugs.

(3) The manufacturer or authorized distributor of record of a drug subject to subsection (b) of this section may, by means other than mail or common carrier, distribute drug samples only if the manufacturer or authorized distributor of record makes the distributions in accordance with subparagraph (A) and carries out the activities described in subparagraphs (B) through (F) as follows:

(A) Drug samples may only be distributed—

(i) to practitioners licensed to prescribe such drugs if they make a written request for the drug samples, or

(ii) at the written request of such a licensed practitioner, to pharmacies of hospitals or other health care entities.

A written request for drug samples shall be made on a form which contains the practitioner's name, address, and professional designation, the identity of the drug sample requested, the quantity of drug samples requested, the name of the manufacturer or authorized distributor of record of the drug sample, the date of the request and signature of the practitioner making the request.

(B) Drug manufacturers or authorized distributors of record shall store drug samples under conditions that will maintain their stability, integrity, and effectiveness and will assure that the drug samples will be free of contamination, deterioration, and adulteration.

(C) Drug manufacturers or authorized distributors of record shall conduct, at least annually, a complete and accurate inventory of all drug samples in the possession of representatives of the manufacturer or authorized distributor of record. Drug manufacturers or authorized distributors of record shall maintain lists of the names and address of each of their representatives who distribute drug samples and of the sites where drug samples are stored. Drug manufacturers or authorized distributors of record shall maintain records for at least 3 years of all drug samples distributed, destroyed, or returned to the manufacturer or authorized distributor of record, of all inventories maintained under this subparagraph, of all thefts or significant losses of drug samples, and of all requests made under subparagraph (A) for drug samples. Records and lists maintained under this subparagraph shall be made available by the drug manufacturer or authorized distributor of record to the Secretary upon request.

(D) Drug manufacturers or authorized distributors of record shall notify the Secretary of any significant loss of drug samples and any known theft of drug samples.

(E) Drug manufacturers or authorized distributors of record shall report to the Secretary any conviction of their representatives for violations of subsection (c)(1) of this section or a State law because of the sale, purchase, or trade of a drug sample or the offer to sell, purchase, or trade a drug sample.

(F) Drug manufacturers or authorized distributors of record shall provide to the Secretary the name and telephone number of the individual responsible for responding to a request for information respecting drug samples.

(e) Wholesale distributors; guidelines for licensing; definitions

(1)(A) Each person who is engaged in the wholesale distribution of a drug subject to subsection (b) of this section and who is not the manufacturer or an authorized distributor of record of such drug shall, before each wholesale distribution of such drug (including each distribution to an authorized distributor of record or to a retail pharmacy), provide to the person who receives the drug a statement (in such form and containing such information as the Secretary may require) identifying each prior sale, purchase, or trade of such drug (including the date of the transaction and the names and addresses of all parties to the transaction).

(B) Each manufacturer of a drug subject to subsection (b) of this section shall maintain at its corporate offices a current list of the authorized distributors of record of such drug.

(2)(A) No person may engage in the wholesale distribution in interstate commerce of drugs subject to subsection (b) of this section in a State unless such person is licensed by the State in accordance with the guidelines issued under subparagraph (B).

(B) The Secretary shall by regulation issue guidelines establishing minimum standards, terms, and conditions for the licensing of persons to make wholesale distributions in interstate commerce of drugs subject to subsection (b) of this section. Such guidelines shall prescribe requirements for the storage and handling of such drugs and for the establishment and maintenance of records of the distributions of such drugs.

(3) For the purposes of this subsection and subsection (d) of this section—

(A) the term "authorized distributors of record" means those distributors with whom a manufacturer has established an ongoing relationship to distribute such manufacturer's products, and

(B) the term "wholesale distribution" means distribution of drugs subject to subsection (b) of this section to other than the consumer or patient but does not include intracompany sales and does not include distributions of drugs described in subsection (c)(3)(B) of this section.

(f) Veterinary prescription drugs

(1)(A) A drug intended for use by animals other than man, other than a veterinary feed directive drug intended for use in animal feed or an animal feed bearing or containing a veterinary feed directive drug, which—

(i) because of its toxicity or other potentiality for harmful effect, or the method of its use, or the collateral measures necessary for its use, is not safe for animal use except under the professional supervision of a licensed veterinarian, or

(ii) is limited by an approved application under subsection (b) of section 360b of this title, a conditionally-approved application under section 360ccc of this title, or an index listing under section 360ccc–1 of this title to use under the professional supervision of a licensed veterinarian,

shall be dispensed only by or upon the lawful written or oral order of a licensed veterinarian in the course of the veterinarian's professional practice.

(B) For purposes of subparagraph (A), an order is lawful if the order—

(i) is a prescription or other order authorized by law,

(ii) is, if an oral order, promptly reduced to writing by the person lawfully filling the order, and filed by that person, and

(iii) is refilled only if authorized in the original order or in a subsequent oral order promptly reduced to writing by the person lawfully filling the order, and filed by that person.

(C) The act of dispensing a drug contrary to the provisions of this paragraph shall be deemed to be an act which results in the drug being misbranded while held for sale.

(2) Any drug when dispensed in accordance with paragraph (1) of this subsection—

(A) shall be exempt from the requirements of section 352 of this title, except subsections (a), (g), (h), (i)(2), (i)(3), and (p) of such section, and

(B) shall be exempt from the packaging requirements of subsections (g), (h), and (p) of such section, if—

(i) when dispensed by a licensed veterinarian, the drug bears a label containing the name and address of the practitioner and any directions for use and cautionary statements specified by the practitioner, or

(ii) when dispensed by filling the lawful order of a licensed veterinarian, the drug bears a label containing the name and address of the dispenser, the serial number and date of the order or of its filling, the name of the licensed veterinarian, and the directions for use and cautionary statements, if any, contained in such order.

The preceding sentence shall not apply to any drug dispensed in the course of the conduct of a business of dispensing drugs pursuant to diagnosis by mail.

(3) The Secretary may by regulation exempt drugs for animals other than man subject to section 360b, 360ccc, or 360ccc–1 of this title from the requirements of paragraph (1) when such requirements are not necessary for the protection of the public health.

(4) A drug which is subject to paragraph (1) shall be deemed to be misbranded if at any time prior to dispensing its label fails to bear the statement "Caution: Federal law restricts this drug to use by or on the order of a licensed veterinarian.". A drug to which paragraph (1) does not apply shall be deemed to be misbranded if at any time prior to dispensing its label bears the statement specified in the preceding sentence.

(g) Regulation of combination products

(1) The Secretary shall in accordance with this subsection assign an agency center to regulate products that constitute a combination of a drug, device, or biological product. The Secretary shall determine the primary mode of action of the combination product. If the Secretary determines that the primary mode of action is that of—

(A) a drug (other than a biological product), the agency center charged with premarket review of drugs shall have primary jurisdiction,

(B) a device, the agency center charged with premarket review of devices shall have primary jurisdiction, or

(C) a biological product, the agency center charged with premarket review of biological products shall have primary jurisdiction.

(2) Nothing in this subsection shall prevent the Secretary from using any agency resources of the Food and Drug Administration necessary to ensure adequate review of the safety, effectiveness, or substantial equivalence of an article.

(3) The Secretary shall promulgate regulations to implement market clearance procedures in accordance with paragraphs (1) and (2) not later than 1 year after November 28, 1990.

(4)(A) Not later than 60 days after October 26, 2002, the Secretary shall establish within the Office of the Commissioner of Food and Drugs an office to ensure the prompt assignment of combination products to agency centers, the timely and effective premarket review of such products, and consistent and appropriate postmarket regulation of like products subject to the same statutory requirements to the extent permitted by law. Additionally, the office shall, in determining whether a product is to be designated a combination product, consult with the component within the Office of the Commissioner of Food and Drugs that is responsible for such determinations. Such office (referred to in this paragraph as the "Office") shall have appropriate scientific and medical expertise, and shall be headed by a director.

(B) In carrying out this subsection, the Office shall, for each combination product, promptly assign an agency center with primary jurisdiction in accordance with paragraph (1) for the premarket review of such product.

(C)(i) In carrying out this subsection, the Office shall ensure timely and effective premarket reviews by overseeing the timeliness of and coordinating reviews involving more than one agency center.

(ii) In order to ensure the timeliness of the premarket review of a combination product, the agency center with primary jurisdiction for the product, and the consulting agency center, shall be responsible to the Office with respect to the timeliness of the premarket review.

(D) In carrying out this subsection, the Office shall ensure the consistency and appropriateness of postmarket regulation of like products subject to the same statutory requirements to the extent permitted by law.

(E)(i) Any dispute regarding the timeliness of the premarket review of a combination product may be presented to the Office for resolution, unless the dispute is clearly premature.

(ii) During the review process, any dispute regarding the substance of the premarket review may be presented to the Commissioner of Food and Drugs after first being considered by the agency center with primary jurisdiction of the premarket review, under the scientific dispute resolution procedures for such center. The Commissioner of Food and Drugs shall consult with the Director of the Office in resolving the substantive dispute.

(F) The Secretary, acting through the Office, shall review each agreement, guidance, or practice of the Secretary that is specific to the assignment of combination products to agency centers and shall determine whether the agreement, guidance, or practice is consistent with the requirements of this subsection. In carrying out such review, the Secretary shall consult with stakeholders and the directors of the agency centers. After such consultation, the Secretary shall determine whether to continue in effect, modify, revise, or eliminate such agreement, guidance, or practice, and shall publish in the Federal Register a notice of the availability of such modified or revised agreement, guidance or practice. Nothing in this paragraph shall be construed as preventing the Secretary from following each agreement, guidance, or practice until continued, modified, revised, or eliminated.

(G) Not later than one year after October 26, 2002, and annually thereafter, the Secretary shall report to the appropriate committees of Congress on the activities and impact of the Office. The report shall include provisions—

(i) describing the numbers and types of combination products under review and the timeliness in days of such assignments, reviews, and dispute resolutions;

(ii) identifying the number of premarket reviews of such products that involved a consulting agency center; and

(iii) describing improvements in the consistency of postmarket regulation of combination products.

(H) Nothing in this paragraph shall be construed to limit the regulatory authority of any agency center.

(5) As used in this subsection:

(A) The term "agency center" means a center or alternative organizational component of the Food and Drug Administration.

(B) The term "biological product" has the meaning given the term in section 262(i) of title 42.

(C) The term "market clearance" includes—

(i) approval of an application under section 355, 357,[1] 360e, or 360j(g) of this title,

(ii) a finding of substantial equivalence under this part, and

(iii) approval of a biologics license application under subsection (a) of section 262 of title 42.

(June 25, 1938, ch. 675, § 503, 52 Stat. 1051; Oct. 26, 1951, ch. 578, § 1, 65 Stat. 648; Pub. L. 87–781, title I, § 104(e)(2), Oct. 10, 1962, 76 Stat. 785; Pub. L. 91–601, § 6(e), formerly § 7(e), Dec. 30, 1970, 84 Stat. 1673, renumbered Pub. L. 97–35, title XII, § 1205(c), Aug. 13, 1981, 95 Stat. 716; Pub. L. 100–293, §§ 4–6, Apr. 22, 1988, 102 Stat. 96–98; Pub. L. 100–670, title I, § 105, Nov. 16, 1988, 102 Stat. 3983; Pub. L. 101–629, § 16(a), Nov. 28, 1990, 104 Stat. 4526; Pub. L. 102–108, § 2(d), Aug. 17, 1991, 105 Stat. 550; Pub. L. 102–300, § 6(d), June 16, 1992, 106 Stat. 240; Pub. L. 102–353, §§ 2(a)–(c), 4, Aug. 26, 1992, 106 Stat. 941, 942; Pub. L. 104–250, § 5(a), Oct. 9, 1996, 110 Stat. 3155; Pub. L. 105–115, title I, §§ 123(e), 126(a), (c)(1), (2), Nov. 21, 1997, 111 Stat. 2324, 2327, 2328; Pub. L. 107–250, title II, § 204, Oct. 26, 2002, 116 Stat. 1611; Pub. L. 108–282, title I, § 102(b)(5)(F), Aug. 2, 2004, 118 Stat. 903.)

References in Text

Section 357 of this title, referred to in subsec. (g)(5)(C)(i), was repealed by Pub. L. 105–115, title I, § 125(b)(1), Nov. 21, 1997, 111 Stat. 2325.

Codification

In subsec. (b)(5), "sections 4721, 6001, and 6151 of title 26" and "section 4761 of title 26" substituted for "section 3220 of the Internal Revenue Code (26 U.S.C. 3220)" and "section 3238(b) of the Internal Revenue Code (26 U.S.C. 3238(b))", respectively, on authority of section 7852(b) of Title 26, Internal Revenue Code.

Amendments

2004—Subsec. (f)(1)(A)(ii). Pub. L. 108–282, § 102(b)(5)(F)(i), substituted "360b of this title, a conditionally-approved application under section 360ccc of this title, or an index listing under section 360ccc–1 of this title" for "360b of this title".

Subsec. (f)(3). Pub. L. 108–282, § 102(b)(5)(F)(ii), substituted "section 360b, 360ccc, or 360ccc–1" for "section 360b".

[1] See References in Text note below.

2002—Subsec. (g)(1). Pub. L. 107–250, §204(1)(A), substituted "shall in accordance with this subsection assign an agency center" for "shall designate a component of the Food and Drug Administration" in first sentence of introductory provisions.

Subsec. (g)(1)(A) to (C). Pub. L. 107–250, §204(1)(B), substituted "the agency center charged" for "the persons charged".

Subsec. (g)(4). Pub. L. 107–250, §204(3), added par. (4). Former par. (4) redesignated (5).

Subsec. (g)(5). Pub. L. 107–250, §204(2), (4), redesignated par. (4) as (5), added subpar. (A), and redesignated former subpars. (A) and (B) as (B) and (C), respectively.

1997—Subsec. (b)(1)(A) to (C). Pub. L. 105–115, §126(c)(1), redesignated subpars. (B) and (C) as (A) and (B), respectively, and struck out former subpar. (A), which read as follows: "is a habit-forming drug to which section 352(d) of this title applies; or".

Subsec. (b)(3). Pub. L. 105–115, §126(c)(2), struck out reference to section 352(d) of this title before "355".

Subsec. (b)(4). Pub. L. 105–115, §126(a), amended par. (4) generally. Prior to amendment, par. (4) read as follows: "A drug which is subject to paragraph (1) of this subsection shall be deemed to be misbranded if at any time prior to dispensing its label fails to bear the statement 'Caution: Federal law prohibits dispensing without prescription'. A drug to which paragraph (1) of this subsection does not apply shall be deemed to be misbranded if at any time prior to dispensing its label bears the caution statement quoted in the preceding sentence."

Subsec. (g)(4)(A). Pub. L. 105–115, §123(e)(1), substituted "section 262(i) of title 42" for "section 262(a) of title 42".

Subsec. (g)(4)(B)(iii). Pub. L. 105–115, §123(e)(2), substituted "biologics license application under subsection (a)" for "product or establishment license under subsection (a) or (d)".

1996—Subsec. (f)(1)(A). Pub. L. 104–250 inserted ", other than a veterinary feed directive drug intended for use in animal feed or an animal feed bearing or containing a veterinary feed directive drug," after "other than man" in introductory provisions.

1992—Subsec. (d)(1). Pub. L. 102–353, §4(1), amended par. (1) generally. Prior to amendment, par. (1) read as follows: "Except as provided in paragraphs (2) and (3), no representative of a drug manufacturer or distributor may distribute any drug sample."

Subsec. (d)(2). Pub. L. 102–353, §4(2), substituted "authorized distributor of record" for "distributor" wherever appearing.

Subsec. (d)(3). Pub. L. 102–353, §4(2), substituted "authorized distributor of record" for "distributor" and "authorized distributors of record" for "distributors" wherever appearing.

Subsec. (e)(1). Pub. L. 102–353, §4(3), amended par. (1) generally. Prior to amendment, par. (1) read as follows: "Each person who is engaged in the wholesale distribution of drugs subject to subsection (b) of this section and who is not an authorized distributor of record of such drugs shall provide to each wholesale distributor of such drugs a statement identifying each sale of the drug (including the date of the sale) before the sale to such wholesale distributor. Each manufacturer shall maintain at its corporate offices a current list of such authorized distributors."

Subsec. (e)(2)(A). Pub. L. 102–353, §2(a), (d), temporarily inserted "or has registered with the Secretary in accordance with paragraph (3)". See Termination Date of 1992 Amendment note below.

Subsec. (e)(3). Pub. L. 102–353, §2(b), (d), temporarily added par. (3). Former par. (3) redesignated (4). See Termination Date of 1992 Amendment note below.

Subsec. (e)(4). Pub. L. 102–353, §4(4), inserted "and subsection (d) of this section" after "For the purposes of this subsection".

Pub. L. 102–353, §2(b), (d), temporarily redesignated par. (3) as (4). See Termination Date of 1992 Amendment note below.

Subsec. (f)(1)(B). Pub. L. 102–353, §2(c), which directed the substitution of "an order" for "and order", could not be executed because "and order" did not appear in subpar. (B).

Subsec. (g)(3). Pub. L. 102–300 substituted "clearance" for "approval".

1991—Subsec. (c). Pub. L. 102–108, §2(d)(3), redesignated subsec. (c), relating to veterinary prescription drugs, as (f). Former subsec. (f) redesignated (g).

Subsec. (c)(2), (3)(B)(v). Pub. L. 102–108, §2(d)(1), made technical amendment to reference to subsection (b) of this section involving corresponding provision of original act.

Subsec. (d)(3)(E). Pub. L. 102–108, §2(d)(2), made technical amendment to reference to subsection (c)(1) of this section involving corresponding provision of original act.

Subsec. (f). Pub. L. 102–108, §2(d)(4), redesignated subsec. (f), relating to regulation of combination products, as (g).

Pub. L. 102–108, §2(d)(3), redesignated subsec. (c), relating to veterinary prescription drugs, as (f).

Subsec. (g). Pub. L. 102–108, §2(d)(4), redesignated subsec. (f), relating to regulation of combination products, as (g).

1990—Pub. L. 101–629, §16(a)(1), substituted "Exemptions and consideration for certain drugs, devices, and biological products" for "Exemptions in case of drugs and devices" in section catchline.

Subsec. (f). Pub. L. 101–629, §16(a)(2), added subsec. (f).

1988—Subsec. (c). Pub. L. 100–670 added subsec. (c) relating to veterinary prescription drugs.

Pub. L. 100–293, §4, added subsec. (c) relating to sales restrictions.

Subsec. (d). Pub. L. 100–293, §5, added subsec. (d).

Subsec. (e). Pub. L. 100–293, §6, added subsec. (e).

1970—Subsec. (b)(2). Pub. L. 91–601 included exemption from packaging requirements of subsec. (p) of section 352 of this title.

1962—Subsec. (b)(1)(C). Pub. L. 87–781 substituted "approved" for "effective".

1951—Subsec. (b). Act Oct. 26, 1951, amended subsec. (b) generally to protect the public from abuses in the sale of potent prescription drugs, and to relieve retail pharmacists and the public from unnecessary restrictions on the dispensation of drugs that are safe to use without supervision of a doctor.

EFFECTIVE DATE OF 1997 AMENDMENT

Amendment by Pub. L. 105–115 effective 90 days after Nov. 21, 1997, except as otherwise provided, see section 501 of Pub. L. 105–115, set out as a note under section 321 of this title.

TERMINATION DATE OF 1992 AMENDMENT

Section 2(d) of Pub. L. 102–353 provided that: "Effective September 14, 1994, the amendments made by subsections (a) and (b) [amending this section] shall no longer be in effect."

EFFECTIVE DATE OF 1988 AMENDMENT

Section 8 of Pub. L. 100–293 provided that:

"(a) GENERAL RULE.—Except as provided in subsection (b), this Act and the amendments made by this Act [amending this section and sections 331, 333, and 381 of this title and enacting provisions set out as notes under this section and section 301 of this title] shall take effect upon the expiration of 90 days after the date of the enactment of this Act [Apr. 22, 1988].

"(b) EXCEPTION.—

"(1) Section 503(d) of the Federal Food, Drug, and Cosmetic Act [21 U.S.C. 353(d)] (as added by section 5 of this Act) shall take effect upon the expiration of 180 days after the date of the enactment of this Act [Apr. 22, 1988].

"(2) The Secretary of Health and Human Services shall by regulation issue the guidelines required by section 503(e)(2)(B) of the Federal Food, Drug, and Cosmetic Act [21 U.S.C. 353(e)(2)(B)] (as added by section 6 of this Act) not later than 180 days after the date of the enactment of this Act. Section 503(e)(2)(A) of such Act shall take effect upon the expiration of 2 years after the date such regulations are promulgated and take effect."

EFFECTIVE DATE OF 1970 AMENDMENT

Amendment by Pub. L. 91–601 effective Dec. 30, 1970, and regulations establishing special packaging standards effective no sooner than 180 days or later than one year from date regulations are final, or an earlier date published in Federal Register, see section 8 of Pub. L. 91–601, set out as an Effective Date note under section 1471 of Title 15, Commerce and Trade.

EFFECTIVE DATE OF 1962 AMENDMENT

Amendment by Pub. L. 87–781 effective Oct. 10, 1962, see section 107 of Pub. L. 87–781, set out as a note under section 321 of this title.

EFFECTIVE DATE OF 1951 AMENDMENT

Amendment by act Oct. 26, 1951, effective six months after Oct. 26, 1951, see section 3 of act Oct. 26, 1951, set out as a note under section 333 of this title.

TRANSFER OF FUNCTIONS

For transfer of functions of Federal Security Administrator to Secretary of Health, Education, and Welfare [now Health and Human Services], and of Food and Drug Administration in the Department of Agriculture to Federal Security Agency, see notes set out under section 321 of this title.

EFFECTIVE MEDICATION GUIDES

Pub. L. 104–180, title VI, §601, Aug. 6, 1996, 110 Stat. 1593, provided that:

"(a) IN GENERAL.—Not later than 30 days after the date of enactment of this Act [Aug. 6, 1996], the Secretary of the Department of Health and Human Services shall request that national organizations representing health care professionals, consumer organizations, voluntary health agencies, the pharmaceutical industry, drug wholesalers, patient drug information database companies, and other relevant parties collaborate to develop a long-range comprehensive action plan to achieve goals consistent with the goals of the proposed rule of the Food and Drug Administration on 'Prescription Drug Product Labeling: Medication Guide Requirements' (60 Fed. Reg. 44182; relating to the provision of oral and written prescription information to consumers).

"(b) GOALS.—Goals consistent with the proposed rule described in subsection (a) are the distribution of useful written information to 75 percent of individuals receiving new precriptions [sic] by the year 2000 and to 95 percent by the year 2006.

"(c) PLAN.—The plan described in subsection (a) shall—

"(1) identify the plan goals;

"(2) assess the effectiveness of the current private-sector approaches used to provide oral and written prescription information to consumers;

"(3) develop guidelines for providing effective oral and written prescription information consistent with the findings of any such assessment;

"(4) contain elements necessary to ensure the transmittal of useful information to the consuming public, including being scientifically accurate, non-promotional in tone and content, sufficiently specific and comprehensive as to adequately inform consumers about the use of the product, and in an understandable, legible format that is readily comprehensible and not confusing to consumers expected to use the product.[;]

"(5) develop a mechanism to assess periodically the quality of the oral and written prescription information and the frequency with which the information is provided to consumers; and

"(6) provide for compliance with relevant State board regulations.

"(d) LIMITATION ON THE AUTHORITY OF THE SECRETARY.—The Secretary of the Department of Health and Human Services shall have no authority to implement the proposed rule described in subsection (a), or to develop any similar regulation, policy statement, or other guideline specifying a uniform content or format for written information voluntarily provided to consumers about prescription drugs if, (1) not later than 120 days after the date of enactment of this Act [Aug. 6, 1996], the national organizations described in subsection (a) develop and submit to the Secretary for Health and Human Services a comprehensive, long-range action plan (as described in subsection (a)) which shall be acceptable to the Secretary of Health and Human Services; (2) the aforementioned plan is submitted to the Secretary of Health and Human Services for review and acceptance: *Provided*, That the Secretary shall give due consideration to the submitted plan and that any such acceptance shall not be arbitrarily withheld; and (3) the implementation of (a) a plan accepted by the Secretary commences within 30 days of the Secretary's acceptance of such plan, or (b) the plan submitted to the Secretary commences within 60 days of the submission of such plan if the Secretary fails to take any action on the plan within 30 days of the submission of the plan. The Secretary shall accept, reject or suggest modifications to the plan submitted within 30 days of its submission. The Secretary may confer with and assist private parties in the development of the plan described in subsections (a) and (b).

"(e) SECRETARY REVIEW.—Not later than January 1, 2001, the Secretary of the Department of Health and Human Services shall review the status of private-sector initiatives designed to achieve the goals of the plan described in subsection (a), and if such goals are not achieved, the limitation in subsection (d) shall not apply, and the Secretary shall seek public comment on other initiatives that may be carried out to meet such goals."

CONGRESSIONAL FINDINGS

Section 2 of Pub. L. 100–293 provided that: "The Congress finds the following:

"(1) American consumers cannot purchase prescription drugs with the certainty that the products are safe and effective.

"(2) The integrity of the distribution system for prescription drugs is insufficient to prevent the introduction and eventual retail sale of substandard, ineffective, or even counterfeit drugs.

"(3) The existence and operation of a wholesale submarket, commonly known as the 'diversion market', prevents effective control over or even routine knowledge of the true sources of prescription drugs in a significant number of cases.

"(4) Large amounts of drugs are being reimported to the United States as American goods returned. These imports are a health and safety risk to American consumers because they may have become subpotent or adulterated during foreign handling and shipping.

"(5) The ready market for prescription drug reimports has been the catalyst for a continuing series of frauds against American manufacturers and has provided the cover for the importation of foreign counterfeit drugs.

"(6) The existing system of providing drug samples to physicians through manufacturer's representatives has been abused for decades and has resulted in the sale to consumers of misbranded, expired, and adulterated pharmaceuticals.

"(7) The bulk resale of below wholesale priced prescription drugs by health care entities, for ultimate sale at retail, helps fuel the diversion market and is an unfair form of competition to wholesalers and retailers that must pay otherwise prevailing market prices.

"(8) The effect of these several practices and conditions is to create an unacceptable risk that counterfeit, adulterated, misbranded, subpotent, or expired drugs will be sold to American consumers."

§353a. Pharmacy compounding

(a) In general

Sections 351(a)(2)(B), 352(f)(1), and 355 of this title shall not apply to a drug product if the drug product is compounded for an identified individual patient based on the unsolicited receipt of a valid prescription order or a notation, approved by the prescribing practitioner, on the prescription order that a compounded product is necessary for the identified patient, if the drug product meets the requirements of this section, and if the compounding—

(1) is by—

(A) a licensed pharmacist in a State licensed pharmacy or a Federal facility, or

(B) a licensed physician,

on the prescription order for such individual patient made by a licensed physician or other licensed practitioner authorized by State law to prescribe drugs; or

(2)(A) is by a licensed pharmacist or licensed physician in limited quantities before the receipt of a valid prescription order for such individual patient; and

(B) is based on a history of the licensed pharmacist or licensed physician receiving valid prescription orders for the compounding of the drug product, which orders have been generated solely within an established relationship between—

(i) the licensed pharmacist or licensed physician; and

(ii)(I) such individual patient for whom the prescription order will be provided; or

(II) the physician or other licensed practitioner who will write such prescription order.

(b) Compounded drug

(1) Licensed pharmacist and licensed physician

A drug product may be compounded under subsection (a) of this section if the licensed pharmacist or licensed physician—

(A) compounds the drug product using bulk drug substances, as defined in regulations of the Secretary published at section 207.3(a)(4) of title 21 of the Code of Federal Regulations—

(i) that—

(I) comply with the standards of an applicable United States Pharmacopoeia or National Formulary monograph, if a monograph exists, and the United States Pharmacopoeia chapter on pharmacy compounding;

(II) if such a monograph does not exist, are drug substances that are components of drugs approved by the Secretary; or

(III) if such a monograph does not exist and the drug substance is not a component of a drug approved by the Secretary, that appear on a list developed by the Secretary through regulations issued by the Secretary under subsection (d) of this section;

(ii) that are manufactured by an establishment that is registered under section 360 of this title (including a foreign establishment that is registered under section 360(i) of this title); and

(iii) that are accompanied by valid certificates of analysis for each bulk drug substance;

(B) compounds the drug product using ingredients (other than bulk drug substances) that comply with the standards of an applicable United States Pharmacopoeia or National Formulary monograph, if a monograph exists, and the United States Pharmacopoeia chapter on pharmacy compounding;

(C) does not compound a drug product that appears on a list published by the Secretary in the Federal Register of drug products that have been withdrawn or removed from the market because such drug products or components of such drug products have been found to be unsafe or not effective; and

(D) does not compound regularly or in inordinate amounts (as defined by the Secretary) any drug products that are essentially copies of a commercially available drug product.

(2) Definition

For purposes of paragraph (1)(D), the term "essentially a copy of a commercially available drug product" does not include a drug product in which there is a change, made for an identified individual patient, which produces for that patient a significant difference, as determined by the prescribing practitioner, between the compounded drug and the comparable commercially available drug product.

(3) Drug product

A drug product may be compounded under subsection (a) only if—

(A) such drug product is not a drug product identified by the Secretary by regulation as a drug product that presents demonstrable difficulties for compounding that reasonably demonstrate an adverse effect on the safety or effectiveness of that drug product; and

(B) such drug product is compounded in a State—

(i) that has entered into a memorandum of understanding with the Secretary which addresses the distribution of inordinate amounts of compounded drug products interstate and provides for appropriate investigation by a State agency of complaints relating to compounded drug products distributed outside such State; or

(ii) that has not entered into the memorandum of understanding described in clause (i) and the licensed pharmacist, licensed pharmacy, or licensed physician distributes (or causes to be distributed) compounded drug products out of the State in which they are compounded in quantities that do not exceed 5 percent of the total prescription orders dispensed or distributed by such pharmacy or physician.

The Secretary shall, in consultation with the National Association of Boards of Pharmacy, develop a standard memorandum of understanding for use by the States in complying with subparagraph (B)(i).

(c) Advertising and promotion

A drug may be compounded under subsection (a) of this section only if the pharmacy, licensed pharmacist, or licensed physician does not advertise or promote the compounding of any particular drug, class of drug, or type of drug. The pharmacy, licensed pharmacist, or licensed physician may advertise and promote the compounding service provided by the licensed pharmacist or licensed physician.

(d) Regulations

(1) In general

The Secretary shall issue regulations to implement this section. Before issuing regulations to implement subsections (b)(1)(A)(i)(III), (b)(1)(C), or (b)(3)(A) of this section, the Secretary shall convene and consult an advisory committee on compounding unless the Secretary determines that the issuance of such regulations before consultation is necessary to protect the public health. The advisory committee shall include representatives from the National Association of Boards of Pharmacy, the United States Pharmacopoeia, pharmacy, physician, and consumer organizations, and other experts selected by the Secretary.

(2) Limiting compounding

The Secretary, in consultation with the United States Pharmacopoeia Convention, Incorporated, shall promulgate regulations identifying drug substances that may be used in compounding under subsection (b)(1)(A)(i)(III) of this section for which a monograph does not exist or which are not components of drug products approved by the Secretary. The Secretary shall include in the regulation the criteria for such substances, which shall include historical use, reports in peer reviewed medical literature, or other criteria the Secretary may identify.

(e) Application

This section shall not apply to—

(1) compounded positron emission tomography drugs as defined in section 321(ii) of this title; or

(2) radiopharmaceuticals.

(f) "Compounding" defined

As used in this section, the term "compounding" does not include mixing, reconstituting, or other such acts that are performed in accordance with directions contained in approved labeling provided by the product's manufacturer and other manufacturer directions consistent with that labeling.

(June 25, 1938, ch. 675, § 503A, as added Pub. L. 105–115, title I, § 127(a), Nov. 21, 1997, 111 Stat. 2328.)

EFFECTIVE DATE

Section 127(b) of Pub. L. 105–115 provided that: "Section 503A of the Federal Food, Drug, and Cosmetic Act [21 U.S.C. 353a], added by subsection (a), shall take effect upon the expiration of the 1-year period beginning on the date of the enactment of this Act [Nov. 21, 1997]."

§ 353b. Prereview of television advertisements

(a) In general

The Secretary may require the submission of any television advertisement for a drug (including any script, story board, rough, or a completed video production of the television advertisement) to the Secretary for review under this section not later than 45 days before dissemination of the television advertisement.

(b) Review

In conducting a review of a television advertisement under this section, the Secretary may make recommendations with respect to information included in the label of the drug—

(1) on changes that are—

(A) necessary to protect the consumer good and well-being; or

(B) consistent with prescribing information for the product under review; and

(2) if appropriate and if information exists, on statements for inclusion in the advertisement to address the specific efficacy of the drug as it relates to specific population groups, including elderly populations, children, and racial and ethnic minorities.

(c) No authority to require changes

Except as provided by subsection (e), this section does not authorize the Secretary to make or direct changes in any material submitted pursuant to subsection (a).

(d) Elderly populations, children, racially and ethnically diverse communities

In formulating recommendations under subsection (b), the Secretary shall take into consideration the impact of the advertised drug on elderly populations, children, and racially and ethnically diverse communities.

(e) Specific disclosures

(1) Serious risk; safety protocol

In conducting a review of a television advertisement under this section, if the Secretary determines that the advertisement would be false or misleading without a specific disclosure about a serious risk listed in the labeling of the drug involved, the Secretary may require inclusion of such disclosure in the advertisement.

(2) Date of approval

In conducting a review of a television advertisement under this section, the Secretary may require the advertisement to include, for a period not to exceed 2 years from the date of the approval of the drug under section 355 of this title or section 262 of title 42, a specific disclosure of such date of approval if the Secretary determines that the advertisement would otherwise be false or misleading.

(f) Rule of construction

Nothing in this section may be construed as having any effect on requirements under section 352(n) of this title or on the authority of the Secretary under section 314.550, 314.640, 601.45, or 601.94 of title 21, Code of Federal Regulations (or successor regulations).

(June 25, 1938, ch. 675, § 503B, as added Pub. L. 110–85, title IX, § 901(d)(2), Sept. 27, 2007, 121 Stat. 939.)

EFFECTIVE DATE

Section effective 180 days after Sept. 27, 2007, see section 909 of Pub. L. 110–85, set out as an Effective Date of 2007 Amendment note under section 331 of this title.

§354. Veterinary feed directive drugs

(a) Lawful veterinary feed directive requirement

(1) A drug intended for use in or on animal feed which is limited by an approved application filed pursuant to section 360b(b) of this title, a conditionally-approved application filed pursuant to section 360ccc of this title, or an index listing pursuant to section 360ccc–1 of this title to use under the professional supervision of a licensed veterinarian is a veterinary feed directive drug. Any animal feed bearing or containing a veterinary feed directive drug shall be fed to animals only by or upon a lawful veterinary feed directive issued by a licensed veterinarian in the course of the veterinarian's professional practice. When labeled, distributed, held, and used in accordance with this section, a veterinary feed directive drug and any animal feed bearing or containing a veterinary feed directive drug shall be exempt from section 352(f) of this title.

(2) A veterinary feed directive is lawful if it—

(A) contains such information as the Secretary may by general regulation or by order require; and

(B) is in compliance with the conditions and indications for use of the drug set forth in the notice published pursuant to section 360b(i) of this title, or the index listing pursuant to section 360ccc–1(e) of this title.

(3)(A) Any persons involved in the distribution or use of animal feed bearing or containing a veterinary feed directive drug and the licensed veterinarian issuing the veterinary feed directive shall maintain a copy of the veterinary feed directive applicable to each such feed, except in the case of a person distributing such feed to another person for further distribution. Such person distributing the feed shall maintain a written acknowledgment from the person to whom the feed is shipped stating that that person shall not ship or move such feed to an animal production facility without a veterinary feed directive or ship such feed to another person for further distribution unless that person has provided the same written acknowledgment to its immediate supplier.

(B) Every person required under subparagraph (A) to maintain records, and every person in charge or custody thereof, shall, upon request of an officer or employee designated by the Secretary, permit such officer or employee at all reasonable times to have access to and copy and verify such records.

(C) Any person who distributes animal feed bearing or containing a veterinary feed directive drug shall upon first engaging in such distribution notify the Secretary of that person's name and place of business. The failure to provide such notification shall be deemed to be an act which results in the drug being misbranded.

(b) Labeling and advertising

A veterinary feed directive drug and any feed bearing or containing a veterinary feed directive drug shall be deemed to be misbranded if their labeling fails to bear such cautionary statement and such other information as the Secretary may by general regulation or by order prescribe, or their advertising fails to conform to the conditions and indications for use published pursuant to section 360b(i) of this title, or the index listing pursuant to section 360ccc–1(e) of this title or fails to contain the general cautionary statement prescribed by the Secretary.

(c) Nonprescription status

Neither a drug subject to this section, nor animal feed bearing or containing such a drug, shall be deemed to be a prescription article under any Federal or State law.

(June 25, 1938, ch. 675, §504, as added Pub. L. 104–250, §5(b), Oct. 9, 1996, 110 Stat. 3155; amended Pub. L. 108–282, title I, §102(b)(5)(G), (H), Aug. 2, 2004, 118 Stat. 903.)

PRIOR PROVISIONS

A prior section 354, act June 25, 1938, ch. 675, §504, 52 Stat. 1052, which directed Secretary to promulgate regulations for listing of coal-tar colors, was repealed effective July 12, 1960, subject to provisions of section 203 of Pub. L. 86–618, by Pub. L. 86–618, title I, §103(a)(2), title II, §202, July 12, 1960, 74 Stat. 398, 404.

AMENDMENTS

2004—Subsec. (a)(1). Pub. L. 108–282, §102(b)(5)(G), substituted "360b(b) of this title, a conditionally-approved application filed pursuant to section 360ccc of this title, or an index listing pursuant to section 360ccc–1 of this title" for "360b(b) of this title".

Subsecs. (a)(2)(B), (b). Pub. L. 108–282, §102(b)(5)(H), substituted "360b(i) of this title, or the index listing pursuant to section 360ccc–1(e) of this title" for "360b(i) of this title".

§355. New drugs

(a) Necessity of effective approval of application

No person shall introduce or deliver for introduction into interstate commerce any new drug, unless an approval of an application filed pursuant to subsection (b) or (j) of this section is effective with respect to such drug.

(b) Filing application; contents

(1) Any person may file with the Secretary an application with respect to any drug subject to the provisions of subsection (a) of this section. Such person shall submit to the Secretary as a part of the application (A) full reports of investigations which have been made to show whether or not such drug is safe for use and whether such drug is effective in use; (B) a full list of the articles used as components of such drug; (C) a full statement of the composition of such drug; (D) a full description of the methods used in, and the facilities and controls used for, the manufacture, processing, and packing of such drug; (E) such samples of such drug and of the articles used as components thereof as the Secretary may require; (F) specimens of the labeling proposed to be used for such drug, and (G) any assessments required under section 355c of this title. The applicant shall file with the application the patent number and the expiration date of any patent which claims the drug for which the applicant submitted the application or which claims a method of using such drug and

with respect to which a claim of patent infringement could reasonably be asserted if a person not licensed by the owner engaged in the manufacture, use, or sale of the drug. If an application is filed under this subsection for a drug and a patent which claims such drug or a method of using such drug is issued after the filing date but before approval of the application, the applicant shall amend the application to include the information required by the preceding sentence. Upon approval of the application, the Secretary shall publish information submitted under the two preceding sentences. The Secretary shall, in consultation with the Director of the National Institutes of Health and with representatives of the drug manufacturing industry, review and develop guidance, as appropriate, on the inclusion of women and minorities in clinical trials required by clause (A).

(2) An application submitted under paragraph (1) for a drug for which the investigations described in clause (A) of such paragraph and relied upon by the applicant for approval of the application were not conducted by or for the applicant and for which the applicant has not obtained a right of reference or use from the person by or for whom the investigations were conducted shall also include—

(A) a certification, in the opinion of the applicant and to the best of his knowledge, with respect to each patent which claims the drug for which such investigations were conducted or which claims a use for such drug for which the applicant is seeking approval under this subsection and for which information is required to be filed under paragraph (1) or subsection (c) of this section—

(i) that such patent information has not been filed,

(ii) that such patent has expired,

(iii) of the date on which such patent will expire, or

(iv) that such patent is invalid or will not be infringed by the manufacture, use, or sale of the new drug for which the application is submitted; and

(B) if with respect to the drug for which investigations described in paragraph (1)(A) were conducted information was filed under paragraph (1) or subsection (c) of this section for a method of use patent which does not claim a use for which the applicant is seeking approval under this subsection, a statement that the method of use patent does not claim such a use.

(3) NOTICE OF OPINION THAT PATENT IS INVALID OR WILL NOT BE INFRINGED.—

(A) AGREEMENT TO GIVE NOTICE.—An applicant that makes a certification described in paragraph (2)(A)(iv) shall include in the application a statement that the applicant will give notice as required by this paragraph.

(B) TIMING OF NOTICE.—An applicant that makes a certification described in paragraph (2)(A)(iv) shall give notice as required under this paragraph—

(i) if the certification is in the application, not later than 20 days after the date of the postmark on the notice with which the Secretary informs the applicant that the application has been filed; or

(ii) if the certification is in an amendment or supplement to the application, at the time at which the applicant submits the amendment or supplement, regardless of whether the applicant has already given notice with respect to another such certification contained in the application or in an amendment or supplement to the application.

(C) RECIPIENTS OF NOTICE.—An applicant required under this paragraph to give notice shall give notice to—

(i) each owner of the patent that is the subject of the certification (or a representative of the owner designated to receive such a notice); and

(ii) the holder of the approved application under this subsection for the drug that is claimed by the patent or a use of which is claimed by the patent (or a representative of the holder designated to receive such a notice).

(D) CONTENTS OF NOTICE.—A notice required under this paragraph shall—

(i) state that an application that contains data from bioavailability or bioequivalence studies has been submitted under this subsection for the drug with respect to which the certification is made to obtain approval to engage in the commercial manufacture, use, or sale of the drug before the expiration of the patent referred to in the certification; and

(ii) include a detailed statement of the factual and legal basis of the opinion of the applicant that the patent is invalid or will not be infringed.

(4)(A) An applicant may not amend or supplement an application referred to in paragraph (2) to seek approval of a drug that is a different drug than the drug identified in the application as submitted to the Secretary.

(B) With respect to the drug for which such an application is submitted, nothing in this subsection or subsection (c)(3) of this section prohibits an applicant from amending or supplementing the application to seek approval of a different strength.

(5)(A) The Secretary shall issue guidance for the individuals who review applications submitted under paragraph (1) or under section 262 of title 42, which shall relate to promptness in conducting the review, technical excellence, lack of bias and conflict of interest, and knowledge of regulatory and scientific standards, and which shall apply equally to all individuals who review such applications.

(B) The Secretary shall meet with a sponsor of an investigation or an applicant for approval for a drug under this subsection or section 262 of title 42 if the sponsor or applicant makes a reasonable written request for a meeting for the purpose of reaching agreement on the design and size of clinical trials intended to form the primary basis of an effectiveness claim. The sponsor or applicant shall provide information necessary for discussion and agreement on the design and size of the clinical trials. Minutes of any such meeting shall be prepared by the Secretary and made available to the sponsor or applicant upon request.

(C) Any agreement regarding the parameters of the design and size of clinical trials of a new drug under this paragraph that is reached between the Secretary and a sponsor or applicant shall be reduced to writing and made part of the administrative record by the Secretary. Such agreement shall not be changed after the testing begins, except—

(i) with the written agreement of the sponsor or applicant; or

(ii) pursuant to a decision, made in accordance with subparagraph (D) by the director of the reviewing division, that a substantial scientific issue essential to determining the safety or effectiveness of the drug has been identified after the testing has begun.

(D) A decision under subparagraph (C)(ii) by the director shall be in writing and the Secretary shall provide to the sponsor or applicant an opportunity for a meeting at which the director and the sponsor or applicant will be present and at which the director will document the scientific issue involved.

(E) The written decisions of the reviewing division shall be binding upon, and may not directly or indirectly be changed by, the field or compliance division personnel unless such field or compliance division personnel demonstrate to the reviewing division why such decision should be modified.

(F) No action by the reviewing division may be delayed because of the unavailability of information from or action by field personnel unless the reviewing division determines that a delay is necessary to assure the marketing of a safe and effective drug.

(G) For purposes of this paragraph, the reviewing division is the division responsible for the review of an application for approval of a drug under this subsection or section 262 of title 42 (including all scientific and medical matters, chemistry, manufacturing, and controls).

(6) An application submitted under this subsection shall be accompanied by the certification required under section 282(j)(5)(B) of title 42. Such certification shall not be considered an element of such application.

(c) Period for approval of application; period for, notice, and expedition of hearing; period for issuance of order

(1) Within one hundred and eighty days after the filing of an application under subsection (b) of this section, or such additional period as may be agreed upon by the Secretary and the applicant, the Secretary shall either—

(A) approve the application if he then finds that none of the grounds for denying approval specified in subsection (d) of this section applies, or

(B) give the applicant notice of an opportunity for a hearing before the Secretary under subsection (d) of this section on the question whether such application is approvable. If the applicant elects to accept the opportunity for hearing by written request within thirty days after such notice, such hearing shall commence not more than ninety days after the expiration of such thirty days unless the Secretary and the applicant otherwise agree. Any such hearing shall thereafter be conducted on an expedited basis and the Secretary's order thereon shall be issued within ninety days after the date fixed by the Secretary for filing final briefs.

(2) If the patent information described in subsection (b) of this section could not be filed with the submission of an application under subsection (b) of this section because the application was filed before the patent information was required under subsection (b) of this section or a patent was issued after the application was approved under such subsection, the holder of an approved application shall file with the Secretary the patent number and the expiration date of any patent which claims the drug for which the application was submitted or which claims a method of using such drug and with respect to which a claim of patent infringement could reasonably be asserted if a person not licensed by the owner engaged in the manufacture, use, or sale of the drug. If the holder of an approved application could not file patent information under subsection (b) of this section because it was not required at the time the application was approved, the holder shall file such information under this subsection not later than thirty days after September 24, 1984, and if the holder of an approved application could not file patent information under subsection (b) of this section because no patent had been issued when an application was filed or approved, the holder shall file such information under this subsection not later than thirty days after the date the patent involved is issued. Upon the submission of patent information under this subsection, the Secretary shall publish it.

(3) The approval of an application filed under subsection (b) of this section which contains a certification required by paragraph (2) of such subsection shall be made effective on the last applicable date determined by applying the following to each certification made under subsection (b)(2)(A) of this section:

(A) If the applicant only made a certification described in clause (i) or (ii) of subsection (b)(2)(A) of this section or in both such clauses, the approval may be made effective immediately.

(B) If the applicant made a certification described in clause (iii) of subsection (b)(2)(A) of this section, the approval may be made effective on the date certified under clause (iii).

(C) If the applicant made a certification described in clause (iv) of subsection (b)(2)(A) of this section, the approval shall be made effective immediately unless, before the expiration of 45 days after the date on which the notice described in subsection (b)(3) of this section is received, an action is brought for infringement of the patent that is the subject of the certification and for which information was submitted to the Secretary under paragraph (2) or subsection (b)(1) of this section before the date on which the application (excluding an amendment or supplement to the application) was submitted. If such an action is brought before the expiration of such days, the approval may be made effective upon the expiration of the thirty-month period beginning on the date of the receipt of the notice provided under subsection (b)(3) of this section or such shorter or longer period as the court may order because either party to the action failed to reasonably cooperate in expediting the action, except that—

(i) if before the expiration of such period the district court decides that the patent is invalid or not infringed (including any substantive determination that there is no cause of action for patent infringement or invalidity), the approval shall be made effective on—

(I) the date on which the court enters judgment reflecting the decision; or

(II) the date of a settlement order or consent decree signed and entered by the court stating that the patent that is the subject of the certification is invalid or not infringed;

(ii) if before the expiration of such period the district court decides that the patent has been infringed—

(I) if the judgment of the district court is appealed, the approval shall be made effective on—

(aa) the date on which the court of appeals decides that the patent is invalid or not infringed (including any substantive determination that there is no cause of action for patent infringement or invalidity); or

(bb) the date of a settlement order or consent decree signed and entered by the court of appeals stating that the patent that is the subject of the certification is invalid or not infringed; or

(II) if the judgment of the district court is not appealed or is affirmed, the approval shall be made effective on the date specified by the district court in a court order under section 271(e)(4)(A) of title 35;

(iii) if before the expiration of such period the court grants a preliminary injunction prohibiting the applicant from engaging in the commercial manufacture or sale of the drug until the court decides the issues of patent validity and infringement and if the court decides that such patent is invalid or not infringed, the approval shall be made effective as provided in clause (i); or

(iv) if before the expiration of such period the court grants a preliminary injunction prohibiting the applicant from engaging in the commercial manufacture or sale of the drug until the court decides the issues of patent validity and infringement and if the court decides that such patent has been infringed, the approval shall be made effective as provided in clause (ii).

In such an action, each of the parties shall reasonably cooperate in expediting the action.

(D) CIVIL ACTION TO OBTAIN PATENT CERTAINTY.—

(i) DECLARATORY JUDGMENT ABSENT INFRINGEMENT ACTION.—

(I) IN GENERAL.—No action may be brought under section 2201 of title 28 by an applicant referred to in subsection (b)(2) of this section for a declaratory judgment with respect to a patent which is the subject of the certification referred to in subparagraph (C) unless—

(aa) the 45-day period referred to in such subparagraph has expired;

(bb) neither the owner of such patent nor the holder of the approved application under subsection (b) of this section for the drug that is claimed by the patent or a use of which is claimed by the patent brought a civil action against the applicant for infringement of the patent before the expiration of such period; and

(cc) in any case in which the notice provided under paragraph (2)(B) relates to noninfringement, the notice was accompanied by a document described in subclause (III).

(II) FILING OF CIVIL ACTION.—If the conditions described in items (aa), (bb), and as applicable, (cc) of subclause (I) have been met, the applicant referred to in such subclause may, in accordance with section 2201 of title 28, bring a civil action under such section against the owner or holder referred to in such subclause (but not against any owner or holder that has brought such a civil action against the applicant, unless that civil action was dismissed without prejudice) for a declaratory judgment that the patent is invalid or will not be infringed by the drug for which the applicant seeks approval, except that such civil action may be brought for a declaratory judgment that the patent will not be infringed only in a case in which the condition described in subclause (I)(cc) is applicable. A civil action referred to in this subclause shall be brought in the judicial district where the defendant has its principal place of business or a regular and established place of business.

(III) OFFER OF CONFIDENTIAL ACCESS TO APPLICATION.—For purposes of subclause (I)(cc), the document described in this subclause is a document providing an offer of confidential access to the application that is in the custody of the applicant referred to in subsection (b)(2) of this section for the purpose of determining whether an action referred to in subparagraph (C) should be brought. The document providing the offer of confidential access shall contain such restrictions as to persons entitled to access, and on the use and disposition of any information accessed, as would apply had a protective order been entered for the purpose of protecting trade secrets and other confidential business information. A request for access to an application under an offer of confidential access shall be considered acceptance of the offer of confidential access with the restrictions as to persons entitled to access, and on the use and disposition of any information accessed, contained in the offer of confidential access, and those restrictions and other terms of the offer of confidential access shall be considered terms of an enforceable contract. Any person provided an offer of confidential access shall review the application for the sole and limited purpose of evaluating possible infringement of the patent that is the subject of the certification under subsection (b)(2)(A)(iv) of this section and for no other purpose, and may not disclose information of no relevance to any issue of patent infringement to any person other than a person provided an offer of confidential access. Further, the application may be redacted by the applicant to remove any information of no relevance to any issue of patent infringement.

(ii) COUNTERCLAIM TO INFRINGEMENT ACTION.—

(I) IN GENERAL.—If an owner of the patent or the holder of the approved application under subsection (b) of this section for the drug that is claimed by the patent or a use of which is claimed by the patent brings a patent infringement action against the applicant, the applicant may assert a counterclaim seeking an order requiring the holder to correct or delete the patent information submitted by the holder under subsection (b) of this section or this subsection on the ground that the patent does not claim either—

(aa) the drug for which the application was approved; or

(bb) an approved method of using the drug.

(II) NO INDEPENDENT CAUSE OF ACTION.—Subclause (I) does not authorize the assertion of a claim described in subclause (I) in any civil action or proceeding other than a counterclaim described in subclause (I).

(iii) NO DAMAGES.—An applicant shall not be entitled to damages in a civil action under clause (i) or a counterclaim under clause (ii).

(E)(i) If an application (other than an abbreviated new drug application) submitted under subsection (b) of this section for a drug, no active ingredient (including any ester or salt of the active ingredient) of which has been approved in any other application under subsection (b) of this section, was approved during the period beginning January 1, 1982, and ending on September 24, 1984, the Secretary may not make the approval of another application for a drug for which the investigations described in clause (A) of subsection (b)(1) of this section and relied upon by the applicant for approval of the application were not conducted by or for the applicant and for which the applicant has not obtained a right of reference or use from the person by or for whom the investigations were conducted effective before the expiration of ten years from the date of the approval of the application previously approved under subsection (b) of this section.

(ii) If an application submitted under subsection (b) of this section for a drug, no active ingredient (including any ester or salt of the active ingredient) of which has been approved in any other application under subsection (b) of this section, is approved after September 24, 1984, no application which refers to the drug for which the subsection (b) application was submitted and for which the investigations described in clause (A) of subsection (b)(1) of this section and relied upon by the applicant for approval of the application were not conducted by or for the applicant and for which the applicant has not obtained a right of reference or use from the person by or for whom the investigations were conducted may be submitted under subsection (b) of this section before the expiration of five years from the date of the approval of the application under subsection (b) of this section, except that such an application may be submitted under subsection (b) of this section after the expiration of four years from the date of the approval of the subsection (b) application if it contains a certification of patent invalidity or noninfringement described in clause (iv) of subsection (b)(2)(A) of this section. The approval of such an application shall be made effective in accordance with this paragraph except that, if an action for patent infringement is commenced during the one-year period beginning forty-eight months after the date of the approval of the subsection (b) application, the thirty-month period referred to in subparagraph (C) shall be extended by such amount of time (if any) which is required for seven and one-half years to have elapsed from the date of approval of the subsection (b) application.

(iii) If an application submitted under subsection (b) of this section for a drug, which includes an active ingredient (including any ester or salt of the active ingredient) that has been approved in another application approved under subsection (b) of this section, is approved after September 24, 1984, and if such application contains reports of new clinical investigations (other than bioavailability studies) essential to the approval of the application and conducted or sponsored by the applicant, the Secretary may not make the approval of an application submitted under subsection (b) of this section for the conditions of approval of such drug in the approved subsection (b) application effective before the expiration of three years from the date of the approval of the application under subsection (b) of this section if the investigations described in clause (A) of subsection (b)(1) of this section and relied upon by the applicant for approval of the application were not conducted by or for the applicant and if the applicant has not obtained a right of reference or use from the person by or for whom the investigations were conducted.

(iv) If a supplement to an application approved under subsection (b) of this section is approved after September 24, 1984, and the supplement contains reports of new clinical investigations (other than bioavailabilty[1] studies) essential to the approval of the supplement and conducted or sponsored by the person submitting the supplement, the Secretary may not make the approval of an application submitted under subsection (b) of this section for a change approved in the supplement effective before the expiration of three years from the

[1] So in original. Probably should be "bioavailability".

date of the approval of the supplement under subsection (b) of this section if the investigations described in clause (A) of subsection (b)(1) of this section and relied upon by the applicant for approval of the application were not conducted by or for the applicant and if the applicant has not obtained a right of reference or use from the person by or for whom the investigations were conducted.

(v) If an application (or supplement to an application) submitted under subsection (b) of this section for a drug, which includes an active ingredient (including any ester or salt of the active ingredient) that has been approved in another application under subsection (b) of this section, was approved during the period beginning January 1, 1982, and ending on September 24, 1984, the Secretary may not make the approval of an application submitted under this subsection and for which the investigations described in clause (A) of subsection (b)(1) of this section and relied upon by the applicant for approval of the application were not conducted by or for the applicant and for which the applicant has not obtained a right of reference or use from the person by or for whom the investigations were conducted and which refers to the drug for which the subsection (b) application was submitted effective before the expiration of two years from September 24, 1984.

(4) A drug manufactured in a pilot or other small facility may be used to demonstrate the safety and effectiveness of the drug and to obtain approval for the drug prior to manufacture of the drug in a larger facility, unless the Secretary makes a determination that a full scale production facility is necessary to ensure the safety or effectiveness of the drug.

(d) Grounds for refusing application; approval of application; "substantial evidence" defined

If the Secretary finds, after due notice to the applicant in accordance with subsection (c) of this section and giving him an opportunity for a hearing, in accordance with said subsection, that (1) the investigations, reports of which are required to be submitted to the Secretary pursuant to subsection (b) of this section, do not include adequate tests by all methods reasonably applicable to show whether or not such drug is safe for use under the conditions prescribed, recommended, or suggested in the proposed labeling thereof; (2) the results of such tests show that such drug is unsafe for use under such conditions or do not show that such drug is safe for use under such conditions; (3) the methods used in, and the facilities and controls used for, the manufacture, processing, and packing of such drug are inadequate to preserve its identity, strength, quality, and purity; (4) upon the basis of the information submitted to him as part of the application, or upon the basis of any other information before him with respect to such drug, he has insufficient information to determine whether such drug is safe for use under such conditions; or (5) evaluated on the basis of the information submitted to him as part of the application and any other information before him with respect to such drug, there is a lack of substantial evidence that the drug will have the effect it purports or is represented to have under the conditions of use prescribed, recommended, or suggested in the proposed labeling thereof; or (6) the application failed to contain the patent information prescribed by subsection (b) of this section; or (7) based on a fair evaluation of all material facts, such labeling is false or misleading in any particular; he shall issue an order refusing to approve the application. If, after such notice and opportunity for hearing, the Secretary finds that clauses (1) through (6) do not apply, he shall issue an order approving the application. As used in this subsection and subsection (e) of this section, the term "substantial evidence" means evidence consisting of adequate and well-controlled investigations, including clinical investigations, by experts qualified by scientific training and experience to evaluate the effectiveness of the drug involved, on the basis of which it could fairly and responsibly be concluded by such experts that the drug will have the effect it purports or is represented to have under the conditions of use prescribed, recommended, or suggested in the labeling or proposed labeling thereof. If the Secretary determines, based on relevant science, that data from one adequate and well-controlled clinical investigation and confirmatory evidence (obtained prior to or after such investigation) are sufficient to establish effectiveness, the Secretary may consider such data and evidence to constitute substantial evidence for purposes of the preceding sentence.

(e) Withdrawal of approval; grounds; immediate suspension upon finding imminent hazard to public health

The Secretary shall, after due notice and opportunity for hearing to the applicant, withdraw approval of an application with respect to any drug under this section if the Secretary finds (1) that clinical or other experience, tests, or other scientific data show that such drug is unsafe for use under the conditions of use upon the basis of which the application was approved; (2) that new evidence of clinical experience, not contained in such application or not available to the Secretary until after such application was approved, or tests by new methods, or tests by methods not deemed reasonably applicable when such application was approved, evaluated together with the evidence available to the Secretary when the application was approved, shows that such drug is not shown to be safe for use under the conditions of use upon the basis of which the application was approved; or (3) on the basis of new information before him with respect to such drug, evaluated together with the evidence available to him when the application was approved, that there is a lack of substantial evidence that the drug will have the effect it purports or is represented to have under the conditions of use prescribed, recommended, or suggested in the labeling thereof; or (4) the patent information prescribed by subsection (c) of this section was not filed within thirty days after the receipt of written notice from the Secretary specifying the failure to file such information; or (5) that the application contains any untrue statement of a material fact: *Provided*, That if the Secretary (or in his absence the officer acting as Secretary) finds that there is an imminent hazard to the public health, he may suspend the approval of such application immediately, and give the applicant prompt notice of his action and afford the applicant the opportunity for an expedited hearing under this subsection; but the authority conferred by this proviso to suspend the approval of an application shall not be delegated. The Secretary may also, after due notice and opportunity for hearing to the applicant, withdraw the approval of an application submitted under subsection (b) or (j) of this section with respect to any drug under this section if the Secretary finds (1) that the applicant has failed to establish a system for maintaining required records, or has repeatedly or deliberately failed to maintain such records or to make required reports, in accordance with a regulation or order under subsection (k) of this section or to comply with the notice requirements of section 360(k)(2) of this title, or the applicant has refused to permit access to, or copying or verification of, such records as required by paragraph (2) of such subsection; or (2) that on the basis of new information before him, evaluated together with the evidence before him when the application was approved, the methods used in, or the facilities and controls used for, the manufacture, processing, and packing of such drug are inadequate to assure and preserve its identity, strength, quality, and purity and were not made adequate within a reasonable time after receipt of written notice from the Secretary specifying the matter complained of; or (3) that on the basis of new information before him, evaluated together with the evidence before him when the application was approved, the labeling of such drug, based on a fair evaluation of all material facts, is false or misleading in any particular and was not corrected within a reasonable time after receipt of written notice from the Secretary specifying the matter complained of. Any order under this subsection shall state the findings upon which it is based. The Secretary may withdraw the approval of an application submitted under this section, or suspend the approval of such an application, as provided under this subsection, without first ordering the applicant to submit an assessment of the approved risk evaluation and mitigation strategy for the drug under section 355–1(g)(2)(D) of this title.

(f) Revocation of order refusing, withdrawing or suspending approval of application

Whenever the Secretary finds that the facts so require, he shall revoke any previous order under subsection (d) or (e) of this section refusing, withdrawing, or suspending approval of an application and shall approve such application or reinstate such approval, as may be appropriate.

(g) Service of orders

Orders of the Secretary issued under this section shall be served (1) in person by any officer or employee of the department designated by the Secretary or (2) by mailing the order by registered mail or by certified mail addressed to the applicant or respondent at his last-known address in the records of the Secretary.

(h) Appeal from order

An appeal may be taken by the applicant from an order of the Secretary refusing or withdrawing approval of an application under this section. Such appeal shall be taken by filing in the United States court of appeals for the circuit wherein such applicant resides or has his principal place of business, or in the United States Court of Appeals for the District of Columbia Circuit, within sixty days after the entry of such order, a written petition praying that the order of the Secretary be set aside. A copy of such petition shall be forthwith transmitted by the clerk of the court to the Secretary, or any officer designated by him for that purpose, and thereupon the Secretary shall certify and file in the court the record upon which the order complained of was entered, as provided in section 2112 of title 28. Upon the filing of such petition such court shall have exclusive jurisdiction to affirm or set aside such order, except that until the filing of the record the Secretary may modify or set aside his order. No objection to the order of the Secretary shall be considered by the court unless such objection shall have been urged before the Secretary or unless there were reasonable grounds for failure so to do. The finding of the Secretary as to the facts, if supported by substantial evidence, shall be conclusive. If any person shall apply to the court for leave to adduce additional evidence, and shall show to the satisfaction of the court that such additional evidence is material and that there were reasonable grounds for failure to adduce such evidence in the proceeding before the Secretary, the court may order such additional evidence to be taken before the Secretary and to be adduced upon the hearing in such manner and upon such terms and conditions as to the court may seem proper. The Secretary may modify his findings as to the facts by reason of the additional evidence so taken, and he shall file with the court such modified findings which, if supported by substantial evidence, shall be conclusive, and his recommendation, if any, for the setting aside of the original order. The judgment of the court affirming or setting aside any such order of the Secretary shall be final, subject to review by the Supreme Court of the United States upon certiorari or certification as provided in section 1254 of title 28. The commencement of proceedings under this subsection shall not, unless specifically ordered by the court to the contrary, operate as a stay of the Secretary's order.

(i) Exemptions of drugs for research; discretionary and mandatory conditions; direct reports to Secretary

(1) The Secretary shall promulgate regulations for exempting from the operation of the foregoing subsections of this section drugs intended solely for investigational use by experts qualified by scientific training and experience to investigate the safety and effectiveness of drugs. Such regulations may, within the discretion of the Secretary, among other conditions relating to the protection of the public health, provide for conditioning such exemption upon—

(A) the submission to the Secretary, before any clinical testing of a new drug is undertaken, of reports, by the manufacturer or the sponsor of the investigation of such drug, of preclinical tests (including tests on animals) of such drug adequate to justify the proposed clinical testing;

(B) the manufacturer or the sponsor of the investigation of a new drug proposed to be distributed to investigators for clinical testing obtaining a signed agreement from each of such investigators that patients to whom the drug is administered will be under his personal supervision, or under the supervision of investigators responsible to him, and that he will not supply such drug to any other investigator, or to clinics, for administration to human beings;

(C) the establishment and maintenance of such records, and the making of such reports to the Secretary, by the manufacturer or the sponsor of the investigation of such drug, of data (including but not limited to analytical reports by investigators) obtained as the result of such investigational use of such drug, as the Secretary finds will enable him to evaluate the safety and effectiveness of such drug in the event of the filing of an application pursuant to subsection (b) of this section; and

(D) the submission to the Secretary by the manufacturer or the sponsor of the investigation of a new drug of a statement of intent regarding whether the manufacturer or sponsor has plans for assessing pediatric safety and efficacy.

(2) Subject to paragraph (3), a clinical investigation of a new drug may begin 30 days after the Secretary has received from the manufacturer or sponsor of the investigation a submission containing such information about the drug and the clinical investigation, including—

(A) information on design of the investigation and adequate reports of basic information, certified by the applicant to be accurate reports, necessary to assess the safety of the drug for use in clinical investigation; and

(B) adequate information on the chemistry and manufacturing of the drug, controls available for the drug, and primary data tabulations from animal or human studies.

(3)(A) At any time, the Secretary may prohibit the sponsor of an investigation from conducting the investigation (referred to in this paragraph as a "clinical hold") if the Secretary makes a determination described in subparagraph (B). The Secretary shall specify the basis for the clinical hold, including the specific information available to the Secretary which served as the basis for such clinical hold, and confirm such determination in writing.

(B) For purposes of subparagraph (A), a determination described in this subparagraph with respect to a clinical hold is that—

(i) the drug involved represents an unreasonable risk to the safety of the persons who are the subjects of the clinical investigation, taking into account the qualifications of the clinical investigators, information about the drug, the design of the clinical investigation, the condition for which the drug is to be investigated, and the health status of the subjects involved; or

(ii) the clinical hold should be issued for such other reasons as the Secretary may by regulation establish (including reasons established by regulation before November 21, 1997).

(C) Any written request to the Secretary from the sponsor of an investigation that a clinical hold be removed shall receive a decision, in writing and specifying the reasons therefor, within 30 days after receipt of such request. Any such request shall include sufficient information to support the removal of such clinical hold.

(4) Regulations under paragraph (1) shall provide that such exemption shall be conditioned upon the manufacturer, or the sponsor of the investigation, requiring that experts using such drugs for investigational purposes certify to such manufacturer or sponsor that they will inform any human beings to whom such drugs, or any controls used in connection therewith, are being administered, or their representatives, that such drugs are being used for investigational purposes and will obtain the consent of such human beings or their representatives, except where it is not feasible or it is contrary to the best interests of such human beings. Nothing in this subsection shall be construed to require any clinical investigator to submit directly to the Secretary reports on the investigational use of drugs. The Secretary shall update such regulations to require inclusion in the informed consent documents and process a statement that clinical trial information for such clinical investigation has been or will be submitted for inclusion in the registry data bank pursuant to subsection (j) of section 282 of title 42.

(j) Abbreviated new drug applications

(1) Any person may file with the Secretary an abbreviated application for the approval of a new drug.

(2)(A) An abbreviated application for a new drug shall contain—

(i) information to show that the conditions of use prescribed, recommended, or suggested in the labeling proposed for the new drug have been previously approved for a drug listed under paragraph (7) (hereinafter in this subsection referred to as a "listed drug");

(ii)(I) if the listed drug referred to in clause (i) has only one active ingredient, information to show that the active ingredient of the new drug is the same as that of the listed drug;

(II) if the listed drug referred to in clause (i) has more than one active ingredient, information to show that the active ingredients of the new drug are the same as those of the listed drug, or

(III) if the listed drug referred to in clause (i) has more than one active ingredient and if one of the active ingredients of the new drug is different and the application is filed pursuant to the approval of a petition filed under subparagraph (C), information to show that the other active ingredients of the new drug are the same as the active ingredients of the listed drug, information to show that the different active ingredient is an active ingredient of a listed drug or of a drug which does not meet the requirements of section 321(p) of this title, and such other information respecting the different active ingredient with respect to which the petition was filed as the Secretary may require;

(iii) information to show that the route of administration, the dosage form, and the strength of the new drug are the same as those of the listed drug referred to in clause (i) or, if the route of administration, the dosage form, or the strength of the new drug is different and the application is filed pursuant to the approval of a petition filed under subparagraph (C), such information respecting the route of administration, dosage form, or strength with respect to which the petition was filed as the Secretary may require;

(iv) information to show that the new drug is bioequivalent to the listed drug referred to in clause (i), except that if the application is filed pursuant to the approval of a petition filed under subparagraph (C), information to show that the active ingredients of the new drug are of the same pharmacological or therapeutic class as those of the listed drug referred to in clause (i) and the new drug can be expected to have the same therapeutic effect as the listed drug when administered to patients for a condition of use referred to in clause (i);

(v) information to show that the labeling proposed for the new drug is the same as the labeling approved for the listed drug referred to in clause (i) except for changes required because of differences approved under a petition filed under subparagraph (C) or because the new drug and the listed drug are produced or distributed by different manufacturers;

(vi) the items specified in clauses (B) through (F) of subsection (b)(1) of this section;

(vii) a certification, in the opinion of the applicant and to the best of his knowledge, with respect to each patent which claims the listed drug referred to in clause (i) or which claims a use for such listed drug for which the applicant is seeking approval under this subsection and for which information is required to be filed under subsection (b) or (c) of this section—

(I) that such patent information has not been filed,

(II) that such patent has expired,

(III) of the date on which such patent will expire, or

(IV) that such patent is invalid or will not be infringed by the manufacture, use, or sale of the new drug for which the application is submitted; and

(viii) if with respect to the listed drug referred to in clause (i) information was filed under subsection (b) or (c) of this section for a method of use patent which does not claim a use for which the applicant is seeking approval under this subsection, a statement that the method of use patent does not claim such a use.

The Secretary may not require that an abbreviated application contain information in addition to that required by clauses (i) through (viii).

(B) NOTICE OF OPINION THAT PATENT IS INVALID OR WILL NOT BE INFRINGED.—

(i) AGREEMENT TO GIVE NOTICE.—An applicant that makes a certification described in subparagraph (A)(vii)(IV) shall include in the application a statement that the applicant will give notice as required by this subparagraph.

(ii) TIMING OF NOTICE.—An applicant that makes a certification described in subparagraph (A)(vii)(IV) shall give notice as required under this subparagraph—

(I) if the certification is in the application, not later than 20 days after the date of the postmark on the notice with which the Secretary informs the applicant that the application has been filed; or

(II) if the certification is in an amendment or supplement to the application, at the time at which the applicant submits the amendment or supplement, regardless of whether the applicant has already given notice with respect to another such certification contained in the application or in an amendment or supplement to the application.

(iii) RECIPIENTS OF NOTICE.—An applicant required under this subparagraph to give notice shall give notice to—

(I) each owner of the patent that is the subject of the certification (or a representative of the owner designated to receive such a notice); and

(II) the holder of the approved application under subsection (b) of this section for the drug that is claimed by the patent or a use of which is claimed by the patent (or a representative of the holder designated to receive such a notice).

(iv) CONTENTS OF NOTICE.—A notice required under this subparagraph shall—

(I) state that an application that contains data from bioavailability or bioequivalence studies has been submitted under this subsection for the drug with respect to which the certification is made to obtain approval to engage in the commercial manufacture, use, or sale of the drug before the expiration of the patent referred to in the certification; and

(II) include a detailed statement of the factual and legal basis of the opinion of the applicant that the patent is invalid or will not be infringed.

(C) If a person wants to submit an abbreviated application for a new drug which has a different active ingredient or whose route of administration, dosage form, or strength differ from that of a listed drug, such person shall submit a petition to the Secretary seeking permission to file such an application. The Secretary shall approve or disapprove a petition submitted under this subparagraph within ninety days of the date the petition is submitted. The Secretary shall approve such a petition unless the Secretary finds—

(i) that investigations must be conducted to show the safety and effectiveness of the drug or of any of its active ingredients, the route of administration, the dosage form, or strength which differ from the listed drug; or

(ii) that any drug with a different active ingredient may not be adequately evaluated for approval as safe and effective on the basis of the information required to be submitted in an abbreviated application.

(D)(i) An applicant may not amend or supplement an application to seek approval of a drug referring to a different listed drug from the listed drug identified in the application as submitted to the Secretary.

(ii) With respect to the drug for which an application is submitted, nothing in this subsection prohibits an applicant from amending or supplementing the application to seek approval of a different strength.

(iii) Within 60 days after December 8, 2003, the Secretary shall issue guidance defining the term "listed drug" for purposes of this subparagraph.

(3)(A) The Secretary shall issue guidance for the individuals who review applications submitted under paragraph (1), which shall relate to promptness in conducting the review, technical excellence, lack of bias and conflict of interest, and knowledge of regulatory and scientific standards, and which shall apply equally to all individuals who review such applications.

(B) The Secretary shall meet with a sponsor of an investigation or an applicant for approval for a drug under this subsection if the sponsor or applicant makes a reasonable written request for a meeting for the purpose of reaching agreement on the design and size of bioavailability and bioequivalence studies needed for approval of such application. The sponsor or applicant shall provide information necessary for discussion and agreement on the design and size of such studies. Minutes of any such meeting shall be prepared by the Secretary and made available to the sponsor or applicant.

(C) Any agreement regarding the parameters of design and size of bioavailability and bioequivalence studies of a drug under this paragraph that is reached between the Secretary and a sponsor or applicant shall be reduced to writing and made part of the administrative record by the Secretary. Such agreement shall not be changed after the testing begins, except—

(i) with the written agreement of the sponsor or applicant; or

(ii) pursuant to a decision, made in accordance with subparagraph (D) by the director of the reviewing division, that a substantial scientific issue essential to determining the safety or effectiveness of the drug has been identified after the testing has begun.

(D) A decision under subparagraph (C)(ii) by the director shall be in writing and the Secretary shall provide to the sponsor or applicant an opportunity for a meeting at which the director and the sponsor or applicant will be present and at which the director will document the scientific issue involved.

(E) The written decisions of the reviewing division shall be binding upon, and may not directly or indirectly be changed by, the field or compliance office personnel unless such field or compliance office personnel demonstrate to the reviewing division why such decision should be modified.

(F) No action by the reviewing division may be delayed because of the unavailability of information from or action by field personnel unless the reviewing division determines that a delay is necessary to assure the marketing of a safe and effective drug.

(G) For purposes of this paragraph, the reviewing division is the division responsible for the review of an application for approval of a drug under this subsection (including scientific matters, chemistry, manufacturing, and controls).

(4) Subject to paragraph (5), the Secretary shall approve an application for a drug unless the Secretary finds—

(A) the methods used in, or the facilities and controls used for, the manufacture, processing, and packing of the drug are inadequate to assure and preserve its identity, strength, quality, and purity;

(B) information submitted with the application is insufficient to show that each of the proposed conditions of use have been previously approved for the listed drug referred to in the application;

(C)(i) if the listed drug has only one active ingredient, information submitted with the application is insufficient to show that the active ingredient is the same as that of the listed drug;

(ii) if the listed drug has more than one active ingredient, information submitted with the application is insufficient to show that the active ingredients are the same as the active ingredients of the listed drug, or

(iii) if the listed drug has more than one active ingredient and if the application is for a drug which has an active ingredient different from the listed drug, information submitted with the application is insufficient to show—

(I) that the other active ingredients are the same as the active ingredients of the listed drug, or

(II) that the different active ingredient is an active ingredient of a listed drug or a drug which does not meet the requirements of section 321(p) of this title,

or no petition to file an application for the drug with the different ingredient was approved under paragraph (2)(C);

(D)(i) if the application is for a drug whose route of administration, dosage form, or strength of the drug is the same as the route of administration, dosage form, or strength of the listed drug referred to in the application, information submitted in the application is insufficient to show that the route of administration, dosage form, or strength is the same as that of the listed drug, or

(ii) if the application is for a drug whose route of administration, dosage form, or strength of the drug is different from that of the listed drug referred to in the application, no petition to file an application for the drug with the different route of administration, dosage form, or strength was approved under paragraph (2)(C);

(E) if the application was filed pursuant to the approval of a petition under paragraph (2)(C), the application did not contain the information required by the Secretary respecting the active ingredient, route of administration, dosage form, or strength which is not the same;

(F) information submitted in the application is insufficient to show that the drug is bioequivalent to the listed drug referred to in the application or, if the application was filed pursuant to a petition approved under paragraph (2)(C), information submitted in the application is insufficient to show that the active ingredients of the new drug are of the same pharmacological or therapeutic class as those of the listed drug referred to in paragraph (2)(A)(i) and that the new drug can be expected to have the same therapeutic effect as the listed drug when administered to patients for a condition of use referred to in such paragraph;

(G) information submitted in the application is insufficient to show that the labeling proposed for the drug is the same as the labeling approved for the listed drug referred to in the application except for changes required because of differences approved under a petition filed under paragraph (2)(C) or because the drug and the listed drug are produced or distributed by different manufacturers;

(H) information submitted in the application or any other information available to the Secretary shows that (i) the inactive ingredients of the drug are unsafe for use under the conditions prescribed, recommended, or suggested in the labeling proposed for the drug, or (ii) the composition of the drug is unsafe under such conditions because of the type or quantity of inactive ingredients included or the manner in which the inactive ingredients are included;

(I) the approval under subsection (c) of this section of the listed drug referred to in the application under this subsection has been withdrawn or suspended for grounds described in the first sentence of subsection (e) of this section, the Secretary has published a notice of opportunity for hearing to withdraw approval of the listed drug under subsection (c) of this section for grounds described in the first sentence of subsection (e) of this section, the approval under this subsection of the listed drug referred to in the application under this subsection has been withdrawn or suspended under paragraph (6), or the Secretary has determined that the listed drug has been withdrawn from sale for safety or effectiveness reasons;

(J) the application does not meet any other requirement of paragraph (2)(A); or

(K) the application contains an untrue statement of material fact.

(5)(A) Within one hundred and eighty days of the initial receipt of an application under paragraph (2) or within such additional period as may be agreed upon by the Secretary and the applicant, the Secretary shall approve or disapprove the application.

(B) The approval of an application submitted under paragraph (2) shall be made effective on the last applicable date determined by applying the following to each certification made under paragraph (2)(A)(vii):

(i) If the applicant only made a certification described in subclause (I) or (II) of paragraph (2)(A)(vii) or in both such subclauses, the approval may be made effective immediately.

(ii) If the applicant made a certification described in subclause (III) of paragraph (2)(A)(vii), the approval may be made effective on the date certified under subclause (III).

(iii) If the applicant made a certification described in subclause (IV) of paragraph (2)(A)(vii), the approval shall be made effective immediately unless, before the expiration of 45 days after the date on which the notice described in paragraph (2)(B) is received, an action is brought for infringement of the patent that is the subject of the certification and for which information was submitted to the Secretary under subsection (b)(1) or (c)(2) of this section before the date on which the application (excluding an amendment or supplement to the application), which the Secretary later determines to be substantially complete, was submitted. If such an action is brought before the expiration of such days, the approval shall be made effective upon the expiration of the thirty-month period beginning on the date of the receipt of the notice provided under paragraph (2)(B)(i) or such shorter or longer period as the court may order because either party to the action failed to reasonably cooperate in expediting the action, except that—

(I) if before the expiration of such period the district court decides that the patent is invalid or not infringed (including any substantive determination that there is no cause of action for patent infringement or invalidity), the approval shall be made effective on—

(aa) the date on which the court enters judgment reflecting the decision; or

(bb) the date of a settlement order or consent decree signed and entered by the court stating that the patent that is the subject of the certification is invalid or not infringed;

(II) if before the expiration of such period the district court decides that the patent has been infringed—

(aa) if the judgment of the district court is appealed, the approval shall be made effective on—

(AA) the date on which the court of appeals decides that the patent is invalid or not infringed (including any substantive determination that there is no cause of action for patent infringement or invalidity); or

(BB) the date of a settlement order or consent decree signed and entered by the court of appeals stating that the patent that is the subject of the certification is invalid or not infringed; or

(bb) if the judgment of the district court is not appealed or is affirmed, the approval shall be made effective on the date specified by the district court in a court order under section 271(e)(4)(A) of title 35;

(III) if before the expiration of such period the court grants a preliminary injunction prohibiting the applicant from engaging in the commercial manufacture or sale of the drug until the court decides the issues of patent validity and infringement and if the court decides that such patent is invalid or not infringed, the approval shall be made effective as provided in subclause (I); or

(IV) if before the expiration of such period the court grants a preliminary injunction prohibiting the applicant from engaging in the commercial manufacture or sale of the drug until the court decides the issues of patent validity and infringement and if the court decides that such patent has been infringed, the approval shall be made effective as provided in subclause (II).

In such an action, each of the parties shall reasonably cooperate in expediting the action.

(iv) 180-DAY EXCLUSIVITY PERIOD.—

(I) EFFECTIVENESS OF APPLICATION.—Subject to subparagraph (D), if the application contains a certification described in paragraph (2)(A)(vii)(IV) and is for a drug for which a first applicant has submitted an application containing such a certification, the application shall be made effective on the date that is 180 days after the date of the first commercial marketing of the drug (including the commercial marketing of the listed drug) by any first applicant.

(II) DEFINITIONS.—In this paragraph:

(aa) 180-DAY EXCLUSIVITY PERIOD.—The term "180-day exclusivity period" means the 180-day period ending on the day before the date on which an application submitted by an applicant other than a first applicant could become effective under this clause.

(bb) FIRST APPLICANT.—As used in this subsection, the term "first applicant" means an applicant that, on the first day on which a substantially complete application containing a certification described in paragraph (2)(A)(vii)(IV) is submitted for approval of a drug, submits a substantially complete application that contains and lawfully maintains a certification described in paragraph (2)(A)(vii)(IV) for the drug.

(cc) SUBSTANTIALLY COMPLETE APPLICATION.—As used in this subsection, the term "substantially complete application" means an application under this subsection that on its face is sufficiently complete to permit a substantive review and contains all the information required by paragraph (2)(A).

(dd) TENTATIVE APPROVAL.—

(AA) IN GENERAL.—The term "tentative approval" means notification to an applicant by the Secretary that an application under this subsection meets the requirements of paragraph (2)(A), but cannot receive effective approval because the application does not meet the requirements of this subparagraph, there is a period of exclusivity for the listed drug under subparagraph (F) or section 355a of this title, or there is a 7-year period of exclusivity for the listed drug under section 360cc of this title.

(BB) LIMITATION.—A drug that is granted tentative approval by the Secretary is not an approved drug and shall not have an effective approval until the Secretary issues an approval after any necessary additional review of the application.

(C) CIVIL ACTION TO OBTAIN PATENT CERTAINTY.—

(i) DECLARATORY JUDGMENT ABSENT INFRINGEMENT ACTION.—

(I) IN GENERAL.—No action may be brought under section 2201 of title 28 by an applicant under paragraph (2) for a declaratory judgment with respect to a patent which is the subject of the certification referred to in subparagraph (B)(iii) unless—

(aa) the 45-day period referred to in such subparagraph has expired;

(bb) neither the owner of such patent nor the holder of the approved application under subsection (b) of this section for the drug that is claimed by the patent or a use of which is claimed by the patent brought a civil action against the applicant for infringement of the patent before the expiration of such period; and

(cc) in any case in which the notice provided under paragraph (2)(B) relates to noninfringement, the notice was accompanied by a document described in subclause (III).

(II) FILING OF CIVIL ACTION.—If the conditions described in items (aa), (bb), and as applicable, (cc) of subclause (I) have been met, the applicant referred to in such subclause may, in accordance with section 2201 of title 28, bring a civil action under such section against the owner or holder referred to in such subclause (but not against any owner or holder that has brought such a civil action against the applicant, unless that civil action was dismissed without prejudice) for a declaratory judgment that the patent is invalid or will not be infringed by the drug for which the applicant seeks approval, except that such civil action may be brought for a declaratory judgment that the patent will not be infringed only in a case in which the condition described in subclause (I)(cc) is applicable. A civil action referred to in this subclause shall be brought in the judicial district where the defendant has its principal place of business or a regular and established place of business.

(III) OFFER OF CONFIDENTIAL ACCESS TO APPLICATION.—For purposes of subclause (I)(cc), the document described in this subclause is a document providing an offer of confidential access to the application that is in the custody of the applicant under paragraph (2) for the purpose of determining whether an action referred to in subparagraph (B)(iii) should be brought. The document providing the offer of confidential access shall contain such restrictions as to persons entitled to access, and on the use and disposition of any information accessed, as would apply had a protective order been entered for the purpose of protecting trade secrets and other confidential business information. A request for access to an application under an offer of confidential access shall be considered acceptance of the offer of confidential access with the restrictions as to persons entitled to access, and on the use and disposition of any information accessed, contained in the offer of confidential access, and those restrictions and other terms of the offer of confidential access shall be considered terms of an enforceable contract. Any person provided an offer of confidential access shall review the application for the sole and limited purpose of evaluating possible infringement of the patent that is the subject of the certification under paragraph (2)(A)(vii)(IV) and for no other purpose, and may not disclose information of no relevance to any issue of patent infringement to any person other than a person provided an offer of confidential access. Further, the application may be redacted by the applicant to remove any information of no relevance to any issue of patent infringement.

(ii) COUNTERCLAIM TO INFRINGEMENT ACTION.—

(I) IN GENERAL.—If an owner of the patent or the holder of the approved application under subsection (b) of this section for the drug that is claimed by the patent or a use of which is claimed by the patent brings a patent infringement action against the applicant, the applicant may assert a counterclaim seeking an order requiring the holder to correct or delete the patent information submitted by the holder under subsection (b) or (c) of this section on the ground that the patent does not claim either—

(aa) the drug for which the application was approved; or

(bb) an approved method of using the drug.

(II) NO INDEPENDENT CAUSE OF ACTION.—Subclause (I) does not authorize the assertion of a claim described in subclause (I) in any civil action or proceeding other than a counterclaim described in subclause (I).

(iii) NO DAMAGES.—An applicant shall not be entitled to damages in a civil action under clause (i) or a counterclaim under clause (ii).

(D) FORFEITURE OF 180-DAY EXCLUSIVITY PERIOD.—

(i) DEFINITION OF FORFEITURE EVENT.—In this subparagraph, the term "forfeiture event", with respect to an application under this subsection, means the occurrence of any of the following:

(I) FAILURE TO MARKET.—The first applicant fails to market the drug by the later of—

(aa) the earlier of the date that is—

(AA) 75 days after the date on which the approval of the application of the first applicant is made effective under subparagraph (B)(iii); or

(BB) 30 months after the date of submission of the application of the first applicant; or

(bb) with respect to the first applicant or any other applicant (which other applicant has received tentative approval), the date that is 75 days after the date as of which, as to each of the patents with respect to which the first applicant submitted and lawfully maintained a certification qualifying the first applicant for the 180-day exclusivity period under subparagraph (B)(iv), at least 1 of the following has occurred:

(AA) In an infringement action brought against that applicant with respect to the patent or in a declaratory judgment action brought by that applicant with respect to the patent, a court enters a final decision from which no appeal (other than a petition to the Supreme Court for a writ of certiorari) has been or can be taken that the patent is invalid or not infringed.

(BB) In an infringement action or a declaratory judgment action described in subitem (AA), a court signs a settlement order or consent decree that enters a final judgment that includes a finding that the patent is invalid or not infringed.

(CC) The patent information submitted under subsection (b) or (c) of this section is withdrawn by the holder of the application approved under subsection (b) of this section.

(II) WITHDRAWAL OF APPLICATION.—The first applicant withdraws the application or the Secretary considers the application to have been withdrawn as a result of a determination by the Secretary that the application does not meet the requirements for approval under paragraph (4).

(III) AMENDMENT OF CERTIFICATION.—The first applicant amends or withdraws the certification for all of the patents with respect to which that applicant submitted a certification qualifying the applicant for the 180-day exclusivity period.

(IV) FAILURE TO OBTAIN TENTATIVE APPROVAL.—The first applicant fails to obtain tentative approval of the application within 30 months after the date on which the application is filed, unless the failure is caused by a change in or a review of the requirements for approval of the application imposed after the date on which the application is filed.

(V) AGREEMENT WITH ANOTHER APPLICANT, THE LISTED DRUG APPLICATION HOLDER, OR A PATENT OWNER.—The first applicant enters into an agreement with another applicant under this subsection for the drug, the holder of the application for the listed drug, or an owner of the patent that is the subject of the certification under paragraph (2)(A)(vii)(IV), the Federal Trade Commission or the Attorney General files a complaint, and there is a final decision of the Federal Trade Commission or the court with regard to the complaint from which no appeal (other than a petition to the Supreme Court for a writ of certiorari) has been or can be taken that the agreement has violated the antitrust laws (as defined in section 12 of title 15, except that the term includes section 45 of title 15 to the extent that that section applies to unfair methods of competition).

(VI) EXPIRATION OF ALL PATENTS.—All of the patents as to which the applicant submitted a certification qualifying it for the 180-day exclusivity period have expired.

(ii) FORFEITURE.—The 180-day exclusivity period described in subparagraph (B)(iv) shall be forfeited by a first applicant if a forfeiture event occurs with respect to that first applicant.

(iii) SUBSEQUENT APPLICANT.—If all first applicants forfeit the 180-day exclusivity period under clause (ii)—

(I) approval of any application containing a certification described in paragraph (2)(A)(vii)(IV) shall be made effective in accordance with subparagraph (B)(iii); and

(II) no applicant shall be eligible for a 180-day exclusivity period.

(E) If the Secretary decides to disapprove an application, the Secretary shall give the applicant notice of an opportunity for a hearing before the Secretary on the question of whether such application is approvable. If the applicant elects to accept the opportunity for hearing by written request within thirty days after such notice, such hearing shall commence not more than ninety days after the expiration of such thirty days unless the Secretary and the applicant otherwise agree. Any such hearing shall thereafter be conducted on an expedited basis and the Secretary's order thereon shall be issued within ninety days after the date fixed by the Secretary for filing final briefs.

(F)(i) If an application (other than an abbreviated new drug application) submitted under subsection (b) of this section for a drug, no active ingredient (including any ester or salt of the active ingredient) of which has been approved in any other application under subsection (b) of this section, was approved during the period beginning January 1, 1982, and ending on September 24, 1984, the Secretary may not make the approval of an application submitted under this subsection which refers to the drug for which the subsection (b) application was submitted effective before the expiration of ten years from the date of the approval of the application under subsection (b) of this section.

(ii) If an application submitted under subsection (b) of this section for a drug, no active ingredient (including any ester or salt of the active ingredient) of which has been approved in any other application under subsection (b) of this section, is approved after September 24, 1984, no application may be submitted under this subsection which refers to the drug for which the subsection (b) application was submitted before the expiration of five years from the date of the approval of the application under subsection (b) of this section, except that such an application may be submitted under this subsection after the expiration of four years from the date of the approval of the subsection (b) application if it contains a certification of patent invalidity or noninfringement described in subclause (IV) of paragraph (2)(A)(vii). The approval of such an application shall be made effective in accordance with subparagraph (B) except that, if an action for patent infringement is commenced during the one-year period beginning forty-eight months after the date of the approval of the subsection (b) application, the thirty-month period referred to in subparagraph (B)(iii) shall be extended by such amount of time (if any) which is required for seven and one-half years to have elapsed from the date of approval of the subsection (b) application.

(iii) If an application submitted under subsection (b) of this section for a drug, which includes an active ingredient (including any ester or salt of the active ingredient) that has been approved in another application approved under subsection (b) of this section, is approved after September 24, 1984, and if such application contains reports of new clinical investigations (other than bioavailability studies) essential to the approval of the application and conducted or sponsored by the applicant, the Secretary may not make the approval of an application submitted under this subsection for the conditions of approval of such drug in the subsection (b) application effective before the expiration of three years from the date of the approval of the application under subsection (b) of this section for such drug.

(iv) If a supplement to an application approved under subsection (b) of this section is approved after September 24, 1984, and the supplement contains reports of new clinical investigations (other than bioavailability studies) essential to the approval of the supplement and conducted or sponsored by the person submitting the supplement, the Secretary may not make the approval of an application submitted under this subsection for a change approved in the supplement effective before the expiration of three years from the date of the approval of the supplement under subsection (b) of this section.

(v) If an application (or supplement to an application) submitted under subsection (b) of this section for a drug, which includes an active ingredient (including any ester or salt of the active ingredient) that has been approved in another application under subsection (b) of this section, was approved during the period beginning January 1, 1982, and ending on September 24, 1984, the Secretary may not make the approval of an application submitted under this subsection which refers to the drug for which the subsection (b) application was submitted or which refers to a change approved in a supplement to the subsection (b) application effective before the expiration of two years from September 24, 1984.

(6) If a drug approved under this subsection refers in its approved application to a drug the approval of which was withdrawn or suspended for grounds described in the first sentence of subsection (e) of this section or was withdrawn or suspended under this paragraph or which, as determined by the Secretary, has been withdrawn from sale for safety or effectiveness reasons, the approval of the drug under this subsection shall be withdrawn or suspended—

(A) for the same period as the withdrawal or suspension under subsection (e) of this section or this paragraph, or

(B) if the listed drug has been withdrawn from sale, for the period of withdrawal from sale or, if earlier, the period ending on the date the Secretary determines that the withdrawal from sale is not for safety or effectiveness reasons.

(7)(A)(i) Within sixty days of September 24, 1984, the Secretary shall publish and make available to the public—

(I) a list in alphabetical order of the official and proprietary name of each drug which has been approved for safety and effectiveness under subsection (c) of this section before September 24, 1984;

(II) the date of approval if the drug is approved after 1981 and the number of the application which was approved; and

(III) whether in vitro or in vivo bioequivalence studies, or both such studies, are required for applications filed under this subsection which will refer to the drug published.

(ii) Every thirty days after the publication of the first list under clause (i) the Secretary shall revise the list to include each drug which has been approved for safety and effectiveness under subsection (c) of this section or approved under this subsection during the thirty-day period.

(iii) When patent information submitted under subsection (b) or (c) of this section respecting a drug included on the list is to be published by the Secretary, the Secretary shall, in revisions made under clause (ii), include such information for such drug.

(B) A drug approved for safety and effectiveness under subsection (c) of this section or approved under this subsection shall, for purposes of this subsection, be considered to have been published under subparagraph (A) on the date of its approval or September 24, 1984, whichever is later.

(C) If the approval of a drug was withdrawn or suspended for grounds described in the first sentence of subsection (e) of this section or was withdrawn or suspended under paragraph (6) or if the Secretary determines that a drug has been withdrawn from sale for safety or effectiveness reasons, it may not be published in the list under subparagraph (A) or, if the withdrawal or suspension occurred after its publication in such list, it shall be immediately removed from such list—

(i) for the same period as the withdrawal or suspension under subsection (e) of this section or paragraph (6), or

(ii) if the listed drug has been withdrawn from sale, for the period of withdrawal from sale or, if earlier, the period ending on the date the Secretary determines that the withdrawal from sale is not for safety or effectiveness reasons.

A notice of the removal shall be published in the Federal Register.

(8) For purposes of this subsection:

(A)(i) The term "bioavailability" means the rate and extent to which the active ingredient or therapeutic ingredient is absorbed from a drug and becomes available at the site of drug action.

(ii) For a drug that is not intended to be absorbed into the bloodstream, the Secretary may assess bioavailability by scientifically valid measurements intended to reflect the rate and extent to which the active ingredient or therapeutic ingredient becomes available at the site of drug action.

(B) A drug shall be considered to be bioequivalent to a listed drug if—

(i) the rate and extent of absorption of the drug do not show a significant difference from the rate and extent of absorption of the listed drug when administered at the same molar dose of the therapeutic ingredient under similar experimental conditions in either a single dose or multiple doses; or

(ii) the extent of absorption of the drug does not show a significant difference from the extent of absorption of the listed drug when administered at the same molar dose of the therapeutic ingredient under similar experimental conditions in either a single dose or multiple doses and the difference from the listed drug in the rate of absorption of the drug is intentional, is reflected in its proposed labeling, is not essential to the attainment of effective body drug concentrations on chronic use, and is considered medically insignificant for the drug.

(C) For a drug that is not intended to be absorbed into the bloodstream, the Secretary may establish alternative, scientifically valid methods to show bioequivalence if the alternative methods are expected to detect a significant difference between the drug and the listed drug in safety and therapeutic effect.

(9) The Secretary shall, with respect to each application submitted under this subsection, maintain a record of—

(A) the name of the applicant,

(B) the name of the drug covered by the application,

(C) the name of each person to whom the review of the chemistry of the application was assigned and the date of such assignment, and

(D) the name of each person to whom the bioequivalence review for such application was assigned and the date of such assignment.

The information the Secretary is required to maintain under this paragraph with respect to an application submitted under this subsection shall be made available to the public after the approval of such application.

(k) Records and reports; required information; regulations and orders; access to records

(1) In the case of any drug for which an approval of an application filed under subsection (b) or (j) of this section is in effect, the applicant shall establish and maintain such records, and make such reports to the Secretary, of data relating to clinical experience and other data or information, received or otherwise obtained by such applicant with respect to such drug, as the Secretary may by general regulation, or by order with respect to such application, prescribe on the basis of a finding that such records and reports are necessary in order to enable the Secretary to determine, or facilitate a determination, whether there is or may be ground for invoking subsection (e) of this section. Regulations and orders issued under this subsection and under subsection (i) of this section shall have due regard for the professional ethics of the medical profession and the interests of patients and shall provide, where the Secretary deems it to be appropriate, for the examination, upon request, by the persons to whom such regulations or orders are applicable, of similar information received or otherwise obtained by the Secretary.

(2) Every person required under this section to maintain records, and every person in charge or

custody thereof, shall, upon request of an officer or employee designated by the Secretary, permit such officer or employee at all reasonable times to have access to and copy and verify such records.

(3) ACTIVE POSTMARKET RISK IDENTIFICATION.—

(A) DEFINITION.—In this paragraph, the term "data" refers to information with respect to a drug approved under this section or under section 262 of title 42, including claims data, patient survey data, standardized analytic files that allow for the pooling and analysis of data from disparate data environments, and any other data deemed appropriate by the Secretary.

(B) DEVELOPMENT OF POSTMARKET RISK IDENTIFICATION AND ANALYSIS METHODS.—The Secretary shall, not later than 2 years after September 27, 2007, in collaboration with public, academic, and private entities—

(i) develop methods to obtain access to disparate data sources including the data sources specified in subparagraph (C);

(ii) develop validated methods for the establishment of a postmarket risk identification and analysis system to link and analyze safety data from multiple sources, with the goals of including, in aggregate—

(I) at least 25,000,000 patients by July 1, 2010; and

(II) at least 100,000,000 patients by July 1, 2012; and

(iii) convene a committee of experts, including individuals who are recognized in the field of protecting data privacy and security, to make recommendations to the Secretary on the development of tools and methods for the ethical and scientific uses for, and communication of, postmarketing data specified under subparagraph (C), including recommendations on the development of effective research methods for the study of drug safety questions.

(C) ESTABLISHMENT OF THE POSTMARKET RISK IDENTIFICATION AND ANALYSIS SYSTEM.—

(i) IN GENERAL.—The Secretary shall, not later than 1 year after the development of the risk identification and analysis methods under subparagraph (B), establish and maintain procedures—

(I) for risk identification and analysis based on electronic health data, in compliance with the regulations promulgated under section 264(c) of the Health Insurance Portability and Accountability Act of 1996, and in a manner that does not disclose individually identifiable health information in violation of paragraph (4)(B);

(II) for the reporting (in a standardized form) of data on all serious adverse drug experiences (as defined in section 355–1(b) of this title) submitted to the Secretary under paragraph (1), and those adverse events submitted by patients, providers, and drug sponsors, when appropriate;

(III) to provide for active adverse event surveillance using the following data sources, as available:

(aa) Federal health-related electronic data (such as data from the Medicare program and the health systems of the Department of Veterans Affairs);

(bb) private sector health-related electronic data (such as pharmaceutical purchase data and health insurance claims data); and

(cc) other data as the Secretary deems necessary to create a robust system to identify adverse events and potential drug safety signals;

(IV) to identify certain trends and patterns with respect to data accessed by the system;

(V) to provide regular reports to the Secretary concerning adverse event trends, adverse event patterns, incidence and prevalence of adverse events, and other information the Secretary determines appropriate, which may include data on comparative national adverse event trends; and

(VI) to enable the program to export data in a form appropriate for further aggregation, statistical analysis, and reporting.

(ii) TIMELINESS OF REPORTING.—The procedures established under clause (i) shall ensure that such data are accessed, analyzed, and reported in a timely, routine, and systematic manner, taking into consideration the need for data completeness, coding, cleansing, and standardized analysis and transmission.

(iii) PRIVATE SECTOR RESOURCES.—To ensure the establishment of the active postmarket risk identification and analysis system under this subsection not later than 1 year after the development of the risk identification and analysis methods under subparagraph (B), as required under clause (i), the Secretary may, on a temporary or permanent basis, implement systems or products developed by private entities.

(iv) COMPLEMENTARY APPROACHES.—To the extent the active postmarket risk identification and analysis system under this subsection is not sufficient to gather data and information relevant to a priority drug safety question, the Secretary shall develop, support, and participate in complementary approaches to gather and analyze such data and information, including—

(I) approaches that are complementary with respect to assessing the safety of use of a drug in domestic populations not included, or underrepresented, in the trials used to approve the drug (such as older people, people with comorbidities, pregnant women, or children); and

(II) existing approaches such as the Vaccine Adverse Event Reporting System and the Vaccine Safety Datalink or successor databases.

(v) AUTHORITY FOR CONTRACTS.—The Secretary may enter into contracts with public and private entities to fulfill the requirements of this subparagraph.

(4) ADVANCED ANALYSIS OF DRUG SAFETY DATA.—

(A) PURPOSE.—The Secretary shall establish collaborations with public, academic, and private entities, which may include the Centers for Education and Research on Therapeutics under section 299b–1 of title 42, to provide for advanced analysis of drug safety data described in paragraph (3)(C) and other information that is publicly available or is provided by the Secretary, in order to—

(i) improve the quality and efficiency of postmarket drug safety risk-benefit analysis;

(ii) provide the Secretary with routine access to outside expertise to study advanced drug safety questions; and

(iii) enhance the ability of the Secretary to make timely assessments based on drug safety data.

(B) PRIVACY.—Such analysis shall not disclose individually identifiable health information when presenting such drug safety signals and trends or when responding to inquiries regarding such drug safety signals and trends.

(C) PUBLIC PROCESS FOR PRIORITY QUESTIONS.—At least biannually, the Secretary shall seek recommendations from the Drug Safety and Risk Management Advisory Committee (or any successor committee) and from other advisory committees, as appropriate, to the Food and Drug Administration on—

(i) priority drug safety questions; and

(ii) mechanisms for answering such questions, including through—

(I) active risk identification under paragraph (3); and

(II) when such risk identification is not sufficient, postapproval studies and clinical trials under subsection (*o*)(3).

(D) PROCEDURES FOR THE DEVELOPMENT OF DRUG SAFETY COLLABORATIONS

(i) IN GENERAL.—Not later than 180 days after the date of the establishment of the active postmarket risk identification and analysis system under this subsection, the Secretary shall establish and implement procedures under which the Secretary may routinely contract with one or more qualified entities to—

(I) classify, analyze, or aggregate data described in paragraph (3)(C) and information that is publicly available or is provided by the Secretary;

(II) allow for prompt investigation of priority drug safety questions, including—

(aa) unresolved safety questions for drugs or classes of drugs; and

(bb) for a newly-approved drugs,[2] safety signals from clinical trials used to approve the drug and other preapproval trials; rare, serious drug side effects; and the safety of use in domestic populations not included, or underrepresented, in the trials used to approve the drug (such as older people, people with comorbidities, pregnant women, or children);

(III) perform advanced research and analysis on identified drug safety risks;

(IV) focus postapproval studies and clinical trials under subsection (*o*)(3) more effectively on cases for which reports under paragraph (1) and other safety signal detection is not sufficient to resolve whether there is an elevated risk of a serious adverse event associated with the use of a drug; and

(V) carry out other activities as the Secretary deems necessary to carry out the purposes of this paragraph.

(ii) REQUEST FOR SPECIFIC METHODOLOGY.—The procedures described in clause (i) shall permit the Secretary to request that a specific methodology be used by the qualified entity. The qualified entity shall work with the Secretary to finalize the methodology to be used.

(E) USE OF ANALYSES.—The Secretary shall provide the analyses described in this paragraph, including the methods and results of such analyses, about a drug to the sponsor or sponsors of such drug.

(F) QUALIFIED ENTITIES.—

(i) IN GENERAL.—The Secretary shall enter into contracts with a sufficient number of qualified entities to develop and provide information to the Secretary in a timely manner.

(ii) QUALIFICATION.—The Secretary shall enter into a contract with an entity under clause (i) only if the Secretary determines that the entity has a significant presence in the United States and has one or more of the following qualifications:

(I) The research, statistical, epidemiologic, or clinical capability and expertise to conduct and complete the activities under this paragraph, including the capability and expertise to provide the Secretary de-identified data consistent with the requirements of this subsection.

(II) An information technology infrastructure in place to support electronic data and operational standards to provide security for such data.

(III) Experience with, and expertise on, the development of drug safety and effectiveness research using electronic population data.

(IV) An understanding of drug development or risk/benefit balancing in a clinical setting.

(V) Other expertise which the Secretary deems necessary to fulfill the activities under this paragraph.

(G) CONTRACT REQUIREMENTS.—Each contract with a qualified entity under subparagraph (F)(i) shall contain the following requirements:

(i) ENSURING PRIVACY.—The qualified entity shall ensure that the entity will not use data under this subsection in a manner that—

(I) violates the regulations promulgated under section 264(c) of the Health Insurance Portability and Accountability Act of 1996;

(II) violates sections 552 or 552a of title 5 with regard to the privacy of individually-identifiable beneficiary health information; or

[2] So in original. Probably should be "drug,".

(III) discloses individually identifiable health information when presenting drug safety signals and trends or when responding to inquiries regarding drug safety signals and trends.

Nothing in this clause prohibits lawful disclosure for other purposes.

(ii) COMPONENT OF ANOTHER ORGANIZATION.—If a qualified entity is a component of another organization—

(I) the qualified entity shall establish appropriate security measures to maintain the confidentiality and privacy of such data; and

(II) the entity shall not make an unauthorized disclosure of such data to the other components of the organization in breach of such confidentiality and privacy requirement.

(iii) TERMINATION OR NONRENEWAL.—If a contract with a qualified entity under this subparagraph is terminated or not renewed, the following requirements shall apply:

(I) CONFIDENTIALITY AND PRIVACY PROTECTIONS.—The entity shall continue to comply with the confidentiality and privacy requirements under this paragraph with respect to all data disclosed to the entity.

(II) DISPOSITION OF DATA.—The entity shall return any data disclosed to such entity under this subsection to which it would not otherwise have access or, if returning the data is not practicable, destroy the data.

(H) COMPETITIVE PROCEDURES.—The Secretary shall use competitive procedures (as defined in section 403(5)[3] of title 41) to enter into contracts under subparagraph (G).

(I) REVIEW OF CONTRACT IN THE EVENT OF A MERGER OR ACQUISITION.—The Secretary shall review the contract with a qualified entity under this paragraph in the event of a merger or acquisition of the entity in order to ensure that the requirements under this paragraph will continue to be met.

(J) COORDINATION.—In carrying out this paragraph, the Secretary shall provide for appropriate communications to the public, scientific, public health, and medical communities, and other key stakeholders, and to the extent practicable shall coordinate with the activities of private entities, professional associations, or other entities that may have sources of drug safety data.

(5) The Secretary shall—

(A) conduct regular, bi-weekly screening of the Adverse Event Reporting System database and post a quarterly report on the Adverse Event Reporting System Web site of any new safety information or potential signal of a serious risk identified by Adverse[4] Event Reporting System within the last quarter;

(B) report to Congress not later than 2 year[5] after September 27, 2007, on procedures and processes of the Food and Drug Administration for addressing ongoing post market safety issues identified by the Office of Surveillance and Epidemiology and how recommendations of the Office of Surveillance and Epidemiology are handled within the agency; and

(C) on an annual basis, review the entire backlog of postmarket safety commitments to determine which commitments require revision or should be eliminated, report to the Congress on these determinations, and assign start dates and estimated completion dates for such commitments.

(*l*) Public disclosure of safety and effectiveness data and action package

(1) Safety and effectiveness data and information which has been submitted in an application under subsection (b) of this section for a drug and which has not previously been disclosed to the public shall be made available to the public, upon request, unless extraordinary circumstances are shown—

(A) if no work is being or will be undertaken to have the application approved,

(B) if the Secretary has determined that the application is not approvable and all legal appeals have been exhausted,

(C) if approval of the application under subsection (c) of this section is withdrawn and all legal appeals have been exhausted,

(D) if the Secretary has determined that such drug is not a new drug, or

(E) upon the effective date of the approval of the first application under subsection (j) of this section which refers to such drug or upon the date upon which the approval of an application under subsection (j) of this section which refers to such drug could be made effective if such an application had been submitted.

(2) ACTION PACKAGE FOR APPROVAL.—

(A) ACTION PACKAGE.—The Secretary shall publish the action package for approval of an application under subsection (b) or section 262 of title 42 on the Internet Web site of the Food and Drug Administration—

(i) not later than 30 days after the date of approval of such application for a drug no active ingredient (including any ester or salt of the active ingredient) of which has been approved in any other application under this section or section 262 of title 42; and

(ii) not later than 30 days after the third request for such action package for approval received under section 552 of title 5 for any other drug.

(B) IMMEDIATE PUBLICATION OF SUMMARY REVIEW.—Notwithstanding subparagraph (A), the Secretary shall publish, on the Internet Web site of the Food and Drug Administration, the materials described in subparagraph (C)(iv) not later than 48 hours after the date of approval of the drug, except where such materials require redaction by the Secretary.

(C) CONTENTS.—An action package for approval of an application under subparagraph (A) shall be dated and shall include the following:

(i) Documents generated by the Food and Drug Administration related to review of the application.

---

[3] See References in Text note below.

[4] So in original. Probably should be preceded by "the".

[5] So in original. Probably should be "years".

(ii) Documents pertaining to the format and content of the application generated during drug development.

(iii) Labeling submitted by the applicant.

(iv) A summary review that documents conclusions from all reviewing disciplines about the drug, noting any critical issues and disagreements with the applicant and within the review team and how they were resolved, recommendations for action, and an explanation of any nonconcurrence with review conclusions.

(v) The Division Director and Office Director's decision document which includes—

(I) a brief statement of concurrence with the summary review;

(II) a separate review or addendum to the review if disagreeing with the summary review; and

(III) a separate review or addendum to the review to add further analysis.

(vi) Identification by name of each officer or employee of the Food and Drug Administration who—

(I) participated in the decision to approve the application; and

(II) consents to have his or her name included in the package.

(D) REVIEW.—A scientific review of an application is considered the work of the reviewer and shall not be altered by management or the reviewer once final.

(E) CONFIDENTIAL INFORMATION.—This paragraph does not authorize the disclosure of any trade secret, confidential commercial or financial information, or other matter listed in section 552(b) of title 5.

(m) "Patent" defined

For purposes of this section, the term "patent" means a patent issued by the United States Patent and Trademark Office.

(n) Scientific advisory panels

(1) For the purpose of providing expert scientific advice and recommendations to the Secretary regarding a clinical investigation of a drug or the approval for marketing of a drug under this section or section 262 of title 42, the Secretary shall establish panels of experts or use panels of experts established before November 21, 1997, or both.

(2) The Secretary may delegate the appointment and oversight authority granted under section 394 of this title to a director of a center or successor entity within the Food and Drug Administration.

(3) The Secretary shall make appointments to each panel established under paragraph (1) so that each panel shall consist of—

(A) members who are qualified by training and experience to evaluate the safety and effectiveness of the drugs to be referred to the panel and who, to the extent feasible, possess skill and experience in the development, manufacture, or utilization of such drugs;

(B) members with diverse expertise in such fields as clinical and administrative medicine, pharmacy, pharmacology, pharmacoeconomics, biological and physical sciences, and other related professions;

(C) a representative of consumer interests, and a representative of interests of the drug manufacturing industry not directly affected by the matter to be brought before the panel; and

(D) two or more members who are specialists or have other expertise in the particular disease or condition for which the drug under review is proposed to be indicated.

Scientific, trade, and consumer organizations shall be afforded an opportunity to nominate individuals for appointment to the panels. No individual who is in the regular full-time employ of the United States and engaged in the administration of this chapter may be a voting member of any panel. The Secretary shall designate one of the members of each panel to serve as chairman thereof.

(4) The Secretary shall, as appropriate, provide education and training to each new panel member before such member participates in a panel's activities, including education regarding requirements under this chapter and related regulations of the Secretary, and the administrative processes and procedures related to panel meetings.

(5) Panel members (other than officers or employees of the United States), while attending meetings or conferences of a panel or otherwise engaged in its business, shall be entitled to receive compensation for each day so engaged, including traveltime, at rates to be fixed by the Secretary, but not to exceed the daily equivalent of the rate in effect for positions classified above grade GS-15 of the General Schedule. While serving away from their homes or regular places of business, panel members may be allowed travel expenses (including per diem in lieu of subsistence) as authorized by section 5703 of title 5, for persons in the Government service employed intermittently.

(6) The Secretary shall ensure that scientific advisory panels meet regularly and at appropriate intervals so that any matter to be reviewed by such a panel can be presented to the panel not more than 60 days after the matter is ready for such review. Meetings of the panel may be held using electronic communication to convene the meetings.

(7) Within 90 days after a scientific advisory panel makes recommendations on any matter under its review, the Food and Drug Administration official responsible for the matter shall review the conclusions and recommendations of the panel, and notify the affected persons of the final decision on the matter, or of the reasons that no such decision has been reached. Each such final decision shall be documented including the rationale for the decision.

(*o*) Postmarket studies and clinical trials; labeling

(1) In general

A responsible person may not introduce or deliver for introduction into interstate commerce the new drug involved if the person is in violation of a requirement established under paragraph (3) or (4) with respect to the drug.

(2) Definitions

For purposes of this subsection:

(A) Responsible person

The term "responsible person" means a person who—

(i) has submitted to the Secretary a covered application that is pending; or

(ii) is the holder of an approved covered application.

(B) Covered application

The term "covered application" means—

(i) an application under subsection (b) for a drug that is subject to section 353(b) of this title; and

(ii) an application under section 262 of title 42.

(C) New safety information; serious risk

The terms "new safety information", "serious risk", and "signal of a serious risk" have the meanings given such terms in section 355–1(b) of this title.

(3) Studies and clinical trials

(A) In general

For any or all of the purposes specified in subparagraph (B), the Secretary may, subject to subparagraph (D), require a responsible person for a drug to conduct a postapproval study or studies of the drug, or a postapproval clinical trial or trials of the drug, on the basis of scientific data deemed appropriate by the Secretary, including information regarding chemically-related or pharmacologically-related drugs.

(B) Purposes of study or clinical trial

The purposes referred to in this subparagraph with respect to a postapproval study or postapproval clinical trial are the following:

(i) To assess a known serious risk related to the use of the drug involved.

(ii) To assess signals of serious risk related to the use of the drug.

(iii) To identify an unexpected serious risk when available data indicates the potential for a serious risk.

(C) Establishment of requirement after approval of covered application

The Secretary may require a postapproval study or studies or postapproval clinical trial or trials for a drug for which an approved covered application is in effect as of the date on which the Secretary seeks to establish such requirement only if the Secretary becomes aware of new safety information.

(D) Determination by Secretary

(i) Postapproval studies

The Secretary may not require the responsible person to conduct a study under this paragraph, unless the Secretary makes a determination that the reports under subsection (k)(1) and the active postmarket risk identification and analysis system as available under subsection (k)(3) will not be sufficient to meet the purposes set forth in subparagraph (B).

(ii) Postapproval clinical trials

The Secretary may not require the responsible person to conduct a clinical trial under this paragraph, unless the Secretary makes a determination that a postapproval study or studies will not be sufficient to meet the purposes set forth in subparagraph (B).

(E) Notification; timetables; periodic reports

(i) Notification

The Secretary shall notify the responsible person regarding a requirement under this paragraph to conduct a postapproval study or clinical trial by the target dates for communication of feedback from the review team to the responsible person regarding proposed labeling and postmarketing study commitments as set forth in the letters described in section 101(c) of the Food and Drug Administration Amendments Act of 2007.

(ii) Timetable; periodic reports

For each study or clinical trial required to be conducted under this paragraph, the Secretary shall require that the responsible person submit a timetable for completion of the study or clinical trial. With respect to each study required to be conducted under this paragraph or otherwise undertaken by the responsible person to investigate a safety issue, the Secretary shall require the responsible person to periodically report to the Secretary on the status of such study including whether any difficulties in completing the study have been encountered. With respect to each clinical trial required to be conducted under this paragraph or otherwise undertaken by the responsible person to investigate a safety issue, the Secretary shall require the responsible person to periodically report to the Secretary on the status of such clinical trial including whether enrollment has begun, the number of participants enrolled, the expected completion date, whether any difficulties completing the clinical trial have been encountered, and registration information with respect to the requirements under section 282(j) of title 42. If the responsible person fails to comply with such timetable or violates any other requirement of this subparagraph, the responsible person shall be considered in violation of this subsection, unless the responsible person demonstrates good cause for such noncompliance or such other violation. The Secretary shall determine what constitutes good cause under the preceding sentence.

(F) Dispute resolution

The responsible person may appeal a requirement to conduct a study or clinical trial under this paragraph using dispute resolution procedures established by the Secretary in regulation and guidance.

(4) Safety labeling changes requested by Secretary

(A) New safety information

If the Secretary becomes aware of new safety information that the Secretary believes should be included in the labeling of the drug, the Secretary shall promptly notify the responsible person or, if the same drug approved under subsection (b) is not currently marketed, the holder of an approved application under subsection (j).

(B) Response to notification

Following notification pursuant to subparagraph (A), the responsible person or the holder of the approved application under subsection (j) shall within 30 days—

(i) submit a supplement proposing changes to the approved labeling to reflect the new safety information, including changes to boxed warnings, contraindications, warnings, precautions, or adverse reactions; or

(ii) notify the Secretary that the responsible person or the holder of the approved application under subsection (j) does not believe a labeling change is warranted and submit a statement detailing the reasons why such a change is not warranted.

(C) Review

Upon receipt of such supplement, the Secretary shall promptly review and act upon such supplement. If the Secretary disagrees with the proposed changes in the supplement or with the statement setting forth the reasons why no labeling change is necessary, the Secretary shall initiate discussions to reach agreement on whether the labeling for the drug should be modified to reflect the new safety information, and if so, the contents of such labeling changes.

(D) Discussions

Such discussions shall not extend for more than 30 days after the response to the notification under subparagraph (B), unless the Secretary determines an extension of such discussion period is warranted.

(E) Order

Within 15 days of the conclusion of the discussions under subparagraph (D), the Secretary may issue an order directing the responsible person or the holder of the approved application under subsection (j) to make such a labeling change as the Secretary deems appropriate to address the new safety information. Within 15 days of such an order, the responsible person or the holder of the approved application under subsection (j) shall submit a supplement containing the labeling change.

(F) Dispute resolution

Within 5 days of receiving an order under subparagraph (E), the responsible person or the holder of the approved application under subsection (j) may appeal using dispute resolution procedures established by the Secretary in regulation and guidance.

(G) Violation

If the responsible person or the holder of the approved application under subsection (j) has not submitted a supplement within 15 days of the date of such order under subparagraph (E), and there is no appeal or dispute resolution proceeding pending, the responsible person or holder shall be considered to be in violation of this subsection. If at the conclusion of any dispute resolution procedures the Secretary determines that a supplement must be submitted and such a supplement is not submitted within 15 days of the date of that determination, the responsible person or holder shall be in violation of this subsection.

(H) Public health threat

Notwithstanding subparagraphs (A) through (F), if the Secretary concludes that such a labeling change is necessary to protect the public health, the Secretary may accelerate the timelines in such subparagraphs.

(I) Rule of construction

This paragraph shall not be construed to affect the responsibility of the responsible person or the holder of the approved application under subsection (j) to maintain its label in accordance with existing requirements, including subpart B of part 201 and sections 314.70 and 601.12 of title 21, Code of Federal Regulations (or any successor regulations).

(5) Non-delegation

Determinations by the Secretary under this subsection for a drug shall be made by individuals at or above the level of individuals empowered to approve a drug (such as division directors within the Center for Drug Evaluation and Research).

(p) Risk evaluation and mitigation strategy

(1) In general

A person may not introduce or deliver for introduction into interstate commerce a new drug if—

(A)(i) the application for such drug is approved under subsection (b) or (j) and is subject to section 353(b) of this title; or

(ii) the application for such drug is approved under section 262 of title 42; and

(B) a risk evaluation and mitigation strategy is required under section 355–1 of this title with respect to the drug and the person fails to maintain compliance with the requirements of the approved strategy or with other requirements under section 355–1 of this title, including requirements regarding assessments of approved strategies.

(2) Certain postmarket studies

The failure to conduct a postmarket study under section 356 of this title, subpart H of part 314, or subpart E of part 601 of title 21, Code of Federal Regulations (or any successor regulations), is deemed to be a violation of paragraph (1).

(q) Petitions and civil actions regarding approval of certain applications

(1) In general

(A) Determination

The Secretary shall not delay approval of a pending application submitted under subsection (b)(2) or (j) because of any request to take any form of action relating to the application, either before or during consideration of the request, unless—

(i) the request is in writing and is a petition submitted to the Secretary pursuant to section 10.30 or 10.35 of title 21, Code of Federal Regulations (or any successor regulations); and

(ii) the Secretary determines, upon reviewing the petition, that a delay is necessary to protect the public health.

Consideration of the petition shall be separate and apart from review and approval of any application.

(B) Notification

If the Secretary determines under subparagraph (A) that a delay is necessary with respect to an application, the Secretary shall provide to the applicant, not later than 30 days after making such determination, the following information:

(i) Notification of the fact that a determination under subparagraph (A) has been made.

(ii) If applicable, any clarification or additional data that the applicant should submit to the docket on the petition to allow the Secretary to review the petition promptly.

(iii) A brief summary of the specific substantive issues raised in the petition which form the basis of the determination.

(C) Format

The information described in subparagraph (B) shall be conveyed via either, at the discretion of the Secretary—

(i) a document; or

(ii) a meeting with the applicant involved.

(D) Public disclosure

Any information conveyed by the Secretary under subparagraph (C) shall be considered part of the application and shall be subject to the disclosure requirements applicable to information in such application.

(E) Denial based on intent to delay

If the Secretary determines that a petition or a supplement to the petition was submitted with the primary purpose of delaying the approval of an application and the petition does not on its face raise valid scientific or regulatory issues, the Secretary may deny the petition at any point based on such determination. The Secretary may issue guidance to describe the factors that will be used to determine under this subparagraph whether a petition is submitted with the primary purpose of delaying the approval of an application.

(F) Final agency action

The Secretary shall take final agency action on a petition not later than 180 days after the date on which the petition is submitted. The Secretary shall not extend such period for any reason, including—

(i) any determination made under subparagraph (A);

(ii) the submission of comments relating to the petition or supplemental information supplied by the petitioner; or

(iii) the consent of the petitioner.

(G) Extension of 30-month period

If the filing of an application resulted in first-applicant status under subsection (j)(5)(D)(i)(IV) and approval of the application was delayed because of a petition, the 30-month period under such subsection is deemed to be extended by a period of time equal to the period beginning on the date on which the Secretary received the petition and ending on the date of final agency action on the petition (inclusive of such beginning and ending dates), without regard to whether the Secretary grants, in whole or in part, or denies, in whole or in part, the petition.

(H) Certification

The Secretary shall not consider a petition for review unless the party submitting such petition does so in written form and the subject document is signed and contains the following certification: "I certify that, to my best knowledge and belief: (a) this petition includes all information and views upon which the petition relies; (b) this petition includes representative data and/or information known to the petitioner which are unfavorable to the petition; and (c) I have taken reasonable steps to ensure that any representative data and/or information which are unfavorable to the petition were disclosed to me. I further certify that the information upon which I have based the action requested herein first became known to the party on whose behalf this petition is submitted on or about the following date: _______________. If I received or expect to receive payments, including cash and other forms of consideration, to file this information or its contents, I received or expect to receive those payments from the following persons or organizations: ____________________. I verify under penalty of perjury that the foregoing is true and correct as of the date of the submission of this petition.", with the date on which such information first became known to such party and the names of such persons or organizations inserted in the first and second blank space, respectively.

(I) Verification

The Secretary shall not accept for review any supplemental information or comments on a petition unless the party submitting such information or comments does so in written form and the subject document is signed and contains the following verification: "I certify that, to my best knowledge and belief: (a) I have not intentionally delayed submission of this document or its contents; and (b) the information upon which I have based the action requested herein first became known to me on or about _______________. If I received or expect to receive payments, including cash and other forms of consideration, to file this information or its contents, I received or expect to receive those payments from the following persons or organizations: _________. I verify under penalty of perjury that the foregoing is true and correct as of the date of the submission of this petition.'', with the date on which such information first became known to the party and the names of such persons or organizations inserted in the first and second blank space, respectively.

(2) Exhaustion of administrative remedies

(A) Final agency action within 180 days

The Secretary shall be considered to have taken final agency action on a petition if—

(i) during the 180-day period referred to in paragraph (1)(F), the Secretary makes a final decision within the meaning of section 10.45(d) of title 21, Code of Federal Regulations (or any successor regulation); or

(ii) such period expires without the Secretary having made such a final decision.

(B) Dismissal of certain civil actions

If a civil action is filed against the Secretary with respect to any issue raised in the petition before the Secretary has taken final agency action on the petition within the meaning of subparagraph (A), the court shall dismiss without prejudice the action for failure to exhaust administrative remedies.

(C) Administrative record

For purposes of judicial review related to the approval of an application for which a petition under paragraph (1) was submitted, the administrative record regarding any issue raised by the petition shall include—

(i) the petition filed under paragraph (1) and any supplements and comments thereto;

(ii) the Secretary's response to such petition, if issued; and

(iii) other information, as designated by the Secretary, related to the Secretary's determinations regarding the issues raised in such petition, as long as the information was considered by the agency no later than the date of final agency action as defined under subparagraph (2)(A), and regardless of whether the Secretary responded to the petition at or before the approval of the application at issue in the petition.

(3) Annual report on delays in approvals per petitions

The Secretary shall annually submit to the Congress a report that specifies—

(A) the number of applications that were approved during the preceding 12-month period;

(B) the number of such applications whose effective dates were delayed by petitions referred to in paragraph (1) during such period;

(C) the number of days by which such applications were so delayed; and

(D) the number of such petitions that were submitted during such period.

(4) Exceptions

This subsection does not apply to—

(A) a petition that relates solely to the timing of the approval of an application pursuant to subsection (j)(5)(B)(iv); or

(B) a petition that is made by the sponsor of an application and that seeks only to have the Secretary take or refrain from taking any form of action with respect to that application.

(5) Definitions

(A) Application

For purposes of this subsection, the term ''application'' means an application submitted under subsection (b)(2) or (j).

(B) Petition

For purposes of this subsection, other than paragraph (1)(A)(i), the term ''petition'' means a request described in paragraph (1)(A)(i).

(r) Postmarket drug safety information for patients and providers

(1) Establishment

Not later than 1 year after September 27, 2007, the Secretary shall improve the transparency of information about drugs and allow patients and health care providers better access to information about drugs by developing and maintaining an Internet Web site that—

(A) provides links to drug safety information listed in paragraph (2) for prescription drugs that are approved under this section or licensed under section 262 of title 42; and

(B) improves communication of drug safety information to patients and providers.

(2) Internet Web site

The Secretary shall carry out paragraph (1) by—

(A) developing and maintaining an accessible, consolidated Internet Web site with easily searchable drug safety information, including the information found on United States Government Internet Web sites, such as the United States National Library of Medicine's Daily Med and Medline Plus Web sites, in addition to other such Web sites maintained by the Secretary;

(B) ensuring that the information provided on the Internet Web site is comprehensive and includes, when available and appropriate—

(i) patient labeling and patient packaging inserts;

(ii) a link to a list of each drug, whether approved under this section or licensed under such section 262, for which a Medication Guide, as provided for under part 208 of title 21, Code of Federal Regulations (or any successor regulations), is required;

(iii) a link to the registry and results data bank provided for under subsections (i) and (j) of section 282 of title 42;

(iv) the most recent safety information and alerts issued by the Food and Drug Administration for drugs approved by the Secretary under this section, such as product recalls, warning letters, and import alerts;

(v) publicly available information about implemented RiskMAPs and risk evaluation and mitigation strategies under subsection (*o*);

(vi) guidance documents and regulations related to drug safety; and

(vii) other material determined appropriate by the Secretary;

(C) providing access to summaries of the assessed and aggregated data collected from the active surveillance infrastructure under subsection (k)(3) to provide information of known and serious side-effects for drugs approved under this section or licensed under such section 262;

(D) preparing, by 18 months after approval of a drug or after use of the drug by 10,000 individuals, whichever is later, a summary analysis of the adverse drug reaction reports received for the drug, including identification of any new risks not previously identified, potential new risks, or known risks reported in unusual number;

(E) enabling patients, providers, and drug sponsors to submit adverse event reports through the Internet Web site;

(F) providing educational materials for patients and providers about the appropriate means of disposing of expired, damaged, or unusable medications; and

(G) supporting initiatives that the Secretary determines to be useful to fulfill the purposes of the Internet Web site.

(3) Posting of drug labeling

The Secretary shall post on the Internet Web site established under paragraph (1) the approved professional labeling and any required patient labeling of a drug approved under this section or licensed under such section 262 not later than 21 days after the date the drug is approved or licensed, including in a supplemental application with respect to a labeling change.

(4) Private sector resources

To ensure development of the Internet Web site by the date described in paragraph (1), the Secretary may, on a temporary or permanent basis, implement systems or products developed by private entities.

(5) Authority for contracts

The Secretary may enter into contracts with public and private entities to fulfill the requirements of this subsection.

(6) Review

The Advisory Committee on Risk Communication under section 360bbb–6 of this title shall, on a regular basis, perform a comprehensive review and evaluation of the types of risk communication information provided on the Internet Web site established under paragraph (1) and, through other means, shall identify, clarify, and define the purposes and types of information available to facilitate the efficient flow of information to patients and providers, and shall recommend ways for the Food and Drug Administration to work with outside entities to help facilitate the dispensing of risk communication information to patients and providers.

(s) Referral to advisory committee

Prior to the approval of a drug no active ingredient (including any ester or salt of the active ingredient) of which has been approved in any other application under this section or section 262 of title 42, the Secretary shall—

(1) refer such drug to a Food and Drug Administration advisory committee for review at a meeting of such advisory committee; or

(2) if the Secretary does not refer such a drug to a Food and Drug Administration advisory committee prior to the approval of the drug, provide in the action letter on the application for the drug a summary of the reasons why the Secretary did not refer the drug to an advisory committee prior to approval.

(t) Database for authorized generic drugs

(1) In general

(A) Publication

The Commissioner shall—

(i) not later than 9 months after September 27, 2007, publish a complete list on the Internet Web site of the Food and Drug Administration of all authorized generic drugs (including drug trade name, brand company manufacturer, and the date the authorized generic drug entered the market); and

(ii) update the list quarterly to include each authorized generic drug included in an annual report submitted to the Secretary by the sponsor of a listed drug during the preceding 3-month period.

(B) Notification

The Commissioner shall notify relevant Federal agencies, including the Centers for Medicare & Medicaid Services and the Federal Trade Commission, when the Commissioner first publishes the information described in subparagraph (A) that the information has been published and that the information will be updated quarterly.

(2) Inclusion

The Commissioner shall include in the list described in paragraph (1) each authorized generic drug included in an annual report submitted to the Secretary by the sponsor of a listed drug after January 1, 1999.

(3) Authorized generic drug

In this section, the term "authorized generic drug" means a listed drug (as that term is used in subsection (j)) that—

(A) has been approved under subsection (c); and

(B) is marketed, sold, or distributed directly or indirectly to retail class of trade under a different labeling, packaging (other than repackaging as the listed drug in blister packs, unit doses, or similar packaging for use in institutions), product code, labeler code, trade name, or trade mark than the listed drug.

(u) Certain drugs containing single enantiomers

(1) In general

For purposes of subsections (c)(3)(E)(ii) and (j)(5)(F)(ii), if an application is submitted under subsection (b) for a non-racemic drug containing as an active ingredient (including any ester or salt of the active ingredient) a single enantiomer that is contained in a racemic drug approved in another application under subsection (b), the applicant may, in the application for such non-racemic drug, elect to have the single enantiomer not be considered the same active ingredient as that contained in the approved racemic drug, if—

(A)(i) the single enantiomer has not been previously approved except in the approved racemic drug; and

(ii) the application submitted under subsection (b) for such non-racemic drug—

(I) includes full reports of new clinical investigations (other than bioavailability studies)—

(aa) necessary for the approval of the application under subsections (c) and (d); and

(bb) conducted or sponsored by the applicant; and

(II) does not rely on any investigations that are part of an application submitted under subsection (b) for approval of the approved racemic drug; and

(B) the application submitted under subsection (b) for such non-racemic drug is not submitted for approval of a condition of use—

(i) in a therapeutic category in which the approved racemic drug has been approved; or

(ii) for which any other enantiomer of the racemic drug has been approved.

(2) Limitation

(A) No approval in certain therapeutic categories

Until the date that is 10 years after the date of approval of a non-racemic drug described in paragraph (1) and with respect to which the applicant has made the election provided for by such paragraph, the Secretary shall not approve such non-racemic drug for any condition of use in the therapeutic category in which the racemic drug has been approved.

(B) Labeling

If applicable, the labeling of a non-racemic drug described in paragraph (1) and with respect to which the applicant has made the election provided for by such paragraph shall include a statement that the non-racemic drug is not approved, and has not been shown to be safe and effective, for any condition of use of the racemic drug.

(3) Definition

(A) In general

For purposes of this subsection, the term "therapeutic category" means a therapeutic category identified in the list developed by the United States Pharmacopeia pursuant to section 1395w–104(b)(3)(C)(ii) of title 42 and as in effect on September 27, 2007.

(B) Publication by Secretary

The Secretary shall publish the list described in subparagraph (A) and may amend such list by regulation.

(4) Availability

The election referred to in paragraph (1) may be made only in an application that is submitted to the Secretary after September 27, 2007, and before October 1, 2012.

(v) Antibiotic drugs submitted before November 21, 1997

(1) Antibiotic drugs approved before November 21, 1997

(A) In general

Notwithstanding any provision of the Food and Drug Administration Modernization Act of 1997 or any other provision of law, a sponsor of a drug that is the subject of an application described in subparagraph (B)(i) shall be eligible for, with respect to the drug, the 3-year exclusivity period referred to under clauses (iii) and (iv) of subsection (c)(3)(E) and under clauses (iii) and (iv) of subsection (j)(5)(F), subject to the requirements of such clauses, as applicable.

(B) Application; antibiotic drug described

(i) Application

An application described in this clause is an application for marketing submitted under this section after October 8, 2008, in which the drug that is the subject of the application contains an antibiotic drug described in clause (ii).

(ii) Antibiotic drug

An antibiotic drug described in this clause is an antibiotic drug that was the subject of an application approved by the Secretary under section 357 of this title (as in effect before November 21, 1997).

(2) Antibiotic drugs submitted before November 21, 1997, but not approved

(A) In general

Notwithstanding any provision of the Food and Drug Administration Modernization Act of 1997 or any other provision of law, a sponsor of a drug that is the subject of an application described in subparagraph (B)(i) may elect to be eligible for, with respect to the drug—

(i)(I) the 3-year exclusivity period referred to under clauses (iii) and (iv) of subsection (c)(3)(E) and under clauses (iii) and (iv) of subsection (j)(5)(F), subject to the requirements of such clauses, as applicable; and

(II) the 5-year exclusivity period referred to under clause (ii) of subsection (c)(3)(E) and under clause (ii) of subsection (j)(5)(F), subject to the requirements of such clauses, as applicable; or

(ii) a patent term extension under section 156 of title 35, subject to the requirements of such section.

(B) Application; antibiotic drug described

(i) Application

An application described in this clause is an application for marketing submitted under this section after October 8, 2008, in which the drug that is the subject of the application contains an antibiotic drug described in clause (ii).

(ii) Antibiotic drug

An antibiotic drug described in this clause is an antibiotic drug that was the subject of 1 or more applications received by the Secretary under section 357 of this title (as in effect before November 21, 1997), none of which was approved by the Secretary under such section.

(3) Limitations

(A) Exclusivities and extensions

Paragraphs (1)(A) and (2)(A) shall not be construed to entitle a drug that is the subject of an approved application described in subparagraphs[6] (1)(B)(i) or (2)(B)(i), as applicable, to any market exclusivities or patent extensions other than those exclusivities or extensions described in paragraph (1)(A) or (2)(A).

(B) Conditions of use

Paragraphs (1)(A) and (2)(A)(i) shall not apply to any condition of use for which the drug referred to in subparagraph (1)(B)(i) or (2)(B)(i), as applicable, was approved before October 8, 2008.

(4) Application of certain provisions

Notwithstanding section 125, or any other provision, of the Food and Drug Administration Modernization Act of 1997, or any other provision of law, and subject to the limitations in paragraphs (1), (2), and (3), the provisions of the Drug Price Competition and Patent Term Restoration Act of 1984 shall apply to any drug subject to paragraph (1) or any drug with respect to which an election is made under paragraph (2)(A).

(June 25, 1938, ch. 675, §505, 52 Stat. 1052; Pub. L. 86–507, §1(18), June 11, 1960, 74 Stat. 201; Pub. L. 87–781, title I, §§102(b)–(d), 103(a), (b), 104(a)–(d)(2), Oct. 10, 1962, 76 Stat. 781–783, 784, 785; Pub. L. 92–387, §4(d), Aug. 16, 1972, 86 Stat. 562; Pub. L. 98–417, title I, §§101, 102(a)–(b)(5), 103, 104, Sept. 24, 1984, 98 Stat. 1585, 1592, 1593, 1597; Pub. L. 102–282, §5, May 13, 1992, 106 Stat. 161; Pub. L. 103–80, §3(n), Aug. 13, 1993, 107 Stat. 777; Pub. L. 105–115, title I, §§115, 117, 119, 120, 124(a), Nov. 21, 1997, 111 Stat. 2313, 2315, 2316, 2318, 2324; Pub. L. 106–113, div. B, §1000(a)(9) [title IV, §4732(b)(11)], Nov. 29, 1999, 113 Stat. 1536, 1501A–584; Pub. L. 107–109, §15(c)(1), Jan. 4, 2002, 115 Stat. 1420; Pub. L. 108–155, §2(b)(1), Dec. 3, 2003, 117 Stat. 1941; Pub. L. 108–173, title XI, §§1101(a), (b), 1102(a), 1103(a), Dec. 8, 2003, 117 Stat. 2448, 2452, 2457, 2460; Pub. L. 110–85, title VII, §701(b), title VIII, §801(b)(3)(A), (B), title IX, §§901(a), 903, 905(a), 914(a), 915, 916, 918, 920, 921, title XI, §1113, Sept. 27, 2007, 121 Stat. 903, 921, 922, 943, 944, 953, 957, 958, 960–962, 976; Pub. L. 110–316, title III, §301, Aug. 14, 2008, 122 Stat. 3524; Pub. L. 110–379, §4(a), Oct. 8, 2008, 122 Stat. 4076.)

REFERENCES IN TEXT

Section 264(c) of the Health Insurance Portability and Accountability Act of 1996, referred to in subsec. (k)(3)(C)(i)(I), (4)(G)(i)(I), is section 264(c) of Pub. L. 104–191, which is set out as a note under section 1320d–2 of Title 42, The Public Health and Welfare.

Section 403(5) of title 41, referred to in subsec. (k)(4)(H), was in the original "section 4(5) of the Federal Procurement Policy Act" and was translated as meaning section 4(5) of the Office of Federal Procurement Policy Act, to reflect the probable intent of Congress.

The General Schedule, referred to in subsec. (n)(5), is set out under section 5332 of Title 5, Government Organization and Employees.

Section 101(c) of the Food and Drug Administration Amendments Act of 2007, referred to in subsec. (*o*)(3)(E)(i), is section 101(c) of Pub. L. 110–85, which is set out as a note under section 379g of this title.

The Food and Drug Administration Modernization Act of 1997, referred to in subsec. (v)(1)(A), (2)(A), (4), is Pub. L. 105–115, Nov. 21, 1997, 111 Stat. 2296. Section 125 of the Act amended sections 321, 331, 335a, 352, 360, 360j, 360aa to 360cc, 360ee, 374, 379g, 381, and 382 of this title, section 45C of Title 26, Internal Revenue Code, section 156 of Title 35, Patents, and section 8126 of Title 38, Veterans' Benefits, repealed sections 356 and 357 of this title, and enacted provisions set out as a note under this section. For complete classification of this Act to the Code, see Short Title of 1997 Amendment note set out under section 301 of this title and Tables.

The Drug Price Competition and Patent Term Restoration Act of 1984, referred to in subsec. (v)(4), is Pub. L. 98–417, Sept. 24, 1984, 98 Stat. 1585. For complete classification of this Act to the Code, see Short Title of 1984 Amendment note set out under section 301 of this title and Tables.

AMENDMENTS

2008—Subsec. (q)(1)(A). Pub. L. 110–316, §301, inserted concluding provisions.

Subsec. (v). Pub. L. 110–379 added subsec. (v).

2007—Subsec. (b)(6). Pub. L. 110–85, §801(b)(3)(B), added par. (6).

Subsec. (e). Pub. L. 110–85, §903, inserted at end "The Secretary may withdraw the approval of an application submitted under this section, or suspend the approval of such an application, as provided under this subsection, without first ordering the applicant to submit an assessment of the approved risk evaluation and mitigation strategy for the drug under section 355–1(g)(2)(D) of this title."

Subsec. (i)(4). Pub. L. 110–85, §801(b)(3)(A), inserted at end "The Secretary shall update such regulations to require inclusion in the informed consent documents and process a statement that clinical trial information for such clinical investigation has been or will be submitted for inclusion in the registry data bank pursuant to subsection (j) of section 282 of title 42."

Subsec. (k)(3), (4). Pub. L. 110–85, §905(a), added pars. (3) and (4).

Subsec. (k)(5). Pub. L. 110–85, §921, added par. (5).

Subsec. (*l*). Pub. L. 110–85, §916, designated existing provisions as par. (1), redesignated former pars. (1) to (5) as subpars. (A) to (E), respectively, of par. (1), and added par. (2).

Subsec. (n)(4) to (8). Pub. L. 110–85, §701(b), redesignated pars. (5) to (8) as (4) to (7), respectively, and struck out former par. (4) which read as follows: "Each member of a panel shall publicly disclose all conflicts of interest that member may have with the work to be undertaken by the panel. No member of a panel may vote on any matter where the member or the immediate family of such member could gain financially from the advice given to the Secretary. The Secretary may grant a waiver of any conflict of interest requirement upon public disclosure of such conflict of interest if such waiver is necessary to afford the panel essential expertise, except that the Secretary may not grant a waiver for a member of a panel when the member's own scientific work is involved."

Subsecs. (*o*), (p). Pub. L. 110–85, §901(a), added subsecs. (*o*) and (p).

Subsec. (q). Pub. L. 110–85, §914(a), added subsec. (q).

Subsec. (r). Pub. L. 110–85, §915, added subsec. (r).

Subsec. (s). Pub. L. 110–85, §918, added subsec. (s).

Subsec. (t). Pub. L. 110–85, §920, added subsec. (t).

Subsec. (u). Pub. L. 110–85, §1113, added subsec. (u).

2003—Subsec. (b)(1). Pub. L. 108–155, in second sentence, substituted "(F)" for "and (F)" and inserted

[6] So in original. Probably should be "subparagraph".

", and (G) any assessments required under section 355c of this title" before period at end.

Subsec. (b)(3). Pub. L. 108–173, § 1101(b)(1)(A), added par. (3) and struck out former par. (3) which, in subpar. (A), required an applicant making a certification under par. (2)(A)(iv) to include statement that applicant will give notice to each owner of the patent which is the subject of the certification and to the holder of the approved application, in subpar. (B), directed that notice state that an application has been submitted and include a detailed statement of the applicant's opinion that the patent is not valid or will not be infringed, and, in subpar. (C), provided that if an application is amended, notice shall be given when the amended application is submitted.

Subsec. (b)(4), (5). Pub. L. 108–173, § 1101(b)(1)(B), added par. (4) and redesignated former par. (4) as (5).

Subsec. (c)(3). Pub. L. 108–173, § 1101(b)(2)(A), substituted "by applying the following to each certification made under subsection (b)(2)(A) of this section" for "under the following" in introductory provisions.

Subsec. (c)(3)(C). Pub. L. 108–173, § 1101(b)(2)(B)(iii), which directed the substitution of "subsection (b)(3) of this section" for "paragraph (3)(B)" in third sentence, could not be executed because such words do not appear. See note below.

Pub. L. 108–173, § 1101(b)(2)(B)(ii)(VI), in concluding provisions, struck out "Until the expiration of forty-five days from the date the notice made under paragraph (3)(B) is received, no action may be brought under section 2201 of title 28 for a declaratory judgment with respect to the patent. Any action brought under such section 2201 shall be brought in the judicial district where the defendant has its principal place of business or a regular and established place of business." after "expediting the action."

Pub. L. 108–173, § 1101(b)(2)(B)(i), (ii)(I), in first sentence of introductory provisions, substituted "unless, before the expiration of 45 days after the date on which the notice described in subsection (b)(3) of this section is received, an action is brought for infringement of the patent that is the subject of the certification and for which information was submitted to the Secretary under paragraph (2) or subsection (b)(1) of this section before the date on which the application (excluding an amendment or supplement to the application) was submitted" for "unless an action is brought for infringement of a patent which is the subject of the certification before the expiration of forty-five days from the date the notice provided under paragraph (3)(B) is received" and, in second sentence of introductory provisions, substituted "subsection (b)(3) of this section" for "paragraph (3)(B)".

Subsec. (c)(3)(C)(i). Pub. L. 108–173, § 1101(b)(2)(B)(ii)(II), added cl. (i) and struck out former cl. (i) which read as follows: "if before the expiration of such period the court decides that such patent is invalid or not infringed, the approval may be made effective on the date of the court decision,".

Subsec. (c)(3)(C)(ii). Pub. L. 108–173, § 1101(b)(2)(B)(ii)(III), added cl. (ii) and struck out former cl. (ii) which read as follows: "if before the expiration of such period the court decides that such patent has been infringed, the approval may be made effective on such date as the court orders under section 271(e)(4)(A) of title 35, or".

Subsec. (c)(3)(C)(iii). Pub. L. 108–173, § 1101(b)(2)(B)(ii)(IV), substituted "as provided in clause (i); or" for "on the date of such court decision."

Subsec. (c)(3)(C)(iv). Pub. L. 108–173, § 1101(b)(2)(B)(ii)(V), added cl. (iv).

Subsec. (c)(3)(D), (E). Pub. L. 108–173, § 1101(b)(2)(C), (D), added subpar. (D) and redesignated former subpar. (D) as (E).

Subsec. (j)(2)(B). Pub. L. 108–173, § 1101(a)(1)(A), added subpar. (B) and struck out former subpar. (B) which, in cl. (i), required that an applicant making a certification under subpar. (A)(vii)(IV) include in the application a statement that notice would be given to each owner of the patent and the holder of the approved application, in cl. (ii), required that notice would state that an application had been submitted and that it would include a detailed statement of the basis of the applicant's opinion, and, in cl. (iii), directed that notice of an amended application be given when the amended application had been submitted.

Subsec. (j)(2)(D). Pub. L. 108–173, § 1101(a)(1)(B), added subpar. (D).

Subsec. (j)(5)(B). Pub. L. 108–173, § 1101(a)(2)(A)(i), substituted "by applying the following to each certification made under paragraph (2)(A)(vii)" for "under the following" in introductory provisions.

Subsec. (j)(5)(B)(iii). Pub. L. 108–173, § 1101(a)(2)(A)(ii)(II)(ee), which directed amendment of the second sentence of subsec. (j)(5)(B)(iii) by striking "Until the expiration" and all that follows in the matter after and below subclause (IV), was executed by striking "Until the expiration of forty-five days from the date the notice made under paragraph (2)(B)(i) is received, no action may be brought under section 2201 of title 28, for a declaratory judgment with respect to the patent. Any action brought under section 2201 shall be brought in the judicial district where the defendant has its principal place of business or a regular and established place of business." after "expediting the action." in concluding provisions, to reflect the probable intent of Congress.

Pub. L. 108–173, § 1101(a)(2)(A)(ii)(I), in introductory provisions, substituted "unless, before the expiration of 45 days after the date on which the notice described in paragraph (2)(B) is received, an action is brought for infringement of the patent that is the subject of the certification and for which information was submitted to the Secretary under subsection (b)(1) or (c)(2) of this section before the date on which the application (excluding an amendment or supplement to the application), which the Secretary later determines to be substantially complete, was submitted" for "unless an action is brought for infringement of a patent which is the subject of the certification before the expiration of forty-five days from the date the notice provided under paragraph (2)(B)(i) is received".

Subsec. (j)(5)(B)(iii)(I). Pub. L. 108–173, § 1101(a)(2)(A)(ii)(II)(aa), added subcl. (I) and struck out former subcl. (I) which read as follows: "if before the expiration of such period the court decides that such patent is invalid or not infringed, the approval shall be made effective on the date of the court decision,".

Subsec. (j)(5)(B)(iii)(II). Pub. L. 108–173, § 1101(a)(2)(A)(ii)(II)(bb), added subcl. (II) and struck out former subcl. (II) which read as follows: "if before the expiration of such period the court decides that such patent has been infringed, the approval shall be made effective on such date as the court orders under section 271(e)(4)(A) of title 35, or".

Subsec. (j)(5)(B)(iii)(III). Pub. L. 108–173, § 1101(a)(2)(A)(ii)(II)(cc), substituted "as provided in subclause (I); or" for "on the date of such court decision."

Subsec. (j)(5)(B)(iii)(IV). Pub. L. 108–173, § 1101(a)(2)(A)(ii)(II)(dd), added subcl. (IV).

Subsec. (j)(5)(B)(iv). Pub. L. 108–173, § 1102(a)(1), added cl. (iv) and struck out former cl. (iv) which read as follows: "If the application contains a certification described in subclause (IV) of paragraph (2)(A)(vii) and is for a drug for which a previous application has been submitted under this subsection continuing such a certification, the application shall be made effective not earlier than one hundred and eighty days after—

"(I) the date the Secretary receives notice from the applicant under the previous application of the first commercial marketing of the drug under the previous application, or

"(II) the date of a decision of a court in an action described in clause (iii) holding the patent which is the subject of the certification to be invalid or not infringed,

whichever is earlier."

Subsec. (j)(5)(C). Pub. L. 108–173, § 1101(a)(2)(B), (C), added subpar. (C). Former subpar. (C) redesignated (E).

Subsec. (j)(5)(D). Pub. L. 108–173, §1102(a)(2), added subpar. (D).

Pub. L. 108–173, §1101(a)(2)(B), redesignated subpar. (D) as (F).

Subsec. (j)(5)(E), (F). Pub. L. 108–173, §1101(a)(2)(B), redesignated subpars. (C) and (D) as (E) and (F), respectively.

Subsec. (j)(8)(A). Pub. L. 108–173, §1103(a)(1), added subpar. (A) and struck out former subpar. (A) which read as follows: "The term 'bioavailability' means the rate and extent to which the active ingredient or therapeutic ingredient is absorbed from a drug and becomes available at the site of drug action."

Subsec. (j)(8)(C). Pub. L. 108–173, §1103(a)(2), added subpar. (C).

2002—Subsec. (i)(1)(D). Pub. L. 107–109 added subpar. (D).

1999—Subsec. (m). Pub. L. 106–113 substituted "United States Patent and Trademark Office" for "Patent and Trademark Office of the Department of Commerce".

1997—Subsec. (b)(1). Pub. L. 105–115, §115(b), inserted at end "The Secretary shall, in consultation with the Director of the National Institutes of Health and with representatives of the drug manufacturing industry, review and develop guidance, as appropriate, on the inclusion of women and minorities in clinical trials required by clause (A)."

Subsec. (b)(4). Pub. L. 105–115, §119(a), added par. (4).

Subsec. (c)(4). Pub. L. 105–115, §124(a), added par. (4).

Subsec. (d). Pub. L. 105–115, §115(a), inserted at end "If the Secretary determines, based on relevant science, that data from one adequate and well-controlled clinical investigation and confirmatory evidence (obtained prior to or after such investigation) are sufficient to establish effectiveness, the Secretary may consider such data and evidence to constitute substantial evidence for purposes of the preceding sentence."

Subsec. (i). Pub. L. 105–115, §117, inserted "(1)" after "(i)", redesignated former pars. (1) to (3) as subpars. (A) to (C), respectively, of par. (1), added pars. (2) to (4), and struck out closing provisions which read as follows: "Such regulations shall provide that such exemption shall be conditioned upon the manufacturer, or the sponsor of the investigation, requiring that experts using such drugs for investigational purposes certify to such manufacturer or sponsor that they will inform any human beings to whom such drugs, or any controls used in connection therewith, are being administered, or their representatives, that such drugs are being used for investigational purposes and will obtain the consent of such human beings or their representatives, except where they deem it not feasible or, in their professional judgment, contrary to the best interests of such human beings. Nothing in this subsection shall be construed to require any clinical investigator to submit directly to the Secretary reports on the investigational use of drugs."

Subsec. (j)(2)(A)(i). Pub. L. 105–115, §119(b)(2)(A), substituted "paragraph (7)" for "paragraph (6)".

Subsec. (j)(3). Pub. L. 105–115, §119(b)(1)(B), added par. (3). Former par. (3) redesignated (4).

Subsec. (j)(4). Pub. L. 105–115, §119(b)(1)(A), (2)(B), redesignated par. (3) as (4) and in introductory provisions substituted "paragraph (5)" for "paragraph (4)". Former par. (4) redesignated (5).

Subsec. (j)(4)(I). Pub. L. 105–115, §119(b)(2)(C), substituted "paragraph (6)" for "paragraph (5)".

Subsec. (j)(5), (6). Pub. L. 105–115, §119(b)(1)(A), redesignated pars. (4) and (5) as (5) and (6), respectively. Former par. (6) redesignated (7).

Subsec. (j)(7). Pub. L. 105–115, §119(b)(1)(A), (2)(D), redesignated par. (6) as (7) and in subpar. (C) substituted "paragraph (6)" for "paragraph (5)" in two places. Former par. (7) redesignated (8).

Subsec. (j)(8), (9). Pub. L. 105–115, §119(b)(1)(A), redesignated pars. (7) and (8) as (8) and (9), respectively.

Subsec. (n). Pub. L. 105–115, §120, added subsec. (n).

1993—Subsec. (j)(6)(A)(ii). Pub. L. 103–80, §3(n)(1)(A), substituted "Secretary" for "Secretry".

Subsec. (j)(6)(A)(iii). Pub. L. 103–80, §3(n)(1)(B), inserted comma after "published by the Secretary".

Subsec. (k)(1). Pub. L. 103–80, §3(n)(2), substituted "section. Regulations" for "section: *Provided, however*, That regulations".

1992—Subsec. (j)(8). Pub. L. 102–282 added par. (8).

1984—Subsec. (a). Pub. L. 98–417, §102(b)(1), inserted "or (j)" after "subsection (b)".

Subsec. (b). Pub. L. 98–417, §§102(a)(1), 103(a), designated existing provisions of subsec. (b) as par. (1) thereof and redesignated existing cls. (1) through (6) of such par. (1) as cls. (A) through (F) thereof, respectively, inserted requirement that the applicant file with the application the patent number and the expiration date of any patent which claims the drug for which the applicant submitted the application or which claims a method of using such drug and with respect to which a claim of patent infringement could reasonably by asserted if a person not licensed by the owner engaged in the manufacture, use, or sale of the drug, that the applicant amend the application to include such information if an application is filed under this subsection for a drug and a patent which claims such drug or a method of using such drug is issued after the filing date but before approval of the application, and that upon approval of the application, the Secretary publish the information submitted, and added pars. (2) and (3).

Subsec. (c). Pub. L. 98–417, §§102(a)(2), (b)(2), 103(b), designated existing provisions of subsec. (c) as par. (1) thereof and in par. (1) as so designated substituted "subsection (b) of this section" for "this subsection" and redesignated former pars. (1) and (2) as subpars. (A) and (B), respectively, and added pars. (2) and (3).

Subsec. (d)(6), (7). Pub. L. 98–417, §102(a)(3)(A), added cl. (6) relating to the failure of the application to contain the patent information prescribed by subsec. (b) of this section, and redesignated former cl. (6) as (7).

Subsec. (e). Pub. L. 98–417, §102(a)(3)(B), in first sentence, added a new cl. (4) relating to the failure to file the patent information prescribed by subsec. (c) of this section within 30 days after the receipt of written notice from the Secretary specifying the failure to file such information, and redesignated former cl. (4) as (5).

Pub. L. 98–417, §102(b)(3), (4), in second sentence, inserted in provisions preceding cl. (1) "submitted under subsection (b) or (j) of this section" and in cl. (1) substituted "under subsection (k) of this section or to comply with the notice requirements of section 360(k)(2) of this title" for "under subsection (j) of this section or to comply with the notice requirements of section 360(j)(2) of this title".

Subsecs. (j), (k). Pub. L. 98–417, §101, added subsec. (j) and redesignated former subsec. (j) as (k).

Subsec. (k)(1). Pub. L. 98–417, §102(b)(5), substituted "under subsection (b) or (j) of this section" for "pursuant to this section".

Subsecs. (*l*), (m). Pub. L. 98–417, §104, added subsecs. (*l*) and (m).

1972—Subsec. (e). Pub. L. 92–387 inserted "or to comply with the notice requirements of section 360(j)(2) of this title" in cl. (1) of second sentence relating to the maintenance of records.

1962—Subsec. (a). Pub. L. 87–781, §104(a), inserted "an approval of" before "an application".

Subsec. (b). Pub. L. 87–781, §102(b), inserted "and whether such drug is effective in use" after "is safe for use".

Subsec. (c). Pub. L. 87–781, §104(b), substituted provisions requiring the Secretary, within 180 days after filing an application, or such additional period as the Secretary and the applicant agree upon, to either approve the application, if meeting the requirements of subsec. (d) of this section, or give notice of opportunity for hearing on question of whether such application is approvable, and providing that if applicant requests hearing in writing within 30 days, the hearing shall begin within 90 days after expiration of said 30 days, unless the Secretary and applicant agree otherwise, that such hearing shall be expedited, and that the Secretary's order shall be issued within 90 days after date for filing final briefs, for provisions which had an application become effective on the sixtieth day after filing thereof unless prior thereto the Secretary postponed the date by written notice to such time, but not more than 180 days after filing, as the Secretary deemed necessary to study and investigate the application.

Subsec. (d). Pub. L. 87–781, §102(c), inserted references to subsec. (c), added cls. (5) and (6), provided that if after notice and opportunity for hearing, the Secretary finds that cls. (1) to (6) do not apply, he shall approve the application, and defined "substantial evidence" as used in this subsection and subsec. (e) of this section.

Subsec. (e). Pub. L. 87–781, §102(d), amended subsec. (e) generally, and among other changes, directed the Secretary to withdraw approval of an application if by tests, other scientific data or experience, or new evidence of clinical experience not contained in the application or available at the time of its approval, the drug is shown to be unsafe, or on the basis of new information, there is shown a lack of substantial evidence that the drug has the effect it is represented to have, and provided that if the Secretary, or acting Secretary, finds there is an imminent hazard to the public health, he may suspend approval immediately, notify the applicant, and give him opportunity for an expedited hearing, that the Secretary may withdraw approval if the applicant fails to establish a system for maintaining required records, or has repeatedly or deliberately failed to maintain records and make reports, or has refused access to, or copying or verification of such records, or if the Secretary finds on new evidence that the methods, facilities and controls in the manufacturing, processing, and packing are inadequate to assure and preserve the drugs' identity, strength, quality and purity, and were not made adequate within a reasonable time after receipt of written notice thereof, or finds on new evidence, that the labeling is false or misleading and was not corrected within a reasonable time after receipt of written notice thereof.

Subsec. (f). Pub. L. 87–781, §104(c), substituted provisions requiring the Secretary to revoke any previous order under subsecs. (d) or (e) of this section refusing, withdrawing, or suspending approval of an application and to approve such application or reinstate such approval, for provisions which required him to revoke an order refusing effectiveness to an application.

Subsec. (h). Pub. L. 87–781, §104(d)(1), (2), inserted "as provided in section 2112 of title 28", and "except that until the filing of the record the Secretary may modify or set aside his order", substituted "or withdrawing approval of an application under this section" for "to permit the application to become effective, or suspending the effectiveness of the application", "United States court of appeals for the circuit" for "district court of the United States within any district", "Court of Appeals for the District of Columbia Circuit" for "District Court for the District of Columbia", "transmitted by the clerk of the court to" for "served upon", and "by the Supreme Court of the United States upon certiorari or certification as provided in section 1254 of title 28" for "as provided in sections 225, 346, and 347 of title 28, as amended, and in section 7, as amended, of the Act entitled 'An Act to establish a Court of Appeals for the District of Columbia', approved February 9, 1893", and eliminated "upon" before "any officer designated", "a transcript of" before "the record" and "and decree" before "of the court affirming".

Subsec. (i). Pub. L. 87–781, §103(b), inserted "the foregoing subsections of" after "operation of", and "and effectiveness" after "safety", and provided that the regulations may condition exemptions upon the submission of reports of preclinical tests to justify the proposed clinical testing, upon the obtaining by the manufacturer or sponsor of the investigation of a new drug of a signed agreement from each of the investigators that patients to whom the drug is administered will be under his supervision or under investigators responsible to him, and that he will not supply such drug to any other investigator, or to clinics, for administration to human beings, or upon the establishment and maintenance of records and reports of data obtained by the investigational use of such drug, as the Secretary finds will enable him to evaluate the safety and effectiveness of such drug, and provided that the regulations shall condition an exemption upon the manufacturer or sponsor of the investigation requiring that experts using such drugs certify that they will inform humans to whom such drugs or any controls connected therewith are administered, or their representatives, and will obtain the consent of such people where feasible and not contrary to the best interests of such people, and that reports on the investigational use of drugs are not required to be submitted directly to the Secretary.

Subsec. (j). Pub. L. 87–781, §103(a), added subsec. (j).

1960—Subsec. (g). Pub. L. 86–507 inserted "or by certified mail" after "registered mail".

EFFECTIVE DATE OF 2007 AMENDMENT

Pub. L. 110–85, title VII, §701(c), Sept. 27, 2007, 121 Stat. 904, provided that: "The amendments made by this section [enacting section 379d–1 of this title and amending this section] shall take effect on October 1, 2007."

Amendment by sections 901(a), 903, and 905(a) of Pub. L. 110–85 effective 180 days after Sept. 27, 2007, see section 909 of Pub. L. 110–85, set out as a note under section 331 of this title.

EFFECTIVE DATE OF 2003 AMENDMENTS

Pub. L. 108–173, title XI, §1101(c), Dec. 8, 2003, 117 Stat. 2456, provided that:

"(1) IN GENERAL.—Except as provided in paragraphs (2) and (3), the amendments made by subsections (a) and (b) [amending this section] apply to any proceeding under section 505 of the Federal Food, Drug, and Cosmetic Act (21 U.S.C. 355) that is pending on or after the date of the enactment of this Act [Dec. 8, 2003] regardless of the date on which the proceeding was commenced or is commenced.

"(2) NOTICE OF OPINION THAT PATENT IS INVALID OR WILL NOT BE INFRINGED.—The amendments made by subsections (a)(1) and (b)(1) apply with respect to any certification under subsection (b)(2)(A)(iv) or (j)(2)(A)(vii)(IV) of section 505 of the Federal Food, Drug, and Cosmetic Act (21 U.S.C. 355) submitted on or after August 18, 2003, in an application filed under subsection (b) or (j) of that section or in an amendment or supplement to an application filed under subsection (b) or (j) of that section.

"(3) EFFECTIVE DATE OF APPROVAL.—The amendments made by subsections (a)(2)(A)(ii)(I) and (b)(2)(B)(i) apply with respect to any patent information submitted under subsection (b)(1) or (c)(2) of section 505 of the Federal Food, Drug, and Cosmetic Act (21 U.S.C. 355) on or after August 18, 2003."

Pub. L. 108–173, title XI, §1102(b), Dec. 8, 2003, 117 Stat. 2460, provided that:

"(1) IN GENERAL.—Except as provided in paragraph (2), the amendment made by subsection (a) [amending this section] shall be effective only with respect to an application filed under section 505(j) of the Federal Food, Drug, and Cosmetic Act (21 U.S.C. 355(j)) after the date of the enactment of this Act [Dec. 8, 2003] for a listed drug for which no certification under section 505(j)(2)(A)(vii)(IV) of that Act was made before the date of the enactment of this Act.

"(2) COLLUSIVE AGREEMENTS.—If a forfeiture event described in section 505(j)(5)(D)(i)(V) of that Act occurs in the case of an applicant, the applicant shall forfeit the 180-day period under section 505(j)(5)(B)(iv) of that Act without regard to when the first certification under section 505(j)(2)(A)(vii)(IV) of that Act for the listed drug was made.

"(3) DECISION OF A COURT WHEN THE 180-DAY EXCLUSIVITY PERIOD HAS NOT BEEN TRIGGERED.—With respect to an application filed before, on, or after the date of the enactment of this Act [Dec. 8, 2003] for a listed drug for which a certification under section 505(j)(2)(A)(vii)(IV) of that Act was made before the date of the enactment of this Act and for which neither of the events described in subclause (I) or (II) of section 505(j)(5)(B)(iv) of that Act (as in effect on the day before the date of the enactment of this Act) has occurred on or before the date of the enactment of this Act, the term 'decision of a court' as used in clause (iv) of section 505(j)(5)(B) of that Act means a final decision of a court from which no appeal (other than a petition to the Supreme Court for a writ of certiorari) has been or can be taken."

Amendment by Pub. L. 108–155 effective Dec. 3, 2003, except as otherwise provided, see section 4 of Pub. L. 108–155, set out as an Effective Date note under section 355c of this title.

EFFECTIVE DATE OF 1999 AMENDMENT

Amendment by Pub. L. 106–113 effective 4 months after Nov. 29, 1999, see section 1000(a)(9) [title IV, § 4731] of Pub. L. 106–113, set out as a note under section 1 of Title 35, Patents.

EFFECTIVE DATE OF 1997 AMENDMENT

Amendment by Pub. L. 105–115 effective 90 days after Nov. 21, 1997, except as otherwise provided, see section 501 of Pub. L. 105–115, set out as a note under section 321 of this title.

EFFECTIVE DATE OF 1984 AMENDMENT

Section 105 of Pub. L. 98–417 provided that:

"(a) The Secretary of Health and Human Services shall promulgate, in accordance with the notice and comment requirements of section 553 of title 5, United States Code, such regulations as may be necessary for the administration of section 505 of the Federal Food, Drug, and Cosmetic Act [this section], as amended by sections 101, 102, and 103 of this Act, within one year of the date of enactment of this Act [Sept. 24, 1984].

"(b) During the period beginning sixty days after the date of the enactment of this Act [Sept. 24, 1984], and ending on the date regulations promulgated under subsection (a) take effect, abbreviated new drug applications may be submitted in accordance with the provisions of section 314.2 of title 21 of the Code of Federal Regulations and shall be considered as suitable for any drug which has been approved for safety and effectiveness under section 505(c) of the Federal Food, Drug, and Cosmetic Act [subsec. (c) of this section] before the date of the enactment of this Act. If any such provision is inconsistent with the requirements of section 505(j) of the Federal Food, Drug, and Cosmetic Act, the Secretary shall consider the application under the applicable requirements of such section. The Secretary of Health and Human Services may not approve such an abbreviated new drug application which is filed for a drug which is described in sections 505(c)(3)(D) and 505(j)(4)(D) of the Federal Food, Drug, and Cosmetic Act, except in accordance with such section."

EFFECTIVE DATE OF 1972 AMENDMENT

Amendment by Pub. L. 92–387 effective on first day of sixth month beginning after Aug. 16, 1972, see section 5 of Pub. L. 92–387, set out as a note under section 360 of this title.

EFFECTIVE DATE OF 1962 AMENDMENT

Amendment by Pub. L. 87–781 effective on first day of seventh calendar month following October 1962, see section 107 of Pub. L. 87–781, set out as a note under section 321 of this title.

CONSTRUCTION OF AMENDMENT BY PUB. L. 110–85

Pub. L. 110–85, title IX, § 905(b), Sept. 27, 2007, 121 Stat. 949, provided that: "Nothing in this section [amending this section] or the amendment made by this section shall be construed to prohibit the lawful disclosure or use of data or information by an entity other than as described in paragraph (4)(B) or (4)(G) of section 505(k) of the Federal Food, Drug, and Cosmetic Act [21 U.S.C. 355(k)], as added by subsection (a)."

CONSTRUCTION OF AMENDMENTS BY PUB. L. 102–282

Amendment by Pub. L. 102–282 not to preclude any other civil, criminal, or administrative remedy provided under Federal or State law, including any private right of action against any person for the same action subject to any action or civil penalty under an amendment made by Pub. L. 102–282, see section 7 of Pub. L. 102–282, set out as a note under section 335a of this title.

TRANSFER OF FUNCTIONS

For transfer of functions of Federal Security Administrator to Secretary of Health, Education, and Welfare [now Health and Human Services], and of Food and Drug Administration in the Department of Agriculture to Federal Security Agency, see notes set out under section 321 of this title.

EFFECT OF AMENDMENTS BY PUB. L. 110–85 ON VETERINARY MEDICINE

Pub. L. 110–85, title IX, § 907, Sept. 27, 2007, 121 Stat. 950, provided that: "This subtitle [subtitle A (§§ 901–909) of title IX of Pub. L. 110–85, enacting sections 353b and 355–1 of this title, amending this section and sections 331, 333, and 352 of this title and section 262 of Title 42, The Public Health and Welfare, and enacting provisions set out as notes under this section and sections 331, 352, and 355a of this title], and the amendments made by this subtitle, shall have no effect on the use of drugs approved under section 505 of the Federal Food, Drug, and Cosmetic Act [21 U.S.C. 355] by, or on the lawful written or oral order of, a licensed veterinarian within the context of a veterinarian-client-patient relationship, as provided for under section 512(a)(5) of such Act [21 U.S.C. 360b(a)(5)]."

EFFECT OF AMENDMENT BY PUB. L. 108–173 ON ABBREVIATED NEW DRUG APPLICATIONS

Pub. L. 108–173, title XI, § 1103(b), Dec. 8, 2003, 117 Stat. 2461, provided that: "The amendment made by subsection (a) [amending this section] does not alter the standards for approval of drugs under section 505(j) of the Federal Food, Drug, and Cosmetic Act (21 U.S.C. 355(j))."

FEDERAL TRADE COMMISSION REVIEW

Pub. L. 108–173, title XI, subtitle B, Dec. 8, 2003, 117 Stat. 2461, provided that:

"SEC. 1111. DEFINITIONS.

"In this subtitle:

"(1) ANDA.—The term 'ANDA' means an abbreviated drug application, as defined under section 201(aa) of the Federal Food, Drug, and Cosmetic Act [21 U.S.C. 321(aa)].

"(2) ASSISTANT ATTORNEY GENERAL.—The term 'Assistant Attorney General' means the Assistant Attorney General in charge of the Antitrust Division of the Department of Justice.

"(3) BRAND NAME DRUG.—The term 'brand name drug' means a drug for which an application is approved under section 505(c) of the Federal Food, Drug, and Cosmetic Act [21 U.S.C. 355(c)], including an application referred to in section 505(b)(2) of such Act [21 U.S.C. 355(b)(2)].

"(4) BRAND NAME DRUG COMPANY.—The term 'brand name drug company' means the party that holds the approved application referred to in paragraph (3) for a brand name drug that is a listed drug in an ANDA, or a party that is the owner of a patent for which information is submitted for such drug under subsection (b) or (c) of section 505 of the Federal Food, Drug, and Cosmetic Act [21 U.S.C. 355(b), (c)].

"(5) COMMISSION.—The term 'Commission' means the Federal Trade Commission.

"(6) GENERIC DRUG.—The term 'generic drug' means a drug for which an application under section 505(j) of the Federal Food, Drug, and Cosmetic Act [21 U.S.C. 355(j)] is approved.

"(7) GENERIC DRUG APPLICANT.—The term 'generic drug applicant' means a person who has filed or received approval for an ANDA under section 505(j) of the Federal Food, Drug, and Cosmetic Act [21 U.S.C. 355(j)].

"(8) LISTED DRUG.—The term 'listed drug' means a brand name drug that is listed under section 505(j)(7) of the Federal Food, Drug, and Cosmetic Act [21 U.S.C. 355(j)(7)].

"SEC. 1112. NOTIFICATION OF AGREEMENTS.

"(a) AGREEMENT WITH BRAND NAME DRUG COMPANY.—

"(1) REQUIREMENT.—A generic drug applicant that has submitted an ANDA containing a certification under section 505(j)(2)(A)(vii)(IV) of the Federal Food, Drug, and Cosmetic Act [21 U.S.C. 355(j)(2)(A)(vii)(IV)] and a brand name drug company that enter into an agreement described in paragraph (2) shall each file the agreement in accordance with subsection (c). The agreement shall be filed prior to the date of the first commercial marketing of the generic drug that is the subject of the ANDA.

"(2) SUBJECT MATTER OF AGREEMENT.—An agreement described in this paragraph between a generic drug applicant and a brand name drug company is an agreement regarding—

"(A) the manufacture, marketing or sale of the brand name drug that is the listed drug in the ANDA involved;

"(B) the manufacture, marketing, or sale of the generic drug for which the ANDA was submitted; or

"(C) the 180-day period referred to in section 505(j)(5)(B)(iv) of the Federal Food, Drug, and Cosmetic Act [21 U.S.C. 355(j)(5)(B)(iv)] as it applies to such ANDA or to any other ANDA based on the same brand name drug.

"(b) AGREEMENT WITH ANOTHER GENERIC DRUG APPLICANT.—

"(1) REQUIREMENT.—A generic drug applicant that has submitted an ANDA containing a certification under section 505(j)(2)(A)(vii)(IV) of the Federal Food, Drug, and Cosmetic Act [21 U.S.C. 355(j)(2)(A)(vii)(IV)] with respect to a listed drug and another generic drug applicant that has submitted an ANDA containing such a certification for the same listed drug shall each file the agreement in accordance with subsection (c). The agreement shall be filed prior to the date of the first commercial marketing of either of the generic drugs for which such ANDAs were submitted.

"(2) SUBJECT MATTER OF AGREEMENT.—An agreement described in this paragraph between two generic drug applicants is an agreement regarding the 180-day period referred to in section 505(j)(5)(B)(iv) of the Federal Food, Drug, and Cosmetic Act [21 U.S.C. 355(j)(5)(B)(iv)] as it applies to the ANDAs with which the agreement is concerned.

"(c) FILING.—

"(1) AGREEMENT.—The parties that are required in subsection (a) or (b) to file an agreement in accordance with this subsection shall file with the Assistant Attorney General and the Commission the text of any such agreement, except that such parties are not required to file an agreement that solely concerns—

"(A) purchase orders for raw material supplies;

"(B) equipment and facility contracts;

"(C) employment or consulting contracts; or

"(D) packaging and labeling contracts.

"(2) OTHER AGREEMENTS.—The parties that are required in subsection (a) or (b) to file an agreement in accordance with this subsection shall file with the Assistant Attorney General and the Commission the text of any agreements between the parties that are not described in such subsections and are contingent upon, provide a contingent condition for, or are otherwise related to an agreement that is required in subsection (a) or (b) to be filed in accordance with this subsection.

"(3) DESCRIPTION.—In the event that any agreement required in subsection (a) or (b) to be filed in accordance with this subsection has not been reduced to text, each of the parties involved shall file written descriptions of such agreement that are sufficient to disclose all the terms and conditions of the agreement.

"SEC. 1113. FILING DEADLINES.

"Any filing required under section 1112 shall be filed with the Assistant Attorney General and the Commission not later than 10 business days after the date the agreements are executed.

"SEC. 1114. DISCLOSURE EXEMPTION.

"Any information or documentary material filed with the Assistant Attorney General or the Commission pursuant to this subtitle shall be exempt from disclosure under section 552 of title 5, United States Code, and no such information or documentary material may be made public, except as may be relevant to any administrative or judicial action or proceeding. Nothing in this section is intended to prevent disclosure to either body of the Congress or to any duly authorized committee or subcommittee of the Congress.

"SEC. 1115. ENFORCEMENT.

"(a) CIVIL PENALTY.—Any brand name drug company or generic drug applicant which fails to comply with any provision of this subtitle shall be liable for a civil penalty of not more than $11,000, for each day during which such entity is in violation of this subtitle. Such penalty may be recovered in a civil action brought by the United States, or brought by the Commission in accordance with the procedures established in section 16(a)(1) of the Federal Trade Commission Act (15 U.S.C. 56(a) [15 U.S.C. 56(a)(1)]).

"(b) COMPLIANCE AND EQUITABLE RELIEF.—If any brand name drug company or generic drug applicant fails to comply with any provision of this subtitle, the United States district court may order compliance, and may grant such other equitable relief as the court in its discretion determines necessary or appropriate, upon application of the Assistant Attorney General or the Commission.

"SEC. 1116. RULEMAKING.

"The Commission, with the concurrence of the Assistant Attorney General and by rule in accordance with section 553 of title 5, United States Code, consistent with the purposes of this subtitle—

"(1) may define the terms used in this subtitle;

"(2) may exempt classes of persons or agreements from the requirements of this subtitle; and

"(3) may prescribe such other rules as may be necessary and appropriate to carry out the purposes of this subtitle.

"SEC. 1117. SAVINGS CLAUSE.

"Any action taken by the Assistant Attorney General or the Commission, or any failure of the Assistant Attorney General or the Commission to take action, under this subtitle shall not at any time bar any proceeding or any action with respect to any agreement between a brand name drug company and a generic drug applicant, or any agreement between generic drug applicants, under any other provision of law, nor shall any filing under this subtitle constitute or create a presumption of any violation of any competition laws.

"SEC. 1118. EFFECTIVE DATE.

"This subtitle shall—

"(1) take effect 30 days after the date of the enactment of this Act [Dec. 8, 2003]; and

"(2) shall apply to agreements described in section 1112 that are entered into 30 days after the date of the enactment of this Act."

REPORT ON PATIENT ACCESS TO NEW THERAPEUTIC AGENTS FOR PEDIATRIC CANCER

Pub. L. 107–109, § 15(d), Jan. 4, 2002, 115 Stat. 1421, provided that: "Not later than January 31, 2003, the Secretary of Health and Human Services, acting through the Commissioner of Food and Drugs and in consultation with the Director of the National Institutes of Health, shall submit to the Committee on Health, Education, Labor, and Pensions of the Senate and the Committee on Energy and Commerce of the House of Representatives a report on patient access to new therapeutic agents for pediatric cancer, including access to single patient use of new therapeutic agents.''

DATA REQUIREMENTS FOR DRUGS AND BIOLOGICS

Section 118 of Pub. L. 105–115 provided that: ''Within 12 months after the date of enactment of this Act [Nov. 21, 1997], the Secretary of Health and Human Services, acting through the Commissioner of Food and Drugs, shall issue guidance that describes when abbreviated study reports may be submitted, in lieu of full reports, with a new drug application under section 505(b) of the Federal Food, Drug, and Cosmetic Act (21 U.S.C. 355(b)) and with a biologics license application under section 351 of the Public Health Service Act (42 U.S.C. 262) for certain types of studies. Such guidance shall describe the kinds of studies for which abbreviated reports are appropriate and the appropriate abbreviated report formats.''

REQUIREMENTS FOR REVIEW OF APPROVAL PROCEDURES AND CURRENT GOOD MANUFACTURING PRACTICES FOR POSITRON EMISSION TECHNOLOGY

Section 121(c) of Pub. L. 105–115 provided that:

''(1) PROCEDURES AND REQUIREMENTS.—

''(A) IN GENERAL.—In order to take account of the special characteristics of positron emission tomography drugs and the special techniques and processes required to produce these drugs, not later than 2 years after the date of enactment of this Act [Nov. 21, 1997], the Secretary of Health and Human Services shall establish—

''(i) appropriate procedures for the approval of positron emission tomography drugs pursuant to section 505 of the Federal Food, Drug, and Cosmetic Act (21 U.S.C. 355); and

''(ii) appropriate current good manufacturing practice requirements for such drugs.

''(B) CONSIDERATIONS AND CONSULTATION.—In establishing the procedures and requirements required by subparagraph (A), the Secretary of Health and Human Services shall take due account of any relevant differences between not-for-profit institutions that compound the drugs for their patients and commercial manufacturers of the drugs. Prior to establishing the procedures and requirements, the Secretary of Health and Human Services shall consult with patient advocacy groups, professional associations, manufacturers, and physicians and scientists licensed to make or use positron emission tomography drugs.

''(2) SUBMISSION OF NEW DRUG APPLICATIONS AND ABBREVIATED NEW DRUG APPLICATIONS.—

''(A) IN GENERAL.—Except as provided in subparagraph (B), the Secretary of Health and Human Services shall not require the submission of new drug applications or abbreviated new drug applications under subsection (b) or (j) of section 505 (21 U.S.C. 355), for compounded positron emission tomography drugs that are not adulterated drugs described in section 501(a)(2)(C) of the Federal Food, Drug, and Cosmetic Act (21 U.S.C. 351(a)(2)(C)) (as amended by subsection (b)), for a period of 4 years after the date of enactment of this Act [Nov. 21, 1997], or for 2 years after the date on which the Secretary establishes procedures and requirements under paragraph (1), whichever is longer.

''(B) EXCEPTION.—Nothing in this Act [see Short Title of 1997 Amendment note set out under section 301 of this title] shall prohibit the voluntary submission of such applications or the review of such applications by the Secretary of Health and Human Services. Nothing in this Act shall constitute an exemption for a positron emission tomography drug from the requirements of regulations issued under section 505(i) of the Federal Food, Drug, and Cosmetic Act (21 U.S.C. 355(i)).''

''COMPOUNDED POSITRON EMISSION TOPOGRAPHY DRUG'' DEFINED

Section 121(e) of Pub. L. 105–115 provided that: ''As used in this section [amending sections 321 and 351 of this title and enacting provisions set out as notes under this section and section 351 of this title], the term 'compounded positron emission tomography drug' has the meaning given the term in section 201 of the Federal Food, Drug, and Cosmetic Act (21 U.S.C. 321).''

REQUIREMENTS FOR RADIOPHARMACEUTICALS

Section 122 of Pub. L. 105–115 provided that:

''(a) REQUIREMENTS.—

''(1) REGULATIONS.—

''(A) PROPOSED REGULATIONS.—Not later than 180 days after the date of enactment of this Act [Nov. 21, 1997], the Secretary of Health and Human Services, after consultation with patient advocacy groups, associations, physicians licensed to use radiopharmaceuticals, and the regulated industry, shall issue proposed regulations governing the approval of radiopharmaceuticals. The regulations shall provide that the determination of the safety and effectiveness of such a radiopharmaceutical under section 505 of the Federal Food, Drug, and Cosmetic Act (21 U.S.C. 355) or section 351 of the Public Health Service Act (42 U.S.C. 262) shall include consideration of the proposed use of the radiopharmaceutical in the practice of medicine, the pharmacological and toxicological activity of the radiopharmaceutical (including any carrier or ligand component of the radiopharmaceutical), and the estimated absorbed radiation dose of the radiopharmaceutical.

''(B) FINAL REGULATIONS.—Not later than 18 months after the date of enactment of this Act, the Secretary shall promulgate final regulations governing the approval of the radiopharmaceuticals.

''(2) SPECIAL RULE.—In the case of a radiopharmaceutical, the indications for which such radiopharmaceutical is approved for marketing may, in appropriate cases, refer to manifestations of disease (such as biochemical, physiological, anatomic, or pathological processes) common to, or present in, one or more disease states.

''(b) DEFINITION.—In this section, the term 'radiopharmaceutical' means—

''(1) an article—

''(A) that is intended for use in the diagnosis or monitoring of a disease or a manifestation of a disease in humans; and

''(B) that exhibits spontaneous disintegration of unstable nuclei with the emission of nuclear particles or photons; or

''(2) any nonradioactive reagent kit or nuclide generator that is intended to be used in the preparation of any such article.''

SPECIAL RULE

Section 123(f) of Pub. L. 105–115 provided that: ''The Secretary of Health and Human Services shall take measures to minimize differences in the review and approval of products required to have approved biologics license applications under section 351 of the Public Health Service Act (42 U.S.C. 262) and products required to have approved new drug applications under section 505(b)(1) of the Federal Food, Drug, and Cosmetic Act (21 U.S.C. 355(b)(1)).''

TRANSITION

Pub. L. 110–379, § 4(b), Oct. 8, 2008, 122 Stat. 4077, provided that:

''(1) With respect to a patent issued on or before the date of the enactment of this Act [Oct. 8, 2008], any patent information required to be filed with the Secretary of Health and Human Services under subsection (b)(1) or (c)(2) of section 505 of the Federal Food, Drug, and Cosmetic Act (21 U.S.C. 355) to be listed on a drug to which subsection (v)(1) of such section 505 (as added by this section) applies shall be filed with the Secretary not later than 60 days after the date of the enactment of this Act.

''(2) With respect to any patent information referred to in paragraph (1) of this subsection that is filed with the Secretary within the 60-day period after the date of the enactment of this Act [Oct. 8, 2008], the Secretary shall publish such information in the electronic version of the list referred to at section 505(j)(7) of the Federal Food, Drug, and Cosmetic Act (21 U.S.C. 355(j)(7)) as soon as it is received, but in no event later than the date that is 90 days after the enactment of this Act.

"(3) With respect to any patent information referred to in paragraph (1) that is filed with the Secretary within the 60-day period after the date of enactment of this Act [Oct. 8, 2008], each applicant that, not later than 120 days after the date of the enactment of this Act, amends an application that is, on or before the date of the enactment of this Act, a substantially complete application (as defined in paragraph (5)(B)(iv) of section 505(j) of the Federal Food, Drug, and Cosmetic Act (21 U.S.C. 355(j))) to contain a certification described in paragraph (2)(A)(vii)(IV) of such section 505(j) with respect to that patent shall be deemed to be a first applicant (as defined in paragraph (5)(B)(iv) of such section 505(j))."

Section 125(d) of Pub. L. 105–115 provided that:

"(1) IN GENERAL.—An application that was approved by the Secretary of Health and Human Services before the date of the enactment of this Act [Nov. 21, 1997] for the marketing of an antibiotic drug under section 507 of the Federal Food, Drug, and Cosmetic Act (21 U.S.C. 357), as in effect on the day before the date of the enactment of this Act, shall, on and after such date of enactment, be considered to be an application that was submitted and filed under section 505(b) of such Act (21 U.S.C. 355(b)) and approved for safety and effectiveness under section 505(c) of such Act (21 U.S.C. 355(c)), except that if such application for marketing was in the form of an abbreviated application, the application shall be considered to have been filed and approved under section 505(j) of such Act (21 U.S.C. 355(j)).

"(2) EXCEPTION.—The following subsections of section 505 (21 U.S.C. 355) shall not apply to any application for marketing in which the drug that is the subject of the application contains an antibiotic drug and the antibiotic drug was the subject of any application for marketing received by the Secretary of Health and Human Services under section 507 of such Act (21 U.S.C. 357) before the date of the enactment of this Act [Nov. 21, 1997]:

"(A)(i) Subsections (c)(2), (d)(6), (e)(4), (j)(2)(A)(vii), (j)(2)(A)(viii), (j)(2)(B), (j)(4)(B), and (j)(4)(D); and

"(ii) The third and fourth sentences of subsection (b)(1) (regarding the filing and publication of patent information); and

"(B) Subsections (b)(2)(A), (b)(2)(B), (b)(3), and (c)(3) if the investigations relied upon by the applicant for approval of the application were not conducted by or for the applicant and for which the applicant has not obtained a right of reference or use from the person by or for whom the investigations were conducted.

"(3) PUBLICATION.—For purposes of this section, the Secretary is authorized to make available to the public the established name of each antibiotic drug that was the subject of any application for marketing received by the Secretary for Health and Human Services under section 507 of the Federal Food, Drug, and Cosmetic Act (21 U.S.C. 357) before the date of enactment of this Act [Nov. 21, 1997]."

TERMINATION OF ADVISORY PANELS

Advisory panels established after Jan. 5, 1973, to terminate not later than the expiration of the 2-year period beginning on the date of their establishment, unless, in the case of a panel established by the President or an officer of the Federal Government, such panel is renewed by appropriate action prior to the expiration of such 2-year period, or in the case of a panel established by Congress, its duration is otherwise provided for by law. See sections 3(2) and 14 of Pub. L. 92–463, Oct. 6, 1972, 86 Stat. 770, 776, set out in the Appendix to Title 5, Government Organization and Employees.

APPEALS TAKEN PRIOR TO OCTOBER 10, 1962

Section 104(d)(3) of Pub. L. 87–781 made amendments to subsec. (h) of this section inapplicable to any appeal taken prior to Oct. 10, 1962.

§ 355–1. Risk evaluation and mitigation strategies

(a) Submission of proposed strategy

(1) Initial approval

If the Secretary, in consultation with the office responsible for reviewing the drug and the office responsible for postapproval safety with respect to the drug, determines that a risk evaluation and mitigation strategy is necessary to ensure that the benefits of the drug outweigh the risks of the drug, and informs the person who submits such application of such determination, then such person shall submit to the Secretary as part of such application a proposed risk evaluation and mitigation strategy. In making such a determination, the Secretary shall consider the following factors:

(A) The estimated size of the population likely to use the drug involved.

(B) The seriousness of the disease or condition that is to be treated with the drug.

(C) The expected benefit of the drug with respect to such disease or condition.

(D) The expected or actual duration of treatment with the drug.

(E) The seriousness of any known or potential adverse events that may be related to the drug and the background incidence of such events in the population likely to use the drug.

(F) Whether the drug is a new molecular entity.

(2) Postapproval requirement

(A) In general

If the Secretary has approved a covered application (including an application approved before the effective date of this section) and did not when approving the application require a risk evaluation and mitigation strategy under paragraph (1), the Secretary, in consultation with the offices described in paragraph (1), may subsequently require such a strategy for the drug involved (including when acting on a supplemental application seeking approval of a new indication for use of the drug) if the Secretary becomes aware of new safety information and makes a determination that such a strategy is necessary to ensure that the benefits of the drug outweigh the risks of the drug.

(B) Submission of proposed strategy

Not later than 120 days after the Secretary notifies the holder of an approved covered application that the Secretary has made a determination under subparagraph (A) with respect to the drug involved, or within such other reasonable time as the Secretary requires to protect the public health, the holder shall submit to the Secretary a proposed risk evaluation and mitigation strategy.

(3) Abbreviated new drug applications

The applicability of this section to an application under section 355(j) of this title is subject to subsection (i).

(4) Non-delegation

Determinations by the Secretary under this subsection for a drug shall be made by individuals at or above the level of individuals empowered to approve a drug (such as division directors within the Center for Drug Evaluation and Research).

(b) Definitions

For purposes of this section:

(1) Adverse drug experience

The term "adverse drug experience" means any adverse event associated with the use of a drug in humans, whether or not considered drug related, including—

(A) an adverse event occurring in the course of the use of the drug in professional practice;

(B) an adverse event occurring from an overdose of the drug, whether accidental or intentional;

(C) an adverse event occurring from abuse of the drug;

(D) an adverse event occurring from withdrawal of the drug; and

(E) any failure of expected pharmacological action of the drug.

(2) Covered application

The term "covered application" means an application referred to in section 355(p)(1)(A) of this title.

(3) New safety information

The term "new safety information", with respect to a drug, means information derived from a clinical trial, an adverse event report, a postapproval study (including a study under section 355(*o*)(3) of this title), or peer-reviewed biomedical literature; data derived from the postmarket risk identification and analysis system under section 355(k) of this title; or other scientific data deemed appropriate by the Secretary about—

(A) a serious risk or an unexpected serious risk associated with use of the drug that the Secretary has become aware of (that may be based on a new analysis of existing information) since the drug was approved, since the risk evaluation and mitigation strategy was required, or since the last assessment of the approved risk evaluation and mitigation strategy for the drug; or

(B) the effectiveness of the approved risk evaluation and mitigation strategy for the drug obtained since the last assessment of such strategy.

(4) Serious adverse drug experience

The term "serious adverse drug experience" is an adverse drug experience that—

(A) results in—

(i) death;

(ii) an adverse drug experience that places the patient at immediate risk of death from the adverse drug experience as it occurred (not including an adverse drug experience that might have caused death had it occurred in a more severe form);

(iii) inpatient hospitalization or prolongation of existing hospitalization;

(iv) a persistent or significant incapacity or substantial disruption of the ability to conduct normal life functions; or

(v) a congenital anomaly or birth defect; or

(B) based on appropriate medical judgment, may jeopardize the patient and may require a medical or surgical intervention to prevent an outcome described under subparagraph (A).

(5) Serious risk

The term "serious risk" means a risk of a serious adverse drug experience.

(6) Signal of a serious risk

The term "signal of a serious risk" means information related to a serious adverse drug experience associated with use of a drug and derived from—

(A) a clinical trial;

(B) adverse event reports;

(C) a postapproval study, including a study under section 355(*o*)(3) of this title;

(D) peer-reviewed biomedical literature;

(E) data derived from the postmarket risk identification and analysis system under section 355(k)(4) of this title; or

(F) other scientific data deemed appropriate by the Secretary.

(7) Responsible person

The term "responsible person" means the person submitting a covered application or the holder of the approved such application.

(8) Unexpected serious risk

The term "unexpected serious risk" means a serious adverse drug experience that is not listed in the labeling of a drug, or that may be symptomatically and pathophysiologically related to an adverse drug experience identified in the labeling, but differs from such adverse drug experience because of greater severity, specificity, or prevalence.

(c) Contents

A proposed risk evaluation and mitigation strategy under subsection (a) shall—

(1) include the timetable required under subsection (d); and

(2) to the extent required by the Secretary, in consultation with the office responsible for reviewing the drug and the office responsible for postapproval safety with respect to the drug, include additional elements described in subsections (e) and (f).

(d) Minimal strategy

For purposes of subsection (c)(1), the risk evaluation and mitigation strategy for a drug shall require a timetable for submission of assessments of the strategy that—

(1) includes an assessment, by the date that is 18 months after the strategy is initially approved;

(2) includes an assessment by the date that is 3 years after the strategy is initially approved;

(3) includes an assessment in the seventh year after the strategy is so approved; and

(4) subject to paragraphs (1), (2), and (3)—

(A) is at a frequency specified in the strategy;

(B) is increased or reduced in frequency as necessary as provided for in subsection (g)(4)(A); and

(C) is eliminated after the 3-year period described in paragraph (1) if the Secretary determines that serious risks of the drug have been adequately identified and assessed and are being adequately managed.

(e) Additional potential elements of strategy

(1) In general

The Secretary, in consultation with the offices described in subsection (c)(2), may under such subsection require that the risk evaluation and mitigation strategy for a drug include 1 or more of the additional elements described in this subsection if the Secretary makes the determination required with respect to each element involved.

(2) Medication guide; patient package insert

The risk evaluation and mitigation strategy for a drug may require that, as applicable, the responsible person develop for distribution to each patient when the drug is dispensed—

(A) a Medication Guide, as provided for under part 208 of title 21, Code of Federal Regulations (or any successor regulations); and

(B) a patient package insert, if the Secretary determines that such insert may help mitigate a serious risk of the drug.

(3) Communication plan

The risk evaluation and mitigation strategy for a drug may require that the responsible person conduct a communication plan to health care providers, if, with respect to such drug, the Secretary determines that such plan may support implementation of an element of the strategy (including under this paragraph). Such plan may include—

(A) sending letters to health care providers;

(B) disseminating information about the elements of the risk evaluation and mitigation strategy to encourage implementation by health care providers of components that apply to such health care providers, or to explain certain safety protocols (such as medical monitoring by periodic laboratory tests); or

(C) disseminating information to health care providers through professional societies about any serious risks of the drug and any protocol to assure safe use.

(f) Providing safe access for patients to drugs with known serious risks that would otherwise be unavailable

(1) Allowing safe access to drugs with known serious risks

The Secretary, in consultation with the offices described in subsection (c)(2), may require that the risk evaluation and mitigation strategy for a drug include such elements as are necessary to assure safe use of the drug, because of its inherent toxicity or potential harmfulness, if the Secretary determines that—

(A) the drug, which has been shown to be effective, but is associated with a serious adverse drug experience, can be approved only if, or would be withdrawn unless, such elements are required as part of such strategy to mitigate a specific serious risk listed in the labeling of the drug; and

(B) for a drug initially approved without elements to assure safe use, other elements under subsections (c), (d), and (e) are not sufficient to mitigate such serious risk.

(2) Assuring access and minimizing burden

Such elements to assure safe use under paragraph (1) shall—

(A) be commensurate with the specific serious risk listed in the labeling of the drug;

(B) within 30 days of the date on which any element under paragraph (1) is imposed, be posted publicly by the Secretary with an explanation of how such elements will mitigate the observed safety risk;

(C) considering such risk, not be unduly burdensome on patient access to the drug, considering in particular—

(i) patients with serious or life-threatening diseases or conditions; and

(ii) patients who have difficulty accessing health care (such as patients in rural or medically underserved areas); and

(D) to the extent practicable, so as to minimize the burden on the health care delivery system—

(i) conform with elements to assure safe use for other drugs with similar, serious risks; and

(ii) be designed to be compatible with established distribution, procurement, and dispensing systems for drugs.

(3) Elements to assure safe use

The elements to assure safe use under paragraph (1) shall include 1 or more goals to mitigate a specific serious risk listed in the labeling of the drug and, to mitigate such risk, may require that—

(A) health care providers who prescribe the drug have particular training or experience, or are specially certified (the opportunity to obtain such training or certification with respect to the drug shall be available to any willing provider from a frontier area in a widely available training or certification method (including an on-line course or via mail) as approved by the Secretary at reasonable cost to the provider);

(B) pharmacies, practitioners, or health care settings that dispense the drug are specially certified (the opportunity to obtain such certification shall be available to any willing provider from a frontier area);

(C) the drug be dispensed to patients only in certain health care settings, such as hospitals;

(D) the drug be dispensed to patients with evidence or other documentation of safe-use conditions, such as laboratory test results;

(E) each patient using the drug be subject to certain monitoring; or

(F) each patient using the drug be enrolled in a registry.

(4) Implementation system

The elements to assure safe use under paragraph (1) that are described in subparagraphs

(B), (C), and (D) of paragraph (3) may include a system through which the applicant is able to take reasonable steps to—

(A) monitor and evaluate implementation of such elements by health care providers, pharmacists, and other parties in the health care system who are responsible for implementing such elements; and

(B) work to improve implementation of such elements by such persons.

(5) Evaluation of elements to assure safe use

The Secretary, through the Drug Safety and Risk Management Advisory Committee (or successor committee) of the Food and Drug Administration, shall—

(A) seek input from patients, physicians, pharmacists, and other health care providers about how elements to assure safe use under this subsection for 1 or more drugs may be standardized so as not to be—

(i) unduly burdensome on patient access to the drug; and

(ii) to the extent practicable, minimize the burden on the health care delivery system;

(B) at least annually, evaluate, for 1 or more drugs, the elements to assure safe use of such drug to assess whether the elements—

(i) assure safe use of the drug;

(ii) are not unduly burdensome on patient access to the drug; and

(iii) to the extent practicable, minimize the burden on the health care delivery system; and

(C) considering such input and evaluations—

(i) issue or modify agency guidance about how to implement the requirements of this subsection; and

(ii) modify elements under this subsection for 1 or more drugs as appropriate.

(6) Additional mechanisms to assure access

The mechanisms under section 360bbb of this title to provide for expanded access for patients with serious or life-threatening diseases or conditions may be used to provide access for patients with a serious or life-threatening disease or condition, the treatment of which is not an approved use for the drug, to a drug that is subject to elements to assure safe use under this subsection. The Secretary shall promulgate regulations for how a physician may provide the drug under the mechanisms of section 360bbb of this title.

(7) Waiver in public health emergencies

The Secretary may waive any requirement of this subsection during the period described in section 247d(a) of title 42 with respect to a qualified countermeasure described under section 247d–6a(a)(2) of such title, to which a requirement under this subsection has been applied, if the Secretary has—

(A) declared a public health emergency under such section 247d; and

(B) determined that such waiver is required to mitigate the effects of, or reduce the severity of, such public health emergency.

(8) Limitation

No holder of an approved covered application shall use any element to assure safe use required by the Secretary under this subsection to block or delay approval of an application under section 355(b)(2) or (j) of this title or to prevent application of such element under subsection (i)(1)(B) to a drug that is the subject of an abbreviated new drug application.

(g) Assessment and modification of approved strategy

(1) Voluntary assessments

After the approval of a risk evaluation and mitigation strategy under subsection (a), the responsible person involved may, subject to paragraph (2), submit to the Secretary an assessment of, and propose a modification to, the approved strategy for the drug involved at any time.

(2) Required assessments

A responsible person shall, subject to paragraph (5), submit an assessment of, and may propose a modification to, the approved risk evaluation and mitigation strategy for a drug—

(A) when submitting a supplemental application for a new indication for use under section 355(b) of this title or under section 262 of title 42, unless the drug is not subject to section 353(b) of this title and the risk evaluation and mitigation strategy for the drug includes only the timetable under subsection (d);

(B) when required by the strategy, as provided for in such timetable under subsection (d);

(C) within a time period to be determined by the Secretary, if the Secretary, in consultation with the offices described in subsection (c)(2), determines that new safety or effectiveness information indicates that—

(i) an element under subsection (d) or (e) should be modified or included in the strategy; or

(ii) an element under subsection (f) should be modified or included in the strategy; or

(D) within 15 days when ordered by the Secretary, in consultation with the offices described in subsection (c)(2), if the Secretary determines that there may be a cause for action by the Secretary under section 355(e) of this title.

(3) Requirements for assessments

An assessment under paragraph (1) or (2) of an approved risk evaluation and mitigation strategy for a drug shall include—

(A) with respect to any goal under subsection (f), an assessment of the extent to which the elements to assure safe use are meeting the goal or whether the goal or such elements should be modified;

(B) with respect to any postapproval study required under section 355(*o*) of this title or otherwise undertaken by the responsible person to investigate a safety issue, the status of such study, including whether any difficulties completing the study have been encountered; and

(C) with respect to any postapproval clinical trial required under section 355(*o*) of this title or otherwise undertaken by the responsible party to investigate a safety issue, the status of such clinical trial, including whether enrollment has begun, the number of participants enrolled, the expected completion date, whether any difficulties completing the clinical trial have been encountered, and registration information with respect to requirements under subsections (i) and (j) of section 282 of title 42.

(4) Modification

A modification (whether an enhancement or a reduction) to the approved risk evaluation and mitigation strategy for a drug may include the addition or modification of any element under subsection (d) or the addition, modification, or removal of any element under subsection (e) or (f), such as—

(A) modifying the timetable for assessments of the strategy as provided in subsection (d)(3), including to eliminate assessments; or

(B) adding, modifying, or removing an element to assure safe use under subsection (f).

(h) Review of proposed strategies; review of assessments of approved strategies

(1) In general

The Secretary, in consultation with the offices described in subsection (c)(2), shall promptly review each proposed risk evaluation and mitigation strategy for a drug submitted under subsection (a) and each assessment of an approved risk evaluation and mitigation strategy for a drug submitted under subsection (g).

(2) Discussion

The Secretary, in consultation with the offices described in subsection (c)(2), shall initiate discussions with the responsible person for purposes of this subsection to determine a strategy not later than 60 days after any such assessment is submitted or, in the case of an assessment submitted under subsection (g)(2)(D), not later than 30 days after such assessment is submitted.

(3) Action

(A) In general

Unless the dispute resolution process described under paragraph (4) or (5) applies, the Secretary, in consultation with the offices described in subsection (c)(2), shall describe any required risk evaluation and mitigation strategy for a drug, or any modification to any required strategy—

(i) as part of the action letter on the application, when a proposed strategy is submitted under subsection (a) or a modification to the strategy is proposed as part of an assessment of the strategy submitted under subsection (g)(1); or

(ii) in an order issued not later than 90 days after the date discussions of such modification begin under paragraph (2), when a modification to the strategy is proposed as part of an assessment of the strategy submitted under subsection (g)(1) or under any of subparagraphs (B) through (D) of subsection (g)(2).

(B) Inaction

An approved risk evaluation and mitigation strategy shall remain in effect until the Secretary acts, if the Secretary fails to act as provided under subparagraph (A).

(C) Public availability

Any action letter described in subparagraph (A)(i) or order described in subparagraph (A)(ii) shall be made publicly available.

(4) Dispute resolution at initial approval

If a proposed risk evaluation and mitigation strategy is submitted under subsection (a)(1) in an application for initial approval of a drug and there is a dispute about the strategy, the responsible person shall use the major dispute resolution procedures as set forth in the letters described in section 101(c) of the Food and Drug Administration Amendments Act of 2007.

(5) Dispute resolution in all other cases

(A) Request for review

(i) In general

Not earlier than 15 days, and not later than 35 days, after discussions under paragraph (2) have begun, the responsible person may request in writing that a dispute about the strategy be reviewed by the Drug Safety Oversight Board under subsection (j), except that the determination of the Secretary to require a risk evaluation and mitigation strategy is not subject to review under this paragraph. The preceding sentence does not prohibit review under this paragraph of the particular elements of such a strategy.

(ii) Scheduling

Upon receipt of a request under clause (i), the Secretary shall schedule the dispute involved for review under subparagraph (B) and, not later than 5 business days of scheduling the dispute for review, shall publish by posting on the Internet or otherwise a notice that the dispute will be reviewed by the Drug Safety Oversight Board.

(B) Scheduling review

If a responsible person requests review under subparagraph (A), the Secretary—

(i) shall schedule the dispute for review at 1 of the next 2 regular meetings of the Drug Safety Oversight Board, whichever meeting date is more practicable; or

(ii) may convene a special meeting of the Drug Safety Oversight Board to review the matter more promptly, including to meet an action deadline on an application (including a supplemental application).

(C) Agreement after discussion or administrative appeals

(i) Further discussion or administrative appeals

A request for review under subparagraph (A) shall not preclude further discussions to reach agreement on the risk evaluation and mitigation strategy, and such a request shall not preclude the use of administrative appeals within the Food and Drug Administration to reach agreement on the strategy, including appeals as described in the letters described in section 101(c) of the Food and Drug Administration Amendments Act of 2007 for procedural or scientific matters involving the review of human drug applications and supplemental applications that cannot be resolved at the divisional level. At the time a review has been scheduled under subparagraph (B) and notice of such review has been posted, the responsible person shall either withdraw the request under subparagraph (A) or terminate the use of such administrative appeals.

(ii) Agreement terminates dispute resolution

At any time before a decision and order is issued under subparagraph (G), the Secretary (in consultation with the offices described in subsection (c)(2)) and the responsible person may reach an agreement on the risk evaluation and mitigation strategy through further discussion or administrative appeals, terminating the dispute resolution process, and the Secretary shall issue an action letter or order, as appropriate, that describes the strategy.

(D) Meeting of the Board

At a meeting of the Drug Safety Oversight Board described in subparagraph (B), the Board shall—

(i) hear from both parties via written or oral presentation; and

(ii) review the dispute.

(E) Record of proceedings

The Secretary shall ensure that the proceedings of any such meeting are recorded, transcribed, and made public within 90 days of the meeting. The Secretary shall redact the transcript to protect any trade secrets and other information that is exempted from disclosure under section 552 of title 5 or section 552a of title 5.

(F) Recommendation of the Board

Not later than 5 days after any such meeting, the Drug Safety Oversight Board shall provide a written recommendation on resolving the dispute to the Secretary. Not later than 5 days after the Board provides such written recommendation to the Secretary, the Secretary shall make the recommendation available to the public.

(G) Action by the Secretary

(i) Action letter

With respect to a proposal or assessment referred to in paragraph (1), the Secretary shall issue an action letter that resolves the dispute not later than the later of—

(I) the action deadline for the action letter on the application; or

(II) 7 days after receiving the recommendation of the Drug Safety Oversight Board.

(ii) Order

With respect to an assessment of an approved risk evaluation and mitigation strategy under subsection (g)(1) or under any of subparagraphs (B) through (D) of subsection (g)(2), the Secretary shall issue an order, which shall be made public, that resolves the dispute not later than 7 days after receiving the recommendation of the Drug Safety Oversight Board.

(H) Inaction

An approved risk evaluation and mitigation strategy shall remain in effect until the Secretary acts, if the Secretary fails to act as provided for under subparagraph (G).

(I) Effect on action deadline

With respect to a proposal or assessment referred to in paragraph (1), the Secretary shall be considered to have met the action deadline for the action letter on the application if the responsible person requests the dispute resolution process described in this paragraph and if the Secretary—

(i) has initiated the discussions described under paragraph (2) not less than 60 days before such action deadline; and

(ii) has complied with the timing requirements of scheduling review by the Drug Safety Oversight Board, providing a written recommendation, and issuing an action letter under subparagraphs (B), (F), and (G), respectively.

(J) Disqualification

No individual who is an employee of the Food and Drug Administration and who reviews a drug or who participated in an administrative appeal under subparagraph (C)(i) with respect to such drug may serve on the Drug Safety Oversight Board at a meeting under subparagraph (D) to review a dispute about the risk evaluation and mitigation strategy for such drug.

(K) Additional expertise

The Drug Safety Oversight Board may add members with relevant expertise from the Food and Drug Administration, including the Office of Pediatrics, the Office of Women's Health, or the Office of Rare Diseases, or from other Federal public health or health care agencies, for a meeting under subparagraph (D) of the Drug Safety Oversight Board.

(6) Use of advisory committees

The Secretary may convene a meeting of 1 or more advisory committees of the Food and Drug Administration to—

(A) review a concern about the safety of a drug or class of drugs, including before an assessment of the risk evaluation and mitigation strategy or strategies of such drug or drugs is required to be submitted under any of subparagraphs (B) through (D) of subsection (g)(2);

(B) review the risk evaluation and mitigation strategy or strategies of a drug or group of drugs; or

(C) review a dispute under paragraph (4) or (5).

(7) Process for addressing drug class effects

(A) In general

When a concern about a serious risk of a drug may be related to the pharmacological class of the drug, the Secretary, in consultation with the offices described in subsection (c)(2), may defer assessments of the approved risk evaluation and mitigation strategies for such drugs until the Secretary has convened 1 or more public meetings to consider possible responses to such concern.

(B) Notice

If the Secretary defers an assessment under subparagraph (A), the Secretary shall—

(i) give notice of the deferral to the holder of the approved covered application not later than 5 days after the deferral;

(ii) publish the deferral in the Federal Register; and

(iii) give notice to the public of any public meetings to be convened under subparagraph (A), including a description of the deferral.

(C) Public meetings

Such public meetings may include—

(i) 1 or more meetings of the responsible person for such drugs;

(ii) 1 or more meetings of 1 or more advisory committees of the Food and Drug Administration, as provided for under paragraph (6); or

(iii) 1 or more workshops of scientific experts and other stakeholders.

(D) Action

After considering the discussions from any meetings under subparagraph (A), the Secretary may—

(i) announce in the Federal Register a planned regulatory action, including a modification to each risk evaluation and mitigation strategy, for drugs in the pharmacological class;

(ii) seek public comment about such action; and

(iii) after seeking such comment, issue an order addressing such regulatory action.

(8) International coordination

The Secretary, in consultation with the offices described in subsection (c)(2), may coordinate the timetable for submission of assessments under subsection (d), or a study or clinical trial under section 355(*o*)(3) of this title, with efforts to identify and assess the serious risks of such drug by the marketing authorities of other countries whose drug approval and risk management processes the Secretary deems comparable to the drug approval and risk management processes of the United States. If the Secretary takes action to coordinate such timetable, the Secretary shall give notice to the responsible person.

(9) Effect

Use of the processes described in paragraphs (7) and (8) shall not be the sole source of delay of action on an application or a supplement to an application for a drug.

(i) Abbreviated new drug applications

(1) In general

A drug that is the subject of an abbreviated new drug application under section 355(j) of this title is subject to only the following elements of the risk evaluation and mitigation strategy required under subsection (a) for the applicable listed drug:

(A) A Medication Guide or patient package insert, if required under subsection (e) for the applicable listed drug.

(B) Elements to assure safe use, if required under subsection (f) for the listed drug. A drug that is the subject of an abbreviated new drug application and the listed drug shall use a single, shared system under subsection (f). The Secretary may waive the requirement under the preceding sentence for a drug that is the subject of an abbreviated new drug application, and permit the applicant to use a different, comparable aspect of the elements to assure safe use, if the Secretary determines that—

(i) the burden of creating a single, shared system outweighs the benefit of a single, system,[1] taking into consideration the impact on health care providers, patients, the applicant for the abbreviated new drug application, and the holder of the reference drug product; or

(ii) an aspect of the elements to assure safe use for the applicable listed drug is claimed by a patent that has not expired or is a method or process that, as a trade secret, is entitled to protection, and the applicant for the abbreviated new drug application certifies that it has sought a license for use of an aspect of the elements to assure safe use for the applicable listed drug and that it was unable to obtain a license.

A certification under clause (ii) shall include a description of the efforts made by the applicant for the abbreviated new drug application to obtain a license. In a case described in clause (ii), the Secretary may seek to negotiate a voluntary agreement with the owner of the patent, method, or process for a license under which the applicant for such abbreviated new drug application may use an aspect of the elements to assure safe use, if required under subsection (f) for the applicable listed drug, that is claimed by a patent that has not expired or is a method or process that as a trade secret is entitled to protection.

(2) Action by Secretary

For an applicable listed drug for which a drug is approved under section 355(j) of this title, the Secretary—

(A) shall undertake any communication plan to health care providers required under subsection (e)(3) for the applicable listed drug; and

(B) shall inform the responsible person for the drug that is so approved if the risk evaluation and mitigation strategy for the applicable listed drug is modified.

(j) Drug Safety Oversight Board

(1) In general

There is established a Drug Safety Oversight Board.

---

[1] So in original. Probably should be "single, shared system,".

(2) Composition; meetings

The Drug Safety Oversight Board shall—

(A) be composed of scientists and health care practitioners appointed by the Secretary, each of whom is an employee of the Federal Government;

(B) include representatives from offices throughout the Food and Drug Administration, including the offices responsible for postapproval safety of drugs;

(C) include at least 1 representative each from the National Institutes of Health and the Department of Health and Human Services (other than the Food and Drug Administration);

(D) include such representatives as the Secretary shall designate from other appropriate agencies that wish to provide representatives; and

(E) meet at least monthly to provide oversight and advice to the Secretary on the management of important drug safety issues.

(June 25, 1938, ch. 675, § 505–1, as added Pub. L. 110–85, title IX, § 901(b), Sept. 27, 2007, 121 Stat. 926.)

REFERENCES IN TEXT

For the effective date of this section, referred to in subsec. (a)(2)(A), see Effective Date note below.

Section 101(c) of the Food and Drug Administration Amendments Act of 2007, referred to in subsec. (h)(4), (5)(C)(i), is section 101(c) of Pub. L. 110–85, which is set out as a note under section 379g of this title.

EFFECTIVE DATE

Section effective 180 days after Sept. 27, 2007, see section 909 of Pub. L. 110–85, set out as an Effective Date of 2007 Amendment note under section 331 of this title.

§ 355a. Pediatric studies of drugs

(a) Definitions

As used in this section, the term "pediatric studies" or "studies" means at least one clinical investigation (that, at the Secretary's discretion, may include pharmacokinetic studies) in pediatric age groups (including neonates in appropriate cases) in which a drug is anticipated to be used, and, at the discretion of the Secretary, may include preclinical studies.

(b) Market exclusivity for new drugs

(1) In general

Except as provided in paragraph (2), if, prior to approval of an application that is submitted under section 355(b)(1) of this title, the Secretary determines that information relating to the use of a new drug in the pediatric population may produce health benefits in that population, the Secretary makes a written request for pediatric studies (which shall include a timeframe for completing such studies), the applicant agrees to the request, such studies are completed using appropriate formulations for each age group for which the study is requested within any such timeframe, and the reports thereof are submitted and accepted in accordance with subsection (d)(3)—

(A)(i)(I) the period referred to in subsection (c)(3)(E)(ii) of section 355 of this title, and in subsection (j)(5)(F)(ii) of such section, is deemed to be five years and six months rather than five years, and the references in subsections (c)(3)(E)(ii) and (j)(5)(F)(ii) of such section to four years, to forty-eight months, and to seven and one-half years are deemed to be four and one-half years, fifty-four months, and eight years, respectively; or

(II) the period referred to in clauses (iii) and (iv) of subsection (c)(3)(E) of such section, and in clauses (iii) and (iv) of subsection (j)(5)(F) of such section, is deemed to be three years and six months rather than three years; and

(ii) if the drug is designated under section 360bb of this title for a rare disease or condition, the period referred to in section 360cc(a) of this title is deemed to be seven years and six months rather than seven years; and

(B)(i) if the drug is the subject of—

(I) a listed patent for which a certification has been submitted under subsection (b)(2)(A)(ii) or (j)(2)(A)(vii)(II) of section 355 of this title and for which pediatric studies were submitted prior to the expiration of the patent (including any patent extensions); or

(II) a listed patent for which a certification has been submitted under subsections (b)(2)(A)(iii) or (j)(2)(A)(vii)(III) of section 355 of this title,

the period during which an application may not be approved under section 355(c)(3) of this title or section 355(j)(5)(B) of this title shall be extended by a period of six months after the date the patent expires (including any patent extensions); or

(ii) if the drug is the subject of a listed patent for which a certification has been submitted under subsection (b)(2)(A)(iv) or (j)(2)(A)(vii)(IV) of section 355 of this title, and in the patent infringement litigation resulting from the certification the court determines that the patent is valid and would be infringed, the period during which an application may not be approved under section 355(c)(3) of this title or section 355(j)(5)(B) of this title shall be extended by a period of six months after the date the patent expires (including any patent extensions).

(2) Exception

The Secretary shall not extend the period referred to in paragraph (1)(A) or (1)(B) if the determination made under subsection (d)(3) is made later than 9 months prior to the expiration of such period.

(c) Market exclusivity for already-marketed drugs

(1) In general

Except as provided in paragraph (2), if the Secretary determines that information relating to the use of an approved drug in the pediatric population may produce health benefits in that population and makes a written request to the holder of an approved application under section 355(b)(1) of this title for pediatric studies (which shall include a timeframe for completing such studies), the holder agrees to the request, such studies are completed using appropriate formulations for each age group for which the study is requested within any such timeframe, and the reports thereof are submitted and accepted in accordance with subsection (d)(3)—

(A)(i)(I) the period referred to in subsection (c)(3)(E)(ii) of section 355 of this title, and in subsection (j)(5)(F)(ii) of such section, is deemed to be five years and six months rather than five years, and the references in subsections (c)(3)(E)(ii) and (j)(5)(F)(ii) of such section to four years, to forty-eight months, and to seven and one-half years are deemed to be four and one-half years, fifty-four months, and eight years, respectively; or

(II) the period referred to in clauses (iii) and (iv) of subsection (c)(3)(D) of such section, and in clauses (iii) and (iv) of subsection (j)(5)(F) of such section, is deemed to be three years and six months rather than three years; and

(ii) if the drug is designated under section 360bb of this title for a rare disease or condition, the period referred to in section 360cc(a) of this title is deemed to be seven years and six months rather than seven years; and

(B)(i) if the drug is the subject of—

(I) a listed patent for which a certification has been submitted under subsection (b)(2)(A)(ii) or (j)(2)(A)(vii)(II) of section 355 of this title and for which pediatric studies were submitted prior to the expiration of the patent (including any patent extensions); or

(II) a listed patent for which a certification has been submitted under subsection (b)(2)(A)(iii) or (j)(2)(A)(vii)(III) of section 355 of this title,

the period during which an application may not be approved under section 355(c)(3) of this title or section 355(j)(5)(B)(ii) of this title shall be extended by a period of six months after the date the patent expires (including any patent extensions); or

(ii) if the drug is the subject of a listed patent for which a certification has been submitted under subsection (b)(2)(A)(iv) or (j)(2)(A)(vii)(IV) of section 355 of this title, and in the patent infringement litigation resulting from the certification the court determines that the patent is valid and would be infringed, the period during which an application may not be approved under section 355(c)(3) of this title or section 355(j)(5)(B) of this title shall be extended by a period of six months after the date the patent expires (including any patent extensions).

(2) Exception

The Secretary shall not extend the period referred to in paragraph (1)(A) or (1)(B) if the determination made under subsection (d)(3) is made later than 9 months prior to the expiration of such period.

(d) Conduct of pediatric studies

(1) Request for studies

(A) In general

The Secretary may, after consultation with the sponsor of an application for an investigational new drug under section 355(i) of this title, the sponsor of an application for a new drug under section 355(b)(1) of this title, or the holder of an approved application for a drug under section 355(b)(1) of this title, issue to the sponsor or holder a written request for the conduct of pediatric studies for such drug. In issuing such request, the Secretary shall take into account adequate representation of children of ethnic and racial minorities. Such request to conduct pediatric studies shall be in writing and shall include a timeframe for such studies and a request to the sponsor or holder to propose pediatric labeling resulting from such studies.

(B) Single written request

A single written request—

(i) may relate to more than one use of a drug; and

(ii) may include uses that are both approved and unapproved.

(2) Written request for pediatric studies

(A) Request and response

(i) In general

If the Secretary makes a written request for pediatric studies (including neonates, as appropriate) under subsection (b) or (c), the applicant or holder, not later than 180 days after receiving the written request, shall respond to the Secretary as to the intention of the applicant or holder to act on the request by—

(I) indicating when the pediatric studies will be initiated, if the applicant or holder agrees to the request; or

(II) indicating that the applicant or holder does not agree to the request and stating the reasons for declining the request.

(ii) Disagree with request

If, on or after September 27, 2007, the applicant or holder does not agree to the request on the grounds that it is not possible to develop the appropriate pediatric formulation, the applicant or holder shall submit to the Secretary the reasons such pediatric formulation cannot be developed.

(B) Adverse event reports

An applicant or holder that, on or after September 27, 2007, agrees to the request for such studies shall provide the Secretary, at the same time as the submission of the reports of such studies, with all postmarket adverse event reports regarding the drug that is the subject of such studies and are available prior to submission of such reports.

(3) Meeting the studies requirement

Not later than 180 days after the submission of the reports of the studies, the Secretary shall accept or reject such reports and so notify the sponsor or holder. The Secretary's only responsibility in accepting or rejecting the reports shall be to determine, within the 180-day period, whether the studies fairly respond to the written request, have been conducted in accordance with commonly accepted scientific principles and protocols, and have been reported in accordance with the requirements of the Secretary for filing.

(4) Effect of subsection

Nothing in this subsection alters or amends section 331(j) of this title or section 552 of title 5 or section 1905 of title 18.

(e) Notice of determinations on studies requirement

(1) In general

The Secretary shall publish a notice of any determination, made on or after September 27, 2007, that the requirements of subsection (d) have been met and that submissions and approvals under subsection (b)(2) or (j) of section 355 of this title for a drug will be subject to the provisions of this section. Such notice shall be published not later than 30 days after the date of the Secretary's determination regarding market exclusivity and shall include a copy of the written request made under subsection (b) or (c).

(2) Identification of certain drugs

The Secretary shall publish a notice identifying any drug for which, on or after September 27, 2007, a pediatric formulation was developed, studied, and found to be safe and effective in the pediatric population (or specified subpopulation) if the pediatric formulation for such drug is not introduced onto the market within one year after the date that the Secretary publishes the notice described in paragraph (1). Such notice identifying such drug shall be published not later than 30 days after the date of the expiration of such one year period.

(f) Internal review of written requests and pediatric studies

(1) Internal review

The Secretary shall utilize the internal review committee established under section 355d of this title to review all written requests issued on or after September 27, 2007, in accordance with paragraph (2).

(2) Review of written requests

The committee referred to in paragraph (1) shall review all written requests issued pursuant to this section prior to being issued.

(3) Review of pediatric studies

The committee referred to in paragraph (1) may review studies conducted pursuant to this section to make a recommendation to the Secretary whether to accept or reject such reports under subsection (d)(3).

(4) Activity by committee

The committee referred to in paragraph (1) may operate using appropriate members of such committee and need not convene all members of the committee.

(5) Documentation of committee action

For each drug, the committee referred to in paragraph (1) shall document, for each activity described in paragraph (2) or (3), which members of the committee participated in such activity.

(6) Tracking pediatric studies and labeling changes

The Secretary, in consultation with the committee referred to in paragraph (1), shall track and make available to the public, in an easily accessible manner, including through posting on the Web site of the Food and Drug Administration—

(A) the number of studies conducted under this section and under section 284m of title 42;

(B) the specific drugs and drug uses, including labeled and off-labeled indications, studied under such sections;

(C) the types of studies conducted under such sections, including trial design, the number of pediatric patients studied, and the number of centers and countries involved;

(D) the number of pediatric formulations developed and the number of pediatric formulations not developed and the reasons such formulations were not developed;

(E) the labeling changes made as a result of studies conducted under such sections;

(F) an annual summary of labeling changes made as a result of studies conducted under such sections for distribution pursuant to subsection (k)(2); and

(G) information regarding reports submitted on or after September 27, 2007.

(g) Limitations

Notwithstanding subsection (c)(2), a drug to which the six-month period under subsection (b) or (c) has already been applied—

(1) may receive an additional six-month period under subsection (c)(1)(A)(i)(II) for a supplemental application if all other requirements under this section are satisfied, except that such drug may not receive any additional such period under subsection (c)(1)(B); and

(2) may not receive any additional such period under subsection (c)(1)(A)(ii).

(h) Relationship to pediatric research requirements

Notwithstanding any other provision of law, if any pediatric study is required by a provision of law (including a regulation) other than this section and such study meets the completeness, timeliness, and other requirements of this section, such study shall be deemed to satisfy the requirement for market exclusivity pursuant to this section.

(i) Labeling changes

(1) Priority status for pediatric applications and supplements

Any application or supplement to an application under section 355 of this title proposing a labeling change as a result of any pediatric study conducted pursuant to this section—

(A) shall be considered to be a priority application or supplement; and

(B) shall be subject to the performance goals established by the Commissioner for priority drugs.

(2) Dispute resolution

(A) Request for labeling change and failure to agree

If, on or after September 27, 2007, the Commissioner determines that the sponsor and the Commissioner have been unable to reach agreement on appropriate changes to the labeling for the drug that is the subject of the application, not later than 180 days after the date of submission of the application—

(i) the Commissioner shall request that the sponsor of the application make any labeling change that the Commissioner determines to be appropriate; and

(ii) if the sponsor of the application does not agree within 30 days after the Commissioner's request to make a labeling change requested by the Commissioner, the Commissioner shall refer the matter to the Pediatric Advisory Committee.

(B) Action by the Pediatric Advisory Committee

Not later than 90 days after receiving a referral under subparagraph (A)(ii), the Pediatric Advisory Committee shall—

(i) review the pediatric study reports; and

(ii) make a recommendation to the Commissioner concerning appropriate labeling changes, if any.

(C) Consideration of recommendations

The Commissioner shall consider the recommendations of the Pediatric Advisory Committee and, if appropriate, not later than 30 days after receiving the recommendation, make a request to the sponsor of the application to make any labeling change that the Commissioner determines to be appropriate.

(D) Misbranding

If the sponsor of the application, within 30 days after receiving a request under subparagraph (C), does not agree to make a labeling change requested by the Commissioner, the Commissioner may deem the drug that is the subject of the application to be misbranded.

(E) No effect on authority

Nothing in this subsection limits the authority of the United States to bring an enforcement action under this chapter when a drug lacks appropriate pediatric labeling. Neither course of action (the Pediatric Advisory Committee process or an enforcement action referred to in the preceding sentence) shall preclude, delay, or serve as the basis to stay the other course of action.

(j) Other labeling changes

If, on or after September 27, 2007, the Secretary determines that a pediatric study conducted under this section does or does not demonstrate that the drug that is the subject of the study is safe and effective, including whether such study results are inconclusive, in pediatric populations or subpopulations, the Secretary shall order the labeling of such product to include information about the results of the study and a statement of the Secretary's determination.

(k) Dissemination of pediatric information

(1) In general

Not later than 210 days after the date of submission of a report on a pediatric study under this section, the Secretary shall make available to the public the medical, statistical, and clinical pharmacology reviews of pediatric studies conducted under subsection (b) or (c).

(2) Dissemination of information regarding labeling changes

Beginning on September 27, 2007, the Secretary shall include as a requirement of a written request that the sponsors of the studies that result in labeling changes that are reflected in the annual summary developed pursuant to subsection (f)(3)(F) distribute, at least annually (or more frequently if the Secretary determines that it would be beneficial to the public health), such information to physicians and other health care providers.

(3) Effect of subsection

Nothing in this subsection alters or amends section 331(j) of this title or section 552 of title 5 or section 1905 of title 18.

(*l*) Adverse event reporting

(1) Reporting in year one

Beginning on September 27, 2007, during the one-year period beginning on the date a labeling change is approved pursuant to subsection (i), the Secretary shall ensure that all adverse event reports that have been received for such drug (regardless of when such report was received) are referred to the Office of Pediatric Therapeutics established under section 393a of this title. In considering the reports, the Director of such Office shall provide for the review of the reports by the Pediatric Advisory Committee, including obtaining any recommendations of such Committee regarding whether the Secretary should take action under this chapter in response to such reports.

(2) Reporting in subsequent years

Following the one-year period described in paragraph (1), the Secretary shall, as appropriate, refer to the Office of Pediatric Therapeutics all pediatric adverse event reports for a drug for which a pediatric study was conducted under this section. In considering such reports, the Director of such Office may provide for the review of such reports by the Pediatric Advisory Committee, including obtaining any recommendation of such Committee regarding whether the Secretary should take action in response to such reports.

(3) Effect

The requirements of this subsection shall supplement, not supplant, other review of such adverse event reports by the Secretary.

(m) Clarification of interaction of market exclusivity under this section and market exclusivity awarded to an applicant for approval of a drug under section 355(j) of this title

If a 180-day period under section 355(j)(5)(B)(iv) of this title overlaps with a 6-month exclusivity period under this section, so that the applicant for approval of a drug under section 355(j) of this title entitled to the 180-day period under that section loses a portion of the 180-day period to which the applicant is entitled for the drug, the 180-day period shall be extended from—

(1) the date on which the 180-day period would have expired by the number of days of the overlap, if the 180-day period would, but for the application of this subsection, expire after the 6-month exclusivity period; or

(2) the date on which the 6-month exclusivity period expires, by the number of days of the overlap if the 180-day period would, but for the application of this subsection, expire during the six-month exclusivity period.

(n) Referral if pediatric studies not completed

(1) In general

Beginning on September 27, 2007, if pediatric studies of a drug have not been completed under subsection (d) and if the Secretary, through the committee established under section 355d of this title, determines that there is a continuing need for information relating to the use of the drug in the pediatric population (including neonates, as appropriate), the Secretary shall carry out the following:

(A) For a drug for which a listed patent has not expired, make a determination regarding whether an assessment shall be required to be submitted under section 355c(b) of this title. Prior to making such a determination, the Secretary may not take more than 30 days to certify whether the Foundation for the National Institutes of Health has sufficient funding at the time of such certification to initiate and fund all of the studies in the written request in their entirety within the timeframes specified within the written request. Only if the Secretary makes such certification in the affirmative, the Secretary shall refer all pediatric studies in the written request to the Foundation for the National Institutes of Health for the conduct of such studies, and such Foundation shall fund such studies. If no certification has been made at the end of the 30-day period, or if the Secretary certifies that funds are not sufficient to initiate and fund all the studies in their entirety, the Secretary shall consider whether assessments shall be required under section 355c(b) of this title for such drug.

(B) For a drug that has no listed patents or has 1 or more listed patents that have expired, the Secretary shall refer the drug for inclusion on the list established under section 284m of title 42 for the conduct of studies.

(2) Public notice

The Secretary shall give the public notice of a decision under paragraph (1)(A) not to require an assessment under section 355c of this title and the basis for such decision.

(3) Effect of subsection

Nothing in this subsection alters or amends section 331(j) of this title or section 552 of title 5 or section 1905 of title 18.

(*o*) Prompt approval of drugs under section 355(j) when pediatric information is added to labeling

(1) General rule

A drug for which an application has been submitted or approved under section 355(j) of this title shall not be considered ineligible for approval under that section or misbranded under section 352 of this title on the basis that the labeling of the drug omits a pediatric indication or any other aspect of labeling pertaining to pediatric use when the omitted indication or other aspect is protected by patent or by exclusivity under clause (iii) or (iv) of section 355(j)(5)(F) of this title.

(2) Labeling

Notwithstanding clauses (iii) and (iv) of section 355(j)(5)(F) of this title, the Secretary may require that the labeling of a drug approved under section 355(j) of this title that omits a pediatric indication or other aspect of labeling as described in paragraph (1) include—

(A) a statement that, because of marketing exclusivity for a manufacturer—

(i) the drug is not labeled for pediatric use; or

(ii) in the case of a drug for which there is an additional pediatric use not referred to in paragraph (1), the drug is not labeled for the pediatric use under paragraph (1); and

(B) a statement of any appropriate pediatric contraindications, warnings, or precautions that the Secretary considers necessary.

(3) Preservation of pediatric exclusivity and other provisions

This subsection does not affect—

(A) the availability or scope of exclusivity under this section;

(B) the availability or scope of exclusivity under section 355 of this title for pediatric formulations;

(C) the question of the eligibility for approval of any application under section 355(j) of this title that omits any other conditions of approval entitled to exclusivity under clause (iii) or (iv) of section 355(j)(5)(F) of this title; or

(D) except as expressly provided in paragraphs (1) and (2), the operation of section 355 of this title.

(p) Institute of Medicine study

Not later than 3 years after September 27, 2007, the Secretary shall enter into a contract with the Institute of Medicine to conduct a study and report to Congress regarding the written requests made and the studies conducted pursuant to this section. The Institute of Medicine may devise an appropriate mechanism to review a representative sample of requests made and studies conducted pursuant to this section in order to conduct such study. Such study shall—

(1) review such representative written requests issued by the Secretary since 1997 under subsections (b) and (c);

(2) review and assess such representative pediatric studies conducted under subsections (b) and (c) since 1997 and labeling changes made as a result of such studies;

(3) review the use of extrapolation for pediatric subpopulations, the use of alternative endpoints for pediatric populations, neonatal assessment tools, and ethical issues in pediatric clinical trials;

(4) review and assess the pediatric studies of biological products as required under subsections (a) and (b) of section 355c of this title; and

(5) make recommendations regarding appropriate incentives for encouraging pediatric studies of biologics.

(q) Sunset

A drug may not receive any 6-month period under subsection (b) or (c) unless—

(1) on or before October 1, 2012, the Secretary makes a written request for pediatric studies of the drug;

(2) on or before October 1, 2012, an application for the drug is accepted for filing under section 355(b) of this title; and

(3) all requirements of this section are met.

(June 25, 1938, ch. 675, §505A, as added Pub. L. 105–115, title I, §111, Nov. 21, 1997, 111 Stat. 2305; amended Pub. L. 107–109, §§2, 4, 5(b)(2), 7–11(a), 18(a), 19, Jan. 4, 2002, 115 Stat. 1408, 1411, 1413–1415, 1423, 1424; Pub. L. 108–155, §§2(b)(2), 3(a), (b)(1), Dec. 3, 2003, 117 Stat. 1941; Pub. L. 108–173, title XI, §1104, Dec. 8, 2003, 117 Stat. 2461; Pub. L. 110–85, title V, §502(a)(1), Sept. 27, 2007, 121 Stat. 876.)

AMENDMENTS

2007—Pub. L. 110–85 amended section generally. Prior to amendment, text consisted of subsecs. (a) to (n) relating to pediatric studies of drugs, including market exclusivity, conduct of pediatric studies, delay of effective date for certain applications, notice of determinations on studies requirement, limitations, research requirements, labeling supplements, dissemination of information, prompt approval of drugs, report to Congress not later than Jan. 1, 2001, and sunset provisions.

2003—Subsec. (b)(1)(A)(i). Pub. L. 108–173, §1104(1), substituted "(j)(5)(F)(ii)" for "(j)(5)(D)(ii)" in two places.

Subsec. (b)(1)(A)(ii). Pub. L. 108–173, §1104(2), substituted "(j)(5)(F)" for "(j)(5)(D)".

Subsec. (b)(2). Pub. L. 108–155, §3(a), substituted "355(j)(5)(B)" for "355(j)(4)(B)" in two places.

Subsec. (c)(1)(A)(i). Pub. L. 108–173, §1104(1), substituted "(j)(5)(F)(ii)" for "(j)(5)(D)(ii)" in two places.

Subsec. (c)(1)(A)(ii). Pub. L. 108–173, §1104(2), substituted "(j)(5)(F)" for "(j)(5)(D)".

Subsec. (c)(2). Pub. L. 108–155, §3(a), substituted "355(j)(5)(B)" for "355(j)(4)(B)" in two places.

Subsec. (e). Pub. L. 108–173, §1104(3), substituted "355(j)(5)(F)" for "355(j)(5)(D)".

Subsec. (h). Pub. L. 108–155, §2(b)(2), substituted "pediatric research requirements" for "regulations" in heading and "by a provision of law (including a regulation) other than this section" for "pursuant to regulations promulgated by the Secretary" in text.

Subsec. (i)(2). Pub. L. 108–155, §3(b)(1), struck out "Advisory Subcommittee of the Anti-Infective Drugs" before "Advisory Committee" wherever appearing.

Subsec. (*l*). Pub. L. 108–173, §1104(3), substituted "355(j)(5)(F)" for "355(j)(5)(D)" wherever appearing.

2002—Subsec. (a). Pub. L. 107–109, §19(2), (3), redesignated subsec. (g) as (a). Former subsec. (a) redesignated (b).

Subsec. (a)(1)(A). Pub. L. 107–109, §19(1)(A), (B), substituted "(j)(5)(D)(ii)" for "(j)(4)(D)(ii)" in two places in cl. (i) and "(j)(5)(D)" for "(j)(4)(D)" in cl. (ii).

Subsec. (b). Pub. L. 107–109, §19(2), (3), redesignated subsec. (a) as (b).

Pub. L. 107–109, §2(1), struck out heading and text of subsec. (b). Text read as follows: "Not later than 180 days after November 21, 1997, the Secretary, after consultation with experts in pediatric research shall develop, prioritize, and publish an initial list of approved drugs for which additional pediatric information may produce health benefits in the pediatric population. The Secretary shall annually update the list."

Subsec. (c). Pub. L. 107–109, §2(2), in introductory provisions, inserted "determines that information relating to the use of an approved drug in the pediatric population may produce health benefits in that population and" after "the Secretary" and struck out "concerning a drug identified in the list described in subsection (b) of this section" after "such studies)".

Subsec. (c)(1)(A). Pub. L. 107–109, §19(1)(A), (B), substituted "(j)(5)(D)(ii)" for "(j)(4)(D)(ii)" in two places in cl. (i) and "(j)(5)(D)" for "(j)(4)(D)" in cl. (ii).

Subsec. (d)(1). Pub. L. 107–109, §19(4), substituted "subsection (b) or (c)" for "subsection (a) or (c)" in introductory provisions.

Subsec. (d)(2). Pub. L. 107–109, §§18(a), 19(4), substituted "subsection (b) or (c)" for "subsection (a) or (c)" and inserted "In reaching an agreement regarding written protocols, the Secretary shall take into account adequate representation of children of ethnic and racial minorities." after first sentence.

Subsec. (d)(3). Pub. L. 107–109, §19(4), substituted "subsection (b) or (c)" for "subsection (a) or (c)".

Subsec. (d)(4). Pub. L. 107–109, §4, added par. (4).

Subsec. (e). Pub. L. 107–109, §19(1)(C), (4), substituted "section 355(j)(5)(D)" for "section 355(j)(4)(D)" and "subsection (b) or (c)" for "subsection (a) or (c)".

Subsec. (g). Pub. L. 107–109, §19(2), (3), (5), redesignated subsec. (h) as (g) and substituted "subsection (b) or (c)" for "subsection (a) or (b)" in introductory provisions. Former subsec. (g) redesignated (a).

Pub. L. 107–109, §7, inserted "(including neonates in appropriate cases)" after "pediatric age groups".

Subsec. (h). Pub. L. 107–109, §19(2), (3), redesignated subsec. (i) as (h). Former subsec. (h) redesignated (g).

Subsec. (i). Pub. L. 107–109, §19(2), (3), redesignated subsec. (*l*) as (i). Former subsec. (i) redesignated (h).

Subsec. (j). Pub. L. 107–109, §19(2), (3), redesignated subsec. (m) as (j). Former subsec. (j) redesignated (n).

Pub. L. 107–109, §8, added subsec. (j) and struck out heading and text of former subsec. (j). Text read as follows: "A drug may not receive any six-month period under subsection (a) or (c) of this section unless the application for the drug under section 355(b)(1) of this title is submitted on or before January 1, 2002. After January 1, 2002, a drug shall receive a six-month period under subsection (c) of this section if—

"(1) the drug was in commercial distribution as of November 21, 1997;

"(2) the drug was included by the Secretary on the list under subsection (b) of this section as of January 1, 2002;

"(3) the Secretary determines that there is a continuing need for information relating to the use of the drug in the pediatric population and that the drug may provide health benefits in that population; and

"(4) all requirements of this section are met."

Subsec. (k). Pub. L. 107–109, §19(2), (3), redesignated subsec. (n) as (k). Former subsec. (k) redesignated (m).

Subsec. (*l*). Pub. L. 107–109, §19(2), (3), redesignated subsec. (*o*) as (*l*). Former subsec. (*l*) redesignated (i).

Pub. L. 107–109, §5(b)(2), added subsec. (*l*).

Subsec. (m). Pub. L. 107–109, §19(2), (3), redesignated subsec. (k) as (m). Former subsec. (m) redesignated (j).

Pub. L. 107–109, §9, added subsec. (m).

Subsec. (n). Pub. L. 107–109, §19(4), which directed substitution of "subsection (b) or (c)" for "subsection (a) or (c)" in subsec. (m), was executed by making the substitution in introductory provisions of subsec. (n), to reflect the probable intent of Congress.

Pub. L. 107–109, § 19(2), (3), redesignated subsec. (j) as (n). Former subsec. (n) redesignated (k).

Pub. L. 107–109, § 10, added subsec. (n).

Subsec. (*o*). Pub. L. 107–109, § 19(2), (3), redesignated subsec. (*o*) as (*l*).

Pub. L. 107–109, § 11(a), added subsec. (*o*).

EFFECTIVE DATE OF 2007 AMENDMENT

Pub. L. 110–85, title V, § 502(a)(2), Sept. 27, 2007, 121 Stat. 885, provided that:

"(A) IN GENERAL.—The amendment made by this subsection [amending this section] shall apply to written requests under section 505A of the Federal Food, Drug, and Cosmetic Act (21 U.S.C. 355a) issued on or after the date of the enactment of this Act [Sept. 27, 2007].

"(B) CERTAIN WRITTEN REQUESTS.—A written request issued under section 505A of the Federal Food, Drug, and Cosmetic Act, as in effect on the day before the date of the enactment of this Act, which has been accepted and for which no determination under subsection (d)(2) of such section has been made before such date of enactment, shall be subject to such section 505A, except that such written requests shall be subject to subsections (d)(2)(A)(ii), (e)(1) and (2), (f), (i)(2)(A), (j), (k)(1), (*l*)(1), and (n) of section 505A of the Federal Food, Drug, and Cosmetic Act, as in effect on or after the date of the enactment of this Act."

EFFECTIVE DATE OF 2003 AMENDMENT

Amendment by Pub. L. 108–155 effective Dec. 3, 2003, except as otherwise provided, see section 4 of Pub. L. 108–155, set out as an Effective Date note under section 355c of this title.

EFFECTIVE DATE OF 2002 AMENDMENT

Pub. L. 107–109, § 11(b), Jan. 4, 2002, 115 Stat. 1416, provided that: "The amendment made by subsection (a) [amending this section] takes effect on the date of enactment of this Act [Jan. 4, 2002], including with respect to applications under section 505(j) of the Federal Food, Drug, and Cosmetic Act (21 U.S.C. 355(j)) that are approved or pending on that date."

CONSTRUCTION OF 2007 AMENDMENTS ON PEDIATRIC STUDIES

Pub. L. 110–85, title IX, § 901(e), Sept. 27, 2007, 121 Stat. 942, provided that: "This title [enacting sections 353b, 355–1, 355e, 360a, and 360bbb–6 of this title, amending sections 331, 333, 334, 352, 355, and 381 of this title and section 262 of Title 42, The Public Health and Welfare, and enacting provisions set out as notes under sections 331, 352, and 355 of this title] and the amendments made by this title may not be construed as affecting the authority of the Secretary of Health and Human Services to request pediatric studies under section 505A of the Federal Food, Drug, and Cosmetic Act [21 U.S.C. 355a] or to require such studies under section 505B of such Act [21 U.S.C. 355c]."

REPORT ON PEDIATRIC EXCLUSIVITY PROGRAM

Pub. L. 107–109, § 16, Jan. 4, 2002, 115 Stat. 1421, as amended by Pub. L. 108–155, § 3(b)(4), Dec. 3, 2003, 117 Stat. 1942, required the Comptroller General, not later than Oct. 1, 2006, and in consultation with the Secretary of Health and Human Services, to submit to Congress a report on specified issues concerning the effectiveness of the pediatric exclusivity program.

STUDY BY GENERAL ACCOUNTING OFFICE

Pub. L. 107–109, § 18(b), Jan. 4, 2002, 115 Stat. 1423, required the Comptroller General, not later than Jan. 10, 2003, to conduct a study relating to the representation of children of ethnic and racial minorities in studies under section 355a of this title and to submit a report to Congress describing the findings of the study.

§ 355b. Adverse-event reporting

(a) Toll-free number in labeling

Not later than one year after January 4, 2002, the Secretary of Health and Human Services shall promulgate a final rule requiring that the labeling of each drug for which an application is approved under section 505 of the Federal Food, Drug, and Cosmetic Act [21 U.S.C. 355] (regardless of the date on which approved) include the toll-free number maintained by the Secretary for the purpose of receiving reports of adverse events regarding drugs and a statement that such number is to be used for reporting purposes only, not to receive medical advice. With respect to the final rule:

(1) The rule shall provide for the implementation of such labeling requirement in a manner that the Secretary considers to be most likely to reach the broadest consumer audience.

(2) In promulgating the rule, the Secretary shall seek to minimize the cost of the rule on the pharmacy profession.

(3) The rule shall take effect not later than 60 days after the date on which the rule is promulgated.

(b) Drugs with pediatric market exclusivity

(1) In general

During the one year beginning on the date on which a drug receives a period of market exclusivity under 505A[1] of the Federal Food, Drug, and Cosmetic Act [21 U.S.C. 355a], any report of an adverse event regarding the drug that the Secretary of Health and Human Services receives shall be referred to the Office of Pediatric Therapeutics established under section 393a of this title. In considering the report, the Director of such Office shall provide for the review of the report by the Pediatric Advisory Committee, including obtaining any recommendations of such subcommittee[2] regarding whether the Secretary should take action under the Federal Food, Drug, and Cosmetic Act [21 U.S.C. 301 et seq.] in response to the report.

(2) Rule of construction

Paragraph (1) may not be construed as restricting the authority of the Secretary of Health and Human Services to continue carrying out the activities described in such paragraph regarding a drug after the one-year period described in such paragraph regarding the drug has expired.

(Pub. L. 107–109, § 17, Jan. 4, 2002, 115 Stat. 1422; Pub. L. 108–155, § 3(b)(5), Dec. 3, 2003, 117 Stat. 1942.)

REFERENCES IN TEXT

The Federal Food, Drug, and Cosmetic Act, referred to in subsec. (b)(1), is act June 25, 1938, ch. 675, 52 Stat. 1040, as amended, which is classified generally to this chapter. For complete classification of this Act to the Code, see section 301 of this title and Tables.

CODIFICATION

Section was enacted as part of the Best Pharmaceuticals for Children Act, and not as part of the Fed-

[1] So in original. Probably should be preceded by "section".

[2] So in original. Probably should be "Committee".

eral Food, Drug, and Cosmetic Act which comprises this chapter.

AMENDMENTS

2003—Subsec. (b)(1). Pub. L. 108–155 struck out "Advisory Subcommittee of the Anti-Infective Drugs" before "Advisory Committee".

EFFECTIVE DATE OF 2003 AMENDMENT

Amendment by Pub. L. 108–155 effective Dec. 3, 2003, except as otherwise provided, see section 4 of Pub. L. 108–155, set out as an Effective Date note under section 355c of this title.

§355c. Research into pediatric uses for drugs and biological products

(a) New drugs and biological products

(1) In general

A person that submits, on or after September 27, 2007, an application (or supplement to an application)—

(A) under section 355 of this title for a new active ingredient, new indication, new dosage form, new dosing regimen, or new route of administration, or

(B) under section 262 of title 42 for a new active ingredient, new indication, new dosage form, new dosing regimen, or new route of administration,

shall submit with the application the assessments described in paragraph (2).

(2) Assessments

(A) In general

The assessments referred to in paragraph (1) shall contain data, gathered using appropriate formulations for each age group for which the assessment is required, that are adequate—

(i) to assess the safety and effectiveness of the drug or the biological product for the claimed indications in all relevant pediatric subpopulations; and

(ii) to support dosing and administration for each pediatric subpopulation for which the drug or the biological product is safe and effective.

(B) Similar course of disease or similar effect of drug or biological product

(i) In general

If the course of the disease and the effects of the drug are sufficiently similar in adults and pediatric patients, the Secretary may conclude that pediatric effectiveness can be extrapolated from adequate and well-controlled studies in adults, usually supplemented with other information obtained in pediatric patients, such as pharmacokinetic studies.

(ii) Extrapolation between age groups

A study may not be needed in each pediatric age group if data from one age group can be extrapolated to another age group.

(iii) Information on extrapolation

A brief documentation of the scientific data supporting the conclusion under clauses (i) and (ii) shall be included in any pertinent reviews for the application under section 355 of this title or section 262 of title 42.

(3) Deferral

(A) In general

On the initiative of the Secretary or at the request of the applicant, the Secretary may defer submission of some or all assessments required under paragraph (1) until a specified date after approval of the drug or issuance of the license for a biological product if—

(i) the Secretary finds that—

(I) the drug or biological product is ready for approval for use in adults before pediatric studies are complete;

(II) pediatric studies should be delayed until additional safety or effectiveness data have been collected; or

(III) there is another appropriate reason for deferral; and

(ii) the applicant submits to the Secretary—

(I) certification of the grounds for deferring the assessments;

(II) a description of the planned or ongoing studies;

(III) evidence that the studies are being conducted or will be conducted with due diligence and at the earliest possible time; and

(IV) a timeline for the completion of such studies.

(B) Annual review

(i) In general

On an annual basis following the approval of a deferral under subparagraph (A), the applicant shall submit to the Secretary the following information:

(I) Information detailing the progress made in conducting pediatric studies.

(II) If no progress has been made in conducting such studies, evidence and documentation that such studies will be conducted with due diligence and at the earliest possible time.

(ii) Public availability

The information submitted through the annual review under clause (i) shall promptly be made available to the public in an easily accessible manner, including through the Web site of the Food and Drug Administration.

(4) Waivers

(A) Full waiver

On the initiative of the Secretary or at the request of an applicant, the Secretary shall grant a full waiver, as appropriate, of the requirement to submit assessments for a drug or biological product under this subsection if the applicant certifies and the Secretary finds that—

(i) necessary studies are impossible or highly impracticable (because, for example, the number of patients is so small or the patients are geographically dispersed);

(ii) there is evidence strongly suggesting that the drug or biological product would be ineffective or unsafe in all pediatric age groups; or

(iii) the drug or biological product—

(I) does not represent a meaningful therapeutic benefit over existing therapies for pediatric patients; and

(II) is not likely to be used in a substantial number of pediatric patients.

(B) Partial waiver

On the initiative of the Secretary or at the request of an applicant, the Secretary shall grant a partial waiver, as appropriate, of the requirement to submit assessments for a drug or biological product under this subsection with respect to a specific pediatric age group if the applicant certifies and the Secretary finds that—

(i) necessary studies are impossible or highly impracticable (because, for example, the number of patients in that age group is so small or patients in that age group are geographically dispersed);

(ii) there is evidence strongly suggesting that the drug or biological product would be ineffective or unsafe in that age group;

(iii) the drug or biological product—

(I) does not represent a meaningful therapeutic benefit over existing therapies for pediatric patients in that age group; and

(II) is not likely to be used by a substantial number of pediatric patients in that age group; or

(iv) the applicant can demonstrate that reasonable attempts to produce a pediatric formulation necessary for that age group have failed.

(C) Pediatric formulation not possible

If a waiver is granted on the ground that it is not possible to develop a pediatric formulation, the waiver shall cover only the pediatric groups requiring that formulation. An applicant seeking either a full or partial waiver shall submit to the Secretary documentation detailing why a pediatric formulation cannot be developed and, if the waiver is granted, the applicant's submission shall promptly be made available to the public in an easily accessible manner, including through posting on the Web site of the Food and Drug Administration.

(D) Labeling requirement

If the Secretary grants a full or partial waiver because there is evidence that a drug or biological product would be ineffective or unsafe in pediatric populations, the information shall be included in the labeling for the drug or biological product.

(b) Marketed drugs and biological products

(1) In general

After providing notice in the form of a letter (that, for a drug approved under section 355 of this title, references a declined written request under section 355a of this title for a labeled indication which written request is not referred under section 355a(n)(1)(A) of this title to the Foundation of the National Institutes of Health for the pediatric studies), the Secretary may (by order in the form of a letter) require the sponsor or holder of an approved application for a drug under section 355 of this title or the holder of a license for a biological product under section 262 of title 42 to submit by a specified date the assessments described in subsection (a)(2), if the Secretary finds that—

(A)(i) the drug or biological product is used for a substantial number of pediatric patients for the labeled indications; and

(ii) adequate pediatric labeling could confer a benefit on pediatric patients;

(B) there is reason to believe that the drug or biological product would represent a meaningful therapeutic benefit over existing therapies for pediatric patients for 1 or more of the claimed indications; or

(C) the absence of adequate pediatric labeling could pose a risk to pediatric patients.

(2) Waivers

(A) Full waiver

At the request of an applicant, the Secretary shall grant a full waiver, as appropriate, of the requirement to submit assessments under this subsection if the applicant certifies and the Secretary finds that—

(i) necessary studies are impossible or highly impracticable (because, for example, the number of patients in that age group is so small or patients in that age group are geographically dispersed); or

(ii) there is evidence strongly suggesting that the drug or biological product would be ineffective or unsafe in all pediatric age groups.

(B) Partial waiver

At the request of an applicant, the Secretary shall grant a partial waiver, as appropriate, of the requirement to submit assessments under this subsection with respect to a specific pediatric age group if the applicant certifies and the Secretary finds that—

(i) necessary studies are impossible or highly impracticable (because, for example, the number of patients in that age group is so small or patients in that age group are geographically dispersed);

(ii) there is evidence strongly suggesting that the drug or biological product would be ineffective or unsafe in that age group;

(iii)(I) the drug or biological product—

(aa) does not represent a meaningful therapeutic benefit over existing therapies for pediatric patients in that age group; and

(bb) is not likely to be used in a substantial number of pediatric patients in that age group; and

(II) the absence of adequate labeling could not pose significant risks to pediatric patients; or

(iv) the applicant can demonstrate that reasonable attempts to produce a pediatric formulation necessary for that age group have failed.

(C) Pediatric formulation not possible

If a waiver is granted on the ground that it is not possible to develop a pediatric formulation, the waiver shall cover only the pediatric groups requiring that formulation. An applicant seeking either a full or partial waiver shall submit to the Secretary documentation detailing why a pediatric formulation cannot be developed and, if the waiver is granted, the applicant's submission shall promptly be made available to the public in an easily accessible manner, including through posting on the Web site of the Food and Drug Administration.

(D) Labeling requirement

If the Secretary grants a full or partial waiver because there is evidence that a drug or biological product would be ineffective or unsafe in pediatric populations, the information shall be included in the labeling for the drug or biological product.

(3) Effect of subsection

Nothing in this subsection alters or amends section 331(j) of this title or section 552 of title 5 or section 1905 of title 18.

(c) Meaningful therapeutic benefit

For the purposes of paragraph (4)(A)(iii)(I) and (4)(B)(iii)(I) of subsection (a) and paragraphs (1)(B) and (2)(B)(iii)(I)(aa) of subsection (b), a drug or biological product shall be considered to represent a meaningful therapeutic benefit over existing therapies if the Secretary determines that—

(1) if approved, the drug or biological product could represent an improvement in the treatment, diagnosis, or prevention of a disease, compared with marketed products adequately labeled for that use in the relevant pediatric population; or

(2) the drug or biological product is in a class of products or for an indication for which there is a need for additional options.

(d) Submission of assessments

If a person fails to submit an assessment described in subsection (a)(2), or a request for approval of a pediatric formulation described in subsection (a) or (b), in accordance with applicable provisions of subsections (a) and (b)—

(1) the drug or biological product that is the subject of the assessment or request may be considered misbranded solely because of that failure and subject to relevant enforcement action (except that the drug or biological product shall not be subject to action under section 333 of this title); but

(2) the failure to submit the assessment or request shall not be the basis for a proceeding—

(A) to withdraw approval for a drug under section 355(e) of this title; or

(B) to revoke the license for a biological product under section 262 of title 42.

(e) Meetings

Before and during the investigational process for a new drug or biological product, the Secretary shall meet at appropriate times with the sponsor of the new drug or biological product to discuss—

(1) information that the sponsor submits on plans and timelines for pediatric studies; or

(2) any planned request by the sponsor for waiver or deferral of pediatric studies.

(f) Review of pediatric plans, assessments, deferrals, and waivers

(1) Review

Beginning not later than 30 days after September 27, 2007, the Secretary shall utilize the internal committee established under section 355d of this title to provide consultation to reviewing divisions on all pediatric plans and assessments prior to approval of an application or supplement for which a pediatric assessment is required under this section and all deferral and waiver requests granted pursuant to this section.

(2) Activity by committee

The committee referred to in paragraph (1) may operate using appropriate members of such committee and need not convene all members of the committee.

(3) Documentation of committee action

For each drug or biological product, the committee referred to in paragraph (1) shall document, for each activity described in paragraph (4) or (5), which members of the committee participated in such activity.

(4) Review of pediatric plans, assessments, deferrals, and waivers

Consultation on pediatric plans and assessments by the committee referred to in paragraph (1) pursuant to this section shall occur prior to approval of an application or supplement for which a pediatric assessment is required under this section. The committee shall review all requests for deferrals and waivers from the requirement to submit a pediatric assessment granted under this section and shall provide recommendations as needed to reviewing divisions, including with respect to whether such a supplement, when submitted, shall be considered for priority review.

(5) Retrospective review of pediatric assessments, deferrals, and waivers

Not later than 1 year after September 27, 2007, the committee referred to in paragraph (1) shall conduct a retrospective review and analysis of a representative sample of assessments submitted and deferrals and waivers approved under this section since December 3, 2003. Such review shall include an analysis of the quality and consistency of pediatric information in pediatric assessments and the appropriateness of waivers and deferrals granted. Based on such review, the Secretary shall issue recommendations to the review divisions for improvements and initiate guidance to industry related to the scope of pediatric studies required under this section.

(6) Tracking of assessments and labeling changes

The Secretary, in consultation with the committee referred to in paragraph (1), shall track and make available to the public in an easily accessible manner, including through posting on the Web site of the Food and Drug Administration—

(A) the number of assessments conducted under this section;

(B) the specific drugs and biological products and their uses assessed under this section;

(C) the types of assessments conducted under this section, including trial design, the number of pediatric patients studied, and the number of centers and countries involved;

(D) the total number of deferrals requested and granted under this section and, if granted, the reasons for such deferrals, the timeline for completion, and the number completed and pending by the specified date, as outlined in subsection (a)(3);

(E) the number of waivers requested and granted under this section and, if granted, the reasons for the waivers;

(F) the number of pediatric formulations developed and the number of pediatric formulations not developed and the reasons any such formulation was not developed;

(G) the labeling changes made as a result of assessments conducted under this section;

(H) an annual summary of labeling changes made as a result of assessments conducted under this section for distribution pursuant to subsection (h)(2);

(I) an annual summary of information submitted pursuant to subsection (a)(3)(B); and

(J) the number of times the committee referred to in paragraph (1) made a recommendation to the Secretary under paragraph (4) regarding priority review, the number of times the Secretary followed or did not follow such a recommendation, and, if not followed, the reasons why such a recommendation was not followed.

(g) Labeling changes

(1) Dispute resolution

(A) Request for labeling change and failure to agree

If, on or after September 27, 2007, the Commissioner determines that a sponsor and the Commissioner have been unable to reach agreement on appropriate changes to the labeling for the drug that is the subject of the application or supplement, not later than 180 days after the date of the submission of the application or supplement—

(i) the Commissioner shall request that the sponsor of the application make any labeling change that the Commissioner determines to be appropriate; and

(ii) if the sponsor does not agree within 30 days after the Commissioner's request to make a labeling change requested by the Commissioner, the Commissioner shall refer the matter to the Pediatric Advisory Committee.

(B) Action by the Pediatric Advisory Committee

Not later than 90 days after receiving a referral under subparagraph (A)(ii), the Pediatric Advisory Committee shall—

(i) review the pediatric study reports; and

(ii) make a recommendation to the Commissioner concerning appropriate labeling changes, if any.

(C) Consideration of recommendations

The Commissioner shall consider the recommendations of the Pediatric Advisory Committee and, if appropriate, not later than 30 days after receiving the recommendation, make a request to the sponsor of the application or supplement to make any labeling changes that the Commissioner determines to be appropriate.

(D) Misbranding

If the sponsor of the application or supplement, within 30 days after receiving a request under subparagraph (C), does not agree to make a labeling change requested by the Commissioner, the Commissioner may deem the drug that is the subject of the application or supplement to be misbranded.

(E) No effect on authority

Nothing in this subsection limits the authority of the United States to bring an enforcement action under this chapter when a drug lacks appropriate pediatric labeling. Neither course of action (the Pediatric Advisory Committee process or an enforcement action referred to in the preceding sentence) shall preclude, delay, or serve as the basis to stay the other course of action.

(2) Other labeling changes

If, on or after September 27, 2007, the Secretary makes a determination that a pediatric assessment conducted under this section does or does not demonstrate that the drug that is the subject of such assessment is safe and effective in pediatric populations or subpopulations, including whether such assessment results are inconclusive, the Secretary shall order the label of such product to include information about the results of the assessment and a statement of the Secretary's determination.

(h) Dissemination of pediatric information

(1) In general

Not later than 210 days after the date of submission of a pediatric assessment under this section, the Secretary shall make available to the public in an easily accessible manner the medical, statistical, and clinical pharmacology reviews of such pediatric assessments, and shall post such assessments on the Web site of the Food and Drug Administration.

(2) Dissemination of information regarding labeling changes

Beginning on September 27, 2007, the Secretary shall require that the sponsors of the assessments that result in labeling changes that are reflected in the annual summary developed pursuant to subsection (f)(6)(H) distribute such information to physicians and other health care providers.

(3) Effect of subsection

Nothing in this subsection shall alter or amend section 331(j) of this title or section 552 of title 5 or section 1905 of title 18.

(i) Adverse event reporting

(1) Reporting in year one

Beginning on September 27, 2007, during the one-year period beginning on the date a labeling change is made pursuant to subsection (g), the Secretary shall ensure that all adverse event reports that have been received for such drug (regardless of when such report was received) are referred to the Office of Pediatric Therapeutics. In considering such reports, the Director of such Office shall provide for the review of such reports by the Pediatric Advisory Committee, including obtaining any recommendations of such committee regarding whether the Secretary should take action under this chapter in response to such reports.

(2) Reporting in subsequent years

Following the one-year period described in paragraph (1), the Secretary shall, as appropriate, refer to the Office of Pediatric Therapeutics all pediatric adverse event reports for a drug for which a pediatric study was conducted under this section. In considering such reports, the Director of such Office may provide for the review of such reports by the Pediatric Advisory Committee, including obtaining any recommendation of such Committee regarding whether the Secretary should take action in response to such reports.

(3) Effect

The requirements of this subsection shall supplement, not supplant, other review of such adverse event reports by the Secretary.

(j) Scope of authority

Nothing in this section provides to the Secretary any authority to require a pediatric assessment of any drug or biological product, or any assessment regarding other populations or uses of a drug or biological product, other than the pediatric assessments described in this section.

(k) Orphan drugs

Unless the Secretary requires otherwise by regulation, this section does not apply to any drug for an indication for which orphan designation has been granted under section 360bb of this title.

(*l*) Institute of Medicine study

(1) In general

Not later than three years after September 27, 2007, the Secretary shall contract with the Institute of Medicine to conduct a study and report to Congress regarding the pediatric studies conducted pursuant to this section or precursor regulations since 1997 and labeling changes made as a result of such studies.

(2) Content of study

The study under paragraph (1) shall review and assess the use of extrapolation for pediatric subpopulations, the use of alternative endpoints for pediatric populations, neonatal assessment tools, the number and type of pediatric adverse events, and ethical issues in pediatric clinical trials.

(3) Representative sample

The Institute of Medicine may devise an appropriate mechanism to review a representative sample of studies conducted pursuant to this section from each review division within the Center for Drug Evaluation and Research in order to make the requested assessment.

(m) Integration with other pediatric studies

The authority under this section shall remain in effect so long as an application subject to this section may be accepted for filing by the Secretary on or before the date specified in section 355a(q) of this title.

(June 25, 1938, ch. 675, § 505B, as added Pub. L. 108–155, § 2(a), Dec. 3, 2003, 117 Stat. 1936; amended Pub. L. 110–85, title IV, § 402(a), Sept. 27, 2007, 121 Stat. 866.)

AMENDMENTS

2007—Pub. L. 110–85 amended section generally. Prior to amendment, section related to required submission of assessments with an application for a new drug or new biological product and by order of the Secretary for certain marketed drugs and biological products used for pediatric patients, a definition of meaningful therapeutic benefit, consequences of failure to submit required assessments, meetings of the Secretary and the sponsor of a new drug or biological product, a limitation of the scope of the Secretary's authority, application to orphan drugs, and integration with other pediatric studies.

EFFECTIVE DATE OF 2007 AMENDMENT

Pub. L. 110–85, title IV, § 402(b), Sept. 27, 2007, 121 Stat. 875, provided that:

"(1) IN GENERAL.—Notwithstanding subsection (h) of section 505B of the Federal Food, Drug and Cosmetic Act [21 U.S.C. 355c(h)], as in effect on the day before the date of the enactment of this Act [Sept. 27, 2007], a pending assessment, including a deferred assessment, required under such section 505B shall be deemed to have been required under section 505B of the Federal Food, Drug and Cosmetic Act as in effect on or after the date of the enactment of this Act.

"(2) CERTAIN ASSESSMENTS AND WAIVER REQUESTS.—An assessment pending on or after the date that is 1 year prior to the date of the enactment of this Act shall be subject to the tracking and disclosure requirements established under such section 505B, as in effect on or after such date of enactment, except that any such assessments submitted or waivers of such assessments requested before such date of enactment shall not be subject to subsections (a)(4)(C), (b)(2)(C), (f)(6)(F), and (h) of such section 505B."

EFFECTIVE DATE

Pub. L. 108–155, § 4, Dec. 3, 2003, 117 Stat. 1942, provided that:

"(a) IN GENERAL.—Subject to subsection (b), this Act [enacting this section, amending sections 355, 355a, and 355b of this title and sections 262 and 284m of Title 42, The Public Health and Welfare, enacting provisions set out as a note under section 301 of this title, and amending provisions set out as notes under section 355a of this title and section 284m of Title 42] and the amendments made by this Act take effect on the date of enactment of this Act [Dec. 3, 2003].

"(b) APPLICABILITY TO NEW DRUGS AND BIOLOGICAL PRODUCTS.—

"(1) IN GENERAL.—Subsection (a) of section 505B of the Federal Food, Drug, and Cosmetic Act [21 U.S.C. 355c(a)] (as added by section 2) shall apply to an application described in paragraph (1) of that subsection submitted to the Secretary of Health and Human Services on or after April 1, 1999.

"(2) WAIVERS AND DEFERRALS.—

"(A) WAIVER OR DEFERRAL GRANTED.—If, with respect to an application submitted to the Secretary of Health and Human Services between April 1, 1999, and the date of enactment of this Act [Dec. 3, 2003], a waiver or deferral of pediatric assessments was granted under regulations of the Secretary then in effect, the waiver or deferral shall be a waiver or deferral under subsection (a) of section 505B of the Federal Food, Drug, and Cosmetic Act [21 U.S.C. 355c(a)], except that any date specified in such a deferral shall be extended by the number of days that is equal to the number of days between October 17, 2002, and the date of enactment of this Act.

"(B) WAIVER AND DEFERRAL NOT GRANTED.—If, with respect to an application submitted to the Secretary of Health and Human Services between April 1, 1999, and the date of enactment of this Act [Dec. 3, 2003], neither a waiver nor deferral of pediatric assessments was granted under regulations of the Secretary then in effect, the person that submitted the application shall be required to submit assessments under subsection (a)(2) of section 505B of the Federal Food, Drug, and Cosmetic Act [21 U.S.C. 355c(a)(2)] on the date that is the later of—

"(i) the date that is 1 year after the date of enactment of this Act; or

"(ii) such date as the Secretary may specify under subsection (a)(3) of that section;

unless the Secretary grants a waiver under subsection (a)(4) of that section.

"(c) NO LIMITATION OF AUTHORITY.—Neither the lack of guidance or regulations to implement this Act or the amendments made by this Act nor the pendency of the process for issuing guidance or regulations shall limit the authority of the Secretary of Health and Human Services under, or defer any requirement under, this Act or those amendments."

§ 355d. Internal committee for review of pediatric plans, assessments, deferrals, and waivers

The Secretary shall establish an internal committee within the Food and Drug Administration to carry out the activities as described in sections 355a(f) and 355c(f) of this title. Such internal committee shall include employees of the Food and Drug Administration, with expertise in pediatrics (including representation from the Office of Pediatric Therapeutics), biopharmacology, statistics, chemistry, legal issues, pediatric ethics, and the appropriate expertise pertaining to the pediatric product under review, such as expertise in child and adolescent psychiatry, and other individuals designated by the Secretary.

(June 25, 1938, ch. 675, § 505C, as added Pub. L. 110–85, title IV, § 403, Sept. 27, 2007, 121 Stat. 875.)

§ 355e. Pharmaceutical security

(a) In general

The Secretary shall develop standards and identify and validate effective technologies for the purpose of securing the drug supply chain against counterfeit, diverted, subpotent, substandard, adulterated, misbranded, or expired drugs.

(b) Standards development

(1) In general

The Secretary shall, in consultation with the agencies specified in paragraph (4), manufacturers, distributors, pharmacies, and other supply chain stakeholders, prioritize and develop standards for the identification, validation, authentication, and tracking and tracing of prescription drugs.

(2) Standardized numeral identifier

Not later than 30 months after September 27, 2007, the Secretary shall develop a standardized numerical identifier (which, to the extent practicable, shall be harmonized with international consensus standards for such an identifier) to be applied to a prescription drug at the point of manufacturing and repackaging (in which case the numerical identifier shall be linked to the numerical identifier applied at the point of manufacturing) at the package or pallet level, sufficient to facilitate the identification, validation, authentication, and tracking and tracing of the prescription drug.

(3) Promising technologies

The standards developed under this subsection shall address promising technologies, which may include—

(A) radio frequency identification technology;

(B) nanotechnology;

(C) encryption technologies; and

(D) other track-and-trace or authentication technologies.

(4) Interagency collaboration

In carrying out this subsection, the Secretary shall consult with Federal health and security agencies, including—

(A) the Department of Justice;

(B) the Department of Homeland Security;

(C) the Department of Commerce; and

(D) other appropriate Federal and State agencies.

(c) Inspection and enforcement

(1) In general

The Secretary shall expand and enhance the resources and facilities of agency components of the Food and Drug Administration involved with regulatory and criminal enforcement of this chapter to secure the drug supply chain against counterfeit, diverted, subpotent, substandard, adulterated, misbranded, or expired drugs including biological products and active pharmaceutical ingredients from domestic and foreign sources.

(2) Activities

The Secretary shall undertake enhanced and joint enforcement activities with other Federal and State agencies, and establish regional capacities for the validation of prescription drugs and the inspection of the prescription drug supply chain.

(d) Definition

In this section, the term "prescription drug" means a drug subject to section 353(b)(1) of this title.

(June 25, 1938, ch. 675, § 505D, as added Pub. L. 110–85, title IX, § 913, Sept. 27, 2007, 121 Stat. 952.)

§ 356. Fast track products

(a) Designation of drug as fast track product

(1) In general

The Secretary shall, at the request of the sponsor of a new drug, facilitate the development and expedite the review of such drug if it is intended for the treatment of a serious or life-threatening condition and it demonstrates the potential to address unmet medical needs for such a condition. (In this section, such a drug is referred to as a "fast track product".)

(2) Request for designation

The sponsor of a new drug may request the Secretary to designate the drug as a fast track product. A request for the designation may be made concurrently with, or at any time after, submission of an application for the investigation of the drug under section 355(i) of this title or section 262(a)(3) of title 42.

(3) Designation

Within 60 calendar days after the receipt of a request under paragraph (2), the Secretary shall determine whether the drug that is the subject of the request meets the criteria described in paragraph (1). If the Secretary finds that the drug meets the criteria, the Secretary shall designate the drug as a fast track product and shall take such actions as are appropriate to expedite the development and review of the application for approval of such product.

(b) Approval of application for fast track product

(1) In general

The Secretary may approve an application for approval of a fast track product under section 355(c) of this title or section 262 of title 42 upon a determination that the product has an effect on a clinical endpoint or on a surrogate endpoint that is reasonably likely to predict clinical benefit.

(2) Limitation

Approval of a fast track product under this subsection may be subject to the requirements—

(A) that the sponsor conduct appropriate post-approval studies to validate the surrogate endpoint or otherwise confirm the effect on the clinical endpoint; and

(B) that the sponsor submit copies of all promotional materials related to the fast track product during the preapproval review period and, following approval and for such period thereafter as the Secretary determines to be appropriate, at least 30 days prior to dissemination of the materials.

(3) Expedited withdrawal of approval

The Secretary may withdraw approval of a fast track product using expedited procedures (as prescribed by the Secretary in regulations which shall include an opportunity for an informal hearing) if—

(A) the sponsor fails to conduct any required post-approval study of the fast track drug with due diligence;

(B) a post-approval study of the fast track product fails to verify clinical benefit of the product;

(C) other evidence demonstrates that the fast track product is not safe or effective under the conditions of use; or

(D) the sponsor disseminates false or misleading promotional materials with respect to the product.

(c) Review of incomplete applications for approval of fast track product

(1) In general

If the Secretary determines, after preliminary evaluation of clinical data submitted by the sponsor, that a fast track product may be effective, the Secretary shall evaluate for filing, and may commence review of portions of, an application for the approval of the product before the sponsor submits a complete application. The Secretary shall commence such review only if the applicant—

(A) provides a schedule for submission of information necessary to make the application complete; and

(B) pays any fee that may be required under section 379h of this title.

(2) Exception

Any time period for review of human drug applications that has been agreed to by the Secretary and that has been set forth in goals identified in letters of the Secretary (relating to the use of fees collected under section 379h of this title to expedite the drug development process and the review of human drug applications) shall not apply to an application submitted under paragraph (1) until the date on which the application is complete.

(d) Awareness efforts

The Secretary shall—

(1) develop and disseminate to physicians, patient organizations, pharmaceutical and biotechnology companies, and other appropriate persons a description of the provisions of this section applicable to fast track products; and

(2) establish a program to encourage the development of surrogate endpoints that are reasonably likely to predict clinical benefit for serious or life-threatening conditions for which there exist significant unmet medical needs.

(June 25, 1938, ch. 675, § 506, as added Pub. L. 105–115, title I, § 112(a), Nov. 21, 1997, 111 Stat. 2309.)

PRIOR PROVISIONS

A prior section 356, act June 25, 1938, ch. 675, § 506, as added Dec. 22, 1941, ch. 613, § 3, 55 Stat. 851; amended Pub. L. 102–300, § 6(b)(2), June 16, 1992, 106 Stat. 240; Pub. L. 103–80, § 3(*o*), Aug. 13, 1993, 107 Stat. 777, related to certification of drugs containing insulin, prior to repeal by Pub. L. 105–115, title I, § 125(a)(1), Nov. 21, 1997, 111 Stat. 2325.

EFFECTIVE DATE

Section effective 90 days after Nov. 21, 1997, except as otherwise provided, see section 501 of Pub. L. 105–115, set out as an Effective Date of 1997 Amendment note under section 321 of this title.

GUIDANCE

Section 112(b) of Pub. L. 105–115 provided that: "Within 1 year after the date of enactment of this Act [Nov. 21, 1997], the Secretary of Health and Human Services shall issue guidance for fast track products (as defined in section 506(a)(1) of the Federal Food, Drug, and Cosmetic Act [21 U.S.C. 356(a)(1)]) that describes the policies and procedures that pertain to section 506 of such Act."

§ 356–1. Accelerated approval of priority countermeasures

(a) In general

The Secretary of Health and Human Services may designate a priority countermeasure as a fast-track product pursuant to section 356 of this title or as a device granted review priority pursuant to section 360e(d)(5) of this title. Such a designation may be made prior to the submission of—

(1) a request for designation by the sponsor or applicant; or

(2) an application for the investigation of the drug under section 355(i) of this title or section 262(a)(3) of title 42.

Nothing in this subsection shall be construed to prohibit a sponsor or applicant from declining such a designation.

(b) Use of animal trials

A drug for which approval is sought under section 355(b) of this title or section 262 of title 42 on the basis of evidence of effectiveness that is derived from animal studies pursuant to section 123[1] may be designated as a fast track product for purposes of this section.

(c) Priority review of drugs and biological products

A priority countermeasure that is a drug or biological product shall be considered a priority drug or biological product for purposes of performance goals for priority drugs or biological products agreed to by the Commissioner of Food and Drugs.

(d) Definitions

For purposes of this title:[1]

(1) The term "priority countermeasure" has the meaning given such term in section 247d–6(h)(4) of title 42.

(2) The term "priority drugs or biological products" means a drug or biological product that is the subject of a drug or biologics application referred to in section 101(4) of the Food and Drug Administration Modernization Act of 1997.

(Pub. L. 107–188, title I, § 122, June 12, 2002, 116 Stat. 613.)

REFERENCES IN TEXT

Section 123, referred to in subsec. (b), is section 123 of Pub. L. 107–188, title I, June 12, 2002, 116 Stat. 613, which is not classified to the Code.

This title, referred to in subsec. (d), is title I of Pub. L. 107–188, June 12, 2002, 116 Stat. 596, which enacted this section, section 669a of Title 29, Labor, and sections 244, 245, 247d–3a, 247d–3b, 247d–7a to 247d–7d, 300hh, 300hh–11 to 300hh–13, 1320b–5, and 7257d of Title 42, The Public Health and Welfare, amended sections 247d to 247d–6, 264, 266, 290hh–1, and 5196b of Title 42, and enacted provisions set out as notes preceding section 8101 of Title 38, Veterans' Benefits, and under sections 201, 244, 247d, 247d–6, 300hh, 300hh–12, and 1320b–5 of Title 42. For complete classification of this title to the Code, see Tables.

Section 101(4) of the Food and Drug Administration Modernization Act of 1997, referred to in subsec. (d)(2), is section 101(4) of Pub. L. 105–115, which is set out as a note under section 379g of this title.

CODIFICATION

Section was enacted as part of the Public Health Security and Bioterrorism Preparedness and Response Act of 2002, and not as part of the Federal Food, Drug, and Cosmetic Act which comprises this chapter.

§ 356a. Manufacturing changes

(a) In general

With respect to a drug for which there is in effect an approved application under section 355 or 360b of this title or a license under section 262 of title 42, a change from the manufacturing process approved pursuant to such application or license may be made, and the drug as made with the change may be distributed, if—

(1) the holder of the approved application or license (referred to in this section as a "holder") has validated the effects of the change in accordance with subsection (b) of this section; and

(2)(A) in the case of a major manufacturing change, the holder has complied with the requirements of subsection (c) of this section; or

(B) in the case of a change that is not a major manufacturing change, the holder complies with the applicable requirements of subsection (d) of this section.

(b) Validation of effects of changes

For purposes of subsection (a)(1) of this section, a drug made with a manufacturing change (whether a major manufacturing change or otherwise) may be distributed only if, before distribution of the drug as so made, the holder involved validates the effects of the change on the identity, strength, quality, purity, and potency of the drug as the identity, strength, quality, purity, and potency may relate to the safety or effectiveness of the drug.

(c) Major manufacturing changes

(1) Requirement of supplemental application

For purposes of subsection (a)(2)(A) of this section, a drug made with a major manufacturing change may be distributed only if, before the distribution of the drug as so made, the holder involved submits to the Secretary a supplemental application for such change and the Secretary approves the application. The application shall contain such information as the Secretary determines to be appropriate, and shall include the information developed under subsection (b) of this section by the holder in validating the effects of the change.

(2) Changes qualifying as major changes

For purposes of subsection (a)(2)(A) of this section, a major manufacturing change is a manufacturing change that is determined by the Secretary to have substantial potential to adversely affect the identity, strength, quality, purity, or potency of the drug as they may relate to the safety or effectiveness of a drug. Such a change includes a change that—

(A) is made in the qualitative or quantitative formulation of the drug involved or in the specifications in the approved application or license referred to in subsection (a) of this section for the drug (unless exempted by the Secretary by regulation or guidance from the requirements of this subsection);

(B) is determined by the Secretary by regulation or guidance to require completion of an appropriate clinical study demonstrating equivalence of the drug to the drug as manufactured without the change; or

(C) is another type of change determined by the Secretary by regulation or guidance to have a substantial potential to adversely affect the safety or effectiveness of the drug.

[1] See References in Text note below.

(d) Other manufacturing changes

(1) In general

For purposes of subsection (a)(2)(B) of this section, the Secretary may regulate drugs made with manufacturing changes that are not major manufacturing changes as follows:

(A) The Secretary may in accordance with paragraph (2) authorize holders to distribute such drugs without submitting a supplemental application for such changes.

(B) The Secretary may in accordance with paragraph (3) require that, prior to the distribution of such drugs, holders submit to the Secretary supplemental applications for such changes.

(C) The Secretary may establish categories of such changes and designate categories to which subparagraph (A) applies and categories to which subparagraph (B) applies.

(2) Changes not requiring supplemental application

(A) Submission of report

A holder making a manufacturing change to which paragraph (1)(A) applies shall submit to the Secretary a report on the change, which shall contain such information as the Secretary determines to be appropriate, and which shall include the information developed under subsection (b) of this section by the holder in validating the effects of the change. The report shall be submitted by such date as the Secretary may specify.

(B) Authority regarding annual reports

In the case of a holder that during a single year makes more than one manufacturing change to which paragraph (1)(A) applies, the Secretary may in carrying out subparagraph (A) authorize the holder to comply with such subparagraph by submitting a single report for the year that provides the information required in such subparagraph for all the changes made by the holder during the year.

(3) Changes requiring supplemental application

(A) Submission of supplemental application

The supplemental application required under paragraph (1)(B) for a manufacturing change shall contain such information as the Secretary determines to be appropriate, which shall include the information developed under subsection (b) of this section by the holder in validating the effects of the change.

(B) Authority for distribution

In the case of a manufacturing change to which paragraph (1)(B) applies:

(i) The holder involved may commence distribution of the drug involved 30 days after the Secretary receives the supplemental application under such paragraph, unless the Secretary notifies the holder within such 30-day period that prior approval of the application is required before distribution may be commenced.

(ii) The Secretary may designate a category of such changes for the purpose of providing that, in the case of a change that is in such category, the holder involved may commence distribution of the drug involved upon the receipt by the Secretary of a supplemental application for the change.

(iii) If the Secretary disapproves the supplemental application, the Secretary may order the manufacturer to cease the distribution of the drugs that have been made with the manufacturing change.

(June 25, 1938, ch. 675, §506A, as added Pub. L. 105–115, title I, §116(a), Nov. 21, 1997, 111 Stat. 2313.)

EFFECTIVE DATE

Section 116(b) of Pub. L. 105–115 provided that: "The amendment made by subsection (a) [enacting this section] takes effect upon the effective date of regulations promulgated by the Secretary of Health and Human Services to implement such amendment, or upon the expiration of the 24-month period beginning on the date of the enactment of this Act [Nov. 21, 1997], whichever occurs first."

§ 356b. Reports of postmarketing studies

(a) Submission

(1) In general

A sponsor of a drug that has entered into an agreement with the Secretary to conduct a postmarketing study of a drug shall submit to the Secretary, within 1 year after the approval of such drug and annually thereafter until the study is completed or terminated, a report of the progress of the study or the reasons for the failure of the sponsor to conduct the study. The report shall be submitted in such form as is prescribed by the Secretary in regulations issued by the Secretary.

(2) Agreements prior to effective date

Any agreement entered into between the Secretary and a sponsor of a drug, prior to November 21, 1997, to conduct a postmarketing study of a drug shall be subject to the requirements of paragraph (1). An initial report for such an agreement shall be submitted within 6 months after the date of the issuance of the regulations under paragraph (1).

(b) Consideration of information as public information

Any information pertaining to a report described in subsection (a) of this section shall be considered to be public information to the extent that the information is necessary—

(1) to identify the sponsor; and

(2) to establish the status of a study described in subsection (a) of this section and the reasons, if any, for any failure to carry out the study.

(c) Status of studies and reports

The Secretary shall annually develop and publish in the Federal Register a report that provides information on the status of the postmarketing studies—

(1) that sponsors have entered into agreements to conduct; and

(2) for which reports have been submitted under subsection (a)(1) of this section.

(d) Disclosure

If a sponsor fails to complete an agreed upon study required by this section by its original or otherwise negotiated deadline, the Secretary shall publish a statement on the Internet site of the Food and Drug Administration stating that the study was not completed and, if the reasons for such failure to complete the study were not satisfactory to the Secretary, a statement that such reasons were not satisfactory to the Secretary.

(e) Notification

With respect to studies of the type required under section 356(b)(2)(A) of this title or under section 314.510 or 601.41 of title 21, Code of Federal Regulations, as each of such sections was in effect on the day before the effective date of this subsection, the Secretary may require that a sponsor who, for reasons not satisfactory to the Secretary, fails to complete by its deadline a study under any of such sections of such type for a drug or biological product (including such a study conducted after such effective date) notify practitioners who prescribe such drug or biological product of the failure to complete such study and the questions of clinical benefit, and, where appropriate, questions of safety, that remain unanswered as a result of the failure to complete such study. Nothing in this subsection shall be construed as altering the requirements of the types of studies required under section 356(b)(2)(A) of this title or under section 314.510 or 601.41 of title 21, Code of Federal Regulations, as so in effect, or as prohibiting the Secretary from modifying such sections of title 21 of such Code to provide for studies in addition to those of such type.

(June 25, 1938, ch. 675, § 506B, as added Pub. L. 105–115, title I, § 130(a), Nov. 21, 1997, 111 Stat. 2331; amended Pub. L. 107–188, title V, § 506, June 12, 2002, 116 Stat. 693.)

REFERENCES IN TEXT

The effective date of this subsection, referred to in subsec. (e), is Oct. 1, 2002, see Effective Date of 2002 Amendment note set out below.

AMENDMENTS

2002—Subsecs. (d), (e). Pub. L. 107–188 added subsecs. (d) and (e).

EFFECTIVE DATE OF 2002 AMENDMENT

Pub. L. 107–188, title V, § 508, June 12, 2002, 116 Stat. 694, provided that: "The amendments made by this subtitle [subtitle A (§§ 501–509) of title V of Pub. L. 107–188, amending this section and sections 379g and 379h of this title] shall take effect October 1, 2002."

EFFECTIVE DATE

Section effective 90 days after Nov. 21, 1997, except as otherwise provided, see section 501 of Pub. L. 105–115, set out as an Effective Date of 1997 Amendment note under section 321 of this title.

REPORT TO CONGRESSIONAL COMMITTEES

Pub. L. 105–115, title I, § 130(b), Nov. 21, 1997, 111 Stat. 2331, provided that not later than Oct. 1, 2001, the Secretary was to submit to Congress a report containing a summary of the reports submitted under section 356b of this title and an evaluation and legislative recommendations relating to postmarketing studies of drugs.

§ 356c. Discontinuance of life saving product

(a) In general

A manufacturer that is the sole manufacturer of a drug—

(1) that is—

(A) life-supporting;

(B) life-sustaining; or

(C) intended for use in the prevention of a debilitating disease or condition;

(2) for which an application has been approved under section 355(b) or 355(j) of this title; and

(3) that is not a product that was originally derived from human tissue and was replaced by a recombinant product,

shall notify the Secretary of a discontinuance of the manufacture of the drug at least 6 months prior to the date of the discontinuance.

(b) Reduction in notification period

The notification period required under subsection (a) of this section for a manufacturer may be reduced if the manufacturer certifies to the Secretary that good cause exists for the reduction, such as a situation in which—

(1) a public health problem may result from continuation of the manufacturing for the 6-month period;

(2) a biomaterials shortage prevents the continuation of the manufacturing for the 6-month period;

(3) a liability problem may exist for the manufacturer if the manufacturing is continued for the 6-month period;

(4) continuation of the manufacturing for the 6-month period may cause substantial economic hardship for the manufacturer;

(5) the manufacturer has filed for bankruptcy under chapter 7 or 11 of title 11; or

(6) the manufacturer can continue the distribution of the drug involved for 6 months.

(c) Distribution

To the maximum extent practicable, the Secretary shall distribute information on the discontinuation of the drugs described in subsection (a) of this section to appropriate physician and patient organizations.

(June 25, 1938, ch. 675, § 506C, as added Pub. L. 105–115, title I, § 131(a), Nov. 21, 1997, 111 Stat. 2332.)

EFFECTIVE DATE

Section effective 90 days after Nov. 21, 1997, except as otherwise provided, see section 501 of Pub. L. 105–115, set out as an Effective Date of 1997 Amendment note under section 321 of this title.

§ 357. Repealed. Pub. L. 105–115, title I, § 125(b)(1), Nov. 21, 1997, 111 Stat. 2325

Section, act June 25, 1938, ch. 675, § 507, as added July 6, 1945, ch. 281, § 3, 59 Stat. 463; amended Mar. 10, 1947, ch. 16, § 3, 61 Stat. 12; July 13, 1949, ch. 305, § 2, 63 Stat. 409; Aug. 5, 1953, ch. 334, § 2, 67 Stat. 389; Pub. L. 87–781, title I, §§ 105(a), (b), (d)–(f), 106(a), (b), Oct. 10, 1962, 76 Stat. 785, 786, 787; Pub. L. 90–399, § 105(b), July 13, 1968, 82 Stat. 352; Pub. L. 102–300, § 6(b)(2), June 16, 1992, 106 Stat. 240; Pub. L. 103–80, § 3(p), Aug. 13, 1993, 107 Stat. 777, related to certification of drugs containing penicillin, streptomycin, chlortetracycline, chloramphenicol, bacitracin, or any other antibiotic drug.

§358. Authority to designate official names

(a) Necessity or desirability; use in official compendiums; infringement of trademarks

The Secretary may designate an official name for any drug or device if he determines that such action is necessary or desirable in the interest of usefulness and simplicity. Any official name designated under this section for any drug or device shall be the only official name of that drug or device used in any official compendium published after such name has been prescribed or for any other purpose of this chapter. In no event, however, shall the Secretary establish an official name so as to infringe a valid trademark.

(b) Review of names in official compendiums

Within a reasonable time after October 10, 1962, and at such other times as he may deem necessary, the Secretary shall cause a review to be made of the official names by which drugs are identified in the official United States Pharmacopoeia, the official Homoeopathic Pharmacopoeia of the United States, and the official National Formulary, and all supplements thereto, and at such times as he may deem necessary shall cause a review to be made of the official names by which devices are identified in any official compendium (and all supplements thereto) to determine whether revision of any of those names is necessary or desirable in the interest of usefulness and simplicity.

(c) Determinations of complexity, usefulness, multiplicity, or lack of name; designation by Secretary

Whenever he determines after any such review that (1) any such official name is unduly complex or is not useful for any other reason, (2) two or more official names have been applied to a single drug or device, or to two or more drugs which are identical in chemical structure and pharmacological action and which are substantially identical in strength, quality, and purity, or to two or more devices which are substantially equivalent in design and purpose or (3) no official name has been applied to a medically useful drug or device, he shall transmit in writing to the compiler of each official compendium in which that drug or drugs or device are identified and recognized his request for the recommendation of a single official name for such drug or drugs or device which will have usefulness and simplicity. Whenever such a single official name has not been recommended within one hundred and eighty days after such request, or the Secretary determines that any name so recommended is not useful for any reason, he shall designate a single official name for such drug or drugs or device. Whenever he determines that the name so recommended is useful, he shall designate that name as the official name of such drug or drugs or device. Such designation shall be made as a regulation upon public notice and in accordance with the procedure set forth in section 553 of title 5.

(d) Revised official names; compilation, publication, and public distribution of listings

After each such review, and at such other times as the Secretary may determine to be necessary or desirable, the Secretary shall cause to be compiled, published, and publicly distributed a list which shall list all revised official names of drugs or devices designated under this section and shall contain such descriptive and explanatory matter as the Secretary may determine to be required for the effective use of those names.

(e) Request by compiler of official compendium for designation of name

Upon a request in writing by any compiler of an official compendium that the Secretary exercise the authority granted to him under subsection (a) of this section, he shall upon public notice and in accordance with the procedure set forth in section 553 of title 5 designate the official name of the drug or device for which the request is made.

(June 25, 1938, ch. 675, §508, as added Pub. L. 87–781, title I, §111(a), Oct. 10, 1962, 76 Stat. 789; amended Pub. L. 94–295, §5(b), May 28, 1976, 90 Stat. 581; Pub. L. 103–80, §3(q), Aug. 13, 1993, 107 Stat. 777.)

AMENDMENTS

1993—Subsecs. (c), (e). Pub. L. 103–80 substituted reference to section 553 of title 5 for "section 4 of the Administrative Procedure Act (5 U.S.C. 1003)".

1976—Subsec. (a). Pub. L. 94–295 substituted "drug or device" for "drug" wherever appearing.

Subsec. (b). Pub. L. 94–295 substituted "National Formulary, and all supplements thereto, and at such times as he may deem necessary shall cause a review to be made of the official names by which devices are identified in any official compendium (and all supplements thereto)" for "National Formulary, and all supplements thereto,".

Subsec. (c)(2). Pub. L. 94–295 inserted "or device" after "single drug", and "or to two or more devices which are substantially equivalent in design and purpose" after "purity,".

Subsec. (c)(3). Pub. L. 94–295 inserted "or device" after "useful drug" and after "drug or drugs" wherever appearing.

Subsec. (d). Pub. L. 94–295 inserted "or devices" after "drugs".

Subsec. (e). Pub. L. 94–295 substituted "drug or device" for "drug".

EFFECTIVE DATE

Section 111(b) of Pub. L. 87–781 provided that: "This section [enacting this section] shall take effect on the date of its enactment [Oct. 10, 1962]."

§359. Nonapplicability of subchapter to cosmetics

This subchapter, as amended by the Drug Amendments of 1962, shall not apply to any cosmetic unless such cosmetic is also a drug or device or component thereof.

(June 25, 1938, ch. 675, §509, as added Pub. L. 87–781, title I, §113, Oct. 10, 1962, 76 Stat. 791.)

REFERENCES IN TEXT

This subchapter, as amended by the Drug Amendments of 1962, referred to in text, means the amendment of this subchapter by Pub. L. 87–781 which enacted sections 358 to 360 of this title, amended sections 351 to 353, 355, and 357 of this title, and enacted provisions set out as notes under sections 352, 355, 358, and 360 of this title.

The Drug Amendments of 1962, referred to in text, is Pub. L. 87–781, Oct. 10, 1962, 76 Stat. 780, as amended. For complete classification of this Act to the Code, see Short Title of 1962 Amendment note set out under section 301 of this title and Tables.

§ 360. Registration of producers of drugs or devices

(a) Definitions

As used in this section—

(1) the term "manufacture, preparation, propagation, compounding, or processing" shall include repackaging or otherwise changing the container, wrapper, or labeling of any drug package or device package in furtherance of the distribution of the drug or device from the original place of manufacture to the person who makes final delivery or sale to the ultimate consumer or user; and

(2) the term "name" shall include in the case of a partnership the name of each partner and, in the case of a corporation, the name of each corporate officer and director, and the State of incorporation.

(b) Annual registration

(1) On or before December 31 of each year every person who owns or operates any establishment in any State engaged in the manufacture, preparation, propagation, compounding, or processing of a drug or drugs shall register with the Secretary his name, places of business, and all such establishments.

(2) During the period beginning on October 1 and ending on December 31 of each year, every person who owns or operates any establishment in any State engaged in the manufacture, preparation, propagation, compounding, or processing of a device or devices shall register with the Secretary his name, places of business, and all such establishments.

(c) New producers

Every person upon first engaging in the manufacture, preparation, propagation, compounding, or processing of a drug or drugs or a device or devices in any establishment which he owns or operates in any State shall immediately register with the Secretary his name, place of business, and such establishment.

(d) Additional establishments

Every person duly registered in accordance with the foregoing subsections of this section shall immediately register with the Secretary any additional establishment which he owns or operates in any State and in which he begins the manufacture, preparation, propagation, compounding, or processing of a drug or drugs or a device or devices.

(e) Registration number; uniform system for identification of devices intended for human use

The Secretary may assign a registration number to any person or any establishment registered in accordance with this section. The Secretary may also assign a listing number to each drug or class of drugs listed under subsection (j) of this section. Any number assigned pursuant to the preceding sentence shall be the same as that assigned pursuant to the National Drug Code. The Secretary may by regulation prescribe a uniform system for the identification of devices intended for human use and may require that persons who are required to list such devices pursuant to subsection (j) of this section shall list such devices in accordance with such system.

(f) Availability of registrations for inspection

The Secretary shall make available for inspection, to any person so requesting, any registration filed pursuant to this section; except that any list submitted pursuant to paragraph (3) of subsection (j) of this section and the information accompanying any list or notice filed under paragraph (1) or (2) of that subsection shall be exempt from such inspection unless the Secretary finds that such an exemption would be inconsistent with protection of the public health.

(g) Exclusions from application of section

The foregoing subsections of this section shall not apply to—

(1) pharmacies which maintain establishments in conformance with any applicable local laws regulating the practice of pharmacy and medicine and which are regularly engaged in dispensing prescription drugs or devices, upon prescriptions of practitioners licensed to administer such drugs or devices to patients under the care of such practitioners in the course of their professional practice, and which do not manufacture, prepare, propagate, compound, or process drugs or devices for sale other than in the regular course of their business of dispensing or selling drugs or devices at retail;

(2) practitioners licensed by law to prescribe or administer drugs or devices and who manufacture, prepare, propagate, compound, or process drugs or devices solely for use in the course of their professional practice;

(3) persons who manufacture, prepare, propagate, compound, or process drugs or devices solely for use in research, teaching, or chemical analysis and not for sale;

(4) any distributor who acts as a wholesale distributor of devices, and who does not manufacture, repackage, process, or relabel a device; or

(5) such other classes of persons as the Secretary may by regulation exempt from the application of this section upon a finding that registration by such classes of persons in accordance with this section is not necessary for the protection of the public health.

In this subsection, the term "wholesale distributor" means any person (other than the manufacturer or the initial importer) who distributes a device from the original place of manufacture to the person who makes the final delivery or sale of the device to the ultimate consumer or user.

(h) Inspection of premises

Every establishment in any State registered with the Secretary pursuant to this section shall be subject to inspection pursuant to section 374 of this title and every such establishment engaged in the manufacture, propagation, compounding, or processing of a drug or drugs or of a device or devices classified in class II or III shall be so inspected by one or more officers or employees duly designated by the Secretary, or by persons accredited to conduct inspections under section 374(g) of this title, at least once in the two-year period beginning with the date of registration of such establishment pursuant to this section and at least once in every successive two-year period thereafter.

(i) Registration of foreign establishments

(1) Any establishment within any foreign country engaged in the manufacture, preparation, propagation, compounding, or processing of a drug or device that is imported or offered for import into the United States shall, through electronic means in accordance with the criteria of the Secretary—

(A) upon first engaging in any such activity, immediately register with the Secretary the name and place of business of the establishment, the name of the United States agent for the establishment, the name of each importer of such drug or device in the United States that is known to the establishment, and the name of each person who imports or offers for import such drug or device to the United States for purposes of importation; and

(B) each establishment subject to the requirements of subparagraph (A) shall thereafter—

(i) with respect to drugs, register with the Secretary on or before December 31 of each year; and

(ii) with respect to devices, register with the Secretary during the period beginning on October 1 and ending on December 31 of each year.

(2) The establishment shall also provide the information required by subsection (j) of this section.

(3) The Secretary is authorized to enter into cooperative arrangements with officials of foreign countries to ensure that adequate and effective means are available for purposes of determining, from time to time, whether drugs or devices manufactured, prepared, propagated, compounded, or processed by an establishment described in paragraph (1), if imported or offered for import into the United States, shall be refused admission on any of the grounds set forth in section 381(a) of this title.

(j) Filing of lists of drugs and devices manufactured, prepared, propagated and compounded by registrants; statements; accompanying disclosures

(1) Every person who registers with the Secretary under subsection (b), (c), (d), or (i) of this section shall, at the time of registration under any such subsection, file with the Secretary a list of all drugs and a list of all devices and a brief statement of the basis for believing that each device included in the list is a device rather than a drug (with each drug and device in each list listed by its established name (as defined in section 352(e) of this title) and by any proprietary name) which are being manufactured, prepared, propagated, compounded, or processed by him for commercial distribution and which he has not included in any list of drugs or devices filed by him with the Secretary under this paragraph or paragraph (2) before such time of registration. Such list shall be prepared in such form and manner as the Secretary may prescribe and shall be accompanied by—

(A) in the case of a drug contained in the applicable list and subject to section 355 or 360b of this title, or a device intended for human use contained in the applicable list with respect to which a performance standard has been established under section 360d of this title or which is subject to section 360e of this title, a reference to the authority for the marketing of such drug or device and a copy of all labeling for such drug or device;

(B) in the case of any other drug or device contained in an applicable list—

(i) which drug is subject to section 353(b)(1) of this title, or which device is a restricted device, a copy of all labeling for such drug or device, a representative sampling of advertisements for such drug or device, and, upon request made by the Secretary for good cause, a copy of all advertisements for a particular drug product or device, or

(ii) which drug is not subject to section 353(b)(1) of this title or which device is not a restricted device, the label and package insert for such drug or device and a representative sampling of any other labeling for such drug or device;

(C) in the case of any drug contained in an applicable list which is described in subparagraph (B), a quantitative listing of its active ingredient or ingredients, except that with respect to a particular drug product the Secretary may require the submission of a quantitative listing of all ingredients if he finds that such submission is necessary to carry out the purposes of this chapter; and

(D) if the registrant filing a list has determined that a particular drug product or device contained in such list is not subject to section 355 or 360b of this title, or the particular device contained in such list is not subject to a performance standard established under section 360d of this title or to section 360e of this title or is not a restricted device a brief statement of the basis upon which the registrant made such determination if the Secretary requests such a statement with respect to that particular drug product or device.

(2) Each person who registers with the Secretary under this section shall report to the Secretary, with regard to drugs once during the month of June of each year and once during the month of December of each year, and with regard to devices once each year during the period beginning on October 1 and ending on December 31, the following information:

(A) A list of each drug or device introduced by the registrant for commercial distribution which has not been included in any list previously filed by him with the Secretary under this subparagraph or paragraph (1) of this subsection. A list under this subparagraph shall list a drug or device by its established name (as defined in section 352(e) of this title), and by any proprietary name it may have and shall be accompanied by the other information required by paragraph (1).

(B) If since the date the registrant last made a report under this paragraph (or if he has not made a report under this paragraph, since February 1, 1973) he has discontinued the manufacture, preparation, propagation, compounding, or processing for commercial distribution of a drug or device included in a list filed by him under subparagraph (A) or paragraph (1); notice of such discontinuance, the date of such discontinuance, and the identity (by established name (as defined in section 352(e) of this title) and by any proprietary name) of such drug or device.

(C) If since the date the registrant reported pursuant to subparagraph (B) a notice of discontinuance he has resumed the manufacture, preparation, propagation, compounding, or processing for commercial distribution of the drug or device with respect to which such notice of discontinuance was reported; notice of such resumption, the date of such resumption, the identity of such drug or device (each by established name (as defined in section 352(e) of this title) and by any proprietary name), and the other information required by paragraph (1), unless the registrant has previously reported such resumption to the Secretary pursuant to this subparagraph.

(D) Any material change in any information previously submitted pursuant to this paragraph or paragraph (1).

(3) The Secretary may also require each registrant under this section to submit a list of each drug product which (A) the registrant is manufacturing, preparing, propagating, compounding, or processing for commercial distribution, and (B) contains a particular ingredient. The Secretary may not require the submission of such a list unless he has made a finding that the submission of such a list is necessary to carry out the purposes of this chapter.

(k) Report preceding introduction of devices into interstate commerce

Each person who is required to register under this section and who proposes to begin the introduction or delivery for introduction into interstate commerce for commercial distribution of a device intended for human use shall, at least ninety days before making such introduction or delivery, report to the Secretary or person who is accredited under section 360m(a) of this title (in such form and manner as the Secretary shall by regulation prescribe)—

(1) the class in which the device is classified under section 360c of this title or if such person determines that the device is not classified under such section, a statement of that determination and the basis for such person's determination that the device is or is not so classified, and

(2) action taken by such person to comply with requirements under section 360d or 360e of this title which are applicable to the device.

A notification submitted under this subsection that contains clinical trial data for an applicable device clinical trial (as defined in section 282(j)(1) of title 42) shall be accompanied by the certification required under section 282(j)(5)(B) of such title. Such certification shall not be considered an element of such notification.

(*l*) Exemption from reporting requirements

A report under subsection (k) of this section is not required for a device intended for human use that is exempted from the requirements of this subsection under subsection (m) of this section or is within a type that has been classified into class I under section 360c of this title. The exception established in the preceding sentence does not apply to any class I device that is intended for a use which is of substantial importance in preventing impairment of human health, or to any class I device that presents a potential unreasonable risk of illness or injury.

(m) List of exempt class II devices; determination by Secretary; publication in Federal Register

(1) Not later than 60 days after November 21, 1997, the Secretary shall publish in the Federal Register a list of each type of class II device that does not require a report under subsection (k) of this section to provide reasonable assurance of safety and effectiveness. Each type of class II device identified by the Secretary as not requiring the report shall be exempt from the requirement to provide a report under subsection (k) of this section as of the date of the publication of the list in the Federal Register. The Secretary shall publish such list on the Internet site of the Food and Drug Administration. The list so published shall be updated not later than 30 days after each revision of the list by the Secretary.

(2) Beginning on the date that is 1 day after the date of the publication of a list under this subsection, the Secretary may exempt a class II device from the requirement to submit a report under subsection (k) of this section, upon the Secretary's own initiative or a petition of an interested person, if the Secretary determines that such report is not necessary to assure the safety and effectiveness of the device. The Secretary shall publish in the Federal Register notice of the intent of the Secretary to exempt the device, or of the petition, and provide a 30-day period for public comment. Within 120 days after the issuance of the notice in the Federal Register, the Secretary shall publish an order in the Federal Register that sets forth the final determination of the Secretary regarding the exemption of the device that was the subject of the notice. If the Secretary fails to respond to a petition within 180 days of receiving it, the petition shall be deemed to be granted.

(n) Review of report; time for determination by Secretary

The Secretary shall review the report required in subsection (k) of this section and make a determination under section 360c(f)(1) of this title not later than 90 days after receiving the report.

(*o*) Reprocessed single-use devices

(1) With respect to reprocessed single-use devices for which reports are required under subsection (k) of this section:

(A) The Secretary shall identify such devices or types of devices for which reports under such subsection must, in order to ensure that the device is substantially equivalent to a predicate device, include validation data, the types of which shall be specified by the Secretary, regarding cleaning and sterilization, and functional performance demonstrating that the single-use device will remain substantially equivalent to its predicate device after the maximum number of times the device is reprocessed as intended by the person submitting the premarket notification. Within six months after October 26, 2002, the Secretary shall publish in the Federal Register a list of the types so identified, and shall revise the list as appropriate. Reports under subsection (k) of this section for devices or types of devices within a type included on the list are, upon publication of the list, required to include such validation data.

(B) In the case of each report under subsection (k) of this section that was submitted to the Secretary before the publication of the initial list under subparagraph (A), or any revision thereof, and was for a device or type of device included on such list, the person who submitted the report under subsection (k) of this section shall submit validation data as described in subparagraph (A) to the Secretary not later than nine months after the publication of the list. During such nine-month period, the Secretary may not take any action under this chapter against such device solely on the basis that the validation data for the device have not been submitted to the Secretary. After the submission of the validation data to the Secretary, the Secretary may not determine that the device is misbranded under section 352(*o*) of this title or adulterated under section 351(f)(1)(B) of this title, or take action against the device under section 331(p) of this title for failure to provide any information required by subsection (k) of this section until (i) the review is terminated by withdrawal of the submission of the report under subsection (k) of this section; (ii) the Secretary finds the data to be acceptable and issues a letter; or (iii) the Secretary determines that the device is not substantially equivalent to a predicate device. Upon a determination that a device is not substantially equivalent to a predicate device, or if such submission is withdrawn, the device can no longer be legally marketed.

(C) In the case of a report under subsection (k) of this section for a device identified under subparagraph (A) that is of a type for which the Secretary has not previously received a report under such subsection, the Secretary may, in advance of revising the list under subparagraph (A) to include such type, require that the report include the validation data specified in subparagraph (A).

(D) Section 352(*o*) of this title applies with respect to the failure of a report under subsection (k) of this section to include validation data required under subparagraph (A).

(2) With respect to critical or semi-critical reprocessed single-use devices that, under subsection (*l*) or (m) of this section, are exempt from the requirement of submitting reports under subsection (k) of this section:

(A) The Secretary shall identify such devices or types of devices for which such exemptions should be terminated in order to provide a reasonable assurance of the safety and effectiveness of the devices. The Secretary shall publish in the Federal Register a list of the devices or types of devices so identified, and shall revise the list as appropriate. The exemption for each device or type included on the list is terminated upon the publication of the list. For each report under subsection (k) of this section submitted pursuant to this subparagraph the Secretary shall require the validation data described in paragraph (1)(A).

(B) For each device or type of device included on the list under subparagraph (A), a report under subsection (k) of this section shall be submitted to the Secretary not later than 15 months after the publication of the initial list, or a revision of the list, whichever terminates the exemption for the device. During such 15-month period, the Secretary may not take any action under this chapter against such device solely on the basis that such report has not been submitted to the Secretary. After the submission of the report to the Secretary the Secretary may not determine that the device is misbranded under section 352(*o*) of this title or adulterated under section 351(f)(1)(B) of this title, or take action against the device under section 331(p) of this title for failure to provide any information required by subsection (k) of this section until (i) the review is terminated by withdrawal of the submission; (ii) the Secretary determines by order that the device is substantially equivalent to a predicate device; or (iii) the Secretary determines by order that the device is not substantially equivalent to a predicate device. Upon a determination that a device is not substantially equivalent to a predicate device, the device can no longer be legally marketed.

(C) In the case of semi-critical devices, the initial list under subparagraph (A) shall be published not later than 18 months after the effective date of this subsection. In the case of critical devices, the initial list under such subparagraph shall be published not later than six months after such effective date.

(D) Section 352(*o*) of this title applies with respect to the failure to submit a report under subsection (k) of this section that is required pursuant to subparagraph (A), including a failure of the report to include validation data required in such subparagraph.

(E) The termination under subparagraph (A) of an exemption under subsection (*l*) or (m) of this section for a critical or semi-critical reprocessed single-use device does not terminate the exemption under subsection (*l*) or (m) of this section for the original device.

(p) Electronic registration

Registrations and listings under this section (including the submission of updated information) shall be submitted to the Secretary by electronic means unless the Secretary grants a request for waiver of such requirement because use of electronic means is not reasonable for the person requesting such waiver.

(June 25, 1938, ch. 675, §510, as added Pub. L. 87–781, title III, §302, Oct. 10, 1962, 76 Stat. 794; amended Pub. L. 89–74, §4, July 15, 1965, 79 Stat. 231; Pub. L. 91–513, title II, §701(e), Oct. 27, 1970, 84 Stat. 1282; Pub. L. 92–387, §§3, 4(a)–(c), Aug. 16, 1972, 86 Stat. 560–562; Pub. L. 94–295, §4(a), May 28, 1976, 90 Stat. 579; Pub. L. 105–115, title I, §125(a)(2)(C), title II, §§206(a), 209(a), 213(b), title IV, §417, Nov. 21, 1997, 111 Stat. 2325, 2338, 2341, 2347, 2379; Pub. L. 107–188, title III, §321(a), June 12, 2002, 116 Stat. 675; Pub. L. 107–250, title II,

§§ 201(e), 207, 211, title III, § 302(b), Oct. 26, 2002, 116 Stat. 1609, 1613, 1614, 1616; Pub. L. 108–214, § 2(c)(2), Apr. 1, 2004, 118 Stat. 576; Pub. L. 110–85, title II, §§ 222–224, title VIII, § 801(b)(3)(C), Sept. 27, 2007, 121 Stat. 853, 921.)

REFERENCES IN TEXT

The effective date of this subsection, referred to in subsec. (*o*)(2)(C), probably means the date of the enactment of Pub. L. 107–250, which enacted subsec. (*o*) of this section and was approved Oct. 26, 2002.

AMENDMENTS

2007—Subsec. (b). Pub. L. 110–85, § 222(a), designated existing provisions as par. (1), struck out "or a device or devices" after "drug or drugs", and added par. (2).

Subsec. (i)(1). Pub. L. 110–85, § 222(b), inserted text of par. (1) and struck out former text of par. (1) which related to registration requirement for foreign establishments engaged in the manufacture, preparation, propagation, compounding, or processing of a drug or device to be imported or offered for import into the United States.

Subsec. (j)(2). Pub. L. 110–85, § 223, in introductory provisions, substituted "Each person who registers with the Secretary under this section shall report to the Secretary, with regard to drugs once during the month of June of each year and once during the month of December of each year, and with regard to devices once each year during the period beginning on October 1 and ending on December 31, the following information:" for "Each person who registers with the Secretary under this section shall report to the Secretary once during the month of June of each year and once during the month of December of each year the following information:".

Subsec. (k). Pub. L. 110–85, § 801(b)(3)(C), inserted concluding provisions.

Subsec. (p). Pub. L. 110–85, § 224, amended subsec. (p) generally. Prior to amendment, subsec. (p) read as follows: "Registrations under subsections (b), (c), (d), and (i) of this section (including the submission of updated information) shall be submitted to the Secretary by electronic means, upon a finding by the Secretary that the electronic receipt of such registrations is feasible, unless the Secretary grants a request for waiver of such requirement because use of electronic means is not reasonable for the person requesting such waiver."

2004—Subsec. (*o*)(1)(B), (2)(B). Pub. L. 108–214, § 2(c)(2)(A), (B)(i), substituted "or adulterated" for ", adulterated".

Subsec. (*o*)(2)(E). Pub. L. 108–214, § 2(c)(2)(B)(ii), substituted "semi-critical" for "semicritical".

2002—Subsec. (h). Pub. L. 107–250, § 201(e), inserted ", or by persons accredited to conduct inspections under section 374(g) of this title," after "duly designated by the Secretary".

Subsec. (i)(1). Pub. L. 107–188, § 321(a)(1), substituted "On or before December 31 of each year, any establishment" for "Any establishment" and "shall, through electronic means in accordance with the criteria of the Secretary, register with the Secretary the name and place of business of the establishment, the name of the United States agent for the establishment, the name of each importer of such drug or device in the United States that is known to the establishment, and the name of each person who imports or offers for import such drug or device to the United States for purposes of importation" for "shall register with the Secretary the name and place of business of the establishment and the name of the United States agent for the establishment".

Subsec. (j)(1). Pub. L. 107–188, § 321(a)(2), substituted "subsection (b), (c), (d), or (i)" for "subsection (b), (c), or (d)" in first sentence.

Subsec. (m)(1). Pub. L. 107–250, § 211, inserted at end "The Secretary shall publish such list on the Internet site of the Food and Drug Administration. The list so published shall be updated not later than 30 days after each revision of the list by the Secretary."

Subsec. (*o*). Pub. L. 107–250, § 302(b), added subsec. (*o*).

Subsec. (p). Pub. L. 107–250, § 207, added subsec. (p).

1997—Subsec. (g). Pub. L. 105–115, § 213(b)(3), inserted at end "In this subsection, the term 'wholesale distributor' means any person (other than the manufacturer or the initial importer) who distributes a device from the original place of manufacture to the person who makes the final delivery or sale of the device to the ultimate consumer or user."

Subsec. (g)(4), (5). Pub. L. 105–115, § 213(b)(1), (2), added par. (4) and redesignated former par. (4) as (5).

Subsec. (i). Pub. L. 105–115, § 417, amended subsec. (i) generally. Prior to amendment, subsec. (i) read as follows: "Any establishment within any foreign country engaged in the manufacture, preparation, propagation, compounding, or processing of a drug or drugs, or a device or devices, shall be permitted to register under this section pursuant to regulations promulgated by the Secretary. Such regulations shall require such establishment to provide the information required by subsection (j) of this section and shall require such establishment to provide the information required by subsection (j) of this section in the case of a device or devices and shall include provisions for registration of any such establishment upon condition that adequate and effective means are available, by arrangement with the government of such foreign country or otherwise, to enable the Secretary to determine from time to time whether drugs or devices manufactured, prepared, propagated, compounded, or processed in such establishment, if imported or offered for import into the United States, shall be refused admission on any of the grounds set forth in section 381(a) of this title."

Subsec. (j)(1)(A), (D). Pub. L. 105–115, § 125(a)(2)(C), struck out ", 356, 357," before "or 360b of this title".

Subsec. (k). Pub. L. 105–115, § 206(a)(1), inserted "or person who is accredited under section 360m(a) of this title" after "report to the Secretary".

Subsecs. (*l*), (m). Pub. L. 105–115, § 206(a)(2), added subsecs. (*l*) and (m).

Subsec. (n). Pub. L. 105–115, § 209(a), added subsec. (n).

1976—Subsec. (a)(1). Pub. L. 94–295, § 4(a)(2), substituted "drug package or device package" for "drug package", "distribution of the drug or device" for "distribution of the drug", and "ultimate consumer or user" for "ultimate consumer".

Subsecs. (b) to (d). Pub. L. 94–295, § 4(a)(3), inserted "or a device or devices" after "drug or drugs".

Subsec. (e). Pub. L. 94–295, § 4(a)(4), authorized the Secretary to prescribe by regulation a uniform system for the identification of devices intended for human use and authorized him, in addition, to require that persons who are required to list devices pursuant to subsec. (j) also list such devices in accordance with the system.

Subsec. (g)(1) to (3). Pub. L. 94–295, § 4(a)(5), substituted "drugs or devices" for "drugs".

Subsec. (h). Pub. L. 94–295, § 4(a)(6), inserted reference to establishments engaged in the manufacture, propagation, compounding, or processing of a drug or drugs or of a device or devices classified in class II or III.

Subsec. (i). Pub. L. 94–295, § 4(a)(7), inserted reference to devices and inserted requirement that regulations require establishments to provide the information required by subsection (j) of this section in the case of a device or devices.

Subsec. (j)(1). Pub. L. 94–295, § 4(a)(8)(A), in introductory provisions substituted "a list of all drugs and a list of all devices and a brief statement of the basis for believing that each device included in the list is a device rather than a drug (with each drug and device in each list listed by its established name" for "a list of all drugs (by established name" and "drugs or devices filed" for "drugs filed".

Subsec. (j)(1)(A). Pub. L. 94–295, § 4(a)(8)(B), substituted "the applicable list" for "such list", inserted "or a device intended for human use contained in the applicable list with respect to which a performance standard has been established under section 360d of this title or which is subject to section 360e of this title," after "360b of this title,", and substituted "such drug or device" for "such drug" wherever appearing.

Subsec. (j)(1)(B). Pub. L. 94–295, §4(a)(8)(C), in introductory provisions substituted "drug or device contained in an applicable list" for "drug contained in such list".

Subsec. (j)(1)(B)(i). Pub. L. 94–295, §4(a)(8)(D), substituted "which drug is subject to section 353(b)(1) of this title, or which device is a restricted device, a copy of all labeling for such drug or device, a representative sampling of advertisements for such drug or device, and, upon request made by the Secretary for good cause, a copy of all advertisements for a particular drug product or device, or" for "which is subject to section 353(b)(1) of this title, a copy of all labeling for such drug, a representative sampling of advertisements for such drug, and, upon request made by the Secretary for good cause, a copy of all advertisements for a particular drug product, or".

Subsec. (j)(1)(B)(ii). Pub. L. 94–295, §4(a)(8)(E), substituted "which drug is not subject to section 353(b)(1) of this title or which device is not a restricted device, the label and package insert for such drug or device and a representative sampling of any other labeling for such drug or device" for "which is not subject to section 353(b)(1) of this title, the label and package insert for such drug and a representative sampling of any other labeling for such drug".

Subsec. (j)(1)(C). Pub. L. 94–295, §4(a)(8)(F), substituted "an applicable list" for "such list".

Subsec. (j)(1)(D). Pub. L. 94–295, §4(a)(8)(G), substituted "a list" for "the list", inserted "or the particular device contained in such list is not subject to a performance standard established under section 360d of this title or to section 360e of this title or is not a restricted device" after "or 360b of this title,", and substituted "particular drug product or device" for "particular drug product" wherever appearing.

Subsec. (j)(2). Pub. L. 94–295, §4(a)(8)(H), substituted "drug or device" for "drug" in subpars. (A), (B), and (C), and substituted "(each by established name" for "(by established name" in subpar. (C).

Subsec. (k). Pub. L. 94–295, §4(a)(9), added subsec. (k).

1972—Subsec. (e). Pub. L. 92–387, §4(a), inserted provision that the Secretary may assign a listing number to each drug or class of drugs listed under subsec. (j).

Subsec. (f). Pub. L. 92–387, §4(b), inserted exception that the list submitted under subsec. (j)(3) and information submitted under subsec. (j)(1), (2) shall be exempt from inspection unless the Secretary determines otherwise.

Subsec. (i). Pub. L. 92–387, §4(c), inserted provision that the regulations shall require such establishment to provide the information required by subsec. (j).

Subsec. (j). Pub. L. 92–387, §3, added subsec. (j).

1970—Subsec. (a). Pub. L. 91–513 struck out provisions defining the wholesaling, jobbing, or distributing of depressant or stimulant drugs.

Subsec. (b). Pub. L. 91–513 struck out provisions covering establishments engaged in the wholesaling, jobbing, or distributing of depressant or stimulant drugs and the inclusion of the fact of such activity in the annual registration.

Subsec. (c). Pub. L. 91–513 struck out provisions covering new registrations of persons first engaging in the wholesaling, jobbing, or distributing of depressant or stimulant drugs and the inclusion of the fact of such activity in the registration.

Subsec. (d). Pub. L. 91–513 struck out number designation "(1)" preceding first sentence, struck out portion of such redesignated provisions covering the wholesaling, jobbing, or distributing of depressant or stimulant drugs, and struck out par. (2) covering the filing of supplemental registration whenever a person not previously engaged or involved with depressant or stimulant drugs goes into the manufacturing, preparation, or processing thereof.

1965—Pub. L. 89–74, §4(e), included certain wholesalers in section catchline.

Subsec. (a)(2), (3). Pub. L. 89–74, §4(a), added par. (2) and redesignated former par. (2) as (3).

Subsecs. (b), (c). Pub. L. 89–74, §4(b), (c), inserted "or in the wholesaling, jobbing, or distributing of any depressant or stimulant drug" after "drug or drugs" and inserted requirement that establishment indicate activity in depressant or stimulant drugs at time of registration.

Subsec. (d). Pub. L. 89–74 §4(d), designated existing provisions as par. (1), inserted "or the wholesaling, jobbing, or distributing of any depressant or stimulant drug" and the requirement that the additional establishment indicate activity in depressant or stimulant drugs at time of registration, and added par. (2).

EFFECTIVE DATE OF 2002 AMENDMENT

Amendment by Pub. L. 107–188 effective upon the expiration of the 180-day period beginning June 12, 2002, see section 321(c) of Pub. L. 107–188, set out as a note under section 331 of this title.

EFFECTIVE DATE OF 1997 AMENDMENT

Amendment by sections 206(a), 209(a), 213(b), and 417 of Pub. L. 105–115 effective 90 days after Nov. 21, 1997, except as otherwise provided, see section 501 of Pub. L. 105–115, set out as a note under section 321 of this title.

EFFECTIVE DATE OF 1972 AMENDMENT

Section 5 of Pub. L. 92–387 provided that: "The amendments made by this Act [amending this section and sections 331 and 335 of this title and enacting provisions set out below] shall take effect on the first day of the sixth month beginning after the date of enactment of this Act [Aug. 16, 1972]."

EFFECTIVE DATE OF 1970 AMENDMENT

Amendment by Pub. L. 91–513 effective on first day of seventh calendar month that begins after Oct. 26, 1970, see section 704 of Pub. L. 91–513, set out as an Effective Date note under section 801 of this title.

EFFECTIVE DATE OF 1965 AMENDMENT

Amendment by Pub. L. 89–74 effective Feb. 1, 1966, subject to registration with Secretary of names, places of business, establishments, and other prescribed information prior to Feb. 1, 1966, see section 11 of Pub. L. 89–74, set out as a note under section 321 of this title.

SAVINGS PROVISION

Amendment by Pub. L. 91–513 not to affect or abate any prosecutions for any violation of law or any civil seizures or forfeitures and injunctive proceedings commenced prior to the effective date of such amendment, and all administrative proceedings pending before the Bureau of Narcotics and Dangerous Drugs [now the Drug Enforcement Administration] on Oct. 27, 1970, to be continued and brought to final determination in accord with laws and regulations in effect prior to Oct. 27, 1970, see section 702 of Pub. L. 91–513, set out as a note under section 321 of this title.

CONGRESSIONAL DECLARATION OF NEED FOR REGISTRATION AND INSPECTION OF DRUG ESTABLISHMENTS

Section 301 of Pub. L. 87–781 provided that: "The Congress hereby finds and declares that in order to make regulation of interstate commerce in drugs effective, it is necessary to provide for registration and inspection of all establishments in which drugs are manufactured, prepared, propagated, compounded, or processed; that the products of all such establishments are likely to enter the channels of interstate commerce and directly affect such commerce; and that the regulation of interstate commerce in drugs without provision for registration and inspection of establishments that may be engaged only in intrastate commerce in such drugs would discriminate against and depress interstate commerce in such drugs, and adversely burden, obstruct, and affect such interstate commerce."

DECLARATION OF POLICY OF DRUG LISTING ACT OF 1972

Section 2 of Pub. L. 92–387 provided that: "The Federal Government which is responsible for regulating drugs has no ready means of determining what drugs are actually being manufactured or packed by establishments registered under the Federal Food, Drug, and Cosmetic Act [this chapter] except by periodic inspection of such registered establishments. Knowledge of which particular drugs are being manufactured or packed by each registered establishment would substantially assist in the enforcement of Federal laws requiring that such drugs be pure, safe, effective, and properly labeled. Information on the discontinuance of a particular drug could serve to alleviate the burden of reviewing and implementing enforcement actions against drugs which, although commercially discontinued, remain active for regulatory purposes. Information on the type and number of different drugs being manufactured or packed by drug establishments could permit more effective and timely regulation by the agencies of the Federal Government responsible for regulating drugs, including identification of which drugs in interstate commerce are subject to section 505 or 507 [section 355 or 357 of this title], or to other provisions of the Federal Food, Drug, and Cosmetic Act."

REGISTRATION OF CERTAIN PERSONS OWNING OR OPERATING DRUG ESTABLISHMENTS PRIOR TO OCT. 10, 1962

Section 303 of Pub. L. 87–781 provided that any person who, on the day immediately preceding Oct. 10, 1962, owned or operated an establishment which manufactured or processed drugs, registered before the first day of the seventh month following October, 1962, would be deemed to be registered in accordance with subsec. (b) of this section for the calendar year 1962 and if registered within this period and effected in 1963, be deemed in compliance for that calendar year.

§ 360a. Clinical trial guidance for antibiotic drugs

(a) In general

Not later than 1 year after September 27, 2007, the Secretary shall issue guidance for the conduct of clinical trials with respect to antibiotic drugs, including antimicrobials to treat acute bacterial sinusitis, acute bacterial otitis media, and acute bacterial exacerbation of chronic bronchitis. Such guidance shall indicate the appropriate models and valid surrogate markers.

(b) Review

Not later than 5 years after September 27, 2007, the Secretary shall review and update the guidance described under subsection (a) to reflect developments in scientific and medical information and technology.

(June 25, 1938, ch. 675, § 511, as added Pub. L. 110–85, title IX, § 911, Sept. 27, 2007, 121 Stat. 951.)

PRIOR PROVISIONS

A prior section 360a, act June 25, 1938, ch. 675, § 511, as added July 15, 1965, Pub. L. 89–74, § 3(b), 79 Stat. 227; amended Oct. 24, 1968, Pub. L. 90–639, § 2(a), 82 Stat. 1361, regulated the manufacture, compounding, and processing of depressant and stimulant drugs and their sale, delivery, disposal, possession, and recordkeeping activities connected therewith, prior to repeal by Pub. L. 91–513, title II, §§ 701(a), 704, Oct. 27, 1970, 84 Stat. 1281, 1284, effective on the first day of the seventh calendar month that began after Oct. 26, 1970.

§ 360b. New animal drugs

(a) Unsafe new animal drugs and animal feed containing such drugs; conditions of safety; exemption of drugs for research; import tolerances

(1) A new animal drug shall, with respect to any particular use or intended use of such drug, be deemed unsafe for purposes of section 351(a)(5) of this title and section 342(a)(2)(C)(ii) of this title unless—

(A) there is in effect an approval of an application filed pursuant to subsection (b) of this section with respect to such use or intended use of such drug, and such drug, its labeling, and such use conform to such approved application;

(B) there is in effect a conditional approval of an application filed pursuant to section 360ccc of this title with respect to such use or intended use of such drug, and such drug, its labeling, and such use conform to such conditionally approved application; or

(C) there is in effect an index listing pursuant to section 360ccc–1 of this title with respect to such use or intended use of such drug in a minor species, and such drug, its labeling, and such use conform to such index listing.

A new animal drug shall also be deemed unsafe for such purposes in the event of removal from the establishment of a manufacturer, packer, or distributor of such drug for use in the manufacture of animal feed in any State unless at the time of such removal such manufacturer, packer, or distributor has an unrevoked written statement from the consignee of such drug, or notice from the Secretary, to the effect that, with respect to the use of such drug in animal feed, such consignee (i) holds a license issued under subsection (m) of this section and has in its possession current approved labeling for such drug in animal feed; or (ii) will, if the consignee is not a user of the drug, ship such drug only to a holder of a license issued under subsection (m) of this section.

(2) An animal feed bearing or containing a new animal drug shall, with respect to any particular use or intended use of such animal feed be deemed unsafe for purposes of section 351(a)(6) of this title unless—

(A) there is in effect—

(i) an approval of an application filed pursuant to subsection (b) of this section with respect to such drug, as used in such animal feed, and such animal feed and its labeling, distribution, holding, and use conform to such approved application;

(ii) a conditional approval of an application filed pursuant to section 360ccc of this title with respect to such drug, as used in such animal feed, and such animal feed and its labeling, distribution, holding, and use conform to such conditionally approved application; or

(iii) an index listing pursuant to section 360ccc–1 of this title with respect to such drug, as used in such animal feed, and such animal feed and its labeling, distribution, holding, and use conform to such index listing; and

(B) such animal feed is manufactured at a site for which there is in effect a license issued pursuant to subsection (m)(1) of this section to manufacture such animal feed.

(3) A new animal drug or an animal feed bearing or containing a new animal drug shall not be deemed unsafe for the purposes of section 351(a)(5) or (6) of this title if such article is for

investigational use and conforms to the terms of an exemption in effect with respect thereto under subsection (j) of this section.

(4)(A) Except as provided in subparagraph (B), if an approval of an application filed under subsection (b) of this section is in effect with respect to a particular use or intended use of a new animal drug, the drug shall not be deemed unsafe for the purposes of paragraph (1) and shall be exempt from the requirements of section 352(f) of this title with respect to a different use or intended use of the drug, other than a use in or on animal feed, if such use or intended use—

(i) is by or on the lawful written or oral order of a licensed veterinarian within the context of a veterinarian-client-patient relationship, as defined by the Secretary; and

(ii) is in compliance with regulations promulgated by the Secretary that establish the conditions for such different use or intended use.

The regulations promulgated by the Secretary under clause (ii) may prohibit particular uses of an animal drug and shall not permit such different use of an animal drug if the labeling of another animal drug that contains the same active ingredient and which is in the same dosage form and concentration provides for such different use.

(B) If the Secretary finds that there is a reasonable probability that a use of an animal drug authorized under subparagraph (A) may present a risk to the public health, the Secretary may—

(i) establish a safe level for a residue of an animal drug when it is used for such different use authorized by subparagraph (A); and

(ii) require the development of a practical, analytical method for the detection of residues of such drug above the safe level established under clause (i).

The use of an animal drug that results in residues exceeding a safe level established under clause (i) shall be considered an unsafe use of such drug under paragraph (1). Safe levels may be established under clause (i) either by regulation or order.

(C) The Secretary may by general regulation provide access to the records of veterinarians to ascertain any use or intended use authorized under subparagraph (A) that the Secretary has determined may present a risk to the public health.

(D) If the Secretary finds, after affording an opportunity for public comment, that a use of an animal drug authorized under subparagraph (A) presents a risk to the public health or that an analytical method required under subparagraph (B) has not been developed and submitted to the Secretary, the Secretary may, by order, prohibit any such use.

(5) If the approval of an application filed under section 355 of this title is in effect, the drug under such application shall not be deemed unsafe for purposes of paragraph (1) and shall be exempt from the requirements of section 352(f) of this title with respect to a use or intended use of the drug in animals if such use or intended use—

(A) is by or on the lawful written or oral order of a licensed veterinarian within the context of a veterinarian-client-patient relationship, as defined by the Secretary; and

(B) is in compliance with regulations promulgated by the Secretary that establish the conditions for the use or intended use of the drug in animals.

(6) For purposes of section 342(a)(2)(D)[1] of this title, a use or intended use of a new animal drug shall not be deemed unsafe under this section if the Secretary establishes a tolerance for such drug and any edible portion of any animal imported into the United States does not contain residues exceeding such tolerance. In establishing such tolerance, the Secretary shall rely on data sufficient to demonstrate that a proposed tolerance is safe based on similar food safety criteria used by the Secretary to establish tolerances for applications for new animal drugs filed under subsection (b)(1) of this section. The Secretary may consider and rely on data submitted by the drug manufacturer, including data submitted to appropriate regulatory authorities in any country where the new animal drug is lawfully used or data available from a relevant international organization, to the extent such data are not inconsistent with the criteria used by the Secretary to establish a tolerance for applications for new animal drugs filed under subsection (b)(1) of this section. For purposes of this paragraph, "relevant international organization" means the Codex Alimenterius[2] Commission or other international organization deemed appropriate by the Secretary. The Secretary may, under procedures specified by regulation, revoke a tolerance established under this paragraph if information demonstrates that the use of the new animal drug under actual use conditions results in food being imported into the United States with residues exceeding the tolerance or if scientific evidence shows the tolerance to be unsafe.

(b) Filing application for uses of new animal drug; contents; patent information; abbreviated application; presubmission conference

(1) Any person may file with the Secretary an application with respect to any intended use or uses of a new animal drug. Such person shall submit to the Secretary as a part of the application (A) full reports of investigations which have been made to show whether or not such drug is safe and effective for use; (B) a full list of the articles used as components of such drug; (C) a full statement of the composition of such drug; (D) a full description of the methods used in, and the facilities and controls used for, the manufacture, processing, and packing of such drug; (E) such samples of such drug and of the articles used as components thereof, of any animal feed for use in or on which such drug is intended, and of the edible portions or products (before or after slaughter) of animals to which such drug (directly or in or on animal feed) is intended to be administered, as the Secretary may require; (F) specimens of the labeling proposed to be used for such drug, or in case such drug is intended for use in animal feed, proposed labeling appropriate for such use, and specimens of

[1] See References in Text note below.

[2] So in original. Probably should be "Alimentarius".

the labeling for the drug to be manufactured, packed, or distributed by the applicant; (G) a description of practicable methods for determining the quantity, if any, of such drug in or on food, and any substance formed in or on food, because of its use; and (H) the proposed tolerance or withdrawal period or other use restrictions for such drug if any tolerance or withdrawal period or other use restrictions are required in order to assure that the proposed use of such drug will be safe. The applicant shall file with the application the patent number and the expiration date of any patent which claims the new animal drug for which the applicant filed the application or which claims a method of using such drug and with respect to which a claim of patent infringement could reasonably be asserted if a person not licensed by the owner engaged in the manufacture, use, or sale of the drug. If an application is filed under this subsection for a drug and a patent which claims such drug or a method of using such drug is issued after the filing date but before approval of the application, the applicant shall amend the application to include the information required by the preceding sentence. Upon approval of the application, the Secretary shall publish information submitted under the two preceding sentences.

(2) Any person may file with the Secretary an abbreviated application for the approval of a new animal drug. An abbreviated application shall contain the information required by subsection (n) of this section.

(3) Any person intending to file an application under paragraph (1), section 360ccc of this title, or a request for an investigational exemption under subsection (j) of this section shall be entitled to one or more conferences prior to such submission to reach an agreement acceptable to the Secretary establishing a submission or an investigational requirement, which may include a requirement for a field investigation. A decision establishing a submission or an investigational requirement shall bind the Secretary and the applicant or requestor unless (A) the Secretary and the applicant or requestor mutually agree to modify the requirement, or (B) the Secretary by written order determines that a substantiated scientific requirement essential to the determination of safety or effectiveness of the animal drug involved has appeared after the conference. No later than 25 calendar days after each such conference, the Secretary shall provide a written order setting forth a scientific justification specific to the animal drug and intended uses under consideration if the agreement referred to in the first sentence requires more than one field investigation as being essential to provide substantial evidence of effectiveness for the intended uses of the drug. Nothing in this paragraph shall be construed as compelling the Secretary to require a field investigation.

(c) Period for submission and approval of application; period for notice and expedition of hearing; period for issuance of order; abbreviated applications; withdrawal periods; effective date of approval; relationship to other applications; withdrawal or suspension of approval; bioequivalence; filing of additional patent information

(1) Within one hundred and eighty days after the filing of an application pursuant to subsection (b) of this section, or such additional period as may be agreed upon by the Secretary and the applicant, the Secretary shall either (A) issue an order approving the application if he then finds that none of the grounds for denying approval specified in subsection (d) of this section applies, or (B) give the applicant notice of an opportunity for a hearing before the Secretary under subsection (d) of this section on the question whether such application is approvable. If the applicant elects to accept the opportunity for a hearing by written request within thirty days after such notice, such hearing shall commence not more than ninety days after the expiration of such thirty days unless the Secretary and the applicant otherwise agree. Any such hearing shall thereafter be conducted on an expedited basis and the Secretary's order thereon shall be issued within ninety days after the date fixed by the Secretary for filing final briefs.

(2)(A) Subject to subparagraph (C), the Secretary shall approve an abbreviated application for a drug unless the Secretary finds—

(i) the methods used in, or the facilities and controls used for, the manufacture, processing, and packing of the drug are inadequate to assure and preserve its identity, strength, quality, and purity;

(ii) the conditions of use prescribed, recommended, or suggested in the proposed labeling are not reasonably certain to be followed in practice or, except as provided in subparagraph (B), information submitted with the application is insufficient to show that each of the proposed conditions of use or similar limitations (whether in the labeling or published pursuant to subsection (i) of this section) have been previously approved for the approved new animal drug referred to in the application;

(iii) information submitted with the application is insufficient to show that the active ingredients are the same as those of the approved new animal drug referred to in the application;

(iv)(I) if the application is for a drug whose active ingredients, route of administration, dosage form, strength, or use with other animal drugs in animal feed is the same as the active ingredients, route of administration, dosage form, strength, or use with other animal drugs in animal feed of the approved new animal drug referred to in the application, information submitted in the application is insufficient to show that the active ingredients, route of administration, dosage form, strength, or use with other animal drugs in animal feed is the same as that of the approved new animal drug, or

(II) if the application is for a drug whose active ingredients, route of administration, dosage form, strength, or use with other animal drugs in animal feed is different from that of the approved new animal drug referred to in the application, no petition to file an application for the drug with the different active ingredients, route of administration, dosage form, strength, or use with other animal drugs in animal feed was approved under subsection (n)(3) of this section;

(v) if the application was filed pursuant to the approval of a petition under subsection (n)(3) of this section, the application did not contain the information required by the Secretary respecting the active ingredients, route of administration, dosage form, strength, or use with other animal drugs in animal feed which is not the same;

(vi) information submitted in the application is insufficient to show that the drug is bioequivalent to the approved new animal drug referred to in the application, or if the application is filed under a petition approved pursuant to subsection (n)(3) of this section, information submitted in the application is insufficient to show that the active ingredients of the new animal drug are of the same pharmacological or therapeutic class as the pharmacological or therapeutic class of the approved new animal drug and that the new animal drug can be expected to have the same therapeutic effect as the approved new animal drug when used in accordance with the labeling;

(vii) information submitted in the application is insufficient to show that the labeling proposed for the drug is the same as the labeling approved for the approved new animal drug referred to in the application except for changes required because of differences approved under a petition filed under subsection (n)(3) of this section, because of a different withdrawal period, or because the drug and the approved new animal drug are produced or distributed by different manufacturers;

(viii) information submitted in the application or any other information available to the Secretary shows that (I) the inactive ingredients of the drug are unsafe for use under the conditions prescribed, recommended, or suggested in the labeling proposed for the drug, (II) the composition of the drug is unsafe under such conditions because of the type or quantity of inactive ingredients included or the manner in which the inactive ingredients are included, or (III) in the case of a drug for food producing animals, the inactive ingredients of the drug or its composition may be unsafe with respect to human food safety;

(ix) the approval under subsection (b)(1) of this section of the approved new animal drug referred to in the application filed under subsection (b)(2) of this section has been withdrawn or suspended for grounds described in paragraph (1) of subsection (e) of this section, the Secretary has published a notice of a hearing to withdraw approval of the approved new animal drug for such grounds, the approval under this paragraph of the new animal drug for which the application under subsection (b)(2) of this section was filed has been withdrawn or suspended under subparagraph (G) for such grounds, or the Secretary has determined that the approved new animal drug has been withdrawn from sale for safety or effectiveness reasons;

(x) the application does not meet any other requirement of subsection (n) of this section; or

(xi) the application contains an untrue statement of material fact.

(B) If the Secretary finds that a new animal drug for which an application is submitted under subsection (b)(2) of this section is bioequivalent to the approved new animal drug referred to in such application and that residues of the new animal drug are consistent with the tolerances established for such approved new animal drug but at a withdrawal period which is different than the withdrawal period approved for such approved new animal drug, the Secretary may establish, on the basis of information submitted, such different withdrawal period as the withdrawal period for the new animal drug for purposes of the approval of such application for such drug.

(C) Within 180 days of the initial receipt of an application under subsection (b)(2) of this section or within such additional period as may be agreed upon by the Secretary and the applicant, the Secretary shall approve or disapprove the application.

(D) The approval of an application filed under subsection (b)(2) of this section shall be made effective on the last applicable date determined under the following:

(i) If the applicant only made a certification described in clause (i) or (ii) of subsection (n)(1)(G) of this section or in both such clauses, the approval may be made effective immediately.

(ii) If the applicant made a certification described in clause (iii) of subsection (n)(1)(G) of this section, the approval may be made effective on the date certified under clause (iii).

(iii) If the applicant made a certification described in clause (iv) of subsection (n)(1)(G) of this section, the approval shall be made effective immediately unless an action is brought for infringement of a patent which is the subject of the certification before the expiration of 45 days from the date the notice provided under subsection (n)(2)(B)(i) of this section is received. If such an action is brought before the expiration of such days, the approval shall be made effective upon the expiration of the 30 month period beginning on the date of the receipt of the notice provided under subsection (n)(2)(B) of this section or such shorter or longer period as the court may order because either party to the action failed to reasonably cooperate in expediting the action, except that if before the expiration of such period—

(I) the court decides that such patent is invalid or not infringed, the approval shall be made effective on the date of the court decision,

(II) the court decides that such patent has been infringed, the approval shall be made effective on such date as the court orders under section 271(e)(4)(A) of title 35, or

(III) the court grants a preliminary injunction prohibiting the applicant from engaging in the commercial manufacture or sale of the drug until the court decides the issues of patent validity and infringement and if the court decides that such patent is invalid or not infringed, the approval shall be made effective on the date of such court decision.

In such an action, each of the parties shall reasonably cooperate in expediting the action. Until the expiration of 45 days from the date the notice made under subsection (n)(2)(B) of this section is received, no action may be brought under section 2201 of title 28 for a declaratory judgment with respect to the patent. Any action brought under section 2201 of title 28 shall be brought in the judicial district where the defendant has its principal place of business or a regular and established place of business.

(iv) If the application contains a certification described in clause (iv) of subsection (n)(1)(G) of this section and is for a drug for which a previous application has been filed under this subsection containing such a certification, the application shall be made effective not earlier than 180 days after—

(I) the date the Secretary receives notice from the applicant under the previous application of the first commercial marketing of the drug under the previous application, or

(II) the date of a decision of a court in an action described in subclause (III)[3] holding the patent which is the subject of the certification to be invalid or not infringed,

whichever is earlier.

(E) If the Secretary decides to disapprove an application, the Secretary shall give the applicant notice of an opportunity for a hearing before the Secretary on the question of whether such application is approvable. If the applicant elects to accept the opportunity for hearing by written request within 30 days after such notice, such hearing shall commence not more than 90 days after the expiration of such 30 days unless the Secretary and the applicant otherwise agree. Any such hearing shall thereafter be conducted on an expedited basis and the Secretary's order thereon shall be issued within 90 days after the date fixed by the Secretary for filing final briefs.

(F)(i) If an application submitted under subsection (b)(1) of this section for a drug, no active ingredient (including any ester or salt of the active ingredient) of which has been approved in any other application under subsection (b)(1) of this section, is approved after November 16, 1988, no application may be submitted under subsection (b)(2) of this section which refers to the drug for which the subsection (b)(1) application was submitted before the expiration of 5 years from the date of the approval of the application under subsection (b)(1) of this section, except that such an application may be submitted under subsection (b)(2) of this section after the expiration of 4 years from the date of the approval of the subsection (b)(1) application if it contains a certification of patent invalidity or noninfringement described in clause (iv) of subsection (n)(1)(G) of this section. The approval of such an application shall be made effective in accordance with subparagraph (B) except that, if an action for patent infringement is commenced during the one-year period beginning 48 months after the date of the approval of the subsection (b) application, the 30 month period referred to in subparagraph (D)(iii) shall be extended by such amount of time (if any) which is required for seven and one-half years to have elapsed from the date of approval of the subsection (b) application.

(ii) If an application submitted under subsection (b)(1) of this section for a drug, which includes an active ingredient (including any ester or salt of the active ingredient) that has been approved in another application approved under such subsection, is approved after November 16, 1988, and if such application contains substantial evidence of the effectiveness of the drug involved, any studies of animal safety, or, in the case of food producing animals, human food safety studies (other than bioequivalence studies or residue depletion studies, except residue depletion studies for minor uses or minor species) required for the approval of the application and conducted or sponsored by the applicant, the Secretary may not make the approval of an application submitted under subsection (b)(2) of this section for the conditions of approval of such drug in the subsection (b)(1) application effective before the expiration of 3 years from the date of the approval of the application under subsection (b)(1) of this section for such drug.

(iii) If a supplement to an application approved under subsection (b)(1) of this section is approved after November 16, 1988, and the supplement contains substantial evidence of the effectiveness of the drug involved, any studies of animal safety, or, in the case of food producing animals, human food safety studies (other than bioequivalence studies or residue depletion studies, except residue depletion studies for minor uses or minor species) required for the approval of the supplement and conducted or sponsored by the person submitting the supplement, the Secretary may not make the approval of an application submitted under subsection (b)(2) of this section for a change approved in the supplement effective before the expiration of 3 years from the date of the approval of the supplement.

(iv) An applicant under subsection (b)(1) of this section who comes within the provisions of clause (i) of this subparagraph as a result of an application which seeks approval for a use solely in non-food producing animals, may elect, within 10 days of receiving such approval, to waive clause (i) of this subparagraph, in which event the limitation on approval of applications submitted under subsection (b)(2) of this section set forth in clause (ii) of this subparagraph shall be applicable to the subsection (b)(1) application.

(v) If an application (including any supplement to a new animal drug application) submitted under subsection (b)(1) of this section for a new animal drug for a food-producing animal use, which includes an active ingredient (including any ester or salt of the active ingredient) which has been the subject of a waiver under clause (iv) is approved after November 16, 1988, and if the application contains substantial evidence of the effectiveness of the drug involved, any studies of animal safety, or human food safety studies (other than bioequivalence stud-

[3] So in original. Probably should be "clause (iii)(III)".

ies or residue depletion studies, except residue depletion studies for minor uses or minor species) required for the new approval of the application and conducted or sponsored by the applicant, the Secretary may not make the approval of an application (including any supplement to such application) submitted under subsection (b)(2) of this section for the new conditions of approval of such drug in the subsection (b)(1) application effective before the expiration of five years from the date of approval of the application under subsection (b)(1) of this section for such drug. The provisions of this paragraph shall apply only to the first approval for a food-producing animal use for the same applicant after the waiver under clause (iv).

(G) If an approved application submitted under subsection (b)(2) of this section for a new animal drug refers to a drug the approval of which was withdrawn or suspended for grounds described in paragraph (1) or (2) of subsection (e) of this section or was withdrawn or suspended under this subparagraph or which, as determined by the Secretary, has been withdrawn from sale for safety or effectiveness reasons, the approval of the drug under this paragraph shall be withdrawn or suspended—

(i) for the same period as the withdrawal or suspension under subsection (e) of this section or this subparagraph, or

(ii) if the approved new animal drug has been withdrawn from sale, for the period of withdrawal from sale or, if earlier, the period ending on the date the Secretary determines that the withdrawal from sale is not for safety or effectiveness reasons.

(H) For purposes of this paragraph:

(i) The term "bioequivalence" means the rate and extent to which the active ingredient or therapeutic ingredient is absorbed from a new animal drug and becomes available at the site of drug action.

(ii) A new animal drug shall be considered to be bioequivalent to the approved new animal drug referred to in its application under subsection (n) of this section if—

(I) the rate and extent of absorption of the drug do not show a significant difference from the rate and extent of absorption of the approved new animal drug referred to in the application when administered at the same dose of the active ingredient under similar experimental conditions in either a single dose or multiple doses;

(II) the extent of absorption of the drug does not show a significant difference from the extent of absorption of the approved new animal drug referred to in the application when administered at the same dose of the active ingredient under similar experimental conditions in either a single dose or multiple doses and the difference from the approved new animal drug in the rate of absorption of the drug is intentional, is reflected in its proposed labeling, is not essential to the attainment of effective drug concentrations in use, and is considered scientifically insignificant for the drug in attaining the intended purposes of its use and preserving human food safety; or

(III) in any case in which the Secretary determines that the measurement of the rate and extent of absorption or excretion of the new animal drug in biological fluids is inappropriate or impractical, an appropriate acute pharmacological effects test or other test of the new animal drug and, when deemed scientifically necessary, of the approved new animal drug referred to in the application in the species to be tested or in an appropriate animal model does not show a significant difference between the new animal drug and such approved new animal drug when administered at the same dose under similar experimental conditions.

If the approved new animal drug referred to in the application for a new animal drug under subsection (n) of this section is approved for use in more than one animal species, the bioequivalency information described in subclauses (I), (II), and (III) shall be obtained for one species, or if the Secretary deems appropriate based on scientific principles, shall be obtained for more than one species. The Secretary may prescribe the dose to be used in determining bioequivalency under subclause (I), (II), or (III). To assure that the residues of the new animal drug will be consistent with the established tolerances for the approved new animal drug referred to in the application under subsection (b)(2) of this section upon the expiration of the withdrawal period contained in the application for the new animal drug, the Secretary shall require bioequivalency data or residue depletion studies of the new animal drug or such other data or studies as the Secretary considers appropriate based on scientific principles. If the Secretary requires one or more residue studies under the preceding sentence, the Secretary may not require that the assay methodology used to determine the withdrawal period of the new animal drug be more rigorous than the methodology used to determine the withdrawal period for the approved new animal drug referred to in the application. If such studies are required and if the approved new animal drug, referred to in the application for the new animal drug for which such studies are required, is approved for use in more than one animal species, such studies shall be conducted for one species, or if the Secretary deems appropriate based on scientific principles, shall be conducted for more than one species.

(3) If the patent information described in subsection (b)(1) of this section could not be filed with the submission of an application under subsection (b)(1) of this section because the application was filed before the patent information was required under subsection (b)(1) of this section or a patent was issued after the application was approved under such subsection, the holder of an approved application shall file with the Secretary the patent number and the expiration date of any patent which claims the new animal drug for which the application was filed or which claims a method of using such drug and with respect to which a claim of patent infringement could reasonably be asserted if a person not licensed by the owner engaged in the manufacture, use, or sale of the drug. If the holder of an approved application could not file patent in-

formation under subsection (b)(1) of this section because it was not required at the time the application was approved, the holder shall file such information under this subsection not later than 30 days after November 16, 1988, and if the holder of an approved application could not file patent information under subsection (b)(1) of this section because no patent had been issued when an application was filed or approved, the holder shall file such information under this subsection not later than 30 days after the date the patent involved is issued. Upon the submission of patent information under this subsection, the Secretary shall publish it.

(4) A drug manufactured in a pilot or other small facility may be used to demonstrate the safety and effectiveness of the drug and to obtain approval for the drug prior to manufacture of the drug in a larger facility, unless the Secretary makes a determination that a full scale production facility is necessary to ensure the safety or effectiveness of the drug.

(d) Grounds for refusing application; approval of application; factors; "substantial evidence" defined; combination drugs

(1) If the Secretary finds, after due notice to the applicant in accordance with subsection (c) of this section and giving him an opportunity for a hearing, in accordance with said subsection, that—

(A) the investigations, reports of which are required to be submitted to the Secretary pursuant to subsection (b) of this section, do not include adequate tests by all methods reasonably applicable to show whether or not such drug is safe for use under the conditions prescribed, recommended, or suggested in the proposed labeling thereof;

(B) the results of such tests show that such drug is unsafe for use under such conditions or do not show that such drug is safe for use under such conditions;

(C) the methods used in, and the facilities and controls used for, the manufacture, processing, and packing of such drug are inadequate to preserve its identity, strength, quality, and purity;

(D) upon the basis of the information submitted to him as part of the application, or upon the basis of any other information before him with respect to such drug, he has insufficient information to determine whether such drug is safe for use under such conditions;

(E) evaluated on the basis of the information submitted to him as part of the application and any other information before him with respect to such drug, there is a lack of substantial evidence that the drug will have the effect it purports or is represented to have under the conditions of use prescribed, recommended, or suggested in the proposed labeling thereof;

(F) upon the basis of information submitted to the Secretary as part of the application or any other information before the Secretary with respect to such drug, any use prescribed, recommended, or suggested in labeling proposed for such drug will result in a residue of such drug in excess of a tolerance found by the Secretary to be safe for such drug;

(G) the application failed to contain the patent information prescribed by subsection (b)(1) of this section;

(H) based on a fair evaluation of all material facts, such labeling is false or misleading in any particular; or

(I) such drug induces cancer when ingested by man or animal or, after tests which are appropriate for the evaluation of the safety of such drug, induces cancer in man or animal, except that the foregoing provisions of this subparagraph shall not apply with respect to such drug if the Secretary finds that, under the conditions of use specified in proposed labeling and reasonably certain to be followed in practice (i) such drug will not adversely affect the animals for which it is intended, and (ii) no residue of such drug will be found (by methods of examination prescribed or approved by the Secretary by regulations, which regulations shall not be subject to subsections (c), (d), and (h) of this section), in any edible portion of such animals after slaughter or in any food yielded by or derived from the living animals;

he shall issue an order refusing to approve the application. If, after such notice and opportunity for hearings, the Secretary finds that subparagraphs (A) through (I) do not apply, he shall issue an order approving the application.

(2) In determining whether such drug is safe for use under the conditions prescribed, recommended, or suggested in the proposed labeling thereof, the Secretary shall consider, among other relevant factors, (A) the probable consumption of such drug and of any substance formed in or on food because of the use of such drug, (B) the cumulative effect on man or animal of such drug, taking into account any chemically or pharmacologically related substance, (C) safety factors which in the opinion of experts, qualified by scientific training and experience to evaluate the safety of such drugs, are appropriate for the use of animal experimentation data, and (D) whether the conditions of use prescribed, recommended, or suggested in the proposed labeling are reasonably certain to be followed in practice. Any order issued under this subsection refusing to approve an application shall state the findings upon which it is based.

(3) As used in this section, the term "substantial evidence" means evidence consisting of one or more adequate and well controlled investigations, such as—

(A) a study in a target species;

(B) a study in laboratory animals;

(C) any field investigation that may be required under this section and that meets the requirements of subsection (b)(3) of this section if a presubmission conference is requested by the applicant;

(D) a bioequivalence study; or

(E) an in vitro study;

by experts qualified by scientific training and experience to evaluate the effectiveness of the drug involved, on the basis of which it could fairly and reasonably be concluded by such experts that the drug will have the effect it purports or is represented to have under the conditions of use prescribed, recommended, or suggested in the labeling or proposed labeling thereof.

(4) In a case in which an animal drug contains more than one active ingredient, or the labeling of the drug prescribes, recommends, or suggests use of the drug in combination with one or more other animal drugs, and the active ingredients or drugs intended for use in the combination have previously been separately approved pursuant to an application submitted under subsection (b)(1) of this section for particular uses and conditions of use for which they are intended for use in the combination—

(A) the Secretary shall not issue an order under paragraph (1)(A), (1)(B), or (1)(D) refusing to approve the application for such combination on human food safety grounds unless the Secretary finds that the application fails to establish that—

(i) none of the active ingredients or drugs intended for use in the combination, respectively, at the longest withdrawal time of any of the active ingredients or drugs in the combination, respectively, exceeds its established tolerance; or

(ii) none of the active ingredients or drugs in the combination interferes with the methods of analysis for another of the active ingredients or drugs in the combination, respectively;

(B) the Secretary shall not issue an order under paragraph (1)(A), (1)(B), or (1)(D) refusing to approve the application for such combination on target animal safety grounds unless the Secretary finds that—

(i)(I) there is a substantiated scientific issue, specific to one or more of the active ingredients or animal drugs in the combination, that cannot adequately be evaluated based on information contained in the application for the combination (including any investigations, studies, or tests for which the applicant has a right of reference or use from the person by or for whom the investigations, studies, or tests were conducted); or

(II) there is a scientific issue raised by target animal observations contained in studies submitted to the Secretary as part of the application; and

(ii) based on the Secretary's evaluation of the information contained in the application with respect to the issues identified in clauses (i)(I) and (II), paragraph (1)(A), (B), or (D) apply;

(C) except in the case of a combination that contains a nontopical antibacterial ingredient or animal drug, the Secretary shall not issue an order under paragraph (1)(E) refusing to approve an application for a combination animal drug intended for use other than in animal feed or drinking water unless the Secretary finds that the application fails to demonstrate that—

(i) there is substantial evidence that any active ingredient or animal drug intended only for the same use as another active ingredient or animal drug in the combination makes a contribution to labeled effectiveness;

(ii) each active ingredient or animal drug intended for at least one use that is different from all other active ingredients or animal drugs used in the combination provides appropriate concurrent use for the intended target population; or

(iii) where based on scientific information the Secretary has reason to believe the active ingredients or animal drugs may be physically incompatible or have disparate dosing regimens, such active ingredients or animal drugs are physically compatible or do not have disparate dosing regimens; and

(D) the Secretary shall not issue an order under paragraph (1)(E) refusing to approve an application for a combination animal drug intended for use in animal feed or drinking water unless the Secretary finds that the application fails to demonstrate that—

(i) there is substantial evidence that any active ingredient or animal drug intended only for the same use as another active ingredient or animal drug in the combination makes a contribution to the labeled effectiveness;

(ii) each of the active ingredients or animal drugs intended for at least one use that is different from all other active ingredients or animal drugs used in the combination provides appropriate concurrent use for the intended target population;

(iii) where a combination contains more than one nontopical antibacterial ingredient or animal drug, there is substantial evidence that each of the nontopical antibacterial ingredients or animal drugs makes a contribution to the labeled effectiveness, except that for purposes of this clause, antibacterial ingredient or animal drug does not include the ionophore or arsenical classes of animal drugs; or

(iv) where based on scientific information the Secretary has reason to believe the active ingredients or animal drugs intended for use in drinking water may be physically incompatible, such active ingredients or animal drugs intended for use in drinking water are physically compatible.

(5) In reviewing an application that proposes a change to add an intended use for a minor use or a minor species to an approved new animal drug application, the Secretary shall reevaluate only the relevant information in the approved application to determine whether the application for the minor use or minor species can be approved. A decision to approve the application for the minor use or minor species is not, implicitly or explicitly, a reaffirmation of the approval of the original application.

(e) Withdrawal of approval; grounds; immediate suspension upon finding imminent hazard to health of man or animals

(1) The Secretary shall, after due notice and opportunity for hearing to the applicant, issue an order withdrawing approval of an application filed pursuant to subsection (b) of this section with respect to any new animal drug if the Secretary finds—

(A) that experience or scientific data show that such drug is unsafe for use under the conditions of use upon the basis of which the application was approved or the condition of use authorized under subsection (a)(4)(A) of this section;

(B) that new evidence not contained in such application or not available to the Secretary until after such application was approved, or tests by new methods, or tests by methods not deemed reasonably applicable when such application was approved, evaluated together with the evidence available to the Secretary when the application was approved, shows that such drug is not shown to be safe for use under the conditions of use upon the basis of which the application was approved or that subparagraph (I) of paragraph (1) of subsection (d) of this section applies to such drug;

(C) on the basis of new information before him with respect to such drug, evaluated together with the evidence available to him when the application was approved, that there is a lack of substantial evidence that such drug will have the effect it purports or is represented to have under the conditions of use prescribed, recommended, or suggested in the labeling thereof;

(D) the patent information prescribed by subsection (c)(3) of this section was not filed within 30 days after the receipt of written notice from the Secretary specifying the failure to file such information;

(E) that the application contains any untrue statement of a material fact; or

(F) that the applicant has made any changes from the standpoint of safety or effectiveness beyond the variations provided for in the application unless he has supplemented the application by filing with the Secretary adequate information respecting all such changes and unless there is in effect an approval of the supplemental application. The supplemental application shall be treated in the same manner as the original application.

If the Secretary (or in his absence the officer acting as Secretary) finds that there is an imminent hazard to the health of man or of the animals for which such drug is intended, he may suspend the approval of such application immediately, and give the applicant prompt notice of his action and afford the applicant the opportunity for an expedited hearing under this subsection; but the authority conferred by this sentence to suspend the approval of an application shall not be delegated.

(2) The Secretary may also, after due notice and opportunity for hearing to the applicant, issue an order withdrawing the approval of an application with respect to any new animal drug under this section if the Secretary finds—

(A) that the applicant has failed to establish a system for maintaining required records, or has repeatedly or deliberately failed to maintain such records or to make required reports in accordance with a regulation or order under subsection (l) of this section, or the applicant has refused to permit access to, or copying or verification of, such records as required by paragraph (2) of such subsection;

(B) that on the basis of new information before him, evaluated together with the evidence before him when the application was approved, the methods used in, or the facilities and controls used for, the manufacture, processing, and packing of such drug are inadequate to assure and preserve its identity, strength, quality, and purity and were not made adequate within a reasonable time after receipt of written notice from the Secretary specifying the matter complained of; or

(C) that on the basis of new information before him, evaluated together with the evidence before him when the application was approved, the labeling of such drug, based on a fair evaluation of all material facts, is false or misleading in any particular and was not corrected within a reasonable time after receipt of written notice from the Secretary specifying the matter complained of.

(3) Any order under this subsection shall state the findings upon which it is based.

(f) Revocation of order refusing, withdrawing or suspending approval of application

Whenever the Secretary finds that the facts so require, he shall revoke any previous order under subsection (d), (e), or (m) of this section, or section 360ccc(c), (d), or (e) of this title refusing, withdrawing, or suspending approval of an application and shall approve such application or reinstate such approval, as may be appropriate.

(g) Service of orders

Orders of the Secretary issued under this section, or section 360ccc of this title (other than orders issuing, amending, or repealing regulations) shall be served (1) in person by any officer or employee of the department designated by the Secretary or (2) by mailing the order by registered mail or by certified mail addressed to the applicant or respondent at his last known address in the records of the Secretary.

(h) Appeal from order

An appeal may be taken by the applicant from an order of the Secretary refusing or withdrawing approval of an application filed under subsection (b) or (m) of this section. The provisions of subsection (h) of section 355 of this title shall govern any such appeal.

(i) Publication in Federal Register; effective date and revocation or suspension of regulation

When a new animal drug application filed pursuant to subsection (b) of this section or section 360ccc of this title is approved, the Secretary shall by notice, which upon publication shall be effective as a regulation, publish in the Federal Register the name and address of the applicant and the conditions and indications of use of the new animal drug covered by such application, including any tolerance and withdrawal period or other use restrictions and, if such new animal drug is intended for use in animal feed, appropriate purposes and conditions of use (including special labeling requirements and any requirement that an animal feed bearing or containing the new animal drug be limited to use under the professional supervision of a licensed veterinarian) applicable to any animal feed for use in which such drug is approved, and such other information, upon the basis of which such application was approved, as the Secretary deems necessary to assure the safe and effective use of such drug. Upon withdrawal of approval of such new animal drug application or upon its suspension or upon failure to renew a conditional approval under section 360ccc of this title, the Secretary shall forthwith revoke or suspend, as the case may be, the regulation published pursuant to this subsection (i) insofar as it is based on the approval of such application.

(j) Exemption of drugs for research; discretionary and mandatory conditions

To the extent consistent with the public health, the Secretary shall promulgate regulations for exempting from the operation of this section new animal drugs, and animal feeds bearing or containing new animal drugs, intended solely for investigational use by experts qualified by scientific training and experience to investigate the safety and effectiveness of animal drugs. Such regulations may, in the discretion of the Secretary, among other conditions relating to the protection of the public health, provide for conditioning such exemption upon the establishment and maintenance of such records, and the making of such reports to the Secretary, by the manufacturer or the sponsor of the investigation of such article, of data (including but not limited to analytical reports by investigators) obtained as a result of such investigational use of such article, as the Secretary finds will enable him to evaluate the safety and effectiveness of such article in the event of the filing of an application pursuant to this section. Such regulations, among other things, shall set forth the conditions (if any) upon which animals treated with such articles, and any products of such animals (before or after slaughter), may be marketed for food use.

(k) Food containing new animal drug considered unadulterated while approval of application for such drug is effective

While approval of an application for a new animal drug is effective, a food shall not, by reason of bearing or containing such drug or any substance formed in or on the food because of its use in accordance with such application (including the conditions and indications of use prescribed pursuant to subsection (i) of this section), be considered adulterated within the meaning of clause (1) of section 342(a) of this title.

(*l*) Records and reports; required information; regulations and orders; examination of data; access to records

(1) In the case of any new animal drug for which an approval of an application filed pursuant to subsection (b) of this section or section 360ccc of this title is in effect, the applicant shall establish and maintain such records, and make such reports to the Secretary, of data relating to experience, including experience with uses authorized under subsection (a)(4)(A) of this section, and other data or information, received or otherwise obtained by such applicant with respect to such drug, or with respect to animal feeds bearing or containing such drug, as the Secretary may by general regulation, or by order with respect to such application, prescribe on the basis of a finding that such records and reports are necessary in order to enable the Secretary to determine, or facilitate a determination, whether there is or may be ground for invoking subsection (e) or subsection (m)(4) of this section. Such regulation or order shall provide, where the Secretary deems it to be appropriate, for the examination, upon request, by the persons to whom such regulation or order is applicable, of similar information received or otherwise obtained by the Secretary.

(2) Every person required under this subsection to maintain records, and every person in charge or custody thereof, shall, upon request of an officer or employee designated by the Secretary, permit such officer or employee at all reasonable times to have access to and copy and verify such records.

(3)(A) In the case of each new animal drug described in paragraph (1) that contains an antimicrobial active ingredient, the sponsor of the drug shall submit an annual report to the Secretary on the amount of each antimicrobial active ingredient in the drug that is sold or distributed for use in food-producing animals, including information on any distributor-labeled product.

(B) Each report under this paragraph shall specify the amount of each antimicrobial active ingredient—

(i) by container size, strength, and dosage form;

(ii) by quantities distributed domestically and quantities exported; and

(iii) by dosage form, including, for each such dosage form, a listing of the target animals, indications, and production classes that are specified on the approved label of the product.

(C) Each report under this paragraph shall—

(i) be submitted not later than March 31 each year;

(ii) cover the period of the preceding calendar year; and

(iii) include separate information for each month of such calendar year.

(D) The Secretary may share information reported under this paragraph with the Antimicrobial Resistance Task Force established under section 247d–5 of title 42.

(E) The Secretary shall make summaries of the information reported under this paragraph publicly available, except that—

(i) the summary data shall be reported by antimicrobial class, and no class with fewer than 3 distinct sponsors of approved applications shall be independently reported; and

(ii) the data shall be reported in a manner consistent with protecting both national security and confidential business information.

(m) Feed mill licenses

(1) Any person may file with the Secretary an application for a license to manufacture animal feeds bearing or containing new animal drugs. Such person shall submit to the Secretary as part of the application (A) a full statement of the business name and address of the specific facility at which the manufacturing is to take place and the facility's registration number, (B) the name and signature of the responsible individual or individuals for that facility, (C) a certification that the animal feeds bearing or con-

taining new animal drugs are manufactured and labeled in accordance with the applicable regulations published pursuant to subsection (i) of this section or for indexed new animal drugs in accordance with the index listing published pursuant to section 360ccc–1(e)(2) of this title and the labeling requirements set forth in section 360ccc–1(h) of this title, and (D) a certification that the methods used in, and the facilities and controls used for, manufacturing, processing, packaging, and holding such animal feeds are in conformity with current good manufacturing practice as described in section 351(a)(2)(B) of this title.

(2) Within 90 days after the filing of an application pursuant to paragraph (1), or such additional period as may be agreed upon by the Secretary and the applicant, the Secretary shall (A) issue an order approving the application if the Secretary then finds that none of the grounds for denying approval specified in paragraph (3) applies, or (B) give the applicant notice of an opportunity for a hearing before the Secretary under paragraph (3) on the question whether such application is approvable. The procedure governing such a hearing shall be the procedure set forth in the last two sentences of subsection (c)(1) of this section.

(3) If the Secretary, after due notice to the applicant in accordance with paragraph (2) and giving the applicant an opportunity for a hearing in accordance with such paragraph, finds, on the basis of information submitted to the Secretary as part of the application, on the basis of a preapproval inspection, or on the basis of any other information before the Secretary—

(A) that the application is incomplete, false, or misleading in any particular;

(B) that the methods used in, and the facilities and controls used for, the manufacture, processing, and packing of such animal feed are inadequate to preserve the identity, strength, quality, and purity of the new animal drug therein; or

(C) that the facility manufactures animal feeds bearing or containing new animal drugs in a manner that does not accord with the specifications for manufacture or labels animal feeds bearing or containing new animal drugs in a manner that does not accord with the conditions or indications of use that are published pursuant to subsection (i) of this section or an index listing pursuant to section 360ccc–1(e) of this title,

the Secretary shall issue an order refusing to approve the application. If, after such notice and opportunity for hearing, the Secretary finds that subparagraphs (A) through (C) do not apply, the Secretary shall issue an order approving the application. An order under this subsection approving an application for a license to manufacture animal feeds bearing or containing new animal drugs shall permit a facility to manufacture only those animal feeds bearing or containing new animal drugs for which there are in effect regulations pursuant to subsection (i) of this section or an index listing pursuant to section 360ccc–1(e) of this title relating to the use of such drugs in or on such animal feed.

(4)(A) The Secretary shall, after due notice and opportunity for hearing to the applicant, revoke a license to manufacture animal feeds bearing or containing new animal drugs under this subsection if the Secretary finds—

(i) that the application for such license contains any untrue statement of a material fact; or

(ii) that the applicant has made changes that would cause the application to contain any untrue statements of material fact or that would affect the safety or effectiveness of the animal feeds manufactured at the facility unless the applicant has supplemented the application by filing with the Secretary adequate information respecting all such changes and unless there is in effect an approval of the supplemental application.

If the Secretary (or in the Secretary's absence the officer acting as the Secretary) finds that there is an imminent hazard to the health of humans or of the animals for which such animal feed is intended, the Secretary may suspend the license immediately, and give the applicant prompt notice of the action and afford the applicant the opportunity for an expedited hearing under this subsection; but the authority conferred by this sentence shall not be delegated.

(B) The Secretary may also, after due notice and opportunity for hearing to the applicant, revoke a license to manufacture animal feed under this subsection if the Secretary finds—

(i) that the applicant has failed to establish a system for maintaining required records, or has repeatedly or deliberately failed to maintain such records or to make required reports in accordance with a regulation or order under paragraph (5)(A) of this subsection or section 354(a)(3)(A) of this title, or the applicant has refused to permit access to, or copying or verification of, such records as required by subparagraph (B) of such paragraph or section 354(a)(3)(B) of this title;

(ii) that on the basis of new information before the Secretary, evaluated together with the evidence before the Secretary when such license was issued, the methods used in, or the facilities and controls used for, the manufacture, processing, packing, and holding of such animal feed are inadequate to assure and preserve the identity, strength, quality, and purity of the new animal drug therein, and were not made adequate within a reasonable time after receipt of written notice from the Secretary, specifying the matter complained of;

(iii) that on the basis of new information before the Secretary, evaluated together with the evidence before the Secretary when such license was issued, the labeling of any animal feeds, based on a fair evaluation of all material facts, is false or misleading in any particular and was not corrected within a reasonable time after receipt of written notice from the Secretary specifying the matter complained of; or

(iv) that on the basis of new information before the Secretary, evaluated together with the evidence before the Secretary when such license was issued, the facility has manufactured, processed, packed, or held animal feed bearing or containing a new animal drug adulterated under section 351(a)(6) of this title and the facility did not discontinue the manufacture, processing, packing, or holding of such animal feed within a reasonable time after receipt of written notice from the Secretary specifying the matter complained of.

(C) The Secretary may also revoke a license to manufacture animal feeds under this subsection if an applicant gives notice to the Secretary of intention to discontinue the manufacture of all animal feed covered under this subsection and waives an opportunity for a hearing on the matter.

(D) Any order under this paragraph shall state the findings upon which it is based.

(5) When a license to manufacture animal feeds bearing or containing new animal drugs has been issued—

(A) the applicant shall establish and maintain such records, and make such reports to the Secretary, or (at the option of the Secretary) to the appropriate person or persons holding an approved application filed under subsection (b) of this section, as the Secretary may by general regulation, or by order with respect to such application, prescribe on the basis of a finding that such records and reports are necessary in order to enable the Secretary to determine, or facilitate a determination, whether there is or may be ground for invoking subsection (e) of this section or paragraph (4); and

(B) every person required under this subsection to maintain records, and every person in charge or custody thereof, shall, upon request of an officer or employee designated by the Secretary, permit such officer or employee at all reasonable times to have access to and copy and verify such records.

(6) To the extent consistent with the public health, the Secretary may promulgate regulations for exempting from the operation of this subsection facilities that manufacture, process, pack, or hold animal feeds bearing or containing new animal drugs.

(n) Abbreviated applications for new animal drugs; contents, filing, etc.; lists of approved drugs

(1) An abbreviated application for a new animal drug shall contain—

(A)(i) except as provided in clause (ii), information to show that the conditions of use or similar limitations (whether in the labeling or published pursuant to subsection (i) of this section) prescribed, recommended, or suggested in the labeling proposed for the new animal drug have been previously approved for a new animal drug listed under paragraph (4) (hereinafter in this subsection referred to as an "approved new animal drug"), and

(ii) information to show that the withdrawal period at which residues of the new animal drug will be consistent with the tolerances established for the approved new animal drug is the same as the withdrawal period previously established for the approved new animal drug or, if the withdrawal period is proposed to be different, information showing that the residues of the new animal drug at the proposed different withdrawal period will be consistent with the tolerances established for the approved new animal drug;

(B)(i) information to show that the active ingredients of the new animal drug are the same as those of the approved new animal drug, and

(ii) if the approved new animal drug has more than one active ingredient, and if one of the active ingredients of the new animal drug is different from one of the active ingredients of the approved new animal drug and the application is filed pursuant to the approval of a petition filed under paragraph (3)—

(I) information to show that the other active ingredients of the new animal drug are the same as the active ingredients of the approved new animal drug,

(II) information to show either that the different active ingredient is an active ingredient of another approved new animal drug or of an animal drug which does not meet the requirements of section 321(v) of this title, and

(III) such other information respecting the different active ingredients as the Secretary may require;

(C)(i) if the approved new animal drug is permitted to be used with one or more animal drugs in animal feed, information to show that the proposed uses of the new animal drug with other animal drugs in animal feed are the same as the uses of the approved new animal drug, and

(ii) if the approved new animal drug is permitted to be used with one or more other animal drugs in animal feed, and one of the other animal drugs proposed for use with the new animal drug in animal feed is different from one of the other animal drugs permitted to be used in animal feed with the approved new animal drug, and the application is filed pursuant to the approval of a petition filed under paragraph (3)—

(I) information to show either that the different animal drug proposed for use with the approved new animal drug in animal feed is an approved new animal drug permitted to be used in animal feed or does not meet the requirements of section 321(v) of this title when used with another animal drug in animal feed,

(II) information to show that other animal drugs proposed for use with the new animal drug in animal feed are the same as the other animal drugs permitted to be used with the approved new animal drug, and

(III) such other information respecting the different animal drug or combination with respect to which the petition was filed as the Secretary may require,

(D) information to show that the route of administration, the dosage form, and the strength of the new animal drug are the same as those of the approved new animal drug or, if the route of administration, the dosage form, or the strength of the new animal drug is different and the application is filed pursuant to the approval of a petition filed under paragraph (3), such information respecting the route of administration, dosage form, or strength with respect to which the petition was filed as the Secretary may require;

(E) information to show that the new animal drug is bioequivalent to the approved new animal drug, except that if the application is filed pursuant to the approval of a petition filed under paragraph (3) for the purposes described in subparagraph (B) or (C), information to show that the active ingredients of the new animal drug are of the same pharmacological or therapeutic class as the pharmacological or therapeutic class of the approved new animal drug and that the new animal drug can be expected to have the same therapeutic effect as the approved new animal drug when used in accordance with the labeling;

(F) information to show that the labeling proposed for the new animal drug is the same as the labeling approved for the approved new animal drug except for changes required because of differences approved under a petition filed under paragraph (3), because of a different withdrawal period, or because the new animal drug and the approved new animal drug are produced or distributed by different manufacturers;

(G) the items specified in clauses (B) through (F) of subsection (b)(1) of this section;

(H) a certification, in the opinion of the applicant and to the best of his knowledge, with respect to each patent which claims the approved new animal drug or which claims a use for such approved new animal drug for which the applicant is seeking approval under this subsection and for which information is required to be filed under subsection (b)(1) or (c)(3) of this section—

(i) that such patent information has not been filed,

(ii) that such patent has expired,

(iii) of the date on which such patent will expire, or

(iv) that such patent is invalid or will not be infringed by the manufacture, use, or sale of the new animal drug for which the application is filed; and

(I) if with respect to the approved new animal drug information was filed under subsection (b)(1) or (c)(3) of this section for a method of use patent which does not claim a use for which the applicant is seeking approval of an application under subsection (c)(2) of this section, a statement that the method of use patent does not claim such a use.

The Secretary may not require that an abbreviated application contain information in addition to that required by subparagraphs (A) through (I).

(2)(A) An applicant who makes a certification described in paragraph (1)(G)(iv) shall include in the application a statement that the applicant will give the notice required by subparagraph (B) to—

(i) each owner of the patent which is the subject of the certification or the representative of such owner designated to receive such notice, and

(ii) the holder of the approved application under subsection (c)(1) of this section for the drug which is claimed by the patent or a use of which is claimed by the patent or the representative of such holder designated to receive such notice.

(B) The notice referred to in subparagraph (A) shall state that an application, which contains data from bioequivalence studies, has been filed under this subsection for the drug with respect to which the certification is made to obtain approval to engage in the commercial manufacture, use, or sale of such drug before the expiration of the patent referred to in the certification. Such notice shall include a detailed statement of the factual and legal basis of the applicant's opinion that the patent is not valid or will not be infringed.

(C) If an application is amended to include a certification described in paragraph (1)(G)(iv), the notice required by subparagraph (B) shall be given when the amended application is filed.

(3) If a person wants to submit an abbreviated application for a new animal drug—

(A) whose active ingredients, route of administration, dosage form, or strength differ from that of an approved new animal drug, or

(B) whose use with other animal drugs in animal feed differs from that of an approved new animal drug,

such person shall submit a petition to the Secretary seeking permission to file such an application. The Secretary shall approve a petition for a new animal drug unless the Secretary finds that—

(C) investigations must be conducted to show the safety and effectiveness, in animals to be treated with the drug, of the active ingredients, route of administration, dosage form, strength, or use with other animal drugs in animal feed which differ from the approved new animal drug, or

(D) investigations must be conducted to show the safety for human consumption of any residues in food resulting from the proposed active ingredients, route of administration, dosage form, strength, or use with other animal drugs in animal feed for the new animal drug which is different from the active ingredients, route of administration, dosage form, strength, or use with other animal drugs in animal feed of the approved new animal drug.

The Secretary shall approve or disapprove a petition submitted under this paragraph within 90 days of the date the petition is submitted.

(4)(A)(i) Within 60 days of November 16, 1988, the Secretary shall publish and make available to the public a list in alphabetical order of the official and proprietary name of each new animal drug which has been approved for safety and effectiveness before November 16, 1988.

(ii) Every 30 days after the publication of the first list under clause (i) the Secretary shall revise the list to include each new animal drug which has been approved for safety and effectiveness under subsection (c) of this section during the 30 day period.

(iii) When patent information submitted under subsection (b)(1) or (c)(3) of this section respecting a new animal drug included on the list is to be published by the Secretary, the Secretary shall, in revisions made under clause (ii), include such information for such drug.

(B) A new animal drug approved for safety and effectiveness before November 16, 1988, or approved for safety and effectiveness under subsection (c) of this section shall, for purposes of this subsection, be considered to have been published under subparagraph (A) on the date of its approval or November 16, 1988, whichever is later.

(C) If the approval of a new animal drug was withdrawn or suspended under subsection (c)(2)(G) of this section or for grounds described in subsection (e) of this section or if the Secretary determines that a drug has been withdrawn from sale for safety or effectiveness reasons, it may not be published in the list under subparagraph (A) or, if the withdrawal or suspension occurred after its publication in such list, it shall be immediately removed from such list—

(i) for the same period as the withdrawal or suspension under subsection (c)(2)(G) or (e) of this section, or

(ii) if the listed drug has been withdrawn from sale, for the period of withdrawal from sale or, if earlier, the period ending on the date the Secretary determines that the withdrawal from sale is not for safety or effectiveness reasons.

A notice of the removal shall be published in the Federal Register.

(5) If an application contains the information required by clauses (A), (G), and (H) of subsection (b)(1) of this section and such information—

(A) is relied on by the applicant for the approval of the application, and

(B) is not information derived either from investigations, studies, or tests conducted by or for the applicant or for which the applicant had obtained a right of reference or use from the person by or for whom the investigations, studies, or tests were conducted,

such application shall be considered to be an application filed under subsection (b)(2) of this section.

(o) "Patent" defined

For purposes of this section, the term "patent" means a patent issued by the United States Patent and Trademark Office.

(p) Safety and effectiveness data

(1) Safety and effectiveness data and information which has been submitted in an application filed under subsection (b)(1) of this section or section 360ccc(a) of this title for a drug and which has not previously been disclosed to the public shall be made available to the public, upon request, unless extraordinary circumstances are shown—

(A) if no work is being or will be undertaken to have the application approved,

(B) if the Secretary has determined that the application is not approvable and all legal appeals have been exhausted,

(C) if approval of the application under subsection (c) of this section is withdrawn and all legal appeals have been exhausted,

(D) if the Secretary has determined that such drug is not a new drug, or

(E) upon the effective date of the approval of the first application filed under subsection (b)(2) of this section which refers to such drug or upon the date upon which the approval of an application filed under subsection (b)(2) of this section which refers to such drug could be made effective if such an application had been filed.

(2) Any request for data and information pursuant to paragraph (1) shall include a verified statement by the person making the request that any data or information received under such paragraph shall not be disclosed by such person to any other person—

(A) for the purpose of, or as part of a plan, scheme, or device for, obtaining the right to make, use, or market, or making, using, or marketing, outside the United States, the drug identified in the application filed under subsection (b)(1) of this section or section 360ccc(a) of this title, and

(B) without obtaining from any person to whom the data and information are disclosed an identical verified statement, a copy of which is to be provided by such person to the Secretary, which meets the requirements of this paragraph.

(June 25, 1938, ch. 675, §512, as added Pub. L. 90–399, §101(b), July 13, 1968, 82 Stat. 343; amended Pub. L. 100–670, title I, §§101, 102, 104, 107(a)(2), Nov. 16, 1988, 102 Stat. 3971, 3981, 3982, 3984; Pub. L. 102–108, §2(e), Aug. 17, 1991, 105 Stat. 550; Pub. L. 103–80, §3(r), Aug. 13, 1993, 107 Stat. 777; Pub. L. 103–396, §2(a), (b)(2), (3), Oct. 22, 1994, 108 Stat. 4153, 4154; Pub. L. 104–250, §§2(a)–(d), 3–5(c), 6(a), (b), Oct. 9, 1996, 110 Stat. 3151–3153, 3155–3157; Pub. L. 105–115, title I, §124(b), Nov. 21, 1997, 111 Stat. 2325; Pub. L. 105–277, div. A, §101(a) [title VII, §737], Oct. 21, 1998, 112 Stat. 2681, 2681–30; Pub. L. 106–113, div. B, §1000(a)(9) [title IV, §4732(b)(11)], Nov. 29, 1999, 113 Stat. 1536, 1501A–584; Pub. L. 108–282, title I, §102(b)(2), (3), (5)(I)–(S), Aug. 2, 2004, 118 Stat. 892, 903, 904; Pub. L. 110–316, title I, §105(a), Aug. 14, 2008, 122 Stat. 3513.)

REFERENCES IN TEXT

Section 342(a)(2) of this title, referred to in subsec. (a)(6), was amended by Pub. L. 104–170, title IV, §404, Aug. 3, 1996, 110 Stat. 1514, and, as so amended, no longer contains a subcl. (D). See section 342(a)(2)(C)(ii) of this title.

AMENDMENTS

2008—Subsec. (*l*)(3). Pub. L. 110–316 added par. (3).

2004—Subsec. (a)(1), (2). Pub. L. 108–282, §102(b)(5)(I), added pars. (1) and (2) and struck out former pars. (1) and (2) which deemed as unsafe new animal drugs and animal feed bearing or containing a new animal drug which did not have in effect certain approvals.

Subsec. (b)(3). Pub. L. 108–282, §102(b)(5)(J), substituted "under paragraph (1), section 360ccc of this title, or a request for an investigational exemption under subsection (j)" for "under paragraph (1) or a request for an investigational exemption under subsection (j)".

Subsec. (c)(2)(F)(ii), (iii), (v). Pub. L. 108–282, §102(b)(2), substituted "(other than bioequivalence studies or residue depletion studies, except residue depletion studies for minor uses or minor species)" for "(other than bioequivalence or residue studies)".

Subsec. (d)(4). Pub. L. 108–282, §102(b)(5)(K), substituted "have previously been separately approved pursuant to an application submitted under subsection (b)(1) of this section" for "have previously been separately approved" in introductory provisions.

Subsec. (d)(5). Pub. L. 108–282, §102(b)(3), added par. (5).

Subsec. (f). Pub. L. 108–282, § 102(b)(5)(L), substituted "subsection (d), (e), or (m) of this section, or section 360ccc(c), (d), or (e) of this title" for "subsection (d), (e), or (m) of this section".

Subsec. (g). Pub. L. 108–282, § 102(b)(5)(M), substituted "this section, or section 360ccc of this title" for "this section".

Subsec. (i). Pub. L. 108–282, § 102(b)(5)(N), substituted "subsection (b) of this section or section 360ccc of this title" for "subsection (b) of this section" and inserted "or upon failure to renew a conditional approval under section 360ccc of this title" after "or upon its suspension".

Subsec. (*l*)(1). Pub. L. 108–282, § 102(b)(5)(O), substituted "subsection (b) of this section or section 360ccc of this title" for "subsection (b) of this section".

Subsec. (m)(1)(C). Pub. L. 108–282, § 102(b)(5)(P), substituted "applicable regulations published pursuant to subsection (i) of this section or for indexed new animal drugs in accordance with the index listing published pursuant to section 360ccc–1(e)(2) of this title and the labeling requirements set forth in section 360ccc–1(h) of this title" for "applicable regulations published pursuant to subsection (i) of this section".

Subsec. (m)(3). Pub. L. 108–282, § 102(b)(5)(Q), inserted "or an index listing pursuant to section 360ccc–1(e) of this title" after "subsection (i) of this section" in subpar. (C) and concluding provisions.

Subsec. (p)(1), (2)(A). Pub. L. 108–282, § 102(b)(5)(R), (S), substituted "subsection (b)(1) of this section or section 360ccc(a) of this title" for "subsection (b)(1) of this section".

1999—Subsec. (*o*). Pub. L. 106–113 substituted "United States Patent and Trademark Office" for "Patent and Trademark Office of the Department of Commerce".

1998—Subsec. (d)(4)(D)(iii). Pub. L. 105–277 inserted before semicolon ", except that for purposes of this clause, antibacterial ingredient or animal drug does not include the ionophore or arsenical classes of animal drugs".

1997—Subsec. (c)(4). Pub. L. 105–115 added par. (4).

1996—Subsec. (a)(1). Pub. L. 104–250, § 6(a), amended par. (1) generally. Prior to amendment, par. (1) read as follows: "A new animal drug shall, with respect to any particular use or intended use of such drug, be deemed unsafe for the purposes of section 351(a)(5) and section 342(a)(2)(D) of this title unless—

"(A) there is in effect an approval of an application filed pursuant to subsection (b) of this section with respect to such use or intended use of such drug, and

"(B) such drug, its labeling, and such use conform to such approved application.

A new animal drug shall also be deemed unsafe for such purposes in the event of removal from the establishment of a manufacturer, packer, or distributor of such drug for use in the manufacture of animal feed in any State unless at the time of such removal such manufacturer, packer, or distributor has an unrevoked written statement from the consignee of such drug, or notice from the Secretary, to the effect that, with respect to the use of such drug in animal feed, such consignee—

"(i) is the holder of an approved application under subsection (m) of this section; or

"(ii) will, if the consignee is not a user of the drug, ship such drug only to a holder of an approved application under subsection (m) of this section."

Subsec. (a)(2). Pub. L. 104–250, § 6(a), amended par. (2) generally. Prior to amendment, par. (2) read as follows: "An animal feed bearing or containing a new animal drug shall, with respect to any particular use or intended use of such animal feed, be deemed unsafe for the purposes of section 351(a)(6) of this title unless—

"(A) there is in effect an approval of an application filed pursuant to subsection (b) of this section with respect to such drugs, as used in such animal feed,

"(B) there is in effect an approval of an application pursuant to subsection (m)(1) of this section with respect to such animal feed, and

"(C) such animal feed, its labeling, and such use conform to the conditions and indications of use published pursuant to subsection (i) of this section and to the application with respect thereto approved under subsection (m) of this section."

Subsec. (a)(6). Pub. L. 104–250, § 4, added par. (6).

Subsec. (b)(3). Pub. L. 104–250, § 2(d), added par. (3).

Subsec. (c)(2)(F)(ii), (iii). Pub. L. 104–250, § 2(b)(1), substituted "substantial evidence of the effectiveness of the drug involved, any studies of animal safety, or," for "reports of new clinical or field investigations (other than bioequivalence or residue studies) and," and "required for the approval" for "essential to the approval".

Subsec. (c)(2)(F)(v). Pub. L. 104–250, § 2(b)(2), substituted "clause (iv)" for "subparagraph (B)(iv)" in two places, "substantial evidence of the effectiveness of the drug involved, any studies of animal safety," for "reports of clinical or field investigations" and "required for the new approval" for "essential to the new approval".

Subsec. (d)(1)(F). Pub. L. 104–250, § 3, amended subpar. (F) generally. Prior to amendment, subpar. (F) read as follows: "upon the basis of the information submitted to him as part of the application or any other information before him with respect to such drug, the tolerance limitation proposed, if any, exceeds that reasonably required to accomplish the physical or other technical effect for which the drug is intended;".

Subsec. (d)(3). Pub. L. 104–250, § 2(a), amended par. (3) generally. Prior to amendment, par. (3) read as follows: "As used in this subsection and subsection (e) of this section, the term 'substantial evidence' means evidence consisting of adequate and well-controlled investigations, including field investigation, by experts qualified by scientific training and experience to evaluate the effectiveness of the drug involved, on the basis of which it could fairly and reasonably be concluded by such experts that the drug will have the effect it purports or is represented to have under the conditions of use prescribed, recommended, or suggested in the labeling or proposed labeling thereof."

Subsec. (d)(4). Pub. L. 104–250, § 2(c), added par. (4).

Subsec. (i). Pub. L. 104–250, § 5(c), inserted "and any requirement that an animal feed bearing or containing the new animal drug be limited to use under the professional supervision of a licensed veterinarian" after "(including special labeling requirements".

Subsec. (m). Pub. L. 104–250, § 6(b), amended subsec. (m) generally, substituting provisions relating to application for feed mill licenses, including approval, refusal, revocation, and suspension of such licenses, and provisions for record and reporting requirements for, as well as exemption from, such licenses, for provisions relating to application for uses of animal feed containing new animal drug, including required contents, approval, refusal, and withdrawal of approval or suspension of such usage applications, and provisions for record and reporting requirements of such usage applications.

1994—Subsec. (a)(4), (5). Pub. L. 103–396, § 2(a), added pars. (4) and (5).

Subsec. (e)(1)(A). Pub. L. 103–396, § 2(b)(2), inserted before semicolon at end "or the condition of use authorized under subsection (a)(4)(A) of this section".

Subsec. (*l*)(1). Pub. L. 103–396, § 2(b)(3), substituted "relating to experience, including experience with uses authorized under subsection (a)(4)(A) of this section," for "relating to experience".

1993—Subsec. (c)(2)(A)(ii). Pub. L. 103–80, § 3(r)(1), inserted "in" after "except as provided".

Subsec. (c)(2)(F)(i). Pub. L. 103–80, § 3(r)(2), substituted "subparagraph (D)(iii)" for "subparagraph (C)(iii)".

Subsec. (c)(2)(H)(ii). Pub. L. 103–80, § 3(r)(3), substituted "subclauses" for "subclause" after "bioequivalency information described in" in concluding provisions.

Subsec. (d)(1). Pub. L. 103–80, § 3(r)(4), substituted "subparagraphs (A) through (I)" for "subparagraphs (A) through (G)" in concluding provisions.

Subsec. (n)(1). Pub. L. 103–80, § 3(r)(5), substituted "section 321(v) of this title" for "section 321(w) of this title" in subpars. (B)(ii)(II) and (C)(ii)(I) and substituted "through (I)" for "through (H)" in concluding provisions.

1991—Subsec. (e)(1)(B). Pub. L. 102–108 substituted "(I)" for "(H)".

1988—Subsec. (a)(1)(C). Pub. L. 100–670, § 107(a)(2), struck out subpar. (C) which read as follows: "in the case of a new animal drug subject to subsection (n) of this section and not exempted therefrom by regulations it is from a batch with respect to which a certificate or release issued pursuant to subsection (n) of this section is in effect with respect to such drug."

Subsec. (b). Pub. L. 100–670, §§ 101(a), 102(a), designated existing provisions as par. (1), redesignated cls. (1) to (8) as cls. (A) to (H), respectively, added par. (2), and inserted provisions at end of par. (1) which require applicant to file with application, patent number and expiration date of any patent which claims new animal drug, to amend application to include such information if patent which claims such drug or method of using such drug is issued after filing date but before approval of application, and to publish such information upon approval.

Subsec. (c). Pub. L. 100–670, §§ 101(c), 102(b)(1), designated existing provisions as par. (1), redesignated cls. (1) and (2) as cls. (A) and (B), respectively, and added pars. (2) and (3).

Subsec. (d)(1). Pub. L. 100–670, § 102(b)(3), substituted "(G)" for "(H)" in last sentence.

Subsec. (d)(1)(G) to (I). Pub. L. 100–670, § 102(b)(2), added subpar. (G) and redesignated former subpars. (G) and (H) as (H) and (I), respectively.

Subsec. (e)(1)(D) to (F). Pub. L. 100–670, § 102(b)(4), added subpar. (D) and redesignated former subpars. (D) and (E) as (E) and (F), respectively.

Subsecs. (n) to (p). Pub. L. 100–670, § 101(b), added subsecs. (n) to (p) and struck out former subsec. (n) which related to certification of new drugs containing penicillin, streptomycin, chlortetracycline, chloramphenicol, or bacitracin, and release prior to certification.

Effective Date of 1999 Amendment

Amendment by Pub. L. 106–113 effective 4 months after Nov. 29, 1999, see section 1000(a)(9) [title IV, § 4731] of Pub. L. 106–113, set out as a note under section 1 of Title 35, Patents.

Effective Date of 1997 Amendment

Amendment by Pub. L. 105–115 effective 90 days after Nov. 21, 1997, except as otherwise provided, see section 501 of Pub. L. 105–115, set out as a note under section 321 of this title.

Effective Date of 1994 Amendment

Section 2(d) of Pub. L. 103–396 provided that: "The amendments made by this section [amending this section and section 331 of this title] shall take effect upon the adoption of the final regulations under subsection (c) [set out below]." [Final regulations were dated Oct. 22, 1996, filed Nov. 6, 1996, published Nov. 7, 1996, 61 F.R. 57732, and effective Dec. 9, 1996.]

Effective Date of 1988 Amendment

Section 108 of Pub. L. 100–670 provided that: "The Secretary of Health and Human Services may not make an approval of an application submitted under section 512(b)(2) of the Federal Food, Drug, and Cosmetic Act (21 U.S.C. 360b(b)(2)) effective before January 1, 1991."

Effective Date and Transitional Provisions

Pub. L. 90–399, § 108, July 13, 1968, 82 Stat. 353, as amended by Pub. L. 108–282, title I, § 102(b)(5)(T), Aug. 2, 2004, 118 Stat. 905, provided that:

"(a) Except as otherwise provided in this section, the amendments made by the foregoing sections [see Short Title of 1968 Amendment note set out under section 301 of this title] shall take effect on the first day of the thirteenth calendar month which begins after the date of enactment of this Act [July 13, 1968].

"(b)(1) As used in this subsection, the term 'effective date' means the effective date specified in subsection (a) of this section; the term 'basic Act' means the Federal Food, Drug, and Cosmetic Act [this chapter]; and other terms used both in this section and the basic Act shall have the same meaning as they have, or had, at the time referred to in the context, under the basic Act.

"(2) Any approval, prior to the effective date, of a new animal drug or of an animal feed bearing or containing a new animal drug, whether granted by approval of a new-drug application, master file, antibiotic regulation, or food additive regulations, shall continue in effect, and shall be subject to change in accordance with the provisions of the basic Act as amended by this Act [see Short Title of 1968 Amendment note set out under section 301 of this title].

"(3) In the case of any drug (other than a drug subject to section 512(n) of the basic Act as amended by this Act) [subsection (n) of this section] intended for use in animals other than man which, on October 9, 1962, (A) was commercially used or sold in the United States, (B) was not a new drug as defined by section 201(p) of the basic Act [section 321(p) of this title] as then in force, and (C) was not covered by an effective application under section 505 of that Act [section 355 of this title], the words 'effectiveness' and 'effective' contained in section 201(v) to the basic Act [sic] [section 321(v) of this title] shall not apply to such drug when intended solely for use under conditions prescribed, recommended, or suggested in labeling with respect to such drug on that day.

"(4) Regulations providing for fees (and advance deposits to cover fees) which on the day preceding the effective date applicable under subsection (a) of this section were in effect pursuant to section 507 of the basic Act [section 357 of this title] shall, except as the Secretary may otherwise prescribe, be deemed to apply also under section 512(n) of the basic Act [subsection (n) of this section], and appropriations of fees (and of advance deposits to cover fees) available for the purposes specified in such section 507 [section 357 of this title] as in effect prior to the effective date shall also be available for the purposes specified in section 512(n) [subsection (n) of this section], including preparatory work or proceedings prior to that date."

Regulations

Section 2(e) of Pub. L. 104–250 provided that:

"(1) In general.—Not later than 6 months after the date of enactment of this Act [Oct. 9, 1996], the Secretary of Health and Human Services shall issue proposed regulations implementing the amendments made by this Act as described in paragraph (2)(A) of this subsection, and not later than 18 months after the date of enactment of this Act, the Secretary shall issue final regulations implementing such amendments. Not later than 12 months after the date of enactment of this Act, the Secretary shall issue proposed regulations implementing the other amendments made by this Act as described in paragraphs (2)(B) and (2)(C) of this subsection, and not later than 24 months after the date of enactment of this Act, the Secretary shall issue final regulations implementing such amendments.

"(2) Contents.—In issuing regulations implementing the amendments made by this Act [see Short Title of 1996 Amendments note set out under section 301 of this title], and in taking an action to review an application for approval of a new animal drug under section 512 of the Federal Food, Drug, and Cosmetic Act (21 U.S.C. 360b), or a request for an investigational exemption for a new animal drug under subsection (j) of such section, that is pending or has been submitted prior to the effective date of the regulations, the Secretary shall—

"(A) further define the term 'adequate and well controlled', as used in subsection (d)(3) of section 512 of such Act, to require that field investigations be designed and conducted in a scientifically sound manner, taking into account practical conditions in the field and differences between field conditions and laboratory conditions;

"(B) further define the term 'substantial evidence', as defined in subsection (d)(3) of such section, in a manner that encourages the submission of applications and supplemental applications; and

"(C) take into account the proposals contained in the citizen petition (FDA Docket No. 91P–0434/CP) jointly submitted by the American Veterinary Medical Association and the Animal Health Institute, dated October 21, 1991.

Until the regulations required by subparagraph (A) are issued, nothing in the regulations published at 21 C.F.R. 514.111(a)(5) (April 1, 1996) shall be construed to compel the Secretary of Health and Human Services to require a field investigation under section 512(d)(1)(E) of the Federal Food, Drug, and Cosmetic Act (21 U.S.C. 360b(d)(1)(E)) or to apply any of its provisions in a manner inconsistent with the considerations for scientifically sound field investigations set forth in subparagraph (A)."

Section 2(c) of Pub. L. 103–396 provided that: "Not later than 2 years after the date of the enactment of this Act [Oct. 22, 1994], the Secretary of Health and Human Services shall promulgate regulations to implement paragraphs (4)(A) and (5) of section 512(a) of the Federal Food, Drug, and Cosmetic Act [21 U.S.C. 360b(a)(4)(A), (5)] (as amended by subsection (a))."

Section 103 of Pub. L. 100–670 provided that:

"(a) GENERAL RULE.—The Secretary of Health and Human Services shall promulgate, in accordance with the notice and comment requirements of section 553 of title 5, United States Code, such regulations as may be necessary for the administration of section 512 of the Federal Food, Drug, and Cosmetic Act [21 U.S.C. 360b], as amended by sections 101 through 103 of this title, within one year of the date of enactment of this Act [Nov. 16, 1988].

"(b) TRANSITION.—During the period beginning 60 days after the date of enactment of this Act [Nov. 16, 1988] and ending on the date regulations promulgated under subsection (a) take effect, abbreviated new animal drug applications may be submitted in accordance with the provisions of section 314.55 and part 320 of title 21 of the Code of Federal Regulations and shall be considered as suitable for any drug which has been approved for safety and effectiveness under section 512(c) of the Federal Food, Drug, and Cosmetic Act [21 U.S.C. 360b(c)] before the date of enactment of this Act. If any such provision of section 314.55 or part 320 is inconsistent with the requirements of section 512 of the Federal Food, Drug, and Cosmetic Act (as amended by this title), the Secretary shall consider the application under the applicable requirements of section 512 (as so amended)."

ANTIMICROBIAL ANIMAL DRUG DISTRIBUTION REPORTS

Pub. L. 110–316, title I, §105(b), (c), Aug. 14, 2008, 122 Stat. 3514, provided that:

"(b) FIRST REPORT.—For each new animal drug that is subject to the reporting requirement under section 512(*l*)(3) of the Federal Food, Drug, and Cosmetic Act [21 U.S.C. 360b(*l*)(3)], as added by subsection (a), and for which an approval of an application filed pursuant to section 512(b) or 571 of such Act [21 U.S.C. 360b(b), 360ccc] is in effect on the date of the enactment of this title [Aug. 14, 2008], the Secretary of Health and Human Services shall require the sponsor of the drug to submit the first report under such section 512(*l*)(3) for the drug not later than March 31, 2010.

"(c) SEPARATE REPORT.—The reports required under section 512(*l*)(3) of the Federal Food, Drug, and Cosmetic Act, as added by subsection (a), shall be separate from periodic drug experience reports that are required under section 514.80(b)(4) of title 21, Code of Federal Regulations (as in effect on the date of the enactment of this title)."

DRUGS INTENDED FOR MINOR SPECIES AND MINOR USES

Section 2(f) of Pub. L. 104–250 provided that: "The Secretary of Health and Human Services shall consider legislative and regulatory options for facilitating the approval under section 512 of the Federal Food, Drug, and Cosmetic Act [21 U.S.C. 360b] of animal drugs intended for minor species and for minor uses and, within 18 months after the date of enactment of this Act [Oct. 9, 1996], announce proposals for legislative or regulatory change to the approval process under such section for animal drugs intended for use in minor species or for minor uses."

TRANSITIONAL PROVISION REGARDING IMPLEMENTATION OF PUB. L. 104–250; APPROVED MEDICATED FEED APPLICATION DEEMED LICENSE

Section 6(c) of Pub. L. 104–250 provided that: "A person engaged in the manufacture of animal feeds bearing or containing new animal drugs who holds at least one approved medicated feed application for an animal feed bearing or containing new animal drugs, the manufacture of which was not otherwise exempt from the requirement for an approved medicated feed application on the date of the enactment of this Act [Oct. 9, 1996], shall be deemed to hold a license for the manufacturing site identified in the approved medicated feed application. The revocation of license provisions of section 512(m)(4) of the Federal Food, Drug, and Cosmetic Act [21 U.S.C. 360b(m)(4)], as amended by this Act, shall apply to such licenses. Such license shall expire within 18 months from the date of enactment of this Act unless the person submits to the Secretary a completed license application for the manufacturing site accompanied by a copy of an approved medicated feed application for such site, which license application shall be deemed to be approved upon receipt by the Secretary."

DRUGS PRIMARILY MANUFACTURED USING BIOTECHNOLOGY

Section 106 of Pub. L. 100–670 provided that: "Notwithstanding section 512(b)(2) of the Federal Food, Drug, and Cosmetic Act [21 U.S.C. 360b(b)(2)], the Secretary of Health and Human Services may not approve an abbreviated application submitted under such section for a new animal drug which is primarily manufactured using recombinant DNA, recombinant RNA, hybridoma technology, or other processes involving site specific genetic manipulation techniques."

§ 360c. Classification of devices intended for human use

(a) Classes of devices

(1) There are established the following classes of devices intended for human use:

(A) CLASS I, GENERAL CONTROLS.—

(i) A device for which the controls authorized by or under section 351, 352, 360, 360f, 360h, 360i, or 360j of this title or any combination of such sections are sufficient to provide reasonable assurance of the safety and effectiveness of the device.

(ii) A device for which insufficient information exists to determine that the controls referred to in clause (i) are sufficient to provide reasonable assurance of the safety and effectiveness of the device or to establish special controls to provide such assurance, but because it—

(I) is not purported or represented to be for a use in supporting or sustaining human life or for a use which is of substantial importance in preventing impairment of human health, and

(II) does not present a potential unreasonable risk of illness or injury,

is to be regulated by the controls referred to in clause (i).

(B) CLASS II, SPECIAL CONTROLS.—A device which cannot be classified as a class I device because the general controls by themselves are insufficient to provide reasonable assurance of the safety and effectiveness of the device, and for which there is sufficient information to establish special controls to provide such assurance, including the promulgation of performance standards, postmarket surveillance, patient registries, development and dissemination of guidelines (including guidelines for the submission of clinical data in premarket notification submissions in accordance with section 360(k) of this title), recommendations, and other appropriate actions as the Secretary deems necessary to provide such assurance. For a device that is purported or represented to be for a use in supporting or sustaining human life, the Secretary shall examine and identify the special controls, if any, that are necessary to provide adequate assurance of safety and effectiveness and describe how such controls provide such assurance.

(C) CLASS III, PREMARKET APPROVAL.—A device which because—

(i) it (I) cannot be classified as a class I device because insufficient information exists to determine that the application of general controls are sufficient to provide reasonable assurance of the safety and effectiveness of the device, and (II) cannot be classified as a class II device because insufficient information exists to determine that the special controls described in subparagraph (B) would provide reasonable assurance of its safety and effectiveness, and

(ii)(I) is purported or represented to be for a use in supporting or sustaining human life or for a use which is of substantial importance in preventing impairment of human health, or

(II) presents a potential unreasonable risk of illness or injury,

is to be subject, in accordance with section 360e of this title, to premarket approval to provide reasonable assurance of its safety and effectiveness.

If there is not sufficient information to establish a performance standard for a device to provide reasonable assurance of its safety and effectiveness, the Secretary may conduct such activities as may be necessary to develop or obtain such information.

(2) For purposes of this section and sections 360d and 360e of this title, the safety and effectiveness of a device are to be determined—

(A) with respect to the persons for whose use the device is represented or intended,

(B) with respect to the conditions of use prescribed, recommended, or suggested in the labeling of the device, and

(C) weighing any probable benefit to health from the use of the device against any probable risk of injury or illness from such use.

(3)(A) Except as authorized by subparagraph (B), the effectiveness of a device is, for purposes of this section and sections 360d and 360e of this title, to be determined, in accordance with regulations promulgated by the Secretary, on the basis of well-controlled investigations, including 1 or more clinical investigations where appropriate, by experts qualified by training and experience to evaluate the effectiveness of the device, from which investigations it can fairly and responsibly be concluded by qualified experts that the device will have the effect it purports or is represented to have under the conditions of use prescribed, recommended, or suggested in the labeling of the device.

(B) If the Secretary determines that there exists valid scientific evidence (other than evidence derived from investigations described in subparagraph (A))—

(i) which is sufficient to determine the effectiveness of a device, and

(ii) from which it can fairly and responsibly be concluded by qualified experts that the device will have the effect it purports or is represented to have under the conditions of use prescribed, recommended, or suggested in the labeling of the device,

then, for purposes of this section and sections 360d and 360e of this title, the Secretary may authorize the effectiveness of the device to be determined on the basis of such evidence.

(C) In making a determination of a reasonable assurance of the effectiveness of a device for which an application under section 360e of this title has been submitted, the Secretary shall consider whether the extent of data that otherwise would be required for approval of the application with respect to effectiveness can be reduced through reliance on postmarket controls.

(D)(i) The Secretary, upon the written request of any person intending to submit an application under section 360e of this title, shall meet with such person to determine the type of valid scientific evidence (within the meaning of subparagraphs (A) and (B)) that will be necessary to demonstrate for purposes of approval of an application the effectiveness of a device for the conditions of use proposed by such person. The written request shall include a detailed description of the device, a detailed description of the proposed conditions of use of the device, a proposed plan for determining whether there is a reasonable assurance of effectiveness, and, if available, information regarding the expected performance from the device. Within 30 days after such meeting, the Secretary shall specify in writing the type of valid scientific evidence that will provide a reasonable assurance that a device is effective under the conditions of use proposed by such person.

(ii) Any clinical data, including one or more well-controlled investigations, specified in writing by the Secretary for demonstrating a reasonable assurance of device effectiveness shall be specified as result of a determination by the Secretary that such data are necessary to establish device effectiveness. The Secretary shall consider, in consultation with the applicant, the least burdensome appropriate means of evaluating device effectiveness that would have a reasonable likelihood of resulting in approval.

(iii) The determination of the Secretary with respect to the specification of valid scientific evidence under clauses (i) and (ii) shall be binding upon the Secretary, unless such determination by the Secretary could be contrary to the public health.

(b) Classification panels

(1) For purposes of—

(A) determining which devices intended for human use should be subject to the requirements of general controls, performance standards, or premarket approval, and

(B) providing notice to the manufacturers and importers of such devices to enable them to prepare for the application of such requirements to devices manufactured or imported by them,

the Secretary shall classify all such devices (other than devices classified by subsection (f) of this section) into the classes established by subsection (a) of this section. For the purpose of securing recommendations with respect to the classification of devices, the Secretary shall establish panels of experts or use panels of experts established before May 28, 1976, or both. Section 14 of the Federal Advisory Committee Act shall not apply to the duration of a panel established under this paragraph.

(2) The Secretary shall appoint to each panel established under paragraph (1) persons who are qualified by training and experience to evaluate the safety and effectiveness of the devices to be referred to the panel and who, to the extent feasible, possess skill in the use of, or experience in the development, manufacture, or utilization of, such devices. The Secretary shall make appointments to each panel so that each panel shall consist of members with adequately diversified expertise in such fields as clinical and administrative medicine, engineering, biological and physical sciences, and other related professions. In addition, each panel shall include as nonvoting members a representative of consumer interests and a representative of interests of the device manufacturing industry. Scientific, trade, and consumer organizations shall be afforded an opportunity to nominate individuals for appointment to the panels. No individual who is in the regular full-time employ of the United States and engaged in the administration of this chapter may be a member of any panel. The Secretary shall designate one of the members of each panel to serve as chairman thereof.

(3) Panel members (other than officers or employees of the United States), while attending meetings or conferences of a panel or otherwise engaged in its business, shall be entitled to receive compensation at rates to be fixed by the Secretary, but not at rates exceeding the daily equivalent of the rate in effect for grade GS–18 of the General Schedule, for each day so engaged, including traveltime; and while so serving away from their homes or regular places of business each member may be allowed travel expenses (including per diem in lieu of subsistence) as authorized by section 5703 of title 5, for persons in the Government service employed intermittently.

(4) The Secretary shall furnish each panel with adequate clerical and other necessary assistance.

(5) Classification panels covering each type of device shall be scheduled to meet at such times as may be appropriate for the Secretary to meet applicable statutory deadlines.

(6)(A) Any person whose device is specifically the subject of review by a classification panel shall have—

(i) the same access to data and information submitted to a classification panel (except for data and information that are not available for public disclosure under section 552 of title 5) as the Secretary;

(ii) the opportunity to submit, for review by a classification panel, information that is based on the data or information provided in the application submitted under section 360e of this title by the person, which information shall be submitted to the Secretary for prompt transmittal to the classification panel; and

(iii) the same opportunity as the Secretary to participate in meetings of the panel.

(B) Any meetings of a classification panel shall provide adequate time for initial presentations and for response to any differing views by persons whose devices are specifically the subject of a classification panel review, and shall encourage free and open participation by all interested persons.

(7) After receiving from a classification panel the conclusions and recommendations of the panel on a matter that the panel has reviewed, the Secretary shall review the conclusions and recommendations, shall make a final decision on the matter in accordance with section 360e(d)(2) of this title, and shall notify the affected persons of the decision in writing and, if the decision differs from the conclusions and recommendations of the panel, shall include the reasons for the difference.

(8) A classification panel under this subsection shall not be subject to the annual chartering and annual report requirements of the Federal Advisory Committee Act.

(c) Classification panel organization and operation

(1) The Secretary shall organize the panels according to the various fields of clinical medicine and fundamental sciences in which devices intended for human use are used. The Secretary shall refer a device to be classified under this section to an appropriate panel established or authorized to be used under subsection (b) of this section for its review and for its recommendation respecting the classification of the device. The Secretary shall by regulation prescribe the procedure to be followed by the panels in making their reviews and recommendations. In making their reviews of devices, the panels, to the maximum extent practicable, shall provide an opportunity for interested persons to submit data and views on the classification of the devices.

(2)(A) Upon completion of a panel's review of a device referred to it under paragraph (1), the panel shall, subject to subparagraphs (B) and (C), submit to the Secretary its recommendation for the classification of the device. Any such recommendation shall (i) contain (I) a summary of the reasons for the recommendation, (II) a summary of the data upon which the recommendation is based, and (III) an identification of the risks to health (if any) presented by the device with respect to which the recommendation is made, and (ii) to the extent practicable, include a recommendation for the assignment of a priority for the application of the requirements of section 360d or 360e of this title to a device recommended to be classified in class II or class III.

(B) A recommendation of a panel for the classification of a device in class I shall include a recommendation as to whether the device should be exempted from the requirements of section 360, 360i, or 360j(f) of this title.

(C) In the case of a device which has been referred under paragraph (1) to a panel, and which—

(i) is intended to be implanted in the human body or is purported or represented to be for a use in supporting or sustaining human life, and

(ii)(I) has been introduced or delivered for introduction into interstate commerce for commercial distribution before May 28, 1976, or

(II) is within a type of device which was so introduced or delivered before such date and is substantially equivalent to another device within that type,

such panel shall recommend to the Secretary that the device be classified in class III unless the panel determines that classification of the device in such class is not necessary to provide reasonable assurance of its safety and effectiveness. If a panel does not recommend that such a device be classified in class III, it shall in its recommendation to the Secretary for the classification of the device set forth the reasons for not recommending classification of the device in such class.

(3) The panels shall submit to the Secretary within one year of the date funds are first appropriated for the implementation of this section their recommendations respecting all devices of a type introduced or delivered for introduction into interstate commerce for commercial distribution before May 28, 1976.

(d) Panel recommendation; publication; priorities

(1) Upon receipt of a recommendation from a panel respecting a device, the Secretary shall publish in the Federal Register the panel's recommendation and a proposed regulation classifying such device and shall provide interested persons an opportunity to submit comments on such recommendation and the proposed regulation. After reviewing such comments, the Secretary shall, subject to paragraph (2), by regulation classify such device.

(2)(A) A regulation under paragraph (1) classifying a device in class I shall prescribe which, if any, of the requirements of section 360, 360i, or 360j(f) of this title shall not apply to the device. A regulation which makes a requirement of section 360, 360i, or 360j(f) of this title inapplicable to a device shall be accompanied by a statement of the reasons of the Secretary for making such requirement inapplicable.

(B) A device described in subsection (c)(2)(C) of this section shall be classified in class III unless the Secretary determines that classification of the device in such class is not necessary to provide reasonable assurance of its safety and effectiveness. A proposed regulation under paragraph (1) classifying such a device in a class other than class III shall be accompanied by a full statement of the reasons of the Secretary (and supporting documentation and data) for not classifying such device in such class and an identification of the risks to health (if any) presented by such device.

(3) In the case of devices classified in class II and devices classified under this subsection in class III and described in section 360e(b)(1) of this title the Secretary may establish priorities which, in his discretion, shall be used in applying sections 360d and 360e of this title, as appropriate, to such devices.

(e) Classification changes

(1) Based on new information respecting a device, the Secretary may, upon his own initiative or upon petition of an interested person, by regulation (A) change such device's classification, and (B) revoke, because of the change in classification, any regulation or requirement in effect under section 360d or 360e of this title with respect to such device. In the promulgation of such a regulation respecting a device's classification, the Secretary may secure from the panel to which the device was last referred pursuant to subsection (c) of this section a recommendation respecting the proposed change in the device's classification and shall publish in the Federal Register any recommendation submitted to the Secretary by the panel respecting such change. A regulation under this subsection changing the classification of a device from class III to class II may provide that such classification shall not take effect until the effective date of a performance standard established under section 360d of this title for such device.

(2) By regulation promulgated under paragraph (1), the Secretary may change the classification of a device from class III—

(A) to class II if the Secretary determines that special controls would provide reasonable assurance of the safety and effectiveness of the device and that general controls would not provide reasonable assurance of the safety and effectiveness of the device, or

(B) to class I if the Secretary determines that general controls would provide reasonable assurance of the safety and effectiveness of the device.

(f) Initial classification and reclassification of certain devices

(1) Any device intended for human use which was not introduced or delivered for introduction into interstate commerce for commercial distribution before May 28, 1976, is classified in class III unless—

(A) the device—

(i) is within a type of device (I) which was introduced or delivered for introduction into interstate commerce for commercial distribution before such date and which is to be classified pursuant to subsection (b) of this section, or (II) which was not so introduced or delivered before such date and has been classified in class I or II, and

(ii) is substantially equivalent to another device within such type, or

(B) the Secretary in response to a petition submitted under paragraph (3) has classified such device in class I or II.

A device classified in class III under this paragraph shall be classified in that class until the effective date of an order of the Secretary under paragraph (2) or (3) classifying the device in class I or II.

(2)(A) Any person who submits a report under section 360(k) of this title for a type of device that has not been previously classified under this chapter, and that is classified into class III under paragraph (1), may request, within 30 days after receiving written notice of such a classification, the Secretary to classify the device under the criteria set forth in subparagraphs (A) through (C) of subsection (a)(1) of this section. The person may, in the request, recommend to the Secretary a classification for the device. Any such request shall describe the device and provide detailed information and reasons for the recommended classification.

(B)(i) Not later than 60 days after the date of the submission of the request under subparagraph (A), the Secretary shall by written order classify the device involved. Such classification shall be the initial classification of the device for purposes of paragraph (1) and any device classified under this paragraph shall be a predicate device for determining substantial equivalence under paragraph (1).

(ii) A device that remains in class III under this subparagraph shall be deemed to be adulterated within the meaning of section 351(f)(1)(B) of this title until approved under section 360e of this title or exempted from such approval under section 360j(g) of this title.

(C) Within 30 days after the issuance of an order classifying a device under this paragraph, the Secretary shall publish a notice in the Federal Register announcing such classification.

(3)(A) The Secretary may initiate the reclassification of a device classified into class III under paragraph (1) of this subsection or the manufacturer or importer of a device classified under paragraph (1) may petition the Secretary (in such form and manner as he shall prescribe) for the issuance of an order classifying the device in class I or class II. Within thirty days of the filing of such a petition, the Secretary shall notify the petitioner of any deficiencies in the petition which prevent the Secretary from making a decision on the petition.

(B)(i) Upon determining that a petition does not contain any deficiency which prevents the Secretary from making a decision on the petition, the Secretary may for good cause shown refer the petition to an appropriate panel established or authorized to be used under subsection (b) of this section. A panel to which such a petition has been referred shall not later than ninety days after the referral of the petition make a recommendation to the Secretary respecting approval or denial of the petition. Any such recommendation shall contain (I) a summary of the reasons for the recommendation, (II) a summary of the data upon which the recommendation is based, and (III) an identification of the risks to health (if any) presented by the device with respect to which the petition was filed. In the case of a petition for a device which is intended to be implanted in the human body or which is purported or represented to be for a use in supporting or sustaining human life, the panel shall recommend that the petition be denied unless the panel determines that the classification in class III of the device is not necessary to provide reasonable assurance of its safety and effectiveness. If the panel recommends that such petition be approved, it shall in its recommendation to the Secretary set forth its reasons for such recommendation.

(ii) The requirements of paragraphs (1) and (2) of subsection (c) of this section (relating to opportunities for submission of data and views and recommendations respecting priorities and exemptions from sections 360, 360i, and 360j(f) of this title) shall apply with respect to consideration by panels of petitions submitted under subparagraph (A).

(C)(i) Within ninety days from the date the Secretary receives the recommendation of a panel respecting a petition (but not later than 210 days after the filing of such petition) the Secretary shall by order deny or approve the petition. If the Secretary approves the petition, the Secretary shall order the classification of the device into class I or class II in accordance with the criteria prescribed by subsection (a)(1)(A) or (a)(1)(B) of this section. In the case of a petition for a device which is intended to be implanted in the human body or which is purported or represented to be for a use in supporting or sustaining human life, the Secretary shall deny the petition unless the Secretary determines that the classification in class III of the device is not necessary to provide reasonable assurance of its safety and effectiveness. An order approving such petition shall be accompanied by a full statement of the reasons of the Secretary (and supporting documentation and data) for approving the petition and an identification of the risks to health (if any) presented by the device to which such order applies.

(ii) The requirements of paragraphs (1) and (2)(A) of subsection (d) of this section (relating to publication of recommendations, opportunity for submission of comments, and exemption from sections 360, 360i, and 360j(f) of this title) shall apply with respect to action by the Secretary on petitions submitted under subparagraph (A).

(4) If a manufacturer reports to the Secretary under section 360(k) of this title that a device is substantially equivalent to another device—

(A) which the Secretary has classified as a class III device under subsection (b) of this section,

(B) which was introduced or delivered for introduction into interstate commerce for commercial distribution before December 1, 1990, and

(C) for which no final regulation requiring premarket approval has been promulgated under section 360e(b) of this title,

the manufacturer shall certify to the Secretary that the manufacturer has conducted a reasonable search of all information known or otherwise available to the manufacturer respecting such other device and has included in the report under section 360(k) of this title a summary of and a citation to all adverse safety and effectiveness data respecting such other device and respecting the device for which the section 360(k) report is being made and which has not been submitted to the Secretary under section 360i of this title. The Secretary may require the manufacturer to submit the adverse safety and effectiveness data described in the report.

(5) The Secretary may not withhold a determination of the initial classification of a device under paragraph (1) because of a failure to comply with any provision of this chapter unrelated to a substantial equivalence decision, including a finding that the facility in which the device is manufactured is not in compliance with good manufacturing requirements as set forth in regulations of the Secretary under section 360j(f) of this title (other than a finding that there is a substantial likelihood that the failure to comply with such regulations will potentially present a serious risk to human health).

(g) Information

Within sixty days of the receipt of a written request of any person for information respecting the class in which a device has been classified or the requirements applicable to a device under this chapter, the Secretary shall provide such person a written statement of the classification (if any) of such device and the requirements of this chapter applicable to the device.

(h) Definitions

For purposes of this section and sections 351, 360, 360d, 360e, 360f, 360i, and 360j of this title

(1) a reference to "general controls" is a reference to the controls authorized by or under sections 351, 352, 360, 360f, 360h, 360i, and 360j of this title,

(2) a reference to "class I", "class II", or "class III" is a reference to a class of medical devices described in subparagraph (A), (B), or (C) of subsection (a)(1) of this section, and

(3) a reference to a "panel under section 360c of this title" is a reference to a panel established or authorized to be used under this section.

(i) Substantial equivalence

(1)(A) For purposes of determinations of substantial equivalence under subsection (f) of this section and section 360j(*l*) of this title, the term "substantially equivalent" or "substantial equivalence" means, with respect to a device being compared to a predicate device, that the device has the same intended use as the predicate device and that the Secretary by order has found that the device—

(i) has the same technological characteristics as the predicate device, or

(ii)(I) has different technological characteristics and the information submitted that the device is substantially equivalent to the predicate device contains information, including appropriate clinical or scientific data if deemed necessary by the Secretary or a person accredited under section 360m of this title, that demonstrates that the device is as safe and effective as a legally marketed device, and (II) does not raise different questions of safety and effectiveness than the predicate device.

(B) For purposes of subparagraph (A), the term "different technological characteristics" means, with respect to a device being compared to a predicate device, that there is a significant change in the materials, design, energy source, or other features of the device from those of the predicate device.

(C) To facilitate reviews of reports submitted to the Secretary under section 360(k) of this title, the Secretary shall consider the extent to which reliance on postmarket controls may expedite the classification of devices under subsection (f)(1) of this section.

(D) Whenever the Secretary requests information to demonstrate that devices with differing technological characteristics are substantially equivalent, the Secretary shall only request information that is necessary to making substantial equivalence determinations. In making such request, the Secretary shall consider the least burdensome means of demonstrating substantial equivalence and request information accordingly.

(E)(i) Any determination by the Secretary of the intended use of a device shall be based upon the proposed labeling submitted in a report for the device under section 360(k) of this title. However, when determining that a device can be found substantially equivalent to a legally marketed device, the director of the organizational unit responsible for regulating devices (in this subparagraph referred to as the "Director") may require a statement in labeling that provides appropriate information regarding a use of the device not identified in the proposed labeling if, after providing an opportunity for consultation with the person who submitted such report, the Director determines and states in writing—

(I) that there is a reasonable likelihood that the device will be used for an intended use not identified in the proposed labeling for the device; and

(II) that such use could cause harm.

(ii) Such determination shall—

(I) be provided to the person who submitted the report within 10 days from the date of the notification of the Director's concerns regarding the proposed labeling;

(II) specify the limitations on the use of the device not included in the proposed labeling; and

(III) find the device substantially equivalent if the requirements of subparagraph (A) are met and if the labeling for such device conforms to the limitations specified in subclause (II).

(iii) The responsibilities of the Director under this subparagraph may not be delegated.

(F) Not later than 270 days after November 21, 1997, the Secretary shall issue guidance specifying the general principles that the Secretary will consider in determining when a specific intended use of a device is not reasonably included within a general use of such device for purposes of a determination of substantial equivalence under subsection (f) of this section or section 360j(*l*) of this title.

(2) A device may not be found to be substantially equivalent to a predicate device that has been removed from the market at the initiative of the Secretary or that has been determined to be misbranded or adulterated by a judicial order.

(3)(A) As part of a submission under section 360(k) of this title respecting a device, the person required to file a premarket notification under such section shall provide an adequate summary of any information respecting safety and effectiveness or state that such information will be made available upon request by any person.

(B) Any summary under subparagraph (A) respecting a device shall contain detailed information regarding data concerning adverse health effects and shall be made available to the public by the Secretary within 30 days of the issuance of a determination that such device is substantially equivalent to another device.

(June 25, 1938, ch. 675, §513, as added Pub. L. 94–295, §2, May 28, 1976, 90 Stat. 540; amended Pub. L. 101–629, §§4(a), 5(a)–(c)(1), (3), 12(a), 18(a), Nov. 28, 1990, 104 Stat. 4515, 4517, 4518, 4523, 4528; Pub. L. 102–300, §6(e), June 16, 1992, 106 Stat. 240; Pub. L. 103–80, §3(s), Aug. 13, 1993, 107 Stat. 778; Pub. L. 105–115, title II, §§205(a), (b), 206(b), (c), 207, 208, 217, Nov. 21, 1997, 111 Stat. 2336, 2337, 2339, 2340, 2350; Pub. L. 107–250, title II, §208, Oct. 26, 2002, 116 Stat. 1613.)

REFERENCES IN TEXT

The Federal Advisory Committee Act, referred to in subsec. (b)(1), (8), is Pub. L. 92–463, Oct. 6, 1972, 86 Stat. 770, as amended, which is set out in the Appendix to Title 5, Government Organization and Employees.

AMENDMENTS

2002—Subsec. (i)(1)(E)(iv). Pub. L. 107–250 struck out cl. (iv) which read as follows: "This subparagraph has no legal effect after the expiration of the five-year period beginning on November 21, 1997."

1997—Subsec. (a)(3)(A). Pub. L. 105–115, §217, substituted "1 or more clinical investigations" for "clinical investigations".

Subsec. (a)(3)(C), (D). Pub. L. 105–115, §205(a), added subpars. (C) and (D).

Subsec. (b)(5) to (8). Pub. L. 105–115, §208, added pars. (5) to (8).

Subsec. (f)(1). Pub. L. 105–115, §207(1)(B), substituted "paragraph (2) or (3)" for "paragraph (2)" in closing provisions.

Subsec. (f)(1)(B). Pub. L. 105–115, §207(1)(A), substituted "paragraph (3)" for "paragraph (2)".

Subsec. (f)(2) to (4). Pub. L. 105–115, §207(2), (3), added par. (2) and redesignated former pars. (2) and (3) as (3) and (4), respectively.

Subsec. (f)(5). Pub. L. 105–115, §206(b), added par. (5).

Subsec. (i)(1)(A)(ii). Pub. L. 105–115, §206(c)(1), substituted "appropriate clinical or scientific data" for "clinical data", inserted "or a person accredited under section 360m of this title" after "Secretary", and substituted "effectiveness" for "efficacy".

Subsec. (i)(1)(C) to (E). Pub. L. 105–115, §205(b), added subpars. (C) to (E).

Subsec. (i)(1)(F). Pub. L. 105–115, §206(c)(2), added subpar. (F).

1993—Subsec. (b)(3). Pub. L. 103–80 substituted "5703" for "5703(b)".

1992—Subsec. (f)(3). Pub. L. 102–300 redesignated clauses (i) to (iii) as subpars. (A) to (C), respectively, and substituted "the section 360(k) report" for "the 360(k) report" in closing provisions.

1990—Subsec. (a)(1)(A)(ii). Pub. L. 101–629, §5(a)(1), substituted "or to establish special controls" for "or to establish a performance standard".

Subsec. (a)(1)(B). Pub. L. 101–629, §5(a)(2), amended subpar. (B) generally. Prior to amendment, subpar. (B) read as follows: "CLASS II, PERFORMANCE STANDARDS.—A device which cannot be classified as a class I device because the controls authorized by or under sections 351, 352, 360, 360f, 360h, 360i, and 360j of this title by themselves are insufficient to provide reasonable assurance of the safety and effectiveness of the device, for which there is sufficient information to establish a performance standard to provide such assurance, and for which it is therefore necessary to establish for the device a performance standard under section 360d of this title to provide reasonable assurance of its safety and effectiveness."

Subsec. (a)(1)(C)(i). Pub. L. 101–629, §5(a)(3), amended cl. (i) generally. Prior to amendment, cl. (i) read as follows: "it (I) cannot be classified as a class I device because insufficient information exists to determine that the controls authorized by or under sections 351, 352, 360, 360f, 360h, 360i, and 360j of this title are sufficient to provide reasonable assurance of the safety and effectiveness of the device and (II) cannot be classified as a class II device because insufficient information exists for the establishment of a performance standard to provide reasonable assurance of its safety and effectiveness, and".

Subsec. (e). Pub. L. 101–629, §5(b), designated existing provisions as par. (1), redesignated cls. (1) and (2) as (A) and (B), respectively, and added par. (2).

Subsec. (f). Pub. L. 101–629, §5(c)(3), inserted "and reclassification" before "of" in heading.

Subsec. (f)(2)(A). Pub. L. 101–629, §5(c)(1), substituted "The Secretary may initiate the reclassification of a device classified into class III under paragraph (1) of this subsection or the manufacturer" for "The manufacturer".

Subsec. (f)(2)(B)(i). Pub. L. 101–629, §18(a), substituted "the Secretary may for good cause shown" for "the Secretary shall".

Subsec. (f)(3). Pub. L. 101–629, §4(a), added par. (3).

Subsec. (i). Pub. L. 101–629, §12(a), added subsec. (i).

EFFECTIVE DATE OF 1997 AMENDMENT

Amendment by Pub. L. 105–115 effective 90 days after Nov. 21, 1997, except as otherwise provided, see section 501 of Pub. L. 105–115, set out as a note under section 321 of this title.

SHORT TITLE OF 1976 AMENDMENT

Pub. L. 94–295, §1(a), May 28, 1976, 90 Stat. 539, provided that: "This Act [enacting sections 360c to 360k, 379, and 379a of this title and section 3512 of Title 42, The Public Health and Welfare, and amending sections 321, 331, 334, 351, 352, 358, 360, 374, 379e, and 381 of this title and section 55 of Title 15, Commerce and Trade] may be cited as the 'Medical Device Amendments of 1976'."

REGULATIONS

Section 12(b) of Pub. L. 101–629 provided that: "Within 12 months of the date of the enactment of this Act [Nov. 28, 1990], the Secretary of Health and Human Services shall issue regulations establishing the requirements of the summaries under section 513(i)(3) of the Federal Food, Drug, and Cosmetic Act [21 U.S.C. 360c(i)(3)], as added by the amendment made by subsection (a)."

DAILY WEAR SOFT OR DAILY WEAR NONHYDROPHILIC PLASTIC CONTACT LENSES

Section 4(b)(3) of Pub. L. 101–629 provided that:

"(A) Notwithstanding section 520(*l*)(5) of the Federal Food, Drug, and Cosmetic Act [21 U.S.C. 360j(*l*)(5)], the Secretary of Health and Human Services shall not retain any daily wear soft or daily wear nonhydrophilic plastic contact lens in class III under such Act [this chapter] unless the Secretary finds that it meets the criteria set forth in section 513(a)(1)(C) of such Act [21 U.S.C. 360c(a)(1)(C)]. The finding and the grounds for the finding shall be published in the Federal Register. For any such lens, the Secretary shall make the determination respecting reclassification required in section 520(*l*)(5)(B) of such Act within 24 months of the date of the enactment of this paragraph [Nov. 28, 1990].

"(B) The Secretary of Health and Human Services may by notice published in the Federal Register extend the two-year period prescribed by subparagraph (A) for a lens for an additional period not to exceed one year.

"(C)(i) Before classifying a lens in class II pursuant to subparagraph (A), the Secretary of Health and Human Services shall pursuant to section 513(a)(1)(B) of such Act assure that appropriate regulatory safeguards are in effect which provide reasonable assurance of the safety and effectiveness of such lens, including clinical and preclinical data if deemed necessary by the Secretary.

"(ii) Prior to classifying a lens in class I pursuant to subparagraph (A), the Secretary shall assure that appropriate regulatory safeguards are in effect which provide reasonable assurance of the safety and effectiveness of such lens, including clinical and preclinical data if deemed necessary by the Secretary.

"(D) Notwithstanding section 520(*l*)(5) of such Act, if the Secretary of Health and Human Services has not made the finding and published the finding required by subparagraph (A) within 36 months of the date of the enactment of this subparagraph [Nov. 28, 1990], the Secretary shall issue an order placing the lens in class II.

"(E) Any person adversely affected by a final regulation under this paragraph revising the classification of a lens may challenge the revision of the classification of such lens only by filing a petition under section 513(e) for a classification change."

REFERENCES IN OTHER LAWS TO GS-16, 17, OR 18 PAY RATES

References in laws to the rates of pay for GS-16, 17, or 18, or to maximum rates of pay under the General Schedule, to be considered references to rates payable under specified sections of Title 5, Government Organization and Employees, see section 529 [title I, § 101(c)(1)] of Pub. L. 101-509, set out in a note under section 5376 of Title 5.

§ 360d. Performance standards

(a) Reasonable assurance of safe and effective performance; periodic evaluation

(1) The special controls required by section 360c(a)(1)(B) of this title shall include performance standards for a class II device if the Secretary determines that a performance standard is necessary to provide reasonable assurance of the safety and effectiveness of the device. A class III device may also be considered a class II device for purposes of establishing a standard for the device under subsection (b) of this section if the device has been reclassified as a class II device under a regulation under section 360c(e) of this title but such regulation provides that the reclassification is not to take effect until the effective date of such a standard for the device.

(2) A performance standard established under subsection (b) of this section for a device—

(A) shall include provisions to provide reasonable assurance of its safe and effective performance;

(B) shall, where necessary to provide reasonable assurance of its safe and effective performance, include—

(i) provisions respecting the construction, components, ingredients, and properties of the device and its compatibility with power systems and connections to such systems,

(ii) provisions for the testing (on a sample basis or, if necessary, on an individual basis) of the device or, if it is determined that no other more practicable means are available to the Secretary to assure the conformity of the device to the standard, provisions for the testing (on a sample basis or, if necessary, on an individual basis) by the Secretary or by another person at the direction of the Secretary,

(iii) provisions for the measurement of the performance characteristics of the device,

(iv) provisions requiring that the results of each or of certain of the tests of the device required to be made under clause (ii) show that the device is in conformity with the portions of the standard for which the test or tests were required, and

(v) a provision requiring that the sale and distribution of the device be restricted but only to the extent that the sale and distribution of a device may be restricted under a regulation under section 360j(e) of this title; and

(C) shall, where appropriate, require the use and prescribe the form and content of labeling for the proper installation, maintenance, operation, and use of the device.

(3) The Secretary shall provide for periodic evaluation of performance standards established under subsection (b) of this section to determine if such standards should be changed to reflect new medical, scientific, or other technological data.

(4) In carrying out his duties under this subsection and subsection (b) of this section, the Secretary shall, to the maximum extent practicable—

(A) use personnel, facilities, and other technical support available in other Federal agencies,

(B) consult with other Federal agencies concerned with standard-setting and other nationally or internationally recognized standard-setting entities, and

(C) invite appropriate participation, through joint or other conferences, workshops, or other means, by informed persons representative of scientific, professional, industry, or consumer organizations who in his judgment can make a significant contribution.

(b) Establishment of a standard

(1)(A) The Secretary shall publish in the Federal Register a notice of proposed rulemaking for the establishment, amendment, or revocation of any performance standard for a device.

(B) A notice of proposed rulemaking for the establishment or amendment of a performance standard for a device shall—

(i) set forth a finding with supporting justification that the performance standard is appropriate and necessary to provide reasonable assurance of the safety and effectiveness of the device,

(ii) set forth proposed findings with respect to the risk of illness or injury that the performance standard is intended to reduce or eliminate,

(iii) invite interested persons to submit to the Secretary, within 30 days of the publication of the notice, requests for changes in the classification of the device pursuant to section 360c(e) of this title based on new information relevant to the classification, and

(iv) invite interested persons to submit an existing performance standard for the device, including a draft or proposed performance standard, for consideration by the Secretary.

(C) A notice of proposed rulemaking for the revocation of a performance standard shall set forth a finding with supporting justification that the performance standard is no longer necessary to provide reasonable assurance of the safety and effectiveness of a device.

(D) The Secretary shall provide for a comment period of not less than 60 days.

(2) If, after publication of a notice in accordance with paragraph (1), the Secretary receives a request for a change in the classification of the device, the Secretary shall, within 60 days of the publication of the notice, after consultation with the appropriate panel under section 360c of this title, either deny the request or give notice of an intent to initiate such change under section 360c(e) of this title.

(3)(A) After the expiration of the period for comment on a notice of proposed rulemaking published under paragraph (1) respecting a performance standard and after consideration of such comments and any report from an advisory committee under paragraph (5), the Secretary shall (i) promulgate a regulation establishing a performance standard and publish in the Federal Register findings on the matters referred to in paragraph (1), or (ii) publish a notice terminating the proceeding for the development of the standard together with the reasons for such termination. If a notice of termination is published, the Secretary shall (unless such notice is issued because the device is a banned device under section 360f of this title) initiate a proceeding under section 360c(e) of this title to reclassify the device subject to the proceeding terminated by such notice.

(B) A regulation establishing a performance standard shall set forth the date or dates upon which the standard shall take effect, but no such regulation may take effect before one year after the date of its publication unless (i) the Secretary determines that an earlier effective date is necessary for the protection of the public health and safety, or (ii) such standard has been established for a device which, effective upon the effective date of the standard, has been reclassified from class III to class II. Such date or dates shall be established so as to minimize, consistent with the public health and safety, economic loss to, and disruption or dislocation of, domestic and international trade.

(4)(A) The Secretary, upon his own initiative or upon petition of an interested person may by regulation, promulgated in accordance with the requirements of paragraphs (1), (2), and (3)(B) of this subsection, amend or revoke a performance standard.

(B) The Secretary may declare a proposed amendment of a performance standard to be effective on and after its publication in the Federal Register and until the effective date of any final action taken on such amendment if he determines that making it so effective is in the public interest. A proposed amendment of a performance standard made so effective under the preceding sentence may not prohibit, during the period in which it is so effective, the introduction or delivery for introduction into interstate commerce of a device which conforms to such standard without the change or changes provided by such proposed amendment.

(5)(A) The Secretary—

(i) may on his own initiative refer a proposed regulation for the establishment, amendment, or revocation of a performance standard, or

(ii) shall, upon the request of an interested person which demonstrates good cause for referral and which is made before the expiration of the period for submission of comments on such proposed regulation refer such proposed regulation,

to an advisory committee of experts, established pursuant to subparagraph (B), for a report and recommendation with respect to any matter involved in the proposed regulation which requires the exercise of scientific judgment. If a proposed regulation is referred under this subparagraph to an advisory committee, the Secretary shall provide the advisory committee with the data and information on which such proposed regulation is based. The advisory committee shall, within sixty days of the referral of a proposed regulation and after independent study of the data and information furnished to it by the Secretary and other data and information before it, submit to the Secretary a report and recommendation respecting such regulation, together with all underlying data and information and a statement of the reason or basis for the recommendation. A copy of such report and recommendation shall be made public by the Secretary.

(B) The Secretary shall establish advisory committees (which may not be panels under section 360c of this title) to receive referrals under subparagraph (A). The Secretary shall appoint as members of any such advisory committee persons qualified in the subject matter to be referred to the committee and of appropriately diversified professional background, except that the Secretary may not appoint to such a committee any individual who is in the regular full-time employ of the United States and engaged in the administration of this chapter. Each such committee shall include as nonvoting members a representative of consumer interests and a representative of interests of the device manufacturing industry. Members of an advisory committee who are not officers or employees of the United States, while attending conferences or meetings of their committee or otherwise serving at the request of the Secretary, shall be entitled to receive compensation at rates to be fixed by the Secretary, which rates may not exceed the daily equivalent of the rate in effect for grade GS–18 of the General Schedule, for each day (including traveltime) they are so engaged; and while so serving away from their homes or regular places of business each member may be allowed travel expenses, including per diem in lieu of subsistence, as authorized by section 5703 of title 5 for persons in the Government service employed intermittently. The Secretary shall designate one of the members of each advisory committee to serve as chairman thereof. The Secretary shall furnish each advisory committee with clerical and other assistance, and shall by regulation prescribe the procedures to be followed by each such committee in acting on referrals made under subparagraph (A).

(c) Recognition of standard

(1)(A) In addition to establishing a performance standard under this section, the Secretary shall, by publication in the Federal Register, recognize all or part of an appropriate standard established by a nationally or internationally recognized standard development organization for which a person may submit a declaration of conformity in order to meet a premarket submission requirement or other requirement under this chapter to which such standard is applicable.

(B) If a person elects to use a standard recognized by the Secretary under subparagraph (A) to meet the requirements described in such subparagraph, the person shall provide a declaration of conformity to the Secretary that certifies that the device is in conformity with such standard. A person may elect to use data, or information, other than data required by a standard recognized under subparagraph (A) to meet any requirement regarding devices under this chapter.

(2) The Secretary may withdraw such recognition of a standard through publication of a notice in the Federal Register if the Secretary determines that the standard is no longer appropriate for meeting a requirement regarding devices under this chapter.

(3)(A) Subject to subparagraph (B), the Secretary shall accept a declaration of conformity that a device is in conformity with a standard recognized under paragraph (1) unless the Secretary finds—

(i) that the data or information submitted to support such declaration does not demonstrate that the device is in conformity with the standard identified in the declaration of conformity; or

(ii) that the standard identified in the declaration of conformity is not applicable to the particular device under review.

(B) The Secretary may request, at any time, the data or information relied on by the person to make a declaration of conformity with respect to a standard recognized under paragraph (1).

(C) A person making a declaration of conformity with respect to a standard recognized under paragraph (1) shall maintain the data and information demonstrating conformity of the device to the standard for a period of two years after the date of the classification or approval of the device by the Secretary or a period equal to the expected design life of the device, whichever is longer.

(June 25, 1938, ch. 675, §514, as added Pub. L. 94–295, §2, May 28, 1976, 90 Stat. 546; amended Pub. L. 94–460, title III, §304, Oct. 8, 1976, 90 Stat. 1960; Pub. L. 101–629, §§6(a), (b)(1), 18(b), Nov. 28, 1990, 104 Stat. 4519, 4528; Pub. L. 102–300, §6(g), June 16, 1992, 106 Stat. 241; Pub. L. 103–80, §4(a)(1), Aug. 13, 1993, 107 Stat. 779; Pub. L. 105–115, title II, §204(a), (d), Nov. 21, 1997, 111 Stat. 2335, 2336.)

AMENDMENTS

1997—Subsec. (a)(1). Pub. L. 105–115, §204(d)(1), substituted "under subsection (b) of this section" for "under this section".

Subsec. (a)(2). Pub. L. 105–115, §204(d)(2), substituted "under subsection (b) of this section" for "under this section" in introductory provisions.

Subsec. (a)(3). Pub. L. 105–115, §204(d)(3), substituted "under subsection (b) of this section" for "under this section".

Subsec. (a)(4). Pub. L. 105–115, §204(d)(4), substituted "this subsection and subsection (b) of this section" for "this section" in introductory provisions.

Subsec. (c). Pub. L. 105–115, §204(a), added subsec. (c).

1993—Subsec. (b)(4)(B), (5)(A)(ii). Pub. L. 103–80 amended directory language of Pub. L. 101–619, §18(b), identical to amendment by Pub. L. 102–300, §6(g)(1). See 1992 and 1990 Amendment notes below.

1992—Subsec. (b)(4)(B), (5)(A)(ii). Pub. L. 102–300 made technical corrections to directory language of Pub. L. 101–629, §18(b)(1), (2). See 1990 Amendment note below.

1990—Subsec. (a)(1). Pub. L. 101–629, §6(a)(1), substituted "The special controls required by section 360c(a)(1)(B) of this title shall include performance standards for a class II device if the Secretary determines that a performance standard is necessary to provide reasonable assurance of the safety and effectiveness of the device." for "The Secretary may by regulation, promulgated in accordance with this section, establish a performance standard for a class II device."

Subsec. (b). Pub. L. 101–629, §6(a)(2), (3), redesignated subsec. (g) as (b) and struck out former subsec. (b) which read as follows:

"(1) A proceeding for the development of a performance standard for a device shall be initiated by the Secretary by the publication in the Federal Register of notice of the opportunity to submit to the Secretary a request (within fifteen days of the date of the publication of the notice) for a change in the classification of the device based on new information relevant to its classification.

"(2) If, after publication of a notice pursuant to paragraph (1) the Secretary receives a request for a change in the device's classification, he shall, within sixty days of the publication of such notice and after consultation with the appropriate panel under section 360c of this title, by order published in the Federal Register, either deny the request for change in classification or give notice of his intent to initiate such a change under section 360c(e) of this title."

Subsec. (b)(1), (2). Pub. L. 101–629, §6(a)(4), amended pars. (1) and (2) generally. Prior to amendment, pars. (1) and (2) read as follows:

"(1)(A) After publication pursuant to subsection (c) of this section of a notice respecting a performance standard for a device, the Secretary shall either—

"(i) publish, in the Federal Register in a notice of proposed rulemaking, a proposed performance standard for the device (I) developed by an offeror under such notice and accepted by the Secretary, (II) developed under subsection (c)(4) of this section, (III) accepted by the Secretary under subsection (d) of this section, or (IV) developed by him under subsection (f) of this section, or

"(ii) issue a notice in the Federal Register that the proceeding is terminated together with the reasons for such termination.

"(B) If the Secretary issues under subparagraph (A)(ii) a notice of termination of a proceeding to establish a performance standard for a device, he shall (unless such notice is issued because the device is a banned device under section 360f of this title) initiate a proceeding under section 360c(e) of this title to reclassify the device subject to the proceeding terminated by such notice.

"(2) A notice of proposed rulemaking for the establishment of a performance standard for a device published under paragraph (1)(A)(i) shall set forth proposed findings with respect to the degree of the risk of illness or injury designed to be eliminated or reduced by the proposed standard and the benefit to the public from the device."

Subsec. (b)(3)(A)(i). Pub. L. 101–629, §6(b)(1)(A), substituted "paragraph (1)" for "paragraph (2)".

Subsec. (b)(4)(A). Pub. L. 101–629, § 6(b)(1)(B), substituted "paragraphs (1), (2), and (3)(B)" for "paragraphs (2) and (3)(B)".

Subsec. (b)(4)(B). Pub. L. 101–629, § 18(b)(1), as amended by Pub. L. 102–300, § 6(g)(1), (2), and Pub. L. 103–80, § 4(a)(1), struck out ", after affording all interested persons an opportunity for an informal hearing," after "if he determines".

Subsec. (b)(5)(A)(ii). Pub. L. 101–629, § 18(b)(2), as amended by Pub. L. 102–300, § 6(g)(1), (3), and Pub. L. 103–80, § 4(a)(1), substituted "which demonstrates good cause for referral and which is made before the expiration of the period for submission of comments on such proposed regulation refer such proposed regulation," for "unless the Secretary finds the request to be without good cause or the request is made after the expiration of the period for submission of comments on such proposed regulation refer such proposed regulation,".

Subsecs. (c) to (f). Pub. L. 101–629, § 6(a)(2), struck out subsec. (c) relating to invitations for standards, subsec. (d) relating to acceptance of certain existing standards, subsec. (e) relating to acceptance of offers to develop standards, and subsec. (f) relating to development of standards by the Secretary after publication of notice inviting submissions or offers of standards.

Subsec. (g). Pub. L. 101–629, § 6(a)(3), redesignated subsec. (g) as (b).

1976—Subsec. (a). Pub. L. 94–460 redesignated pars. (4) and (5) as (3) and (4), respectively. Section as originally enacted contained no par. (3).

EFFECTIVE DATE OF 1997 AMENDMENT

Amendment by Pub. L. 105–115 effective 90 days after Nov. 21, 1997, except as otherwise provided, see section 501 of Pub. L. 105–115, set out as a note under section 321 of this title.

REFERENCES IN OTHER LAWS TO GS–16, 17, OR 18 PAY RATES

References in laws to the rates of pay for GS–16, 17, or 18, or to maximum rates of pay under the General Schedule, to be considered references to rates payable under specified sections of Title 5, Government Organization and Employees, see section 529 [title I, § 101(c)(1)] of Pub. L. 101–509, set out in a note under section 5376 of Title 5.

TERMINATION OF ADVISORY COMMITTEES

Advisory committees in existence on Jan. 5, 1973, to terminate not later than the expiration of the 2-year period following Jan. 5, 1973, and advisory committees established after Jan. 5, 1973, to terminate not later than the expiration of the 2-year period beginning on the date of their establishment, unless in the case of a committee established by the President or an officer of the Federal Government, such committee is renewed by appropriate action prior to the expiration of such 2-year period, or in the case of a committee established by Congress, its duration is otherwise provided by law. See section 14 of Pub. L. 92–463, Oct. 6, 1972, 86 Stat. 776, set out in the Appendix to Title 5, Government Organization and Employees.

§ 360e. Premarket approval

(a) General requirement

A class III device—

(1) which is subject to a regulation promulgated under subsection (b) of this section; or

(2) which is a class III device because of section 360c(f) of this title,

is required to have, unless exempt under section 360j(g) of this title, an approval under this section of an application for premarket approval or, as applicable, an approval under subsection (c)(2) of this section of a report seeking premarket approval.

(b) Regulation to require premarket approval

(1) In the case of a class III device which—

(A) was introduced or delivered for introduction into interstate commerce for commercial distribution before May 28, 1976; or

(B) is (i) of a type so introduced or delivered, and (ii) is substantially equivalent to another device within that type,

the Secretary shall by regulation, promulgated in accordance with this subsection, require that such device have an approval under this section of an application for premarket approval.

(2)(A) A proceeding for the promulgation of a regulation under paragraph (1) respecting a device shall be initiated by the publication in the Federal Register of a notice of proposed rulemaking. Such notice shall contain—

(i) the proposed regulation;

(ii) proposed findings with respect to the degree of risk of illness or injury designed to be eliminated or reduced by requiring the device to have an approved application for premarket approval and the benefit to the public from use of the device;

(iii) opportunity for the submission of comments on the proposed regulation and the proposed findings; and

(iv) opportunity to request a change in the classification of the device based on new information relevant to the classification of the device.

(B) If, within fifteen days after publication of a notice under subparagraph (A), the Secretary receives a request for a change in the classification of a device, he shall, within sixty days of the publication of such notice and after consultation with the appropriate panel under section 360c of this title, by order published in the Federal Register, either deny the request for change in classification or give notice of his intent to initiate such a change under section 360c(e) of this title.

(3) After the expiration of the period for comment on a proposed regulation and proposed findings published under paragraph (2) and after consideration of comments submitted on such proposed regulation and findings, the Secretary shall (A) promulgate such regulation and publish in the Federal Register findings on the matters referred to in paragraph (2)(A)(ii), or (B) publish a notice terminating the proceeding for the promulgation of the regulation together with the reasons for such termination. If a notice of termination is published, the Secretary shall (unless such notice is issued because the device is a banned device under section 360f of this title) initiate a proceeding under section 360c(e) of this title to reclassify the device subject to the proceeding terminated by such notice.

(4) The Secretary, upon his own initiative or upon petition of an interested person, may by regulation amend or revoke any regulation promulgated under this subsection. A regulation to amend or revoke a regulation under this subsection shall be promulgated in accordance with the requirements prescribed by this subsection for the promulgation of the regulation to be amended or revoked.

(c) Application for premarket approval

(1) Any person may file with the Secretary an application for premarket approval for a class III device. Such an application for a device shall contain—

(A) full reports of all information, published or known to or which should reasonably be known to the applicant, concerning investigations which have been made to show whether or not such device is safe and effective;

(B) a full statement of the components, ingredients, and properties and of the principle or principles of operation, of such device;

(C) a full description of the methods used in, and the facilities and controls used for, the manufacture, processing, and, when relevant, packing and installation of, such device;

(D) an identifying reference to any performance standard under section 360d of this title which would be applicable to any aspect of such device if it were a class II device, and either adequate information to show that such aspect of such device fully meets such performance standard or adequate information to justify any deviation from such standard;

(E) such samples of such device and of components thereof as the Secretary may reasonably require, except that where the submission of such samples is impracticable or unduly burdensome, the requirement of this subparagraph may be met by the submission of complete information concerning the location of one or more such devices readily available for examination and testing;

(F) specimens of the labeling proposed to be used for such device;

(G) the certification required under section 282(j)(5)(B) of title 42 (which shall not be considered an element of such application); and

(H) such other information relevant to the subject matter of the application as the Secretary, with the concurrence of the appropriate panel under section 360c of this title, may require.

(2)(A) Any person may file with the Secretary a report seeking premarket approval for a class III device referred to in subsection (a) of this section that is a reprocessed single-use device. Such a report shall contain the following:

(i) The device name, including both the trade or proprietary name and the common or usual name.

(ii) The establishment registration number of the owner or operator submitting the report.

(iii) Actions taken to comply with performance standards under section 360d of this title.

(iv) Proposed labels, labeling, and advertising sufficient to describe the device, its intended use, and directions for use.

(v) Full reports of all information, published or known to or which should be reasonably known to the applicant, concerning investigations which have been made to show whether or not the device is safe or effective.

(vi) A description of the device's components, ingredients, and properties.

(vii) A full description of the methods used in, and the facilities and controls used for, the reprocessing and packing of the device.

(viii) Such samples of the device that the Secretary may reasonably require.

(ix) A financial certification or disclosure statement or both, as required by part 54 of title 21, Code of Federal Regulations.

(x) A statement that the applicant believes to the best of the applicant's knowledge that all data and information submitted to the Secretary are truthful and accurate and that no material fact has been omitted in the report.

(xi) Any additional data and information, including information of the type required in paragraph (1) for an application under such paragraph, that the Secretary determines is necessary to determine whether there is reasonable assurance of safety and effectiveness for the reprocessed device.

(xii) Validation data described in section 360(*o*)(1)(A) of this title that demonstrates that the reasonable assurance of the safety or effectiveness of the device will remain after the maximum number of times the device is reprocessed as intended by the person submitting such report.

(B) In the case of a class III device referred to in subsection (a) of this section that is a reprocessed single-use device:

(i) Subparagraph (A) of this paragraph applies in lieu of paragraph (1).

(ii) Subject to clause (i), the provisions of this section apply to a report under subparagraph (A) to the same extent and in the same manner as such provisions apply to an application under paragraph (1).

(iii) Each reference in other sections of this chapter to an application under this section, other than such a reference in section 379i or 379j of this title, shall be considered to be a reference to a report under subparagraph (A).

(iv) Each reference in other sections of this chapter to a device for which an application under this section has been approved, or has been denied, suspended, or withdrawn, other than such a reference in section 379i or 379j of this title, shall be considered to be a reference to a device for which a report under subparagraph (A) has been approved, or has been denied, suspended, or withdrawn, respectively.

(3) Upon receipt of an application meeting the requirements set forth in paragraph (1), the Secretary—

(A) may on the Secretary's own initiative, or

(B) shall, upon the request of an applicant unless the Secretary finds that the information in the application which would be reviewed by a panel substantially duplicates information which has previously been reviewed by a panel appointed under section 360c of this title,

refer such application to the appropriate panel under section 360c of this title for study and for submission (within such period as he may establish) of a report and recommendation respecting approval of the application, together with all underlying data and the reasons or basis for the recommendation. Where appropriate, the Secretary shall ensure that such panel includes, or consults with, one or more pediatric experts.

(4)(A) Prior to the submission of an application under this subsection, the Secretary shall accept and review any portion of the application that the applicant and the Secretary agree is complete, ready, and appropriate for review, except that such requirement does not apply, and the Secretary has discretion whether to accept and review such portion, during any period in which, under section 379j(g) of this title, the Secretary does not have the authority to collect fees under section 379j(a) of this title.

(B) Each portion of a submission reviewed under subparagraph (A) and found acceptable by the Secretary shall not be further reviewed after receipt of an application that satisfies the requirements of paragraph (1), unless a significant issue of safety or effectiveness provides the Secretary reason to review such accepted portion.

(C) Whenever the Secretary determines that a portion of a submission under subparagraph (A) is unacceptable, the Secretary shall, in writing, provide to the applicant a description of any deficiencies in such portion and identify the information that is required to correct these deficiencies, unless the applicant is no longer pursuing the application.

(d) Action on application for premarket approval

(1)(A) As promptly as possible, but in no event later than one hundred and eighty days after the receipt of an application under subsection (c) of this section (except as provided in section 360j(*l*)(3)(D)(ii) of this title or unless, in accordance with subparagraph (B)(i), an additional period as agreed upon by the Secretary and the applicant), the Secretary, after considering the report and recommendation submitted under paragraph (2) of such subsection, shall—

(i) issue an order approving the application if he finds that none of the grounds for denying approval specified in paragraph (2) of this subsection applies; or

(ii) deny approval of the application if he finds (and sets forth the basis for such finding as part of or accompanying such denial) that one or more grounds for denial specified in paragraph (2) of this subsection apply.

In making the determination whether to approve or deny the application, the Secretary shall rely on the conditions of use included in the proposed labeling as the basis for determining whether or not there is a reasonable assurance of safety and effectiveness, if the proposed labeling is neither false nor misleading. In determining whether or not such labeling is false or misleading, the Secretary shall fairly evaluate all material facts pertinent to the proposed labeling.

(B)(i) The Secretary may not enter into an agreement to extend the period in which to take action with respect to an application submitted for a device subject to a regulation promulgated under subsection (b) of this section unless he finds that the continued availability of the device is necessary for the public health.

(ii) An order approving an application for a device may require as a condition to such approval that the sale and distribution of the device be restricted but only to the extent that the sale and distribution of a device may be restricted under a regulation under section 360j(e) of this title.

(iii) The Secretary shall accept and review statistically valid and reliable data and any other information from investigations conducted under the authority of regulations required by section 360j(g) of this title to make a determination of whether there is a reasonable assurance of safety and effectiveness of a device subject to a pending application under this section if—

(I) the data or information is derived from investigations of an earlier version of the device, the device has been modified during or after the investigations (but prior to submission of an application under subsection (c) of this section) and such a modification of the device does not constitute a significant change in the design or in the basic principles of operation of the device that would invalidate the data or information; or

(II) the data or information relates to a device approved under this section, is available for use under this chapter, and is relevant to the design and intended use of the device for which the application is pending.

(2) The Secretary shall deny approval of an application for a device if, upon the basis of the information submitted to the Secretary as part of the application and any other information before him with respect to such device, the Secretary finds that—

(A) there is a lack of a showing of reasonable assurance that such device is safe under the conditions of use prescribed, recommended, or suggested in the proposed labeling thereof;

(B) there is a lack of a showing of reasonable assurance that the device is effective under the conditions of use prescribed, recommended, or suggested in the proposed labeling thereof;

(C) the methods used in, or the facilities or controls used for, the manufacture, processing, packing, or installation of such device do not conform to the requirements of section 360j(f) of this title;

(D) based on a fair evaluation of all material facts, the proposed labeling is false or misleading in any particular; or

(E) such device is not shown to conform in all respects to a performance standard in effect under section 360d of this title compliance with which is a condition to approval of the application and there is a lack of adequate information to justify the deviation from such standard.

Any denial of an application shall, insofar as the Secretary determines to be practicable, be accompanied by a statement informing the applicant of the measures required to place such application in approvable form (which measures may include further research by the applicant in accordance with one or more protocols prescribed by the Secretary).

(3)(A)(i) The Secretary shall, upon the written request of an applicant, meet with the applicant, not later than 100 days after the receipt of an application that has been filed as complete under subsection (c) of this section, to discuss the review status of the application.

(ii) The Secretary shall, in writing and prior to the meeting, provide to the applicant a description of any deficiencies in the application that, at that point, have been identified by the Secretary based on an interim review of the entire application and identify the information that is required to correct those deficiencies.

(iii) The Secretary shall notify the applicant promptly of—

(I) any additional deficiency identified in the application, or

(II) any additional information required to achieve completion of the review and final action on the application,

that was not described as a deficiency in the written description provided by the Secretary under clause (ii).

(B) The Secretary and the applicant may, by mutual consent, establish a different schedule for a meeting required under this paragraph.

(4) An applicant whose application has been denied approval may, by petition filed on or before the thirtieth day after the date upon which he receives notice of such denial, obtain review thereof in accordance with either paragraph (1) or (2) of subsection (g) of this section, and any interested person may obtain review, in accordance with paragraph (1) or (2) of subsection (g) of this section, of an order of the Secretary approving an application.

(5) In order to provide for more effective treatment or diagnosis of life-threatening or irreversibly debilitating human diseases or conditions, the Secretary shall provide review priority for devices—

(A) representing breakthrough technologies,

(B) for which no approved alternatives exist,

(C) which offer significant advantages over existing approved alternatives, or

(D) the availability of which is in the best interest of the patients.

(6)(A)(i) A supplemental application shall be required for any change to a device subject to an approved application under this subsection that affects safety or effectiveness, unless such change is a modification in a manufacturing procedure or method of manufacturing and the holder of the approved application submits a written notice to the Secretary that describes in detail the change, summarizes the data or information supporting the change, and informs the Secretary that the change has been made under the requirements of section 360j(f) of this title.

(ii) The holder of an approved application who submits a notice under clause (i) with respect to a manufacturing change of a device may distribute the device 30 days after the date on which the Secretary receives the notice, unless the Secretary within such 30-day period notifies the holder that the notice is not adequate and describes such further information or action that is required for acceptance of such change. If the Secretary notifies the holder that a supplemental application is required, the Secretary shall review the supplement within 135 days after the receipt of the supplement. The time used by the Secretary to review the notice of the manufacturing change shall be deducted from the 135-day review period if the notice meets appropriate content requirements for premarket approval supplements.

(B)(i) Subject to clause (ii), in reviewing a supplement to an approved application, for an incremental change to the design of a device that affects safety or effectiveness, the Secretary shall approve such supplement if—

(I) nonclinical data demonstrate that the design modification creates the intended additional capacity, function, or performance of the device; and

(II) clinical data from the approved application and any supplement to the approved application provide a reasonable assurance of safety and effectiveness for the changed device.

(ii) The Secretary may require, when necessary, additional clinical data to evaluate the design modification of the device to provide a reasonable assurance of safety and effectiveness.

(e) Withdrawal and temporary suspension of approval of application

(1) The Secretary shall, upon obtaining, where appropriate, advice on scientific matters from a panel or panels under section 360c of this title, and after due notice and opportunity for informal hearing to the holder of an approved application for a device, issue an order withdrawing approval of the application if the Secretary finds—

(A) that such device is unsafe or ineffective under the conditions of use prescribed, recommended, or suggested in the labeling thereof;

(B) on the basis of new information before him with respect to such device, evaluated together with the evidence available to him when the application was approved, that there is a lack of a showing of reasonable assurance that the device is safe or effective under the conditions of use prescribed, recommended, or suggested in the labeling thereof;

(C) that the application contained or was accompanied by an untrue statement of a material fact;

(D) that the applicant (i) has failed to establish a system for maintaining records, or has repeatedly or deliberately failed to maintain records or to make reports, required by an applicable regulation under section 360i(a) of this title, (ii) has refused to permit access to, or copying or verification of, such records as required by section 374 of this title, or (iii) has not complied with the requirements of section 360 of this title;

(E) on the basis of new information before him with respect to such device, evaluated together with the evidence before him when the application was approved, that the methods used in, or the facilities and controls used for, the manufacture, processing, packing, or installation of such device do not conform with the requirements of section 360j(f) of this title and were not brought into conformity with such requirements within a reasonable time after receipt of written notice from the Secretary of nonconformity;

(F) on the basis of new information before him, evaluated together with the evidence before him when the application was approved, that the labeling of such device, based on a fair evaluation of all material facts, is false or misleading in any particular and was not corrected within a reasonable time after receipt of written notice from the Secretary of such fact; or

(G) on the basis of new information before him, evaluated together with the evidence before him when the application was approved, that such device is not shown to conform in all respects to a performance standard which is in effect under section 360d of this title compliance with which was a condition to approval of the application and that there is a lack of adequate information to justify the deviation from such standard.

(2) The holder of an application subject to an order issued under paragraph (1) withdrawing approval of the application may, by petition filed on or before the thirtieth day after the date upon which he receives notice of such withdrawal, obtain review thereof in accordance with either paragraph (1) or (2) of subsection (g) of this section.

(3) If, after providing an opportunity for an informal hearing, the Secretary determines there is reasonable probability that the continuation of distribution of a device under an approved application would cause serious, adverse health consequences or death, the Secretary shall by order temporarily suspend the approval of the application approved under this section. If the Secretary issues such an order, the Secretary shall proceed expeditiously under paragraph (1) to withdraw such application.

(f) Product development protocol

(1) In the case of a class III device which is required to have an approval of an application submitted under subsection (c) of this section, such device shall be considered as having such an approval if a notice of completion of testing conducted in accordance with a product development protocol approved under paragraph (4) has been declared completed under paragraph (6).

(2) Any person may submit to the Secretary a proposed product development protocol with respect to a device. Such a protocol shall be accompanied by data supporting it. If, within thirty days of the receipt of such a protocol, the Secretary determines that it appears to be appropriate to apply the requirements of this subsection to the device with respect to which the protocol is submitted, the Secretary—

(A) may, at the initiative of the Secretary, refer the proposed protocol to the appropriate panel under section 360c of this title for its recommendation respecting approval of the protocol; or

(B) shall so refer such protocol upon the request of the submitter, unless the Secretary finds that the proposed protocol and accompanying data which would be reviewed by such panel substantially duplicate a product development protocol and accompanying data which have previously been reviewed by such a panel.

(3) A proposed product development protocol for a device may be approved only if—

(A) the Secretary determines that it is appropriate to apply the requirements of this subsection to the device in lieu of the requirement of approval of an application submitted under subsection (c) of this section; and

(B) the Secretary determines that the proposed protocol provides—

(i) a description of the device and the changes which may be made in the device,

(ii) a description of the preclinical trials (if any) of the device and a specification of (I) the results from such trials to be required before the commencement of clinical trials of the device, and (II) any permissible variations in preclinical trials and the results therefrom,

(iii) a description of the clinical trials (if any) of the device and a specification of (I) the results from such trials to be required before the filing of a notice of completion of the requirements of the protocol, and (II) any permissible variations in such trials and the results therefrom,

(iv) a description of the methods to be used in, and the facilities and controls to be used for, the manufacture, processing, and, when relevant, packing and installation of the device,

(v) an identifying reference to any performance standard under section 360d of this title to be applicable to any aspect of such device,

(vi) if appropriate, specimens of the labeling proposed to be used for such device,

(vii) such other information relevant to the subject matter of the protocol as the Secretary, with the concurrence of the appropriate panel or panels under section 360c of this title, may require, and

(viii) a requirement for submission of progress reports and, when completed, records of the trials conducted under the protocol which records are adequate to show compliance with the protocol.

(4) The Secretary shall approve or disapprove a proposed product development protocol submitted under paragraph (2) within one hundred and twenty days of its receipt unless an additional period is agreed upon by the Secretary and the person who submitted the protocol. Approval of a protocol or denial of approval of a protocol is final agency action subject to judicial review under chapter 7 of title 5.

(5) At any time after a product development protocol for a device has been approved pursuant to paragraph (4), the person for whom the protocol was approved may submit a notice of completion—

(A) stating (i) his determination that the requirements of the protocol have been fulfilled and that, to the best of his knowledge, there is no reason bearing on safety or effectiveness why the notice of completion should not become effective, and (ii) the data and other information upon which such determination was made, and

(B) setting forth the results of the trials required by the protocol and all the information required by subsection (c)(1) of this section.

(6)(A) The Secretary may, after providing the person who has an approved protocol and opportunity for an informal hearing and at any time prior to receipt of notice of completion of such protocol, issue a final order to revoke such protocol if he finds that—

(i) such person has failed substantially to comply with the requirements of the protocol,

(ii) the results of the trials obtained under the protocol differ so substantially from the results required by the protocol that further trials cannot be justified, or

(iii) the results of the trials conducted under the protocol or available new information do not demonstrate that the device tested under the protocol does not present an unreasonable risk to health and safety.

(B) After the receipt of a notice of completion of an approved protocol the Secretary shall, within the ninety-day period beginning on the date such notice is received, by order either declare the protocol completed or declare it not completed. An order declaring a protocol not completed may take effect only after the Secretary has provided the person who has the protocol opportunity for an informal hearing on the order. Such an order may be issued only if the Secretary finds—

(i) such person has failed substantially to comply with the requirements of the protocol,

(ii) the results of the trials obtained under the protocol differ substantially from the results required by the protocol, or

(iii) there is a lack of a showing of reasonable assurance of the safety and effectiveness of the device under the conditions of use prescribed, recommended, or suggested in the proposed labeling thereof.

(C) A final order issued under subparagraph (A) or (B) shall be in writing and shall contain the reasons to support the conclusions thereof.

(7) At any time after a notice of completion has become effective, the Secretary may issue an order (after due notice and opportunity for an informal hearing to the person for whom the notice is effective) revoking the approval of a device provided by a notice of completion which has become effective as provided in subparagraph (B) if he finds that any of the grounds listed in subparagraphs (A) through (G) of subsection (e)(1) of this section apply. Each reference in such subparagraphs to an application shall be considered for purposes of this paragraph as a reference to a protocol and the notice of completion of such protocol, and each reference to the time when an application was approved shall be considered for purposes of this paragraph as a reference to the time when a notice of completion took effect.

(8) A person who has an approved protocol subject to an order issued under paragraph (6)(A) revoking such protocol, a person who has an approved protocol with respect to which an order under paragraph (6)(B) was issued declaring that the protocol had not been completed, or a person subject to an order issued under paragraph (7) revoking the approval of a device may, by petition filed on or before the thirtieth day after the date upon which he receives notice of such order, obtain review thereof in accordance with either paragraph (1) or (2) of subsection (g) of this section.

(g) Review

(1) Upon petition for review of—

(A) an order under subsection (d) of this section approving or denying approval of an application or an order under subsection (e) of this section withdrawing approval of an application, or

(B) an order under subsection (f)(6)(A) of this section revoking an approved protocol, under subsection (f)(6)(B) of this section declaring that an approved protocol has not been completed, or under subsection (f)(7) of this section revoking the approval of a device,

the Secretary shall, unless he finds the petition to be without good cause or unless a petition for review of such order has been submitted under paragraph (2), hold a hearing, in accordance with section 554 of title 5, on the order. The panel or panels which considered the application, protocol, or device subject to such order shall designate a member to appear and testify at any such hearing upon request of the Secretary, the petitioner, or the officer conducting the hearing, but this requirement does not preclude any other member of the panel or panels from appearing and testifying at any such hearing. Upon completion of such hearing and after considering the record established in such hearing, the Secretary shall issue an order either affirming the order subject to the hearing or reversing such order and, as appropriate, approving or denying approval of the application, reinstating the application's approval, approving the protocol, or placing in effect a notice of completion.

(2)(A) Upon petition for review of—

(i) an order under subsection (d) of this section approving or denying approval of an application or an order under subsection (e) of this section withdrawing approval of an application, or

(ii) an order under subsection (f)(6)(A) of this section revoking an approved protocol, under subsection (f)(6)(B) of this section declaring that an approved protocol has not been completed, or under subsection (f)(7) of this section revoking the approval of a device,

the Secretary shall refer the application or protocol subject to the order and the basis for the order to an advisory committee of experts established pursuant to subparagraph (B) for a report and recommendation with respect to the order. The advisory committee shall, after independent study of the data and information furnished to it by the Secretary and other data and information before it, submit to the Secretary a report and recommendation, together with all underlying data and information and a statement of the reasons or basis for the recommendation. A copy of such report shall be promptly supplied by the Secretary to any person who petitioned for such referral to the advisory committee.

(B) The Secretary shall establish advisory committees (which may not be panels under section 360c of this title) to receive referrals under subparagraph (A). The Secretary shall appoint as members of any such advisory committee persons qualified in the subject matter to be referred to the committee and of appropriately diversified professional backgrounds, except that the Secretary may not appoint to such a committee any individual who is in the regular full-time employ of the United States and engaged in the administration of this chapter. Members of an advisory committee (other than officers or employees of the United States), while attending conferences or meetings of their committee or otherwise serving at the request of the Secretary, shall be entitled to receive compensation at rates to be fixed by the Secretary, which rates may not exceed the daily equivalent for grade GS–18 of the General Schedule for each day (including traveltime) they are so engaged; and while so serving away from their homes or regular places of business each member may be allowed travel expenses, including per diem in lieu of subsistence, as authorized by section 5703 of title 5 for persons in the Government service employed intermittently. The Secretary shall designate the chairman of an advisory committee from its members. The Secretary shall furnish each advisory committee with clerical and other assistance, and shall by regulation prescribe the procedures to be followed by each such committee in acting on referrals made under subparagraph (A).

(C) The Secretary shall make public the report and recommendation made by an advisory committee with respect to an application and shall by order, stating the reasons therefor, either affirm the order referred to the advisory committee or reverse such order and, if appropriate, approve or deny approval of the application, reinstate the application's approval, approve the protocol, or place in effect a notice of completion.

(h) Service of orders

Orders of the Secretary under this section shall be served (1) in person by any officer or employee of the department designated by the Secretary, or (2) by mailing the order by registered mail or certified mail addressed to the applicant at his last known address in the records of the Secretary.

(i) Revision

(1) Before December 1, 1995, the Secretary shall by order require manufacturers of devices, which were introduced or delivered for introduction into interstate commerce for commercial distribution before May 28, 1976, and which are subject to revision of classification under paragraph (2), to submit to the Secretary a summary of and citation to any information known or otherwise available to the manufacturer respecting such devices, including adverse safety or effectiveness information which has not been submitted under section 360i of this title. The Secretary may require the manufacturer to submit the adverse safety or effectiveness data for which a summary and citation were submitted, if such data are available to the manufacturer.

(2) After the issuance of an order under paragraph (1) but before December 1, 1995, the Secretary shall publish a regulation in the Federal Register for each device—

(A) which the Secretary has classified as a class III device, and

(B) for which no final regulation has been promulgated under subsection (b) of this section,

revising the classification of the device so that the device is classified into class I or class II, unless the regulation requires the device to remain in class III. In determining whether to revise the classification of a device or to require a device to remain in class III, the Secretary shall apply the criteria set forth in section 360c(a) of this title. Before the publication of a regulation requiring a device to remain in class III or revising its classification, the Secretary shall publish a proposed regulation respecting the classification of a device under this paragraph and provide reasonable opportunity for the submission of comments on any such regulation. No regulation requiring a device to remain in class III or revising its classification may take effect before the expiration of 90 days from the date of its publication in the Federal Register as a proposed regulation.

(3) The Secretary shall, as promptly as is reasonably achievable, but not later than 12 months after the effective date of the regulation requiring a device to remain in class III, establish a schedule for the promulgation of a subsection (b) of this section regulation for each device which is subject to the regulation requiring the device to remain in class III.

(June 25, 1938, ch. 675, § 515, as added Pub. L. 94–295, § 2, May 28, 1976, 90 Stat. 552; amended Pub. L. 101–629, §§ 4(b)(1), 9(a), 18(c), Nov. 28, 1990, 104 Stat. 4515, 4521, 4528; Pub. L. 103–80, § 3(t), Aug. 13, 1993, 107 Stat. 778; Pub. L. 105–115, title II, §§ 201(b), 202, 205(c), 209(b), 216(b), Nov. 21, 1997, 111 Stat. 2334, 2338, 2341, 2349; Pub. L. 107–250, title II, §§ 209, 210, title III, § 302(c), Oct. 26, 2002, 116 Stat. 1613, 1614, 1618; Pub. L. 108–214, § 2(d)(1), Apr. 1, 2004, 118 Stat. 576; Pub. L. 110–85, title VIII, § 801(b)(3)(D), Sept. 27, 2007, 121 Stat. 921.)

AMENDMENTS

2007—Subsec. (c)(1)(G), (H). Pub. L. 110–85 added subpar. (G) and redesignated former subpar. (G) as (H).

2004—Subsec. (c)(3). Pub. L. 108–214, § 2(d)(1)(B), amended directory language of Pub. L. 107–250, § 210. See 2002 Amendment note below.

Pub. L. 108–214, § 2(d)(1)(A)(i), redesignated par. (3) relating to acceptance and review of any portion of the application prior to submission as (4).

Subsec. (c)(4). Pub. L. 108–214, § 2(d)(1)(A), redesignated par. (3) relating to acceptance and review of any portion of the application prior to submission as (4) and substituted "unless a significant issue of safety" for "unless an issue of safety" in subpar. (B).

2002—Subsec. (a). Pub. L. 107–250, § 302(c)(1), inserted "or, as applicable, an approval under subsection (c)(2) of this section of a report seeking premarket approval" before period in concluding provisions.

Subsec. (c)(2). Pub. L. 107–250, § 302(c)(2)(B), added par. (2). Former par. (2) redesignated (3).

Subsec. (c)(3). Pub. L. 107–250, § 302(c)(2)(A), redesignated par. (2) relating to Secretary's referral of application to appropriate panel as (3).

Pub. L. 107–250, § 210, as amended by Pub. L. 108–214, § 2(d)(1)(B), inserted "Where appropriate, the Secretary shall ensure that such panel includes, or consults with, one or more pediatric experts." at the end of the concluding provisions of par. (3) as redesignated by Pub. L. 107–250, § 302(c)(2)(A).

Pub. L. 107–250, § 209, added par. (3) relating to acceptance and review of any portion of the application prior to submission.

1997—Subsec. (d)(1)(A). Pub. L. 105–115, § 205(c)(1), inserted at end "In making the determination whether to approve or deny the application, the Secretary shall rely on the conditions of use included in the proposed labeling as the basis for determining whether or not there is a reasonable assurance of safety and effectiveness, if the proposed labeling is neither false nor misleading. In determining whether or not such labeling is false or misleading, the Secretary shall fairly evaluate all material facts pertinent to the proposed labeling."

Subsec. (d)(1)(B)(iii). Pub. L. 105–115, § 201(b), added cl. (iii).

Subsec. (d)(3), (4). Pub. L. 105–115, § 202(1), 209(b), added par. (3) and redesignated former par. (3) as (4).

Subsec. (d)(5). Pub. L. 105–115, § 202(2), added par. (5).

Subsec. (d)(6). Pub. L. 105–115, § 205(c)(2), added par. (6).

Subsec. (f)(2). Pub. L. 105–115, § 216(b), substituted "the Secretary—" and subpars. (A) and (B) for "he shall refer the proposed protocol to the appropriate panel under section 360c of this title for its recommendation respecting approval of the protocol."

1993—Subsec. (c)(2)(A). Pub. L. 103–80 struck out "refer such application" after "own initiative".

1990—Subsec. (c)(2). Pub. L. 101–629, § 18(c), substituted "the Secretary—" for "the Secretary shall" and added subpars. (A) and (B).

Subsec. (e). Pub. L. 101–629, § 9(a)(2), inserted "and temporary suspension" after "Withdrawal" in heading.

Subsec. (e)(3). Pub. L. 101–629, § 9(a)(1), added par. (3).

Subsec. (i). Pub. L. 101–629, § 4(b)(1), added subsec. (i).

EFFECTIVE DATE OF 1997 AMENDMENT

Amendment by Pub. L. 105–115 effective 90 days after Nov. 21, 1997, except as otherwise provided, see section 501 of Pub. L. 105–115, set out as a note under section 321 of this title.

TERMINATION OF ADVISORY COMMITTEES

Advisory committees in existence on Jan. 5, 1973, to terminate not later than the expiration of the 2-year period following Jan. 5, 1973, and advisory committees established after Jan. 5, 1973, to terminate not later than the expiration of the 2-year period beginning on the date of their establishment, unless in the case of a committee established by the President or an officer of the Federal Government, such committee is renewed by appropriate action prior to the expiration of such 2-year period, or in the case of a committee established by Congress, its duration is otherwise provided by law. See section 14 of Pub. L. 92–463, Oct. 6, 1972, 86 Stat. 776, set out in the Appendix to Title 5, Government Organization and Employees.

REPORT ON CERTAIN DEVICES

Pub. L. 107–250, title II, § 205, Oct. 26, 2002, 116 Stat. 1612, directed the Secretary of Health and Human Services, not later than one year after Oct. 26, 2002, to report to the appropriate committees of Congress on the timeliness and effectiveness of device premarket reviews by centers other than the Center for Devices and Radiological Health, including information on the times required to log in and review original submissions and supplements, times required to review manufacturers' replies to submissions, times to approve or clear such devices, and recommendations on improvement of performance and reassignment of responsibility for regulating such devices.

REFERENCES IN OTHER LAWS TO GS–16, 17, OR 18 PAY RATES

References in laws to the rates of pay for GS–16, 17, or 18, or to maximum rates of pay under the General Schedule, to be considered references to rates payable under specified sections of Title 5, Government Organization and Employees, see section 529 [title I, § 101(c)(1)] of Pub. L. 101–509, set out in a note under section 5376 of Title 5.

§ 360e–1. Pediatric uses of devices

(a) New devices

(1) In general

A person that submits to the Secretary an application under section 360j(m) of this title, or an application (or supplement to an application) or a product development protocol under section 360e of this title, shall include in the application or protocol the information described in paragraph (2).

(2) Required information

The application or protocol described in paragraph (1) shall include, with respect to the device for which approval is sought and if readily available—

(A) a description of any pediatric subpopulations that suffer from the disease or condition that the device is intended to treat, diagnose, or cure; and

(B) the number of affected pediatric patients.

(3) Annual report

Not later than 18 months after September 27, 2007, and annually thereafter, the Secretary shall submit to the Committee on Health, Education, Labor, and Pensions of the Senate and the Committee on Energy and Commerce of the House of Representatives a report that includes—

(A) the number of devices approved in the year preceding the year in which the report is submitted, for which there is a pediatric subpopulation that suffers from the disease or condition that the device is intended to treat, diagnose, or cure;

(B) the number of devices approved in the year preceding the year in which the report is submitted, labeled for use in pediatric patients;

(C) the number of pediatric devices approved in the year preceding the year in which the report is submitted, exempted from a fee pursuant to section 379j(a)(2)(B)(v) of this title; and

(D) the review time for each device described in subparagraphs (A), (B), and (C).

(b) Determination of pediatric effectiveness based on similar course of disease or condition or similar effect of device on adults

(1) In general

If the course of the disease or condition and the effects of the device are sufficiently similar in adults and pediatric patients, the Secretary may conclude that adult data may be used to support a determination of a reasonable assurance of effectiveness in pediatric populations, as appropriate.

(2) Extrapolation between subpopulations

A study may not be needed in each pediatric subpopulation if data from one subpopulation can be extrapolated to another subpopulation.

(c) Pediatric subpopulation

For purposes of this section, the term "pediatric subpopulation" has the meaning given the term in section 360j(m)(6)(E)(ii) of this title.

(June 25, 1938, ch. 675, § 515A, as added Pub. L. 110–85, title III, § 302, Sept. 27, 2007, 121 Stat. 859.)

§ 360f. Banned devices

(a) General rule

Whenever the Secretary finds, on the basis of all available data and information, that—

(1) a device intended for human use presents substantial deception or an unreasonable and substantial risk of illness or injury; and

(2) in the case of substantial deception or an unreasonable and substantial risk of illness or injury which the Secretary determined could be corrected or eliminated by labeling or change in labeling and with respect to which the Secretary provided written notice to the manufacturer specifying the deception or risk of illness or injury, the labeling or change in labeling to correct the deception or eliminate or reduce such risk, and the period within which such labeling or change in labeling was to be done, such labeling or change in labeling was not done within such period;

he may initiate a proceeding to promulgate a regulation to make such device a banned device.

(b) Special effective date

The Secretary may declare a proposed regulation under subsection (a) of this section to be effective upon its publication in the Federal Register and until the effective date of any final action taken respecting such regulation if (1) he determines, on the basis of all available data and information, that the deception or risk of illness or injury associated with the use of the device which is subject to the regulation presents an unreasonable, direct, and substantial danger to the health of individuals, and (2) before the date of the publication of such regulation, the Secretary notifies the manufacturer of such device that such regulation is to be made so effective. If the Secretary makes a proposed regulation so effective, he shall, as expeditiously as possible, give interested persons prompt notice of his action under this subsection, provide reasonable opportunity for an informal hearing on the proposed regulation, and either affirm, modify, or revoke such proposed regulation.

(June 25, 1938, ch. 675, § 516, as added Pub. L. 94–295, § 2, May 28, 1976, 90 Stat. 560; amended Pub. L. 101–629, § 18(d), Nov. 28, 1990, 104 Stat. 4529.)

AMENDMENTS

1990—Subsec. (a). Pub. L. 101–629 struck out "and after consultation with the appropriate panel or panels under section 360c of this title" after "data and information" in introductory provisions and struck out at end "The Secretary shall afford all interested persons opportunity for an informal hearing on a regulation proposed under this subsection."

§ 360g. Judicial review

(a) Petition; record

Not later than thirty days after—

(1) the promulgation of a regulation under section 360c of this title classifying a device in class I or changing the classification of a device to class I or an order under subsection (f)(2) of such section reclassifying a device or denying a petition for reclassification of a device,

(2) the promulgation of a regulation under section 360d of this title establishing, amending, or revoking a performance standard for a device,

(3) the issuance of an order under section 360d(b)(2) or 360e(b)(2)(B) of this title denying a request for reclassification of a device,

(4) the promulgation of a regulation under paragraph (3) of section 360e(b) of this title requiring a device to have an approval of a premarket application, a regulation under paragraph (4) of that section amending or revoking a regulation under paragraph (3), or an order pursuant to section 360e(g)(1) or 360e(g)(2)(C) of this title,

(5) the promulgation of a regulation under section 360f of this title (other than a proposed regulation made effective under subsection (b) of such section upon the regulation's publication) making a device a banned device,

(6) the issuance of an order under section 360j(f)(2) of this title,

(7) an order under section 360j(g)(4) of this title disapproving an application for an exemption of a device for investigational use or an order under section 360j(g)(5) of this title withdrawing such an exemption for a device,

(8) an order pursuant to section 360c(i) of this title, or

(9) a regulation under section 360e(i)(2) or 360j(*l*)(5)(B) of this title,

any person adversely affected by such regulation or order may file a petition with the United States Court of Appeals for the District of Columbia or for the circuit wherein such person resides or has his principal place of business for judicial review of such regulation or order. A copy of the petition shall be transmitted by the clerk of the court to the Secretary or other officer designated by him for that purpose. The Secretary shall file in the court the record of the proceedings on which the Secretary based his regulation or order as provided in section 2112 of title 28. For purposes of this section, the term "record" means all notices and other matter published in the Federal Register with respect to the regulation or order reviewed, all information submitted to the Secretary with respect to such regulation or order, proceedings of any panel or advisory committee with respect to such regulation or order, any hearing held with respect to such regulation or order, and any other information identified by the Secretary, in the administrative proceeding held with respect to such regulation or order, as being relevant to such regulation or order.

(b) Additional data, views, and arguments

If the petitioner applies to the court for leave to adduce additional data, views, or arguments respecting the regulation or order being reviewed and shows to the satisfaction of the court that such additional data, views, or arguments are material and that there were reasonable grounds for the petitioner's failure to adduce such data, views, or arguments in the proceedings before the Secretary, the court may order the Secretary to provide additional opportunity for the oral presentation of data, views, or arguments and for written submissions. The Secretary may modify his findings, or make new findings by reason of the additional data, views, or arguments so taken and shall file with the court such modified or new findings, and his recommendation, if any, for the modification or setting aside of the regulation or order being reviewed, with the return of such additional data, views, or arguments.

(c) Standard for review

Upon the filing of the petition under subsection (a) of this section for judicial review of a regulation or order, the court shall have jurisdiction to review the regulation or order in accordance with chapter 7 of title 5 and to grant appropriate relief, including interim relief, as provided in such chapter. A regulation described in paragraph (2) or (5) of subsection (a) of this section and an order issued after the review provided by section 360e(g) of this title shall not be affirmed if it is found to be unsupported by substantial evidence on the record taken as a whole.

(d) Finality of judgments

The judgment of the court affirming or setting aside, in whole or in part, any regulation or order shall be final, subject to review by the Supreme Court of the United States upon certiorari or certification, as provided in section 1254 of title 28.

(e) Remedies

The remedies provided for in this section shall be in addition to and not in lieu of any other remedies provided by law.

(f) Statement of reasons

To facilitate judicial review under this section or under any other provision of law of a regulation or order issued under section 360c, 360d, 360e, 360f, 360h, 360i, 360j, or 360k of this title each such regulation or order shall contain a statement of the reasons for its issuance and the basis, in the record of the proceedings held in connection with its issuance, for its issuance.

(June 25, 1938, ch. 675, §517, as added Pub. L. 94–295, §2, May 28, 1976, 90 Stat. 560; amended Pub. L. 101–629, §13, Nov. 28, 1990, 104 Stat. 4524; Pub. L. 102–300, §6(f), June 16, 1992, 106 Stat. 240; Pub. L. 105–115, title II, §216(a)(2), Nov. 21, 1997, 111 Stat. 2349.)

AMENDMENTS

1997—Subsec. (a)(8). Pub. L. 105–115, §216(a)(2)(A), inserted "or" at end.

Subsec. (a)(9). Pub. L. 105–115, §216(a)(2)(B), substituted comma for ", or" at end.

Subsec. (a)(10). Pub. L. 105–115, §216(a)(2)(C), struck out par. (10) which read as follows: "an order under section 360j(h)(4)(B) of this title,".

1992—Subsec. (a)(10). Pub. L. 102–300 substituted "360j(h)(4)(B)" for "360j(c)(4)(B)".

1990—Subsec. (a)(8) to (10). Pub. L. 101–629 added pars. (8) to (10).

EFFECTIVE DATE OF 1997 AMENDMENT

Amendment by Pub. L. 105–115 effective 90 days after Nov. 21, 1997, except as otherwise provided, see section 501 of Pub. L. 105–115, set out as a note under section 321 of this title.

§360h. Notification and other remedies

(a) Notification

If the Secretary determines that—

(1) a device intended for human use which is introduced or delivered for introduction into interstate commerce for commercial distribution presents an unreasonable risk of substantial harm to the public health, and

(2) notification under this subsection is necessary to eliminate the unreasonable risk of such harm and no more practicable means is available under the provisions of this chapter (other than this section) to eliminate such risk,

the Secretary may issue such order as may be necessary to assure that adequate notification is provided in an appropriate form, by the persons and means best suited under the circumstances involved, to all health professionals who prescribe or use the device and to any other person (including manufacturers, importers, distributors, retailers, and device users) who should properly receive such notification in order to eliminate such risk. An order under this subsection shall require that the individuals subject to the risk with respect to which the order is to be issued be included in the persons to be notified of the risk unless the Secretary determines that notice to such individuals would present a greater danger to the health of such individuals than no such notification. If the Secretary makes such a determination with respect to such individuals, the order shall require that the health professionals who prescribe or use the device provide for the notification of the individuals whom the health professionals treated with the device of the risk presented by the device and of any action which may be taken by or on behalf of such individuals to eliminate or reduce such risk. Before issuing an order under this subsection, the Secretary shall consult with the persons who are to give notice under the order.

(b) Repair, replacement, or refund

(1)(A) If, after affording opportunity for an informal hearing, the Secretary determines that—

(i) a device intended for human use which is introduced or delivered for introduction into interstate commerce for commercial distribution presents an unreasonable risk of substantial harm to the public health,

(ii) there are reasonable grounds to believe that the device was not properly designed or manufactured with reference to the state of the art as it existed at the time of its design or manufacture,

(iii) there are reasonable grounds to believe that the unreasonable risk was not caused by failure of a person other than a manufacturer, importer, distributor, or retailer of the device to exercise due care in the installation, maintenance, repair, or use of the device, and

(iv) the notification authorized by subsection (a) of this section would not by itself be sufficient to eliminate the unreasonable risk and action described in paragraph (2) of this subsection is necessary to eliminate such risk,

the Secretary may order the manufacturer, importer, or any distributor of such device, or any combination of such persons, to submit to him within a reasonable time a plan for taking one or more of the actions described in paragraph (2). An order issued under the preceding sentence which is directed to more than one person shall specify which person may decide which action shall be taken under such plan and the person specified shall be the person who the Secretary determines bears the principal, ultimate financial responsibility for action taken under the plan unless the Secretary cannot determine who bears such responsibility or the Secretary determines that the protection of the public health requires that such decision be made by a person (including a device user or health professional) other than the person he determines bears such responsibility.

(B) The Secretary shall approve a plan submitted pursuant to an order issued under subparagraph (A) unless he determines (after affording opportunity for an informal hearing) that the action or actions to be taken under the plan or the manner in which such action or actions are to be taken under the plan will not assure that the unreasonable risk with respect to which such order was issued will be eliminated. If the Secretary disapproves a plan, he shall order a revised plan to be submitted to him within a reasonable time. If the Secretary determines (after affording opportunity for an informal hearing) that the revised plan is unsatisfactory or if no revised plan or no initial plan has been submitted to the Secretary within the prescribed time, the Secretary shall (i) prescribe a plan to be carried out by the person or persons to whom the order issued under subparagraph (A) was directed, or (ii) after affording an opportunity for an informal hearing, by order prescribe a plan to be carried out by a person who is a manufacturer, importer, distributor, or retailer of the device with respect to which the order was issued but to whom the order under subparagraph (A) was not directed.

(2) The actions which may be taken under a plan submitted under an order issued under paragraph (1) are as follows:

(A) To repair the device so that it does not present the unreasonable risk of substantial harm with respect to which the order under paragraph (1) was issued.

(B) To replace the device with a like or equivalent device which is in conformity with all applicable requirements of this chapter.

(C) To refund the purchase price of the device (less a reasonable allowance for use if such device has been in the possession of the device user for one year or more—

(i) at the time of notification ordered under subsection (a) of this section, or

(ii) at the time the device user receives actual notice of the unreasonable risk with respect to which the order was issued under paragraph (1),

whichever first occurs).

(3) No charge shall be made to any person (other than a manufacturer, importer, distributor or retailer) for availing himself of any remedy, described in paragraph (2) and provided under an order issued under paragraph (1), and the person subject to the order shall reimburse each person (other than a manufacturer, importer, distributor, or retailer) who is entitled to such a remedy for any reasonable and foreseeable expenses actually incurred by such person in availing himself of such remedy.

(c) Reimbursement

An order issued under subsection (b) of this section with respect to a device may require any person who is a manufacturer, importer, distributor, or retailer of the device to reimburse any other person who is a manufacturer, importer, distributor, or retailer of such device for such other person's expenses actually incurred in connection with carrying out the order if the Secretary determines such reimbursement is required for the protection of the public health. Any such requirement shall not affect any rights or obligations under any contract to which the person receiving reimbursement or the person making such reimbursement is a party.

(d) Effect on other liability

Compliance with an order issued under this section shall not relieve any person from liability under Federal or State law. In awarding damages for economic loss in an action brought for the enforcement of any such liability, the value to the plaintiff in such action of any remedy provided him under such order shall be taken into account.

(e) Recall authority

(1) If the Secretary finds that there is a reasonable probability that a device intended for human use would cause serious, adverse health consequences or death, the Secretary shall issue an order requiring the appropriate person (including the manufacturers, importers, distributors, or retailers of the device)—

(A) to immediately cease distribution of such device, and

(B) to immediately notify health professionals and device user facilities of the order and to instruct such professionals and facilities to cease use of such device.

The order shall provide the person subject to the order with an opportunity for an informal hearing, to be held not later than 10 days after the date of the issuance of the order, on the actions required by the order and on whether the order should be amended to require a recall of such device. If, after providing an opportunity for such a hearing, the Secretary determines that inadequate grounds exist to support the actions required by the order, the Secretary shall vacate the order.

(2)(A) If, after providing an opportunity for an informal hearing under paragraph (1), the Secretary determines that the order should be amended to include a recall of the device with respect to which the order was issued, the Secretary shall, except as provided in subparagraphs (B) and (C), amend the order to require a recall. The Secretary shall specify a timetable in which the device recall will occur and shall require periodic reports to the Secretary describing the progress of the recall.

(B) An amended order under subparagraph (A)—

(i) shall—

(I) not include recall of a device from individuals, and

(II) not include recall of a device from device user facilities if the Secretary determines that the risk of recalling such device from the facilities presents a greater health risk than the health risk of not recalling the device from use, and

(ii) shall provide for notice to individuals subject to the risks associated with the use of such device.

In providing the notice required by clause (ii), the Secretary may use the assistance of health professionals who prescribed or used such a device for individuals. If a significant number of such individuals cannot be identified, the Secretary shall notify such individuals pursuant to section 375(b) of this title.

(3) The remedy provided by this subsection shall be in addition to remedies provided by subsections (a), (b), and (c) of this section.

(June 25, 1938, ch. 675, § 518, as added Pub. L. 94–295, § 2, May 28, 1976, 90 Stat. 562; amended Pub. L. 101–629, § 8, Nov. 28, 1990, 104 Stat. 4520; Pub. L. 102–300, § 4, June 16, 1992, 106 Stat. 239.)

AMENDMENTS

1992—Subsec. (b)(1)(A)(ii). Pub. L. 102–300 substituted "or" for "and" after "properly designed" and "time of its design".

1990—Subsec. (e). Pub. L. 101–629 added subsec. (e).

§ 360i. Records and reports on devices

(a) General rule

Every person who is a manufacturer or importer of a device intended for human use shall establish and maintain such records, make such reports, and provide such information, as the Secretary may by regulation reasonably require to assure that such device is not adulterated or misbranded and to otherwise assure its safety and effectiveness. Regulations prescribed under the preceding sentence—

(1) shall require a device manufacturer or importer to report to the Secretary whenever the manufacturer or importer receives or otherwise becomes aware of information that reasonably suggests that one of its marketed devices—

(A) may have caused or contributed to a death or serious injury, or

(B) has malfunctioned and that such device or a similar device marketed by the manufacturer or importer would be likely to cause or contribute to a death or serious injury if the malfunction were to recur, which report under this subparagraph—

(i) shall be submitted in accordance with part 803 of title 21, Code of Federal Regulations (or successor regulations), unless the Secretary grants an exemption or variance from, or an alternative to, a requirement under such regulations pursuant to section 803.19 of such part, if the device involved is—

(I) a class III device;

(II) a class II device that is permanently implantable, is life supporting, or is life sustaining; or

(III) a type of device which the Secretary has, by notice published in the Federal Register or letter to the person who is the manufacturer or importer of the device, indicated should be subject to such part 803 in order to protect the public health;

(ii) shall, if the device is not subject to clause (i), be submitted in accordance with criteria established by the Secretary for reports made pursuant to this clause, which criteria shall require the reports to be in summary form and made on a quarterly basis; or

(iii) shall, if the device is imported into the United States and for which part 803 of title 21, Code of Federal Regulations (or successor regulations) requires an importer to submit a report to the manufacturer, be submitted by the importer to the manufacturer in accordance with part 803 of title 21, Code of Federal Regulations (or successor regulations) [1]

(2) shall define the term "serious injury" to mean an injury that—

(A) is life threatening,

(B) results in permanent impairment of a body function or permanent damage to a body structure, or

(C) necessitates medical or surgical intervention to preclude permanent impairment of a body function or permanent damage to a body structure;

(3) shall require reporting of other significant adverse device experiences as determined by the Secretary to be necessary to be reported;

(4) shall not impose requirements unduly burdensome to a device manufacturer or importer taking into account his cost of complying with such requirements and the need for the protection of the public health and the implementation of this chapter;

(5) which prescribe the procedure for making requests for reports or information shall require that each request made under such regulations for submission of a report or information to the Secretary state the reason or purpose for such request and identify to the fullest extent practicable such report or information;

(6) which require submission of a report or information to the Secretary shall state the reason or purpose for the submission of such report or information and identify to the fullest extent practicable such report or information;

(7) may not require that the identity of any patient be disclosed in records, reports, or information required under this subsection unless required for the medical welfare of an individual, to determine the safety or effectiveness of a device, or to verify a record, report, or information submitted under this chapter; and

(8) may not require a manufacturer or importer of a class I device to—

(A) maintain for such a device records respecting information not in the possession of the manufacturer or importer, or

(B) to submit for such a device to the Secretary any report or information—

(i) not in the possession of the manufacturer or importer, or

(ii) on a periodic basis,

unless such report or information is necessary to determine if the device should be reclassified or if the device is adulterated or misbranded. and [2]

In prescribing such regulations, the Secretary shall have due regard for the professional ethics

---

[1] So in original. Probably should be followed by a semicolon.

[2] So in original. The word "and" probably should not appear.

of the medical profession and the interests of patients. The prohibitions of paragraph (7) of this subsection continue to apply to records, reports, and information concerning any individual who has been a patient, irrespective of whether or when he ceases to be a patient. The Secretary shall by regulation require distributors to keep records and make such records available to the Secretary upon request. Paragraphs (4) and (8) apply to distributors to the same extent and in the same manner as such paragraphs apply to manufacturers and importers.

(b) User reports

(1)(A) Whenever a device user facility receives or otherwise becomes aware of information that reasonably suggests that a device has or may have caused or contributed to the death of a patient of the facility, the facility shall, as soon as practicable but not later than 10 working days after becoming aware of the information, report the information to the Secretary and, if the identity of the manufacturer is known, to the manufacturer of the device. In the case of deaths, the Secretary may by regulation prescribe a shorter period for the reporting of such information.

(B) Whenever a device user facility receives or otherwise becomes aware of—

(i) information that reasonably suggests that a device has or may have caused or contributed to the serious illness of, or serious injury to, a patient of the facility, or

(ii) other significant adverse device experiences as determined by the Secretary by regulation to be necessary to be reported,

the facility shall, as soon as practicable but not later than 10 working days after becoming aware of the information, report the information to the manufacturer of the device or to the Secretary if the identity of the manufacturer is not known.

(C) Each device user facility shall submit to the Secretary on an annual basis a summary of the reports made under subparagraphs (A) and (B). Such summary shall be submitted on January 1 of each year. The summary shall be in such form and contain such information from such reports as the Secretary may require and shall include—

(i) sufficient information to identify the facility which made the reports for which the summary is submitted,

(ii) in the case of any product which was the subject of a report, the product name, serial number, and model number,

(iii) the name and the address of the manufacturer of such device, and

(iv) a brief description of the event reported to the manufacturer.

(D) For purposes of subparagraphs (A), (B), and (C), a device user facility shall be treated as having received or otherwise become aware of information with respect to a device of that facility when medical personnel who are employed by or otherwise formally affiliated with the facility receive or otherwise become aware of information with respect to that device in the course of their duties.

(2) The Secretary may not disclose the identity of a device user facility which makes a report under paragraph (1) except in connection with—

(A) an action brought to enforce section 331(q) of this title, or

(B) a communication to a manufacturer of a device which is the subject of a report under paragraph (1).

This paragraph does not prohibit the Secretary from disclosing the identity of a device user facility making a report under paragraph (1) or any information in such a report to employees of the Department of Health and Human Services, to the Department of Justice, or to the duly authorized committees and subcommittees of the Congress.

(3) No report made under paragraph (1) by—

(A) a device user facility,

(B) an individual who is employed by or otherwise formally affiliated with such a facility, or

(C) a physician who is not required to make such a report,

shall be admissible into evidence or otherwise used in any civil action involving private parties unless the facility, individual, or physician who made the report had knowledge of the falsity of the information contained in the report.

(4) A report made under paragraph (1) does not affect any obligation of a manufacturer who receives the report to file a report as required under subsection (a) of this section.

(5) With respect to device user facilities:

(A) The Secretary shall by regulation plan and implement a program under which the Secretary limits user reporting under paragraphs (1) through (4) to a subset of user facilities that constitutes a representative profile of user reports for device deaths and serious illnesses or serious injuries.

(B) During the period of planning the program under subparagraph (A), paragraphs (1) through (4) continue to apply.

(C) During the period in which the Secretary is providing for a transition to the full implementation of the program, paragraphs (1) through (4) apply except to the extent that the Secretary determines otherwise.

(D) On and after the date on which the program is fully implemented, paragraphs (1) through (4) do not apply to a user facility unless the facility is included in the subset referred to in subparagraph (A).

(E) Not later than 2 years after November 21, 1997, the Secretary shall submit to the Committee on Commerce of the House of Representatives, and to the Committee on Labor and Human Resources of the Senate, a report describing the plan developed by the Secretary under subparagraph (A) and the progress that has been made toward the implementation of the plan.

(6) For purposes of this subsection:

(A) The term "device user facility" means a hospital, ambulatory surgical facility, nursing home, or outpatient treatment facility which is not a physician's office. The Secretary may by regulation include an outpatient diagnostic facility which is not a physician's office in such term.

(B) The terms "serious illness" and "serious injury" mean illness or injury, respectively, that—

(i) is life threatening,

(ii) results in permanent impairment of a body function or permanent damage to a body structure, or

(iii) necessitates medical or surgical intervention to preclude permanent impairment of a body function or permanent damage to a body structure.

(c) Persons exempt

Subsection (a) of this section shall not apply to—

(1) any practitioner who is licensed by law to prescribe or administer devices intended for use in humans and who manufactures or imports devices solely for use in the course of his professional practice;

(2) any person who manufactures or imports devices intended for use in humans solely for such person's use in research or teaching and not for sale (including any person who uses a device under an exemption granted under section 360j(g) of this title); and

(3) any other class of persons as the Secretary may by regulation exempt from subsection (a) of this section upon a finding that compliance with the requirements of such subsection by such class with respect to a device is not necessary to (A) assure that a device is not adulterated or misbranded or (B) otherwise to assure its safety and effectiveness.

(d) Repealed. Pub. L. 105–115, title II, § 213(a)(2), Nov. 21, 1997, 111 Stat. 2347

(e) Device tracking

(1) The Secretary may by order require a manufacturer to adopt a method of tracking a class II or class III device—

(A) the failure of which would be reasonably likely to have serious adverse health consequences; or

(B) which is—

(i) intended to be implanted in the human body for more than one year, or

(ii) a life sustaining or life supporting device used outside a device user facility.

(2) Any patient receiving a device subject to tracking under paragraph (1) may refuse to release, or refuse permission to release, the patient's name, address, social security number, or other identifying information for the purpose of tracking.

(f) Unique device identification system

The Secretary shall promulgate regulations establishing a unique device identification system for medical devices requiring the label of devices to bear a unique identifier, unless the Secretary requires an alternative placement or provides an exception for a particular device or type of device. The unique identifier shall adequately identify the device through distribution and use, and may include information on the lot or serial number.

(g) Reports of removals and corrections

(1) Except as provided in paragraph (2), the Secretary shall by regulation require a manufacturer or importer of a device to report promptly to the Secretary any correction or removal of a device undertaken by such manufacturer or importer if the removal or correction was undertaken—

(A) to reduce a risk to health posed by the device, or

(B) to remedy a violation of this chapter caused by the device which may present a risk to health.

A manufacturer or importer of a device who undertakes a correction or removal of a device which is not required to be reported under this paragraph shall keep a record of such correction or removal.

(2) No report of the corrective action or removal of a device may be required under paragraph (1) if a report of the corrective action or removal is required and has been submitted under subsection (a) of this section.

(3) For purposes of paragraphs (1) and (2), the terms "correction" and "removal" do not include routine servicing.

(June 25, 1938, ch. 675, § 519, as added Pub. L. 94–295, § 2, May 28, 1976, 90 Stat. 564; amended Pub. L. 101–629, §§ 2(a), 3(a)(1), (b)(1), 7, Nov. 28, 1990, 104 Stat. 4511, 4513, 4514, 4520; Pub. L. 102–300, § 5(a), June 16, 1992, 106 Stat. 239; Pub. L. 103–80, § 3(u), Aug. 13, 1993, 107 Stat. 778; Pub. L. 105–115, title II, §§ 211, 213(a), (c), Nov. 21, 1997, 111 Stat. 2345–2347; Pub. L. 110–85, title II, §§ 226(a), 227, Sept. 27, 2007, 121 Stat. 854.)

AMENDMENTS

2007—Subsec. (a)(1)(B). Pub. L. 110–85, § 227, substituted "were to recur, which report under this subparagraph—" for "were to recur;" and added cls. (i) to (iii).

Subsecs. (f), (g). Pub. L. 110–85, § 226(a), added subsec. (f) and redesignated former subsec. (f) as (g).

1997—Subsec. (a). Pub. L. 105–115, § 213(a)(1)(A), (F), in introductory provisions, substituted "manufacturer or importer" for "manufacturer, importer, or distributor" and, in closing provisions, inserted at end "The Secretary shall by regulation require distributors to keep records and make such records available to the Secretary upon request. Paragraphs (4) and (8) apply to distributors to the same extent and in the same manner as such paragraphs apply to manufacturers and importers."

Subsec. (a)(4). Pub. L. 105–115, § 213(a)(1)(B), substituted "manufacturer or importer" for "manufacturer, importer, or distributor".

Subsec. (a)(7). Pub. L. 105–115, § 213(a)(1)(C), inserted "and" after semicolon at end.

Subsec. (a)(8). Pub. L. 105–115, § 213(a)(1)(D), substituted "manufacturer or importer" for "manufacturer, importer, or distributor" wherever appearing and substituted period for semicolon after "misbranded".

Subsec. (a)(9). Pub. L. 105–115, § 213(a)(1)(E), struck out par. (9) which read as follows: "shall require distributors who submit such reports to submit copies of the reports to the manufacturer of the device for which the report was made."

Subsec. (b)(1)(C). Pub. L. 105–115, § 213(c)(1)(A), in introductory provisions, substituted "on an annual basis" for "on a semi-annual basis" and struck out "and July 1" after "January 1" and struck out closing provisions which read as follows: "The Secretary may by regulation alter the frequency and timing of reports required by this subparagraph."

Subsec. (b)(2)(A). Pub. L. 105–115, § 213(c)(1)(B)(i), inserted "or" after comma at end.

Subsec. (b)(2)(B). Pub. L. 105–115, § 213(c)(1)(B)(ii), substituted period for ", or" at end.

Subsec. (b)(2)(C). Pub. L. 105–115, § 213(c)(1)(B)(iii), struck out subpar. (C) which read as follows: "a disclosure required under subsection (a) of this section."

Subsec. (b)(5), (6). Pub. L. 105–115, §213(c)(2), added par. (5) and redesignated former par. (5) as (6).

Subsec. (d). Pub. L. 105–115, §213(a)(2), struck out heading and text of subsec. (d). Text read as follows: "Each manufacturer, importer, and distributor required to make reports under subsection (a) of this section shall submit to the Secretary annually a statement certifying that—

"(1) the manufacturer, importer, or distributor did file a certain number of such reports, or

"(2) the manufacturer, importer, or distributor did not file any report under subsection (a) of this section."

Subsec. (e). Pub. L. 105–115, §211, amended heading and text of subsec. (e) generally. Prior to amendment, text read as follows: "Every person who registers under section 360 of this title and is engaged in the manufacture of—

"(1) a device the failure of which would be reasonably likely to have serious adverse health consequences and which is (A) a permanently implantable device, or (B) a life sustaining or life supporting device used outside a device user facility, or

"(2) any other device which the Secretary may designate,

shall adopt a method of device tracking."

Subsec. (f)(1). Pub. L. 105–115, §213(a)(3), substituted "or importer" for ", importer, or distributor" wherever appearing.

1993—Subsec. (a). Pub. L. 103–80 substituted "paragraph (7)" for "paragraph (4)" in last sentence.

1992—Subsec. (a). Pub. L. 102–300, §5(a)(1), added pars. (1) to (3) and redesignated former pars. (1) to (6) as (4) to (9), respectively.

Subsec. (b)(1)(A). Pub. L. 102–300, §5(a)(2)(A), substituted "a device has or may have" for "there is a probability that a device has".

Subsec. (b)(1)(B). Pub. L. 102–300, §5(a)(2)(A), (B), substituted "a device has or may have" for "there is a probability that a device has", designated existing provisions as cl. (i), and added cl. (ii).

Subsec. (b)(5)(B)(iii). Pub. L. 102–300, §5(a)(2)(C), struck out "immediate" before "medical".

1990—Subsec. (a)(6). Pub. L. 101–629, §3(a)(1), added par. (6).

Subsecs. (b), (c). Pub. L. 101–629, §2(a), added subsec. (b) and redesignated former subsec. (b) as (c).

Subsecs. (d), (e). Pub. L. 101–629, §3(b)(1), added subsecs. (d) and (e).

Subsec. (f). Pub. L. 101–629, §7, added subsec. (f).

CHANGE OF NAME

Committee on Labor and Human Resources of Senate changed to Committee on Health, Education, Labor, and Pensions of Senate by Senate Resolution No. 20, One Hundred Sixth Congress, Jan. 19, 1999.

EFFECTIVE DATE OF 1997 AMENDMENT

Section 211 of Pub. L. 105–115 provided in part that the amendment made by that section is effective 90 days after Nov. 21, 1997.

Amendment by section 213(a), (c) of Pub. L. 105–115 effective 90 days after Nov. 21, 1997, except as otherwise provided, see section 501 of Pub. L. 105–115, set out as a note under section 321 of this title.

EFFECTIVE DATE OF 1992 AMENDMENT

Section 2(b) of Pub. L. 102–300 provided that: "The amendments made by subsection (a) [amending sections 3(b)(3) and 3(c) of Pub. L. 101–629, set out as notes below] shall take effect as of May 27, 1992 and any rule to implement section 519(e) of the Federal Food, Drug, and Cosmetic Act [21 U.S.C. 360i(e)] proposed under section 3(c)(2) of the Safe Medical Devices Act of 1990 [Pub. L. 101–629, set out as a note below] shall revert to its proposed status as of such date."

Section 5(b) of Pub. L. 102–300 provided that: "The amendments made by subsection (a) [amending this section] shall take effect—

"(1) 1 year after the date of the enactment of this Act [June 16, 1992]; or

"(2) on the effective date of regulations of the Secretary to implement such amendments,

whichever occurs first."

EFFECTIVE DATE OF 1990 AMENDMENT

Section 2(c) of Pub. L. 101–629 provided that: "Section 519(b) of the Federal Food, Drug, and Cosmetic Act [21 U.S.C. 360i(b)], as added by the amendment made by subsection (a), shall take effect—

"(1) upon the effective date of regulations promulgated under subsection (b) [set out below], or

"(2) upon the expiration of 12 months from the date of the enactment of this Act [Nov. 28, 1990],

whichever occurs first."

Section 3(a)(2) of Pub. L. 101–629 provided that: "Section 519(a)(6) [21 U.S.C. 360i(a)(6)], as added by the amendment made by paragraph (1), shall take effect upon the effective date of final regulations under subsection (c) [set out below]."

Section 3(b)(3) of Pub. L. 101–629, as amended by Pub. L. 102–300, §2(a)(1), June 16, 1992, 106 Stat. 238, provided that: "Section 519(e) [21 U.S.C. 360i(e)], as added by the amendment made by paragraph (1), shall take effect upon the expiration of 9 months after the issuance of final regulations under subsection (c) [set out below]."

[For effective date of amendment by Pub. L. 102–300, see section 2(b) of Pub. L. 102–300, set out above as an Effective Date of 1992 Amendment note.]

REGULATIONS

Section 2(b) of Pub. L. 101–629 provided that: "The Secretary of Health and Human Services shall promulgate regulations to implement section 519(b) of the Federal Food, Drug, and Cosmetic Act [21 U.S.C. 360i(b)], as added by the amendment made by subsection (a) (including a definition of the summary required by paragraph (1)(C) of such section) not later than 12 months after the date of enactment of this Act [Nov. 28, 1990]. In promulgating the regulations, the Secretary shall minimize the administrative burdens on device user facilities consistent with the need to assure adequate information."

Section 3(c) of Pub. L. 101–629, as amended by Pub. L. 102–300, §2(a)(2), (3), June 16, 1992, 106 Stat. 238, provided that:

"(1)(A) Not later than 9 months after the date of the enactment of this Act [Nov. 28, 1990], the Secretary of Health and Human Services shall issue proposed regulations—

"(i) to require distributors of devices to establish and maintain records and to make reports (including reports required by part 803 of title 21 of the Code of Federal Regulations) under section 519(a)(6) of the Federal Food, Drug, and Cosmetic Act [21 U.S.C. 360i(a)(6)], and

"(ii) to implement section 519(e) of such Act.

The Secretary may exempt from regulations described in clause (i) classes of distributors of class I and class II devices from whom reports are not necessary for the protection of the public health.

"(B) Regulations under subparagraph (A) shall—

"(i) require appropriate methods for maintenance of records to ensure that patients who receive devices can be provided the notification required by such Act [this chapter],

"(ii) require that manufacturers adopt effective methods of tracking devices,

"(iii) take into account the position of distributors in the device distribution process, and

"(iv) include such other requirements as the Secretary deems necessary for the adoption of an effective user tracking program under section 519(e) of such Act.

"(2) Not later than 18 months after the date of the enactment of this Act, the Secretary shall issue final regulations to implement sections [sic] 519(a)(6) of the Federal Food, Drug, and Cosmetic Act. If the Secretary does not promulgate such final regulations upon the expiration of such 18 months, the Congress finds that there is good cause for the proposed regulations to be considered as the final regulations without response to comment because the implementation of sections [sic] 519(a)(6) of such Act is essential to protect the health of patients who use such devices. Consequently, in such event, the proposed regulations issued under paragraph (1) shall become final regulations as of the expiration of such 18 months. There shall be promptly published in the Federal Register notice of the new status of the proposed regulations.

"(3) Not later than November 28, 1992, the Secretary shall issue final regulations to implement section 519(e) of the Federal Food, Drug, and Cosmetic Act. If the Secretary does not promulgate such final regulations by November 28, 1992, the Congress finds that there is good cause for the proposed regulations to be considered as the final regulations without response to comment because the implementation of section 519(e) of such Act is essential to protect the health of patients who use devices. In such event, the proposed regulations issued under paragraph (1) shall become the issued final regulations on November 29, 1992. There shall be promptly published in the Federal Register notice of the new status of the proposed regulations."

[For effective date of amendment by Pub. L. 102–300, see section 2(b) of Pub. L. 102–300, set out above as an Effective Date of 1992 Amendment note.]

INFORMATION CONCERNING REPORTING REQUIREMENTS FOR DEVICE USER FACILITIES

Section 2(d) of Pub. L. 101–629 directed Secretary of Health and Human Services, during the 18-month period beginning on Nov. 28, 1990, to inform device user facilities (as defined in 21 U.S.C. 360i(b)(5)(A)) and manufacturers and distributors of devices respecting the requirements of 21 U.S.C. 360i(b), and, to the extent practicable, provide persons subject to such requirements assistance in the form of publications regarding such requirements.

STUDY OF REPORTING REQUIREMENTS; COMPLIANCE BY DEVICE USER FACILITIES; ACTIONS BY MANUFACTURERS; COST EFFECTIVENESS; RECOMMENDATIONS

Section 2(e) of Pub. L. 101–629 directed Comptroller General of the United States, not more than 36 months after Nov. 28, 1990, to conduct a study of compliance by device user facilities with the requirements of 21 U.S.C. 360i(b), actions taken by manufacturers of devices in response to reports made to them, cost effectiveness of such requirements and their implementation, and any recommendations for improvements to such requirements, with Comptroller General to complete the study and submit a report on the study not later than 45 months from Nov. 28, 1990, to appropriate committees of Congress.

REPORT TO CONGRESS ON REPORTING REQUIREMENTS FOR DEVICE USER FACILITIES

Section 2(f) of Pub. L. 101–629 directed Secretary of Health and Human Services, not later than 36 months after Nov. 28, 1990, to prepare and submit to appropriate committees of Congress a report containing an evaluation of the requirements of 21 U.S.C. 360i(b), consisting of an evaluation of the safety benefits of the requirements, the burdens placed on the Food and Drug Administration and on device user facilities by the requirements, and the cost-effectiveness of the requirements and recommendations for legislative reform.

§ 360j. General provisions respecting control of devices intended for human use

(a) General rule

Any requirement authorized by or under section 351, 352, 360, or 360i of this title applicable to a device intended for human use shall apply to such device until the applicability of the requirement to the device has been changed by action taken under section 360c, 360d, or 360e of this title or under subsection (g) of this section, and any requirement established by or under section 351, 352, 360, or 360i of this title which is inconsistent with a requirement imposed on such device under section 360d or 360e of this title or under subsection (g) of this section shall not apply to such device.

(b) Custom devices

Sections 360d and 360e of this title do not apply to any device which, in order to comply with the order of an individual physician or dentist (or any other specially qualified person designated under regulations promulgated by the Secretary after an opportunity for an oral hearing) necessarily deviates from an otherwise applicable performance standard or requirement prescribed by or under section 360e of this title if (1) the device is not generally available in finished form for purchase or for dispensing upon prescription and is not offered through labeling or advertising by the manufacturer, importer, or distributor thereof for commercial distribution, and (2) such device—

(A)(i) is intended for use by an individual patient named in such order of such physician or dentist (or other specially qualified person so designated) and is to be made in a specific form for such patient, or

(ii) is intended to meet the special needs of such physician or dentist (or other specially qualified person so designated) in the course of the professional practice of such physician or dentist (or other specially qualified person so designated), and

(B) is not generally available to or generally used by other physicians or dentists (or other specially qualified persons so designated).

(c) Trade secrets

Any information reported to or otherwise obtained by the Secretary or his representative under section 360c, 360d, 360e, 360f, 360h, 360i, or 374 of this title or under subsection (f) or (g) of this section which is exempt from disclosure pursuant to subsection (a) of section 552 of title 5 by reason of subsection (b)(4) of such section shall be considered confidential and shall not be disclosed and may not be used by the Secretary as the basis for the reclassification of a device from class III to class II or class I or as the basis for the establishment or amendment of a performance standard under section 360d of this title for a device reclassified from class III to class II, except (1) in accordance with subsection (h) of this section, and (2) that such information may be disclosed to other officers or employees concerned with carrying out this chapter or when relevant in any proceeding under this chapter (other than section 360c or 360d of this title).

(d) Notices and findings

Each notice of proposed rulemaking under section 360c, 360d, 360e, 360f, 360h, or 360i of this title, or under this section, any other notice which is published in the Federal Register with respect to any other action taken under any such section and which states the reasons for such action, and each publication of findings required to be made in connection with rulemaking under any such section shall set forth—

(1) the manner in which interested persons may examine data and other information on which the notice or findings is based, and

(2) the period within which interested persons may present their comments on the notice or findings (including the need therefor) orally or in writing, which period shall be at least sixty days but may not exceed ninety days unless the time is extended by the Secretary by a notice published in the Federal Register stating good cause therefor.

(e) Restricted devices

(1) The Secretary may by regulation require that a device be restricted to sale, distribution, or use—

(A) only upon the written or oral authorization of a practitioner licensed by law to administer or use such device, or

(B) upon such other conditions as the Secretary may prescribe in such regulation,

if, because of its potentiality for harmful effect or the collateral measures necessary to its use, the Secretary determines that there cannot otherwise be reasonable assurance of its safety and effectiveness. No condition prescribed under subparagraph (B) may restrict the use of a device to persons with specific training or experience in its use or to persons for use in certain facilities unless the Secretary determines that such a restriction is required for the safe and effective use of the device. No such condition may exclude a person from using a device solely because the person does not have the training or experience to make him eligible for certification by a certifying board recognized by the American Board of Medical Specialties or has not been certified by such a Board. A device subject to a regulation under this subsection is a restricted device.

(2) The label of a restricted device shall bear such appropriate statements of the restrictions required by a regulation under paragraph (1) as the Secretary may in such regulation prescribe.

(f) Good manufacturing practice requirements

(1)(A) The Secretary may, in accordance with subparagraph (B), prescribe regulations requiring that the methods used in, and the facilities and controls used for, the manufacture, pre-production design validation (including a process to assess the performance of a device but not including an evaluation of the safety or effectiveness of a device), packing, storage, and installation of a device conform to current good manufacturing practice, as prescribed in such regulations, to assure that the device will be safe and effective and otherwise in compliance with this chapter.

(B) Before the Secretary may promulgate any regulation under subparagraph (A) he shall—

(i) afford the advisory committee established under paragraph (3) an opportunity to submit recommendations to him with respect to the regulation proposed to be promulgated;

(ii) afford opportunity for an oral hearing; and

(iii) ensure that such regulation conforms, to the extent practicable, with internationally recognized standards defining quality systems, or parts of the standards, for medical devices.

The Secretary shall provide the advisory committee a reasonable time to make its recommendation with respect to proposed regulations under subparagraph (A).

(2)(A) Any person subject to any requirement prescribed by regulations under paragraph (1) may petition the Secretary for an exemption or variance from such requirement. Such a petition shall be submitted to the Secretary in such form and manner as he shall prescribe and shall—

(i) in the case of a petition for an exemption from a requirement, set forth the basis for the petitioner's determination that compliance with the requirement is not required to assure that the device will be safe and effective and otherwise in compliance with this chapter,

(ii) in the case of a petition for a variance from a requirement, set forth the methods proposed to be used in, and the facilities and controls proposed to be used for, the manufacture, packing, storage, and installation of the device in lieu of the methods, facilities, and controls prescribed by the requirement, and

(iii) contain such other information as the Secretary shall prescribe.

(B) The Secretary may refer to the advisory committee established under paragraph (3) any petition submitted under subparagraph (A). The advisory committee shall report its recommendations to the Secretary with respect to a petition referred to it within sixty days of the date of the petition's referral. Within sixty days after—

(i) the date the petition was submitted to the Secretary under subparagraph (A), or

(ii) if the petition was referred to an advisory committee, the expiration of the sixty-day period beginning on the date the petition was referred to the advisory committee,

whichever occurs later, the Secretary shall by order either deny the petition or approve it.

(C) The Secretary may approve—

(i) a petition for an exemption for a device from a requirement if he determines that compliance with such requirement is not required to assure that the device will be safe and effective and otherwise in compliance with this chapter, and

(ii) a petition for a variance for a device from a requirement if he determines that the methods to be used in, and the facilities and controls to be used for, the manufacture, packing, storage, and installation of the device in lieu of the methods, controls, and facilities prescribed by the requirement are sufficient to assure that the device will be safe and effective and otherwise in compliance with this chapter.

An order of the Secretary approving a petition for a variance shall prescribe such conditions respecting the methods used in, and the facilities and controls used for, the manufacture, packing, storage, and installation of the device to be granted the variance under the petition as may be necessary to assure that the device will be safe and effective and otherwise in compliance with this chapter.

(D) After the issuance of an order under subparagraph (B) respecting a petition, the petitioner shall have an opportunity for an informal hearing on such order.

(3) The Secretary shall establish an advisory committee for the purpose of advising and making recommendations to him with respect to regulations proposed to be promulgated under paragraph (1)(A) and the approval or disapproval of petitions submitted under paragraph (2). The advisory committee shall be composed of nine members as follows:

(A) Three of the members shall be appointed from persons who are officers or employees of any State or local government or of the Federal Government.

(B) Two of the members shall be appointed from persons who are representative of interests of the device manufacturing industry; two of the members shall be appointed from persons who are representative of the interests of physicians and other health professionals; and two of the members shall be representative of the interests of the general public.

Members of the advisory committee who are not officers or employees of the United States, while attending conferences or meetings of the committee or otherwise engaged in its business, shall be entitled to receive compensation at rates to be fixed by the Secretary, which rates may not exceed the daily equivalent of the rate in effect for grade GS–18 of the General Schedule, for each day (including traveltime) they are so engaged; and while so serving away from their homes or regular places of business each member may be allowed travel expenses, including per diem in lieu of subsistence, as authorized by section 5703 of title 5 for persons in the Government service employed intermittently. The Secretary shall designate one of the members of the advisory committee to serve as its chairman. The Secretary shall furnish the advisory committee with clerical and other assistance. Section 14 of the Federal Advisory Committee Act shall not apply with respect to the duration of the advisory committee established under this paragraph.

(g) Exemption for devices for investigational use

(1) It is the purpose of this subsection to encourage, to the extent consistent with the protection of the public health and safety and with ethical standards, the discovery and development of useful devices intended for human use and to that end to maintain optimum freedom for scientific investigators in their pursuit of that purpose.

(2)(A) The Secretary shall, within the one hundred and twenty-day period beginning on May 28, 1976, by regulation prescribe procedures and conditions under which devices intended for human use may upon application be granted an exemption from the requirements of section 352, 360, 360d, 360e, 360f, 360i, or 379e of this title or subsection (e) or (f) of this section or from any combination of such requirements to permit the investigational use of such devices by experts qualified by scientific training and experience to investigate the safety and effectiveness of such devices.

(B) The conditions prescribed pursuant to subparagraph (A) shall include the following:

(i) A requirement that an application be submitted to the Secretary before an exemption may be granted and that the application be submitted in such form and manner as the Secretary shall specify.

(ii) A requirement that the person applying for an exemption for a device assure the establishment and maintenance of such records, and the making of such reports to the Secretary of data obtained as a result of the investigational use of the device during the exemption, as the Secretary determines will enable him to assure compliance with such conditions, review the progress of the investigation, and evaluate the safety and effectiveness of the device.

(iii) Such other requirements as the Secretary may determine to be necessary for the protection of the public health and safety.

(C) Procedures and conditions prescribed pursuant to subparagraph (A) for an exemption may appropriately vary depending on (i) the scope and duration of clinical testing to be conducted under such exemption, (ii) the number of human subjects that are to be involved in such testing, (iii) the need to permit changes to be made in the device subject to the exemption during testing conducted in accordance with a clinical testing plan required under paragraph (3)(A), and (iv) whether the clinical testing of such device is for the purpose of developing data to obtain approval for the commercial distribution of such device.

(3) Procedures and conditions prescribed pursuant to paragraph (2)(A) shall require, as a condition to the exemption of any device to be the subject of testing involving human subjects, that the person applying for the exemption—

(A) submit a plan for any proposed clinical testing of the device and a report of prior investigations of the device (including, where appropriate, tests on animals) adequate to justify the proposed clinical testing—

(i) to the local institutional review committee which has been established in accordance with regulations of the Secretary to supervise clinical testing of devices in the facilities where the proposed clinical testing is to be conducted, or

(ii) to the Secretary, if—

(I) no such committee exists, or

(II) the Secretary finds that the process of review by such committee is inadequate (whether or not the plan for such testing has been approved by such committee),

for review for adequacy to justify the commencement of such testing; and, unless the plan and report are submitted to the Secretary, submit to the Secretary a summary of the plan and a report of prior investigations of the device (including, where appropriate, tests on animals);

(B) promptly notify the Secretary (under such circumstances and in such manner as the Secretary prescribes) of approval by a local institutional review committee of any clinical testing plan submitted to it in accordance with subparagraph (A);

(C) in the case of a device to be distributed to investigators for testing, obtain signed agreements from each of such investigators that any testing of the device involving human subjects will be under such investigator's supervision and in accordance with subparagraph (D) and submit such agreements to the Secretary; and

(D) assure that informed consent will be obtained from each human subject (or his representative) of proposed clinical testing involving such device, except where subject to such conditions as the Secretary may prescribe, the investigator conducting or supervising the proposed clinical testing of the device determines in writing that there exists a life threatening situation involving the human subject of such testing which necessitates the use of such device and it is not feasible to obtain informed consent from the subject and there is not sufficient time to obtain such consent from his representative.

The determination required by subparagraph (D) shall be concurred in by a licensed physician who is not involved in the testing of the human subject with respect to which such determination is made unless immediate use of the device is required to save the life of the human subject of such testing and there is not sufficient time to obtain such concurrence.

(4)(A) An application, submitted in accordance with the procedures prescribed by regulations under paragraph (2), for an exemption for a device (other than an exemption from section 360f of this title) shall be deemed approved on the thirtieth day after the submission of the application to the Secretary unless on or before such day the Secretary by order disapproves the application and notifies the applicant of the disapproval of the application.

(B) The Secretary may disapprove an application only if he finds that the investigation with respect to which the application is submitted does not conform to procedures and conditions prescribed under regulations under paragraph (2). Such a notification shall contain the order of disapproval and a complete statement of the reasons for the Secretary's disapproval of the application and afford the applicant opportunity for an informal hearing on the disapproval order.

(5) The Secretary may by order withdraw an exemption granted under this subsection for a device if the Secretary determines that the conditions applicable to the device under this subsection for such exemption are not met. Such an order may be issued only after opportunity for an informal hearing, except that such an order may be issued before the provision of an opportunity for an informal hearing if the Secretary determines that the continuation of testing under the exemption with respect to which the order is to be issued will result in an unreasonable risk to the public health.

(6)(A) Not later than 1 year after November 21, 1997, the Secretary shall by regulation establish, with respect to a device for which an exemption under this subsection is in effect, procedures and conditions that, without requiring an additional approval of an application for an exemption or the approval of a supplement to such an application, permit—

(i) developmental changes in the device (including manufacturing changes) that do not constitute a significant change in design or in basic principles of operation and that are made in response to information gathered during the course of an investigation; and

(ii) changes or modifications to clinical protocols that do not affect—

(I) the validity of data or information resulting from the completion of an approved protocol, or the relationship of likely patient risk to benefit relied upon to approve a protocol;

(II) the scientific soundness of an investigational plan submitted under paragraph (3)(A); or

(III) the rights, safety, or welfare of the human subjects involved in the investigation.

(B) Regulations under subparagraph (A) shall provide that a change or modification described in such subparagraph may be made if—

(i) the sponsor of the investigation determines, on the basis of credible information (as defined by the Secretary) that the applicable conditions under subparagraph (A) are met; and

(ii) the sponsor submits to the Secretary, not later than 5 days after making the change or modification, a notice of the change or modification.

(7)(A) In the case of a person intending to investigate the safety or effectiveness of a class III device or any implantable device, the Secretary shall ensure that the person has an opportunity, prior to submitting an application to the Secretary or to an institutional review committee, to submit to the Secretary, for review, an investigational plan (including a clinical protocol). If the applicant submits a written request for a meeting with the Secretary regarding such review, the Secretary shall, not later than 30 days after receiving the request, meet with the applicant for the purpose of reaching agreement regarding the investigational plan (including a clinical protocol). The written request shall include a detailed description of the device, a detailed description of the proposed conditions of use of the device, a proposed plan (including a clinical protocol) for determining whether there is a reasonable assurance of effectiveness, and, if available, information regarding the expected performance from the device.

(B) Any agreement regarding the parameters of an investigational plan (including a clinical protocol) that is reached between the Secretary and a sponsor or applicant shall be reduced to writing and made part of the administrative record by the Secretary. Any such agreement shall not be changed, except—

(i) with the written agreement of the sponsor or applicant; or

(ii) pursuant to a decision, made in accordance with subparagraph (C) by the director of the office in which the device involved is reviewed, that a substantial scientific issue essential to determining the safety or effectiveness of the device involved has been identified.

(C) A decision under subparagraph (B)(ii) by the director shall be in writing, and may be made only after the Secretary has provided to the sponsor or applicant an opportunity for a meeting at which the director and the sponsor or applicant are present and at which the director documents the scientific issue involved.

(h) Release of information respecting safety and effectiveness

(1) The Secretary shall promulgate regulations under which a detailed summary of information respecting the safety and effectiveness of a device which information was submitted to the Secretary and which was the basis for—

(A) an order under section 360e(d)(1)(A) of this title approving an application for premarket approval for the device or denying approval of such an application or an order under section 360e(e) of this title withdrawing approval of such an application for the device,

(B) an order under section 360e(f)(6)(A) of this title revoking an approved protocol for the device, an order under section 360e(f)(6)(B) of this title declaring a protocol for the device completed or not completed, or an order under section 360e(f)(7) of this title revoking the approval of the device, or

(C) an order approving an application under subsection (g) of this section for an exemption for the device from section 360f of this title or an order disapproving, or withdrawing approval of, an application for an exemption under such subsection for the device,

shall be made available to the public upon issuance of the order. Summaries of information made available pursuant to this paragraph respecting a device shall include information respecting any adverse effects on health of the device.

(2) The Secretary shall promulgate regulations under which each advisory committee established under section 360e(g)(2)(B) of this title shall make available to the public a detailed summary of information respecting the safety and effectiveness of a device which information was submitted to the advisory committee and which was the basis for its recommendation to the Secretary made pursuant to section 360e(g)(2)(A) of this title. A summary of information upon which such a recommendation is based shall be made available pursuant to this paragraph only after the issuance of the order with respect to which the recommendation was made and each summary shall include information respecting any adverse effect on health of the device subject to such order.

(3) Except as provided in paragraph (4), any information respecting a device which is made available pursuant to paragraph (1) or (2) of this subsection (A) may not be used to establish the safety or effectiveness of another device for purposes of this chapter by any person other than the person who submitted the information so made available, and (B) shall be made available subject to subsection (c) of this section.

(4)(A) Any information contained in an application for premarket approval filed with the Secretary pursuant to section 360e(c) of this title (including information from clinical and preclinical tests or studies that demonstrate the safety and effectiveness of a device, but excluding descriptions of methods of manufacture and product composition and other trade secrets) shall be available, 6 years after the application has been approved by the Secretary, for use by the Secretary in—

(i) approving another device;

(ii) determining whether a product development protocol has been completed, under section 360e of this title for another device;

(iii) establishing a performance standard or special control under this chapter; or

(iv) classifying or reclassifying another device under section 360c of this title and subsection (*l*)(2) of this section.

(B) The publicly available detailed summaries of information respecting the safety and effectiveness of devices required by paragraph (1)(A) shall be available for use by the Secretary as the evidentiary basis for the agency actions described in subparagraph (A).

(i) Proceedings of advisory panels and committees

Each panel under section 360c of this title and each advisory committee established under section 360d(b)(5)(B) or 360e(g) of this title or under subsection (f) of this section shall make and maintain a transcript of any proceeding of the panel or committee. Each such panel and committee shall delete from any transcript made pursuant to this subsection information which under subsection (c) of this section is to be considered confidential.

(j) Traceability

Except as provided in section 360i(e) of this title, no regulation under this chapter may impose on a type or class of device requirements for the traceability of such type or class of device unless such requirements are necessary to assure the protection of the public health.

(k) Research and development

The Secretary may enter into contracts for research, testing, and demonstrations respecting devices and may obtain devices for research, testing, and demonstration purposes without regard to section 3324(a) and (b) of title 31 and section 5 of title 41.

(*l*) Transitional provisions for devices considered as new drugs

(1) Any device intended for human use—

(A) for which on May 28, 1976 (hereinafter in this subsection referred to as the "enactment date") an approval of an application submitted under section 355(b) of this title was in effect;

(B) for which such an application was filed on or before the enactment date and with respect to which application no order of approval or refusing to approve had been issued on such date under subsection (c) or (d) of such section;

(C) for which on the enactment date an exemption under subsection (i) of such section was in effect;

(D) which is within a type of device described in subparagraph (A), (B), or (C) and is substantially equivalent to another device within that type;

(E) which the Secretary in a notice published in the Federal Register before the enactment date has declared to be a new drug subject to section 355 of this title; or

(F) with respect to which on the enactment date an action is pending in a United States court under section 332, 333, or 334 of this title for an alleged violation of a provision of section 331 of this title which enforces a requirement of section 355 of this title or for an alleged violation of section 355(a) of this title,

is classified in class III unless the Secretary in response to a petition submitted under paragraph (2) has classified such device in class I or II.

(2) The Secretary may initiate the reclassification of a device classified into class III under paragraph (1) of this subsection or the manufacturer or importer of a device classified under paragraph (1) may petition the Secretary (in such form and manner as he shall prescribe) for the issuance of an order classifying the device in class I or class II. Within thirty days of the filing of such a petition, the Secretary shall notify the petitioner of any deficiencies in the petition which prevent the Secretary from making a decision on the petition. Except as provided in paragraph (3)(D)(ii), within one hundred and eighty days after the filing of a petition under this paragraph, the Secretary shall, after consultation with the appropriate panel under section 360c of this title, by order either deny the petition or order the classification, in accordance with the criteria prescribed by section 360c(a)(1)(A) of this title or 360c(a)(1)(B) of this title, of the device in class I or class II.

(3)(A) In the case of a device which is described in paragraph (1)(A) and which is in class III—

(i) such device shall on the enactment date be considered a device with an approved application under section 360e of this title, and

(ii) the requirements applicable to such device before the enactment date under section 355 of this title shall continue to apply to such device until changed by the Secretary as authorized by this chapter.

(B) In the case of a device which is described in paragraph (1)(B) and which is in class III, an application for such device shall be considered as having been filed under section 360e of this title on the enactment date. The period in which the Secretary shall act on such application in accordance with section 360e(d)(1) of this title shall be one hundred and eighty days from the enactment date (or such greater period as the Secretary and the applicant may agree upon after the Secretary has made the finding required by section 360e(d)(1)(B)(i) of this title) less the number of days in the period beginning on the date an application for such device was filed under section 355 of this title and ending on the enactment date. After the expiration of such period such device is required, unless exempt under subsection (g) of this section, to have in effect an approved application under section 360e of this title.

(C) A device which is described in paragraph (1)(C) and which is in class III shall be considered a new drug until the expiration of the ninety-day period beginning on the date of the promulgation of regulations under subsection (g) of this section. After the expiration of such period such device is required, unless exempt under subsection (g) of this section, to have in effect an approved application under section 360e of this title.

(D)(i) Except as provided in clauses (ii) and (iii), a device which is described in subparagraph (D), (E), or (F) of paragraph (1) and which is in class III is required, unless exempt under subsection (g) of this section, to have on and after sixty days after the enactment date in effect an approved application under section 360e of this title.

(ii) If—

(I) a petition is filed under paragraph (2) for a device described in subparagraph (D), (E), or (F) of paragraph (1), or

(II) an application for premarket approval is filed under section 360e of this title for such a device,

within the sixty-day period beginning on the enactment date (or within such greater period as the Secretary, after making the finding required under section 360e(d)(1)(B) of this title, and the petitioner or applicant may agree upon), the Secretary shall act on such petition or application in accordance with paragraph (2) or section 360e of this title except that the period within which the Secretary must act on the petition or application shall be within the one hundred and twenty-day period beginning on the date the petition or application is filed. If such a petition or application is filed within such sixty-day (or greater) period, clause (i) of this subparagraph shall not apply to such device before the expiration of such one hundred and twenty-day period, or if such petition is denied or such application is denied approval, before the date of such denial, whichever occurs first.

(iii) In the case of a device which is described in subparagraph (E) of paragraph (1), which the Secretary in a notice published in the Federal Register after March 31, 1976, declared to be a new drug subject to section 355 of this title, and which is in class III—

(I) the device shall, after eighteen months after the enactment date, have in effect an approved application under section 360e of this title unless exempt under subsection (g) of this section, and

(II) the Secretary may, during the period beginning one hundred and eighty days after the enactment date and ending eighteen months after such date, restrict the use of the device to investigational use by experts qualified by scientific training and experience to investigate the safety and effectiveness of such device, and to investigational use in accordance with the requirements applicable under regulations under subsection (g) of this section to investigational use of devices granted an exemption under such subsection.

If the requirements under subsection (g) of this section are made applicable to the investigational use of such a device, they shall be made applicable in such a manner that the device shall be made reasonably available to physicians meeting appropriate qualifications prescribed by the Secretary.

(4) Repealed. Pub. L. 105–115, title I, § 125(b)(2)(E), Nov. 21, 1997, 111 Stat. 2325.

(5)(A) Before December 1, 1991, the Secretary shall by order require manufacturers of devices described in paragraph (1), which are subject to revision of classification under subparagraph

(B), to submit to the Secretary a summary of and citation to any information known or otherwise available to the manufacturers respecting the devices, including adverse safety or effectiveness information which has not been submitted under section 360i of this title. The Secretary may require a manufacturer to submit the adverse safety or effectiveness data for which a summary and citation were submitted, if such data are available to the manufacturer.

(B) Except as provided in subparagraph (C), after the issuance of an order under subparagraph (A) but before December 1, 1992, the Secretary shall publish a regulation in the Federal Register for each device which is classified in class III under paragraph (1) revising the classification of the device so that the device is classified into class I or class II, unless the regulation requires the device to remain in class III. In determining whether to revise the classification of a device or to require a device to remain in class III, the Secretary shall apply the criteria set forth in section 360c(a) of this title. Before the publication of a regulation requiring a device to remain in class III or revising its classification, the Secretary shall publish a proposed regulation respecting the classification of a device under this subparagraph and provide an opportunity for the submission of comments on any such regulation. No regulation under this subparagraph requiring a device to remain in class III or revising its classification may take effect before the expiration of 90 days from the date of the publication in the Federal Register of the proposed regulation.

(C) The Secretary may by notice published in the Federal Register extend the period prescribed by subparagraph (B) for a device for an additional period not to exceed 1 year.

(m) Humanitarian device exemption

(1) To the extent consistent with the protection of the public health and safety and with ethical standards, it is the purpose of this subsection to encourage the discovery and use of devices intended to benefit patients in the treatment and diagnosis of diseases or conditions that affect fewer than 4,000 individuals in the United States.

(2) The Secretary may grant a request for an exemption from the effectiveness requirements of sections 360d and 360e of this title for a device for which the Secretary finds that—

(A) the device is designed to treat or diagnose a disease or condition that affects fewer than 4,000 individuals in the United States,

(B) the device would not be available to a person with a disease or condition referred to in subparagraph (A) unless the Secretary grants such an exemption and there is no comparable device, other than under this exemption, available to treat or diagnose such disease or condition, and

(C) the device will not expose patients to an unreasonable or significant risk of illness or injury and the probable benefit to health from the use of the device outweighs the risk of injury or illness from its use, taking into account the probable risks and benefits of currently available devices or alternative forms of treatment.

The request shall be in the form of an application submitted to the Secretary and such application shall include the certification required under section 282(j)(5)(B) of title 42 (which shall not be considered an element of such application). Not later than 75 days after the date of the receipt of the application, the Secretary shall issue an order approving or denying the application.

(3) Except as provided in paragraph (6), no person granted an exemption under paragraph (2) with respect to a device may sell the device for an amount that exceeds the costs of research and development, fabrication, and distribution of the device.

(4) Devices granted an exemption under paragraph (2) may only be used—

(A) in facilities that have established, in accordance with regulations of the Secretary, a local institutional review committee to supervise clinical testing of devices in the facilities, and

(B) if, before the use of a device, an institutional review committee approves the use in the treatment or diagnosis of a disease or condition referred to in paragraph (2)(A), unless a physician determines in an emergency situation that approval from a local institutional review committee can not be obtained in time to prevent serious harm or death to a patient.

In a case described in subparagraph (B) in which a physician uses a device without an approval from an institutional review committee, the physician shall, after the use of the device, notify the chairperson of the local institutional review committee of such use. Such notification shall include the identification of the patient involved, the date on which the device was used, and the reason for the use.

(5) The Secretary may require a person granted an exemption under paragraph (2) to demonstrate continued compliance with the requirements of this subsection if the Secretary believes such demonstration to be necessary to protect the public health, if the Secretary has reason to believe that the requirements of paragraph (6) are no longer met, or if the Secretary has reason to believe that the criteria for the exemption are no longer met. If the person granted an exemption under paragraph (2) fails to demonstrate continued compliance with the requirements of this subsection, the Secretary may suspend or withdraw the exemption from the effectiveness requirements of sections 360d and 360e of this title for a humanitarian device only after providing notice and an opportunity for an informal hearing.

(6)(A) Except as provided in subparagraph (D), the prohibition in paragraph (3) shall not apply with respect to a person granted an exemption under paragraph (2) if each of the following conditions apply:

(i)(I) The device with respect to which the exemption is granted is intended for the treatment or diagnosis of a disease or condition that occurs in pediatric patients or in a pediatric subpopulation, and such device is labeled for use in pediatric patients or in a pediatric subpopulation in which the disease or condition occurs.

(II) The device was not previously approved under this subsection for the pediatric patients or the pediatric subpopulation described in subclause (I) prior to September 27, 2007.

(ii) During any calendar year, the number of such devices distributed during that year does not exceed the annual distribution number specified by the Secretary when the Secretary grants such exemption. The annual distribution number shall be based on the number of individuals affected by the disease or condition that such device is intended to treat, diagnose, or cure, and of that number, the number of individuals likely to use the device, and the number of devices reasonably necessary to treat such individuals. In no case shall the annual distribution number exceed the number identified in paragraph (2)(A).

(iii) Such person immediately notifies the Secretary if the number of such devices distributed during any calendar year exceeds the annual distribution number referred to in clause (ii).

(iv) The request for such exemption is submitted on or before October 1, 2012.

(B) The Secretary may inspect the records relating to the number of devices distributed during any calendar year of a person granted an exemption under paragraph (2) for which the prohibition in paragraph (3) does not apply.

(C) A person may petition the Secretary to modify the annual distribution number specified by the Secretary under subparagraph (A)(ii) with respect to a device if additional information on the number of individuals affected by the disease or condition arises, and the Secretary may modify such number but in no case shall the annual distribution number exceed the number identified in paragraph (2)(A).

(D) If a person notifies the Secretary, or the Secretary determines through an inspection under subparagraph (B), that the number of devices distributed during any calendar year exceeds the annual distribution number, as required under subparagraph (A)(iii), and modified under subparagraph (C), if applicable, then the prohibition in paragraph (3) shall apply with respect to such person for such device for any sales of such device after such notification.

(E)(i) In this subsection, the term "pediatric patients" means patients who are 21 years of age or younger at the time of the diagnosis or treatment.

(ii) In this subsection, the term "pediatric subpopulation" means 1 of the following populations:

(I) Neonates.

(II) Infants.

(III) Children.

(IV) Adolescents.

(7) The Secretary shall refer any report of an adverse event regarding a device for which the prohibition under paragraph (3) does not apply pursuant to paragraph (6)(A) that the Secretary receives to the Office of Pediatric Therapeutics, established under section 393a of this title. In considering the report, the Director of the Office of Pediatric Therapeutics, in consultation with experts in the Center for Devices and Radiological Health, shall provide for periodic review of the report by the Pediatric Advisory Committee, including obtaining any recommendations of such committee regarding whether the Secretary should take action under this chapter in response to the report.

(8) The Secretary, acting through the Office of Pediatric Therapeutics and the Center for Devices and Radiological Health, shall provide for an annual review by the Pediatric Advisory Committee of all devices described in paragraph (6) to ensure that the exemption under paragraph (2) remains appropriate for the pediatric populations for which it is granted.

(n) Regulation of contact lenses as devices

(1) All contact lenses shall be deemed to be devices under section 321(h) of this title.

(2) Paragraph (1) shall not be construed as bearing on or being relevant to the question of whether any product other than a contact lens is a device as defined by section 321(h) of this title or a drug as defined by section 321(g) of this title.

(June 25, 1938, ch. 675, § 520, as added Pub. L. 94–295, § 2, May 28, 1976, 90 Stat. 565; amended Pub. L. 101–629, §§ 3(b)(2), 4(b)(2), 5(c)(2), 6(b)(2), 11, 14(a), 18(e), (f), Nov. 28, 1990, 104 Stat. 4514, 4516, 4518, 4519, 4522, 4524, 4529; Pub. L. 102–571, title I, § 107(10), Oct. 29, 1992, 106 Stat. 4499; Pub. L. 105–115, title I, § 125(b)(2)(E), title II, §§ 201(a), 203, 216(a)(1), title IV, § 410(a), Nov. 21, 1997, 111 Stat. 2325, 2332, 2334, 2349, 2372; Pub. L. 109–96, § 1, Nov. 9, 2005, 119 Stat. 2119; Pub. L. 110–85, title III, § 303(a), title VIII, § 801(b)(3)(E), Sept. 27, 2007, 121 Stat. 860, 921.)

REFERENCES IN TEXT

Section 14 of the Federal Advisory Committee Act, referred to in subsec. (f)(3), is section 14 of Pub. L. 92–463, which is set out in the Appendix to Title 5, Government Organization and Employees.

CODIFICATION

In subsec. (k), "section 3324(a) and (b) of title 31" substituted for reference to section 3648 of the Revised Statutes (31 U.S.C. 529) on authority of Pub. L. 97–258, § 4(b), Sept. 13, 1982, 96 Stat. 1067, the first section of which enacted Title 31, Money and Finance.

AMENDMENTS

2007—Subsec. (m)(2). Pub. L. 110–85, § 801(b)(3)(E), inserted before period at end of first sentence of concluding provisions "and such application shall include the certification required under section 282(j)(5)(B) of title 42 (which shall not be considered an element of such application)".

Subsec. (m)(3). Pub. L. 110–85, § 303(a)(1), substituted "Except as provided in paragraph (6), no" for "No".

Subsec. (m)(5). Pub. L. 110–85, § 303(a)(2), inserted ", if the Secretary has reason to believe that the requirements of paragraph (6) are no longer met," after "public health" and inserted at end "If the person granted an exemption under paragraph (2) fails to demonstrate continued compliance with the requirements of this subsection, the Secretary may suspend or withdraw the exemption from the effectiveness requirements of sections 360d and 360e of this title for a humanitarian device only after providing notice and an opportunity for an informal hearing."

Subsec. (m)(6) to (8). Pub. L. 110–85, § 303(a)(3), added pars. (6) to (8) and struck out former par. (6) which read as follows: "The Secretary may suspend or withdraw an exemption from the effectiveness requirements of sections 360d and 360e of this title for a humanitarian device only after providing notice and an opportunity for an informal hearing."

2005—Subsec. (n). Pub. L. 109–96 added subsec. (n).

1997—Subsec. (f)(1)(B)(iii). Pub. L. 105–115, §410(a), added cl. (iii).

Subsec. (g)(6), (7). Pub. L. 105–115, §201(a), added pars. (6) and (7).

Subsec. (h)(4). Pub. L. 105–115, §216(a)(1), amended par. (4) generally. Prior to amendment, par. (4) related to premarket approval of devices.

Subsec. (*l*). Pub. L. 105–115, §125(b)(2)(E), struck out "or antibiotic drugs" after "new drugs" in heading.

Subsec. (*l*)(4). Pub. L. 105–115, §125(b)(2)(E), struck out par. (4) which read as follows: "Any device intended for human use which on the enactment date was subject to the requirements of section 357 of this title shall be subject to such requirements as follows:

"(A) In the case of such a device which is classified into class I, such requirements shall apply to such device until the effective date of the regulation classifying the device into such class.

"(B) In the case of such a device which is classified into class II, such requirements shall apply to such device until the effective date of a performance standard applicable to the device under section 360d of this title.

"(C) In the case of such a device which is classified into class III, such requirements shall apply to such device until the date on which the device is required to have in effect an approved application under section 360e of this title."

Subsec. (m)(2). Pub. L. 105–115, §203(1), inserted at end "The request shall be in the form of an application submitted to the Secretary. Not later than 75 days after the date of the receipt of the application, the Secretary shall issue an order approving or denying the application."

Subsec. (m)(4). Pub. L. 105–115, §203(2)(B), inserted at end "In a case described in subparagraph (B) in which a physician uses a device without an approval from an institutional review committee, the physician shall, after the use of the device, notify the chairperson of the local institutional review committee of such use. Such notification shall include the identification of the patient involved, the date on which the device was used, and the reason for the use."

Subsec. (m)(4)(B). Pub. L. 105–115, §203(2)(A), inserted before period at end ", unless a physician determines in an emergency situation that approval from a local institutional review committee can not be obtained in time to prevent serious harm or death to a patient".

Subsec. (m)(5). Pub. L. 105–115, §203(3), amended par. (5) generally. Prior to amendment, par. (5) read as follows: "An exemption under paragraph (2) shall be for a term of 18 months and may only be initially granted in the 5-year period beginning on the date regulations under paragraph (6) take effect. The Secretary may extend such an exemption for a period of 18 months if the Secretary is able to make the findings set forth in paragraph (2) and if the applicant supplies information demonstrating compliance with paragraph (3). An exemption may be extended more than once and may be extended after the expiration of such 5-year period."

Subsec. (m)(6). Pub. L. 105–115, §203(4), amended par. (6) generally. Prior to amendment, par. (6) read as follows: "Within one year of November 28, 1990, the Secretary shall issue regulations to implement this subsection."

1992—Subsec. (g)(2)(A). Pub. L. 102–571 substituted "379e" for "376".

1990—Subsec. (c). Pub. L. 101–629, §11(1), substituted "from class III to class II or class I" for "under section 360c of this title from class III to class II" and inserted "(1) in accordance with subsection (h) of this section, and (2)" after "except".

Subsec. (f)(1)(A). Pub. L. 101–629, §18(e), inserted "preproduction design validation (including a process to assess the performance of a device but not including an evaluation of the safety or effectiveness of a device)," after "manufacture,".

Subsec. (h)(3). Pub. L. 101–629, §11(2)(A), substituted "Except as provided in paragraph (4), any" for "Any".

Subsec. (h)(4). Pub. L. 101–629, §11(2)(B), added par. (4).

Subsec. (i). Pub. L. 101–629, §6(b)(2), substituted "section 360d(b)(5)(B)" for "section 360d(g)(5)(B)".

Subsec. (j). Pub. L. 101–629, §3(b)(2), substituted "Except as provided in section 360i(e) of this title, no" for "No".

Subsec. (*l*)(2). Pub. L. 101–629, §18(f), struck out "and after affording the petitioner an opportunity for an informal hearing" after "under this paragraph".

Pub. L. 101–629, §5(c)(2), substituted "The Secretary may initiate the reclassification of a device classified into class III under paragraph (1) of this subsection or the manufacturer" for "The manufacturer".

Subsec. (*l*)(5). Pub. L. 101–629, §4(b)(2), added par. (5).

Subsec. (m). Pub. L. 101–629, §14(a), added subsec. (m).

EFFECTIVE DATE OF 1997 AMENDMENT

Amendment by sections 201(a), 203, 216(a)(1), and 410(a) of Pub. L. 105–115 effective 90 days after Nov. 21, 1997, except as otherwise provided, see section 501 of Pub. L. 105–115, set out as a note under section 321 of this title.

EFFECTIVE DATE OF 1990 AMENDMENT

Section 14(b) of Pub. L. 101–629 provided that: "Subsection (m) of section 520 of the Federal Food, Drug, and Cosmetic Act [21 U.S.C. 360j(m)], as added by the amendment made by subsection (a), shall take effect on the effective date of the regulations issued by the Secretary under paragraph (6) of such subsection."

GUIDANCE

Pub. L. 110–85, title III, §303(c), Sept. 27, 2007, 121 Stat. 862, provided that: "Not later than 180 days after the date of the enactment of this Act [Sept. 27, 2007], the Commissioner of Food and Drugs shall issue guidance for institutional review committees on how to evaluate requests for approval for devices for which a humanitarian device exemption under section 520(m)(2) of the Federal Food, Drug, and Cosmetic Act (21 U.S.C. 360j(m)(2)) has been granted."

Pub. L. 107–250, title II, §213, Oct. 26, 2002, 116 Stat. 1614, provided that: "Not later than 270 days after the date of the enactment of this Act [Oct. 26, 2002], the Secretary of Health and Human Services shall issue guidance on the following:

"(1) The type of information necessary to provide reasonable assurance of the safety and effectiveness of medical devices intended for use in pediatric populations.

"(2) Protections for pediatric subjects in clinical investigations of the safety or effectiveness of such devices."

REPORT ON HUMANITARIAN DEVICE EXEMPTIONS

Section 14(c) of Pub. L. 101–629 directed Secretary of Health and Human Services, within 4 years after issuance of regulations under 21 U.S.C. 360j(m)(6), to report to Congress on types of devices exempted, an evaluation of effects of such section, and a recommendation on extension of the section.

REFERENCES IN OTHER LAWS TO GS–16, 17, OR 18 PAY RATES

References in laws to the rates of pay for GS–16, 17, or 18, or to maximum rates of pay under the General Schedule, to be considered references to rates payable under specified sections of Title 5, Government Organization and Employees, see section 529 [title I, §101(c)(1)] of Pub. L. 101–509, set out in a note under section 5376 of Title 5.

§ 360k. State and local requirements respecting devices

(a) General rule

Except as provided in subsection (b) of this section, no State or political subdivision of a State may establish or continue in effect with respect to a device intended for human use any requirement—

(1) which is different from, or in addition to, any requirement applicable under this chapter to the device, and

(2) which relates to the safety or effectiveness of the device or to any other matter included in a requirement applicable to the device under this chapter.

(b) Exempt requirements

Upon application of a State or a political subdivision thereof, the Secretary may, by regulation promulgated after notice and opportunity for an oral hearing, exempt from subsection (a) of this section, under such conditions as may be prescribed in such regulation, a requirement of such State or political subdivision applicable to a device intended for human use if—

(1) the requirement is more stringent than a requirement under this chapter which would be applicable to the device if an exemption were not in effect under this subsection; or

(2) the requirement—

(A) is required by compelling local conditions, and

(B) compliance with the requirement would not cause the device to be in violation of any applicable requirement under this chapter.

(June 25, 1938, ch. 675, § 521, as added Pub. L. 94–295, § 2, May 28, 1976, 90 Stat. 574.)

§ 360l. Postmarket surveillance

(a) Postmarket surveillance

(1) In general

(A) Conduct

The Secretary may by order require a manufacturer to conduct postmarket surveillance for any device of the manufacturer that is a class II or class III device—

(i) the failure of which would be reasonably likely to have serious adverse health consequences;

(ii) that is expected to have significant use in pediatric populations; or

(iii) that is intended to be—

(I) implanted in the human body for more than 1 year; or

(II) a life-sustaining or life-supporting device used outside a device user facility.

(B) Condition

The Secretary may order a postmarket surveillance under subparagraph (A) as a condition to approval or clearance of a device described in subparagraph (A)(ii).

(2) Rule of construction

The provisions of paragraph (1) shall have no effect on authorities otherwise provided under the[1] chapter or regulations issued under this chapter.

(b) Surveillance approval

(1) In general

Each manufacturer required to conduct a surveillance of a device shall, within 30 days of receiving an order from the Secretary prescribing that the manufacturer is required under this section to conduct such surveillance, submit, for the approval of the Secretary, a plan for the required surveillance. The Secretary, within 60 days of the receipt of such plan, shall determine if the person designated to conduct the surveillance has appropriate qualifications and experience to undertake such surveillance and if the plan will result in the collection of useful data that can reveal unforeseen adverse events or other information necessary to protect the public health. Except as provided in paragraph (2), the Secretary, in consultation with the manufacturer, may by order require a prospective surveillance period of up to 36 months. Except as provided in paragraph (2), any determination by the Secretary that a longer period is necessary shall be made by mutual agreement between the Secretary and the manufacturer or, if no agreement can be reached, after the completion of a dispute resolution process as described in section 360bbb–1 of this title.

(2) Longer surveillance for pediatric devices

The Secretary may by order require a prospective surveillance period of more than 36 months with respect to a device that is expected to have significant use in pediatric populations if such period of more than 36 months is necessary in order to assess the impact of the device on growth and development, or the effects of growth, development, activity level, or other factors on the safety or efficacy of the device.

(c) Dispute resolution

A manufacturer may request review under section 360bbb–1 of this title of any order or condition requiring postmarket surveillance under this section. During the pendency of such review, the device subject to such a postmarket surveillance order or condition shall not, because of noncompliance with such order or condition, be deemed in violation of section 331(q)(1)(C) of this title, adulterated under section 351(f)(1) of this title, misbranded under section 352(t)(3) of this title, or in violation of, as applicable, section 360(k) of this title or section 360e of this title, unless deemed necessary to protect the public health.

(June 25, 1938, ch. 675, § 522, as added Pub. L. 101–629, § 10, Nov. 28, 1990, 104 Stat. 4521; amended Pub. L. 102–300, § 3(b), June 16, 1992, 106 Stat. 239; Pub. L. 105–115, title II, § 212, Nov. 21, 1997, 111 Stat. 2346; Pub. L. 110–85, title III, § 307, Sept. 27, 2007, 121 Stat. 865.)

AMENDMENTS

2007—Pub. L. 110–85, § 307(1), made technical amendment to section catchline.

Subsec. (a). Pub. L. 110–85, § 307(2), added subsec. (a) and struck out former subsec. (a). Prior to amendment, text read as follows: "The Secretary may by order require a manufacturer to conduct postmarket surveillance for any device of the manufacturer which is a class II or class III device the failure of which would be reasonably likely to have serious adverse health consequences or which is intended to be—

"(1) implanted in the human body for more than one year, or

"(2) a life sustaining or life supporting device used outside a device user facility."

[1] So in original. Probably should be "this".

Subsec. (b). Pub. L. 110–85, § 307(3), designated existing provisions as par. (1), inserted par. heading, substituted "Except as provided in paragraph (2), the Secretary, in consultation" for "The Secretary, in consultation" and "Except as provided in paragraph (2), any determination" for "Any determination", and added par. (2).

Subsec. (c). Pub. L. 110–85, § 307(3)(D), added subsec. (c).

1997—Pub. L. 105–115 amended section generally, substituting present provisions for former provisions which related to required surveillance, discretionary surveillance, and surveillance approval.

1992—Subsec. (b). Pub. L. 102–300 substituted "(a)(1)" for "(a)", inserted comma after "commerce", and inserted after first sentence "Each manufacturer required to conduct a surveillance of a device under subsection (a)(2) of this section shall, within 30 days after receiving notice that the manufacturer is required to conduct such surveillance, submit, for the approval of the Secretary, a protocol for the required surveillance."

EFFECTIVE DATE OF 1997 AMENDMENT

Section 212 of Pub. L. 105–115 provided in part that the amendment made by that section is effective 90 days after Nov. 21, 1997.

STUDY BY INSTITUTE OF MEDICINE OF POSTMARKET SURVEILLANCE REGARDING PEDIATRIC POPULATIONS

Pub. L. 107–250, title II, § 212, Oct. 26, 2002, 116 Stat. 1614, as amended by Pub. L. 108–214, § 2(d)(3)(C), Apr. 1, 2004, 118 Stat. 577, provided that:

"(a) IN GENERAL.—The Secretary of Health and Human Services (referred to in this section as the 'Secretary') shall request the Institute of Medicine to enter into an agreement with the Secretary under which such Institute conducts a study for the purpose of determining whether the system under the Federal Food, Drug, and Cosmetic Act [21 U.S.C. 301 et seq.] for the postmarket surveillance of medical devices provides adequate safeguards regarding the use of devices in pediatric populations.

"(b) CERTAIN MATTERS.—The Secretary shall ensure that determinations made in the study under subsection (a) include determinations of—

"(1) whether postmarket surveillance studies of implanted medical devices are of long enough duration to evaluate the impact of growth and development for the number of years that the child will have the implant, and whether the studies are adequate to evaluate how children's active lifestyles may affect the failure rate and longevity of the implant; and

"(2) whether the postmarket surveillance by the Food and Drug Administration of medical devices used in pediatric populations is sufficient to provide adequate safeguards for such populations, taking into account the Secretary's monitoring of commitments made at the time of approval of medical devices and the Secretary's monitoring and use of adverse reaction reports, registries, and other postmarket surveillance activities.

"(c) REPORT TO CONGRESS.—The Secretary shall ensure that, not later than four years after the date of the enactment of this Act [Oct. 26, 2002], a report describing the findings of the study under subsection (a) is submitted to the Congress. The report shall include any recommendations of the Secretary for administrative or legislative changes to the system of postmarket surveillance referred to in such subsection."

§ 360m. Accredited persons

(a) In general

(1) Review and classification of devices

Not later than 1 year after November 21, 1997, the Secretary shall, subject to paragraph (3), accredit persons for the purpose of reviewing reports submitted under section 360(k) of this title and making recommendations to the Secretary regarding the initial classification of devices under section 360c(f)(1) of this title.

(2) Requirements regarding review

(A) In general

In making a recommendation to the Secretary under paragraph (1), an accredited person shall notify the Secretary in writing of the reasons for the recommendation.

(B) Time period for review

Not later than 30 days after the date on which the Secretary is notified under subparagraph (A) by an accredited person with respect to a recommendation of an initial classification of a device, the Secretary shall make a determination with respect to the initial classification.

(C) Special rule

The Secretary may change the initial classification under section 360c(f)(1) of this title that is recommended under paragraph (1) by an accredited person, and in such case shall provide to such person, and the person who submitted the report under section 360(k) of this title for the device, a statement explaining in detail the reasons for the change.

(3) Certain devices

(A) In general

An accredited person may not be used to perform a review of—

(i) a class III device;

(ii) a class II device which is intended to be permanently implantable or life sustaining or life supporting; or

(iii) a class II device which requires clinical data in the report submitted under section 360(k) of this title for the device, except that the number of class II devices to which the Secretary applies this clause for a year, less the number of such reports to which clauses (i) and (ii) apply, may not exceed 6 percent of the number that is equal to the total number of reports submitted to the Secretary under such section for such year less the number of such reports to which such clauses apply for such year.

(B) Adjustment

In determining for a year the ratio described in subparagraph (A)(iii), the Secretary shall not include in the numerator class III devices that the Secretary reclassified into class II, and the Secretary shall include in the denominator class II devices for which reports under section 360(k) of this title were not required to be submitted by reason of the operation of section 360(m) of this title.

(b) Accreditation

(1) Programs

The Secretary shall provide for such accreditation through programs administered by the Food and Drug Administration, other government agencies, or by other qualified nongovernment organizations.

(2) Accreditation

(A) In general

Not later than 180 days after November 21, 1997, the Secretary shall establish and publish in the Federal Register criteria to accredit or deny accreditation to persons who request to perform the duties specified in subsection (a) of this section. The Secretary shall respond to a request for accreditation within 60 days of the receipt of the request. The accreditation of such person shall specify the particular activities under subsection (a) of this section for which such person is accredited.

(B) Withdrawal of accreditation

The Secretary may suspend or withdraw accreditation of any person accredited under this paragraph, after providing notice and an opportunity for an informal hearing, when such person is substantially not in compliance with the requirements of this section or poses a threat to public health or fails to act in a manner that is consistent with the purposes of this section.

(C) Performance auditing

To ensure that persons accredited under this section will continue to meet the standards of accreditation, the Secretary shall—

(i) make onsite visits on a periodic basis to each accredited person to audit the performance of such person; and

(ii) take such additional measures as the Secretary determines to be appropriate.

(D) Annual report

The Secretary shall include in the annual report required under section 393(g) of this title the names of all accredited persons and the particular activities under subsection (a) of this section for which each such person is accredited and the name of each accredited person whose accreditation has been withdrawn during the year.

(3) Qualifications

An accredited person shall, at a minimum, meet the following requirements:

(A) Such person may not be an employee of the Federal Government.

(B) Such person shall be an independent organization which is not owned or controlled by a manufacturer, supplier, or vendor of devices and which has no organizational, material, or financial affiliation with such a manufacturer, supplier, or vendor.

(C) Such person shall be a legally constituted entity permitted to conduct the activities for which it seeks accreditation.

(D) Such person shall not engage in the design, manufacture, promotion, or sale of devices.

(E) The operations of such person shall be in accordance with generally accepted professional and ethical business practices and shall agree in writing that as a minimum it will—

(i) certify that reported information accurately reflects data reviewed;

(ii) limit work to that for which competence and capacity are available;

(iii) treat information received, records, reports, and recommendations as proprietary information;

(iv) promptly respond and attempt to resolve complaints regarding its activities for which it is accredited; and

(v) protect against the use, in carrying out subsection (a) of this section with respect to a device, of any officer or employee of the person who has a financial conflict of interest regarding the device, and annually make available to the public disclosures of the extent to which the person, and the officers and employees of the person, have maintained compliance with requirements under this clause relating to financial conflicts of interest.

(4) Selection of accredited persons

The Secretary shall provide each person who chooses to use an accredited person to receive a section 360(k) of this title report a panel of at least two or more accredited persons from which the regulated person may select one for a specific regulatory function.

(5) Compensation of accredited persons

Compensation for an accredited person shall be determined by agreement between the accredited person and the person who engages the services of the accredited person, and shall be paid by the person who engages such services.

(c) Duration

The authority provided by this section terminates October 1, 2012.

(d) Report

Not later than January 10, 2007, the Secretary shall conduct a study based on the experience under the program under this section and submit to the Committee on Energy and Commerce of the House of Representatives, and the Committee on Health, Education, Labor, and Pensions of the Senate, a report describing the findings of the study. The objectives of the study shall include determining—

(1) the number of devices reviewed under this section;

(2) the number of devices reviewed under this section that were ultimately cleared by the Secretary;

(3) the number of devices reviewed under this section that were ultimately not cleared by the Secretary;

(4) the average time period for a review under this section (including the time it takes for the Secretary to review a recommendation of an accredited person under subsection (a) of this section and determine the initial device classification);

(5) the average time period identified in paragraph (4) compared to the average time period for review of devices solely by the Secretary pursuant to section 360(k) of this title;

(6) if there is a difference in the average time period under paragraph (4) and the average time period under paragraph (5), the reasons for such difference;

(7) whether the quality of reviews under this section for devices for which no guidance has

been issued is qualitatively inferior to reviews by the Secretary for devices for which no guidance has been issued;

(8) whether the quality of reviews under this section of devices for which no guidance has been issued is qualitatively inferior to reviews under this section of devices for which guidance has been issued;

(9) whether this section has in any way jeopardized or improved the public health;

(10) any impact of this section on resources available to the Secretary to review reports under section 360(k) of this title; and

(11) any suggestions for continuation, modification (including contraction or expansion of device eligibility), or termination of this section that the Secretary determines to be appropriate.

(June 25, 1938, ch. 675, §523, as added Pub. L. 105–115, title II, §210(a), Nov. 21, 1997, 111 Stat. 2342; amended Pub. L. 107–250, title II, §202, Oct. 26, 2002, 116 Stat. 1609; Pub. L. 110–85, title II, §221, Sept. 27, 2007, 121 Stat. 852.)

AMENDMENTS

2007—Subsec. (c). Pub. L. 110–85 substituted "2012" for "2007".

2002—Subsec. (c). Pub. L. 107–250, §202(1), substituted "The authority provided by this section terminates October 1, 2007." for "The authority provided by this section terminates—

"(1) 5 years after the date on which the Secretary notifies Congress that at least 2 persons accredited under subsection (b) of this section are available to review at least 60 percent of the submissions under section 360(k) of this title, or

"(2) 4 years after the date on which the Secretary notifies Congress that the Secretary has made a determination described in paragraph (2)(B) of subsection (a) of this section for at least 35 percent of the devices that are subject to review under paragraph (1) of such subsection,

whichever occurs first."

Subsec. (d). Pub. L. 107–250, §202(2), added subsec. (d).

EFFECTIVE DATE

Section effective 90 days after Nov. 21, 1997, except as otherwise provided, see section 501 of Pub. L. 105–115, set out as a note under section 321 of this title.

REPORTS ON PROGRAM OF ACCREDITATION

Pub. L. 105–115, title II, §210(d), Nov. 21, 1997, 111 Stat. 2345, provided that:

"(1) COMPTROLLER GENERAL.—

"(A) IMPLEMENTATION OF PROGRAM.—Not later than 5 years after the date of the enactment of this Act [Nov. 21, 1997], the Comptroller General of the United States shall submit to the Committee on Commerce [now Committee on Energy and Commerce] of the House of Representatives and the Committee on Labor and Human Resources [now Committee on Health, Education, Labor, and Pensions] of the Senate a report describing the extent to which the program of accreditation required by the amendment made by subsection (a) [enacting this section] has been implemented.

"(B) EVALUATION OF PROGRAM.—Not later than 6 months prior to the date on which, pursuant to subsection (c) of section 523 of the Federal Food, Drug, and Cosmetic Act [21 U.S.C. 360m(c)] (as added by subsection (a)), the authority provided under subsection (a) of such section will terminate, the Comptroller General shall submit to the Committee on Commerce [now Committee on Energy and Commerce] of the House of Representatives and the Committee on Labor and Human Resources [now Committee on Health, Education, Labor, and Pensions] of the Senate a report describing the use of accredited persons under such section 523, including an evaluation of the extent to which such use assisted the Secretary in carrying out the duties of the Secretary under such Act [21 U.S.C. 301 et seq.] with respect to devices, and the extent to which such use promoted actions which are contrary to the purposes of such Act.

"(2) INCLUSION OF CERTAIN DEVICES WITHIN PROGRAM.—Not later than 3 years after the date of the enactment of this Act [Nov. 21, 1997], the Secretary of Health and Human Services shall submit to the Committee on Commerce of the House of Representatives and the Committee on Labor and Human Resources [now Committee on Health, Education, Labor, and Pensions] of the Senate a report providing a determination by the Secretary of whether, in the program of accreditation established pursuant to the amendment made by subsection (a), the limitation established in clause (iii) of section 523(a)(3)(A) of the Federal Food, Drug, and Cosmetic Act [21 U.S.C. 360m(a)(3)(A)] (relating to class II devices for which clinical data are required in reports under section 510(k) [21 U.S.C. 360(k)]) should be removed."

§ 360n. Priority review to encourage treatments for tropical diseases

(a) Definitions

In this section:

(1) Priority review

The term "priority review", with respect to a human drug application as defined in section 379g(1) of this title, means review and action by the Secretary on such application not later than 6 months after receipt by the Secretary of such application, as described in the Manual of Policies and Procedures of the Food and Drug Administration and goals identified in the letters described in section 101(c) of the Food and Drug Administration Amendments Act of 2007.

(2) Priority review voucher

The term "priority review voucher" means a voucher issued by the Secretary to the sponsor of a tropical disease product application that entitles the holder of such voucher to priority review of a single human drug application submitted under section 355(b)(1) of this title or section 262 of title 42 after the date of approval of the tropical disease product application.

(3) Tropical disease

The term "tropical disease" means any of the following:

(A) Tuberculosis.
(B) Malaria.
(C) Blinding trachoma.
(D) Buruli Ulcer.
(E) Cholera.
(F) Dengue/dengue haemorrhagic fever.
(G) Dracunculiasis (guinea-worm disease).
(H) Fascioliasis.
(I) Human African trypanosomiasis.
(J) Leishmaniasis.
(K) Leprosy.
(L) Lymphatic filariasis.
(M) Onchocerciasis.
(N) Schistosomiasis.
(O) Soil transmitted helmithiasis.
(P) Yaws.
(Q) Any other infectious disease for which there is no significant market in developed

nations and that disproportionately affects poor and marginalized populations, designated by regulation by the Secretary.

(4) Tropical disease product application

The term "tropical disease product application" means an application that—

(A) is a human drug application as defined in section 379g(1) of this title—

(i) for prevention or treatment of a tropical disease; and

(ii) the Secretary deems eligible for priority review;

(B) is approved after September 27, 2007, by the Secretary for use in the prevention, detection, or treatment of a tropical disease; and

(C) is for a human drug, no active ingredient (including any ester or salt of the active ingredient) of which has been approved in any other application under section 355(b)(1) of this title or section 262 of title 42.

(b) Priority review voucher

(1) In general

The Secretary shall award a priority review voucher to the sponsor of a tropical disease product application upon approval by the Secretary of such tropical disease product application.

(2) Transferability

The sponsor of a tropical disease product that receives a priority review voucher under this section may transfer (including by sale) the entitlement to such voucher to a sponsor of a human drug for which an application under section 355(b)(1) of this title or section 262 of title 42 will be submitted after the date of the approval of the tropical disease product application.

(3) Limitation

(A) No award for prior approved application

A sponsor of a tropical disease product may not receive a priority review voucher under this section if the tropical disease product application was submitted to the Secretary prior to September 27, 2007.

(B) One-year waiting period

The Secretary shall issue a priority review voucher to the sponsor of a tropical disease product no earlier than the date that is 1 year after September 27, 2007.

(4) Notification

The sponsor of a human drug application shall notify the Secretary not later than 365 days prior to submission of the human drug application that is the subject of a priority review voucher of an intent to submit the human drug application, including the date on which the sponsor intends to submit the application. Such notification shall be a legally binding commitment to pay for the user fee to be assessed in accordance with this section.

(c) Priority review user fee

(1) In general

The Secretary shall establish a user fee program under which a sponsor of a human drug application that is the subject of a priority review voucher shall pay to the Secretary a fee determined under paragraph (2). Such fee shall be in addition to any fee required to be submitted by the sponsor under subchapter VII.

(2) Fee amount

The amount of the priority review user fee shall be determined each fiscal year by the Secretary and based on the average cost incurred by the agency in the review of a human drug application subject to priority review in the previous fiscal year.

(3) Annual fee setting

The Secretary shall establish, before the beginning of each fiscal year beginning after September 30, 2007, for that fiscal year, the amount of the priority review user fee.

(4) Payment

(A) In general

The priority review user fee required by this subsection shall be due upon the submission of a human drug application under section 355(b)(1) of this title or section 262 of title 42 for which the priority review voucher is used.

(B) Complete application

An application described under subparagraph (A) for which the sponsor requests the use of a priority review voucher shall be considered incomplete if the fee required by this subsection and all other applicable user fees are not paid in accordance with the Secretary's procedures for paying such fees.

(C) No waivers, exemptions, reductions, or refunds

The Secretary may not grant a waiver, exemption, reduction, or refund of any fees due and payable under this section.

(5) Offsetting collections

Fees collected pursuant to this subsection for any fiscal year—

(A) shall be deposited and credited as offsetting collections to the account providing appropriations to the Food and Drug Administration; and

(B) shall not be collected for any fiscal year except to the extent provided in advance in appropriation Acts.

(June 25, 1938, ch. 675, § 524, as added Pub. L. 110–85, title XI, § 1102, Sept. 27, 2007, 121 Stat. 972.)

REFERENCES IN TEXT

Section 101(c) of the Food and Drug Administration Amendments Act of 2007, referred to in subsec. (a)(1), is section 101(c) of Pub. L. 110–85, which is set out as a note under section 379g of this title.

PART B—DRUGS FOR RARE DISEASES OR CONDITIONS

§ 360aa. Recommendations for investigations of drugs for rare diseases or conditions

(a) Request by sponsor; response by Secretary

The sponsor of a drug for a disease or condition which is rare in the States may request the

Secretary to provide written recommendations for the non-clinical and clinical investigations which must be conducted with the drug before—

(1) it may be approved for such disease or condition under section 355 of this title, or

(2) if the drug is a biological product, it may be licensed for such disease or condition under section 262 of title 42.

If the Secretary has reason to believe that a drug for which a request is made under this section is a drug for a disease or condition which is rare in the States, the Secretary shall provide the person making the request written recommendations for the non-clinical and clinical investigations which the Secretary believes, on the basis of information available to the Secretary at the time of the request under this section, would be necessary for approval of such drug for such disease or condition under section 355 of this title or licensing of such drug for such disease or condition under section 262 of title 42.

(b) Regulations

The Secretary shall by regulation promulgate procedures for the implementation of subsection (a) of this section.

(June 25, 1938, ch. 675, §525, as added Pub. L. 97–414, §2(a), Jan. 4, 1983, 96 Stat. 2049; amended Pub. L. 99–91, §3(a)(1), Aug. 15, 1985, 99 Stat. 387; Pub. L. 105–115, title I, §125(b)(2)(F), (G), Nov. 21, 1997, 111 Stat. 2325, 2326.)

AMENDMENTS

1997—Subsec. (a). Pub. L. 105–115, §125(b)(2)(G), struck out ", certification of such drug for such disease or condition under section 357 of this title," before "or licensing of such drug" in closing provisions.

Subsec. (a)(1) to (3). Pub. L. 105–115, §125(b)(2)(F), inserted "or" at end of par. (1), redesignated par. (3) as (2), and struck out former par. (2), which read as follows: "if the drug is an antibiotic, it may be certified for such disease or condition under section 357 of this title, or".

1985—Subsec. (a). Pub. L. 99–91 struck out "or" at end of par. (1), inserted par. (2), redesignated former par. (2) as (3) and struck out "before" after "product,", and in last sentence inserted provisions relating to certification of such drug for disease or condition under section 357 of this title and substituted "licensing of such drug for such disease or condition under section 262 of title 42" for "licensing under section 262 of title 42 for such disease or condition".

EFFECTIVE DATE OF 1985 AMENDMENT

Section 8 of Pub. L. 99–91 provided that:

"(a) GENERAL RULE.—Except as provided in subsection (b), this Act and the amendments made by this Act [amending this section, sections 360bb, 360cc, and 360ee of this title, and sections 295g–1 and 6022 of Title 42, The Public Health and Welfare, and enacting provisions set out as notes under section 301 of this title and section 236 of Title 42] shall take effect October 1, 1985.

"(b) EXCEPTION.—The amendments made by sections 2, 3, and 6(a) [amending this section and sections 360bb and 360cc of this title] shall take effect on the date of the enactment of this Act [Aug. 15, 1985]. The amendment made by section 6(b) [amending section 6022 of Title 42] shall take effect October 19, 1984. The amendments made by section 7 [amending section 295g–1 of Title 42] shall take effect October 1, 1984 and shall cease to be in effect after September 30, 1985."

STUDY

Pub. L. 100–290, §3(d), Apr. 18, 1988, 102 Stat. 91, directed Secretary of Health and Human Services to conduct a study to determine whether the application of subchapter B of chapter V of the Federal Food, Drug, and Cosmetic Act, 21 U.S.C. 360aa et seq. (relating to drugs for rare diseases and conditions), and 26 U.S.C. 28 (relating to tax credit) to medical devices or medical foods for rare diseases or conditions or to both was needed to encourage development of such devices and foods and report results of the study to Congress not later than one year after Apr. 18, 1988.

CONGRESSIONAL FINDINGS

Section 1(b) of Pub. L. 97–414 provided that: "The Congress finds that—

"(1) there are many diseases and conditions, such as Huntington's disease, myoclonus, ALS (Lou Gehrig's disease), Tourette syndrome, and muscular dystrophy which affect such small numbers of individuals residing in the United States that the diseases and conditions are considered rare in the United States;

"(2) adequate drugs for many of such diseases and conditions have not been developed;

"(3) drugs for these diseases and conditions are commonly referred to as 'orphan drugs';

"(4) because so few individuals are affected by any one rare disease or condition, a pharmaceutical company which develops an orphan drug may reasonably expect the drug to generate relatively small sales in comparison to the cost of developing the drug and consequently to incur a financial loss;

"(5) there is reason to believe that some promising orphan drugs will not be developed unless changes are made in the applicable Federal laws to reduce the costs of developing such drugs and to provide financial incentives to develop such drugs; and

"(6) it is in the public interest to provide such changes and incentives for the development of orphan drugs."

§ 360bb. Designation of drugs for rare diseases or conditions

(a) Request by sponsor; preconditions; "rare disease or condition" defined

(1) The manufacturer or the sponsor of a drug may request the Secretary to designate the drug as a drug for a rare disease or condition. A request for designation of a drug shall be made before the submission of an application under section 355(b) of this title for the drug, or the submission of an application for licensing of the drug under section 262 of title 42. If the Secretary finds that a drug for which a request is submitted under this subsection is being or will be investigated for a rare disease or condition and—

(A) if an application for such drug is approved under section 355 of this title, or

(B) if a license for such drug is issued under section 262 of title 42,

the approval, certification, or license would be for use for such disease or condition, the Secretary shall designate the drug as a drug for such disease or condition. A request for a designation of a drug under this subsection shall contain the consent of the applicant to notice being given by the Secretary under subsection (b) of this section respecting the designation of the drug.

(2) For purposes of paragraph (1), the term "rare disease or condition" means any disease or condition which (A) affects less than 200,000 persons in the United States, or (B) affects more than 200,000 in the United States and for which there is no reasonable expectation that the cost of developing and making available in the

United States a drug for such disease or condition will be recovered from sales in the United States of such drug. Determinations under the preceding sentence with respect to any drug shall be made on the basis of the facts and circumstances as of the date the request for designation of the drug under this subsection is made.

(b) Notification of discontinuance of drug or application as condition

A designation of a drug under subsection (a) of this section shall be subject to the condition that—

(1) if an application was approved for the drug under section 355(b) of this title or a license was issued for the drug under section 262 of title 42, the manufacturer of the drug will notify the Secretary of any discontinuance of the production of the drug at least one year before discontinuance, and

(2) if an application has not been approved for the drug under section 355(b) of this title or a license has not been issued for the drug under section 262 of title 42 and if preclinical investigations or investigations under section 355(i) of this title are being conducted with the drug, the manufacturer or sponsor of the drug will notify the Secretary of any decision to discontinue active pursuit of approval of an application under section 355(b) of this title or approval of a license under section 262 of title 42.

(c) Notice to public

Notice respecting the designation of a drug under subsection (a) of this section shall be made available to the public.

(d) Regulations

The Secretary shall by regulation promulgate procedures for the implementation of subsection (a) of this section.

(June 25, 1938, ch. 675, § 526, as added Pub. L. 97–414, § 2(a), Jan. 4, 1983, 96 Stat. 2050; amended Pub. L. 98–551, § 4(a), Oct. 30, 1984, 98 Stat. 2817; Pub. L. 99–91, § 3(a)(2), Aug. 15, 1985, 99 Stat. 387; Pub. L. 100–290, § 2, Apr. 18, 1988, 102 Stat. 90; Pub. L. 105–115, title I, § 125(b)(2)(H), (I), Nov. 21, 1997, 111 Stat. 2326.)

AMENDMENTS

1997—Subsec. (a)(1). Pub. L. 105–115, § 125(b)(2)(H), struck out "the submission of an application for certification of the drug under section 357 of this title," before "or the submission of an application for licensing of the drug" in introductory provisions, inserted "or" at end of subpar. (A), redesignated subpar. (C) as (B), and struck out former subpar. (B) which read as follows: "if a certification for such drug is issued under section 357 of this title, or".

Subsec. (b)(1). Pub. L. 105–115, § 125(b)(2)(I)(i), struck out ", a certificate was issued for the drug under section 357 of this title," before "or a license was issued".

Subsec. (b)(2). Pub. L. 105–115, § 125(b)(2)(I)(ii), struck out ", a certificate has not been issued for the drug under section 357 of this title," before "or a license has not been issued" and ", approval of an application for certification under section 357 of this title," before "or approval of a license".

1988—Subsec. (a)(1). Pub. L. 100–290, § 2(a), inserted after first sentence "A request for designation of a drug shall be made before the submission of an application under section 355(b) of this title for the drug, the submission of an application for certification of the drug under section 357 of this title, or the submission of an application for licensing of the drug under section 262 of title 42."

Subsecs. (b) to (d). Pub. L. 100–290, § 2(b), added subsec. (b) and redesignated former subsecs. (b) and (c) as (c) and (d), respectively.

1985—Subsec. (a)(1). Pub. L. 99–91 struck out "or" at end of subpar. (A), struck out subpar. (B) and substituted subpars. (B) and (C), and inserted ", certification," after "approval".

1984—Subsec. (a)(2). Pub. L. 98–551 substituted "which (A) affects less than 200,000 persons in the United States, or (B) affects more than 200,000 in the United States and for which" for "which occurs so infrequently in the United States that".

EFFECTIVE DATE OF 1985 AMENDMENT

Amendment by Pub. L. 99–91 effective Aug. 15, 1985, see section 8(b) of Pub. L. 99–91, set out as a note under section 360aa of this title.

§ 360cc. Protection for drugs for rare diseases or conditions

(a) Exclusive approval, certification, or license

Except as provided in subsection (b) of this section, if the Secretary—

(1) approves an application filed pursuant to section 355 of this title, or

(2) issues a license under section 262 of title 42

for a drug designated under section 360bb of this title for a rare disease or condition, the Secretary may not approve another application under section 355 of this title or issue another license under section 262 of title 42 for such drug for such disease or condition for a person who is not the holder of such approved application or of such license until the expiration of seven years from the date of the approval of the approved application or the issuance of the license. Section 355(c)(2) of this title does not apply to the refusal to approve an application under the preceding sentence.

(b) Exceptions

If an application filed pursuant to section 355 of this title is approved for a drug designated under section 360bb of this title for a rare disease or condition or if a license is issued under section 262 of title 42 for such a drug, the Secretary may, during the seven-year period beginning on the date of the application approval or of the issuance of the license, approve another application under section 355 of this title or issue a license under section 262 of title 42, for such drug for such disease or condition for a person who is not the holder of such approved application or of such license if—

(1) the Secretary finds, after providing the holder notice and opportunity for the submission of views, that in such period the holder of the approved application or of the license cannot assure the availability of sufficient quantities of the drug to meet the needs of persons with the disease or condition for which the drug was designated; or

(2) such holder provides the Secretary in writing the consent of such holder for the approval of other applications or the issuance of other licenses before the expiration of such seven-year period.

(June 25, 1938, ch. 675, § 527, as added Pub. L. 97–414, § 2(a), Jan. 4, 1983, 96 Stat. 2050; amended Pub. L. 98–417, title I, § 102(b)(6), Sept. 24, 1984, 98 Stat. 1593; Pub. L. 99–91, §§ 2, 3(a)(3), Aug. 15, 1985, 99 Stat. 387, 388; Pub. L. 103–80, § 3(v), Aug. 13, 1993, 107 Stat. 778; Pub. L. 105–115, title I, § 125(b)(2)(J), (K), Nov. 21, 1997, 111 Stat. 2326; Pub. L. 107–281, § 4, Nov. 6, 2002, 116 Stat. 1993.)

AMENDMENTS

2002—Subsec. (a). Pub. L. 107–281, in concluding provisions, struck out ", of such certification," after "such approved application" and ", the issuance of the certification," after "approval of the approved application".

1997—Subsec. (a). Pub. L. 105–115, § 125(b)(2)(J), struck out ", issue another certification under section 357 of this title," before "or issue another license" in closing provisions, inserted "or" at end of par. (1), redesignated par. (3) as (2), and struck out former par. (2) which read as follows: "issues a certification under section 357 of this title, or".

Subsec. (b). Pub. L. 105–115, § 125(b)(2)(K), in introductory provisions, struck out ", if a certification is issued under section 357 of this title for such a drug," after "rare disease or condition", ", of the issuance of the certification under section 357 of this title," after "application approval", ", issue another certification under section 357 of this title," after "application under section 355 of this title", and ", of such certification," after "approved application".

Subsec. (b)(1). Pub. L. 105–115, § 125(b)(2)(K), struck out ", of the certification," after "holder of the approved application".

Subsec. (b)(2). Pub. L. 105–115, § 125(b)(2)(K), struck out ", issuance of other certifications," after "approval of other applications".

1993—Subsec. (b). Pub. L. 103–80 struck out extraneous comma before "or issue a license under section 262" in introductory provisions and substituted "the" for "The" at beginning of par. (1).

1985—Pub. L. 99–91, § 2(3), struck out "unpatented" before "drugs" in section catchline.

Subsec. (a). Pub. L. 99–91, §§ 2(1), 3(a)(3)(A)–(D), struck out "or" at end of par. (1), added par. (2), redesignated former par. (2) as (3), struck out "and for which a United States Letter of Patent may not be issued" after "rare disease or condition", inserted in first sentence ", issue another certification under section 357 of this title," after "section 355 of this title" the second time it appeared, inserted ", of such certification," after "holder of such approved application", and inserted ", the issuance of the certification," after "approval of the approved application".

Subsec. (b). Pub. L. 99–91, §§ 2(2), 3(a)(3)(E)–(K), struck out "and if a United States Letter of Patent may not be issued for the drug" after "such a drug", substituted ", if a certification is issued under section 357 of this title for such a drug, or if a license" for "or a license", inserted ", of the issuance of the certification under section 357 of this title," after "application approval", struck out ", if the drug is a biological product," before "issue a license", inserted ", issue another certification under section 357 of this title," after "section 355 of this title", inserted ", of such certification," after "holder of such approved application", inserted ", of such certification," after "application" in par. (1), and inserted ", issuance of other certifications," after "other applications" in par. (2).

1984—Subsecs. (a), (b). Pub. L. 98–417 substituted "section 355" for "section 355(b)" wherever appearing.

EFFECTIVE DATE OF 1985 AMENDMENT

Amendment by Pub. L. 99–91 effective Aug. 15, 1985, see section 8(b) of Pub. L. 99–91, set out as a note under section 360aa of this title.

§ 360dd. Open protocols for investigations of drugs for rare diseases or conditions

If a drug is designated under section 360bb of this title as a drug for a rare disease or condition and if notice of a claimed exemption under section 355(i) of this title or regulations issued thereunder is filed for such drug, the Secretary shall encourage the sponsor of such drug to design protocols for clinical investigations of the drug which may be conducted under the exemption to permit the addition to the investigations of persons with the disease or condition who need the drug to treat the disease or condition and who cannot be satisfactorily treated by available alternative drugs.

(June 25, 1938, ch. 675, § 528, as added Pub. L. 97–414, § 2(a), Jan. 4, 1983, 96 Stat. 2051.)

§ 360ee. Grants and contracts for development of drugs for rare diseases and conditions

(a) Authority of Secretary

The Secretary may make grants to and enter into contracts with public and private entities and individuals to assist in (1) defraying the costs of qualified testing expenses incurred in connection with the development of drugs for rare diseases and conditions, (2) defraying the costs of developing medical devices for rare diseases or conditions, and (3) defraying the costs of developing medical foods for rare diseases or conditions.

(b) Definitions

For purposes of subsection (a) of this section:

(1) The term "qualified testing" means—

(A) human clinical testing—

(i) which is carried out under an exemption for a drug for a rare disease or condition under section 355(i) of this title (or regulations issued under such section); and

(ii) which occurs after the date such drug is designated under section 360bb of this title and before the date on which an application with respect to such drug is submitted under section 355(b) of this title or under section 262 of title 42; and

(B) preclinical testing involving a drug for a rare disease or condition which occurs after the date such drug is designated under section 360bb of this title and before the date on which an application with respect to such drug is submitted under section 355(b) of this title or under section 262 of title 42.

(2) The term "rare disease or condition" means (1) in the case of a drug, any disease or condition which (A) affects less than 200,000 persons in the United States, or (B) affects more than 200,000 in the United States and for which there is no reasonable expectation that the cost of developing and making available in the United States a drug for such disease or condition will be recovered from sales in the United States of such drug, (2) in the case of a medical device, any disease or condition that occurs so infrequently in the United States that there is no reasonable expectation that a medical device for such disease or condition will be developed without assistance under subsection (a) of this section, and (3) in the

case of a medical food, any disease or condition that occurs so infrequently in the United States that there is no reasonable expectation that a medical food for such disease or condition will be developed without assistance under subsection (a) of this section. Determinations under the preceding sentence with respect to any drug shall be made on the basis of the facts and circumstances as of the date the request for designation of the drug under section 360bb of this title is made.

(3) The term "medical food" means a food which is formulated to be consumed or administered enterally under the supervision of a physician and which is intended for the specific dietary management of a disease or condition for which distinctive nutritional requirements, based on recognized scientific principles, are established by medical evaluation.

(c) Authorization of appropriations

For grants and contracts under subsection (a), there is authorized to be appropriated $30,000,000 for each of fiscal years 2008 through 2012.

(Pub. L. 97–414, § 5, Jan. 4, 1983, 96 Stat. 2056; Pub. L. 98–551, § 4(b), Oct. 30, 1984, 98 Stat. 2817; Pub. L. 99–91, § 5, Aug. 15, 1985, 99 Stat. 391; Pub. L. 100–290, § 3(a)–(c), Apr. 18, 1988, 102 Stat. 90, 91; Pub. L. 105–115, title I, § 125(b)(2)(N), Nov. 21, 1997, 111 Stat. 2326; Pub. L. 107–281, § 3, Nov. 6, 2002, 116 Stat. 1993; Pub. L. 110–85, title XI, § 1112(b), Sept. 27, 2007, 121 Stat. 976.)

CODIFICATION

Section was enacted as part of the Orphan Drug Act, and not as part of the Federal Food, Drug, and Cosmetic Act which comprises this chapter.

AMENDMENTS

2007—Subsec. (c). Pub. L. 110–85 amended subsec. (c) generally. Prior to amendment, subsec. (c) read as follows: "For grants and contracts under subsection (a) of this section, there are authorized to be appropriated such sums as already have been appropriated for fiscal year 2002, and $25,000,000 for each of the fiscal years 2003 through 2006."

2002—Subsec. (c). Pub. L. 107–281 amended subsec. (c) generally. Prior to amendment, subsec. (c) read as follows: "For grants and contracts under subsection (a) of this section there are authorized to be appropriated $10,000,000 for fiscal year 1988, $12,000,000 for fiscal year 1989, $14,000,000 for fiscal year 1990."

1997—Subsec. (b)(1)(A)(ii), (B). Pub. L. 105–115 struck out "or 357" after "355(b)".

1988—Subsec. (a). Pub. L. 100–290, § 3(a)(1), (b)(1), inserted "(1)" after "assist in" and added cls. (2) and (3).

Subsec. (b)(2). Pub. L. 100–290, § 3(a)(2), (b)(2), inserted "(1) in the case of a drug," after "means", added cls. (2) and (3), and substituted "under section 360bb of this title" for "under this subsection" in last sentence.

Subsec. (b)(3). Pub. L. 100–290, § 3(b)(3), added par. (3).

Subsec. (c). Pub. L. 100–290, § 3(c), amended subsec. (c) generally. Prior to amendment, subsec. (c) read as follows: "For grants and contracts under subsection (a) of this section there are authorized to be appropriated $4,000,000 for fiscal year 1986, $4,000,000 for fiscal year 1987, and $4,000,000 for fiscal year 1988."

1985—Subsec. (a). Pub. L. 99–91, § 5(a)(1), struck out "clinical" before "testing".

Subsec. (b)(1). Pub. L. 99–91, § 5(a)(2), substituted provisions defining "qualified testing" for provisions defining "qualified clinical testing".

Subsec. (c). Pub. L. 99–91, § 5(b), substituted provisions authorizing appropriations for fiscal years 1986 to 1988, for provisions authorizing appropriations for fiscal years 1983 and the two succeeding fiscal years.

1984—Subsec. (b)(2). Pub. L. 98–551 substituted "which (A) affects less than 200,000 persons in the United States, or (B) affects more than 200,000 in the United States and for which" for "which occurs so infrequently in the United States that".

EFFECTIVE DATE OF 1985 AMENDMENT

Amendment by Pub. L. 99–91 effective Oct. 1, 1985, see section 8(a) of Pub. L. 99–91, set out as a note under section 360aa of this title.

FINDINGS AND PURPOSES

Pub. L. 107–281, § 2, Nov. 6, 2002, 116 Stat. 1992, provided that:

"(a) FINDINGS.—Congress makes the following findings:

"(1) Rare diseases and disorders are those which affect small patient populations, typically populations smaller than 200,000 individuals in the United States. Such diseases and conditions include Huntington's disease, amyotrophic lateral sclerosis (Lou Gehrig's disease), Tourette syndrome, Crohn's disease, cystic fibrosis, cystinosis, and Duchenne muscular dystrophy.

"(2) For many years, the 25,000,000 Americans suffering from the over 6,000 rare diseases and disorders were denied access to effective medicines because prescription drug manufacturers could rarely make a profit from marketing drugs for such small groups of patients. The prescription drug industry did not adequately fund research into such treatments. Despite the urgent health need for these medicines, they came to be known as 'orphan drugs' because no companies would commercialize them.

"(3) During the 1970s, an organization called the National Organization for Rare Disorders (NORD) was founded to provide services and to lobby on behalf of patients with rare diseases and disorders. NORD was instrumental in pressing Congress for legislation to encourage the development of orphan drugs.

"(4) The Orphan Drug Act [see Short Title of 1983 Amendments note set out under section 301 of this title] created financial incentives for the research and production of such orphan drugs. New Federal programs at the National Institutes of Health and the Food and Drug Administration encouraged clinical research and commercial product development for products that target rare diseases. An Orphan Products Board was established to promote the development of drugs and devices for rare diseases or disorders.

"(5) Before 1983, some 38 orphan drugs had been developed. Since the enactment of the Orphan Drug Act [Jan. 4, 1983], more than 220 new orphan drugs have been approved and marketed in the United States and more than 800 additional drugs are in the research pipeline.

"(6) Despite the tremendous success of the Orphan Drug Act, rare diseases and disorders deserve greater emphasis in the national biomedical research enterprise.

"(7) The Food and Drug Administration supports small clinical trials through Orphan Products Research Grants. Such grants embody successful partnerships of government and industry, and have led to the development of at least 23 drugs and four medical devices for rare diseases and disorders. Yet the appropriations in fiscal year 2001 for such grants were less than in fiscal year 1995.

"(b) PURPOSES.—The purpose of this Act [see Short Title of 2002 Amendments note set out under section 301 of this title] is to increase the national investment in the development of diagnostics and treatments for patients with rare diseases and disorders."

PART C—ELECTRONIC PRODUCT RADIATION CONTROL

CODIFICATION

This part was classified to subpart 3 (§ 263c et seq.) of part F of subchapter II of chapter 6A of Title 42, The Public Health and Welfare, prior to its renumbering by Pub. L. 101–629, § 19(a)(4), Nov. 28, 1990, 104 Stat. 4530, as amended by Pub. L. 103–80, § 4(a)(2), Aug. 13, 1993, 107 Stat. 779.

§ 360hh. Definitions

As used in this part—

(1) the term "electronic product radiation" means—

(A) any ionizing or non-ionizing electromagnetic or particulate radiation, or

(B) any sonic, infrasonic, or ultrasonic wave, which is emitted from an electronic product as the result of the operation of an electronic circuit in such product;

(2) the term "electronic product" means (A) any manufactured or assembled product which, when in operation, (i) contains or acts as part of an electronic circuit and (ii) emits (or in the absence of effective shielding or other controls would emit) electronic product radiation, or (B) any manufactured or assembled article which is intended for use as a component, part, or accessory of a product described in clause (A) and which when in operation emits (or in the absence of effective shielding or other controls would emit) such radiation;

(3) the term "manufacturer" means any person engaged in the business of manufacturing, assembling, or importing of electronic products;

(4) the term "commerce" means (A) commerce between any place in any State and any place outside thereof; and (B) commerce wholly within the District of Columbia; and

(5) the term "State" includes the District of Columbia, the Commonwealth of Puerto Rico, the Northern Mariana Islands, the Virgin Islands, Guam, and American Samoa.

(June 25, 1938, ch. 675, § 531, formerly act July 1, 1944, ch. 373, title III, § 531, formerly § 355, as added Pub. L. 90–602, § 2(3), Oct. 18, 1968, 82 Stat. 1174; amended Pub. L. 94–484, title IX, § 905(b)(1), Oct. 12, 1976, 90 Stat. 2325; renumbered § 531 and amended Pub. L. 101–629, § 19(a)(1)(B), (3), (4), Nov. 28, 1990, 104 Stat. 4529, 4530; Pub. L. 103–80, § 4(a)(2), Aug. 13, 1993, 107 Stat. 779.)

CODIFICATION

Section was classified to section 263c of Title 42, The Public Health and Welfare, prior to renumbering by Pub. L. 101–629.

AMENDMENTS

1993—Pub. L. 103–80 amended directory language of Pub. L. 101–629, § 19(a)(4), which renumbered section 263c of Title 42, The Public Health and Welfare, as this section.

1990—Pub. L. 101–629, § 19(a)(1)(B), substituted "this part" for "this subpart" in introductory provisions.

1976—Par. (5). Pub. L. 94–484 defined "State" to include Northern Mariana Islands.

SHORT TITLE

For short title of Pub. L. 90–602, which enacted provisions now comprising this part (§§ 360hh to 360ss), as the "Radiation Control for Health and Safety Act of 1968", see section 1 of Pub. L. 90–602, set out as a Short Title of 1968 Amendments note under section 301 of this title.

TRANSFER OF SUBPART; CONSTRUCTION

Section 19(c) of Pub. L. 101–629 provided that: "The transfer of subpart 3 of part F of title III of the Public Health Service Act [42 U.S.C. 263b et seq.] to the Federal Food, Drug, and Cosmetic Act [this chapter] does not change the application of the requirements of such subpart and such Act to electronic products which were in effect on the date of the enactment of this Act [Nov. 28, 1990]."

DEFINITION OF "SECRETARY" AND "DEPARTMENT"

Section 3 of Pub. L. 90–602, as amended Pub. L. 96–88, title V, § 509(b), Oct. 17, 1979, 93 Stat. 695, provided that: "As used in the amendments made by section 2 of this Act [enacting provisions now comprising sections 360hh to 360ss of this title], except when otherwise specified, the term 'Secretary' means the Secretary of Health and Human Services, and the term 'Department' means the Department of Health and Human Services."

NONINTERFERENCE WITH OTHER FEDERAL AGENCIES

Section 4 of Pub. L. 90–602 provided that: "The amendments made by section 2 of this Act [enacting provisions now comprising sections 360hh to 360ss of this title] shall not be construed as superseding or limiting the functions, under any other provision of law, of any officer or agency of the United States."

§ 360ii. Program of control

(a) Establishment

The Secretary shall establish and carry out an electronic product radiation control program designed to protect the public health and safety from electronic product radiation. As a part of such program, he shall—

(1) pursuant to section 360kk of this title, develop and administer performance standards for electronic products;

(2) plan, conduct, coordinate, and support research, development, training, and operational activities to minimize the emissions of and the exposure of people to, unnecessary electronic product radiation;

(3) maintain liaison with and receive information from other Federal and State departments and agencies with related interests, professional organizations, industry, industry and labor associations, and other organizations on present and future potential electronic product radiation;

(4) study and evaluate emissions of, and conditions of exposure to, electronic product radiation and intense magnetic fields;

(5) develop, test, and evaluate the effectiveness of procedures and techniques for minimizing exposure to electronic product radiation; and

(6) consult and maintain liaison with the Secretary of Commerce, the Secretary of Defense, the Secretary of Labor, the Atomic Energy Commission, and other appropriate Federal departments and agencies on (A) techniques, equipment, and programs for testing and evaluating electronic product radiation, and (B) the development of performance standards pursuant to section 360kk of this title to control such radiation emissions.

(b) Powers of Secretary

In carrying out the purposes of subsection (a) of this section, the Secretary is authorized to—

(1)(A) collect and make available, through publications and other appropriate means, the results of, and other information concerning, research and studies relating to the nature and extent of the hazards and control of electronic product radiation; and (B) make such recommendations relating to such hazards and control as he considers appropriate;

(2) make grants to public and private agencies, organizations, and institutions, and to individuals for the purposes stated in paragraphs (2), (4), and (5) of subsection (a) of this section;

(3) contract with public or private agencies, institutions, and organizations, and with individuals, without regard to section 3324 of title 31 and section 5 of title 41; and

(4) procure (by negotiation or otherwise) electronic products for research and testing purposes, and sell or otherwise dispose of such products.

(c) Record keeping

(1) Each recipient of assistance under this part pursuant to grants or contracts entered into under other than competitive bidding procedures shall keep such records as the Secretary shall prescribe, including records which fully disclose the amount and disposition by such recipient of the proceeds of such assistance, the total cost of the project or undertaking in connection with which such assistance is given or used, and the amount of that portion of the cost of the project or undertaking supplied by other sources, and such other records as will facilitate an effective audit.

(2) The Secretary and the Comptroller General of the United States, or any of their duly authorized representatives, shall have access for the purpose of audit and examination to any books, documents, papers, and records of the recipients that are pertinent to the grants or contracts entered into under this part under other than competitive bidding procedures.

(June 25, 1938, ch. 675, § 532, formerly act July 1, 1944, ch. 373, title III, § 532, formerly § 356, as added Pub. L. 90–602, § 2(3), Oct. 18, 1968, 82 Stat. 1174; renumbered § 532 and amended Pub. L. 101–629, § 19(a)(1)(B), (2)(A), (3), (4), Nov. 28, 1990, 104 Stat. 4529, 4530; Pub. L. 103–80, § 4(a)(2), Aug. 13, 1993, 107 Stat. 779.)

CODIFICATION

Section was classified to section 263d of Title 42, The Public Health and Welfare, prior to renumbering by Pub. L. 101–629.

AMENDMENTS

1993—Pub. L. 103–80 amended directory language of Pub. L. 101–629, § 19(a)(4), which renumbered section 263d of Title 42, The Public Health and Welfare, as this section.

1990—Subsec. (a)(1), (6). Pub. L. 101–629, § 19(a)(2)(A)(i), substituted "section 360kk" for "section 263f".

Subsec. (b)(3). Pub. L. 101–629, § 19(a)(2)(A)(ii), substituted reference to section 3324 of title 31 for reference to section 3648 of the Revised Statutes (31 U.S.C. 529).

Subsec. (c)(1), (2). Pub. L. 101–629, § 19(a)(1)(B), substituted "this part" for "this subpart".

TRANSFER OF FUNCTIONS

Atomic Energy Commission abolished and functions transferred by sections 5814 and 5841 of Title 42, The Public Health and Welfare. See also Transfer of Functions notes set out under those sections.

NONINTERFERENCE WITH OTHER FEDERAL AGENCIES

Enactment of this section not to be construed to supersede or limit the functions under any other provision of law or any officer or agency of the United States, see section 4 of Pub. L. 90–602, set out as a note under section 360hh of this title.

§ 360jj. Studies by Secretary

(a) Report to Congress

The Secretary shall conduct the following studies, and shall make a report or reports of the results of such studies to the Congress on or before January 1, 1970, and from time to time thereafter as he may find necessary, together with such recommendations for legislation as he may deem appropriate:

(1) A study of present State and Federal control of health hazards from electronic product radiation and other types of ionizing radiation, which study shall include, but not be limited to—

(A) control of health hazards from radioactive materials other than materials regulated under the Atomic Energy Act of 1954 [42 U.S.C. 2011 et seq.];

(B) any gaps and inconsistencies in present controls;

(C) the need for controlling the sale of certain used electronic products, particularly antiquated X-ray equipment, without upgrading such products to meet the standards for new products or separate standards for used products;

(D) measures to assure consistent and effective control of the aforementioned health hazards;

(E) measures to strengthen radiological health programs of State governments; and

(F) the feasibility of authorizing the Secretary to enter into arrangements with individual States or groups of States to define their respective functions and responsibilities for the control of electronic product radiation and other ionizing radiation;

(2) A study to determine the necessity for the development of standards for the use of nonmedical electronic products for commercial and industrial purposes; and

(3) A study of the development of practicable procedures for the detection and measurement of electronic product radiation which may be emitted from electronic products manufactured or imported prior to the effective date of any applicable standard established pursuant to this part.

(b) Participation of other Federal agencies

In carrying out these studies, the Secretary shall invite the participation of other Federal departments and agencies having related responsibilities and interests, State governments—particularly those of States which regulate radioactive materials under section 274 of the Atomic Energy Act of 1954, as amended [42 U.S.C. 2021], and interested professional, labor, and industrial organizations. Upon request from congressional committees interested in these studies, the Secretary shall keep these committees currently informed as to the progress of the studies and shall permit the committees to send observers to meetings of the study groups.

(c) Organization of studies and participation

The Secretary or his designee shall organize the studies and the participation of the invited participants as he deems best. Any dissent from the findings and recommendations of the Secretary shall be included in the report if so requested by the dissenter.

(June 25, 1938, ch. 675, §533, formerly act July 1, 1944, ch. 373, title III, §533, formerly §357, as added Pub. L. 90–602, §2(3), Oct. 18, 1968, 82 Stat. 1176; renumbered §533 and amended Pub. L. 101–629, §19(a)(1)(B), (3), (4), Nov. 28, 1990, 104 Stat. 4529, 4530; Pub. L. 103–80, §4(a)(2), Aug. 13, 1993, 107 Stat. 779.)

REFERENCES IN TEXT

The Atomic Energy Act of 1954, referred to in subsec. (a)(1)(A), is act Aug. 1, 1946, ch. 724, as added by act Aug. 30, 1954, ch. 1073, §1, 68 Stat. 921, and amended, which is classified generally to chapter 23 (§2011 et seq.) of Title 42, The Public Health and Welfare. For complete classification of this Act to the Code, see Short Title note set out under section 2011 of Title 42 and Tables.

CODIFICATION

Section was classified to section 263e of Title 42, The Public Health and Welfare, prior to renumbering by Pub. L. 101–629.

AMENDMENTS

1993—Pub. L. 103–80 amended directory language of Pub. L. 101–629, §19(a)(4), which renumbered section 263e of Title 42, The Public Health and Welfare, as this section.

1990—Subsec. (a)(3). Pub. L. 101–629, §19(a)(1)(B), substituted "this part" for "this subpart".

NONINTERFERENCE WITH OTHER FEDERAL AGENCIES

Enactment of this section not to be construed to supersede or limit the functions under any other provision of law of any officer or agency of the United States, see section 4 of Pub. L. 90–602, set out as a note under section 360hh of this title.

§360kk. Performance standards for electronic products

(a) Promulgation of regulations

(1) The Secretary shall by regulation prescribe performance standards for electronic products to control the emission of electronic product radiation from such products if he determines that such standards are necessary for the protection of the public health and safety. Such standards may include provisions for the testing of such products and the measurement of their electronic product radiation emissions, may require the attachment of warning signs and labels, and may require the provision of instructions for the installation, operation, and use of such products. Such standards may be prescribed from time to time whenever such determinations are made, but the first of such standards shall be prescribed prior to January 1, 1970. In the development of such standards, the Secretary shall consult with Federal and State departments and agencies having related responsibilities or interests and with appropriate professional organizations and interested persons, including representatives of industries and labor organizations which would be affected by such standards, and shall give consideration to—

(A) the latest available scientific and medical data in the field of electronic product radiation;

(B) the standards currently recommended by (i) other Federal agencies having responsibilities relating to the control and measurement of electronic product radiation, and (ii) public or private groups having an expertise in the field of electronic product radiation;

(C) the reasonableness and technical feasibility of such standards as applied to a particular electronic product;

(D) the adaptability of such standards to the need for uniformity and reliability of testing and measuring procedures and equipment; and

(E) in the case of a component, or accessory described in paragraph (2)(B) of section 360hh of this title, the performance of such article in the manufactured or assembled product for which it is designed.

(2) The Secretary may prescribe different and individual performance standards, to the extent appropriate and feasible, for different electronic products so as to recognize their different operating characteristics and uses.

(3) The performance standards prescribed under this section shall not apply to any electronic product which is intended solely for export if (A) such product and the outside of any shipping container used in the export of such product are labeled or tagged to show that such product is intended for export, and (B) such product meets all the applicable requirements of the country to which such product is intended for export.

(4) The Secretary may by regulation amend or revoke any performance standard prescribed under this section.

(5) The Secretary may exempt from the provisions of this section any electronic product intended for use by departments or agencies of the United States provided such department or agency has prescribed procurement specifications governing emissions of electronic product radiation and provided further that such product is of a type used solely or predominantly by departments or agencies of the United States.

(b) Administrative procedure

The provisions of subchapter II of chapter 5 of title 5 (relating to the administrative procedure for rulemaking), and of chapter 7 of title 5 (relating to judicial review), shall apply with respect to any regulation prescribing, amending, or revoking any standard prescribed under this section.

(c) Publication in Federal Register

Each regulation prescribing, amending, or revoking a standard shall specify the date on which it shall take effect which, in the case of any regulation prescribing, or amending any standard, may not be sooner than one year or not later than two years after the date on which such regulation is issued, unless the Secretary finds, for good cause shown, that an earlier or later effective date is in the public interest and publishes in the Federal Register his reason for such finding, in which case such earlier or later date shall apply.

(d) Judicial review

(1) In a case of actual controversy as to the validity of any regulation issued under this section prescribing, amending, or revoking a performance standard, any person who will be adversely affected by such regulation when it is effective may at any time prior to the sixtieth day after such regulation is issued file a petition with the United States court of appeals for the circuit wherein such person resides or has his principal place of business, for a judicial review of such regulation. A copy of the petition shall be forthwith transmitted by the clerk of the court to the Secretary or other officer designated by him for that purpose. The Secretary thereupon shall file in the court the record of the proceedings on which the Secretary based the regulation, as provided in section 2112 of title 28.

(2) If the petitioner applies to the court for leave to adduce additional evidence, and shows to the satisfaction of the court that such additional evidence is material and that there were reasonable grounds for the failure to adduce such evidence in the proceeding before the Secretary, the court may order such additional evidence (and evidence in rebuttal thereof) to be taken before the Secretary, and to be adduced upon the hearing, in such manner and upon such terms and conditions as to the court may seem proper. The Secretary may modify his findings, or make new findings, by reason of the additional evidence so taken, and he shall file such modified or new findings, and his recommendations, if any, for the modification or setting aside of his original regulation, with the return of such additional evidence.

(3) Upon the filing of the petition referred to in paragraph (1) of this subsection, the court shall have jurisdiction to review the regulation in accordance with chapter 7 of title 5 and to grant appropriate relief as provided in such chapter.

(4) The judgment of the court affirming or setting aside, in whole or in part, any such regulation of the Secretary shall be final, subject to review by the Supreme Court of the United States upon certiorari or certification as provided in section 1254 of title 28.

(5) Any action instituted under this subsection shall survive, notwithstanding any change in the person occupying the office of Secretary or any vacancy in such office.

(6) The remedies provided for in this subsection shall be in addition to and not in substitution for any other remedies provided by law.

(e) Availability of record

A certified copy of the transcript of the record and administrative proceedings under this section shall be furnished by the Secretary to any interested party at his request, and payment of the costs thereof, and shall be admissible in any criminal, exclusion of imports, or other proceeding arising under or in respect of this part irrespective of whether proceedings with respect to the regulation have previously been initiated or become final under this section.

(f) Technical Electronic Product Radiation Safety Standards Committee

(1)(A) The Secretary shall establish a Technical Electronic Product Radiation Safety Standards Committee (hereafter in this part referred to as the "Committee") which he shall consult before prescribing any standard under this section. The Committee shall be appointed by the Secretary, after consultation with public and private agencies concerned with the technical aspect of electronic product radiation safety, and shall be composed of fifteen members each of whom shall be technically qualified by training and experience in one or more fields of science or engineering applicable to electronic product radiation safety, as follows:

(i) Five members shall be selected from governmental agencies, including State and Federal Governments;

(ii) Five members shall be selected from the affected industries after consultation with industry representatives; and

(iii) Five members shall be selected from the general public, of which at least one shall be a representative of organized labor.

(B) The Committee may propose electronic product radiation safety standards to the Secretary for his consideration. All proceedings of the Committee shall be recorded and the record of each such proceeding shall be available for public inspection.

(2) Payments to members of the Committee who are not officers or employees of the United States pursuant to subsection (c) of section 210 of title 42 shall not render members of the Committee officers or employees of the United States for any purpose.

(g) Review and evaluation

The Secretary shall review and evaluate on a continuing basis testing programs carried out by industry to assure the adequacy of safeguards against hazardous electronic product radiation and to assure that electronic products comply with standards prescribed under this section.

(h) Product certification

Every manufacturer of an electronic product to which is applicable a standard in effect under this section shall furnish to the distributor or dealer at the time of delivery of such product, in the form of a label or tag permanently affixed to such product or in such manner as approved by the Secretary, the certification that such product conforms to all applicable standards under this section. Such certification shall be based upon a test, in accordance with such standard, of the individual article to which it is attached or upon a testing program which is in accord with good manufacturing practice and which has not been disapproved by the Secretary (in such manner as he shall prescribe by regulation) on the grounds that it does not assure the adequacy of safeguards against hazardous electronic product radiation or that it does not assure that electronic products comply with the standards prescribed under this section.

(June 25, 1938, ch. 675, § 534, formerly act July 1, 1944, ch. 373, title III, § 534, formerly § 358, as added Pub. L. 90–602, § 2(3), Oct. 18, 1968, 82 Stat.

1177; amended Pub. L. 91–515, title VI, § 601(b)(2), (3), Oct. 30, 1970, 84 Stat. 1311; renumbered § 534 and amended Pub. L. 101–629, § 19(a)(1)(B), (2)(B), (3), (4), Nov. 28, 1990, 104 Stat. 4529, 4530; Pub. L. 103–80, §§ 3(w), 4(a)(2), Aug. 13, 1993, 107 Stat. 778, 779.)

CODIFICATION

Section was classified to section 263f of Title 42, The Public Health and Welfare, prior to renumbering by Pub. L. 101–629.

AMENDMENTS

1993—Pub. L. 103–80, § 4(a)(2), amended directory language of Pub. L. 101–629, § 19(a)(4), which renumbered section 263f of Title 42, The Public Health and Welfare, as this section.

Subsec. (f)(2). Pub. L. 103–80, § 3(w), made technical amendment to reference to section 210 of title 42 to reflect correction of corresponding provision of original act.

1990—Subsec. (a)(1)(E). Pub. L. 101–629, § 19(a)(2)(B), substituted "section 360hh" for "section 263c".

Subsecs. (e), (f)(1)(A). Pub. L. 101–629, § 19(a)(1)(B), substituted "this part" for "this subpart".

1970—Subsec. (f)(2). Pub. L. 91–515 struck out provisions related to payment of compensation and travel expenses of members of the Committee who are not officers or employees of the United States, and substituted "to members of the Committee who are not officers or employees of the United States pursuant to subsection (c) of section 210 of title 42" for "under this subsection".

NONINTERFERENCE WITH OTHER FEDERAL AGENCIES

Enactment of this section not to be construed to supersede or limit the functions under any other provision of law of any officer or agency of the United States, see section 4 of Pub. L. 90–602, set out as a note under section 360hh of this title.

§ 360*ll*. Notification of defects in and repair or replacement of electronic products

(a) Notification; exemption

(1) Every manufacturer of electronic products who discovers that an electronic product produced, assembled, or imported by him has a defect which relates to the safety of use of such product by reason of the emission of electronic product radiation, or that an electronic product produced, assembled, or imported by him on or after the effective date of an applicable standard prescribed pursuant to section 360kk of this title fails to comply with such standard, shall immediately notify the Secretary of such defect or failure to comply if such product has left the place of manufacture and shall (except as authorized by paragraph (2)) with reasonable promptness furnish notification of such defect or failure to the persons (where known to the manufacturer) specified in subsection (b) of this section.

(2) If, in the opinion of such manufacturer, the defect or failure to comply is not such as to create a significant risk of injury, including genetic injury, to any person, he may, at the time of giving notice to the Secretary of such defect or failure to comply, apply to the Secretary for an exemption from the requirement of notice to the persons specified in subsection (b) of this section. If such application states reasonable grounds for such exemption, the Secretary shall afford such manufacturer an opportunity to present his views and evidence in support of the application, the burden of proof being on the manufacturer. If, after such presentation, the Secretary is satisfied that such defect or failure to comply is not such as to create a significant risk of injury, including genetic injury, to any person, he shall exempt such manufacturer from the requirement of notice to the persons specified in subsection (b) of this section and from the requirements of repair or replacement imposed by subsection (f) of this section.

(b) Method of notification

The notification (other than to the Secretary) required by paragraph (1) of subsection (a) of this section shall be accomplished—

(1) by certified mail to the first purchaser of such product for purposes other than resale, and to any subsequent transferee of such product; and

(2) by certified mail or other more expeditious means to the dealers or distributors of such manufacturer to whom such product was delivered.

(c) Requisite elements of notification

The notifications required by paragraph (1) of subsection (a) of this section shall contain a clear description of such defect or failure to comply with an applicable standard, an evaluation of the hazard reasonably related to such defect or failure to comply, and a statement of the measures to be taken to repair such defect. In the case of a notification to a person referred to in subsection (b) of this section, the notification shall also advise the person of his rights under subsection (f) of this section.

(d) Copies to Secretary of communications by manufacturers to dealers or distributors regarding defects

Every manufacturer of electronic products shall furnish to the Secretary a true or representative copy of all notices, bulletins, and other communications to the dealers or distributors of such manufacturer or to purchasers (or subsequent transferees) of electronic products of such manufacturer regarding any such defect in such product or any such failure to comply with a standard applicable to such product. The Secretary shall disclose to the public so much of the information contained in such notice or other information obtained under section 360nn of this title as he deems will assist in carrying out the purposes of this part, but he shall not disclose any information which contains or relates to a trade secret or other matter referred to in section 1905 of title 18 unless he determines that it is necessary to carry out the purposes of this part.

(e) Notice from Secretary to manufacturer of defects or failure to comply with standards

If through testing, inspection, investigation, or research carried out pursuant to this part, or examination of reports submitted pursuant to section 360nn of this title, or otherwise, the Secretary determines that any electronic product—

(1) does not comply with an applicable standard prescribed pursuant to section 360kk of this title; or

(2) contains a defect which relates to the safety of use of such product by reason of the emission of electronic product radiation;

he shall immediately notify the manufacturer of such product of such defect or failure to comply. The notice shall contain the findings of the Secretary and shall include all information upon which the findings are based. The Secretary shall afford such manufacturer an opportunity to present his views and evidence in support thereof, to establish that there is no failure of compliance or that the alleged defect does not exist or does not relate to safety of use of the product by reason of the emission of such radiation hazard. If after such presentation by the manufacturer the Secretary determines that such product does not comply with an applicable standard prescribed pursuant to section 360kk of this title, or that it contains a defect which relates to the safety of use of such product by reason of the emission of electronic product radiation, the Secretary shall direct the manufacturer to furnish the notification specified in subsection (c) of this section to the persons specified in paragraphs (1) and (2) of subsection (b) of this section (where known to the manufacturer), unless the manufacturer has applied for an exemption from the requirement of such notification on the ground specified in paragraph (2) of subsection (a) of this section and the Secretary is satisfied that such noncompliance or defect is not such as to create a significant risk of injury, including genetic injury, to any person.

(f) Correction of defects

If any electronic product is found under subsection (a) or (e) of this section to fail to comply with an applicable standard prescribed under this part or to have a defect which relates to the safety of use of such product, and the notification specified in subsection (c) of this section is required to be furnished on account of such failure or defect, the manufacturer of such product shall (1) without charge, bring such product into conformity with such standard or remedy such defect and provide reimbursement for any expenses for transportation of such product incurred in connection with having such product brought into conformity or having such defect remedied, (2) replace such product with a like or equivalent product which complies with each applicable standard prescribed under this part and which has no defect relating to the safety of its use, or (3) make a refund of the cost of such product. The manufacturer shall take the action required by this subsection in such manner, and with respect to such persons, as the Secretary by regulations shall prescribe.

(g) Effective date

This section shall not apply to any electronic product that was manufactured before October 18, 1968.

(June 25, 1938, ch. 675, § 535, formerly act July 1, 1944, ch. 373, title III, § 535, formerly § 359, as added Pub. L. 90–602, § 2(3), Oct. 18, 1968, 82 Stat. 1180; renumbered § 535 and amended Pub. L. 101–629, § 19(a)(1)(B), (2)(C), (3), (4), Nov. 28, 1990, 104 Stat. 4529, 4530; Pub. L. 103–80, § 4(a)(2), Aug. 13, 1993, 107 Stat. 779.)

CODIFICATION

Section was classified to section 263g of Title 42, The Public Health and Welfare, prior to renumbering by Pub. L. 101–629.

AMENDMENTS

1993—Pub. L. 103–80 amended directory language of Pub. L. 101–629, § 19(a)(4), which renumbered section 263g of Title 42, The Public Health and Welfare, as this section.

1990—Subsec. (a)(1). Pub. L. 101–629, § 19(a)(2)(C)(i), substituted "section 360kk" for "section 263f".

Subsec. (d). Pub. L. 101–629, § 19(a)(1)(B), (2)(C)(ii), substituted "section 360nn" for "section 263i" and "this part" for "this subpart" in two places.

Subsec. (e). Pub. L. 101–629, § 19(a)(1)(B), (2)(C), substituted "this part" for "this subpart" and "section 360nn" for "section 263i" in introductory provisions and "section 360kk" for "section 263f" in par. (1) and concluding provisions.

Subsec. (f). Pub. L. 101–629, § 19(a)(1)(B), substituted "this part" for "this subpart" in two places.

NONINTERFERENCE WITH OTHER FEDERAL AGENCIES

Enactment of this section not to be construed to supersede or limit the functions under any other provision of law of any officer or agency of the United States, see section 4 of Pub. L. 90–602, set out as a note under section 360hh of this title.

§ 360mm. Imports

(a) Refusal of admission to noncomplying electronic products

Any electronic product offered for importation into the United States which fails to comply with an applicable standard prescribed under this part, or to which is not affixed a certification in the form of a label or tag in conformity with section 360kk(h) of this title shall be refused admission into the United States. The Secretary of the Treasury shall deliver to the Secretary of Health and Human Services, upon the latter's request, samples of electronic products which are being imported or offered for import into the United States, giving notice thereof to the owner or consignee, who may have a hearing before the Secretary of Health and Human Services. If it appears from an examination of such samples or otherwise that any electronic product fails to comply with applicable standards prescribed pursuant to section 360kk of this title, then, unless subsection (b) of this section applies and is complied with, (1) such electronic product shall be refused admission, and (2) the Secretary of the Treasury shall cause the destruction of such electronic product unless such article is exported, under regulations prescribed by the Secretary of the Treasury, within 90 days after the date of notice of refusal of admission or within such additional time as may be permitted by such regulations.

(b) Bond

If it appears to the Secretary of Health and Human Services that any electronic product refused admission pursuant to subsection (a) of this section can be brought into compliance with applicable standards prescribed pursuant to section 360kk of this title, final determination as to admission of such electronic product may be deferred upon filing of timely written application by the owner or consignee and the execution by him of a good and sufficient bond providing for the payment of such liquidated damages in the event of default as the Secretary of Health and Human Services may by regulation prescribe. If such application is filed and such bond is executed the Secretary of Health and

Human Services may, in accordance with rules prescribed by him, permit the applicant to perform such operations with respect to such electronic product as may be specified in the notice of permission.

(c) Liability of owner or consignee for expenses connected with refusal of admission

All expenses (including travel, per diem or subsistence, and salaries of officers or employees of the United States) in connection with the destruction provided for in subsection (a) of this section and the supervision of operations provided for in subsection (b) of this section, and all expenses in connection with the storage, cartage, or labor with respect to any electronic product refused admission pursuant to subsection (a) of this section, shall be paid by the owner or consignee, and, in event of default, shall constitute a lien against any future importations made by such owner or consignee.

(d) Designation of agent for purposes of service

It shall be the duty of every manufacturer offering an electronic product for importation into the United States to designate in writing an agent upon whom service of all administrative and judicial processes, notices, orders, decisions, and requirements may be made for and on behalf of said manufacturer, and to file such designation with the Secretary, which designation may from time to time be changed by like writing, similarly filed. Service of all administrative and judicial processes, notices, orders, decisions, and requirements may be made upon said manufacturer by service upon such designated agent at his office or usual place of residence with like effect as if made personally upon said manufacturer, and in default of such designation of such agent, service of process, notice, order, requirement, or decision in any proceeding before the Secretary or in any judicial proceeding for enforcement of this part or any standards prescribed pursuant to this part may be made by posting such process, notice, order, requirement, or decision in the Office of the Secretary or in a place designated by him by regulation.

(June 25, 1938, ch. 675, § 536, formerly act July 1, 1944, ch. 373, title III, § 536, formerly § 360, as added Pub. L. 90–602, § 2(3), Oct. 18, 1968, 82 Stat. 1181; renumbered § 536 and amended Pub. L. 101–629, § 19(a)(1)(B), (2)(D), (3), (4), Nov. 28, 1990, 104 Stat. 4529, 4530; Pub. L. 102–300, § 6(b)(1), June 16, 1992, 106 Stat. 240; Pub. L. 103–80, § 4(a)(2), Aug. 13, 1993, 107 Stat. 779.)

CODIFICATION

Section was classified to section 263h of Title 42, The Public Health and Welfare, prior to renumbering by Pub. L. 101–629.

AMENDMENTS

1993—Pub. L. 103–80 amended directory language of Pub. L. 101–629, § 19(a)(4), which renumbered section 263h of Title 42, The Public Health and Welfare, as this section.

1992—Subsecs. (a), (b). Pub. L. 102–300 substituted "Health and Human Services" for "Health, Education, and Welfare" wherever appearing.

1990—Subsec. (a). Pub. L. 101–629, § 19(a)(1)(B), (2)(D), substituted "this part" for "this subpart", "section 360kk(h)" for "section 263f(h)", and "section 360kk" for "section 263f".

Subsec. (b). Pub. L. 101–629, § 19(a)(2)(D), substituted "section 360kk" for "section 263f".

Subsec. (d). Pub. L. 101–629, § 19(a)(1)(B), substituted "this part" for "this subpart" in two places.

NONINTERFERENCE WITH OTHER FEDERAL AGENCIES

Enactment of this section not to be construed to supersede or limit the functions under any other provision of law of any officer or agency of the United States, see section 4 of Pub. L. 90–602, set out as a note under section 360hh of this title.

§ 360nn. Inspection, records, and reports

(a) Inspection of premises

If the Secretary finds for good cause that the methods, tests, or programs related to electronic product radiation safety in a particular factory, warehouse, or establishment in which electronic products are manufactured or held, may not be adequate or reliable, officers or employees duly designated by the Secretary, upon presenting appropriate credentials and a written notice to the owner, operator, or agent in charge, are thereafter authorized (1) to enter, at reasonable times, any area in such factory, warehouse, or establishment in which the manufacturer's tests (or testing programs) required by section 360kk(h) of this title are carried out, and (2) to inspect, at reasonable times and within reasonable limits and in a reasonable manner, the facilities and procedures within such area which are related to electronic product radiation safety. Each such inspection shall be commenced and completed with reasonable promptness. In addition to other grounds upon which good cause may be found for purposes of this subsection, good cause will be considered to exist in any case where the manufacturer has introduced into commerce any electronic product which does not comply with an applicable standard prescribed under this part and with respect to which no exemption from the notification requirements has been granted by the Secretary under section 360*ll*(a)(2) or 360*ll*(e) of this title.

(b) Record keeping

Every manufacturer of electronic products shall establish and maintain such records (including testing records), make such reports, and provide such information, as the Secretary may reasonably require to enable him to determine whether such manufacturer has acted or is acting in compliance with this part and standards prescribed pursuant to this part and shall, upon request of an officer or employee duly designated by the Secretary, permit such officer or employee to inspect appropriate books, papers, records, and documents relevant to determining whether such manufacturer has acted or is acting in compliance with standards prescribed pursuant to this part.

(c) Disclosure of technical data

Every manufacturer of electronic products shall provide to the Secretary such performance data and other technical data related to safety as may be required to carry out the purposes of this part. The Secretary is authorized to require the manufacturer to give such notification of such performance and technical data at the time of original purchase to the ultimate purchaser of the electronic product, as he determines necessary to carry out the purposes of this part after consulting with the affected industry.

(d) Public nature of reports

Accident and investigation reports made under this part by any officer, employee, or agent of the Secretary shall be available for use in any civil, criminal, or other judicial proceeding arising out of such accident. Any such officer, employee, or agent may be required to testify in such proceedings as to the facts developed in such investigations. Any such report shall be made available to the public in a manner which need not identify individuals. All reports on research projects, demonstration projects, and other related activities shall be public information.

(e) Trade secrets

The Secretary or his representative shall not disclose any information reported to or otherwise obtained by him, pursuant to subsection (a) or (b) of this section, which concerns any information which contains or relates to a trade secret or other matter referred to in section 1905 of title 18, except that such information may be disclosed to other officers or employees of the Department and of other agencies concerned with carrying out this part or when relevant in any proceeding under this part. Nothing in this section shall authorize the withholding of information by the Secretary, or by any officers or employees under his control, from the duly authorized committees of the Congress.

(f) Information required to identify and locate first purchasers of electronic products

The Secretary may by regulation (1) require dealers and distributors of electronic products, to which there are applicable standards prescribed under this part and the retail prices of which is not less than $50, to furnish manufacturers of such products such information as may be necessary to identify and locate, for purposes of section 360*ll* of this title, the first purchasers of such products for purposes other than resale, and (2) require manufacturers to preserve such information. Any regulation establishing a requirement pursuant to clause (1) of the preceding sentence shall (A) authorize such dealers and distributors to elect, in lieu of immediately furnishing such information to the manufacturer, to hold and preserve such information until advised by the manufacturer or Secretary that such information is needed by the manufacturer for purposes of section 360*ll* of this title, and (B) provide that the dealer or distributor shall, upon making such election, give prompt notice of such election (together with information identifying the notifier and the product) to the manufacturer and shall, when advised by the manufacturer or Secretary, of the need therefor for the purposes of section 360*ll* of this title, immediately furnish the manufacturer with the required information. If a dealer or distributor discontinues the dealing in or distribution of electronic products, he shall turn the information over to the manufacturer. Any manufacturer receiving information pursuant to this subsection concerning first purchasers of products for purposes other than resale shall treat it as confidential and may use it only if necessary for the purpose of notifying persons pursuant to section 360*ll*(a) of this title.

(June 25, 1938, ch. 675, § 537, formerly act July 1, 1944, ch. 373, title III, § 537, formerly § 360A, as added Pub. L. 90–602, § 2(3), Oct. 18, 1968, 82 Stat. 1182; renumbered § 537 and amended Pub. L. 101–629, § 19(a)(1)(B), (2)(E), (3), (4), Nov. 28, 1990, 104 Stat. 4529, 4530; Pub. L. 103–80, § 4(a)(2), Aug. 13, 1993, 107 Stat. 779.)

CODIFICATION

Section was classified to section 263i of Title 42, The Public Health and Welfare, prior to renumbering by Pub. L. 101–629.

AMENDMENTS

1993—Pub. L. 103–80 amended directory language of Pub. L. 101–629, § 19(a)(4), which renumbered section 263i of Title 42, The Public Health and Welfare, as this section.

1990—Subsec. (a). Pub. L. 101–629, § 19(a)(1)(B), (2)(E), substituted "section 360kk(h)" for "section 263f(h)", "this part" for "this subpart", and "section 360*ll*(a)(2) or 360*ll*(e)" for "section 263g(a)(2) or 263g(e)".

Subsecs. (b) to (e). Pub. L. 101–629, § 19(a)(1)(B), substituted "this part" for "this subpart" wherever appearing.

Subsec. (f). Pub. L. 101–629, § 19(a)(1)(B), (2)(E)(ii), substituted "this part" for "this subpart", "section 360*ll*" for "section 263g" in three places, and "section 360*ll*(a)" for "section 263g(a)".

NONINTERFERENCE WITH OTHER FEDERAL AGENCIES

Enactment of this section not to be construed to supersede or limit the functions under any other provision of law of any officer or agency of the United States, see section 4 of Pub. L. 90–602, set out as a note under section 360hh of this title.

§ 360oo. Prohibited acts

(a) It shall be unlawful—

(1) for any manufacturer to introduce, or to deliver for introduction, into commerce, or to import into the United States, any electronic product which does not comply with an applicable standard prescribed pursuant to section 360kk of this title;

(2) for any person to fail to furnish any notification or other material or information required by section 360*ll* or 360nn of this title; or to fail to comply with the requirements of section 360*ll*(f) of this title;

(3) for any person to fail or to refuse to establish or maintain records required by this part or to permit access by the Secretary or any of his duly authorized representatives to, or the copying of, such records, or to permit entry or inspection, as required by or pursuant to section 360nn of this title;

(4) for any person to fail or to refuse to make any report required pursuant to section 360nn(b) of this title or to furnish or preserve any information required pursuant to section 360nn(f) of this title; or

(5) for any person (A) to fail to issue a certification as required by section 360kk(h) of this title, or (B) to issue such a certification when such certification is not based upon a test or testing program meeting the requirements of section 360kk(h) of this title or when the issuer, in the exercise of due care, would have reason to know that such certification is false or misleading in a material respect.

(b) The Secretary may exempt any electronic product, or class thereof, from all or part of subsection (a) of this section, upon such conditions as he may find necessary to protect the public health or welfare, for the purpose of research, investigations, studies, demonstrations, or training, or for reasons of national security.

(June 25, 1938, ch. 675, §538, formerly act July 1, 1944, ch. 373, title III, §538, formerly §360B, as added Pub. L. 90–602, §2(3), Oct. 18, 1968, 82 Stat. 1184; renumbered §538 and amended Pub. L. 101–629, §19(a)(1)(B), (2)(F), (3), (4), Nov. 28, 1990, 104 Stat. 4529, 4530; Pub. L. 103–80, §4(a)(2), Aug. 13, 1993, 107 Stat. 779.)

CODIFICATION

Section was classified to section 263j of Title 42, The Public Health and Welfare, prior to renumbering by Pub. L. 101–629.

AMENDMENTS

1993—Pub. L. 103–80 amended directory language of Pub. L. 101–629, §19(a)(4), which renumbered section 263j of Title 42, The Public Health and Welfare, as this section.

1990—Subsec. (a)(1). Pub. L. 101–629, §19(a)(2)(F)(i), substituted "section 360kk" for "section 263f".

Subsec. (a)(2). Pub. L. 101–629, §19(a)(2)(F)(ii), (iii), substituted "section 360*ll* or 360nn" for "section 263g or 263i" and "section 360*ll*(f)" for "section 263g(f)".

Subsec. (a)(3). Pub. L. 101–629, §19(a)(1)(B), (2)(F)(iii), substituted "this part" for "this subpart" and "section 360nn" for "section 263i".

Subsec. (a)(4). Pub. L. 101–629, §19(a)(2)(F)(iii), substituted "section 360nn(b)" for "section 263i(b)" and "section 360nn(f)" for "section 263i(f)".

Subsec. (a)(5). Pub. L. 101–629, §19(a)(2)(F)(i), substituted "section 360kk(h)" for "section 263f(h)" in two places.

NONINTERFERENCE WITH OTHER FEDERAL AGENCIES

Enactment of this section not to be construed to supersede or limit the functions under any other provision of law of any officer or agency of the United States, see section 4 of Pub. L. 90–602, set out as a note under section 360hh of this title.

§ 360pp. Enforcement

(a) Jurisdiction of courts

The district courts of the United States shall have jurisdiction, for cause shown, to restrain violations of section 360*oo* of this title and to restrain dealers and distributors of electronic products from selling or otherwise disposing of electronic products which do not conform to an applicable standard prescribed pursuant to section 360kk of this title except when such products are disposed of by returning them to the distributor or manufacturer from whom they were obtained. The district courts of the United States shall also have jurisdiction in accordance with section 1355 of title 28 to enforce the provisions of subsection (b) of this section.

(b) Penalties

(1) Any person who violates section 360*oo* of this title shall be subject to a civil penalty of not more than $1,000. For purposes of this subsection, any such violation shall with respect to each electronic product involved, or with respect to each act or omission made unlawful by section 360*oo* of this title, constitute a separate violation, except that the maximum civil penalty imposed on any person under this subsection for any related series of violations shall not exceed $300,000.

(2) Any such civil penalty may on application be remitted or mitigated by the Secretary. In determining the amount of such penalty, or whether it should be remitted or mitigated and in what amount, the appropriateness of such penalty to the size of the business of the person charged and the gravity of the violation shall be considered. The amount of such penalty, when finally determined, may be deducted from any sums owing by the United States to the person charged.

(c) Venue; process

Actions under subsections (a) and (b) of this section may be brought in the district court of the United States for the district wherein any act or omission or transaction constituting the violation occurred, or in such court for the district where the defendant is found or transacts business, and process in such cases may be served in any other district of which the defendant is an inhabitant or wherever the defendant may be found.

(d) Warnings

Nothing in this part shall be construed as requiring the Secretary to report for the institution of proceedings minor violations of this part whenever he believes that the public interest will be adequately served by a suitable written notice or warning.

(e) Compliance with regulations

Except as provided in the first sentence of section 360ss of this title, compliance with this part or any regulations issued thereunder shall not relieve any person from liability at common law or under statutory law.

(f) Additional remedies

The remedies provided for in this part shall be in addition to and not in substitution for any other remedies provided by law.

(June 25, 1938, ch. 675, §539, formerly act July 1, 1944, ch. 373, title III, §539, formerly §360C, as added Pub. L. 90–602, §2(3), Oct. 18, 1968, 82 Stat. 1184; renumbered §539 and amended Pub. L. 101–629, §19(a)(1)(B), (2)(G), (3), (4), Nov. 28, 1990, 104 Stat. 4529, 4530; Pub. L. 103–80, §4(a)(2), Aug. 13, 1993, 107 Stat. 779.)

CODIFICATION

Section was classified to section 263k of Title 42, The Public Health and Welfare, prior to renumbering by Pub. L. 101–629.

AMENDMENTS

1993—Pub. L. 103–80 amended directory language of Pub. L. 101–629, §19(a)(4), which renumbered section 263k of Title 42, The Public Health and Welfare, as this section.

1990—Subsec. (a). Pub. L. 101–629, §19(a)(2)(G)(i), (ii), substituted "section 360*oo*" for "section 263j" and "section 360kk" for "section 263f".

Subsec. (b)(1). Pub. L. 101–629, §19(a)(2)(G)(ii), substituted "section 360*oo*" for "section 263j" in two places.

Subsec. (d). Pub. L. 101–629, §19(a)(1)(B), substituted "this part" for "this subpart" in two places.

Subsec. (e). Pub. L. 101–629, §19(a)(1)(B), (2)(G)(iii), substituted "section 360ss" for "section 263n" and "this part" for "this subpart".

Subsec. (f). Pub. L. 101–629, § 19(a)(1)(B), substituted "this part" for "this subpart".

NONINTERFERENCE WITH OTHER FEDERAL AGENCIES

Enactment of this section not to be construed to supersede or limit the functions under any other provision of law of any officer or agency of the United States, see section 4 of Pub. L. 90–602, set out as a note under section 360hh of this title.

§ 360qq. Repealed. Pub. L. 105–362, title VI, § 601(a)(2)(A), Nov. 10, 1998, 112 Stat. 3285

Section, act June 25, 1938, ch. 675, § 540, formerly act July 1, 1944, ch. 373, title III, § 540, formerly § 360D, as added Pub. L. 90–602, § 2(3), Oct. 18, 1968, 82 Stat. 1185; renumbered § 540 and amended Pub. L. 101–629, § 19(a)(1)(B), (3), (4), Nov. 28, 1990, 104 Stat. 4529, 4530; Pub. L. 103–80, § 4(a)(2), Aug. 13, 1993, 107 Stat. 779, related to annual report on administration of electronic product radiation control program.

§ 360rr. Federal-State cooperation

The Secretary is authorized (1) to accept from State and local authorities engaged in activities related to health or safety or consumer protection, on a reimbursable basis or otherwise, any assistance in the administration and enforcement of this part which he may request and which they may be able and willing to provide and, if so agreed, may pay in advance or otherwise for the reasonable cost of such assistance, and (2) he may, for the purpose of conducting examinations, investigations, and inspections, commission any officer or employee of any such authority as an officer of the Department.

(June 25, 1938, ch. 675, § 541, formerly act July 1, 1944, ch. 373, title III, § 541, formerly § 360E, as added Pub. L. 90–602, § 2(3), Oct. 18, 1968, 82 Stat. 1186; renumbered § 541 and amended Pub. L. 101–629, § 19(a)(1)(B), (3), (4), Nov. 28, 1990, 104 Stat. 4529, 4530; Pub. L. 103–80, § 4(a)(2), Aug. 13, 1993, 107 Stat. 779.)

CODIFICATION

Section was classified to section 263m of Title 42, The Public Health and Welfare, prior to renumbering by Pub. L. 101–629.

AMENDMENTS

1993—Pub. L. 103–80 amended directory language of Pub. L. 101–629, § 19(a)(4), which renumbered section 263m of Title 42, The Public Health and Welfare, as this section.

1990—Pub. L. 101–629, § 19(a)(1)(B), substituted "this part" for "this subpart".

NONINTERFERENCE WITH OTHER FEDERAL AGENCIES

Enactment of this section not to be construed to supersede or limit the functions under any other provision of law of any officer or agency of the United States, see section 4 of Pub. L. 90–602, set out as a note under section 360hh of this title.

§ 360ss. State standards

Whenever any standard prescribed pursuant to section 360kk of this title with respect to an aspect of performance of an electronic product is in effect, no State or political subdivision of a State shall have any authority either to establish, or to continue in effect, any standard which is applicable to the same aspect of performance of such product and which is not identical to the Federal standard. Nothing in this part shall be construed to prevent the Federal Government or the government of any State or political subdivision thereof from establishing a requirement with respect to emission of radiation from electronic products procured for its own use if such requirement imposes a more restrictive standard than that required to comply with the otherwise applicable Federal standard.

(June 25, 1938, ch. 675, § 542, formerly act July 1, 1944, ch. 373, title III, § 542, formerly § 360F, as added Pub. L. 90–602, § 2(3), Oct. 18, 1968, 82 Stat. 1186; renumbered § 542 and amended Pub. L. 101–629, § 19(a)(1)(B), (2)(H), (3), (4), Nov. 28, 1990, 104 Stat. 4529, 4530; Pub. L. 103–80, § 4(a)(2), Aug. 13, 1993, 107 Stat. 779.)

CODIFICATION

Section was classified to section 263n of Title 42, The Public Health and Welfare, prior to renumbering by Pub. L. 101–629.

AMENDMENTS

1993—Pub. L. 103–80 amended directory language of Pub. L. 101–629, § 19(a)(4), which renumbered section 263n of Title 42, The Public Health and Welfare, as this section.

1990—Pub. L. 101–629, § 19(a)(1)(B), (2)(H), substituted "section 360kk" for "section 263f" and "this part" for "this subpart".

NONINTERFERENCE WITH OTHER FEDERAL AGENCIES

Enactment of this section not to be construed to supersede or limit the functions under any other provision of law of any officer or agency of the United States, see section 4 of Pub. L. 90–602, set out as a note under section 360hh of this title.

PART D—DISSEMINATION OF TREATMENT INFORMATION

§§ 360aaa to 360aaa–6. Omitted

CODIFICATION

Sections 360aaa to 360aaa–6 ceased to be effective pursuant to section 401(e) of Pub. L. 105–115, set out as an Effective and Termination Dates note below.

Section 360aaa, act June 25, 1938, ch. 675, § 551, as added Pub. L. 105–115, title IV, § 401(a), Nov. 21, 1997, 111 Stat. 2356, related to requirements for dissemination of treatment information on drugs or devices.

Section 360aaa–1, act June 25, 1938, ch. 675, § 552, as added Pub. L. 105–115, title IV, § 401(a), Nov. 21, 1997, 111 Stat. 2358, related to information authorized to be disseminated under section 360aaa.

Section 360aaa–2, act June 25, 1938, ch. 675, § 553, as added Pub. L. 105–115, title IV, § 401(a), Nov. 21, 1997, 111 Stat. 2359, related to establishment of list of articles and publications disseminated and list of providers that received articles and reference publications.

Section 360aaa–3, act June 25, 1938, ch. 675, § 554, as added Pub. L. 105–115, title IV, § 401(a), Nov. 21, 1997, 111 Stat. 2359, related to requirement regarding submission of supplemental application for new use and an exemption from that requirement.

Section 360aaa–4, act June 25, 1938, ch. 675, § 555, as added Pub. L. 105–115, title IV, § 401(a), Nov. 21, 1997, 111 Stat. 2361, related to corrective actions and cessation of dissemination.

Section 360aaa–5, act June 25, 1938, ch. 675, § 556, as added Pub. L. 105–115, title IV, § 401(a), Nov. 21, 1997, 111 Stat. 2362, related to definitions.

Section 360aaa–6, act June 25, 1938, ch. 675, § 557, as added Pub. L. 105–115, title IV, § 401(a), Nov. 21, 1997, 111 Stat. 2363, related to rules of construction.

EFFECTIVE AND TERMINATION DATES

Pub. L. 105–115, title IV, § 401(d), Nov. 21, 1997, 111 Stat. 2364, provided that: "The amendments made by this section [enacting this part and amending section 331 of this title] shall take effect 1 year after the date of enactment of this Act [Nov. 21, 1997], or upon the Secretary's issuance of final regulations pursuant to subsection (c) [section 401(c) of Pub. L. 105–115 set out below] [Such regulations were issued effective Nov. 20, 1998. See 63 F.R. 64556.], whichever is sooner."

Pub. L. 105–115, title IV, §401(e), Nov. 21, 1997, 111 Stat. 2364, provided that: "The amendments made by this section [enacting this part and amending section 331 of this title] cease to be effective September 30, 2006, or 7 years after the date on which the Secretary promulgates the regulations described in subsection (c) [section 401(c) of Pub. L. 105–115 set out below] [Such regulations were issued effective Nov. 20, 1998. See 63 F.R. 64556.], whichever is later."

REGULATIONS

Pub. L. 105–115, title IV, §401(c), Nov. 21, 1997, 111 Stat. 2364, provided that: "Not later than 1 year after the date of enactment of this Act [Nov. 21, 1997], the Secretary of Health and Human Services shall promulgate regulations to implement the amendments made by this section [enacting this part and amending section 331 of this title]."

PART E—GENERAL PROVISIONS RELATING TO DRUGS AND DEVICES

§ 360bbb. Expanded access to unapproved therapies and diagnostics

(a) Emergency situations

The Secretary may, under appropriate conditions determined by the Secretary, authorize the shipment of investigational drugs or investigational devices for the diagnosis, monitoring, or treatment of a serious disease or condition in emergency situations.

(b) Individual patient access to investigational products intended for serious diseases

Any person, acting through a physician licensed in accordance with State law, may request from a manufacturer or distributor, and any manufacturer or distributor may, after complying with the provisions of this subsection, provide to such physician an investigational drug or investigational device for the diagnosis, monitoring, or treatment of a serious disease or condition if—

(1) the licensed physician determines that the person has no comparable or satisfactory alternative therapy available to diagnose, monitor, or treat the disease or condition involved, and that the probable risk to the person from the investigational drug or investigational device is not greater than the probable risk from the disease or condition;

(2) the Secretary determines that there is sufficient evidence of safety and effectiveness to support the use of the investigational drug or investigational device in the case described in paragraph (1);

(3) the Secretary determines that provision of the investigational drug or investigational device will not interfere with the initiation, conduct, or completion of clinical investigations to support marketing approval; and

(4) the sponsor, or clinical investigator, of the investigational drug or investigational device submits to the Secretary a clinical protocol consistent with the provisions of section 355(i) or 360j(g) of this title, including any regulations promulgated under section 355(i) or 360j(g) of this title, describing the use of the investigational drug or investigational device in a single patient or a small group of patients.

(c) Treatment investigational new drug applications and treatment investigational device exemptions

Upon submission by a sponsor or a physician of a protocol intended to provide widespread access to an investigational drug or investigational device for eligible patients (referred to in this subsection as an "expanded access protocol"), the Secretary shall permit such investigational drug or investigational device to be made available for expanded access under a treatment investigational new drug application or treatment investigational device exemption if the Secretary determines that—

(1) under the treatment investigational new drug application or treatment investigational device exemption, the investigational drug or investigational device is intended for use in the diagnosis, monitoring, or treatment of a serious or immediately life-threatening disease or condition;

(2) there is no comparable or satisfactory alternative therapy available to diagnose, monitor, or treat that stage of disease or condition in the population of patients to which the investigational drug or investigational device is intended to be administered;

(3)(A) the investigational drug or investigational device is under investigation in a controlled clinical trial for the use described in paragraph (1) under an investigational drug application in effect under section 355(i) of this title or investigational device exemption in effect under section 360j(g) of this title; or

(B) all clinical trials necessary for approval of that use of the investigational drug or investigational device have been completed;

(4) the sponsor of the controlled clinical trials is actively pursuing marketing approval of the investigational drug or investigational device for the use described in paragraph (1) with due diligence;

(5) in the case of an investigational drug or investigational device described in paragraph (3)(A), the provision of the investigational drug or investigational device will not interfere with the enrollment of patients in ongoing clinical investigations under section 355(i) or 360j(g) of this title;

(6) in the case of serious diseases, there is sufficient evidence of safety and effectiveness to support the use described in paragraph (1); and

(7) in the case of immediately life-threatening diseases, the available scientific evidence, taken as a whole, provides a reasonable basis to conclude that the investigational drug or investigational device may be effective for its intended use and would not expose patients to an unreasonable and significant risk of illness or injury.

A protocol submitted under this subsection shall be subject to the provisions of section 355(i) or 360j(g) of this title, including regulations promulgated under section 355(i) or 360j(g) of this title. The Secretary may inform national, State, and local medical associations and societies, voluntary health associations, and other appropriate persons about the availability of an investigational drug or investigational device under expanded access protocols submitted under this subsection. The information provided by the Secretary, in accordance with the preceding sentence, shall be the same type of information that is required by section 282(i)(3) of title 42.

(d) Termination

The Secretary may, at any time, with respect to a sponsor, physician, manufacturer, or distributor described in this section, terminate expanded access provided under this section for an investigational drug or investigational device if the requirements under this section are no longer met.

(e) Definitions

In this section, the terms "investigational drug", "investigational device", "treatment investigational new drug application", and "treatment investigational device exemption" shall have the meanings given the terms in regulations prescribed by the Secretary.

(June 25, 1938, ch. 675, §561, as added Pub. L. 105–115, title IV, §402, Nov. 21, 1997, 111 Stat. 2365; amended Pub. L. 109–482, title I, §102(f)(2), Jan. 15, 2007, 120 Stat. 3685.)

AMENDMENTS

2007—Subsec. (c). Pub. L. 109–482 substituted "section 282(i)(3)" for "section 282(j)(3)" in concluding provisions.

EFFECTIVE DATE OF 2007 AMENDMENT

Amendment by Pub. L. 109–482 applicable only with respect to amounts appropriated for fiscal year 2007 or subsequent fiscal years, see section 109 of Pub. L. 109–482, set out as a note under section 281 of Title 42, The Public Health and Welfare.

EFFECTIVE DATE

Section effective 90 days after Nov. 21, 1997, except as otherwise provided, see section 501 of Pub. L. 105–115, set out as an Effective Date of 1997 Amendment note under section 321 of this title.

§ 360bbb–1. Dispute resolution

If, regarding an obligation concerning drugs or devices under this Act or section 351 of the Public Health Service Act [42 U.S.C. 262], there is a scientific controversy between the Secretary and a person who is a sponsor, applicant, or manufacturer and no specific provision of the Act involved, including a regulation promulgated under such Act, provides a right of review of the matter in controversy, the Secretary shall, by regulation, establish a procedure under which such sponsor, applicant, or manufacturer may request a review of such controversy, including a review by an appropriate scientific advisory panel described in section 355(n) of this title or an advisory committee described in section 360e(g)(2)(B) of this title. Any such review shall take place in a timely manner. The Secretary shall promulgate such regulations within 1 year after November 21, 1997.

(June 25, 1938, ch. 675, §562, as added Pub. L. 105–115, title IV, §404, Nov. 21, 1997, 111 Stat. 2368.)

REFERENCES IN TEXT

This Act, referred to in text, is the Federal Food, Drug, and Cosmetic Act, act June 25, 1938, ch. 675, 52 Stat. 1040, as amended, which is classified generally to this chapter. For complete classification of this Act to the Code, see section 301 of this title and Tables.

EFFECTIVE DATE

Section effective 90 days after Nov. 21, 1997, except as otherwise provided, see section 501 of Pub. L. 105–115, set out as an Effective Date of 1997 Amendment note under section 321 of this title.

§ 360bbb–2. Classification of products

(a) Request

A person who submits an application or submission (including a petition, notification, and any other similar form of request) under this chapter for a product, may submit a request to the Secretary respecting the classification of the product as a drug, biological product, device, or a combination product subject to section 353(g) of this title or respecting the component of the Food and Drug Administration that will regulate the product. In submitting the request, the person shall recommend a classification for the product, or a component to regulate the product, as appropriate.

(b) Statement

Not later than 60 days after the receipt of the request described in subsection (a) of this section, the Secretary shall determine the classification of the product under subsection (a) of this section, or the component of the Food and Drug Administration that will regulate the product, and shall provide to the person a written statement that identifies such classification or such component, and the reasons for such determination. The Secretary may not modify such statement except with the written consent of the person, or for public health reasons based on scientific evidence.

(c) Inaction of Secretary

If the Secretary does not provide the statement within the 60-day period described in subsection (b) of this section, the recommendation made by the person under subsection (a) of this section shall be considered to be a final determination by the Secretary of such classification of the product, or the component of the Food and Drug Administration that will regulate the product, as applicable, and may not be modified by the Secretary except with the written consent of the person, or for public health reasons based on scientific evidence.

(June 25, 1938, ch. 675, §563, as added Pub. L. 105–115, title IV, §416, Nov. 21, 1997, 111 Stat. 2378.)

EFFECTIVE DATE

Section effective 90 days after Nov. 21, 1997, except as otherwise provided, see section 501 of Pub. L. 105–115, set out as an Effective Date of 1997 Amendment note under section 321 of this title.

§ 360bbb–3. Authorization for medical products for use in emergencies

(a) In general

(1) Emergency uses

Notwithstanding sections 355, 360(k), and 360e of this title and section 262 of title 42, and subject to the provisions of this section, the Secretary may authorize the introduction into interstate commerce, during the effective period of a declaration under subsection (b) of this section, of a drug, device, or biological product intended for use in an actual or potential emergency (referred to in this section as an "emergency use").

(2) Approval status of product

An authorization under paragraph (1) may authorize an emergency use of a product that—

(A) is not approved, licensed, or cleared for commercial distribution under a provision of law referred to in such paragraph (referred to in this section as an "unapproved product"); or

(B) is approved, licensed, or cleared under such a provision, but which use is not under such provision an approved, licensed, or cleared use of the product (referred to in this section as an "unapproved use of an approved product").

(3) Relation to other uses

An emergency use authorized under paragraph (1) for a product is in addition to any other use that is authorized for the product under a provision of law referred to in such paragraph.

(4) Definitions

For purposes of this section:

(A) The term "biological product" has the meaning given such term in section 262 of title 42.

(B) The term "emergency use" has the meaning indicated for such term in paragraph (1).

(C) The term "product" means a drug, device, or biological product.

(D) The term "unapproved product" has the meaning indicated for such term in paragraph (2)(A).

(E) The term "unapproved use of an approved product" has the meaning indicated for such term in paragraph (2)(B).

(b) Declaration of emergency

(1) In general

The Secretary may declare an emergency justifying the authorization under this subsection for a product on the basis of—

(A) a determination by the Secretary of Homeland Security that there is a domestic emergency, or a significant potential for a domestic emergency, involving a heightened risk of attack with a specified biological, chemical, radiological, or nuclear agent or agents;

(B) a determination by the Secretary of Defense that there is a military emergency, or a significant potential for a military emergency, involving a heightened risk to United States military forces of attack with a specified biological, chemical, radiological, or nuclear agent or agents; or

(C) a determination by the Secretary of a public health emergency under section 247d of title 42 that affects, or has a significant potential to affect, national security, and that involves a specified biological, chemical, radiological, or nuclear agent or agents, or a specified disease or condition that may be attributable to such agent or agents.

(2) Termination of declaration

(A) In general

A declaration under this subsection shall terminate upon the earlier of—

(i) a determination by the Secretary, in consultation as appropriate with the Secretary of Homeland Security or the Secretary of Defense, that the circumstances described in paragraph (1) have ceased to exist; or

(ii) the expiration of the one-year period beginning on the date on which the declaration is made.

(B) Renewal

Notwithstanding subparagraph (A), the Secretary may renew a declaration under this subsection, and this paragraph shall apply to any such renewal.

(C) Disposition of product

If an authorization under this section with respect to an unapproved product ceases to be effective as a result of a termination under subparagraph (A) of this paragraph, the Secretary shall consult with the manufacturer of such product with respect to the appropriate disposition of the product.

(3) Advance notice of termination

The Secretary shall provide advance notice that a declaration under this subsection will be terminated. The period of advance notice shall be a period reasonably determined to provide—

(A) in the case of an unapproved product, a sufficient period for disposition of the product, including the return of such product (except such quantities of product as are necessary to provide for continued use consistent with subsection (f)(2) of this section) to the manufacturer (in the case of a manufacturer that chooses to have such product returned); and

(B) in the case of an unapproved use of an approved product, a sufficient period for the disposition of any labeling, or any information under subsection (e)(2)(B)(ii) of this section, as the case may be, that was provided with respect to the emergency use involved.

(4) Publication

The Secretary shall promptly publish in the Federal Register each declaration, determination, advance notice of termination, and renewal under this subsection.

(c) Criteria for issuance of authorization

The Secretary may issue an authorization under this section with respect to the emergency use of a product only if, after consultation with the Director of the National Institutes of Health and the Director of the Centers for Disease Control and Prevention (to the extent feasible and appropriate given the circumstances of the emergency involved), the Secretary concludes—

(1) that an agent specified in a declaration under subsection (b) of this section can cause

a serious or life-threatening disease or condition;

(2) that, based on the totality of scientific evidence available to the Secretary, including data from adequate and well-controlled clinical trials, if available, it is reasonable to believe that—

(A) the product may be effective in diagnosing, treating, or preventing—

(i) such disease or condition; or

(ii) a serious or life-threatening disease or condition caused by a product authorized under this section, approved or cleared under this chapter, or licensed under section 262 of title 42, for diagnosing, treating, or preventing such a disease or condition caused by such an agent; and

(B) the known and potential benefits of the product, when used to diagnose, prevent, or treat such disease or condition, outweigh the known and potential risks of the product;

(3) that there is no adequate, approved, and available alternative to the product for diagnosing, preventing, or treating such disease or condition; and

(4) that such other criteria as the Secretary may by regulation prescribe are satisfied.

(d) Scope of authorization

An authorization of a product under this section shall state—

(1) each disease or condition that the product may be used to diagnose, prevent, or treat within the scope of the authorization;

(2) the Secretary's conclusions, made under subsection (c)(2)(B) of this section, that the known and potential benefits of the product, when used to diagnose, prevent, or treat such disease or condition, outweigh the known and potential risks of the product; and

(3) the Secretary's conclusions, made under subsection (c) of this section, concerning the safety and potential effectiveness of the product in diagnosing, preventing, or treating such diseases or conditions, including an assessment of the available scientific evidence.

(e) Conditions of authorization

(1) Unapproved product

(A) Required conditions

With respect to the emergency use of an unapproved product, the Secretary, to the extent practicable given the circumstances of the emergency, shall, for a person who carries out any activity for which the authorization is issued, establish such conditions on an authorization under this section as the Secretary finds necessary or appropriate to protect the public health, including the following:

(i) Appropriate conditions designed to ensure that health care professionals administering the product are informed—

(I) that the Secretary has authorized the emergency use of the product;

(II) of the significant known and potential benefits and risks of the emergency use of the product, and of the extent to which such benefits and risks are unknown; and

(III) of the alternatives to the product that are available, and of their benefits and risks.

(ii) Appropriate conditions designed to ensure that individuals to whom the product is administered are informed—

(I) that the Secretary has authorized the emergency use of the product;

(II) of the significant known and potential benefits and risks of such use, and of the extent to which such benefits and risks are unknown; and

(III) of the option to accept or refuse administration of the product, of the consequences, if any, of refusing administration of the product, and of the alternatives to the product that are available and of their benefits and risks.

(iii) Appropriate conditions for the monitoring and reporting of adverse events associated with the emergency use of the product.

(iv) For manufacturers of the product, appropriate conditions concerning recordkeeping and reporting, including records access by the Secretary, with respect to the emergency use of the product.

(B) Authority for additional conditions

With respect to the emergency use of an unapproved product, the Secretary may, for a person who carries out any activity for which the authorization is issued, establish such conditions on an authorization under this section as the Secretary finds necessary or appropriate to protect the public health, including the following:

(i) Appropriate conditions on which entities may distribute the product with respect to the emergency use of the product (including limitation to distribution by government entities), and on how distribution is to be performed.

(ii) Appropriate conditions on who may administer the product with respect to the emergency use of the product, and on the categories of individuals to whom, and the circumstances under which, the product may be administered with respect to such use.

(iii) Appropriate conditions with respect to the collection and analysis of information, during the period when the authorization is in effect, concerning the safety and effectiveness of the product with respect to the emergency use of such product.

(iv) For persons other than manufacturers of the product, appropriate conditions concerning recordkeeping and reporting, including records access by the Secretary, with respect to the emergency use of the product.

(2) Unapproved use

With respect to the emergency use of a product that is an unapproved use of an approved product:

(A) For a manufacturer of the product who carries out any activity for which the authorization is issued, the Secretary shall, to the extent practicable given the circumstances of the emergency, establish conditions described in clauses (i) and (ii) of paragraph (1)(A), and may establish conditions described in clauses (iii) and (iv) of such paragraph.

(B)(i) If the authorization under this section regarding the emergency use authorizes a change in the labeling of the product, but the manufacturer of the product chooses not to make such change, such authorization may not authorize distributors of the product or any other person to alter or obscure the labeling provided by the manufacturer.

(ii) In the circumstances described in clause (i), for a person who does not manufacture the product and who chooses to act under this clause, an authorization under this section regarding the emergency use shall, to the extent practicable given the circumstances of the emergency, authorize such person to provide appropriate information with respect to such product in addition to the labeling provided by the manufacturer, subject to compliance with clause (i). While the authorization under this section is effective, such additional information shall not be considered labeling for purposes of section 352 of this title.

(C) The Secretary may establish with respect to the distribution and administration of the product for the unapproved use conditions no more restrictive than those established by the Secretary with respect to the distribution and administration of the product for the approved use.

(3) Good manufacturing practice

With respect to the emergency use of a product for which an authorization under this section is issued (whether an unapproved product or an unapproved use of an approved product), the Secretary may waive or limit, to the extent appropriate given the circumstances of the emergency, requirements regarding current good manufacturing practice otherwise applicable to the manufacture, processing, packing, or holding of products subject to regulation under this chapter, including such requirements established under section 351 of this title.

(4) Advertising

The Secretary may establish conditions on advertisements and other promotional descriptive printed matter that relate to the emergency use of a product for which an authorization under this section is issued (whether an unapproved product or an unapproved use of an approved product), including, as appropriate—

(A) with respect to drugs and biological products, requirements applicable to prescription drugs pursuant to section 352(n) of this title; or

(B) with respect to devices, requirements applicable to restricted devices pursuant to section 352(r) of this title.

(f) Duration of authorization

(1) In general

Except as provided in paragraph (2), an authorization under this section shall be effective until the earlier of the termination of the declaration under subsection (b) of this section or a revocation under subsection (g) of this section.

(2) Continued use after end of effective period

Notwithstanding the termination of the declaration under subsection (b) of this section or a revocation under subsection (g) of this section, an authorization shall continue to be effective to provide for continued use of an unapproved product with respect to a patient to whom it was administered during the period described by paragraph (1), to the extent found necessary by such patient's attending physician.

(g) Revocation of authorization

(1) Review

The Secretary shall periodically review the circumstances and the appropriateness of an authorization under this section.

(2) Revocation

The Secretary may revoke an authorization under this section if the criteria under subsection (c) of this section for issuance of such authorization are no longer met or other circumstances make such revocation appropriate to protect the public health or safety.

(h) Publication; confidential information

(1) Publication

The Secretary shall promptly publish in the Federal Register a notice of each authorization, and each termination or revocation of an authorization under this section, and an explanation of the reasons therefor (which may include a summary of data or information that has been submitted to the Secretary in an application under section 355(i) of this title or section 360j(g) of this title, even if such summary may indirectly reveal the existence of such application).

(2) Confidential information

Nothing in this section alters or amends section 1905 of title 18 or section 552(b)(4) of title 5.

(i) Actions committed to agency discretion

Actions under the authority of this section by the Secretary, by the Secretary of Defense, or by the Secretary of Homeland Security are committed to agency discretion.

(j) Rules of construction

The following applies with respect to this section:

(1) Nothing in this section impairs the authority of the President as Commander in Chief of the Armed Forces of the United States under article II, section 2 of the United States Constitution.

(2) Nothing in this section impairs the authority of the Secretary of Defense with respect to the Department of Defense, including the armed forces, under other provisions of Federal law.

(3) Nothing in this section (including any exercise of authority by a manufacturer under subsection (e)(2)) impairs the authority of the United States to use or manage quantities of

a product that are owned or controlled by the United States (including quantities in the stockpile maintained under section 247d–6b of title 42).

(k) Relation to other provisions

If a product is the subject of an authorization under this section, the use of such product within the scope of the authorization shall not be considered to constitute a clinical investigation for purposes of section 355(i) of this title, section 360j(g) of this title, or any other provision of this chapter or section 262 of title 42.

(*l*) Option to carry out authorized activities

Nothing in this section provides the Secretary any authority to require any person to carry out any activity that becomes lawful pursuant to an authorization under this section, and no person is required to inform the Secretary that the person will not be carrying out such activity, except that a manufacturer of a sole-source unapproved product authorized for emergency use shall report to the Secretary within a reasonable period of time after the issuance by the Secretary of such authorization if such manufacturer does not intend to carry out any activity under the authorization. This section only has legal effect on a person who carries out an activity for which an authorization under this section is issued. This section does not modify or affect activities carried out pursuant to other provisions of this chapter or section 262 of title 42. Nothing in this subsection may be construed as restricting the Secretary from imposing conditions on persons who carry out any activity pursuant to an authorization under this section.

(June 25, 1938, ch. 675, § 564, as added Pub. L. 108–136, div. A, title XVI, § 1603(a), Nov. 24, 2003, 117 Stat. 1684; amended Pub. L. 108–276, § 4(a), July 21, 2004, 118 Stat. 853.)

AMENDMENTS

2004—Pub. L. 108–276 amended section generally, substituting provisions of subsecs. (a) to (*l*) for similar former provisions, except for additional provisions in subsec. (b)(1) allowing Secretary to authorize use of medical products in actual or potential domestic and public health emergencies in addition to actual or potential military emergencies.

§ 360bbb–4. Technical assistance

The Secretary, in consultation with the Commissioner of Food and Drugs, shall establish within the Food and Drug Administration a team of experts on manufacturing and regulatory activities (including compliance with current Good Manufacturing Practice) to provide both off-site and on-site technical assistance to the manufacturers of qualified countermeasures (as defined in section 247d–6a of title 42), security countermeasures (as defined in section 247d–6b of title 42), or vaccines, at the request of such a manufacturer and at the discretion of the Secretary, if the Secretary determines that a shortage or potential shortage may occur in the United States in the supply of such vaccines or countermeasures and that the provision of such assistance would be beneficial in helping alleviate or avert such shortage.

(June 25, 1938, ch. 675, § 565, as added Pub. L. 109–417, title IV, § 404, Dec. 19, 2006, 120 Stat. 2875.)

§ 360bbb–5. Critical Path Public-Private Partnerships

(a) Establishment

The Secretary, acting through the Commissioner of Food and Drugs, may enter into collaborative agreements, to be known as Critical Path Public-Private Partnerships, with one or more eligible entities to implement the Critical Path Initiative of the Food and Drug Administration by developing innovative, collaborative projects in research, education, and outreach for the purpose of fostering medical product innovation, enabling the acceleration of medical product development, manufacturing, and translational therapeutics, and enhancing medical product safety.

(b) Eligible entity

In this section, the term "eligible entity" means an entity that meets each of the following:

(1) The entity is—

(A) an institution of higher education (as such term is defined in section 1001 of title 20) or a consortium of such institutions; or

(B) an organization described in section 501(c)(3) of title 26 and exempt from tax under section 501(a) of such title.

(2) The entity has experienced personnel and clinical and other technical expertise in the biomedical sciences, which may include graduate training programs in areas relevant to priorities of the Critical Path Initiative.

(3) The entity demonstrates to the Secretary's satisfaction that the entity is capable of—

(A) developing and critically evaluating tools, methods, and processes—

(i) to increase efficiency, predictability, and productivity of medical product development; and

(ii) to more accurately identify the benefits and risks of new and existing medical products;

(B) establishing partnerships, consortia, and collaborations with health care practitioners and other providers of health care goods or services; pharmacists; pharmacy benefit managers and purchasers; health maintenance organizations and other managed health care organizations; health care insurers; government agencies; patients and consumers; manufacturers of prescription drugs, biological products, diagnostic technologies, and devices; and academic scientists; and

(C) securing funding for the projects of a Critical Path Public-Private Partnership from Federal and nonfederal governmental sources, foundations, and private individuals.

(c) Funding

The Secretary may not enter into a collaborative agreement under subsection (a) unless the eligible entity involved provides an assurance that the entity will not accept funding for a Critical Path Public-Private Partnership project from any organization that manufactures or distributes products regulated by the Food and

Drug Administration unless the entity provides assurances in its agreement with the Food and Drug Administration that the results of the Critical Path Public-Private Partnership project will not be influenced by any source of funding.

(d) Annual report

Not later than 18 months after September 27, 2007, and annually thereafter, the Secretary, in collaboration with the parties to each Critical Path Public-Private Partnership, shall submit a report to the Committee on Health, Education, Labor, and Pensions of the Senate and the Committee on Energy and Commerce of the House of Representatives—

(1) reviewing the operations and activities of the Partnerships in the previous year; and

(2) addressing such other issues relating to this section as the Secretary determines to be appropriate.

(e) Definition

In this section, the term "medical product" includes a drug, a biological product as defined in section 262 of title 42, a device, and any combination of such products.

(f) Authorization of appropriations

To carry out this section, there are authorized to be appropriated $5,000,000 for fiscal year 2008 and such sums as may be necessary for each of fiscal years 2009 through 2012.

(June 25, 1938, ch. 675, § 566, as added Pub. L. 110–85, title VI, § 603, Sept. 27, 2007, 121 Stat. 898.)

§ 360bbb–6. Risk communication

(a) Advisory Committee on Risk Communication

(1) In general

The Secretary shall establish an advisory committee to be known as the "Advisory Committee on Risk Communication" (referred to in this section as the "Committee").

(2) Duties of Committee

The Committee shall advise the Commissioner on methods to effectively communicate risks associated with the products regulated by the Food and Drug Administration.

(3) Members

The Secretary shall ensure that the Committee is composed of experts on risk communication, experts on the risks described in subsection (b), and representatives of patient, consumer, and health professional organizations.

(4) Permanence of Committee

Section 14 of the Federal Advisory Committee Act shall not apply to the Committee established under this subsection.

(b) Partnerships for risk communication

(1) In general

The Secretary shall partner with professional medical societies, medical schools, academic medical centers, and other stakeholders to develop robust and multi-faceted systems for communication to health care providers about emerging postmarket drug risks.

(2) Partnerships

The systems developed under paragraph (1) shall—

(A) account for the diversity among physicians in terms of practice, willingness to adopt technology, and medical specialty; and

(B) include the use of existing communication channels, including electronic communications, in place at the Food and Drug Administration.

(June 25, 1938, ch. 675, § 567, as added Pub. L. 110–85, title IX, § 917, Sept. 27, 2007, 121 Stat. 960.)

REFERENCES IN TEXT

Section 14 of the Federal Advisory Committee Act, referred to in subsec. (a)(4), is section 14 of Pub. L. 92–463, which is set out in the Appendix to Title 5, Government Organization and Employees.

PART F—NEW ANIMAL DRUGS FOR MINOR USE AND MINOR SPECIES

§ 360ccc. Conditional approval of new animal drugs for minor use and minor species

(a) Application requirements; contents; restrictions

(1) Except as provided in paragraph (3) of this section,[1] any person may file with the Secretary an application for conditional approval of a new animal drug intended for a minor use or a minor species. Such an application may not be a supplement to an application approved under section 360b of this title. Such application must comply in all respects with the provisions of section 360b of this title except sections 360b(a)(4), 360b(b)(2), 360b(c)(1), 360b(c)(2), 360b(c)(3), 360b(d)(1), 360b(e), 360b(h), and 360b(n) of this title unless otherwise stated in this section, and any additional provisions of this section. New animal drugs are subject to application of the same safety standards that would be applied to such drugs under section 360b(d) of this title (including, for antimicrobial new animal drugs, with respect to antimicrobial resistance).

(2) The applicant shall submit to the Secretary as part of an application for the conditional approval of a new animal drug—

(A) all information necessary to meet the requirements of section 360b(b)(1) of this title except section 360b(b)(1)(A) of this title;

(B) full reports of investigations which have been made to show whether or not such drug is safe under section 360b(d) of this title (including, for an antimicrobial new animal drug, with respect to antimicrobial resistance) and there is a reasonable expectation of effectiveness for use;

(C) data for establishing a conditional dose;

(D) projections of expected need and the justification for that expectation based on the best information available;

(E) information regarding the quantity of drug expected to be distributed on an annual basis to meet the expected need; and

(F) a commitment that the applicant will conduct additional investigations to meet the requirements for the full demonstration of effectiveness under section 360b(d)(1)(E) of this title within 5 years.

(3) A person may not file an application under paragraph (1) if—

[1] So in original. Probably should be "this subsection,".

(A) the application seeks conditional approval of a new animal drug that is contained in, or is a product of, a transgenic animal.[2]

(B) the person has previously filed an application for conditional approval under paragraph (1) for the same drug in the same dosage form for the same intended use whether or not subsequently conditionally approved by the Secretary under subsection (b) of this section, or

(C) the person obtained the application, or data or other information contained therein, directly or indirectly from the person who filed for conditional approval under paragraph (1) for the same drug in the same dosage form for the same intended use whether or not subsequently conditionally approved by the Secretary under subsection (b) of this section.

(b) Order of approval or hearing

Within 180 days after the filing of an application pursuant to subsection (a) of this section, or such additional period as may be agreed upon by the Secretary and the applicant, the Secretary shall either—

(1) issue an order, effective for one year, conditionally approving the application if the Secretary finds that none of the grounds for denying conditional approval, specified in subsection (c) of this section applies and publish a Federal Register notice of the conditional approval, or

(2) give the applicant notice of an opportunity for an informal hearing on the question whether such application can be conditionally approved.

(c) Order of approval or refusal after hearing

If the Secretary finds, after giving the applicant notice and an opportunity for an informal hearing, that—

(1) any of the provisions of section 360b(d)(1)(A) through (D) or (F) through (I) of this title are applicable;

(2) the information submitted to the Secretary as part of the application and any other information before the Secretary with respect to such drug, is insufficient to show that there is a reasonable expectation that the drug will have the effect it purports or is represented to have under the conditions of use prescribed, recommended, or suggested in the proposed labeling thereof; or

(3) another person has received approval under section 360b of this title for the same drug in the same dosage form for the same intended use, and that person is able to assure the availability of sufficient quantities of the drug to meet the needs for which the drug is intended;

the Secretary shall issue an order refusing to conditionally approve the application. If, after such notice and opportunity for an informal hearing, the Secretary finds that paragraphs (1) through (3) do not apply, the Secretary shall issue an order conditionally approving the application effective for one year and publish a Federal Register notice of the conditional approval. Any order issued under this subsection refusing to conditionally approve an application shall state the findings upon which it is based.

(d) Effective period; renewal; refusal of renewal

A conditional approval under this section is effective for a 1-year period and is thereafter renewable by the Secretary annually for up to 4 additional 1-year terms. A conditional approval shall be in effect for no more than 5 years from the date of approval under subsection (b)(1) or (c) of this section unless extended as provided for in subsection (h) of this section. The following shall also apply:

(1) No later than 90 days from the end of the 1-year period for which the original or renewed conditional approval is effective, the applicant may submit a request to renew a conditional approval for an additional 1-year term.

(2) A conditional approval shall be deemed renewed at the end of the 1-year period, or at the end of a 90-day extension that the Secretary may, at the Secretary's discretion, grant by letter in order to complete review of the renewal request, unless the Secretary determines before the expiration of the 1-year period or the 90-day extension that—

(A) the applicant failed to submit a timely renewal request;

(B) the request fails to contain sufficient information to show that—

(i) the applicant is making sufficient progress toward meeting approval requirements under section 360b(d)(1)(E) of this title, and is likely to be able to fulfill those requirements and obtain an approval under section 360b of this title before the expiration of the 5-year maximum term of the conditional approval;

(ii) the quantity of the drug that has been distributed is consistent with the conditionally approved intended use and conditions of use, unless there is adequate explanation that ensures that the drug is only used for its intended purpose; or

(iii) the same drug in the same dosage form for the same intended use has not received approval under section 360b of this title, or if such a drug has been approved, that the holder of the approved application is unable to assure the availability of sufficient quantities of the drug to meet the needs for which the drug is intended; or

(C) any of the provisions of section 360b(e)(1)(A) through (B) or (D) through (F) of this title are applicable.

(3) If the Secretary determines before the end of the 1-year period or the 90-day extension, if granted, that a conditional approval should not be renewed, the Secretary shall issue an order refusing to renew the conditional approval, and such conditional approval shall be deemed withdrawn and no longer in effect. The Secretary shall thereafter provide an opportunity for an informal hearing to the applicant on the issue whether the conditional approval shall be reinstated.

(e) Withdrawal of conditional approval

(1) The Secretary shall issue an order withdrawing conditional approval of an application filed pursuant to subsection (a) of this section if

---
[2] So in original. The period probably should be a comma.

the Secretary finds that another person has received approval under section 360b of this title for the same drug in the same dosage form for the same intended use and that person is able to assure the availability of sufficient quantities of the drug to meet the needs for which the drug is intended.

(2) The Secretary shall, after due notice and opportunity for an informal hearing to the applicant, issue an order withdrawing conditional approval of an application filed pursuant to subsection (a) of this section if the Secretary finds that—

(A) any of the provisions of section 360b(e)(1)(A) through (B) or (D) through (F) of this title are applicable; or

(B) on the basis of new information before the Secretary with respect to such drug, evaluated together with the evidence available to the Secretary when the application was conditionally approved, that there is not a reasonable expectation that such drug will have the effect it purports or is represented to have under the conditions of use prescribed, recommended, or suggested in the labeling thereof.

(3) The Secretary may also, after due notice and opportunity for an informal hearing to the applicant, issue an order withdrawing conditional approval of an application filed pursuant to subsection (a) of this section if the Secretary finds that any of the provisions of section 360b(e)(2) of this title are applicable.

(f) Labeling

(1) The label and labeling of a new animal drug with a conditional approval under this section shall—

(A) bear the statement, "conditionally approved by FDA pending a full demonstration of effectiveness under application number"; and

(B) contain such other information as prescribed by the Secretary.

(2) An intended use that is the subject of a conditional approval under this section shall not be included in the same product label with any intended use approved under section 360b of this title.

(g) Amendment of application

A conditionally approved new animal drug application may not be amended or supplemented to add indications for use.

(h) Order of approval after conditional approval period termination

180 days prior to the termination date established under subsection (d) of this section, an applicant shall have submitted all the information necessary to support a complete new animal drug application in accordance with section 360b(b)(1) of this title or the conditional approval issued under this section is no longer in effect. Following review of this information, the Secretary shall either—

(1) issue an order approving the application under section 360b(c) of this title if the Secretary finds that none of the grounds for denying approval specified in section 360b(d)(1) of this title applies, or

(2) give the applicant an opportunity for a hearing before the Secretary under section 360b(d) of this title on the question whether such application can be approved.

Upon issuance of an order approving the application, product labeling and administrative records of approval shall be modified accordingly. If the Secretary has not issued an order under section 360b(c) of this title approving such application prior to the termination date established under subsection (d) of this section, the conditional approval issued under this section is no longer in effect unless the Secretary grants an extension of an additional 180-day period so that the Secretary can complete review of the application. The decision to grant an extension is committed to the discretion of the Secretary and not subject to judicial review.

(i) Judicial review

The decision of the Secretary under subsection (c), (d), or (e) of this section refusing or withdrawing conditional approval of an application shall constitute final agency action subject to judicial review.

(j) Definition

In this section and section 360ccc–1 of this title, the term "transgenic animal" means an animal whose genome contains a nucleotide sequence that has been intentionally modified in vitro, and the progeny of such an animal; Provided that the term "transgenic animal" does not include an animal of which the nucleotide sequence of the genome has been modified solely by selective breeding.

(June 25, 1938, ch. 675, §571, as added Pub. L. 108–282, title I, §102(b)(4), Aug. 2, 2004, 118 Stat. 892.)

FINDINGS

Pub. L. 108–282, title I, §102(a), Aug. 2, 2004, 118 Stat. 891, provided that: "Congress makes the following findings:

"(1) There is a severe shortage of approved new animal drugs for use in minor species.

"(2) There is a severe shortage of approved new animal drugs for treating animal diseases and conditions that occur infrequently or in limited geographic areas.

"(3) Because of the small market shares, low-profit margins involved, and capital investment required, it is generally not economically feasible for new animal drug applicants to pursue approvals for these species, diseases, and conditions.

"(4) Because the populations for which such new animal drugs are intended may be small and conditions of animal management may vary widely, it is often difficult to design and conduct studies to establish drug safety and effectiveness under traditional new animal drug approval processes.

"(5) It is in the public interest and in the interest of animal welfare to provide for special procedures to allow the lawful use and marketing of certain new animal drugs for minor species and minor uses that take into account these special circumstances and that ensure that such drugs do not endanger animal or public health.

"(6) Exclusive marketing rights for clinical testing expenses have helped encourage the development of 'orphan' drugs for human use, and comparable incentives should encourage the development of new animal drugs for minor species and minor uses."

REGULATIONS

Pub. L. 108–282, title I, §102(b)(6), Aug. 2, 2004, 118 Stat. 905, provided that: "On the date of enactment of this Act [Aug. 2, 2004], the Secretary of Health and Human Services shall implement sections 571 and 573 of the Federal Food, Drug, and Cosmetic Act [21 U.S.C. 360ccc, 360ccc–2] and subsequently publish implementing regulations. Not later than 12 months after the date of enactment of this Act, the Secretary shall issue proposed regulations to implement section 573 of the Federal Food, Drug, and Cosmetic Act (as added by this Act), and not later than 24 months after the date of enactment of this Act, the Secretary shall issue final regulations implementing section 573 of the Federal Food, Drug, and Cosmetic Act. Not later than 18 months after the date of enactment of this Act, the Secretary shall issue proposed regulations to implement section 572 of the Federal Food, Drug, and Cosmetic Act (as added by this Act) [21 U.S.C. 360ccc–1], and not later than 36 months after the date of enactment of this Act, the Secretary shall issue final regulations implementing section 572 of the Federal Food, Drug, and Cosmetic Act. Not later than 30 months after the date of enactment of this Act, the Secretary shall issue proposed regulations to implement section 571 of the Federal Food, Drug, and Cosmetic Act (as added by this Act), and not later than 42 months after the date of enactment of this Act, the Secretary shall issue final regulations implementing section 571 of the Federal Food, Drug, and Cosmetic Act. These timeframes shall be extended by 12 months for each fiscal year, in which the funds authorized to be appropriated under subsection (i) [no subsection (i) of section 102 has been enacted] are not in fact appropriated."

§ 360ccc–1. Index of legally marketed unapproved new animal drugs for minor species

(a) Establishment and content

(1) The Secretary shall establish an index limited to—

(A) new animal drugs intended for use in a minor species for which there is a reasonable certainty that the animal or edible products from the animal will not be consumed by humans or food-producing animals; and

(B) new animal drugs intended for use only in a hatchery, tank, pond, or other similar contained man-made structure in an early, non-food life stage of a food-producing minor species, where safety for humans is demonstrated in accordance with the standard of section 360b(d) of this title (including, for an antimicrobial new animal drug, with respect to antimicrobial resistance).

(2) The index shall not include a new animal drug that is contained in or a product of a transgenic animal.

(b) Conferences

Any person intending to file a request under this section shall be entitled to one or more conferences to discuss the requirements for indexing a new animal drug.

(c) Request for determination of eligibility for inclusion in index

(1) Any person may submit a request to the Secretary for a determination whether a new animal drug may be eligible for inclusion in the index. Such a request shall include—

(A) information regarding the need for the new animal drug, the species for which the new animal drug is intended, the proposed intended use and conditions of use, and anticipated annual distribution;

(B) information to support the conclusion that the proposed use meets the conditions of subparagraph (A) or (B) of subsection (a)(1) of this section;

(C) information regarding the components and composition of the new animal drug;

(D) a description of the methods used in, and the facilities and controls used for, the manufacture, processing, and packing of such new animal drug;

(E) an environmental assessment that meets the requirements of the National Environmental Policy Act of 1969 [42 U.S.C. 4321 et seq.], as amended, and as defined in 21 CFR Part 25, as it appears on August 2, 2004, and amended thereafter or information to support a categorical exclusion from the requirement to prepare an environmental assessment;

(F) information sufficient to support the conclusion that the proposed use of the new animal drug is safe under section 360b(d) of this title with respect to individuals exposed to the new animal drug through its manufacture or use; and

(G) such other information as the Secretary may deem necessary to make this eligibility determination.

(2) Within 90 days after the submission of a request for a determination of eligibility for indexing based on subsection (a)(1)(A) of this section, or 180 days for a request submitted based on subsection (a)(1)(B) of this section, the Secretary shall grant or deny the request, and notify the person who requested such determination of the Secretary's decision. The Secretary shall grant the request if the Secretary finds that—

(A) the same drug in the same dosage form for the same intended use is not approved or conditionally approved;

(B) the proposed use of the drug meets the conditions of subparagraph (A) or (B) of subsection (a)(1) of this section, as appropriate;

(C) the person requesting the determination has established appropriate specifications for the manufacture and control of the new animal drug and has demonstrated an understanding of the requirements of current good manufacturing practices;

(D) the new animal drug will not significantly affect the human environment; and

(E) the new animal drug is safe with respect to individuals exposed to the new animal drug through its manufacture or use.

If the Secretary denies the request, the Secretary shall thereafter provide due notice and an opportunity for an informal conference. A decision of the Secretary to deny an eligibility request following an informal conference shall constitute final agency action subject to judicial review.

(d) Request for addition to index

(1) With respect to a new animal drug for which the Secretary has made a determination of eligibility under subsection (c) of this section, the person who made such a request may ask that the Secretary add the new animal drug to the index established under subsection (a) of this section. The request for addition to the index shall include—

(A) a copy of the Secretary's determination of eligibility issued under subsection (c) of this section;

(B) a written report that meets the requirements in subsection (d)(2) of this section;

(C) a proposed index entry;

(D) facsimile labeling;

(E) anticipated annual distribution of the new animal drug;

(F) a written commitment to manufacture the new animal drug and animal feeds bearing or containing such new animal drug according to current good manufacturing practices;

(G) a written commitment to label, distribute, and promote the new animal drug only in accordance with the index entry;

(H) upon specific request of the Secretary, information submitted to the expert panel described in paragraph (3); and

(I) any additional requirements that the Secretary may prescribe by general regulation or specific order.

(2) The report required in paragraph (1) shall—

(A) be authored by a qualified expert panel;

(B) include an evaluation of all available target animal safety and effectiveness information, including anecdotal information;

(C) state the expert panel's opinion regarding whether the benefits of using the new animal drug for the proposed use in a minor species outweigh its risks to the target animal, taking into account the harm being caused by the absence of an approved or conditionally approved new animal drug for the minor species in question;

(D) include information from which labeling can be written; and

(E) include a recommendation regarding whether the new animal drug should be limited to use under the professional supervision of a licensed veterinarian.

(3) A qualified expert panel, as used in this section, is a panel that—

(A) is composed of experts qualified by scientific training and experience to evaluate the target animal safety and effectiveness of the new animal drug under consideration;

(B) operates external to FDA; and

(C) is not subject to the Federal Advisory Committee Act.

The Secretary shall define the criteria for selection of a qualified expert panel and the procedures for the operation of the panel by regulation.

(4) Within 180 days after the receipt of a request for listing a new animal drug in the index, the Secretary shall grant or deny the request. The Secretary shall grant the request if the request for indexing continues to meet the eligibility criteria in subsection (a) of this section and the Secretary finds, on the basis of the report of the qualified expert panel and other information available to the Secretary, that the benefits of using the new animal drug for the proposed use in a minor species outweigh its risks to the target animal, taking into account the harm caused by the absence of an approved or conditionally-approved new animal drug for the minor species in question. If the Secretary denies the request, the Secretary shall thereafter provide due notice and the opportunity for an informal conference. The decision of the Secretary following an informal conference shall constitute final agency action subject to judicial review.

(e) Index contents; publication

(1) The index established under subsection (a) of this section shall include the following information for each listed drug—

(A) the name and address of the person who holds the index listing;

(B) the name of the drug and the intended use and conditions of use for which it is being indexed;

(C) product labeling; and

(D) conditions and any limitations that the Secretary deems necessary regarding use of the drug.

(2) The Secretary shall publish the index, and revise it periodically.

(3) The Secretary may establish by regulation a process for reporting changes in the conditions of manufacturing or labeling of indexed products.

(f) Removal from index; suspended listing

(1) If the Secretary finds, after due notice to the person who requested the index listing and an opportunity for an informal conference, that—

(A) the expert panel failed to meet the requirements as set forth by the Secretary by regulation;

(B) on the basis of new information before the Secretary, evaluated together with the evidence available to the Secretary when the new animal drug was listed in the index, the benefits of using the new animal drug for the indexed use do not outweigh its risks to the target animal;

(C) the conditions of subsection (c)(2) of this section are no longer satisfied;

(D) the manufacture of the new animal drug is not in accordance with current good manufacturing practices;

(E) the labeling, distribution, or promotion of the new animal drug is not in accordance with the index entry;

(F) the conditions and limitations of use associated with the index listing have not been followed; or

(G) the request for indexing contains any untrue statement of material fact,

the Secretary shall remove the new animal drug from the index. The decision of the Secretary following an informal conference shall constitute final agency action subject to judicial review.

(2) If the Secretary finds that there is a reasonable probability that the use of the drug would present a risk to the health of humans or other animals, the Secretary may—

(A) suspend the listing of such drug immediately;

(B) give the person listed in the index prompt notice of the Secretary's action; and

(C) afford that person the opportunity for an informal conference.

The decision of the Secretary following an informal conference shall constitute final agency action subject to judicial review.

(g) Regulations concerning exemptions for investigational use

For purposes of indexing new animal drugs under this section, to the extent consistent with the public health, the Secretary shall promulgate regulations for exempting from the operation of section 360b of this title minor species new animal drugs and animal feeds bearing or containing new animal drugs intended solely for investigational use by experts qualified by scientific training and experience to investigate the safety and effectiveness of minor species animal drugs. Such regulations may, at the discretion of the Secretary, among other conditions relating to the protection of the public health, provide for conditioning such exemption upon the establishment and maintenance of such records, and the making of such reports to the Secretary, by the manufacturer or the sponsor of the investigation of such article, of data (including but not limited to analytical reports by investigators) obtained as a result of such investigational use of such article, as the Secretary finds will enable the Secretary to evaluate the safety and effectiveness of such article in the event of the filing of a request for an index listing pursuant to this section.

(h) Labeling contents

The labeling of a new animal drug that is the subject of an index listing shall state, prominently and conspicuously—

(1) "NOT APPROVED BY FDA.—Legally marketed as an FDA indexed product. Extra-label use is prohibited.";

(2) except in the case of new animal drugs indexed for use in an early life stage of a food-producing animal, "This product is not to be used in animals intended for use as food for humans or other animals."; and

(3) such other information as may be prescribed by the Secretary in the index listing.

(i) Records and reports

(1) In the case of any new animal drug for which an index listing pursuant to subsection (a) of this section is in effect, the person who has an index listing shall establish and maintain such records, and make such reports to the Secretary, of data relating to experience, and other data or information, received or otherwise obtained by such person with respect to such drug, or with respect to animal feeds bearing or containing such drug, as the Secretary may by general regulation, or by order with respect to such listing, prescribe on the basis of a finding that such records and reports are necessary in order to enable the Secretary to determine, or facilitate a determination, whether there is or may be ground for invoking subsection (f) of this section. Such regulation or order shall provide, where the Secretary deems it to be appropriate, for the examination, upon request, by the persons to whom such regulation or order is applicable, of similar information received or otherwise obtained by the Secretary.

(2) Every person required under this subsection to maintain records, and every person in charge or custody thereof, shall, upon request of an officer or employee designated by the Secretary, permit such officer or employee at all reasonable times to have access to and copy and verify such records.

(j) Public disclosure of safety and effectiveness data

(1) Safety and effectiveness data and information which has been submitted in support of a request for a new animal drug to be indexed under this section and which has not been previously disclosed to the public shall be made available to the public, upon request, unless extraordinary circumstances are shown—

(A) if no work is being or will be undertaken to have the drug indexed in accordance with the request,

(B) if the Secretary has determined that such drug cannot be indexed and all legal appeals have been exhausted,

(C) if the indexing of such drug is terminated and all legal appeals have been exhausted, or

(D) if the Secretary has determined that such drug is not a new animal drug.

(2) Any request for data and information pursuant to paragraph (1) shall include a verified statement by the person making the request that any data or information received under such paragraph shall not be disclosed by such person to any other person—

(A) for the purpose of, or as part of a plan, scheme, or device for, obtaining the right to make, use, or market, or making, using, or marketing, outside the United States, the drug identified in the request for indexing; and

(B) without obtaining from any person to whom the data and information are disclosed an identical verified statement, a copy of which is to be provided by such person to the Secretary, which meets the requirements of this paragraph.

(June 25, 1938, ch. 675, § 572, as added Pub. L. 108–282, title I, § 102(b)(4), Aug. 2, 2004, 118 Stat. 896.)

REFERENCES IN TEXT

The National Environmental Policy Act of 1969, referred to in subsec. (c)(1)(E), is Pub. L. 91–190, Jan. 1, 1970, 83 Stat. 852, as amended, which is classified generally to chapter 55 (§ 4321 et seq.) of Title 42, The Public Health and Welfare. For complete classification of this Act to the Code, see Short Title note set out under section 4321 of Title 42 and Tables.

The Federal Advisory Committee Act, referred to in subsec. (d)(3)(C), is Pub. L. 92–463, Oct. 6, 1972, 86 Stat. 770, as amended, which is set out in the Appendix to Title 5, Government Organization and Employees.

§ 360ccc–2. Designated new animal drugs for minor use or minor species

(a) Designation

(1) The manufacturer or the sponsor of a new animal drug for a minor use or use in a minor species may request that the Secretary declare that drug a "designated new animal drug". A request for designation of a new animal drug shall be made before the submission of an application under section 360b(b) of this title or section 360ccc of this title for the new animal drug.

(2) The Secretary may declare a new animal drug a "designated new animal drug" if—

(A) it is intended for a minor use or use in a minor species; and

(B) the same drug in the same dosage form for the same intended use is not approved under section 360b or 360ccc of this title or designated under this section at the time the request is made.

(3) Regarding the termination of a designation—

(A) the sponsor of a new animal drug shall notify the Secretary of any decision to discontinue active pursuit of approval under section 360b or 360ccc of this title of an application for a designated new animal drug. The Secretary shall terminate the designation upon such notification;

(B) the Secretary may also terminate designation if the Secretary independently determines that the sponsor is not actively pursuing approval under section 360b or 360ccc of this title with due diligence;

(C) the sponsor of an approved designated new animal drug shall notify the Secretary of any discontinuance of the manufacture of such new animal drug at least one year before discontinuance. The Secretary shall terminate the designation upon such notification; and

(D) the designation shall terminate upon the expiration of any applicable exclusivity period under subsection (c) of this section.

(4) Notice respecting the designation or termination of designation of a new animal drug shall be made available to the public.

(b) Grants and contracts for development of designated new animal drugs

(1) The Secretary may make grants to and enter into contracts with public and private entities and individuals to assist in defraying the costs of qualified safety and effectiveness testing expenses and manufacturing expenses incurred in connection with the development of designated new animal drugs.

(2) For purposes of paragraph (1) of this section—

(A) The term "qualified safety and effectiveness testing" means testing—

(i) which occurs after the date such new animal drug is designated under this section and before the date on which an application with respect to such drug is submitted under section 360b of this title; and

(ii) which is carried out under an investigational exemption under section 360b(j) of this title.

(B) The term "manufacturing expenses" means expenses incurred in developing processes and procedures associated with manufacture of the designated new animal drug which occur after the new animal drug is designated under this section and before the date on which an application with respect to such new animal drug is submitted under section 360b or 360ccc of this title.

(c) Exclusivity for designated new animal drugs

(1) Except as provided in subsection (c)(2) of this section, if the Secretary approves or conditionally approves an application for a designated new animal drug, the Secretary may not approve or conditionally approve another application submitted for such new animal drug with the same intended use as the designated new animal drug for another applicant before the expiration of seven years from the date of approval or conditional approval of the application.

(2) If an application filed pursuant to section 360b of this title or section 360ccc of this title is approved for a designated new animal drug, the Secretary may, during the 7-year exclusivity period beginning on the date of the application approval or conditional approval, approve or conditionally approve another application under section 360b of this title or section 360ccc of this title for such drug for such minor use or minor species for another applicant if—

(A) the Secretary finds, after providing the holder of such an approved application notice and opportunity for the submission of views, that in the granted exclusivity period the holder of the approved application cannot assure the availability of sufficient quantities of the drug to meet the needs for which the drug was designated; or

(B) such holder provides written consent to the Secretary for the approval or conditional approval of other applications before the expiration of such exclusivity period.

(June 25, 1938, ch. 675, § 573, as added Pub. L. 108–282, title I, § 102(b)(4), Aug. 2, 2004, 118 Stat. 900.)

SUBCHAPTER VI—COSMETICS

§ 361. Adulterated cosmetics

A cosmetic shall be deemed to be adulterated—

(a) If it bears or contains any poisonous or deleterious substance which may render it injurious to users under the conditions of use prescribed in the labeling thereof, or under such conditions of use as are customary or usual, except that this provision shall not apply to coal-tar hair dye, the label of which bears the following legend conspicuously displayed thereon: "Caution—This product contains ingredients which may cause skin irritation on certain individuals and a preliminary test according to accompanying directions should first be made. This product must not be used for dyeing the eyelashes or eyebrows; to do so may cause blindness.", and the labeling of which bears adequate directions for such preliminary testing. For the purposes of this paragraph and paragraph (e) the term "hair dye" shall not include eyelash dyes or eyebrow dyes.

(b) If it consists in whole or in part of any filthy, putrid, or decomposed substance.

(c) If it has been prepared, packed, or held under insanitary conditions whereby it may have become contaminated with filth, or whereby it may have been rendered injurious to health.

(d) If its container is composed, in whole or in part, of any poisonous or deleterious substance which may render the contents injurious to health.

(e) If it is not a hair dye and it is, or it bears or contains, a color additive which is unsafe within the meaning of section 379e(a) of this title.

(June 25, 1938, ch. 675, § 601, 52 Stat. 1054; Pub. L. 86–618, title I, § 102(c)(1), July 12, 1960, 74 Stat.

398; Pub. L. 102–571, title I, § 107(11), Oct. 29, 1992, 106 Stat. 4499; Pub. L. 103–80, § 3(x), Aug. 13, 1993, 107 Stat. 778.)

AMENDMENTS

1993—Subsec. (a). Pub. L. 103–80 substituted "usual, except that this" for "usual: *Provided*, That this".

1992—Par. (e). Pub. L. 102–571 substituted "379e(a)" for "376(a)".

1960—Par. (e). Pub. L. 86–618 substituted "and it is, or it bears or contains, a color additive which is unsafe within the meaning of section 376(a) of this title" for "and it bears or contains a coal-tar color other than one from a batch that has been certified in accordance with regulations as provided by section 364 of this title".

EFFECTIVE DATE OF 1960 AMENDMENT

Amendment by Pub. L. 86–618 effective July 12, 1960, subject to the provisions of section 203 of Pub. L. 86–618, see section 202 of Pub. L. 86–618, set out as a note under section 379e of this title.

EFFECTIVE DATE; POSTPONEMENT

Par. (e) effective Jan. 1, 1940, see act June 23, 1939, ch. 242, 53 Stat. 853, set out as an Effective Date; Postponement in Certain Cases note under section 301 of this title.

EFFECTIVE DATE

Section effective twelve months after June 25, 1938, except par. (a), which, with certain exceptions, became effective on June 25, 1938, see section 902(a) of act June 25, 1938, set out as a note under section 301 of this title.

§ 362. Misbranded cosmetics

A cosmetic shall be deemed to be misbranded—

(a) If its labeling is false or misleading in any particular.

(b) If in package form unless it bears a label containing (1) the name and place of business of the manufacturer, packer, or distributor; and (2) an accurate statement of the quantity of the contents in terms of weight, measure, or numerical count: *Provided*, That under clause (2) of this paragraph reasonable variations shall be permitted, and exemptions as to small packages shall be established, by regulations prescribed by the Secretary.

(c) If any word, statement, or other information required by or under authority of this chapter to appear on the label or labeling is not prominently placed thereon with such conspicuousness (as compared with other words, statements, designs, or devices, in the labeling) and in such terms as to render it likely to be read and understood by the ordinary individual under customary conditions of purchase and use.

(d) If its container is so made, formed, or filled as to be misleading.

(e) If it is a color additive, unless its packaging and labeling are in conformity with such packaging and labeling requirements, applicable to such color additive, as may be contained in regulations issued under section 379e of this title. This paragraph shall not apply to packages of color additives which, with respect to their use for cosmetics, are marketed and intended for use only in or on hair dyes (as defined in the last sentence of section 361(a) of this title).

(f) If its packaging or labeling is in violation of an applicable regulation issued pursuant to section 1472 or 1473 of title 15.

(June 25, 1938, ch. 675, § 602, 52 Stat. 1054; Pub. L. 86–618, title I, § 102(c)(2), July 12, 1960, 74 Stat. 398; Pub. L. 91–601, § 6(f), formerly § 7(f), Dec. 30, 1970, 84 Stat. 1673, renumbered Pub. L. 97–35, title XII, § 1205(c), Aug. 13, 1981, 95 Stat. 716; Pub. L. 102–571, title I, § 107(12), Oct. 29, 1992, 106 Stat. 4499.)

AMENDMENTS

1992—Par. (e). Pub. L. 102–571 substituted "379e" for "376".

1970—Par. (f). Pub. L. 91–601 added par. (f).

1960—Par. (e). Pub. L. 86–618 added par. (e).

EFFECTIVE DATE OF 1970 AMENDMENT

Amendment by Pub. L. 91–601 effective Dec. 30, 1970, and regulations establishing special packaging standards effective no sooner than 180 days or later than one year from date regulations are final, or an earlier date published in Federal Register, see section 8 of Pub. L. 91–601, set out as an Effective Date note under section 1471 of Title 15, Commerce and Trade.

EFFECTIVE DATE OF 1960 AMENDMENT

Amendment by Pub. L. 86–618 effective July 12, 1960, subject to the provisions of section 203 of Pub. L. 86–618, see section 202 of Pub. L. 86–618, set out as a note under section 379e of this title.

EFFECTIVE DATE; POSTPONEMENT

Par. (b) effective Jan. 1, 1940, and such subsection effective July 1, 1940, as provided by regulations for certain lithographed labeling and containers bearing certain labeling, see act June 23, 1939, ch. 242, 53 Stat. 853, set out as an Effective Date; Postponement in Certain Cases note under section 301 of this title.

TRANSFER OF FUNCTIONS

For transfer of functions of Federal Security Administrator to Secretary of Health, Education, and Welfare [now Health and Human Services], and of Food and Drug Administration in the Department of Agriculture to Federal Security Agency, see notes set out under section 321 of this title.

§ 363. Regulations making exemptions

The Secretary shall promulgate regulations exempting from any labeling requirement of this chapter cosmetics which are, in accordance with the practice of the trade, to be processed, labeled, or repacked in substantial quantities at establishments other than those where originally processed or packed, on condition that such cosmetics are not adulterated or misbranded under the provisions of this chapter upon removal from such processing, labeling, or repacking establishment.

(June 25, 1938, ch. 675, § 603, 52 Stat. 1054.)

TRANSFER OF FUNCTIONS

For transfer of functions of Federal Security Administrator to Secretary of Health, Education, and Welfare [now Health and Human Services], and of Food and Drug Administration in the Department of Agriculture to Federal Security Agency, see notes set out under section 321 of this title.

§ 364. Repealed. Pub. L. 86–618, title I, § 103(a)(3), July 12, 1960, 74 Stat. 398

Section, act June 25, 1938, ch. 675, § 604, 52 Stat. 1055, directed Secretary to promulgate regulations for listing of coal-tar colors for cosmetics. See section 379e of this title.

EFFECTIVE DATE OF REPEAL

Repeal effective July 12, 1960, subject to the provisions of section 203 of Pub. L. 86–618, see section 202 of

Pub. L. 86–618, set out as an Effective Date of 1960 Amendment note under section 379e of this title.

SUBCHAPTER VII—GENERAL AUTHORITY

PART A—GENERAL ADMINISTRATIVE PROVISIONS

§371. Regulations and hearings

(a) Authority to promulgate regulations

The authority to promulgate regulations for the efficient enforcement of this chapter, except as otherwise provided in this section, is vested in the Secretary.

(b) Regulations for imports and exports

The Secretary of the Treasury and the Secretary of Health and Human Services shall jointly prescribe regulations for the efficient enforcement of the provisions of section 381 of this title, except as otherwise provided therein. Such regulations shall be promulgated in such manner and take effect at such time, after due notice, as the Secretary of Health and Human Services shall determine.

(c) Conduct of hearings

Hearings authorized or required by this chapter shall be conducted by the Secretary or such officer or employee as he may designate for the purpose.

(d) Effectiveness of definitions and standards of identity

The definitions and standards of identity promulgated in accordance with the provisions of this chapter shall be effective for the purposes of the enforcement of this chapter, notwithstanding such definitions and standards as may be contained in other laws of the United States and regulations promulgated thereunder.

(e) Procedure for establishment

(1) Any action for the issuance, amendment, or repeal of any regulation under section 343(j), 344(a), 346, 351(b), or 352(d) or (h) of this title, and any action for the amendment or repeal of any definition and standard of identity under section 341 of this title for any dairy product (including products regulated under parts 131, 133 and 135 of title 21, Code of Federal Regulations) shall be begun by a proposal made (A) by the Secretary on his own initiative, or (B) by petition of any interested person, showing reasonable grounds therefor, filed with the Secretary. The Secretary shall publish such proposal and shall afford all interested persons an opportunity to present their views thereon, orally or in writing. As soon as practicable thereafter, the Secretary shall by order act upon such proposal and shall make such order public. Except as provided in paragraph (2), the order shall become effective at such time as may be specified therein, but not prior to the day following the last day on which objections may be filed under such paragraph.

(2) On or before the thirtieth day after the date on which an order entered under paragraph (1) is made public, any person who will be adversely affected by such order if placed in effect may file objections thereto with the Secretary, specifying with particularity the provisions of the order deemed objectionable, stating the grounds therefor, and requesting a public hearing upon such objections. Until final action upon such objections is taken by the Secretary under paragraph (3), the filing of such objections shall operate to stay the effectiveness of those provisions of the order to which the objections are made. As soon as practicable after the time for filing objections has expired the Secretary shall publish a notice in the Federal Register specifying those parts of the order which have been stayed by the filing of objections and, if no objections have been filed, stating that fact.

(3) As soon as practicable after such request for a public hearing, the Secretary, after due notice, shall hold such a public hearing for the purpose of receiving evidence relevant and material to the issues raised by such objections. At the hearing, any interested person may be heard in person or by representative. As soon as practicable after completion of the hearing, the Secretary shall by order act upon such objections and make such order public. Such order shall be based only on substantial evidence of record at such hearing and shall set forth, as part of the order, detailed findings of fact on which the order is based. The Secretary shall specify in the order the date on which it shall take effect, except that it shall not be made to take effect prior to the ninetieth day after its publication unless the Secretary finds that emergency conditions exist necessitating an earlier effective date, in which event the Secretary shall specify in the order his findings as to such conditions.

(f) Review of order

(1) In a case of actual controversy as to the validity of any order under subsection (e) of this section, any person who will be adversely affected by such order if placed in effect may at any time prior to the ninetieth day after such order is issued file a petition with the United States court of appeals for the circuit wherein such person resides or has his principal place of business, for a judicial review of such order. A copy of the petition shall be forthwith transmitted by the clerk of the court to the Secretary or other officer designated by him for that purpose. The Secretary thereupon shall file in the court the record of the proceedings on which the Secretary based his order, as provided in section 2112 of title 28.

(2) If the petitioner applies to the court for leave to adduce additional evidence, and shows to the satisfaction of the court that such additional evidence is material and that there were reasonable grounds for the failure to adduce such evidence in the proceeding before the Secretary, the court may order such additional evidence (and evidence in rebuttal thereof) to be taken before the Secretary, and to be adduced upon the hearing, in such manner and upon such terms and conditions as to the court may seem proper. The Secretary may modify his findings as to the facts, or make new findings, by reason of the additional evidence so taken, and he shall file such modified or new findings, and his recommendation, if any, for the modification or setting aside of his original order, with the return of such additional evidence.

(3) Upon the filing of the petition referred to in paragraph (1) of this subsection, the court

shall have jurisdiction to affirm the order, or to set it aside in whole or in part, temporarily or permanently. If the order of the Secretary refuses to issue, amend, or repeal a regulation and such order is not in accordance with law the court shall by its judgment order the Secretary to take action, with respect to such regulation, in accordance with law. The findings of the Secretary as to the facts, if supported by substantial evidence, shall be conclusive.

(4) The judgment of the court affirming or setting aside, in whole or in part, any such order of the Secretary shall be final, subject to review by the Supreme Court of the United States upon certiorari or certification as provided in section 1254 of title 28.

(5) Any action instituted under this subsection shall survive notwithstanding any change in the person occupying the office of Secretary or any vacancy in such office.

(6) The remedies provided for in this subsection shall be in addition to and not in substitution for any other remedies provided by law.

(g) Copies of records of hearings

A certified copy of the transcript of the record and proceedings under subsection (e) of this section shall be furnished by the Secretary to any interested party at his request, and payment of the costs thereof, and shall be admissible in any criminal, libel for condemnation, exclusion of imports, or other proceeding arising under or in respect to this chapter, irrespective of whether proceedings with respect to the order have previously been instituted or become final under subsection (f) of this section.

(h) Guidance documents

(1)(A) The Secretary shall develop guidance documents with public participation and ensure that information identifying the existence of such documents and the documents themselves are made available to the public both in written form and, as feasible, through electronic means. Such documents shall not create or confer any rights for or on any person, although they present the views of the Secretary on matters under the jurisdiction of the Food and Drug Administration.

(B) Although guidance documents shall not be binding on the Secretary, the Secretary shall ensure that employees of the Food and Drug Administration do not deviate from such guidances without appropriate justification and supervisory concurrence. The Secretary shall provide training to employees in how to develop and use guidance documents and shall monitor the development and issuance of such documents.

(C) For guidance documents that set forth initial interpretations of a statute or regulation, changes in interpretation or policy that are of more than a minor nature, complex scientific issues, or highly controversial issues, the Secretary shall ensure public participation prior to implementation of guidance documents, unless the Secretary determines that such prior public participation is not feasible or appropriate. In such cases, the Secretary shall provide for public comment upon implementation and take such comment into account.

(D) For guidance documents that set forth existing practices or minor changes in policy, the Secretary shall provide for public comment upon implementation.

(2) In developing guidance documents, the Secretary shall ensure uniform nomenclature for such documents and uniform internal procedures for approval of such documents. The Secretary shall ensure that guidance documents and revisions of such documents are properly dated and indicate the nonbinding nature of the documents. The Secretary shall periodically review all guidance documents and, where appropriate, revise such documents.

(3) The Secretary, acting through the Commissioner, shall maintain electronically and update and publish periodically in the Federal Register a list of guidance documents. All such documents shall be made available to the public.

(4) The Secretary shall ensure that an effective appeals mechanism is in place to address complaints that the Food and Drug Administration is not developing and using guidance documents in accordance with this subsection.

(5) Not later than July 1, 2000, the Secretary after evaluating the effectiveness of the Good Guidance Practices document, published in the Federal Register at 62 Fed. Reg. 8961, shall promulgate a regulation consistent with this subsection specifying the policies and procedures of the Food and Drug Administration for the development, issuance, and use of guidance documents.

(June 25, 1938, ch. 675, §701, 52 Stat. 1055; June 25, 1948, ch. 646, §32, 62 Stat. 991; Apr. 15, 1954, ch. 143, §2, 68 Stat. 55; Aug. 1, 1956, ch. 861, §2, 70 Stat. 919; Pub. L. 85–791, §21, Aug. 28, 1958, 72 Stat. 948; Pub. L. 86–618, title I, §103(a)(4), July 12, 1960, 74 Stat. 398; Pub. L. 101–535, §8, Nov. 8, 1990, 104 Stat. 2365; Pub. L. 102–300, §6(b)(1), June 16, 1992, 106 Stat. 240; Pub. L. 103–80, §§3(y), (dd)(1), 4(c), Aug. 13, 1993, 107 Stat. 778, 779; Pub. L. 103–396, §3(b), Oct. 22, 1994, 108 Stat. 4155; Pub. L. 105–115, title IV, §405, Nov. 21, 1997, 111 Stat. 2368.)

AMENDMENTS

1997—Subsec. (h). Pub. L. 105–115 added subsec. (h).

1994—Subsec. (e)(1). Pub. L. 103–396 which directed the amendment of par. (1) by striking out "or maple syrup (regulated under section 168.140 of title 21, Code of Federal Regulations).", was executed by striking out "or maple sirup (regulated under section 168.140 of title 21, Code of Federal Regulations)" before "shall be begun by a proposal", to reflect the probable intent of Congress.

1993—Subsec. (b). Pub. L. 103–80, §3(dd)(1), substituted "Health and Human Services" for "Agriculture" in two places.

Subsec. (e)(1). Pub. L. 103–80, §4(c), made technical correction to directory language of Pub. L. 101–535, §8. See 1990 Amendment note below.

Pub. L. 103–80, §3(y)(1), struck out period after second reference to "Regulations)".

Subsec. (f)(4). Pub. L. 103–80, §3(y)(2), substituted reference to section 1254 of title 28 for "sections 239 and 240 of the Judicial Code, as amended".

1992—Subsec. (b). Pub. L. 102–300, which directed the substitution of "Health and Human Services" for "Health, Education, and Welfare", could not be executed because such words did not appear in the original statutory text. See 1993 Amendment note above and Transfer of Functions note below.

1990—Subsec. (e)(1). Pub. L. 101–535, §8, as amended by Pub. L. 103–80, §4(c), substituted "Any action for the issuance, amendment, or repeal of any regulation under section 343(j), 344(a), 346, 351(b), or 352(d) or (h) of this title, and any action for the amendment or repeal of any definition and standard of identity under section 341 of this title for any dairy product (including products regulated under parts 131, 133 and 135 of title 21, Code of Federal Regulations) or maple sirup (regulated under section 168.140 of title 21, Code of Federal Regulations)" for "Any action for the issuance, amendment, or repeal of any regulation under section 341, 343(j), 344(a), 346, 351(b), or 352(d) or (h) of this title".

1960—Subsec. (e). Pub. L. 86–618 substituted "section 341, 343(j), 344(a), 346, 351(b), or 352(d) or (h), of this title" for "section 341, 343(j), 344(a), 346(a) or (b), 351(b), 352(d) or (h), 354 or 364 of this title".

1958—Subsec. (f)(1). Pub. L. 85–791, §21(a), substituted provisions requiring transmission of a copy of the petition by clerk to Secretary, and filing of the record by Secretary, for provisions which permitted service of summons and petition any place in United States and required Secretary to certify and file transcript of the proceedings and record upon service.

Subsec. (f)(3). Pub. L. 85–791, §21(b), inserted "Upon the filing of the petition referred to in paragraph (1) of this subsection".

1956—Subsec. (e). Act Aug. 1, 1956, simplified procedures governing prescribing of regulations under certain provisions of this chapter.

1954—Subsec. (e). Act Apr. 15, 1954, struck out reference to section 341 of this title, before "343(j)", such section 341 now containing its own provisions with respect to hearings regarding the establishment of food standards.

CHANGE OF NAME

Circuit Court of Appeals of the United States changed to United States court of appeals by act June 25, 1948, eff. Sept. 1, 1948.

EFFECTIVE DATE OF 1997 AMENDMENT

Amendment by Pub. L. 105–115 effective 90 days after Nov. 21, 1997, except as otherwise provided, see section 501 of Pub. L. 105–115, set out as a note under section 321 of this title.

EFFECTIVE DATE OF 1960 AMENDMENT

Amendment by Pub. L. 86–618 effective July 12, 1960, subject to the provisions of section 203 of Pub. L. 86–618, see section 202 of Pub. L. 86–618, set out as a note under section 379e of this title.

CONSTRUCTION OF AMENDMENTS BY PUB. L. 101–535

Amendments by Pub. L. 101–535 not to be construed to alter the authority of the Secretary of Health and Human Services and the Secretary of Agriculture under the Federal Food, Drug, and Cosmetic Act (21 U.S.C. 301 et seq.), the Federal Meat Inspection Act (21 U.S.C. 601 et seq.), the Poultry Products Inspection Act (21 U.S.C. 451 et seq.), and the Egg Products Inspection Act (21 U.S.C. 1031 et seq.), see section 9 of Pub. L. 101–535, set out as a note under section 343 of this title.

SAVINGS PROVISION

Savings clause of act Aug. 1, 1956, see note set out under section 341 of this title.

TRANSFER OF FUNCTIONS

Secretary and Department of Health, Education, and Welfare redesignated Secretary and Department of Health and Human Services by Pub. L. 96–88, title V, §509(b), Oct. 17, 1979, 93 Stat. 695, which is classified to section 3508(b) of Title 20, Education.

For transfer of functions of Federal Security Administrator to Secretary of Health, Education, and Welfare [now Health and Human Services], and of Food and Drug Administration in the Department of Agriculture to Federal Security Agency, see notes set out under section 321 of this title.

APPROVAL OF SUPPLEMENTAL APPLICATIONS FOR APPROVED PRODUCTS

Section 403 of Pub. L. 105–115 provided that:

"(a) STANDARDS.—Not later than 180 days after the date of enactment of this Act [Nov. 21, 1997], the Secretary of Health and Human Services shall publish in the Federal Register standards for the prompt review of supplemental applications submitted for approved articles under the Federal Food, Drug, and Cosmetic Act (21 U.S.C. 301 et seq.) or section 351 of the Public Health Service Act (42 U.S.C. 262).

"(b) GUIDANCE TO INDUSTRY.—Not later than 180 days after the date of enactment of this Act [Nov. 21, 1997], the Secretary shall issue final guidances to clarify the requirements for, and facilitate the submission of data to support, the approval of supplemental applications for the approved articles described in subsection (a). The guidances shall—

"(1) clarify circumstances in which published matter may be the basis for approval of a supplemental application;

"(2) specify data requirements that will avoid duplication of previously submitted data by recognizing the availability of data previously submitted in support of an original application; and

"(3) define supplemental applications that are eligible for priority review.

"(c) RESPONSIBILITIES OF CENTERS.—The Secretary shall designate an individual in each center within the Food and Drug Administration (except the Center for Food Safety and Applied Nutrition) to be responsible for—

"(1) encouraging the prompt review of supplemental applications for approved articles; and

"(2) working with sponsors to facilitate the development and submission of data to support supplemental applications.

"(d) COLLABORATION.—The Secretary shall implement programs and policies that will foster collaboration between the Food and Drug Administration, the National Institutes of Health, professional medical and scientific societies, and other persons, to identify published and unpublished studies that may support a supplemental application, and to encourage sponsors to make supplemental applications or conduct further research in support of a supplemental application based, in whole or in part, on such studies."

HEARINGS PENDING ON APRIL 15, 1954, WITH RESPECT TO FOOD STANDARDS

Provisions of this chapter in effect prior to Apr. 15, 1954, as applicable with respect to hearings begun prior to such date under subsection (e) of this section, regarding food standards, see Savings Provisions note set out under section 341 of this title.

§ 372. Examinations and investigations

(a) Authority to conduct

(1) The Secretary is authorized to conduct examinations and investigations for the purposes of this chapter through officers and employees of the Department or through any health, food, or drug officer or employee of any State, Territory, or political subdivision thereof, duly commissioned by the Secretary as an officer of the Department.

(2)(A) In addition to the authority established in paragraph (1), the Secretary, pursuant to a memorandum of understanding between the Secretary and the head of another Federal department or agency, is authorized to conduct examinations and investigations for the purposes of this chapter through the officers and employees of such other department or agency, subject to subparagraph (B). Such a memorandum shall include provisions to ensure adequate training of such officers and employees to conduct the examinations and investigations. The memorandum of understanding shall contain provisions regarding reimbursement. Such provisions may, at the sole discretion of the head of the other department or agency, require reimbursement, in whole or in part, from the Secretary for the examinations or investigations performed under this section by the officers or employees of the other department or agency.

(B) A memorandum of understanding under subparagraph (A) between the Secretary and another Federal department or agency is effective only in the case of examinations or inspections at facilities or other locations that are jointly regulated by the Secretary and such department or agency.

(C) For any fiscal year in which the Secretary and the head of another Federal department or agency carries out one or more examinations or inspections under a memorandum of understanding under subparagraph (A), the Secretary and the head of such department or agency shall with respect to their respective departments or agencies submit to the committees of jurisdiction (authorizing and appropriating) in the House of Representatives and the Senate a report that provides, for such year—

(i) the number of officers or employees that carried out one or more programs, projects, or activities under such memorandum;

(ii) the number of additional articles that were inspected or examined as a result of such memorandum; and

(iii) the number of additional examinations or investigations that were carried out pursuant to such memorandum.

(3) In the case of food packed in the Commonwealth of Puerto Rico or a Territory the Secretary shall attempt to make inspection of such food at the first point of entry within the United States when, in his opinion and with due regard to the enforcement of all the provisions of this chapter, the facilities at his disposal will permit of such inspection.

(4) For the purposes of this subsection, the term "United States" means the States and the District of Columbia.

(b) Availability to owner of part of analysis samples

Where a sample of a food, drug, or cosmetic is collected for analysis under this chapter the Secretary shall, upon request, provide a part of such official sample for examination or analysis by any person named on the label of the article, or the owner thereof, or his attorney or agent; except that the Secretary is authorized, by regulations, to make such reasonable exceptions from, and impose such reasonable terms and conditions relating to, the operation of this subsection as he finds necessary for the proper administration of the provisions of this chapter.

(c) Records of other departments and agencies

For purposes of enforcement of this chapter, records of any department or independent establishment in the executive branch of the Government shall be open to inspection by any official of the Department duly authorized by the Secretary to make such inspection.

(d) Information on patents for drugs

The Secretary is authorized and directed, upon request from the Under Secretary of Commerce for Intellectual Property and Director of the United States Patent and Trademark Office, to furnish full and complete information with respect to such questions relating to drugs as the Director may submit concerning any patent application. The Secretary is further authorized, upon receipt of any such request, to conduct or cause to be conducted, such research as may be required.

(e) Powers of enforcement personnel

Any officer or employee of the Department designated by the Secretary to conduct examinations, investigations, or inspections under this chapter relating to counterfeit drugs may, when so authorized by the Secretary—

(1) carry firearms;

(2) execute and serve search warrants and arrest warrants;

(3) execute seizure by process issued pursuant to libel under section 334 of this title;

(4) make arrests without warrant for offenses under this chapter with respect to such drugs if the offense is committed in his presence or, in the case of a felony, if he has probable cause to believe that the person so arrested has committed, or is committing, such offense; and

(5) make, prior to the institution of libel proceedings under section 334(a)(2) of this title, seizures of drugs or containers or of equipment, punches, dies, plates, stones, labeling, or other things, if they are, or he has reasonable grounds to believe that they are, subject to seizure and condemnation under such section 334(a)(2). In the event of seizure pursuant to this paragraph (5), libel proceedings under section 334(a)(2) of this title shall be instituted promptly and the property seized be placed under the jurisdiction of the court.

(June 25, 1938, ch. 675, §702, 52 Stat. 1056; Pub. L. 87–781, title III, §§307(b), 308, Oct. 10, 1962, 76 Stat. 796; Pub. L. 89–74, §8(a), July 15, 1965, 79 Stat. 234; Pub. L. 91–513, title II, §701(f), Oct. 27, 1970, 84 Stat. 1282; Pub. L. 102–300, §6(b)(2), June 16, 1992, 106 Stat. 240; Pub. L. 103–80, §3(dd)(2), Aug. 13, 1993, 107 Stat. 779; Pub. L. 106–113, div. B, §1000(a)(9) [title IV, §4732(b)(12)], Nov. 29, 1999, 113 Stat. 1536, 1501A-584; Pub. L. 107–188, title III, §314, June 12, 2002, 116 Stat. 674.)

AMENDMENTS

2002—Subsec. (a). Pub. L. 107–188 inserted "(1)" before "The Secretary is authorized to conduct", added par. (2), inserted "(3)" before "In the case of food packed", and substituted "(4) For the purposes of this subsection," for "For the purposes of this subsection".

1999—Subsec. (d). Pub. L. 106–113, in first sentence, substituted "Under Secretary of Commerce for Intellectual Property and Director of the United States Patent and Trademark Office" for "Commissioner of Patents" and "Director" for "Commissioner".

1993—Subsec. (c). Pub. L. 103–80 struck out "of Agriculture" after "Department".

1992—Subsec. (c). Pub. L. 102–300, which directed the amendment of subsec. (c) by striking out "of Health, Education, and Welfare", could not be executed because such words did not appear in the original statutory text. See 1993 Amendment note above and Transfer of Functions note below.

1970—Subsec. (e). Pub. L. 91–513 struck out reference to depressant or stimulant drugs.

1965—Subsec. (e). Pub. L. 89–74 added subsec. (e).

1962—Subsec. (a). Pub. L. 87–781, §307(b), inserted "the Commonwealth of Puerto Rico or" before "a Territory the Secretary".

Subsec. (d). Pub. L. 87–781, §308, added subsec. (d).

EFFECTIVE DATE OF 1999 AMENDMENT

Amendment by Pub. L. 106–113 effective 4 months after Nov. 29, 1999, see section 1000(a)(9) [title IV, §4731] of Pub. L. 106–113, set out as a note under section 1 of Title 35, Patents.

EFFECTIVE DATE OF 1970 AMENDMENT

Amendment by Pub. L. 91–513 effective on first day of seventh calendar month that begins after Oct. 26, 1970, see section 704 of Pub. L. 91–513, set out as an Effective Date note under section 801 of this title.

EFFECTIVE DATE OF 1965 AMENDMENT

Amendment by Pub. L. 89–74 effective July 15, 1965, see section 11 of Pub. L. 89–74, set out as a note under section 321 of this title.

SAVINGS PROVISION

Amendment by Pub. L. 91–513 not to affect or abate any prosecutions for any violation of law or any civil seizures or forfeitures and injunctive proceedings commenced prior to the effective date of such amendment, and all administrative proceedings pending before the Bureau of Narcotics and Dangerous Drugs [now Drug Enforcement Administration] on Oct. 27, 1970, to be continued and brought to final determination in accord with laws and regulations in effect prior to Oct. 27, 1970, see section 702 of Pub. L. 91–513, set out as a note under section 321 of this title.

TRANSFER OF FUNCTIONS

For transfer of functions of Federal Security Administrator to Secretary of Health, Education, and Welfare [now Health and Human Services], and of Food and Drug Administration in the Department of Agriculture to Federal Security Agency, see note set out under section 41 of this title.

§372a. Transferred

CODIFICATION

Section, act June 25, 1938, ch. 675, §702A, formerly June 30, 1906, ch. 3915, §10A, as added June 22, 1934, ch. 712, 48 Stat. 1204, and amended, which related to examination of sea food, was renumbered section 706 of act June 25, 1938, by Pub. L. 102–571, title I, §106(3), Oct. 29, 1992, 106 Stat. 4498, and transferred to section 376 of this title.

§373. Records

(a) In general

For the purpose of enforcing the provisions of this chapter, carriers engaged in interstate commerce, and persons receiving food, drugs, devices, or cosmetics in interstate commerce or holding such articles so received, shall, upon the request of an officer or employee duly designated by the Secretary, permit such officer or employee, at reasonable times, to have access to and to copy all records showing the movement in interstate commerce of any food, drug, device, or cosmetic, or the holding thereof during or after such movement, and the quantity, shipper, and consignee thereof; and it shall be unlawful for any such carrier or person to fail to permit such access to and copying of any such record so requested when such request is accompanied by a statement in writing specifying the nature or kind of food, drug, device, or cosmetic to which such request relates, except that evidence obtained under this section, or any evidence which is directly or indirectly derived from such evidence, shall not be used in a criminal prosecution of the person from whom obtained, and except that carriers shall not be subject to the other provisions of this chapter by reason of their receipt, carriage, holding, or delivery of food, drugs, devices, or cosmetics in the usual course of business as carriers, except as provided in subsection (b) of this section.

(b) Food transportation records

A shipper, carrier by motor vehicle or rail vehicle, receiver, or other person subject to section 350e of this title shall, on request of an officer or employee designated by the Secretary, permit the officer or employee, at reasonable times, to have access to and to copy all records that the Secretary requires to be kept under section 350e(c)(1)(E) of this title.

(June 25, 1938, ch. 675, §703, 52 Stat. 1057; Pub. L. 91–452, title II, §230, Oct. 15, 1970, 84 Stat. 930; Pub. L. 103–80, §3(z), Aug. 13, 1993, 107 Stat. 778; Pub. L. 109–59, title VII, §7202(c), Aug. 10, 2005, 119 Stat. 1913.)

AMENDMENTS

2005—Pub. L. 109–59 struck out "of interstate shipment" after "Records" in section catchline, designated existing provisions as subsec. (a), inserted subsec. heading, substituted "carriers, except as provided in subsection (b) of this section" for "carriers" before period at end, and added subsec. (b).

1993—Pub. L. 103–80 substituted ", except that" for ": *Provided*, That" and ", and except that" for ": *Provided further*, That".

1970—Pub. L. 91–452 inserted ", or any evidence which is directly or indirectly derived from such evidence," after "under this section".

EFFECTIVE DATE OF 2005 AMENDMENT

Amendment by Pub. L. 109–59 effective Oct. 1, 2005, see section 7204 of Pub. L. 109–59, set out as a note under section 331 of this title.

EFFECTIVE DATE OF 1970 AMENDMENT

Amendment by Pub. L. 91–452 effective on sixtieth day following Oct. 15, 1970, and not to affect any immunity to which any individual is entitled under this section by reason of any testimony given before sixtieth day following Oct. 15, 1970, see section 260 of Pub. L. 91–452, set out as an Effective Date; Savings Provision note under section 6001 of Title 18, Crimes and Criminal Procedure.

TRANSFER OF FUNCTIONS

For transfer of functions of Federal Security Administrator to Secretary of Health, Education, and Welfare [now Health and Human Services], and of Food and Drug Administration in the Department of Agriculture to Federal Security Agency, see notes set out under section 321 of this title.

§374. Inspection

(a) Right of agents to enter; scope of inspection; notice; promptness; exclusions

(1) For purposes of enforcement of this chapter, officers or employees duly designated by the Secretary, upon presenting appropriate credentials and a written notice to the owner, operator, or agent in charge, are authorized (A) to enter, at reasonable times, any factory, warehouse, or establishment in which food, drugs, de-

vices, or cosmetics are manufactured, processed, packed, or held, for introduction into interstate commerce or after such introduction, or to enter any vehicle being used to transport or hold such food, drugs, devices, or cosmetics in interstate commerce; and (B) to inspect, at reasonable times and within reasonable limits and in a reasonable manner, such factory, warehouse, establishment, or vehicle and all pertinent equipment, finished and unfinished materials, containers, and labeling therein. In the case of any person (excluding farms and restaurants) who manufactures, processes, packs, transports, distributes, holds, or imports foods, the inspection shall extend to all records and other information described in section 350c of this title when the Secretary has a reasonable belief that an article of food is adulterated and presents a threat of serious adverse health consequences or death to humans or animals, subject to the limitations established in section 350c(d) of this title. In the case of any factory, warehouse, establishment, or consulting laboratory in which prescription drugs, nonprescription drugs intended for human use, or restricted devices are manufactured, processed, packed, or held, the inspection shall extend to all things therein (including records, files, papers, processes, controls, and facilities) bearing on whether prescription drugs, nonprescription drugs intended for human use, or restricted devices which are adulterated or misbranded within the meaning of this chapter, or which may not be manufactured, introduced into interstate commerce, or sold, or offered for sale by reason of any provision of this chapter, have been or are being manufactured, processed, packed, transported, or held in any such place, or otherwise bearing on violation of this chapter. No inspection authorized by the preceding sentence or by paragraph (3) shall extend to financial data, sales data other than shipment data, pricing data, personnel data (other than data as to qualification of technical and professional personnel performing functions subject to this chapter), and research data (other than data relating to new drugs, antibiotic drugs, and devices and subject to reporting and inspection under regulations lawfully issued pursuant to section 355(i) or (k)[1] section 360i, or 360j(g) of this title, and data relating to other drugs or devices which in the case of a new drug would be subject to reporting or inspection under lawful regulations issued pursuant to section 355(j) of this title). A separate notice shall be given for each such inspection, but a notice shall not be required for each entry made during the period covered by the inspection. Each such inspection shall be commenced and completed with reasonable promptness.

(2) The provisions of the third sentence of paragraph (1) shall not apply to—

(A) pharmacies which maintain establishments in conformance with any applicable local laws regulating the practice of pharmacy and medicine and which are regularly engaged in dispensing prescription drugs or devices, upon prescriptions of practitioners licensed to administer such drugs or devices to patients under the care of such practitioners in the course of their professional practice, and which do not, either through a subsidiary or otherwise, manufacture, prepare, propagate, compound, or process drugs or devices for sale other than in the regular course of their business of dispensing or selling drugs or devices at retail;

(B) practitioners licensed by law to prescribe or administer drugs, or prescribe or use devices, as the case may be, and who manufacture, prepare, propagate, compound, or process drugs, or manufacture or process devices, solely for use in the course of their professional practice;

(C) persons who manufacture, prepare, propagate, compound, or process drugs or manufacture or process devices, solely for use in research, teaching, or chemical analysis and not for sale;

(D) such other classes of persons as the Secretary may by regulation exempt from the application of this section upon a finding that inspection as applied to such classes of persons in accordance with this section is not necessary for the protection of the public health.

(3) An officer or employee making an inspection under paragraph (1) for purposes of enforcing the requirements of section 350a of this title applicable to infant formulas shall be permitted, at all reasonable times, to have access to and to copy and verify any records—

(A) bearing on whether the infant formula manufactured or held in the facility inspected meets the requirements of section 350a of this title, or

(B) required to be maintained under section 350a of this title.

(b) Written report to owner; copy to Secretary

Upon completion of any such inspection of a factory, warehouse, consulting laboratory, or other establishment, and prior to leaving the premises, the officer or employee making the inspection shall give to the owner, operator, or agent in charge a report in writing setting forth any conditions or practices observed by him which, in his judgment, indicate that any food, drug, device, or cosmetic in such establishment (1) consists in whole or in part of any filthy, putrid, or decomposed substance, or (2) has been prepared, packed, or held under insanitary conditions whereby it may have become contaminated with filth, or whereby it may have been rendered injurious to health. A copy of such report shall be sent promptly to the Secretary.

(c) Receipt for samples taken

If the officer or employee making any such inspection of a factory, warehouse, or other establishment has obtained any sample in the course of the inspection, upon completion of the inspection and prior to leaving the premises he shall give to the owner, operator, or agent in charge a receipt describing the samples obtained.

(d) Analysis of samples furnished owner

Whenever in the course of any such inspection of a factory or other establishment where food is manufactured, processed, or packed, the officer or employee making the inspection obtains a sample of any such food, and an analysis is made of such sample for the purpose of ascertaining

[1] So in original. Probably should be followed by a comma.

whether such food consists in whole or in part of any filthy, putrid, or decomposed substance, or is otherwise unfit for food, a copy of the results of such analysis shall be furnished promptly to the owner, operator, or agent in charge.

(e) Accessibility of records

Every person required under section 360i or 360j(g) of this title to maintain records and every person who is in charge or custody of such records shall, upon request of an officer or employee designated by the Secretary, permit such officer or employee at all reasonable times to have access to, and to copy and verify, such records.

(f) Recordkeeping

(1) An accredited person described in paragraph (3) shall maintain records documenting the training qualifications of the person and the employees of the person, the procedures used by the person for handling confidential information, the compensation arrangements made by the person, and the procedures used by the person to identify and avoid conflicts of interest. Upon the request of an officer or employee designated by the Secretary, the person shall permit the officer or employee, at all reasonable times, to have access to, to copy, and to verify, the records.

(2) Within 15 days after the receipt of a written request from the Secretary to an accredited person described in paragraph (3) for copies of records described in paragraph (1), the person shall produce the copies of the records at the place designated by the Secretary.

(3) For purposes of paragraphs (1) and (2), an accredited person described in this paragraph is a person who—

(A) is accredited under subsection (g) of this section; or

(B) is accredited under section 360m of this title.

(g) Inspections by accredited persons

(1) The Secretary shall, subject to the provisions of this subsection, accredit persons for the purpose of conducting inspections of establishments that manufacture, prepare, propagate, compound, or process class II or class III devices, which inspections are required under section 360(h) of this title or are inspections of such establishments required to register under section 360(i) of this title. The owner or operator of such an establishment that is eligible under paragraph (6) may, from the list published under paragraph (4), select an accredited person to conduct such inspections.

(2) The Secretary shall publish in the Federal Register criteria to accredit or deny accreditation to persons who request to perform the duties specified in paragraph (1). Thereafter, the Secretary shall inform those requesting accreditation, within 60 days after the receipt of such request, whether the request for accreditation is adequate for review, and the Secretary shall promptly act on the request for accreditation. Any resulting accreditation shall state that such person is accredited to conduct inspections at device establishments identified in paragraph (1). The accreditation of such person shall specify the particular activities under this subsection for which such person is accredited.

(3) An accredited person shall, at a minimum, meet the following requirements:

(A) Such person may not be an employee of the Federal Government.

(B) Such person shall be an independent organization which is not owned or controlled by a manufacturer, supplier, or vendor of articles regulated under this chapter and which has no organizational, material, or financial affiliation (including a consultative affiliation) with such a manufacturer, supplier, or vendor.

(C) Such person shall be a legally constituted entity permitted to conduct the activities for which it seeks accreditation.

(D) Such person shall not engage in the design, manufacture, promotion, or sale of articles regulated under this chapter.

(E) The operations of such person shall be in accordance with generally accepted professional and ethical business practices, and such person shall agree in writing that at a minimum the person will—

(i) certify that reported information accurately reflects data reviewed, inspection observations made, other matters that relate to or may influence compliance with this chapter, and recommendations made during an inspection or at an inspection's closing meeting;

(ii) limit work to that for which competence and capacity are available;

(iii) treat information received, records, reports, and recommendations as confidential commercial or financial information or trade secret information, except such information may be made available to the Secretary;

(iv) promptly respond and attempt to resolve complaints regarding its activities for which it is accredited; and

(v) protect against the use, in carrying out paragraph (1), of any officer or employee of the accredited person who has a financial conflict of interest regarding any product regulated under this chapter, and annually make available to the public disclosures of the extent to which the accredited person, and the officers and employees of the person, have maintained compliance with requirements under this clause relating to financial conflicts of interest.

(F) Such person shall notify the Secretary of any withdrawal, suspension, restriction, or expiration of certificate of conformance with the quality systems standard referred to in paragraph (7) for any device establishment that such person inspects under this subsection not later than 30 days after such withdrawal, suspension, restriction, or expiration.

(G) Such person may conduct audits to establish conformance with the quality systems standard referred to in paragraph (7).

(4) The Secretary shall publish on the Internet site of the Food and Drug Administration a list of persons who are accredited under paragraph (2). Such list shall be updated to ensure that the identity of each accredited person, and the particular activities for which the person is accredited, is known to the public. The updating of such list shall be no later than one month after

the accreditation of a person under this subsection or the suspension or withdrawal of accreditation, or the modification of the particular activities for which the person is accredited.

(5)(A) To ensure that persons accredited under this subsection continue to meet the standards of accreditation, the Secretary shall (i) audit the performance of such persons on a periodic basis through the review of inspection reports and inspections by persons designated by the Secretary to evaluate the compliance status of a device establishment and the performance of accredited persons, and (ii) take such additional measures as the Secretary determines to be appropriate.

(B) The Secretary may withdraw accreditation of any person accredited under paragraph (2), after providing notice and an opportunity for an informal hearing, when such person is substantially not in compliance with the standards of accreditation, poses a threat to public health, fails to act in a manner that is consistent with the purposes of this subsection, or where the Secretary determines that there is a financial conflict of interest in the relationship between the accredited person and the owner or operator of a device establishment that the accredited person has inspected under this subsection. The Secretary may suspend the accreditation of such person during the pendency of the process under the preceding sentence.

(6)(A) Subject to subparagraphs (B) and (C), a device establishment is eligible for inspection by persons accredited under paragraph (2) if the following conditions are met:

(i) The Secretary classified the results of the most recent inspection of the establishment as "no action indicated" or "voluntary action indicated".

(ii) With respect to inspections of the establishment to be conducted by an accredited person, the owner or operator of the establishment submits to the Secretary a notice that—

(I) provides the date of the last inspection of the establishment by the Secretary and the classification of that inspection;

(II) states the intention of the owner or operator to use an accredited person to conduct inspections of the establishment;

(III) identifies the particular accredited person the owner or operator intends to select to conduct such inspections; and

(IV) includes a certification that, with respect to the devices that are manufactured, prepared, propagated, compounded, or processed in the establishment—

(aa) at least 1 of such devices is marketed in the United States; and

(bb) at least 1 of such devices is marketed, or is intended to be marketed, in 1 or more foreign countries, 1 of which countries certifies, accredits, or otherwise recognizes the person accredited under paragraph (2) and identified under subclause (III) as a person authorized to conduct inspections of device establishments.

(B)(i) Except with respect to the requirement of subparagraph (A)(i), a device establishment is deemed to have clearance to participate in the program and to use the accredited person identified in the notice under subparagraph (A)(ii) for inspections of the establishment unless the Secretary, not later than 30 days after receiving such notice, issues a response that—

(I) denies clearance to participate as provided under subparagraph (C); or

(II) makes a request under clause (ii).

(ii) The Secretary may request from the owner or operator of a device establishment in response to the notice under subparagraph (A)(ii) with respect to the establishment, or from the particular accredited person identified in such notice—

(I) compliance data for the establishment in accordance with clause (iii)(I); or

(II) information concerning the relationship between the owner or operator of the establishment and the accredited person identified in such notice in accordance with clause (iii)(II).

The owner or operator of the establishment, or such accredited person, as the case may be, shall respond to such a request not later than 60 days after receiving such request.

(iii)(I) The compliance data to be submitted by the owner or operator of a device establishment in response to a request under clause (ii)(I) are data describing whether the quality controls of the establishment have been sufficient for ensuring consistent compliance with current good manufacturing practice within the meaning of section 351(h) of this title and with other applicable provisions of this chapter. Such data shall include complete reports of inspectional findings regarding good manufacturing practice or other quality control audits that, during the preceding 2-year period, were conducted at the establishment by persons other than the owner or operator of the establishment, together with all other compliance data the Secretary deems necessary. Data under the preceding sentence shall demonstrate to the Secretary whether the establishment has facilitated consistent compliance by promptly correcting any compliance problems identified in such inspections.

(II) A request to an accredited person under clause (ii)(II) may not seek any information that is not required to be maintained by such person in records under subsection (f)(1).

(iv) A device establishment is deemed to have clearance to participate in the program and to use the accredited person identified in the notice under subparagraph (A)(ii) for inspections of the establishment unless the Secretary, not later than 60 days after receiving the information requested under clause (ii), issues a response that denies clearance to participate as provided under subparagraph (C).

(C)(i) The Secretary may deny clearance to a device establishment if the Secretary has evidence that the certification under subparagraph (A)(ii)(IV) is untrue and the Secretary provides to the owner or operator of the establishment a statement summarizing such evidence.

(ii) The Secretary may deny clearance to a device establishment if the Secretary determines that the establishment has failed to demonstrate consistent compliance for purposes of subparagraph (B)(iii)(I) and the Secretary provides to the owner or operator of the establishment a statement of the reasons for such determination.

(iii)(I) The Secretary may reject the selection of the accredited person identified in the notice under subparagraph (A)(ii) if the Secretary provides to the owner or operator of the establishment a statement of the reasons for such rejection. Reasons for the rejection may include that the establishment or the accredited person, as the case may be, has failed to fully respond to the request, or that the Secretary has concerns regarding the relationship between the establishment and such accredited person.

(II) If the Secretary rejects the selection of an accredited person by the owner or operator of a device establishment, the owner or operator may make an additional selection of an accredited person by submitting to the Secretary a notice that identifies the additional selection. Clauses (i) and (ii) of subparagraph (B), and subclause (I) of this clause, apply to the selection of an accredited person through a notice under the preceding sentence in the same manner and to the same extent as such provisions apply to a selection of an accredited person through a notice under subparagraph (A)(ii).

(iv) In the case of a device establishment that is denied clearance under clause (i) or (ii) or with respect to which the selection of the accredited person is rejected under clause (iii), the Secretary shall designate a person to review the statement of reasons, or statement summarizing such evidence, as the case may be, of the Secretary under such clause if, during the 30-day period beginning on the date on which the owner or operator of the establishment receives such statement, the owner or operator requests the review. The review shall commence not later than 30 days after the owner or operator requests the review, unless the Secretary and the owner or operator otherwise agree.

(7)(A) Persons accredited under paragraph (2) to conduct inspections shall record in writing their inspection observations and shall present the observations to the device establishment's designated representative and describe each observation. Additionally, such accredited person shall prepare an inspection report in a form and manner designated by the Secretary to conduct inspections, taking into consideration the goals of international harmonization of quality systems standards. Any official classification of the inspection shall be determined by the Secretary.

(B) At a minimum, an inspection report under subparagraph (A) shall identify the persons responsible for good manufacturing practice compliance at the inspected device establishment, the dates of the inspection, the scope of the inspection, and shall describe in detail each observation identified by the accredited person, identify other matters that relate to or may influence compliance with this chapter, and describe any recommendations during the inspection or at the inspection's closing meeting.

(C) An inspection report under subparagraph (A) shall be sent to the Secretary and to the designated representative of the inspected device establishment at the same time, but under no circumstances later than three weeks after the last day of the inspection. The report to the Secretary shall be accompanied by all written inspection observations previously provided to the designated representative of the establishment.

(D) Any statement or representation made by an employee or agent of a device establishment to a person accredited under paragraph (2) to conduct inspections shall be subject to section 1001 of title 18.

(E) If at any time during an inspection by an accredited person the accredited person discovers a condition that could cause or contribute to an unreasonable risk to the public health, the accredited person shall immediately notify the Secretary of the identification of the device establishment subject to inspection and such condition.

(F) For the purpose of setting risk-based inspectional priorities, the Secretary shall accept voluntary submissions of reports of audits assessing conformance with appropriate quality systems standards set by the International Organization for Standardization (ISO) and identified by the Secretary in public notice. If the owner or operator of an establishment elects to submit audit reports under this subparagraph, the owner or operator shall submit all such audit reports with respect to the establishment during the preceding 2-year periods.

(8) Compensation for an accredited person shall be determined by agreement between the accredited person and the person who engages the services of the accredited person, and shall be paid by the person who engages such services.

(9) Nothing in this subsection affects the authority of the Secretary to inspect any device establishment pursuant to this chapter.

(10)(A) For fiscal year 2005 and each subsequent fiscal year, no device establishment may be inspected during the fiscal year involved by a person accredited under paragraph (2) if—

(i) of the amounts appropriated for salaries and expenses of the Food and Drug Administration for the preceding fiscal year (referred to in this subparagraph as the "first prior fiscal year"), the amount obligated by the Secretary for inspections of device establishments by the Secretary was less than the adjusted base amount applicable to such first prior fiscal year; and

(ii) of the amounts appropriated for salaries and expenses of the Food and Drug Administration for the fiscal year preceding the first prior fiscal year (referred to in this subparagraph as the "second prior fiscal year"), the amount obligated by the Secretary for inspections of device establishments by the Secretary was less than the adjusted base amount applicable to such second prior fiscal year.

(B)(i) Subject to clause (ii), the Comptroller General of the United States shall determine the amount that was obligated by the Secretary for fiscal year 2002 for compliance activities of the Food and Drug Administration with respect to devices (referred to in this subparagraph as the "compliance budget"), and of such amount, the amount that was obligated for inspections by the Secretary of device establishments (referred to in this subparagraph as the "inspection budget").

(ii) For purposes of determinations under clause (i), the Comptroller General shall not include in the compliance budget or the inspection budget any amounts obligated for inspections of device establishments conducted as part of the process of reviewing applications under section 360e of this title.

(iii) Not later than March 31, 2003, the Comptroller General shall complete the determinations required in this subparagraph and submit to the Secretary and the Congress a report describing the findings made through such determinations.

(C) For purposes of this paragraph:

(i) The term "base amount" means the inspection budget determined under subparagraph (B) for fiscal year 2002.

(ii) The term "adjusted base amount", in the case of applicability to fiscal year 2003, means an amount equal to the base amount increased by 5 percent.

(iii) The term "adjusted base amount", with respect to applicability to fiscal year 2004 or any subsequent fiscal year, means the adjusted base amount applicable to the preceding year increased by 5 percent.

(11) The authority provided by this subsection terminates on October 1, 2012.

(12) No later than four years after October 26, 2002, the Comptroller General shall report to the Committee on Energy and Commerce of the House of Representatives and the Committee on Health, Education, Labor and Pensions of the Senate—

(A) the number of inspections conducted by accredited persons pursuant to this subsection and the number of inspections conducted by Federal employees pursuant to section 360(h) of this title and of device establishments required to register under section 360(i) of this title;

(B) the number of persons who sought accreditation under this subsection, as well as the number of persons who were accredited under this subsection;

(C) the reasons why persons who sought accreditation, but were denied accreditation, were denied;

(D) the number of audits conducted by the Secretary of accredited persons, the quality of inspections conducted by accredited persons, whether accredited persons are meeting their obligations under this chapter, and whether the number of audits conducted is sufficient to permit these assessments;

(E) whether this subsection is achieving the goal of ensuring more information about device establishment compliance is being presented to the Secretary, and whether that information is of a quality consistent with information obtained by the Secretary pursuant to inspections conducted by Federal employees;

(F) whether this subsection is advancing efforts to allow device establishments to rely upon third-party inspections for purposes of compliance with the laws of foreign governments; and

(G) whether the Congress should continue, modify, or terminate the program under this subsection.

(13) The Secretary shall include in the annual report required under section 393(g) of this title the names of all accredited persons and the particular activities under this subsection for which each such person is accredited and the name of each accredited person whose accreditation has been withdrawn during the year.

(14) Notwithstanding any provision of this subsection, this subsection does not have any legal effect on any agreement described in section 383(b) of this title between the Secretary and a foreign country.

(June 25, 1938, ch. 675, § 704, 52 Stat. 1057; Aug. 7, 1953, ch. 350, § 1, 67 Stat. 476; Pub. L. 87–781, title II, § 201(a), (b), Oct. 10, 1962, 76 Stat. 792, 793; Pub. L. 94–295, § 6, May 28, 1976, 90 Stat. 581; Pub. L. 96–359, § 4, Sept. 26, 1980, 94 Stat. 1193; Pub. L. 103–80, § 3(aa), Aug. 13, 1993, 107 Stat. 778; Pub. L. 105–115, title I, § 125(b)(2)(L), title II, § 210(b), title IV, § 412(b), Nov. 21, 1997, 111 Stat. 2326, 2344, 2375; Pub. L. 107–188, title III, § 306(b), June 12, 2002, 116 Stat. 670; Pub. L. 107–250, title II, § 201(a), (b), Oct. 26, 2002, 116 Stat. 1602, 1609; Pub. L. 108–214, § 2(b)(1), Apr. 1, 2004, 118 Stat. 573; Pub. L. 110–85, title II, § 228, Sept. 27, 2007, 121 Stat. 855.)

AMENDMENTS

2007—Subsec. (g)(1). Pub. L. 110–85, § 228(1), substituted "The Secretary" for "Not later than one year after October 26, 2002, the Secretary".

Subsec. (g)(2). Pub. L. 110–85, § 228(2), substituted "The Secretary" for "Not later than 180 days after October 26, 2002, the Secretary" and struck out at end "In the first year following the publication in the Federal Register of criteria to accredit or deny accreditation to persons who request to perform the duties specified in paragraph (1), the Secretary shall accredit no more than 15 persons who request to perform duties specified in paragraph (1)."

Subsec. (g)(3)(F), (G). Pub. L. 110–85, § 228(3), added subpars. (F) and (G).

Subsec. (g)(6). Pub. L. 110–85, § 228(4), amended par. (6) generally, revising and restating provisions of former subpars. (A) to (C).

Subsec. (g)(7)(A). Pub. L. 110–85, § 228(5)(A), added subpar. (A) and struck out former subpar. (A) which read as follows: "Persons accredited under paragraph (2) to conduct inspections shall record in writing their inspection observations and shall present the observations to the device establishment's designated representative and describe each observation. Additionally, such accredited person shall prepare an inspection report (including for inspections classified as 'no action indicated') in a form and manner consistent with such reports prepared by employees and officials designated by the Secretary to conduct inspections."

Subsec. (g)(7)(F). Pub. L. 110–85, § 228(5)(B), added subpar. (F).

Subsec. (g)(10)(C)(iii). Pub. L. 110–85, § 228(6), substituted "base amount applicable" for "based amount applicable".

2004—Subsec. (g)(1). Pub. L. 108–214, § 2(b)(1)(A), in first sentence, substituted "conducting inspections of establishments that manufacture, prepare, propagate, compound, or process class II or class III devices, which inspections are required under section 360(h) of this title or are inspections of such establishments required to register under section 360(i) of this title." for "conducting inspections of establishments that manufacture, prepare, propagate, compound, or process class II or class III devices that are required in section 360(h) of this title, or inspections of such establishments required to register pursuant to section 360(i) of this title."

Subsec. (g)(5)(B). Pub. L. 108–214, § 2(b)(1)(B), in first sentence, substituted "poses a threat to public health, fails to act in a manner that is consistent with the purposes of this subsection, or where the Secretary determines that there is a financial conflict of interest in the relationship between the accredited person and the owner or operator of a device establishment that the accredited person has inspected under this subsection."

for "or poses a threat to public health or fails to act in a manner that is consistent with the purposes of this subsection."

Subsec. (g)(6)(A)(i). Pub. L. 108–214, §2(b)(1)(C)(i), substituted "described in paragraph (1)" for "of the establishment pursuant to subsection (h) or (i) of section 360 of this title".

Subsec. (g)(6)(A)(ii). Pub. L. 108–214, §2(b)(1)(C)(ii)(I), substituted "inspections" for "each inspection" and inserted "during a 2-year period" after "person" in introductory provisions.

Subsec. (g)(6)(A)(ii)(I). Pub. L. 108–214, §2(b)(1)(C)(ii)(II), substituted "an accredited person" for "such a person".

Subsec. (g)(6)(A)(iii). Pub. L. 108–214, §2(b)(1)(C)(iii)(I), substituted "and 1 or both of the following additional conditions are met:" for "and the following additional conditions are met:" in introductory provisions.

Subsec. (g)(6)(A)(iii)(I). Pub. L. 108–214, §2(b)(1)(C)(iii)(II), substituted "(accredited under paragraph (2) and identified under clause (ii)(II)) as a person authorized to conduct such inspections of device establishments." for "accredited under paragraph (2) and identified under subclause (II) of this clause."

Subsec. (g)(6)(A)(iii)(II). Pub. L. 108–214, §2(b)(1)(C)(iii)(III), inserted "or by a person accredited under paragraph (2)" after "by the Secretary".

Subsec. (g)(6)(A)(iv)(I). Pub. L. 108–214, §2(b)(1)(C)(iv), in first sentence, inserted "section" after "pursuant to" and substituted "inspections of the establishment during the previous 4 years" for "the two immediately preceding inspections of the establishment", in third sentence, struck out "the petition states a commercial reason for the waiver;" after "granted only if" and inserted "not" after "the Secretary has not determined that the public health would", and, in last sentence, substituted "granted or deemed to be granted until" for "granted until".

Subsec. (g)(6)(A)(iv)(II). Pub. L. 108–214, §2(b)(1)(C)(v), inserted "of a device establishment required to register" after "to be conducted" and "section" after "pursuant to".

Subsec. (g)(6)(B)(iii). Pub. L. 108–214, §2(b)(1)(D), in first sentence, substituted "and with other" for ", and data otherwise describing whether the establishment has consistently been in compliance with sections 351 and 352 of this title and other" and, in second sentence, substituted "inspectional findings" for "inspections" and inserted "relevant" after "together with all other".

Subsec. (g)(6)(B)(iv). Pub. L. 108–214, §2(b)(1)(E), designated existing provisions as subcl. (I) and added subcl. (II).

Subsec. (g)(6)(C)(ii). Pub. L. 108–214, §2(b)(1)(F), struck out "in accordance with section 360(h) of this title, or has not during such period been inspected pursuant to section 360(i) of this title, as applicable" after "inspected by the Secretary".

Subsec. (g)(10)(B)(iii). Pub. L. 108–214, §2(b)(1)(G), substituted "a report" for "a reporting".

Subsec. (g)(12)(A). Pub. L. 108–214, §2(b)(1)(H)(i), added subpar. (A) and struck out former subpar. (A) which read as follows: "the number of inspections pursuant to subsections (h) and (i) of section 360 of this title conducted by accredited persons and the number of inspections pursuant to such subsections conducted by Federal employees;".

Subsec. (g)(12)(E). Pub. L. 108–214, §2(b)(1)(H)(ii), substituted "obtained by the Secretary pursuant to inspections conducted by Federal employees;" for "obtained by the Secretary pursuant to subsection (h) or (i) of section 360 of this title;".

2002—Subsec. (a)(1). Pub. L. 107–188, §306(b)(1), inserted after first sentence "In the case of any person (excluding farms and restaurants) who manufactures, processes, packs, transports, distributes, holds, or imports foods, the inspection shall extend to all records and other information described in section 350c of this title when the Secretary has a reasonable belief that an article of food is adulterated and presents a threat of serious adverse health consequences or death to humans or animals, subject to the limitations established in section 350c(d) of this title."

Subsec. (a)(2). Pub. L. 107–188, §306(b)(2), substituted "third sentence" for "second sentence" in introductory provisions.

Subsec. (f)(1). Pub. L. 107–250, §201(b)(1), in first sentence, substituted "An accredited person described in paragraph (3) shall maintain records" for "A person accredited under section 360m of this title to review reports made under section 360(k) of this title and make recommendations of initial classifications of devices to the Secretary shall maintain records".

Subsec. (f)(2). Pub. L. 107–250, §201(b)(2), substituted "an accredited person described in paragraph (3)" for "a person accredited under section 360m of this title".

Subsec. (f)(3). Pub. L. 107–250, §201(b)(3), added par. (3).

Subsec. (g). Pub. L. 107–250, §201(a), added subsec. (g).

1997—Subsec. (a)(1). Pub. L. 105–115, §412(b), substituted "prescription drugs, nonprescription drugs intended for human use," for "prescription drugs" in two places.

Pub. L. 105–115, §125(b)(2)(L), struck out ", section 357(d) or (g)," before "section 360i".

Subsec. (f). Pub. L. 105–115, §210(b), added subsec. (f).

1993—Subsec. (a)(1). Pub. L. 103–80 substituted a comma for semicolon after "finished and unfinished materials" and "section 355(i) or (k)" for "section 355(i) or (j)".

1980—Subsec. (a)(1). Pub. L. 96–359, §4(1), (2), restructured first five sentences of former subsec. (a) as par. (1) and, as so restructured, inserted reference to paragraph (3) and substituted "(A)" and "(B)" for "(1)" and "(2)", respectively.

Subsec. (a)(2). Pub. L. 96–359, §4(3), redesignated sixth sentence of former subsec. (a) as par. (2) and, as so redesignated, substituted reference to second sentence of paragraph (1) for reference to former second sentence of this subsection, and "(A)", "(B)", "(C)", and "(D)", for "(1)", "(2)", "(3)", and "(4)", respectively.

Subsec. (a)(3). Pub. L. 96–359, §4(4), added par. (3).

1976—Subsec. (a). Pub. L. 94–295, §6(a)–(c), expanded existing provisions to encompass medical devices by inserting references to factories, warehouses, establishments, and consulting laboratories in which restricted devices are manufactured, processed, packed, or held, inspections relating to devices, reporting and inspection regulations issued pursuant to sections 360i and 360j(g) of this title, and the manufacture and processing of devices.

Subsec. (e). Pub. L. 94–295, §6(d), added subsec. (e).

1962—Subsec. (a). Pub. L. 87–781, §201(a), extended the inspection, where prescription drugs are manufactured, processed, packed, or held, to all things bearing on whether adulterated or misbranded drugs, or any which may not be manufactured, introduced in interstate commerce, or sold or offered for sale under any provision of this chapter, have been or are being manufactured, processed, packed, transported or held in any such place, or otherwise bearing on violation of this chapter, but excluded from such inspection, data concerning finance, sales other than shipment, pricing, personnel other than qualifications of technical and professional personnel, research other than relating to new drugs subject to reporting, provided that provisions of second sentence of this subsection shall be inapplicable to pharmacies, practitioners and other persons enumerated in pars. (1) to (4), and struck out "are held" before "after such introduction".

Subsec. (b). Pub. L. 87–781, §201(b), inserted "consulting laboratory" after "warehouse".

1953—Act Aug. 7, 1953, designated existing provisions as subsec. (a) and amended them by substituting provisions permitting entry and inspection upon presentation of appropriate credentials and a written notice to the owner, operator, or agent in charge for provisions which authorized entry and inspection only after making a request and obtaining permission from the owner, operator, or custodian, and inserting provisions requiring a separate written notice for each inspection but not for each entry made during the period covered by the inspection, and directing that the inspection shall be conducted within reasonable limits, in a reasonable manner and completed with reasonable promptness, and added subsecs. (b) to (d).

EFFECTIVE DATE OF 1997 AMENDMENT

Amendment by sections 210(b) and 412(b) of Pub. L. 105–115 effective 90 days after Nov. 21, 1997, except as otherwise provided, see section 501 of Pub. L. 105–115, set out as a note under section 321 of this title.

EFFECTIVE DATE OF 1962 AMENDMENT

Amendment by Pub. L. 87–781 effective Oct. 10, 1962, see section 203 of Pub. L. 87–781, set out as a note under section 332 of this title.

TRANSFER OF FUNCTIONS

For transfer of functions of Federal Security Administrator to Secretary of Health, Education, and Welfare [now Health and Human Services], and of Food and Drug Administration in the Department of Agriculture to Federal Security Agency, see notes set out under section 321 of this title.

AUTHORITY OF SECRETARY PRIOR TO OCTOBER 10, 1962

Section 201(d) of Pub. L. 87–781 provided that: "Nothing in the amendments made by subsections (a) and (b) of this section [amending this section] shall be construed to negate or derogate from any authority of the Secretary existing prior to the enactment of this Act [Oct. 10, 1962]."

§ 374a. Inspections relating to food allergens

The Secretary of Health and Human Services shall conduct inspections consistent with the authority under section 374 of this title of facilities in which foods are manufactured, processed, packed, or held—

(1) to ensure that the entities operating the facilities comply with practices to reduce or eliminate cross-contact of a food with residues of major food allergens that are not intentional ingredients of the food; and

(2) to ensure that major food allergens are properly labeled on foods.

(Pub. L. 108–282, title II, § 205, Aug. 2, 2004, 118 Stat. 909.)

CODIFICATION

Section was enacted as a part of the Food Allergen Labeling and Consumer Protection Act of 2004, and not as part of the Federal Food, Drug, and Cosmetic Act which comprises this chapter.

§ 375. Publicity

(a) Reports

The Secretary shall cause to be published from time to time reports summarizing all judgments, decrees, and court orders which have been rendered under this chapter, including the nature of the charge and the disposition thereof.

(b) Information regarding certain goods

The Secretary may also cause to be disseminated information regarding food, drugs, devices, or cosmetics in situations involving, in the opinion of the Secretary, imminent danger to health or gross deception of the consumer. Nothing in this section shall be construed to prohibit the Secretary from collecting, reporting, and illustrating the results of the investigations of the Department.

(June 25, 1938, ch. 675, § 705, 52 Stat. 1057.)

TRANSFER OF FUNCTIONS

For transfer of functions of Federal Security Administrator to Secretary of Health, Education, and Welfare [now Health and Human Services], and of Food and Drug Administration in the Department of Agriculture to Federal Security Agency, see notes set out under section 321 of this title.

§ 376. Examination of sea food on request of packer; marking food with results; fees; penalties

The Secretary, upon application of any packer of any sea food for shipment or sale within the jurisdiction of this chapter, may, at his discretion, designate inspectors to examine and inspect such food and the production, packing, and labeling thereof. If on such examination and inspection compliance is found with the provisions of this chapter and regulations promulgated thereunder, the applicant shall be authorized or required to mark the food as provided by regulation to show such compliance. Services under this section shall be rendered only upon payment by the applicant of fees fixed by regulation in such amounts as may be necessary to provide, equip, and maintain an adequate and efficient inspection service. Receipts from such fees shall be covered into the Treasury and shall be available to the Secretary for expenditures incurred in carrying out the purposes of this section, including expenditures for salaries of additional inspectors when necessary to supplement the number of inspectors for whose salaries Congress has appropriated. The Secretary is authorized to promulgate regulations governing the sanitary and other conditions under which the service herein provided shall be granted and maintained, and for otherwise carrying out the purposes of this section. Any person who forges, counterfeits, simulates, or falsely represents, or without proper authority uses any mark, stamp, tag, label, or other identification devices authorized or required by the provisions of this section or regulations thereunder, shall be guilty of a misdemeanor, and shall on conviction thereof be subject to imprisonment for not more than one year or a fine of not less than $1,000 nor more than $5,000, or both such imprisonment and fine.

(June 25, 1938, ch. 675, § 706, formerly § 702A, formerly June 30, 1906, ch. 3915, § 10A, as added June 22, 1934, ch. 712, 48 Stat. 1204; amended Aug. 27, 1935, ch. 739, 49 Stat. 871; June 25, 1938, ch. 675, § 902(a), 52 Stat. 1059; renumbered § 702A of act June 25, 1938, July 12, 1943, ch. 221, title II, 57 Stat. 500; Pub. L. 102–300, § 6(b)(2), June 16, 1992, 106 Stat. 240; renumbered § 706, Pub. L. 102–571, title I, § 106(3), Oct. 29, 1992, 106 Stat. 4498; Pub. L. 103–80, § 3(dd)(2), Aug. 13, 1993, 107 Stat. 779.)

CODIFICATION

Section was formerly classified to section 372a of this title prior to renumbering by Pub. L. 102–571.

Section, which formerly was not a part of the Federal Food, Drug, and Cosmetic Act, originally was classified to section 14a of this title. Section 902(a) of act June 25, 1938, set out as an Effective Date note under section 301 of this title, provided that the section should remain in force and effect and be applicable to the provisions of this chapter. Act July 12, 1943, renumbered this section as 702A of the Federal Food, Drug, and Cosmetic Act.

PRIOR PROVISIONS

A prior section 376, act June 25, 1938, ch. 675, §706, 52 Stat. 1058, as amended, which related to listing and certification of color additives for foods, drugs, devices, and cosmetics, was renumbered section 721 of act June 25, 1938, by Pub. L. 102–571, title I, §106(4), Oct. 29, 1992, 106 Stat. 4498, and transferred to section 379e of this title.

AMENDMENTS

1993—Pub. L. 103–80 struck out "of Agriculture" after "Secretary" in two places.

1992—Pub. L. 102–300, which directed the amendment of the section by striking out "of Health, Education, and Welfare" wherever appearing, could not be executed because such words did not appear in the original statutory text. See 1993 Amendment note above and Transfer of Functions note below.

TRANSFER OF FUNCTIONS

Secretary and Department of Health, Education, and Welfare redesignated Secretary and Department of Health and Human Services by Pub. L. 96–88, title V, §509(b), Oct. 17, 1979, 93 Stat. 695, which is classified to section 3508(b) of Title 20, Education.

For transfer of functions of Federal Security Administrator to Secretary of Health, Education, and Welfare [now Health and Human Services], and of Food and Drug Administration in the Department of Agriculture to Federal Security Agency, see notes set out under section 321 of this title.

§377. Revision of United States Pharmacopoeia; development of analysis and mechanical and physical tests

The Secretary, in carrying into effect the provisions of this chapter, is authorized on and after July 12, 1943, to cooperate with associations and scientific societies in the revision of the United States Pharmacopoeia and in the development of methods of analysis and mechanical and physical tests necessary to carry out the work of the Food and Drug Administration.

(July 12, 1943, ch. 221, title II, 57 Stat. 500; 1953 Reorg. Plan No. 1, §5, eff. Apr. 11, 1953, 18 F.R. 2053, 67 Stat. 631.)

CODIFICATION

Section was enacted as part of the Labor-Federal Security Appropriation Act, 1944, and not as part of the Federal Food, Drug, and Cosmetic Act which comprises this chapter.

TRANSFER OF FUNCTIONS

For transfer of functions of Federal Security Administrator to Secretary of Health, Education, and Welfare [now Health and Human Services], and of Food and Drug Administration in the Department of Agriculture to Federal Security Agency, see notes set out under section 321 of this title.

§378. Advertising of foods

(a) Determination of misbranding; notification of Federal Trade Commission by Secretary; contents

(1) Except as provided in subsection (c) of this section, before the Secretary may initiate any action under subchapter III of this chapter—

(A) with respect to any food which the Secretary determines is misbranded under section 343(a)(2) of this title because of its advertising, or

(B) with respect to a food's advertising which the Secretary determines causes the food to be so misbranded,

the Secretary shall, in accordance with paragraph (2), notify in writing the Federal Trade Commission of the action the Secretary proposes to take respecting such food or advertising.

(2) The notice required by paragraph (1) shall—

(A) contain (i) a description of the action the Secretary proposes to take and of the advertising which the Secretary has determined causes a food to be misbranded, (ii) a statement of the reasons for the Secretary's determination that such advertising has caused such food to be misbranded, and

(B) be accompanied by the records, documents, and other written materials which the Secretary determines supports his determination that such food is misbranded because of such advertising.

(b) Action by Federal Trade Commission precluding action by Secretary; exception

(1) If the Secretary notifies the Federal Trade Commission under subsection (a) of this section of action proposed to be taken under subchapter III of this chapter with respect to a food or food advertising and the Commission notifies the Secretary in writing, within the 30-day period beginning on the date of the receipt of such notice, that—

(A) it has initiated under the Federal Trade Commission Act [15 U.S.C. 41 et seq.] an investigation of such advertising to determine if it is prohibited by such Act or any order or rule under such Act,

(B) it has commenced (or intends to commence) a civil action under section 5, 13, or 19 [15 U.S.C. 45, 53, or 57b] with respect to such advertising or the Attorney General has commenced (or intends to commence) a civil action under section 5 [15 U.S.C. 45] with respect to such advertising,

(C) it has issued and served (or intends to issue and serve) a complaint under section 5(b) of such Act [15 U.S.C. 45(b)] respecting such advertising, or

(D) pursuant to section 16(b) of such Act [15 U.S.C. 56(b)] it has made a certification to the Attorney General respecting such advertising,

the Secretary may not, except as provided by paragraph (2), initiate the action described in the Secretary's notice to the Federal Trade Commission.

(2) If, before the expiration of the 60-day period beginning on the date the Secretary receives a notice described in paragraph (1) from the Federal Trade Commission in response to a notice of the Secretary under subsection (a) of this section—

(A) the Commission or the Attorney General does not commence a civil action described in subparagraph (B) of paragraph (1) of this subsection respecting the advertising described in the Secretary's notice,

(B) the Commission does not issue and serve a complaint described in subparagraph (C) of such paragraph respecting such advertising, or

(C) the Commission does not (as described in subparagraph (D) of such paragraph) make a certification to the Attorney General respecting such advertising, or, if the Commission does make such a certification to the Attorney General respecting such advertising, the Attorney General, before the expiration of such period, does not cause appropriate criminal proceedings to be brought against such advertising,

the Secretary may, after the expiration of such period, initiate the action described in the notice to the Commission pursuant to subsection (a) of this section. The Commission shall promptly notify the Secretary of the commencement by the Commission of such a civil action, the issuance and service by it of such a complaint, or the causing by the Attorney General of criminal proceedings to be brought against such advertising.

(c) Secretary's determination of imminent hazard to health as suspending applicability of provisions

The requirements of subsections (a) and (b) of this section do not apply with respect to action under subchapter III of this chapter with respect to any food or food advertising if the Secretary determines that such action is required to eliminate an imminent hazard to health.

(d) Coordination of action by Secretary with Federal Trade Commission

For the purpose of avoiding unnecessary duplication, the Secretary shall coordinate any action taken under subchapter III of this chapter because of advertising which the Secretary determines causes a food to be misbranded with any action of the Federal Trade Commission under the Federal Trade Commission Act [15 U.S.C. 41 et seq.] with respect to such advertising.

(June 25, 1938, ch. 675, § 707, as added Pub. L. 94–278, title V, § 502(b), Apr. 22, 1976, 90 Stat. 412.)

REFERENCES IN TEXT

The Federal Trade Commission Act, referred to in subsecs. (b) and (d), is act Sept. 26, 1914, ch. 311, 38 Stat. 717, as amended, which is classified generally to subchapter I (§ 41 et seq.) of chapter 2 of Title 15, Commerce and Trade. For complete classification of this Act to the Code, see section 58 of Title 15 and Tables.

§ 379. Confidential information

The Secretary may provide any information which is exempt from disclosure pursuant to subsection (a) of section 552 of title 5 by reason of subsection (b)(4) of such section to a person other than an officer or employee of the Department if the Secretary determines such other person requires the information in connection with an activity which is undertaken under contract with the Secretary, which relates to the administration of this chapter, and with respect to which the Secretary (or an officer or employee of the Department) is not prohibited from using such information. The Secretary shall require as a condition to the provision of information under this section that the person receiving it take such security precautions respecting the information as the Secretary may by regulation prescribe.

(June 25, 1938, ch. 675, § 708, as added Pub. L. 94–295, § 8, May 28, 1976, 90 Stat. 582.)

§ 379a. Presumption of existence of jurisdiction

In any action to enforce the requirements of this chapter respecting a device, food, drug, or cosmetic the connection with interstate commerce required for jurisdiction in such action shall be presumed to exist.

(June 25, 1938, ch. 675, § 709, as added Pub. L. 94–295, § 8, May 28, 1976, 90 Stat. 583; amended Pub. L. 105–115, title IV, § 419, Nov. 21, 1997, 111 Stat. 2379.)

AMENDMENTS

1997—Pub. L. 105–115 substituted "a device, food, drug, or cosmetic" for "a device".

EFFECTIVE DATE OF 1997 AMENDMENT

Amendment by Pub. L. 105–115 effective 90 days after Nov. 21, 1997, except as otherwise provided, see section 501 of Pub. L. 105–115, set out as a note under section 321 of this title.

§ 379b. Consolidated administrative and laboratory facility

(a) Authority

The Secretary, in consultation with the Administrator of the General Services Administration, shall enter into contracts for the design, construction, and operation of a consolidated Food and Drug Administration administrative and laboratory facility.

(b) Awarding of contract

The Secretary shall solicit contract proposals under subsection (a) of this section from interested parties. In awarding contracts under such subsection, the Secretary shall review such proposals and give priority to those alternatives that are the most cost effective for the Federal Government and that allow for the use of donated land, federally owned property, or lease-purchase arrangements. A contract under this subsection shall not be entered into unless such contract results in a net cost savings to the Federal Government over the duration of the contract, as compared to the Government purchase price including borrowing by the Secretary of the Treasury.

(c) Donations

In carrying out this section, the Secretary shall have the power, in connection with real property, buildings, and facilities, to accept on behalf of the Food and Drug Administration gifts or donations of services or property, real or personal, as the Secretary determines to be necessary.

(d) Authorization of appropriations

There are authorized to be appropriated to carry out this section $100,000,000 for fiscal year 1991, and such sums as may be necessary for each of the subsequent fiscal years, to remain available until expended.

(June 25, 1938, ch. 675, § 710, as added Pub. L. 101–635, title I, § 101, Nov. 28, 1990, 104 Stat. 4583.)

§ 379c. Transferred

CODIFICATION

Section, act June 25, 1938, ch. 675, § 711, as added Nov. 28, 1990, Pub. L. 101–635, title II, § 201, 104 Stat. 4584, which related to recovery and retention of fees for freedom of information requests, was renumbered section 731 of act June 25, 1938, by Pub. L. 102–571, title I, §106(6), Oct. 29, 1992, 106 Stat. 4499, and transferred to section 379f of this title.

§379d. Automation of Food and Drug Administration

(a) In general

The Secretary, acting through the Commissioner of Food and Drugs, shall automate appropriate activities of the Food and Drug Administration to ensure timely review of activities regulated under this chapter.

(b) Authorization of appropriations

There are authorized to be appropriated each fiscal year such sums as are necessary to carry out this section.

(June 25, 1938, ch. 675, §711, formerly §712, as added Pub. L. 101–635, title IV, §401, Nov. 28, 1990, 104 Stat. 4585; renumbered §711, Pub. L. 102–571, title I, §106(3), Oct. 29, 1992, 106 Stat. 4498.)

PRIOR PROVISIONS

A prior section 711 of act June 25, 1938, was renumbered section 731 by Pub. L. 102–571 and is classified to section 379f of this title.

§379d–1. Conflicts of interest

(a) Definitions

For purposes of this section:

(1) Advisory committee

The term "advisory committee" means an advisory committee under the Federal Advisory Committee Act that provides advice or recommendations to the Secretary regarding activities of the Food and Drug Administration.

(2) Financial interest

The term "financial interest" means a financial interest under section 208(a) of title 18.

(b) Appointments to advisory committees

(1) Recruitment

(A) In general

The Secretary shall—

(i) develop and implement strategies on effective outreach to potential members of advisory committees at universities, colleges, other academic research centers, professional and medical societies, and patient and consumer groups;

(ii) seek input from professional medical and scientific societies to determine the most effective informational and recruitment activities; and

(iii) take into account the advisory committees with the greatest number of vacancies.

(B) Recruitment activities

The recruitment activities under subparagraph (A) may include—

(i) advertising the process for becoming an advisory committee member at medical and scientific society conferences;

(ii) making widely available, including by using existing electronic communications channels, the contact information for the Food and Drug Administration point of contact regarding advisory committee nominations; and

(iii) developing a method through which an entity receiving funding from the National Institutes of Health, the Agency for Healthcare Research and Quality, the Centers for Disease Control and Prevention, or the Veterans Health Administration can identify a person who the Food and Drug Administration can contact regarding the nomination of individuals to serve on advisory committees.

(2) Evaluation and criteria

When considering a term appointment to an advisory committee, the Secretary shall review the expertise of the individual and the financial disclosure report filed by the individual pursuant to the Ethics in Government Act of 1978 for each individual under consideration for the appointment, so as to reduce the likelihood that an appointed individual will later require a written determination as referred to in section 208(b)(1) of title 18, a written certification as referred to in section 208(b)(3) of title 18, or a waiver as referred to in subsection (c)(2) of this section for service on the committee at a meeting of the committee.

(c) Disclosures; prohibitions on participation; waivers

(1) Disclosure of financial interest

Prior to a meeting of an advisory committee regarding a "particular matter" (as that term is used in section 208 of title 18), each member of the committee who is a full-time Government employee or special Government employee shall disclose to the Secretary financial interests in accordance with subsection (b) of such section 208.

(2) Prohibitions and waivers on participation

(A) In general

Except as provided under subparagraph (B), a member of an advisory committee may not participate with respect to a particular matter considered in an advisory committee meeting if such member (or an immediate family member of such member) has a financial interest that could be affected by the advice given to the Secretary with respect to such matter, excluding interests exempted in regulations issued by the Director of the Office of Government Ethics as too remote or inconsequential to affect the integrity of the services of the Government officers or employees to which such regulations apply.

(B) Waiver

If the Secretary determines it necessary to afford the advisory committee essential expertise, the Secretary may grant a waiver of the prohibition in subparagraph (A) to permit a member described in such subparagraph to—

(i) participate as a non-voting member with respect to a particular matter considered in a committee meeting; or

(ii) participate as a voting member with respect to a particular matter considered in a committee meeting.

(C) Limitation on waivers and other exceptions

(i) Definition

For purposes of this subparagraph, the term "exception" means each of the following with respect to members of advisory committees:

(I) A waiver under section 355(n)(4) of this title (as in effect on the day before September 27, 2007).

(II) A written determination under section 208(b) of title 18.

(III) A written certification under section 208(b)(3) of such title.

(ii) Determination of total number of members slots and member exceptions during fiscal year 2007

The Secretary shall determine—

(I)(aa) for each meeting held by any advisory committee during fiscal year 2007, the number of members who participated in the meeting; and

(bb) the sum of the respective numbers determined under item (aa) (referred to in this subparagraph as the "total number of 2007 meeting slots"); and

(II)(aa) for each meeting held by any advisory committee during fiscal year 2007, the number of members who received an exception for the meeting; and

(bb) the sum of the respective numbers determined under item (aa) (referred to in this subparagraph as the "total number of 2007 meeting exceptions").

(iii) Determination of percentage regarding exceptions during fiscal year 2007

The Secretary shall determine the percentage constituted by—

(I) the total number of 2007 meeting exceptions; divided by

(II) the total number of 2007 meeting slots.

(iv) Limitation for fiscal years 2008 through 2012

The number of exceptions at the Food and Drug Administration for members of advisory committees for a fiscal year may not exceed the following:

(I) For fiscal year 2008, 95 percent of the percentage determined under clause (iii) (referred to in this clause as the "base percentage").

(II) For fiscal year 2009, 90 percent of the base percentage.

(III) For fiscal year 2010, 85 percent of the base percentage.

(IV) For fiscal year 2011, 80 percent of the base percentage.

(V) For fiscal year 2012, 75 percent of the base percentage.

(v) Allocation of exceptions

The exceptions authorized under clause (iv) for a fiscal year may be allocated within the centers or other organizational units of the Food and Drug Administration as determined appropriate by the Secretary.

(3) Disclosure of waiver

Notwithstanding section 107(a)(2) of the Ethics in Government Act (5 U.S.C. App.), the following shall apply:

(A) 15 or more days in advance

As soon as practicable, but (except as provided in subparagraph (B)) not later than 15 days prior to a meeting of an advisory committee to which a written determination as referred to in section 208(b)(1) of title 18, a written certification as referred to in section 208(b)(3) of title 18, or a waiver as referred to in paragraph (2)(B) applies, the Secretary shall disclose (other than information exempted from disclosure under section 552 of title 5 and section 552a of title 5 (popularly known as the Freedom of Information Act and the Privacy Act of 1974, respectively)) on the Internet Web site of the Food and Drug Administration—

(i) the type, nature, and magnitude of the financial interests of the advisory committee member to which such determination, certification, or waiver applies; and

(ii) the reasons of the Secretary for such determination, certification, or waiver.

(B) Less than 30 days in advance

In the case of a financial interest that becomes known to the Secretary less than 30 days prior to a meeting of an advisory committee to which a written determination as referred to in section 208(b)(1) of title 18, a written certification as referred to in section 208(b)(3) of title 18, or a waiver as referred to in paragraph (2)(B) applies, the Secretary shall disclose (other than information exempted from disclosure under section 552 of title 5 and section 552a of title 5) on the Internet Web site of the Food and Drug Administration, the information described in clauses (i) and (ii) of subparagraph (A) as soon as practicable after the Secretary makes such determination, certification, or waiver, but in no case later than the date of such meeting.

(d) Public record

The Secretary shall ensure that the public record and transcript of each meeting of an advisory committee includes the disclosure required under subsection (c)(3) (other than information exempted from disclosure under section 552 of title 5 and section 552a of title 5).

(e) Annual report

Not later than February 1 of each year, the Secretary shall submit to the Committee on Appropriations and the Committee on Health, Education, Labor, and Pensions of the Senate, and the Committee on Appropriations and the Committee on Energy and Commerce of the House of Representatives a report that describes—

(1) with respect to the fiscal year that ended on September 30 of the previous year, the number of vacancies on each advisory committee, the number of nominees received for each committee, and the number of such nominees willing to serve;

(2) with respect to such year, the aggregate number of disclosures required under sub-

section (c)(3) for each meeting of each advisory committee and the percentage of individuals to whom such disclosures did not apply who served on such committee for each such meeting;

(3) with respect to such year, the number of times the disclosures required under subsection (c)(3) occurred under subparagraph (B) of such subsection; and

(4) how the Secretary plans to reduce the number of vacancies reported under paragraph (1) during the fiscal year following such year, and mechanisms to encourage the nomination of individuals for service on an advisory committee, including those who are classified by the Food and Drug Administration as academicians or practitioners.

(f) Periodic review of guidance

Not less than once every 5 years, the Secretary shall review guidance of the Food and Drug Administration regarding conflict of interest waiver determinations with respect to advisory committees and update such guidance as necessary.

(June 25, 1938, ch. 675, § 712, as added Pub. L. 110–85, title VII, § 701(a), Sept. 27, 2007, 121 Stat. 900.)

REFERENCES IN TEXT

The Federal Advisory Committee Act, referred to in subsec. (a)(1), is Pub. L. 92–463, Oct. 6, 1972, 86 Stat. 770, which is set out in the Appendix to Title 5, Government Organization and Employees.

The Ethics in Government Act of 1978, referred to in subsecs. (b)(2) and (c)(3), is Pub. L. 95–521, Oct. 26, 1978, 92 Stat. 1824. For complete classification of this Act to the Code, see Short Title note set out under section 101 of Pub. L. 95–521 in the Appendix to Title 5, Government Organization and Employees, and Tables.

The Privacy Act of 1974, referred to in subsec. (c)(3)(A), is Pub. L. 93–579, Dec. 31, 1974, 88 Stat. 1896, which enacted section 552a of Title 5, Government Organization and Employees, and provisions set out as notes under section 552a of Title 5. For complete classification of this Act to the Code, see Short Title of 1974 Amendment note set out under section 552a of Title 5 and Tables.

PRIOR PROVISIONS

A prior section 712 of act June 25, 1938, was renumbered section 711 by Pub. L. 102–571 and is classified to section 379d of this title.

EFFECTIVE DATE

Section effective Oct. 1, 2007, see section 701(c) of Pub. L. 110–85, set out as an Effective Date of 2007 Amendment note under section 355 of this title.

§ 379d–2. Policy on the review and clearance of scientific articles published by FDA employees

(a) Definition

In this section, the term "article" means a paper, poster, abstract, book, book chapter, or other published writing.

(b) Policies

The Secretary, through the Commissioner of Food and Drugs, shall establish and make publicly available clear written policies to implement this section and govern the timely submission, review, clearance, and disclaimer requirements for articles.

(c) Timing of submission for review

If an officer or employee, including a Staff Fellow and a contractor who performs staff work, of the Food and Drug Administration is directed by the policies established under subsection (b) to submit an article to the supervisor of such officer or employee, or to some other official of the Food and Drug Administration, for review and clearance before such officer or employee may seek to publish or present such an article at a conference, such officer or employee shall submit such article for such review and clearance not less than 30 days before submitting the article for publication or presentation.

(d) Timing for review and clearance

The supervisor or other reviewing official shall review such article and provide written clearance, or written clearance on the condition of specified changes being made, to such officer or employee not later than 30 days after such officer or employee submitted such article for review.

(e) Non-timely review

If, 31 days after such submission under subsection (c), the supervisor or other reviewing official has not cleared or has not reviewed such article and provided written clearance, such officer or employee may consider such article not to have been cleared and may submit the article for publication or presentation with an appropriate disclaimer as specified in the policies established under subsection (b).

(f) Effect

Nothing in this section shall be construed as affecting any restrictions on such publication or presentation provided by other provisions of law.

(June 25, 1938, ch. 675, § 713, as added Pub. L. 110–85, title XI, § 1101, Sept. 27, 2007, 121 Stat. 971.)

PART B—COLORS

§ 379e. Listing and certification of color additives for foods, drugs, devices, and cosmetics

(a) Unsafe color additives

A color additive shall, with respect to any particular use (for which it is being used or intended to be used or is represented as suitable) in or on food or drugs or devices or cosmetics, be deemed unsafe for the purposes of the application of section 342(c), 351(a)(4), or 361(e) of this title, as the case may be, unless—

(1)(A) there is in effect, and such additive and such use are in conformity with, a regulation issued under subsection (b) of this section listing such additive for such use, including any provision of such regulation prescribing the conditions under which such additive may be safely used, and (B) such additive either (i) is from a batch certified, in accordance with regulations issued pursuant to subsection (c) of this section, for such use, or (ii) has, with respect to such use, been exempted by the Secretary from the requirement of certification; or

(2) such additive and such use thereof conform to the terms of an exemption which is in

effect pursuant to subsection (f) of this section.

While there are in effect regulations under subsections (b) and (c) of this section relating to a color additive or an exemption pursuant to subsection (f) of this section with respect to such additive, an article shall not, by reason of bearing or containing such additive in all respects in accordance with such regulations or such exemption, be considered adulterated within the meaning of clause (1) of section 342(a) of this title if such article is a food, or within the meaning of section 361(a) of this title if such article is a cosmetic other than a hair dye (as defined in the last sentence of section 361(a) of this title). A color additive for use in or on a device shall be subject to this section only if the color additive comes in direct contact with the body of man or other animals for a significant period of time. The Secretary may by regulation designate the uses of color additives in or on devices which are subject to this section.

(b) Listing of colors; regulations; issuance, amendment or repeal; referral to advisory committee; report and recommendations; appointment and compensation of advisory committee

(1) The Secretary shall, by regulation, provide for separately listing color additives for use in or on food, color additives for use in or on drugs, or devices, and color additives for use in or on cosmetics, if and to the extent that such additives are suitable and safe for any such use when employed in accordance with such regulations.

(2)(A) Such regulations may list any color additive for use generally in or on food, or in or on drugs or devices, or in or on cosmetics, if the Secretary finds that such additive is suitable and may safely be employed for such general use.

(B) If the data before the Secretary do not establish that the additive satisfies the requirements for listing such additive on the applicable list pursuant to subparagraph (A) of this paragraph, or if the proposal is for listing such additive for a more limited use or uses, such regulations may list such additive only for any more limited use or uses for which it is suitable and may safely be employed.

(3) Such regulations shall, to the extent deemed necessary by the Secretary to assure the safety of the use or uses for which a particular color additive is listed, prescribe the conditions under which such additive may be safely employed for such use or uses (including, but not limited to, specifications, hereafter in this section referred to as tolerance limitations, as to the maximum quantity or quantities which may be used or permitted to remain in or on the article or articles in or on which it is used; specifications as to the manner in which such additive may be added to or used in or on such article or articles; and directions or other labeling or packaging requirements for such additive).

(4) The Secretary shall not list a color additive under this section for a proposed use unless the data before him establish that such use, under the conditions of use specified in the regulations, will be safe: *Provided, however*, That a color additive shall be deemed to be suitable and safe for the purpose of listing under this subsection for use generally in or on food, while there is in effect a published finding of the Secretary declaring such substance exempt from the term "food additive" because of its being generally recognized by qualified experts as safe for its intended use, as provided in section 321(s) of this title.

(5)(A) In determining, for the purposes of this section, whether a proposed use of a color additive is safe, the Secretary shall consider, among other relevant factors—

(i) the probable consumption of, or other relevant exposure from, the additive and of any substance formed in or on food, drugs or devices, or cosmetics because of the use of the additive;

(ii) the cumulative effect, if any, of such additive in the diet of man or animals, taking into account the same or any chemically or pharmacologically related substance or substances in such diet;

(iii) safety factors which, in the opinion of experts qualified by scientific training and experience to evaluate the safety of color additives for the use or uses for which the additive is proposed to be listed, are generally recognized as appropriate for the use of animal experimentation data; and

(iv) the availability of any needed practicable methods of analysis for determining the identity and quantity of (I) the pure dye and all intermediates and other impurities contained in such color additive, (II) such additive in or on any article of food, drug or device, or cosmetic, and (III) any substance formed in or on such article because of the use of such additive.

(B) A color additive (i) shall be deemed unsafe, and shall not be listed, for any use which will or may result in ingestion of all or part of such additive, if the additive is found by the Secretary to induce cancer when ingested by man or animal, or if it is found by the Secretary, after tests which are appropriate for the evaluation of the safety of additives for use in food, to induce cancer in man or animal, and (ii) shall be deemed unsafe, and shall not be listed, for any use which will not result in ingestion of any part of such additive, if, after tests which are appropriate for the evaluation of the safety of additives for such use, or after other relevant exposure of man or animal to such additive, it is found by the Secretary to induce cancer in man or animal: *Provided*, That clause (i) of this subparagraph (B) shall not apply with respect to the use of a color additive as an ingredient of feed for animals which are raised for food production, if the Secretary finds that, under the conditions of use and feeding specified in proposed labeling and reasonably certain to be followed in practice, such additive will not adversely affect the animals for which such feed is intended, and that no residue of the additive will be found (by methods of examination prescribed or approved by the Secretary by regulations, which regulations shall not be subject to subsection (d) of this section) in any edible portion of such animals after slaughter or in any food yielded by or derived from the living animal.

(C)(i) In any proceeding for the issuance, amendment, or repeal of a regulation listing a color additive, whether commenced by a proposal of the Secretary on his own initiative or by a proposal contained in a petition, the petitioner, or any other person who will be adversely affected by such proposal or by the Secretary's order issued in accordance with paragraph (1) of section 371(e) of this title if placed in effect, may request, within the time specified in this subparagraph, that the petition or order thereon, or the Secretary's proposal, be referred to an advisory committee for a report and recommendations with respect to any matter arising under subparagraph (B) of this paragraph, which is involved in such proposal or order and which requires the exercise of scientific judgment. Upon such request, or if the Secretary within such time deems such a referral necessary, the Secretary shall forthwith appoint an advisory committee under subparagraph (D) of this paragraph and shall refer to it, together with all the data before him, such matter arising under subparagraph (B) for study thereof and for a report and recommendations on such matter. A person who has filed a petition or who has requested the referral of a matter to an advisory committee pursuant to this subparagraph (C), as well as representatives of the Department, shall have the right to consult with such advisory committee in connection with the matter referred to it. The request for referral under this subparagraph, or the Secretary's referral on his own initiative, may be made at any time before, or within thirty days after, publication of an order of the Secretary acting upon the petition or proposal.

(ii) Within sixty days after the date of such referral, or within an additional thirty days if the committee deems such additional time necessary, the committee shall, after independent study of the data furnished to it by the Secretary and other data before it, certify to the Secretary a report and recommendations, together with all underlying data and a statement of the reasons or basis for the recommendations. A copy of the foregoing shall be promptly supplied by the Secretary to any person who has filed a petition, or who has requested such referral to the advisory committee. Within thirty days after such certification, and after giving due consideration to all data then before him, including such report, recommendations, underlying data, and statement, and to any prior order issued by him in connection with such matter, the Secretary shall by order confirm or modify any order theretofore issued or, if no such prior order has been issued, shall by order act upon the petition or other proposal.

(iii) Where—

(I) by reason of subparagraph (B) of this paragraph, the Secretary has initiated a proposal to remove from listing a color additive previously listed pursuant to this section; and

(II) a request has been made for referral of such proposal to an advisory committee;

the Secretary may not act by order on such proposal until the advisory committee has made a report and recommendations to him under clause (ii) of this subparagraph and he has considered such recommendations, unless the Secretary finds that emergency conditions exist necessitating the issuance of an order notwithstanding this clause.

(D) The advisory committee referred to in subparagraph (C) of this paragraph shall be composed of experts selected by the National Academy of Sciences, qualified in the subject matter referred to the committee and of adequately diversified professional background, except that in the event of the inability or refusal of the National Academy of Sciences to act, the Secretary shall select the members of the committee. The size of the committee shall be determined by the Secretary. Members of any advisory committee established under this chapter, while attending conferences or meetings of their committees or otherwise serving at the request of the Secretary, shall be entitled to receive compensation at rates to be fixed by the Secretary but at rates not exceeding the daily equivalent of the rate specified at the time of such service for grade GS–18 of the General Schedule, including traveltime; and while away from their homes or regular places of business they may be allowed travel expenses, including per diem in lieu of subsistence, as authorized by section 5703 of title 5 for persons in the Government service employed intermittently. The members shall not be subject to any other provisions of law regarding the appointment and compensation of employees of the United States. The Secretary shall furnish the committee with adequate clerical and other assistance, and shall by rules and regulations prescribe the procedure to be followed by the committee.

(6) The Secretary shall not list a color additive under this subsection for a proposed use if the data before him show that such proposed use would promote deception of the consumer in violation of this chapter or would otherwise result in misbranding or adulteration within the meaning of this chapter.

(7) If, in the judgment of the Secretary, a tolerance limitation is required in order to assure that a proposed use of a color additive will be safe, the Secretary—

(A) shall not list the additive for such use if he finds that the data before him do not establish that such additive, if used within a safe tolerance limitation, would achieve the intended physical or other technical effect; and

(B) shall not fix such tolerance limitation at a level higher than he finds to be reasonably required to accomplish the intended physical or other technical effect.

(8) If, having regard to the aggregate quantity of color additive likely to be consumed in the diet or to be applied to the human body, the Secretary finds that the data before him fail to show that it would be safe and otherwise permissible to list a color additive (or pharmacologically related color additives) for all the uses proposed therefor and at the levels of concentration proposed, the Secretary shall, in determining for which use or uses such additive (or such related additives) shall be or remain listed, or how the aggregate allowable safe tolerance for such additive or additives shall be allocated by him among the uses under consideration, take into account, among other relevant factors (and subject to the paramount criterion of safety), (A) the relative marketability of the articles involved as affected by the proposed uses of the color additive (or of such related additives) in or

on such articles, and the relative dependence of the industries concerned on such uses; (B) the relative aggregate amounts of such color additive which he estimates would be consumed in the diet or applied to the human body by reason of the various uses and levels of concentration proposed; and (C) the availability, if any, of other color additives suitable and safe for one or more of the uses proposed.

(c) Certification of colors

The Secretary shall further, by regulation, provide (1) for the certification, with safe diluents or without diluents, of batches of color additives listed pursuant to subsection (b) of this section and conforming to the requirements for such additives established by regulations under such subsection and this subsection, and (2) for exemption from the requirement of certification in the case of any such additive, or any listing or use thereof, for which he finds such requirement not to be necessary in the interest of the protection of the public health: *Provided*, That, with respect to any use in or on food for which a listed color additive is deemed to be safe by reason of the proviso to paragraph (4) of subsection (b), the requirement of certification shall be deemed not to be necessary in the interest of public health protection.

(d) Procedure for issuance, amendment, or repeal of regulations

The provisions of section 371(e), (f), and (g) of this title shall, subject to the provisions of subparagraph (C) of subsection (b)(5) of this section, apply to and in all respects govern proceedings for the issuance, amendment, or repeal of regulations under subsection (b) or (c) of this section (including judicial review of the Secretary's action in such proceedings) and the admissibility of transcripts of the record of such proceedings in other proceedings, except that—

(1) if the proceeding is commenced by the filing of a petition, notice of the proposal made by the petition shall be published in general terms by the Secretary within thirty days after such filing, and the Secretary's order (required by paragraph (1) of section 371(e) of this title) acting upon such proposal shall, in the absence of prior referral (or request for referral) to an advisory committee, be issued within ninety days after the date of such filing, except that the Secretary may (prior to such ninetieth day), by written notice to the petitioner, extend such ninety-day period to such time (not more than one hundred and eighty days after the date of filing of the petition) as the Secretary deems necessary to enable him to study and investigate the petition;

(2) any report, recommendations, underlying data, and reasons certified to the Secretary by an advisory committee appointed pursuant to subparagraph (D) of subsection (b)(5) of this section, shall be made a part of the record of any hearing if relevant and material, subject to the provisions of section 556(d) of title 5. The advisory committee shall designate a member to appear and testify at any such hearing with respect to the report and recommendations of such committee upon request of the Secretary, the petitioner, or the officer conducting the hearing, but this shall not preclude any other member of the advisory committee from appearing and testifying at such hearing;

(3) the Secretary's order after public hearing (acting upon objections filed to an order made prior to hearing) shall be subject to the requirements of section 348(f)(2) of this title; and

(4) the scope of judicial review of such order shall be in accordance with the fourth sentence of paragraph (2), and with the provisions of paragraph (3), of section 348(g) of this title.

(e) Fees

The admitting to listing and certification of color additives, in accordance with regulations prescribed under this chapter, shall be performed only upon payment of such fees, which shall be specified in such regulations, as may be necessary to provide, maintain, and equip an adequate service for such purposes.

(f) Exemptions

The Secretary shall by regulations (issued without regard to subsection (d) of this section) provide for exempting from the requirements of this section any color additive or any specific type of use thereof, and any article of food, drug, or device, or cosmetic bearing or containing such additive, intended solely for investigational use by qualified experts when in his opinion such exemption is consistent with the public health.

(June 25, 1938, ch. 675, §721, formerly §706, 52 Stat. 1058; Pub. L. 86–618, title I, §103(b), July 12, 1960, 74 Stat. 399; Pub. L. 87–781, title I, §104(f)(2), Oct. 10, 1962, 76 Stat. 785; Pub. L. 91–515, title VI, §601(d)(2), Oct. 30, 1970, 84 Stat. 1311; Pub. L. 94–295, §9(a), May 28, 1976, 90 Stat. 583; Pub. L. 96–88, title V, §509(b), Oct. 17, 1979, 93 Stat. 695; Pub. L. 102–300, §6(b)(2), June 16, 1992, 106 Stat. 240; renumbered §721, Pub. L. 102–571, title I, §106(4), Oct. 29, 1992, 106 Stat. 4498; Pub. L. 103–80, §3(bb), Aug. 13, 1993, 107 Stat. 778.)

CODIFICATION

Section was formerly classified to section 376 of this title prior to renumbering by Pub. L. 102–571.

In subsec. (d)(2), "section 556(d) of title 5" substituted for "section 7(c) of the Administrative Procedure Act (5 U.S.C., sec. 1006(c))" on authority of Pub. L. 89–554, §7(b), Sept. 6, 1966, 80 Stat. 631, the first section of which enacted Title 5, Government Organization and Employees.

AMENDMENTS

1993—Subsec. (b)(5)(D). Pub. L. 103–80 substituted "section 5703" for "section 5703(b)".

1992—Subsec. (b)(5)(C)(i). Pub. L. 102–300 struck out "of Health, Education, and Welfare" after "representatives of the Department".

1976—Subsec. (a). Pub. L. 94–295, §9(a)(2), (3), inserted reference to devices and inserted provisions directing that color additives for use in or on devices be subject to this section only if the color additives come in direct contact with the body of man or other animals for a significant period of time and authorizing the Secretary to designate by regulation the uses of color additives in or on devices which are subject to this section.

Subsec. (b). Pub. L. 94–295, §9(a)(1), (2), substituted "drug or device" for "drug" and "drugs or devices" for "drugs" wherever appearing.

Subsec. (f). Pub. L. 94–295, §9(a)(1), substituted "drug or device" for "drug".

1970—Subsec. (b)(5)(D). Pub. L. 91–515 substituted provisions authorizing members of an advisory committee to receive compensation at rates fixed by the Secretary, with a specific maximum amount, and travel expenses, including per diem in lieu of subsistence, as authorized by section 5703(b) of Title 5, for provisions authorizing such members to receive as compensation a reasonable per diem for time actually spent on committee work, and necessary traveling and subsistence expenses while serving away from their places of residence.

1962—Subsec. (b)(5)(B). Pub. L. 87–781 provided that clause (i) of this subparagraph shall not apply to a color additive in feed of animals raised for food production, if under the conditions of use specified in proposed labeling, and which conditions are reasonably certain to be followed in practice, such additive will not adversely affect the animals and no residue will be found in any edible portion of such animal after slaughter or in any food from the living animal.

1960—Pub. L. 86–618 amended section generally. Prior to amendment, section read as follows: "The admitting to listing and certification of coal-tar colors, in accordance with regulations prescribed under this chapter, shall be performed only upon payment of such fees, which shall be specified in such regulations, as may be necessary to provide, maintain, and equip an adequate service for such purposes."

EFFECTIVE DATE OF 1962 AMENDMENT

Amendment by Pub. L. 87–781 effective Oct. 10, 1962, see section 107 of Pub. L. 87–781, set out as a note under section 321 of this title.

EFFECTIVE DATE OF 1960 AMENDMENT, TRANSITIONAL PROVISIONS, AND EFFECT ON OTHER LAWS

Title II of Pub. L. 86–618 provided that:

"SEC. 201. [DEFINITIONS.] As used in this title, the term 'basic Act' means the Federal Food, Drug, and Cosmetic Act [this chapter]; the term 'enactment date' means the date of enactment of this Act [July 12, 1960]; and other terms, insofar as also used in the basic Act (whether before or after enactment of this Act) shall have the same meaning as they have, or had when in effect, under the basic Act.

"SEC. 202. [EFFECTIVE DATE.] This Act [amending this section and sections 321, 331, 333, 342, 343, 346, 351, 352, 361, 362, and 371 of this title and repealing sections 354 and 364 of this title] shall, subject to the provisions of section 203, take effect on the enactment date [July 12, 1960].

"SEC. 203. [PROVISIONAL LISTINGS OF COMMERCIALLY ESTABLISHED COLORS.] (a)(1) The purpose of this section is to make possible, on an interim basis for a reasonable period, through provisional listings, the use of commercially established color additives to the extent consistent with the public health, pending the completion of the scientific investigations needed as a basis for making determinations as to listing of such additives under the basic Act as amended by this Act. A provisional listing (including a deemed provisional listing) of a color additive under this section for any use shall, unless sooner terminated or expiring under the provisions of this section, expire (A) on the closing date (as defined in paragraph (2) of this subsection) or (B) on the effective date of a listing of such additive for such use under section 706 [now 721] of the basic Act, [this section], whichever date first occurs.

"(2) For the purposes of this section, the term 'closing date' means (A) the last day of the two and one-half year period beginning on the enactment date [July 12, 1960] or (B), with respect to a particular provisional listing (or deemed provisional listing) of a color additive or use thereof, such later closing date as the Secretary may from time to time establish pursuant to the authority of this paragraph. The Secretary may by regulation, upon application of an interested person or on his own initiative, from time to time postpone the original closing date with respect to a provisional listing (or deemed provisional listing) under this section of a specified color additive, or of a specified use or uses of such additive, for such period or periods as he finds necessary to carry out the purpose of this section, if in the Secretary's judgment such action is consistent with the objective of carrying to completion in good faith, as soon as reasonably practicable, the scientific investigations necessary for making a determination as to listing such additive, or such specified use or uses thereof, under section 706 [now 721] of the basic Act [this section]. The Secretary may terminate a postponement of the closing date at any time if he finds that such postponement should not have been granted, or that by reason of a change in circumstances the basis for such postponement no longer exists, or that there has been a failure to comply with a requirement for submission of progress reports or with other conditions attached to such postponement.

"(b) Subject to the other provisions of this section—

"(1) any color additive which, on the day preceding the enactment date [July 12, 1960], was listed and certifiable for any use or uses under section 406(b), 504, or 604 [section 346(b), 354, or 364 of this title], or under the third proviso of section 402(c) [section 342(c) of this title], of the basic Act, and of which a batch or batches had been certified for such use or uses prior to the enactment date [July 12, 1960], and

"(2) any color additive which was commercially used or sold prior to the enactment date [July 12, 1960] for any use or uses in or on any food, drug, or cosmetic, and which either, (A), on the day preceding the enactment date [July 12, 1960], was not a material within the purview of any of the provisions of the basic Act enumerated in paragraph (1) of this subsection, or (B) is the color additive known as synthetic beta-carotene,

shall, beginning on the enactment date [July 12, 1960], be deemed to be provisionally listed under this section as a color additive for such use or uses.

"(c) Upon request of any person, the Secretary, by regulations issued under subsection (d), shall without delay, if on the basis of the data before him he deems such action consistent with the protection of the public health, provisionally list a material as a color additive for any use for which it was listed, and for which a batch or batches of such material had been certified, under section 406(b), 504, or 604 of the basic Act [section 346(b), 354, or 364 of this title] prior to the enactment date [July 12, 1960], although such color was no longer listed and certifiable for such use under such sections on the day preceding the enactment date. Such provisional listing shall take effect on the date of publication.

"(d)(1) The Secretary shall, by regulations issued or amended from time to time under this section—

"(A) insofar as practicable promulgate and keep current a list or lists of the color additives, and of the particular uses thereof, which he finds are deemed provisionally listed under subsection (b), and the presence of a color additive on such a list with respect to a particular use shall, in any proceeding under the basic Act, be conclusive evidence that such provisional listing is in effect;

"(B) provide for the provisional listing of the color additives and particular uses thereof specified in subsection (c);

"(C) provide, with respect to particular uses for which color additives are or are deemed to be provisionally listed, such temporary tolerance limitations (including such limitations at zero level) and other conditions of use and labeling or packaging requirements, if any, as in his judgment are necessary to protect the public health pending listing under section 706 [now 721] of the basic Act [this section];

"(D) provide for the certification of batches of such color additives (with or without diluents) for the uses for which they are so listed or deemed to be listed under this section, except that such an additive which is a color additive deemed provisionally listed under subsection (b)(2) of this section shall be deemed exempt from the requirement of such certification while not subject to a tolerance limitation; and

"(E) provide for the termination of a provisional listing (or deemed provisional listing) of a color additive or particular use thereof forthwith whenever in his judgment such action is necessary to protect the public health.

"(2)(A) Except as provided in subparagraph (C) of this paragraph, regulations under this section shall, from time to time, be issued, amended, or repealed by the Secretary without regard to the requirements of the basic Act [subsec. (e) of this section], but for the purposes of the application of section 706(e) [now 721(e)] of the basic Act (relating to fees) and of determining the availability of appropriations of fees (and of advance deposits to cover fees), proceedings, regulations, and certifications under this section shall be deemed to be proceedings, regulations, and certifications under such section 706 [now 721, this section]. Regulations providing for fees (and advance deposits to cover fees), which on the day preceding the enactment date [July 12, 1960] were in effect pursuant to section 706 [now 721] of the basic Act [this section], shall be deemed to be regulations under such section 706 [now 721, this section] as amended by this Act, and appropriations of fees (and advance deposits) available for the purposes specified in such section 706 [now 721] as in effect prior to the enactment date [July 12, 1960] shall be available for the purposes specified in such section 706 [now 721, this section] as so amended.

"(B) If the Secretary, by regulation—

"(i) has terminated a provisional listing (or deemed provisional listing) of a color additive or particular use thereof pursuant to paragraph (1)(E) of this subsection; or

"(ii) has, pursuant to paragraph (1)(C) or paragraph (3) of this subsection, initially established or rendered more restrictive a tolerance limitation or other restriction or requirement with respect to a provisional listing (or deemed provisional listing) which listing had become effective prior to such action,

any person adversely affected by such action may, prior to the expiration of the period specified in clause (A) of subsection (a)(2) of this section, file with the Secretary a petition for amendment of such regulation so as to revoke or modify such action of the Secretary, but the filing of such petition shall not operate to stay or suspend the effectiveness of such action. Such petition shall, in accordance with regulations, set forth the proposed amendment and shall contain data (or refer to data which are before the Secretary or of which he will take official notice), which show that the revocation or modification proposed is consistent with the protection of the public health. The Secretary shall, after publishing such proposal and affording all interested persons an opportunity to present their views thereon orally or in writing, act upon such proposal by published order.

"(C) Any person adversely affected by an order entered under subparagraph (B) of this paragraph may, within thirty days after its publication, file objections thereto with the Secretary, specifying with particularity the provisions of the order deemed objectionable, stating reasonable grounds for such objections, and requesting a public hearing upon such objections. The Secretary shall hold a public hearing on such objections and shall, on the basis of the evidence adduced at such hearing, act on such objections by published order. Such order may reinstate a terminated provisional listing, or increase or dispense with a previously established temporary tolerance limitation, or make less restrictive any other limitation established by him under paragraph (1) or (3) of this subsection, only if in his judgment the evidence so adduced shows that such action will be consistent with the protection of the public health. An order entered under this subparagraph shall be subject to judicial review in accordance with section 701(f) of the basic Act [section 371(f) of this title] except that the findings and order of the Secretary shall be sustained only if based upon a fair evaluation of the entire record at such hearing. No stay or suspension of such order shall be ordered by the court pending conclusion of such judicial review.

"(D) On and after the enactment date [July 12, 1960], regulations, provisional listings, and certifications (or exemptions from certification) in effect under this section shall, for the purpose of determining whether an article is adulterated or misbranded within the meaning of the basic Act by reason of its being, bearing, or containing a color additive, have the same effect as would regulations, listings, and certifications (or exemptions from certification) under section 706 [now 721] of the basic Act [this section]. A regulation, provisional listing or termination thereof, tolerance limitation, or certification or exemption therefrom, under this section shall not be the basis for any presumption or inference in any proceeding under section 706(b) or (c) [now 721(b), (c)] of the basic Act [subsec. (b) or (c) of this section].

"(3) For the purpose of enabling the Secretary to carry out his functions under paragraphs (1)(A) and (C) of this subsection with respect to color additives deemed provisionally listed, he shall, as soon as practicable after enactment of this Act [July 12, 1960], afford by public notice a reasonable opportunity to interested persons to submit data relevant thereto. If the data so submitted or otherwise before him do not, in his judgment, establish a reliable basis for including such a color additive or particular use or uses thereof in a list or lists promulgated under paragraph (1)(A), or for determining the prevailing level or levels of use thereof prior to the enactment date [July 12, 1960] with a view to prescribing a temporary tolerance or tolerances for such use or uses under paragraph (1)(C), the Secretary shall establish a temporary tolerance limitation at zero level for such use or uses until such time as he finds that it would not be inconsistent with the protection of the public health to increase or dispense with such temporary tolerance limitation.

"SEC. 204. [EFFECT ON MEAT INSPECTION AND POULTRY PRODUCTS INSPECTION ACTS.] Nothing in this Act [amending this section and sections 321, 331, 333, 342, 343, 346, 351, 352, 361, 362, and 371 of this title and repealing sections 354 and 364 of this title] shall be construed to exempt any meat or meat food product, poultry or poultry product, or any person from any requirement imposed by or pursuant to the Meat Inspection Act of March 4, 1907, 34 Stat. 1260, as amended or extended (21 U.S.C. 71 and the following) [see section 601 et seq. of this title] or the Poultry Products Inspection Act (21 U.S.C. 451 and the following)."

EFFECTIVE DATE; ACCELERATION

This section was made "immediately effective" by act May 2, 1939, ch. 107, title I, §1, 53 Stat. 631.

TERMINATION OF ADVISORY COMMITTEES

Advisory committees in existence on Jan. 5, 1973, to terminate not later than the expiration of the 2-year period following Jan. 5, 1973, and advisory committees established after Jan. 5, 1973, to terminate not later than the expiration of the 2-year period beginning on the date of their establishment, unless in the case of a committee established by the President or an officer of the Federal Government, such committee is renewed by appropriate action prior to the expiration of such 2-year period, or in the case of a committee established by Congress, its duration is otherwise provided by law. See section 14 of Pub. L. 92–463, Oct. 6, 1972, 86 Stat. 776, set out in the Appendix to Title 5, Government Organization and Employees.

REFERENCES IN OTHER LAWS TO GS–16, 17, OR 18 PAY RATES

References in laws to the rates of pay for GS–16, 17, or 18, or to maximum rates of pay under the General Schedule, to be considered references to rates payable under specified sections of Title 5, Government Organization and Employees, see section 529 [title I, §101(c)(1)] of Pub. L. 101–509, set out in a note under section 5376 of Title 5.

PART C—FEES

SUBPART 1—FREEDOM OF INFORMATION FEES

§379f. Recovery and retention of fees for freedom of information requests

(a) In general

The Secretary, acting through the Commissioner of Food and Drugs, may—

(1) set and charge fees, in accordance with section 552(a)(4)(A) of title 5, to recover all reasonable costs incurred in processing requests made under section 552 of title 5 for records obtained or created under this chapter or any other Federal law for which responsibility for administration has been delegated to the Commissioner by the Secretary;

(2) retain all fees charged for such requests; and

(3) establish an accounting system and procedures to control receipts and expenditures of fees received under this section.

(b) Use of fees

The Secretary and the Commissioner of Food and Drugs shall not use fees received under this section for any purpose other than funding the processing of requests described in subsection (a)(1) of this section. Such fees shall not be used to reduce the amount of funds made to carry out other provisions of this chapter.

(c) Waiver of fees

Nothing in this section shall supersede the right of a requester to obtain a waiver of fees pursuant to section 552(a)(4)(A) of title 5.

(June 25, 1938, ch. 675, §731, formerly §711, as added Pub. L. 101–635, title II, §201, Nov. 28, 1990, 104 Stat. 4584; renumbered §731, Pub. L. 102–571, title I, §106(6), Oct. 29, 1992, 106 Stat. 4499.)

CODIFICATION

Section was formerly classified to section 379c of this title prior to renumbering by Pub. L. 102–571.

SUBPART 2—FEES RELATING TO DRUGS

TERMINATION OF SUBPART

For termination of subpart by section 105 of Pub. L. 102–571, see Termination Date note set out under section 379g of this title.

§379g. Definitions

For purposes of this subpart:

(1) The term "human drug application" means an application for—

(A) approval of a new drug submitted under section 355(b) of this title, or

(B) licensure of a biological product under section 262 of title 42.

Such term does not include a supplement to such an application, does not include an application with respect to whole blood or a blood component for transfusion, does not include an application with respect to a bovine blood product for topical application licensed before September 1, 1992, an allergenic extract product, or an in vitro diagnostic biologic product licensed under section 262 of title 42, does not include an application with respect to a large volume parenteral drug product approved before September 1, 1992, does not include an application for a licensure of a biological product for further manufacturing use only, and does not include an application or supplement submitted by a State or Federal Government entity for a drug that is not distributed commercially. Such term does include an application for licensure, as described in subparagraph (B), of a large volume biological product intended for single dose injection for intravenous use or infusion.

(2) The term "supplement" means a request to the Secretary to approve a change in a human drug application which has been approved.

(3) The term "prescription drug product" means a specific strength or potency of a drug in final dosage form—

(A) for which a human drug application has been approved,

(B) which may be dispensed only under prescription pursuant to section 353(b) of this title, and

(C) which is on the list of products described in section 355(j)(7)(A) of this title (not including the discontinued section of such list) or is on a list created and maintained by the Secretary of products approved under human drug applications under section 262 of title 42 (not including the discontinued section of such list).

Such term does not include whole blood or a blood component for transfusion, does not include a bovine blood product for topical application licensed before September 1, 1992, an allergenic extract product, or an in vitro diagnostic biologic product licensed under section 262 of title 42. Such term does not include a biological product that is licensed for further manufacturing use only, and does not include a drug that is not distributed commercially and is the subject of an application or supplement submitted by a State or Federal Government entity. Such term does include a large volume biological product intended for single dose injection for intravenous use or infusion.

(4) The term "final dosage form" means, with respect to a prescription drug product, a finished dosage form which is approved for administration to a patient without substantial further manufacturing (such as capsules, tablets, or lyophilized products before reconstitution).

(5) The term "prescription drug establishment" means a foreign or domestic place of business which is at one general physical location consisting of one or more buildings all of which are within five miles of each other and at which one or more prescription drug products are manufactured in final dosage form. For purposes of this paragraph, the term "manufactured" does not include packaging.

(6) The term "process for the review of human drug applications" means the following activities of the Secretary with respect to the review of human drug applications and supplements:

(A) The activities necessary for the review of human drug applications and supplements.

(B) The issuance of action letters which approve human drug applications or which set forth in detail the specific deficiencies in such applications and, where appropriate, the actions necessary to place such applications in condition for approval.

(C) The inspection of prescription drug establishments and other facilities undertaken as part of the Secretary's review of pending human drug applications and supplements.

(D) Activities necessary for the review of applications for licensure of establishments subject to section 262 of title 42 and for the release of lots of biologics under such section.

(E) Monitoring of research conducted in connection with the review of human drug applications.

(F) Postmarket safety activities with respect to drugs approved under human drug applications or supplements, including the following activities:

(i) Collecting, developing, and reviewing safety information on approved drugs, including adverse event reports.

(ii) Developing and using improved adverse-event data-collection systems, including information technology systems.

(iii) Developing and using improved analytical tools to assess potential safety problems, including access to external data bases.

(iv) Implementing and enforcing section 355(*o*) of this title (relating to postapproval studies and clinical trials and labeling changes) and section 355(p) of this title (relating to risk evaluation and mitigation strategies).

(v) Carrying out section 355(k)(5) of this title (relating to adverse event reports and postmarket safety activities).

(7) The term "costs of resources allocated for the process for the review of human drug applications" means the expenses incurred in connection with the process for the review of human drug applications for—

(A) officers and employees of the Food and Drug Administration, contractors of the Food and Drug Administration, advisory committees, and costs related to such officers, employees, and committees and to contracts with such contractors,

(B) management of information, and the acquisition, maintenance, and repair of computer resources,

(C) leasing, maintenance, renovation, and repair of facilities and acquisition, maintenance, and repair of fixtures, furniture, scientific equipment, and other necessary materials and supplies, and

(D) collecting fees under section 379h of this title and accounting for resources allocated for the review of human drug applications and supplements.

(8) The term "adjustment factor" applicable to a fiscal year is the Consumer Price Index for all urban consumers (all items; United States city average) for October of the preceding fiscal year divided by such Index for October 1996.

(9) The term "person" includes an affiliate thereof.

(10) The term "active", with respect to a commercial investigational new drug application, means such an application to which information was submitted during the relevant period.

(11) The term "affiliate" means a business entity that has a relationship with a second business entity if, directly or indirectly—

(A) one business entity controls, or has the power to control, the other business entity; or

(B) a third party controls, or has power to control, both of the business entities.

(June 25, 1938, ch. 675, §735, as added Pub. L. 102–571, title I, §103, Oct. 29, 1992, 106 Stat. 4491; amended Pub. L. 105–115, title I, §§102, 125(b)(2)(M), Nov. 21, 1997, 111 Stat. 2298, 2326; Pub. L. 107–188, title V, §503, June 12, 2002, 116 Stat. 688; Pub. L. 110–85, title I, §102, Sept. 27, 2007, 121 Stat. 825.)

Amendment of Section

For termination of amendment by section 106(a) of Pub. L. 110–85, see Effective and Termination Dates of 2007 Amendment note below.

For termination of amendment by section 509 of Pub. L. 107–188, see Effective and Termination Dates of 2002 Amendment note below.

For termination of amendment by section 107 of Pub. L. 105–115, see Effective and Termination Dates of 1997 Amendment note below.

Termination of Section

For termination of section by section 105 of Pub. L. 102–571, see Termination Date note below.

Amendments

2007—Pub. L. 110–85, §§102(1), 106(a), in introductory provisions, temporarily substituted "For purposes of this subpart" for "For purposes of this part". See Effective and Termination Dates of 2007 Amendment note below.

Par. (1). Pub. L. 110–85, §§102(2)(D), 106(a), temporarily substituted "subparagraph (B)" for "subparagraph (C)" in concluding provisions. See Effective and Termination Dates of 2007 Amendment note below.

Par. (1)(A). Pub. L. 110–85, §§102(2)(A), 106(a), temporarily substituted "355(b) of this title, or" for "355(b)(1) of this title,". See Effective and Termination Dates of 2007 Amendment note below.

Par. (1)(B), (C). Pub. L. 110–85, §§102(2)(B), (C), 106(a), temporarily redesignated subpar. (C) as (B) and struck out former subpar. (B) which read as follows: "approval of a new drug submitted under section 355(b)(2) of this title after September 30, 1992, which requests approval of—

"(i) a molecular entity which is an active ingredient (including any salt or ester of an active ingredient), or

"(ii) an indication for a use,

that had not been approved under an application submitted under section 355(b) of this title, or". See Effective and Termination Dates of 2007 Amendment note below.

Par. (3)(C). Pub. L. 110–85, §§102(3), 106(a), temporarily substituted "355(j)(7)(A) of this title (not including the discontinued section of such list)" for "355(j)(7)(A) of this title" and inserted "(not including the discontinued section of such list)" before period at end. See Effective and Termination Dates of 2007 Amendment note below.

Par. (4). Pub. L. 110–85, §§102(4), 106(a), temporarily inserted "(such as capsules, tablets, or lyophilized products before reconstitution)" before period at end.

See Effective and Termination Dates of 2007 Amendment note below.

Par. (6)(F). Pub. L. 110–85, §§102(5), 106(a), temporarily amended subpar. (F) generally. Prior to amendment, subpar. (F) read as follows: "In the case of drugs approved after October 1, 2002, under human drug applications or supplements: collecting, developing, and reviewing safety information on the drugs, including adverse event reports, during a period of time after approval of such applications or supplements, not to exceed three years." See Effective and Termination Dates of 2007 Amendment note below.

Par. (8). Pub. L. 110–85, §§102(6), 106(a), temporarily substituted "October of the preceding fiscal year" for "April of the preceding fiscal year" and "October 1996" for "April 1997". See Effective and Termination Dates of 2007 Amendment note below.

Pars. (9) to (11). Pub. L. 110–85, §§102(7), (8), 106(a), temporarily added pars. (9) and (10) and redesignated former par. (9) as (11). See Effective and Termination Dates of 2007 Amendment note below.

2002—Par. (1). Pub. L. 107–188, §§503(1), 509, temporarily substituted "licensure, as described in subparagraph (C)" for "licensure, as described in subparagraph (D)" in concluding provisions. See Effective and Termination Dates of 2002 Amendment note below.

Par. (3). Pub. L. 107–188, §§503(2)(D), 509, which directed the temporary amendment of concluding provisions of par. (3) by striking "section 262 of title 42" and all that follows through "biological product" and inserting "section 262 of title 42. Such term does not include a biological product", was executed by striking language ending with "biological product" the first time appearing, thereby making the substitution for "section 262 of title 42, does not include a large volume parenteral drug product approved before September 1, 1992, does not include a biological product", to reflect the probable intent of Congress. See Effective and Termination Dates of 2002 Amendment note below.

Par. (3)(C). Pub. L. 107–188, §§503(2)(A)–(C), 509, temporarily added subpar. (C). See Effective and Termination Dates of 2002 Amendment note below.

Par. (6)(F). Pub. L. 107–188, §§503(3), 509, temporarily added subpar. (F). See Effective and Termination Dates of 2002 Amendment note below.

Par. (8). Pub. L. 107–188, §§503(4), 509, temporarily struck out designations of subpars. (A) and (B) and text of subpar. (B) and concluding provisions, substituting definition of "adjustment factor" as the Consumer Price Index for definition of Index as the lower of the Consumer Price Index or the total of discretionary budget authority provided for programs in the domestic category for the immediately preceding fiscal year divided by such budget authority for fiscal year 1997. See Effective and Termination Dates of 2002 Amendment note below.

1997—Par. (1). Pub. L. 105–115, §§102(1), 107, in closing provisions, temporarily struck out "and" before "does not include an application" and substituted "September 1, 1992, does not include an application for a licensure of a biological product for further manufacturing use only, and does not include an application or supplement submitted by a State or Federal Government entity for a drug that is not distributed commercially. Such term does include an application for licensure, as described in subparagraph (D), of a large volume biological product intended for single dose injection for intravenous use or infusion" for "September 1, 1992" before period at end. See Effective and Termination Dates of 1997 Amendment note below.

Par. (1)(B) to (D). Pub. L. 105–115, §125(b)(2)(M), inserted "or" at end of subpar. (B), redesignated subpar. (D) as (C), and struck out former subpar. (C) which read as follows: "initial certification or initial approval of an antibiotic drug under section 357 of this title, or".

Par. (3). Pub. L. 105–115, §§102(2), 107, in closing provisions, temporarily struck out "and" before "does not include a large volume parenteral drug" and substituted "September 1, 1992, does not include a biological product that is licensed for further manufacturing use only, and does not include a drug that is not distributed commercially and is the subject of an application or supplement submitted by a State or Federal Government entity. Such term does include a large volume biological product intended for single dose injection for intravenous use or infusion" for "September 1, 1992" before period at end. See Effective and Termination Dates of 1997 Amendment note below.

Par. (4). Pub. L. 105–115, §§102(3), 107, temporarily substituted "without substantial further manufacturing" for "without further manufacturing". See Effective and Termination Dates of 1997 Amendment note below.

Par. (5). Pub. L. 105–115, §§102(4), 107, temporarily amended first sentence generally. Prior to amendment, first sentence read as follows: "The term 'prescription drug establishment' means a foreign or domestic place of business which is—

"(A) at one general physical location consisting of one or more buildings all of which are within 5 miles of each other, at which one or more prescription drug products are manufactured in final dosage form, and

"(B) under the management of a person that is listed as the applicant in a human drug application for a prescription drug product with respect to at least one such product."

See Effective and Termination Dates of 1997 Amendment note below.

Par. (7)(A). Pub. L. 105–115, §§102(5), 107, temporarily substituted "contractors of the Food and Drug Administration," for "employees under contract with the Food and Drug Administration who work in facilities owned or leased for the Food and Drug Administration," and "and committees and to contracts with such contractors," for "and committees,". See Effective and Termination Dates of 1997 Amendment note below.

Par. (8)(A). Pub. L. 105–115, §§102(6)(A), 107, temporarily substituted "April of the preceding fiscal year" for "August of the preceding fiscal year" and "April 1997" for "August 1992". See Effective and Termination Dates of 1997 Amendment note below.

Par. (8)(B). Pub. L. 105–115, §§102(6)(B), 107, temporarily substituted "section 254(c)" for "section 254(d)", "fiscal year 1997" for "fiscal year 1992", and "105th Congress, 1st Session" for "102d Congress, 2d Session". See Effective and Termination Dates of 1997 Amendment note below.

Par. (9). Pub. L. 105–115, §§102(7), 107, temporarily added par. (9). See Effective and Termination Dates of 1997 Amendment note below.

Effective and Termination Dates of 2007 Amendment

Pub. L. 110–85, title I, §106(a), Sept. 27, 2007, 121 Stat. 842, provided that: "The amendments made by sections 102, 103, and 104 [enacting section 379h–1 of this title and amending this section and section 379h of this title] cease to be effective October 1, 2012."

Pub. L. 110–85, title I, §107, Sept. 27, 2007, 121 Stat. 842, provided that: "The amendments made by this title [enacting sections 379h–1 and 379h–2 of this title and amending this section and sections 379h and 379j–11 of this title] shall take effect on October 1, 2007, or the date of the enactment of this Act [Sept. 27, 2007], whichever is later, except that fees under part 2 of subchapter C of chapter VII of the Federal Food, Drug, and Cosmetic Act [this subpart] shall be assessed for all human drug applications received on or after October 1, 2007, regardless of the date of the enactment of this Act."

Effective and Termination Dates of 2002 Amendment

Amendment by Pub. L. 107–188 effective Oct. 1, 2002, see section 508 of Pub. L. 107–188, set out as an Effective Date of 2002 Amendment note under section 356b of this title.

Pub. L. 107–188, title V, §509, June 12, 2002, 116 Stat. 694, provided that: "The amendments made by sections 503 and 504 [amending this section and section 379h of this title] cease to be effective October 1, 2007, and section 505 [enacting provisions set out as a note below] ceases to be effective 120 days after such date."

EFFECTIVE AND TERMINATION DATES OF 1997 AMENDMENT

Pub. L. 105–115, title I, §106, Nov. 21, 1997, 111 Stat. 2305, provided that: "The amendments made by this subtitle [subtitle A (§§101–107) of title I of Pub. L. 105–115, amending this section and section 379h of this title] shall take effect October 1, 1997."

Pub. L. 105–115, title I, §107, Nov. 21, 1997, 111 Stat. 2305, provided that: "The amendments made by sections 102 and 103 [amending this section and section 379h of this title] cease to be effective October 1, 2002, and section 104 [enacting provisions formerly set out as a note below] ceases to be effective 120 days after such date."

TERMINATION DATE

Pub. L. 102–571, title I, §105, Oct. 29, 1992, 106 Stat. 4498, provided that: "The amendments made by section 103 [enacting this subpart] shall not be in effect after October 1, 1997 and section 104 [enacting provisions set out as a note below] shall not be in effect after 120 days after such date."

SAVINGS PROVISION

Pub. L. 110–85, title I, §108, Sept. 27, 2007, 121 Stat. 842, provided that: "Notwithstanding section 509 of the Prescription Drug User Fee Amendments of 2002 (21 U.S.C. 379g note) [Pub. L. 107–188], and notwithstanding the amendments made by this title [enacting sections 379h–1 and 379h–2 of this title and amending this section and sections 379h and 379j–11 of this title], part 2 of subchapter C of chapter VII of the Federal Food, Drug, and Cosmetic Act [this subpart], as in effect on the day before the date of the enactment of this title [Sept. 27, 2007], shall continue to be in effect with respect to human drug applications and supplements (as defined in such part as of such day) that on or after October 1, 2002, but before October 1, 2007, were accepted by the Food and Drug Administration for filing with respect to assessing and collecting any fee required by such part for a fiscal year prior to fiscal year 2008."

Pub. L. 107–188, title V, §507, June 12, 2002, 116 Stat. 694, provided that: "Notwithstanding section 107 of the Food and Drug Administration Modernization Act of 1997 [section 107 of Pub. L. 105–115, set out as an Effective and Termination Dates of 1997 Amendment note above], and notwithstanding the amendments made by this subtitle [subtitle A (§§501–509) of title V of Pub. L. 107–188, amending this section and sections 356b and 379h of this title], part 2 of subchapter C of chapter VII of the Federal Food, Drug, and Cosmetic Act [this subpart], as in effect on the day before the date of the enactment of this Act [June 12, 2002], continues to be in effect with respect to human drug applications and supplements (as defined in such part as of such day) that, on or after October 1, 1997, but before October 1, 2002, were accepted by the Food and Drug Administration for filing and with respect to assessing and collecting any fee required by such Act for a fiscal year prior to fiscal year 2003."

Pub. L. 105–115, title I, §105, Nov. 21, 1997, 111 Stat. 2305, provided that: "Notwithstanding section 105 of the Prescription Drug User Fee Act of 1992 [section 105 of Pub. L. 102–571, set out above], the Secretary shall retain the authority to assess and collect any fee required by part 2 of subchapter C of chapter VII of the Federal Food, Drug, and Cosmetic Act [this subpart] for a human drug application or supplement accepted for filing prior to October 1, 1997, and to assess and collect any product or establishment fee required by such Act for a fiscal year prior to fiscal year 1998."

ACCOUNTABILITY AND REPORTS

Pub. L. 107–188, title V, §505, June 12, 2002, 116 Stat. 692, which required the Secretary of Health and Human Services to consult with various congressional committees and health care professionals and provide for public commentary when developing recommendations to Congress regarding review of human drug applications for fiscal years after 2007, and which required the Secretary to submit performance and fiscal reports on certain goals and fees beginning with fiscal year 2003, ceased to be effective 120 days after Oct. 1, 2007. See Effective and Termination Dates of 2002 Amendment note above.

CONGRESSIONAL FINDINGS CONCERNING FEES RELATING TO DRUGS

Pub. L. 110–85, title I, §101(c), Sept. 27, 2007, 121 Stat. 825, provided that: "The Congress finds that the fees authorized by the amendments made in this title [enacting sections 379h–1 and 379h–2 of this title and amending this section and sections 379h and 379j–11 of this title] will be dedicated toward expediting the drug development process and the process for the review of human drug applications, including postmarket drug safety activities, as set forth in the goals identified for purposes of part 2 of subchapter C of chapter VII of the Federal Food, Drug, and Cosmetic Act [this subpart], in the letters from the Secretary of Health and Human Services to the Chairman of the Committee on Health, Education, Labor, and Pensions of the Senate and the Chairman of the Committee on Energy and Commerce of the House of Representatives, as set forth in the Congressional Record."

Pub. L. 107–188, title V, §502, June 12, 2002, 116 Stat. 687, provided that: "The Congress finds that—

"(1) prompt approval of safe and effective new drugs and other therapies is critical to the improvement of the public health so that patients may enjoy the benefits provided by these therapies to treat and prevent illness and disease;

"(2) the public health will be served by making additional funds available for the purpose of augmenting the resources of the Food and Drug Administration that are devoted to the process for the review of human drug applications and the assurance of drug safety;

"(3) the provisions added by the Prescription Drug User Fee Act of 1992 [see section 101(a) of Pub. L. 102–571, set out as a Short Title of 1992 Amendment note under section 301 of this title], as amended by the Food and Drug Administration Modernization Act of 1997 [see Short Title of 1997 Amendment note set out under section 301 of this title], have been successful in substantially reducing review times for human drug applications and should be—

"(A) reauthorized for an additional 5 years, with certain technical improvements; and

"(B) carried out by the Food and Drug Administration with new commitments to implement more ambitious and comprehensive improvements in regulatory processes of the Food and Drug Administration, including—

"(i) strengthening and improving the review and monitoring of drug safety;

"(ii) considering greater interaction between the agency and sponsors during the review of drugs and biologics intended to treat serious diseases and life-threatening diseases; and

"(iii) developing principles for improving first-cycle reviews; and

"(4) the fees authorized by amendments made in this subtitle [subtitle A (§§501–509) of title V of Pub. L. 107–188, amending this section and sections 356b and 379h of this title] will be dedicated towards expediting the drug development process and the process for the review of human drug applications as set forth in the goals identified for purposes of part 2 of subchapter C of chapter VII of the Federal Food, Drug, and Cosmetic Act [this subpart], in the letters from the Secretary of Health and Human Services to the chairman of the Committee on Energy and Commerce of the House of Representatives and the chairman of the Committee on Health, Education, Labor and Pensions of the Senate, as set forth in the Congressional Record."

Pub. L. 105–115, title I, §101, Nov. 21, 1997, 111 Stat. 2298, provided that: "Congress finds that—

"(1) prompt approval of safe and effective new drugs and other therapies is critical to the improvement of the public health so that patients may enjoy the benefits provided by these therapies to treat and prevent illness and disease;

"(2) the public health will be served by making additional funds available for the purpose of augmenting the resources of the Food and Drug Administration that are devoted to the process for review of human drug applications;

"(3) the provisions added by the Prescription Drug User Fee Act of 1992 [see section 101(a) of Pub. L. 102–571, set out as a Short Title of 1992 Amendment note under section 301 of this title] have been successful in substantially reducing review times for human drug applications and should be—

"(A) reauthorized for an additional 5 years, with certain technical improvements; and

"(B) carried out by the Food and Drug Administration with new commitments to implement more ambitious and comprehensive improvements in regulatory processes of the Food and Drug Administration; and

"(4) the fees authorized by amendments made in this subtitle [subtitle A (§§101–107) of title I of Pub. L. 105–115, amending this section and section 379h of this title] will be dedicated toward expediting the drug development process and the review of human drug applications as set forth in the goals identified, for purposes of part 2 of subchapter C of chapter VII of the Federal Food, Drug, and Cosmetic Act [this subpart], in the letters from the Secretary of Health and Human Services to the chairman of the Committee on Commerce of the House of Representatives and the chairman of the Committee on Labor and Human Resources [now Committee on Health, Education, Labor, and Pensions] of the Senate, as set forth in the Congressional Record."

Pub. L. 102–571, title I, §102, Oct. 29, 1992, 106 Stat. 4491, provided that: "The Congress finds that—

"(1) prompt approval of safe and effective new drugs is critical to the improvement of the public health so that patients may enjoy the benefits provided by these therapies to treat and prevent illness and disease;

"(2) the public health will be served by making additional funds available for the purpose of augmenting the resources of the Food and Drug Administration that are devoted to the process for review of human drug applications; and

"(3) the fees authorized by this title [see Short Title of 1992 Amendment note, set out under section 301 of this title] will be dedicated toward expediting the review of human drug applications as set forth in the goals identified in the letters of September 14, 1992, and September 21, 1992, from the Commissioner of Food and Drugs to the Chairman of the Energy and Commerce Committee of the House of Representatives and the Chairman of the Labor and Human Resources Committee of the Senate, as set forth at 138 Cong. Rec. H9099–H9100 (daily ed. September 22, 1992)."

ANNUAL REPORTS

Pub. L. 105–115, title I, §104, Nov. 21, 1997, 111 Stat. 2304, which directed the Secretary of Health and Human Services to prepare and submit to Committee on Commerce of the House of Representatives and the Committee on Labor and Human Resources of the Senate, within 60 days after the end of each fiscal year during which fees are collected under this subpart, a report stating the Food and Drug Administration's progress in achieving the goals identified in the letters described in section 101(4) of Pub. L. 105–115, set out above, during such fiscal year and the Administration's future plans for meeting the goals, and within 120 days after the end of each fiscal year during which fees are collected, to prepare and submit a report on the implementation of the authority for such fees during such fiscal year and on the use the Administration made of the fees collected during such fiscal year, ceased to be effective 120 days after Oct. 1, 2002. See section 107 of Pub. L. 105–115, set out as an Effective and Termination Dates of 1997 Amendment note above.

Pub. L. 102–571, title I, §104, Oct. 29, 1992, 106 Stat. 4498, which provided that the Secretary of Health and Human Services submit to Committee on Energy and Commerce of the House of Representatives and Committee on Labor and Human Resources of the Senate, within 60 days after the end of each fiscal year during which fees were collected under this subpart, a report stating the Food and Drug Administration's progress in achieving the goals identified in section 102(3) of Pub. L. 102–571, set out as a note above, during such fiscal year and that agency's future plans for meeting such goals, and within 120 days after the end of each fiscal year during which such fees were collected, a report on the implementation of the authority for such fees during such fiscal year and on the use the Food and Drug Administration made of the fees collected during such fiscal year, ceased to be in effect 120 days after Oct. 1, 1997. See Termination Date note above.

ANIMAL DRUG USER FEE STUDY

Pub. L. 102–571, title I, §108, Oct. 29, 1992, 106 Stat. 4500, directed Secretary, in consultation with manufacturers of animal drug products and other interested persons, to undertake study to evaluate whether, and under what conditions, to impose user fees to supplement appropriated funds in order to improve process of reviewing applications (including abbreviated and supplemental applications) for new animal drugs under section 360b of this title, and further provided for submission of study to Congress no later than Jan. 4, 1994.

§379h. Authority to assess and use drug fees

(a) Types of fees

Beginning in fiscal year 2008, the Secretary shall assess and collect fees in accordance with this section as follows:

(1) Human drug application and supplement fee

(A) In general

Each person that submits, on or after September 1, 1992, a human drug application or a supplement shall be subject to a fee as follows:

(i) A fee established under subsection (c)(5) of this section for a human drug application for which clinical data (other than bioavailability or bioequivalence studies) with respect to safety or effectiveness are required for approval.

(ii) A fee established under subsection (c)(5) of this section for a human drug application for which clinical data with respect to safety or effectiveness are not required or a supplement for which clinical data (other than bioavailability or bioequivalence studies) with respect to safety or effectiveness are required. Such fee shall be half of the amount of the fee established under clause (i).

(B) Payment

The fee required by subparagraph (A) shall be due upon submission of the application or supplement.

(C) Exception for previously filed application or supplement

If a human drug application or supplement was submitted by a person that paid the fee for such application or supplement, was accepted for filing, and was not approved or was withdrawn (without a waiver), the submission of a human drug application or a supplement for the same product by the same person (or the person's licensee, assignee, or successor) shall not be subject to a fee under subparagraph (A).

(D) Refund of fee if application refused for filing or withdrawn before filing

The Secretary shall refund 75 percent of the fee paid under subparagraph (B) for any application or supplement which is refused for filing or withdrawn without a waiver before filing.

(E) Fees for applications previously refused for filing or withdrawn before filing

A human drug application or supplement that was submitted but was refused for filing, or was withdrawn before being accepted or refused for filing, shall be subject to the full fee under subparagraph (A) upon being resubmitted or filed over protest, unless the fee is waived or reduced under subsection (d).

(F) Exception for designated orphan drug or indication

A human drug application for a prescription drug product that has been designated as a drug for a rare disease or condition pursuant to section 360bb of this title shall not be subject to a fee under subparagraph (A), unless the human drug application includes an indication for other than a rare disease or condition. A supplement proposing to include a new indication for a rare disease or condition in a human drug application shall not be subject to a fee under subparagraph (A), if the drug has been designated pursuant to section 360bb of this title as a drug for a rare disease or condition with regard to the indication proposed in such supplement.

(G) Refund of fee if application withdrawn

If an application or supplement is withdrawn after the application or supplement was filed, the Secretary may refund the fee or a portion of the fee if no substantial work was performed on the application or supplement after the application or supplement was filed. The Secretary shall have the sole discretion to refund a fee or a portion of the fee under this subparagraph. A determination by the Secretary concerning a refund under this paragraph shall not be reviewable.

(2) Prescription drug establishment fee

(A) In general

Except as provided in subparagraphs (B) and (C), each person that—

(i) is named as the applicant in a human drug application; and

(ii) after September 1, 1992, had pending before the Secretary a human drug application or supplement,

shall be assessed an annual fee established under subsection (c)(5) of this section for each prescription drug establishment listed in its approved human drug application as an establishment that manufactures the prescription drug product named in the application. The annual establishment fee shall be assessed in each fiscal year in which the prescription drug product named in the application is assessed a fee under paragraph (3) unless the prescription drug establishment listed in the application does not engage in the manufacture of the prescription drug product during the fiscal year. The establishment fee shall be payable on or before October 1 of each year. Each such establishment shall be assessed only one fee per establishment, notwithstanding the number of prescription drug products manufactured at the establishment. In the event an establishment is listed in a human drug application by more than one applicant, the establishment fee for the fiscal year shall be divided equally and assessed among the applicants whose prescription drug products are manufactured by the establishment during the fiscal year and assessed product fees under paragraph (3).

(B) Exception

If, during the fiscal year, an applicant initiates or causes to be initiated the manufacture of a prescription drug product at an establishment listed in its human drug application—

(i) that did not manufacture the product in the previous fiscal year; and

(ii) for which the full establishment fee has been assessed in the fiscal year at a time before manufacture of the prescription drug product was begun;

the applicant will not be assessed a share of the establishment fee for the fiscal year in which the manufacture of the product began.

(C) Special rules for positron emission tomography drugs

(i) In general

Except as provided in clause (ii), each person who is named as the applicant in an approved human drug application for a positron emission tomography drug shall be subject under subparagraph (A) to one-sixth of an annual establishment fee with respect to each such establishment identified in the application as producing positron emission tomography drugs under the approved application.

(ii) Exception from annual establishment fee

Each person who is named as the applicant in an application described in clause (i) shall not be assessed an annual establishment fee for a fiscal year if the person certifies to the Secretary, at a time specified by the Secretary and using procedures specified by the Secretary, that—

(I) the person is a not-for-profit medical center that has only 1 establishment for the production of positron emission tomography drugs; and

(II) at least 95 percent of the total number of doses of each positron emission tomography drug produced by such establishment during such fiscal year will be used within the medical center.

(iii) Definition

For purposes of this subparagraph, the term "positron emission tomography drug" has the meaning given to the term "compounded positron emission tomography drug" in section 321(ii) of this title, except that paragraph (1)(B) of such section shall not apply.

(3) Prescription drug product fee

(A) In general

Except as provided in subparagraph (B), each person who is named as the applicant in a human drug application, and who, after September 1, 1992, had pending before the Secretary a human drug application or supplement, shall pay for each such prescription drug product the annual fee established under subsection (c)(5) of this section. Such fee shall be payable on or before October 1 of each year. Such fee shall be paid only once for each product for a fiscal year in which the fee is payable.

(B) Exception

A prescription drug product shall not be assessed a fee under subparagraph (A) if such product is identified on the list compiled under section 355(j)(7)(A) of this title with a potency described in terms of per 100 mL, or if such product is the same product as another product approved under an application filed under section 355(b) or 355(j) of this title, under an abbreviated application filed under section 357 of this title (as in effect on the day before November 21, 1997), or under an abbreviated new drug application pursuant to regulations in effect prior to the implementation of the Drug Price Competition and Patent Term Restoration Act of 1984.

(b) Fee revenue amounts

(1) In general

For each of the fiscal years 2008 through 2012, fees under subsection (a) shall, except as provided in subsections (c), (d), (f), and (g), be established to generate a total revenue amount under such subsection that is equal to the sum of—

(A) $392,783,000; and

(B) an amount equal to the modified workload adjustment factor for fiscal year 2007 (as determined under paragraph (3)).

(2) Types of fees

Of the total revenue amount determined for a fiscal year under paragraph (1)—

(A) one-third shall be derived from fees under subsection (a)(1) (relating to human drug applications and supplements);

(B) one-third shall be derived from fees under subsection (a)(2) (relating to prescription drug establishments); and

(C) one-third shall be derived from fees under subsection (a)(3) (relating to prescription drug products).

(3) Modified workload adjustment factor for fiscal year 2007

For purposes of paragraph (1)(B), the Secretary shall determine the modified workload adjustment factor by determining the dollar amount that results from applying the methodology that was in effect under subsection (c)(2) for fiscal year 2007 to the amount $354,893,000, except that, with respect to the portion of such determination that is based on the change in the total number of commercial investigational new drug applications, the Secretary shall count the number of such applications that were active during the most recent 12-month period for which data on such submissions is available.

(4) Additional fee revenues for drug safety

(A) In general

For each of the fiscal years 2008 through 2012, paragraph (1)(A) shall be applied by substituting the amount determined under subparagraph (B) for "$392,783,000".

(B) Amount determined

For each of the fiscal years 2008 through 2012, the amount determined under this subparagraph is the sum of—

(i) $392,783,000; plus

(ii)(I) for fiscal year 2008, $25,000,000;

(II) for fiscal year 2009, $35,000,000;

(III) for fiscal year 2010, $45,000,000;

(IV) for fiscal year 2011, $55,000,000; and

(V) for fiscal year 2012, $65,000,000.

(c) Adjustments

(1) Inflation adjustment

For fiscal year 2009 and subsequent fiscal years, the revenues established in subsection (b) shall be adjusted by the Secretary by notice, published in the Federal Register, for a fiscal year to reflect the greater of—

(A) the total percentage change that occurred in the Consumer Price Index for all urban consumers (all items; U.S. city average) for the 12 month period ending June 30 preceding the fiscal year for which fees are being established,

(B) the total percentage change for the previous fiscal year in basic pay under the General Schedule in accordance with section 5332 of title 5, as adjusted by any locality-based comparability payment pursuant to section 5304 of such title for Federal employees stationed in the District of Columbia, or

(C) the average annual change in the cost, per full-time equivalent position of the Food and Drug Administration, of all personnel compensation and benefits paid with respect to such positions for the first 5 years of the preceding 6 fiscal years.

The adjustment made each fiscal year by this subsection will be added on a compounded basis to the sum of all adjustments made each fiscal year after fiscal year 2008 under this subsection.

(2) Workload adjustment

For fiscal year 2009 and subsequent fiscal years, after the fee revenues established in subsection (b) of this section are adjusted for a fiscal year for inflation in accordance with paragraph (1), the fee revenues shall be adjusted further for such fiscal year to reflect changes in the workload of the Secretary for the process for the review of human drug applications. With respect to such adjustment:

(A) The adjustment shall be determined by the Secretary based on a weighted average of the change in the total number of human drug applications (adjusted for changes in review activities, as described in the notice that the Secretary is required to publish in the Federal Register under this subparagraph), efficacy supplements, and manufacturing supplements submitted to the Secretary, and the change in the total number of active commercial investigational new drug applications (adjusted for changes in review activities, as so described) during the most recent 12-month period for which data on such submissions is available. The Secretary shall publish in the Federal Register the fee revenues and fees resulting from the adjustment and the supporting methodologies.

(B) Under no circumstances shall the adjustment result in fee revenues for a fiscal year that are less than the fee revenues for the fiscal year established in subsection (b) of this section, as adjusted for inflation under paragraph (1). Any adjustment for changes in review activities made in setting fees and revenue amounts for fiscal year 2009 may not result in the total workload adjustment being more than 2 percentage points higher than it would have been in the absence of the adjustment for changes in review activities.

(C) The Secretary shall contract with an independent accounting firm to study the adjustment for changes in review activities applied in setting fees and revenue amounts for fiscal year 2009 and to make recommendations, if warranted, for future changes in the methodology for calculating the adjustment. After review of the recommendations, the Secretary shall, if warranted, make appropriate changes to the methodology, and the changes shall be effective for each of the fiscal years 2010 through 2012. The Secretary shall not make any adjustment for changes in review activities for any fiscal year after 2009 unless such study has been completed.

(3) Rent and rent-related cost adjustment

For fiscal year 2010 and each subsequent fiscal year, the Secretary shall, before making adjustments under paragraphs (1) and (2), decrease the fee revenue amount established in subsection (b) if actual costs paid for rent and rent-related expenses for the preceding fiscal year are less than estimates made for such year in fiscal year 2006. Any reduction made under this paragraph shall not exceed the amount by which such costs fall below the estimates made in fiscal year 2006 for such fiscal year, and shall not exceed $11,721,000 for any fiscal year.

(4) Final year adjustment

(A) Increase in fees

For fiscal year 2012, the Secretary may, in addition to adjustments under this paragraph and paragraphs (1), (2), and (3), further increase the fee revenues and fees established in subsection (b) if such an adjustment is necessary to provide for not more than 3 months of operating reserves of carryover user fees for the process for the review of human drug applications for the first 3 months of fiscal year 2013. If such an adjustment is necessary, the rationale for the amount of the increase shall be contained in the annual notice establishing fee revenues and fees for fiscal year 2012. If the Secretary has carryover balances for such process in excess of 3 months of such operating reserves, the adjustment under this subparagraph shall not be made.

(B) Decrease in fees

(i) In general

For fiscal year 2012, the Secretary may, in addition to adjustments under this paragraph and paragraphs (1), (2), and (3), decrease the fee revenues and fees established in subsection (b) by the amount determined in clause (ii), if, for fiscal year 2009 or 2010—

(I) the amount of the total appropriations for the Food and Drug Administration for such fiscal year (excluding the amount of fees appropriated for such fiscal year) exceeds the amount of the total appropriations for the Food and Drug Administration for fiscal year 2008 (excluding the amount of fees appropriated for such fiscal year), adjusted as provided under paragraph (1); and

(II) the amount of the total appropriations expended for the process for the review of human drug applications at the Food and Drug Administration for such fiscal year (excluding the amount of fees appropriated for such fiscal year) exceeds the amount of appropriations expended for the process for the review of human drug applications at the Food and Drug Administration for fiscal year 2008 (excluding the amount of fees appropriated for such fiscal year), adjusted as provided under paragraph (1).

(ii) Amount of decrease

The amount determined in this clause is the lesser of—

(I) the amount equal to the sum of the amounts that, for each of fiscal years 2009 and 2010, is the lesser of—

(aa) the excess amount described in clause (i)(II) for such fiscal year; or

(bb) the amount specified in subsection (b)(4)(B)(ii) for such fiscal year; or

(II) $65,000,000.

(iii) Limitations

(I) Fiscal year condition

In making the determination under clause (ii), an amount described in subclause (I) of such clause for fiscal year 2009 or 2010 shall be taken into account only if subclauses (I) and (II) of clause (i) apply to such fiscal year.

(II) Relation to subparagraph (A)

The Secretary shall limit any decrease under this paragraph if such a limitation is necessary to provide for the 3 months of operating reserves described in subparagraph (A).

(5) Annual fee setting

The Secretary shall, 60 days before the start of each fiscal year that begins after September 30, 2007, establish, for the next fiscal year, application, product, and establishment fees under subsection (a) of this section, based on the revenue amounts established under subsection (b) of this section and the adjustments provided under this subsection.

(6) Limit

The total amount of fees charged, as adjusted under this subsection, for a fiscal year may not exceed the total costs for such fiscal year for the resources allocated for the process for the review of human drug applications.

(d) Fee waiver or reduction

(1) In general

The Secretary shall grant to a person who is named as the applicant in a human drug application a waiver from or a reduction of one or more fees assessed to that person under subsection (a) of this section where the Secretary finds that—

(A) such waiver or reduction is necessary to protect the public health,

(B) the assessment of the fee would present a significant barrier to innovation because of limited resources available to such person or other circumstances,

(C) the fees to be paid by such person will exceed the anticipated present and future costs incurred by the Secretary in conducting the process for the review of human drug applications for such person, or

(D) the applicant involved is a small business submitting its first human drug application to the Secretary for review.

(2) Considerations

In determining whether to grant a waiver or reduction of a fee under paragraph (1), the Secretary shall consider only the circumstances and assets of the applicant involved and any affiliate of the applicant.

(3) Use of standard costs

In making the finding in paragraph (1)(C), the Secretary may use standard costs.

(4) Rules relating to small businesses

(A) "Small business" defined

In paragraph (1)(D), the term "small business" means an entity that has fewer than 500 employees, including employees of affiliates, and that does not have a drug product that has been approved under a human drug application and introduced or delivered for introduction into interstate commerce.

(B) Waiver of application fee

The Secretary shall waive under paragraph (1)(D) the application fee for the first human drug application that a small business or its affiliate submits to the Secretary for review. After a small business or its affiliate is granted such a waiver, the small business or its affiliate shall pay—

(i) application fees for all subsequent human drug applications submitted to the Secretary for review in the same manner as an entity that does not qualify as a small business; and

(ii) all supplement fees for all supplements to human drug applications submitted to the Secretary for review in the same manner as an entity that does not qualify as a small business.

(e) Effect of failure to pay fees

A human drug application or supplement submitted by a person subject to fees under subsection (a) of this section shall be considered incomplete and shall not be accepted for filing by the Secretary until all fees owed by such person have been paid.

(f) Limitations

(1) In general

Fees under subsection (a) of this section shall be refunded for a fiscal year beginning after fiscal year 1997 unless appropriations for salaries and expenses of the Food and Drug Administration for such fiscal year (excluding the amount of fees appropriated for such fiscal year) are equal to or greater than the amount of appropriations for the salaries and expenses of the Food and Drug Administration for the fiscal year 1997 (excluding the amount of fees appropriated for such fiscal year) multiplied by the adjustment factor applicable to the fiscal year involved.

(2) Authority

If the Secretary does not assess fees under subsection (a) of this section during any portion of a fiscal year because of paragraph (1) and if at a later date in such fiscal year the Secretary may assess such fees, the Secretary may assess and collect such fees, without any modification in the rate, for human drug applications and supplements, prescription drug establishments, and prescription drug products at any time in such fiscal year notwithstanding the provisions of subsection (a) of this section relating to the date fees are to be paid.

(g) Crediting and availability of fees

(1) In general

Fees authorized under subsection (a) shall be collected and available for obligation only to the extent and in the amount provided in advance in appropriations Acts. Such fees are authorized to remain available until expended. Such sums as may be necessary may be transferred from the Food and Drug Administration salaries and expenses appropriation account without fiscal year limitation to such appropriation account for salaries and expenses with such fiscal year limitation. The sums transferred shall be available solely for the process for the review of human drug applications.

(2) Collections and appropriation acts

(A) In general

The fees authorized by this section—

(i) shall be retained in each fiscal year in an amount not to exceed the amount specified in appropriation Acts, or otherwise made available for obligation, for such fiscal year, and

(ii) shall only be collected and available to defray increases in the costs of the resources allocated for the process for the review of human drug applications (including increases in such costs for an additional number of full-time equivalent positions in the Department of Health and Human Services to be engaged in such process) over such costs, excluding costs paid from fees collected under this section, for fiscal year 1997 multiplied by the adjustment factor.

(B) Compliance

The Secretary shall be considered to have met the requirements of subparagraph (A)(ii) in any fiscal year if the costs funded by appropriations and allocated for the process for the review of human drug applications—

(i) are not more than 3 percent below the level specified in subparagraph (A)(ii); or

(ii)(I) are more than 3 percent below the level specified in subparagraph (A)(ii), and fees assessed for the fiscal year following the subsequent fiscal year are decreased by the amount in excess of 3 percent by which such costs fell below the level specified in such subparagraph; and

(II) such costs are not more than 5 percent below the level specified in such subparagraph.

(3) Authorization of appropriations

For each of the fiscal years 2008 through 2012, there is authorized to be appropriated for fees under this section an amount equal to the total revenue amount determined under subsection (b) for the fiscal year, as adjusted or otherwise affected under subsection (c) and paragraph (4) of this subsection.

(4) Offset

If the sum of the cumulative amount of fees collected under this section for the fiscal years 2008 through 2010 and the amount of fees estimated to be collected under this section for fiscal year 2011 exceeds the cumulative amount appropriated under paragraph (3) for the fiscal years 2008 through 2011, the excess shall be credited to the appropriation account of the Food and Drug Administration as provided in paragraph (1), and shall be subtracted from the amount of fees that would otherwise be authorized to be collected under this section pursuant to appropriation Acts for fiscal year 2012.

(h) Collection of unpaid fees

In any case where the Secretary does not receive payment of a fee assessed under subsection (a) of this section within 30 days after it is due, such fee shall be treated as a claim of the United States Government subject to subchapter II of chapter 37 of title 31.

(i) Written requests for waivers, reductions, and refunds

To qualify for consideration for a waiver or reduction under subsection (d) of this section, or for a refund of any fee collected in accordance with subsection (a) of this section, a person shall submit to the Secretary a written request for such waiver, reduction, or refund not later than 180 days after such fee is due.

(j) Construction

This section may not be construed to require that the number of full-time equivalent positions in the Department of Health and Human Services, for officers, employers, and advisory committees not engaged in the process of the review of human drug applications, be reduced to offset the number of officers, employees, and advisory committees so engaged.

(k) Orphan drugs

(1) Exemption

A drug designated under section 360bb of this title for a rare disease or condition and approved under section 355 of this title or under section 262 of title 42 shall be exempt from product and establishment fees under this section, if the drug meets all of the following conditions:

(A) The drug meets the public health requirements contained in this chapter as such requirements are applied to requests for waivers for product and establishment fees.

(B) The drug is owned or licensed and is marketed by a company that had less than $50,000,000 in gross worldwide revenue during the previous year.

(2) Evidence of qualification

An exemption under paragraph (1) applies with respect to a drug only if the applicant involved submits a certification that its gross annual revenues did not exceed $50,000,000 for the preceding 12 months before the exemption was requested.

(June 25, 1938, ch. 675, § 736, as added Pub. L. 102–571, title I, § 103, Oct. 29, 1992, 106 Stat. 4494; amended Pub. L. 105–115, title I, § 103(a)–(g), Nov. 21, 1997, 111 Stat. 2299–2304; Pub. L. 107–109, § 5(a), Jan. 4, 2002, 115 Stat. 1413; Pub. L. 107–188, title V, § 504, June 12, 2002, 116 Stat. 689; Pub. L. 110–85, title I, § 103(a)–(h)(1), Sept. 27, 2007, 121 Stat. 826–832.)

AMENDMENT OF SECTION

For termination of amendment by section 106(a) of Pub. L. 110–85, see Effective and Termination Dates of 2007 Amendment note below.

For termination of amendment by section 509 of Pub. L. 107–188, see Effective and Termination Date of 2002 Amendments note below.

For termination of amendment by section 107 of Pub. L. 105–115, see Effective and Termination Dates of 1997 Amendment note below.

TERMINATION OF SECTION

For termination of section by section 105 of Pub. L. 102–571, see Termination Date note below.

REFERENCES IN TEXT

Section 357 of this title, referred to in subsec. (a)(3)(B), was repealed by Pub. L. 105–115, title I, § 125(b)(1), Nov. 21, 1997, 111 Stat. 2325.

The Drug Price Competition and Patent Term Restoration Act of 1984, referred to in subsec. (a)(3)(B), is

Pub. L. 98–417, Sept. 24, 1984, 98 Stat. 1585. For complete classification of this Act to the Code, see Short Title of 1984 Amendment note set out under section 301 of this title and Tables.

AMENDMENTS

2007—Subsec. (a). Pub. L. 110–85, §§103(a)(1), 106(a), temporarily substituted "2008" for "2003" in introductory provisions. See Effective and Termination Dates of 2007 Amendment note below.

Subsec. (a)(1)(A). Pub. L. 110–85, §§103(g), 106(a), temporarily substituted "(c)(5)" for "(c)(4)" in cls. (i) and (ii). See Effective and Termination Dates of 2007 Amendment note below.

Subsec. (a)(1)(D). Pub. L. 110–85, §§103(a)(2)(A), 106(a), temporarily inserted "or withdrawn before filing" after "refused for filing" in heading and "or withdrawn without a waiver before filing" before period at end of text. See Effective and Termination Dates of 2007 Amendment note below.

Subsec. (a)(1)(E) to (G). Pub. L. 110–85, §§103(a)(2)(B), (C), 106(a), temporarily added subpar. (E) and redesignated former subpars. (E) and (F) as (F) and (G), respectively. See Effective and Termination Dates of 2007 Amendment note below.

Subsec. (a)(2)(A). Pub. L. 110–85, §§103(a)(3)(A), (g), 106(a), temporarily substituted "subparagraphs (B) and (C)" for "subparagraph (B)" in introductory provisions and "(c)(5)" for "(c)(4)" in concluding provisions. See Effective and Termination Dates of 2007 Amendment note below.

Subsec. (a)(2)(C). Pub. L. 110–85, §§103(a)(3)(B), 106(a), temporarily added subpar. (C). See Effective and Termination Dates of 2007 Amendment note below.

Subsec. (a)(3)(A). Pub. L. 110–85, §§103(g), 106(a), temporarily substituted "(c)(5)" for "(c)(4)". See Effective and Termination Dates of 2007 Amendment note below.

Subsec. (b). Pub. L. 110–85, §§103(b), 106(a), temporarily amended subsec. (b) generally, substituting provisions contained in pars. (1) to (4) relating to fee revenue amounts for fiscal years 2008 through 2012 for undesignated provisions relating to fee schedules for fiscal years 2003 to 2007. See Effective and Termination Dates of 2007 Amendment note below.

Subsec. (c)(1). Pub. L. 110–85, §§103(c)(1), 106(a), temporarily amended par. (1) by substituting "For fiscal year 2009 and subsequent fiscal years, the revenues established in subsection (b)" for "The revenues established in subsection (b)" in introductory provisions, adding subpar. (C), and substituting "fiscal year 2008" for "fiscal year 2003" in concluding provisions. See Effective and Termination Dates of 2007 Amendment note below.

Subsec. (c)(2). Pub. L. 110–85, §§103(c)(2)(A), 106(a), temporarily substituted "For fiscal year 2009 and subsequent fiscal years," for "Beginning with fiscal year 2004," in introductory provisions. See Effective and Termination Dates of 2007 Amendment note below.

Subsec. (c)(2)(A). Pub. L. 110–85, §§103(c)(2)(B), 106(a), temporarily substituted "human drug applications (adjusted for changes in review activities, as described in the notice that the Secretary is required to publish in the Federal Register under this subparagraph), efficacy supplements, and manufacturing supplements submitted to the Secretary, and the change in the total number of active commercial investigational new drug applications (adjusted for changes in review activities, as so described) during the most recent 12-month period for which data on such submissions is available." for "human drug applications, commercial investigational new drug applications, efficacy supplements, and manufacturing supplements submitted to the Secretary." in first sentence. See Effective and Termination Dates of 2007 Amendment note below.

Subsec. (c)(2)(B). Pub. L. 110–85, §§103(c)(2)(C), 106(a), temporarily inserted at end "Any adjustment for changes in review activities made in setting fees and revenue amounts for fiscal year 2009 may not result in the total workload adjustment being more than 2 percentage points higher than it would have been in the absence of the adjustment for changes in review activities." See Effective and Termination Dates of 2007 Amendment note below.

Subsec. (c)(2)(C). Pub. L. 110–85, §§103(c)(2)(D), 106(a), temporarily added subpar. (C). See Effective and Termination Dates of 2007 Amendment note below.

Subsec. (c)(3). Pub. L. 110–85, §§103(c)(3), 106(a), temporarily added par. (3). Former par. (3) redesignated (4). See Effective and Termination Dates of 2007 Amendment note below.

Subsec. (c)(4). Pub. L. 110–85, §§103(c)(3)(A), (4), 106(a), temporarily redesignated par. (3) as (4) and amended it generally. Prior to amendment, text read as follows: "For fiscal year 2007, the Secretary may, in addition to adjustments under paragraphs (1) and (2), further increase the fee revenues and fees established in subsection (b) of this section if such an adjustment is necessary to provide for not more than three months of operating reserves of carryover user fees for the process for the review of human drug applications for the first three months of fiscal year 2008. If such an adjustment is necessary, the rationale for the amount of the increase shall be contained in the annual notice establishing fee revenues and fees for fiscal year 2007. If the Secretary has carryover balances for such process in excess of three months of such operating reserves, the adjustment under this paragraph shall not be made." Former par. (4) redesignated (5). See Effective and Termination Dates of 2007 Amendment note below.

Subsec. (c)(5). Pub. L. 110–85, §§103(c)(3)(A), (5), 106(a), temporarily redesignated par. (4) as (5) and substituted "2007" for "2002". Former par. (5) redesignated (6). See Effective and Termination Dates of 2007 Amendment note below.

Subsec. (c)(6). Pub. L. 110–85, §§103(c)(3)(A), 106(a), temporarily redesignated par. (5) as (6). See Effective and Termination Dates of 2007 Amendment note below.

Subsec. (d)(1). Pub. L. 110–85, §§103(d)(1), 106(a), temporarily inserted "to a person who is named as the applicant in a human drug application" after "The Secretary shall grant" and "to that person" after "one or more fees assessed" in introductory provisions. See Effective and Termination Dates of 2007 Amendment note below.

Subsec. (d)(2), (3). Pub. L. 110–85, §§103(d)(2), (3), 106(a), temporarily added par. (2) and redesignated former par. (2) as (3). Former par. (3) redesignated (4). See Effective and Termination Dates of 2007 Amendment note below.

Subsec. (d)(4). Pub. L. 110–85, §§103(d)(2), 106(a), temporarily redesignated par. (3) as (4). See Effective and Termination Dates of 2007 Amendment note below.

Subsec. (d)(4)(A). Pub. L. 110–85, §§103(d)(4), 106(a), temporarily inserted before period at end ", and that does not have a drug product that has been approved under a human drug application and introduced or delivered for introduction into interstate commerce". See Effective and Termination Dates of 2007 Amendment note below.

Subsec. (g)(1). Pub. L. 110–85, §§103(h)(1), 106(a), temporarily substituted "Fees authorized under subsection (a) shall be collected and available for obligation only to the extent and in the amount provided in advance in appropriations Acts. Such fees are authorized to remain available until expended." for "Fees collected for a fiscal year pursuant to subsection (a) of this section shall be credited to the appropriation account for salaries and expenses of the Food and Drug Administration and shall be available in accordance with appropriation Acts until expended without fiscal year limitation." See Effective and Termination Dates of 2007 Amendment note below.

Subsec. (g)(3). Pub. L. 110–85, §§103(e)(1), 106(a), temporarily amended par. (3) generally. Prior to amendment, par. (3) authorized appropriations for fiscal years 2003 to 2007. See Effective and Termination Dates of 2007 Amendment note below.

Subsec. (g)(4). Pub. L. 110–85, §§103(e)(2), 106(a), temporarily reenacted heading without change and amended text generally. Prior to amendment, text read as follows: "Any amount of fees collected for a fiscal year under this section that exceeds the amount of fees specified in appropriation Acts for such fiscal year shall be credited to the appropriation account of the Food and Drug Administration as provided in paragraph (1), and shall be subtracted from the amount of fees that would otherwise be authorized to be collected under this section pursuant to appropriation Acts for a subsequent fiscal year." See Effective and Termination Dates of 2007 Amendment note below.

Subsec. (k). Pub. L. 110–85, §§ 103(f), 106(a), temporarily added subsec. (k). See Effective and Termination Dates of 2007 Amendment note below.

2002—Subsec. (a). Pub. L. 107–188, §§ 504(a)(1), 509, temporarily substituted "fiscal year 2003" for "fiscal year 1998" in introductory provisions. See Effective and Termination Dates of 2002 Amendment note below.

Subsec. (a)(1)(A)(i). Pub. L. 107–188, §§ 504(a)(2)(A), 509, temporarily substituted "under subsection (c)(4)" for "in subsection (b)". See Effective and Termination Dates of 2002 Amendment note below.

Subsec. (a)(1)(A)(ii). Pub. L. 107–188, §§ 504(a)(2), 509, temporarily substituted "under subsection (c)(4)" for "in subsection (b)" and inserted "Such fee shall be half of the amount of the fee established under clause (i)." at end. See Effective and Termination Dates of 2002 Amendment note below.

Subsec. (a)(1)(F), (G). Pub. L. 107–109 redesignated subpar. (G) as (F) and struck out heading and text of former subpar. (F). Text read as follows: "A supplement to a human drug application proposing to include a new indication for use in pediatric populations shall not be assessed a fee under subparagraph (A)."

Subsec. (a)(2)(A). Pub. L. 107–188, §§ 504(a)(3), 509, in concluding provisions, temporarily substituted "under subsection (c)(4)" for "in subsection (b)" and "payable on or before October 1" for "payable on or before January 31". See Effective and Termination Dates of 2002 Amendment note below.

Subsec. (a)(3)(A). Pub. L. 107–188, §§ 504(a)(4)(A), 509, temporarily amended heading and text of subpar. (A) generally. Prior to amendment, text read as follows: "Except as provided in subparagraph (B), each person—

"(i) who is named as the applicant in a human drug application for a prescription drug product which has been submitted for listing under section 360 of this title, and

"(ii) who, after September 1, 1992, had pending before the Secretary a human drug application or supplement,

shall pay for each such prescription drug product the annual fee established in subsection (b) of this section. Such fee shall be payable for the fiscal year in which the product is first submitted for listing under section 360 of this title, or is submitted for relisting under section 360 of this title if the product has been withdrawn from listing and relisted. After such fee is paid for that fiscal year, such fee shall be payable on or before January 31 of each year. Such fee shall be paid only once for each product for a fiscal year in which the fee is payable." See Effective and Termination Dates of 2002 Amendment note below.

Subsec. (a)(3)(B). Pub. L. 107–188, §§ 504(a)(4)(B), 509, temporarily substituted "A prescription drug product shall not be assessed a fee under subparagraph (A) if such product is identified on the list compiled under section 355(j)(7)(A) of this title with a potency described in terms of per 100 mL, or if such product is the same product as another product approved under an application filed under section 355(b)" for "The listing of a prescription drug product under section 360 of this title shall not require the person who listed such product to pay the fee prescribed by subparagraph (A) if such product is the same product as a product approved under an application filed under section 355(b)(2)". See Effective and Termination Dates of 2002 Amendment note below.

Subsec. (b). Pub. L. 107–188, §§ 504(b), 509, temporarily amended heading and text of subsec. (b) generally, substituting "Fee revenue amounts" for "Fee amounts" in heading and substituting fee schedules for fiscal years 2003 to 2007 for fee provisions relating to fiscal years 1998 to 2002. See Effective and Termination Dates of 2002 Amendment note below.

Subsec. (c)(1). Pub. L. 107–188, §§ 504(c)(1)(A), (D), 509, temporarily substituted "revenues" for "fees and total fee revenues" in introductory provisions and "fiscal year 2003" for "fiscal year 1997" in concluding provisions. See Effective and Termination Dates of 2002 Amendment note below.

Subsec. (c)(1)(A). Pub. L. 107–188, §§ 504(c)(1)(B), 509, temporarily struck out "during the preceding fiscal year" before "in the Consumer Price Index" and substituted "for the 12 month period ending June 30 preceding the fiscal year for which fees are being established, or" for ", or". See Effective and Termination Dates of 2002 Amendment note below.

Subsec. (c)(1)(B). Pub. L. 107–188, §§ 504(c)(1)(C), 509, temporarily substituted "for the previous fiscal year" for "for such fiscal year". See Effective and Termination Dates of 2002 Amendment note below.

Subsec. (c)(2) to (5). Pub. L. 107–188, §§ 504(c)(2)–(4), 509, temporarily added pars. (2) and (3), redesignated former pars. (2) and (3) as (4) and (5), respectively, and amended heading and text of par. (4) generally. Prior to amendment, text of par. (4) read as follows: "Subject to the amount appropriated for a fiscal year under subsection (g) of this section, the Secretary shall, within 60 days after the end of each fiscal year beginning after September 30, 1997, adjust the establishment and product fees described in subsection (b) of this section for the fiscal year in which the adjustment occurs so that the revenues collected from each of the categories of fees described in paragraphs (2) and (3) of subsection (b) of this section shall be set to be equal to the revenues collected from the category of application and supplement fees described in paragraph (1) of subsection (b) of this section." See Effective and Termination Dates of 2002 Amendment note below.

Subsec. (d)(1)(C) to (E). Pub. L. 107–188, §§ 504(d)(1), 509, temporarily inserted "or" at end of subpar. (C), redesignated subpar. (E) as (D), and struck out former subpar. (D) which read as follows: "assessment of the fee for an application or a supplement filed under section 355(b)(1) of this title pertaining to a drug containing an active ingredient would be inequitable because an application for a product containing the same active ingredient filed by another person under section 355(b)(2) of this title could not be assessed fees under subsection (a)(1) of this section, or". See Effective and Termination Dates of 2002 Amendment note below.

Subsec. (d)(3)(A), (B). Pub. L. 107–188, §§ 504(d)(2), 509, temporarily substituted "paragraph (1)(D)" for "paragraph (1)(E)". See Effective and Termination Dates of 2002 Amendment note below.

Subsec. (f). Pub. L. 107–188, §§ 504(e)(1), 509, temporarily substituted "Limitations" for "Assessment of fees" in heading. See Effective and Termination Dates of 2002 Amendment note below.

Subsec. (f)(1). Pub. L. 107–188, §§ 504(e)(2), 509, temporarily substituted "In general" for "Limitation" in heading and "Fees under subsection (a) of this section shall be refunded for a fiscal year beginning" for "Fees may not be assessed under subsection (a) of this section for a fiscal year beginning" in text. See Effective and Termination Dates of 2002 Amendment note below.

Subsec. (g)(1). Pub. L. 107–188, §§ 504(f)(1), 509, which directed the temporary amendment of par. (1) by striking "Fees collected for a fiscal year" and all that follows through "fiscal year limitation." and inserting "Fees authorized under subsection (a) shall be collected and available for obligation only to the extent and in the amount provided in advance in appropriations Acts. Such fees are authorized to remain available until expended.", was not executed because the phrase "fiscal year limitation." appeared in two places and because of the corrective amendment by Pub. L. 110–85, § 103(h)(1), which is effective as if included in Pub. L. 107–188, § 504. See 2007 Amendment note above and Effective and Termination Dates of 2002 Amendment note and Effective and Termination Dates of 2007 Amendment note below.

Subsec. (g)(2). Pub. L. 107–188, §§ 504(f)(2), 509, temporarily amended par. (2) by designating existing provisions as subpar. (A), inserting subpar. (A) heading, adding subpar. (B), redesignating former subpars. (A) and (B) as cls. (i) and (ii), respectively, of subpar. (A), substituting "shall be retained in each fiscal year in an amount not to exceed the amount specified" for "shall be collected in each fiscal year in an amount equal to the amount specified" in cl. (i), and realigning margin of cl. (ii). See Effective and Termination Dates of 2002 Amendment note below.

Subsec. (g)(3)(A) to (E). Pub. L. 107–188, §§504(f)(3), 509, temporarily added subpars. (A) to (E) and struck out former subpars. (A) to (E) which read as follows:

"(A) $106,800,000 for fiscal year 1998;

"(B) $109,200,000 for fiscal year 1999;

"(C) $109,200,000 for fiscal year 2000;

"(D) $114,000,000 for fiscal year 2001; and

"(E) $110,100,000 for fiscal year 2002.".

See Effective and Termination Dates of 2002 Amendment note below.

1997—Subsec. (a). Pub. L. 105–115, §§103(a)(1), 107, temporarily substituted "Beginning in fiscal year 1998" for "Beginning in fiscal year 1993" in introductory provisions. See Effective and Termination Dates of 1997 Amendment note below.

Subsec. (a)(1)(B). Pub. L. 105–115, §§103(a)(2)(A), 107, temporarily amended heading and text of subpar. (B) generally. Prior to amendment, text read as follows:

"(i) FIRST PAYMENT.—50 percent of the fee required by subparagraph (A) shall be due upon submission of the application or supplement.

"(ii) FINAL PAYMENT.—The remaining 50 percent of the fee required by subparagraph (A) shall be due upon—

"(I) the expiration of 30 days from the date the Secretary sends to the applicant a letter designated by the Secretary as an action letter described in section 379g(6)(B) of this title, or

"(II) the withdrawal of the application or supplement after it is filed unless the Secretary waives the fee or a portion of the fee because no substantial work was performed on such application or supplement after it was filed.

The designation under subclause (I) or the waiver under subclause (II) shall be solely in the discretion of the Secretary and shall not be reviewable." See Effective and Termination Dates of 1997 Amendment note below.

Subsec. (a)(1)(D). Pub. L. 105–115, §§103(a)(2)(B), 107, temporarily substituted "refused" for "not accepted" in heading and "75 percent" for "50 percent", "subparagraph (B)" for "subparagraph (B)(i)", and "refused" for "not accepted" in text. See Effective and Termination Dates of 1997 Amendment note below.

Subsec. (a)(1)(E) to (G). Pub. L. 105–115, §§103(a)(2)(C), 107, temporarily added subpars. (E) to (G). See Effective and Termination Dates of 1997 Amendment note below.

Subsec. (a)(2). Pub. L. 105–115, §§103(a)(3), 107, temporarily reenacted heading without change and amended text generally. Prior to amendment, text read as follows: "Each person that—

"(A) owns a prescription drug establishment, at which is manufactured at least 1 prescription drug product which is not the, or not the same as a, product approved under an application filed under section 355(b)(2) or 355(j) of this title, and

"(B) after September 1, 1992, had pending before the Secretary a human drug application or supplement,

shall be subject to the annual fee established in subsection (b) of this section for each such establishment, payable on or before January 31 of each year." See Effective and Termination Dates of 1997 Amendment note below.

Subsec. (a)(3)(A). Pub. L. 105–115, §§103(a)(4)(A), 107, temporarily substituted, in cl. (i), "has been submitted for listing" for "is listed" and, in closing provisions, "Such fee shall be payable for the fiscal year in which the product is first submitted for listing under section 360 of this title, or is submitted for relisting under section 360 of this title if the product has been withdrawn from listing and relisted. After such fee is paid for that fiscal year, such fee shall be payable on or before January 31 of each year. Such fee shall be paid only once for each product for a fiscal year in which the fee is payable." for "Such fee shall be payable at the time of the first such listing of such product in each calendar year. Such fee shall be paid only once each year for each listed prescription drug product irrespective of the number of times such product is listed under section 360 of this title." See Effective and Termination Dates of 1997 Amendment note below.

Subsec. (a)(3)(B). Pub. L. 105–115, §§103(a)(4)(B), 107, temporarily substituted "355(j) of this title, under an abbreviated application filed under section 357 of this title (as in effect on the day before November 21, 1997), or under an abbreviated new drug application pursuant to regulations in effect prior to the implementation of the Drug Price Competition and Patent Term Restoration Act of 1984." for "355(j) of this title.". See Effective and Termination Dates of 1997 Amendment note below.

Subsec. (b). Pub. L. 105–115, §§103(b), 107, temporarily amended subsec. (b) generally. Prior to amendment, subsec. (b) related to fee amounts, including a schedule of fees in par. (1) and fee exceptions for certain small businesses in par. (2). See Effective and Termination Dates of 1997 Amendment note below.

Subsec. (c). Pub. L. 105–115, §§103(c)(1), 107, temporarily substituted "Adjustments" for "Increases and adjustments" in heading. See Effective and Termination Dates of 1997 Amendment note below.

Subsec. (c)(1). Pub. L. 105–115, §§103(c)(2), 107, temporarily substituted "Inflation adjustment" for "Revenue increase" in heading, "The fees and total fee revenues established in subsection (b) of this section shall be adjusted by the Secretary" for "The total fee revenues established by the schedule in subsection (b)(1) of this section shall be increased by the Secretary" in introductory provisions, and "change" for "increase" after "total percentage" in subpars. (A) and (B), and inserted at end "The adjustment made each fiscal year by this subsection will be added on a compounded basis to the sum of all adjustments made each fiscal year after fiscal year 1997 under this subsection." See Effective and Termination Dates of 1997 Amendment note below.

Subsec. (c)(2). Pub. L. 105–115, §§103(c)(3), 107, temporarily substituted "September 30, 1997, adjust the establishment and product fees described in subsection (b) of this section for the fiscal year in which the adjustment occurs so that the revenues collected from each of the categories of fees described in paragraphs (2) and (3) of subsection (b) of this section shall be set to be equal to the revenues collected from the category of application and supplement fees described in paragraph (1) of subsection (b) of this section." for "October 1, 1992, adjust the fees established by the schedule in subsection (b)(1) of this section for the following fiscal year to achieve the total fee revenues, as may be increased under paragraph (1). Such fees shall be adjusted under this paragraph to maintain the proportions established in such schedule." See Effective and Termination Dates of 1997 Amendment note below.

Subsec. (c)(3). Pub. L. 105–115, §§103(c)(4), 107, temporarily substituted "this subsection" for "paragraph (2)". See Effective and Termination Dates of 1997 Amendment note below.

Subsec. (d). Pub. L. 105–115, §§103(d), 107, temporarily struck out introductory provisions which read "The Secretary shall grant a waiver from or a reduction of 1 or more fees under subsection (a) of this section where the Secretary finds that—" and closing provisions which read "In making the finding in paragraph (3), the Secretary may use standard costs.", inserted designation, heading, and introductory provisions of par. (1), redesignated former pars. (1) to (4) as subpars. (A) to (D), respectively, of par. (1), and added pars. (1)(E), (2), and (3). See Effective and Termination Dates of 1997 Amendment note below.

Subsec. (f)(1). Pub. L. 105–115, §§103(e), 107, temporarily substituted "fiscal year 1997" for "fiscal year 1993" and "fiscal year 1997 (excluding the amount of fees appropriated for such fiscal year)" for "fiscal year

1992". See Effective and Termination Dates of 1997 Amendment note below.

Subsec. (g)(1). Pub. L. 105-115, §§103(f)(1), 107, temporarily inserted at end "Such sums as may be necessary may be transferred from the Food and Drug Administration salaries and expenses appropriation account without fiscal year limitation to such appropriation account for salaries and expenses with such fiscal year limitation. The sums transferred shall be available solely for the process for the review of human drug applications." See Effective and Termination Dates of 1997 Amendment note below.

Subsec. (g)(2)(A). Pub. L. 105-115, §§103(f)(2)(A), 107, temporarily substituted "Acts, or otherwise made available for obligation," for "Acts". See Effective and Termination Dates of 1997 Amendment note below.

Subsec. (g)(2)(B). Pub. L. 105-115, §§103(f)(2)(B), 107, temporarily substituted "over such costs, excluding costs paid from fees collected under this section, for fiscal year 1997" for "over such costs for fiscal year 1992". See Effective and Termination Dates of 1997 Amendment note below.

Subsec. (g)(3), (4). Pub. L. 105-115, §§103(f)(3), 107, temporarily added pars. (3) and (4) and struck out heading and text of former par. (3). Text read as follows: "There are authorized to be appropriated for fees under this section—

"(A) $36,000,000 for fiscal year 1993,

"(B) $54,000,000 for fiscal year 1994,

"(C) $75,000,000 for fiscal year 1995,

"(D) $78,000,000 for fiscal year 1996, and

"(E) $84,000,000 for fiscal year 1997,

as adjusted to reflect increases in the total fee revenues made under subsection (c)(1) of this section." See Effective and Termination Dates of 1997 Amendment note below.

Subsecs. (i), (j). Pub. L. 105-115, §§103(g), 107, temporarily added subsec. (i) and redesignated former subsec. (i) as (j). See Effective and Termination Dates of 1997 Amendment note below.

EFFECTIVE AND TERMINATION DATES OF 2007 AMENDMENT

Pub. L. 110-85, title I, §103(h)(2), Sept. 27, 2007, 121 Stat. 832, provided that: "Paragraph (1) [amending this section] shall take effect as if included in section 504 of the Prescription Drug User Fee Amendments of 2002 (Public Law 107-188; 116 Stat. 687) [amending this section]."

Amendment by Pub. L. 110-85 to cease to be effective Oct. 1, 2012, see section 106(a) of Pub. L. 110-85, set out as a note under section 379g of this title.

Amendment by Pub. L. 110-85 effective Oct. 1, 2007, with fees under this subpart to be assessed for all human drug applications received on or after Oct. 1, 2007, see section 107 of Pub. L. 110-85, set out as a note under section 379g of this title.

EFFECTIVE AND TERMINATION DATES OF 2002 AMENDMENT

Amendment by Pub. L. 107-188 effective Oct. 1, 2002, see section 508 of Pub. L. 107-188, set out as an Effective Date of 2002 Amendment note under section 356b of this title.

Amendment by Pub. L. 107-188 to cease to be effective Oct. 1, 2007, see section 509 of Pub. L. 107-188, set out as a note under section 379g of this title.

EFFECTIVE AND TERMINATION DATES OF 1997 AMENDMENT

Amendment by Pub. L. 105-115 effective Oct. 1, 1997, and ceases to be effective Oct. 1, 2002, see sections 106 and 107 of Pub. L. 105-115, set out as notes under section 379g of this title.

TERMINATION DATE

Section not in effect after Oct. 1, 1997, see section 105 of Pub. L. 102-571, set out as a note under section 379g of this title.

SPECIAL RULE FOR WAIVERS AND REFUNDS

Section 103(h) of Pub. L. 105-115 provided that: "Any requests for waivers or refunds for fees assessed under section 736 of the Federal Food, Drug, and Cosmetic Act (42 U.S.C. 379h) prior to the date of enactment of this Act [Nov. 21, 1997] shall be submitted in writing to the Secretary of Health and Human Services within 1 year after the date of enactment of this Act. Any requests for waivers or refunds pertaining to a fee for a human drug application or supplement accepted for filing prior to October 1, 1997 or to a product or establishment fee required by such Act for a fiscal year prior to fiscal year 1998, shall be evaluated according to the terms of the Prescription Drug User Fee Act of 1992 [see section 101(a) of Pub. L. 102-571, set out as a Short Title of 1992 Amendment note under section 301 of this title] (as in effect on September 30, 1997) and part 2 of subchapter C of chapter VII of the Federal Food, Drug, and Cosmetic Act [21 U.S.C. 379g et seq.] (as in effect on September 30, 1997). The term "person" in such Acts shall continue to include an affiliate thereof."

§379h-1. Fees relating to advisory review of prescription-drug television advertising

(a) Types of direct-to-consumer television advertisement review fees

Beginning in fiscal year 2008, the Secretary shall assess and collect fees in accordance with this section as follows:

(1) Advisory review fee

(A) In general

With respect to a proposed direct-to-consumer television advertisement (referred to in this section as a "DTC advertisement"), each person that on or after October 1, 2007, submits such an advertisement for advisory review by the Secretary prior to its initial public dissemination shall, except as provided in subparagraph (B), be subject to a fee established under subsection (c)(3).

(B) Exception for required submissions

A DTC advertisement that is required to be submitted to the Secretary prior to initial public dissemination is not subject to a fee under subparagraph (A) unless the sponsor designates the submission as a submission for advisory review.

(C) Notice to Secretary of number of advertisements

Not later than June 1 of each fiscal year, the Secretary shall publish a notice in the Federal Register requesting any person to notify the Secretary within 30 days of the number of DTC advertisements the person intends to submit for advisory review in the next fiscal year. Notwithstanding the preceding sentence, for fiscal year 2008, the Secretary shall publish such a notice in the Federal Register not later than 30 days after September 27, 2007.

(D) Payment

(i) In general

The fee required by subparagraph (A) (referred to in this section as "an advisory review fee") shall be due not later than October 1 of the fiscal year in which the DTC advertisement involved is intended to be submitted for advisory review, subject to subparagraph (F)(i). Notwithstanding the preceding sentence, the advisory review fee for any DTC advertisement that is intended to be submitted for advisory review during fiscal year 2008 shall be due not later than 120 days after September 27, 2007, or an earlier date as specified by the Secretary.

(ii) Effect of submission

Notification of the Secretary under subparagraph (C) of the number of DTC advertisements a person intends to submit for advisory review is a legally binding commitment by that person to pay the annual advisory review fee for that number of submissions on or before October 1 of the fiscal year in which the advertisement is intended to be submitted. Notwithstanding the preceding sentence, the commitment shall be a legally binding commitment by that person to pay the annual advisory review fee for that number of submissions for fiscal year 2008 by the date specified in clause (i).

(iii) Notice regarding carryover submissions

In making a notification under subparagraph (C), the person involved shall in addition notify the Secretary if under subparagraph (F)(i) the person intends to submit a DTC advertisement for which the advisory review fee has already been paid. If the person does not so notify the Secretary, each DTC advertisement submitted by the person for advisory review in the fiscal year involved shall be subject to the advisory review fee.

(E) Modification of advisory review fee

(i) Late payment

If a person has submitted a notification under subparagraph (C) with respect to a fiscal year and has not paid all advisory review fees due under subparagraph (D) not later than November 1 of such fiscal year (or, in the case of such a notification submitted with respect to fiscal year 2008, not later than 150 days after September 27, 2007, or an earlier date specified by the Secretary), the fees shall be regarded as late and an increase in the amount of fees applies in accordance with this clause, notwithstanding any other provision of this section. For such person, all advisory review fees for such fiscal year shall be due and payable 20 days before any direct-to-consumer advertisement is submitted to the Secretary for advisory review, and each such fee shall be equal to 150 percent of the fee that otherwise would have applied pursuant to subsection (c)(3).

(ii) Exceeding identified number of submissions

If a person submits a number of DTC advertisements for advisory review in a fiscal year that exceeds the number identified by the person under subparagraph (C), an increase in the amount of fees applies under this clause for each submission in excess of such number, notwithstanding any other provision of this section. For each such DTC advertisement, the advisory review fee shall be due and payable 20 days before the advertisement is submitted to the Secretary, and the fee shall be equal to 150 percent of the fee that otherwise would have applied pursuant to subsection (c)(3).

(F) Limits

(i) Submissions

For each advisory review fee paid by a person for a fiscal year, the person is entitled to acceptance for advisory review by the Secretary of one DTC advertisement and acceptance of one resubmission for advisory review of the same advertisement. The advertisement shall be submitted for review in the fiscal year for which the fee was assessed, except that a person may carry over not more than one paid advisory review submission to the next fiscal year. Resubmissions may be submitted without regard to the fiscal year of the initial advisory review submission.

(ii) No refunds

Except as provided by subsections (d)(4) and (f), fees paid under this section shall not be refunded.

(iii) No waivers, exemptions, or reductions

The Secretary shall not grant a waiver, exemption, or reduction of any fees due or payable under this section.

(iv) Right to advisory review not transferable

The right to an advisory review under this paragraph is not transferable, except to a successor in interest.

(2) Operating reserve fee

(A) In general

Each person that on or after October 1, 2007, is assessed an advisory review fee under paragraph (1) shall be subject to fee[1] established under subsection (d)(2) (referred to in this section as an "operating reserve fee") for the first fiscal year in which an advisory review fee is assessed to such person. The person is not subject to an operating reserve fee for any other fiscal year.

(B) Payment

Except as provided in subparagraph (C), the operating reserve fee shall be due no later than—

(i) October 1 of the first fiscal year in which the person is required to pay an advisory review fee under paragraph (1); or

(ii) for fiscal year 2008, 120 days after September 27, 2007, or an earlier date specified by the Secretary.

(C) Late notice of submission

If, in the first fiscal year of a person's participation in the program under this section, that person submits any DTC advertisements for advisory review that are in excess of the number identified by that person in

[1] So in original. Probably should be "the fee".

response to the Federal Register notice described in subsection (a)(1)(C), that person shall pay an operating reserve fee for each of those advisory reviews equal to the advisory review fee for each submission established under paragraph (1)(E)(ii). Fees required by this subparagraph shall be in addition to any fees required by subparagraph (A). Fees under this subparagraph shall be due 20 days before any DTC advertisement is submitted by such person to the Secretary for advisory review.

(D) Late payment

(i) In general

Notwithstanding subparagraph (B), and subject to clause (ii), an operating reserve fee shall be regarded as late if the person required to pay the fee has not paid the complete operating reserve fee by—

(I) for fiscal year 2008, 150 days after September 27, 2007, or an earlier date specified by the Secretary; or

(II) in any subsequent year, November 1.

(ii) Complete payment

The complete operating reserve fee shall be due and payable 20 days before any DTC advertisement is submitted by such person to the Secretary for advisory review.

(iii) Amount

Notwithstanding any other provision of this section, an operating reserve fee that is regarded as late under this subparagraph shall be equal to 150 percent of the operating reserve fee that otherwise would have applied pursuant to subsection (d).

(b) Advisory review fee revenue amounts

Fees under subsection (a)(1) shall be established to generate revenue amounts of $6,250,000 for each of fiscal years 2008 through 2012, as adjusted pursuant to subsections (c) and (g)(4).

(c) Adjustments

(1) Inflation adjustment

Beginning with fiscal year 2009, the revenues established in subsection (b) shall be adjusted by the Secretary by notice, published in the Federal Register, for a fiscal year to reflect the greater of—

(A) the total percentage change that occurred in the Consumer Price Index for all urban consumers (all items; U.S. city average), for the 12-month period ending June 30 preceding the fiscal year for which fees are being established;

(B) the total percentage change for the previous fiscal year in basic pay under the General Schedule in accordance with section 5332 of title 5, as adjusted by any locality-based comparability payment pursuant to section 5304 of such title for Federal employees stationed in the District of Columbia; or

(C) the average annual change in the cost, per full-time equivalent position of the Food and Drug Administration, of all personnel compensation and benefits paid with respect to such positions for the first 5 fiscal years of the previous 6 fiscal years.

The adjustment made each fiscal year by this subsection shall be added on a compounded basis to the sum of all adjustments made each fiscal year after fiscal year 2008 under this subsection.

(2) Workload adjustment

Beginning with fiscal year 2009, after the fee revenues established in subsection (b) are adjusted for a fiscal year for inflation in accordance with paragraph (1), the fee revenues shall be adjusted further for such fiscal year to reflect changes in the workload of the Secretary with respect to the submission of DTC advertisements for advisory review prior to initial dissemination. With respect to such adjustment:

(A) The adjustment shall be determined by the Secretary based upon the number of DTC advertisements identified pursuant to subsection (a)(1)(C) for the upcoming fiscal year, excluding allowable previously paid carry over submissions. The adjustment shall be determined by multiplying the number of such advertisements projected for that fiscal year that exceeds 150 by $27,600 (adjusted each year beginning with fiscal year 2009 for inflation in accordance with paragraph (1)). The Secretary shall publish in the Federal Register the fee revenues and fees resulting from the adjustment and the supporting methodologies.

(B) Under no circumstances shall the adjustment result in fee revenues for a fiscal year that are less than the fee revenues established for the prior fiscal year.

(3) Annual fee setting for advisory review

(A) In general

Not later than August 1 of each fiscal year (or, with respect to fiscal year 2008, not later than 90 days after September 27, 2007), the Secretary shall establish for the next fiscal year the DTC advertisement advisory review fee under subsection (a)(1), based on the revenue amounts established under subsection (b), the adjustments provided under paragraphs (1) and (2), and the number of DTC advertisements identified pursuant to subsection (a)(1)(C), excluding allowable previously-paid carry over submissions. The annual advisory review fee shall be established by dividing the fee revenue for a fiscal year (as adjusted pursuant to this subsection) by the number of DTC advertisements so identified, excluding allowable previously-paid carry over submissions under subsection (a)(1)(F)(i).

(B) Fiscal year 2008 fee limit

Notwithstanding subsection (b) and the adjustments pursuant to this subsection, the fee established under subparagraph (A) for fiscal year 2008 may not be more than $83,000 per submission for advisory review.

(C) Annual fee limit

Notwithstanding subsection (b) and the adjustments pursuant to this subsection, the fee established under subparagraph (A) for a fiscal year after fiscal year 2008 may not be more than 50 percent more than the fee established for the prior fiscal year.

(D) Limit

The total amount of fees obligated for a fiscal year may not exceed the total costs for such fiscal year for the resources allocated for the process for the advisory review of prescription drug advertising.

(d) Operating reserves

(1) In general

The Secretary shall establish in the Food and Drug Administration salaries and expenses appropriation account without fiscal year limitation a Direct-to-Consumer Advisory Review Operating Reserve, of at least $6,250,000 in fiscal year 2008, to continue the program under this section in the event the fees collected in any subsequent fiscal year pursuant to subsection (a)(1) do not generate the fee revenue amount established for that fiscal year.

(2) Fee setting

The Secretary shall establish the operating reserve fee under subsection (a)(2)(A) for each person required to pay the fee by multiplying the number of DTC advertisements identified by that person pursuant to subsection (a)(1)(C) by the advisory review fee established pursuant to subsection (c)(3) for that fiscal year, except that in no case shall the operating reserve fee assessed be less than the operating reserve fee assessed if the person had first participated in the program under this section in fiscal year 2008.

(3) Use of operating reserve

The Secretary may use funds from the reserves only to the extent necessary in any fiscal year to make up the difference between the fee revenue amount established for that fiscal year under subsections (b) and (c) and the amount of fees actually collected for that fiscal year pursuant to subsection (a)(1), or to pay costs of ending the program under this section if it is terminated pursuant to subsection (f) or not reauthorized beyond fiscal year 2012.

(4) Refund of operating reserves

Within 120 days after the end of fiscal year 2012, or if the program under this section ends early pursuant to subsection (f), the Secretary, after setting aside sufficient operating reserve amounts to terminate the program under this section, shall refund all amounts remaining in the operating reserve on a pro rata basis to each person that paid an operating reserve fee assessment. In no event shall the refund to any person exceed the total amount of operating reserve fees paid by such person pursuant to subsection (a)(2).

(e) Effect of failure to pay fees

Notwithstanding any other requirement, a submission for advisory review of a DTC advertisement submitted by a person subject to fees under subsection (a) shall be considered incomplete and shall not be accepted for review by the Secretary until all fees owed by such person under this section have been paid.

(f) Effect of inadequate funding of program

(1) Initial funding

If on November 1, 2007, or 120 days after September 27, 2007, whichever is later, the Secretary has not received at least $11,250,000 in advisory review fees and operating reserve fees combined, the program under this section shall not commence and all collected fees shall be refunded.

(2) Later fiscal years

Beginning in fiscal year 2009, if, on November 1 of the fiscal year, the combination of the operating reserves, annual fee revenues from that fiscal year, and unobligated fee revenues from prior fiscal years falls below $9,000,000, adjusted for inflation (as described in subsection (c)(1)), the program under this section shall terminate, and the Secretary shall notify all participants, retain any money from the unused advisory review fees and the operating reserves needed to terminate the program, and refund the remainder of the unused fees and operating reserves. To the extent required to terminate the program, the Secretary shall first use unobligated advisory review fee revenues from prior fiscal years, then the operating reserves, and finally, unused advisory review fees from the relevant fiscal year.

(g) Crediting and availability of fees

(1) In general

Fees authorized under subsection (a) shall be collected and available for obligation only to the extent and in the amount provided in advance in appropriations Acts. Such fees are authorized to remain available until expended. Such sums as may be necessary may be transferred from the Food and Drug Administration salaries and expenses appropriation account without fiscal year limitation to such appropriation account for salaries and expenses with such fiscal year limitation. The sums transferred shall be available solely for the process for the advisory review of prescription drug advertising.

(2) Collections and appropriation acts

(A) In general

The fees authorized by this section—

(i) shall be retained in each fiscal year in an amount not to exceed the amount specified in appropriation Acts, or otherwise made available for obligation for such fiscal year; and

(ii) shall be available for obligation only if the amounts appropriated as budget authority for such fiscal year are sufficient to support a number of full-time equivalent review employees that is not fewer than the number of such employees supported in fiscal year 2007.

(B) Review employees

For purposes of subparagraph (A)(ii), the term "full-time equivalent review employees" means the total combined number of full-time equivalent employees in—

(i) the Center for Drug Evaluation and Research, Division of Drug Marketing, Advertising, and Communications, Food and Drug Administration; and

(ii) the Center for Biologics Evaluation and Research, Advertising and Promotional Labeling Branch, Food and Drug Administration.

(3) Authorization of appropriations

For each of the fiscal years 2008 through 2012, there is authorized to be appropriated for fees under this section an amount equal to the total revenue amount determined under subsection (b) for the fiscal year, as adjusted pursuant to subsection (c) and paragraph (4) of this subsection, plus amounts collected for the reserve fund under subsection (d).

(4) Offset

Any amount of fees collected for a fiscal year under this section that exceeds the amount of fees specified in appropriation Acts for such fiscal year shall be credited to the appropriation account of the Food and Drug Administration as provided in paragraph (1), and shall be subtracted from the amount of fees that would otherwise be collected under this section pursuant to appropriation Acts for a subsequent fiscal year.

(h) Definitions

For purposes of this section:

(1) The term "advisory review" means reviewing and providing advisory comments on DTC advertisements regarding compliance of a proposed advertisement with the requirements of this chapter prior to its initial public dissemination.

(2) The term "advisory review fee" has the meaning indicated for such term in subsection (a)(1)(D).

(3) The term "carry over submission" means a submission for an advisory review for which a fee was paid in one fiscal year that is submitted for review in the following fiscal year.

(4) The term "direct-to-consumer television advertisement" means an advertisement for a prescription drug product (as defined in section 379g(3) of this title) intended to be displayed on any television channel for less than 3 minutes.

(5) The term "DTC advertisement" has the meaning indicated for such term in subsection (a)(1)(A).

(6) The term "operating reserve fee" has the meaning indicated for such term in subsection (a)(2)(A).

(7) The term "person" includes an individual, partnership, corporation, and association, and any affiliate thereof or successor in interest.

(8) The term "process for the advisory review of prescription drug advertising" means the activities necessary to review and provide advisory comments on DTC advertisements prior to public dissemination and, to the extent the Secretary has additional staff resources available under the program under this section that are not necessary for the advisory review of DTC advertisements, the activities necessary to review and provide advisory comments on other proposed advertisements and promotional material prior to public dissemination.

(9) The term "resources allocated for the process for the advisory review of prescription drug advertising" means the expenses incurred in connection with the process for the advisory review of prescription drug advertising for—

(A) officers and employees of the Food and Drug Administration, contractors of the Food and Drug Administration, advisory committees, and costs related to such officers, employees, and committees, and to contracts with such contractors;

(B) management of information, and the acquisition, maintenance, and repair of computer resources;

(C) leasing, maintenance, renovation, and repair of facilities and acquisition, maintenance, and repair of fixtures, furniture, scientific equipment, and other necessary materials and supplies;

(D) collection of fees under this section and accounting for resources allocated for the advisory review of prescription drug advertising; and

(E) terminating the program under this section pursuant to subsection (f)(2) if that becomes necessary.

(10) The term "resubmission" means a subsequent submission for advisory review of a direct-to-consumer television advertisement that has been revised in response to the Secretary's comments on an original submission. A resubmission may not introduce significant new concepts or creative themes into the television advertisement.

(11) The term "submission for advisory review" means an original submission of a direct-to-consumer television advertisement for which the sponsor voluntarily requests advisory comments before the advertisement is publicly disseminated.

(June 25, 1938, ch. 675, § 736A, as added Pub. L. 110–85, title I, § 104, Sept. 27, 2007, 121 Stat. 832.)

TERMINATION OF SECTION

For termination of section by section 106(a) of Pub. L. 110–85, see Effective and Termination Dates note below.

EFFECTIVE AND TERMINATION DATES

Section effective Oct. 1, 2007, with fees under this subpart to be assessed for all human drug applications received on or after Oct. 1, 2007, and ceases to be effective Oct. 1, 2012, see sections 106(a) and 107 of Pub. L. 110–85, set out as Effective and Termination Dates of 2007 Amendment notes under section 379g of this title.

§ 379h–2. Reauthorization; reporting requirements

(a) Performance report

Beginning with fiscal year 2008, not later than 120 days after the end of each fiscal year for which fees are collected under this subpart, the Secretary shall prepare and submit to the Committee on Energy and Commerce of the House of Representatives and the Committee on Health, Education, Labor, and Pensions of the Senate a report concerning the progress of the Food and Drug Administration in achieving the goals identified in the letters described in section 101(c) of the Food and Drug Administration Amendments Act of 2007 during such fiscal year and the future plans of the Food and Drug Administration for meeting the goals. The report for a fiscal year shall include information on all previous cohorts for which the Secretary has not given a complete response on all human drug applications and supplements in the cohort.

(b) Fiscal report

Beginning with fiscal year 2008, not later than 120 days after the end of each fiscal year for which fees are collected under this subpart, the Secretary shall prepare and submit to the Committee on Energy and Commerce of the House of Representatives and the Committee on Health, Education, Labor, and Pensions of the Senate a report on the implementation of the authority for such fees during such fiscal year and the use, by the Food and Drug Administration, of the fees collected for such fiscal year.

(c) Public availability

The Secretary shall make the reports required under subsections (a) and (b) available to the public on the Internet Web site of the Food and Drug Administration.

(d) Reauthorization

(1) Consultation

In developing recommendations to present to the Congress with respect to the goals, and plans for meeting the goals, for the process for the review of human drug applications for the first 5 fiscal years after fiscal year 2012, and for the reauthorization of this subpart for such fiscal years, the Secretary shall consult with—

(A) the Committee on Energy and Commerce of the House of Representatives;

(B) the Committee on Health, Education, Labor, and Pensions of the Senate;

(C) scientific and academic experts;

(D) health care professionals;

(E) representatives of patient and consumer advocacy groups; and

(F) the regulated industry.

(2) Prior public input

Prior to beginning negotiations with the regulated industry on the reauthorization of this subpart, the Secretary shall—

(A) publish a notice in the Federal Register requesting public input on the reauthorization;

(B) hold a public meeting at which the public may present its views on the reauthorization, including specific suggestions for changes to the goals referred to in subsection (a);

(C) provide a period of 30 days after the public meeting to obtain written comments from the public suggesting changes to this subpart; and

(D) publish the comments on the Food and Drug Administration's Internet Web site.

(3) Periodic consultation

Not less frequently than once every month during negotiations with the regulated industry, the Secretary shall hold discussions with representatives of patient and consumer advocacy groups to continue discussions of their views on the reauthorization and their suggestions for changes to this subpart as expressed under paragraph (2).

(4) Public review of recommendations

After negotiations with the regulated industry, the Secretary shall—

(A) present the recommendations developed under paragraph (1) to the Congressional committees specified in such paragraph;

(B) publish such recommendations in the Federal Register;

(C) provide for a period of 30 days for the public to provide written comments on such recommendations;

(D) hold a meeting at which the public may present its views on such recommendations; and

(E) after consideration of such public views and comments, revise such recommendations as necessary.

(5) Transmittal of recommendations

Not later than January 15, 2012, the Secretary shall transmit to the Congress the revised recommendations under paragraph (4), a summary of the views and comments received under such paragraph, and any changes made to the recommendations in response to such views and comments.

(6) Minutes of negotiation meetings

(A) Public availability

Before presenting the recommendations developed under paragraphs (1) through (5) to the Congress, the Secretary shall make publicly available, on the public Web site of the Food and Drug Administration, minutes of all negotiation meetings conducted under this subsection between the Food and Drug Administration and the regulated industry.

(B) Content

The minutes described under subparagraph (A) shall summarize any substantive proposal made by any party to the negotiations as well as significant controversies or differences of opinion during the negotiations and their resolution.

(June 25, 1938, ch. 675, §736B, as added Pub. L. 110–85, title I, §105, Sept. 27, 2007, 121 Stat. 840.)

TERMINATION OF SECTION

For termination of section by section 106(b) of Pub. L. 110–85, see Effective and Termination Dates note below.

REFERENCES IN TEXT

Section 101(c) of the Food and Drug Administration Amendments Act of 2007, referred to in subsec. (a), is section 101(c) of Pub. L. 110–85, which is set out as a note under section 379g of this title.

EFFECTIVE AND TERMINATION DATES

Pub. L. 110–85, title I, §106(b), Sept. 27, 2007, 121 Stat. 842, provided that: "The amendment made by section 105 [enacting this section] ceases to be effective January 31, 2013."

Section effective Oct. 1, 2007, with fees under this subpart to be assessed for all human drug applications received on or after Oct. 1, 2007, see section 107 of Pub. L. 110–85, set out as an Effective and Termination Dates of 2007 Amendment note under section 379g of this title.

SUBPART 3—FEES RELATING TO DEVICES

TERMINATION OF SUBPART

For termination of subpart by section 107 of Pub. L. 107–250, see Effective and Termination

Dates note set out under section 379i of this title.

§ 379i. Definitions

For purposes of this subpart:

(1) The term "premarket application" means—

(A) an application for approval of a device submitted under section 360e(c) of this title or section 262 of title 42; or

(B) a product development protocol described in section 360e(f) of this title.

Such term does not include a supplement, a premarket report, or a premarket notification submission.

(2) The term "premarket report" means a report submitted under section 360e(c)(2) of this title.

(3) The term "premarket notification submission" means a report submitted under section 360(k) of this title.

(4)(A) The term "supplement", with respect to a panel-track supplement, a 180-day supplement, a real-time supplement, or an efficacy supplement, means a request to the Secretary to approve a change in a device for which—

(i) an application or report has been approved under section 360e(d) of this title, or an application has been approved under section 262 of title 42; or

(ii) a notice of completion has become effective under section 360e(f) of this title.

(B) The term "panel-track supplement" means a supplement to an approved premarket application or premarket report under section 360e of this title that requests a significant change in design or performance of the device, or a new indication for use of the device, and for which substantial clinical data are necessary to provide a reasonable assurance of safety and effectiveness.

(C) The term "180-day supplement" means a supplement to an approved premarket application or premarket report under section 360e of this title that is not a panel-track supplement and requests a significant change in components, materials, design, specification, software, color additives, or labeling.

(D) The term "real-time supplement" means a supplement to an approved premarket application or premarket report under section 360e of this title that requests a minor change to the device, such as a minor change to the design of the device, software, sterilization, or labeling, and for which the applicant has requested and the agency has granted a meeting or similar forum to jointly review and determine the status of the supplement.

(E) The term "efficacy supplement" means a supplement to an approved premarket application under section 262 of title 42 that requires substantive clinical data.

(5) The term "30-day notice" means a notice under section 360e(d)(6) of this title that is limited to a request to make modifications to manufacturing procedures or methods of manufacture affecting the safety and effectiveness of the device.

(6) The term "request for classification information" means a request made under section 360c(g) of this title for information respecting the class in which a device has been classified or the requirements applicable to a device.

(7) The term "annual fee", for periodic reporting concerning a class III device, means the annual fee associated with periodic reports required by a premarket application approval order.

(8) The term "process for the review of device applications" means the following activities of the Secretary with respect to the review of premarket applications, premarket reports, supplements, and premarket notification submissions:

(A) The activities necessary for the review of premarket applications, premarket reports, supplements, and premarket notification submissions.

(B) The issuance of action letters that allow the marketing of devices or which set forth in detail the specific deficiencies in such applications, reports, supplements, or submissions and, where appropriate, the actions necessary to place them in condition for approval.

(C) The inspection of manufacturing establishments and other facilities undertaken as part of the Secretary's review of pending premarket applications, premarket reports, and supplements.

(D) Monitoring of research conducted in connection with the review of such applications, reports, supplements, and submissions.

(E) Review of device applications subject to section 262 of title 42 for an investigational new drug application under section 355(i) of this title or for an investigational device exemption under section 360j(g) of this title and activities conducted in anticipation of the submission of such applications under section 355(i) or 360j(g) of this title.

(F) The development of guidance, policy documents, or regulations to improve the process for the review of premarket applications, premarket reports, supplements, and premarket notification submissions.

(G) The development of voluntary test methods, consensus standards, or mandatory performance standards under section 360d of this title in connection with the review of such applications, reports, supplements, or submissions and related activities.

(H) The provision of technical assistance to device manufacturers in connection with the submission of such applications, reports, supplements, or submissions.

(I) Any activity undertaken under section 360c or 360e(i) of this title in connection with the initial classification or reclassification of a device or under section 360e(b) of this title in connection with any requirement for approval of a device.

(J) Evaluation of postmarket studies required as a condition of an approval of a premarket application or premarket report under section 360e of this title or a premarket application under section 262 of title 42.

(K) Compiling, developing, and reviewing information on relevant devices to identify safety and effectiveness issues for devices subject to premarket applications, premarket reports, supplements, or premarket notification submissions.

(9) The term "costs of resources allocated for the process for the review of device applications" means the expenses incurred in connection with the process for the review of device applications for—

(A) officers and employees of the Food and Drug Administration, contractors of the Food and Drug Administration, advisory committees, and costs related to such officers, employees, and committees and to contracts with such contractors;

(B) management of information, and the acquisition, maintenance, and repair of computer resources;

(C) leasing, maintenance, renovation, and repair of facilities and acquisition, maintenance, and repair of fixtures, furniture, scientific equipment, and other necessary materials and supplies; and

(D) collecting fees and accounting for resources allocated for the review of premarket applications, premarket reports, supplements, and submissions.

(10) The term "adjustment factor" applicable to a fiscal year is the Consumer Price Index for all urban consumers (all items; United States city average) for October of the preceding fiscal year divided by such Index for October 2001.

(11) The term "person" includes an affiliate thereof.

(12) The term "affiliate" means a business entity that has a relationship with a second business entity (whether domestic or international) if, directly or indirectly—

(A) one business entity controls, or has the power to control, the other business entity; or

(B) a third party controls, or has power to control, both of the business entities.

(13) The term "establishment subject to a registration fee" means an establishment that is required to register with the Secretary under section 360 of this title and is one of the following types of establishments:

(A) Manufacturer

An establishment that makes by any means any article that is a device, including an establishment that sterilizes or otherwise makes such article for or on behalf of a specification developer or any other person.

(B) Single-use device reprocessor

An establishment that, within the meaning of section 321(*ll*)(2)(A) of this title, performs additional processing and manufacturing operations on a single-use device that has previously been used on a patient.

(C) Specification developer

An establishment that develops specifications for a device that is distributed under the establishment's name but which performs no manufacturing, including an establishment that, in addition to developing specifications, also arranges for the manufacturing of devices labeled with another establishment's name by a contract manufacturer.

(June 25, 1938, ch. 675, § 737, as added Pub. L. 107–250, title I, § 102(a), Oct. 26, 2002, 116 Stat. 1589; amended Pub. L. 108–214, § 2(a)(1), (d)(3)(A), Apr. 1, 2004, 118 Stat. 572, 577; Pub. L. 110–85, title II, § 211, Sept. 27, 2007, 121 Stat. 843.)

AMENDMENT OF SECTION

For termination of amendment by section 217 of Pub. L. 110–85, see Effective and Termination Dates of 2007 Amendment note below.

TERMINATION OF SECTION

For termination of section by section 107 of Pub. L. 107–250, see Effective and Termination Dates note set out below.

AMENDMENTS

2007—Pub. L. 110–85, §§ 211(1), 217, temporarily substituted "For purposes of this subpart" for "For purposes of this part" in introductory provisions. See Effective and Termination Dates of 2007 Amendment note below.

Pars. (5) to (9). Pub. L. 110–85, §§ 211(2), (3), 217, temporarily added pars. (5) to (7) and redesignated former pars. (5) and (6) as (8) and (9), respectively. Former pars. (7) and (8) redesignated (10) and (12), respectively. See Effective and Termination Dates of 2007 Amendment note below.

Par. (10). Pub. L. 110–85, §§ 211(2), (4), 217, temporarily redesignated par. (7) as (10) and substituted "October of the preceding fiscal year" for "April of the preceding fiscal year" and "October 2001" for "April 2002". See Effective and Termination Dates of 2007 Amendment note below.

Par. (11). Pub. L. 110–85, §§ 211(5), 217, temporarily added par. (11). See Effective and Termination Dates of 2007 Amendment note below.

Par. (12). Pub. L. 110–85, §§ 211(2), 217, temporarily redesignated par. (8) as (12). See Effective and Termination Dates of 2007 Amendment note below.

Par. (13). Pub. L. 110–85, §§ 211(6), 217, temporarily added par. (13). See Effective and Termination Dates of 2007 Amendment note below.

2004—Pub. L. 108–214, § 2(d)(3)(A), made technical correction to directory language of Pub. L. 107–250, § 102(a), which enacted this section.

Par. (4)(B). Pub. L. 108–214, § 2(a)(1)(A), substituted "and for which substantial clinical data are necessary to provide a reasonable assurance of safety and effectiveness" for "and for which clinical data are generally necessary to provide a reasonable assurance of safety and effectiveness".

Par. (4)(D). Pub. L. 108–214, § 2(a)(1)(B), struck out "manufacturing," after "software,".

Par. (5)(J). Pub. L. 108–214, § 2(a)(1)(C), substituted "a premarket application or premarket report under section 360e of this title or a premarket application under section 262 of title 42." for "a premarket application under section 360e of this title or section 262 of title 42."

Par. (8). Pub. L. 108–214, § 2(a)(1)(D), substituted "The term 'affiliate' means a business entity that has a relationship with a second business entity (whether domestic or international)" for "The term 'affiliate' means a business entity that has a relationship with a second business entity".

EFFECTIVE AND TERMINATION DATES OF 2007 AMENDMENT

Pub. L. 110–85, title II, § 216, Sept. 27, 2007, 121 Stat. 852, provided that: "The amendments made by this subtitle [subtitle A (§§ 211–217) of title II of Pub. L. 110–85, enacting section 379j–1 of this title and amending this section and section 379j of this title] shall take effect on October 1, 2007, or the date of the enactment of this Act [Sept. 27, 2007], whichever is later, except that fees under part 3 of subchapter C of chapter VII of the Federal Food, Drug, and Cosmetic Act [this subpart] shall be assessed for all premarket applications, premarket reports, supplements, 30-day notices, and premarket notification submissions received on or after October 1, 2007, regardless of the date of the enactment of this Act."

Pub. L. 110–85, title II, § 217, Sept. 27, 2007, 121 Stat. 852, provided that: "The amendments made by this subtitle [subtitle A (§§ 211–217) of title II of Pub. L. 110–85, enacting section 379j–1 of this title and amending this section and section 379j of this title] cease to be effective October 1, 2012, except that section 738A of the Federal Food, Drug, and Cosmetic Act [21 U.S.C. 379j–1] (regarding annual performance and financial reports) ceases to be effective January 31, 2013."

EFFECTIVE AND TERMINATION DATES

Pub. L. 107–250, title I, § 106, Oct. 26, 2002, 116 Stat. 1602, provided that: "The amendments made by this title [enacting this subpart] shall take effect on the date of the enactment of this Act [Oct. 26, 2002], except that fees shall be assessed for all premarket applications, premarket reports, supplements, and premarket notification submissions received on or after October 1, 2002, regardless of the date of enactment."

Pub. L. 107–250, title I, § 107, Oct. 26, 2002, 116 Stat. 1602, provided that: "The amendments made by this title [enacting this subpart] cease to be effective October 1, 2007, except that section 103 [set out as a note below] with respect to annual reports ceases to be effective January 31, 2008."

SAVINGS PROVISION

Pub. L. 110–85, title II, § 214, Sept. 27, 2007, 121 Stat. 852, provided that: "Notwithstanding section 107 of the Medical Device User Fee and Modernization Act of 2002 (Public Law 107–250) [set out as an Effective and Termination Dates note above], and notwithstanding the amendments made by this subtitle [subtitle A (§§ 211–217) of title II of Pub. L. 110–85, enacting section 379j–1 of this title and amending this section and section 379j of this title], part 3 of subchapter C of chapter VII of the Federal Food, Drug, and Cosmetic Act (21 U.S.C. 379i et seq.), as in effect on the day before the date of the enactment of this subtitle [Sept. 27, 2007], shall continue to be in effect with respect to premarket applications, premarket reports, premarket notification submissions, and supplements (as defined in such part as of such day) that on or after October 1, 2002, but before October 1, 2007, were accepted by the Food and Drug Administration for filing with respect to assessing and collecting any fee required by such part for a fiscal year prior to fiscal year 2008."

FINDINGS

Pub. L. 110–85, title II, § 201(c), Sept. 27, 2007, 121 Stat. 842, provided that: "The Congress finds that the fees authorized under the amendments made by this title [enacting section 379j–1 of this title and amending this section and sections 333, 360, 360i, 360m, 374, and 379j of this title] will be dedicated toward expediting the process for the review of device applications and for assuring the safety and effectiveness of devices, as set forth in the goals identified for purposes of part 3 of subchapter C of chapter VII of the Federal Food, Drug, and Cosmetic Act [this subpart] in the letters from the Secretary of Health and Human Services to the Chairman of the Committee on Health, Education, Labor, and Pensions of the Senate and the Chairman of the Committee on Energy and Commerce of the House of Representatives, as set forth in the Congressional Record."

Pub. L. 107–250, title I, § 101, Oct. 26, 2002, 116 Stat. 1589, provided that: "The Congress finds that—

"(1) prompt approval and clearance of safe and effective devices is critical to the improvement of the public health so that patients may enjoy the benefits of devices to diagnose, treat, and prevent disease;

"(2) the public health will be served by making additional funds available for the purpose of augmenting the resources of the Food and Drug Administration that are devoted to the process for the review of devices and the assurance of device safety and effectiveness so that statutorily mandated deadlines may be met; and

"(3) the fees authorized by this title [enacting this subpart and provisions set out as notes under this section and section 379j of this title] will be dedicated to meeting the goals identified in the letters from the Secretary of Health and Human Services to the Committee on Energy and Commerce of the House of Representatives and the Committee on Health, Education, Labor, and Pensions of the Senate, as set forth in the Congressional Record."

ANNUAL REPORTS

Pub. L. 107–250, title I, § 103, Oct. 26, 2002, 116 Stat. 1600, as amended by Pub. L. 109–43, § 2(b), Aug. 1, 2005, 119 Stat. 441, which directed the Secretary of Health and Human Services to submit annual reports to Congress on progress in achieving goals identified in section 101(3), set out above, and implementation of authority for and use of fees collected under the medical device user-fee program established under this subpart, ceased to be effective Jan. 31, 2008. See Effective and Termination Dates note above.

STUDY

Pub. L. 107–250, title I, § 104(b), Oct. 26, 2002, 116 Stat. 1601, directed the Secretary of Health and Human Services to conduct a study for the purpose of making certain determinations regarding the medical device user-fee program established under the amendment made by section 102 of Pub. L. 107–250 and to submit a report to Congress by Jan. 10, 2007.

CONSULTATION

Pub. L. 107–250, title I, § 105, Oct. 26, 2002, 116 Stat. 1601, provided that:

"(a) IN GENERAL.—In developing recommendations to the Congress for the goals and plans for meeting the goals for the process for the review of medical device applications for fiscal years after fiscal year 2007, and for the reauthorization of sections 737 and 738 of the Federal Food, Drug, and Cosmetic Act [21 U.S.C. 379i, 379j], the Secretary of Health and Human Services (referred to in this section as the 'Secretary') shall consult with the Committee on Energy and Commerce of the House of Representatives, the Committee on Health, Education, Labor, and Pensions of the Senate, appropriate scientific and academic experts, health care professionals, representatives of patient and consumer advocacy groups, and the regulated industry.

"(b) RECOMMENDATIONS.—The Secretary shall publish in the Federal Register recommendations under subsection (a), after negotiations with the regulated industry; shall present such recommendations to the congressional committees specified in such paragraph; shall hold a meeting at which the public may present its views on such recommendations; and shall provide for a period of 30 days for the public to provide written comments on such recommendations."

§ 379j. Authority to assess and use device fees

(a) Types of fees

(1) In general

Beginning in fiscal year 2008, the Secretary shall assess and collect fees in accordance with this section.

(2) Premarket application, premarket report, supplement, and submission fee, and annual fee for periodic reporting concerning a class III device

(A) In general

Except as provided in subparagraph (B) and subsections (d) and (e) of this section, each person who submits any of the following, on or after October 1, 2002, shall be subject to a fee established under subsection (c)(1) of this section for the fiscal year involved in accordance with the following:

(i) A premarket application.

(ii) For a premarket report, a fee equal to the fee that applies under clause (i).

(iii) For a panel track supplement, a fee equal to 75 percent of the fee that applies under clause (i).

(iv) For a 180-day supplement, a fee equal to 15 percent of the fee that applies under clause (i).

(v) For a real-time supplement, a fee equal to 7 percent of the fee that applies under clause (i).

(vi) For a 30-day notice, a fee equal to 1.6 percent of the fee that applies under clause (i).

(vii) For an efficacy supplement, a fee equal to the fee that applies under clause (i).

(viii) For a premarket notification submission, a fee equal to 1.84 percent of the fee that applies under clause (i).

(ix) For a request for classification information, a fee equal to 1.35 percent of the fee that applies under clause (i).

(x) For periodic reporting concerning a class III device, an annual fee equal to 3.5 percent of the fee that applies under clause (i).

(B) Exceptions

(i) Humanitarian device exemption

An application under section 360j(m) of this title is not subject to any fee under subparagraph (A).

(ii) Further manufacturing use

No fee shall be required under subparagraph (A) for the submission of a premarket application under section 262 of title 42 for a product licensed for further manufacturing use only.

(iii) State or Federal Government sponsors

No fee shall be required under subparagraph (A) for a premarket application, premarket report, supplement, or premarket notification submission submitted by a State or Federal Government entity unless the device involved is to be distributed commercially.

(iv) Premarket notifications by third parties

No fee shall be required under subparagraph (A) for a premarket notification submission reviewed by an accredited person pursuant to section 360m of this title.

(v) Pediatric conditions of use

(I) In general

No fee shall be required under subparagraph (A) for a premarket application, premarket report, or premarket notification submission if the proposed conditions of use for the device involved are solely for a pediatric population. No fee shall be required under such subparagraph for a supplement if the sole purpose of the supplement is to propose conditions of use for a pediatric population.

(II) Subsequent proposal of adult conditions of use

In the case of a person who submits a premarket application or premarket report for which, under subclause (I), a fee under subparagraph (A) is not required, any supplement to such application that proposes conditions of use for any adult population is subject to the fee that applies under such subparagraph for a premarket application.

(C) Payment

The fee required by subparagraph (A) shall be due upon submission of the premarket application, premarket report, supplement, premarket notification submission, 30-day notice, request for classification information, or periodic reporting concerning a class III device. Applicants submitting portions of applications pursuant to section 360e(c)(4) of this title shall pay such fees upon submission of the first portion of such applications.

(D) Refunds

(i) Application refused for filing

The Secretary shall refund 75 percent of the fee paid under subparagraph (A) for any application, report, or supplement that is refused for filing.

(ii) Application withdrawn before filing

The Secretary shall refund 75 percent of the fee paid under subparagraph (A) for any application, report, or supplement that is withdrawn prior to the filing decision of the Secretary.

(iii) Application withdrawn before first action

After receipt of a request for a refund of the fee paid under subparagraph (A) for a premarket application, premarket report, or supplement that is withdrawn after filing but before a first action, the Secretary may return some or all of the fee. The amount of refund, if any, shall be based on the level of effort already expended on the review of such application, report, or supplement.

(iv) Modular applications withdrawn before first action

The Secretary shall refund 75 percent of the application fee paid for an application submitted under section 360e(c)(4) of this title that is withdrawn before a second portion is submitted and before a first action on the first portion.

(v) Later withdrawn modular applications

If an application submitted under section 360e(c)(4) of this title is withdrawn after a second or subsequent portion is submitted but before any first action, the Secretary may return a portion of the fee. The amount of refund, if any, shall be based on the level of effort already expended on the review of the portions submitted.

(vi) Sole discretion to refund

The Secretary shall have sole discretion to refund a fee or portion of the fee under clause (iii) or (v). A determination by the Secretary concerning a refund under clause (iii) or (v) shall not be reviewable.

(3) Annual establishment registration fee

(A) In general

Except as provided in subparagraph (B), each establishment subject to a registration fee shall be subject to a fee for each initial or annual registration under section 360 of this title beginning with its registration for fiscal year 2008.

(B) Exception

No fee shall be required under subparagraph (A) for an establishment operated by a State or Federal governmental entity or an Indian tribe (as defined in the Indian Self Determination and Educational Assistance Act[1] [25 U.S.C. 450 et seq.]), unless a device manufactured by the establishment is to be distributed commercially.

(C) Payment

The fee required under subparagraph (A) shall be due once each fiscal year, upon the initial registration of the establishment or upon the annual registration under section 360 of this title.

(b) Fee amounts

Except as provided in subsections (c), (d), (e), and (h) the fees under subsection (a) shall be based on the following fee amounts:

Fee Type	Fiscal Year 2008	Fiscal Year 2009	Fiscal Year 2010	Fiscal Year 2011	Fiscal Year 2012
Premarket Application	$185,000	$200,725	$217,787	$236,298	$256,384
Establishment Registration	$1,706	$1,851	$2,008	$2,179	$2,364.

(c) Annual fee setting

(1) In general

The Secretary shall, 60 days before the start of each fiscal year after September 30, 2002, publish in the Federal Register fees under subsection (a) of this section.

(2) Adjustment

(A) In general

When setting fees for fiscal year 2010, the Secretary may increase the fee under subsection (a)(3)(A) (applicable to establishments subject to registration) only if the Secretary estimates that the number of establishments submitting fees for fiscal year 2009 is fewer than 12,250. The percentage increase shall be the percentage by which the estimate of establishments submitting fees in fiscal year 2009 is fewer than 12,750, but in no case may the percentage increase be more than 8.5 percent over that specified in subsection (b) for fiscal year 2010. If the Secretary makes any adjustment to the fee under subsection (a)(3)(A) for fiscal year 2010, then such fee for fiscal years 2011 and 2012 shall be adjusted so that such fee for fiscal year 2011 is equal to the adjusted fee for fiscal year 2010 increased by 8.5 percent, and such fee for fiscal year 2012 is equal to the adjusted fee for fiscal year 2011 increased by 8.5 percent.

(B) Publication

For any adjustment made under subparagraph (A), the Secretary shall publish in the Federal Register the Secretary's determination to make the adjustment and the rationale for the determination.

(3) Limit

The total amount of fees charged, as adjusted under this subsection, for a fiscal year may not exceed the total costs for such fiscal year for the resources allocated for the process for the review of device applications.

(4) Supplement

(A) In general

The Secretary may use unobligated carryover balances from fees collected in previous fiscal years to ensure that sufficient fee revenues are available in that fiscal year, so long as the Secretary maintains unobligated carryover balances of not less than 1 month of operating reserves for the first month of the next fiscal year.

(B) Notice to Congress

Not later than 14 days before the Secretary anticipates the use of funds described in subparagraph (A), the Secretary shall provide notice to the Committee on Health, Education, Labor, and Pensions and the Committee on Appropriations of the Senate and the Committee on Energy and Commerce and the Committee on Appropriations of the House of Representatives.

(d) Small businesses; fee waiver and fee reduction regarding premarket approval fees

(1) In general

The Secretary shall grant a waiver of the fee required under subsection (a) of this section for one premarket application, or one premarket report, where the Secretary finds that the applicant involved is a small business submitting its first premarket application to the Secretary, or its first premarket report, re-

[1] See References in Text note below.

spectively, for review. For the purposes of this paragraph, the term "small business" means an entity that reported $30,000,000 or less of gross receipts or sales in its most recent Federal income tax return for a taxable year, including such returns of all of its affiliates. In addition, for subsequent premarket applications, premarket reports, and supplements where the Secretary finds that the applicant involved is a small business, the fees specified in clauses (i) through (v) and clauses (vii), (ix), and (x) of subsection (a)(2)(A) may be paid at a reduced rate in accordance with paragraph (2)(C).

(2) Rules relating to premarket approval fees

(A) Definition

For purposes of this paragraph, the term "small business" means an entity that reported $100,000,000 or less of gross receipts or sales in its most recent Federal income tax return for a taxable year, including such returns of all of its affiliates.

(B) Evidence of qualification

(i) In general

An applicant shall pay the higher fees established by the Secretary each year unless the applicant submits evidence that it qualifies for a waiver of the fee or the lower fee rate.

(ii) Firms submitting tax returns to the United States Internal Revenue Service

The applicant shall support its claim that it meets the definition under subparagraph (A) by submission of a copy of its most recent Federal income tax return for a taxable year, and a copy of such returns of its affiliates, which show an amount of gross sales or receipts that is less than the maximum established in subparagraph (A). The applicant, and each of such affiliates, shall certify that the information provided is a true and accurate copy of the actual tax forms they submitted to the Internal Revenue Service. If no tax forms are submitted for any affiliate, the applicant shall certify that the applicant has no affiliates.

(iii) Firms not submitting tax returns to the United States Internal Revenue Service

In the case of an applicant that has not previously submitted a Federal income tax return, the applicant and each of its affiliates shall demonstrate that it meets the definition under subparagraph (A) by submission of a signed certification, in such form as the Secretary may direct through a notice published in the Federal Register, that the applicant or affiliate meets the criteria for a small business and a certification, in English, from the national taxing authority of the country in which the applicant or, if applicable, affiliate is headquartered. The certification from such taxing authority shall bear the official seal of such taxing authority and shall provide the applicant's or affiliate's gross receipts or sales for the most recent year in both the local currency of such country and in United States dollars, the exchange rate used in converting such local currency to dollars, and the dates during which these receipts or sales were collected. The applicant shall also submit a statement signed by the head of the applicant's firm or by its chief financial officer that the applicant has submitted certifications for all of its affiliates, or that the applicant has no affiliates.

(C) Reduced fees

Where the Secretary finds that the applicant involved meets the definition under subparagraph (A), the fees established under subsection (c)(1) may be paid at a reduced rate of—

(i) 25 percent of the fee established under such subsection for a premarket application, a premarket report, a supplement, or periodic reporting concerning a class III device; and

(ii) 50 percent of the fee established under such subsection for a 30-day notice or a request for classification information.

(D) Request for fee waiver or reduction

An applicant seeking a fee waiver or reduction under this subsection shall submit supporting information to the Secretary at least 60 days before the fee is required pursuant to subsection (a) of this section. The decision of the Secretary regarding whether an entity qualifies for such a waiver or reduction is not reviewable.

(e) Small businesses; fee reduction regarding premarket notification submissions

(1) In general

For fiscal year 2008 and each subsequent fiscal year, where the Secretary finds that the applicant involved is a small business, the fee specified in subsection (a)(2)(A)(viii) of this section may be paid at a reduced rate in accordance with paragraph (2)(C).

(2) Rules relating to premarket notification submissions

(A) Definition

For purposes of this subsection, the term "small business" means an entity that reported $100,000,000 or less of gross receipts or sales in its most recent Federal income tax return for a taxable year, including such returns of all of its affiliates.

(B) Evidence of qualification

(i) In general

An applicant shall pay the higher fees established by the Secretary each year unless the applicant submits evidence that it qualifies for the lower fee rate.

(ii) Firms submitting tax returns to the United States Internal Revenue Service

The applicant shall support its claim that it meets the definition under subparagraph (A) by submission of a copy of its most recent Federal income tax return for a taxable year, and a copy of such returns of its affiliates, which show an amount of gross sales or receipts that is less than the maximum established in subparagraph (A). The applicant, and each of such affiliates, shall certify that the information provided is a true and accurate copy of the actual tax forms they submitted to the Internal Revenue Service. If no tax forms are submitted for any affiliate, the applicant shall certify that the applicant has no affiliates.

(iii) Firms not submitting tax returns to the United States Internal Revenue Service

In the case of an applicant that has not previously submitted a Federal income tax return, the applicant and each of its affiliates shall demonstrate that it meets the definition under subparagraph (A) by submission of a signed certification, in such form as the Secretary may direct through a notice published in the Federal Register, that the applicant or affiliate meets the criteria for a small business and a certification, in English, from the national taxing authority of the country in which the applicant or, if applicable, affiliate is headquartered. The certification from such taxing authority shall bear the official seal of such taxing authority and shall provide the applicant's or affiliate's gross receipts or sales for the most recent year in both the local currency of such country and in United States dollars, the exchange rate used in converting such local currency to dollars, and the dates during which these receipts or sales were collected. The applicant shall also submit a statement signed by the head of the applicant's firm or by its chief financial officer that the applicant has submitted certifications for all of its affiliates, or that the applicant has no affiliates.

(C) Reduced fees

For fiscal year 2008 and each subsequent fiscal year, where the Secretary finds that the applicant involved meets the definition under subparagraph (A), the fee for a premarket notification submission may be paid at 50 percent of the fee that applies under subsection (a)(2)(A)(viii), and as established under subsection (c)(1).

(D) Request for reduction

An applicant seeking a fee reduction under this subsection shall submit supporting information to the Secretary at least 60 days before the fee is required pursuant to subsection (a) of this section. The decision of the Secretary regarding whether an entity qualifies for such a reduction is not reviewable.

(f) Effect of failure to pay fees

(1) No acceptance of submissions

A premarket application, premarket report, supplement, premarket notification submission, 30-day notice, request for classification information, or periodic reporting concerning a class III device submitted by a person subject to fees under subsections (a)(2) and (a)(3) shall be considered incomplete and shall not be accepted by the Secretary until all fees owed by such person have been paid.

(2) No registration

Registration information submitted under section 360 of this title by an establishment subject to a registration fee shall be considered incomplete and shall not be accepted by the Secretary until the registration fee under subsection (a)(3) owed for the establishment has been paid. Until the fee is paid and the registration is complete, the establishment is deemed to have failed to register in accordance with section 360 of this title.

(g) Conditions

(1) Performance goals; termination of program

With respect to the amount that, under the salaries and expenses account of the Food and Drug Administration, is appropriated for a fiscal year for devices and radiological products, fees may not be assessed under subsection (a) for the fiscal year, and the Secretary is not expected to meet any performance goals identified for the fiscal year, if—

(A) the amount so appropriated for the fiscal year, excluding the amount of fees appropriated for the fiscal year, is more than 1 percent less than $205,720,000 multiplied by the adjustment factor applicable to such fiscal year; or

(B) fees were not assessed under subsection (a) for the previous fiscal year.

(2) Authority

If the Secretary does not assess fees under subsection (a) during any portion of a fiscal year because of paragraph (1) and if at a later date in such fiscal year the Secretary may assess such fees, the Secretary may assess and collect such fees, without any modification in the rate for premarket applications, supplements, premarket reports, premarket notification submissions, 30-day notices, requests for classification information, periodic reporting concerning a class III device, and establishment registrations at any time in such fiscal year, notwithstanding the provisions of subsection (a) relating to the date fees are to be paid.

(h) Crediting and availability of fees

(1) In general

Fees authorized under subsection (a) of this section shall be collected and available for obligation only to the extent and in the amount provided in advance in appropriation Acts. Such fees are authorized to be appropriated to remain available until expended. Such sums as may be necessary may be transferred from the Food and Drug Administration salaries and expenses appropriation account without fiscal year limitation to such appropriation account for salaries and expenses with such fiscal year limitation. The sums transferred shall be available solely for the process for the review of device applications.

(2) Collections and appropriation acts

(A) In general

The fees authorized by this section—

(i) shall be retained in each fiscal year in an amount not to exceed the amount specified in appropriation Acts, or otherwise made available for obligation, for such fiscal year, and

(ii) shall only be collected and available to defray increases in the costs of the resources allocated for the process for the review of device applications (including increases in such costs for an additional number of full-time equivalent positions in the Department of Health and Human Services to be engaged in such process) over such costs, excluding costs paid from fees collected under this section, for fiscal year 2002 multiplied by the adjustment factor.

(B) Compliance

(i) In general

The Secretary shall be considered to have met the requirements of subparagraph (A)(ii) in any fiscal year if the costs funded by appropriations and allocated for the process for the review of device applications—

(I) are not more than 3 percent below the level specified in subparagraph (A)(ii); or

(II)(aa) are more than 3 percent below the level specified in subparagraph (A)(ii), and fees assessed for a subsequent fiscal year are decreased by the amount in excess of 3 percent by which such costs fell below the level specified in such subparagraph; and

(bb) such costs are not more than 5 percent below the level specified in such subparagraph.

(ii) More than 5 percent

To the extent such costs are more than 5 percent below the specified level in subparagraph (A)(ii), fees may not be collected under this section for that fiscal year.

(3) Authorizations of appropriations

There are authorized to be appropriated for fees under this section—

(A) $48,431,000 for fiscal year 2008;

(B) $52,547,000 for fiscal year 2009;

(C) $57,014,000 for fiscal year 2010;

(D) $61,860,000 for fiscal year 2011; and

(E) $67,118,000 for fiscal year 2012.

(4) Offset

If the cumulative amount of fees collected during fiscal years 2008, 2009, and 2010, added to the amount estimated to be collected for fiscal year 2011, which estimate shall be based upon the amount of fees received by the Secretary through June 30, 2011, exceeds the amount of fees specified in aggregate in paragraph (3) for these four fiscal years, the aggregate amount in excess shall be credited to the appropriation account of the Food and Drug Administration as provided in paragraph (1), and shall be subtracted from the amount of fees that would otherwise be authorized to be collected under this section pursuant to appropriation Acts for fiscal year 2012.

(i) Collection of unpaid fees

In any case where the Secretary does not receive payment of a fee assessed under subsection (a) of this section within 30 days after it is due, such fee shall be treated as a claim of the United States Government subject to subchapter II of chapter 37 of title 31.

(j) Written requests for refunds

To qualify for consideration for a refund under subsection (a)(2)(D) of this section, a person shall submit to the Secretary a written request for such refund not later than 180 days after such fee is due.

(k) Construction

This section may not be construed to require that the number of full-time equivalent positions in the Department of Health and Human Services, for officers, employees, and advisory committees not engaged in the process of the review of device applications, be reduced to offset the number of officers, employees, and advisory committees so engaged.

(June 25, 1938, ch. 675, §738, as added Pub. L. 107–250, title I, §102(a), Oct. 26, 2002, 116 Stat. 1591; amended Pub. L. 108–214, §2(a)(2), (d)(2)(A), (B), (3)(A), Apr. 1, 2004, 118 Stat. 572, 576, 577; Pub. L. 109–43, §2(a), Aug. 1, 2005, 119 Stat. 439; Pub. L. 110–85, title II, §212, Sept. 27, 2007, 121 Stat. 844.)

AMENDMENT OF SECTION

For termination of amendment by section 217 of Pub. L. 110–85, see Effective and Termination Dates of 2007 Amendment note below.

TERMINATION OF SECTION

For termination of section by section 107 of Pub. L. 107–250, see Effective and Termination Dates note set out under section 379i of this title.

REFERENCES IN TEXT

The Indian Self Determination and Educational Assistance Act, referred to in subsec. (a)(3)(B), probably means the Indian Self-Determination and Education Assistance Act, Pub. L. 93–638, Jan. 4, 1975, 88 Stat. 2203, which is classified principally to subchapter II (§450 et seq.) of chapter 14 of Title 25, Indians. For complete classification of this Act to the Code, see Short Title note set out under section 450 of Title 25 and Tables.

AMENDMENTS

2007—Subsec. (a)(1). Pub. L. 110–85, §§212(a)(1)(A), 217, temporarily substituted "Beginning in fiscal year 2008" for "Beginning on October 26, 2002". See Effective and Termination Dates of 2007 Amendment note below.

Subsec. (a)(2). Pub. L. 110–85, §§212(a)(1)(B), 217, temporarily amended heading generally. Prior to amendment, heading read as follows: "Premarket application, premarket report, supplement, and submission fee". See Effective and Termination Dates of 2007 Amendment note below.

Subsec. (a)(2)(A)(iii). Pub. L. 110–85, §§212(a)(2)(A), 217, temporarily substituted "a fee equal to 75 percent of the fee that applies" for "a fee equal to the fee that applies". See Effective and Termination Dates of 2007 Amendment note below.

Subsec. (a)(2)(A)(iv). Pub. L. 110–85, §§212(a)(2)(B), 217, temporarily substituted "15 percent" for "21.5 percent". See Effective and Termination Dates of 2007 Amendment note below.

Subsec. (a)(2)(A)(v). Pub. L. 110–85, §§212(a)(2)(C), 217, temporarily substituted "7 percent" for "7.2 percent".

See Effective and Termination Dates of 2007 Amendment note below.

Subsec. (a)(2)(A)(vi), (vii). Pub. L. 110–85, §§ 212(a)(2)(D), (E), 217, temporarily added cl. (vi) and redesignated former cl. (vi) as (vii). Former cl. (vii) redesignated (viii). See Effective and Termination Dates of 2007 Amendment note below.

Subsec. (a)(2)(A)(viii). Pub. L. 110–85, §§ 212(a)(2)(D), (F), 217, temporarily redesignated cl. (vii) as (viii), substituted "1.84 percent" for "1.42 percent", and struck out ", subject to any adjustment under subsection (e)(2)(C)(ii) of this section" before period at end. See Effective and Termination Dates of 2007 Amendment note below.

Subsec. (a)(2)(A)(ix), (x). Pub. L. 110–85, §§ 212(a)(2)(G), 217, temporarily added cls. (ix) and (x). See Effective and Termination Dates of 2007 Amendment note below.

Subsec. (a)(2)(C). Pub. L. 110–85, §§ 212(a)(3), 217, temporarily amended subpar. (C) generally. Prior to amendment, text read as follows: "The fee required by subparagraph (A) shall be due upon submission of the premarket application, premarket report, supplement, or premarket notification submission except that invoices for applications submitted between October 1, 2002, and October 26, 2002, shall be payable on October 30, 2002. Applicants submitting portions of applications pursuant to section 360e(c)(3) of this title shall pay such fees upon submission of the first portion of such applications. The fees credited to fiscal year 2003 under this section shall include all fees payable from October 1, 2002, through September 30, 2003." See Effective and Termination Dates of 2007 Amendment note below.

Subsec. (a)(2)(D)(iii). Pub. L. 110–85, §§ 212(a)(4)(A), 217, temporarily struck out at end "The Secretary shall have sole discretion to refund a fee or portion of the fee under this subparagraph. A determination by the Secretary concerning a refund under this paragraph shall not be reviewable." See Effective and Termination Dates of 2007 Amendment note below.

Subsec. (a)(2)(D)(iv) to (vi). Pub. L. 110–85, §§ 212(a)(4)(B), 217, temporarily added cls. (iv) to (vi). See Effective and Termination Dates of 2007 Amendment note below.

Subsec. (a)(3). Pub. L. 110–85, §§ 212(a)(5), 217, temporarily added par. (3). See Effective and Termination Dates of 2007 Amendment note below.

Subsec. (b). Pub. L. 110–85, §§ 212(b), 217, temporarily amended subsec. (b) generally. Prior to amendment, text read as follows: "Except as provided in subsections (c), (d), (e), (g), and (h) of this section, the fees under subsection (a) of this section shall be established to generate the following revenue amounts: $25,125,000 in fiscal year 2003; $27,255,000 in fiscal year 2004; and $29,785,000 in fiscal year 2005. If legislation is enacted after October 26, 2002, requiring the Secretary to fund additional costs of the retirement of Federal personnel, fee revenue amounts under this subsection shall be increased in each year by the amount necessary to fully fund the portion of such additional costs that are attributable to the process for the review of device applications." See Effective and Termination Dates of 2007 Amendment note below.

Subsec. (c). Pub. L. 110–85, §§ 212(c)(1)(A), 217, temporarily made technical amendment to heading. See Effective and Termination Dates of 2007 Amendment note below.

Subsec. (c)(1). Pub. L. 110–85, §§ 212(c)(1)(B), 217, temporarily struck out at end "The fees established for fiscal year 2006 shall be based on a premarket application fee of $259,600, and the fees established for fiscal year 2007 shall be based on a premarket application fee of $281,600.". See Effective and Termination Dates of 2007 Amendment note below.

Subsec. (c)(2), (3). Pub. L. 110–85, §§ 212(c)(2)(A), (B), 217, temporarily added par. (2) and redesignated former par. (2) as (3). Former par. (3) redesignated (4). See Effective and Termination Dates of 2007 Amendment note below.

Subsec. (c)(4). Pub. L. 110–85, §§ 212(c)(2)(A), (C), 217, temporarily redesignated par. (3) as (4) and substituted in subpar. (A) "The Secretary" for "For fiscal years 2006 and 2007, the Secretary" and "for the first month of the next fiscal year" for "for the first month of fiscal year 2008". See Effective and Termination Dates of 2007 Amendment note below.

Subsec. (d)(1). Pub. L. 110–85, §§ 212(d)(1), 217, temporarily struck out ", partners, and parent firms" after "affiliates" and substituted "clauses (i) through (v) and clauses (vii), (ix), and (x) of subsection (a)(2)(A)" for "clauses (i) through (vi) of subsection (a)(2)(A) of this section". See Effective and Termination Dates of 2007 Amendment note below.

Subsec. (d)(2)(A). Pub. L. 110–85, §§ 212(d)(2)(A), 217, temporarily struck out ", partners, and parent firms" before period at end. See Effective and Termination Dates of 2007 Amendment note below.

Subsec. (d)(2)(B). Pub. L. 110–85, §§ 212(d)(2)(B)(i), (ii), 217, temporarily designated first sentence as cl. (i) and second to fourth sentences as cl. (ii) and inserted cl. headings. See Effective and Termination Dates of 2007 Amendment note below.

Subsec. (d)(2)(B)(ii). Pub. L. 110–85, §§ 212(d)(2)(B)(iii), (iv), 217, temporarily struck out ", partners, and parent firms" after "its affiliates" and after "such affiliates" and substituted "If no tax forms are submitted for any affiliate, the applicant shall certify that the applicant has no affiliates." for "If no tax forms are submitted for affiliates, partners, or parent firms, the applicant shall certify that the applicant has no affiliates, partners, or parent firms, respectively." See Effective and Termination Dates of 2007 Amendment note below.

Subsec. (d)(2)(B)(iii). Pub. L. 110–85, §§ 212(d)(2)(B)(v), 217, temporarily added cl. (iii). See Effective and Termination Dates of 2007 Amendment note below.

Subsec. (d)(2)(C). Pub. L. 110–85, §§ 212(d)(3), 217, temporarily amended subpar. (C) generally. Prior to amendment, text read as follows: "Where the Secretary finds that the applicant involved meets the definition under subparagraph (A), the fees established under subsection (c)(1) of this section may be paid at a reduced rate of 38 percent of the fee established under such subsection for a premarket application, a premarket report, or a supplement." See Effective and Termination Dates of 2007 Amendment note below.

Subsec. (e)(1). Pub. L. 110–85, §§ 212(e)(1), 217, temporarily substituted "2008" for "2004" and "(a)(2)(A)(viii)" for "(a)(2)(A)(vii)". See Effective and Termination Dates of 2007 Amendment note below.

Subsec. (e)(2)(A). Pub. L. 110–85, §§ 212(e)(2)(A), 217, temporarily struck out ", partners, and parent firms" before period at end. See Effective and Termination Dates of 2007 Amendment note below.

Subsec. (e)(2)(B). Pub. L. 110–85, §§ 212(e)(2)(B)(i), (ii), 217, temporarily inserted cl. headings and designated first sentence as cl. (i) and second to fourth sentences as cl. (ii). See Effective and Termination Dates of 2007 Amendment note below.

Subsec. (e)(2)(B)(ii). Pub. L. 110–85, §§ 212(e)(2)(B)(iii), (iv), 217, temporarily struck out ", partners, and parent firms" after "its affiliates" and after "such affiliates" and substituted "If no tax forms are submitted for any affiliate, the applicant shall certify that the applicant has no affiliates." for "If no tax forms are submitted for affiliates, partners, or parent firms, the applicant shall certify that the applicant has no affiliates, partners, or parent firms, respectively." See Effective and Termination Dates of 2007 Amendment note below.

Subsec. (e)(2)(B)(iii). Pub. L. 110–85, §§ 212(e)(2)(B)(v), 217, temporarily added cl. (iii). See Effective and Termination Dates of 2007 Amendment note below.

Subsec. (e)(2)(C). Pub. L. 110–85, §§ 212(e)(3), 217, temporarily amended subpar. (C) generally. Prior to amendment, subpar. (C) contained provisions, for fiscal year 2004 and each subsequent fiscal year, authorizing in cl. (i) a reduced fee for a premarket notification submission, and directing in cl. (ii) the Secretary how to determine an adjustment per fee revenue amount. See Effective and Termination Dates of 2007 Amendment note below.

Subsec. (f). Pub. L. 110–85, §§ 212(f), 217, temporarily amended subsec. (f) generally. Prior to amendment, text read as follows: "A premarket application, premarket report, supplement, or premarket notification submission submitted by a person subject to fees under subsection (a) of this section shall be considered incomplete and shall not be accepted by the Secretary until all fees owed by such person have been paid." See Effective and Termination Dates of 2007 Amendment note below.

Subsec. (g)(1). Pub. L. 110–85, §§ 212(g)(1), 217, temporarily added par. (1) and struck out former par. (1). Prior to amendment, par. (1) related to performance goals for fiscal years 2003 through 2005, with respect to the amount appropriated under the salaries and expenses account of the Food and Drug Administration, for devices and radiological products, and termination of the program after fiscal year 2005. See Effective and Termination Dates of 2007 Amendment note below.

Subsec. (g)(2). Pub. L. 110–85, §§ 212(g)(2), 217, temporarily amended par. (2) generally. Prior to amendment, text read as follows: "If the Secretary does not assess fees under subsection (a) of this section during any portion of a fiscal year because of subparagraph (C) or (D) of paragraph (1) and if at a later date in such fiscal year the Secretary may assess such fees, the Secretary may assess and collect such fees, without any modification in the rate for premarket applications, supplements, premarket reports, and premarket notification submissions, and at any time in such fiscal year, notwithstanding the provisions of subsection (a) of this section relating to the date fees are to be paid." See Effective and Termination Dates of 2007 Amendment note below.

Subsec. (h)(3). Pub. L. 110–85, §§ 212(h)(1), 217, temporarily amended par. (3) generally, substituting provisions authorizing appropriations for fiscal years 2008 to 2012 for provisions authorizing appropriations for fiscal years 2003 to 2007. See Effective and Termination Dates of 2007 Amendment note below.

Subsec. (h)(4). Pub. L. 110–85, §§ 212(h)(2), 217, temporarily amended par. (4) generally. Prior to amendment, text read as follows: "Any amount of fees collected for a fiscal year under this section that exceeds the amount of fees specified in appropriation Acts for such fiscal year shall be credited to the appropriation account of the Food and Drug Administration as provided in paragraph (1), and shall be subtracted from the amount of fees that would otherwise be authorized to be collected under this section pursuant to appropriation Acts for a subsequent fiscal year." See Effective and Termination Dates of 2007 Amendment note below.

2005—Subsec. (a)(2)(A). Pub. L. 109–43, § 2(a)(7), substituted "subsection (c)(1)" for "subsection (c)(5)".

Subsec. (b). Pub. L. 109–43, § 2(a)(1), inserted "and" after "2004;" and substituted "2005" for "2005; $32,615,000 in fiscal year 2006, and $35,000,000 in fiscal year 2007".

Subsec. (c). Pub. L. 109–43, § 2(a)(2)(A), substituted "Annual fee setting" for "Adjustments" in heading.

Subsec. (c)(1). Pub. L. 109–43, § 2(a)(2)(B)–(D), redesignated par. (5) as (1), substituted "In general" for "Annual fee setting" in heading, "publish in the Federal Register fees under subsection (a) of this section. The fees" for "establish, for the next fiscal year, and publish in the Federal Register, fees under subsection (a) of this section, based on the revenue amounts established under subsection (b) of this section and the adjustment provided under this subsection and subsection (e)(2)(C)(ii) of this section, except that the fees", "2006" for "2003", and "$259,600, and the fees established for fiscal year 2007 shall be based on a premarket application fee of $281,600." for "$154,000." in text, and struck out former par. (1) which required an annual inflation adjustment of the revenues established in subsec. (b).

Subsec. (c)(2). Pub. L. 109–43, § 2(a)(2)(B), (C), redesignated par. (6) as (2) and struck out former par. (2) which required an annual adjustment of the fee revenues established in subsec. (b) to reflect changes in the workload of the Secretary for the process for the review of device applications.

Subsec. (c)(3). Pub. L. 109–43, § 2(a)(2)(B), (E), added par. (3) and struck out former par. (3) which required an annual compensating adjustment of the fee revenues established in subsec. (b).

Subsec. (c)(4). Pub. L. 109–43, § 2(a)(2)(B), struck out par. (4) which provided for a fiscal year 2007 adjustment of the fee revenues established in subsec. (b) to provide for operating reserves of carryover user fees.

Subsec. (c)(5), (6). Pub. L. 109–43, § 2(a)(2)(C), redesignated pars. (5) and (6) as (1) and (2), respectively.

Subsec. (d)(1). Pub. L. 109–43, § 2(a)(3)(A), inserted after first sentence "For the purposes of this paragraph, the term 'small business' means an entity that reported $30,000,000 or less of gross receipts or sales in its most recent Federal income tax return for a taxable year, including such returns of all of its affiliates, partners, and parent firms."

Subsec. (d)(2)(A). Pub. L. 109–43, § 2(a)(3)(B), struck out cl. (i) designation and heading before "For purposes", substituted "paragraph," for "subsection," and "$100,000,000" for "$30,000,000", and struck out heading and text of clause (ii). Text read as follows: "The Secretary may adjust the $30,000,000 threshold established in clause (i) if the Secretary has evidence from actual experience that this threshold results in a reduction in revenues from premarket applications, premarket reports, and supplements that is 16 percent or more than would occur without small business exemptions and lower fee rates. To adjust this threshold, the Secretary shall publish a notice in the Federal Register setting out the rationale for the adjustment, and the new threshold."

Subsec. (d)(2)(C). Pub. L. 109–43, § 2(a)(7), substituted "subsection (c)(1)" for "subsection (c)(5)".

Subsec. (e)(2)(A). Pub. L. 109–43, § 2(a)(4), substituted "$100,000,000" for "$30,000,000".

Subsec. (e)(2)(C). Pub. L. 109–43, § 2(a)(7), substituted "subsection (c)(1)" for "subsection (c)(5)" in cls. (i) and (ii).

Subsec. (g)(1)(B)(i). Pub. L. 109–43, § 2(a)(5)(A)(i), added cl. (i) and struck out former cl. (i) which read as follows: "For fiscal year 2005, the Secretary is expected to meet all of the performance goals identified for the fiscal year if the total of the amounts so appropriated for fiscal years 2003 through 2005, excluding the amount of fees appropriated for such fiscal years, is equal to or greater than the sum of—

"(I) $205,720,000 multiplied by the adjustment factor applicable to fiscal year 2003;

"(II) $205,720,000 multiplied by the adjustment factor applicable to fiscal year 2004; and

"(III) $205,720,000 multiplied by the adjustment factor applicable to fiscal year 2005."

Subsec. (g)(1)(B)(ii). Pub. L. 109–43, § 2(a)(5)(A)(ii), added introductory provisions and struck out former introductory provisions which read as follows: "For fiscal year 2005, if the total of the amounts so appropriated for fiscal years 2003 through 2005, excluding the amount of fees appropriated for such fiscal years, is less than the sum that applies under clause (i) for fiscal year 2005, the following applies:".

Subsec. (g)(1)(C). Pub. L. 109–43, § 2(a)(5)(B)(i), substituted "2005 and" for "2003 through" and inserted "more than 1 percent" after "years, is".

Subsec. (g)(1)(C)(ii). Pub. L. 109–43, § 2(a)(5)(B)(ii), substituted "amount that applies" for "sum that applies".

Subsec. (g)(1)(D)(i). Pub. L. 109–43, § 2(a)(5)(C), inserted "more than 1 percent" after "year, is".

Subsec. (h)(3)(D), (E). Pub. L. 109–43, § 2(a)(6), added subpar. (D) and struck out former subpars. (D) and (E) which read as follows:

"(D) $32,615,000 for fiscal year 2006; and

"(E) $35,000,000 for fiscal year 2007.".

2004—Pub. L. 108–214, § 2(d)(3)(A), made technical correction to directory language of Pub. L. 107–250, § 102(a), which enacted this section.

Subsec. (a). Pub. L. 108–214, § 2(d)(2)(A), designated introductory provisions of subsec. (a) as par. (1), inserted heading, substituted "this section." for "this section as follows:", and redesignated former par. (1) as (2).

Subsec. (a)(1)(A). Pub. L. 108–214, § 2(a)(2)(A)(i), substituted, in introductory provisions, "subsections (d) and (e)" for "subsection (d)", in cl. (iv), "clause (i)" for "clause (i), subject to any adjustment under subsection (c)(3) of this section", and, in cl. (vii), "clause (i), subject to any adjustment under subsection (e)(2)(C)(ii)" for "clause (i), subject to any adjustment under subsection (c)(3) of this section and any adjustment under subsection (e)(2)(C)(ii)".

Subsec. (a)(1)(D)(i), (ii). Pub. L. 108–214, §2(a)(2)(A)(ii), substituted "application, report," for "application".

Subsec. (d)(1). Pub. L. 108–214, §2(d)(2)(B)(i), substituted "subsection (a)(2)(A)" for "subsection (a)(1)(A)" in last sentence.

Subsec. (d)(2)(B). Pub. L. 108–214, §2(a)(2)(B), substituted "firms, which show" for "firms. which show" in second sentence.

Subsec. (e)(1). Pub. L. 108–214, §2(a)(2)(C)(i), (d)(2)(B)(ii), substituted "For fiscal year 2004 and each subsequent fiscal year, where" for "Where" and "subsection (a)(2)(A)(vii)" for "subsection (a)(1)(A)(vii)".

Subsec. (e)(2)(B). Pub. L. 108–214, §2(a)(2)(C)(ii)(I), substituted "firms, which show" for "firms. which show".

Subsec. (e)(2)(C). Pub. L. 108–214, §2(a)(2)(C)(ii)(II), (d)(2)(B)(iii), substituted "For fiscal year 2004 and each subsequent fiscal year, where" for "Where" in cl. (i), "subsection (a)(2)(A)(vii)" for "subsection (a)(1)(A)(vii)" in cls. (i) and (ii), and "subsection (a)(2)(A)(i)" for "subsection (a)(1)(A)(i)" in cl. (ii).

Subsec. (f). Pub. L. 108–214, §2(a)(2)(D), struck out "for filing" after "accepted".

Subsec. (h)(2)(B). Pub. L. 108–214, §2(a)(2)(E), designated existing provisions as cl. (i), inserted heading, redesignated former cls. (i) and (ii) as subcls. (I) and (II), respectively, of cl. (i), redesignated former subcls. (I) and (II) of cl. (i) as items (aa) and (bb), respectively, of cl. (i)(II), and added cl. (ii).

Subsec. (j). Pub. L. 108–214, §2(d)(2)(B)(iv), substituted "subsection (a)(2)(D)" for "subsection (a)(1)(D)".

EFFECTIVE AND TERMINATION DATES OF 2007 AMENDMENT

Amendment by Pub. L. 110–85 effective Oct. 1, 2007, except for certain premarket fees under this subpart, and ceases to be effective Oct. 1, 2012, see sections 216 and 217 of Pub. L. 110–85, set out as notes under section 379i of this title.

EFFECTIVE AND TERMINATION DATES

Section effective Oct. 26, 2002, except for certain premarket fees, and ceases to be effective Oct. 1, 2007, see sections 106 and 107 of Pub. L. 107–250, set out as notes under section 379i of this title.

FEE EXEMPTION FOR CERTAIN ENTITIES SUBMITTING PREMARKET REPORTS

Pub. L. 107–250, title I, §102(b), Oct. 26, 2002, 116 Stat. 1600, as amended by Pub. L. 108–214, §2(d)(2)(C), (3)(B), Apr. 1, 2004, 118 Stat. 577, provided that: "A person submitting a premarket report to the Secretary of Health and Human Services is exempt from the fee under section 738(a)(2)(A)(ii) of the Federal Food, Drug, and Cosmetic Act [21 U.S.C. 379j(a)(2)(A)(ii)] (as added by subsection (a) of this section) if—

"(1) the premarket report is the first such report submitted to the Secretary by the person; and

"(2) before October 1, 2002, the person submitted a premarket application to the Secretary for the same device as the device for which the person is submitting the premarket report."

§ 379j–1. Reauthorization; reporting requirements

(a) Reports

(1) Performance report

For fiscal years 2008 through 2012, not later than 120 days after the end of each fiscal year during which fees are collected under this subpart, the Secretary shall prepare and submit to the Committee on Health, Education, Labor, and Pensions of the Senate and the Committee on Energy and Commerce of the House of Representatives, a report concerning the progress of the Food and Drug Administration in achieving the goals identified in the letters described in section 201(c) of the Food and Drug Administration Amendments Act of 2007 during such fiscal year and the future plans of the Food and Drug Administration for meeting the goals. The report for a fiscal year shall include information on all previous cohorts for which the Secretary has not given a complete response on all device premarket applications and reports, supplements, and premarket notifications in the cohort.

(2) Fiscal report

For fiscal years 2008 through 2012, not later than 120 days after the end of each fiscal year during which fees are collected under this subpart, the Secretary shall prepare and submit to the Committee on Health, Education, Labor, and Pensions of the Senate and the Committee on Energy and Commerce of the House of Representatives, a report on the implementation of the authority for such fees during such fiscal year and the use, by the Food and Drug Administration, of the fees collected during such fiscal year for which the report is made.

(3) Public availability

The Secretary shall make the reports required under paragraphs (1) and (2) available to the public on the Internet Web site of the Food and Drug Administration.

(b) Reauthorization

(1) Consultation

In developing recommendations to present to Congress with respect to the goals, and plans for meeting the goals, for the process for the review of device applications for the first 5 fiscal years after fiscal year 2012, and for the reauthorization of this subpart for such fiscal years, the Secretary shall consult with—

(A) the Committee on Energy and Commerce of the House of Representatives;

(B) the Committee on Health, Education, Labor, and Pensions of the Senate;

(C) scientific and academic experts;

(D) health care professionals;

(E) representatives of patient and consumer advocacy groups; and

(F) the regulated industry.

(2) Prior public input

Prior to beginning negotiations with the regulated industry on the reauthorization of this subpart, the Secretary shall—

(A) publish a notice in the Federal Register requesting public input on the reauthorization;

(B) hold a public meeting at which the public may present its views on the reauthorization, including specific suggestions for changes to the goals referred to in subsection (a)(1);

(C) provide a period of 30 days after the public meeting to obtain written comments from the public suggesting changes to this subpart; and

(D) publish the comments on the Food and Drug Administration's Internet Web site.

(3) Periodic consultation

Not less frequently than once every month during negotiations with the regulated industry, the Secretary shall hold discussions with representatives of patient and consumer advocacy groups to continue discussions of their views on the reauthorization and their suggestions for changes to this subpart as expressed under paragraph (2).

(4) Public review of recommendations

After negotiations with the regulated industry, the Secretary shall—

(A) present the recommendations developed under paragraph (1) to the Congressional committees specified in such paragraph;

(B) publish such recommendations in the Federal Register;

(C) provide for a period of 30 days for the public to provide written comments on such recommendations;

(D) hold a meeting at which the public may present its views on such recommendations; and

(E) after consideration of such public views and comments, revise such recommendations as necessary.

(5) Transmittal of recommendations

Not later than January 15, 2012, the Secretary shall transmit to Congress the revised recommendations under paragraph (4), a summary of the views and comments received under such paragraph, and any changes made to the recommendations in response to such views and comments.

(6) Minutes of negotiation meetings

(A) Public availability

Before presenting the recommendations developed under paragraphs (1) through (5) to the Congress, the Secretary shall make publicly available, on the public Web site of the Food and Drug Administration, minutes of all negotiation meetings conducted under this subsection between the Food and Drug Administration and the regulated industry.

(B) Content

The minutes described under subparagraph (A) shall summarize any substantive proposal made by any party to the negotiations as well as significant controversies or differences of opinion during the negotiations and their resolution.

(June 25, 1938, ch. 675, §738A, as added Pub. L. 110–85, title II, §213, Sept. 27, 2007, 121 Stat. 850.)

TERMINATION OF SECTION

For termination of section by section 217 of Pub. L. 110–85, see Effective and Termination Dates note below.

REFERENCES IN TEXT

Section 201(c) of the Food and Drug Administration Amendments Act of 2007, referred to in subsec. (a)(1), is section 201(c) of Pub. L. 110–85, which is set out as a note under section 379i of this title.

EFFECTIVE AND TERMINATION DATES

Section effective Oct. 1, 2007, except for certain premarket fees under this subpart, and ceases to be effective Jan. 31, 2013, see sections 216 and 217 of Pub. L. 110–85, set out as Effective and Termination Dates of 2007 Amendment notes under section 379i of this title.

SUBPART 4—FEES RELATING TO ANIMAL DRUGS

TERMINATION OF SUBPART

For termination of subpart by section 5 of Pub. L. 108–130, see Termination Date note set out under section 379j–11 of this title.

For savings provisions, see section 106 of Pub. L. 110–316, set out as a note under section 379j–11 of this title.

§379j–11. Definitions

For purposes of this subpart:

(1) The term "animal drug application" means an application for approval of any new animal drug submitted under section 360b(b)(1) of this title. Such term does not include either a new animal drug application submitted under section 360b(b)(2) of this title or a supplemental animal drug application.

(2) The term "supplemental animal drug application" means—

(A) a request to the Secretary to approve a change in an animal drug application which has been approved; or

(B) a request to the Secretary to approve a change to an application approved under section 360b(c)(2) of this title for which data with respect to safety or effectiveness are required.

(3) The term "animal drug product" means each specific strength or potency of a particular active ingredient or ingredients in final dosage form marketed by a particular manufacturer or distributor, which is uniquely identified by the labeler code and product code portions of the national drug code, and for which an animal drug application or a supplemental animal drug application has been approved.

(4) The term "animal drug establishment" means a foreign or domestic place of business which is at one general physical location consisting of one or more buildings all of which are within 5 miles of each other, at which one or more animal drug products are manufactured in final dosage form.

(5) The term "investigational animal drug submission" means—

(A) the filing of a claim for an investigational exemption under section 360b(j) of this title for a new animal drug intended to be the subject of an animal drug application or a supplemental animal drug application, or

(B) the submission of information for the purpose of enabling the Secretary to evaluate the safety or effectiveness of an animal drug application or supplemental animal drug application in the event of their filing.

(6) The term "animal drug sponsor" means either an applicant named in an animal drug application that has not been withdrawn by the applicant and for which approval has not been withdrawn by the Secretary, or a person who has submitted an investigational animal drug submission that has not been terminated

or otherwise rendered inactive by the Secretary.

(7) The term "final dosage form" means, with respect to an animal drug product, a finished dosage form which is approved for administration to an animal without substantial further manufacturing. Such term includes animal drug products intended for mixing in animal feeds.

(8) The term "process for the review of animal drug applications" means the following activities of the Secretary with respect to the review of animal drug applications, supplemental animal drug applications, and investigational animal drug submissions:

(A) The activities necessary for the review of animal drug applications, supplemental animal drug applications, and investigational animal drug submissions.

(B) The issuance of action letters which approve animal drug applications or supplemental animal drug applications or which set forth in detail the specific deficiencies in animal drug applications, supplemental animal drug applications, or investigational animal drug submissions and, where appropriate, the actions necessary to place such applications, supplements or submissions in condition for approval.

(C) The inspection of animal drug establishments and other facilities undertaken as part of the Secretary's review of pending animal drug applications, supplemental animal drug applications, and investigational animal drug submissions.

(D) Monitoring of research conducted in connection with the review of animal drug applications, supplemental animal drug applications, and investigational animal drug submissions.

(E) The development of regulations and policy related to the review of animal drug applications, supplemental animal drug applications, and investigational animal drug submissions.

(F) Development of standards for products subject to review.

(G) Meetings between the agency and the animal drug sponsor.

(H) Review of advertising and labeling prior to approval of an animal drug application or supplemental animal drug application, but not after such application has been approved.

(9) The term "costs of resources allocated for the process for the review of animal drug applications" means the expenses incurred in connection with the process for the review of animal drug applications for—

(A) officers and employees of the Food and Drug Administration, contractors of the Food and Drug Administration, advisory committees consulted with respect to the review of specific animal drug applications, supplemental animal drug applications, or investigational animal drug submissions, and costs related to such officers, employees, committees, and contractors, including costs for travel, education, and recruitment and other personnel activities,

(B) management of information, and the acquisition, maintenance, and repair of computer resources,

(C) leasing, maintenance, renovation, and repair of facilities and acquisition, maintenance, and repair of fixtures, furniture, scientific equipment, and other necessary materials and supplies, and

(D) collecting fees under section 379j–12 of this title and accounting for resources allocated for the review of animal drug applications, supplemental animal drug applications, and investigational animal drug submissions.

(10) The term "adjustment factor" applicable to a fiscal year refers to the formula set forth in section 379g(8) of this title with the base or comparator month being October 2002.

(11) The term "person" includes an affiliate thereof.

(12) The term "affiliate" refers to the definition set forth in section 379g(11) of this title.

(June 25, 1938, ch. 675, § 739, as added Pub. L. 108–130, § 3, Nov. 18, 2003, 117 Stat. 1361; amended Pub. L. 110–85, title I, § 109, Sept. 27, 2007, 121 Stat. 842; Pub. L. 110–316, title I, § 102, Aug. 14, 2008, 122 Stat. 3510.)

AMENDMENT OF SECTION

For termination of amendment by section 108(a) of Pub. L. 110–316, see Effective and Termination Dates of 2008 Amendment note below.

TERMINATION OF SECTION

For termination of section by section 5 of Pub. L. 108–130, see Termination Date note below.

For savings provisions, see section 106 of Pub. L. 110–316, set out as a note below.

AMENDMENTS

2008—Par. (6). Pub. L. 110–316, §§ 102(1), 108(a), temporarily substituted "that has not been withdrawn by the applicant and for which approval has not been withdrawn by the Secretary" for ", except for an approved application for which all subject products have been removed from listing under section 360 of this title". See Effective and Termination Dates of 2008 Amendment note below.

Par. (8)(H). Pub. L. 110–316, §§ 102(2), 108(a), temporarily substituted "but not after such application has been approved" for "but not such activities after an animal drug has been approved". See Effective and Termination Dates of 2008 Amendment note below.

Par. (10). Pub. L. 110–316, §§ 102(3), 108(a), temporarily substituted "month being October 2002" for "year being 2003". See Effective and Termination Dates of 2008 Amendment note below.

Pars. (11), (12). Pub. L. 110–316, §§ 102(4), (5), 108(a), temporarily added par. (11) and redesignated former par. (11) as (12). See Effective and Termination Dates of 2008 Amendment note below.

2007—Pub. L. 110–85, § 109(a), substituted "subpart" for "part" in introductory provisions.

Par. (11). Pub. L. 110–85, § 109(b), substituted "379g(11)" for "379g(9)".

EFFECTIVE AND TERMINATION DATES OF 2008 AMENDMENT

Pub. L. 110–316, title I, § 107, Aug. 14, 2008, 122 Stat. 3514, provided that: "The amendments made by sections 102, 103, and 104 [enacting section 379j–13 of this title and amending this section and section 379j–12 of this title] shall take effect on October 1, 2008, and fees under part 4 of subchapter C of chapter VII of the Federal

Food, Drug, and Cosmetic Act [21 U.S.C. 379j–11 et seq.], as amended by this title, shall be assessed for all animal drug applications and supplemental animal drug applications received on or after such date, regardless of the date of the enactment of this title [Aug. 14, 2008].''

Pub. L. 110–316, title I, §108, Aug. 14, 2008, 122 Stat. 3515, provided that:

''(a) AUTHORIZATION.—The amendments made by sections 102 and 103 [amending this section and section 379j–12 of this title] cease to be effective October 1, 2013.

''(b) REPORTING REQUIREMENTS.—The amendment made by section 104 [enacting section 379j–13 of this title] ceases to be effective January 31, 2014.''

EFFECTIVE DATE OF 2007 AMENDMENT

Amendment by Pub. L. 110–85 effective Oct. 1, 2007, see section 107 of Pub. L. 110–85, set out as an Effective and Termination Dates of 2007 Amendment note under section 379g of this title.

TERMINATION DATE

Pub. L. 108–130, §5, Nov. 18, 2003, 117 Stat. 1371, provided that: ''The amendments made by section 3 [enacting this subpart] shall not be in effect after October 1, 2008, and section 4 [enacting provisions set out as a note below] shall not be in effect after 120 days after such date.''

SAVINGS PROVISIONS

Pub. L. 110–316, title I, §106, Aug. 14, 2008, 122 Stat. 3514, provided that: ''Notwithstanding section 5 of the Animal Drug User Fee Act of 2003 [Pub. L. 108–130] (21 U.S.C. 379j–11 note), and notwithstanding the amendments made by this title [enacting section 379j–13 of this title and amending this section and sections 360b and 379j–12 of this title], part 4 of subchapter C of chapter VII of the Federal Food, Drug, and Cosmetic Act (21 U.S.C. 379j–11 et seq.), as in effect on the day before the date of the enactment of this title [Aug. 14, 2008], shall continue to be in effect with respect to animal drug applications and supplemental animal drug applications (as defined in such part as of such day) that on or after September 1, 2003, but before October 1, 2008, were accepted by the Food and Drug Administration for filing with respect to assessing and collecting any fee required by such part for a fiscal year prior to fiscal year 2009.''

FINDINGS

Pub. L. 110–316, title I, §101(b), Aug. 14, 2008, 122 Stat. 3509, provided that: ''Congress finds that the fees authorized by the amendments made in this title [enacting section 379j–13 of this title and amending this section and sections 360b and 379j–12 of this title] will be dedicated toward expediting the animal drug development process and the review of new and supplemental animal drug applications and investigational animal drug submissions as set forth in the goals identified, for purposes of part 4 of subchapter C of chapter VII of the Federal Food, Drug, and Cosmetic Act [21 U.S.C. 379j–11 et seq.], in the letters from the Secretary of Health and Human Services to the Chairman of the Committee on Energy and Commerce of the House of Representatives and the Chairman of the Committee on Health, Education, Labor, and Pensions of the Senate as set forth in the Congressional Record.''

Pub. L. 108–130, §2, Nov. 18, 2003, 117 Stat. 1361, provided that: ''Congress finds as follows:

''(1) Prompt approval of safe and effective new animal drugs is critical to the improvement of animal health and the public health.

''(2) Animal health and the public health will be served by making additional funds available for the purpose of augmenting the resources of the Food and Drug Administration that are devoted to the process for review of new animal drug applications.

''(3) The fees authorized by this Act [enacting this subpart and provisions set out as notes under this section and section 301 of this title] will be dedicated toward expediting the animal drug development process and the review of new and supplemental animal drug applications and investigational animal drug submissions as set forth in the goals identified, for purposes of part 4 of subchapter C of chapter VII of the Federal Food, Drug, and Cosmetic Act [this subpart], in the letters from the Secretary of Health and Human Services to the Chairman of the Committee on Energy and Commerce of the House of Representatives and the Chairman of the Committee on Health, Education, Labor, and Pensions of the Senate as set forth in the Congressional Record.''

ACCOUNTABILITY AND REPORTS

Pub. L. 108–130, §4, Nov. 18, 2003, 117 Stat. 1370, which required the Secretary of Health and Human Services, after certain consultations, to develop recommendations relating to the review of animal drug applications after fiscal year 2008, to submit to congressional committees a report each fiscal year concerning the progress of the Food and Drug Administration in achieving certain goals toward expediting the animal drug development process and the review of the animal drug applications and investigational animal drug submissions, and to submit a report for each fiscal year to congressional committees on the implementation of the authority for the fees collected under this subpart during the fiscal year and the use, by the Food and Drug Administration, of the fees collected, ceased to be effective 120 days after Oct. 1, 2008. See Termination Date note above.

§ 379j–12. Authority to assess and use animal drug fees

(a) Types of fees

Beginning in fiscal year 2004, the Secretary shall assess and collect fees in accordance with this section as follows:

(1) Animal drug application and supplement fee

(A) In general

Each person that submits, on or after September 1, 2003, an animal drug application or a supplemental animal drug application shall be subject to a fee as follows:

(i) A fee established in subsection (b) of this section for an animal drug application, except an animal drug application subject to the criteria set forth in section 360b(d)(4) of this title; and

(ii) A fee established in subsection (b), in an amount that is equal to 50 percent of the amount of the fee under clause (i), for—

(I) a supplemental animal drug application for which safety or effectiveness data are required; and

(II) an animal drug application subject to the criteria set forth in section 360b(d)(4) of this title.

(B) Payment

The fee required by subparagraph (A) shall be due upon submission of the animal drug application or supplemental animal drug application.

(C) Exception for previously filed application or supplement

If an animal drug application or a supplemental animal drug application was submitted by a person that paid the fee for such application or supplement, was accepted for filing, and was not approved or was withdrawn (without a waiver or refund), the submission of an animal drug application or a supplemental animal drug application for the same product by the same person (or the person's licensee, assignee, or successor) shall not be subject to a fee under subparagraph (A).

(D) Refund of fee if application refused for filing

The Secretary shall refund 75 percent of the fee paid under subparagraph (B) for any animal drug application or supplemental animal drug application which is refused for filing.

(E) Refund of fee if application withdrawn

If an animal drug application or a supplemental animal drug application is withdrawn after the application or supplement was filed, the Secretary may refund the fee or portion of the fee paid under subparagraph (B) if no substantial work was performed on the application or supplement after the application or supplement was filed. The Secretary shall have the sole discretion to refund the fee under this paragraph. A determination by the Secretary concerning a refund under this paragraph shall not be reviewable.

(2) Animal drug product fee

Each person—

(A) who is named as the applicant in an animal drug application or supplemental animal drug application for an animal drug product which has been submitted for listing under section 360 of this title, and

(B) who, after September 1, 2003, had pending before the Secretary an animal drug application or supplemental animal drug application;

shall pay for each such animal drug product the annual fee established in subsection (b) of this section. Such fee shall be payable for the fiscal year in which the animal drug product is first submitted for listing under section 360 of this title, or is submitted for relisting under section 360 of this title if the animal drug product has been withdrawn from listing and relisted. After such fee is paid for that fiscal year, such fee shall be payable on or before January 31 of each year. Such fee shall be paid only once for each animal drug product for a fiscal year in which the fee is payable.

(3) Animal drug establishment fee

Each person—

(A) who owns or operates, directly or through an affiliate, an animal drug establishment, and

(B) who is named as the applicant in an animal drug application or supplemental animal drug application for an animal drug product which has been submitted for listing under section 360 of this title, and

(C) who, after September 1, 2003, had pending before the Secretary an animal drug application or supplemental animal drug application,

shall be assessed an annual fee established in subsection (b) of this section for each animal drug establishment listed in its approved animal drug application as an establishment that manufactures the animal drug product named in the application. The annual establishment fee shall be assessed in each fiscal year in which the animal drug product named in the application is assessed a fee under paragraph (2) unless the animal drug establishment listed in the application does not engage in the manufacture of the animal drug product during the fiscal year. The fee shall be paid on or before January 31 of each year. The establishment shall be assessed only one fee per fiscal year under this section: *Provided, however*, that where a single establishment manufactures both animal drug products and prescription drug products, as defined in section 379g(3) of this title, such establishment shall be assessed both the animal drug establishment fee and the prescription drug establishment fee, as set forth in section 379h(a)(2) of this title, within a single fiscal year.

(4) Animal drug sponsor fee

Each person—

(A) who meets the definition of an animal drug sponsor within a fiscal year; and

(B) who, after September 1, 2003, had pending before the Secretary an animal drug application, a supplemental animal drug application, or an investigational animal drug submission,

shall be assessed an annual fee established under subsection (b) of this section. The fee shall be paid on or before January 31 of each year. Each animal drug sponsor shall pay only one such fee each fiscal year.

(b) Fee amounts

Except as provided in subsection (a)(1) of this section and subsections (c), (d), (f), and (g) of this section, the fees required under subsection (a) of this section shall be established to generate fee revenue amounts as follows:

(1) Total fee revenues for application and supplement fees

The total fee revenues to be collected in animal drug application fees under subsection (a)(1)(A)(i) of this section and supplemental and other animal drug application fees under subsection (a)(1)(A)(ii) of this section shall be $3,815,000 for fiscal year 2009, $4,320,000 for fiscal year 2010, $4,862,000 for fiscal year 2011, $5,442,000 for fiscal year 2012, and $6,061,000 for fiscal year 2013.

(2) Total fee revenues for product fees

The total fee revenues to be collected in product fees under subsection (a)(2) of this section shall be $3,815,000 for fiscal year 2009, $4,320,000 for fiscal year 2010, $4,862,000 for fiscal year 2011, $5,442,000 for fiscal year 2012, and $6,061,000 for fiscal year 2013.

(3) Total fee revenues for establishment fees

The total fee revenues to be collected in establishment fees under subsection (a)(3) of this section shall be $3,815,000 for fiscal year 2009, $4,320,000 for fiscal year 2010, $4,862,000 for fiscal year 2011, $5,442,000 for fiscal year 2012, and $6,061,000 for fiscal year 2013.

(4) Total fee revenues for sponsor fees

The total fee revenues to be collected in sponsor fees under subsection (a)(4) of this section shall be $3,815,000 for fiscal year 2009, $4,320,000 for fiscal year 2010, $4,862,000 for fiscal year 2011, $5,442,000 for fiscal year 2012, and $6,061,000 for fiscal year 2013.

(c) Adjustments

(1) Workload adjustment

The fee revenues shall be adjusted each fiscal year after fiscal year 2009 to reflect changes in review workload. With respect to such adjustment:

(A) This adjustment shall be determined by the Secretary based on a weighted average of the change in the total number of animal drug applications, supplemental animal drug applications for which data with respect to safety or effectiveness are required, manufacturing supplemental animal drug applications, investigational animal drug study submissions, and investigational animal drug protocol submissions submitted to the Secretary. The Secretary shall publish in the Federal Register the fees resulting from this adjustment and the supporting methodologies.

(B) Under no circumstances shall this workload adjustment result in fee revenues for a fiscal year that are less than the fee revenues for that fiscal year established in subsection (b) of this section.

(2) Final year adjustment

For fiscal year 2013, the Secretary may further increase the fees to provide for up to 3 months of operating reserves of carryover user fees for the process for the review of animal drug applications for the first 3 months of fiscal year 2014. If the Food and Drug Administration has carryover balances for the process for the review of animal drug applications in excess of 3 months of such operating reserves, then this adjustment will not be made. If this adjustment is necessary, then the rationale for the amount of the increase shall be contained in the annual notice setting fees for fiscal year 2013.

(3) Annual fee setting

The Secretary shall establish, 60 days before the start of each fiscal year beginning after September 30, 2003, for that fiscal year, animal drug application fees, supplemental animal drug application fees, animal drug sponsor fees, animal drug establishment fees, and animal drug product fees based on the revenue amounts established under subsection (b) of this section and the adjustments provided under this subsection.

(4) Limit

The total amount of fees charged, as adjusted under this subsection, for a fiscal year may not exceed the total costs for such fiscal year for the resources allocated for the process for the review of animal drug applications.

(d) Fee waiver or reduction

(1) In general

The Secretary shall grant a waiver from or a reduction of 1 or more fees assessed under subsection (a) of this section where the Secretary finds that—

(A) the assessment of the fee would present a significant barrier to innovation because of limited resources available to such person or other circumstances,

(B) the fees to be paid by such person will exceed the anticipated present and future costs incurred by the Secretary in conducting the process for the review of animal drug applications for such person,

(C) the animal drug application or supplemental animal drug application is intended solely to provide for use of the animal drug in—

(i) a Type B medicated feed (as defined in section 558.3(b)(3) of title 21, Code of Federal Regulations (or any successor regulation)) intended for use in the manufacture of Type C free-choice medicated feeds, or

(ii) a Type C free-choice medicated feed (as defined in section 558.3(b)(4) of title 21, Code of Federal Regulations (or any successor regulation)),

(D) the animal drug application or supplemental animal drug application is intended solely to provide for a minor use or minor species indication, or

(E) the sponsor involved is a small business submitting its first animal drug application to the Secretary for review.

(2) Use of standard costs

In making the finding in paragraph (1)(B), the Secretary may use standard costs.

(3) Rules for small businesses

(A) Definition

In paragraph (1)(E), the term "small business" means an entity that has fewer than 500 employees, including employees of affiliates.

(B) Waiver of application fee

The Secretary shall waive under paragraph (1)(E) the application fee for the first animal drug application that a small business or its affiliate submits to the Secretary for review. After a small business or its affiliate is granted such a waiver, the small business or its affiliate shall pay application fees for all subsequent animal drug applications and supplemental animal drug applications for which safety or effectiveness data are required in the same manner as an entity that does not qualify as a small business.

(C) Certification

The Secretary shall require any person who applies for a waiver under paragraph (1)(E) to certify their qualification for the waiver. The Secretary shall periodically publish in the Federal Register a list of persons making such certifications.

(e) Effect of failure to pay fees

An animal drug application or supplemental animal drug application submitted by a person subject to fees under subsection (a) of this section shall be considered incomplete and shall not be accepted for filing by the Secretary until all fees owed by such person have been paid. An investigational animal drug submission under section 379j–11(5)(B) of this title that is submitted by a person subject to fees under subsection (a) of this section shall be considered incomplete and shall not be accepted for review by the Secretary until all fees owed by such person have been paid. The Secretary may discontinue review of any animal drug application, supplemental animal drug application or investigational animal drug submission from a person if such person has not submitted for payment all fees owed under this section by 30 days after the date upon which they are due.

(f) Assessment of fees

(1) Limitation

Fees may not be assessed under subsection (a) of this section for a fiscal year beginning after fiscal year 2003 unless appropriations for salaries and expenses of the Food and Drug Administration for such fiscal year (excluding the amount of fees appropriated for such fiscal year) are equal to or greater than the amount of appropriations for the salaries and expenses of the Food and Drug Administration for the fiscal year 2003 (excluding the amount of fees appropriated for such fiscal year) multiplied by the adjustment factor applicable to the fiscal year involved.

(2) Authority

If the Secretary does not assess fees under subsection (a) of this section during any portion of a fiscal year because of paragraph (1) and if at a later date in such fiscal year the Secretary may assess such fees, the Secretary may assess and collect such fees, without any modification in the rate, for animal drug applications, supplemental animal drug applications, investigational animal drug submissions, animal drug sponsors, animal drug establishments and animal drug products at any time in such fiscal year notwithstanding the provisions of subsection (a) of this section relating to the date fees are to be paid.

(g) Crediting and availability of fees

(1) In general

Fees authorized under subsection (a) of this section shall be collected and available for obligation only to the extent and in the amount provided in advance in appropriations Acts. Such fees are authorized to be appropriated to remain available until expended. Such sums as may be necessary may be transferred from the Food and Drug Administration salaries and expenses appropriation account without fiscal year limitation to such appropriation account for salary and expenses with such fiscal year limitation. The sums transferred shall be available solely for the process for the review of animal drug applications.

(2) Collections and appropriation acts

(A) In general

The fees authorized by this section—

(i) shall be retained in each fiscal year in an amount not to exceed the amount specified in appropriation Acts, or otherwise made available for obligation for such fiscal year, and

(ii) shall only be collected and available to defray increases in the costs of the resources allocated for the process for the review of animal drug applications (including increases in such costs for an additional number of full-time equivalent positions in the Department of Health and Human Services to be engaged in such process) over such costs, excluding costs paid from fees collected under this section, for fiscal year 2003 multiplied by the adjustment factor.

(B) Compliance

The Secretary shall be considered to have met the requirements of subparagraph (A)(ii) in any fiscal year if the costs funded by appropriations and allocated for the process for the review of animal drug applications—

(i) are not more than 3 percent below the level specified in subparagraph (A)(ii); or

(ii)(I) are more than 3 percent below the level specified in subparagraph (A)(ii), and fees assessed for the fiscal year following the subsequent fiscal year are decreased by the amount in excess of 3 percent by which such costs fell below the level specified in subparagraph (A)(ii); and

(II) such costs are not more than 5 percent below the level specified in subparagraph (A)(ii).

(3) Authorization of appropriations

There are authorized to be appropriated for fees under this section—

(A) $15,260,000 for fiscal year 2009;
(B) $17,280,000 for fiscal year 2010;
(C) $19,448,000 for fiscal year 2011;
(D) $21,768,000 for fiscal year 2012; and
(E) $24,244,000 for fiscal year 2013;

as adjusted to reflect adjustments in the total fee revenues made under this section and changes in the total amounts collected by animal drug application fees, supplemental animal drug application fees, animal drug sponsor fees, animal drug establishment fees, and animal drug product fees.

(4) Offset

If the sum of the cumulative amount of fees collected under this section for fiscal years 2009 through 2011 and the amount of fees estimated to be collected under this section for fiscal year 2012 exceeds the cumulative amount appropriated under paragraph (3) for the fiscal years 2009 through 2012, the excess amount shall be credited to the appropriation account of the Food and Drug Administration as provided in paragraph (1), and shall be subtracted from the amount of fees that would otherwise be authorized to be collected under this section pursuant to appropriation Acts for fiscal year 2013.

(h) Collection of unpaid fees

In any case where the Secretary does not receive payment of a fee assessed under subsection (a) of this section within 30 days after it is due, such fee shall be treated as a claim of the United

States Government subject to subchapter II of chapter 37 of title 31.

(i) Written requests for waivers, reductions, and refunds

To qualify for consideration for a waiver or reduction under subsection (d) of this section, or for a refund of any fee collected in accordance with subsection (a) of this section, a person shall submit to the Secretary a written request for such waiver, reduction, or refund not later than 180 days after such fee is due.

(j) Construction

This section may not be construed to require that the number of full-time equivalent positions in the Department of Health and Human Services, for officers, employees, and advisory committees not engaged in the process of the review of animal drug applications, be reduced to offset the number of officers, employees, and advisory committees so engaged.

(k) Abbreviated new animal drug applications

The Secretary shall—

(1) to the extent practicable, segregate the review of abbreviated new animal drug applications from the process for the review of animal drug applications, and

(2) adopt other administrative procedures to ensure that review times of abbreviated new animal drug applications do not increase from their current level due to activities under the user fee program.

(June 25, 1938, ch. 675, § 740, as added Pub. L. 108–130, § 3, Nov. 18, 2003, 117 Stat. 1363; amended Pub. L. 110–316, title I, § 103, Aug. 14, 2008, 122 Stat. 3510.)

AMENDMENT OF SECTION

For termination of amendment by section 108(a) of Pub. L. 110–316, see Effective and Termination Dates of 2008 Amendment note below.

TERMINATION OF SECTION

For termination of section by section 5 of Pub. L. 108–130, see Termination Date note below.

For savings provisions, see section 106 of Pub. L. 110–316, set out as a note under section 379j–11 of this title.

AMENDMENTS

2008—Subsec. (a)(1)(A)(i). Pub. L. 110–316, §§ 103(a)(1), 108(a), temporarily inserted “, except an animal drug application subject to the criteria set forth in section 360b(d)(4) of this title” after “for an animal drug application”. See Effective and Termination Dates of 2008 Amendment note below.

Subsec. (a)(1)(A)(ii). Pub. L. 110–316, §§ 103(a)(2), 108(a), temporarily amended cl. (ii) generally. Prior to amendment, cl. (ii) read as follows: “A fee established in subsection (b) of this section for a supplemental animal drug application for which safety or effectiveness data are required, in an amount that is equal to 50 percent of the amount of the fee under clause (i).” See Effective and Termination Dates of 2008 Amendment note below.

Subsec. (b)(1). Pub. L. 110–316, §§ 103(b)(1), 108(a), temporarily substituted “and supplemental and other animal drug application fees” for “and supplemental animal drug application fees” and “$3,815,000 for fiscal year 2009, $4,320,000 for fiscal year 2010, $4,862,000 for fiscal year 2011, $5,442,000 for fiscal year 2012, and $6,061,000 for fiscal year 2013.” for “$1,250,000 in fiscal year 2004, $2,000,000 in fiscal year 2005, and $2,500,000 in fiscal years 2006, 2007, and 2008.” See Effective and Termination Dates of 2008 Amendment note below.

Subsec. (b)(2). Pub. L. 110–316, §§ 103(b)(2), 108(a), temporarily substituted “$3,815,000 for fiscal year 2009, $4,320,000 for fiscal year 2010, $4,862,000 for fiscal year 2011, $5,442,000 for fiscal year 2012, and $6,061,000 for fiscal year 2013.” for “$1,250,000 in fiscal year 2004, $2,000,000 in fiscal year 2005, and $2,500,000 in fiscal years 2006, 2007, and 2008.” See Effective and Termination Dates of 2008 Amendment note below.

Subsec. (b)(3). Pub. L. 110–316, §§ 103(b)(3), 108(a), temporarily substituted “$3,815,000 for fiscal year 2009, $4,320,000 for fiscal year 2010, $4,862,000 for fiscal year 2011, $5,442,000 for fiscal year 2012, and $6,061,000 for fiscal year 2013.” for “$1,250,000 in fiscal year 2004, $2,000,000 in fiscal year 2005, and $2,500,000 in fiscal years 2006, 2007, and 2008.” See Effective and Termination Dates of 2008 Amendment note below.

Subsec. (b)(4). Pub. L. 110–316, §§ 103(b)(4), 108(a), temporarily substituted “$3,815,000 for fiscal year 2009, $4,320,000 for fiscal year 2010, $4,862,000 for fiscal year 2011, $5,442,000 for fiscal year 2012, and $6,061,000 for fiscal year 2013.” for “$1,250,000 in fiscal year 2004, $2,000,000 in fiscal year 2005, and $2,500,000 in fiscal years 2006, 2007, and 2008.” See Effective and Termination Dates of 2008 Amendment note below.

Subsec. (c)(1). Pub. L. 110–316, §§ 103(c)(1)–(3), 108(a), temporarily redesignated par. (2) as (1), substituted “The fee revenues shall be adjusted each fiscal year after fiscal year 2009” for “After the fee revenues are adjusted for inflation in accordance with paragraph (1), the fee revenues shall be further adjusted each fiscal year after fiscal year 2004” in introductory provisions, struck out “, as adjusted for inflation under paragraph (1)” before period in subpar. (B), and struck out former par. (1) relating to inflation adjustment. See Effective and Termination Dates of 2008 Amendment note below.

Subsec. (c)(2). Pub. L. 110–316, §§ 103(c)(2), (4), 108(a), temporarily redesignated par. (3) as (2) and substituted “2013” for “2008” in two places and “2014” for “2009”. Former par. (2) redesignated (1). See Effective and Termination Dates of 2008 Amendment note below.

Subsec. (c)(3) to (5). Pub. L. 110–316, §§ 103(c)(2), 108(a), temporarily redesignated pars. (4) and (5) as (3) and (4), respectively. Former par. (3) redesignated (2). See Effective and Termination Dates of 2008 Amendment note below.

Subsec. (g)(3)(A) to (E). Pub. L. 110–316, §§ 103(d), 108(a), temporarily amended subpars. (A) to (E) generally. Prior to amendment, subpars. (A) to (E) read as follows:

“(A) $5,000,000 for fiscal year 2004;

“(B) $8,000,000 for fiscal year 2005;

“(C) $10,000,000 for fiscal year 2006;

“(D) $10,000,000 for fiscal year 2007; and

“(E) $10,000,000 for fiscal year 2008;”.

See Effective and Termination Dates of 2008 Amendment note below.

Subsec. (g)(4). Pub. L. 110–316, §§ 103(e), 108(a), temporarily amended par. (4) generally. Prior to amendment, par. (4) read as follows: “Any amount of fees collected for a fiscal year under this section that exceeds the amount of fees specified in appropriations Acts for such fiscal year shall be credited to the appropriation account of the Food and Drug Administration as provided in paragraph (1), and shall be subtracted from the amount of fees that would otherwise be authorized to be collected under this section pursuant to appropriation Acts for a subsequent fiscal year.” See Effective and Termination Dates of 2008 Amendment note below.

EFFECTIVE AND TERMINATION DATES OF 2008 AMENDMENT

Amendment by Pub. L. 110–316 effective Oct. 1, 2008, with fees under this subpart to be assessed for all animal drug applications and supplemental animal drug applications received on or after Oct. 1, 2008, and ceases to be effective Oct. 1, 2013, see sections 107 and 108(a) of Pub. L. 110–316, set out as notes under section 379j–11 of this title.

TERMINATION DATE

Section not effective after Oct. 1, 2008, see section 5 of Pub. L. 108–130, set out as a note under section 379j–11 of this title.

§ 379j–13. Reauthorization; reporting requirements

(a) Performance report

Beginning with fiscal year 2009, not later than 60 days after the end of each fiscal year during which fees are collected under this subpart, the Secretary shall prepare and submit to the Committee on Energy and Commerce of the House of Representatives and the Committee on Health, Education, Labor, and Pensions of the Senate a report concerning the progress of the Food and Drug Administration in achieving the goals identified in the letters described in section 101(b) of the Animal Drug User Fee Amendments of 2008 toward expediting the animal drug development process and the review of the new and supplemental animal drug applications and investigational animal drug submissions during such fiscal year, the future plans of the Food and Drug Administration for meeting the goals, the review times for abbreviated new animal drug applications, and the administrative procedures adopted by the Food and Drug Administration to ensure that review times for abbreviated new animal drug applications are not increased from their current level due to activities under the user fee program.

(b) Fiscal report

Beginning with fiscal year 2009, not later than 120 days after the end of each fiscal year during which fees are collected under this subpart, the Secretary shall prepare and submit to the Committee on Energy and Commerce of the House of Representatives and the Committee on Health, Education, Labor, and Pensions of the Senate a report on the implementation of the authority for such fees during such fiscal year and the use, by the Food and Drug Administration, of the fees collected during such fiscal year for which the report is made.

(c) Public availability

The Secretary shall make the reports required under subsections (a) and (b) available to the public on the Internet Web site of the Food and Drug Administration.

(d) Reauthorization

(1) Consultation

In developing recommendations to present to the Congress with respect to the goals, and plans for meeting the goals, for the process for the review of animal drug applications for the first 5 fiscal years after fiscal year 2013, and for the reauthorization of this subpart for such fiscal years, the Secretary shall consult with—

(A) the Committee on Energy and Commerce of the House of Representatives;

(B) the Committee on Health, Education, Labor, and Pensions of the Senate;

(C) scientific and academic experts;

(D) veterinary professionals;

(E) representatives of patient and consumer advocacy groups; and

(F) the regulated industry.

(2) Prior public input

Prior to beginning negotiations with the regulated industry on the reauthorization of this subpart, the Secretary shall—

(A) publish a notice in the Federal Register requesting public input on the reauthorization;

(B) hold a public meeting at which the public may present its views on the reauthorization, including specific suggestions for changes to the goals referred to in subsection (a);

(C) provide a period of 30 days after the public meeting to obtain written comments from the public suggesting changes to this subpart; and

(D) publish the comments on the Food and Drug Administration's Internet Web site.

(3) Periodic consultation

Not less frequently than once every 4 months during negotiations with the regulated industry, the Secretary shall hold discussions with representatives of veterinary, patient, and consumer advocacy groups to continue discussions of their views on the reauthorization and their suggestions for changes to this subpart as expressed under paragraph (2).

(4) Public review of recommendations

After negotiations with the regulated industry, the Secretary shall—

(A) present the recommendations developed under paragraph (1) to the Congressional committees specified in such paragraph;

(B) publish such recommendations in the Federal Register;

(C) provide for a period of 30 days for the public to provide written comments on such recommendations;

(D) hold a meeting at which the public may present its views on such recommendations; and

(E) after consideration of such public views and comments, revise such recommendations as necessary.

(5) Transmittal of recommendations

Not later than January 15, 2013, the Secretary shall transmit to the Congress the revised recommendations under paragraph (4), a summary of the views and comments received under such paragraph, and any changes made to the recommendations in response to such views and comments.

(6) Minutes of negotiation meetings

(A) Public availability

Before presenting the recommendations developed under paragraphs (1) through (5) to the Congress, the Secretary shall make publicly available, on the Internet Web site of the Food and Drug Administration, minutes of all negotiation meetings conducted under this subsection between the Food and Drug Administration and the regulated industry.

(B) Content

The minutes described under subparagraph (A) shall summarize any substantive proposal made by any party to the negotiations as well as significant controversies or differences of opinion during the negotiations and their resolution.

(June 25, 1938, ch. 675, §740A, as added Pub. L. 110–316, title I, §104, Aug. 14, 2008, 122 Stat. 3511.)

TERMINATION OF SECTION

For termination of section by section 108(b) of Pub. L. 110–316, see Effective and Termination Dates note below.

REFERENCES IN TEXT

Section 101(b) of the Animal Drug User Fee Amendments of 2008, referred to in subsec. (a), is section 101(b) of Pub. L. 110–316, which is set out as a note under section 379j–11 of this title.

EFFECTIVE AND TERMINATION DATES

Section effective Oct. 1, 2008, with fees under this subpart to be assessed for all animal drug applications and supplemental animal drug applications received on or after Oct. 1, 2008, and ceases to be effective Jan. 31, 2014, see sections 107 and 108(b) of Pub. L. 110–316, set out as Effective and Termination Dates of 2008 Amendment notes under section 379j–11 of this title.

SUBPART 5—FEES RELATING TO GENERIC NEW ANIMAL DRUGS

TERMINATION OF SUBPART

For termination of subpart by section 204 of Pub. L. 110–316, see Termination Date notes set out under sections 379j–21 and 379j–22 of this title.

§379j–21. Authority to assess and use generic new animal drug fees

(a) Types of fees

Beginning with respect to fiscal year 2009, the Secretary shall assess and collect fees in accordance with this section as follows:

(1) Abbreviated application fee

(A) In general

Each person that submits, on or after July 1, 2008, an abbreviated application for a generic new animal drug shall be subject to a fee as established in subsection (b) for such an application.

(B) Payment

The fee required by subparagraph (A) shall be due upon submission of the abbreviated application.

(C) Exception for previously filed application

If an abbreviated application was submitted by a person that paid the fee for such application, was accepted for filing, and was not approved or was withdrawn (without a waiver or refund), the submission of an abbreviated application for the same product by the same person (or the person's licensee, assignee, or successor) shall not be subject to a fee under subparagraph (A).

(D) Refund of fee if application refused for filing

The Secretary shall refund 75 percent of the fee paid under subparagraph (B) for any abbreviated application which is refused for filing.

(E) Refund of fee if application withdrawn

If an abbreviated application is withdrawn after the application was filed, the Secretary may refund the fee or portion of the fee paid under subparagraph (B) if no substantial work was performed on the application after the application was filed. The Secretary shall have the sole discretion to refund the fee under this subparagraph. A determination by the Secretary concerning a refund under this subparagraph shall not be reviewable.

(2) Generic new animal drug product fee

Each person—

(A) who is named as the applicant in an abbreviated application or supplemental abbreviated application for a generic new animal drug product which has been submitted for listing under section 360 of this title, and

(B) who, after September 1, 2008, had pending before the Secretary an abbreviated application or supplemental abbreviated application,

shall pay for each such generic new animal drug product the annual fee established in subsection (b). Such fee shall be payable for the fiscal year in which the generic new animal drug product is first submitted for listing under section 360 of this title, or is submitted for relisting under section 360 of this title if the generic new animal drug product has been withdrawn from listing and relisted. After such fee is paid for that fiscal year, such fee shall be payable on or before January 31 of each year. Such fee shall be paid only once for each generic new animal drug product for a fiscal year in which the fee is payable.

(3) Generic new animal drug sponsor fee

(A) In general

Each person—

(i) who meets the definition of a generic new animal drug sponsor within a fiscal year, and

(ii) who, after September 1, 2008, had pending before the Secretary an abbreviated application, a supplemental abbreviated application, or an investigational submission,

shall be assessed an annual fee established under subsection (b). The fee shall be paid on or before January 31 of each year.

(B) Amount of fee

Each generic new animal drug sponsor shall pay only 1 such fee each fiscal year, as follows:

(i) 100 percent of the amount of the generic new animal drug sponsor fee published for that fiscal year under subsection (c)(3) for an applicant with more than 6 approved abbreviated applications.

(ii) 75 percent of the amount of the generic new animal drug sponsor fee published for that fiscal year under subsection (c)(3) for an applicant with more than 1 and fewer than 7 approved abbreviated applications.

(iii) 50 percent of the amount of the generic new animal drug sponsor fee published for that fiscal year under subsection (c)(3) for an applicant with 1 or fewer approved abbreviated applications.

(b) Fee amounts

Except as provided in subsection (a)(1) and subsections (c), (d), (f), and (g), the fees required under subsection (a) shall be established to generate fee revenue amounts as follows:

(1) Total fee revenues for application fees

The total fee revenues to be collected in abbreviated application fees under subsection (a)(1) shall be $1,449,000 for fiscal year 2009, $1,532,000 for fiscal year 2010, $1,619,000 for fiscal year 2011, $1,712,000 for fiscal year 2012, and $1,809,000 for fiscal year 2013.

(2) Total fee revenues for product fees

The total fee revenues to be collected in generic new animal drug product fees under subsection (a)(2) shall be $1,691,000 for fiscal year 2009, $1,787,000 for fiscal year 2010, $1,889,000 for fiscal year 2011, $1,997,000 for fiscal year 2012, and $2,111,000 for fiscal year 2013.

(3) Total fee revenues for sponsor fees

The total fee revenues to be collected in generic new animal drug sponsor fees under subsection (a)(3) shall be $1,691,000 for fiscal year 2009, $1,787,000 for fiscal year 2010, $1,889,000 for fiscal year 2011, $1,997,000 for fiscal year 2012, and $2,111,000 for fiscal year 2013.

(c) Adjustments

(1) Workload adjustment

The fee revenues shall be adjusted each fiscal year after fiscal year 2009 to reflect changes in review workload. With respect to such adjustment:

(A) This adjustment shall be determined by the Secretary based on a weighted average of the change in the total number of abbreviated applications for generic new animal drugs, manufacturing supplemental abbreviated applications for generic new animal drugs, investigational generic new animal drug study submissions, and investigational generic new animal drug protocol submissions submitted to the Secretary. The Secretary shall publish in the Federal Register the fees resulting from this adjustment and the supporting methodologies.

(B) Under no circumstances shall this workload adjustment result in fee revenues for a fiscal year that are less than the fee revenues for that fiscal year established in subsection (b).

(2) Final year adjustment

For fiscal year 2013, the Secretary may further increase the fees to provide for up to 3 months of operating reserves of carryover user fees for the process for the review of abbreviated applications for generic new animal drugs for the first 3 months of fiscal year 2014. If the Food and Drug Administration has carryover balances for the process for the review of abbreviated applications for generic new animal drugs in excess of 3 months of such operating reserves, then this adjustment shall not be made. If this adjustment is necessary, then the rationale for the amount of the increase shall be contained in the annual notice setting fees for fiscal year 2013.

(3) Annual fee setting

The Secretary shall establish, 60 days before the start of each fiscal year beginning after September 30, 2008, for that fiscal year, abbreviated application fees, generic new animal drug sponsor fees, and generic new animal drug product fees based on the revenue amounts established under subsection (b) and the adjustments provided under this subsection.

(4) Limit

The total amount of fees charged, as adjusted under this subsection, for a fiscal year may not exceed the total costs for such fiscal year for the resources allocated for the process for the review of abbreviated applications for generic new animal drugs.

(d) Fee waiver or reduction

The Secretary shall grant a waiver from or a reduction of 1 or more fees assessed under subsection (a) where the Secretary finds that the generic new animal drug is intended solely to provide for a minor use or minor species indication.

(e) Effect of failure to pay fees

An abbreviated application for a generic new animal drug submitted by a person subject to fees under subsection (a) shall be considered incomplete and shall not be accepted for filing by the Secretary until all fees owed by such person have been paid. An investigational submission for a generic new animal drug that is submitted by a person subject to fees under subsection (a) shall be considered incomplete and shall not be accepted for review by the Secretary until all fees owed by such person have been paid. The Secretary may discontinue review of any abbreviated application for a generic new animal drug, supplemental abbreviated application for a generic new animal drug, or investigational submission for a generic new animal drug from a person if such person has not submitted for payment all fees owed under this section by 30 days after the date upon which they are due.

(f) Assessment of fees

(1) Limitation

Fees may not be assessed under subsection (a) for a fiscal year beginning after fiscal year 2008 unless appropriations for salaries and expenses of the Food and Drug Administration for such fiscal year (excluding the amount of fees appropriated for such fiscal year) are equal to or greater than the amount of appropriations for the salaries and expenses of the Food and Drug Administration for the fiscal year 2003 (excluding the amount of fees appropriated for such fiscal year) multiplied by the adjustment factor applicable to the fiscal year involved.

(2) Authority

If the Secretary does not assess fees under subsection (a) during any portion of a fiscal year because of paragraph (1) and if at a later date in such fiscal year the Secretary may assess such fees, the Secretary may assess and collect such fees, without any modification in the rate, for abbreviated applications, generic new animal drug sponsors, and generic new animal drug products at any time in such fiscal year notwithstanding the provisions of subsection (a) relating to the date fees are to be paid.

(g) Crediting and availability of fees

(1) In general

Fees authorized under subsection (a) shall be collected and available for obligation only to the extent and in the amount provided in advance in appropriations Acts. Such fees are authorized to be appropriated to remain available until expended. Such sums as may be necessary may be transferred from the Food and Drug Administration salaries and expenses appropriation account without fiscal year limitation to such appropriation account for salary and expenses with such fiscal year limitation. The sums transferred shall be available solely for the process for the review of abbreviated applications for generic new animal drugs.

(2) Collections and appropriation acts

(A) In general

The fees authorized by this section—

(i) shall be retained in each fiscal year in an amount not to exceed the amount specified in appropriation Acts, or otherwise made available for obligation for such fiscal year; and

(ii) shall only be collected and available to defray increases in the costs of the resources allocated for the process for the review of abbreviated applications for generic new animal drugs (including increases in such costs for an additional number of full-time equivalent positions in the Department of Health and Human Services to be engaged in such process) over such costs, excluding costs paid from fees collected under this section, for fiscal year 2008 multiplied by the adjustment factor.

(B) Compliance

The Secretary shall be considered to have met the requirements of subparagraph (A)(ii) in any fiscal year if the costs funded by appropriations and allocated for the process for the review of abbreviated applications for generic new animal drugs—

(i) are not more than 3 percent below the level specified in subparagraph (A)(ii); or

(ii)(I) are more than 3 percent below the level specified in subparagraph (A)(ii), and fees assessed for the fiscal year following the subsequent fiscal year are decreased by the amount in excess of 3 percent by which such costs fell below the level specified in subparagraph (A)(ii); and

(II) such costs are not more than 5 percent below the level specified in subparagraph (A)(ii).

(3) Authorization of appropriations

There are authorized to be appropriated for fees under this section—

(A) $4,831,000 for fiscal year 2009;

(B) $5,106,000 for fiscal year 2010;

(C) $5,397,000 for fiscal year 2011;

(D) $5,706,000 for fiscal year 2012; and

(E) $6,031,000 for fiscal year 2013;

as adjusted to reflect adjustments in the total fee revenues made under this section and changes in the total amounts collected by abbreviated application fees, generic new animal drug sponsor fees, and generic new animal drug product fees.

(4) Offset

If the sum of the cumulative amount of fees collected under this section for the fiscal years 2009 through 2011 and the amount of fees estimated to be collected under this section for fiscal year 2012 exceeds the cumulative amount appropriated under paragraph (3) for the fiscal years 2009 through 2012, the excess amount shall be credited to the appropriation account of the Food and Drug Administration as provided in paragraph (1), and shall be subtracted from the amount of fees that would otherwise be authorized to be collected under this section pursuant to appropriation Acts for fiscal year 2013.

(h) Collection of unpaid fees

In any case where the Secretary does not receive payment of a fee assessed under subsection (a) within 30 days after it is due, such fee shall be treated as a claim of the United States Government subject to subchapter II of chapter 37 of title 31.

(i) Written requests for waivers, reductions, and refunds

To qualify for consideration for a waiver or reduction under subsection (d), or for a refund of any fee collected in accordance with subsection (a), a person shall submit to the Secretary a written request for such waiver, reduction, or refund not later than 180 days after such fee is due.

(j) Construction

This section may not be construed to require that the number of full-time equivalent positions in the Department of Health and Human Services, for officers, employees, and advisory committees not engaged in the process of the review of abbreviated applications for generic new animal drugs, be reduced to offset the number of officers, employees, and advisory committees so engaged.

(k) Definitions

In this section and section 379j–22 of this title:

(1) Abbreviated application for a generic new animal drug

The terms "abbreviated application for a generic new animal drug" and "abbreviated application" mean an abbreviated application for the approval of any generic new animal drug submitted under section 360b(b)(2) of this title. Such term does not include a supplemental abbreviated application for a generic new animal drug.

(2) Adjustment factor

The term "adjustment factor" applicable to a fiscal year is the Consumer Price Index for all urban consumers (all items; United States city average) for October of the preceding fiscal year divided by—

(A) for purposes of subsection (f)(1), such Index for October 2002; and

(B) for purposes of subsection (g)(2)(A)(ii), such Index for October 2007.

(3) Costs of resources allocated for the process for the review of abbreviated applications for generic new animal drugs

The term "costs of resources allocated for the process for the review of abbreviated applications for generic new animal drugs" means the expenses incurred in connection with the process for the review of abbreviated applications for generic new animal drugs for—

(A) officers and employees of the Food and Drug Administration, contractors of the Food and Drug Administration, advisory committees consulted with respect to the review of specific abbreviated applications, supplemental abbreviated applications, or investigational submissions, and costs related to such officers, employees, committees, and contractors, including costs for travel, education, and recruitment and other personnel activities;

(B) management of information, and the acquisition, maintenance, and repair of computer resources;

(C) leasing, maintenance, renovation, and repair of facilities and acquisition, maintenance, and repair of fixtures, furniture, scientific equipment, and other necessary materials and supplies; and

(D) collecting fees under this section and accounting for resources allocated for the review of abbreviated applications, supplemental abbreviated applications, and investigational submissions.

(4) Final dosage form

The term "final dosage form" means, with respect to a generic new animal drug product, a finished dosage form which is approved for administration to an animal without substantial further manufacturing. Such term includes generic new animal drug products intended for mixing in animal feeds.

(5) Generic new animal drug

The term "generic new animal drug" means a new animal drug that is the subject of an abbreviated application.

(6) Generic new animal drug product

The term "generic new animal drug product" means each specific strength or potency of a particular active ingredient or ingredients in final dosage form marketed by a particular manufacturer or distributor, which is uniquely identified by the labeler code and product code portions of the national drug code, and for which an abbreviated application for a generic new animal drug or a supplemental abbreviated application has been approved.

(7) Generic new animal drug sponsor

The term "generic new animal drug sponsor" means either an applicant named in an abbreviated application for a generic new animal drug that has not been withdrawn by the applicant and for which approval has not been withdrawn by the Secretary, or a person who has submitted an investigational submission for a generic new animal drug that has not been terminated or otherwise rendered inactive by the Secretary.

(8) Investigational submission for a generic new animal drug

The terms "investigational submission for a generic new animal drug" and "investigational submission" mean—

(A) the filing of a claim for an investigational exemption under section 360b(j) of this title for a generic new animal drug intended to be the subject of an abbreviated application or a supplemental abbreviated application; or

(B) the submission of information for the purpose of enabling the Secretary to evaluate the safety or effectiveness of a generic new animal drug in the event of the filing of an abbreviated application or supplemental abbreviated application for such drug.

(9) Person

The term "person" includes an affiliate thereof (as such term is defined in section 379g(11) of this title).

(10) Process for the review of abbreviated applications for generic new animal drugs

The term "process for the review of abbreviated applications for generic new animal drugs" means the following activities of the Secretary with respect to the review of abbreviated applications, supplemental abbreviated applications, and investigational submissions:

(A) The activities necessary for the review of abbreviated applications, supplemental abbreviated applications, and investigational submissions.

(B) The issuance of action letters which approve abbreviated applications or supplemental abbreviated applications or which set forth in detail the specific deficiencies in abbreviated applications, supplemental abbreviated applications, or investigational submissions and, where appropriate, the actions necessary to place such applications, supplemental applications, or submissions in condition for approval.

(C) The inspection of generic new animal drug establishments and other facilities undertaken as part of the Secretary's review of pending abbreviated applications, supplemental abbreviated applications, and investigational submissions.

(D) Monitoring of research conducted in connection with the review of abbreviated applications, supplemental abbreviated applications, and investigational submissions.

(E) The development of regulations and policy related to the review of abbreviated applications, supplemental abbreviated applications, and investigational submissions.

(F) Development of standards for products subject to review.

(G) Meetings between the agency and the generic new animal drug sponsor.

(H) Review of advertising and labeling prior to approval of an abbreviated application or supplemental abbreviated application, but not after such application has been approved.

(11) Supplemental abbreviated application for generic new animal drug

The terms "supplemental abbreviated application for a generic new animal drug" and "supplemental abbreviated application" mean a request to the Secretary to approve a change in an approved abbreviated application.

(June 25, 1938, ch. 675, § 741, as added Pub. L. 110–316, title II, § 202(b), Aug. 14, 2008, 122 Stat. 3515.)

TERMINATION OF SECTION

For termination of section by section 204(a) of Pub. L. 110–316, see Termination Date note below.

PRIOR PROVISIONS

A prior section 741 of act June 25, 1938, was renumbered section 745 and is classified to section 379k of this title.

TERMINATION DATE

Pub. L. 110–316, title II, § 204(a), Aug. 14, 2008, 122 Stat. 3524, provided that: "The amendments made by section 202 [enacting this section and amending sections 379k, 379*l*, and 379*o* of this title] shall cease to be effective October 1, 2013."

FINDINGS

Pub. L. 110–316, title II, § 201(b), Aug. 14, 2008, 122 Stat. 3515, provided that: "Congress finds as follows:

"(1) Prompt approval of abbreviated applications for safe and effective generic new animal drugs will reduce animal healthcare costs and promote the well-being of animal health and the public health.

"(2) Animal health and the public health will be served by making additional funds available for the purpose of augmenting the resources of the Food and Drug Administration that are devoted to the process for the review of abbreviated applications for the approval of generic new animal drugs.

"(3) The fees authorized by this title [see Short Title of 2008 Amendment note set out under section 301 of this title] will be dedicated toward expediting the generic new animal drug development process and the review of abbreviated applications for generic new animal drugs, supplemental abbreviated applications for generic new animal drugs, and investigational submissions for generic new animal drugs as set forth in the goals identified in the letters from the Secretary of Health and Human Services to the Chairman of the Committee on Energy and Commerce of the House of Representatives and the Chairman of the Committee on Health, Education, Labor, and Pensions of the Senate as set forth in the Congressional Record."

§ 379j–22. Reauthorization; reporting requirements

(a) Performance reports

Beginning with fiscal year 2009, not later than 60 days after the end of each fiscal year during which fees are collected under this subpart, the Secretary shall prepare and submit to the Committee on Health, Education, Labor, and Pensions of the Senate, and the Committee on Energy and Commerce of the House of Representatives a report concerning the progress of the Food and Drug Administration in achieving the goals identified in the letters described in section 201(3)[1] of the Animal Generic Drug User Fee Act of 2008 toward expediting the generic new animal drug development process and the review of abbreviated applications for generic new animal drugs, supplemental abbreviated applications for generic new animal drugs, and investigational submissions for generic new animal drugs during such fiscal year.

(b) Fiscal report

Beginning with fiscal year 2009, not later than 120 days after the end of each fiscal year during which fees are collected under this subpart, the Secretary shall prepare and submit to Committee on Health, Education, Labor, and Pensions of the Senate and the Committee on Energy and Commerce of the House of Representatives a report on the implementation of the authority for such fees during such fiscal year and the use, by the Food and Drug Administration, of the fees collected during such fiscal year for which the report is made.

(c) Public availability

The Secretary shall make the reports required under subsections (a) and (b) available to the public on the Internet Web site of the Food and Drug Administration.

(d) Reauthorization

(1) Consultation

In developing recommendations to present to Congress with respect to the goals, and plans for meeting the goals, for the process for the review of abbreviated applications for generic new animal drugs for the first 5 fiscal years after fiscal year 2013, and for the reauthorization of this subpart for such fiscal years, the Secretary shall consult with—

(A) the Committee on Energy and Commerce of the House of Representatives;

(B) the Committee on Health, Education, Labor, and Pensions of the Senate;

(C) scientific and academic experts;

(D) veterinary professionals;

(E) representatives of patient and consumer advocacy groups; and

(F) the regulated industry.

(2) Prior public input

Prior to beginning negotiations with the regulated industry on the reauthorization of this subpart, the Secretary shall—

(A) publish a notice in the Federal Register requesting public input on the reauthorization;

(B) hold a public meeting at which the public may present its views on the reauthorization, including specific suggestions for changes to the goals referred to in subsection (a);

(C) provide a period of 30 days after the public meeting to obtain written comments from the public suggesting changes to this subpart; and

(D) publish the comments on the Food and Drug Administration's Internet Web site.

(3) Periodic consultation

Not less frequently than once every 4 months during negotiations with the regulated

[1] See References in Text note below.

industry, the Secretary shall hold discussions with representatives of veterinary, patient, and consumer advocacy groups to continue discussions of their views on the reauthorization and their suggestions for changes to this subpart as expressed under paragraph (2).

(4) Public review of recommendations

After negotiations with the regulated industry, the Secretary shall—

(A) present the recommendations developed under paragraph (1) to the congressional committees specified in such paragraph;

(B) publish such recommendations in the Federal Register;

(C) provide for a period of 30 days for the public to provide written comments on such recommendations;

(D) hold a meeting at which the public may present its views on such recommendations; and

(E) after consideration of such public views and comments, revise such recommendations as necessary.

(5) Transmittal of recommendations

Not later than January 15, 2013, the Secretary shall transmit to Congress the revised recommendations under paragraph (4), a summary of the views and comments received under such paragraph, and any changes made to the recommendations in response to such views and comments.

(6) Minutes of negotiation meetings

(A) Public availability

Before presenting the recommendations developed under paragraphs (1) through (5) to Congress, the Secretary shall make publicly available, on the Internet Web site of the Food and Drug Administration, minutes of all negotiation meetings conducted under this subsection between the Food and Drug Administration and the regulated industry.

(B) Content

The minutes described under subparagraph (A) shall summarize any substantive proposal made by any party to the negotiations as well as significant controversies or differences of opinion during the negotiations and their resolution.

(June 25, 1938, ch. 675, § 742, as added Pub. L. 110–316, title II, § 203, Aug. 14, 2008, 122 Stat. 3522.)

TERMINATION OF SECTION

For termination of section by section 204(b) of Pub. L. 110–316, see Termination Date note below.

REFERENCES IN TEXT

Section 201(3) of the Animal Generic Drug User Fee Act of 2008, referred to in subsec. (a), probably means section 201(b)(3) of Pub. L. 110–316, which is set out as a note under section 379j–21 of this title.

PRIOR PROVISIONS

A prior section 742 of act June 25, 1938, was renumbered section 746 and is classified to section 379*l* of this title.

TERMINATION DATE

Pub. L. 110–316, title II, § 204(b), Aug. 14, 2008, 122 Stat. 3524, provided that: "The amendment made by section 203 [enacting this section] shall cease to be effective January 31, 2014."

PART D—INFORMATION AND EDUCATION

§ 379k. Information system

The Secretary shall establish and maintain an information system to track the status and progress of each application or submission (including a petition, notification, or other similar form of request) submitted to the Food and Drug Administration requesting agency action.

(June 25, 1938, ch. 675, § 745, formerly § 741, as added Pub. L. 105–115, title IV, § 407(a), Nov. 21, 1997, 111 Stat. 2370; renumbered § 745, Pub. L. 110–316, title II, § 202(a), Aug. 14, 2008, 122 Stat. 3515.)

AMENDMENT OF SECTION

For termination of amendment renumbering this section by section 204(a) of Pub. L. 110–316, see Termination Date of 2008 Amendment note below.

TERMINATION DATE OF 2008 AMENDMENT

Amendment by Pub. L. 110–316 to cease to be effective Oct. 1, 2013, see section 204(a) of Pub. L. 110–316, set out as a Termination Date note under section 379j–21 of this title.

EFFECTIVE DATE

Section effective 90 days after Nov. 21, 1997, except as otherwise provided, see section 501 of Pub. L. 105–115, set out as an Effective Date of 1997 Amendment note under section 321 of this title.

REPORT ON STATUS OF SYSTEM

Section 407(b) of Pub. L. 105–115 provided that not later than 1 year after Nov. 21, 1997, Secretary of Health and Human Services was to submit report to Congress on status of system to be established under this section, including projected costs of system and concerns about confidentiality.

§ 379*l*. Education

(a) In general

The Secretary shall conduct training and education programs for the employees of the Food and Drug Administration relating to the regulatory responsibilities and policies established by this chapter, including programs for—

(1) scientific training;

(2) training to improve the skill of officers and employees authorized to conduct inspections under section 374 of this title;

(3) training to achieve product specialization in such inspections; and

(4) training in administrative process and procedure and integrity issues.

(b) Intramural fellowships and other training programs

The Secretary, acting through the Commissioner, may, through fellowships and other training programs, conduct and support intramural research training for predoctoral and postdoctoral scientists and physicians. Any such fellowships and training programs under this section or under section 379dd(d)(2)(A)(ix) of this title may include provision by such scientists and physicians of services on a voluntary and uncompensated basis, as the Secretary determines appropriate. Such scientists and physicians shall be subject to all legal and ethical requirements otherwise applicable to officers or employees of the Department of Health and Human Services.

(June 25, 1938, ch. 675, § 746, formerly § 742, as added Pub. L. 105–115, title IV, § 408(a), Nov. 21, 1997, 111 Stat. 2371; amended Pub. L. 110–85, title VI, § 601(c), Sept. 27, 2007, 121 Stat. 897; renumbered § 746, Pub. L. 110–316, title II, § 202(a), Aug. 14, 2008, 122 Stat. 3515.)

AMENDMENT OF SECTION

For termination of amendment renumbering this section by section 204(a) of Pub. L. 110–316, see Termination Date of 2008 Amendment note below.

PRIOR PROVISIONS

A prior section 746 of act June 25, 1938, was renumbered section 749 and is classified to section 379*o* of this title.

AMENDMENTS

2007—Subsec. (b). Pub. L. 110–85 inserted at end "Any such fellowships and training programs under this section or under section 379dd(d)(2)(A)(ix) of this title may include provision by such scientists and physicians of services on a voluntary and uncompensated basis, as the Secretary determines appropriate. Such scientists and physicians shall be subject to all legal and ethical requirements otherwise applicable to officers or employees of the Department of Health and Human Services."

TERMINATION DATE OF 2008 AMENDMENT

Amendment by Pub. L. 110–316 to cease to be effective Oct. 1, 2013, see section 204(a) of Pub. L. 110–316, set out as a Termination Date note under section 379j–21 of this title.

EFFECTIVE DATE

Section effective 90 days after Nov. 21, 1997, except as otherwise provided, see section 501 of Pub. L. 105–115, set out as an Effective Date of 1997 Amendment note under section 321 of this title.

PART E—ENVIRONMENTAL IMPACT REVIEW

§ 379*o*. Environmental impact

Notwithstanding any other provision of law, an environmental impact statement prepared in accordance with the regulations published in part 25 of title 21, Code of Federal Regulations (as in effect on August 31, 1997) in connection with an action carried out under (or a recommendation or report relating to) this chapter, shall be considered to meet the requirements for a detailed statement under section 4332(2)(C) of title 42.

(June 25, 1938, ch. 675, § 749, formerly § 746, as added Pub. L. 105–115, title IV, § 411, Nov. 21, 1997, 111 Stat. 2373; renumbered § 749, Pub. L. 110–316, title II, § 202(a), Aug. 14, 2008, 122 Stat. 3515.)

AMENDMENT OF SECTION

For termination of amendment renumbering this section by section 204(a) of Pub. L. 110–316, see Termination Date of 2008 Amendment note below.

TERMINATION DATE OF 2008 AMENDMENT

Amendment by Pub. L. 110–316 to cease to be effective Oct. 1, 2013, see section 204(a) of Pub. L. 110–316, set out as a Termination Date note under section 379j–21 of this title.

EFFECTIVE DATE

Section effective 90 days after Nov. 21, 1997, except as otherwise provided, see section 501 of Pub. L. 105–115, set out as an Effective Date of 1997 Amendment note under section 321 of this title.

PART F—NATIONAL UNIFORMITY FOR NONPRESCRIPTION DRUGS AND PREEMPTION FOR LABELING OR PACKAGING OF COSMETICS

§ 379r. National uniformity for nonprescription drugs

(a) In general

Except as provided in subsection (b), (c)(1), (d), (e), or (f) of this section, no State or political subdivision of a State may establish or continue in effect any requirement—

(1) that relates to the regulation of a drug that is not subject to the requirements of section 353(b)(1) or 353(f)(1)(A) of this title; and

(2) that is different from or in addition to, or that is otherwise not identical with, a requirement under this chapter, the Poison Prevention Packaging Act of 1970 (15 U.S.C. 1471 et seq.), or the Fair Packaging and Labeling Act (15 U.S.C. 1451 et seq.).

(b) Exemption

(1) In general

Upon application of a State or political subdivision thereof, the Secretary may by regulation, after notice and opportunity for written and oral presentation of views, exempt from subsection (a) of this section, under such conditions as may be prescribed in such regulation, a State or political subdivision requirement that—

(A) protects an important public interest that would otherwise be unprotected, including the health and safety of children;

(B) would not cause any drug to be in violation of any applicable requirement or prohibition under Federal law; and

(C) would not unduly burden interstate commerce.

(2) Timely action

The Secretary shall make a decision on the exemption of a State or political subdivision requirement under paragraph (1) not later than 120 days after receiving the application of the State or political subdivision under paragraph (1).

(c) Scope

(1) In general

This section shall not apply to—

(A) any State or political subdivision requirement that relates to the practice of pharmacy; or

(B) any State or political subdivision requirement that a drug be dispensed only upon the prescription of a practitioner licensed by law to administer such drug.

(2) Safety or effectiveness

For purposes of subsection (a) of this section, a requirement that relates to the regulation of a drug shall be deemed to include any requirement relating to public information or any other form of public communication relating to a warning of any kind for a drug.

(d) Exceptions

(1) In general

In the case of a drug described in subsection (a)(1) of this section that is not the subject of an application approved under section 355 of this title or section 357 of this title (as in effect on the day before November 21, 1997) or a final regulation promulgated by the Secretary establishing conditions under which the drug is generally recognized as safe and effective and not misbranded, subsection (a) of this section shall apply only with respect to a requirement of a State or political subdivision of a State that relates to the same subject as, but is different from or in addition to, or that is otherwise not identical with—

(A) a regulation in effect with respect to the drug pursuant to a statute described in subsection (a)(2) of this section; or

(B) any other requirement in effect with respect to the drug pursuant to an amendment to such a statute made on or after November 21, 1997.

(2) State initiatives

This section shall not apply to a State requirement adopted by a State public initiative or referendum enacted prior to September 1, 1997.

(e) No effect on product liability law

Nothing in this section shall be construed to modify or otherwise affect any action or the liability of any person under the product liability law of any State.

(f) State enforcement authority

Nothing in this section shall prevent a State or political subdivision thereof from enforcing, under any relevant civil or other enforcement authority, a requirement that is identical to a requirement of this chapter.

(June 25, 1938, ch. 675, § 751, as added Pub. L. 105–115, title IV, § 412(a), Nov. 21, 1997, 111 Stat. 2373.)

REFERENCES IN TEXT

The Poison Prevention Packaging Act of 1970, referred to in subsec. (a)(2), is Pub. L. 91–601, Dec. 30, 1970, 84 Stat. 1670, as amended, which is classified principally to chapter 39A (§ 1471 et seq.) of Title 15, Commerce and Trade. For complete classification of this Act to the Code, see Short Title note set out under section 1471 of Title 15 and Tables.

The Fair Packaging and Labeling Act, referred to in subsec. (a)(2), is Pub. L. 89–755, Nov. 3, 1966, 80 Stat. 1296, as amended, which is classified generally to chapter 39 (§ 1451 et seq.) of Title 15, Commerce and Trade. For complete classification of this Act to the Code, see Short Title note set out under section 1451 of Title 15 and Tables.

EFFECTIVE DATE

Section effective 90 days after Nov. 21, 1997, except as otherwise provided, see section 501 of Pub. L. 105–115, set out as an Effective Date of 1997 Amendment note under section 321 of this title.

§ 379s. Preemption for labeling or packaging of cosmetics

(a) In general

Except as provided in subsection (b), (d), or (e) of this section, no State or political subdivision of a State may establish or continue in effect any requirement for labeling or packaging of a cosmetic that is different from or in addition to, or that is otherwise not identical with, a requirement specifically applicable to a particular cosmetic or class of cosmetics under this chapter, the Poison Prevention Packaging Act of 1970 (15 U.S.C. 1471 et seq.), or the Fair Packaging and Labeling Act (15 U.S.C. 1451 et seq.).

(b) Exemption

Upon application of a State or political subdivision thereof, the Secretary may by regulation, after notice and opportunity for written and oral presentation of views, exempt from subsection (a) of this section, under such conditions as may be prescribed in such regulation, a State or political subdivision requirement for labeling or packaging that—

(1) protects an important public interest that would otherwise be unprotected;

(2) would not cause a cosmetic to be in violation of any applicable requirement or prohibition under Federal law; and

(3) would not unduly burden interstate commerce.

(c) Scope

For purposes of subsection (a) of this section, a reference to a State requirement that relates to the packaging or labeling of a cosmetic means any specific requirement relating to the same aspect of such cosmetic as a requirement specifically applicable to that particular cosmetic or class of cosmetics under this chapter for packaging or labeling, including any State requirement relating to public information or any other form of public communication.

(d) No effect on product liability law

Nothing in this section shall be construed to modify or otherwise affect any action or the liability of any person under the product liability law of any State.

(e) State initiative

This section shall not apply to a State requirement adopted by a State public initiative or referendum enacted prior to September 1, 1997.

(June 25, 1938, ch. 675, § 752, as added Pub. L. 105–115, title IV, § 412(d), Nov. 21, 1997, 111 Stat. 2376.)

REFERENCES IN TEXT

The Poison Prevention Packaging Act of 1970, referred to in subsec. (a), is Pub. L. 91–601, Dec. 30, 1970, 84 Stat. 1670, as amended, which is classified principally to chapter 39A (§ 1471 et seq.) of Title 15, Commerce and Trade. For complete classification of this Act to the Code, see Short Title note set out under section 1471 of Title 15 and Tables.

The Fair Packaging and Labeling Act, referred to in subsec. (a), is Pub. L. 89–755, Nov. 3, 1966, 80 Stat. 1296, as amended, which is classified generally to chapter 39 (§ 1451 et seq.) of Title 15, Commerce and Trade. For complete classification of this Act to the Code, see

Short Title note set out under section 1451 of Title 15 and Tables.

EFFECTIVE DATE

Section effective 90 days after Nov. 21, 1997, except as otherwise provided, see section 501 of Pub. L. 105–115, set out as an Effective Date of 1997 Amendment note under section 321 of this title.

PART G—SAFETY REPORTS

§379v. Safety report disclaimers

With respect to any entity that submits or is required to submit a safety report or other information in connection with the safety of a product (including a product that is a food, drug, device, dietary supplement, or cosmetic) under this chapter (and any release by the Secretary of that report or information), such report or information shall not be construed to reflect necessarily a conclusion by the entity or the Secretary that the report or information constitutes an admission that the product involved malfunctioned, caused or contributed to an adverse experience, or otherwise caused or contributed to a death, serious injury, or serious illness. Such an entity need not admit, and may deny, that the report or information submitted by the entity constitutes an admission that the product involved malfunctioned, caused or contributed to an adverse experience, or caused or contributed to a death, serious injury, or serious illness.

(June 25, 1938, ch. 675, §756, as added Pub. L. 105–115, title IV, §420, Nov. 21, 1997, 111 Stat. 2379.)

EFFECTIVE DATE

Section effective 90 days after Nov. 21, 1997, except as otherwise provided, see section 501 of Pub. L. 105–115, set out as an Effective Date of 1997 Amendment note under section 321 of this title.

PART H—SERIOUS ADVERSE EVENT REPORTS

§379aa. Serious adverse event reporting for nonprescription drugs

(a) Definitions

In this section:

(1) Adverse event

The term "adverse event" means any health-related event associated with the use of a nonprescription drug that is adverse, including—

(A) an event occurring from an overdose of the drug, whether accidental or intentional;

(B) an event occurring from abuse of the drug;

(C) an event occurring from withdrawal from the drug; and

(D) any failure of expected pharmacological action of the drug.

(2) Nonprescription drug

The term "nonprescription drug" means a drug that is—

(A) not subject to section 353(b) of this title; and

(B) not subject to approval in an application submitted under section 355 of this title.

(3) Serious adverse event

The term "serious adverse event" is an adverse event that—

(A) results in—

(i) death;

(ii) a life-threatening experience;

(iii) inpatient hospitalization;

(iv) a persistent or significant disability or incapacity; or

(v) a congenital anomaly or birth defect; or

(B) requires, based on reasonable medical judgment, a medical or surgical intervention to prevent an outcome described under subparagraph (A).

(4) Serious adverse event report

The term "serious adverse event report" means a report that is required to be submitted to the Secretary under subsection (b).

(b) Reporting requirement

(1) In general

The manufacturer, packer, or distributor whose name (pursuant to section 352(b)(1) of this title) appears on the label of a nonprescription drug marketed in the United States (referred to in this section as the "responsible person") shall submit to the Secretary any report received of a serious adverse event associated with such drug when used in the United States, accompanied by a copy of the label on or within the retail package of such drug.

(2) Retailer

A retailer whose name appears on the label described in paragraph (1) as a distributor may, by agreement, authorize the manufacturer or packer of the nonprescription drug to submit the required reports for such drugs to the Secretary so long as the retailer directs to the manufacturer or packer all adverse events associated with such drug that are reported to the retailer through the address or telephone number described in section 352(x) of this title.

(c) Submission of reports

(1) Timing of reports

The responsible person shall submit to the Secretary a serious adverse event report no later than 15 business days after the report is received through the address or phone number described in section 352(x) of this title.

(2) New medical information

The responsible person shall submit to the Secretary any new medical information, related to a submitted serious adverse event report that is received by the responsible person within 1 year of the initial report, no later than 15 business days after the new information is received by the responsible person.

(3) Consolidation of reports

The Secretary shall develop systems to ensure that duplicate reports of, and new medical information related to, a serious adverse event shall be consolidated into a single report.

(4) Exemption

The Secretary, after providing notice and an opportunity for comment from interested parties, may establish an exemption to the requirements under paragraphs (1) and (2) if the Secretary determines that such exemption would have no adverse effect on public health.

(d) Contents of reports

Each serious adverse event report under this section shall be submitted to the Secretary using the MedWatch form, which may be modified by the Secretary for nonprescription drugs, and may be accompanied by additional information.

(e) Maintenance and inspection of records

(1) Maintenance

The responsible person shall maintain records related to each report of an adverse event received by the responsible person for a period of 6 years.

(2) Records inspection

(A) In general

The responsible person shall permit an authorized person to have access to records required to be maintained under this section, during an inspection pursuant to section 374 of this title.

(B) Authorized person

For purposes of this paragraph, the term "authorized person" means an officer or employee of the Department of Health and Human Services who has—

(i) appropriate credentials, as determined by the Secretary; and

(ii) been duly designated by the Secretary to have access to the records required under this section.

(f) Protected information

A serious adverse event report submitted to the Secretary under this section, including any new medical information submitted under subsection (c)(2), or an adverse event report voluntarily submitted to the Secretary shall be considered to be—

(1) a safety report under section 379v of this title and may be accompanied by a statement, which shall be a part of any report that is released for public disclosure, that denies that the report or the records constitute an admission that the product involved caused or contributed to the adverse event; and

(2) a record about an individual under section 552a of title 5 (commonly referred to as the "Privacy Act of 1974") and a medical or similar file the disclosure of which would constitute a violation of section 552 of such title 5 (commonly referred to as the "Freedom of Information Act"), and shall not be publicly disclosed unless all personally identifiable information is redacted.

(g) Rule of construction

The submission of any adverse event report in compliance with this section shall not be construed as an admission that the nonprescription drug involved caused or contributed to the adverse event.

(h) Preemption

(1) In general

No State or local government shall establish or continue in effect any law, regulation, order, or other requirement, related to a mandatory system for adverse event reports for nonprescription drugs, that is different from, in addition to, or otherwise not identical to, this section.

(2) Effect of section

(A) In general

Nothing in this section shall affect the authority of the Secretary to provide adverse event reports and information to any health, food, or drug officer or employee of any State, territory, or political subdivision of a State or territory, under a memorandum of understanding between the Secretary and such State, territory, or political subdivision.

(B) Personally-identifiable information

Notwithstanding any other provision of law, personally-identifiable information in adverse event reports provided by the Secretary to any health, food, or drug officer or employee of any State, territory, or political subdivision of a State or territory, shall not—

(i) be made publicly available pursuant to any State or other law requiring disclosure of information or records; or

(ii) otherwise be disclosed or distributed to any party without the written consent of the Secretary and the person submitting such information to the Secretary.

(C) Use of safety reports

Nothing in this section shall permit a State, territory, or political subdivision of a State or territory, to use any safety report received from the Secretary in a manner inconsistent with subsection (g) or section 379v of this title.

(i) Authorization of appropriations

There are authorized to be appropriated to carry out this section such sums as may be necessary.

(June 25, 1938, ch. 675, § 760, as added Pub. L. 109–462, § 2(a), Dec. 22, 2006, 120 Stat. 3469.)

EFFECTIVE DATE

Section effective 1 year after Dec. 22, 2006, see section 2(e)(1) of Pub. L. 109–462, set out as an Effective Date of 2006 Amendment note under section 352 of this title.

MODIFICATIONS

Pub. L. 109–462, § 2(b), Dec. 22, 2006, 120 Stat. 3472, provided that: "The Secretary of Health and Human Services may modify requirements under the amendments made by this section [enacting this section and amending sections 331 and 352 of this title] in accordance with section 553 of title 5, United States Code, to maintain consistency with international harmonization efforts over time."

GUIDANCE

Pub. L. 109–462, § 2(e)(3), Dec. 22, 2006, 120 Stat. 3472, provided that: "Not later than 270 days after the date of enactment of this Act [Dec. 22, 2006], the Secretary of Health and Human Services shall issue guidance on the minimum data elements that should be included in a serious adverse event report described under the amendments made by this Act [see Short Title of 2006 Amendment note set out under section 301 of this title]."

Pub. L. 109–462, § 3(d)(3), Dec. 22, 2006, 120 Stat. 3475, enacted provisions substantially identical to those enacted by Pub. L. 109–462, § 2(b), set out above.

§ 379aa–1. Serious adverse event reporting for dietary supplements

(a) Definitions

In this section:

(1) Adverse event

The term "adverse event" means any health-related event associated with the use of a dietary supplement that is adverse.

(2) Serious adverse event

The term "serious adverse event" is an adverse event that—

(A) results in—

(i) death;

(ii) a life-threatening experience;

(iii) inpatient hospitalization;

(iv) a persistent or significant disability or incapacity; or

(v) a congenital anomaly or birth defect; or

(B) requires, based on reasonable medical judgment, a medical or surgical intervention to prevent an outcome described under subparagraph (A).

(3) Serious adverse event report

The term "serious adverse event report" means a report that is required to be submitted to the Secretary under subsection (b).

(b) Reporting requirement

(1) In general

The manufacturer, packer, or distributor of a dietary supplement whose name (pursuant to section 343(e)(1) of this title) appears on the label of a dietary supplement marketed in the United States (referred to in this section as the "responsible person") shall submit to the Secretary any report received of a serious adverse event associated with such dietary supplement when used in the United States, accompanied by a copy of the label on or within the retail packaging of such dietary supplement.

(2) Retailer

A retailer whose name appears on the label described in paragraph (1) as a distributor may, by agreement, authorize the manufacturer or packer of the dietary supplement to submit the required reports for such dietary supplements to the Secretary so long as the retailer directs to the manufacturer or packer all adverse events associated with such dietary supplement that are reported to the retailer through the address or telephone number described in section 343(y) of this title.

(c) Submission of reports

(1) Timing of reports

The responsible person shall submit to the Secretary a serious adverse event report no later than 15 business days after the report is received through the address or phone number described in section 343(y) of this title.

(2) New medical information

The responsible person shall submit to the Secretary any new medical information, related to a submitted serious adverse event report that is received by the responsible person within 1 year of the initial report, no later than 15 business days after the new information is received by the responsible person.

(3) Consolidation of reports

The Secretary shall develop systems to ensure that duplicate reports of, and new medical information related to, a serious adverse event shall be consolidated into a single report.

(4) Exemption

The Secretary, after providing notice and an opportunity for comment from interested parties, may establish an exemption to the requirements under paragraphs (1) and (2) if the Secretary determines that such exemption would have no adverse effect on public health.

(d) Contents of reports

Each serious adverse event report under this section shall be submitted to the Secretary using the MedWatch form, which may be modified by the Secretary for dietary supplements, and may be accompanied by additional information.

(e) Maintenance and inspection of records

(1) Maintenance

The responsible person shall maintain records related to each report of an adverse event received by the responsible person for a period of 6 years.

(2) Records inspection

(A) In general

The responsible person shall permit an authorized person to have access to records required to be maintained under this section during an inspection pursuant to section 374 of this title.

(B) Authorized person

For purposes of this paragraph, the term "authorized person" means an officer or employee of the Department of Health and Human Services, who has—

(i) appropriate credentials, as determined by the Secretary; and

(ii) been duly designated by the Secretary to have access to the records required under this section.

(f) Protected information

A serious adverse event report submitted to the Secretary under this section, including any new medical information submitted under subsection (c)(2), or an adverse event report voluntarily submitted to the Secretary shall be considered to be—

(1) a safety report under section 379v of this title and may be accompanied by a statement, which shall be a part of any report that is released for public disclosure, that denies that the report or the records constitute an admission that the product involved caused or contributed to the adverse event; and

(2) a record about an individual under section 552a of title 5 (commonly referred to as the "Privacy Act of 1974") and a medical or similar file the disclosure of which would con-

stitute a violation of section 552 of such title 5 (commonly referred to as the "Freedom of Information Act"), and shall not be publicly disclosed unless all personally identifiable information is redacted.

(g) Rule of construction

The submission of any adverse event report in compliance with this section shall not be construed as an admission that the dietary supplement involved caused or contributed to the adverse event.

(h) Preemption

(1) In general

No State or local government shall establish or continue in effect any law, regulation, order, or other requirement, related to a mandatory system for adverse event reports for dietary supplements, that is different from, in addition to, or otherwise not identical to, this section.

(2) Effect of section

(A) In general

Nothing in this section shall affect the authority of the Secretary to provide adverse event reports and information to any health, food, or drug officer or employee of any State, territory, or political subdivision of a State or territory, under a memorandum of understanding between the Secretary and such State, territory, or political subdivision.

(B) Personally-identifiable information

Notwithstanding any other provision of law, personally-identifiable information in adverse event reports provided by the Secretary to any health, food, or drug officer or employee of any State, territory, or political subdivision of a State or territory, shall not—

(i) be made publicly available pursuant to any State or other law requiring disclosure of information or records; or

(ii) otherwise be disclosed or distributed to any party without the written consent of the Secretary and the person submitting such information to the Secretary.

(C) Use of safety reports

Nothing in this section shall permit a State, territory, or political subdivision of a State or territory, to use any safety report received from the Secretary in a manner inconsistent with subsection (g) or section 379v of this title.

(i) Authorization of appropriations

There are authorized to be appropriated to carry out this section such sums as may be necessary.

(June 25, 1938, ch. 675, § 761, as added Pub. L. 109–462, § 3(a), Dec. 22, 2006, 120 Stat. 3472.)

EFFECTIVE DATE

Section effective 1 year after Dec. 22, 2006, see section 3(d)(1) of Pub. L. 109–462, set out as an Effective Date of 2006 Amendment note under section 343 of this title.

PART I—REAGAN-UDALL FOUNDATION FOR THE FOOD AND DRUG ADMINISTRATION

§ 379dd. Establishment and functions of the Foundation

(a) In general

A nonprofit corporation to be known as the Reagan-Udall Foundation for the Food and Drug Administration (referred to in this part as the "Foundation") shall be established in accordance with this section. The Foundation shall be headed by an Executive Director, appointed by the members of the Board of Directors under subsection (e).[1] The Foundation shall not be an agency or instrumentality of the United States Government.

(b) Purpose of Foundation

The purpose of the Foundation is to advance the mission of the Food and Drug Administration to modernize medical, veterinary, food, food ingredient, and cosmetic product development, accelerate innovation, and enhance product safety.

(c) Duties of the Foundation

The Foundation shall—

(1) taking into consideration the Critical Path reports and priorities published by the Food and Drug Administration, identify unmet needs in the development, manufacture, and evaluation of the safety and effectiveness, including postapproval, of devices, including diagnostics, biologics, and drugs, and the safety of food, food ingredients, and cosmetics, and including the incorporation of more sensitive and predictive tools and devices to measure safety;

(2) establish goals and priorities in order to meet the unmet needs identified in paragraph (1);

(3) in consultation with the Secretary, identify existing and proposed Federal intramural and extramural research and development programs relating to the goals and priorities established under paragraph (2), coordinate Foundation activities with such programs, and minimize Foundation duplication of existing efforts;

(4) award grants to, or enter into contracts, memoranda of understanding, or cooperative agreements with, scientists and entities, which may include the Food and Drug Administration, university consortia, public-private partnerships, institutions of higher education, entities described in section 501(c)(3) of title 26 (and exempt from tax under section 501(a) of such title), and industry, to efficiently and effectively advance the goals and priorities established under paragraph (2);

(5) recruit meeting participants and hold or sponsor (in whole or in part) meetings as appropriate to further the goals and priorities established under paragraph (2);

(6) release and publish information and data and, to the extent practicable, license, distribute, and release material, reagents, and techniques to maximize, promote, and coordinate the availability of such material, reagents,

[1] So in original. Probably should be "subsection (g)."

and techniques for use by the Food and Drug Administration, nonprofit organizations, and academic and industrial researchers to further the goals and priorities established under paragraph (2);

(7) ensure that—

(A) action is taken as necessary to obtain patents for inventions developed by the Foundation or with funds from the Foundation;

(B) action is taken as necessary to enable the licensing of inventions developed by the Foundation or with funds from the Foundation; and

(C) executed licenses, memoranda of understanding, material transfer agreements, contracts, and other such instruments, promote, to the maximum extent practicable, the broadest conversion to commercial and noncommercial applications of licensed and patented inventions of the Foundation to further the goals and priorities established under paragraph (2);

(8) provide objective clinical and scientific information to the Food and Drug Administration and, upon request, to other Federal agencies to assist in agency determinations of how to ensure that regulatory policy accommodates scientific advances and meets the agency's public health mission;

(9) conduct annual assessments of the unmet needs identified in paragraph (1); and

(10) carry out such other activities consistent with the purposes of the Foundation as the Board determines appropriate.

(d) Board of Directors

(1) Establishment

(A) In general

The Foundation shall have a Board of Directors (referred to in this part as the "Board"), which shall be composed of ex officio and appointed members in accordance with this subsection. All appointed members of the Board shall be voting members.

(B) Ex officio members

The ex officio members of the Board shall be the following individuals or their designees:

(i) The Commissioner.

(ii) The Director of the National Institutes of Health.

(iii) The Director of the Centers for Disease Control and Prevention.

(iv) The Director of the Agency for Healthcare Research and Quality.

(C) Appointed members

(i) In general

The ex officio members of the Board under subparagraph (B) shall, by majority vote, appoint to the Board 14 individuals, of which 9 shall be from a list of candidates to be provided by the National Academy of Sciences and 5 shall be from lists of candidates provided by patient and consumer advocacy groups, professional scientific and medical societies, and industry trade organizations. Of such appointed members—

(I) 4 shall be representatives of the general pharmaceutical, device, food, cosmetic, and biotechnology industries;

(II) 3 shall be representatives of academic research organizations;

(III) 2 shall be representatives of patient or consumer advocacy organizations;

(IV) 1 shall be a representative of health care providers; and

(V) 4 shall be at-large members with expertise or experience relevant to the purpose of the Foundation.

(ii) Requirements

(I) Expertise

The ex officio members shall ensure the Board membership includes individuals with expertise in areas including the sciences of developing, manufacturing, and evaluating the safety and effectiveness of devices, including diagnostics, biologics, and drugs, and the safety of food, food ingredients, and cosmetics.

(II) Federal employees

No employee of the Federal Government shall be appointed as a member of the Board under this subparagraph or under paragraph (3)(B).

(D) Initial meeting

(i) In general

Not later than 30 days after September 27, 2007, the Secretary shall convene a meeting of the ex officio members of the Board to—

(I) incorporate the Foundation; and

(II) appoint the members of the Board in accordance with subparagraph (C).

(ii) Service of ex officio members

Upon the appointment of the members of the Board under clause (i)(II)—

(I) the terms of service of the Director of the Centers for Disease Control and Prevention and of the Director of the Agency for Healthcare Research and Quality as ex officio members of the Board shall terminate; and

(II) the Commissioner and the Director of the National Institutes of Health shall continue to serve as ex officio members of the Board, but shall be nonvoting members.

(iii) Chair

The ex officio members of the Board under subparagraph (B) shall designate an appointed member of the Board to serve as the Chair of the Board.

(2) Duties of Board

The Board shall—

(A) establish bylaws for the Foundation that—

(i) are published in the Federal Register and available for public comment;

(ii) establish policies for the selection of the officers, employees, agents, and contractors of the Foundation;

(iii) establish policies, including ethical standards, for the acceptance, solicitation, and disposition of donations and grants to the Foundation and for the disposition of the assets of the Foundation, including appropriate limits on the ability of donors to designate, by stipulation or restriction, the use or recipient of donated funds;

(iv) establish policies that would subject all employees, fellows, and trainees of the Foundation to the conflict of interest standards under section 208 of title 18;

(v) establish licensing, distribution, and publication policies that support the widest and least restrictive use by the public of information and inventions developed by the Foundation or with Foundation funds to carry out the duties described in paragraphs (6) and (7) of subsection (c), and may include charging cost-based fees for published material produced by the Foundation;

(vi) specify principles for the review of proposals and awarding of grants and contracts that include peer review and that are consistent with those of the Foundation for the National Institutes of Health, to the extent determined practicable and appropriate by the Board;

(vii) specify a cap on administrative expenses for recipients of a grant, contract, or cooperative agreement from the Foundation;

(viii) establish policies for the execution of memoranda of understanding and cooperative agreements between the Foundation and other entities, including the Food and Drug Administration;

(ix) establish policies for funding training fellowships, whether at the Foundation, academic or scientific institutions, or the Food and Drug Administration, for scientists, doctors, and other professionals who are not employees of regulated industry, to foster greater understanding of and expertise in new scientific tools, diagnostics, manufacturing techniques, and potential barriers to translating basic research into clinical and regulatory practice;

(x) specify a process for annual Board review of the operations of the Foundation; and

(xi) establish specific duties of the Executive Director;

(B) prioritize and provide overall direction to the activities of the Foundation;

(C) evaluate the performance of the Executive Director; and

(D) carry out any other necessary activities regarding the functioning of the Foundation.

(3) Terms and vacancies

(A) Term

The term of office of each member of the Board appointed under paragraph (1)(C) shall be 4 years, except that the terms of offices for the initial appointed members of the Board shall expire on a staggered basis as determined by the ex officio members.

(B) Vacancy

Any vacancy in the membership of the Board—

(i) shall not affect the power of the remaining members to execute the duties of the Board; and

(ii) shall be filled by appointment by the appointed members described in paragraph (1)(C) by majority vote.

(C) Partial term

If a member of the Board does not serve the full term applicable under subparagraph (A), the individual appointed under subparagraph (B) to fill the resulting vacancy shall be appointed for the remainder of the term of the predecessor of the individual.

(D) Serving past term

A member of the Board may continue to serve after the expiration of the term of the member until a successor is appointed.

(4) Compensation

Members of the Board may not receive compensation for service on the Board. Such members may be reimbursed for travel, subsistence, and other necessary expenses incurred in carrying out the duties of the Board, as set forth in the bylaws issued by the Board.

(e) Incorporation

The ex officio members of the Board shall serve as incorporators and shall take whatever actions necessary to incorporate the Foundation.

(f) Nonprofit status

In carrying out subsection (b), the Board shall establish such policies and bylaws under subsection (d), and the Executive Director shall carry out such activities under subsection (g), as may be necessary to ensure that the Foundation maintains status as an organization that—

(1) is described in subsection (c)(3) of section 501 of title 26; and

(2) is, under subsection (a) of such section, exempt from taxation.

(g) Executive Director

(1) In general

The Board shall appoint an Executive Director who shall serve at the pleasure of the Board. The Executive Director shall be responsible for the day-to-day operations of the Foundation and shall have such specific duties and responsibilities as the Board shall prescribe.

(2) Compensation

The compensation of the Executive Director shall be fixed by the Board but shall not be greater than the compensation of the Commissioner.

(h) Administrative powers

In carrying out this part, the Board, acting through the Executive Director, may—

(1) adopt, alter, and use a corporate seal, which shall be judicially noticed;

(2) hire, promote, compensate, and discharge 1 or more officers, employees, and agents, as may be necessary, and define their duties;

(3) prescribe the manner in which—

(A) real or personal property of the Foundation is acquired, held, and transferred;

(B) general operations of the Foundation are to be conducted; and

(C) the privileges granted to the Board by law are exercised and enjoyed;

(4) with the consent of the applicable executive department or independent agency, use the information, services, and facilities of such department or agencies in carrying out this section;

(5) enter into contracts with public and private organizations for the writing, editing, printing, and publishing of books and other material;

(6) hold, administer, invest, and spend any gift, devise, or bequest of real or personal property made to the Foundation under subsection (i);

(7) enter into such other contracts, leases, cooperative agreements, and other transactions as the Board considers appropriate to conduct the activities of the Foundation;

(8) modify or consent to the modification of any contract or agreement to which it is a party or in which it has an interest under this part;

(9) take such action as may be necessary to obtain patents and licenses for devices and procedures developed by the Foundation and its employees;

(10) sue and be sued in its corporate name, and complain and defend in courts of competent jurisdiction;

(11) appoint other groups of advisors as may be determined necessary to carry out the functions of the Foundation; and

(12) exercise other powers as set forth in this section, and such other incidental powers as are necessary to carry out its powers, duties, and functions in accordance with this part.

(i) Acceptance of funds from other sources

The Executive Director may solicit and accept on behalf of the Foundation, any funds, gifts, grants, devises, or bequests of real or personal property made to the Foundation, including from private entities, for the purposes of carrying out the duties of the Foundation.

(j) Service of Federal employees

Federal Government employees may serve on committees advisory to the Foundation and otherwise cooperate with and assist the Foundation in carrying out its functions, so long as such employees do not direct or control Foundation activities.

(k) Detail of Government employees; fellowships

(1) Detail from Federal agencies

Federal Government employees may be detailed from Federal agencies with or without reimbursement to those agencies to the Foundation at any time, and such detail shall be without interruption or loss of civil service status or privilege. Each such employee shall abide by the statutory, regulatory, ethical, and procedural standards applicable to the employees of the agency from which such employee is detailed and those of the Foundation.

(2) Voluntary service; acceptance of Federal employees

(A) Foundation

The Executive Director of the Foundation may accept the services of employees detailed from Federal agencies with or without reimbursement to those agencies.

(B) Food and Drug Administration

The Commissioner may accept the uncompensated services of Foundation fellows or trainees. Such services shall be considered to be undertaking an activity under contract with the Secretary as described in section 379 of this title.

(*l*) Annual reports

(1) Reports to Foundation

Any recipient of a grant, contract, fellowship, memorandum of understanding, or cooperative agreement from the Foundation under this section shall submit to the Foundation a report on an annual basis for the duration of such grant, contract, fellowship, memorandum of understanding, or cooperative agreement, that describes the activities carried out under such grant, contract, fellowship, memorandum of understanding, or cooperative agreement.

(2) Report to Congress and the FDA

Beginning with fiscal year 2009, the Executive Director shall submit to Congress and the Commissioner an annual report that—

(A) describes the activities of the Foundation and the progress of the Foundation in furthering the goals and priorities established under subsection (c)(2), including the practical impact of the Foundation on regulated product development;

(B) provides a specific accounting of the source and use of all funds used by the Foundation to carry out such activities; and

(C) provides information on how the results of Foundation activities could be incorporated into the regulatory and product review activities of the Food and Drug Administration.

(m) Separation of funds

The Executive Director shall ensure that the funds received from the Treasury are held in separate accounts from funds received from entities under subsection (i).

(n) Funding

From amounts appropriated to the Food and Drug Administration for each fiscal year, the Commissioner shall transfer not less than $500,000 and not more than $1,250,000, to the Foundation to carry out subsections (a), (b), and (d) through (m).

(June 25, 1938, ch. 675, §770, as added Pub. L. 110–85, title VI, §601(a), Sept. 27, 2007, 121 Stat. 890.)

§379dd–1. Location of Foundation

The Foundation shall, if practicable, be located not more than 20 miles from the District of Columbia.

(June 25, 1938, ch. 675, §771, as added Pub. L. 110–85, title VI, §601(b), Sept. 27, 2007, 121 Stat. 897.)

§ 379dd–2. Activities of the Food and Drug Administration

(a) In general

The Commissioner shall receive and assess the report submitted to the Commissioner by the Executive Director of the Foundation under section 379dd(*l*)(2) of this title.

(b) Report to Congress

Beginning with fiscal year 2009, the Commissioner shall submit to Congress an annual report summarizing the incorporation of the information provided by the Foundation in the report described under section 379dd(*l*)(2) of this title and by other recipients of grants, contracts, memoranda of understanding, or cooperative agreements into regulatory and product review activities of the Food and Drug Administration.

(c) Extramural grants

The provisions of this part and section 360bbb–5 of this title shall have no effect on any grant, contract, memorandum of understanding, or cooperative agreement between the Food and Drug Administration and any other entity entered into before, on, or after September 27, 2007.

(June 25, 1938, ch. 675, § 772, as added Pub. L. 110–85, title VI, § 601(b), Sept. 27, 2007, 121 Stat. 897.)

SUBCHAPTER VIII—IMPORTS AND EXPORTS

§ 381. Imports and exports

(a) Imports; list of registered foreign establishments; samples from unregistered foreign establishments; examination and refusal of admission

The Secretary of the Treasury shall deliver to the Secretary of Health and Human Services, upon his request, samples of food, drugs, devices, and cosmetics which are being imported or offered for import into the United States, giving notice thereof to the owner or consignee, who may appear before the Secretary of Health and Human Services and have the right to introduce testimony. The Secretary of Health and Human Services shall furnish to the Secretary of the Treasury a list of establishments registered pursuant to subsection (i) of section 360 of this title and shall request that if any drugs and devices manufactured, prepared, propagated, compounded, or processed in an establishment not so registered are imported or offered for import into the United States, samples of such drugs and devices be delivered to the Secretary of Health and Human Services, with notice of such delivery to the owner or consignee, who may appear before the Secretary of Health and Human Services and have the right to introduce testimony. If it appears from the examination of such samples or otherwise that (1) such article has been manufactured, processed, or packed under insanitary conditions or, in the case of a device, the methods used in, or the facilities or controls used for, the manufacture, packing, storage, or installation of the device do not conform to the requirements of section 360j(f) of this title, or (2) such article is forbidden or restricted in sale in the country in which it was produced or from which it was exported, or (3) such article is adulterated, misbranded, or in violation of section 355 of this title, or prohibited from introduction or delivery for introduction into interstate commerce under section 331(*ll*) of this title, then such article shall be refused admission, except as provided in subsection (b) of this section. If such article is subject to a requirement under section 379aa or 379aa–1 of this title and if the Secretary has credible evidence or information indicating that the responsible person (as defined in such section 379aa or 379aa–1 of this title) has not complied with a requirement of such section 379aa or 379aa–1 of this title with respect to any such article, or has not allowed access to records described in such section 379aa or 379aa–1 of this title, then such article shall be refused admission, except as provided in subsection (b) of this section. The Secretary of the Treasury shall cause the destruction of any such article refused admission unless such article is exported, under regulations prescribed by the Secretary of the Treasury, within ninety days of the date of notice of such refusal or within such additional time as may be permitted pursuant to such regulations. Clause (2) of the third sentence of this paragraph[1] shall not be construed to prohibit the admission of narcotic drugs the importation of which is permitted under the Controlled Substances Import and Export Act [21 U.S.C. 951 et seq.].

(b) Disposition of refused articles

Pending decision as to the admission of an article being imported or offered for import, the Secretary of the Treasury may authorize delivery of such article to the owner or consignee upon the execution by him of a good and sufficient bond providing for the payment of such liquidated damages in the event of default as may be required pursuant to regulations of the Secretary of the Treasury. If it appears to the Secretary of Health and Human Services that (1) an article included within the provisions of clause (3) of subsection (a) of this section can, by relabeling or other action, be brought into compliance with this chapter or rendered other than a food, drug, device, or cosmetic, or (2) with respect to an article included within the provision of the fourth sentence of subsection (a), the responsible person (as defined in section 379aa or 379aa–1 of this title) can take action that would assure that the responsible person is in compliance with section 379aa or 379aa–1 of this title, as the case may be, final determination as to admission of such article may be deferred and, upon filing of timely written application by the owner or consignee and the execution by him of a bond as provided in the preceding provisions of this subsection, the Secretary may, in accordance with regulations, authorize the applicant, or, with respect to clause (2), the responsible person, to perform such relabeling or other action specified in such authorization (including destruction or export of rejected articles or portions thereof, as may be specified in the Secretary's authorization). All such relabeling or other action pursuant to such authorization

[1] So in original. Probably should be "subsection".

shall in accordance with regulations be under the supervision of an officer or employee of the Department of Health and Human Services designated by the Secretary, or an officer or employee of the Department of the Treasury designated by the Secretary of the Treasury.

(c) Charges concerning refused articles

All expenses (including travel, per diem or subsistence, and salaries of officers or employees of the United States) in connection with the destruction provided for in subsection (a) of this section and the supervision of the relabeling or other action authorized under the provisions of subsection (b) of this section, the amount of such expenses to be determined in accordance with regulations, and all expenses in connection with the storage, cartage, or labor with respect to any article refused admission under subsection (a) of this section, shall be paid by the owner or consignee and, in default of such payment, shall constitute a lien against any future importations made by such owner or consignee.

(d) Reimportation

(1) Except as provided in paragraph (2) and section 384 of this title, no drug subject to section 353(b) of this title or composed wholly or partly of insulin which is manufactured in a State and exported may be imported into the United States unless the drug is imported by the manufacturer of the drug.

(2) The Secretary may authorize the importation of a drug the importation of which is prohibited by paragraph (1) if the drug is required for emergency medical care.

(3)(A) Subject to subparagraph (B), no component of a drug, no component part or accessory of a device, or other article of device requiring further processing, which is ready or suitable for use for health-related purposes, and no article of a food additive, color additive, or dietary supplement, including a product in bulk form, shall be excluded from importation into the United States under subsection (a) of this section if each of the following conditions is met:

(i) The importer of such article of a drug or device or importer of such article of a food additive, color additive, or dietary supplement submits to the Secretary, at the time of initial importation, a statement in accordance with the following:

(I) Such statement provides that such article is intended to be further processed by the initial owner or consignee, or incorporated by the initial owner or consignee, into a drug, biological product, device, food, food additive, color additive, or dietary supplement that will be exported by the initial owner or consignee from the United States in accordance with subsection (e) of this section or section 382 of this title, or with section 262(h) of title 42.

(II) The statement identifies the manufacturer of such article and each processor, packer, distributor, or other entity that had possession of the article in the chain of possession of the article from the manufacturer to such importer of the article.

(III) The statement is accompanied by such certificates of analysis as are necessary to identify such article, unless the article is a device or is an article described in paragraph (4).

(ii) At the time of initial importation and before the delivery of such article to the importer or the initial owner or consignee, such owner or consignee executes a good and sufficient bond providing for the payment of such liquidated damages in the event of default as may be required pursuant to regulations of the Secretary of the Treasury.

(iii) Such article is used and exported by the initial owner or consignee in accordance with the intent described under clause (i)(I), except for any portions of the article that are destroyed.

(iv) The initial owner or consignee maintains records on the use or destruction of such article or portions thereof, as the case may be, and submits to the Secretary any such records requested by the Secretary.

(v) Upon request of the Secretary, the initial owner or consignee submits a report that provides an accounting of the exportation or destruction of such article or portions thereof, and the manner in which such owner or consignee complied with the requirements of this subparagraph.

(B) Notwithstanding subparagraph (A), the Secretary may refuse admission to an article that otherwise would be imported into the United States under such subparagraph if the Secretary determines that there is credible evidence or information indicating that such article is not intended to be further processed by the initial owner or consignee, or incorporated by the initial owner or consignee, into a drug, biological product, device, food, food additive, color additive, or dietary supplement that will be exported by the initial owner or consignee from the United States in accordance with subsection (e) of this section or section 382 of this title, or with section 262(h) of title 42.

(C) This section may not be construed as affecting the responsibility of the Secretary to ensure that articles imported into the United States under authority of subparagraph (A) meet each of the conditions established in such subparagraph for importation.

(4) The importation into the United States of blood, blood components, source plasma, or source leukocytes or of a component, accessory, or part thereof is not permitted pursuant to paragraph (3) unless the importation complies with section 262(a) of title 42 or the Secretary permits the importation under appropriate circumstances and conditions, as determined by the Secretary. The importation of tissue or a component or part of tissue is not permitted pursuant to paragraph (3) unless the importation complies with section 264 of title 42.

(e) Exports

(1) A food, drug, device, or cosmetic intended for export shall not be deemed to be adulterated or misbranded under this chapter if it—

(A) accords to the specifications of the foreign purchaser,

(B) is not in conflict with the laws of the country to which it is intended for export,

(C) is labeled on the outside of the shipping package that it is intended for export, and

(D) is not sold or offered for sale in domestic commerce.

(2) Paragraph (1) does not apply to any device—

(A) which does not comply with an applicable requirement of section 360d or 360e of this title,

(B) which under section 360j(g) of this title is exempt from either such section, or

(C) which is a banned device under section 360f of this title,

unless, in addition to the requirements of paragraph (1), either (i) the Secretary has determined that the exportation of the device is not contrary to public health and safety and has the approval of the country to which it is intended for export or (ii) the device is eligible for export under section 382 of this title.

(3) A new animal drug that requires approval under section 360b of this title shall not be exported pursuant to paragraph (1) if such drug has been banned in the United States.

(4)(A) Any person who exports a drug, animal drug, or device may request that the Secretary—

(i) certify in writing that the exported drug, animal drug, or device meets the requirements of paragraph (1) or section 382 of this title; or

(ii) certify in writing that the drug, animal drug, or device being exported meets the applicable requirements of this chapter upon a showing that the drug or device meets the applicable requirements of this chapter.

The Secretary shall issue such a certification within 20 days of the receipt of a request for such certification.

(B) If the Secretary issues a written export certification within the 20 days prescribed by subparagraph (A), a fee for such certification may be charged but shall not exceed $175 for each certification. Fees collected for a fiscal year pursuant to this subparagraph shall be credited to the appropriation account for salaries and expenses of the Food and Drug Administration and shall be available in accordance with appropriations Acts until expended without fiscal year limitation. Such fees shall be collected in each fiscal year in an amount equal to the amount specified in appropriations Acts for such fiscal year and shall only be collected and available for the costs of the Food and Drug Administration.

(f) Labeling of exported drugs

(1) If a drug (other than insulin, an antibiotic drug, an animal drug, or a drug exported under section 382 of this title) being exported in accordance with subsection (e) of this section is being exported to a country that has different or additional labeling requirements or conditions for use and such country requires the drug to be labeled in accordance with those requirements or uses, such drug may be labeled in accordance with such requirements and conditions for use in the country to which such drug is being exported if it also is labeled in accordance with the requirements of this chapter.

(2) If, pursuant to paragraph (1), the labeling of an exported drug includes conditions for use that have not been approved under this chapter, the labeling must state that such conditions for use have not been approved under this chapter. A drug exported under section 382 of this title is exempt from this section.

(g) Warning notice of importation in violation of chapter

(1) With respect to a prescription drug being imported or offered for import into the United States, the Secretary, in the case of an individual who is not in the business of such importations, may not send a warning notice to the individual unless the following conditions are met:

(A) The notice specifies, as applicable to the importation of the drug, that the Secretary has made a determination that—

(i) importation is in violation of subsection (a) of this section because the drug is or appears to be adulterated, misbranded, or in violation of section 355 of this title;

(ii) importation is in violation of subsection (a) of this section because the drug is or appears to be forbidden or restricted in sale in the country in which it was produced or from which it was exported;

(iii) importation is or appears to be in violation of subsection (d)(1) of this section; or

(iv) importation otherwise is or appears to be in violation of Federal law.

(B) The notice does not specify any provision described in subparagraph (A) that is not applicable to the importation of the drug.

(C) The notice states the reasons underlying such determination by the Secretary, including a brief application to the principal facts involved of the provision of law described in subparagraph (A) that is the basis of the determination by the Secretary.

(2) For purposes of this section, the term "warning notice", with respect to the importation of a drug, means a communication from the Secretary (written or otherwise) notifying a person, or clearly suggesting to the person, that importing the drug for personal use is, or appears to be, a violation of this chapter.

(h) Protection against adulteration of food

(1) The Secretary shall give high priority to increasing the number of inspections under this section for the purpose of enabling the Secretary to inspect food offered for import at ports of entry into the United States, with the greatest priority given to inspections to detect the intentional adulteration of food.

(2) The Secretary shall give high priority to making necessary improvements to the information management systems of the Food and Drug Administration that contain information related to foods imported or offered for import into the United States for purposes of improving the ability of the Secretary to allocate resources, detect the intentional adulteration of food, and facilitate the importation of food that is in compliance with this chapter.

(3) The Secretary shall improve linkages with other regulatory agencies of the Federal Government that share responsibility for food safety, and shall with respect to such safety improve linkages with the States and Indian tribes (as defined in section 450b(e) of title 25).

(i) Testing for rapid detection of adulteration of food

(1) For use in inspections of food under this section, the Secretary shall provide for research on the development of tests and sampling methodologies—

(A) whose purpose is to test food in order to rapidly detect the adulteration of the food, with the greatest priority given to detect the intentional adulteration of food; and

(B) whose results offer significant improvements over the available technology in terms of accuracy, timing, or costs.

(2) In providing for research under paragraph (1), the Secretary shall give priority to conducting research on the development of tests that are suitable for inspections of food at ports of entry into the United States.

(3) In providing for research under paragraph (1), the Secretary shall as appropriate coordinate with the Director of the Centers for Disease Control and Prevention, the Director of the National Institutes of Health, the Administrator of the Environmental Protection Agency, and the Secretary of Agriculture.

(4) The Secretary shall annually submit to the Committee on Energy and Commerce of the House of Representatives, and the Committee on Health, Education, Labor, and Pensions of the Senate, a report describing the progress made in research under paragraph (1), including progress regarding paragraph (2).

(j) Temporary holds at ports of entry

(1) If an officer or qualified employee of the Food and Drug Administration has credible evidence or information indicating that an article of food presents a threat of serious adverse health consequences or death to humans or animals, and such officer or qualified employee is unable to inspect, examine, or investigate such article upon the article being offered for import at a port of entry into the United States, the officer or qualified employee shall request the Secretary of Treasury to hold the food at the port of entry for a reasonable period of time, not to exceed 24 hours, for the purpose of enabling the Secretary to inspect, examine, or investigate the article as appropriate.

(2) The Secretary shall request the Secretary of Treasury to remove an article held pursuant to paragraph (1) to a secure facility, as appropriate. During the period of time that such article is so held, the article shall not be transferred by any person from the port of entry into the United States for the article, or from the secure facility to which the article has been removed, as the case may be. Subsection (b) of this section does not authorize the delivery of the article pursuant to the execution of a bond while the article is so held.

(3) An officer or qualified employee of the Food and Drug Administration may make a request under paragraph (1) only if the Secretary or an official designated by the Secretary approves the request. An official may not be so designated unless the official is the director of the district under this chapter in which the article involved is located, or is an official senior to such director.

(4) With respect to an article of food for which a request under paragraph (1) is made, the Secretary, promptly after the request is made, shall notify the State in which the port of entry involved is located that the request has been made, and as applicable, that such article is being held under this subsection.

(k) Importation by debarred persons

(1) If an article of food is being imported or offered for import into the United States, and the importer, owner, or consignee of the article is a person who has been debarred under section 335a(b)(3) of this title, such article shall be held at the port of entry for the article, and may not be delivered to such person. Subsection (b) of this section does not authorize the delivery of the article pursuant to the execution of a bond while the article is so held. The article shall be removed to a secure facility, as appropriate. During the period of time that such article is so held, the article shall not be transferred by any person from the port of entry into the United States for the article, or from the secure facility to which the article has been removed, as the case may be.

(2) An article of food held under paragraph (1) may be delivered to a person who is not a debarred person under section 335a(b)(3) of this title if such person affirmatively establishes, at the expense of the person, that the article complies with the requirements of this chapter, as determined by the Secretary.

(*l*) Failure to register

(1)[2] If an article of food is being imported or offered for import into the United States, and such article is from a foreign facility for which a registration has not been submitted to the Secretary under section 350d of this title, such article shall be held at the port of entry for the article, and may not be delivered to the importer, owner, or consignee of the article, until the foreign facility is so registered. Subsection (b) of this section does not authorize the delivery of the article pursuant to the execution of a bond while the article is so held. The article shall be removed to a secure facility, as appropriate. During the period of time that such article is so held, the article shall not be transferred by any person from the port of entry into the United States for the article, or from the secure facility to which the article has been removed, as the case may be.

(m) Prior notice of imported food shipments

(1) In the case of an article of food that is being imported or offered for import into the United States, the Secretary, after consultation with the Secretary of the Treasury, shall by regulation require, for the purpose of enabling such article to be inspected at ports of entry into the United States, the submission to the Secretary of a notice providing the identity of each of the following: The article; the manufacturer and shipper of the article; if known within the specified period of time that notice is required to be provided, the grower of the article; the country from which the article originates; the country from which the article is shipped; and the anticipated port of entry for the article. An article of food imported or offered for import without

[2] So in original. No par. (2) has been enacted.

submission of such notice in accordance with the requirements under this paragraph shall be refused admission into the United States. Nothing in this section may be construed as a limitation on the port of entry for an article of food.

(2)(A) Regulations under paragraph (1) shall require that a notice under such paragraph be provided by a specified period of time in advance of the time of the importation of the article of food involved or the offering of the food for import, which period shall be no less than the minimum amount of time necessary for the Secretary to receive, review, and appropriately respond to such notification, but may not exceed five days. In determining the specified period of time required under this subparagraph, the Secretary may consider, but is not limited to consideration of, the effect on commerce of such period of time, the locations of the various ports of entry into the United States, the various modes of transportation, the types of food imported into the United States, and any other such consideration. Nothing in the preceding sentence may be construed as a limitation on the obligation of the Secretary to receive, review, and appropriately respond to any notice under paragraph (1).

(B)(i) If an article of food is being imported or offered for import into the United States and a notice under paragraph (1) is not provided in advance in accordance with the requirements under paragraph (1), such article shall be held at the port of entry for the article, and may not be delivered to the importer, owner, or consignee of the article, until such notice is submitted to the Secretary, and the Secretary examines the notice and determines that the notice is in accordance with the requirements under paragraph (1). Subsection (b) of this section does not authorize the delivery of the article pursuant to the execution of a bond while the article is so held. The article shall be removed to a secure facility, as appropriate. During the period of time that such article is so held, the article shall not be transferred by any person from the port of entry into the United States for the article, or from the secure facility to which the article has been removed, as the case may be.

(ii) In carrying out clause (i) with respect to an article of food, the Secretary shall determine whether there is in the possession of the Secretary any credible evidence or information indicating that such article presents a threat of serious adverse health consequences or death to humans or animals.

(3)(A) This subsection may not be construed as limiting the authority of the Secretary to obtain information under any other provision of this chapter.

(B) This subsection may not be construed as authorizing the Secretary to impose any requirements with respect to a food to the extent that it is within the exclusive jurisdiction of the Secretary of Agriculture pursuant to the Federal Meat Inspection Act (21 U.S.C. 601 et seq.), the Poultry Products Inspection Act (21 U.S.C. 451 et seq.), or the Egg Products Inspection Act (21 U.S.C. 1031 et seq.).

(n) Labeling of food refused admission

(1) If a food has been refused admission under subsection (a) of this section, other than such a food that is required to be destroyed, the Secretary may require the owner or consignee of the food to affix to the container of the food a label that clearly and conspicuously bears the statement: "UNITED STATES: REFUSED ENTRY".

(2) All expenses in connection with affixing a label under paragraph (1) shall be paid by the owner or consignee of the food involved, and in default of such payment, shall constitute a lien against future importations made by such owner or consignee.

(3) A requirement under paragraph (1) remains in effect until the Secretary determines that the food involved has been brought into compliance with this chapter.

(*o*) Registration statement

If an article that is a drug or device is being imported or offered for import into the United States, and the importer, owner, or consignee of such article does not, at the time of offering the article for import, submit to the Secretary a statement that identifies the registration under section 360(i) of this title of each establishment that with respect to such article is required under such section to register with the Secretary, the article may be refused admission. If the article is refused admission for failure to submit such a statement, the article shall be held at the port of entry for the article, and may not be delivered to the importer, owner, or consignee of the article, until such a statement is submitted to the Secretary. Subsection (b) of this section does not authorize the delivery of the article pursuant to the execution of a bond while the article is so held. The article shall be removed to a secure facility, as appropriate. During the period of time that such article is so held, the article shall not be transferred by any person from the port of entry into the United States for the article, or from the secure facility to which the article has been removed, as the case may be.

(June 25, 1938, ch. 675, §801, 52 Stat. 1058; Oct. 18, 1949, ch. 696, §§1–3, 63 Stat. 882; Pub. L. 87–781, title III, §306, Oct. 10, 1962, 76 Stat. 796; Pub. L. 90–399, §106, July 13, 1968, 82 Stat. 353; Pub. L. 91–513, title II, §701(h), Oct. 27, 1970, 84 Stat. 1282; Pub. L. 94–295, §§3(f), 4(b)(3), May 28, 1976, 90 Stat. 578, 580; Pub. L. 100–293, §3, Apr. 22, 1988, 102 Stat. 96; Pub. L. 102–300, §6(b)(1), June 16, 1992, 106 Stat. 240; Pub. L. 102–353, §5, Aug. 26, 1992, 106 Stat. 943; Pub. L. 103–80, §3(cc), (dd)(1), Aug. 13, 1993, 107 Stat. 778, 779; Pub. L. 104–134, title II, §2102(a)–(c), Apr. 26, 1996, 110 Stat. 1321–313, 1321–314; Pub. L. 104–180, title VI, §603(a), (b), Aug. 6, 1996, 110 Stat. 1594, 1595; Pub. L. 105–115, title I, §125(a)(2)(D), Nov. 21, 1997, 111 Stat. 2325; Pub. L. 106–387, §1(a) [title VII, §§745(c)(1), 746(c)], Oct. 28, 2000, 114 Stat. 1549, 1549A–36, 1549A–40; Pub. L. 107–188, title III, §§302(a)–(d), 303(c), 304(e), 305(c), 307(a), 308(a), 321(b)(1), 322(a), June 12, 2002, 116 Stat. 662, 663, 665, 667, 668, 670, 672, 676; Pub. L. 109–462, §5(a), Dec. 22, 2006, 120 Stat. 3475; Pub. L. 110–85, title IX, §912(b)(2), Sept. 27, 2007, 121 Stat. 952.)

REFERENCES IN TEXT

The Controlled Substances Import and Export Act, referred to in subsec. (a), is title III of Pub. L. 91–513,

Oct. 27, 1970, 84 Stat. 1285, as amended, which is classified principally to subchapter II (§951 et seq.) of chapter 13 of this title. For complete classification of this Act to the Code, see Short Title note set out under section 951 of this title and Tables.

The Federal Meat Inspection Act, referred to in subsec. (m)(3)(B), is titles I to IV of act Mar. 4, 1907, ch. 2907, as added Pub. L. 90–201, Dec. 15, 1967, 81 Stat. 584, and amended, which are classified generally to subchapters I to IV (§601 et seq.) of chapter 12 of this title. For complete classification of this Act to the Code, see Short Title note set out under section 601 of this title and Tables.

The Poultry Products Inspection Act, referred to in subsec. (m)(3)(B), is Pub. L. 85–172, Aug. 28, 1957, 71 Stat. 441, as amended, which is classified generally to chapter 10 (§451 et seq.) of this title. For complete classification of this Act to the Code, see Short Title note set out under section 451 of this title and Tables.

The Egg Products Inspection Act, referred to in subsec. (m)(3)(B), is Pub. L. 91–597, Dec. 29, 1970, 84 Stat. 1620, as amended, which is classified generally to chapter 15 (§1031 et seq.) of this title. For complete classification of this Act to the Code, see Short Title note set out under section 1031 of this title and Tables.

AMENDMENTS

2007—Subsec. (a). Pub. L. 110–85 substituted "is adulterated, misbranded, or in violation of section 355 of this title, or prohibited from introduction or delivery for introduction into interstate commerce under section 331(*ll*) of this title," for "is adulterated, misbranded, or in violation of section 355 of this title,".

2006—Subsec. (a). Pub. L. 109–462, §5(a)(1), inserted after third sentence "If such article is subject to a requirement under section 379aa or 379aa–1 of this title and if the Secretary has credible evidence or information indicating that the responsible person (as defined in such section 379aa or 379aa–1 of this title) has not complied with a requirement of such section 379aa or 379aa–1 of this title with respect to any such article, or has not allowed access to records described in such section 379aa or 379aa–1 of this title, then such article shall be refused admission, except as provided in subsection (b) of this section."

Subsec. (b). Pub. L. 109–462, §5(a)(2), in second sentence, inserted "(1)" before "an article included", "or (2) with respect to an article included within the provision of the fourth sentence of subsection (a), the responsible person (as defined in section 379aa or 379aa–1 of this title) can take action that would assure that the responsible person is in compliance with section 379aa or 379aa–1 of this title, as the case may be," before "final determination", and ", or, with respect to clause (2), the responsible person," before "to perform".

2002—Subsec. (d)(3). Pub. L. 107–188, §322(a), amended par. (3) generally. Prior to amendment, par. (3) read as follows: "No component of a drug, no component part or accessory of a device, or other article of device requiring further processing, which is ready or suitable for use for health-related purposes, and no food additive, color additive, or dietary supplement, including a product in bulk form, shall be excluded from importation into the United States under subsection (a) of this section if—

"(A) the importer of such article of a drug or device or importer of the food additive, color additive, or dietary supplement submits a statement to the Secretary, at the time of initial importation, that such article of a drug or device, food additive, color additive, or dietary supplement is intended to be further processed by the initial owner or consignee, or incorporated by the initial owner or consignee into a drug, biological product, device, food, food additive, color additive, or dietary supplement that will be exported by such owner or consignee from the United States in accordance with subsection (e) of this section or section 382 of this title or section 262(h) of title 42;

"(B) the initial owner or consignee responsible for such imported article maintains records that identify the use of such imported article and upon request of the Secretary submits a report that provides an accounting of the exportation or the disposition of the imported article, including portions that have been destroyed, and the manner in which such person complied with the requirements of this paragraph; and

"(C) any imported component, part, article, or accessory of a drug or device and any food additive, color additive, or dietary supplement not incorporated or further processed as described in subparagraph (A) is destroyed or exported by the owner or consignee."

Subsec. (h). Pub. L. 107–188, §302(a)–(c), added subsec. (h).

Subsec. (i). Pub. L. 107–188, §302(d), added subsec. (i).

Subsec. (j). Pub. L. 107–188, §303(c), added subsec. (j).

Subsec. (k). Pub. L. 107–188, §304(e), added subsec. (k).

Subsec. (*l*). Pub. L. 107–188, §305(c), added subsec. (*l*).

Subsec. (m). Pub. L. 107–188, §307(a), added subsec. (m).

Subsec. (n). Pub. L. 107–188, §308(a), added subsec. (n).

Subsec. (*o*). Pub. L. 107–188, §321(b)(1), added subsec. (*o*).

2000—Subsec. (d)(1). Pub. L. 106–387, §1(a) [title VII, §745(c)(1)], inserted "and section 384 of this title" after "paragraph (2)".

Subsec. (g). Pub. L. 106–387, §1(a) [title VII, §746(c)], added subsec. (g).

1997—Subsec. (d)(1). Pub. L. 105–115 inserted "or composed wholly or partly of insulin" after "353(b) of this title".

1996—Subsec. (d)(3). Pub. L. 104–180, §603(a), substituted "accessory of a device, or other article of device requiring further processing, which is ready" for "accessory of a device which is ready" in introductory provisions, inserted "further processed by the initial owner or consignee, or" after "is intended to be" in subpar. (A), and inserted "article," after "part," and "or further processed" after "incorporated" in subpar. (C).

Pub. L. 104–134, §2102(a)(1), added par. (3)

Subsec. (d)(4). Pub. L. 104–134, §2102(a)(1), added par. (4).

Subsec. (e)(1). Pub. L. 104–134, §2102(b)(1), struck out concluding provisions which read as follows: "This paragraph does not authorize the exportation of any new animal drug, or an animal feed bearing or containing a new animal drug, which is unsafe within the meaning of section 360b of this title."

Subsec. (e)(2). Pub. L. 104–134, §2102(b)(2), in concluding provisions, substituted "either (i) the Secretary" for "the Secretary" and added cl. (ii).

Subsec. (e)(3), (4). Pub. L. 104–134, §2102(b)(3), added pars. (3) and (4).

Subsec. (f). Pub. L. 104–180, §603(b), inserted "(other than insulin, an antibiotic drug, an animal drug, or a drug exported under section 382 of this title)" after "If a drug" in par. (1) and "A drug exported under section 382 of this title is exempt from this section." at end of par. (2).

Pub. L. 104–134, §2102(c), added subsec. (f).

1993—Subsec. (a). Pub. L. 103–80, §3(dd)(1), substituted "Health and Human Services" for "Agriculture" after "Secretary of" in two places in first sentence.

Subsec. (b). Pub. L. 103–80, §3(cc), substituted "Secretary of Health and Human Services" for "Administrator" after "If it appears to the", "Secretary" for "Administrator" after "provisions of this subsection, the", "Secretary's" for "Administrator's" after "as may be specified in the", "Department of Health and Human Services" for "Federal Security Agency", and "Secretary" for "Administrator" after "designated by the".

1992—Subsecs. (a), (b). Pub. L. 102–300, which directed the substitution of "Health and Human Services" for "Health, Education, and Welfare" wherever appearing, was executed in second sentence of subsec. (a), but could not be executed in first sentence of subsec. (a) or in subsec. (b) because such words did not appear. See 1993 Amendment note above and Transfer of Functions note below.

Subsec. (d)(1). Pub. L. 102–353 substituted "manufacturer of" for "person who manufactured".

1988—Subsecs. (d), (e). Pub. L. 100–293 added subsec. (d) and redesignated former subsec. (d) as (e).

1976—Subsec. (a). Pub. L. 94–295, §§ 3(f)(2), 4(b)(3), expanded provisions requiring the Secretary of Health, Education, and Welfare to request that the Secretary of the Treasury deliver to the Secretary of Health, Education, and Welfare items imported or offered for import into the United States that were manufactured, prepared, propagated, compounded, or processed in nonregistered establishments by extending the provisions to include devices imported or offered for import, and, in cl. (1), inserted reference to devices which were manufactured, packed, stored, or installed using methods, facilities, or controls not conforming to the requirements of section 360j(f) of this title.

Subsec. (d). Pub. L. 94–295, § 3(f)(1), designated existing provisions as par. (1) and added par. (2).

1970—Subsec. (a). Pub. L. 91–513 substituted "Clause (2) of the third sentence of this paragraph" for "This paragraph" and "the Controlled Substances Import and Export Act" for "section 173 of this title" in last sentence.

1968—Subsec. (d). Pub. L. 90–399 provided that nothing in subsec. (d) shall authorize the exportation of any new animal drug, or an animal feed bearing or containing a new animal drug, which is unsafe within the meaning of section 360b of this title.

1962—Subsec. (a). Pub. L. 87–781 inserted provisions requiring the Secretary of Health, Education, and Welfare to furnish the Secretary of the Treasury a list of establishments registered under section 360(i) of this title, and to request that samples of any drugs from any establishments not so registered be delivered to the Secretary of Health, Education, and Welfare, with notice of delivery to the consignee who may appear before the Secretary to testify.

1949—Subsec. (a). Act Oct. 18, 1949, § 1, inserted before period at end of second sentence ", except as provided in subsection (b) of this section. The Secretary of the Treasury shall cause the destruction of any such article refused admission unless such article is exported, under regulations prescribed by the Secretary of the Treasury within ninety days of the notice of such refusal or within such additional time as may be permitted pursuant to such regulations".

Subsec. (b). Act Oct. 18, 1949, § 2, provided for express statutory authority for the long-standing administrative practice of releasing imported articles that do not comply with the requirements of the law so that they may be relabeled or given appropriate treatment to bring them into compliance.

Subsec. (c). Act Oct. 18, 1949, § 3, charged all costs, including salaries and travel and subsistence expenses of officers and employees, against importers.

Effective Date of 2006 Amendment

Pub. L. 109–462, § 5(b), Dec. 22, 2006, 120 Stat. 3476, provided that: "The amendments made by this section [amending this section] shall take effect 1 year after the date of enactment of this Act [Dec. 22, 2006]."

Effective Date of 2002 Amendment

Amendment by section 321(b)(1) of Pub. L. 107–188 effective upon the expiration of the 180-day period beginning June 12, 2002, see section 321(c) of Pub. L. 107–188, set out as a note under section 331 of this title.

Amendment by section 322(a) of Pub. L. 107–188 effective upon the expiration of the 90-day period beginning June 12, 2002, see section 322(c) of Pub. L. 107–188, set out as a note under section 331 of this title.

Effective Date of 1988 Amendment

Amendment by Pub. L. 100–293 effective upon expiration of 90 days after Apr. 22, 1988, see section 8(a) of Pub. L. 100–293, set out as a note under section 353 of this title.

Effective Date of 1970 Amendment

Amendment by Pub. L. 91–513 effective on first day of seventh calendar month that begins after Oct. 26, 1970, see section 704 of Pub. L. 91–513, set out as an Effective Date note under section 801 of this title.

Effective Date of 1968 Amendment

Amendment of subsec. (d) by Pub. L. 90–399 effective on first day of thirteenth calendar month after July 13, 1968, see section 108(a) of Pub. L. 90–399, set out as an Effective Date and Transitional Provisions note under section 360b of this title.

Regulations

Pub. L. 107–188, title III, § 307(c), June 12, 2002, 116 Stat. 672, provided that:

"(1) In general.—Not later than 18 months after the date of the enactment of this Act [June 12, 2002], the Secretary of Health and Human Services shall promulgate proposed and final regulations for the requirement of providing notice in accordance with section 801(m) of the Federal Food, Drug, and Cosmetic Act [21 U.S.C. 381(m)] (as added by subsection (a) of this section). Such requirement of notification takes effect—

"(A) upon the effective date of such final regulations; or

"(B) upon the expiration of such 18-month period if the final regulations have not been made effective as of the expiration of such period, subject to compliance with the final regulations when the final regulations are made effective.

"(2) Default; minimum period of advance notice.—If under paragraph (1) the requirement for providing notice in accordance with section 801(m) of the Federal Food, Drug, and Cosmetic Act [21 U.S.C. 381(m)] takes effect without final regulations having been made effective, then for purposes of such requirement, the specified period of time that the notice is required to be made in advance of the time of the importation of the article of food involved or the offering of the food for import shall be not fewer than eight hours and not more than five days, which shall remain in effect until the final regulations are made effective."

Savings Provision

Amendment by Pub. L. 91–513 not to affect or abate any prosecutions for violation of law or any civil seizure or forfeitures and injunctive proceedings commenced prior to the effective date of such amendment, and all administrative proceedings pending before the Bureau of Narcotic and Dangerous Drugs [now Drug Enforcement Administration] on Oct. 27, 1970, to be continued and brought to final determination in accord with laws and regulations in effect prior to Oct. 27, 1970, see section 702 of Pub. L. 91–513, set out as a note under section 321 of this title.

Construction of Amendments by Pub. L. 107–188

Pub. L. 107–188, title III, § 308(c), June 12, 2002, 116 Stat. 673, provided that: "With respect to articles of food that are imported or offered for import into the United States, nothing in this section [amending this section and section 343 of this title] shall be construed to limit the authority of the Secretary of Health and Human Services or the Secretary of the Treasury to require the marking of refused articles of food under any other provision of law."

Transfer of Functions

Secretary and Department of Health, Education, and Welfare redesignated Secretary and Department of Health and Human Services by Pub. L. 96–88, title V, § 509(b), Oct. 17, 1979, 93 Stat. 695, which is classified to section 3508(b) of Title 20, Education.

For transfer of functions of Federal Security Administrator to Secretary of Health, Education, and Welfare [now Health and Human Services], and of Food and Drug Administration in the Department of Agriculture to Federal Security Agency, see notes set out under section 321 of this title.

Study and Report on Trade in Pharmaceuticals

Pub. L. 108–173, title XI, § 1123, Dec. 8, 2003, 117 Stat. 2469, provided that: "The President's designees shall conduct a study and report on issues related to trade and pharmaceuticals."

FINDINGS

Pub. L. 106–387, § 1(a) [title VII, § 746(b)], Oct. 28, 2000, 114 Stat. 1549, 1549A–40, provided that: "The Congress finds as follows:

"(1) Patients and their families sometimes have reason to import into the United States drugs that have been approved by the Food and Drug Administration ('FDA').

"(2) There have been circumstances in which—

"(A) an individual seeking to import such a drug has received a notice from FDA that importing the drug violates or may violate the Federal Food, Drug, and Cosmetic Act [21 U.S.C. 301 et seq.]; and

"(B) the notice failed to inform the individual of the reasons underlying the decision to send the notice.

"(3) FDA should not send a warning notice regarding the importation of a drug without providing to the individual involved a statement of the underlying reasons for the notice."

§ 382. Exports of certain unapproved products

(a) Drugs or devices intended for human or animal use which require approval or licensing

A drug or device—

(1) which, in the case of a drug—

(A)(i) requires approval by the Secretary under section 355 of this title before such drug may be introduced or delivered for introduction into interstate commerce; or

(ii) requires licensing by the Secretary under section 262 of title 42 or by the Secretary of Agriculture under the Act of March 4, 1913 [21 U.S.C. 151 et seq.] (known as the Virus-Serum Toxin Act) before it may be introduced or delivered for introduction into interstate commerce;

(B) does not have such approval or license; and

(C) is not exempt from such sections or Act; and

(2) which, in the case of a device—

(A) does not comply with an applicable requirement under section 360d or 360e of this title;

(B) under section 360j(g) of this title is exempt from either such section; or

(C) is a banned device under section 360f of this title, is adulterated, misbranded, and in violation of such sections or Act unless the export of the drug or device is, except as provided in subsection (f) of this section, authorized under subsection (b), (c), (d), or (e) of this section or section 381(e)(2) of this title. If a drug or device described in paragraphs (1) and (2) may be exported under subsection (b) of this section and if an application for such drug or device under section 355 or 360e of this title or section 262 of title 42 was disapproved, the Secretary shall notify the appropriate public health official of the country to which such drug will be exported of such disapproval.

(b) List of eligible countries for export; criteria for addition to list; direct export; petition for exemption

(1)(A) A drug or device described in subsection (a) of this section may be exported to any country, if the drug or device complies with the laws of that country and has valid marketing authorization by the appropriate authority—

(i) in Australia, Canada, Israel, Japan, New Zealand, Switzerland, or South Africa; or

(ii) in the European Union or a country in the European Economic Area (the countries in the European Union and the European Free Trade Association) if the drug or device is marketed in that country or the drug or device is authorized for general marketing in the European Economic Area.

(B) The Secretary may designate an additional country to be included in the list of countries described in clauses (i) and (ii) of subparagraph (A) if all of the following requirements are met in such country:

(i) Statutory or regulatory requirements which require the review of drugs and devices for safety and effectiveness by an entity of the government of such country and which authorize the approval of only those drugs and devices which have been determined to be safe and effective by experts employed by or acting on behalf of such entity and qualified by scientific training and experience to evaluate the safety and effectiveness of drugs and devices on the basis of adequate and well-controlled investigations, including clinical investigations, conducted by experts qualified by scientific training and experience to evaluate the safety and effectiveness of drugs and devices.

(ii) Statutory or regulatory requirements that the methods used in, and the facilities and controls used for—

(I) the manufacture, processing, and packing of drugs in the country are adequate to preserve their identity, quality, purity, and strength; and

(II) the manufacture, preproduction design validation, packing, storage, and installation of a device are adequate to assure that the device will be safe and effective.

(iii) Statutory or regulatory requirements for the reporting of adverse reactions to drugs and devices and procedures to withdraw approval and remove drugs and devices found not to be safe or effective.

(iv) Statutory or regulatory requirements that the labeling and promotion of drugs and devices must be in accordance with the approval of the drug or device.

(v) The valid marketing authorization system in such country or countries is equivalent to the systems in the countries described in clauses (i) and (ii) of subparagraph (A).

The Secretary shall not delegate the authority granted under this subparagraph.

(C) An appropriate country official, manufacturer, or exporter may request the Secretary to take action under subparagraph (B) to designate an additional country or countries to be added to the list of countries described in clauses (i) and (ii) of subparagraph (A) by submitting documentation to the Secretary in support of such designation. Any person other than a country requesting such designation shall include, along with the request, a letter from the country indicating the desire of such country to be designated.

(2) A drug described in subsection (a) of this section may be directly exported to a country

which is not listed in clause (i) or (ii) of paragraph (1)(A) if—

(A) the drug complies with the laws of that country and has valid marketing authorization by the responsible authority in that country; and

(B) the Secretary determines that all of the following requirements are met in that country:

(i) Statutory or regulatory requirements which require the review of drugs for safety and effectiveness by an entity of the government of such country and which authorize the approval of only those drugs which have been determined to be safe and effective by experts employed by or acting on behalf of such entity and qualified by scientific training and experience to evaluate the safety and effectiveness of drugs on the basis of adequate and well-controlled investigations, including clinical investigations, conducted by experts qualified by scientific training and experience to evaluate the safety and effectiveness of drugs.

(ii) Statutory or regulatory requirements that the methods used in, and the facilities and controls used for the manufacture, processing, and packing of drugs in the country are adequate to preserve their identity, quality, purity, and strength.

(iii) Statutory or regulatory requirements for the reporting of adverse reactions to drugs and procedures to withdraw approval and remove drugs found not to be safe or effective.

(iv) Statutory or regulatory requirements that the labeling and promotion of drugs must be in accordance with the approval of the drug.

(3) The exporter of a drug described in subsection (a) of this section which would not meet the conditions for approval under this chapter or conditions for approval of a country described in clause (i) or (ii) of paragraph (1)(A) may petition the Secretary for authorization to export such drug to a country which is not described in clause (i) or (ii) of paragraph (1)(A) or which is not described in paragraph (2). The Secretary shall permit such export if—

(A) the person exporting the drug—

(i) certifies that the drug would not meet the conditions for approval under this chapter or the conditions for approval of a country described in clause (i) or (ii) of paragraph (1)(A); and

(ii) provides the Secretary with credible scientific evidence, acceptable to the Secretary, that the drug would be safe and effective under the conditions of use in the country to which it is being exported; and

(B) the appropriate health authority in the country to which the drug is being exported—

(i) requests approval of the export of the drug to such country;

(ii) certifies that the health authority understands that the drug is not approved under this chapter or in a country described in clause (i) or (ii) of paragraph (1)(A); and

(iii) concurs that the scientific evidence provided pursuant to subparagraph (A) is credible scientific evidence that the drug would be reasonably safe and effective in such country.

The Secretary shall take action on a request for export of a drug under this paragraph within 60 days of receiving such request.

(c) Investigational use exemption

A drug or device intended for investigational use in any country described in clause (i) or (ii) of subsection (b)(1)(A) of this section may be exported in accordance with the laws of that country and shall be exempt from regulation under section 355(i) or 360j(g) of this title.

(d) Anticipation of market authorization

A drug or device intended for formulation, filling, packaging, labeling, or further processing in anticipation of market authorization in any country described in clause (i) or (ii) of subsection (b)(1)(A) of this section may be exported for use in accordance with the laws of that country.

(e) Diagnosis, prevention, or treatment of tropical disease

(1) A drug or device which is used in the diagnosis, prevention, or treatment of a tropical disease or another disease not of significant prevalence in the United States and which does not otherwise qualify for export under this section shall, upon approval of an application, be permitted to be exported if the Secretary finds that the drug or device will not expose patients in such country to an unreasonable risk of illness or injury and the probable benefit to health from the use of the drug or device (under conditions of use prescribed, recommended, or suggested in the labeling or proposed labeling of the drug or device) outweighs the risk of injury or illness from its use, taking into account the probable risks and benefits of currently available drug or device treatment.

(2) The holder of an approved application for the export of a drug or device under this subsection shall report to the Secretary—

(A) the receipt of any credible information indicating that the drug or device is being or may have been exported from a country for which the Secretary made a finding under paragraph (1)(A) to a country for which the Secretary cannot make such a finding; and

(B) the receipt of any information indicating adverse reactions to such drug.

(3)(A) If the Secretary determines that—

(i) a drug or device for which an application is approved under paragraph (1) does not continue to meet the requirements of such paragraph; or

(ii) the holder of an approved application under paragraph (1) has not made the report required by paragraph (2),

the Secretary may, after providing the holder of the application an opportunity for an informal hearing, withdraw the approved application.

(B) If the Secretary determines that the holder of an approved application under paragraph (1) or an importer is exporting a drug or device from the United States to an importer and such importer is exporting the drug or device to a country for which the Secretary cannot make a finding under paragraph (1) and such export presents an imminent hazard, the Secretary shall immediately prohibit the export of the drug or device to such importer, provide the person exporting the drug or device from the United States prompt notice of the prohibition, and afford such person an opportunity for an expedited hearing.

(f) Prohibition of export of drug or device

A drug or device may not be exported under this section—

(1) if the drug or device is not manufactured, processed, packaged, and held in substantial conformity with current good manufacturing practice requirements or does not meet international standards as certified by an international standards organization recognized by the Secretary;

(2) if the drug or device is adulterated under clause (1), (2)(A), or (3) of section 351(a) or subsection (c) or (d) of section 351 of this title;

(3) if the requirements of subparagraphs (A) through (D) of section 381(e)(1) of this title have not been met;

(4)(A) if the drug or device is the subject of a notice by the Secretary or the Secretary of Agriculture of a determination that the probability of reimportation of the exported drug or device would present an imminent hazard to the public health and safety of the United States and the only means of limiting the hazard is to prohibit the export of the drug or device; or

(B) if the drug or device presents an imminent hazard to the public health of the country to which the drug or device would be exported;

(5) if the labeling of the drug or device is not—

(A) in accordance with the requirements and conditions for use in—

(i) the country in which the drug or device received valid marketing authorization under subsection (b) of this section; and

(ii) the country to which the drug or device would be exported; and

(B) in the language and units of measurement of the country to which the drug or device would be exported or in the language designated by such country; or

(6) if the drug or device is not promoted in accordance with the labeling requirements set forth in paragraph (5).

In making a finding under paragraph (4)(B), (5), or (6) the Secretary shall consult with the appropriate public health official in the affected country.

(g) Notification of Secretary

The exporter of a drug or device exported under subsection (b)(1) of this section shall provide a simple notification to the Secretary identifying the drug or device when the exporter first begins to export such drug or device to any country listed in clause (i) or (ii) of subsection (b)(1)(A) of this section. When an exporter of a drug or device first begins to export a drug or device to a country which is not listed in clause (i) or (ii) of subsection (b)(1)A)[1] of this section, the exporter shall provide a simple notification to the Secretary identifying the drug or device and the country to which such drug or device is being exported. Any exporter of a drug or device shall maintain records of all drugs or devices exported and the countries to which they were exported.

(h) References to Secretary and term "drug"

For purposes of this section—

(1) a reference to the Secretary shall in the case of a biological product which is required to be licensed under the Act of March 4, 1913 [21 U.S.C. 151 et seq.] (37 Stat. 832–833) (commonly known as the Virus-Serum Toxin Act) be considered to be a reference to the Secretary of Agriculture, and

(2) the term "drug" includes drugs for human use as well as biologicals under section 262 of title 42 or the Act of March 4, 1913 (37 Stat. 832–833) (commonly known as the Virus-Serum Toxin Act).

(i) Exportation

Insulin and antibiotic drugs may be exported without regard to the requirements in this section if the insulin and antibiotic drugs meet the requirements of section 381(e)(1) of this title.

(June 25, 1938, ch. 675, §802, as added Pub. L. 99–660, title I, §102(2), Nov. 14, 1986, 100 Stat. 3743; amended Pub. L. 104–134, title III, §2102(d)(1), Apr. 26, 1996, 110 Stat. 1321–315; Pub. L. 104–180, title VI, §603(c), Aug. 6, 1996, 110 Stat. 1595; Pub. L. 105–115, title I, §125(c), Nov. 21, 1997, 111 Stat. 2326.)

REFERENCES IN TEXT

Act of March 4, 1913 (known as the Virus-Serum Toxin Act), referred to in subsecs. (a)(1)(A)(ii), (C), (2)(C) and (h), is the eighth paragraph under the heading "Bureau of Animal Industry" of act Mar. 4, 1913, ch. 145, 37 Stat. 832, as amended, which is classified generally to chapter 5 (§151 et seq.) of this title. For complete classification of this Act to the Code, see Short Title note set out under section 151 of this title and Tables.

AMENDMENTS

1997—Subsec. (i). Pub. L. 105–115 added subsec. (i).

1996—Pub. L. 104–134 reenacted section catchline without change and amended text generally. Prior to amendment, text related to exports of certain unapproved products, including provisions relating to drugs intended for human or animal use which required approval or licensing, conditions for export, active pursuit of drug approval or licensing, application for export, contents, approval or disapproval, list of eligible countries for export, and criteria for list change, report to Secretary by holder of approved application, events requiring report, and annual report to Secretary on pursuit of approval of drug, export of drug under approved application prohibited under certain conditions, determination by Secretary of noncompliance, failure of active pursuit of drug approval, imminent hazard of drug to public health, or exportation of drug to non-eligible country, notices, hearings, and prohibition on exportation of drug under certain circumstances, drugs used in prevention or treatment of tropical disease, and reference to Secretary and holder of application.

Subsec. (f)(5). Pub. L. 104–180 substituted "if the labeling of the drug or device is not" for "if the drug or device is not labeled".

[1] So in original. Probably should be subsection "(b)(1)(A)".

§383. Office of International Relations

(a) Establishment

There is established in the Department of Health and Human Services an Office of International Relations.

(b) Agreements with foreign countries

In carrying out the functions of the office under subsection (a) of this section, the Secretary may enter into agreements with foreign countries to facilitate commerce in devices between the United States and such countries consistent with the requirements of this chapter. In such agreements, the Secretary shall encourage the mutual recognition of—

(1) good manufacturing practice regulations promulgated under section 360j(f) of this title, and

(2) other regulations and testing protocols as the Secretary determines to be appropriate.

(c) Harmonizing regulatory requirements

(1) The Secretary shall support the Office of the United States Trade Representative, in consultation with the Secretary of Commerce, in meetings with representatives of other countries to discuss methods and approaches to reduce the burden of regulation and harmonize regulatory requirements if the Secretary determines that such harmonization continues consumer protections consistent with the purposes of this chapter.

(2) The Secretary shall support the Office of the United States Trade Representative, in consultation with the Secretary of Commerce, in efforts to move toward the acceptance of mutual recognition agreements relating to the regulation of drugs, biological products, devices, foods, food additives, and color additives, and the regulation of good manufacturing practices, between the European Union and the United States.

(3) The Secretary shall regularly participate in meetings with representatives of other foreign governments to discuss and reach agreement on methods and approaches to harmonize regulatory requirements.

(4) The Secretary shall, not later than 180 days after November 21, 1997, make public a plan that establishes a framework for achieving mutual recognition of good manufacturing practices inspections.

(5) Paragraphs (1) through (4) shall not apply with respect to products defined in section 321(ff) of this title.

(June 25, 1938, ch. 675, §803, as added Pub. L. 101–629, §15(a), Nov. 28, 1990, 104 Stat. 4525; amended Pub. L. 105–115, title IV, §410(b), Nov. 21, 1997, 111 Stat. 2373.)

AMENDMENTS

1997—Subsec. (c). Pub. L. 105–115 added subsec. (c).

EFFECTIVE DATE OF 1997 AMENDMENT

Amendment by Pub. L. 105–115 effective 90 days after Nov. 21, 1997, except as otherwise provided, see section 501 of Pub. L. 105–115, set out as a note under section 321 of this title.

REPORT ON ACTIVITIES OF OFFICE OF INTERNATIONAL RELATIONS

Section 15(b) of Pub. L. 101–629 directed Secretary of Health and Human Services, not later than 2 years after Nov. 28, 1990, to prepare and submit to the appropriate committees of Congress a report on the activities of the Office of International Relations under 21 U.S.C. 383.

§384. Importation of prescription drugs

(a) Definitions

In this section:

(1) Importer

The term "importer" means a pharmacist or wholesaler.

(2) Pharmacist

The term "pharmacist" means a person licensed by a State to practice pharmacy, including the dispensing and selling of prescription drugs.

(3) Prescription drug

The term "prescription drug" means a drug subject to section 353(b) of this title, other than—

(A) a controlled substance (as defined in section 802 of this title);

(B) a biological product (as defined in section 262 of title 42);

(C) an infused drug (including a peritoneal dialysis solution);

(D) an intravenously injected drug;

(E) a drug that is inhaled during surgery; or

(F) a drug which is a parenteral drug, the importation of which pursuant to subsection (b) of this section is determined by the Secretary to pose a threat to the public health, in which case section 381(d)(1) of this title shall continue to apply.

(4) Qualifying laboratory

The term "qualifying laboratory" means a laboratory in the United States that has been approved by the Secretary for the purposes of this section.

(5) Wholesaler

(A) In general

The term "wholesaler" means a person licensed as a wholesaler or distributor of prescription drugs in the United States under section 353(e)(2)(A) of this title.

(B) Exclusion

The term "wholesaler" does not include a person authorized to import drugs under section 381(d)(1) of this title.

(b) Regulations

The Secretary, after consultation with the United States Trade Representative and the Commissioner of Customs, shall promulgate regulations permitting pharmacists and wholesalers to import prescription drugs from Canada into the United States.

(c) Limitation

The regulations under subsection (b) of this section shall—

(1) require that safeguards be in place to ensure that each prescription drug imported under the regulations complies with section 355 of this title (including with respect to being safe and effective for the intended use of

the prescription drug), with sections 351 and 352 of this title, and with other applicable requirements of this chapter;

(2) require that an importer of a prescription drug under the regulations comply with subsections (d)(1) and (e) of this section; and

(3) contain any additional provisions determined by the Secretary to be appropriate as a safeguard to protect the public health or as a means to facilitate the importation of prescription drugs.

(d) Information and records

(1) In general

The regulations under subsection (b) of this section shall require an importer of a prescription drug under subsection (b) of this section to submit to the Secretary the following information and documentation:

(A) The name and quantity of the active ingredient of the prescription drug.

(B) A description of the dosage form of the prescription drug.

(C) The date on which the prescription drug is shipped.

(D) The quantity of the prescription drug that is shipped.

(E) The point of origin and destination of the prescription drug.

(F) The price paid by the importer for the prescription drug.

(G) Documentation from the foreign seller specifying—

(i) the original source of the prescription drug; and

(ii) the quantity of each lot of the prescription drug originally received by the seller from that source.

(H) The lot or control number assigned to the prescription drug by the manufacturer of the prescription drug.

(I) The name, address, telephone number, and professional license number (if any) of the importer.

(J)(i) In the case of a prescription drug that is shipped directly from the first foreign recipient of the prescription drug from the manufacturer:

(I) Documentation demonstrating that the prescription drug was received by the recipient from the manufacturer and subsequently shipped by the first foreign recipient to the importer.

(II) Documentation of the quantity of each lot of the prescription drug received by the first foreign recipient demonstrating that the quantity being imported into the United States is not more than the quantity that was received by the first foreign recipient.

(III)(aa) In the case of an initial imported shipment, documentation demonstrating that each batch of the prescription drug in the shipment was statistically sampled and tested for authenticity and degradation.

(bb) In the case of any subsequent shipment, documentation demonstrating that a statistically valid sample of the shipment was tested for authenticity and degradation.

(ii) In the case of a prescription drug that is not shipped directly from the first foreign recipient of the prescription drug from the manufacturer, documentation demonstrating that each batch in each shipment offered for importation into the United States was statistically sampled and tested for authenticity and degradation.

(K) Certification from the importer or manufacturer of the prescription drug that the prescription drug—

(i) is approved for marketing in the United States and is not adulterated or misbranded; and

(ii) meets all labeling requirements under this chapter.

(L) Laboratory records, including complete data derived from all tests necessary to ensure that the prescription drug is in compliance with established specifications and standards.

(M) Documentation demonstrating that the testing required by subparagraphs (J) and (L) was conducted at a qualifying laboratory.

(N) Any other information that the Secretary determines is necessary to ensure the protection of the public health.

(2) Maintenance by the Secretary

The Secretary shall maintain information and documentation submitted under paragraph (1) for such period of time as the Secretary determines to be necessary.

(e) Testing

The regulations under subsection (b) of this section shall require—

(1) that testing described in subparagraphs (J) and (L) of subsection (d)(1) of this section be conducted by the importer or by the manufacturer of the prescription drug at a qualified laboratory;

(2) if the tests are conducted by the importer—

(A) that information needed to—

(i) authenticate the prescription drug being tested; and

(ii) confirm that the labeling of the prescription drug complies with labeling requirements under this chapter;

be supplied by the manufacturer of the prescription drug to the pharmacist or wholesaler; and

(B) that the information supplied under subparagraph (A) be kept in strict confidence and used only for purposes of testing or otherwise complying with this chapter; and

(3) may include such additional provisions as the Secretary determines to be appropriate to provide for the protection of trade secrets and commercial or financial information that is privileged or confidential.

(f) Registration of foreign sellers

Any establishment within Canada engaged in the distribution of a prescription drug that is imported or offered for importation into the United States shall register with the Secretary the name and place of business of the establishment and the name of the United States agent for the establishment.

(g) Suspension of importation

The Secretary shall require that importations of a specific prescription drug or importations by a specific importer under subsection (b) of this section be immediately suspended on discovery of a pattern of importation of that specific prescription drug or by that specific importer of drugs that are counterfeit or in violation of any requirement under this section, until an investigation is completed and the Secretary determines that the public is adequately protected from counterfeit and violative prescription drugs being imported under subsection (b) of this section.

(h) Approved labeling

The manufacturer of a prescription drug shall provide an importer written authorization for the importer to use, at no cost, the approved labeling for the prescription drug.

(i) Charitable contributions

Notwithstanding any other provision of this section, section 381(d)(1) of this title continues to apply to a prescription drug that is donated or otherwise supplied at no charge by the manufacturer of the drug to a charitable or humanitarian organization (including the United Nations and affiliates) or to a government of a foreign country.

(j) Waiver authority for importation by individuals

(1) Declarations

Congress declares that in the enforcement against individuals of the prohibition of importation of prescription drugs and devices, the Secretary should—

(A) focus enforcement on cases in which the importation by an individual poses a significant threat to public health; and

(B) exercise discretion to permit individuals to make such importations in circumstances in which—

(i) the importation is clearly for personal use; and

(ii) the prescription drug or device imported does not appear to present an unreasonable risk to the individual.

(2) Waiver authority

(A) In general

The Secretary may grant to individuals, by regulation or on a case-by-case basis, a waiver of the prohibition of importation of a prescription drug or device or class of prescription drugs or devices, under such conditions as the Secretary determines to be appropriate.

(B) Guidance on case-by-case waivers

The Secretary shall publish, and update as necessary, guidance that accurately describes circumstances in which the Secretary will consistently grant waivers on a case-by-case basis under subparagraph (A), so that individuals may know with the greatest practicable degree of certainty whether a particular importation for personal use will be permitted.

(3) Drugs imported from Canada

In particular, the Secretary shall by regulation grant individuals a waiver to permit individuals to import into the United States a prescription drug that—

(A) is imported from a licensed pharmacy for personal use by an individual, not for resale, in quantities that do not exceed a 90-day supply;

(B) is accompanied by a copy of a valid prescription;

(C) is imported from Canada, from a seller registered with the Secretary;

(D) is a prescription drug approved by the Secretary under subchapter V of this chapter;

(E) is in the form of a final finished dosage that was manufactured in an establishment registered under section 360 of this title; and

(F) is imported under such other conditions as the Secretary determines to be necessary to ensure public safety.

(k) Construction

Nothing in this section limits the authority of the Secretary relating to the importation of prescription drugs, other than with respect to section 381(d)(1) of this title as provided in this section.

(*l*) Effectiveness of section

(1) Commencement of program

This section shall become effective only if the Secretary certifies to the Congress that the implementation of this section will—

(A) pose no additional risk to the public's health and safety; and

(B) result in a significant reduction in the cost of covered products to the American consumer.

(2) Termination of program

(A) In general

If, after the date that is 1 year after the effective date of the regulations under subsection (b) of this section and before the date that is 18 months after the effective date, the Secretary submits to Congress a certification that, in the opinion of the Secretary, based on substantial evidence obtained after the effective date, the benefits of implementation of this section do not outweigh any detriment of implementation of this section, this section shall cease to be effective as of the date that is 30 days after the date on which the Secretary submits the certification.

(B) Procedure

The Secretary shall not submit a certification under subparagraph (A) unless, after a hearing on the record under sections 556 and 557 of title 5, the Secretary—

(i)(I) determines that it is more likely than not that implementation of this section would result in an increase in the risk to the public health and safety;

(II) identifies specifically, in qualitative and quantitative terms, the nature of the increased risk;

(III) identifies specifically the causes of the increased risk; and

(IV)(aa) considers whether any measures can be taken to avoid, reduce, or mitigate the increased risk; and

(bb) if the Secretary determines that any measures described in item (aa) would require additional statutory authority, submits to Congress a report describing the legislation that would be required;

(ii) identifies specifically, in qualitative and quantitative terms, the benefits that would result from implementation of this section (including the benefit of reductions in the cost of covered products to consumers in the United States, allowing consumers to procure needed medication that consumers might not otherwise be able to procure without foregoing other necessities of life); and

(iii)(I) compares in specific terms the detriment identified under clause (i) with the benefits identified under clause (ii); and

(II) determines that the benefits do not outweigh the detriment.

(m) Authorization of appropriations

There are authorized to be appropriated such sums as are necessary to carry out this section.

(June 25, 1938, ch. 675, § 804, as added Pub. L. 108–173, title XI, § 1121(a), Dec. 8, 2003, 117 Stat. 2464.)

PRIOR PROVISIONS

A prior section 384, act June 25, 1938, ch. 675, § 804, as added Pub. L. 106–387, § 1(a) [title VII, § 745(c)(2)], Oct. 28, 2000, 114 Stat. 1549, 1549A–36, related to importation of covered products, prior to repeal by Pub. L. 108–173, title XI, § 1121(a), Dec. 8, 2003, 117 Stat. 2464.

TRANSFER OF FUNCTIONS

For transfer of functions, personnel, assets, and liabilities of the United States Customs Service of the Department of the Treasury, including functions of the Secretary of the Treasury relating thereto, to the Secretary of Homeland Security, and for treatment of related references, see sections 203(1), 551(d), 552(d), and 557 of Title 6, Domestic Security, and the Department of Homeland Security Reorganization Plan of November 25, 2002, as modified, set out as a note under section 542 of Title 6.

STUDY AND REPORT ON IMPORTATION OF DRUGS

Pub. L. 108–173, title XI, § 1122, Dec. 8, 2003, 117 Stat. 2469, directed the Secretary of Health and Human Services to conduct a study on the importation of drugs into the United States pursuant to this section and to submit to Congress, not later than 12 months after Dec. 8, 2003, a report providing the findings of such study.

SUBCHAPTER IX—MISCELLANEOUS

§ 391. Separability clause

If any provision of this chapter is declared unconstitutional, or the applicability thereof to any person or circumstances is held invalid, the constitutionality of the remainder of the chapter and the applicability thereof to other persons and circumstances shall not be affected thereby.

(June 25, 1938, ch. 675, § 901, 52 Stat. 1059.)

§ 392. Exemption of meats and meat food products

(a) Law determinative of exemption

Meats and meat food products shall be exempt from the provisions of this chapter to the extent of the application or the extension thereto of the Meat Inspection Act, approved March 4, 1907, as amended [21 U.S.C. 601 et seq.].

(b) Laws unaffected

Nothing contained in this chapter shall be construed as in any way affecting, modifying, repealing, or superseding the provisions of section 351 of Public Health Service Act [42 U.S.C. 262] (relating to viruses, serums, toxins, and analogous products applicable to man); the virus, serum, toxin, and analogous products provisions, applicable to domestic animals, of the Act of Congress approved March 4, 1913 (37 Stat. 832–833) [21 U.S.C. 151 et seq.]; the Filled Cheese Act of June 6, 1896 (U.S.C., 1934 ed., title 26, ch. 10), the Filled Milk Act of March 4, 1923 [21 U.S.C. 61 et seq.]; or the Import Milk Act of February 15, 1927 [21 U.S.C. 141 et seq.].

(June 25, 1938, ch. 675, § 902(b), (c), 52 Stat. 1059; Pub. L. 90–399, § 107, July 13, 1968, 82 Stat. 353.)

REFERENCES IN TEXT

The Meat Inspection Act, approved March 4, 1907, as amended, referred to in subsec. (a), is act Mar. 4, 1907, ch. 2907, titles I to IV, as added Dec. 15, 1967, Pub. L. 90–201, 81 Stat. 584, which are classified generally to subchapters I to IV (§ 601 et seq.) of chapter 12 of this title. For complete classification of this Act to the Code, see Short Title note set out under section 601 of this title and Tables.

Act of March 4, 1913, referred to in subsec. (b), is act Mar. 4, 1913, ch. 145, 37 Stat. 828, as amended. The provisions of such act referred to relating to viruses, etc., applicable to domestic animals, are contained in the eighth paragraph under the heading "Bureau of Animal Industry", 37 Stat. 832, as amended, popularly known as the Virus-Serum-Toxin Act, which is classified generally to chapter 5 (§ 151 et seq.) of this title. For complete classification of this Act to the Code, see Short Title note set out under section 151 of this title and Tables.

The Filled Cheese Act of June 6, 1896 (U.S.C., 1934 ed., title 26, ch. 10), referred to in subsec. (b), is act June 6, 1896, ch. 337, 29 Stat. 253, as amended, which had been classified to chapter 10 (§ 1000 et seq.) of Title 26, Internal Revenue, and included as chapter 17 (§ 2350 et seq.) of Title 26, Internal Revenue Code of 1939. Such chapter 17 was covered by section 4831 et seq. of Title 26, Internal Revenue Code, prior to the repeal of section 4831 et seq. of Title 26 by Pub. L. 93–490, § 3(a)(1), Oct. 26, 1974, 88 Stat. 1466.

The Filled Milk Act of March 4, 1923, referred to in subsec. (b), is act Mar. 4, 1923, ch. 262, 42 Stat. 1486, as amended, which is classified generally to chapter 3 (§ 61 et seq.) of this title. For complete classification of this Act to the Code, see Short Title note set out under section 61 of this title and Tables.

The Import Milk Act of February 15, 1927, referred to in subsec. (b), is act Feb. 15, 1927, ch. 155, 44 Stat. 1101, as amended, which is classified generally to subchapter IV (§ 141 et seq.) of chapter 4 of this title. For complete classification of this Act to the Code, see Short Title note set out under section 141 of this title and Tables.

CODIFICATION

Subsecs. (a) and (b) of this section comprise respectively subsecs. (b) and (c) of section 902 of act June 25, 1938. Subsecs. (a) and (d) of section 902 of act June 25, 1938, which prescribed the effective date of this chapter and made appropriations available, are set out as notes under section 301 of this title and this section, respectively.

AMENDMENTS

1968—Subsec. (b). Pub. L. 90–399 substituted "section 262 of title 42 (relating to viruses, serums, toxins, and analogous products applicable to man)" for "the virus serum, and toxin Act of July 1, 1902" and inserted reference to "the virus, serum, toxin, and analogous products provisions, applicable to domestic animals, of the Act of Congress approved March 4, 1913".

EFFECTIVE DATE OF 1968 AMENDMENT

Amendment by Pub. L. 90–399 effective on first day of thirteenth calendar month after July 13, 1968, see section 108(a) of Pub. L. 90–399, set out as an Effective Date and Transitional Provisions note under section 360b of this title.

AVAILABILITY OF APPROPRIATIONS

Section 902(d) of act June 25, 1938, provided that: "In order to carry out the provisions of this Act which take effect [see section 902(a) of act June 25, 1938, set out as an Effective Date note under section 301 of this title] prior to the repeal of the Food and Drugs Act of June 30, 1906, as amended [sections 1 to 15 of this title], appropriations available for the enforcement of such Act of June 30, 1906, are also authorized to be made available to carry out such provisions."

§393. Food and Drug Administration

(a) In general

There is established in the Department of Health and Human Services the Food and Drug Administration (hereinafter in this section referred to as the "Administration").

(b) Mission

The Administration shall—

(1) promote the public health by promptly and efficiently reviewing clinical research and taking appropriate action on the marketing of regulated products in a timely manner;

(2) with respect to such products, protect the public health by ensuring that—

(A) foods are safe, wholesome, sanitary, and properly labeled;

(B) human and veterinary drugs are safe and effective;

(C) there is reasonable assurance of the safety and effectiveness of devices intended for human use;

(D) cosmetics are safe and properly labeled; and

(E) public health and safety are protected from electronic product radiation;

(3) participate through appropriate processes with representatives of other countries to reduce the burden of regulation, harmonize regulatory requirements, and achieve appropriate reciprocal arrangements; and

(4) as determined to be appropriate by the Secretary, carry out paragraphs (1) through (3) in consultation with experts in science, medicine, and public health, and in cooperation with consumers, users, manufacturers, importers, packers, distributors, and retailers of regulated products.

(c) Interagency collaboration

The Secretary shall implement programs and policies that will foster collaboration between the Administration, the National Institutes of Health, and other science-based Federal agencies, to enhance the scientific and technical expertise available to the Secretary in the conduct of the duties of the Secretary with respect to the development, clinical investigation, evaluation, and postmarket monitoring of emerging medical therapies, including complementary therapies, and advances in nutrition and food science.

(d) Commissioner

(1) Appointment

There shall be in the Administration a Commissioner of Food and Drugs (hereinafter in this section referred to as the "Commissioner") who shall be appointed by the President by and with the advice and consent of the Senate.

(2) General powers

The Secretary, through the Commissioner, shall be responsible for executing this chapter and for—

(A) providing overall direction to the Food and Drug Administration and establishing and implementing general policies respecting the management and operation of programs and activities of the Food and Drug Administration;

(B) coordinating and overseeing the operation of all administrative entities within the Administration;

(C) research relating to foods, drugs, cosmetics, and devices in carrying out this chapter;

(D) conducting educational and public information programs relating to the responsibilities of the Food and Drug Administration; and

(E) performing such other functions as the Secretary may prescribe.

(e) Technical and scientific review groups

The Secretary through the Commissioner of Food and Drugs may, without regard to the provisions of title 5 governing appointments in the competitive service and without regard to the provisions of chapter 51 and subchapter III of chapter 53 of such title relating to classification and General Schedule pay rates, establish such technical and scientific review groups as are needed to carry out the functions of the Administration, including functions under this chapter, and appoint and pay the members of such groups, except that officers and employees of the United States shall not receive additional compensation for service as members of such groups.

(f) Agency plan for statutory compliance

(1) In general

Not later than 1 year after November 21, 1997, the Secretary, after consultation with appropriate scientific and academic experts, health care professionals, representatives of patient and consumer advocacy groups, and the regulated industry, shall develop and publish in the Federal Register a plan bringing the Secretary into compliance with each of the obligations of the Secretary under this chapter. The Secretary shall review the plan biannually and shall revise the plan as necessary, in consultation with such persons.

(2) Objectives of agency plan

The plan required by paragraph (1) shall establish objectives and mechanisms to achieve such objectives, including objectives related to—

(A) maximizing the availability and clarity of information about the process for review of applications and submissions (including petitions, notifications, and any other similar forms of request) made under this chapter;

(B) maximizing the availability and clarity of information for consumers and patients concerning new products;

(C) implementing inspection and postmarket monitoring provisions of this chapter;

(D) ensuring access to the scientific and technical expertise needed by the Secretary to meet obligations described in paragraph (1);

(E) establishing mechanisms, by July 1, 1999, for meeting the time periods specified in this chapter for the review of all applications and submissions described in subparagraph (A) and submitted after November 21, 1997; and

(F) eliminating backlogs in the review of applications and submissions described in subparagraph (A), by January 1, 2000.

(g) Annual report

The Secretary shall annually prepare and publish in the Federal Register and solicit public comment on a report that—

(1) provides detailed statistical information on the performance of the Secretary under the plan described in subsection (f) of this section;

(2) compares such performance of the Secretary with the objectives of the plan and with the statutory obligations of the Secretary; and

(3) identifies any regulatory policy that has a significant negative impact on compliance with any objective of the plan or any statutory obligation and sets forth any proposed revision to any such regulatory policy.

(June 25, 1938, ch. 675, § 903, as added Pub. L. 100–607, title V, § 503(a), Nov. 4, 1988, 102 Stat. 3121; amended Pub. L. 100–690, title II, § 2631, Nov. 18, 1988, 102 Stat. 4244; Pub. L. 105–115, title IV, §§ 406, 414, Nov. 21, 1997, 111 Stat. 2369, 2377.)

REFERENCES IN TEXT

The provisions of title 5 governing appointments in the competitive service, referred to in subsec. (e), are classified generally to section 3301 et seq. of Title 5, Government Organization and Employees.

CODIFICATION

Another section 903 of the Federal Food, Drug, and Cosmetic Act was renumbered section 904 and is classified to section 394 of this title.

AMENDMENTS

1997—Subsec. (b). Pub. L. 105–115, § 406(a)(2), added subsec. (b). Former subsec. (b) redesignated (d).

Subsec. (c). Pub. L. 105–115, § 414, added subsec. (c). Former subsec. (c) redesignated (e).

Subsecs. (d), (e). Pub. L. 105–115, § 406(a)(1), redesignated subsecs. (b) and (c) as (d) and (e), respectively.

Subsecs. (f), (g). Pub. L. 105–115, § 406(b), added subsecs. (f) and (g).

1988—Subsec. (b)(2). Pub. L. 100–690 substituted "shall be responsible for executing this chapter and" for "shall be responsible".

EFFECTIVE DATE OF 1997 AMENDMENT

Amendment by Pub. L. 105–115 effective 90 days after Nov. 21, 1997, except as otherwise provided, see section 501 of Pub. L. 105–115, set out as a note under section 321 of this title.

EFFECTIVE DATE

Section 503(c) of title V of Pub. L. 100–607 provided that:

"(1) Except as provided in paragraph (2), the amendments made by this title [enacting this section and amending sections 5315 and 5316 of Title 5, Government Organization and Employees] shall take effect on the date of enactment of this Act [Nov. 4, 1988].

"(2) Section 903(b)(1) of the Federal Food, Drug, and Cosmetic Act [21 U.S.C. 393(b)(1)] (as added by subsection (a) of this section) shall apply to the appointments of Commissioners of Food and Drugs made after the date of enactment of this Act."

OFFICE OF MINOR USE AND MINOR SPECIES ANIMAL DRUG DEVELOPMENT

Pub. L. 108–282, title I, § 102(b)(7), Aug. 2, 2004, 118 Stat. 905, provided that: "The Secretary of Health and Human Services shall establish within the Center for Veterinary Medicine (of the Food and Drug Administration), an Office of Minor Use and Minor Species Animal Drug Development that reports directly to the Director of the Center for Veterinary Medicine. This office shall be responsible for overseeing the development and legal marketing of new animal drugs for minor uses and minor species. There is authorized to be appropriated to carry out this subsection $1,200,000 for fiscal year 2004 and such sums as may be necessary for each fiscal year thereafter."

REGULATIONS FOR SUNSCREEN PRODUCTS

Section 129 of Pub. L. 105–115 provided that: "Not later than 18 months after the date of enactment of this Act [Nov. 21, 1997], the Secretary of Health and Human Services shall issue regulations for over-the-counter sunscreen products for the prevention or treatment of sunburn."

FDA STUDY OF MERCURY COMPOUNDS IN DRUGS AND FOOD

Section 413 of Pub. L. 105–115 provided that:

"(a) LIST AND ANALYSIS.—The Secretary of Health and Human Services shall, acting through the Food and Drug Administration—

"(1) compile a list of drugs and foods that contain intentionally introduced mercury compounds, and

"(2) provide a quantitative and qualitative analysis of the mercury compounds in the list under paragraph (1).

The Secretary shall compile the list required by paragraph (1) within 2 years after the date of enactment of the Food and Drug Administration Modernization Act of 1997 [Nov. 21, 1997] and shall provide the analysis required by paragraph (2) within 2 years after such date of enactment.

"(b) STUDY.—The Secretary of Health and Human Services, acting through the Food and Drug Administration, shall conduct a study of the effect on humans of the use of mercury compounds in nasal sprays. Such study shall include data from other studies that have been made of such use.

"(c) STUDY OF MERCURY SALES.—

"(1) STUDY.—The Secretary of Health and Human Services, acting through the Food and Drug Administration and subject to appropriations, shall conduct, or shall contract with the Institute of Medicine of the National Academy of Sciences to conduct, a study of the effect on humans of the use of elemental, organic, or inorganic mercury when offered for sale as a drug or dietary supplement. Such study shall, among other things, evaluate—

"(A) the scope of mercury use as a drug or dietary supplement; and

"(B) the adverse effects on health of children and other sensitive populations resulting from exposure to, or ingestion or inhalation of, mercury when so used.

In conducting such study, the Secretary shall consult with the Administrator of the Environmental Protection Agency, the Chair of the Consumer Product Safety Commission, and the Administrator of the Agency for Toxic Substances and Disease Registry, and, to the extent the Secretary believes necessary or appropriate, with any other Federal or private entity.

"(2) REGULATIONS.—If, in the opinion of the Secretary, the use of elemental, organic, or inorganic mercury offered for sale as a drug or dietary supplement poses a threat to human health, the Secretary shall promulgate regulations restricting the sale of mercury intended for such use. At a minimum, such regulations shall be designed to protect the health of children and other sensitive populations from adverse effects resulting from exposure to, or ingestion or inhalation of, mercury. Such regulations, to the extent feasible, should not unnecessarily interfere with the availability of mercury for use in religious ceremonies."

MANAGEMENT ACTIVITIES STUDY

Pub. L. 102–571, title II, §205, Oct. 29, 1992, 106 Stat. 4502, directed Comptroller General to conduct a study of management of activities of the Food and Drug Administration that are related to dietary supplements of vitamins, minerals, herbs, or other similar nutritional substances and submit an interim report to Congress, not later than 6 months after Oct. 29, 1992, with a final report to be submitted not later than 12 months after Oct. 29, 1992.

CONGRESSIONAL FINDINGS

Section 502 of Pub. L. 100–607 provided that: "Congress finds that—

"(1) the public health has been effectively protected by the presence of the Food and Drug Administration during the last eighty years;

"(2) the presence and importance of the Food and Drug Administration must be guaranteed; and

"(3) the independence and integrity of the Food and Drug Administration need to be enhanced in order to ensure the continuing protection of the public health."

§ 393a. Office of Pediatric Therapeutics

(a) Establishment

The Secretary of Health and Human Services shall establish an Office of Pediatric Therapeutics within the Food and Drug Administration.

(b) Duties

The Office of Pediatric Therapeutics shall be responsible for coordination and facilitation of all activities of the Food and Drug Administration that may have any effect on a pediatric population or the practice of pediatrics or may in any other way involve pediatric issues, including increasing pediatric access to medical devices.

(c) Staff

The staff of the Office of Pediatric Therapeutics shall coordinate with employees of the Department of Health and Human Services who exercise responsibilities relating to pediatric therapeutics and shall include—

(1) one or more additional individuals with expertise concerning ethical issues presented by the conduct of clinical research in the pediatric population; and

(2) one or more additional individuals with expertise in pediatrics as may be necessary to perform the activities described in subsection (b) of this section.

(Pub. L. 107–109, §6, Jan. 4, 2002, 115 Stat. 1414; Pub. L. 110–85, title III, §306(a), Sept. 27, 2007, 121 Stat. 864.)

CODIFICATION

Section was enacted as part of the Best Pharmaceuticals for Children Act, and not as part of the Federal Food, Drug, and Cosmetic Act which comprises this chapter.

AMENDMENTS

2007—Subsec. (b). Pub. L. 110–85 inserted ", including increasing pediatric access to medical devices" before period at end.

§ 394. Scientific review groups

Without regard to the provisions of title 5 governing appointments in the competitive service and without regard to the provisions of chapter 51 and subchapter III of chapter 53 of such title relating to classification and General Schedule pay rates, the Commissioner of Food and Drugs may—

(1) establish such technical and scientific review groups as are needed to carry out the functions of the Food and Drug Administration (including functions prescribed under this chapter); and

(2) appoint and pay the members of such groups, except that officers and employees of the United States shall not receive additional compensation for service as members of such groups.

(June 25, 1938, ch. 675, §904, formerly §903, as added Pub. L. 101–635, title III, §301, Nov. 28, 1990, 104 Stat. 4584; renumbered §904, Pub. L. 103–43, title XX, §2006(1), June 10, 1993, 107 Stat. 209.)

REFERENCES IN TEXT

The provisions of title 5 governing appointments in the competitive service, referred to in text, are classified generally to section 3301 et seq. of Title 5, Government Organization and Employees.

§ 395. Loan repayment program

(a) In general

(1) Authority for program

Subject to paragraph (2), the Secretary shall carry out a program of entering into contracts with appropriately qualified health professionals under which such health professionals agree to conduct research, as employees of the Food and Drug Administration, in consideration of the Federal Government agreeing to repay, for each year of such service, not more than $20,000 of the principal and interest of the educational loans of such health professionals.

(2) Limitation

The Secretary may not enter into an agreement with a health professional pursuant to paragraph (1) unless such professional—

(A) has a substantial amount of educational loans relative to income; and

(B) agrees to serve as an employee of the Food and Drug Administration for purposes of paragraph (1) for a period of not less than 3 years.

(b) Applicability of certain provisions

With respect to the National Health Service Corps Loan Repayment Program established in subpart III of part D of title III of the Public Health Service Act [42 U.S.C. 254l et seq.], the provisions of such subpart shall, except as inconsistent with subsection (a) of this section, apply to the program established in such subsection in the same manner and to the same extent as such provisions apply to the National Health Service Corps Loan Repayment Program.

(c) Authorization of appropriations

For the purpose of carrying out this section, there are authorized to be appropriated such sums as may be necessary for each of the fiscal years 1994 through 1996.

(June 25, 1938, ch. 675, § 905, as added Pub. L. 103–43, title XX, § 2006(2), June 10, 1993, 107 Stat. 210.)

REFERENCES IN TEXT

The Public Health Service Act, referred to in subsec. (b), is act July 1, 1944, ch. 373, 58 Stat. 682, as amended. Subpart III of part D of title III of the Act is classified generally to subpart III [§ 254l et seq.] of part D of subchapter II of chapter 6A of Title 42, The Public Health and Welfare. For complete classification of this Act to the Code, see Short Title note set out under section 201 of Title 42 and Tables.

§ 396. Practice of medicine

Nothing in this chapter shall be construed to limit or interfere with the authority of a health care practitioner to prescribe or administer any legally marketed device to a patient for any condition or disease within a legitimate health care practitioner-patient relationship. This section shall not limit any existing authority of the Secretary to establish and enforce restrictions on the sale or distribution, or in the labeling, of a device that are part of a determination of substantial equivalence, established as a condition of approval, or promulgated through regulations. Further, this section shall not change any existing prohibition on the promotion of unapproved uses of legally marketed devices.

(June 25, 1938, ch. 675, § 906, as added Pub. L. 105–115, title II, § 214, Nov. 21, 1997, 111 Stat. 2348.)

EFFECTIVE DATE

Section effective 90 days after Nov. 21, 1997, except as otherwise provided, see section 501 of Pub. L. 105–115, set out as an Effective Date of 1997 Amendment note under section 321 of this title.

§ 397. Contracts for expert review

(a) In general

(1) Authority

The Secretary may enter into a contract with any organization or any individual (who is not an employee of the Department) with relevant expertise, to review and evaluate, for the purpose of making recommendations to the Secretary on, part or all of any application or submission (including a petition, notification, and any other similar form of request) made under this chapter for the approval or classification of an article or made under section 351(a) of the Public Health Service Act (42 U.S.C. 262(a)) with respect to a biological product. Any such contract shall be subject to the requirements of section 379 of this title relating to the confidentiality of information.

(2) Increased efficiency and expertise through contracts

The Secretary may use the authority granted in paragraph (1) whenever the Secretary determines that use of a contract described in paragraph (1) will improve the timeliness of the review of an application or submission described in paragraph (1), unless using such authority would reduce the quality, or unduly increase the cost, of such review. The Secretary may use such authority whenever the Secretary determines that use of such a contract will improve the quality of the review of an application or submission described in paragraph (1), unless using such authority would unduly increase the cost of such review. Such improvement in timeliness or quality may include providing the Secretary increased scientific or technical expertise that is necessary to review or evaluate new therapies and technologies.

(b) Review of expert review

(1) In general

Subject to paragraph (2), the official of the Food and Drug Administration responsible for any matter for which expert review is used pursuant to subsection (a) of this section shall review the recommendations of the organization or individual who conducted the expert review and shall make a final decision regarding the matter in a timely manner.

(2) Limitation

A final decision by the Secretary on any such application or submission shall be made within the applicable prescribed time period for review of the matter as set forth in this chapter or in the Public Health Service Act (42 U.S.C. 201 et seq.).

(June 25, 1938, ch. 675, § 907, as added Pub. L. 105–115, title IV, § 415, Nov. 21, 1997, 111 Stat. 2377.)

REFERENCES IN TEXT

The Public Health Service Act, referred to in subsec. (b)(2), is act July 1, 1944, ch. 373, 58 Stat. 682, as amended, which is classified generally to chapter 6A (§ 201 et seq.) of Title 42, The Public Health and Welfare. For complete classification of this Act to the Code, see Short Title note set out under section 201 of Title 42 and Tables.

EFFECTIVE DATE

Section effective 90 days after Nov. 21, 1997, except as otherwise provided, see section 501 of Pub. L. 105–115, set out as an Effective Date of 1997 Amendment note under section 321 of this title.

§ 398. Notices to States regarding imported food

(a) In general

If the Secretary has credible evidence or information indicating that a shipment of imported food or portion thereof presents a threat of serious adverse health consequences or death to humans or animals, the Secretary shall provide notice regarding such threat to the States in which the food is held or will be held, and to the States in which the manufacturer, packer, or distributor of the food is located, to the extent that the Secretary has knowledge of which States are so involved. In providing notice to a State, the Secretary shall request the State to take such action as the State considers appropriate, if any, to protect the public health regarding the food involved.

(b) Rule of construction

Subsection (a) of this section may not be construed as limiting the authority of the Secretary with respect to food under any other provision of this chapter.

(June 25, 1938, ch. 675, § 908, as added Pub. L. 107–188, title III, § 310, June 12, 2002, 116 Stat. 673.)

§ 399. Grants to States for inspections

(a) In general

The Secretary is authorized to make grants to States, territories, and Indian tribes (as defined in section 450b(e) of title 25) that undertake examinations, inspections, and investigations, and related activities under section 372 of this title. The funds provided under such grants shall only be available for the costs of conducting such examinations, inspections, investigations, and related activities.

(b) Notices regarding adulterated imported food

The Secretary may make grants to the States for the purpose of assisting the States with the costs of taking appropriate action to protect the public health in response to notification under section 398 of this title, including planning and otherwise preparing to take such action.

(c) Authorization of appropriations

For the purpose of carrying out this section, there are authorized to be appropriated $10,000,000 for fiscal year 2002, and such sums as may be necessary for each of the fiscal years 2003 through 2006.

(June 25, 1938, ch. 675, § 909, as added Pub. L. 107–188, title III, § 311, June 12, 2002, 116 Stat. 673.)

§ 399a. Office of the Chief Scientist

(a) Establishment; appointment

The Secretary shall establish within the Office of the Commissioner an office to be known as the Office of the Chief Scientist. The Secretary shall appoint a Chief Scientist to lead such Office.

(b) Duties of the Office

The Office of the Chief Scientist shall—

(1) oversee, coordinate, and ensure quality and regulatory focus of the intramural research programs of the Food and Drug Administration;

(2) track and, to the extent necessary, coordinate intramural research awards made by each center of the Administration or science-based office within the Office of the Commissioner, and ensure that there is no duplication of research efforts supported by the Reagan-Udall Foundation for the Food and Drug Administration;

(3) develop and advocate for a budget to support intramural research;

(4) develop a peer review process by which intramural research can be evaluated;

(5) identify and solicit intramural research proposals from across the Food and Drug Administration through an advisory board composed of employees of the Administration that shall include—

(A) representatives of each of the centers and the science-based offices within the Office of the Commissioner; and

(B) experts on trial design, epidemiology, demographics, pharmacovigilance, basic science, and public health; and

(6) develop postmarket safety performance measures that are as measurable and rigorous as the ones already developed for premarket review.

(June 25, 1938, ch. 675, § 910, as added Pub. L. 110–85, title VI, § 602, Sept. 27, 2007, 121 Stat. 898.)

CHAPTER 10—POULTRY AND POULTRY PRODUCTS INSPECTION

§ 451. Congressional statement of findings

Poultry and poultry products are an important source of the Nation's total supply of food. They are consumed throughout the Nation and the major portion thereof moves in interstate or foreign commerce. It is essential in the public interest that the health and welfare of consumers be protected by assuring that poultry products distributed to them are wholesome, not adulterated, and properly marked, labeled, and packaged. Unwholesome, adulterated, or misbranded poultry products impair the effective regulation of poultry products in interstate or foreign commerce, are injurious to the public welfare, destroy markets for wholesome, not adulterated, and properly labeled and packaged poultry products, and result in sundry losses to poultry producers and processors of poultry and poultry products, as well as injury to consumers. It is hereby found that all articles and poultry which are regulated under this chapter are either in interstate or foreign commerce or substantially affect such commerce, and that regulation by the Secretary of Agriculture and cooperation by the States and other jurisdictions as contemplated by this chapter are appropriate to prevent and eliminate burdens upon such commerce, to effectively regulate such commerce, and to protect the health and welfare of consumers.

(Pub. L. 85–172, §2, Aug. 28, 1957, 71 Stat. 441; Pub. L. 90–492, §2, Aug. 18, 1968, 82 Stat. 791.)

Amendments

1968—Pub. L. 90–492 inserted provisions stating it to be necessary that the health and welfare of consumers be protected by assuring that poultry products distributed to them are wholesome, not adulterated, and properly marked, labeled, and packaged, provisions that misbranded poultry products impair the effective regulation of poultry products and destroy markets for wholesome, not adulterated, and properly labeled and packaged poultry products, and result in sundry losses to poultry producers and processors of poultry and poultry products, as well as injury to consumers, and provisions that all articles and poultry which are regulated by this chapter are either in interstate or foreign commerce or substantially affect such commerce and that regulation by the Secretary of Agriculture and cooperation by the states and other jurisdictions as contemplated by this chapter are appropriate to serve the specified aims, and struck out provisions that all poultry and poultry products which have or are required to have inspection under this chapter are either in the current of interstate or foreign commerce or directly affect such commerce, provisions that that part entering directly into the current of interstate or foreign commerce cannot be effectively inspected and regulated without also inspecting and regulating all poultry and poultry products in the same establishment, and provisions authorizing the Secretary to designate major consuming areas.

Effective Date of 1968 Amendment

Section 20 of Pub. L. 90–492 provided that: "This Act [see Short Title of 1968 Amendment note below] shall become effective upon enactment [Aug. 18, 1968] except as provided in paragraphs (a) through (c):

"(a) The provisions of subparagraphs (a)(2)(A) and (a)(3) of section 9 of the Poultry Products Inspection Act, as amended by section 9 of this Act [section 458(a)(2)(A) and (a)(3) of this title], shall become effective upon the expiration of sixty days after enactment hereof [Aug. 18, 1968].

"(b) Section 14 of this Act, amending section 15 of the Poultry Products Inspection Act [section 464 of this title], shall become effective upon the expiration of sixty days after enactment hereof [Aug. 18, 1968].

"(c) Paragraph 11(d) of the Poultry Products Inspection Act, as added by section 11 of this Act [section 460(d) of this title], shall become effective upon the expiration of sixty days after enactment hereof [Aug. 18, 1968]."

Effective Date

Section 29, formerly section 22, of Pub. L. 85–172, as renumbered by Pub. L. 90–492, §17, Aug. 18, 1968, 82 Stat. 805, provided that: "This Act [this chapter] shall take effect upon enactment [Aug. 28, 1957], except that no person shall be subject to the provisions of this Act [this chapter] prior to January 1, 1959, unless such person after January 1, 1958, applies for and receives inspection for poultry or poultry products in accordance with the provisions of this Act [this chapter] and pursuant to regulations promulgated by the Secretary hereunder, in any establishment processing poultry or poultry products in commerce or in a designated major consuming area. Any person who voluntarily applies for and receives such inspection after January 1, 1958, shall be subject, on and after the date he commences to receive such inspection, to all of the provisions and penalties provided for in this Act [this chapter] with respect to all poultry or poultry products handled in the establishment for which such said application for inspection is made."

Short Title of 1968 Amendment

Section 1 of Pub. L. 90–492 provided: "That this Act [enacting sections 467a to 467f and 470 of this title, amending this section and sections 452 to 461, 463 to 465, and 467 of this title, and enacting provisions set out as notes under this section] may be cited as the 'Wholesome Poultry Products Act'."

Short Title

Section 1 of Pub. L. 85–172 provided: "That this Act [enacting this chapter and provisions set out as notes under this section] may be cited as the 'Poultry Products Inspection Act'."

Separability

Section 19 of Pub. L. 90–492 provided that: "If any provisions of this Act or of the amendments made hereby [see Short Title of 1968 Amendment note above] or the application thereof to any person or circumstances is held invalid, the validity of the remainder of the Act and the remaining amendments and of the application of such provision to other persons and circumstances shall not be affected thereby."

Section 28, formerly section 21, of Pub. L. 85–172, as renumbered by Pub. L. 90–492, §17, Aug. 18, 1968, 82 Stat. 805, provided that: "If any provision of this Act [this chapter] or the application thereof to any person or circumstances is held invalid, the validity of the remainder of the Act and of the application of such provision to other persons and circumstances shall not be affected thereby."

FOOD ADDITIVES AMENDMENT OF 1958

Pub. L. 85–929, §7, Sept. 6, 1958, 72 Stat. 1789, provided that: "Nothing in this Act [amending sections 321, 331, 342, 346, and 348 of this title and section 210 of Title 42, The Public Health and Welfare, and enacting provisions set out as notes under sections 321 and 342 of this title] shall be construed to exempt any meat or meat food product or any person from any requirement imposed by or pursuant to the Poultry Products Inspection Act (21 U.S.C. 451 and the following) [this chapter] or the Meat Inspection Act of March 4, 1907, 34 Stat. 1260, as amended and extended (21 U.S.C. 71 and the following) [see section 601 et seq. of this title]."

§452. Congressional declaration of policy

It is hereby declared to be the policy of the Congress to provide for the inspection of poultry and poultry products and otherwise regulate the processing and distribution of such articles as hereinafter prescribed to prevent the movement or sale in interstate or foreign commerce of, or the burdening of such commerce by, poultry products which are adulterated or misbranded. It is the intent of Congress that when poultry and poultry products are condemned because of disease, the reason for condemnation in such instances shall be supported by scientific fact, information, or criteria, and such condemnation under this chapter shall be achieved through uniform inspection standards and uniform applications thereof.

(Pub. L. 85–172, §3, Aug. 28, 1957, 71 Stat. 441; Pub. L. 90–492, §3, Aug. 18, 1968, 82 Stat. 792.)

AMENDMENTS

1968—Pub. L. 90–492 inserted provisions declaring the policy of Congress to be to otherwise regulate the processing and distribution of poultry and poultry products as hereinafter prescribed so as to prevent the movement or sale in interstate commerce of, or the burdening of such commerce by poultry products which are adulterated or misbranded, and provisions that declared the policy of Congress to be that condemnation of diseased poultry and poultry products shall be achieved through uniform inspection standards and supported by scientific fact or criteria, and struck out provisions that declared the policy of Congress to be to provide for inspection by the inspection service to prevent the movement in interstate commerce or foreign commerce or in a designated major consuming area of poultry products which are unwholesome, adulterated, or otherwise unfit for human food.

EFFECTIVE DATE OF 1968 AMENDMENT

Amendment by Pub. L. 90–492 effective Aug. 18, 1968, see section 20 of Pub. L. 90–492, set out as a note under section 451 of this title.

§453. Definitions

For purposes of this chapter—

(a) The term "commerce" means commerce between any State, any territory, or the District of Columbia, and any place outside thereof; or within any territory not organized with a legislative body, or the District of Columbia.

(b) Except as otherwise provided in this chapter, the term "State" means any State of the United States and the Commonwealth of Puerto Rico.

(c) The term "territory" means Guam, the Virgin Islands of the United States, American Samoa, and any other territory or possession of the United States, excluding the Canal Zone.

(d) The term "United States" means the States, the District of Columbia, and the territories of the United States.

(e) The term "poultry" means any domesticated bird, whether live or dead.

(f) The term "poultry product" means any poultry carcass, or part thereof; or any product which is made wholly or in part from any poultry carcass or part thereof, excepting products which contain poultry ingredients only in a relatively small proportion or historically have not been considered by consumers as products of the poultry food industry, and which are exempted by the Secretary from definition as a poultry product under such conditions as the Secretary may prescribe to assure that the poultry ingredients in such products are not adulterated and that such products are not represented as poultry products.

(g) The term "adulterated" shall apply to any poultry product under one or more of the following circumstances:

(1) if it bears or contains any poisonous or deleterious substance which may render it injurious to health; but in case the substance is not an added substance, such article shall not be considered adulterated under this clause if the quantity of such substance in or on such article does not ordinarily render it injurious to health;

(2)(A) if it bears or contains (by reason of administration of any substance to the live poultry or otherwise) any added poisonous or added deleterious substance (other than one which is (i) a pesticide chemical in or on a raw agricultural commodity; (ii) a food additive; or (iii) a color additive) which may, in the judgment of the Secretary, make such article unfit for human food;

(B) if it is, in whole or in part, a raw agricultural commodity and such commodity bears or contains a pesticide chemical which is unsafe within the meaning of section 346a of this title;

(C) if it bears or contains any food additive which is unsafe within the meaning of section 348 of this title;

(D) if it bears or contains any color additive which is unsafe within the meaning of section 379e of this title: *Provided*, That an article which is not otherwise deemed adulterated under clause (B), (C), or (D) shall nevertheless be deemed adulterated if use of the pesticide chemical, food additive, or color additive in or on such article is prohibited by regulations of the Secretary in official establishments;

(3) if it consists in whole or in part of any filthy, putrid, or decomposed substance or is for any other reason unsound, unhealthful, unwholesome, or otherwise unfit for human food;

(4) if it has been prepared, packed, or held under insanitary conditions whereby it may have become contaminated with filth, or whereby it may have been rendered injurious to health;

(5) if it is, in whole or in part, the product of any poultry which has died otherwise than by slaughter;

(6) if its container is composed, in whole or in part, of any poisonous or deleterious substance which may render the contents injurious to health;

(7) if it has been intentionally subjected to radiation, unless the use of the radiation was in conformity with a regulation or exemption in effect pursuant to section 348 of this title;

(8) if any valuable constituent has been in whole or in part omitted or abstracted therefrom; or if any substance has been substituted, wholly or in part therefor; or if damage or inferiority has been concealed in any manner; or if any substance has been added thereto or mixed or packed therewith so as to increase its bulk or weight, or reduce its quality or strength, or make it appear better or of greater value than it is.

(h) The term "misbranded" shall apply to any poultry product under one or more of the following circumstances:

(1) if its labeling is false or misleading in any particular;

(2) if it is offered for sale under the name of another food;

(3) if it is an imitation of another food, unless its label bears, in type of uniform size and prominence, the word "imitation" and immediately thereafter, the name of the food imitated;

(4) if its container is so made, formed, or filled as to be misleading;

(5) unless it bears a label showing (A) the name and the place of business of the manufacturer, packer, or distributor; and (B) an accurate statement of the quantity of the product in terms of weight, measure, or numerical count: *Provided*, That under clause (B) of this subparagraph (5), reasonable variations may be permitted, and exemptions as to small packages or articles not in packages or other containers may be established by regulations prescribed by the Secretary;

(6) if any word, statement, or other information required by or under authority of this chapter to appear on the label or other labeling is not prominently placed thereon with such conspicuousness (as compared with other words, statements, designs, or devices, in the labeling) and in such terms as to render it likely to be read and understood by the ordinary individual under customary conditions of purchase and use;

(7) if it purports to be or is represented as a food for which a definition and standard of identity or composition has been prescribed by regulations of the Secretary under section 457 of this title unless (A) it conforms to such definition and standard, and (B) its label bears the name of the food specified in the definition and standard and, insofar as may be required by such regulations, the common names of optional ingredients (other than spices, flavoring, and coloring) present in such food;

(8) if it purports to be or is represented as a food for which a standard or standards of fill of container have been prescribed by regulations of the Secretary under section 457 of this title, and it falls below the standard of fill of container applicable thereto, unless its label bears, in such manner and form as such regulations specify, a statement that it falls below such standard;

(9) if it is not subject to the provisions of subparagraph (7), unless its label bears (A) the common or usual name of the food, if any there be, and (B) in case it is fabricated from two or more ingredients, the common or usual name of each such ingredient; except that spices, flavorings, and colorings may, when authorized by the Secretary, be designated as spices, flavorings, and colorings without naming each: *Provided*, That to the extent that compliance with the requirements of clause (B) of this subparagraph (9) is impracticable or results in deception or unfair competition, exemptions shall be established by regulations promulgated by the Secretary;

(10) if it purports to be or is represented for special dietary uses unless its label bears such information concerning its vitamin, mineral, and other dietary properties as the Secretary, after consultation with the Secretary of Health and Human Services, determines to be, and by regulations prescribes as, necessary in order fully to inform purchasers as to its value for such uses;

(11) if it bears or contains any artificial flavoring, artificial coloring, or chemical preservative unless it bears labeling stating that fact: *Provided*, That, to the extent that compliance with the requirements of this subparagraph (11) is impracticable, exemptions shall be established by regulations promulgated by the Secretary; or

(12) if it fails to bear on its containers, and in the case of nonconsumer packaged carcasses (if the Secretary so requires) directly thereon, as the Secretary may by regulations prescribe, the official inspection legend and official establishment number of the establishment where the article was processed, and, unrestricted by any of the foregoing, such other information as the Secretary may require in such regulations to assure that it will not have false or misleading labeling and that the public will be informed of the manner of handling required to maintain the article in a wholesome condition.

(i) The term "Secretary" means the Secretary of Agriculture or his delegate.

(j) The term "person" means any individual, partnership, corporation, association, or other business unit.

(k) The term "inspector" means: (1) an employee or official of the United States Government authorized by the Secretary to inspect poultry and poultry products under the authority of this chapter, or (2) any employee or official of the government of any State or territory or the District of Columbia authorized by the Secretary to inspect poultry and poultry products under authority of this chapter, under an agreement entered into between the Secretary and the appropriate State or other agency.

(*l*) The term "official mark" means the official inspection legend or any other symbol prescribed by regulation of the Secretary to identify the status of any article or poultry under this chapter.

(m) The term "official inspection legend" means any symbol prescribed by regulations of the Secretary showing that an article was inspected for wholesomeness in accordance with this chapter.

(n) The term "official certificate" means any certificate prescribed by regulations of the Secretary for issuance by an inspector or other person performing official functions under this chapter.

(*o*) The term "official device" means any device prescribed or authorized by the Secretary for use in applying any official mark.

(p) The term "official establishment" means any establishment as determined by the Secretary at which inspection of the slaughter of poultry, or the processing of poultry products, is maintained under the authority of this chapter.

(q) The term "inspection service" means the official Government service within the Department of Agriculture designated by the Secretary as having the responsibility for carrying out the provisions of this chapter.

(r) The term "container" or "package" includes any box, can, tin, cloth, plastic, or other receptacle, wrapper, or cover.

(s) The term "label" means a display of written, printed, or graphic matter upon any article or the immediate container (not including package liners) of any article; and the term "labeling" means all labels and other written, printed, or graphic matter (1) upon any article or any of its containers or wrappers, or (2) accompanying such article.

(t) The term "shipping container" means any container used or intended for use in packaging the product packed in an immediate container.

(u) The term "immediate container" includes any consumer package; or any other container in which poultry products, not consumer packaged, are packed.

(v) The term "capable of use as human food" shall apply to any carcass, or part or product of a carcass, of any poultry, unless it is denatured or otherwise identified as required by regulations prescribed by the Secretary to deter its use as human food, or it is naturally inedible by humans.

(w) The term "processed" means slaughtered, canned, salted, stuffed, rendered, boned, cut up, or otherwise manufactured or processed.

(x) The term "Federal Food, Drug, and Cosmetic Act" means the Act so entitled, approved June 25, 1938 (52 Stat. 1040) [21 U.S.C. 301 et seq.], and Acts amendatory thereof or supplementary thereto.

(y) The terms "pesticide chemical", "food additive", "color additive", and "raw agricultural commodity" shall have the same meanings for purposes of this chapter as under the Federal Food, Drug, and Cosmetic Act [21 U.S.C. 301 et seq.].

(z) The term "poultry products broker" means any person engaged in the business of buying or selling poultry products on commission, or otherwise negotiating purchases or sales of such articles other than for his own account or as an employee of another person.

(aa) The term "renderer" means any person engaged in the business of rendering carcasses, or parts or products of the carcasses, of poultry, except rendering conducted under inspection or exemption under this chapter.

(bb) The term "animal food manufacturer" means any person engaged in the business of manufacturing or processing animal food derived wholly or in part from carcasses, or parts or products of the carcasses, of poultry.

(Pub. L. 85–172, §4, Aug. 28, 1957, 71 Stat. 441; Pub. L. 87–498, June 25, 1962, 76 Stat. 110; Pub. L. 90–492, §4, Aug. 18, 1968, 82 Stat. 792; Pub. L. 96–88, title V, §509(b), Oct. 17, 1979, 93 Stat. 695; Pub. L. 102–571, title I, §107(13), Oct. 29, 1992, 106 Stat. 4499.)

REFERENCES IN TEXT

The Federal Food, Drug, and Cosmetic Act, referred to in pars. (x) and (y), is act June 25, 1938, ch. 675, 52 Stat. 1040, as amended, which is classified generally to chapter 9 (§301 et seq.) of this title. For complete classification of this Act to the Code, see section 301 of this title and Tables.

AMENDMENTS

1992—Subsec. (g)(2)(D). Pub. L. 102–571 substituted "379e" for "376".

1968—Pub. L. 90–492 inserted definitions of "State", "territory", "United States", "misbranded", "official mark", "official inspection legend", "official certificate", "official device", "capable of use as human food", "processed", "Federal Food, Drug, and Cosmetic Act", "pesticide chemical", "poultry products broker", "renderer", and "animal food manufacturer", revised definitions of "commerce", "poultry", "poultry product", "adulterated", "Secretary", "inspector", "container" or "package", "label", and "immediate container", reenacted without change definitions of "person", "official establishment", "inspection service", and "shipping container", and deleted definition of "wholesome", "unwholesome", and "official inspection mark".

1962—Par. (a). Pub. L. 87–498 struck out references to Territories or possessions, and inserted definition of "State".

CHANGE OF NAME

"Secretary of Health and Human Services" substituted for "Secretary of Health, Education, and Welfare" in par. (h)(10) pursuant to section 509(b) of Pub. L. 96–88, which is classified to section 3508(b) of Title 20, Education.

EFFECTIVE DATE OF 1968 AMENDMENT

Amendment by Pub. L. 90–492 effective Aug. 18, 1968, see section 20 of Pub. L. 90–492, set out as a note under section 451 of this title.

§454. Federal and State cooperation in development and administration of State poultry product inspection programs

(a) State laws; planning, technical and financial assistance; advisory committees

It is the policy of the Congress to protect the consuming public from poultry products that are adulterated or misbranded and to assist in efforts by State and other government agencies to accomplish this objective. In furtherance of this policy—

(1) The Secretary is authorized, whenever he determines that it would effectuate the purposes of this chapter, to cooperate with the appropriate State agency in developing and administering a State poultry product inspection program in any State which has enacted a mandatory State poultry product inspection law that imposes ante mortem and post mortem inspection, reinspection and sanita-

tion requirements that are at least equal to those under this chapter, with respect to all or certain classes of persons engaged in the State in slaughtering poultry or processing poultry products for use as human food solely for distribution within such State.

(2) The Secretary is further authorized, whenever he determines that it would effectuate the purposes of this chapter, to cooperate with appropriate State agencies in developing and administering State programs under State laws containing authorities at least equal to those provided in section 460 of this title; and to cooperate with other agencies of the United States in carrying out any provisions of this chapter. In carrying out the provisions of this chapter, the Secretary may conduct such examinations, investigations, and inspections as he determines practicable through any officer or employee of any State or Territory or the District of Columbia commissioned by the Secretary for such purpose.

(3) Cooperation with State agencies under this section may include furnishing to the appropriate State agency (i) advisory assistance in planning and otherwise developing an adequate State program under the State law; and (ii) technical and laboratory assistance and training (including necessary curricular and instructional materials and equipment), and financial and other aid for administration of such a program. The amount to be contributed to any State by the Secretary under this section from Federal funds for any year shall not exceed 50 per centum of the estimated total cost of the cooperative program; and the Federal funds shall be allocated among the States desiring to cooperate on an equitable basis. Such cooperation and payment shall be contingent at all times upon the administration of the State program in a manner which the Secretary, in consultation with the appropriate advisory committee appointed under subparagraph (4), deems adequate to effectuate the purposes of this section.

(4) The Secretary may appoint advisory committees consisting of such representatives of appropriate State agencies as the Secretary and the State agencies may designate to consult with him concerning State and Federal programs with respect to poultry product inspection and other matters within the scope of this chapter, including evaluating State programs for purposes of this chapter, and obtaining better coordination and more uniformity among the State programs and between the Federal and State programs and adequate protection of consumers.

(b) Appropriate State agency; performance of functions by subordinate governmental unit

The appropriate State agency with which the Secretary may cooperate under this chapter shall be a single agency in the State which is primarily responsible for the coordination of the State programs having objectives similar to those under this chapter. When the State program includes performance of certain functions by a municipality or other subordinate governmental unit, such unit shall be deemed to be a part of the State agency for purposes of this section.

(c) Intrastate activities; designation of State for regulation; publication of designation; exempted operations; termination of designation; review of operations in nondesignated States; annual report

(1) If the Secretary has reason to believe, by thirty days prior to the expiration of two years after August 18, 1968, that a State has failed to develop or is not enforcing, with respect to all establishments within its jurisdiction (except those that would be exempted from Federal inspection under subparagraph (2) of this paragraph (c)) at which poultry are slaughtered, or poultry products are processed for use as human food, solely for distribution within such State, and the products of such establishments, requirements at least equal to those imposed under sections 451 to 453, 455 to 459, 461 to 467d of this title, he shall promptly notify the Governor of the State of this fact. If the Secretary determines, after consultation with the Governor of the State, or representative selected by him, that such requirements have not been developed and activated, he shall promptly after the expiration of such two-year period designate such State as one in which the provisions of said sections of this chapter shall apply to operations and transactions wholly within such State: *Provided*, That if the Secretary has reason to believe that the State will activate such requirements within one additional year, he may delay such designation for said period, and not designate the State, if he determines at the end of the year that the State then has such requirements in effective operation. The Secretary shall publish any such designation in the Federal Register and, upon the expiration of thirty days after such publication, the provisions of said sections of this chapter shall apply to operations and transactions and to persons engaged therein in the State to the same extent and in the same manner as if such operations and transactions were conducted in or for commerce. However, notwithstanding any other provision of this section, if the Secretary determines that any establishment within a State is producing adulterated poultry products for distribution within such State which would clearly endanger the public health he shall notify the Governor of the State and the appropriate advisory committee provided for by subparagraph (a)(4) of this section of such fact for effective action under State or local law. If the State does not take action to prevent such endangering of the public health within a reasonable time after such notice, as determined by the Secretary, in light of the risk to public health, the Secretary may forthwith designate any such establishment as subject to the provisions of said sections of this chapter, and thereupon the establishment and operator thereof shall be subject to such provisions as though engaged in commerce until such time as the Secretary determines that such State has developed and will enforce requirements at least equal to those imposed under said sections.

(2) The provisions of this chapter requiring inspection of the slaughter of poultry and the processing of poultry products shall not apply to operations of types traditionally and usually conducted at retail stores and restaurants, when

conducted at any retail store or restaurant or similar retail-type establishment for sale in normal retail quantities or service of such articles to consumers at such establishments if such establishments are subject to such inspection provisions only under this paragraph (c). For the purposes of this subparagraph, operations conducted at a restaurant central kitchen facility shall be considered as being conducted at a restaurant if the restaurant central kitchen prepares poultry products that are ready to eat when they leave such facility and are served in meals or as entrees only to customers at restaurants owned or operated by the same person owning or operating such facility: *Provided*, That such facility shall be subject to the provisions of section 460(b) of this title: *Provided further*, That the facility may be subject to the inspection requirements of this chapter for as long as the Secretary deems necessary, if the Secretary determines that the sanitary conditions or practices of the facility or the processing procedures or methods at the facility are such that any of its poultry products are rendered adulterated.

(3) Whenever the Secretary determines that any State designated under this paragraph (c) has developed and will enforce State poultry products inspection requirements at least equal to those imposed under the aforesaid sections of this chapter, with respect to the operations and transactions within such State which are regulated under subparagraph (1) of this paragraph (c), he shall terminate the designation of such State under this paragraph (c), but this shall not preclude the subsequent redesignation of the State at any time upon thirty days' notice to the Governor and publication in the Federal Register in accordance with this paragraph, and any State may be designated upon such notice and publication, at any time after the period specified in this paragraph whether or not the State has theretofore been designated, upon the Secretary determining that it is not effectively enforcing requirements at least equal to those imposed under said sections.

(4) The Secretary shall promptly upon August 18, 1968, and periodically thereafter, but at least annually, review the requirements, including the enforcement thereof, of the several States not designated under this paragraph (c), with respect to the slaughter, and the processing, storage, handling, and distribution of poultry products, and inspection of such operations, and annually report thereon to the Committee on Agriculture of the House of Representatives and the Committee on Agriculture, Nutrition, and Forestry of the Senate in the report required in section 470[1] of this title.

(d) "State" defined

As used in this section, the term "State" means any State (including the Commonwealth of Puerto Rico) or organized territory.

(Pub. L. 85–172, §5, Aug. 28, 1957, 71 Stat. 443; Pub. L. 90–492, §5, Aug. 18, 1968, 82 Stat. 796; Pub. L. 98–487, §2, Oct. 17, 1984, 98 Stat. 2264; Pub. L. 103–437, §8(1), Nov. 2, 1994, 108 Stat. 4588.)

[1] See References in Text note below.

REFERENCES IN TEXT

Section 470 of this title, referred to in subsec. (c)(4), was omitted from the Code.

CODIFICATION

In par. (c)(1), (4), "August 18, 1968" substituted for "enactment of the Wholesome Poultry Products Act".

AMENDMENTS

1994—Subsec. (c)(4). Pub. L. 103–437 substituted "Agriculture, Nutrition, and Forestry" for "Agriculture and Forestry".

1984—Par. (c)(2). Pub. L. 98–487 inserted provisions relating to operations conducted at a restaurant central kitchen facility.

1968—Pub. L. 90–492 substituted provisions authorizing the Secretary to cooperate with the appropriate state agency in the development and administration of state poultry product inspection programs in those states having mandatory poultry product inspection laws and those states having laws at least equal to the provisions of section 460 of this title, provisions authorizing planning, technical and financial assistance and the appointment of advisory committees, provisions designating the appropriate state agency with which the Secretary may cooperate, provisions authorizing the Secretary to designate states as subject to the regulatory provisions of this chapter when the requirements of the specified section have not been complied with or when the specified intrastate activities are present, provisions exempting from the requirements of this chapter operations of the types traditionally and usually conducted at retail stores and restaurants, provisions authorizing the Secretary to terminate the aforementioned designation of states as subject to the regulatory provisions of this chapter, and provisions authorizing the Secretary to review the operations in nondesignated states and make an annual report thereon, for provisions authorizing the Secretary, upon application by any appropriate state or local official or agency or by any appropriate local poultry industry group and after public hearing, to designate major consuming areas as subject to the regulatory provisions of this chapter where the Secretary finds that poultry or poultry products are handled or consumed in such volume as to affect, burden or obstruct the movement of inspected poultry products in interstate commerce.

EFFECTIVE DATE OF 1968 AMENDMENT

Amendment by Pub. L. 90–492 effective Aug. 18, 1968, see section 20 of Pub. L. 90–492, set out as a note under section 451 of this title.

§ 455. Inspection in official establishments

(a) Ante mortem inspection

For the purpose of preventing the entry into or flow or movement in commerce of, or the burdening of commerce by, any poultry product which is capable of use as human food and is adulterated, the Secretary shall, where and to the extent considered by him necessary, cause to be made by inspectors ante mortem inspection of poultry in each official establishment processing poultry or poultry products for commerce or otherwise subject to inspection under this chapter.

(b) Post mortem inspection; quarantine, segregation, and reinspection

The Secretary, whenever processing operations are being conducted, shall cause to be made by inspectors post mortem inspection of the carcass of each bird processed, and at any time such quarantine, segregation, and reinspection as he deems necessary of poultry and poultry products capable of use as human food in each official establishment processing such poultry or poultry products for commerce or otherwise subject to inspection under this chapter.

(c) Condemnation; appeal; reprocessing

All poultry carcasses and parts thereof and other poultry products found to be adulterated shall be condemned and shall, if no appeal be taken from such determination of condemnation, be destroyed for human food purposes under the supervision of an inspector: *Provided*, That carcasses, parts, and products, which may by reprocessing be made not adulterated, need not be so condemned and destroyed if so reprocessed under the supervision of an inspector and thereafter found to be not adulterated. If an appeal be taken from such determination, the carcasses, parts, or products shall be appropriately marked and segregated pending completion of an appeal inspection, which appeal shall be at the cost of the appellant if the Secretary determines that the appeal is frivolous. If the determination of condemnation is sustained the carcasses, parts, and products shall be destroyed for human food purposes under the supervision of an inspector.

(Pub. L. 85–172, §6, Aug. 28, 1957, 71 Stat. 443; Pub. L. 90–492, §6, Aug. 18, 1968, 82 Stat. 798.)

AMENDMENTS

1968—Par. (a). Pub. L. 90–492, §6(a), substituted "of, or the burdening of commerce by, any poultry product which is capable of use as human food and is adulterated," for "or a designated major consuming area of any poultry product which is unwholesome or adulterated," "each official establishment" for "any official establishment", and "otherwise subject to inspection under this chapter" for "in, or for marketing in a designated city or area".

Par. (b). Pub. L. 90–492, §6(b), substituted "segregation, and reinspection" for "segregation, reinspection", and "otherwise subject to inspection under this chapter" for "in, or for marketing in a designated city or area", and inserted "capable of use as human food" after "necessary of poultry and poultry products".

Par. (c). Pub. L. 90–492, §6(c), inserted "other" before "poultry products", and substituted "to be adulterated" for "to be unwholesome or adulterated", "made not adulterated" for "made not unwholesome and not adulterated", and "to be not adulterated" for "to be not unwholesome and not adulterated".

EFFECTIVE DATE OF 1968 AMENDMENT

Amendment by Pub. L. 90–492 effective Aug. 18, 1968, see section 20 of Pub. L. 90–492, set out as a note under section 451 of this title.

APPLICABILITY OF CHAPTER REQUIREMENTS TO BIRDS OF THE ORDER RATITAE

Pub. L. 106–387, §1(a) [title VII, §752], Oct. 28, 2000, 114 Stat. 1549, 1549A–41, provided that: "Effective 180 days after the date of the enactment of this Act [Oct. 28, 2000] and continuing for the remainder of fiscal year 2001 and each subsequent fiscal year, establishments in the United States that slaughter or process birds of the order Ratitae, such as ostriches, emus and rheas, and squab, for distribution in commerce as human food shall be subject to the ante mortem and post mortem inspection, reinspection, and sanitation requirements of the Poultry Products Inspection Act (21 U.S.C. 451 et seq.) rather than the voluntary poultry inspection program of the Department of Agriculture under section 203 of the Agricultural Marketing Act of 1946 (7 U.S.C. 1622)."

§456. Operation of premises, facilities and equipment

(a) Sanitary practices

Each official establishment slaughtering poultry or processing poultry products for commerce or otherwise subject to inspection under this chapter shall have such premises, facilities, and equipment, and be operated in accordance with such sanitary practices, as are required by regulations promulgated by the Secretary for the purpose of preventing the entry into or flow or movement in commerce or burdensome effect upon commerce, of poultry products which are adulterated.

(b) Refusal of inspection

The Secretary shall refuse to render inspection to any establishment whose premises, facilities, or equipment, or the operation thereof, fail to meet the requirements of this section.

(Pub. L. 85–172, §7, Aug. 28, 1957, 71 Stat. 444; Pub. L. 90–492, §7, Aug. 18, 1968, 82 Stat. 799.)

AMENDMENTS

1968—Par. (a). Pub. L. 90–492 substituted "otherwise subject to inspection under this chapter" for "in or for marketing in a designated major consuming area", "burdensome effect upon commerce" for "in a designated major consuming area", and "which are adulterated" for "which are unwholesome or adulterated".

EFFECTIVE DATE OF 1968 AMENDMENT

Amendment by Pub. L. 90–492 effective Aug. 18, 1968, see section 20 of Pub. L. 90–492, set out as a note under section 451 of this title.

§457. Labeling and container standards

(a) Requirements for shipping containers and immediate containers; nonconsumer packaged carcasses

All poultry products inspected at any official establishment under the authority of this chapter and found to be not adulterated, shall at the time they leave the establishment bear, in distinctly legible form, on their shipping containers and immediate containers as the Secretary may require, the information required under paragraph (h) of section 453 of this title. In addition, the Secretary whenever he determines such action is practicable and necessary for the protection of the public, may require nonconsumer packaged carcasses at the time they leave the establishment to bear directly thereon in distinctly legible form any information required under such paragraph (h).

(b) Labeling requirements; definitions and standards of identity or composition or articles and standards of fill of container; standards consistent with Federal Food, Drug, and Cosmetic Act; consistency between Federal and State standards

The Secretary, whenever he determines such action is necessary for the protection of the public, may prescribe: (1) the styles and sizes of type to be used with respect to material required to be incorporated in labeling to avoid false or misleading labeling in marketing and labeling any articles or poultry subject to this chapter; (2) definitions and standards of identity or composition or articles subject to this chapter and standards of fill of container for such articles not inconsistent with any such standards established under the Federal Food, Drug, and Cosmetic Act [21 U.S.C. 301 et seq.], and there shall be consultation between the Secretary and the Secretary of Health and Human Services prior to the issuance of such standards under either Act relating to articles subject to this chapter to avoid inconsistency in such standards and possible impairment of the coordinated effective administration of this chapter and the Federal Food, Drug, and Cosmetic Act. There shall also be consultation between the Secretary and an appropriate advisory committee provided for in section 454 of this title, prior to the issuance of such standards under this chapter, to avoid, insofar as feasible, inconsistency between Federal and State standards.

(c) Use of trade names; false or misleading marking or labeling; misleading form or size of container

No article subject to this chapter shall be sold or offered for sale by any person in commerce, under any name or other marking or labeling which is false or misleading, or in any container of a misleading form or size, but established trade names and other marking and labeling and containers which are not false or misleading and which are approved by the Secretary are permitted.

(d) Withholding use of false or misleading mark, label, or container size or form; modification; hearing; conclusiveness of determination; appeal

If the Secretary has reason to believe that any marking or labeling or the size or form of any container in use or proposed for use with respect to any article subject to this chapter is false or misleading in any particular, he may direct that such use be withheld unless the marking, labeling, or container is modified in such manner as he may prescribe so that it will not be false or misleading. If the person using or proposing to use the marketing, labeling, or container does not accept the determination of the Secretary, such person may request a hearing, but the use of the marking, labeling, or container shall, if the Secretary so directs, be withheld pending hearing and final determination by the Secretary. Any such determination by the Secretary shall be conclusive unless, within thirty days after receipt of notice of such final determination, the person adversely affected thereby appeals to the United States Court of Appeals for the circuit in which such person has its principal place of business or to the United States Court of Appeals for the District of Columbia Circuit. The provisions of section 194 of title 7 shall be applicable to appeals taken under this section.

(Pub. L. 85–172, §8, Aug. 28, 1957, 71 Stat. 444; Pub. L. 90–492, §8, Aug. 18, 1968, 82 Stat. 799; Pub. L. 96–88, title V, §509(b), Oct. 17, 1979, 93 Stat. 695.)

REFERENCES IN TEXT

The Federal Food, Drug, and Cosmetic Act, referred to in par. (b), is act June 25, 1938, ch. 675, 52 Stat. 1040, as amended, which is classified generally to chapter 9 (§301 et seq.) of this title. For complete classification of this Act to the Code, see section 301 of this title and Tables.

AMENDMENTS

1968—Par. (a). Pub. L. 90–492 substituted provisions requiring shipping containers and immediate containers, as the Secretary may order, to bear the information required under section 453(h) of this title, and provisions, whenever the Secretary determines such action to be practicable and necessary, requiring nonconsumer packaged carcasses at the time they leave the official establishment to bear the information required under the aforementioned section, for provisions requiring shipping containers to bear the official mark and the approved plant number of the official establishment in which the contents were processed, provisions requiring immediate containers to bear the official inspection mark, the name of the product, a statement of ingredients, the net weight or other appropriate measure of the contents, the name and address of the processor, and the approved plant number of the official establishment in which the contents were processed, and provisions authorizing the Secretary to make reasonable variations and grant exemptions from the foregoing labeling requirements.

Par. (b). Pub. L. 90–492 added par. (b). Provisions of former par. (b) were redesignated as pars. (c) and (d).

Par. (c). Pub. L. 90–492 redesignated part of provisions of former par. (b) as (c) and made changes in phraseology.

Par. (d). Pub. L. 90–492 redesignated part of provisions of former par. (b) as (d) and extended the authority of the Secretary to withhold from use products which have false or misleading markings or containers.

CHANGE OF NAME

"Secretary of Health and Human Services" substituted for "Secretary of Health, Education, and Welfare" in par. (b) pursuant to section 509(b) of Pub. L. 96–88, which is classified to section 3508(b) of Title 20, Education.

EFFECTIVE DATE OF 1968 AMENDMENT

Amendment by Pub. L. 90–492 effective Aug. 18, 1968, see section 20 of Pub. L. 90–492, set out as a note under section 451 of this title.

§ 458. Prohibited acts

(a) No person shall—

(1) slaughter any poultry or process any poultry products which are capable of use as human food at any establishment processing any such articles for commerce, except in compliance with the requirements of this chapter;

(2) sell, transport, offer for sale or transportation, or receive for transportation, in commerce, (A) any poultry products which are capable of use as human food and are adulterated or misbranded at the time of such sale, transportation, offer for sale or transportation, or receipt for transportation; or (B) any poultry products required to be inspected under this chapter unless they have been so inspected and passed;

(3) do, with respect to any poultry products which are capable of use as human food, any act while they are being transported in commerce or held for sale after such transportation, which is intended to cause or has the effect of causing such products to be adulterated or misbranded;

(4) sell, transport, offer for sale or transportation, or receive for transportation, in commerce or from an official establishment, any

slaughtered poultry from which the blood, feathers, feet, head, or viscera have not been removed in accordance with regulations promulgated by the Secretary, except as may be authorized by regulations of the Secretary;

(5) use to his own advantage, or reveal other than to the authorized representatives of the United States Government or any State or other government in their official capacity, or as ordered by a court in any judicial proceedings, any information acquired under the authority of this chapter concerning any matter which is entitled to protection as a trade secret.

(b) No brand manufacturer, printer, or other person shall cast, print, lithograph, or otherwise make any device containing any official mark or simulation thereof, or any label bearing any such mark or simulation, or any form of official certificate or simulation thereof, except as authorized by the Secretary.

(c) No person shall—

(1) forge any official device, mark, or certificate;

(2) without authorization from the Secretary use any official device, mark, or certificate, or simulation thereof, or alter, detach, deface, or destroy any official device, mark, or certificate;

(3) contrary to the regulations prescribed by the Secretary, fail to use, or to detach, deface, or destroy any official device, mark, or certificate;

(4) knowingly possess, without promptly notifying the Secretary or his representative, any official device or any counterfeit, simulated, forged, or improperly altered official certificate or any device or label or any carcass of any poultry, or part or product thereof, bearing any counterfeit, simulated, forged, or improperly altered official mark;

(5) knowingly make any false statement in any shipper's certificate or other nonofficial or official certificate provided for in the regulations prescribed by the Secretary; or

(6) knowingly represent that any article has been inspected and passed, or exempted, under this chapter when, in fact, it has respectively, not been so inspected and passed, or exempted.

(Pub. L. 85–172, §9, Aug. 28, 1957, 71 Stat. 445; Pub. L. 90–492, §9, Aug. 18, 1968, 82 Stat. 800.)

AMENDMENTS

1968—Pub. L. 90–492 made revisions in form and phraseology, added to the enumerated prohibited acts slaughtering poultry or processing any poultry products capable of use as human food, except in compliance with the requirements of this chapter, selling and transporting adulterated or misbranded poultry products or uninspected poultry products, adulterating or misbranding poultry products while they are being transported in commerce or held for sale after such transportation, treating carcasses not in accordance with regulations promulgated by the Secretary, possessing, without notifying the Secretary, any official device or any counterfeit, simulated, etc., official certificate, or any device or label bearing any counterfeit, simulated, etc., official mark, and making false representations and statements, and clarified application to brand manufacturers and printers of existing provisions prohibiting the counterfeiting of official marks, labels, or certificates.

EFFECTIVE DATE OF 1968 AMENDMENT

Amendment by Pub. L. 90–492 effective Aug. 18, 1968, except that amendment of pars. (a)(2)(A) and (a)(3) effective upon the expiration of sixty days after Aug. 18, 1968, see section 20 of Pub. L. 90–492, set out as a note under section 451 of this title.

§ 459. Compliance by all establishments

(a) In general

No establishment processing poultry or poultry products for commerce otherwise subject to this chapter shall process any poultry or poultry product except in compliance with the requirements of this chapter.

(b) Notification

Any establishment subject to inspection under this chapter that believes, or has reason to believe, that an adulterated or misbranded poultry or poultry product received by or originating from the establishment has entered into commerce shall promptly notify the Secretary with regard to the type, amount, origin, and destination of the poultry or poultry product.

(c) Plans and reassessments

The Secretary shall require that each establishment subject to inspection under this chapter shall, at a minimum—

(1) prepare and maintain current procedures for the recall of all poultry or poultry products produced and shipped by the establishment;

(2) document each reassessment of the process control plans of the establishment; and

(3) upon request, make the procedures and reassessed process control plans available to inspectors appointed by the Secretary for review and copying.

(Pub. L. 85–172, §10, Aug. 28, 1957, 71 Stat. 446; Pub. L. 90–492, §10, Aug. 18, 1968, 82 Stat. 801; Pub. L. 110–234, title XI, §11017(b), May 22, 2008, 122 Stat. 1370; Pub. L. 110–246, §4(a), title XI, §11017(b), June 18, 2008, 122 Stat. 1664, 2132.)

CODIFICATION

Pub. L. 110–234 and Pub. L. 110–246 made identical amendments to this section. The amendments by Pub. L. 110–234 were repealed by section 4(a) of Pub. L. 110–246.

AMENDMENTS

2008—Pub. L. 110–246, §11017(b), inserted section catchline, designated existing provisions as subsec. (a), inserted heading, and added subsecs. (b) and (c).

1968—Pub. L. 90–492 substituted "otherwise subject to this chapter" for "in or for marketing in a designated major consuming area".

EFFECTIVE DATE OF 2008 AMENDMENT

Amendment of this section and repeal of Pub. L. 110–234 by Pub. L. 110–246 effective May 22, 2008, the date of enactment of Pub. L. 110–234, see section 4 of Pub. L. 110–246, set out as an Effective Date note under section 8701 of Title 7, Agriculture.

EFFECTIVE DATE OF 1968 AMENDMENT

Amendment by Pub. L. 90–492 effective Aug. 18, 1968, see section 20 of Pub. L. 90–492, set out as a note under section 451 of this title.

§ 460. Miscellaneous activities subject to regulation

(a) Prohibition of inspection of articles not intended for use as human food; denaturation or other identification prior to distribution in commerce; inedible articles

Inspection shall not be provided under this chapter at any establishment for the slaughter of poultry or the processing of any carcasses or parts or products of poultry, which are not intended for use as human food, but such articles shall, prior to their offer for sale or transportation in commerce, unless naturally inedible by humans, be denatured or otherwise identified as prescribed by regulations of the Secretary to deter their use for human food. No person shall buy, sell, transport, or offer for sale or transportation, or receive for transportation, in commerce, or import, any poultry carcasses or parts or products thereof which are not intended for use as human food unless they are denatured or otherwise identified as required by the regulations of the Secretary or are naturally inedible by humans.

(b) Recordkeeping requirements; persons liable; scope of disclosure; access to places of business; examination of records, facilities, and inventories; copies; samples

The following classes of persons shall, for such period of time as the Secretary may by regulations prescribe, not to exceed two years unless otherwise directed by the Secretary for good cause shown, keep such records as are properly necessary for the effective enforcement of this chapter in order to insure against adulterated or misbranded poultry products for the American consumer; and all persons subject to such requirements shall, at all reasonable times, upon notice by a duly authorized representative of the Secretary, afford such representative access to their places of business and opportunity to examine the facilities, inventory, and records thereof, to copy all such records, and to take reasonable samples of their inventory upon payment of the fair market value therefor—

(1) Any person that engages in the business of slaughtering any poultry or processing, freezing, packaging, or labeling any carcasses, or parts or products of carcasses, of any poultry, for commerce, for use as human food or animal food;

(2) Any person that engages in the business of buying or selling (as poultry products brokers, wholesalers or otherwise), or transporting, in commerce, or storing in or for commerce, or importing, any carcasses, or parts or products of carcasses, of any poultry;

(3) Any person that engages in business, in or for commerce, as a renderer, or engages in the business of buying, selling, or transporting, in commerce, or importing, any dead, dying, disabled, or diseased poultry or parts of the carcasses of any poultry that died otherwise than by slaughter.

(c) Registration of business, name of person, and trade names

No person shall engage in business, in or for commerce, as a poultry products broker, renderer, or animal food manufacturer, or engage in business in commerce as a wholesaler of any carcasses, or parts or products of the carcasses, of any poultry, whether intended for human food or other purposes, or engage in business as a public warehouseman storing any such articles in or for commerce, or engage in the business of buying, selling, or transporting in commerce, or importing, any dead, dying, disabled, or diseased poultry, or parts of the carcasses of any poultry that died otherwise than by slaughter, unless when required by regulations of the Secretary, he has registered with the Secretary his name, and the address of each place of business at which, and all trade names under which, he conducts such business.

(d) Regulation of transactions, transportation, or importation of dead, dying, disabled or diseased poultry or carcasses to prevent use as human food

No person engaged in the business of buying, selling, or transporting in commerce, or importing, dead, dying, disabled, or diseased poultry, or any parts of the carcasses of any poultry that died otherwise than by slaughter, shall buy, sell, transport, offer for sale or transportation, or receive for transportation, in commerce, or import, any dead, dying, disabled, or diseased poultry or parts of the carcasses of any poultry that died otherwise than by slaughter, unless such transaction, transportation or importation is made in accordance with such regulations as the Secretary may prescribe to assure that such poultry, or the unwholesome parts or products thereof, will be prevented from being used for human food.

(e) Federal provisions applicable to State or Territorial business transactions of a local nature and not subject to local authority

The authority conferred on the Secretary by paragraph (b), (c), or (d) of this section with respect to persons engaged in the specified kinds of business in or for commerce may be exercised with respect to persons engaged, in any State or organized territory, in such kinds of business but not in or for commerce, whenever the Secretary determines, after consultation with an appropriate advisory committee provided for in section 454 of this title, that the State or territory does not have at least equal authority under its laws or such authority is not exercised in a manner to effectuate the purposes of this chapter, including the State or territory providing for the Secretary or his representative being afforded access to such places of business and the facilities, inventories, and records thereof, and the taking of reasonable samples, where he determines necessary in carrying out his responsibilities under this chapter; and in such case the provisions of paragraph (b), (c), or (d) of this section, respectively, shall apply to such persons to the same extent and in the same manner as if they were engaged in such business in or for commerce and the transactions involved were in commerce.

(Pub. L. 85–172, § 11, Aug. 28, 1957, 71 Stat. 446; Pub. L. 90–492, § 11, Aug. 18, 1968, 82 Stat. 801.)

AMENDMENTS

1968—Pub. L. 90–492 designated existing provisions as par. (b), added pars. (a), and (c) to (e), and in par. (b), as so designated, extended the types of persons required to maintain records necessary for the enforcement of this chapter, required such persons to give representatives of the Secretary access to their places of business, and opportunity to examine records, facilities, and inventories and to copy records and take inventory samples upon payment.

EFFECTIVE DATE OF 1968 AMENDMENT

Amendment by Pub. L. 90–492 effective Aug. 18, 1968, except that par. (d) effective upon the expiration of sixty days after Aug. 18, 1968, see section 20 of Pub. L. 90–492, set out as a note under section 451 of this title.

§461. Offenses and punishment

(a) Violations; liability of agents, employees, and employers

Any person who violates the provisions of section 458, 459, 460, 463, or 466 of this title shall be fined not more than $1,000 or imprisoned not more than one year, or both; but if such violation involves intent to defraud, or any distribution or attempted distribution of an article that is adulterated (except as defined in section 453(g)(8) of this title), such person shall be fined not more than $10,000 or imprisoned not more than three years, or both. When construing or enforcing the provisions of said sections the act, omission, or failure of any person acting for or employed by any individual, partnership, corporation, or association within the scope of his employment or office shall in every case be deemed the act, omission, or failure of such individual, partnership, corporation, or association, as well as of such person.

(b) Liability of carrier

No carrier shall be subject to the penalties of this chapter, other than the penalties for violation of section 460 of this title, by reason of his receipt, carriage, holding, or delivery, in the usual course of business, as a carrier, of poultry or poultry products, owned by another person unless the carrier has knowledge, or is in possession of facts which would cause a reasonable person to believe that such poultry or poultry products were not inspected or marked in accordance with the provisions of this chapter or were otherwise not eligible for transportation under this chapter or unless the carrier refuses to furnish on request of a representative of the Secretary the name and address of the person from whom he received such poultry or poultry products, and copies of all documents, if any there be, pertaining to the delivery of the poultry or poultry products to such carrier.

(c) Assaulting, resisting, or impeding certain persons; murder; punishments

Any person who forcibly assaults, resists, opposes, impedes, intimidates, or interferes with any person while engaged in or on account of the performance of his official duties under this chapter shall be fined not more than $5,000 or imprisoned not more than three years, or both. Whoever, in the commission of any such acts, uses a deadly or dangerous weapon, shall be fined not more than $10,000 or imprisoned not more than ten years, or both. Whoever kills any person while engaged in or on account of the performance of his official duties under this chapter shall be punished as provided under sections 1111 and 1114 of title 18.

(Pub. L. 85–172, §12, Aug. 28, 1957, 71 Stat. 446; Pub. L. 90–492, §12, Aug. 18, 1968, 82 Stat. 802.)

AMENDMENTS

1968—Par. (a). Pub. L. 90–492, §12(a), inserted reference to violations of section 463 of this title, and substituted provisions that violators of the enumerated sections shall be fined not more than $1,000 or imprisoned not more than one year, or both, but that in cases involving intent to defraud, or any distribution or attempt to distribute adulterated articles, except as defined in section 453(g) of this title, the violators shall be fined not more than $10,000 or imprisoned not more than three years, or both, for provisions that violators shall be guilty of a misdemeanor and subject to imprisonment for not more than six months or a fine of not more than $3,000, or both, with increased fines and imprisonment for any subsequent violations.

Par. (b). Pub. L. 90–492, §12(b), substituted "of poultry" for "of slaughtered poultry", "such poultry" for "such slaughtered poultry", and "otherwise not eligible" for "not otherwise eligible", and inserted provision that no carrier shall be subject to punishment unless the carrier refuses to furnish the name and address of the person from whom he received such poultry or poultry products, and copies of any documents pertaining to the delivery of the poultry or poultry products to such carrier.

Par. (c). Pub. L. 90–492, §12(c), added par. (c).

EFFECTIVE DATE OF 1968 AMENDMENT

Amendment by Pub. L. 90–492 effective Aug. 18, 1968, see section 20 of Pub. L. 90–492, set out as a note under section 451 of this title.

§462. Reporting of violations; notice; opportunity to present views

Before any violation of this chapter is reported by the Secretary to any United States attorney for institution of a criminal proceeding, the person against whom such proceeding is contemplated shall be given reasonable notice of the alleged violation and opportunity to present his views orally or in writing with regard to such contemplated proceeding. Nothing in this chapter shall be construed as requiring the Secretary to report for criminal prosecution violations of this chapter whenever he believes that the public interest will be adequately served and compliance with the chapter obtained by a suitable written notice or warning.

(Pub. L. 85–172, §13, Aug. 28, 1957, 71 Stat. 447.)

§463. Rules and regulations

(a) Storage and handling of poultry products; violation of regulations

The Secretary may by regulations prescribe conditions under which poultry products capable of use as human food, shall be stored or otherwise handled by any person engaged in the business of buying, selling, freezing, storing, or transporting, in or for commerce, or importing, such articles, whenever the Secretary deems such action necessary to assure that such articles will not be adulterated or misbranded when delivered to the consumer. Violation of any such regulation is prohibited.

(b) Other necessary rules and regulations

The Secretary shall promulgate such other rules and regulations as are necessary to carry out the provisions of this chapter.

(c) Oral presentation of views

In applying the provisions of section 553(c) of title 5 to proposed rule making under this chapter, an opportunity for the oral presentation of views shall be accorded all interested persons.

(Pub. L. 85–172, § 14, Aug. 28, 1957, 71 Stat. 447; Pub. L. 90–492, § 13, Aug. 18, 1968, 82 Stat. 803.)

AMENDMENTS

1968—Pub. L. 90–492 designated existing provisions as par. (b), added pars. (a) and (c), and in par. (b), as so designated, substituted "such other rules" for "such rules".

EFFECTIVE DATE OF 1968 AMENDMENT

Amendment by Pub. L. 90–492 effective Aug. 18, 1968, see section 20 of Pub. L. 90–492, set out as a note under section 451 of this title.

§ 464. Exemptions

(a) Persons exempted

The Secretary shall, by regulation and under such conditions as to sanitary standards, practices, and procedures as he may prescribe, exempt from specific provisions of this chapter—

(1) retail dealers with respect to poultry products sold directly to consumers in individual retail stores, if the only processing operation performed by such retail dealers is the cutting up of poultry products on the premises where such sales to consumers are made;

(2) for such period of time as the Secretary determines that it would be impracticable to provide inspection and the exemption will aid in the effective administration of this chapter, any person engaged in the processing of poultry or poultry products for commerce and the poultry or poultry products processed by such person: *Provided, however*, That no such exemption shall continue in effect on and after January 1, 1970; and

(3) persons slaughtering, processing, or otherwise handling poultry or poultry products which have been or are to be processed as required by recognized religious dietary laws, to the extent that the Secretary determines necessary to avoid conflict with such requirements while still effectuating the purposes of this chapter.

(b) Territorial exemption

The Secretary may, under such sanitary conditions as he may by regulations prescribe, exempt from the inspection requirements of this chapter the slaughter of poultry, and the processing of poultry products, by any person in any Territory not organized with a legislative body, solely for distribution within such Territory, when the Secretary determines that it is impracticable to provide such inspection within the limits of funds appropriated for administration of this chapter and that such exemption will aid in the effective administration of this chapter.

(c) Personal slaughtering; custom slaughtering; name and address of the poultry producer or processor in lieu of other labeling requirements; small enterprises; slaughterers or processors of specified number of turkeys; poultry producers raising poultry on own farms

(1) The Secretary shall, by regulation and under such conditions, including sanitary standards, practices, and procedures, as he may prescribe, exempt from specific provisions of this chapter—

(A) the slaughtering by any person of poultry of his own raising, and the processing by him and transportation in commerce of the poultry products exclusively for use by him and members of his household and his nonpaying guests and employees;

(B) the custom slaughter by any person of poultry delivered by the owner thereof for such slaughter, and the processing by such slaughterer and transportation in commerce of the poultry products exclusively for use, in the household of such owner, by him and members of his household and his nonpaying guests and employees: *Provided*, That such custom slaughterer does not engage in the business of buying or selling any poultry products capable of use as human food;

(C) the slaughtering and processing of poultry products in any State or Territory or the District of Columbia by any poultry producer on his own premises with respect to sound and healthy poultry raised on his premises and the distribution by any person solely within such jurisdiction of the poultry products derived from such operations, if, in lieu of other labeling requirements, such poultry products are identified with the name and address of such poultry producer, and if they are not otherwise misbranded, and are sound, clean, and fit for human food when so distributed; and

(D) the slaughtering of sound and healthy poultry or the processing of poultry products of such poultry in any State or territory or the District of Columbia by any poultry producer or other person for distribution by him solely within such jurisdiction directly to household consumers, restaurants, hotels, and boarding houses, for use in their own dining rooms, or in the preparation of meals for sales direct to consumers, if, in lieu of other labeling requirements, such poultry products are identified with the name and address of the processor, and if they are not otherwise misbranded and are sound, clean, and fit for human food when distributed by such processor.

The exemptions provided for in clauses (C) and (D) above shall not apply if the poultry producer or other person engages in the current calendar year in the business of buying or selling any poultry or poultry products other than as specified in such clauses.

(2) In addition to the specific exemptions provided herein, the Secretary shall, when he determines that the protection of consumers from adulterated or misbranded poultry products will not be impaired by such action, provide by regulation, consistent with subparagraph (3), for the exemption of the operation and products of small enterprises (including poultry producers), not exempted under subparagraph (1), which are engaged in any State or Territory or the District of Columbia in slaughtering and/or cutting up poultry for distribution as carcasses or parts thereof solely for distribution within such jurisdiction, from such provisions of this chapter as he deems appropriate, while still protecting the public from adulterated or misbranded products,

under such conditions, including sanitary requirements, as he shall prescribe to effectuate the purposes of this chapter.

(3) No exemption under subparagraph (1)(C) or (D) or subparagraph (2) shall apply to any poultry producer or other person who, in the current calendar year—

(A) slaughters or processes the products of more than 20,000 poultry; or

(B) slaughters or processes the products of poultry at a facility used for slaughtering or processing of the products of poultry by any other poultry producer or person.

Notwithstanding clause (B), the Secretary may grant such exemption to any poultry producer or other person if the Secretary determines, upon application of such poultry producer or other person, that granting such exemption will not impair effectuating the purposes of this chapter.

(4) The provisions of this chapter shall not apply to poultry producers with respect to poultry of their own raising on their own farms if (i) such producers slaughter not more than 1,000 poultry during the calendar year for which this exemption is being determined; (ii) such poultry producers do not engage in buying or selling poultry products other than those produced from poultry raised on their own farms; and (iii) none of such poultry moves in commerce (as defined in section 453(a) of this title).

(d) Pizzas containing poultry products

(1) Under such terms and conditions as the Secretary shall prescribe through rules and regulations issued under this section that may be necessary to ensure food safety and protect public health such as special handling procedures, the Secretary shall exempt pizzas containing a poultry product from the inspection requirements of this chapter if—

(A) the poultry product components of the pizzas have been prepared, inspected, and passed in a cured or cooked form as ready-to-eat in compliance with the requirements of this chapter; and

(B) the pizzas are to be served in public or private nonprofit institutions.

(2) The Secretary may withdraw or modify any exemption under this subsection whenever the Secretary determines such action is necessary to ensure food safety and to protect public health. The Secretary may reinstate or further modify any exemption withdrawn or modified under this subsection.

(e) Applicability of adulteration and misbranding provisions to articles exempted from inspection

The adulteration and misbranding provisions of this chapter, other than the requirement of the inspection legend, shall apply to articles which are exempted from inspection under this section, except as otherwise specified under paragraphs (a) and (d).

(f) Suspension or termination of exemption

The Secretary may by order suspend or terminate any exemption under this section with respect to any person whenever he finds that such action will aid in effectuating the purposes of this chapter.

(Pub. L. 85–172, §15, Aug. 28, 1957, 71 Stat. 447; Pub. L. 90–492, §14, Aug. 18, 1968, 82 Stat. 803; Pub. L. 97–206, June 30, 1982, 96 Stat. 136; Pub. L. 102–237, title X, §1016(b), Dec. 13, 1991, 105 Stat. 1903.)

AMENDMENTS

1991—Subsecs. (d) to (f). Pub. L. 102–237 added subsec. (d), redesignated former subsec. (d) as (e) and substituted "(d)" for "(c)", and redesignated former subsec. (e) as (f).

1982—Par. (c)(3). Pub. L. 97–206, §1, substituted provisions that no exemption would be given to persons who during the current calendar year either slaughter or process the products of more than 20,000 poultry, or slaughter or process such poultry at a facility of another poultry producer or person, but that, in the latter case, the Secretary may grant the exemption upon application of such poultry producer or person if granting such exemption would not impair the purposes of this chapter, for provisions that an exemption would not be granted to those who slaughter or process the products of more than 5,000 turkeys or an equivalent number of poultry of all species in the current calendar year (four birds of other species being deemed equivalent of one turkey).

Par. (c)(4)(i). Pub. L. 97–206, §2, substituted "1,000 poultry during the calendar year for which this exemption is being determined" for "250 turkeys, or not more than an equivalent number of birds of all species during the calendar year for which this exemption is being determined (four birds of other species being deemed the equivalent of one turkey)".

1968—Par. (a). Pub. L. 90–492, §14(a), (b), redesignated subpars. (2) to (4) as (1) to (3), respectively, and in subpar. (2), as so redesignated, substituted "January 1, 1970" for "July 1, 1960". Former subpar. (1), which exempted poultry producers with respect to poultry of their own raising on their own farms which they sold directly to household consumers, hotels, etc., for use in their own dining rooms or in the preparation of meals for sales direct to consumers only, provided that such producers did not engage in buying or selling poultry products other than those produced from poultry raised on their own farms, was struck out.

Pars. (b) to (e). Pub. L. 90–492, §14(c), added pars. (b) to (d) and redesignated former par. (b) as (e).

EFFECTIVE DATE OF 1968 AMENDMENT

Amendment by Pub. L. 90–492 effective upon the expiration of sixty days after Aug. 18, 1968, see section 20(b) of Pub. L. 90–492, set out as a note under section 451 of this title.

REGULATIONS

Section 1016(c) of Pub. L. 102–237 provided that: "No later than August 1, 1992, the Secretary of Agriculture shall issue final rules, through prior notice and comment rulemaking procedures, to implement the exemption authorized by section 23(c) of the Federal Meat Inspection Act [21 U.S.C. 623(c)] (as added by subsection (a)) and the exemption authorized by section 15(d) of the Poultry Products Inspection Act [21 U.S.C. 464(d)] (as added by subsection (b)). Prior to the issuance of the final rules, the Secretary shall hold at least one public hearing examining the public health and food safety issues raised by the granting of each of the exemptions."

STUDIES CONCERNING GRANT OF FUTURE EXEMPTIONS FOR POULTRY AND MEAT FOOD PRODUCTS

Section 1016(d) of Pub. L. 102–237 directed Secretary of Agriculture in consultation with National Academy of Sciences to conduct a study on meat food and poultry products inspection exemptions under Federal Meat Inspection Act and Poultry Products Inspection Act and a study on an exemption from requirements of such Acts for certain wholesale meat outlets selling to hotels and other similar institutional users not later than 24 months after Dec. 13, 1991, and on completion of each study to provide the results to Committee on Agriculture of House of Representatives and Committee on Agriculture, Nutrition, and Forestry of Senate.

§ 465. Limitations upon entry of poultry products and other materials into official establishments

The Secretary may limit the entry of poultry products and other materials into any official establishment, under such conditions as he may prescribe to assure that allowing the entry of such articles into such inspected establishments will be consistent with the purposes of this chapter.

(Pub. L. 85–172, § 16, Aug. 28, 1957, 71 Stat. 448; Pub. L. 90–492, § 15, Aug. 18, 1968, 82 Stat. 805.)

AMENDMENTS

1968—Pub. L. 90–492 substituted provisions authorizing the Secretary to limit the entry of poultry products and other materials into any official establishment for provisions that any person distributing unwholesome or adulterated exempted poultry or poultry products intended for human consumption shall be guilty of a misdemeanor and subject to penalties upon conviction thereof.

EFFECTIVE DATE OF 1968 AMENDMENT

Amendment by Pub. L. 90–492 effective Aug. 18, 1968, see section 20 of Pub. L. 90–492, set out as a note under section 451 of this title.

§ 466. Imports

(a) Compliance with standards and regulations; status after importation

No slaughtered poultry, or parts or products thereof, of any kind shall be imported into the United States unless they are healthful, wholesome, fit for human food, not adulterated, and contain no dye, chemical, preservative, or ingredient which renders them unhealthful, unwholesome, adulterated, or unfit for human food and unless they also comply with the rules and regulations made by the Secretary of Agriculture to assure that imported poultry or poultry products comply with the standards provided for in this chapter. All imported, slaughtered poultry, or parts or products thereof, shall after entry into the United States in compliance with such rules and regulations be deemed and treated as domestic slaughtered poultry, or parts or products thereof, within the meaning and subject to the provisions of this chapter and the Federal Food, Drug, and Cosmetic Act [21 U.S.C. 301 et seq.], and Acts amendatory of, supplemental to, or in substitution for such chapter and Act.

(b) Rules and regulations; destruction and exportation of refused imports

The Secretary of Agriculture is authorized to make rules and regulations to carry out the purposes of this section and in such rules and regulations the Secretary of Agriculture may prescribe the terms and conditions for the destruction of all slaughtered poultry, or parts or products thereof, offered for entry and refused admission into the United States unless such slaughtered poultry, or parts or products thereof, be exported by the consignee within the time fixed therefor in such rules and regulations.

(c) Storage, cartage and labor charges for imports refused admission

All charges for storage, cartage, and labor with respect to any product which is refused admission pursuant to this section shall be paid by the owner or consignee, and in default of such payment shall constitute a lien against any other products imported thereafter by or for such owner or consignee.

(d) Domestic standards and processing facilities applicable; enforcement

(1) Notwithstanding any other provision of law, all poultry, or parts or products of poultry, capable of use as human food offered for importation into the United States shall—

(A) be subject to inspection, sanitary, quality, species verification, and residue standards that achieve a level of sanitary protection equivalent to that achieved under United States standards; and

(B) have been processed in facilities and under conditions that achieve a level of sanitary protection equivalent to that achieved under United States standards.

(2)(A) The Secretary may treat as equivalent to a United States standard a standard of an exporting country described in paragraph (1) if the exporting country provides the Secretary with scientific evidence or other information, in accordance with risk assessment methodologies determined appropriate by the Secretary, to demonstrate that the standard of the exporting country achieves the level of sanitary protection achieved under the United States standard. For the purposes of this subsection, the term "sanitary protection" means protection to safeguard public health.

(B) The Secretary may—

(i) determine, on a scientific basis, that the standard of the exporting country does not achieve the level of protection that the Secretary considers appropriate; and

(ii) provide the basis for the determination in writing to the exporting country on request.

(3) Any such imported poultry article that does not meet such standards shall not be permitted entry into the United States.

(4) The Secretary shall enforce this subsection through—

(A) random inspections for such species verification and for residues; and

(B) random sampling and testing of internal organs and fat of carcasses for residues at the point of slaughter by the exporting country, in accordance with methods approved by the Secretary.

(Pub. L. 85–172, § 17, Aug. 28, 1957, 71 Stat. 448; Pub. L. 99–198, title XVII, § 1701(a), Dec. 23, 1985, 99 Stat. 1633; Pub. L. 103–182, title III, § 361(e), Dec. 8, 1993, 107 Stat. 2123; Pub. L. 103–465, title IV, § 431(k), Dec. 8, 1994, 108 Stat. 4969.)

REFERENCES IN TEXT

The Federal Food, Drug, and Cosmetic Act, referred to in subsec. (a), is act June 25, 1938, ch. 675, 52 Stat. 1040, as amended, which is classified generally to chapter 9 (§ 301 et seq.) of this title. For complete classification of this Act to the Code, see section 301 of this title and Tables.

AMENDMENTS

1994—Subsec. (d)(1). Pub. L. 103–465, § 431(k)(1), amended par. (1) generally. Prior to amendment, par. (1) read as follows: "Notwithstanding any other provision of law, except as provided in paragraph (2), all poultry, or parts or products thereof, capable of use as human food offered for importation into the United States shall—

"(A) be subject to the same inspection, sanitary, quality, species verification, and residue standards applied to products produced in the United States; and

"(B) have been processed in facilities and under conditions that are the same as those under which similar products are processed in the United States."

Subsec. (d)(2)(A). Pub. L. 103–465, § 431(k)(2)(A), amended subpar. (A) generally. Prior to amendment, subpar. (A) read as follows: "Notwithstanding any other provision of law, all poultry, or parts or products of poultry, capable of use as human food offered for importation into the United States from Canada and Mexico shall—

"(i) comply with paragraph (1); or

"(ii)(I) be subject to inspection, sanitary, quality, species verification, and residue standards that are equivalent to United States standards; and

"(II) have been processed in facilities and under conditions that meet standards that are equivalent to United States standards."

Subsec. (d)(2)(B), (C). Pub. L. 103–465, § 431(k)(2)(B), (C), redesignated subpar. (C) as (B) and struck out former subpar. (B) which read as follows: "The Secretary may treat as equivalent to a United States standard a standard of Canada or Mexico described in subparagraph (A)(ii) if the exporting country provides the Secretary with scientific evidence or other information, in accordance with risk assessment methodologies agreed to by the Secretary and the exporting country, to demonstrate that the standard of the exporting country achieves the level of protection that the Secretary considers appropriate."

1993—Subsec. (d). Pub. L. 103–182, in par. (1), inserted "except as provided in paragraph (2)," before "all poultry" in introductory provisions, added par. (2), and redesignated former pars. (2) and (3) as (3) and (4), respectively.

1985—Par. (d). Pub. L. 99–198 added par. (d).

EFFECTIVE DATE OF 1994 AMENDMENT

Amendment by Pub. L. 103–465 effective, except as otherwise provided, on the date of entry into force of the World Trade Organization Agreement with respect to the United States [Jan. 1, 1995], see section 451 of Pub. L. 103–465, set out as an Effective Date note under section 3601 of Title 19, Customs Duties.

EFFECTIVE DATE OF 1985 AMENDMENT

Section 1701(b) of Pub. L. 99–198 proved that: "The amendment made by this section [amending this section] shall become effective 6 months after the date of enactment of this Act [Dec. 23, 1985]."

§ 467. Inspection services

(a) Refusal or withdrawal; hearing; business unfitness based upon certain convictions; persons responsibly connected with the business

The Secretary may (for such period, or indefinitely, as he deems necessary to effectuate the purposes of this chapter) refuse to provide, or withdraw, inspection service under this chapter with respect to any establishment if he determines, after opportunity for a hearing is accorded to the applicant for, or recipient of, such service, that such applicant or recipient is unfit to engage in any business requiring inspection upon this chapter because the applicant or recipient or anyone responsibly connected with the applicant or recipient, has been convicted, in any Federal or State court, within the previous ten years of (1) any felony or more than one misdemeanor under any law based upon the acquiring, handling, or distributing of adulterated, mislabeled, or deceptively packaged food or fraud in connection with transactions in food; or (2) any felony, involving fraud, bribery, extortion, or any other act or circumstances indicating a lack of the integrity needed for the conduct of operations affecting the public health. For the purpose of this paragraph a person shall be deemed to be responsibly connected with the business if he was a partner, officer, director, holder, or owner of 10 per centum or more of its voting stock or employee in a managerial or executive capacity.

(b) Hearing to determine validity of withdrawal or refusal of inspection services; continuation of withdrawal or refusal

Upon the withdrawal of inspection service from any official establishment for failure to destroy condemned poultry products as required under section 455 of this title, or other failure of an official establishment to comply with the requirements as to premises, facilities, or equipment, or the operation thereof, as provided in section 456 of this title, or the refusal of inspection service to any applicant therefor because of failure to comply with any requirements under section 456 of this title, the applicant for, or recipient of, the service shall, upon request, be afforded opportunity for a hearing with respect to the merits or validity of such action; but such withdrawal or refusal shall continue in effect unless otherwise ordered by the Secretary.

(c) Finality and conclusiveness of determination; judicial review; record

The determination and order of the Secretary when made after opportunity for hearing, with respect to withdrawal or refusal of inspection service under this chapter shall be final and conclusive unless the affected applicant for, or recipient of, inspection service files application for judicial review within thirty days after the effective date of such order in the United States Court of Appeals as provided in section 457 of this title. Judicial review of any such order shall be upon the record upon which the determination and order are based. The provisions of section 194 of title 7 shall be applicable to appeals taken under this section.

(Pub. L. 85–172, § 18, Aug. 28, 1957, 71 Stat. 448; Pub. L. 90–492, § 16, Aug. 18, 1968, 82 Stat. 805.)

AMENDMENTS

1968—Par. (a). Pub. L. 90–492 substituted provisions authorizing the Secretary to refuse or withdraw inspection services subsequent to a hearing determining that the applicant or recipient is unfit to engage in any business requiring inspection under this chapter based upon the specified considerations, for provisions granting the Secretary exclusive jurisdiction within the scope of this chapter and exempting poultry and poultry products from the provisions of the Federal Food, Drug, and Cosmetic Act, as amended, to the extent of the application or the extension thereof of the provisions of this chapter.

Par. (b). Pub. L. 90–492 substituted provisions granting a hearing, upon request by the applicant or recipient, to determine the merits and validity of the withdrawal or refusal of inspection services and continuing such withdrawal or refusal in effect, unless otherwise ordered by the Secretary, for provisions authorizing the Secretary to cooperate with other branches of government and with State agencies and to conduct examinations, investigations, and inspections through any officer or employee of a State commissioned by the Secretary for such purpose.

Par. (c). Pub. L. 90–492 added par. (c).

EFFECTIVE DATE OF 1968 AMENDMENT

Amendment by Pub. L. 90–492 effective Aug. 18, 1968, see section 20 of Pub. L. 90–492, set out as a note under section 451 of this title.

§467a. Administrative detention; duration; pending judicial proceedings; notification of government authorities; release; removal of official marks

Whenever any poultry product, or any product exempted from the definition of a poultry product, or any dead, dying, disabled, or diseased poultry is found by any authorized representative of the Secretary upon any premises where it is held for purposes of, or during or after distribution in, commerce or otherwise subject to this chapter, and there is reason to believe that any such article is adulterated or misbranded and is capable of use as human food, or that it has not been inspected, in violation of the provisions of this chapter or of any other Federal law or the laws of any State or Territory, or the District of Columbia, or that it has been or is intended to be, distributed in violation of any such provisions, it may be detained by such representative for a period not to exceed twenty days, pending action under section 467b of this title or notification of any Federal, State, or other governmental authorities having jurisdiction over such article or poultry, and shall not be moved by any person, from the place at which it is located when so detained, until released by such representative. All official marks may be required by such representative to be removed from such article or poultry before it is released unless it appears to the satisfaction of the Secretary that the article or poultry is eligible to retain such marks.

(Pub. L. 85–172, §19, as added Pub. L. 90–492, §17, Aug. 18, 1968, 82 Stat. 805.)

§467b. Seizure and condemnation

(a) Proceedings in rem; libel of information; jurisdiction; disposal by destruction or sale; proceeds into the Treasury; sales restrictions; bonds; court costs and fees, storage, and other expenses against claimants; jury trial; United States as plaintiff

(1) Any poultry product, or any dead, dying, disabled, or diseased poultry, that is being transported in commerce or otherwise subject to this chapter, or is held for sale in the United States after such transportation, and that (A) is or has been processed, sold, transported, or otherwise distributed or offered or received for distribution in violation of this chapter, or (B) is capable of use as human food and is adulterated or misbranded, or (C) in any other way is in violation of this chapter, shall be liable to be proceeded against and seized and condemned, at any time, on a libel of information in any United States district court or other proper court as provided in section 467c of this title within the jurisdiction of which the article or poultry is found.

(2) If the article or poultry is condemned it shall, after entry of the decree, (A) be distributed in accordance with paragraph (5), or (B) be disposed of by destruction or sale as the court may direct and the proceeds, if sold, less the court costs and fees, and storage and other proper expenses, shall be paid into the Treasury of the United States, but the article or poultry shall not be sold contrary to the provisions of this chapter, or the laws of the jurisdiction in which it is sold: *Provided*, That upon the execution and delivery of a good and sufficient bond conditioned that the article or poultry shall not be sold or otherwise disposed of contrary to the provisions of this chapter, or the laws of the jurisdiction in which disposal is made, the court may direct that such article or poultry be delivered to the owner thereof subject to such supervision by authorized representatives of the Secretary as is necessary to insure compliance with the applicable laws.

(3) When a decree of condemnation is entered against the article or poultry and it is released under bond, or destroyed, court costs and fees, and storage and other proper expenses shall be awarded against the person, if any, intervening as claimant of the article or poultry.

(4) The proceedings in such libel cases shall conform, as nearly as may be, to the proceedings in admiralty, except that either party may demand trial by jury of any issue of fact joined in any case, and all such proceedings shall be at the suit of and in the name of the United States.

(5)(A) An article that is condemned under paragraph (1) may as the court may direct, after entry of the decree, be distributed without charge to nonprofit, private entities or to Federal, State, or local government entities engaged in the distribution of food without charge to individuals, if such article—

(i) is capable of use as a human food;

(ii) has been inspected under this chapter and found to be wholesome and not to be adulterated within the meaning of paragraphs (1) through (7) of section 453(g) of this title and a determination is made at the time of the entry of the decree that such article is wholesome and not so adulterated; and

(iii) is plainly marked "Not for Sale" on such article or its container.

(B) The United States may not be held legally responsible for any article that is distributed under subparagraph (A) to a nonprofit, private entity or to a Federal, State, or local government entity, if such article—

(i) was found after inspection under this chapter to be wholesome and not adulterated within the meaning of paragraphs (1) through (7) of section 453(g) of this title and a determination was made at the time of the entry of the decree that such article was wholesome and not so adulterated; and

(ii) was plainly marked "Not for Sale" on such article or its container.

(C) The person from whom such article was seized and condemned may not be held legally responsible for such article, if such article—

(i) was found after inspection under this chapter to be wholesome and not adulterated within the meaning of paragraphs (1) through (7) of section 453(g) of this title and a determination was made at the time of entry of the decree that such article was wholesome and not so adulterated; and

(ii) was plainly marked "Not for Sale" on such article or its container.

(b) Condemnation or seizure under other provisions unaffected

The provisions of this section shall in no way derogate from authority for condemnation or seizure conferred by other provisions of this chapter, or other laws.

(Pub. L. 85–172, § 20, as added Pub. L. 90–492, § 17, Aug. 18, 1968, 82 Stat. 806; amended Pub. L. 101–205, § 2, Dec. 7, 1989, 103 Stat. 1830.)

AMENDMENTS

1989—Subsec. (a). Pub. L. 101–205 designated first sentence as par. (1) and redesignated cls. (1) to (3) as cls. (A) to (C), respectively, designated second sentence as par. (2) and inserted "(A) be distributed in accordance with paragraph (5), or (B)" after "entry of the decree,", designated third and fourth sentences as pars. (3) and (4), respectively, and added par. (5).

§ 467c. Federal court jurisdiction of enforcement and injunction proceedings and other kinds of cases; limitations; United States as plaintiff; subpenas

The United States district courts, the District Court of Guam, the District Court of the Virgin Islands, the highest court of American Samoa, and the United States courts of the other territories, are vested with jurisdiction specifically to enforce, and to prevent and restrain violations of, this chapter, and shall have jurisdiction in all other kinds of cases arising under this chapter, except as provided in section 457(d) or 467 of this title. All proceedings for the enforcement or to restrain violations of this chapter shall be by and in the name of the United States. Subpenas for witnesses who are required to attend a court of the United States, in any district, may run into any other district in any such proceeding.

(Pub. L. 85–172, § 21, as added Pub. L. 90–492, § 17, Aug. 18, 1968, 82 Stat. 806.)

§ 467d. Administration and enforcement; applicability of penalty provisions; conduct of inquiries; power and jurisdiction of courts

For the efficient administration and enforcement of this chapter, the provision (including penalties) of sections 46, 48, 49 and 50 of title 15 (except paragraphs (c) through (h) of section 46 and the last paragraph of section 49[1] of title 15), and the provisions of section 409(*l*)[1] of title 47, are made applicable to the jurisdiction, powers, and duties of the Secretary in administering and enforcing the provisions of this chapter and to any person with respect to whom such authority is exercised. The Secretary, in person or by such agents as he may designate, may prosecute any inquiry necessary to his duties under this chapter in any part of the United States, and the powers conferred by said sections 49 and 50 of title 15 on the district courts of the United States may be exercised for the purposes of this chapter by any court designated in section 467c of this title.

(Pub. L. 85–172, § 22, as added Pub. L. 90–492, § 17, Aug. 18, 1968, 82 Stat. 807.)

REFERENCES IN TEXT

The last paragraph of section 49 of title 15, and the provisions of section 409(*l*) of title 47, referred to in text, which related to immunity of witnesses, were repealed by sections 211 and 242, respectively, of Pub. L. 91–452, Oct. 15, 1970, title II, 84 Stat. 929, 930. For provisions relating to immunity of witnesses, see section 6001 et seq. of Title 18, Crimes and Criminal Procedure.

§ 467e. Non-Federal jurisdiction of federally regulated matters; prohibition of additional or different requirements for establishments with inspection services and as to marking, labeling, packaging, and ingredients; recordkeeping and related requirements; concurrent jurisdiction over distribution for human food purposes of adulterated or misbranded and imported articles; other matters

Requirements within the scope of this chapter with respect to premises, facilities and operations of any official establishment which are in addition to, or different than those made under this chapter may not be imposed by any State or Territory or the District of Columbia, except that any such jurisdiction may impose recordkeeping and other requirements within the scope of paragraph (b) of section 460 of this title, if consistent therewith, with respect to any such establishment. Marking, labeling, packaging, or ingredient requirements (or storage or handling requirements found by the Secretary to unduly interfere with the free flow of poultry products in commerce) in addition to, or different than, those made under this chapter may not be imposed by any State or Territory or the District of Columbia with respect to articles prepared at any official establishment in accordance with the requirements under this chapter, but any State or Territory or the District of Columbia may, consistent with the requirements under this chapter exercise concurrent jurisdiction with the Secretary over articles required to be inspected under this chapter for the purpose of preventing the distribution for human food purposes of any such articles which are adulterated or misbranded and are outside of such an establishment, or, in the case of imported articles which are not at such an establishment, after their entry into the United States. This chapter shall not preclude any State or Territory or the District of Columbia from making requirement or taking other action, consistent with this chapter, with respect to any other matters regulated under this chapter.

(Pub. L. 85–172, § 23, as added Pub. L. 90–492, § 17, Aug. 18, 1968, 82 Stat. 807.)

[1] See References in Text note below.

§ 467f. Federal Food, Drug, and Cosmetic Act applications

(a) Exemptions; authorities under food, drug, and cosmetic provisions unaffected

Poultry and poultry products shall be exempt from the provisions of the Federal Food, Drug, and Cosmetic Act [21 U.S.C. 301 et seq.] to the extent of the application or extension thereto of the provisions of this chapter, except that the provisions of this chapter shall not derogate from any authority conferred by the Federal Food, Drug, and Cosmetic Act prior to August 18, 1968.

(b) Enforcement proceedings; detainer authority of representatives of Secretary of Health and Human Services

The detainer authority conferred by section 467a of this title shall apply to any authorized representative of the Secretary of Health and Human Services for purposes of the enforcement of the Federal Food, Drug, and Cosmetic Act [21 U.S.C. 301 et seq.] with respect to any poultry carcass, or part or product thereof, that is outside any official establishment, and for such purposes the first reference to the Secretary in section 467a of this title shall be deemed to refer to the Secretary of Health and Human Services.

(Pub. L. 85–172, § 24, as added Pub. L. 90–492, § 17, Aug. 18, 1968, 82 Stat. 807; amended Pub. L. 96–88, title V, § 509(b), Oct. 17, 1979, 93 Stat. 695.)

REFERENCES IN TEXT

The Federal Food, Drug, and Cosmetic Act, referred to in text, is act June 25, 1938, ch. 675, 52 Stat. 1040, as amended, which is classified generally to chapter 9 (§ 301 et seq.) of this title. For complete classification of this Act to the Code, see section 301 of this title and Tables.

CHANGE OF NAME

"Secretary of Health and Human Services" substituted for "Secretary of Health, Education, and Welfare" in par. (b) pursuant to section 509(b) of Pub. L. 96–88, which is classified to section 3508(b) of Title 20, Education.

§ 468. Cost of inspection; overtime

The cost of inspection rendered under the requirements of this chapter, shall be borne by the United States, except the cost of overtime and holiday pay paid pursuant to the[1] section 2219a of title 7.

(Pub. L. 85–172, § 25, formerly § 19, Aug. 28, 1957, 71 Stat. 448, renumbered Pub. L. 90–492, § 17, Aug. 18, 1968, 82 Stat. 805; Pub. L. 107–171, title X, § 10703(c)(1), May 13, 2002, 116 Stat. 517.)

REFERENCES IN TEXT

Section 2219a of title 7, referred to in text, was in the original "section 10703 of the Farm Security and Rural Investment Act of 2002", meaning section 10703 of Pub. L. 107–171, which enacted section 2219a of Title 7, Agriculture, amended this section, section 695 of this title, and section 5549 of Title 5, Government Organization and Employees, and repealed section 394 of Title 7.

AMENDMENTS

2002—Pub. L. 107–171 substituted "except the cost of overtime and holiday pay paid pursuant to the section 2219a of title 7." for "except that the cost of overtime and holiday work performed in establishments subject to the provisions of this chapter at such rates as the Secretary may determine shall be borne by such establishments. Sums received by the Secretary in reimbursement for sums paid out by him for such premium pay work shall be available without fiscal year limitation to carry out the purposes of this section."

[1] So in original. The word "the" probably should not appear.

§ 469. Authorization of appropriations

There is authorized to be appropriated such sums as are necessary to carry out the provisions of this chapter.

(Pub. L. 85–172, § 26, formerly § 20, Aug. 28, 1957, 71 Stat. 449, renumbered Pub. L. 90–492, § 17, Aug. 18, 1968, 82 Stat. 805.)

§ 470. Omitted

CODIFICATION

Section, Pub. L. 85–172, § 27, as added Pub. L. 90–492, § 17, Aug. 18, 1968, 82 Stat. 807; amended Pub. L. 103–437, § 8(1), Nov. 2, 1994, 108 Stat. 4588, which required the Secretary of Agriculture to report annually to the Committee on Agriculture of the House of Representatives and the Committee on Agriculture, Nutrition, and Forestry of the Senate on the slaughter of poultry and the processing and distribution of poultry parts and products, terminated, effective May 15, 2000, pursuant to section 3003 of Pub. L. 104–66, as amended, set out as a note under section 1113 of Title 31, Money and Finance. See, also, page 46 of House Document No. 103–7.

§ 471. Safe Meat and Poultry Inspection Panel

(a) Review and evaluation

The advisory panel known as the "Safe Meat and Poultry Inspection Panel" established by section 679a of this title shall review and evaluate, as the panel considers necessary, the adequacy, necessity, safety, cost-effectiveness, and scientific merit of—

(1) inspection procedures of, and work rules and worker relations involving Federal employees employed in, plants inspected under this chapter;

(2) informal petitions or proposals for changes in inspection procedures, processes, and techniques of plants inspected under this chapter;

(3) formal changes in poultry inspection regulations promulgated under this chapter, whether in notice, proposed, or final form; and

(4) such other matters as may be referred to the panel by the Secretary regarding the quality or effectiveness of a safe and cost-effective poultry inspection system under this chapter.

(b) Reports

(1) In general

The Safe Meat and Poultry Inspection Panel shall submit to the Secretary a report on the results of each review and evaluation carried out under paragraph (1), including such recommendations as the panel considers appropriate.

(2) Reports on formal changes

In the case of a report concerning a formal change in poultry inspection regulations, the report shall be made within the time limits prescribed for formal comments on such changes.

(Pub. L. 85–172, § 30, as added Pub. L. 104–127, title IX, § 918(a)(2), Apr. 4, 1996, 110 Stat. 1190.)

§ 472. Interstate shipment of poultry inspected by Federal and State agencies for certain small establishments

(a) Definitions

(1) Appropriate State agency

The term "appropriate State agency" means a State agency described in section 454(a)(1) of this title.

(2) Designated personnel

The term "designated personnel" means inspection personnel of a State agency that have undergone all necessary inspection training and certification to assist the Secretary in the administration and enforcement of this chapter, including rules and regulations issued under this chapter.

(3) Eligible establishment

The term "eligible establishment" means an establishment that is in compliance with—

(A) the State inspection program of the State in which the establishment is located; and

(B) this chapter, including rules and regulations issued under this chapter.

(4) Poultry item

The term "poultry item" means—

(A) a portion of poultry; and

(B) a poultry product.

(5) Selected establishment

The term "selected establishment" means an eligible establishment that is selected by the Secretary, in coordination with the appropriate State agency of the State in which the eligible establishment is located, under subsection (b) to ship poultry items in interstate commerce.

(b) Authority of Secretary to allow shipments

(1) In general

Subject to paragraph (2), the Secretary, in coordination with the appropriate State agency of the State in which an establishment is located, may select the establishment to ship poultry items in interstate commerce, and place on each poultry item shipped in interstate commerce a Federal mark, stamp, tag, or label of inspection, if—

(A) the poultry item qualifies for the Federal mark, stamp, tag, or label of inspection under the requirements of this chapter;

(B) the establishment is an eligible establishment; and

(C) inspection services for the establishment are provided by designated personnel.

(2) Prohibited establishments

In carrying out paragraph (1), the Secretary, in coordination with an appropriate State agency, shall not select an establishment that—

(A) on average, employs more than 25 employees (including supervisory and nonsupervisory employees), as defined by the Secretary;

(B) as of the date of the enactment of this section, ships in interstate commerce carcasses, portions of carcasses, or poultry items that are inspected by the Secretary in accordance with this chapter;

(C)(i) is a Federal establishment;

(ii) was a Federal establishment as of the date of the enactment of this section, and was reorganized on a later date under the same name or a different name or person by the person, firm, or corporation that controlled the establishment as of the date of the enactment of this section; or

(iii) was a State establishment as of the date of the enactment of this section that—

(I) as of the date of the enactment of this section, employed more than 25 employees; and

(II) was reorganized on a later date by the person, firm, or corporation that controlled the establishment as of the date of the enactment of this section;

(D) is in violation of this chapter;

(E) is located in a State that does not have a State inspection program; or

(F) is the subject of a transition carried out in accordance with a procedure developed by the Secretary under paragraph (3)(A).

(3) Establishments that employ more than 25 employees

(A) Development of procedure

The Secretary may develop a procedure to transition to a Federal establishment any establishment under this section that, on average, consistently employs more than 25 employees.

(B) Eligibility of certain establishments

(i) In general

A State establishment that employs more than 25 employees but less than 35 employees as of the date of the enactment of this section may be selected as a selected establishment under this subsection.

(ii) Procedures

A State establishment shall be subject to the procedures established under subparagraph (A) beginning on the date that is 3 years after the effective date described in subsection (i).

(c) Reimbursement of State costs

The Secretary shall reimburse a State for costs related to the inspection of selected establishments in the State in accordance with Federal requirements in an amount of not less than 60 percent of eligible State costs.

(d) Coordination between Federal and State agencies

(1) In general

The Secretary shall designate an employee of the Federal Government as State coordinator for each appropriate State agency—

(A) to provide oversight and enforcement of this section; and

(B) to oversee the training and inspection activities of designated personnel of the State agency.

(2) Supervision

A State coordinator shall be under the direct supervision of the Secretary.

(3) Duties of State coordinator

(A) In general

A State coordinator shall visit selected establishments with a frequency that is appropriate to ensure that selected establishments are operating in a manner that is consistent with this chapter (including regulations and policies under this chapter).

(B) Quarterly reports

A State coordinator shall, on a quarterly basis, submit to the Secretary a report that describes the status of each selected establishment that is under the jurisdiction of the State coordinator with respect to the level of compliance of each selected establishment with the requirements of this chapter.

(C) Immediate notification requirement

If a State coordinator determines that any selected establishment that is under the jurisdiction of the State coordinator is in violation of any requirement of this chapter, the State coordinator shall—

(i) immediately notify the Secretary of the violation; and

(ii) deselect the selected establishment or suspend inspection at the selected establishment.

(4) Performance evaluations

Performance evaluations of State coordinators designated under this subsection shall be conducted by the Secretary as part of the Federal agency management control system.

(e) Audits

(1) Periodic audits conducted by Inspector General of the Department of Agriculture

Not later than 2 years after the effective date described in subsection (i), and not less often than every 3 years thereafter, the Inspector General of the Department of Agriculture shall conduct an audit of each activity taken by the Secretary under this section for the period covered by the audit to determine compliance with this section.

(2) Audit conducted by Comptroller General of the United States

Not earlier than 3 years, nor later than 5 years, after the date of the enactment of this section, the Comptroller General of the United States shall conduct an audit of the implementation of this section to determine—

(A) the effectiveness of the implementation of this section; and

(B) the number of selected establishments selected by the Secretary to ship poultry items under this section.

(f) Transition grants

The Secretary may provide grants to appropriate State agencies to assist the appropriate State agencies in helping establishments covered by this chapter to transition to selected establishments.

(g) Violations

Any selected establishment that the Secretary determines to be in violation of any requirement of this chapter shall be transitioned to a Federal establishment in accordance with a procedure developed by the Secretary under subsection (b)(3)(A).

(h) Effect

Nothing in this section limits the jurisdiction of the Secretary with respect to the regulation of poultry and poultry products under this chapter.

(i) Effective date

(1) In general

This section takes effect on the date on which the Secretary, after providing a period of public comment (including through the conduct of public meetings or hearings), promulgates final regulations to carry out this section.

(2) Requirement

Not later than 18 months after the date of the enactment of this section, the Secretary shall promulgate final regulations in accordance with paragraph (1).

(Pub. L. 85–172, § 31, as added Pub. L. 110–234, title XI, § 11015(b), May 22, 2008, 122 Stat. 1365, and Pub. L. 110–246, § 4(a), title XI, § 11015(b), June 18, 2008, 122 Stat. 1664, 2127.)

REFERENCES IN TEXT

The date of the enactment of this section, referred to in subsecs. (b)(2)(B), (C)(ii), (iii), (3)(B)(i), (e)(2), and (i)(2), is the date of enactment of Pub. L. 110–246, which was approved June 18, 2008.

CODIFICATION

Pub. L. 110–234 and Pub. L. 110–246 enacted identical sections. Pub. L. 110–234 was repealed by section 4(a) of Pub. L. 110–246.

EFFECTIVE DATE

Enactment of this section and repeal of Pub. L. 110–234 by Pub. L. 110–246 effective May 22, 2008, the date of enactment of Pub. L. 110–234, see section 4 of Pub. L. 110–246, set out as a note under section 8701 of Title 7, Agriculture.

CHAPTER 11—MANUFACTURE OF NARCOTIC DRUGS

§§ 501 to 517. Repealed. Pub. L. 91–513, title III, § 1101(a)(10), Oct. 27, 1970, 84 Stat. 1292

Sections, Pub. L. 86–429, Apr. 22, 1960, 74 Stat. 55, provided for licensing and control of the manufacture of all narcotic drugs and was known as the "Narcotic Manufacturing Act of 1960". Sections 1 to 3 and 5 to 22 of said Pub. L. 86–429 were classified respectively to sections 501, 501 notes, and 502 to 517 of this title. Section 4 of Pub. L. 86–429 was classified to sections 4702, 4731, and 4731 note of Title 26, Internal Revenue Code. See section 801 et seq. of this title.

EFFECTIVE DATE OF REPEAL

Repeal effective on first day of seventh calendar month that begins after Oct. 26, 1970, see section 1105(a) of Pub. L. 91–513, set out as a note under section 951 of this title. For provisions postponing such effective date if the Attorney General postpones the effective date of section 826 of this title, see section 1105(c) of Pub. L. 91–513, set out as an Effective Date note under section 951 of this title.

SAVINGS PROVISION

Prosecutions for any violation of law occurring, and civil seizures or forfeitures and injunctive proceedings commenced, prior to the effective date of repeal of these sections by section 1101 of Pub. L. 91–513 not to be affected or abated by reason thereof, see section 1103 of Pub. L. 91–513, set out as a note under sections 171 to 174 of this title.

CHAPTER 12—MEAT INSPECTION

SUBCHAPTER I—INSPECTION REQUIREMENTS; ADULTERATION AND MISBRANDING

§ 601. Definitions

As used in this chapter, except as otherwise specified, the following terms shall have the meanings stated below:

(a) The term "Secretary" means the Secretary of Agriculture of the United States or his delegate.

(b) The term "firm" means any partnership, association, or other unincorporated business organization.

(c) The term "meat broker" means any person, firm, or corporation engaged in the business of buying or selling carcasses, parts of carcasses, meat, or meat food products of cattle, sheep, swine, goats, horses, mules, or other equines on commission, or otherwise negotiating purchases or sales of such articles other than for his own account or as an employee of another person, firm, or corporation.

(d) The term "renderer" means any person, firm, or corporation engaged in the business of rendering carcasses or parts or products of the carcasses, of cattle, sheep, swine, goats, horses, mules, or other equines, except rendering conducted under inspection or exemption under this subchapter.

(e) The term "animal food manufacturer" means any person, firm, or corporation engaged in the business of manufacturing or processing animal food derived wholly or in part from carcasses, or parts or products of the carcasses, of cattle, sheep, swine, goats, horses, mules, or other equines.

(f) The term "State" means any State of the United States and the Commonwealth of Puerto Rico.

(g) The term "Territory" means Guam, the Virgin Islands of the United States, American Samoa, and any other territory or possession of the United States, excluding the Canal Zone.

(h) The term "commerce" means commerce between any State, any Territory, or the District of Columbia, and any place outside thereof; or within any Territory not organized with a legislative body, or the District of Columbia.

(i) The term "United States" means the States, the District of Columbia, and the Territories of the United States.

(j) The term "meat food product" means any product capable of use as human food which is made wholly or in part from any meat or other portion of the carcass of any cattle, sheep, swine, or goats, excepting products which contain meat or other portions of such carcasses only in a relatively small proportion or historically have not been considered by consumers as products of the meat food industry, and which are exempted from definition as a meat food product by the Secretary under such conditions as he may prescribe to assure that the meat or other portions of such carcasses contained in such product are not adulterated and that such products are not represented as meat food products. This term as applied to food products of equines shall have a meaning comparable to that provided in this paragraph with respect to cattle, sheep, swine, and goats.

(k) The term "capable of use as human food" shall apply to any carcass, or part or product of a carcass, of any animal, unless it is denatured or otherwise identified as required by regulations prescribed by the Secretary to deter its use as human food, or it is naturally inedible by humans.

(*l*) The term "prepared" means slaughtered, canned, salted, rendered, boned, cut up, or otherwise manufactured or processed.

(m) The term "adulterated" shall apply to any carcass, part thereof, meat or meat food product under one or more of the following circumstances:

(1) if it bears or contains any poisonous or deleterious substance which may render it injurious to health; but in case the substance is not an added substance, such article shall not be considered adulterated under this clause if the quantity of such substance in or on such article does not ordinarily render it injurious to health;

(2)(A) if it bears or contains (by reason of administration of any substance to the live animal or otherwise) any added poisonous or added deleterious substance (other than one which is (i) a pesticide chemical in or on a raw agricultural commodity; (ii) a food additive; or (iii) a color additive) which may, in the judgment of the Secretary, make such article unfit for human food;

(B) if it is, in whole or in part, a raw agricultural commodity and such commodity bears or contains a pesticide chemical which is unsafe within the meaning of section 346a of this title,

(C) if it bears or contains any food additive which is unsafe within the meaning of section 348 of this title,

(D) if it bears or contains any color additive which is unsafe within the meaning of section 379e of this title: *Provided*, That an article which is not adulterated under clause (B), (C), or (D) shall nevertheless be deemed adulterated if use of the pesticide chemical, food additive, or color additive in or on such article is prohibited by regulations of the Secretary in establishments at which inspection is maintained under this subchapter;

(3) if it consists in whole or in part of any filthy, putrid, or decomposed substance or is for any other reason unsound, unhealthful, unwholesome, or otherwise unfit for human food;

(4) if it has been prepared, packed, or held under insanitary conditions whereby it may have become contaminated with filth, or whereby it may have been rendered injurious to health;

(5) if it is, in whole or in part, the product of an animal which has died otherwise than by slaughter;

(6) if its container is composed, in whole or in part, of any poisonous or deleterious substance which may render the contents injurious to health;

(7) if it has been intentionally subjected to radiation, unless the use of the radiation was in conformity with a regulation or exemption in effect pursuant to section 348 of this title;

(8) if any valuable constituent has been in whole or in part omitted or abstracted therefrom; or if any substance has been substituted, wholly or in part therefor; or if damage or inferiority has been concealed in any manner; or if any substance has been added thereto or mixed or packed therewith so as to increase its bulk or weight, or reduce its quality or strength, or make it appear better or of greater value than it is; or

(9) if it is margarine containing animal fat and any of the raw material used therein consisted in whole or in part of any filthy, putrid, or decomposed substance.

(n) The term "misbranded" shall apply to any carcass, part thereof, meat or meat food product under one or more of the following circumstances:

(1) if its labeling is false or misleading in any particular;

(2) if it is offered for sale under the name of another food;

(3) if it is an imitation of another food, unless its label bears, in type of uniform size and prominence, the word "imitation" and immediately thereafter, the name of the food imitated;

(4) if its container is so made, formed, or filled as to be misleading;

(5) if in a package or other container unless it bears a label showing (A) the name and place of business of the manufacturer, packer, or distributor; and (B) an accurate statement of the quantity of the contents in terms of weight, measure, or numerical count: *Provided*, That under clause (B) of this subparagraph (5), reasonable variations may be permitted, and exemptions as to small packages may be established, by regulations prescribed by the Secretary;

(6) if any word, statement, or other information required by or under authority of this chapter to appear on the label or other labeling is not prominently placed thereon with such conspicuousness (as compared with other words, statements, designs, or devices, in the labeling) and in such terms as to render it likely to be read and understood by the ordinary individual under customary conditions of purchase and use;

(7) if it purports to be or is represented as a food for which a definition and standard of identity or composition has been prescribed by regulations of the Secretary under section 607 of this title unless (A) it conforms to such definition and standard, and (B) its label bears the name of the food specified in the definition and standard and, insofar as may be required by such regulations, the common names of optional ingredients (other than spices, flavoring, and coloring) present in such food;

(8) if it purports to be or is represented as a food for which a standard or standards of fill of container have been prescribed by regulations of the Secretary under section 607 of this title, and it falls below the standard of fill of container applicable thereto, unless its label bears, in such manner and form as such regulations specify, a statement that it falls below such standard;

(9) if it is not subject to the provisions of subparagraph (7), unless its label bears (A) the common or usual name of the food, if any there be, and (B) in case it is fabricated from two or more ingredients, the common or usual name of each such ingredient; except that spices, flavorings, and colorings may, when authorized by the Secretary, be designated as spices, flavorings, and colorings without naming each: *Provided*, That to the extent that compliance with the requirements of clause (B) of this subparagraph (9) is impracticable, or results in deception or unfair competition, exemptions shall be established by regulations promulgated by the Secretary;

(10) if it purports to be or is represented for special dietary uses, unless its label bears such information concerning its vitamin, mineral, and other dietary properties as the Secretary, after consultation with the Secretary of Health and Human Services, determines to be, and by regulations prescribes as, necessary in order fully to inform purchasers as to its value for such uses;

(11) if it bears or contains any artificial flavoring, artificial coloring, or chemical preservative, unless it bears labeling stating that fact: *Provided*, That, to the extent that compliance with the requirements of this subparagraph (11) is impracticable, exemptions shall be established by regulations promulgated by the Secretary; or

(12) if it fails to bear, directly thereon or on its container, as the Secretary may by regulations prescribe, the inspection legend and, unrestricted by any of the foregoing, such other information as the Secretary may require in such regulations to assure that it will not have false or misleading labeling and that the public will be informed of the manner of handling required to maintain the article in a wholesome condition.

(*o*) The term "label" means a display of written, printed, or graphic matter upon the immediate container (not including package liners) of any article.

(p) The term "labeling" means all labels and other written, printed, or graphic matter (1) upon any article or any of its containers or wrappers, or (2) accompanying such article.

(q) The term "Federal Food, Drug, and Cosmetic Act [21 U.S.C. 301 et seq.]" means the Act so entitled, approved June 25, 1938 (52 Stat. 1040), and Acts amendatory thereof or supplementary thereto.

(r) The terms "pesticide chemical," "food additive," "color additive," and "raw agricultural commodity" shall have the same meanings for purposes of this chapter as under the Federal Food, Drug, and Cosmetic Act [21 U.S.C. 301 et seq.].

(s) The term "official mark" means the official inspection legend or any other symbol prescribed by regulations of the Secretary to identify the status of any article or animal under this chapter.

(t) The term "official inspection legend" means any symbol prescribed by regulations of the Secretary showing that an article was inspected and passed in accordance with this chapter.

(u) The term "official certificate" means any certificate prescribed by regulations of the Secretary for issuance by an inspector or other person performing official functions under this chapter.

(v) The term "official device" means any device prescribed or authorized by the Secretary for use in applying any official mark.

(w) The term "amenable species" means—

(1) those species subject to the provisions of this chapter on the day before November 10, 2005;

(2) catfish, as defined by the Secretary; and

(3) any additional species of livestock that the Secretary considers appropriate.

(Mar. 4, 1907, ch. 2907, title I, §1, as added Pub. L. 90–201, §2, Dec. 15, 1967, 81 Stat. 584; amended Pub. L. 96–88, title V, §509(b), Oct. 17, 1979, 93 Stat. 695; Pub. L. 102–571, title I, §107(14), Oct. 29, 1992, 106 Stat. 4499; Pub. L. 109–97, title VII, §798[(a)](2), Nov. 10, 2005, 119 Stat. 2166; Pub. L. 110–234, title XI, §11016(b)(1)(A), May 22, 2008, 122 Stat. 1369; Pub. L. 110–246, §4(a), title XI, §11016(b)(1)(A), June 18, 2008, 122 Stat. 1664, 2130.)

REFERENCES IN TEXT

The Federal Food, Drug, and Cosmetic Act, referred to in pars. (q) and (r), is act June 25, 1938, ch. 675, 52

Stat. 1040, as amended, which is classified generally to chapter 9 (§ 301 et seq.) of this title. For complete classification of this Act to the Code, see section 301 of this title and Tables.

CODIFICATION

Pub. L. 110–234 and Pub. L. 110–246 made identical amendments to this section. The amendments by Pub. L. 110–234 were repealed by section 4(a) of Pub. L. 110–246.

AMENDMENTS

2008—Subsec. (w)(2), (3). Pub. L. 110–246, § 11016(b)(1)(A), added par. (2) and redesignated former par. (2) as (3).

2005—Par. (w). Pub. L. 109–97 added par. (w).

1992—Par. (m)(2)(D). Pub. L. 102–571 substituted "379e" for "376".

CHANGE OF NAME

"Secretary of Health and Human Services" substituted for "Secretary of Health, Education, and Welfare" in par. (n)(10) pursuant to section 509(b) of Pub. L. 96–88, which is classified to section 3508(b) of Title 20, Education.

EFFECTIVE DATE OF 2008 AMENDMENT

Amendment of this section and repeal of Pub. L. 110–234 by Pub. L. 110–246 effective May 22, 2008, the date of enactment of Pub. L. 110–234, except as otherwise provided, see section 4 of Pub. L. 110–246, set out as an Effective Date note under section 8701 of Title 7, Agriculture.

Pub. L. 110–234, title XI, § 11016(b)(2)(A), May 22, 2008, 122 Stat. 1369, and Pub. L. 110–246, § 4(a), title XI, § 11016(b)(2)(A), June 18, 2008, 122 Stat. 1664, 2131, provided that: "The amendments made by paragraph (1) [enacting sections 606 and 625 of this title, amending this section, and repealing former section 606 of this title] shall not apply until the date on which the Secretary of Agriculture issues final regulations (after providing a period of public comment, including through the conduct of public meetings or hearings, in accordance with chapter 5 of title 5, United States Code) to carry out such amendments."

[Pub. L. 110–234 and Pub. L. 110–246 enacted identical provisions. Pub. L. 110–234 was repealed by section 4(a) of Pub. L. 110–246, set out as a note under section 8701 of Title 7, Agriculture.]

EFFECTIVE DATE OF 2005 AMENDMENT

Pub. L. 109–97, title VII, § 798(b), Nov. 10, 2005, 119 Stat. 2166, provided that: "The amendments made by subsection (a) [amending this section and sections 603 to 605, 608, 609, 615, and 617 to 621 of this title] shall take effect on the day after the effective date of section 794 of the Agriculture, Rural Development, Food and Drug Administration, and Related Agencies Appropriations Act, 2006 [section 794 of Pub. L. 109–97, 119 Stat. 2164, effective 120 days after Nov. 10, 2005]."

EFFECTIVE DATE

Section 20 of Pub. L. 90–201 provided that: "This Act [see Short Title note below] shall become effective upon enactment [Dec. 15, 1967] except as provided in paragraphs (a) through (d):

"(a) The provisions of paragraph (b)(1) and (c) of section 10 and the provisions of section 20 of the Federal Meat Inspection Act, as amended by sections 7 and 10 of this Act [sections 610 and 620 of this title], and the provisions of section 18 of this Act repealing paragraph (b) of section 306 of the Tariff Act of 1930 [section 1306(b) of Title 19, Customs Duties], shall become effective upon the expiration of sixty days after enactment [Dec. 15, 1967], hereof.

"(b) The provisions of title I of the Federal Meat Inspection Act, as amended by this Act [this subchapter], shall become effective with respect to equines (other than horses) and their carcasses and parts thereof, meat, and meat food products thereof upon the expiration of sixty days after enactment [Dec. 15, 1967] hereof.

"(c) Section 11 of this Act, amending section 23, of the Federal Meat Inspection Act [section 623 of this title], shall become effective upon the expiration of sixty days after enactment hereof [Dec. 15, 1967].

"(d) Section 204 of the Federal Meat Inspection Act, as added by section 14 of this Act [section 644 of this title], shall become effective upon the expiration of sixty days after enactment hereof [Dec. 15, 1967]."

SHORT TITLE OF 1986 AMENDMENT

Pub. L. 99–641, title IV, § 401, Nov. 10, 1986, 100 Stat. 3567, provided that: "This title [amending sections 606, 609, 621, 671, and 676 of this title and enacting provisions set out as notes under sections 606, 609, 621, 671, and 676 of this title] may be cited as the 'Processed Products Inspection Improvement Act of 1986'."

SHORT TITLE OF 1978 AMENDMENT

Pub. L. 95–445, § 1, Oct. 10, 1978, 92 Stat. 1069, provided: "That this Act [amending sections 603, 610, and 620 of this title and sections 1902 and 1904 of Title 7, Agriculture, repealing sections 1903 and 1905 of Title 7, and enacting provisions set out as notes under this section and section 603 of this title] may be cited as the 'Humane Methods of Slaughter Act of 1978'."

SHORT TITLE

Section 1 of Pub. L. 90–201 provided in part: "That this Act [enacting this section and sections 602, 624, 641 to 645, 661, 671 to 680, and 691 of this title, amending sections 603 to 623 of this title, repealing section 96 of this title and section 1306(b) of Title 19, Customs Duties, and enacting provisions set out as notes under this section] may be cited as the 'Wholesome Meat Act'."

Section 1 of Pub. L. 90–201 provided in part that the provisions of act Mar. 4, 1907, as amended, classified to subchapters I to IV–A of this chapter, are designated as the "Federal Meat Inspection Act".

REGULATIONS

Pub. L. 110–234, title XI, § 11016(b)(2)(B), May 22, 2008, 122 Stat. 1370, and Pub. L. 110–246, § 4(a), title XI, § 11016(b)(2)(B), June 18, 2008, 122 Stat. 1664, 2131, provided that: "Not later than 18 months after the date of the enactment of this Act [June 18, 2008], the Secretary of Agriculture, in consultation with the Commissioner of Food and Drugs, shall issue final regulations to carry out the amendments made by paragraph (1) [enacting sections 606 and 625 of this title, amending this section, and repealing former section 606 of this title]."

[Pub. L. 110–234 and Pub. L. 110–246 enacted identical provisions. Pub. L. 110–234 was repealed by section 4(a) of Pub. L. 110–246, set out as a note under section 8701 of Title 7, Agriculture.]

SEPARABILITY

Section 19 of Pub. L. 90–201 provided that: "If any provision of this Act or of the amendments made hereby [see Short Title note above] or the application thereof to any person or circumstances is held invalid, the validity of the remainder of the Act and the remaining amendments [see Short Title note above] and of the application of such provision to other persons and circumstances shall not be affected thereby."

§ 602. Congressional statement of findings

Meat and meat food products are an important source of the Nation's total supply of food. They are consumed throughout the Nation and the major portion thereof moves in interstate or foreign commerce. It is essential in the public interest that the health and welfare of consumers be protected by assuring that meat and meat food products distributed to them are wholesome, not adulterated, and properly marked, labeled, and packaged. Unwholesome, adulterated, or misbranded meat or meat food products impair the effective regulation of meat and meat food products in interstate or foreign commerce, are injurious to the public welfare, destroy markets for wholesome, not adulterated, and properly labeled and packaged meat and meat food products, and result in sundry losses to livestock producers and processors of meat and meat food products, as well as injury to consumers. The unwholesome, adulterated, mislabeled, or deceptively packaged articles can be sold at lower prices and compete unfairly with the wholesome, not adulterated, and properly labeled and packaged articles, to the detriment of consumers and the public generally. It is hereby found that all articles and animals which are regulated under this chapter are either in interstate or foreign commerce or substantially affect such commerce, and that regulation by the Secretary and cooperation by the States and other jurisdictions as contemplated by this chapter are appropriate to prevent and eliminate burdens upon such commerce, to effectively regulate such commerce, and to protect the health and welfare of consumers.

(Mar. 4, 1907, ch. 2907, title I, §2, as added Pub. L. 90–201, §2, Dec. 15, 1967, 81 Stat. 587.)

§603. Examination of animals prior to slaughter; use of humane methods

(a) Examination of animals before slaughtering; diseased animals slaughtered separately and carcasses examined

For the purpose of preventing the use in commerce of meat and meat food products which are adulterated, the Secretary shall cause to be made, by inspectors appointed for that purpose, an examination and inspection of all amenable species before they shall be allowed to enter into any slaughtering, packing, meat-canning, rendering, or similar establishment, in which they are to be slaughtered and the meat and meat food products thereof are to be used in commerce; and all amenable species found on such inspection to show symptoms of disease shall be set apart and slaughtered separately from all other cattle, sheep, swine, goats, horses, mules, or other equines, and when so slaughtered the carcasses of said cattle, sheep, swine, goats, horses, mules, or other equines shall be subject to a careful examination and inspection, all as provided by the rules and regulations to be prescribed by the Secretary, as provided for in this subchapter.

(b) Humane methods of slaughter

For the purpose of preventing the inhumane slaughtering of livestock, the Secretary shall cause to be made, by inspectors appointed for that purpose, an examination and inspection of the method by which amenable species are slaughtered and handled in connection with slaughter in the slaughtering establishments inspected under this chapter. The Secretary may refuse to provide inspection to a new slaughtering establishment or may cause inspection to be temporarily suspended at a slaughtering establishment if the Secretary finds that any cattle, sheep, swine, goats, horses, mules, or other equines have been slaughtered or handled in connection with slaughter at such establishment by any method not in accordance with the Act of August 27, 1958 (72 Stat. 862; 7 U.S.C. 1901–1906) until the establishment furnishes assurances satisfactory to the Secretary that all slaughtering and handling in connection with slaughter of livestock shall be in accordance with such a method.

(Mar. 4, 1907, ch. 2907, title I, §3, formerly 1st par., 34 Stat. 1260; renumbered §3 and amended Pub. L. 90–201, §§1, 3, 12(a), (b), Dec. 15, 1967, 81 Stat. 584, 588, 592; Pub. L. 95–445, §2, Oct. 10, 1978, 92 Stat. 1069; Pub. L. 109–97, title VII, §798[(a)](1), Nov. 10, 2005, 119 Stat. 2166.)

References in Text

Act of August 27, 1958, referred to in subsec. (b), is Pub. L. 85–765, Aug. 27, 1958, 72 Stat. 862, as amended, which is classified generally to chapter 48 (§1901 et seq.) of Title 7, Agriculture. For complete classification of this Act to the Code, see Tables.

Sections 1903 and 1905 of Title 7, included within reference to Act of August 27, 1958, were repealed by Pub. L. 95–445, §5(b), Oct. 10, 1978, 92 Stat. 1069, effective as set forth in section 7 of Pub. L. 95–445, set out as an Effective Date of 1978 Amendment note below.

Codification

Section was formerly classified to section 71 of this title.

Amendments

2005—Pub. L. 109–97 substituted "amenable species" for "cattle, sheep, swine, goats, horses, mules, and other equines" wherever appearing.

1978—Pub. L. 95–445 designated existing provisions as subsec. (a) and added subsec. (b).

1967—Pub. L. 90–201, §§3, 12(a), (b), struck out "interstate or foreign" before "commerce" in two places, substituted "Secretary shall" for "Secretary, at his discretion, may", and struck out "of Agriculture" after "Secretary", included horses, mules, and other equines, and horses, mules, or other equines in the list of animals, and substituted "adulterated" for "unsound, unhealthful, unwholesome, or otherwise unfit for human food", respectively.

Effective Date of 2005 Amendment

Amendment by Pub. L. 109–97 effective the day after 120 days after Nov. 10, 2005, see section 798(b) of Pub. L. 109–97, set out as a note under section 601 of this title.

Effective Date of 1978 Amendment

Section 7 of Pub. L. 95–445 provided that: "The provisions of this Act [see Short Title of 1978 Amendment note set out under section 601 of this title] shall become effective one year after the date of enactment [Oct. 10, 1978]. However, such provisions shall not apply to a person, firm, or corporation for such additional period of time, not to exceed eighteen months, as may be determined by the Secretary, if the Secretary, upon application, finds that compliance with the provisions of this Act on its effective date would cause undue hardship on such person, firm, or corporation."

Effective Date of 1967 Amendment

Amendment by Pub. L. 90–201 effective Dec. 15, 1967, except that with respect to equines (other than horses) and their carcasses and parts thereof, meat, and meat food products thereof, amendment effective upon expiration of sixty days after Dec. 15, 1967, see section 20(b) of Pub. L. 90–201, set out as an Effective Date note under section 601 of this title.

RELIGIOUS FREEDOM; RITUAL SLAUGHTER

Section 6 of Pub. L. 95–445 provided that: "Nothing in this Act [see Short Title of 1978 Amendment note set out under section 601 of this title] shall be construed to prohibit, abridge, or in any way hinder the religious freedom of any person or group. Notwithstanding any other provision of this Act, in order to protect freedom of religion, ritual slaughter and the handling or other preparation of livestock for ritual slaughter are exempted from the terms of this Act. For the purposes of this section the term 'ritual slaughter' means slaughter in accordance with section 2(b) of the Act of August 27, 1958 (72 Stat. 862; 7 U.S.C. 1902(b))."

§ 604. Post mortem examination of carcasses and marking or labeling; destruction of carcasses condemned; reinspection

For the purposes hereinbefore set forth the Secretary shall cause to be made by inspectors appointed for that purpose a post mortem examination and inspection of the carcasses and parts thereof of all amenable species to be prepared at any slaughtering, meat-canning, salting, packing, rendering, or similar establishment in any State, Territory, or the District of Columbia as articles of commerce which are capable of use as human food; and the carcasses and parts thereof of all such animals found to be not adulterated shall be marked, stamped, tagged, or labeled as "Inspected and passed"; and said inspectors shall label, mark, stamp, or tag as "Inspected and condemned" all carcasses and parts thereof of animals found to be adulterated; and all carcasses and parts thereof thus inspected and condemned shall be destroyed for food purposes by the said establishment in the presence of an inspector, and the Secretary may remove inspectors from any such establishment which fails to so destroy any such condemned carcass or part thereof, and said inspectors, after said first inspection, shall, when they deem it necessary, reinspect said carcasses or parts thereof to determine whether since the first inspection the same have become adulterated, and if any carcass or any part thereof shall, upon examination and inspection subsequent to the first examination and inspection, be found to be adulterated, it shall be destroyed for food purposes by the said establishment in the presence of an inspector, and the Secretary may remove inspectors from any establishment which fails to so destroy any such condemned carcass or part thereof.

(Mar. 4, 1907, ch. 2907, title I, § 4, formerly 2nd par., 34 Stat. 1260; renumbered § 4 and amended Pub. L. 90–201, §§ 1, 3, 4, 12(a)–(d), Dec. 15, 1967, 81 Stat. 584, 588, 592; Pub. L. 109–97, title VII, § 798[(a)](1), Nov. 10, 2005, 119 Stat. 2166.)

CODIFICATION

Section was formerly classified to section 72 of this title.

AMENDMENTS

2005—Pub. L. 109–97 substituted "amenable species" for "cattle, sheep, swine, goats, horses, mules, and other equines".

1967—Pub. L. 90–201, §§ 3, 4, 12(a)–(d), struck out "interstate or foreign" before "commerce" and "of Agriculture" after "Secretary" in three places; struck out "for human consumption" before "at any slaughtering" and "for transportation or sale" after "District of Columbia" and inserted "which are capable of use as human food" after "commerce"; included horses, mules, and other equines in the list of animals; substituted "adulterated" for "unsound, unhealthful, unwholesome, or otherwise unfit for human food" after "'Inspected and condemned,' all carcasses and parts thereof of animals found to be" and before ", it shall be destroyed"; substituted "not adulterated" for "sound, healthful, wholesome, and fit for human food"; and substituted "adulterated" for "unsound, unhealthful, unwholesome, or in any way unfit for human food" before "and if any carcass", respectively.

EFFECTIVE DATE OF 2005 AMENDMENT

Amendment by Pub. L. 109–97 effective the day after 120 days after Nov. 10, 2005, see section 798(b) of Pub. L. 109–97, set out as a note under section 601 of this title.

EFFECTIVE DATE OF 1967 AMENDMENT

Amendment by Pub. L. 90–201 effective Dec. 15, 1967, except that with respect to equines (other than horses) and their carcasses and parts thereof, meat, and meat food products thereof, amendment effective upon expiration of sixty days after Dec. 15, 1967, see section 20(b) of Pub. L. 90–201, set out as an Effective Date note under section 601 of this title.

§ 605. Examination of carcasses brought into slaughtering or packing establishments, and of meat food products issued from and returned thereto; conditions for entry

The foregoing provisions shall apply to all carcasses or parts of carcasses of amenable species or the meat or meat products thereof which may be brought into any slaughtering, meat-canning, salting, packing, rendering, or similar establishment, and such examination and inspection shall be had before the said carcasses or parts thereof shall be allowed to enter into any department wherein the same are to be treated and prepared for meat food products; and the foregoing provisions shall also apply to all such products, which, after having been issued from any slaughtering, meat-canning, salting, packing, rendering, or similar establishment, shall be returned to the same or to any similar establishment where such inspection is maintained. The Secretary may limit the entry of carcasses, parts of carcasses, meat and meat food products, and other materials into any establishment at which inspection under this subchapter is maintained, under such conditions as he may prescribe to assure that allowing the entry of such articles into such inspected establishments will be consistent with the purposes of this chapter.

(Mar. 4, 1907, ch. 2907, title I, § 5, formerly 3rd par., 34 Stat. 1261; renumbered § 5 and amended Pub. L. 90–201, §§ 1, 5, 12(a), Dec. 15, 1967, 81 Stat. 584, 588, 592; Pub. L. 109–97, title VII, § 798[(a)](1), Nov. 10, 2005, 119 Stat. 2166.)

CODIFICATION

Section was formerly classified to section 73 of this title.

AMENDMENTS

2005—Pub. L. 109–97 substituted "amenable species" for "cattle, sheep, swine, goats, horses, mules, and other equines".

1967—Pub. L. 90–201, §§ 5, 12(a), limited entry of articles into establishments under such prescribed conditions as would be consistent with the purpose of this chapter and included horses, mules, and other equines in the list of animals, respectively.

EFFECTIVE DATE OF 2005 AMENDMENT

Amendment by Pub. L. 109–97 effective the day after 120 days after Nov. 10, 2005, see section 798(b) of Pub. L. 109–97, set out as a note under section 601 of this title.

EFFECTIVE DATE OF 1967 AMENDMENT

Amendment by Pub. L. 90–201 effective Dec. 15, 1967, except that with respect to equines (other than horses) and their carcasses and parts thereof, meat, and meat food products thereof, amendment effective upon expiration of sixty days after Dec. 15, 1967, see section 20(b) of Pub. L. 90–201, set out as an Effective Date note under section 601 of this title.

§ 606. Inspection and labeling of meat food products

(a) In general

For the purposes hereinbefore set forth the Secretary shall cause to be made, by inspectors appointed for that purpose, an examination and inspection of all meat food products prepared for commerce in any slaughtering, meat-canning, salting, packing, rendering, or similar establishment, and for the purposes of any examination and inspection and inspectors shall have access at all times, by day or night, whether the establishment be operated or not, to every part of said establishment; and said inspectors shall mark, stamp, tag, or label as "Inspected and passed" all such products found to be not adulterated; and said inspectors shall label, mark, stamp, or tag as "Inspected and condemned" all such products found adulterated, and all such condemned meat food products shall be destroyed for food purposes, as hereinbefore provided, and the Secretary may remove inspectors from any establishment which fails to so destroy such condemned meat food products: *Provided*, That subject to the rules and regulations of the Secretary the provisions of this section in regard to preservatives shall not apply to meat food products for export to any foreign country and which are prepared or packed according to the specifications or directions of the foreign purchaser, when no substance is used in the preparation or packing thereof in conflict with the laws of the foreign country to which said article is to be exported; but if said article shall be in fact sold or offered for sale for domestic use or consumption then this proviso shall not exempt said article from the operation of all the other provisions of this chapter.[1]

(b) Catfish

In the case of an examination and inspection under subsection (a) of a meat food product derived from catfish, the Secretary shall take into account the conditions under which the catfish is raised and transported to a processing establishment.

(Mar. 4, 1907, ch. 2907, title I, §6, as added Pub. L. 110–234, title XI, §11016(b)(1)(B), May 22, 2008, 122 Stat. 1369, and Pub. L. 110–246, §4(a), title XI, §11016(b)(1)(B), June 18, 2008, 122 Stat. 1664, 2131.)

REFERENCES IN TEXT

This chapter, referred to in subsec. (a), probably should have been a reference to this Act in the original, meaning the Federal Meat Inspection Act, titles I to V of act Mar. 4, 1907, ch. 2907, as added Dec. 15, 1967, Pub. L. 90–201, 81 Stat. 584, which are classified generally to subchapters I to IV–A of this chapter.

CODIFICATION

Pub. L. 110–234 and Pub. L. 110–246 enacted identical sections and repealed former section 6 of act Mar. 4, 1907. Pub. L. 110–234 was repealed by section 4(a) of Pub. L. 110–246.

PRIOR PROVISIONS

A prior section 606, acts Mar. 4, 1907, ch. 2907, title I, §6, formerly 4th par., 34 Stat. 1261; renumbered §6 and amended Pub. L. 90–201, §§1, 3, 12(e), Dec. 15, 1967, 81 Stat. 584, 588, 592; Pub. L. 99–641, title IV, §403(a), Nov. 10, 1986, 100 Stat. 3567, was formerly classified to section 74 of this title and was repealed by Pub. L. 110–234, title XI, §11016(b)(1)(B), May 22, 2008, 122 Stat. 1369, and Pub. L. 110–246, §4(a), title XI, §11016(b)(1)(B), June 18, 2008, 122 Stat. 1664, 2131. Prior to repeal, section read as follows: "For the purposes hereinbefore set forth the Secretary shall cause to be made, by inspectors appointed for that purpose, an examination and inspection of all meat food products prepared for commerce in any slaughtering, meat-canning, salting, packing, rendering, or similar establishment, and for the purposes of any examination and inspection and inspectors shall have access at all times, by day or night, whether the establishment be operated or not, to every part of said establishment; and said inspectors shall mark, stamp, tag, or label as 'Inspected and passed' all such products found to be not adulterated; and said inspectors shall label, mark, stamp, or tag as 'Inspected and condemned' all such products found adulterated, and all such condemned meat food products shall be destroyed for food purposes, as hereinbefore provided, and the Secretary may remove inspectors from any establishment which fails to so destroy such condemned meat food products: *Provided*, That subject to the rules and regulations of the Secretary the provisions of this section in regard to preservatives shall not apply to meat food products for export to any foreign country and which are prepared or packed according to the specifications or directions of the foreign purchaser, when no substance is used in the preparation or packing thereof in conflict with the laws of the foreign country to which said article is to be exported; but if said article shall be in fact sold or offered for sale for domestic use or consumption then this proviso shall not exempt said article from the operation of all the other provisions of this chapter."

EFFECTIVE DATE

Enactment of this section and repeal of former section 6 of act Mar. 4, 1907, and Pub. L. 110–234 by Pub. L. 110–246 effective May 22, 2008, the date of enactment of Pub. L. 110–234, except as otherwise provided, see section 4 of Pub. L. 110–246, set out as a note under section 8701 of Title 7, Agriculture.

Section and repeal of former section 6 of act Mar. 4, 1907, inapplicable until date on which the Secretary of Agriculture issues final regulations to carry out amendments by Pub. L. 110–246, §11016(b)(1), see section 11016(b)(2)(A) of Pub. L. 110–246, set out as an Effective Date of 2008 Amendment note under section 601 of this title.

§ 607. Labeling, marking, and container requirements

(a) Labeling receptacles or coverings of meat or meat food products inspected and passed; supervision by inspectors

When any meat or meat food product prepared for commerce which has been inspected as hereinbefore provided and marked "Inspected and passed" shall be placed or packed in any can, pot, tin, canvas, or other receptacle or covering

[1] See References in Text note below.

in any establishment where inspection under the provisions of this chapter is maintained, the person, firm, or corporation preparing said product shall cause a label to be attached to said can, pot, tin, canvas, or other receptacle or covering, under the supervision of an inspector, which label shall state that the contents thereof have been "inspected and passed" under the provisions of this chapter; and no inspection and examination of meat or meat food products deposited or inclosed in cans, tins, pots, canvas, or other receptacle or covering in any establishment where inspection under the provisions of this chapter is maintained shall be deemed to be complete until such meat or meat food products have been sealed or inclosed in said can, tin, pot, canvas, or other receptacle or covering under the supervision of an inspector.

(b) Information on articles or containers; legible form

All carcasses, parts of carcasses, meat and meat food products inspected at any establishment under the authority of this subchapter and found to be not adulterated, shall at the time they leave the establishment bear, in distinctly legible form, directly thereon or on their containers, as the Secretary may require, the information required under paragraph (n) of section 601 of this title.

(c) Labeling: type styles and sizes; definitions and standards of identity or composition; standards of fill of container; consistency of Federal and Federal-State standards

The Secretary, whenever he determines such action is necessary for the protection of the public, may prescribe: (1) the styles and sizes of type to be used with respect to material required to be incorporated in labeling to avoid false or misleading labeling in marketing and labeling any articles or animals subject to this subchapter or subchapter II of this chapter; (2) definitions and standards of identity or composition for articles subject to this subchapter and standards of fill of container for such articles not inconsistent with any such standards established under the Federal Food, Drug, and Cosmetic Act [21 U.S.C. 301 et seq.], and there shall be consultation between the Secretary and the Secretary of Health and Human Services prior to the issuance of such standards under either Act relating to articles subject to this chapter to avoid inconsistency in such standards and possible impairment of the coordinated effective administration of these Acts. There shall also be consultation between the Secretary and an appropriate advisory committee provided for in section 661 of this title, prior to the issuance of such standards under this chapter, to avoid, insofar as feasible, inconsistency between Federal and State standards.

(d) Sales under false or misleading name, other marking or labeling or in containers of misleading form or size; trade names, and other marking, labeling, and containers approved by Secretary

No article subject to this subchapter shall be sold or offered for sale by any person, firm, or corporation, in commerce, under any name or other marking or labeling which is false or misleading, or in any container of a misleading form or size, but established trade names and other marking and labeling and containers which are not false or misleading and which are approved by the Secretary are permitted.

(e) Use withholding directive respecting false or misleading marking, labeling, or container; modification of false or misleading matter; hearing; withholding use pending proceedings; finality of Secretary's action; judicial review; application of section 194 of title 7

If the Secretary has reason to believe that any marking or labeling or the size or form of any container in use or proposed for use with respect to any article subject to this subchapter is false or misleading in any particular, he may direct that such use be withheld unless the marking, labeling, or container is modified in such manner as he may prescribe so that it will not be false or misleading. If the person, firm, or corporation using or proposing to use the marking, labeling or container does not accept the determination of the Secretary, such person, firm, or corporation may request a hearing, but the use of the marking, labeling, or container shall, if the Secretary so directs, be withheld pending hearing and final determination by the Secretary. Any such determination by the Secretary shall be conclusive unless, within thirty days after receipt of notice of such final determination, the person, firm, or corporation adversely affected thereby appeals to the United States court of appeals for the circuit in which such person, firm, or corporation has its principal place of business or to the United States Court of Appeals for the District of Columbia Circuit. The provisions of section 194 of title 7 shall be applicable to appeals taken under this section.

(f) Lamb and mutton

The Secretary, consistent with United States international obligations, shall establish standards for the labeling of sheep carcasses, parts of sheep carcasses, sheepmeat, and sheepmeat food products.

(Mar. 4, 1907, ch. 2907, title I, §7, formerly 5th par., 34 Stat. 1262; renumbered §7 and amended Pub. L. 90–201, §§1, 3(a), 6, Dec. 15, 1967, 81 Stat. 584, 588; Pub. L. 96–88, title V, §509(b), Oct. 17, 1979, 93 Stat. 695; Pub. L. 104–127, title II, §279, Apr. 4, 1996, 110 Stat. 979.)

REFERENCES IN TEXT

The Federal Food, Drug, and Cosmetic Act, referred to in subsec. (c)(2), is act June 25, 1938, ch. 675, 52 Stat. 1040, as amended, which is classified generally to chapter 9 (§301 et seq.) of this title. For complete classification of this Act to the Code, see section 301 of this title and Tables.

Either Act and these Acts, referred to in subsec. (c)(2), mean the Federal Meat Inspection Act and the Federal Food, Drug, and Cosmetic Act. The Federal Meat Inspection Act is act Mar. 4, 1907, ch. 2907, titles I to IV, as added Dec. 15, 1967, Pub. L. 90–201, 81 Stat. 584, and amended, which are classified generally to subchapters I to IV (§601 et seq.), respectively, of this chapter. For complete classification of this Act to the Code, see Short Title note under section 601 of this title and Tables.

CODIFICATION

Section was formerly classified to section 75 of this title.

AMENDMENTS

1996—Subsec. (f). Pub. L. 104–127 added subsec. (f).

1967—Subsec. (a). Pub. L. 90–201, §§3(a), 6(a), (b), struck out "interstate or foreign" before "commerce" and provisions prohibiting sales of meat or meat food products in interstate or foreign commerce under any false or deceptive names and permitting trade names or names which are usual to such products and are not false and deceptive and are approved by the Secretary of Agriculture, now incorporated in subsec. (d), and designated remaining provisions as subsecs. (a), respectively.

Subsecs. (b) to (e). Pub. L. 90–201, §6(c), added subsecs. (b) to (e).

CHANGE OF NAME

"Secretary of Health and Human Services" substituted for "Secretary of Health, Education, and Welfare" in subsec. (c)(2) pursuant to section 509(b) of Pub. L. 96–88, which is classified to section 3508(b) of Title 20, Education.

EFFECTIVE DATE OF 1967 AMENDMENT

Amendment by Pub. L. 90–201 effective Dec. 15, 1967, except that with respect to equines (other than horses) and their carcasses and parts thereof, meat, and meat food products thereof, amendment effective upon expiration of sixty days after Dec. 15, 1967, see section 20(b) of Pub. L. 90–201, set out as an Effective Date note under section 601 of this title.

§ 608. Sanitary inspection and regulation of slaughtering and packing establishments; rejection of adulterated meat or meat food products

The Secretary shall cause to be made, by experts in sanitation or by other competent inspectors, such inspection of all slaughtering, meat canning, salting, packing, rendering, or similar establishments in which amenable species are slaughtered and the meat and meat food products thereof are prepared for commerce as may be necessary to inform himself concerning the sanitary conditions of the same, and to prescribe the rules and regulations of sanitation under which such establishments shall be maintained; and where the sanitary conditions of any such establishment are such that the meat or meat food products are rendered adulterated, he shall refuse to allow said meat or meat food products to be labeled, marked, stamped or tagged as "inspected and passed."

(Mar. 4, 1907, ch. 2907, title I, §8, formerly 6th par., 34 Stat. 1262; renumbered §8 and amended Pub. L. 90–201, §§1, 3, 12(a), (f), Dec. 15, 1967, 81 Stat. 584, 588, 592; Pub. L. 109–97, title VII, §798[(a)](1), Nov. 10, 2005, 119 Stat. 2166.)

CODIFICATION

Section was formerly classified to section 76 of this title.

AMENDMENTS

2005—Pub. L. 109–97 substituted "amenable species" for "cattle, sheep, swine, goats, horses, mules, and other equines".

1967—Pub. L. 90–201, §§3, 12(a), (f), struck out "interstate or foreign" before "commerce" and "of Agriculture" after "Secretary", included horses, mules, and other equines in the list of animals, and substituted "adulterated" for "unclean, unsound, unhealthful, unwholesome, or otherwise unfit for human food", respectively.

EFFECTIVE DATE OF 2005 AMENDMENT

Amendment by Pub. L. 109–97 effective the day after 120 days after Nov. 10, 2005, see section 798(b) of Pub. L. 109–97, set out as a note under section 601 of this title.

EFFECTIVE DATE OF 1967 AMENDMENT

Amendment by Pub. L. 90–201 effective Dec. 15, 1967, except that with respect to equines (other than horses) and their carcasses and parts thereof, meat, and meat food products thereof, amendment effective upon expiration of sixty days after Dec. 15, 1967, see section 20(b) of Pub. L. 90–201, set out as an Effective Date note under section 601 of this title.

§ 609. Examination of animals and food products thereof, slaughtered and prepared during nighttime

The Secretary shall cause an examination and inspection of all amenable species, and the food products thereof, slaughtered and prepared in the establishments hereinbefore described for the purposes of commerce to be made during the nighttime as well as during the daytime when the slaughtering of said amenable species, or the preparation of said food products is conducted during the nighttime.

(Mar. 4, 1907, ch. 2907, title I, §9, formerly 7th par., 34 Stat. 1262; renumbered §9 and amended Pub. L. 90–201, §§1, 3, 12(a), Dec. 15, 1967, 81 Stat. 584, 588, 592; Pub. L. 99–641, title IV, §403(d)(1), Nov. 10, 1986, 100 Stat. 3570; Pub. L. 109–97, title VII, §798[(a)](1), Nov. 10, 2005, 119 Stat. 2166.)

CODIFICATION

Section was formerly classified to section 77 of this title.

AMENDMENTS

2005—Pub. L. 109–97 substituted "amenable species" for "cattle, sheep, swine, goats, horses, mules, and other equines" in two places.

1986—Pub. L. 99–641 temporarily inserted ", except as provided in section 606 of this title," after first reference to "other equines, and". See Effective and Termination Dates of 1986 Amendment note below.

1967—Pub. L. 90–201, §§3, 12(a), struck out "interstate or foreign" before "commerce" and "of Agriculture" after "Secretary" and included horses, mules, and other equines in the list of animals, respectively.

EFFECTIVE DATE OF 2005 AMENDMENT

Amendment by Pub. L. 109–97 effective the day after 120 days after Nov. 10, 2005, see section 798(b) of Pub. L. 109–97, set out as a note under section 601 of this title.

EFFECTIVE AND TERMINATION DATES OF 1986 AMENDMENT

Section 403(d)(1) of Pub. L. 99–641 provided that the amendment made by that section is effective only during the 6-year period beginning Nov. 10, 1986.

Pub. L. 99–641, title IV, §408, Nov. 10, 1986, 100 Stat. 3571, provided that:

"(a) GENERAL EFFECTIVE DATE.—Except as provided in subsection (b) of this section, this title and the amendments made by this title [amending this section and sections 606, 621, 671, and 676 of this title and enacting provisions set out as notes under this section and sections 606, 621, 671, and 676 of this title] shall become effective on the date of the enactment of this Act [Nov. 10, 1986].

"(b) TEMPORARY APPLICATION OF EXISTING LAW.—Sections 6, 9, and 21 of the Federal Meat Inspection Act (21 U.S.C. 606, 609, and 621), as in effect immediately before the date of the enactment of this Act [Nov. 10, 1986], shall apply with respect to establishments until the

Secretary of Agriculture first issues rules and regulations to implement the amendments made by section 403(a) [amending section 606 of this title]."

EFFECTIVE DATE OF 1967 AMENDMENT

Amendment by Pub. L. 90–201 effective Dec. 15, 1967, except that with respect to equines (other than horses) and their carcasses and parts thereof, meat, and meat food products thereof, amendment effective upon expiration of sixty days after Dec. 15, 1967, see section 20(b) of Pub. L. 90–201, set out as an Effective Date note under section 601 of this title.

SAVINGS PROVISION

Section 404 of Pub. L. 99–641 provided that: "The expiration date provisions of section 403 [enacting provisions set out as notes under this section and sections 606, 621, 671, and 676 of this title] shall not have the effect of releasing or extinguishing any penalty, forfeiture, or liability incurred under the Federal Meat Inspection Act (21 U.S.C. 601 et seq.), as amended by section 403 [amending this section and sections 606, 621, 671, and 676 of this title], or under the rules or regulations issued under such Act."

INSPECTION SERVICES FOR ESTABLISHMENTS NOT PARTICIPATING IN TOTAL PLANT QUALITY-CONTROL PROGRAM

Section 403(e) of Pub. L. 99–641 provided that: "The amendments made by this section [amending this section and sections 606, 621, 671, and 676 of this title] shall not be construed to authorize the Secretary of Agriculture to refuse to provide inspection under the Federal Meat Inspection Act (21 U.S.C. 601 et seq.) at an establishment solely because such establishment does not participate in a total plant quality-control program."

§ 610. Prohibited acts

No person, firm, or corporation shall, with respect to any cattle, sheep, swine, goats, horses, mules, or other equines, or any carcasses, parts of carcasses, meat or meat food products of any such animals—

(a) Slaughtering animals or preparation of articles capable of use as human food

slaughter any such animals or prepare any such articles which are capable of use as human food at any establishment preparing any such articles for commerce, except in compliance with the requirements of this chapter;

(b) Humane methods of slaughter

slaughter or handle in connection with slaughter any such animals in any manner not in accordance with the Act of August 27, 1958 (72 Stat. 862; 7 U.S.C. 1901–1906);

(c) Sales, transportation, and other transactions

sell, transport, offer for sale or transportation, or receive for transportation, in commerce, (1) any such articles which (A) are capable of use as human food and (B) are adulterated or misbranded at the time of such sale, transportation, offer for sale or transportation, or receipt for transportation; or (2) any articles required to be inspected under this subchapter unless they have been so inspected and passed;

(d) Adulteration or misbranding

do, with respect to any such articles which are capable of use as human food, any act while they are being transported in commerce or held for sale after such transportation, which is intended to cause or has the effect of causing such articles to be adulterated or misbranded.

(Mar. 4, 1907, ch. 2907, title I, § 10, formerly 8th par., 34 Stat. 1262; renumbered § 10 and amended Pub. L. 90–201, §§ 1, 7, Dec. 15, 1967, 81 Stat. 584, 589; Pub. L. 95–445, § 3, Oct. 10, 1978, 92 Stat. 1069.)

REFERENCES IN TEXT

Act of August 27, 1958, referred to in subsec. (b), is Pub. L. 85–765, Aug. 27, 1958, 72 Stat. 862, as amended, which is classified generally to chapter 48 (§ 1901 et seq.) of Title 7, Agriculture. For complete classification of this Act to the Code, see Tables.

Sections 1903 and 1905 of Title 7, included within reference to Act of August 27, 1958, were repealed by Pub. L. 95–445, § 5(b), Oct. 10, 1978, 92 Stat. 1069, effective as set forth in section 7 of Pub. L. 95–445, set out as an Effective Date of 1978 Amendment note under section 603 of this title.

CODIFICATION

Section was formerly classified to section 78 of this title.

AMENDMENTS

1978—Subsecs. (b) to (d). Pub. L. 95–445 added subsec. (b) and redesignated former subsecs. (b) and (c) as (c) and (d), respectively.

1967—Pub. L. 90–201, § 7, included the list of animals and prohibited, except in compliance with requirements of this chapter, slaughtering animals or preparation of articles capable of use as human food, sales, transportation, and other transactions, and acts of adulteration or misbranding, incorporating in subsec. (b)(2) existing prohibition on distributions in interstate or foreign commerce of noninspected articles.

EFFECTIVE DATE OF 1978 AMENDMENT

Amendment by Pub. L. 95–445 effective one year after Oct. 10, 1978, and an additional eighteen month period thereafter in hardship cases, see section 7 of Pub. L. 95–445, set out as an Effective Date of 1978 Amendment note under section 603 of this title.

EFFECTIVE DATE OF 1967 AMENDMENT

Amendment by Pub. L. 90–201 effective Dec. 15, 1967, except that subsecs. (b)(1) and (c) of this section effective upon expiration of sixty days after Dec. 15, 1967, see section 20(a) of Pub. L. 90–201, set out as an Effective Date note under section 601 of this title.

§ 611. Devices, marks, labels, and certificates; simulations

(a) Devices to be made under authorization of Secretary

No brand manufacturer, printer, or other person, firm, or corporation shall cast, print, lithograph, or otherwise make any device containing any official mark or simulation thereof, or any label bearing any such mark or simulation, or any form of official certificate or simulation thereof, except as authorized by the Secretary.

(b) Other misconduct

No person, firm, or corporation shall—

(1) forge any official device, mark, or certificate;

(2) without authorization from the Secretary use any official device, mark, or certificate, or simulation thereof, or alter, detach, deface, or destroy any official device, mark, or certificate;

(3) contrary to the regulations prescribed by the Secretary, fail to use, or to detach, deface, or destroy any official device, mark, or certificate;

(4) knowingly possess, without promptly notifying the Secretary or his representative, any official device or any counterfeit, simulated, forged, or improperly altered official certificate or any device or label or any carcass of any animal, or part or product thereof, bearing any counterfeit, simulated, forged, or improperly altered official mark;

(5) knowingly make any false statement in any shipper's certificate or other nonofficial or official certificate provided for in the regulations prescribed by the Secretary; or

(6) knowingly represent that any article has been inspected and passed, or exempted, under this chapter when, in fact, it has, respectively, not been so inspected and passed, or exempted.

(Mar. 4, 1907, ch. 2907, title I, §11, formerly 9th par., 34 Stat. 1263; renumbered §11 and amended Pub. L. 90–201, §§1, 8, Dec. 15, 1967, 81 Stat. 584, 589.)

CODIFICATION

Section was formerly classified to section 79 of this title.

AMENDMENTS

1967—Pub. L. 90–201, §8, clarified application to brand manufacturers and printers of existing prohibition against counterfeiting official marks, labels or certificates, the provisions with respect to forgery, unauthorized use or failure to use official marks, or similar items, and similar offenses, and existing prohibitions with respect to false statements in official or nonofficial certificates, and added restriction upon possession of official devices, or devices, labels, meat, or other articles bearing counterfeit official marks, counterfeit official certificates, or similar items, and prohibition against false representations.

EFFECTIVE DATE OF 1967 AMENDMENT

Amendment by Pub. L. 90–201 effective Dec. 15, 1967, except that with respect to equines (other than horses) and their carcasses and parts thereof, meat, and meat food products thereof, amendment effective upon expiration of sixty days after Dec. 15, 1967, see section 20(b) of Pub. L. 90–201, set out as an Effective Date note under section 601 of this title.

§612. Notification

Any establishment subject to inspection under this chapter that believes, or has reason to believe, that an adulterated or misbranded meat or meat food product received by or originating from the establishment has entered into commerce shall promptly notify the Secretary with regard to the type, amount, origin, and destination of the meat or meat food product.

(Mar. 4, 1907, ch. 2907, title I, §12, as added Pub. L. 110–234, title XI, §11017(a), May 22, 2008, 122 Stat. 1370, and Pub. L. 110–246, §4(a), title XI, §11017(a), June 18, 2008, 122 Stat. 1664, 2132.)

CODIFICATION

Pub. L. 110–234 and Pub. L. 110–246 enacted identical sections. Pub. L. 110–234 was repealed by section 4(a) of Pub. L. 110–246.

PRIOR PROVISIONS

A prior section 612, acts Mar. 4, 1907, ch. 2907, title I, §12, formerly 10th par., 34 Stat. 1263; renumbered §12 and amended Pub. L. 90–201, §§1, 3(b), 12(a), Dec. 15, 1967, 81 Stat. 584, 588, 592, related to inspection of animals for export, prior to repeal by Pub. L. 107–171, title X, §10418(a)(19), May 13, 2002, 116 Stat. 508. Section was formerly classified to section 80 of this title.

EFFECTIVE DATE

Enactment of this section and repeal of Pub. L. 110–234 by Pub. L. 110–246 effective May 22, 2008, the date of enactment of Pub. L. 110–234, see section 4 of Pub. L. 110–246, set out as a note under section 8701 of Title 7, Agriculture.

§613. Plans and reassessments

The Secretary shall require that each establishment subject to inspection under this chapter shall, at a minimum—

(1) prepare and maintain current procedures for the recall of all meat or meat food products produced and shipped by the establishment;

(2) document each reassessment of the process control plans of the establishment; and

(3) upon request, make the procedures and reassessed process control plans available to inspectors appointed by the Secretary for review and copying.

(Mar. 4, 1907, ch. 2907, title I, §13, as added Pub. L. 110–234, title XI, §11017(a), May 22, 2008, 122 Stat. 1370, and Pub. L. 110–246, §4(a), title XI, §11017(a), June 18, 2008, 122 Stat. 1664, 2132.)

CODIFICATION

Pub. L. 110–234 and Pub. L. 110–246 enacted identical sections. Pub. L. 110–234 was repealed by section 4(a) of Pub. L. 110–246.

PRIOR PROVISIONS

A prior section 613, acts Mar. 4, 1907, ch. 2907, title I, §13, formerly 11th par., 34 Stat. 1263; renumbered §13 and amended Pub. L. 90–201, §§1, 3(b), 12(a), Dec. 15, 1967, 81 Stat. 584, 588, 592, related to inspectors of animals for export and certificates of condition, prior to repeal by Pub. L. 107–171, title X, §10418(a)(19), May 13, 2002, 116 Stat. 508. Section was formerly classified to section 81 of this title.

EFFECTIVE DATE

Enactment of this section and repeal of Pub. L. 110–234 by Pub. L. 110–246 effective May 22, 2008, the date of enactment of Pub. L. 110–234, see section 4 of Pub. L. 110–246, set out as a note under section 8701 of Title 7, Agriculture.

§614. Repealed. Pub. L. 107–171, title X, §10418(a)(19), May 13, 2002, 116 Stat. 508

Section, acts Mar. 4, 1907, ch. 2907, title I, §14, formerly 12th par., 34 Stat. 1263; renumbered §14 and amended Pub. L. 90–201, §§1, 3(b), 12(a), Dec. 15, 1967, 81 Stat. 584, 588, 592, prohibited clearance to vessel carrying animals for export without inspector's certificate. Section was formerly classified to section 82 of this title.

§615. Inspection of carcasses, meat of which is intended for export

The Secretary shall also cause to be made a careful inspection of the carcasses and parts thereof of all amenable species, the meat of which, fresh, salted, canned, corned, packed, cured, or otherwise prepared, is intended and offered for export to any foreign country, at such times and places and in such manner as he may deem proper.

(Mar. 4, 1907, ch. 2907, title I, §15, formerly 13th par., 34 Stat. 1263; renumbered §15 and amended Pub. L. 90–201, §§1, 3(b), 12(a), Dec. 15, 1967, 81 Stat. 584, 588, 592; Pub. L. 109–97, title VII, §798[(a)](1), Nov. 10, 2005, 119 Stat. 2166.)

CODIFICATION

Section was formerly classified to section 83 of this title.

AMENDMENTS

2005—Pub. L. 109–97 substituted "amenable species" for "cattle, sheep, swine, goats, horses, mules, and other equines".

1967—Pub. L. 90–201, §§3(b), 12(a), struck out "of Agriculture" after "Secretary" and included horses, mules, and other equines in the list of animals, respectively.

EFFECTIVE DATE OF 2005 AMENDMENT

Amendment by Pub. L. 109–97 effective the day after 120 days after Nov. 10, 2005, see section 798(b) of Pub. L. 109–97, set out as a note under section 601 of this title.

EFFECTIVE DATE OF 1967 AMENDMENT

Amendment by Pub. L. 90–201 effective Dec. 15, 1967, except that with respect to equines (other than horses) and their carcasses and parts thereof, meat, and meat food products thereof, amendment effective upon expiration of sixty days after Dec. 15, 1967, see section 20(b) of Pub. L. 90–201, set out as an Effective Date note under section 601 of this title.

§616. Inspectors of carcasses, etc., meat of which is intended for export; certificates of condition

For the purpose of section 615 of this title the Secretary may appoint inspectors who shall be authorized to give an official certificate stating the condition in which said cattle, sheep, swine, goats, horses, mules, or other equines, and the meat thereof, are found.

(Mar. 4, 1907, ch. 2907, title I, §16, formerly 14th par., 34 Stat. 1263; renumbered §16 and amended Pub. L. 90–201, §§1, 3(b), 12(a), Dec. 15, 1967, 81 Stat. 584, 588, 592.)

CODIFICATION

Section was formerly classified to section 84 of this title.

AMENDMENTS

1967—Pub. L. 90–201, §§3(b), 12(a), struck out "of Agriculture" after "Secretary", and included horses, mules, or other equines in the list of animals.

EFFECTIVE DATE OF 1967 AMENDMENT

Amendment by Pub. L. 90–201 effective Dec. 15, 1967, except that with respect to equines (other than horses) and their carcasses and parts thereof, meat, and meat food products thereof, amendment effective upon expiration of sixty days after Dec. 15, 1967, see section 20(b) of Pub. L. 90–201, set out as an Effective Date note under section 601 of this title.

§617. Clearance prohibited to vessel carrying meat for export without inspector's certificate

No clearance shall be given to any vessel having on board any fresh, salted, canned, corned, or packed beef, mutton, pork, goat or equine meat for export to and sale in a foreign country from any port in the United States, until the owner or shipper thereof shall obtain from an inspector appointed under the provisions of this chapter a certificate that the said amenable species were sound and healthy at the time of inspection, and that their meat is sound and wholesome, unless the Secretary shall have waived the requirements of such certificate for the country to which said amenable species or meats are to be exported.

(Mar. 4, 1907, ch. 2907, title I, §17, formerly 15th par., 34 Stat. 1263; renumbered §17 and amended Pub. L. 90–201, §§1, 3(b), 12(a), (g), Dec. 15, 1967, 81 Stat. 584, 588, 592; Pub. L. 109–97, title VII, §798[(a)](1), Nov. 10, 2005, 119 Stat. 2166.)

CODIFICATION

Section was formerly classified to section 85 of this title.

AMENDMENTS

2005—Pub. L. 109–97 substituted "amenable species" for "cattle, sheep, swine, goats, horses, mules, and other equines" in two places.

1967—Pub. L. 90–201, §§3(b), 12(a), (g), struck out "of Agriculture" after "Secretary", included horses, mules, and other equines in the list of animals, and substituted "goat or equine meat" for "or goat meat, being the meat of animals killed after March 4, 1907, or except as hereinbefore provided", respectively.

EFFECTIVE DATE OF 2005 AMENDMENT

Amendment by Pub. L. 109–97 effective the day after 120 days after Nov. 10, 2005, see section 798(b) of Pub. L. 109–97, set out as a note under section 601 of this title.

EFFECTIVE DATE OF 1967 AMENDMENT

Amendment by Pub. L. 90–201 effective Dec. 15, 1967, except that with respect to equines (other than horses) and their carcasses and parts thereof, meat, and meat food products thereof, amendment effective upon expiration of sixty days after Dec. 15, 1967, see section 20(b) of Pub. L. 90–201, set out as an Effective Date note under section 601 of this title.

§618. Delivery of inspectors' certificates, and of copies

The inspectors provided for under this subchapter shall be authorized to give official certificates of the condition of the carcasses and products of amenable species; and one copy of every certificate granted under the provisions of this chapter shall be filed in the Department of Agriculture, another copy shall be delivered to the owner or shipper, and when the amenable species, or their carcasses and products are sent abroad, a third copy shall be delivered to the chief officer of the vessel on which the shipment shall be made.

(Mar. 4, 1907, ch. 2907, title I, §18, formerly 16th par., 34 Stat. 1263; renumbered §18 and amended Pub. L. 90–201, §§1, 12(a), (h), Dec. 15, 1967, 81 Stat. 584, 592; Pub. L. 107–171, title X, §10418(b)(4), May 13, 2002, 116 Stat. 508; Pub. L. 109–97, title VII, §798[(a)](1), Nov. 10, 2005, 119 Stat. 2166.)

CODIFICATION

"Provided for under this subchapter" was in the original "provided for herein".

Section was formerly classified to section 86 of this title.

AMENDMENTS

2005—Pub. L. 109–97 substituted "amenable species" for "cattle, sheep, swine, goats, horses, mules, and other equines" in two places.

2002—Pub. L. 107–171 substituted "of the carcasses and products of cattle, sheep, swine, goats, horses, mules, and other equines" for "of the cattle, sheep, swine, goats, horses, mules, and other equines, their carcasses and products as described in this subchapter".

1967—Pub. L. 90–201, §12(a), (h), included horses, mules, and other equines in the list of animals and struck out "sound and wholesome" before "conditions", respectively.

EFFECTIVE DATE OF 2005 AMENDMENT

Amendment by Pub. L. 109–97 effective the day after 120 days after Nov. 10, 2005, see section 798(b) of Pub. L. 109–97, set out as a note under section 601 of this title.

EFFECTIVE DATE OF 1967 AMENDMENT

Amendment by Pub. L. 90–201 effective Dec. 15, 1967, except that with respect to equines (other than horses) and their carcasses and parts thereof, meat, and meat food products thereof, amendment effective upon expiration of sixty days after Dec. 15, 1967, see section 20(b) of Pub. L. 90–201, set out as an Effective Date note under section 601 of this title.

§619. Marking, labeling, or other identification to show kinds of animals from which derived; separate establishments for preparation and slaughtering activities

No person, firm, or corporation shall sell, transport, offer for sale or transportation, or receive for transportation, in commerce, any carcasses of species designated by regulations in effect on the day before November 10, 2005, or parts of such carcasses, or the meat or meat food products thereof, unless they are plainly and conspicuously marked or labeled or otherwise identified as required by regulations prescribed by the Secretary to show the kinds of animals from which they were derived. When required by the Secretary, with respect to establishments at which inspection is maintained under this subchapter, such animals and their carcasses, parts thereof, meat and meat food products shall be prepared in establishments separate from those in which other amenable species are slaughtered or their carcasses, parts thereof, meat or meat food products are prepared.

(Mar. 4, 1907, ch. 2907, title I, §19, formerly 17th par., 34 Stat. 1264; renumbered §19 and amended Pub. L. 90–201, §§1, 9, Dec. 15, 1967, 81 Stat. 584, 590; Pub. L. 109–97, title VII, §798[(a)](3), Nov. 10, 2005, 119 Stat. 2166.)

CODIFICATION

Section was formerly classified to section 87 of this title.

AMENDMENTS

2005—Pub. L. 109–97 substituted "species designated by regulations in effect on the day before November 10, 2005," for "horses, mules, or other equines" and "other amenable species" for "cattle, sheep, swine, or goats".

1967—Pub. L. 90–201, §9, substituted provisions for marking, labeling, or other identification of kinds of animals whence the articles are derived and for separate establishments for preparation and slaughtering activities for prohibition against transportation or sale of meat or meat food products without complying with inspection provisions. See section 610(b) of this title.

EFFECTIVE DATE OF 2005 AMENDMENT

Amendment by Pub. L. 109–97 effective the day after 120 days after Nov. 10, 2005, see section 798(b) of Pub. L. 109–97, set out as a note under section 601 of this title.

EFFECTIVE DATE OF 1967 AMENDMENT

Amendment by Pub. L. 90–201 effective Dec. 15, 1967, except that with respect to equines (other than horses) and their carcasses and parts thereof, meat, and meat food products thereof, amendment effective upon expiration, of sixty days after Dec. 15, 1967, see section 20(b) of Pub. L. 90–201, set out as an Effective Date note under section 601 of this title.

§620. Imports

(a) Adulteration or misbranding prohibition; compliance with inspection, building construction standards, and other provisions; humane methods of slaughter; treatment as domestic articles subject to this chapter and food, drug, and cosmetic provisions; marking and labeling; personal consumption exemption

No carcasses, parts of carcasses, meat or meat food products of cattle, sheep, swine, goats, horses, mules, or other equines which are capable of use as human food, shall be imported into the United States if such articles are adulterated or misbranded and unless they comply with all the inspection, building, construction standards, and all other provisions of this chapter and regulations issued thereunder applicable to such articles in commerce within the United States. No such carcasses, parts of carcasses, meat or meat food products shall be imported into the United States unless the livestock from which they were produced was slaughtered and handled in connection with slaughter in accordance with the Act of August 27, 1958 (72 Stat. 862; 7 U.S.C. 1901–1906). All such imported articles shall, upon entry into the United States, be deemed and treated as domestic articles subject to the other provisions of this chapter and the Federal Food, Drug, and Cosmetic Act [21 U.S.C. 301 et seq.]: *Provided*, That they shall be marked and labeled as required by such regulations for imported articles: *Provided further*, That nothing in this section shall apply to any individual who purchases meat or meat products outside the United States for his own consumption except that the total amount of such meat or meat products shall not exceed fifty pounds.

(b) Terms and conditions for destruction

The Secretary may prescribe the terms and conditions for the destruction of all such articles which are imported contrary to this section, unless (1) they are exported by the consignee within the time fixed therefor by the Secretary, or (2) in the case of articles which are not in compliance with the chapter solely because of misbranding, such articles are brought into compliance with the chapter under supervision of authorized representatives of the Secretary.

(c) Payment of storage, cartage, and labor charges by owner or consignee; liens

All charges for storage, cartage, and labor with respect to any article which is imported contrary to this section shall be paid by the owner or consignee, and in default of such payment shall constitute a lien against such article and any other article thereafter imported under this chapter by or for such owner or consignee.

(d) Prohibition

The knowing importation of any article contrary to this section is prohibited.

(e) Omitted

(f) Inspection and other standards; applicability, enforcement, etc.; certifications

Notwithstanding any other provision of law, all carcasses, parts of carcasses, meat, and meat food products of cattle, sheep, swine, goats, horses, mules, or other equines, capable of use as human food, offered for importation into the United States shall be subject to the inspection, sanitary, quality, species verification, and residue standards applied to products produced in the United States. Any such imported meat articles that do not meet such standards shall not be permitted entry in to the United States. The Secretary shall enforce this provision through (1) the imposition of random inspections for such species verification and for residues, and (2) random sampling and testing of internal organs and fat of the carcasses for residues at the point of slaughter by the exporting country in accordance with methods approved by the Secretary. Each foreign country from which such meat articles are offered for importation into the United States shall obtain a certification issued by the Secretary stating that the country maintains a program using reliable analytical methods to ensure compliance with the United States standards for residues in such meat articles. No such meat article shall be permitted entry into the United States from a country for which the Secretary has not issued such certification. The Secretary shall periodically review such certifications and shall revoke any certification if the Secretary determines that the country involved is not maintaining a program that uses reliable analytical methods to ensure compliance with United States standards for residues in such meat articles. The consideration of any application for a certification under this subsection and the review of any such certification, by the Secretary, shall include the inspection of individual establishments to ensure that the inspection program of the foreign country involved is meeting such United States standards.

(g) Administration of animal drugs or antibiotics; terms and conditions; entry order violations

The Secretary may prescribe terms and conditions under which amenable species that have been administered an animal drug or antibiotic banned for use in the United States may be imported for slaughter and human consumption. No person shall enter amenable species into the United States in violation of any order issued under this subsection by the Secretary.

(h) Reciprocal meat inspection requirement

(1) As used in this subsection:

(A) The term "meat articles" means carcasses, meat and meat food products of cattle, sheep, swine, goats, horses, mules, or other equines, that are capable of use as human food.

(B) The term "standards" means inspection, building construction, sanitary, quality, species verification, residue, and other standards that are applicable to meat articles.

(2) On request of the Committee on Agriculture or the Committee on Ways and Means of the House of Representatives or the Committee on Agriculture, Nutrition, and Forestry or the Committee on Finance of the Senate, or at the initiative of the Secretary, the Secretary shall, as soon as practicable, determine whether a particular foreign country applies standards for the importation of meat articles from the United States that are not related to public health concerns about end-product quality that can be substantiated by reliable analytical methods.

(3) If the Secretary determines that a foreign country applies standards described in paragraph (2)—

(A) the Secretary shall consult with the United States Trade Representative; and

(B) within 30 days after the determination of the Secretary under paragraph (2), the Secretary and the United States Trade Representative shall recommend to the President whether action should be taken under paragraph (4).

(4) Within 30 days after receiving a recommendation for action under paragraph (3), the President shall, if and for such time as the President considers appropriate, prohibit imports into the United States of any meat articles produced in such foreign country unless it is determined that the meat articles produced in that country meet the standards applicable to meat articles in commerce within the United States.

(5) The action authorized under paragraph (4) may be used instead of, or in addition to, any other action taken under any other law.

(Mar. 4, 1907, ch. 2907, title I, §20, formerly 18th par., 34 Stat. 1264; renumbered §20 and amended Pub. L. 90–201, §§1, 10, Dec. 15, 1967, 81 Stat. 584, 590; Pub. L. 95–445, §4, Oct. 10, 1978, 92 Stat. 1069; Pub. L. 97–98, title XI, §1122, Dec. 22, 1981, 95 Stat. 1273; Pub. L. 99–198, title XVII, §1702, Dec. 23, 1985, 99 Stat. 1634; Pub. L. 100–418, title IV, §4604, Aug. 23, 1988, 102 Stat. 1408; Pub. L. 103–182, title III, §361(f), Dec. 8, 1993, 107 Stat. 2124; Pub. L. 103–437, §8(2), Nov. 2, 1994, 108 Stat. 4588; Pub. L. 103–465, title IV, §431(*l*), Dec. 8, 1994, 108 Stat. 4970; Pub. L. 109–97, title VII, §798[(a)](1), Nov. 10, 2005, 119 Stat. 2166.)

REFERENCES IN TEXT

Act of August 27, 1958, referred to in subsec. (a), is Pub. L. 85–765, Aug. 27, 1958, 72 Stat. 862, as amended, which is classified generally to chapter 48 (§1901 et seq.) of Title 7, Agriculture. Sections 1903 and 1905 of Title 7, included within reference to Act of August 27, 1958, were repealed by Pub. L. 95–445, §5(b), Oct. 10, 1978, 92 Stat. 1069, effective as set forth in section 7 of Pub. L. 95–445, set out as an Effective Date of 1978 Amendment note under section 603 of this title. For complete classification of this Act to the Code, see Tables.

The Federal Food, Drug, and Cosmetic Act, referred to in subsec. (a), is act June 25, 1938, ch. 675, 52 Stat. 1040, as amended, which is classified generally to chapter 9 (§301 et seq.) of this title. For complete classification of this act to the Code, see section 301 of this title and Tables.

CODIFICATION

Subsec. (e) of this section, which required the Secretary to submit to the Committee on Agriculture of the House of Representatives and the Committee on

Agriculture, Nutrition, and Forestry of the Senate a comprehensive and detailed written annual report on the administration of this section, terminated, effective May 15, 2000, pursuant to section 3003 of Pub. L. 104–66, as amended, set out as a note under section 1113 of Title 31, Money and Finance. See, also, page 46 of House Document No. 103–7.

Section was formerly classified to section 88 of this title.

AMENDMENTS

2005—Subsec. (g). Pub. L. 109–97 substituted "amenable species" for "cattle, sheep, swine, goats, horses, mules, and other equines" in two places.

1994—Subsec. (e). Pub. L. 103–437 substituted "Agriculture, Nutrition, and Forestry" for "Agriculture and Forestry" in introductory provisions.

Subsec. (e)(1)(A), (B). Pub. L. 103–465, §431(*l*)(1), amended subpars. (A) and (B) generally. Prior to amendment, subpars. (A) and (B) read as follows:

"(A) Subject to subparagraphs (B) and (C), a certification by the Secretary that foreign plants in Canada and Mexico that export carcasses or meat or meat products referred to in subsection (a) of this section have complied with paragraph (2) or with requirements that are equivalent to United States requirements with regard to all inspection and building construction standards, and all other provisions of this chapter and regulations issued under this chapter.

"(B) Subject to subparagraph (C), the Secretary may treat as equivalent to a United States requirement a requirement described in subparagraph (A) if the exporting country provides the Secretary with scientific evidence or other information, in accordance with risk assessment methodologies agreed to by the Secretary and the exporting country, to demonstrate that the requirement or standard of the exporting country achieves the level of protection that the Secretary considers appropriate."

Subsec. (e)(2) to (7). Pub. L. 103–465, §431(*l*)(2), (3), redesignated pars. (3) to (7) as (2) to (6), respectively, and struck out former par. (2) which read as follows: "A certification by the Secretary that, except as provided in paragraph (1), foreign plants that export carcasses or meat or meat products referred to in subsection (a) of this section have complied with requirements that are at least equal to all inspection and building construction standards and all other provisions of this chapter and regulations issued under this chapter."

1993—Subsec. (e). Pub. L. 103–182, §361(f)(1), substituted "not be limited to the following:" for "not be limited to—" in introductory provisions.

Subsec. (e)(1) to (7). Pub. L. 103–182, §361(f)(2)–(7), added pars. (1) and (2), struck out former par. (1), redesignated pars. (2) to (6) as (3) to (7), respectively, substituted "The" for "the" at beginning of each par., substituted period for semicolon at end of pars. (3) to (5), and substituted period for "; and" at end of par. (6). Prior to amendment, former par. (1) read as follows: "a certification by the Secretary that foreign plants exporting carcasses or meat or meat products referred to in subsection (a) of this section have complied with requirements at least equal to all the inspection, building construction standards, and all other provisions of this chapter and regulations issued thereunder;".

1988—Subsec. (e)(6). Pub. L. 100–418, §4604(b), added par. (6).

Subsec. (h). Pub. L. 100–418, §4604(a), added subsec. (h).

1985—Subsec. (f). Pub. L. 99–198, §1702(a), struck out provision which had made this subsection effective six months after Dec. 22, 1981, and inserted provisions requiring that each foreign country from which meat articles are offered for importation into the United States obtain a certification issued by the Secretary stating that the country maintains a program using reliable analytical methods to ensure compliance with the United States standards for residues in such meat articles, that no meat article be permitted entry into the United States from a country for which the Secretary has not issued such certification, that the Secretary periodically review such certifications and revoke any certification if the Secretary determines that the country involved is not maintaining a program that uses reliable analytical methods to ensure compliance with United States standards for residues in such meat articles, and that the consideration of any application for a certification under this subsection and the review of any such certification, by the Secretary, include the inspection of individual establishments to ensure that the inspection program of the foreign country involved is meeting such United States standards.

Subsec. (g). Pub. L. 99–198, §1702(b), added subsec. (g).

1981—Subsec. (f). Pub. L. 97–98 added subsec. (f).

1978—Subsec. (a). Pub. L. 95–445 prohibited imports which do not comply with humane methods of slaughter.

1967—Pub. L. 90–201, §10, substituted imported articles provisions for penalty provisions deeming offenses as misdemeanors and punishable by fine of $10,000 or imprisonment for two years or both. See section 676(a) of this title.

EFFECTIVE DATE OF 2005 AMENDMENT

Amendment by Pub. L. 109–97 effective the day after 120 days after Nov. 10, 2005, see section 798(b) of Pub. L. 109–97, set out as a note under section 601 of this title.

EFFECTIVE DATE OF 1994 AMENDMENT

Amendment by Pub. L. 103–465 effective, except as otherwise provided, on the date of entry into force of the World Trade Organization Agreement with respect to the United States [Jan. 1, 1995], see section 451 of Pub. L. 103–465, set out as an Effective Date note under section 3601 of Title 19, Customs Duties.

EFFECTIVE DATE OF 1981 AMENDMENT

Amendment by Pub. L. 97–98 effective Dec. 22, 1981, see section 1801 of Pub. L. 97–98, set out as an Effective Date note under section 4301 of Title 7, Agriculture.

EFFECTIVE DATE OF 1978 AMENDMENT

Amendment by Pub. L. 95–445 effective one year after Oct. 10, 1978, and an additional eighteen-month period thereafter in hardship cases, see section 7 of Pub. L. 95–445, set out as a note under section 603 of this title.

EFFECTIVE DATE OF 1967 AMENDMENT

Amendment by Pub. L. 90–201 effective upon expiration of sixty days after Dec. 15, 1967, see section 20(a) of Pub. L. 90–201, set out as an Effective Date note under section 601 of this title.

§621. Inspectors to make examinations provided for; appointment; duties; regulations

The Secretary shall appoint from time to time inspectors to make examination and inspection of all amenable species, inspection of which is hereby provided for and of all carcasses and parts thereof, and of all meats and meat food products thereof, and of the sanitary conditions of all establishments in which such meat and meat food products hereinbefore described are prepared; and said inspectors shall refuse to stamp, mark, tag, or label any carcass or any part thereof, or meat food product therefrom, prepared in any establishment hereinbefore mentioned, until the same shall have actually been inspected and found to be not adulterated; and shall perform such other duties as are provided by this chapter and by the rules and regulations to be prescribed by said Secretary; and said Secretary shall, from time to time, make such rules and regulations as are necessary for the efficient execution of the provisions of this chapter, and all inspections and examinations made under this chapter, shall be such and made in such manner as described in the rules and regulations prescribed by said Secretary not inconsistent with provisions of this chapter.

(Mar. 4, 1907, ch. 2907, title I, § 21, formerly 19th par., 34 Stat. 1264; renumbered § 21 and amended Pub. L. 90–201, §§ 1, 3(b), 12(a), (i), Dec. 15, 1967, 81 Stat. 584, 588, 592, 593; Pub. L. 99–641, title IV, § 403(d)(2), Nov. 10, 1986, 100 Stat. 3570; Pub. L. 109–97, title VII, § 798[(a)](1), Nov. 10, 2005, 119 Stat. 2166.)

CODIFICATION

Section was formerly classified to section 89 of this title.

AMENDMENTS

2005—Pub. L. 109–97 substituted "amenable species" for "cattle, sheep, swine, goats, horses, mules, and other equines".

1986—Pub. L. 99–641 temporarily substituted "thereof, and of meat food products" for "and meat food products", which substitution was made for the first such reference as the probable intent of Congress. See Effective and Termination Dates of 1986 Amendment note below.

1967—Pub. L. 90–201, §§ 3(b), 12(a), (i), struck out "of Agriculture" after "Secretary" in four places, included horses, mules, and other equines in the list of animals, and substituted "not adulterated" for "sound, healthful, wholesome, and fit for human food, and to contain no dyes, chemicals, preservatives, or ingredients which render such meat food product unsound, unhealthful, unwholesome, or unfit for human food; and to have been prepared under proper sanitary conditions, hereinbefore provided for", respectively.

EFFECTIVE DATE OF 2005 AMENDMENT

Amendment by Pub. L. 109–97 effective the day after 120 days after Nov. 10, 2005, see section 798(b) of Pub. L. 109–97, set out as a note under section 601 of this title.

EFFECTIVE AND TERMINATION DATES OF 1986 AMENDMENT

Section 403(d)(2) of Pub. L. 99–641 provided that the amendment made by that section is effective only during the 6-year period beginning on Nov. 10, 1986.

Amendment by Pub. L. 99–641 effective Nov. 10, 1986, except that this section as in effect immediately before Nov. 10, 1986, applies with respect to establishments until the Secretary of Agriculture first issues rules and regulations to implement the amendments made by section 403(a) of Pub. L. 99–641 to section 606 of this title, see section 408 of Pub. L. 99–641, set out as a note under section 609 of this title.

EFFECTIVE DATE OF 1967 AMENDMENT

Amendment by Pub. L. 90–201 effective Dec. 15, 1967, except that with respect to equines (other than horses) and their carcasses and parts thereof, meat, and meat food products thereof, amendment effective upon expiration of sixty days after Dec. 15, 1967, see section 20(b) of Pub. L. 90–201, set out as an Effective Date note under section 601 of this title.

CONSTRUCTION AND EFFECT OF AMENDMENTS BY PUB. L. 99–641

For provisions relating to construction and effect of temporary amendments by section 403 of Pub. L. 99–641, see sections 403(e) and 404 of Pub. L. 99–641, set out as notes entitled "Inspection Services for Establishments Not Participating in Total Plant Quality-Control Program" and "Savings Provision", respectively, under section 609 of this title.

§ 622. Bribery of or gifts to inspectors or other officers and acceptance of gifts

Any person, firm, or corporation, or any agent or employee of any person, firm, or corporation, who shall give, pay, or offer, directly or indirectly, to any inspector, deputy inspector, chief inspector, or any other officer or employee of the United States authorized to perform any of the duties prescribed by this chapter or by the rules and regulations of the Secretary any money or other thing of value, with intent to influence said inspector, deputy inspector, chief inspector, or other officer or employee of the United States in the discharge of any duty provided for in this chapter, shall be deemed guilty of a felony, and, upon conviction thereof, shall be punished by a fine not less than $5,000 nor more than $10,000 and by imprisonment not less than one year nor more than three years; and any inspector, deputy inspector, chief inspector, or other officer or employee of the United States authorized to perform any of the duties prescribed by this chapter who shall accept any money, gift, or other thing of value from any person, firm, or corporation, or officers, agents, or employees thereof, given with intent to influence his official action, or who shall receive or accept from any person, firm, or corporation engaged in commerce any gift, money, or other thing of value, given with any purpose or intent whatsoever, shall be deemed guilty of a felony and shall, upon conviction thereof, be summarily discharged from office and shall be punished by a fine not less than $1,000 nor more than $10,000 and by imprisonment not less than one year nor more than three years.

(Mar. 4, 1907, ch. 2907, title I, § 22, formerly 20th par., 34 Stat. 1264; renumbered § 22 and amended Pub. L. 90–201, §§ 1, 3, Dec. 15, 1967, 81 Stat. 584, 588.)

CODIFICATION

Section was formerly classified to section 90 of this title.

AMENDMENTS

1967—Pub. L. 90–201, § 3, struck out "interstate or foreign" before "commerce" and "of Agriculture" after "Secretary".

EFFECTIVE DATE OF 1967 AMENDMENT

Amendment by Pub. L. 90–201 effective Dec. 15, 1967, except that with respect to equines (other than horses) and their carcasses and parts thereof, meat, and meat food products thereof, amendment effective upon expiration of sixty days after Dec. 15, 1967, see section 20(b) of Pub. L. 90–201, set out as an Effective Date note under section 601 of this title.

§ 623. Exemptions from inspection requirements

(a) Personal slaughtering and custom slaughtering for personal, household, guest, and employee uses

The provisions of this subchapter requiring inspection of the slaughter of animals and the preparation of the carcasses, parts thereof, meat and meat food products at establishments conducting such operations for commerce shall not apply to the slaughtering by any person of animals of his own raising, and the preparation by him and transportation in commerce of the carcasses, parts thereof, meat and meat food products of such animals exclusively for use by him and members of his household and his nonpaying guests and employees; nor to the custom slaughter by any person, firm, or corporation of cattle, sheep, swine or goats delivered by the owner thereof for such slaughter, and the preparation by such slaughterer and transportation in commerce of the carcasses, parts thereof, meat and meat food products of such animals, exclusively for use, in the household of such owner, by him and members of his household and his nonpaying guests and employees; nor to the custom preparation by any person, firm, or corporation of carcasses, parts thereof, meat or meat food products, derived from the slaughter by any person of cattle, sheep, swine, or goats of his own raising, or from game animals, delivered by the owner thereof for such custom preparation, and transportation in commerce of such custom prepared articles, exclusively for use in the household of such owner, by him and members of his household and his nonpaying guests and employees: *Provided*, That in cases where such person, firm, or corporation engages in such custom operations at an establishment at which inspection under this subchapter is maintained, the Secretary may exempt from such inspection at such establishment any animals slaughtered or any meat or meat food products otherwise prepared on such custom basis: *Provided further*, That custom operations at any establishment shall be exempt from inspection requirements as provided by this section only if the establishment complies with regulations which the Secretary is hereby authorized to promulgate to assure that any carcasses, parts thereof, meat or meat food products wherever handled on a custom basis, or any containers or packages containing such articles, are separated at all times from carcasses, parts thereof, meat or meat food products prepared for sale, and that all such articles prepared on a custom basis, or any containers or packages containing such articles, are plainly marked "Not for Sale" immediately after being prepared and kept so identified until delivered to the owner and that the establishment conducting the custom operation is maintained and operated in a sanitary manner.

(b) Territorial exemption; refusal, withdrawal, or modification

The Secretary may, under such sanitary conditions as he may by regulations prescribe, exempt from the inspection requirements of this subchapter the slaughter of animals, and the preparation of carcasses, parts thereof, meat and meat food products, by any person, firm, or corporation in any Territory not organized with a legislative body solely for distribution within such Territory when the Secretary determines that it is impracticable to provide such inspection within the limits of funds appropriated for administration of this chapter and that such exemption will otherwise facilitate enforcement of this chapter. The Secretary may refuse, withdraw, or modify any exemption under this subsection in his discretion whenever he determines such action is necessary to effectuate the purposes of this chapter.

(c) Pizzas containing meat food products

(1) Under such terms and conditions as the Secretary shall prescribe through rules and regulations issued under section 624 of this title that may be necessary to ensure food safety and protect public health such as special handling procedures, the Secretary shall exempt pizzas containing a meat food product from the inspection requirements of this chapter if—

(A) the meat food product components of the pizzas have been prepared, inspected, and passed in a cured or cooked form as ready-to-eat in compliance with the requirements of this chapter; and

(B) the pizzas are to be served in public or private nonprofit institutions.

(2) The Secretary may withdraw or modify any exemption under this subsection whenever the Secretary determines such action is necessary to ensure food safety and to protect public health. The Secretary may reinstate or further modify any exemption withdrawn or modified under this subsection.

(d) Adulteration and misbranding provisions applicable to inspection-free articles

The adulteration and misbranding provisions of this subchapter, other than the requirement of the inspection legend, shall apply to articles which are exempted from inspection or not required to be inspected under this section.

(Mar. 4, 1907, ch. 2907, title I, §23, formerly 21st, 22nd pars., 34 Stat. 1265; June 29, 1938, ch. 810, 52 Stat. 1235; renumbered §23 and amended Pub. L. 90–201, §§1, 11, Dec. 15, 1967, 81 Stat. 584, 591; Pub. L. 91–342, July 18, 1970, 84 Stat. 438; Pub. L. 102–237, title X, §1016(a), Dec. 13, 1991, 105 Stat. 1902.)

CODIFICATION

Section was formerly classified to sections 91 and 92 of this title.

AMENDMENTS

1991—Subsecs. (c), (d). Pub. L. 102–237 added subsec. (c) and redesignated former subsec. (c) as (d).

1970—Subsec. (a). Pub. L. 91–342 changed proviso so as to permit custom slaughterers to conduct a separate inspected meat business, continued the exemption for owners to slaughter and process their own animals for their own use, authorized the Secretary to exempt custom slaughtering and processing performed by an inspected establishment, and required that custom slaughtered articles be clearly marked "not for sale".

1967—Pub. L. 90–201, §11, substituted provisions for personal, custom, and territorial slaughtering exemptions and for application of adulteration and misbranding provisions to inspection-free articles for farmer definition and retail butcher and retail dealer exemption provisions.

1938—Act June 29, 1948, amended section generally.

EFFECTIVE DATE OF 1967 AMENDMENT

Amendment by Pub. L. 90–201 effective upon expiration of sixty days after Dec. 15, 1967, see section 20(c) of Pub. L. 90–201, set out as an Effective Date note under section 601 of this title.

REGULATIONS

Secretary to issue final rules no later than Aug. 1, 1992, to implement exemption authorized by subsec. (c) of this section, see section 1016(c) of Pub. L. 102–237, set out as a note under section 464 of this title.

§ 624. Storage and handling regulations; violations; exemption of establishments subject to non-Federal jurisdiction

The Secretary may by regulations prescribe conditions under which carcasses, parts of carcasses, meat, and meat food products of cattle, sheep, swine, goats, horses, mules, or other equines, capable of use as human food, shall be stored or otherwise handled by any person, firm, or corporation engaged in the business of buying, selling, freezing, storing, or transporting, in or for commerce, or importing, such articles, whenever the Secretary deems such action necessary to assure that such articles will not be adulterated or misbranded when delivered to the consumer. Violation of any such regulation is prohibited. However, such regulations shall not apply to the storage or handling of such articles at any retail store or other establishment in any State or organized Territory that would be subject to this section only because of purchases in commerce, if the storage and handling of such articles at such establishment is regulated under the laws of the State or Territory in which such establishment is located, in a manner which the Secretary, after consultation with the appropriate advisory committee provided for in section 661 of this title, determines is adequate to effectuate the purposes of this section.

(Mar. 4, 1907, ch. 2907, title I, § 24, as added Pub. L. 90–201, § 13, Dec. 15, 1967, 81 Stat. 593.)

§ 625. Inapplicability of certain requirements to catfish

Notwithstanding any other provision of this chapter, the requirements of sections 603, 604, 605, 610(b), and 623 of this title shall not apply to catfish.

(Mar. 4, 1907, ch. 2907, title I, § 25, as added Pub. L. 110–234, title XI, § 11016(b)(1)(C), May 22, 2008, 122 Stat. 1369, and Pub. L. 110–246, § 4(a), title XI, § 11016(b)(1)(C), June 18, 2008, 122 Stat. 1664, 2131.)

CODIFICATION

Pub. L. 110–234 and Pub. L. 110–246 enacted identical sections. Pub. L. 110–234 was repealed by section 4(a) of Pub. L. 110–246.

EFFECTIVE DATE

Enactment of this section and repeal of Pub. L. 110–234 by Pub. L. 110–246 effective May 22, 2008, the date of enactment of Pub. L. 110–234, except as otherwise provided, see section 4 of Pub. L. 110–246, set out as a note under section 8701 of Title 7, Agriculture.

Section inapplicable until date on which the Secretary of Agriculture issues final regulations to carry out amendments by Pub. L. 110–246, § 11016(b)(1), see section 11016(b)(2)(A) of Pub. L. 110–246, set out as an Effective Date of 2008 Amendment note under section 601 of this title.

SUBCHAPTER II—MEAT PROCESSORS AND RELATED INDUSTRIES

§ 641. Prohibition of subchapter I inspection of articles not intended for use as human food; denaturation or other identification prior to distribution in commerce; inedible articles

Inspection shall not be provided under subchapter I of this chapter at any establishment for the slaughter of cattle, sheep, swine, goats, horses, mules, or other equines, or the preparation of any carcasses or parts or products of such animals, which are not intended for use as human food, but such articles shall, prior to their offer for sale or transportation in commerce, unless naturally inedible by humans, be denatured or otherwise identified as prescribed by regulations of the Secretary to deter their use for human food. No person, firm, or corporation shall buy, sell, transport, or offer for sale or transportation, or receive for transportation, in commerce, or import, any carcasses, parts thereof, meat or meat food products of any such animals, which are not intended for use as human food unless they are denatured or otherwise identified as required by the regulations of the Secretary or are naturally inedible by humans.

(Mar. 4, 1907, ch. 2907, title II, § 201, as added Pub. L. 90–201, § 14, Dec. 15, 1967, 81 Stat. 593.)

EFFECTIVE DATE

Subchapter effective Dec. 15, 1967, see section 20 of Pub. L. 90–201, set out as a note under section 601 of this title.

§ 642. Recordkeeping requirements

(a) Classes of persons bound; scope of disclosure; access to places of business; examination of records, facilities, and inventories; copies; samples

The following classes of persons, firms, and corporations shall keep such records as will fully and correctly disclose all transactions involved in their businesses; and all persons, firms, and corporations subject to such requirements shall, at all reasonable times upon notice by a duly authorized representative of the Secretary, afford such representative access to their places of business and opportunity to examine the facilities, inventory, and records thereof, to copy all such records, and to take reasonable samples of their inventory upon payment of the fair market value therefor—

(1) Any persons, firms, or corporations that engage, for commerce, in the business of slaughtering any cattle, sheep, swine, goats, horses, mules, or other equines, or preparing, freezing, packaging, or labeling any carcasses, or parts or products of carcasses, of any such animals, for use as human food or animal food;

(2) Any persons, firms, or corporations that engage in the business of buying or selling (as meat brokers, wholesalers or otherwise), or transporting in commerce, or storing in or for commerce, or importing, any carcasses, or parts or products of carcasses, of any such animals;

(3) Any persons, firms, or corporations that engage in business, in or for commerce, as renderers, or engage in the business of buying, selling, or transporting, in commerce, or importing, any dead, dying, disabled, or diseased cattle, sheep, swine, goats, horses, mules, or other equines, or parts of the carcasses of any such animals that died otherwise than by slaughter.

(b) Period of maintenance

Any record required to be maintained by this section shall be maintained for such period of time as the Secretary may by regulations prescribe.

(Mar. 4, 1907, ch. 2907, title II, §202, as added Pub. L. 90–201, §14, Dec. 15, 1967, 81 Stat. 593.)

§643. Registration of business, name of person, and trade names

No person, firm, or corporation shall engage in business, in or for commerce, as a meat broker, renderer, or animal food manufacturer, or engage in business in commerce as a wholesaler of any carcasses, or parts or products of the carcasses, of any cattle, sheep, swine, goats, horses, mules, or other equines, whether intended for human food or other purposes, or engage in business as a public warehouseman storing any such articles in or for commerce, or engage in the business of buying, selling, or transporting in commerce, or importing, any dead, dying, disabled, or diseased animals of the specified kinds, or parts of the carcasses of any such animals that died otherwise than by slaughter, unless, when required by regulations of the Secretary, he has registered with the Secretary his name, and the address of each place of business at which, and all trade names under which, he conducts such business.

(Mar. 4, 1907, ch. 2907, title II, §203, as added Pub. L. 90–201, §14, Dec. 15, 1967, 81 Stat. 594.)

§644. Regulation of transactions, transportation, or importation of 4–D animals to prevent use as human food

No person, firm, or corporation engaged in the business of buying, selling, or transporting in commerce, or importing, dead, dying, disabled, or diseased animals, or any parts of the carcasses of any animals that died otherwise than by slaughter, shall buy, sell, transport, offer for sale or transportation, or receive for transportation, in commerce, or import, any dead, dying, disabled, or diseased cattle, sheep, swine, goats, horses, mules or other equines, or parts of the carcasses of any such animals that died otherwise than by slaughter, unless such transaction, transportation or importation is made in accordance with such regulations as the Secretary may prescribe to assure that such animals, or the unwholesome parts or products thereof, will be prevented from being used for human food purposes.

(Mar. 4, 1907, ch. 2907, title II, §204, as added Pub. L. 90–201, §14, Dec. 15, 1967, 81 Stat. 594.)

§645. Federal provisions applicable to State or Territorial business transactions of a local nature and not subject to local authority

The authority conferred on the Secretary by section 642, 643, or 644 of this title with respect to persons, firms, and corporations engaged in the specified kinds of business in or for commerce may be exercised with respect to persons, firms, or corporations engaged, in any State or organized Territory, in such kinds of business but not in or for commerce, whenever the Secretary determines, after consultation with an appropriate advisory committee provided for in section 661 of this title, that the State or territory does not have at least equal authority under its laws or such authority is not exercised in a manner to effectuate the purposes of this chapter including the State providing for the Secretary or his representative being afforded access to such places of business and the facilities, inventories, and records thereof, and the taking of reasonable samples, where he determines necessary in carrying out his responsibilities under this chapter; and in such case the provisions of section 642, 643, or 644 of this title, respectively, shall apply to such persons, firms, and corporations to the same extent and in the same manner as if they were engaged in such business in or for commerce and the transactions involved were in commerce.

(Mar. 4, 1907, ch. 2907, title II, §205, as added Pub. L. 90–201, §14, Dec. 15, 1967, 81 Stat. 594.)

SUBCHAPTER III—FEDERAL AND STATE COOPERATION

§661. Federal and State cooperation

(a) Congressional statement of policy

It is the policy of the Congress to protect the consuming public from meat and meat food products that are adulterated or misbranded and to assist in efforts by State and other Government agencies to accomplish this objective. In furtherance of this policy—

(1) Development and administration of State meat inspection program equal to subchapter I ante and post mortem inspection, reinspection, and sanitation requirements

The Secretary is authorized, whenever he determines that it would effectuate the purposes of this chapter, to cooperate with the appropriate State agency in developing and administering a State meat inspection program in any State which has enacted a State meat inspection law that imposes mandatory ante mortem and post mortem inspection, reinspection and sanitation requirements that are at least equal to those under subchapter I of this chapter, with respect to all or certain classes of persons engaged in the State in slaughtering cattle, sheep, swine, goats, or equines, or preparing the carcasses, parts thereof, meat or meat food products, of any such animals for use as human food solely for distribution within such State.

(2) Development and administration of State program with authorities equal to subchapter II authorities; cooperation with Federal agencies

The Secretary is further authorized, whenever he determines that it would effectuate the purposes of this chapter, to cooperate with appropriate State agencies in developing and administering State programs under State laws containing authorities at least equal to those provided in subchapter II of this chapter; and to cooperate with other agencies of the United States in carrying out any provisions of this chapter.

(3) Scope of cooperation: advisory assistance, technical and laboratory assistance and training, and financial and other aid; limitation on amount; equitable allocation of Federal funds; adequacy of State program to obtain Federal cooperation and payments

Cooperation with State agencies under this section may include furnishing to the appropriate State agency (i) advisory assistance in planning and otherwise developing an adequate State program under the State law; and (ii) technical and laboratory assistance and training (including necessary curricular and instructional materials and equipment), and financial and other aid for administration of such a program. The amount to be contributed to any State by the Secretary under this section from Federal funds for any year shall not exceed 50 per centum of the estimated total cost of the cooperative program; and the Federal funds shall be allocated among the States desiring to cooperate on an equitable basis. Such cooperation and payment shall be contingent at all times upon the administration of the State program in a manner which the Secretary, in consultation with the appropriate advisory committee appointed under paragraph (4), deems adequate to effectuate the purposes of this section.

(4) Advisory committees

The Secretary may appoint advisory committees consisting of such representatives of appropriate State agencies as the Secretary and the State agencies may designate to consult with him concerning State and Federal programs with respect to meat inspection and other matters within the scope of this chapter, including evaluating State programs for purposes of this chapter and obtaining better coordination and more uniformity among the State programs and between the Federal and State programs and adequate protection of consumers.

(b) Single State agency; subordinate governmental unit as part of State agency

The appropriate State agency with which the Secretary may cooperate under this chapter shall be a single agency in the State which is primarily responsible for the coordination of the State programs having objectives similar to those under this chapter. When the State program includes performance of certain functions by a municipality or other subordinate governmental unit, such unit shall be deemed to be a part of the State agency for purposes of this section.

(c) State meat inspection requirements

(1) Notice to Governor of nondevelopment or nonenforcement; designation of State as subject to subchapters I and IV; delay and revocation of designation; publication in Federal Register; notice of production of adulterated meat or meat food products; designation of State

If the Secretary has reason to believe, by thirty days prior to the expiration of two years after December 15, 1967, that a State has failed to develop or is not enforcing, with respect to all establishments within its jurisdiction (except those that would be exempted from Federal inspection under subparagraph (2)) at which cattle, sheep, swine, goats, or equines are slaughtered, or their carcasses, or parts or products thereof, are prepared for use as human food, solely for distribution within such State, and the products of such establishments, requirements at least equal to those imposed under subchapter I and IV of this chapter, he shall promptly notify the Governor of the State of this fact. If the Secretary determines, after consultation with the Governor of the State, or representative selected by him, that such requirements have not been developed and activated, he shall promptly after the expiration of such two-year period designate such State as one in which the provisions of subchapters I and IV of this chapter shall apply to operations and transactions wholly within such State: *Provided*, That if the Secretary has reason to believe that the State will activate such requirements within one additional year, he may delay such designation for said period, and not designate the State, if he determines at the end of the year that the State then has such requirements in effective operation. The Secretary shall publish any such designation in the Federal Register and, upon the expiration of thirty days after such publication, the provisions of subchapters I and IV shall apply to operations and transactions and to persons, firms, and corporations engaged therein in the State to the same extent and in the same manner as if such operations and transactions were conducted in or for commerce. Thereafter, upon request of the Governor, the Secretary shall revoke such designation if the Secretary determines that such State has developed and will enforce requirements at least equal to those imposed under subchapter I and subchapter IV of this chapter: *And provided further*, That, notwithstanding any other provision of this section, if the Secretary determines that any establishment within a State is producing adulterated meat or meat food products for distribution within such State which would clearly endanger the public health he shall notify the Governor of the State and the appropriate Advisory Committee provided by section 661 of this title of such fact for effective action under State or local law. If the State does not take action to prevent such endangering of the public health within a reasonable time after such notice, as determined by the Secretary, in light of the risk to public health, the Secretary may forthwith designate any such establishment as subject to the provisions of subchapters I and IV of this chapter, and thereupon the establishment and operator thereof shall be subject to such provisions as though engaged in commerce until such time as the Secretary determines that such State has developed and will enforce requirements at least equal to those imposed under subchapter I and subchapter IV of this chapter.

(2) Exemptions of retail stores, restaurants, and similar retail-type establishments; operations conducted at a restaurant central kitchen facility

The provisions of this chapter requiring inspection of the slaughter of animals and the preparation of carcasses, parts thereof, meat and meat food products shall not apply to operations of types traditionally and usually conducted at retail stores and restaurants, when conducted at any retail store or restaurant or similar retail-type establishment for sale in normal retail quantities or service of such articles to consumers at such establishments if such establishments are subject to such inspection provisions only under this paragraph (c). For the purposes of this subparagraph, operations conducted at a restaurant central kitchen facility shall be considered as being conducted at a restaurant if the restaurant central kitchen prepares meat or meat food products that are ready to eat when they leave such facility and are served in meals or as entrees only to customers at restaurants owned or operated by the same person, firm, or corporation owning or operating such facility: *Provided*, That such facility shall be subject to the provisions of section 642 of this title: *Provided further*, That the facility may be subject to the inspection requirements under subchapter I of this chapter for as long as the Secretary deems necessary, if the Secretary determines that the sanitary conditions or practices of the facility or the processing procedures or methods at the facility are such that any of its meat or meat food products are rendered adulterated.

(3) Termination of designation of State upon development and enforcement of minimum requirements; redesignation; designation for nonenforcement of minimum requirements: notice and publication in Federal Register

Whenever the Secretary determines that any State designated under this paragraph (c) has developed and will enforce State meat inspection requirements at least equal to those imposed under subchapters I and IV of this chapter with respect to the operations and transactions within such State which are regulated under paragraph (1), he shall terminate the designation of such State under this paragraph (c), but this shall not preclude the subsequent redesignation of the State at any time upon thirty days notice to the Governor and publication in the Federal Register in accordance with this paragraph, and any State may be designated upon such notice and publication at any time after the period specified in this paragraph whether or not the State has theretofore been designated upon the Secretary determining that it is not effectively enforcing requirements at least equal to those imposed under subchapters I and IV of this chapter.

(4) Periodic review; report to Congressional committees

The Secretary shall promptly upon December 15, 1967, and periodically thereafter, but at least annually, review the requirements, including the enforcement thereof, of the several States not designated under this paragraph (c), with respect to the slaughter, and the preparation, storage, handling and distribution of carcasses, parts thereof, meat and meat food products, of such animals, and inspection of such operations and annually report thereon to the Committee on Agriculture of the House of Representatives and the Committee on Agriculture, Nutrition, and Forestry of the Senate in the report required under section 691[1] of this title.

(d) "State" defined

As used in this section, the term "State" means any State (including the Commonwealth of Puerto Rico) or organized Territory.

(Mar. 4, 1907, ch. 2907, title III §301, as added Pub. L. 90–201, §15, Dec. 15, 1967, 81 Stat. 595; amended Pub. L. 98–487, §1, Oct. 17, 1984, 98 Stat. 2264; Pub. L. 103–437, §8(2), Nov. 2, 1994, 108 Stat. 4588.)

REFERENCES IN TEXT

Section 691 of this title, referred to in subsec. (c)(4), was omitted from the Code.

CODIFICATION

In subsec. (c)(1), (4), "December 15, 1967" substituted for "enactment of the Wholesome Meat Act".

AMENDMENTS

1994—Subsec. (c)(4). Pub. L. 103–437 substituted "Agriculture, Nutrition, and Forestry" for "Agriculture and Forestry".

1984—Subsec. (c)(2). Pub. L. 98–487 inserted provisions relating to operations conducted at a restaurant central kitchen facility.

EFFECTIVE DATE

Section effective Dec. 15, 1967, see section 20 of Pub. L. 90–201, set out as a note under section 601 of this title.

TERMINATION OF ADVISORY COMMITTEES

Advisory committees in existence on Jan. 5, 1973, to terminate not later than the expiration of the 2-year period following Jan. 5, 1973, and advisory committees established after Jan. 5, 1973, to terminate not later than the expiration of the 2-year period beginning on the date of their establishment, unless in the case of a committee established by the President or an officer of the Federal Government, such committee is renewed by appropriate action prior to the expiration of such 2-year period, or in the case of a committee established by Congress, its duration is otherwise provided by law. See section 14 of Pub. L. 92–463, Oct. 6, 1972, 86 Stat. 776, set out in the Appendix to Title 5, Government Organization and Employees.

SUBCHAPTER IV—AUXILIARY PROVISIONS

§671. Inspection services; refusal or withdrawal; hearing; business unfitness based upon certain convictions; other provisions for withdrawal of services unaffected; responsible connection with business; finality of Secretary's actions; judicial review; record

The Secretary may (for such period, or indefinitely, as he deems necessary to effectuate the purposes of this chapter) refuse to provide, or withdraw, inspection service under subchapter I of this chapter with respect to any establishment if he determines, after opportunity for a hearing is accorded to the applicant for, or recipient of, such service, that such applicant or recipient is unfit to engage in any business requiring inspection under subchapter I because the applicant or recipient, or anyone responsibly connected with the applicant or recipient, has been convicted, in any Federal or State court, of (1) any felony, or (2) more than one violation of

[1] See References in Text note below.

any law, other than a felony, based upon the acquiring, handling, or distributing of unwholesome, mislabeled, or deceptively packaged food or upon fraud in connection with transactions in food. This section shall not affect in any way other provisions of this chapter for withdrawal of inspection services under subchapter I from establishments failing to maintain sanitary conditions or to destroy condemned carcasses, parts, meat or meat food products.

For the purpose of this section a person shall be deemed to be responsibly connected with the business if he was a partner, officer, director, holder, or owner of 10 per centum or more of its voting stock or employee in a managerial or executive capacity.

The determination and order of the Secretary with respect thereto under this section shall be final and conclusive unless the affected applicant for, or recipient of, inspection service files application for judicial review within thirty days after the effective date of such order in the appropriate court as provided in section 674 of this title. Judicial review of any such order shall be upon the record upon which the determination and order are based.

(Mar. 4, 1907, ch. 2907, title IV, § 401, as added Pub. L. 90–201, § 16, Dec. 15, 1967, 81 Stat. 597; amended Pub. L. 99–641, title IV, § 403(b), Nov. 10, 1986, 100 Stat. 3568.)

AMENDMENTS

1986—Subsec. (a). Pub. L. 99–641, § 403(b)(1), (2)(B), (C), temporarily designated provisions which related to authority to refuse or withdraw inspection service as subsec. (a), struck out "any felony, or (2)" after "of (1)", and inserted "or (2) any felony" after "transactions in food". See Effective and Termination Dates of 1986 Amendment note below.

Pub. L. 99–641, § 403(b)(2)(A), which directed that subsec. (a) be amended by substituting "applicant for" for "applicant, for", could not be executed because "applicant, for" does not appear.

Subsecs. (b) to (e). Pub. L. 99–641, § 403(b)(6), temporarily added subsecs. (b) to (e). See Effective and Termination Dates of 1986 Amendment note below.

Subsec. (f). Pub. L. 99–641, § 403(b)(3), temporarily designated provisions which related to other provisions for withdrawal of inspection services as subsec. (f). See Effective and Termination Dates of 1986 Amendment note below.

Subsec. (g). Pub. L. 99–641, § 403(b)(4), temporarily designated provisions which related to responsible connection with business as subsec. (g). See Effective and Termination Dates of 1986 Amendment note below.

Subsec. (h). Pub. L. 99–641, § 403(b)(5), temporarily designated provisions which related to finality of determination by Secretary and to judicial review as subsec. (h), substituted "Except as provided in subsection (e)(2) of this section, the determination" for "The determination" and "subsection (e) of this section" for "this section". See Effective and Termination Dates of 1986 Amendment note below.

EFFECTIVE AND TERMINATION DATES OF 1986 AMENDMENT

Section 403(b) of Pub. L. 99–641 provided that the amendment made by that section is effective only during the 6-year period beginning Nov. 10, 1986.

EFFECTIVE DATE

Subchapter effective Dec. 15, 1967, see section 20 of Pub. L. 90–201, set out as a note under section 601 of this title.

CONSTRUCTION AND EFFECT OF AMENDMENTS BY PUB. L. 99–641

For provisions relating to construction and effect of temporary amendments by section 403 of Pub. L. 99–641, see sections 403(e) and 404 of Pub. L. 99–641, set out as notes entitled "Inspection Services for Establishments Not Participating in Total Plant Quality-Control Program" and "Savings Provision", respectively, under section 609 of this title.

§ 672. Administrative detention; duration; pending judicial proceedings; notification of governmental authorities; release

Whenever any carcass, part of a carcass, meat or meat food product of cattle, sheep, swine, goats, horses, mules, or other equines, or any product exempted from the definition of a meat food product, or any dead, dying, disabled, or diseased cattle, sheep, swine, goat, or equine is found by any authorized representative of the Secretary upon any premises where it is held for purposes of, or during or after distribution in, commerce or otherwise subject to subchapter I or II of this chapter, and there is reason to believe that any such article is adulterated or misbranded and is capable of use as human food, or that it has not been inspected, in violation of the provisions of subchapter I of this chapter or of any other Federal law or the laws of any State or Territory, or the District of Columbia, or that such article or animal has been or is intended to be, distributed in violation of any such provisions, it may be detained by such representative for a period not to exceed twenty days, pending action under section 673 of this title or notification of any Federal, State, or other governmental authorities having jurisdiction over such article or animal, and shall not be moved by any person, firm, or corporation from the place at which it is located when so detained, until released by such representative. All official marks may be required by such representative to be removed from such article or animal before it is released unless it appears to the satisfaction of the Secretary that the article or animal is eligible to retain such marks.

(Mar. 4, 1907, ch. 2907, title IV, § 402, as added Pub. L. 90–201, § 16, Dec. 15, 1967, 81 Stat. 598.)

§ 673. Seizure and condemnation

(a) Proceedings in rem; libel of information; jurisdiction; disposal by destruction or sale; proceeds into the Treasury; sales restrictions; bond; court costs and fees, storage, and other expenses against claimants; proceedings in admiralty; jury trial; United States as plaintiff

(1) Any carcass, part of a carcass, meat or meat food product of cattle, sheep, swine, goats, horses, mules or other equines, or any dead, dying, disabled, or diseased cattle, sheep, swine, goat, or equine, that is being transported in commerce or otherwise subject to subchapter I or II of this chapter, or is held for sale in the United States after such transportation, and that (A) is or has been prepared, sold, transported, or otherwise distributed or offered or received for distribution in violation of this chapter, or (B) is capable of use as human food and is adulterated or misbranded, or (C) in any other

way is in violation of this chapter, shall be liable to be proceeded against and seized and condemned, at any time, on a libel of information in any United States district court or other proper court as provided in section 674 of this title within the jurisdiction of which the article or animal is found.

(2) If the article or animal is condemned it shall, after entry of the decree, (A) be distributed in accordance with paragraph (5), or (B) be disposed of by destruction or sale as the court may direct and the proceeds, if sold, less the court costs and fees, and storage and other proper expenses, shall be paid into the Treasury of the United States, but the article or animal shall not be sold contrary to the provisions of this chapter, or the laws of the jurisdiction in which it is sold: *Provided*, That upon the execution and delivery of a good and sufficient bond conditioned that the article or animal shall not be sold or otherwise disposed of contrary to the provisions of this chapter, or the laws of the jurisdiction in which disposal is made, the court may direct that such article or animal be delivered to the owner thereof subject to such supervision by authorized representatives of the Secretary as is necessary to insure compliance with the applicable laws.

(3) When a decree of condemnation is entered against the article or animal and it is released under bond, or destroyed, court costs and fees, and storage and other proper expenses shall be awarded against the person, if any, intervening as claimant of the article or animal.

(4) The proceedings in such libel cases shall conform, as nearly as may be, to the proceedings in admiralty, except that either party may demand trial by jury of any issue of fact joined in any case, and all such proceedings shall be at the suit of and in the name of the United States.

(5)(A) An article that is condemned under paragraph (1) may as the court may direct, after entry of the decree, be distributed without charge to nonprofit, private entities or to Federal, State, or local government entities engaged in the distribution of food without charge to individuals, if such article—

(i) has been inspected under this chapter and found to be wholesome and not to be adulterated within the meaning of paragraphs (1) through (7) and (9) of section 601(m) of this title and a determination is made at the time of the entry of the decree that such article is wholesome and not so adulterated; and

(ii) is plainly marked "Not for Sale" on such article or its container.

(B) The United States may not be held legally responsible for any article that is distributed under subparagraph (A) to a nonprofit, private entity or to a Federal, State, or local government entity, if such article—

(i) was found after inspection under this chapter to be wholesome and not adulterated within the meaning of paragraphs (1) through (7) and (9) of section 601(m) of this title and a determination was made at the time of the entry of the decree that such article was wholesome and not so adulterated; and

(ii) was plainly marked "Not for Sale" on such article or its container.

(C) The person from whom such article was seized and condemned may not be held legally responsible for such article, if such article—

(i) was found after inspection under this chapter to be wholesome and not adulterated within the meaning of paragraphs (1) through (7) and (9) of section 601(m) of this title and a determination was made at the time of the entry of the decree that such article was wholesome and not so adulterated; and

(ii) was plainly marked "Not for Sale" on such article or its container.

(b) Condemnation or seizure under other provisions unaffected

The provisions of this section shall in no way derogate from authority for condemnation or seizure conferred by other provisions of this chapter, or other laws.

(Mar. 4, 1907, ch. 2907, title IV, § 403, as added Pub. L. 90–201, § 16, Dec. 15, 1967, 81 Stat. 598; amended Pub. L. 101–205, § 1, Dec. 7, 1989, 103 Stat. 1829.)

AMENDMENTS

1989—Subsec. (a). Pub. L. 101–205 designated first sentence as par. (1) and redesignated cls. (1) to (3) as cls. (A) to (C), respectively, designated second sentence as par. (2) and inserted "(A) to be distributed in accordance with paragraph (5), or (B)" after "entry of the decree,", designated third and fourth sentences as pars. (3) and (4), respectively, and added par. (5).

§ 674. Federal court jurisdiction of enforcement and injunction proceedings and other kinds of cases; limitations of section 607(e) of this title

The United States district courts, the District Court of Guam, the District Court of the Virgin Islands, the highest court of American Samoa, and the United States courts of the other Territories, are vested with jurisdiction specifically to enforce, and to prevent and restrain violations of, this chapter, and shall have jurisdiction in all other kinds of cases arising under this chapter, except as provided in section 607(e) of this title.

(Mar. 4, 1907, ch. 2907, title IV, § 404, as added Pub. L. 90–201, § 16, Dec. 15, 1967, 81 Stat. 599.)

§ 675. Assaulting, resisting, or impeding certain persons; murder; protection of such persons

Any person who forcibly assaults, resists, opposes, impedes, intimidates, or interferes with any person while engaged in or on account of the performance of his official duties under this chapter shall be fined not more than $5,000 or imprisoned not more than three years, or both. Whoever, in the commission of any such acts, uses a deadly or dangerous weapon, shall be fined not more than $10,000 or imprisoned not more than ten years, or both. Whoever kills any person while engaged in or on account of the performance of his official duties under this chapter shall be punished as provided under sections 1111 and 1114 of title 18.

(Mar. 4, 1907, ch. 2907, title IV, § 405, as added Pub. L. 90–201, § 16, Dec. 15, 1967, 81 Stat. 599.)

§676. Violations

(a) Misdemeanors; felonies: intent to defraud and distribution of adulterated articles; good faith

Any person, firm, or corporation who violates any provision of this chapter for which no other criminal penalty is provided by this chapter shall upon conviction be subject to imprisonment for not more than one year, or a fine of not more than $1,000, or both such imprisonment and fine; but if such violation involves intent to defraud, or any distribution or attempted distribution of an article that is adulterated (except as defined in section 601(m)(8) of this title), such person, firm, or corporation shall be subject to imprisonment for not more than three years or a fine of not more than $10,000, or both: *Provided*, That no person, firm, or corporation, shall be subject to penalties under this section for receiving for transportation any article or animal in violation of this chapter if such receipt was made in good faith, unless such person, firm, or corporation refuses to furnish on request of a representative of the Secretary the name and address of the person from whom he received such article or animal, and copies of all documents, if any there be, pertaining to the delivery of the article or animal to him.

(b) Minor violations; written notice of warning of criminal and civil proceedings

Nothing in this chapter shall be construed as requiring the Secretary to report for prosecution or for the institution of libel or injunction proceedings, minor violations of this chapter whenever he believes that the public interest will be adequately served by a suitable written notice of warning.

(Mar. 4, 1907, ch. 2907, title IV, §406, as added Pub. L. 90–201, §16, Dec. 15, 1967, 81 Stat. 599; amended Pub. L. 99–641, title IV, §403(c), Nov. 10, 1986, 100 Stat. 3570.)

Amendments

1986—Subsec. (b). Pub. L. 99–641, §403(c)(1), temporarily inserted provisions which related to factors required to be considered by Secretary in determining whether public interest is served by written notice of warning. See Effective and Termination Dates of 1986 Amendment note below.

Subsec. (c). Pub. L. 99–641, §403(c)(2), temporarily added subsec. (c). See Effective and Termination Dates of 1986 Amendment note below.

Effective and Termination Dates of 1986 Amendment

Section 403(c) of Pub. L. 99–641 provided that the amendment made by that section is effective only during the 6-year period beginning Nov. 10, 1986.

Construction and Effect of Amendments by Pub. L. 99–641

For provisions relating to construction and effect of temporary amendments by section 403 of Pub. L. 99–641, see sections 403(e) and 404 of Pub. L. 99–641, set out as notes entitled "Inspection Services for Establishments Not Participating in Total Plant Quality-Control Program" and "Savings Provision", respectively, under section 609 of this title.

§677. Other Federal laws applicable for administration and enforcement of chapter; location of inquiries; jurisdiction of Federal courts

For the efficient administration and enforcement of this chapter, the provisions (including penalties) of sections 46, 48, 49 and 50 of title 15 (except paragraphs (c) through (h) of section 46 and the last paragraph of section 49[1] of title 15), and the provisions of section 409(*l*)[1] of title 47; are made applicable to the jurisdiction, powers, and duties of the Secretary in administering and enforcing the provisions of this chapter and to any person, firm, or corporation with respect to whom such authority is exercised. The Secretary, in person or by such agents as he may designate, may prosecute any inquiry necessary to his duties under this chapter in any part of the United States, and the powers conferred by said sections 49 and 50 of title 15 on the district courts of the United States may be exercised for the purposes of this chapter by any court designated in section 674 of this title.

(Mar. 4, 1907, ch. 2907, title IV, §407, as added Pub. L. 90–201, §16, Dec. 15, 1967, 81 Stat. 599.)

References in Text

The last paragraph of section 49 of title 15, and the provisions of section 409(*l*) of title 47, referred to in text, which related to immunity of witnesses, were repealed by sections 211 and 242, respectively, of Pub. L. 91–452, Oct. 15, 1970, title II, 84 Stat. 929, 930. For provisions relating to immunity of witnesses, see section 6001 et seq. of Title 18, Crimes and Criminal Procedure.

§678. Non-Federal jurisdiction of federally regulated matters; prohibition of additional or different requirements for establishments with inspection services and as to marking, labeling, packaging, and ingredients; recordkeeping and related requirements; concurrent jurisdiction over distribution for human food purposes of adulterated or misbranded and imported articles; other matters

Requirements within the scope of this chapter with respect to premises, facilities and operations of any establishment at which inspection is provided under subchapter I of this chapter, which are in addition to, or different than those made under this chapter may not be imposed by any State or Territory or the District of Columbia, except that any such jurisdiction may impose recordkeeping and other requirements within the scope of section 642 of this title, if consistent therewith, with respect to any such establishment. Marking, labeling, packaging, or ingredient requirements in addition to, or different than, those made under this chapter may not be imposed by any State or Territory or the District of Columbia with respect to articles prepared at any establishment under inspection in accordance with the requirements under subchapter I of this chapter, but any State or Territory or the District of Columbia may, consistent with the requirements under this chapter, exercise concurrent jurisdiction with the Secretary over articles required to be inspected under said subchapter I, for the purpose of preventing the distribution for human food purposes of any

[1] See References in Text note below.

such articles which are adulterated or misbranded and are outside of such an establishment, or, in the case of imported articles which are not at such an establishment, after their entry into the United States. This chapter shall not preclude any State or Territory or the District of Columbia from making requirement[1] or taking other action, consistent with this chapter, with respect to any other matters regulated under this chapter.

(Mar. 4, 1907, ch. 2907, title IV, §408, as added Pub. L. 90–201, §16, Dec. 15, 1967, 81 Stat. 600.)

§679. Application of Federal Food, Drug, and Cosmetic Act

(a) Authorities under food, drug, and cosmetic provisions unaffected

Notwithstanding any other provisions of law, including section 902(b) of the Federal Food, Drug, and Cosmetic Act (21 U.S.C. 392(a)), the provisions of this chapter shall not derogate from any authority conferred by the Federal Food, Drug, and Cosmetic Act [21 U.S.C. 301 et seq.] prior to December 15, 1967.

(b) Enforcement proceedings; detainer authority of representatives of Secretary of Health and Human Services

The detainer authority conferred by section 672 of this title shall apply to any authorized representative of the Secretary of Health and Human Services for purposes of the enforcement of the Federal Food, Drug, and Cosmetic Act [21 U.S.C. 301 et seq.] with respect to any carcass, part thereof, meat, or meat food product of cattle, sheep, swine, goats, or equines that is outside any premises at which inspection is being maintained under this chapter, and for such purposes the first reference to the Secretary in section 672 of this title shall be deemed to refer to the Secretary of Health and Human Services.

(Mar. 4, 1907, ch. 2907, title IV, §409, as added Pub. L. 90–201, §16, Dec. 15, 1967, 81 Stat. 600; amended Pub. L. 96–88, title V, §509(b), Oct. 17, 1979, 93 Stat. 695.)

REFERENCES IN TEXT

The Federal Food, Drug, and Cosmetic Act, referred to in subsec. (b), is act June 25, 1938, ch. 675, 52 Stat. 1040, as amended, which is classified generally to chapter 9 (§301 et seq.) of this title. For complete classification of this Act to the Code, see section 301 of this title and Tables.

CHANGE OF NAME

"Secretary of Health and Human Services" substituted for "Secretary of Health, Education, and Welfare" in subsec. (b) pursuant to section 509(b) of Pub. L. 96–88, which is classified to section 3508(b) of Title 20, Education.

§679a. Safe Meat and Poultry Inspection Panel

(a) Establishment

There is established in the Department of Agriculture a permanent advisory panel to be known as the "Safe Meat and Poultry Inspection Panel" (referred to in this section as the "panel").

(b) Duties

(1) Review and evaluation

The panel shall review and evaluate, as the panel considers necessary, the adequacy, necessity, safety, cost-effectiveness, and scientific merit of—

(A) inspection procedures of, and work rules and worker relations involving Federal employees employed in, plants inspected under this chapter;

(B) informal petitions or proposals for changes in inspection procedures, processes, and techniques of plants inspected under this chapter;

(C) formal changes in meat inspection regulations promulgated under this chapter, whether in notice, proposed, or final form; and

(D) such other matters as may be referred to the panel by the Secretary regarding the quality or effectiveness of a safe and cost-effective meat inspection system under this chapter.

(2) Reports

(A) In general

The panel shall submit to the Secretary a report on the results of each review and evaluation carried out under paragraph (1), including such recommendations as the panel considers appropriate.

(B) Reports on formal changes

In the case of a report concerning a formal change in meat inspection regulations, the report shall be made within the time limits prescribed for formal comments on such changes.

(C) Publication in Federal Register

Each report of the panel to the Secretary shall be published in the Federal Register.

(c) Secretarial response

Not later than 90 days after the publication of a panel report under subsection (b)(2)(C) of this section, the Secretary shall publish in the Federal Register any response required of the Secretary to the report.

(d) Composition of panel

The panel shall be composed of 7 members, not fewer than 5 of whom shall be from the food science, meat science, or poultry science profession, appointed to staggered terms not to exceed 3 years by the Secretary from nominations received from the National Institutes of Health and the Federation of American Societies of Food Animal Science and based on the professional qualifications of the nominees.

(e) Nominations

(1) Initial panel

In constituting the initial panel, the Secretary shall solicit 6 nominees from the National Institutes of Health and 6 nominees from the Federation of American Societies of Food Animal Science for membership on the panel.

(2) Vacancies

Any subsequent vacancy on the panel shall be filled by the Secretary after soliciting 2

[1] So in original. Probably should be "requirements".

nominees from the National Institutes of Health and 2 nominees from the Federation of American Societies of Food Animal Science.

(3) Requirements for nominees

(A) In general

Each nominee provided under paragraph (1) or (2) shall have a background in public health issues and a scientific expertise in food, meat, or poultry science or in veterinary science.

(B) Submission of information

The Secretary may require nominees to submit such information as the Secretary considers necessary prior to completing the selection process.

(4) Additional nominees

If any list of nominees provided under paragraph (1) or (2) is unsatisfactory to the Secretary, the Secretary may request the nominating entities to submit an additional list of nominees.

(f) Travel expenses

While away from the home or regular place of business of a member of the panel in the performance of services for the panel, the member shall be allowed travel expenses, including per diem in lieu of subsistence, at the same rate as a person employed intermittently in the Government service would be allowed under section 5703 of title 5.

(g) Conflicts of interest

The Secretary shall promulgate regulations regarding conflicts of interest with respect to the members of the panel.

(h) Exemption

The Federal Advisory Committee Act (5 U.S.C. App.) and title XVIII of the Food and Agriculture Act of 1977 (7 U.S.C. 2281 et seq.) shall not apply to the panel.

(i) Funding

From funds available to the Secretary to carry out this chapter and the Poultry Products Inspection Act (21 U.S.C. 451 et seq.), the Secretary shall allocate such sums as may be necessary to carry out this section.

(Mar. 4, 1907, ch. 2907, title IV, § 410, as added Pub. L. 104–127, title IX, § 918(a)(1)(B), Apr. 4, 1996, 110 Stat. 1188.)

REFERENCES IN TEXT

The Federal Advisory Committee Act, referred to in subsec. (h), is Pub. L. 92–463, Oct. 6, 1972, 86 Stat. 770, as amended, which is set out in the Appendix to Title 5, Government Organization and Employees.

The Food and Agriculture Act of 1977, referred to in subsec. (h), is Pub. L. 95–113, Sept. 29, 1977, 91 Stat. 913, as amended. Title XVIII of the Act is classified generally to chapter 55A (§ 2281 et seq.) of Title 7, Agriculture. For complete classification of this Act to the Code, see Short Title of 1977 Amendment note set out under section 1281 of Title 7 and Tables.

The Poultry Products Inspection Act, referred to in subsec. (i), is Pub. L. 85–172, Aug. 28, 1957, 71 Stat. 441, as amended, which is classified generally to chapter 10 (§ 451 et seq.) of this title. For complete classification of this Act to the Code, see Short Title note set out under section 451 of this title and Tables.

PRIOR PROVISIONS

A prior section 410 of act Mar. 4, 1907, was renumbered section 411, and is classified to section 680 of this title.

§ 679b. Pasteurization of meat and poultry

(1) In general

Effective beginning not later than 30 days after May 13, 2002, the Secretary of Agriculture shall conduct an education program regarding the availability and safety of processes and treatments that eliminate or substantially reduce the level of pathogens on meat, meat food products, poultry, and poultry products.

(2) Authorization of appropriations

There is authorized to be appropriated such sums as are necessary to carry out this section.

(Pub. L. 107–171, title X, § 10808(a), May 13, 2002, 116 Stat. 530.)

CODIFICATION

Section was enacted as part of the Farm Security and Rural Investment Act of 2002, and not as part of the Federal Meat Inspection Act which is classified to subchapters I to IV of this chapter.

§ 679c. Expansion of Food Safety Inspection Service activities

(a) In general

The Secretary of Agriculture may utilize existing authorities to give high priority to enhancing and expanding the capacity of the Food Safety Inspection Service to conduct activities to—

(1) enhance the ability of the Service to inspect and ensure the safety and wholesomeness of meat and poultry products;

(2) improve the capacity of the Service to inspect international meat and meat products, poultry and poultry products, and egg products at points of origin and at ports of entry;

(3) strengthen the ability of the Service to collaborate with relevant agencies within the Department of Agriculture and with other entities in the Federal Government, the States, and Indian tribes (as defined in section 450b(e) of title 25) through the sharing of information and technology; and

(4) otherwise expand the capacity of the Service to protect against the threat of bioterrorism.

(b) Authorization of appropriations

There is authorized to be appropriated to carry out this section, $15,000,000 for fiscal year 2002, and such sums as may be necessary for each subsequent fiscal year.

(Pub. L. 107–188, title III, § 332, June 12, 2002, 116 Stat. 679.)

CODIFICATION

Section was enacted as part of the Public Health Security and Bioterrorism Preparedness and Response Act of 2002, and not as part of the Federal Meat Inspection Act which is classified to subchapters I to IV of this chapter.

§ 680. Authorization of appropriations

There are hereby authorized to be appropriated such sums as may be necessary to carry out the provisions of this chapter.

(Mar. 4, 1907, ch. 2907, title IV, §411, formerly §410, as added Pub. L. 90–201, §16, Dec. 15, 1967, 81 Stat. 600; renumbered §411, Pub. L. 104–127, title IX, §918(a)(1)(A), Apr. 4, 1996, 110 Stat. 1188.)

SUBCHAPTER IV–A—INSPECTIONS BY FEDERAL AND STATE AGENCIES

§683. Interstate shipment of meat inspected by Federal and State agencies for certain small establishments

(a) Definitions

(1) Appropriate State agency

The term "appropriate State agency" means a State agency described in section 661(b) of this title.

(2) Designated personnel

The term "designated personnel" means inspection personnel of a State agency that have undergone all necessary inspection training and certification to assist the Secretary in the administration and enforcement of this chapter, including rules and regulations issued under this chapter.

(3) Eligible establishment

The term "eligible establishment" means an establishment that is in compliance with—

(A) the State inspection program of the State in which the establishment is located; and

(B) this chapter, including rules and regulations issued under this chapter.

(4) Meat item

The term "meat item" means—

(A) a portion of meat; and

(B) a meat food product.

(5) Selected establishment

The term "selected establishment" means an eligible establishment that is selected by the Secretary, in coordination with the appropriate State agency of the State in which the eligible establishment is located, under subsection (b) to ship carcasses, portions of carcasses, and meat items in interstate commerce.

(b) Authority of Secretary to allow shipments

(1) In general

Subject to paragraph (2), the Secretary, in coordination with the appropriate State agency of the State in which an establishment is located, may select the establishment to ship carcasses, portions of carcasses, and meat items in interstate commerce, and place on each carcass, portion of a carcass, and meat item shipped in interstate commerce a Federal mark, stamp, tag, or label of inspection, if—

(A) the carcass, portion of carcass, or meat item qualifies for the mark, stamp, tag, or label of inspection under the requirements of this chapter;

(B) the establishment is an eligible establishment; and

(C) inspection services for the establishment are provided by designated personnel.

(2) Prohibited establishments

In carrying out paragraph (1), the Secretary, in coordination with an appropriate State agency, shall not select an establishment that—

(A) on average, employs more than 25 employees (including supervisory and nonsupervisory employees), as defined by the Secretary;

(B) as of the date of the enactment of this section, ships in interstate commerce carcasses, portions of carcasses, or meat items that are inspected by the Secretary in accordance with this chapter;

(C)(i) is a Federal establishment;

(ii) was a Federal establishment that was reorganized on a later date under the same name or a different name or person by the person, firm, or corporation that controlled the establishment as of the date of the enactment of this section; or

(iii) was a State establishment as of the date of the enactment of this section that—

(I) as of the date of the enactment of this section, employed more than 25 employees; and

(II) was reorganized on a later date by the person, firm, or corporation that controlled the establishment as of the date of the enactment of this section;

(D) is in violation of this chapter;

(E) is located in a State that does not have a State inspection program; or

(F) is the subject of a transition carried out in accordance with a procedure developed by the Secretary under paragraph (3)(A).

(3) Establishments that employ more than 25 employees

(A) Development of procedure

The Secretary may develop a procedure to transition to a Federal establishment any establishment under this section that, on average, consistently employs more than 25 employees.

(B) Eligibility of certain establishments

(i) In general

A State establishment that employs more than 25 employees but less than 35 employees as of the date of the enactment of this section may be selected as a selected establishment under this subsection.

(ii) Procedures

A State establishment shall be subject to the procedures established under subparagraph (A) beginning on the date that is 3 years after the effective date described in subsection (j).

(c) Reimbursement of State costs

The Secretary shall reimburse a State for costs related to the inspection of selected establishments in the State in accordance with Federal requirements in an amount of not less than 60 percent of eligible State costs.

(d) Coordination between Federal and State agencies

(1) In general

The Secretary shall designate an employee of the Federal Government as State coordinator for each appropriate State agency—

(A) to provide oversight and enforcement of this subchapter; and

(B) to oversee the training and inspection activities of designated personnel of the State agency.

(2) Supervision

A State coordinator shall be under the direct supervision of the Secretary.

(3) Duties of State coordinator

(A) In general

A State coordinator shall visit selected establishments with a frequency that is appropriate to ensure that selected establishments are operating in a manner that is consistent with this chapter (including regulations and policies under this chapter).

(B) Quarterly reports

A State coordinator shall, on a quarterly basis, submit to the Secretary a report that describes the status of each selected establishment that is under the jurisdiction of the State coordinator with respect to the level of compliance of each selected establishment with the requirements of this chapter.

(C) Immediate notification requirement

If a State coordinator determines that any selected establishment that is under the jurisdiction of the State coordinator is in violation of any requirement of this chapter, the State coordinator shall—

(i) immediately notify the Secretary of the violation; and

(ii) deselect the selected establishment or suspend inspection at the selected establishment.

(4) Performance evaluations

Performance evaluations of State coordinators designated under this subsection shall be conducted by the Secretary as part of the Federal agency management control system.

(e) Audits

(1) Periodic audits conducted by Inspector General of the Department of Agriculture

Not later than 2 years after the effective date described in subsection (j), and not less often than every 3 years thereafter, the Inspector General of the Department of Agriculture shall conduct an audit of each activity taken by the Secretary under this section for the period covered by the audit to determine compliance with this section.

(2) Audit conducted by Comptroller General of the United States

Not earlier than 3 years, nor later than 5 years, after the date of the enactment of this section, the Comptroller General of the United States shall conduct an audit of the implementation of this section to determine—

(A) the effectiveness of the implementation of this section; and

(B) the number of selected establishments selected by the Secretary to ship carcasses, portions of carcasses, or meat items under this section.

(f) Technical assistance division

(1) Establishment

Not later than 180 days after the effective date described in subsection (j), the Secretary shall establish in the Food Safety and Inspection Service of the Department of Agriculture a technical assistance division to coordinate the initiatives of any other appropriate agency of the Department of Agriculture to provide—

(A) outreach, education, and training to very small or certain small establishments (as defined by the Secretary); and

(B) grants to appropriate State agencies to provide outreach, technical assistance, education, and training to very small or certain small establishments (as defined by the Secretary).

(2) Personnel

The technical assistance division shall be comprised of individuals that, as determined by the Secretary—

(A) are of a quantity sufficient to carry out the duties of the technical assistance division; and

(B) possess appropriate qualifications and expertise relating to the duties of the technical assistance division.

(g) Transition grants

The Secretary may provide grants to appropriate State agencies to assist the appropriate State agencies in helping establishments covered by subchapter III to transition to selected establishments.

(h) Violations

Any selected establishment that the Secretary determines to be in violation of any requirement of this chapter shall be transitioned to a Federal establishment in accordance with a procedure developed by the Secretary under subsection (b)(3)(A).

(i) Effect

Nothing in this section limits the jurisdiction of the Secretary with respect to the regulation of meat and meat products under this chapter.

(j) Effective date

(1) In general

This section takes effect on the date on which the Secretary, after providing a period of public comment (including through the conduct of public meetings or hearings), promulgates final regulations to carry out this section.

(2) Requirement

Not later than 18 months after the date of the enactment of this section, the Secretary shall promulgate final regulations in accordance with paragraph (1).

(Mar. 4, 1907, ch. 2907, title V, § 501, as added Pub. L. 110–234, title XI, § 11015(a), May 22, 2008, 122 Stat. 1362, and Pub. L. 110–246, § 4(a), title XI, § 11015(a), June 18, 2008, 122 Stat. 1664, 2124.)

REFERENCES IN TEXT

The date of the enactment of this section, referred to in subsecs. (b)(2)(B), (C)(ii), (iii), (3)(B)(i), (e)(2), and (j)(2), is the date of enactment of Pub. L. 110–246, which was approved June 18, 2008.

CODIFICATION

Pub. L. 110–234 and Pub. L. 110–246 enacted identical sections. Pub. L. 110–234 was repealed by section 4(a) of Pub. L. 110–246.

EFFECTIVE DATE

Enactment of this section and repeal of Pub. L. 110–234 by Pub. L. 110–246 effective May 22, 2008, the date of enactment of Pub. L. 110–234, see section 4 of Pub. L. 110–246, set out as a note under section 8701 of Title 7, Agriculture.

SUBCHAPTER V—MISCELLANEOUS PROVISIONS

§ 691. Omitted

CODIFICATION

Section, Pub. L. 90–201, § 17, Dec. 15, 1967, 81 Stat. 600; Pub. L. 103–437, § 8(3), Nov. 2, 1994, 108 Stat. 4588, which required the Secretary of Agriculture to report annually to the Committee on Agriculture of the House of Representatives and the Committee on Agriculture, Nutrition, and Forestry of the Senate on the slaughter of animals and the processing and distribution of carcasses and products, terminated, effective May 15, 2000, pursuant to section 3003 of Pub. L. 104–66, as amended, set out as a note under section 1113 of Title 31, Money and Finance. See, also, page 46 of House Document No. 103–7.

§ 692. Inspection extended to reindeer

The provisions of the meat inspection law may be extended to the inspection of reindeer.

(June 30, 1914, ch. 131, 38 Stat. 420.)

REFERENCES IN TEXT

The meat inspection law, referred to in text, is classified generally to this chapter. At the time of enactment, such reference probably meant the Act of Mar. 4, 1907, ch. 2907, 34 Stat. 1260, as amended. That Act (formerly classified to section 71 et seq. of this title), was generally revised by Pub. L. 90–201, Dec. 15, 1967, 81 Stat. 584, and is classified to this chapter. For complete classification of this Act to the Code, see Tables.

CODIFICATION

Section was not enacted as part of the Federal Meat Inspection Act which is classified to subchapters I to IV–A of this chapter.

Section was formerly classified to section 94 of this title.

§ 693. Inspection of dairy products for export

The act of March 3, 1891, as amended, for the inspection of live cattle and products thereof, shall be deemed to include dairy products intended for exportation to any foreign country, and the Secretary of Agriculture may apply, under rules and regulations to be prescribed by him, the provisions of said act for inspection and certification appropriate for ascertaining the purity and quality of such products, and may cause the same to be so marked, stamped, or labeled as to secure their identity and make known in the markets of foreign countries to which they may be sent from the United States their purity, quality, and grade; and all the provisions of said act relating to live cattle and products thereof for export shall apply to dairy products so inspected and certified.

(May 23, 1908, ch. 192, 35 Stat. 254.)

REFERENCES IN TEXT

Act of March 3, 1891, referred to in text, is act Mar. 3, 1891, ch. 555, 26 Stat. 1089, which was superseded by act Mar. 4, 1907, ch. 2907, 34 Stat. 1260, as amended by act June 29, 1938, ch. 810, 52 Stat. 1235 (formerly classified to section 71 et seq. of this title). Act Mar. 4, 1907, ch. 2907, was generally revised by Pub. L. 90–201, Dec. 15, 1967, 81 Stat. 584, and is classified to this chapter.

CODIFICATION

Section was not enacted as part of the Federal Meat Inspection Act which is classified to subchapters I to IV–A of this chapter.

Section was formerly classified to sections 94a and 132 of this title.

§ 694. Authorization of appropriations

Annual appropriations of the sum of $3,000,000 from the general fund of the Treasury are authorized for the expenses of the inspection of cattle, sheep, swine, and goats and the meat and meat food products thereof which enter into interstate or foreign commerce and for all expenses necessary to carry into effect the provisions of this Act relating to meat inspection, including rent and the employment of labor in Washington and elsewhere, for each year, and in addition there is authorized to be appropriated such other sums as may be necessary in the enforcement of the meat inspection laws.

(June 30, 1906, ch. 3913, 34 Stat. 679; June 26, 1934, ch. 756, § 2, 48 Stat. 1225.)

REFERENCES IN TEXT

This Act, referred to in text, is act June 30, 1906, ch. 3913, 34 Stat. 669, which made appropriations for the Department of Agriculture for the fiscal year ending June 30, 1907.

CODIFICATION

Section 2 of act June 26, 1934, which was classified to section 725a of former Title 31, Money and Finance, repealed the permanent appropriation under the title "Meat inspection, Bureau of Animal Industry (fiscal year) (3–114)" effective July 1, 1935, provided that such portions of any Acts as make permanent appropriations to be expended under such account are amended so as to authorize, in lieu thereof, annual appropriations from the general fund of the Treasury in identical terms and in such amounts as now provided by the laws providing such permanent appropriations, and authorized, in addition thereto, the appropriation of "such other sums as may be necessary in the enforcement of the meat inspection laws." In the original, the parenthetical "(U.S.C., title 21, secs. 71 to 96, inclusive)" followed the phrase "meat inspection laws". The "meat inspection laws" are classified generally to this chapter.

Section was not enacted as part of the Federal Meat Inspection Act which is classified to subchapters I to IV–A of this chapter.

Section was formerly classified to section 95 of this title.

§ 695. Payment of cost of meat-inspection service; exception

The cost of inspection rendered on and after July 1, 1948, under the requirements of laws relating to Federal inspection of meat and meat food products shall be borne by the United States except the cost of overtime and holiday pay paid pursuant to section 2219a of title 7.

(June 5, 1948, ch. 423, 62 Stat. 344; Pub. L. 107–171, title X, § 10703(c)(2), May 13, 2002, 116 Stat. 517.)

REFERENCES IN TEXT

Section 2219a of title 7, referred to in text, was in the original "section 10703 of the Farm Security and Rural Investment Act of 2002", meaning section 10703 of Pub.

L. 107–171, which enacted section 2219a of Title 7, Agriculture, amended this section, section 468 of this title, and section 5549 of Title 5, Government Organization and Employees, and repealed section 394 of Title 7.

CODIFICATION

Section was formerly classified to section 98 of this title.

Section was not enacted as part of the Federal Meat Inspection Act which is classified to subchapters I to IV–A of this chapter.

AMENDMENTS

2002—Pub. L. 107–171 substituted "overtime and holiday pay paid pursuant to section 2219a of title 7." for "overtime pursuant to section 394 of title 7."

CHAPTER 13—DRUG ABUSE PREVENTION AND CONTROL

SUBCHAPTER I—CONTROL AND ENFORCEMENT

PART A—INTRODUCTORY PROVISIONS

SUBCHAPTER I—CONTROL AND ENFORCEMENT

PART A—INTRODUCTORY PROVISIONS

§801. Congressional findings and declarations: controlled substances

The Congress makes the following findings and declarations:

(1) Many of the drugs included within this subchapter have a useful and legitimate medical purpose and are necessary to maintain the health and general welfare of the American people.

(2) The illegal importation, manufacture, distribution, and possession and improper use of controlled substances have a substantial and detrimental effect on the health and general welfare of the American people.

(3) A major portion of the traffic in controlled substances flows through interstate and foreign commerce. Incidents of the traffic which are not an integral part of the interstate or foreign flow, such as manufacture, local distribution, and possession, nonetheless have a substantial and direct effect upon interstate commerce because—

(A) after manufacture, many controlled substances are transported in interstate commerce,

(B) controlled substances distributed locally usually have been transported in interstate commerce immediately before their distribution, and

(C) controlled substances possessed commonly flow through interstate commerce immediately prior to such possession.

(4) Local distribution and possession of controlled substances contribute to swelling the interstate traffic in such substances.

(5) Controlled substances manufactured and distributed intrastate cannot be differentiated from controlled substances manufactured and distributed interstate. Thus, it is not feasible to distinguish, in terms of controls, between controlled substances manufactured and distributed interstate and controlled substances manufactured and distributed intrastate.

(6) Federal control of the intrastate incidents of the traffic in controlled substances is essential to the effective control of the interstate incidents of such traffic.

(7) The United States is a party to the Single Convention on Narcotic Drugs, 1961, and other international conventions designed to establish effective control over international and domestic traffic in controlled substances.

(Pub. L. 91–513, title II, §101, Oct. 27, 1970, 84 Stat. 1242.)

REFERENCES IN TEXT

This subchapter, referred to in par. (1), was in the original "this title", meaning title II of Pub. L. 91–513, Oct. 27, 1970, 84 Stat. 1242, as amended, and is popularly known as the "Controlled Substances Act". For complete classification of title II to the Code, see second paragraph of Short Title note set out below and Tables.

EFFECTIVE DATE

Section 704 of title II of Pub. L. 91–513 provided that:

"(a) Except as otherwise provided in this section, this title [see Short Title note below] shall become effective on the first day of the seventh calendar month that begins after the day immediately preceding the date of enactment [Oct. 27, 1970].

"(b) Parts A, B, E, and F of this title [Parts A, B, E, and F of this subchapter], section 702 [set out as a note under section 321 of this title], this section, and sections 705 through 709 [sections 901 to 904 of this title and note set out below], shall become effective upon enactment [Oct. 27, 1970].

"(c) Sections 305 (relating to labels and labeling) [section 825 of this title], and 306 (relating to manufacturing quotas) [section 826 of this title] shall become effective on the date specified in subsection (a) of this section, except that the Attorney General may by order published in the Federal Register postpone the effective date of either or both of these sections for such period as he may determine to be necessary for the efficient administration of this title [see Short Title note below]."

SHORT TITLE OF 2008 AMENDMENT

Pub. L. 110–425, §1, Oct. 15, 2008, 122 Stat. 4820, provided that: "This Act [enacting section 831 of this title, amending sections 802, 823, 827, 829, 841, 843, 882, and 960 of this title, and enacting provisions set out as notes under section 802 of this title and listed in a table relating to sentencing guidelines set out as a note under section 994 of Title 28, Judiciary and Judicial Procedure] may be cited as the 'Ryan Haight Online Pharmacy Consumer Protection Act of 2008'."

Pub. L. 110–415, §1, Oct. 14, 2008, 122 Stat. 4349, provided that: "This Act [amending section 830 of this title] may be cited as the 'Methamphetamine Production Prevention Act of 2008'."

SHORT TITLE OF 2006 AMENDMENT

Pub. L. 109–177, title VII, §701, Mar. 9, 2006, 120 Stat. 256, provided that: "This title [see Tables for classification] may be cited as the 'Combat Methamphetamine Epidemic Act of 2005'."

SHORT TITLE OF 2005 AMENDMENT

Pub. L. 109–57, §1(a), Aug. 2, 2005, 119 Stat. 592, provided that: "This Act [amending section 953 of this title] may be cited as the 'Controlled Substances Export Reform Act of 2005'."

SHORT TITLE OF 2004 AMENDMENT

Pub. L. 108–358, §1, Oct. 22, 2004, 118 Stat. 1661, provided that: "This Act [enacting section 290bb–25f of Title 42, The Public Health and Welfare, amending sections 802 and 811 of this title, enacting provisions set out as notes under section 802 of this title and section 290aa–4 of Title 42 and listed in a table relating to sentencing guidelines set out as a note under section 994 of Title 28, Judiciary and Judicial Procedure, and amending provisions set out as a note under section 802 of this title] may be cited as the 'Anabolic Steroid Control Act of 2004'."

SHORT TITLE OF 2003 AMENDMENT

Pub. L. 108–21, title VI, § 608(a), Apr. 30, 2003, 117 Stat. 691, provided that: "This section [amending sections 843 and 856 of this title and enacting provisions listed in a table relating to sentencing guidelines set out as a note under section 994 of Title 28, Judiciary and Judicial Procedure] may be cited as the 'Illicit Drug Anti-Proliferation Act of 2003'."

SHORT TITLE OF 2000 AMENDMENTS

Pub. L. 106–310, div. B, title XXXV, § 3501, Oct. 17, 2000, 114 Stat. 1222, provided that: "This title [amending sections 823 and 824 of this title] may be cited as the 'Drug Addiction Treatment Act of 2000'."

Pub. L. 106–310, div. B, title XXXVI, § 3601, Oct. 17, 2000, 114 Stat. 1227, provided that: "This title [enacting section 864 of this title and sections 290aa–5b and 290bb–9 of Title 42, The Public Health and Welfare, amending sections 802, 830, 853, 856, and 863 of this title, sections 3663 and 3663A of Title 18, Crimes and Criminal Procedure, section 524 of Title 28, Judiciary and Judicial Procedure, and sections 285o–2 and 3751 of Title 42, and enacting provisions set out as notes under this section and sections 802, 872, 873, 886, and 1706 of this title, sections 524 and 994 of Title 28, and sections 201, 290aa–4, 290aa–5b and 3751 of Title 42] may be cited as the 'Methamphetamine Anti-Proliferation Act of 2000'."

Pub. L. 106–172, § 1, Feb. 18, 2000, 114 Stat. 7, provided that: "This Act [amending sections 802, 827, 841 and 960 of this title and enacting provisions set out as notes under this section and section 812 of this title] may be cited as the 'Hillory J. Farias and Samantha Reid Date-Rape Drug Prohibition Act of 2000'."

SHORT TITLE OF 1998 AMENDMENT

Pub. L. 105–277, div. C, title VIII, § 801(a), Oct. 21, 1998, 112 Stat. 2681–693, provided that: "This title [enacting section 1713 of this title and section 2291–5 of Title 22, Foreign Relations and Intercourse, amending section 956 of this title, and enacting provisions set out as notes under sections 801 and 956 of this title and section 2291 of Title 22] may be cited as the 'Western Hemisphere Drug Elimination Act'."

Pub. L. 105–277, div. C, title VIII, subtitle G (§§ 871, 872), § 871, Oct. 21, 1998, 112 Stat. 2681–707, and Pub. L. 105–357, § 1, Nov. 10, 1998, 112 Stat. 3271, provided that such subtitle and such Act, which amended section 956 of this title and enacted provisions set out as notes under section 956 of this title "may be cited as the 'Controlled Substances Trafficking Prohibition Act'."

Pub. L. 105–277, div. E, § 1, Oct. 21, 1998, 112 Stat. 2681–759, provided that: "This division [amending sections 841 and 960 of this title and section 13705 of Title 42, The Public Health and Welfare] may be cited as the 'Methamphetamine Trafficking Penalty Enhancement Act of 1998'."

SHORT TITLE OF 1996 AMENDMENTS

Pub. L. 104–305, § 1, Oct. 13, 1996, 110 Stat. 3807, provided that: "This Act [amending sections 841, 844, 959, and 960 of this title and enacting provisions set out as notes under section 872 of this title and section 994 of Title 28, Judiciary and Judicial Procedure] may be cited as the 'Drug-Induced Rape Prevention and Punishment Act of 1996'."

Pub. L. 104–237, § 1(a), Oct. 3, 1996, 110 Stat. 3099, provided that: "This Act [enacting section 872a of this title, amending sections 802, 814, 830, 841 to 844, 853, 881, 959, and 960 of this title and section 1607 of Title 19, Customs Duties, and enacting provisions set out as notes under this section and sections 802, 872, and 971 of this title, section 994 of Title 28, Judiciary and Judicial Procedure, and section 290aa–4 of Title 42, The Public Health and Welfare] may be cited as the 'Comprehensive Methamphetamine Control Act of 1996'."

SHORT TITLE OF 1994 AMENDMENT

Pub. L. 103–322, title XVIII, § 180201(a), Sept. 13, 1994, 108 Stat. 2046, provided that: "This section [enacting section 849 of this title, amending section 841 of this title, and enacting provisions set out as a note under section 994 of Title 28, Judiciary and Judicial Procedure] may be cited as the 'Drug Free Truck Stop Act'."

SHORT TITLE OF 1993 AMENDMENT

Pub. L. 103–200, § 1, Dec. 17, 1993, 107 Stat. 2333, provided that: "This Act [enacting section 814 of this title, amending sections 802, 821 to 824, 830, 843, 880, 957, 958, 960, and 971 of this title, and enacting provisions set out as a note under section 802 of this title] may be cited as the 'Domestic Chemical Diversion Control Act of 1993'."

SHORT TITLE OF 1990 AMENDMENT

Pub. L. 101–647, title XIX, § 1901, Nov. 29, 1990, 104 Stat. 4851, provided that: "This Act [probably means title XIX of Pub. L. 101–647, which amended sections 333, 802, 812, and 844 of this title and section 290aa–6 of Title 42, The Public Health and Welfare, repealed section 333a of this title, and enacted provisions set out as notes under sections 802 and 829 of this title] may be cited as the 'Anabolic Steroids Control Act of 1990'."

SHORT TITLE OF 1988 AMENDMENT

Pub. L. 100–690, title VI, § 6001, Nov. 18, 1988, 102 Stat. 4312, provided that: "This title [see Tables for classification] may be cited as the 'Anti-Drug Abuse Amendments Act of 1988'."

Pub. L. 100–690, title VI, § 6051, Nov. 18, 1988, 102 Stat. 4312, provided that: "This subtitle [subtitle A (§§ 6051–6061) of title VI of Pub. L. 100–690, enacting section 971 of this title, amending sections 802, 830, 841 to 843, 872, 876, 881, 960, and 961 of this title, and enacting provisions set out as notes under sections 802 and 971 of this title] may be cited as the 'Chemical Diversion and Trafficking Act of 1988'."

Pub. L. 100–690, title VI, § 6071, Nov. 18, 1988, 102 Stat. 4320, provided that: "This subtitle [subtitle B (§§ 6071–6080) of title VI of Pub. L. 100–690, enacting sections 881–1, 887, and 1509 of this title, amending section 881 of this title, section 1594 of Title 19, Customs Duties, section 524 of Title 28, Judiciary and Judicial Procedure, and section 782 of former Title 49, Transportation, and enacting provisions set out as notes under section 881 of this title] may be cited as the 'Asset Forfeiture Amendments Act of 1988'."

SHORT TITLE OF 1986 AMENDMENT

Pub. L. 99–570, § 1, Oct. 27, 1986, 100 Stat. 3207, provided that: "This Act [see Tables for classification] may be cited as the 'Anti-Drug Abuse Act of 1986'."

Pub. L. 99–570, title I, § 1001, Oct. 27, 1986, 100 Stat. 3207–2, provided that: "This subtitle [subtitle A (§§ 1001–1009) of title I of Pub. L. 99–570, amending sections 802, 841, 845, 845a, 848, 881, 960, and 962 of this title, sections 3553 and 3583 of Title 18, Crimes and Criminal Procedure, rule 35 of the Federal Rules of Criminal Procedure, Title 18, Appendix, and section 994 of Title 28, Judiciary and Judicial Procedure, and enacting provisions set out as notes under section 841 of this title, sections 3553 and 3583 of Title 18, and rule 35 of the Federal Rules of Criminal Procedure] may be cited as the 'Narcotics Penalties and Enforcement Act of 1986'."

Pub. L. 99–570, title I, § 1051, Oct. 27, 1986, 100 Stat. 3207–8, provided that: "This subtitle [subtitle B (§§ 1051, 1052) of title I of Pub. L. 99–570, amending section 844 of this title] may be cited as the 'Drug Possession Penalty Act of 1986'."

Pub. L. 99–570, title I, § 1101, Oct. 27, 1986, 100 Stat. 3207–10, provided that: "This subtitle [subtitle C (§§ 1101–1105) of title I of Pub. L. 99–570, enacting section 845b of this title and amending sections 841, 845, and 845a of this title] may be cited as the 'Juvenile Drug Trafficking Act of 1986'."

Pub. L. 99–570, title I, §1201, Oct. 27, 1986, 100 Stat. 3207–13, provided that: "This subtitle [subtitle E (§§1201–1204) of title I of Pub. L. 99–570, enacting section 813 of this title and amending section 802 of this title] may be cited as the 'Controlled Substance Analogue Enforcement Act of 1986'."

Pub. L. 99–570, title I, §1251, Oct. 27, 1986, 100 Stat. 3207–14, provided that: "This subtitle [subtitle F (§§1251–1253) of title I of Pub. L. 99–570, amending section 848 of this title] may be cited as the 'Continuing Drug Enterprises Act of 1986'."

Pub. L. 99–570, title I, §1301, Oct. 27, 1986, 100 Stat. 3207–15, provided that: "This subtitle [subtitle G (§§1301, 1302) of title I of Pub. L. 99–570, amending section 960 of this title] may be cited as the 'Controlled Substances Import and Export Penalties Enhancement Act of 1986'."

Pub. L. 99–570, title I, §1821, Oct. 27, 1986, 100 Stat. 3207–51, which provided that subtitle O (§§1821–1823) of title I of Pub. L. 99–570, enacting section 857 of this title and provisions set out as a note under section 857 of this title, was to be cited as the "Mail Order Drug Paraphernalia Control Act", was repealed by Pub. L. 101–647, title XXIV, §2401(d), Nov. 29, 1990, 104 Stat. 4859.

Pub. L. 99–570, title I, §1991, Oct. 27, 1986, 100 Stat. 3207–59, provided that: "This subtitle [subtitle U (§§1991, 1992) of title I of Pub. L. 99–570, amending section 881 of this title] may be cited as the 'Federal Drug Law Enforcement Agent Protection Act of 1986'."

SHORT TITLE OF 1984 AMENDMENT

Pub. L. 98–473, title II, §501, Oct. 12, 1984, 98 Stat. 2068, provided that: "This chapter [chapter V (§§501–525) of title II of Pub. L. 98–473, enacting section 845a of this title, amending sections 802, 811, 812, 822–824, 827, 841, 843, 845, 873, 881, 952, 953, 957, 958, 960, and 962 of this title, and enacting provisions set out as a note under this section] may be cited as the 'Controlled Substances Penalties Amendments Act of 1984'."

Pub. L. 98–473, title II, §506(a), Oct. 12, 1984, 98 Stat. 2070, provided that: "This part [part B of chapter V (§§506–525) of title II of Pub. L. 98–473, amending sections 802, 811, 812, 822–824, 827, 843, 873, 881, 952, 953, 957, and 958 of this title] may be cited as the 'Dangerous Drug Diversion Control Act of 1984'."

SHORT TITLE OF 1978 AMENDMENT

Pub. L. 95–633, §1, Nov. 10, 1978, 92 Stat. 3768, provided: "That this Act [enacting sections 801a, 830, and 852 of this title, amending sections 352, 802, 811, 812, 823, 827, 841 to 843, 872, 881, 952, 953, and 965 of this title and section 242a of Title 42, The Public Health and Welfare, repealing section 830 of this title (effective Jan. 1, 1981), and enacting provisions set out as notes under sections 801a, 812, and 830 of this title] may be cited as the 'Psychotropic Substances Act of 1978'."

SHORT TITLE OF 1974 AMENDMENT

Pub. L. 93–281, §1, May 14, 1974, 88 Stat. 124, provided: "That this Act [amending sections 802, 823, 824, and 827 of this title] may be cited as the 'Narcotic Addict Treatment Act of 1974'."

SHORT TITLE

Pub. L. 91–513, in the provisions preceding section 1 immediately following the enacting clause, provided: "That this Act [enacting this chapter and sections 257a, 2688*l*–1, 2688n–1, and 3509 of Title 42, The Public Health and Welfare, amending sections 162, 198a, 321, 331, 333, 334, 360, 372, and 381 of this title, sections 1114, 1952, and 4251 of Title 18, Crimes and Criminal Procedure, sections 1584, 2078, 2079, and 2080 of Title 19, Customs Duties, sections 4901, 4905, 6808, 7012, 7103, 7326, 7607, 7609, 7641, 7651, and 7655 of Title 26, Internal Revenue Code, section 2901 of Title 28, Judiciary and Judicial Procedure, section 304m of former Title 40, Public Buildings, Property, and Works, sections 201, 225a, 242, 242a, 246, 257, 258, 259, 260, 261, 261a, 2688k, 2688*l*, 2688m, 2688n, 2688*o*, 2688r, and 3411 of Title 42, The Public Health and Welfare, section 239a of former Title 46, Shipping, and section 787 of Title 49, Appendix, Transportation, repealing sections 171 to 174, 176 to 185, 188 to 188n, 191 to 193, 197, 198, 199, 360a, and 501 to 517 of this title, sections 1401 to 1407 and 3616 of Title 18, sections 4701 to 4707, 4711 to 4716, 4721 to 4726, 4731 to 4736, 4741 to 4746, 4751 to 4757, 4761, 4762, 4771 to 4776, 7237, 7238, and 7491 of Title 26, sections 529a and 529g of former Title 31, Money and Finance, and section 1421m of Title 48, Territories and Insular Possessions, and enacting provisions set out as notes under this section and sections 171, 321, 822, 951, and 957 of this title] may be cited as the 'Comprehensive Drug Abuse Prevention and Control Act of 1970'."

Section 100 of title II of Pub. L. 91–513 provided that: "This title [enacting this subchapter, repealing section 360a of this title, amending sections 321, 331, 333, 334, 360, 372, and 381 of this title, sections 1114 and 1952 of Title 18, Crimes and Criminal Procedure, and section 242 of Title 42, The Public Health and Welfare, and enacting provisions set out as notes under this section and sections 321 and 822 of this title] may be cited as the 'Controlled Substances Act'."

For short title and complete classification of title III of Pub. L. 91–513, which enacted subchapter II of this chapter, as the "Controlled Substances Import and Export Act", see section 1000 of Pub. L. 91–513, set out as a note under section 951 of this title.

SEVERABILITY

Pub. L. 106–310, div. B, title XXXVI, §3673, Oct. 17, 2000, 114 Stat. 1246, provided that: "Any provision of this title [see Short Title of 2000 Amendments note above] held to be invalid or unenforceable by its terms, or as applied to any person or circumstance, shall be construed as to give the maximum effect permitted by law, unless such provision is held to be utterly invalid or unenforceable, in which event such provision shall be severed from this title and shall not affect the applicability of the remainder of this title, or of such provision, to other persons not similarly situated or to other, dissimilar circumstances."

CONTINUATION OF ORDERS, RULES, AND REGULATIONS

Section 705 of title II of Pub. L. 91–513 provided that: "Any orders, rules, and regulations which have been promulgated under any law affected by this title [see Short Title note above] and which are in effect on the day preceding enactment of this title [Oct. 27, 1970] shall continue in effect until modified, superseded, or repealed."

ANTI-DRUG MESSAGES ON FEDERAL GOVERNMENT INTERNET SITES

Pub. L. 106–391, title III, §320, Oct. 30, 2000, 114 Stat. 1597, provided that: "Not later than 90 days after the date of the enactment of this Act [Oct. 30, 2000], the Administrator [of the National Aeronautics and Space Administration], in consultation with the Director of the Office of National Drug Control Policy, shall place anti-drug messages on Internet sites controlled by the National Aeronautics and Space Administration."

Pub. L. 106–310, div. B, title XXXVI, §3671, Oct. 17, 2000, 114 Stat. 1245, provided that: "Not later than 90 days after the date of the enactment of this Act [Oct. 17, 2000], the head of each department, agency, and establishment of the Federal Government shall, in consultation with the Director of the Office of National Drug Control Policy, place antidrug messages on appropriate Internet websites controlled by such department, agency, or establishment which messages shall, where appropriate, contain an electronic hyperlink to the Internet website, if any, of the Office."

PROTOCOLS FOR INVESTIGATIONS AND PROSECUTIONS RELATING TO DATE-RAPE DRUGS AND OTHER CONTROLLED SUBSTANCES; ANNUAL REPORT; NATIONAL AWARENESS CAMPAIGN

Pub. L. 106–172, §§6, 7, Feb. 18, 2000, 114 Stat. 11, provided that:

"SEC. 6. DEVELOPMENT OF MODEL PROTOCOLS, TRAINING MATERIALS, FORENSIC FIELD TESTS, AND COORDINATION MECHANISM FOR INVESTIGATIONS AND PROSECUTIONS RELATING TO GAMMA HYDROXYBUTYRIC ACID, OTHER CONTROLLED SUBSTANCES, AND DESIGNER DRUGS.

"(a) IN GENERAL.—The Attorney General, in consultation with the Administrator of the Drug Enforcement Administration and the Director of the Federal Bureau of Investigation, shall—

"(1) develop—

"(A) model protocols for the collection of toxicology specimens and the taking of victim statements in connection with investigations into and prosecutions related to possible violations of the Controlled Substances Act [21 U.S.C. 801 et seq.] or other Federal or State laws that result in or contribute to rape, other crimes of violence, or other crimes involving abuse of gamma hydroxybutyric acid, other controlled substances, or so-called 'designer drugs'; and

"(B) model training materials for law enforcement personnel involved in such investigations; and

"(2) make such protocols and training materials available to Federal, State, and local personnel responsible for such investigations.

"(b) GRANT.—

"(1) IN GENERAL.—The Attorney General shall make a grant, in such amount and to such public or private person or entity as the Attorney General considers appropriate, for the development of forensic field tests to assist law enforcement officials in detecting the presence of gamma hydroxybutyric acid and related substances.

"(2) AUTHORIZATION OF APPROPRIATIONS.—There are authorized to be appropriated such sums as may be necessary to carry out this subsection.

"(c) REPORT.—Not later than 180 days after the date of the enactment of this Act [Feb. 18, 2000], the Attorney General shall submit to the Committees on the Judiciary of the Senate and House of Representatives a report on current mechanisms for coordinating Federal, State, and local investigations into and prosecutions related to possible violations of the Controlled Substances Act [21 U.S.C. 801 et seq.] or other Federal or State laws that result in or contribute to rape, other crimes of violence, or other crimes involving the abuse of gamma hydroxybutyric acid, other controlled substances, or so-called 'designer drugs'. The report shall also include recommendations for the improvement of such mechanisms.

"SEC. 7. ANNUAL REPORT REGARDING DATE-RAPE DRUGS; NATIONAL AWARENESS CAMPAIGN.

"(a) ANNUAL REPORT.—The Secretary of Health and Human Services (in this section referred to as the 'Secretary') shall periodically submit to Congress reports each of which provides an estimate of the number of incidents of the abuse of date-rape drugs (as defined in subsection (c)) that occurred during the most recent 1-year period for which data are available. The first such report shall be submitted not later than January 15, 2000, and subsequent reports shall be submitted annually thereafter.

"(b) NATIONAL AWARENESS CAMPAIGN.—

"(1) DEVELOPMENT OF PLAN; RECOMMENDATIONS OF ADVISORY COMMITTEE.—

"(A) IN GENERAL.—The Secretary, in consultation with the Attorney General, shall develop a plan for carrying out a national campaign to educate individuals described in subparagraph (B) on the following:

"(i) The dangers of date-rape drugs.

"(ii) The applicability of the Controlled Substances Act [21 U.S.C. 801 et seq.] to such drugs, including penalties under such Act.

"(iii) Recognizing the symptoms that indicate an individual may be a victim of such drugs, including symptoms with respect to sexual assault.

"(iv) Appropriately responding when an individual has such symptoms.

"(B) INTENDED POPULATION.—The individuals referred to in subparagraph (A) are young adults, youths, law enforcement personnel, educators, school nurses, counselors of rape victims, and emergency room personnel in hospitals.

"(C) ADVISORY COMMITTEE.—Not later than 180 days after the date of the enactment of this Act [Feb. 18, 2000], the Secretary shall establish an advisory committee to make recommendations to the Secretary regarding the plan under subparagraph (A). The committee shall be composed of individuals who collectively possess expertise on the effects of date-rape drugs and on detecting and controlling the drugs.

"(2) IMPLEMENTATION OF PLAN.—Not later than 180 days after the date on which the advisory committee under paragraph (1) is established, the Secretary, in consultation with the Attorney General, shall commence carrying out the national campaign under such paragraph in accordance with the plan developed under such paragraph. The campaign may be carried out directly by the Secretary and through grants and contracts.

"(3) EVALUATION BY GENERAL ACCOUNTING OFFICE [now Government Accountability Office].—Not later than 2 years after the date on which the national campaign under paragraph (1) is commenced, the Comptroller General of the United States shall submit to Congress an evaluation of the effects with respect to date-rape drugs of the national campaign.

"(c) DEFINITION.—For purposes of this section, the term 'date-rape drugs' means gamma hydroxybutyric acid and its salts, isomers, and salts of isomers and such other drugs or substances as the Secretary, after consultation with the Attorney General, determines to be appropriate."

CONGRESSIONAL FINDINGS REGARDING METHAMPHETAMINE MANUFACTURE AND ABUSE

Pub. L. 104–237, § 2, Oct. 3, 1996, 110 Stat. 3100, provided that: "The Congress finds the following:

"(1) Methamphetamine is a very dangerous and harmful drug. It is highly addictive and is associated with permanent brain damage in long-term users.

"(2) The abuse of methamphetamine has increased dramatically since 1990. This increased use has led to devastating effects on individuals and the community, including—

"(A) a dramatic increase in deaths associated with methamphetamine ingestion;

"(B) an increase in the number of violent crimes associated with methamphetamine ingestion; and

"(C) an increase in criminal activity associated with the illegal importation of methamphetamine and precursor compounds to support the growing appetite for this drug in the United States.

"(3) Illegal methamphetamine manufacture and abuse presents an imminent public health threat that warrants aggressive law enforcement action, increased research on methamphetamine and other substance abuse, increased coordinated efforts to prevent methamphetamine abuse, and increased monitoring of the public health threat methamphetamine presents to the communities of the United States."

SUPPORT FOR INTERNATIONAL EFFORTS TO CONTROL METHAMPHETAMINE AND PRECURSORS

Pub. L. 104–237, title I, § 101, Oct. 3, 1996, 110 Stat. 3100, provided that: "The Attorney General, in consultation with the Secretary of State, shall coordinate international drug enforcement efforts to decrease the movement of methamphetamine and methamphetamine precursors into the United States."

INTERAGENCY METHAMPHETAMINE TASK FORCE

Pub. L. 104–237, title V, § 501, Oct. 3, 1996, 110 Stat. 3111, provided that:

"(a) ESTABLISHMENT.—There is established a 'Methamphetamine Interagency Task Force' (referred to as the 'interagency task force') which shall consist of the following members:

"(1) The Attorney General, or a designee, who shall serve as chair.

"(2) 2 representatives selected by the Attorney General.

"(3) The Secretary of Education or a designee.

"(4) The Secretary of Health and Human Services or a designee.

"(5) 2 representatives of State and local law enforcement and regulatory agencies, to be selected by the Attorney General.

"(6) 2 representatives selected by the Secretary of Health and Human Services.

"(7) 5 nongovernmental experts in drug abuse prevention and treatment to be selected by the Attorney General.

"(b) RESPONSIBILITIES.—The interagency task force shall be responsible for designing, implementing, and evaluating the education and prevention and treatment practices and strategies of the Federal Government with respect to methamphetamine and other synthetic stimulants.

"(c) MEETINGS.—The interagency task force shall meet at least once every 6 months.

"(d) FUNDING.—The administrative expenses of the interagency task force shall be paid out of existing Department of Justice appropriations.

"(e) FACA.—The Federal Advisory Committee Act (5 U.S.C. App. 2) [5 U.S.C. App.] shall apply to the interagency task force.

"(f) TERMINATION.—The interagency task force shall terminate 4 years after the date of enactment of this Act [Oct. 3, 1996]."

SUSPICIOUS ORDERS TASK FORCE

Pub. L. 104–237, title V, §504, Oct. 3, 1996, 110 Stat. 3112, provided that:

"(a) IN GENERAL.—The Attorney General shall establish a 'Suspicious Orders Task Force' (the 'Task Force') which shall consist of—

"(1) appropriate personnel from the Drug Enforcement Administration (the 'DEA') and other Federal, State, and local law enforcement and regulatory agencies with the experience in investigating and prosecuting illegal transactions of listed chemicals and supplies; and

"(2) representatives from the chemical and pharmaceutical industry.

"(b) RESPONSIBILITIES.—The Task Force shall be responsible for developing proposals to define suspicious orders of listed chemicals, and particularly to develop quantifiable parameters which can be used by registrants in determining if an order is a suspicious order which must be reported to DEA. The quantifiable parameters to be addressed will include frequency of orders, deviations from prior orders, and size of orders. The Task Force shall also recommend provisions as to what types of payment practices or unusual business practices shall constitute prima facie suspicious orders. In evaluating the proposals, the Task Force shall consider effectiveness, cost and feasibility for industry and government, and other relevant factors.

"(c) MEETINGS.—The Task Force shall meet at least two times per year and at such other times as may be determined necessary by the Task Force.

"(d) REPORT.—The Task Force shall present a report to the Attorney General on its proposals with regard to suspicious orders and the electronic reporting of suspicious orders within one year of the date of enactment of this Act [Oct. 3, 1996]. Copies of the report shall be forwarded to the Committees of the Senate and House of Representatives having jurisdiction over the regulation of listed chemical and controlled substances.

"(e) FUNDING.—The administrative expenses of the Task Force shall be paid out of existing Department of Justice funds or appropriations.

"(f) FACA.—The Federal Advisory Committee Act (5 U.S.C. App. 2) [5 U.S.C. App.] shall apply to the Task Force.

"(g) TERMINATION.—The Task Force shall terminate upon presentation of its report to the Attorney General, or two years after the date of enactment of this Act [Oct. 3, 1996], whichever is sooner."

JOINT FEDERAL TASK FORCE ON ILLEGAL DRUG LABORATORIES

Pub. L. 100–690, title II, §2405, Nov. 18, 1988, 102 Stat. 4231, provided that:

"(a) ESTABLISHMENT OF TASK FORCE.—There is established the Joint Federal Task Force on Illegal Drug Laboratories (hereafter in this section referred to as the 'Task Force').

"(b) APPOINTMENT AND MEMBERSHIP OF TASK FORCE.—The members of the Task Force shall be appointed by the Administrators of the Environmental Protection Agency and the Drug Enforcement Administration (hereafter in this section referred to as the 'Administrators'). The Task Force shall consist of at least 6 and not more than 20 members. Each Administrator shall appoint one-half of the members as follows: (1) the Administrator of the Environmental Protection Agency shall appoint members from among Emergency Response Technicians and other appropriate employees of the Agency; and (2) the Administrator of the Drug Enforcement Administration shall appoint members from among Special Agents assigned to field divisions and other appropriate employees of the Administration.

"(c) DUTIES OF TASK FORCE.—The Task Force shall formulate, establish, and implement a program for the cleanup and disposal of hazardous waste produced by illegal drug laboratories. In formulating such program, the Task Force shall consider the following factors:

"(1) The volume of hazardous waste produced by illegal drug laboratories.

"(2) The cost of cleaning up and disposing of hazardous waste produced by illegal drug laboratories.

"(3) The effectiveness of the various methods of cleaning up and disposing of hazardous waste produced by illegal drug laboratories.

"(4) The coordination of the efforts of the Environmental Protection Agency and the Drug Enforcement Administration in cleaning up and disposing of hazardous waste produced by illegal drug laboratories.

"(5) The dissemination of information to law enforcement agencies that have responsibility for enforcement of drug laws.

"(d) GUIDELINES.—The Task Force shall recommend to the Administrators guidelines for cleanup of illegal drug laboratories to protect the public health and environment. Not later than 180 days after the date of the enactment of this subtitle [Nov. 18, 1988], the Administrators shall formulate and publish such guidelines.

"(e) DEMONSTRATION PROJECTS.—

"(1) The Attorney General shall make grants to, and enter into contracts with, State and local governments for demonstration projects to clean up and safely dispose of substances associated with illegal drug laboratories which may present a danger to public health or the environment.

"(2) The Attorney General may not under this subsection make a grant or enter into a contract unless the applicant for such assistance agrees to comply with the guidelines issued pursuant to subsection (d).

"(3) The Attorney General shall, through grant or contract, provide for independent evaluations of the activities carried out pursuant to this subsection and shall recommend appropriate legislation to the Congress.

"(f) FUNDING.—Of the amounts made available to carry out the Controlled Substances Act [21 U.S.C. 801 et seq.] for fiscal year 1989, not less than $5,000,000 shall be made available to carry out subsections (d) and (e).

"(g) REPORTS.—After consultation with the Task Force, the Administrators shall—

"(1) transmit to the President and to each House of Congress not later than 270 days after the date of the enactment of this subtitle [Nov. 18, 1988] a report describing the program established by the Task Force under subsection (c) (including an analysis of the factors specified in paragraphs (1) through (5) of that subsection);

"(2) periodically transmit to the President and to each House of Congress reports describing the implementation of the program established by the Task Force under subsection (c) (including an analysis of the factors specified in paragraphs (1) through (5) of that subsection) and the progress made in the cleanup and disposal of hazardous waste produced by illegal drug laboratories; and

"(3) transmit to each House of Congress a report describing the findings made as a result of the evaluations referred to in subsection (e)(3)."

GREAT LAKES DRUG INTERDICTION

Pub. L. 100–690, title VII, §7404, Nov. 18, 1988, 102 Stat. 4484, provided that:

"(a) INTERAGENCY AGREEMENT.—The Secretary of Transportation and the Secretary of the Treasury shall enter into an agreement for the purpose of increasing the effectiveness of maritime drug interdiction activities of the Coast Guard and the Customs Service in the Great Lakes area.

"(b) NEGOTIATIONS WITH CANADA ON DRUG ENFORCEMENT COOPERATION.—The Secretary of State is encouraged to enter into negotiations with appropriate officials of the Government of Canada for the purpose of establishing an agreement between the United States and Canada which provides for increased cooperation and sharing of information between United States and Canadian law enforcement officials with respect to law enforcement efforts conducted on the Great Lakes between the United States and Canada."

[For transfer of authorities, functions, personnel, and assets of the Coast Guard, including the authorities and functions of the Secretary of Transportation relating thereto, to the Department of Homeland Security, and for treatment of related references, see sections 468(b), 551(d), 552(d), and 557 of Title 6, Domestic Security, and the Department of Homeland Security Reorganization Plan of November 25, 2002, as modified, set out as a note under section 542 of Title 6.]

[For transfer of functions, personnel, assets, and liabilities of the United States Customs Service of the Department of the Treasury, including functions of the Secretary of the Treasury relating thereto, to the Secretary of Homeland Security, and for treatment of related references, see sections 203(1), 551(d), 552(d), and 557 of Title 6, Domestic Security, and the Department of Homeland Security Reorganization Plan of November 25, 2002, as modified, set out as a note under section 542 of Title 6.]

GAO STUDY OF CAPABILITIES OF UNITED STATES TO CONTROL DRUG SMUGGLING INTO UNITED STATES

Pub. L. 100–180, div. A, title XII, §1241, Dec. 4, 1987, 101 Stat. 1162, directed Comptroller General of the United States to conduct a comprehensive study regarding smuggling of illegal drugs into United States and current capabilities of United States to deter such smuggling, with special consideration given to issues involving use of military and National Guard units along with Customs Service in cooperative drug smuggling interdiction efforts, and to issue, not later than Apr. 30, 1988, and Mar. 31, 1989, reports to Congress outlining results of this study.

COMPLIANCE WITH BUDGET ACT

Pub. L. 99–570, §3, Oct. 27, 1986, 100 Stat. 3207–1, provided that: "Notwithstanding any other provision of this Act [see Tables for classification], any spending authority and any credit authority provided under this Act shall be effective for any fiscal year only to such extent or in such amounts as are provided in appropriation Acts. For purposes of this Act, the term 'spending authority' has the meaning provided in section 401(c)(2) of the Congressional Budget Act of 1974 [2 U.S.C. 651(c)(2)] and the term 'credit authority' has the meaning provided in section 3(10) of the Congresssional [sic] Budget Act of 1974 [2 U.S.C. 622(10)]."

DRUG INTERDICTION

Pub. L. 99–570, title III, §§3001–3003, 3301, Oct. 27, 1986, 100 Stat. 3207–73, 3207–74, 3207–98, as amended by Pub. L. 104–66, title I, §1091(a), Dec. 21, 1995, 109 Stat. 722, provided that:

"SEC. 3001. SHORT TITLE.

"This title [enacting section 379 of Title 10, Armed Forces, sections 1590, 1628, 1629, and 2081 of Title 19, Customs Duties, and section 312a of Title 47, Telegraphs, Telephones, and Radiotelegraphs, amending section 959 of this title, sections 374 and 911 of Title 10, sections 507, 1401, 1433, 1436, 1454, 1459, 1497, 1509, 1584 to 1586, 1594 to 1595a, 1613, 1613b, 1619, and 1622 of Title 19, section 5316 of Title 31, Money and Finance, section 12109 of Title 46, Shipping, sections 1901 to 1904 of Title 46, Appendix, Shipping, and sections 1401, 1472, 1474, and 1509 of former Title 49, Transportation, repealing section 1460 of Title 19, enacting provisions set out as notes under section 801 of this title, sections 371, 374, 525, and 9441 of Title 10, sections 1613b and 1654 of Title 19, section 403 of Title 23, Highways, section 1901 of Title 46, Appendix, section 11344 of Title 49, and section 1509 of former Title 49, and repealing provisions set out as a note under section 89 of Title 14, Coast Guard] may be cited as the 'National Drug Interdiction Improvement Act of 1986'.

"SEC. 3002. FINDINGS.

"The Congress hereby finds that—

"(1) a balanced, coordinated, multifaceted strategy for combating the growing drug abuse and drug trafficking problem in the United States is essential in order to stop the flow and abuse of drugs within our borders;

"(2) a balanced, coordinated, multifaceted strategy for combating the narcotics drug abuse and trafficking in the United States should include—

"(A) increased investigations of large networks of drug smuggler organizations;

"(B) source country drug eradication;

"(C) increased emphasis on stopping narcotics traffickers in countries through which drugs are transshipped;

"(D) increased emphasis on drug education programs in the schools and workplace;

"(E) increased Federal Government assistance to State and local agencies, civic groups, school systems, and officials in their efforts to combat the drug abuse and trafficking problem at the local level; and

"(F) increased emphasis on the interdiction of drugs and drug smugglers at the borders of the United States, in the air, at sea, and on the land;

"(3) funds to support the interdiction of narcotics smugglers who threaten the transport of drugs through the air, on the sea, and across the land borders of the United States should be emphasized in the Federal Government budget process to the same extent as the other elements of a comprehensive anti-drug effort are emphasized;

"(4) the Department of Defense and the use of its resources should be an integral part of a comprehensive, natonal [national] drug interdiction program;

"(5) the Federal Government civilian agencies engaged in drug interdiction, particularly the United States Customs Service and the Coast Guard, currently lack the aircraft, ships, radar, command, control, communications, and intelligence (C3I) system, and manpower resources necessary to mount a comprehensive attack on the narcotics traffickers who threaten the United States;

"(6) the civilian drug interdiction agencies of the United States are currently interdicting only a small percentage of the illegal, drug smuggler penetrations in the United States every year;

"(7) the budgets for our civilian drug interdiction agencies, primarily the United States Customs Service and the Coast Guard, have not kept pace with those of the traditional investigative law enforcement agencies of the Department of Justice; and

"(8) since the amendment of the Posse Comitatus Act (18 U.S.C. 1385) in 1981, the Department of Defense has assisted in the effort to interdict drugs, but they can do more.

"SEC. 3003. PURPOSES.

"It is the purpose of this title—

"(1) to increase the level of funding and resources available to civilian drug interdiction agencies of the Federal Government;

"(2) to increase the level of support from the Department of Defense as consistent with the Posse Comitatus Act [18 U.S.C. 1385], for interdiction of the narcotics traffickers before such traffickers penetrate the borders of the United States; and

"(3) to improve other drug interdiction programs of the Federal Government.

"SEC. 3301. ESTABLISHMENT OF A UNITED STATES-BAHAMAS DRUG INTERDICTION TASK FORCE

"(a) AUTHORIZATION OF APPROPRIATIONS.—

"(1) ESTABLISHMENT OF A UNITED STATES-BAHAMAS DRUG INTERDICTION TASK FORCE.—(A) There is authorized to be established a United States-Bahamas Drug Interdiction Task Force to be operated jointly by the United States Government and the Government of the Bahamas.

"(B) The Secretary of State, the Commandant of the Coast Guard, the Commissioner of Customs, the Attorney General, and the head of the National Narcotics Border Interdiction System (NNBIS), shall upon enactment of this Act [Oct. 27, 1986], immediately commence negotiations with the Government of the Bahamas to enter into a detailed agreement for the establishment and operation of a new drug interdiction task force, including plans for (i) the joint operation and maintenance of any drug interdiction assets authorized for the task force in this section and section 3141 [see 19 U.S.C. 2075], and (ii) any training and personnel enhancements authorized in this section and section 3141.

"(2) AMOUNTS AUTHORIZED.—There are authorized to be appropriated, in addition to any other amounts authorized to be appropriated in this title [see section 3001 of Pub. L. 99–570 set out above], $10,000,000 for the following:

"(A) $9,000,000 for 3 drug interdiction pursuit helicopters for use primarily for operations of the United States-Bahamas Drug Interdiction Task Force established under this section; and

"(B) $1,000,000 to enhance communications capabilities for the operation of a United States-Bahamas Drug Interdiction Task Force established under this section.

"(3) COAST GUARD-BAHAMAS DRUG INTERDICTION DOCKING FACILITY.—(A) There is authorized to be appropriated for acquisition, construction, and improvements for the Coast Guard for fiscal year 1987, $5,000,000, to be used for initial design engineering, and other activities for construction of a drug interdiction docking facility in the Bahamas to facilitate Coast Guard and Bahamian drug interdiction operations in and through the Bahama Islands. Of the amounts authorized to be appropriated in this subsection, such sums as may be necessary shall be available for necessary communication and air support.

"(B) The Commandant of the Coast Guard shall use such amounts appropriated pursuant to the authorization in this paragraph as may be necessary to establish a repair, maintenance, and boat lift facility to provide repair and maintenance services for both Coast Guard and Bahamian marine drug interdiction equipment, vessels, and related assets.

"(b) CONCURRENCE BY SECRETARY OF STATE.—Programs authorized by this section may be carried out only with the concurrence of the Secretary of State."

INFORMATION ON DRUG ABUSE AT THE WORKPLACE

Pub. L. 99–570, title IV, §4303, Oct. 27, 1986, 100 Stat. 3207–154, directed Secretary of Labor to collect such information as is available on the incidence of drug abuse in the workplace and efforts to assist workers, including counseling, rehabilitation and employee assistance programs, to conduct such additional research as is necessary to assess the impact and extent of drug abuse and remediation efforts, and submit the findings of such collection and research to Congress no later than two years from Oct. 27, 1986.

INTERAGENCY COORDINATION

Pub. L. 99–570, title IV, §4304, Oct. 27, 1986, 100 Stat. 3207–154, provided that:

"(a) The Secretary of Education, the Secretary of Health and Human Services, and the Secretary of Labor shall each designate an officer or employee of the Departments of Education, Health and Human Services, and Labor, respectively, to coordinate interagency drug abuse prevention activities to prevent duplication of effort.

"(b) Within one year after enactment of this Act [Oct. 27, 1986], a report shall be jointly submitted to the Congress by such Secretaries concerning the extent to which States and localities have been able to implement non-duplicative drug abuse prevention activities."

SUBSTANCE ABUSE COVERAGE STUDY

Pub. L. 99–570, title VI, §6005, Oct. 27, 1986, 100 Stat. 3207–160, as amended by Pub. L. 100–690, title II, §2058(c), Nov. 18, 1988, 102 Stat. 4214, directed Secretary of Health and Human Services to contract with Institute of Medicine of National Academy of Sciences to conduct a study of extent to which cost of drug abuse treatment is covered by private insurance, public programs, and other sources of payment, and adequacy of such coverage for the rehabilitation of drug abusers, and not later than 18 months after execution of such contract to transmit to Congress a report of results of study, including recommendations of means to meet the needs identified in such study.

HEALTH INSURANCE COVERAGE FOR DRUG AND ALCOHOL TREATMENT

Pub. L. 99–570, title VI, §6006, Oct. 27, 1986, 100 Stat. 3207–160, provided that:

"(a) FINDINGS.—The Congress finds that—

"(1) drug and alcohol abuse are problems of grave concern and consequence in American society;

"(2) over 500,000 individuals are known heroin addicts; 5 million individuals use cocaine; and at least 7 million individuals regularly use prescription drugs, mostly addictive ones, without medical supervision;

"(3) 10 million adults and 3 million children and adolescents abuse alcohol, and an additional 30 to 40 million people are adversely affected because of close family ties to alcoholics;

"(4) the total cost of drug abuse to the Nation in 1983 was over $60,000,000,000; and

"(5) the vast majority of health benefits plans provide only limited coverage for treatment of drug and alcohol addiction, which is a fact that can discourage the abuser from seeking treatment or, if the abuser does seek treatment, can cause the abuser to face significant out of pocket expenses for the treatment.

"(b) SENSE OF CONGRESS.—It is the sense of Congress that—

"(1) all employers providing health insurance policies should ensure that the policies provide adequate coverage for treatment of drug and alcohol addiction in recognition that the health consequences and costs for individuals and society can be as formidable as those resulting from other diseases and illnesses for which insurance coverage is much more adequate; and

"(2) State insurance commissioners should encourage employers providing health benefits plans to ensure that the policies provide more adequate coverage for treatment of drug and alcohol addiction."

COMMISSION ON MARIHUANA AND DRUG ABUSE

Section 601 of Pub. L. 91–513, as amended by Pub. L. 92–13, May 14, 1971, 85 Stat. 37, provided that:

"(a) [ESTABLISHMENT; COMPOSITION] There is established a commission to be known as the Commission on Marihuana and Drug Abuse (hereafter in this section referred to as the 'Commission'). The Commission shall be composed of—

"(1) two Members of the Senate appointed by the President of the Senate;

"(2) two Members of the House of Representatives appointed by the Speaker of the House of Representatives; and

"(3) nine members appointed by the President of the United States.

At no time shall more than one of the members appointed under paragraph (1), or more than one of the members appointed under paragraph (2), or more than five of the members appointed under paragraph (3) be members of the same political party.

"(b) [CHAIRMAN; VICE CHAIRMAN; COMPENSATION OF MEMBERS; MEETINGS] (1) The President shall designate one of the members of the Commission as Chairman and one as Vice Chairman. Seven members of the Commission shall constitute a quorum, but a lesser number may conduct hearings.

"(2) Members of the Commission who are Members of Congress or full-time officers or employees of the United States shall serve without additional compensation but shall be reimbursed for travel, subsistence, and other necessary expenses incurred in the performance of the duties vested in the Commission. Members of the Commission from private life shall receive $100 per diem while engaged in the actual performance of the duties vested in the Commission, plus reimbursement for travel, subsistence, and other necessary expenses incurred in the performance of such duties.

"(3) The Commission shall meet at the call of the Chairman or at the call of a majority of the members thereof.

"(c) [PERSONNEL; EXPERTS; INFORMATION FROM DEPARTMENTS AND AGENCIES] (1) The Commission shall have the power to appoint and fix the compensation of such personnel as it deems advisable, without regard to the provisions of title 5, United States Code, governing appointments in the competitive service, and the provisions of chapter 51 and subchapter III of chapter 53 of such title, relating to classification and General Schedule pay rates.

"(2) The Commission may procure, in accordance with the provisions of section 3109 of title 5, United States Code, the temporary or intermittent services of experts or consultants. Persons so employed shall receive compensation at a rate to be fixed by the Commission, but not in excess of $75 per diem, including traveltime. While away from his home or regular place of business in the performance of services for the Commission, any such person may be allowed travel expenses, including per diem in lieu of subsistence, as authorized by section 5703(b) of title 5, United States Code, for persons in the Government service employed intermittently.

"(3) The Commission may secure directly from any department or agency of the United States information necessary to enable it to carry out its duties under this section. Upon request of the Chairman of the Commission, such department or agency shall furnish such information to the Commission.

"(d) [MARIHUANA STUDY; REPORT TO THE PRESIDENT AND THE CONGRESS] (1) The Commission shall conduct a study of marihuana including, but not limited to, the following areas:

"(A) the extent of use of marihuana in the United States to include its various sources of users, number of arrests, number of convictions, amount of marihuana seized, type of user, nature of use;

"(B) an evaluation of the efficacy of existing marihuana laws;

"(C) a study of the pharmacology of marihuana and its immediate and long-term effects, both physiological and psychological;

"(D) the relationship of marihuana use to aggressive behavior and crime;

"(E) the relationship between marihuana and the use of other drugs; and

"(F) the international control of marihuana.

"(2) Within one year after the date on which funds first become available to carry out this section, the Commission shall submit to the President and the Congress a comprehensive report on its study and investigation under this subsection which shall include its recommendations and such proposals for legislation and administrative action as may be necessary to carry out its recommendations.

"(e) [STUDY AND INVESTIGATION OF CAUSES OF DRUG ABUSE; REPORT TO THE PRESIDENT AND THE CONGRESS; TERMINATION OF COMMISSION] The Commission shall conduct a comprehensive study and investigation of the causes of drug abuse and their relative significance. The Commission shall submit to the President and the Congress such interim reports as it deems advisable and shall within two years after the date on which funds first become available to carry out this section submit to the President and the Congress a final report which shall contain a detailed statement of its findings and conclusions and also such recommendations for legislation and administrative actions as it deems appropriate. The Commission shall cease to exist sixty days after the final report is submitted under this subsection.

"(f) [LIMITATION ON EXPENDITURES] Total expenditures of the Commission shall not exceed $4,000,000."

EXECUTIVE ORDER NO. 11599

Ex. Ord. No. 11599, June 17, 1971, 36 F.R. 11793, which established the Special Action Office for Drug Abuse Prevention, was superseded. See Prior Provisions notes set out under section 1111 of this title.

EXECUTIVE ORDER NO. 11641

Ex. Ord. No. 11641, Jan. 28, 1972, 37 F.R. 2421, which established the Office for Drug Abuse Law Enforcement, was revoked by Ex. Ord. No. 11727, July 6, 1973, 38 F.R. 18357, set out below.

EXECUTIVE ORDER NO. 11676

Ex. Ord. No. 11676, July 27, 1972, 37 F.R. 15125, which established the Office of National Narcotics Intelligence, was revoked by Ex. Ord. No. 11727, July 6, 1973, 38 F.R. 18357, set out below.

EX. ORD. NO. 11727. DRUG LAW ENFORCEMENT

Ex. Ord. No. 11727, July 6, 1973, 38 F.R. 18357, provided:

Reorganization Plan No. 2 of 1973 [set out in the Appendix to Title 5, Government Organization and Employees], which becomes effective on July 1, 1973, among other things establishes a Drug Enforcement Administration in the Department of Justice. In my message to the Congress transmitting that plan, I stated that all functions of the Office for Drug Abuse Law Enforcement (established pursuant to Executive Order No. 11641 of January 28, 1972) and the Office of National Narcotics Intelligence (established pursuant to Executive Order No. 11676 of July 27, 1972) would, together with other related functions, be merged in the new Drug Enforcement Administration.

NOW, THEREFORE, by virtue of the authority vested in me by the Constitution and laws of the United States, including section 5317 of title 5 of the United States Code, as amended, it is hereby ordered as follows:

SECTION 1. The Attorney General, to the extent permitted by law, is authorized to coordinate all activities of executive branch departments and agencies which are directly related to the enforcement of laws respecting narcotics and dangerous drugs. Each department and agency of the Federal Government shall, upon request and to the extent permitted by law, assist the Attorney General in the performance of functions assigned to him pursuant to this order, and the Attorney General may, in carrying out those functions, utilize the services of any other agencies, Federal and State, as may be available and appropriate.

SEC. 2. Executive Order No. 11641 of January 28, 1972, is revoked and the Attorney General shall provide for the reassignment of the functions of the Office for Drug Abuse Law Enforcement and for the abolishment of that Office.

SEC. 3. Executive Order No. 11676 of July 27, 1972, is hereby revoked and the Attorney General shall provide for the reassignment of the functions of the Office of National Narcotics Intelligence and for the abolishment of that Office.

SEC. 4. Section 1 of Executive Order No. 11708 of March 23, 1973, as amended [set out as a note under section 5317 of Title 5, Government Organization and Employees], placing certain positions in level IV of the Executive Schedule is hereby further amended by deleting—

(1) "(6) Director, Office for Drug Abuse Law Enforcement, Department of Justice."; and

(2) "(7) Director, Office of National Narcotics Intelligence, Department of Justice."

SEC. 5. The Attorney General shall provide for the winding up of the affairs of the two offices and for the reassignment of their functions.

SEC. 6. This order shall be effective as of July 1, 1973.

RICHARD NIXON.

§801a. Congressional findings and declarations: psychotropic substances

The Congress makes the following findings and declarations:

(1) The Congress has long recognized the danger involved in the manufacture, distribution, and use of certain psychotropic substances for nonscientific and nonmedical purposes, and has provided strong and effective legislation to control illicit trafficking and to regulate legitimate uses of psychotropic substances in this country. Abuse of psychotropic substances has become a phenomenon common to many countries, however, and is not confined to national borders. It is, therefore, essential that the United States cooperate with other nations in establishing effective controls over international traffic in such substances.

(2) The United States has joined with other countries in executing an international treaty, entitled the Convention on Psychotropic Substances and signed at Vienna, Austria, on February 21, 1971, which is designed to establish suitable controls over the manufacture, distribution, transfer, and use of certain psychotropic substances. The Convention is not self-executing, and the obligations of the United States thereunder may only be performed pursuant to appropriate legislation. It is the intent of the Congress that the amendments made by this Act, together with existing law, will enable the United States to meet all of its obligations under the Convention and that no further legislation will be necessary for that purpose.

(3) In implementing the Convention on Psychotropic Substances, the Congress intends that, consistent with the obligations of the United States under the Convention, control of psychotropic substances in the United States should be accomplished within the framework of the procedures and criteria for classification of substances provided in the Comprehensive Drug Abuse Prevention and Control Act of 1970 [21 U.S.C. 801 et seq.]. This will insure that (A) the availability of psychotropic substances to manufacturers, distributors, dispensers, and researchers for useful and legitimate medical and scientific purposes will not be unduly restricted; (B) nothing in the Convention will interfere with bona fide research activities; and (C) nothing in the Convention will interfere with ethical medical practice in this country as determined by the Secretary of Health and Human Services on the basis of a consensus of the views of the American medical and scientific community.

(Pub. L. 95–633, title I, §101, Nov. 10, 1978, 92 Stat. 3768; Pub. L. 96–88, title V, §509(b), Oct. 17, 1979, 93 Stat. 695.)

REFERENCES IN TEXT

This Act, referred to in par. (2), is Pub. L. 95–633, Nov. 10, 1978, 92 Stat. 2768, as amended, known as the Psychotropic Substances Act of 1978, which enacted sections 801a, 830, and 852 of this title, amended sections 352, 802, 811, 812, 823, 827, 841 to 843, 872, 881, 952, 953, and 965 of this title and section 242a of Title 42, The Public Health and Welfare, repealed section 830 of this title effective Jan. 1, 1981, and enacted provisions set out as notes under sections 801, 801a, 812, and 830 of this title. For complete classification of this Act to the Code, see Short Title of 1978 Amendment note set out under section 801 of this title and Tables.

The Comprehensive Drug Abuse Prevention and Control Act of 1970, referred to in par. (3), is Pub. L. 91–513, Oct. 27, 1970, 84 Stat. 1236, as amended, which is classified principally to this chapter [§801 et seq.]. For complete classification of this Act to the Code, see Short Title note set out under section 801 of this title and Tables.

CODIFICATION

Section was enacted as a part of the Psychotropic Substances Act of 1978, and not as a part of the Controlled Substances Act which comprises this subchapter.

CHANGE OF NAME

"Secretary of Health and Human Services" substituted for "Secretary of Health, Education, and Welfare" in par. (3) pursuant to section 509(b) of Pub. L. 96–88, which is classified to section 3508(b) of Title 20, Education.

EFFECTIVE DATE

Section 112 of title I of Pub. L. 95–633 provided that: "This title [enacting this section and section 852 of this title, amending sections 352, 802, 811, 812, 823, 827, 872, 952, and 953 of this title and section 242a of Title 42, The Public Health and Welfare, and enacting provisions set out as notes under sections 801 and 812 of this title] and the amendments made by this title shall take effect on the date the Convention on Psychotropic Substances, signed at Vienna, Austria on February 21, 1971, enters into force in respect to the United States." [The Convention entered into force in respect to the United States on July 15, 1980.]

§802. Definitions

As used in this subchapter:

(1) The term "addict" means any individual who habitually uses any narcotic drug so as to endanger the public morals, health, safety, or welfare, or who is so far addicted to the use of narcotic drugs as to have lost the power of self-control with reference to his addiction.

(2) The term "administer" refers to the direct application of a controlled substance to the body of a patient or research subject by—

(A) a practitioner (or, in his presence, by his authorized agent), or

(B) the patient or research subject at the direction and in the presence of the practitioner,

whether such application be by injection, inhalation, ingestion, or any other means.

(3) The term "agent" means an authorized person who acts on behalf of or at the direction of a manufacturer, distributor, or dispenser; except that such term does not include a common or contract carrier, public warehouseman, or employee of the carrier or warehouseman, when acting in the usual and lawful course of the carrier's or warehouseman's business.

(4) The term "Drug Enforcement Administration" means the Drug Enforcement Administration in the Department of Justice.

(5) The term "control" means to add a drug or other substance, or immediate precursor, to a schedule under part B of this subchapter, whether by transfer from another schedule or otherwise.

(6) The term "controlled substance" means a drug or other substance, or immediate precursor, included in schedule I, II, III, IV, or V of part B of this subchapter. The term does not include distilled spirits, wine, malt beverages, or tobacco, as those terms are defined or used in subtitle E of the Internal Revenue Code of 1986.

(7) The term "counterfeit substance" means a controlled substance which, or the container or labeling of which, without authorization, bears the trademark, trade name, or other identifying mark, imprint, number, or device, or any likeness thereof, of a manufacturer, distributor, or dispenser other than the person or persons who in fact manufactured, distributed, or dispensed such substance and which thereby falsely purports or is represented to be the product of, or to have been distributed by, such other manufacturer, distributor, or dispenser.

(8) The terms "deliver" or "delivery" mean the actual, constructive, or attempted transfer of a controlled substance or a listed chemical, whether or not there exists an agency relationship.

(9) The term "depressant or stimulant substance" means—

(A) a drug which contains any quantity of barbituric acid or any of the salts of barbituric acid; or

(B) a drug which contains any quantity of (i) amphetamine or any of its optical isomers; (ii) any salt of amphetamine or any salt of an optical isomer of amphetamine; or (iii) any substance which the Attorney General, after investigation, has found to be, and by regulation designated as, habit forming because of its stimulant effect on the central nervous system; or

(C) lysergic acid diethylamide; or

(D) any drug which contains any quantity of a substance which the Attorney General, after investigation, has found to have, and by regulation designated as having, a potential for abuse because of its depressant or stimulant effect on the central nervous system or its hallucinogenic effect.

(10) The term "dispense" means to deliver a controlled substance to an ultimate user or research subject by, or pursuant to the lawful order of, a practitioner, including the prescribing and administering of a controlled substance and the packaging, labeling or compounding necessary to prepare the substance for such delivery. The term "dispenser" means a practitioner who so delivers a controlled substance to an ultimate user or research subject.

(11) The term "distribute" means to deliver (other than by administering or dispensing) a controlled substance or a listed chemical. The term "distributor" means a person who so delivers a controlled substance or a listed chemical.

(12) The term "drug" has the meaning given that term by section 321(g)(1) of this title.

(13) The term "felony" means any Federal or State offense classified by applicable Federal or State law as a felony.

(14) The term "isomer" means the optical isomer, except as used in schedule I(c) and schedule II(a)(4). As used in schedule I(c), the term "isomer" means any optical, positional, or geometric isomer. As used in schedule II(a)(4), the term "isomer" means any optical or geometric isomer.

(15) The term "manufacture" means the production, preparation, propagation, compounding, or processing of a drug or other substance, either directly or indirectly or by extraction from substances of natural origin, or independently by means of chemical synthesis or by a combination of extraction and chemical synthesis, and includes any packaging or repackaging of such substance or labeling or relabeling of its container; except that such term does not include the preparation, compounding, packaging, or labeling of a drug or other substance in conformity with applicable State or local law by a practitioner as an incident to his administration or dispensing of such drug or substance in the course of his professional practice. The term "manufacturer" means a person who manufactures a drug or other substance.

(16) The term "marihuana" means all parts of the plant Cannabis sativa L., whether growing or not; the seeds thereof; the resin extracted from any part of such plant; and every compound, manufacture, salt, derivative, mixture, or preparation of such plant, its seeds or resin. Such term does not include the mature stalks of such plant, fiber produced from such stalks, oil or cake made from the seeds of such plant, any other compound, manufacture, salt, derivative, mixture, or preparation of such mature stalks (except the resin extracted therefrom), fiber, oil, or cake, or the sterilized seed of such plant which is incapable of germination.

(17) The term "narcotic drug" means any of the following whether produced directly or indirectly by extraction from substances of vegetable origin, or independently by means of chemical synthesis, or by a combination of extraction and chemical synthesis:

(A) Opium, opiates, derivatives of opium and opiates, including their isomers, esters, ethers, salts, and salts of isomers, esters, and ethers, whenever the existence of such isomers, esters, ethers, and salts is possible within the specific chemical designation. Such term does not include the isoquinoline alkaloids of opium.

(B) Poppy straw and concentrate of poppy straw.

(C) Coca leaves, except coca leaves and extracts of coca leaves from which cocaine, ecgonine, and derivatives of ecgonine or their salts have been removed.

(D) Cocaine, its salts, optical and geometric isomers, and salts of isomers.

(E) Ecgonine, its derivatives, their salts, isomers, and salts of isomers.

(F) Any compound, mixture, or preparation which contains any quantity of any of the substances referred to in subparagraphs (A) through (E).

(18) The term "opiate" means any drug or other substance having an addiction-forming or addiction-sustaining liability similar to morphine or being capable of conversion into a drug having such addiction-forming or addiction-sustaining liability.

(19) The term "opium poppy" means the plant of the species Papaver somniferum L., except the seed thereof.

(20) The term "poppy straw" means all parts, except the seeds, of the opium poppy, after mowing.

(21) The term "practitioner" means a physician, dentist, veterinarian, scientific investigator, pharmacy, hospital, or other person licensed, registered, or otherwise permitted, by the United States or the jurisdiction in which he practices or does research, to distribute, dispense, conduct research with respect to, administer, or use in teaching or chemical analysis, a controlled substance in the course of professional practice or research.

(22) The term "production" includes the manufacture, planting, cultivation, growing, or harvesting of a controlled substance.

(23) The term "immediate precursor" means a substance—

(A) which the Attorney General has found to be and by regulation designated as being the principal compound used, or produced primarily for use, in the manufacture of a controlled substance;

(B) which is an immediate chemical intermediary used or likely to be used in the manufacture of such controlled substance; and

(C) the control of which is necessary to prevent, curtail, or limit the manufacture of such controlled substance.

(24) The term "Secretary", unless the context otherwise indicates, means the Secretary of Health and Human Services.

(25) The term "serious bodily injury" means bodily injury which involves—

(A) a substantial risk of death;

(B) protracted and obvious disfigurement; or

(C) protracted loss or impairment of the function of a bodily member, organ, or mental faculty.

(26) The term "State" means a State of the United States, the District of Columbia, and any commonwealth, territory, or possession of the United States.

(27) The term "ultimate user" means a person who has lawfully obtained, and who possesses, a controlled substance for his own use or for the use of a member of his household or for an animal owned by him or by a member of his household.

(28) The term "United States", when used in a geographic sense, means all places and waters, continental or insular, subject to the jurisdiction of the United States.

(29) The term "maintenance treatment" means the dispensing, for a period in excess of twenty-one days, of a narcotic drug in the treatment of an individual for dependence upon heroin or other morphine-like drugs.

(30) The term "detoxification treatment" means the dispensing, for a period not in excess of one hundred and eighty days, of a narcotic drug in decreasing doses to an individual in order to alleviate adverse physiological or psychological effects incident to withdrawal from the continuous or sustained use of a narcotic drug and as a method of bringing the individual to a narcotic drug-free state within such period.

(31) The term "Convention on Psychotropic Substances" means the Convention on Psychotropic Substances signed at Vienna, Austria, on February 21, 1971; and the term "Single Convention on Narcotic Drugs" means the Single Convention on Narcotic Drugs signed at New York, New York, on March 30, 1961.

(32)(A) Except as provided in subparagraph (C), the term "controlled substance analogue" means a substance—

(i) the chemical structure of which is substantially similar to the chemical structure of a controlled substance in schedule I or II;

(ii) which has a stimulant, depressant, or hallucinogenic effect on the central nervous system that is substantially similar to or greater than the stimulant, depressant, or hallucinogenic effect on the central nervous system of a controlled substance in schedule I or II; or

(iii) with respect to a particular person, which such person represents or intends to have a stimulant, depressant, or hallucinogenic effect on the central nervous system that is substantially similar to or greater than the stimulant, depressant, or hallucinogenic effect on the central nervous system of a controlled substance in schedule I or II.

(B) The designation of gamma butyrolactone or any other chemical as a listed chemical pursuant to paragraph (34) or (35) does not preclude a finding pursuant to subparagraph (A) of this paragraph that the chemical is a controlled substance analogue.

(C) Such term does not include—

(i) a controlled substance;

(ii) any substance for which there is an approved new drug application;

(iii) with respect to a particular person any substance, if an exemption is in effect for investigational use, for that person, under section 355 of this title to the extent conduct with respect to such substance is pursuant to such exemption; or

(iv) any substance to the extent not intended for human consumption before such an exemption takes effect with respect to that substance.

(33) The term "listed chemical" means any list I chemical or any list II chemical.

(34) The term "list I chemical" means a chemical specified by regulation of the Attorney Gen-

eral as a chemical that is used in manufacturing a controlled substance in violation of this subchapter and is important to the manufacture of the controlled substances, and such term includes (until otherwise specified by regulation of the Attorney General, as considered appropriate by the Attorney General or upon petition to the Attorney General by any person) the following:

(A) Anthranilic acid, its esters, and its salts.

(B) Benzyl cyanide.

(C) Ephedrine, its salts, optical isomers, and salts of optical isomers.

(D) Ergonovine and its salts.

(E) Ergotamine and its salts.

(F) N-Acetylanthranilic acid, its esters, and its salts.

(G) Norpseudoephedrine, its salts, optical isomers, and salts of optical isomers.

(H) Phenylacetic acid, its esters, and its salts.

(I) Phenylpropanolamine, its salts, optical isomers, and salts of optical isomers.

(J) Piperidine and its salts.

(K) Pseudoephedrine, its salts, optical isomers, and salts of optical isomers.

(L) 3,4-Methylenedioxyphenyl-2-propanone.

(M) Methylamine.

(N) Ethylamine.

(O) Propionic anhydride.

(P) Isosafrole.

(Q) Safrole.

(R) Piperonal.

(S) N-Methylephedrine.

(T) N-methylpseudoephedrine.

(U) Hydriodic acid.

(V) Benzaldehyde.

(W) Nitroethane.

(X) Gamma butyrolactone.

(Y) Any salt, optical isomer, or salt of an optical isomer of the chemicals listed in subparagraphs (M) through (U) of this paragraph.

(35) The term "list II chemical" means a chemical (other than a list I chemical) specified by regulation of the Attorney General as a chemical that is used in manufacturing a controlled substance in violation of this subchapter, and such term includes (until otherwise specified by regulation of the Attorney General, as considered appropriate by the Attorney General or upon petition to the Attorney General by any person) the following chemicals:

(A) Acetic anhydride.

(B) Acetone.

(C) Benzyl chloride.

(D) Ethyl ether.

(E) Repealed. Pub. L. 101–647, title XXIII, §2301(b), Nov. 29, 1990, 104 Stat. 4858.

(F) Potassium permanganate.

(G) 2-Butanone (or Methyl Ethyl Ketone).

(H) Toluene.

(I) Iodine.

(J) Hydrochloric gas.

(36) The term "regular customer" means, with respect to a regulated person, a customer with whom the regulated person has an established business relationship that is reported to the Attorney General.

(37) The term "regular importer" means, with respect to a listed chemical, a person that has an established record as an importer of that listed chemical that is reported to the Attorney General.

(38) The term "regulated person" means a person who manufactures, distributes, imports, or exports a listed chemical, a tableting machine, or an encapsulating machine or who acts as a broker or trader for an international transaction involving a listed chemical, a tableting machine, or an encapsulating machine.

(39) The term "regulated transaction" means—

(A) a distribution, receipt, sale, importation, or exportation of, or an international transaction involving shipment of, a listed chemical, or if the Attorney General establishes a threshold amount for a specific listed chemical, a threshold amount, including a cumulative threshold amount for multiple transactions (as determined by the Attorney General, in consultation with the chemical industry and taking into consideration the quantities normally used for lawful purposes), of a listed chemical, except that such term does not include—

(i) a domestic lawful distribution in the usual course of business between agents or employees of a single regulated person;

(ii) a delivery of a listed chemical to or by a common or contract carrier for carriage in the lawful and usual course of the business of the common or contract carrier, or to or by a warehouseman for storage in the lawful and usual course of the business of the warehouseman, except that if the carriage or storage is in connection with the distribution, importation, or exportation of a listed chemical to a third person, this clause does not relieve a distributor, importer, or exporter from compliance with section 830 of this title;

(iii) any category of transaction or any category of transaction for a specific listed chemical or chemicals specified by regulation of the Attorney General as excluded from this definition as unnecessary for enforcement of this subchapter or subchapter II of this chapter;

(iv) any transaction in a listed chemical that is contained in a drug that may be marketed or distributed lawfully in the United States under the Federal Food, Drug, and Cosmetic Act [21 U.S.C. 301 et seq.], subject to clause (v), unless—

(I) the Attorney General has determined under section 814 of this title that the drug or group of drugs is being diverted to obtain the listed chemical for use in the illicit production of a controlled substance; and

(II) the quantity of the listed chemical contained in the drug included in the transaction or multiple transactions equals or exceeds the threshold established for that chemical by the Attorney General;

(v) any transaction in a scheduled listed chemical product that is a sale at retail by a regulated seller or a distributor required to submit reports under section 830(b)(3) of this title; or

(vi) any transaction in a chemical mixture which the Attorney General has by regulation designated as exempt from the application of this subchapter and subchapter II of this chapter based on a finding that the mixture is formulated in such a way that it cannot be easily used in the illicit production of a controlled substance and that the listed chemical or chemicals contained in the mixture cannot be readily recovered; and

(B) a distribution, importation, or exportation of a tableting machine or encapsulating machine.

(40) The term "chemical mixture" means a combination of two or more chemical substances, at least one of which is not a list I chemical or a list II chemical, except that such term does not include any combination of a list I chemical or a list II chemical with another chemical that is present solely as an impurity.

(41)(A) The term "anabolic steroid" means any drug or hormonal substance, chemically and pharmacologically related to testosterone (other than estrogens, progestins, corticosteroids, and dehydroepiandrosterone), and includes—

(i) androstanediol—

(I) 3β,17β-dihydroxy-5α-androstane; and

(II) 3α,17β-dihydroxy-5α-androstane;

(ii) androstanedione (5α-androstan-3,17-dione);

(iii) androstenediol—

(I) 1-androstenediol (3β,17β-dihydroxy-5α-androst-1-ene);

(II) 1-androstenediol (3α,17β-dihydroxy-5α-androst-1-ene);

(III) 4-androstenediol (3β,17β-dihydroxy-androst-4-ene); and

(IV) 5-androstenediol (3β,17β-dihydroxy-androst-5-ene);

(iv) androstenedione—

(I) 1-androstenedione ([5α]-androst-1-en-3,17-dione);

(II) 4-androstenedione (androst-4-en-3,17-dione); and

(III) 5-androstenedione (androst-5-en-3,17-dione);

(v) bolasterone (7α,17α-dimethyl-17β-hydroxyandrost-4-en-3-one);

(vi) boldenone (17β-hydroxyandrost-1,4,-diene-3-one);

(vii) calusterone (7β,17α-dimethyl-17β-hydroxyandrost-4-en-3-one);

(viii) clostebol (4-chloro-17β-hydroxyandrost-4-en-3-one);

(ix) dehydrochloromethyltestosterone (4-chloro-17β-hydroxy-17α-methyl-androst-1,4-dien-3-one);

(x) Δ 1-dihydrotestosterone (a.k.a. "1-testosterone") (17β-hydroxy-5α-androst-1-en-3-one);

(xi) 4-dihydrotestosterone (17β-hydroxy-androstan-3-one);

(xii) drostanolone (17β-hydroxy-2α-methyl-5α-androstan-3-one);

(xiii) ethylestrenol (17α-ethyl-17β-hydroxyestr-4-ene);

(xiv) fluoxymesterone (9-fluoro-17α-methyl-11β,17β-dihydroxyandrost-4-en-3-one);

(xv) formebolone (2-formyl-17α-methyl-11α,17β-dihydroxyandrost-1,4-dien-3-one);

(xvi) furazabol (17α-methyl-17β-hydroxyandrostano[2,3-c]-furazan);

(xvii) 13β-ethyl-17β-hydroxygon-4-en-3-one;

(xviii) 4-hydroxytestosterone (4,17β-dihydroxy-androst-4-en-3-one);

(xix) 4-hydroxy-19-nortestosterone (4,17β-dihydroxy-estr-4-en-3-one);

(xx) mestanolone (17α-methyl-17β-hydroxy-5α-androstan-3-one);

(xxi) mesterolone (1α-methyl-17β-hydroxy-[5α]-androstan-3-one);

(xxii) methandienone (17α-methyl-17β-hydroxyandrost-1,4-dien-3-one);

(xxiii) methandriol (17α-methyl-3β,17β-dihydroxyandrost-5-ene);

(xxiv) methenolone (1-methyl-17β-hydroxy-5α-androst-1-en-3-one);

(xxv) 17α-methyl-3β, 17β-dihydroxy-5α-androstane;

(xxvi) 17α-methyl-3α,17β-dihydroxy-5α-androstane;

(xxvii) 17α-methyl-3β,17β-dihydroxyandrost-4-ene.

(xxviii) 17α-methyl-4-hydroxynandrolone (17α-methyl-4-hydroxy-17β-hydroxyestr-4-en-3-one);

(xxix) methyldienolone (17α-methyl-17β-hydroxyestra-4,9(10)-dien-3-one);

(xxx) methyltrienolone (17α-methyl-17β-hydroxyestra-4,9-11-trien-3-one);

(xxxi) methyltestosterone (17α-methyl-17β-hydroxyandrost-4-en-3-one);

(xxxii) mibolerone (7α,17α-dimethyl-17β-hydroxyestr-4-en-3-one);

(xxxiii) 17α-methyl-Δ 1-dihydrotestosterone (17β-hydroxy-17α-methyl-5α-androst-1-en-3-one) (a.k.a. "17-α-methyl-1-testosterone");

(xxxiv) nandrolone (17β-hydroxyestr-4-en-3-one);

(xxxv) norandrostenediol—

(I) 19-nor-4-androstenediol (3β, 17β-dihydroxyestr-4-ene);

(II) 19-nor-4-androstenediol (3α, 17β-dihydroxyestr-4-ene);

(III) 19-nor-5-androstenediol (3β, 17β-dihydroxyestr-5-ene); and

(IV) 19-nor-5-androstenediol (3α, 17β-dihydroxyestr-5-ene);

(xxxvi) norandrostenedione—

(I) 19-nor-4-androstenedione (estr-4-en-3,17-dione); and

(II) 19-nor-5-androstenedione (estr-5-en-3,17-dione;

(xxxvii) norbolethone (13β,17α-diethyl-17β-hydroxygon-4-en-3-one);

(xxxviii) norclostebol (4-chloro-17β-hydroxyestr-4-en-3-one);

(xxxix) norethandrolone (17α-ethyl-17β-hydroxyestr-4-en-3-one);

(xl) normethandrolone (17α-methyl-17β-hydroxyestr-4-en-3-one);

(xli) oxandrolone (17α-methyl-17β-hydroxy-2-oxa-[5α]-androstan-3-one);

(xlii) oxymesterone (17α-methyl-4,17β-dihydroxyandrost-4-en-3-one);

(xliii) oxymetholone (17α-methyl-2-hydroxymethylene-17β-hydroxy-[5α]-androstan-3-one);

(xliv) stanozolol (17α-methyl-17β-hydroxy-[5α]-androst-2-eno[3,2-c]-pyrazole);

(xlv) stenbolone (17β-hydroxy-2-methyl-[5α]-androst-1-en-3-one);

(xlvi) testolactone (13-hydroxy-3-oxo-13,17-secoandrosta-1,4-dien-17-oic acid lactone);

(xlvii) testosterone (17β-hydroxyandrost-4-en-3-one);

(xlviii) tetrahydrogestrinone (13β,17α-diethyl-17β-hydroxygon-4,9,11-trien-3-one);

(xlix) trenbolone (17β-hydroxyestr-4,9,11-trien-3-one); and

(xlx)[1] any salt, ester, or ether of a drug or substance described in this paragraph.

The substances excluded under this subparagraph may at any time be scheduled by the Attorney General in accordance with the authority and requirements of subsections (a) through (c) of section 811 of this title.

(B)(i) Except as provided in clause (ii), such term does not include an anabolic steroid which is expressly intended for administration through implants to cattle or other nonhuman species and which has been approved by the Secretary of Health and Human Services for such administration.

(ii) If any person prescribes, dispenses, or distributes such steroid for human use, such person shall be considered to have prescribed, dispensed, or distributed an anabolic steroid within the meaning of subparagraph (A).

(42) The term "international transaction" means a transaction involving the shipment of a listed chemical across an international border (other than a United States border) in which a broker or trader located in the United States participates.

(43) The terms "broker" and "trader" mean a person that assists in arranging an international transaction in a listed chemical by—

(A) negotiating contracts;

(B) serving as an agent or intermediary; or

(C) bringing together a buyer and seller, a buyer and transporter, or a seller and transporter.

(44) The term "felony drug offense" means an offense that is punishable by imprisonment for more than one year under any law of the United States or of a State or foreign country that prohibits or restricts conduct relating to narcotic drugs, marihuana, anabolic steroids, or depressant or stimulant substances.

(45)(A) The term "scheduled listed chemical product" means, subject to subparagraph (B), a product that—

(i) contains ephedrine, pseudoephedrine, or phenylpropanolamine; and

(ii) may be marketed or distributed lawfully in the United States under the Federal, Food, Drug, and Cosmetic Act [21 U.S.C. 301 et seq.] as a nonprescription drug.

Each reference in clause (i) to ephedrine, pseudoephedrine, or phenylpropanolamine includes each of the salts, optical isomers, and salts of optical isomers of such chemical.

(B) Such term does not include a product described in subparagraph (A) if the product contains a chemical specified in such subparagraph that the Attorney General has under section 811(a) of this title added to any of the schedules under section 812(c) of this title. In the absence of such scheduling by the Attorney General, a chemical specified in such subparagraph may not be considered to be a controlled substance.

(46) The term "regulated seller" means a retail distributor (including a pharmacy or a mobile retail vendor), except that such term does not include an employee or agent of such distributor.

(47) The term "mobile retail vendor" means a person or entity that makes sales at retail from a stand that is intended to be temporary, or is capable of being moved from one location to another, whether the stand is located within or on the premises of a fixed facility (such as a kiosk at a shopping center or an airport) or whether the stand is located on unimproved real estate (such as a lot or field leased for retail purposes).

(48) The term "at retail", with respect to the sale or purchase of a scheduled listed chemical product, means a sale or purchase for personal use, respectively.

(49)(A) The term "retail distributor" means a grocery store, general merchandise store, drug store, or other entity or person whose activities as a distributor relating to ephedrine, pseudoephedrine, or phenylpropanolamine products are limited almost exclusively to sales for personal use, both in number of sales and volume of sales, either directly to walk-in customers or in face-to-face transactions by direct sales.

(B) For purposes of this paragraph, entities are defined by reference to the Standard Industrial Classification (SIC) code, as follows:

(i) A grocery store is an entity within SIC code 5411.

(ii) A general merchandise store is an entity within SIC codes 5300 through 5399 and 5499.

(iii) A drug store is an entity within SIC code 5912.

(50) The term "Internet" means collectively the myriad of computer and telecommunications facilities, including equipment and operating software, which comprise the interconnected worldwide network of networks that employ the Transmission Control Protocol/Internet Protocol, or any predecessor or successor protocol to such protocol, to communicate information of all kinds by wire or radio.

(51) The term "deliver, distribute, or dispense by means of the Internet" refers, respectively, to any delivery, distribution, or dispensing of a controlled substance that is caused or facilitated by means of the Internet.

(52) The term "online pharmacy"—

(A) means a person, entity, or Internet site, whether in the United States or abroad, that knowingly or intentionally delivers, distributes, or dispenses, or offers or attempts to deliver, distribute, or dispense, a controlled substance by means of the Internet; and

(B) does not include—

(i) manufacturers or distributors registered under subsection (a), (b), (d), or (e) of section 823 of this title who do not dispense controlled substances to an unregistered individual or entity;

(ii) nonpharmacy practitioners who are registered under section 823(f) of this title and whose activities are authorized by that registration;

(iii) any hospital or other medical facility that is operated by an agency of the United

[1] So in original. Probably should be "(l)".

States (including the Armed Forces), provided such hospital or other facility is registered under section 823(f) of this title;

(iv) a health care facility owned or operated by an Indian tribe or tribal organization, only to the extent such facility is carrying out a contract or compact under the Indian Self-Determination and Education Assistance Act [25 U.S.C. 450 et seq.];

(v) any agent or employee of any hospital or facility referred to in clause (iii) or (iv), provided such agent or employee is lawfully acting in the usual course of business or employment, and within the scope of the official duties of such agent or employee, with such hospital or facility, and, with respect to agents or employees of health care facilities specified in clause (iv), only to the extent such individuals are furnishing services pursuant to the contracts or compacts described in such clause;

(vi) mere advertisements that do not attempt to facilitate an actual transaction involving a controlled substance;

(vii) a person, entity, or Internet site that is not in the United States and does not facilitate the delivery, distribution, or dispensing of a controlled substance by means of the Internet to any person in the United States;

(viii) a pharmacy registered under section 823(f) of this title whose dispensing of controlled substances via the Internet consists solely of—

(I) refilling prescriptions for controlled substances in schedule III, IV, or V, as defined in paragraph (55); or

(II) filling new prescriptions for controlled substances in schedule III, IV, or V, as defined in paragraph (56); or

(ix) any other persons for whom the Attorney General and the Secretary have jointly, by regulation, found it to be consistent with effective controls against diversion and otherwise consistent with the public health and safety to exempt from the definition of an "online pharmacy".

(53) The term "homepage" means the opening or main page or screen of the website of an online pharmacy that is viewable on the Internet.

(54) The term "practice of telemedicine" means, for purposes of this subchapter, the practice of medicine in accordance with applicable Federal and State laws by a practitioner (other than a pharmacist) who is at a location remote from the patient and is communicating with the patient, or health care professional who is treating the patient, using a telecommunications system referred to in section 1395m(m) of title 42, which practice—

(A) is being conducted—

(i) while the patient is being treated by, and physically located in, a hospital or clinic registered under section 823(f) of this title; and

(ii) by a practitioner—

(I) acting in the usual course of professional practice;

(II) acting in accordance with applicable State law; and

(III) registered under section 823(f) of this title in the State in which the patient is located, unless the practitioner—

(aa) is exempted from such registration in all States under section 822(d) of this title; or

(bb) is—

(AA) an employee or contractor of the Department of Veterans Affairs who is acting in the scope of such employment or contract; and

(BB) registered under section 823(f) of this title in any State or is utilizing the registration of a hospital or clinic operated by the Department of Veterans Affairs registered under section 823(f) of this title;

(B) is being conducted while the patient is being treated by, and in the physical presence of, a practitioner—

(i) acting in the usual course of professional practice;

(ii) acting in accordance with applicable State law; and

(iii) registered under section 823(f) of this title in the State in which the patient is located, unless the practitioner—

(I) is exempted from such registration in all States under section 822(d) of this title; or

(II) is—

(aa) an employee or contractor of the Department of Veterans Affairs who is acting in the scope of such employment or contract; and

(bb) registered under section 823(f) of this title in any State or is using the registration of a hospital or clinic operated by the Department of Veterans Affairs registered under section 823(f) of this title;

(C) is being conducted by a practitioner—

(i) who is an employee or contractor of the Indian Health Service, or is working for an Indian tribe or tribal organization under its contract or compact with the Indian Health Service under the Indian Self-Determination and Education Assistance Act [25 U.S.C. 450 et seq.];

(ii) acting within the scope of the employment, contract, or compact described in clause (i); and

(iii) who is designated as an Internet Eligible Controlled Substances Provider by the Secretary under section 831(g)(2) of this title;

(D)(i) is being conducted during a public health emergency declared by the Secretary under section 247d of title 42; and

(ii) involves patients located in such areas, and such controlled substances, as the Secretary, with the concurrence of the Attorney General, designates, provided that such designation shall not be subject to the procedures prescribed by subchapter II of chapter 5 of title 5;

(E) is being conducted by a practitioner who has obtained from the Attorney General a special registration under section 831(h) of this title;

(F) is being conducted—

(i) in a medical emergency situation—

(I) that prevents the patient from being in the physical presence of a practitioner registered under section 823(f) of this title who is an employee or contractor of the Veterans Health Administration acting in the usual course of business and employment and within the scope of the official duties or contract of that employee or contractor;

(II) that prevents the patient from being physically present at a hospital or clinic operated by the Department of Veterans Affairs registered under section 823(f) of this title;

(III) during which the primary care practitioner of the patient or a practitioner otherwise practicing telemedicine within the meaning of this paragraph is unable to provide care or consultation; and

(IV) that requires immediate intervention by a health care practitioner using controlled substances to prevent what the practitioner reasonably believes in good faith will be imminent and serious clinical consequences, such as further injury or death; and

(ii) by a practitioner that—

(I) is an employee or contractor of the Veterans Health Administration acting within the scope of that employment or contract;

(II) is registered under section 823(f) of this title in any State or is utilizing the registration of a hospital or clinic operated by the Department of Veterans Affairs registered under section 823(f) of this title; and

(III) issues a controlled substance prescription in this emergency context that is limited to a maximum of a 5-day supply which may not be extended or refilled; or

(G) is being conducted under any other circumstances that the Attorney General and the Secretary have jointly, by regulation, determined to be consistent with effective controls against diversion and otherwise consistent with the public health and safety.

(55) The term "refilling prescriptions for controlled substances in schedule III, IV, or V"—

(A) means the dispensing of a controlled substance in schedule III, IV, or V in accordance with refill instructions issued by a practitioner as part of a valid prescription that meets the requirements of subsections (b) and (c) of section 829 of this title, as appropriate; and

(B) does not include the issuance of a new prescription to an individual for a controlled substance that individual was previously prescribed.

(56) The term "filling new prescriptions for controlled substances in schedule III, IV, or V" means filling a prescription for an individual for a controlled substance in schedule III, IV, or V, if—

(A) the pharmacy dispensing that prescription has previously dispensed to the patient a controlled substance other than by means of the Internet and pursuant to the valid prescription of a practitioner that meets the applicable requirements of subsections (b) and (c) of section 829 of this title (in this paragraph referred to as the "original prescription");

(B) the pharmacy contacts the practitioner who issued the original prescription at the request of that individual to determine whether the practitioner will authorize the issuance of a new prescription for that individual for the controlled substance described in subparagraph (A); and

(C) the practitioner, acting in the usual course of professional practice, determines there is a legitimate medical purpose for the issuance of the new prescription.

(Pub. L. 91–513, title II, § 102, Oct. 27, 1970, 84 Stat. 1242; Pub. L. 93–281, § 2, May 14, 1974, 88 Stat. 124; Pub. L. 95–633, title I, § 102(b), Nov. 10, 1978, 92 Stat. 3772; Pub. L. 96–88, title V, § 509(b), Oct. 17, 1979, 93 Stat. 695; Pub. L. 96–132, § 16(a), Nov. 30, 1979, 93 Stat. 1049; Pub. L. 98–473, title II, § 507(a), (b), Oct. 12, 1984, 98 Stat. 2071; Pub. L. 98–509, title III, § 301(a), Oct. 19, 1984, 98 Stat. 2364; Pub. L. 99–514, § 2, Oct. 22, 1986, 100 Stat. 2095; Pub. L. 99–570, title I, §§ 1003(b), 1203, 1870, Oct. 27, 1986, 100 Stat. 3207–6, 3207–13, 3207–56; Pub. L. 99–646, § 83, Nov. 10, 1986, 100 Stat. 3619; Pub. L. 100–690, title VI, § 6054, Nov. 18, 1988, 102 Stat. 4316; Pub. L. 101–647, title XIX, § 1902(b), title XXIII, § 2301, title XXXV, § 3599I, Nov. 29, 1990, 104 Stat. 4852, 4858, 4932; Pub. L. 103–200, §§ 2(a), 7–9(a), Dec. 17, 1993, 107 Stat. 2333, 2340; Pub. L. 103–322, title IX, § 90105(d), title XXXIII, § 330024(a), (b), (d)(1), Sept. 13, 1994, 108 Stat. 1988, 2150; Pub. L. 104–237, title II, §§ 204(a), 209, title IV, § 401(a), (b), Oct. 3, 1996, 110 Stat. 3102, 3104, 3106, 3107; Pub. L. 104–294, title VI, §§ 604(b)(4), 607(j), Oct. 11, 1996, 110 Stat. 3506, 3512; Pub. L. 105–115, title I, § 126(c)(3), Nov. 21, 1997, 111 Stat. 2328; Pub. L. 106–172, §§ 3(c), 5(a), Feb. 18, 2000, 114 Stat. 9, 10; Pub. L. 106–310, div. B, title XXXVI, § 3622(a), Oct. 17, 2000, 114 Stat. 1231; Pub. L. 107–273, div. B, title IV, § 4002(c)(1), Nov. 2, 2002, 116 Stat. 1808; Pub. L. 108–358, § 2(a), Oct. 22, 2004, 118 Stat. 1661; Pub. L. 109–162, title XI, § 1180, Jan. 5, 2006, 119 Stat. 3126; Pub. L. 109–177, title VII, §§ 711(a)(1), (2)(A), 712(a)(1), Mar. 9, 2006, 120 Stat. 256, 257, 263; Pub. L. 110–425, § 3(a), Oct. 15, 2008, 122 Stat. 4821.)

References in Text

Schedules I, II, III, IV, and V, referred to in pars. (6), (14), (32)(A), (52)(B)(viii), (55), and (56), are set out in section 812(c) of this title.

This subchapter, referred to in introductory provisions and in pars. (34), (35), (39)(A)(iii), (vi), and (54), was in the original "this title", meaning title II of Pub. L. 91–513, Oct. 27, 1970, 84 Stat. 1242, and is popularly known as the "Controlled Substances Act". For complete classification of title II to the Code, see second paragraph of Short Title note set out under section 801 of this title and Tables.

Subchapter II of this chapter, referred to in par. (39)(A)(iii), (vi), was in the original "title III", meaning title III of Pub. L. 91–513, Oct. 27, 1970, 84 Stat. 1285. Part A of title III comprises subchapter II of this chapter. For classification of Part B, consisting of sections 1101 to 1105 of title III, see Tables.

The Federal Food, Drug, and Cosmetic Act, referred to in pars. (39)(A)(iv) and (45)(A)(ii), is act June 25, 1938, ch. 675, 52 Stat. 1040, as amended, which is classified generally to chapter 9 (§301 et seq.) of this title. For complete classification of this Act to the Code, see section 301 of this title and Tables.

The Indian Self-Determination and Education Assistance Act, referred to in pars. (52)(B)(iv) and (54)(C)(i), is Pub. L. 93–638, Jan. 4, 1975, 88 Stat. 2203, which is classified principally to subchapter II (§450 et seq.) of chapter 14 of Title 25, Indians. For complete classification of this Act to the Code, see Short Title note set out under section 450 of Title 25 and Tables.

AMENDMENTS

2008—Pars. (50) to (56). Pub. L. 110–425 added pars. (50) to (56).

2006—Par. (39)(A)(iv). Pub. L. 109–177, §712(a)(1)(A)(i), amended cl. (iv) generally. Prior to amendment, cl. (iv) related to transactions involving drugs containing ephedrine, pseudoephedrine, or phenylpropanolamine.

Par. (39)(A)(v), (vi). Pub. L. 109–177, §712(a)(1)(A)(ii), (iii), added cl. (v) and redesignated former cl. (v) as (vi).

Par. (41)(A)(xvii). Pub. L. 109–162, §1180(1), substituted "13β-ethyl-17β-hydroxygon-4-en-3-one;" for "13β-ethyl-17α-hydroxygon-4-en-3-one;".

Par. (41)(A)(xliv). Pub. L. 109–162, §1180(2), substituted "(17α-methyl-17β-hydroxy-[5α]-androst-2-eno[3,2-c]-pyrazole);" for "(17α-methyl-17α-hydroxy-[5α]-androst-2-eno[3,2-c]-pyrazole);".

Par. (45). Pub. L. 109–177, §§711(a)(1)(B), 712(a)(1)(B), added par. (45) and struck out former par. (45) which defined "ordinary over-the-counter pseudoephedrine or phenylpropanolamine product".

Pars. (46) to (48). Pub. L. 109–177, §§711(a)(1)(B), added pars. (46) to (48). Former par. (46) redesignated (49).

Par. (49). Pub. L. 109–177, §711(a)(1)(A), (2)(A), redesignated par. (46) as (49), substituted "ephedrine, pseudoephedrine, or" for "pseudoephedrine or" in subpar. (A), redesignated subpar. (C) as (B), and struck out former subpar. (B) which read as follows: "For purposes of this paragraph, sale for personal use means the sale of below-threshold quantities in a single transaction to an individual for legitimate medical use."

2004—Par. (41). Pub. L. 108–358, §2(a)(1), realigned margins, added subpar. (A), and struck out former subpar. (A) which defined "anabolic steroid".

Par. (44). Pub. L. 108–358, §2(a)(2), inserted "anabolic steroids," after "marihuana,".

2002—Pars. (43), (44). Pub. L. 107–273 repealed Pub. L. 104–294, §§604(b)(4), 607(j)(2). See 1996 Amendment note below.

2000—Par. (32)(A). Pub. L. 106–172, §5(a)(1), substituted "subparagraph (C)" for "subparagraph (B)" in introductory provisions.

Par. (32)(B), (C). Pub. L. 106–172, §5(a)(2), (3), added subpar. (B) and redesignated former subpar. (B) as (C).

Par. (34)(X), (Y). Pub. L. 106–172, §3(c), added subpar. (X) and redesignated former subpar. (X) as (Y).

Par. (39)(A)(iv)(II). Pub. L. 106–310 substituted "9 grams" for "24 grams" in two places and inserted before semicolon at end "and sold in package sizes of not more than 3 grams of pseudoephedrine base or 3 grams of phenylpropanolamine base".

1997—Par. (9)(A). Pub. L. 105–115 redesignated cl. (i) as subpar. (A) and struck out cl. (ii) which read as follows: "any derivative of barbituric acid which has been designated by the Secretary as habit forming under section 352(d) of this title; or".

1996—Par. (26). Pub. L. 104–294, §607(j)(1), amended par. (26) generally. Prior to amendment, par. (26) read as follows: "The term 'State' means any State, territory, or possession of the United States, the District of Columbia, the Commonwealth of Puerto Rico, the Trust Territory of the Pacific Islands, and the Canal Zone."

Par. (34)(P), (S), (U). Pub. L. 104–237, §209(1), substituted "Isosafrole" for "Insosafrole" in subpar. (P), "N-Methylephedrine" for "N-Methylepherdrine" in subpar. (S), and "Hydriodic acid" for "Hydriotic acid" in subpar. (U).

Par. (35)(G). Pub. L. 104–237, §209(2), amended subpar. (G) generally, inserting "(or Methyl Ethyl Ketone)" before period at end.

Par. (35)(I), (J). Pub. L. 104–237, §204(a), added subpars. (I) and (J).

Par. (39)(A)(iv)(I)(aa). Pub. L. 104–237, §401(a)(1), (b)(1), substituted ", pseudoephedrine or its salts, optical isomers, or salts of optical isomers, or phenylpropanolamine or its salts, optical isomers, or salts of optical isomers unless otherwise provided by regulation of the Attorney General issued pursuant to section 814(e) of this title, except that any sale of ordinary over-the-counter pseudoephedrine or phenylpropanolamine products by retail distributors shall not be a regulated transaction (except as provided in section 401(d) of the Comprehensive Methamphetamine Control Act of 1996);" for "as the only active medicinal ingredient or contains ephedrine or its salts, optical isomers, or salts of optical isomers and therapeutically insignificant quantities of another active medicinal ingredient;".

Par. (39)(A)(iv)(II). Pub. L. 104–237, §401(a)(2), (b)(2), inserted ", pseudoephedrine, phenylpropanolamine," after "ephedrine" and inserted before semicolon ", except that the threshold for any sale of products containing pseudoephedrine or phenylpropanolamine products by retail distributors or by distributors required to submit reports by section 830(b)(3) of this title shall be 24 grams of pseudoephedrine or 24 grams of phenylpropanolamine in a single transaction".

Pars. (43), (44). Pub. L. 104–294, §§604(b)(4), 607(j)(2), which provided for amendment to section identical to Pub. L. 104–237, §401(b)(3), below, were repealed by Pub. L. 107–273, §4002(c)(1).

Pub. L. 104–237, §401(b)(3), redesignated par. (43), relating to felony drug offense, as (44).

Pars. (45), (46). Pub. L. 104–237, §401(b)(4), added pars. (45) and (46).

1994—Par. (34)(V), (W). Pub. L. 103–322, §330024(b), realigned margins and capitalized first letter.

Par. (35). Pub. L. 103–322, §330024(d)(1), made technical correction to directory language of Pub. L. 103–200, §2(a)(4)(B). See 1993 Amendment note below.

Par. (39)(A)(iv)(II). Pub. L. 103–322, §330024(a), substituted "; or" for period at end.

Par. (43). Pub. L. 103–322, §90105(d), added par. (43) defining "felony drug offense".

1993—Par. (33). Pub. L. 103–200, §2(a)(1), substituted "any list I chemical or any list II chemical" for "any listed precursor chemical or listed essential chemical".

Par. (34). Pub. L. 103–200, §2(a)(2), substituted "list I chemical" for "listed precursor chemical" and "important to the manufacture" for "critical to the creation" in introductory provisions.

Par. (34)(A), (F), (H). Pub. L. 103–200, §2(a)(3), inserted ", its esters," before "and".

Par. (34)(O). Pub. L. 103–200, §8(1), (2), redesignated subpar. (P) as (O) and struck out former subpar. (O) which read as follows: "D-lysergic acid."

Par. (34)(P) to (S). Pub. L. 103–200, §8(2), redesignated subpars. (Q) to (T) as (P) to (S), respectively. Former subpar. (P) redesignated (O).

Par. (34)(T). Pub. L. 103–200, §8(2), redesignated subpar. (V) as (T). Former subpar. (T) redesignated (S).

Par. (34)(U). Pub. L. 103–200, §8(1), (2), redesignated subpar. (X) as (U) and struck out former subpar. (U) which read as follows: "N-ethylephedrine."

Par. (34)(V). Pub. L. 103–200, §8(2), (4), added subpar. (V) and redesignated former subpar. (V) as (T).

Par. (34)(W). Pub. L. 103–200, §8(1), (4), added subpar. (W) and struck out former subpar. (W) which read as follows: "N-ethylpseudoephedrine."

Par. (34)(X). Pub. L. 103–200, §8(2), (3), redesignated subpar. (Y) as (X) and substituted "through (U)" for "through (X)".

Par. (34)(Y). Pub. L. 103–200, §8(2), redesignated subpar. (Y) as (X).

Par. (35). Pub. L. 103–200, §2(a)(4)(A), (C), substituted "list II chemical" for "listed essential chemical" and struck out "as a solvent, reagent, or catalyst" before "in manufacturing".

Pub. L. 103–200, §2(a)(4)(B), as amended by Pub. L. 103–322, §330024(d)(1), inserted "(other than a list I chemical)" before "specified" the first time appearing.

Par. (37). Pub. L. 103–200, §9(a), amended par. (37) generally. Prior to amendment, par. (37) read as follows: "The term 'regular supplier' means, with respect to a regulated person, a supplier with whom the regulated person has an established business relationship that is reported to the Attorney General."

Par. (38). Pub. L. 103–200, §2(a)(5), inserted before period at end "or who acts as a broker or trader for an international transaction involving a listed chemical, a tableting machine, or an encapsulating machine".

Par. (39)(A). Pub. L. 103–200, §§2(a)(6)(A), 7, in introductory provisions, substituted "importation, or exportation of, or an international transaction involving shipment of," for "importation or exportation of" and inserted "a listed chemical, or if the Attorney General establishes a threshold amount for a specific listed chemical," before "a threshold amount,".

Par. (39)(A)(iii). Pub. L. 103–200, §2(a)(6)(B), inserted "or any category of transaction for a specific listed chemical or chemicals" after "transaction".

Par. (39)(A)(iv). Pub. L. 103–200, §2(a)(6)(C), amended cl. (iv) generally. Prior to amendment, cl. (iv) read as follows: "any transaction in a listed chemical that is contained in a drug that may be marketed or distributed lawfully in the United States under the Federal Food, Drug, and Cosmetic Act; or".

Par. (39)(A)(v). Pub. L. 103–200, §2(a)(6)(D), inserted before semicolon at end "which the Attorney General has by regulation designated as exempt from the application of this subchapter and subchapter II of this chapter based on a finding that the mixture is formulated in such a way that it cannot be easily used in the illicit production of a controlled substance and that the listed chemical or chemicals contained in the mixture cannot be readily recovered".

Par. (40). Pub. L. 103–200, §2(a)(7), substituted "list I chemical or a list II chemical" for "listed precursor chemical or a listed essential chemical" in two places.

Pars. (42), (43). Pub. L. 103–200, §2(a)(8), added pars. (42) and (43).

1990—Par. (32)(A). Pub. L. 101–647, §3599I, substituted "the stimulant" for "the stimulent" in cl. (ii) and "a stimulant" for "a stimulent" in cl. (iii).

Par. (34)(M) to (Y). Pub. L. 101–647, §2301(a), added subpars. (M) to (Y).

Par. (35)(E). Pub. L. 101–647, §2301(b), struck out subpar. (E) "Hydriodic acid."

Par. (41). Pub. L. 101–647, §1902(b), added par. (41).

1988—Par. (8). Pub. L. 100–690, §6054(1), inserted "or a listed chemical" after "a controlled substance".

Par. (11). Pub. L. 100–690, §6054(2), inserted "or a listed chemical" after "a controlled substance" in two places.

Pars. (33) to (40). Pub. L. 100–690, §6054(3), added pars. (33) to (40).

1986—Par. (6). Pub. L. 99–514 substituted "Internal Revenue Code of 1986" for "Internal Revenue Code of 1954".

Par. (14). Pub. L. 99–570, §1870, and Pub. L. 99–646 amended par. (14) identically, substituting "any optical" for "the optical" in second and third sentences.

Par. (25). Pub. L. 99–570, §1003(b)(1), added par. (25). Former par. (25) redesignated (26).

Pars. (26) to (31). Pub. L. 99–570, §1003(b)(2), redesignated pars. (25) to (30) as (26) to (31), respectively.

Par. (32). Pub. L. 99–570, §1203, added par. (32).

1984—Pars. (14) to (16). Pub. L. 98–473, §507(a), added par. (14) and redesignated former pars. (14) to (16) as (15) to (17), respectively.

Par. (17). Pub. L. 98–473, §507, redesignated former par. (16) as (17), and expanded and revised definition of "narcotic drug", including within term poppy straw, cocaine, and ecgonine. Former par. (17) redesignated (18).

Pars. (18) to (28). Pub. L. 98–473, §507(a), redesignated former pars. (17) to (27) as (18) to (28), respectively.

Par. (29). Pub. L. 98–509 which directed the substitution of "one hundred and eighty" for "twenty-one" in par. (28), was executed to par. (29) in view of the redesignation of par. (28) as par. (29) by Pub. L. 98–473.

Pub. L. 98–473, §507(a), redesignated former par. (28) as (29). Former par. (29) redesignated (30).

Par. (30). Pub. L. 98–473, §507(a), redesignated former par. (29) as (30).

1979—Par. (4). Pub. L. 96–132 substituted provisions defining "Drug Enforcement Administration" for provisions defining "Bureau of Narcotics and Dangerous Drugs".

1978—Par. (29). Pub. L. 95–633 added par. (29).

1974—Pars. (27), (28). Pub. L. 93–281 added pars. (27) and (28).

Change of Name

"Secretary of Health and Human Services" substituted for "Secretary of Health, Education, and Welfare" in par. (24) pursuant to section 509(b) of Pub. L. 96–88, which is classified to section 3508(b) of Title 20, Education.

Effective Date of 2008 Amendment

Pub. L. 110–425, §3(j), Oct. 15, 2008, 122 Stat. 4832, provided that:

"(1) In general.—Except as provided in paragraph (2), the amendments made by this Act [enacting section 831 of this title and amending this section and sections 823, 827, 829, 841, 843, 882 and 960 of this title] shall take effect 180 days after the date of enactment of this Act [Oct. 15, 2008].

"(2) Definition of practice of telemedicine.—

"(A) In general.—Until the earlier of 3 months after the date on which regulations are promulgated to carry out section 311(h) of the Controlled Substances Act [21 U.S.C. 831(h)], as amended by this Act, or 15 months after the date of enactment of this Act—

"(i) the definition of the term 'practice of telemedicine' in subparagraph (B) of this paragraph shall apply for purposes of the Controlled Substances Act [21 U.S.C. 801 et seq.]; and

"(ii) the definition of the term 'practice of telemedicine' in section 102(54) of the Controlled Substances Act [21 U.S.C. 802(54)], as amended by this Act, shall not apply.

"(B) Temporary phase-in of telemedicine regulation.—During the period specified in subparagraph (A), the term 'practice of telemedicine' means the practice of medicine in accordance with applicable Federal and State laws by a practitioner (as that term is defined in section 102 of the Controlled Substances Act (21 U.S.C. 802)) (other than a pharmacist) who is at a location remote from the patient and is communicating with the patient, or health care professional who is treating the patient, using a telecommunications system referred to in section 1834(m) of the Social Security Act (42 U.S.C. 1395m(m)), if the practitioner is using an interactive telecommunications system that satisfies the requirements of section 410.78(a)(3) of title 42, Code of Federal Regulations.

"(C) Rule of construction.—Nothing in this subsection may be construed to create a precedent that any specific course of conduct constitutes the 'practice of telemedicine' (as that term is defined in section 102(54) of the Controlled Substances Act, as amended by this Act) after the end of the period specified in subparagraph (A)."

Effective Date of 2004 Amendment

Pub. L. 108–358, §2(d), Oct. 22, 2004, 118 Stat. 1664, provided that: "The amendments made by this section [amending this section, section 811 of this title, and provisions set out as a note under this section] shall take effect 90 days after the date of enactment of this Act [Oct. 22, 2004]."

Effective Date of 2002 Amendment

Pub. L. 107–273, div. B, title IV, §4002(c)(1), Nov. 2, 2002, 116 Stat. 1808, provided that the amendment made by section 4002(c)(1) is effective Oct. 11, 1996.

Effective Date of 2000 Amendment

Pub. L. 106–310, div. B, title XXXVI, §3622(b), Oct. 17, 2000, 114 Stat. 1231, provided that: "The amendments made by subsection (a) [amending this section] shall take effect 1 year after the date of the enactment of this Act [Oct. 17, 2000].''

EFFECTIVE DATE OF 1997 AMENDMENT

Amendment by Pub. L. 105–115 effective 90 days after Nov. 21, 1997, except as otherwise provided, see section 501 of Pub. L. 105–115, set out as a note under section 321 of this title.

EFFECTIVE DATE OF 1996 AMENDMENTS

Amendment by section 604(b)(4) of Pub. L. 104–294 effective Sept. 13, 1994, see section 604(d) of Pub. L. 104–294, set out as a note under section 13 of Title 18, Crimes and Criminal Procedure.

Section 401(g) of Pub. L. 104–237 provided that: ''Notwithstanding any other provision of this Act [see section 1(a) of Pub. L. 104–237, set out as a Short Title of 1996 Amendments note under section 801 of this title], this section [amending this section and section 814 of this title and enacting provisions set out as a note below] shall not apply to the sale of any pseudoephedrine or phenylpropanolamine product prior to 12 months after the date of enactment of this Act [Oct. 3, 1996], except that, on application of a manufacturer of a particular pseudoephedrine or phenylpropanolamine drug product, the Attorney General may, in her sole discretion, extend such effective date up to an additional six months. Notwithstanding any other provision of law, the decision of the Attorney General on such an application shall not be subject to judicial review.''

EFFECTIVE DATE OF 1994 AMENDMENT

Section 330024(f) of Pub. L. 103–322 provided that: ''The amendments made by this section [amending this section and sections 824, 960, and 971 of this title] shall take effect as of the date that is 120 days after the date of enactment of the Domestic Chemical Diversion Control Act of 1993 [Dec. 17, 1993].''

EFFECTIVE DATE OF 1993 AMENDMENT

Section 11 of Pub. L. 103–200 provided that: ''This Act [enacting section 814 of this title, amending this section and sections 821 to 824, 830, 843, 880, 957, 958, 960, and 971 of this title, and enacting provisions set out as a note under section 801 of this title] and the amendments made by this Act shall take effect on the date that is 120 days after the date of enactment of this Act [Dec. 17, 1993].''

EFFECTIVE DATE OF 1990 AMENDMENT

Section 1902(d) of Pub. L. 101–647 provided that: ''This section [amending this section and section 812 of this title and enacting provisions set out as a note under section 829 of this title] and the amendment made by this section shall take effect 90 days after the date of enactment of this Act [Nov. 29, 1990].''

EFFECTIVE DATE OF 1988 AMENDMENT

Section 6061 of title VI of Pub. L. 100–690 provided that: ''Except as otherwise provided in this subtitle, this subtitle [subtitle A (§§6051–6061) of title VI of Pub. L. 100–690, enacting section 971 of this title, amending this section and sections 830, 841 to 843, 872, 876, 881, 960, and 961 of this title, and enacting provisions set out as notes under this section and section 971 of this title] shall take effect 120 days after the enactment of this Act [Nov. 18, 1988].''

EFFECTIVE DATE OF 1978 AMENDMENT

Amendment by Pub. L. 95–633 effective on date the Convention on Psychotropic Substances enters into force in the United States [July 15, 1980], see section 112 of Pub. L. 95–633, set out as an Effective Date note under section 801a of this title.

REGULATIONS

Pub. L. 110–425, §3(k)(1), Oct. 15, 2008, 122 Stat. 4833, provided that: ''The Attorney General may promulgate and enforce any rules, regulations, and procedures which may be necessary and appropriate for the efficient execution of functions under this Act [see Short Title of 2008 Amendment note set out under section 801 of this title] or the amendments made by this Act, and, with the concurrence of the Secretary of Health and Human Services where this Act or the amendments made by this Act so provide, promulgate any interim rules necessary for the implementation of this Act or the amendments made by this Act, prior to its effective date [see Effective Date of 2008 Amendment note above].''

Section 301(b) of Pub. L. 98–509 provided that: ''The Secretary of Health and Human Services shall, within ninety days of the date of the enactment of this Act [Oct. 19, 1984], promulgate regulations for the administration of section 102(28) of the Controlled Substances Act [21 U.S.C. 802(29)] as amended by subsection (a) and shall include in the first report submitted under section 505(b) [503(b)] of the Public Health Service Act [former 42 U.S.C. 290aa–2(b)] after the expiration of such ninety days the findings of the Secretary with respect to the effect of the amendment made by subsection (a).''

CONSTRUCTION OF 2008 AMENDMENT

Pub. L. 110–425, §4, Oct. 15, 2008, 122 Stat. 4834, provided that: ''Nothing in this Act [see Short Title of 2008 Amendment note set out under section 801 of this title] or the amendments made by this Act shall be construed as authorizing, prohibiting, or limiting the use of electronic prescriptions for controlled substances.''

PRESERVATION OF STATE AUTHORITY TO REGULATE SCHEDULED LISTED CHEMICALS

Pub. L. 109–177, title VII, §711(g), Mar. 9, 2006, 120 Stat. 263, provided that: ''This section [amending this section and sections 830, 841, 842, and 844 of this title and enacting provisions set out as notes under sections 830 and 844 of this title] and the amendments made by this section may not be construed as having any legal effect on section 708 of the Controlled Substances Act [21 U.S.C. 903] as applied to the regulation of scheduled listed chemicals (as defined in section 102(45) of such Act [21 U.S.C. 802(45)]).''

REPORT ON DIVERSION OF ORDINARY, OVER-THE-COUNTER PSEUDOEPHEDRINE AND PHENYLPROPANOLAMINE PRODUCTS

Pub. L. 106–310, div. B, title XXXVI, §3642, Oct. 17, 2000, 114 Stat. 1237, provided that:

''(a) STUDY.—The Attorney General shall conduct a study of the use of ordinary, over-the-counter pseudoephedrine and phenylpropanolamine products in the clandestine production of illicit drugs. Sources of data for the study shall include the following:

''(1) Information from Federal, State, and local clandestine laboratory seizures and related investigations identifying the source, type, or brand of drug products being utilized and how they were obtained for the illicit production of methamphetamine and amphetamine.

''(2) Information submitted voluntarily from the pharmaceutical and retail industries involved in the manufacture, distribution, and sale of drug products containing ephedrine, pseudoephedrine, and phenylpropanolamine, including information on changes in the pattern, volume, or both, of sales of ordinary, over-the-counter pseudoephedrine and phenylpropanolamine products.

''(b) REPORT.—

''(1) REQUIREMENT.—Not later than 1 year after the date of the enactment of this Act [Oct. 17, 2000], the Attorney General shall submit to Congress a report on the study conducted under subsection (a).

''(2) ELEMENTS.—The report shall include—

''(A) the findings of the Attorney General as a result of the study; and

''(B) such recommendations on the need to establish additional measures to prevent diversion of ordinary, over-the-counter pseudoephedrine and phenylpropanolamine (such as a threshold on ordinary, over-the-counter pseudoephedrine and phenylpropanolamine products) as the Attorney General considers appropriate.

"(3) MATTERS CONSIDERED.—In preparing the report, the Attorney General shall consider the comments and recommendations including the comments on the Attorney General's proposed findings and recommendations, of State and local law enforcement and regulatory officials and of representatives of the industry described in subsection (a)(2).

"(c) REGULATION OF RETAIL SALES.—

"(1) IN GENERAL.—Notwithstanding section 401(d) of the Comprehensive Methamphetamine Control Act of 1996 [Pub. L. 104–237] (21 U.S.C. 802 note) and subject to paragraph (2), the Attorney General shall establish by regulation a single-transaction limit of not less than 24 grams of ordinary, over-the-counter pseudoephedrine or phenylpropanolamine (as the case may be) for retail distributors, if the Attorney General finds, in the report under subsection (b), that—

"(A) there is a significant number of instances (as set forth in paragraph (3)(A) of such section 401(d) for purposes of such section) where ordinary, over-the-counter pseudoephedrine products, phenylpropanolamine products, or both such products that were purchased from retail distributors were widely used in the clandestine production of illicit drugs; and

"(B) the best practical method of preventing such use is the establishment of single-transaction limits for retail distributors of either or both of such products.

"(2) DUE PROCESS.—The Attorney General shall establish the single-transaction limit under paragraph (1) only after notice, comment, and an informal hearing."

REGULATION OF RETAIL SALES OF CERTAIN PRECURSOR CHEMICALS; EFFECT ON THRESHOLDS; COMBINATION EPHEDRINE PRODUCTS

Pub. L. 104–237, title IV, §401(d)–(f), Oct. 3, 1996, 110 Stat. 3108, which authorized the Attorney General to establish a single-transaction limit of 24 grams for pseudoephedrine, phenylpropanolamine, and combination ephedrine products for retail distributors, was repealed by Pub. L. 109–177, title VII, §712(b), Mar. 9, 2006, 120 Stat. 264.

EXEMPTION FOR SUBSTANCES IN PARAGRAPH (41)

Pub. L. 101–647, title XIX, §1903, Nov. 29, 1990, 104 Stat. 4853, as amended by Pub. L. 108–358, §2(c), Oct. 22, 2004, 118 Stat. 1663, provided that:

"(a) DRUGS FOR TREATMENT OF RARE DISEASES.—If the Attorney General finds that a drug listed in paragraph (41) of section 102 of the Controlled Substances Act (as added by section 2 [1902] of this Act) is—

"(1) approved by the Food and Drug Administration as an accepted treatment for a rare disease or condition, as defined in section 526 of the Federal Food, Drug, and Cosmetic Act (21 U.S.C. 360bb); and

"(2) does not have a significant potential for abuse, the Attorney General may exempt such drug from any production regulations otherwise issued under the Controlled Substances Act as may be necessary to ensure adequate supplies of such drug for medical purposes.

"(b) DATE OF ISSUANCE OF REGULATIONS.—The Attorney General shall issue regulations implementing this section not later than 45 days after the date of enactment of this Act [Nov. 29, 1990], except that the regulations required under section 3(a) [former 1903(a)] shall be issued not later than 180 days after the date of enactment of this Act."

§ 803. Repealed. Pub. L. 95–137, § 1(b), Oct. 18, 1977, 91 Stat. 1169

Section, Pub. L. 91–513, title II, §103, Oct. 27, 1970, 84 Stat. 1245, authorized Bureau of Narcotics and Dangerous Drugs to add, during fiscal year 1971, 300 agents, together with necessary supporting personnel, and provided for appropriations of $6,000,000 to carry out such addition.

PART B—AUTHORITY TO CONTROL; STANDARDS AND SCHEDULES

§ 811. Authority and criteria for classification of substances

(a) Rules and regulations of Attorney General; hearing

The Attorney General shall apply the provisions of this subchapter to the controlled substances listed in the schedules established by section 812 of this title and to any other drug or other substance added to such schedules under this subchapter. Except as provided in subsections (d) and (e) of this section, the Attorney General may by rule—

(1) add to such a schedule or transfer between such schedules any drug or other substance if he—

(A) finds that such drug or other substance has a potential for abuse, and

(B) makes with respect to such drug or other substance the findings prescribed by subsection (b) of section 812 of this title for the schedule in which such drug is to be placed; or

(2) remove any drug or other substance from the schedules if he finds that the drug or other substance does not meet the requirements for inclusion in any schedule.

Rules of the Attorney General under this subsection shall be made on the record after opportunity for a hearing pursuant to the rulemaking procedures prescribed by subchapter II of chapter 5 of title 5. Proceedings for the issuance, amendment, or repeal of such rules may be initiated by the Attorney General (1) on his own motion, (2) at the request of the Secretary, or (3) on the petition of any interested party.

(b) Evaluation of drugs and other substances

The Attorney General shall, before initiating proceedings under subsection (a) of this section to control a drug or other substance or to remove a drug or other substance entirely from the schedules, and after gathering the necessary data, request from the Secretary a scientific and medical evaluation, and his recommendations, as to whether such drug or other substance should be so controlled or removed as a controlled substance. In making such evaluation and recommendations, the Secretary shall consider the factors listed in paragraphs (2), (3), (6), (7), and (8) of subsection (c) of this section and any scientific or medical considerations involved in paragraphs (1), (4), and (5) of such subsection. The recommendations of the Secretary shall include recommendations with respect to the appropriate schedule, if any, under which such drug or other substance should be listed. The evaluation and the recommendations of the Secretary shall be made in writing and submitted to the Attorney General within a reasonable time. The recommendations of the Secretary to the Attorney General shall be binding on the Attorney General as to such scientific and medical matters, and if the Secretary recommends that a drug or other substance not be controlled, the Attorney General shall not control the drug or other substance. If the Attorney General determines that these facts and all other relevant data constitute substantial evidence of potential for abuse such as to warrant control or substantial evidence that the drug or other substance should be removed entirely from the schedules, he shall initiate proceedings for control or removal, as the case may be, under subsection (a) of this section.

(c) Factors determinative of control or removal from schedules

In making any finding under subsection (a) of this section or under subsection (b) of section 812 of this title, the Attorney General shall consider the following factors with respect to each drug or other substance proposed to be controlled or removed from the schedules:

(1) Its actual or relative potential for abuse.

(2) Scientific evidence of its pharmacological effect, if known.

(3) The state of current scientific knowledge regarding the drug or other substance.

(4) Its history and current pattern of abuse.

(5) The scope, duration, and significance of abuse.

(6) What, if any, risk there is to the public health.

(7) Its psychic or physiological dependence liability.

(8) Whether the substance is an immediate precursor of a substance already controlled under this subchapter.

(d) International treaties, conventions, and protocols requiring control; procedures respecting changes in drug schedules of Convention on Psychotropic Substances

(1) If control is required by United States obligations under international treaties, conventions, or protocols in effect on October 27, 1970, the Attorney General shall issue an order controlling such drug under the schedule he deems most appropriate to carry out such obligations, without regard to the findings required by subsection (a) of this section or section 812(b) of this title and without regard to the procedures prescribed by subsections (a) and (b) of this section.

(2)(A) Whenever the Secretary of State receives notification from the Secretary-General of the United Nations that information has been transmitted by or to the World Health Organization, pursuant to article 2 of the Convention on Psychotropic Substances, which may justify adding a drug or other substance to one of the schedules of the Convention, transferring a drug or substance from one schedule to another, or deleting it from the schedules, the Secretary of State shall immediately transmit the notice to the Secretary of Health and Human Services who shall publish it in the Federal Register and provide opportunity to interested persons to submit to him comments respecting the scientific and medical evaluations which he is to prepare respecting such drug or substance. The Secretary of Health and Human Services shall prepare for transmission through the Secretary of State to the World Health Organization such medical and scientific evaluations as may be appropriate regarding the possible action that could be proposed by the World Health Organization respecting the drug or substance with respect to which a notice was transmitted under this subparagraph.

(B) Whenever the Secretary of State receives information that the Commission on Narcotic Drugs of the United Nations proposes to decide whether to add a drug or other substance to one of the schedules of the Convention, transfer a drug or substance from one schedule to another, or delete it from the schedules, the Secretary of State shall transmit timely notice to the Secretary of Health and Human Services of such information who shall publish a summary of such information in the Federal Register and provide opportunity to interested persons to submit to him comments respecting the recommendation which he is to furnish, pursuant to this subparagraph, respecting such proposal. The Secretary of Health and Human Services shall evaluate the proposal and furnish a recommendation to the Secretary of State which shall be binding on the representative of the United States in discussions and negotiations relating to the proposal.

(3) When the United States receives notification of a scheduling decision pursuant to article 2 of the Convention on Psychotropic Substances that a drug or other substance has been added or transferred to a schedule specified in the notification or receives notification (referred to in this subsection as a "schedule notice") that existing legal controls applicable under this subchapter to a drug or substance and the controls required by the Federal Food, Drug, and Cosmetic Act [21 U.S.C. 301 et seq.] do not meet the requirements of the schedule of the Convention in which such drug or substance has been placed, the Secretary of Health and Human Services after consultation with the Attorney General, shall first determine whether existing legal controls under this subchapter applicable to the drug or substance and the controls required by the Federal Food, Drug, and Cosmetic Act, meet the requirements of the schedule specified in the notification or schedule notice and shall take the following action:

(A) If such requirements are met by such existing controls but the Secretary of Health and Human Services nonetheless believes that more stringent controls should be applied to the drug or substance, the Secretary shall recommend to the Attorney General that he initiate proceedings for scheduling the drug or substance, pursuant to subsections (a) and (b) of this section, to apply to such controls.

(B) If such requirements are not met by such existing controls and the Secretary of Health and Human Services concurs in the scheduling decision or schedule notice transmitted by the notification, the Secretary shall recommend to the Attorney General that he initiate proceedings for scheduling the drug or substance under the appropriate schedule pursuant to subsections (a) and (b) of this section.

(C) If such requirements are not met by such existing controls and the Secretary of Health and Human Services does not concur in the scheduling decision or schedule notice transmitted by the notification, the Secretary shall—

(i) if he deems that additional controls are necessary to protect the public health and safety, recommend to the Attorney General that he initiate proceedings for scheduling the drug or substance pursuant to subsections (a) and (b) of this section, to apply such additional controls;

(ii) request the Secretary of State to transmit a notice of qualified acceptance, within the period specified in the Convention, pursuant to paragraph 7 of article 2 of the Convention, to the Secretary-General of the United Nations;

(iii) request the Secretary of State to transmit a notice of qualified acceptance as prescribed in clause (ii) and request the Secretary of State to ask for a review by the Economic and Social Council of the United Nations, in accordance with paragraph 8 of article 2 of the Convention, of the scheduling decision; or

(iv) in the case of a schedule notice, request the Secretary of State to take appropriate action under the Convention to initiate proceedings to remove the drug or substance from the schedules under the Convention or to transfer the drug or substance to a schedule under the Convention different from the one specified in the schedule notice.

(4)(A) If the Attorney General determines, after consultation with the Secretary of Health and Human Services, that proceedings initiated under recommendations made under paragraph[1] (B) or (C)(i) of paragraph (3) will not be completed within the time period required by paragraph 7 of article 2 of the Convention, the Attorney General, after consultation with the Secretary and after providing interested persons opportunity to submit comments respecting the requirements of the temporary order to be issued under this sentence, shall issue a temporary order controlling the drug or substance under schedule IV or V, whichever is most appropriate to carry out the minimum United States obligations under paragraph 7 of article 2 of the Convention. As a part of such order, the Attorney General shall, after consultation with the Secretary, except such drug or substance from the application of any provision of part C of this subchapter which he finds is not required to carry out the United States obligations under paragraph 7 of article 2 of the Convention. In the case of proceedings initiated under subparagraph (B) of paragraph (3), the Attorney General, concurrently with the issuance of such order, shall request the Secretary of State to transmit a notice of qualified acceptance to the Secretary-General of the United Nations pursuant to paragraph 7 of article 2 of the Convention. A temporary order issued under this subparagraph controlling a drug or other substance subject to proceedings initiated under subsections (a) and (b) of this section shall expire upon the effective date of the application to the drug or substance of the controls resulting from such proceedings.

(B) After a notice of qualified acceptance of a scheduling decision with respect to a drug or other substance is transmitted to the Secretary-General of the United Nations in accordance with clause (ii) or (iii) of paragraph (3)(C) or after a request has been made under clause (iv) of such paragraph with respect to a drug or substance described in a schedule notice, the Attorney General, after consultation with the Secretary of Health and Human Services and after providing interested persons opportunity to submit comments respecting the requirements of the order to be issued under this sentence, shall issue an order controlling the drug or substance under schedule IV or V, whichever is most appropriate to carry out the minimum United States obligations under paragraph 7 of article 2 of the Convention in the case of a drug or substance for which a notice of qualified acceptance was transmitted or whichever the Attorney General determines is appropriate in the case of a drug or substance described in a schedule notice. As a part of such order, the Attorney General shall, after consultation with the Secretary, except such drug or substance from the application of any provision of part C of this subchapter which he finds is not required to carry out the United States obligations under paragraph 7 of article 2 of the Convention. If, as a result of a review under paragraph 8 of article 2 of the Convention of the scheduling decision with respect to which a notice of qualified acceptance was transmitted in accordance with clause (ii) or (iii) of paragraph (3)(C)—

(i) the decision is reversed, and

(ii) the drug or substance subject to such decision is not required to be controlled under schedule IV or V to carry out the minimum United States obligations under paragraph 7 of article 2 of the Convention,

the order issued under this subparagraph with respect to such drug or substance shall expire upon receipt by the United States of the review decision. If, as a result of action taken pursuant to action initiated under a request transmitted under clause (iv) of paragraph (3)(C), the drug or substance with respect to which such action was taken is not required to be controlled under schedule IV or V, the order issued under this paragraph with respect to such drug or substance shall expire upon receipt by the United States of a notice of the action taken with respect to such drug or substance under the Convention.

(C) An order issued under subparagraph (A) or (B) may be issued without regard to the findings required by subsection (a) of this section or by section 812(b) of this title and without regard to the procedures prescribed by subsection (a) or (b) of this section.

(5) Nothing in the amendments made by the Psychotropic Substances Act of 1978 or the regulations or orders promulgated thereunder shall be construed to preclude requests by the Secretary of Health and Human Services or the Attorney General through the Secretary of State, pursuant to article 2 or other applicable provisions of the Convention, for review of scheduling decisions under such Convention, based on new or additional information.

(e) Immediate precursors

The Attorney General may, without regard to the findings required by subsection (a) of this

[1] So in original. Probably should be "subparagraph".

section or section 812(b) of this title and without regard to the procedures prescribed by subsections (a) and (b) of this section, place an immediate precursor in the same schedule in which the controlled substance of which it is an immediate precursor is placed or in any other schedule with a higher numerical designation. If the Attorney General designates a substance as an immediate precursor and places it in a schedule, other substances shall not be placed in a schedule solely because they are its precursors.

(f) Abuse potential

If, at the time a new-drug application is submitted to the Secretary for any drug having a stimulant, depressant, or hallucinogenic effect on the central nervous system, it appears that such drug has an abuse potential, such information shall be forwarded by the Secretary to the Attorney General.

(g) Exclusion of non-narcotic substances sold over the counter without a prescription; dextromethorphan; exemption of substances lacking abuse potential

(1) The Attorney General shall by regulation exclude any non-narcotic drug which contains a controlled substance from the application of this subchapter and subchapter II of this chapter if such drug may, under the Federal Food, Drug, and Cosmetic Act [21 U.S.C. 301 et seq.], be lawfully sold over the counter without a prescription.

(2) Dextromethorphan shall not be deemed to be included in any schedule by reason of enactment of this subchapter unless controlled after October 27, 1970 pursuant to the foregoing provisions of this section.

(3) The Attorney General may, by regulation, exempt any compound, mixture, or preparation containing a controlled substance from the application of all or any part of this subchapter if he finds such compound, mixture, or preparation meets the requirements of one of the following categories:

(A) A mixture, or preparation containing a nonnarcotic controlled substance, which mixture or preparation is approved for prescription use, and which contains one or more other active ingredients which are not listed in any schedule and which are included therein in such combinations, quantity, proportion, or concentration as to vitiate the potential for abuse.

(B) A compound, mixture, or preparation which contains any controlled substance, which is not for administration to a human being or animal, and which is packaged in such form or concentration, or with adulterants or denaturants, so that as packaged it does not present any significant potential for abuse.

(C) Upon the recommendation of the Secretary of Health and Human Services, a compound, mixture, or preparation which contains any anabolic steroid, which is intended for administration to a human being or an animal, and which, because of its concentration, preparation, formulation or delivery system, does not present any significant potential for abuse.

(h) Temporary scheduling to avoid imminent hazards to public safety

(1) If the Attorney General finds that the scheduling of a substance in schedule I on a temporary basis is necessary to avoid an imminent hazard to the public safety, he may, by order and without regard to the requirements of subsection (b) of this section relating to the Secretary of Health and Human Services, schedule such substance in schedule I if the substance is not listed in any other schedule in section 812 of this title or if no exemption or approval is in effect for the substance under section 505 of the Federal Food, Drug, and Cosmetic Act [21 U.S.C. 355]. Such an order may not be issued before the expiration of thirty days from—

(A) the date of the publication by the Attorney General of a notice in the Federal Register of the intention to issue such order and the grounds upon which such order is to be issued, and

(B) the date the Attorney General has transmitted the notice required by paragraph (4).

(2) The scheduling of a substance under this subsection shall expire at the end of one year from the date of the issuance of the order scheduling such substance, except that the Attorney General may, during the pendency of proceedings under subsection (a)(1) of this section with respect to the substance, extend the temporary scheduling for up to six months.

(3) When issuing an order under paragraph (1), the Attorney General shall be required to consider, with respect to the finding of an imminent hazard to the public safety, only those factors set forth in paragraphs (4), (5), and (6) of subsection (c) of this section, including actual abuse, diversion from legitimate channels, and clandestine importation, manufacture, or distribution.

(4) The Attorney General shall transmit notice of an order proposed to be issued under paragraph (1) to the Secretary of Health and Human Services. In issuing an order under paragraph (1), the Attorney General shall take into consideration any comments submitted by the Secretary in response to a notice transmitted pursuant to this paragraph.

(5) An order issued under paragraph (1) with respect to a substance shall be vacated upon the conclusion of a subsequent rulemaking proceeding initiated under subsection (a) of this section with respect to such substance.

(6) An order issued under paragraph (1) is not subject to judicial review.

(Pub. L. 91–513, title II, §201, Oct. 27, 1970, 84 Stat. 1245; Pub. L. 95–633, title I, §102(a), Nov. 10, 1978, 92 Stat. 3769; Pub. L. 96–88, title V, §509(b), Oct. 17, 1979, 93 Stat. 695; Pub. L. 98–473, title II, §§508, 509(a), Oct. 12, 1984, 98 Stat. 2071, 2072; Pub. L. 108–358, §2(b), Oct. 22, 2004, 118 Stat. 1663.)

REFERENCES IN TEXT

This subchapter, referred to in subsecs. (a), (c)(8), (d)(3), (4)(A), (B), and (g)(2), (3), was in the original "this title", meaning title II of Pub. L. 91–513, Oct. 27, 1970, 84 Stat. 1242, as amended, and is popularly known as the "Controlled Substances Act". For complete classification of title II to the Code, see second paragraph of Short Title note set out under section 801 of this title and Tables.

The Federal Food, Drug, and Cosmetic Act, referred to in subsecs. (d)(3) and (g)(1), is act June 25, 1938, ch. 675, 52 Stat. 1040, as amended, which is classified generally to chapter 9 (§301 et seq.) of this title. For complete classification of this Act to the Code, see section 301 of this title and Tables.

Schedules I, IV, and V, referred to in subsecs. (d)(4)(A), (B), and (h)(1), are set out in section 812(c) of this title.

The Psychotropic Substances Act of 1978, referred to in subsec. (d)(5), is Pub. L. 95–633, Nov. 10, 1978, 92 Stat. 3768, which enacted sections 801a, 830, and 852 of this title, amended sections 352, 802, 811, 812, 823, 827, 841 to 843, 872, 881, 952, 953, and 965 of this title and section 242a of Title 42, The Public Health and Welfare, repealed section 830 of this title effective Jan. 1, 1981, and enacted provisions set out as notes under sections 801, 801a, 812, and 830 of this title. For complete classification of this Act to the Code, see Short Title of 1978 Amendment note set out under section 801 of this title and Tables.

This subchapter and subchapter II of this chapter, referred to in subsec. (g)(1), was in the original "titles II and III of the Comprehensive Drug Abuse Prevention and Control Act", which was translated as meaning titles II and III of the Comprehensive Drug Abuse Prevention and Control Act of 1970, Pub. L. 91–513, Oct. 27, 1970, 84 Stat. 1242, 1285, as amended, to reflect the probable intent of Congress. Title II is classified principally to this subchapter and part A of title III comprises subchapter II of this chapter. For complete classification of this Act to the Code, see Short Title notes set out under section 801 of this title and Tables.

AMENDMENTS

2004—Subsec. (g)(1). Pub. L. 108–358, §2(b)(1), substituted "drug which contains a controlled substance from the application of this subchapter and subchapter II of this chapter if such drug" for "substance from a schedule if such substance".

Subsec. (g)(3)(C). Pub. L. 108–358, §2(b)(2), added subpar. (C).

1984—Subsec. (g)(3). Pub. L. 98–473, §509(a), added par. (3).

Subsec. (h). Pub. L. 98–473, §508, added subsec. (h).

1978—Subsec. (d). Pub. L. 95–633 designated existing provisions as par. (1) and added pars. (2) to (5).

CHANGE OF NAME

"Secretary of Health and Human Services" substituted for "Secretary of Health, Education, and Welfare" in subsec. (d)(2), (3), (4)(A), (B), (5) pursuant to section 509(b) of Pub. L. 96–88 which is classified to section 3508(b) of Title 20, Education.

EFFECTIVE DATE OF 2004 AMENDMENT

Amendment by Pub. L. 108–358 effective 90 days after Oct. 22, 2004, see section 2(d) of Pub. L. 108–358, set out as a note under section 802 of this title.

EFFECTIVE DATE OF 1978 AMENDMENT

Amendment by Pub. L. 95–633 effective on date the Convention on Psychotropic Substances enters into force in the United States [July 15, 1980], see section 112 of Pub. L. 95–633, set out as an Effective Date note under section 801a of this title.

§812. Schedules of controlled substances

(a) Establishment

There are established five schedules of controlled substances, to be known as schedules I, II, III, IV, and V. Such schedules shall initially consist of the substances listed in this section. The schedules established by this section shall be updated and republished on a semiannual basis during the two-year period beginning one year after October 27, 1970, and shall be updated and republished on an annual basis thereafter.

(b) Placement on schedules; findings required

Except where control is required by United States obligations under an international treaty, convention, or protocol, in effect on October 27, 1970, and except in the case of an immediate precursor, a drug or other substance may not be placed in any schedule unless the findings required for such schedule are made with respect to such drug or other substance. The findings required for each of the schedules are as follows:

(1) SCHEDULE I.—

(A) The drug or other substance has a high potential for abuse.

(B) The drug or other substance has no currently accepted medical use in treatment in the United States.

(C) There is a lack of accepted safety for use of the drug or other substance under medical supervision.

(2) SCHEDULE II.—

(A) The drug or other substance has a high potential for abuse.

(B) The drug or other substance has a currently accepted medical use in treatment in the United States or a currently accepted medical use with severe restrictions.

(C) Abuse of the drug or other substances may lead to severe psychological or physical dependence.

(3) SCHEDULE III.—

(A) The drug or other substance has a potential for abuse less than the drugs or other substances in schedules I and II.

(B) The drug or other substance has a currently accepted medical use in treatment in the United States.

(C) Abuse of the drug or other substance may lead to moderate or low physical dependence or high psychological dependence.

(4) SCHEDULE IV.—

(A) The drug or other substance has a low potential for abuse relative to the drugs or other substances in schedule III.

(B) The drug or other substance has a currently accepted medical use in treatment in the United States.

(C) Abuse of the drug or other substance may lead to limited physical dependence or psychological dependence relative to the drugs or other substances in schedule III.

(5) SCHEDULE V.—

(A) The drug or other substance has a low potential for abuse relative to the drugs or other substances in schedule IV.

(B) The drug or other substance has a currently accepted medical use in treatment in the United States.

(C) Abuse of the drug or other substance may lead to limited physical dependence or psychological dependence relative to the drugs or other substances in schedule IV.

(c) Initial schedules of controlled substances

Schedules I, II, III, IV, and V shall, unless and until amended[1] pursuant to section 811 of this title, consist of the following drugs or other sub-

[1] Revised schedules are published in the Code of Federal Regulations, Part 1308 of Title 21, Food and Drugs.

stances, by whatever official name, common or usual name, chemical name, or brand name designated:

SCHEDULE I

(a) Unless specifically excepted or unless listed in another schedule, any of the following opiates, including their isomers, esters, ethers, salts, and salts of isomers, esters, and ethers, whenever the existence of such isomers, esters, ethers, and salts is possible within the specific chemical designation:

(1) Acetylmethadol.
(2) Allylprodine.
(3) Alphacetylmathadol.[2]
(4) Alphameprodine.
(5) Alphamethadol.
(6) Benzethidine.
(7) Betacetylmethadol.
(8) Betameprodine.
(9) Betamethadol.
(10) Betaprodine.
(11) Clonitazene.
(12) Dextromoramide.
(13) Dextrorphan.
(14) Diampromide.
(15) Diethylthiambutene.
(16) Dimenoxadol.
(17) Dimepheptanol.
(18) Dimethylthiambutene.
(19) Dioxaphetyl butyrate.
(20) Dipipanone.
(21) Ethylmethylthiambutene.
(22) Etonitazene.
(23) Etoxeridine.
(24) Furethidine.
(25) Hydroxypethidine.
(26) Ketobemidone.
(27) Levomoramide.
(28) Levophenacylmorphan.
(29) Morpheridine.
(30) Noracymethadol.
(31) Norlevorphanol.
(32) Normethadone.
(33) Norpipanone.
(34) Phenadoxone.
(35) Phenampromide.
(36) Phenomorphan.
(37) Phenoperidine.
(38) Piritramide.
(39) Propheptazine.
(40) Properidine.
(41) Racemoramide.
(42) Trimeperidine.

(b) Unless specifically excepted or unless listed in another schedule, any of the following opium derivatives, their salts, isomers, and salts of isomers whenever the existence of such salts, isomers, and salts of isomers is possible within the specific chemical designation:

(1) Acetorphine.
(2) Acetyldihydrocodeine.
(3) Benzylmorphine.
(4) Codeine methylbromide.
(5) Codeine-N-Oxide.
(6) Cyprenorphine.
(7) Desomorphine.
(8) Dihydromorphine.
(9) Etorphine.
(10) Heroin.
(11) Hydromorphinol.
(12) Methyldesorphine.
(13) Methylhydromorphine.
(14) Morphine methylbromide.
(15) Morphine methylsulfonate.
(16) Morphine-N-Oxide.
(17) Myrophine.
(18) Nicocodeine.
(19) Nicomorphine.
(20) Normorphine.
(21) Pholcodine.
(22) Thebacon.

(c) Unless specifically excepted or unless listed in another schedule, any material, compound, mixture, or preparation, which contains any quantity of the following hallucinogenic substances, or which contains any of their salts, isomers, and salts of isomers whenever the existence of such salts, isomers, and salts of isomers is possible within the specific chemical designation:

(1) 3,4-methylenedioxy amphetamine.
(2) 5-methoxy-3,4-methylenedioxy amphetamine.
(3) 3,4,5-trimethoxy amphetamine.
(4) Bufotenine.
(5) Diethyltryptamine.
(6) Dimethyltryptamine.
(7) 4-methyl-2,5-diamethoxyamphetamine.
(8) Ibogaine.
(9) Lysergic acid diethylamide.
(10) Marihuana.
(11) Mescaline.
(12) Peyote.
(13) N-ethyl-3-piperidyl benzilate.
(14) N-methyl-3-piperidyl benzilate.
(15) Psilocybin.
(16) Psilocyn.
(17) Tetrahydrocannabinols.

SCHEDULE II

(a) Unless specifically excepted or unless listed in another schedule, any of the following substances whether produced directly or indirectly by extraction from substances of vegetable origin, or independently by means of chemical synthesis, or by a combination of extraction and chemical synthesis:

(1) Opium and opiate, and any salt, compound, derivative, or preparation of opium or opiate.

(2) Any salt, compound, derivative, or preparation thereof which is chemically equivalent or identical with any of the substances referred to in clause (1), except that these substances shall not include the isoquinoline alkaloids of opium.

(3) Opium poppy and poppy straw.

(4) coca[3] leaves, except coca leaves and extracts of coca leaves from which cocaine, ecgonine, and derivatives of ecgonine or their salts have been removed; cocaine, its salts, optical and geometric isomers, and salts of isomers; ecgonine, its derivatives, their salts, isomers, and salts of isomers; or any compound, mixture, or preparation which contains any quan-

[2] So in original. Probably should be "Alphacetylmethadol."

[3] So in original. Probably should be capitalized.

tity of any of the substances referred to in this paragraph.

(b) Unless specifically excepted or unless listed in another schedule, any of the following opiates, including their isomers, esters, ethers, salts, and salts of isomers, esters and ethers, whenever the existence of such isomers, esters, ethers, and salts is possible within the specific chemical designation:

(1) Alphaprodine.
(2) Anileridine.
(3) Bezitramide.
(4) Dihydrocodeine.
(5) Diphenoxylate.
(6) Fentanyl.
(7) Isomethadone.
(8) Levomethorphan.
(9) Levorphanol.
(10) Metazocine.
(11) Methadone.
(12) Methadone-Intermediate, 4-cyano-2-dimethylamino-4,4-diphenyl butane.
(13) Moramide-Intermediate, 2-methyl-3-morpholino-1, 1-diphenylpropane-carboxylic acid.
(14) Pethidine.
(15) Pethidine-Intermediate-A, 4-cyano-1-methyl-4-phenylpiperidine.
(16) Pethidine-Intermediate-B, ethyl-4-phenylpiperidine-4-carboxylate.
(17) Pethidine-Intermediate-C, 1-methyl-4-phenylpiperidine-4-carboxylic acid.
(18) Phenazocine.
(19) Piminodine.
(20) Racemethorphan.
(21) Racemorphan.

(c) Unless specifically excepted or unless listed in another schedule, any injectable liquid which contains any quantity of methamphetamine, including its salts, isomers, and salts of isomers.

SCHEDULE III

(a) Unless specifically excepted or unless listed in another schedule, any material, compound, mixture, or preparation which contains any quantity of the following substances having a stimulant effect on the central nervous system:

(1) Amphetamine, its salts, optical isomers, and salts of its optical isomers.
(2) Phenmetrazine and its salts.
(3) Any substance (except an injectable liquid) which contains any quantity of methamphetamine, including its salts, isomers, and salts of isomers.
(4) Methylphenidate.

(b) Unless specifically excepted or unless listed in another schedule, any material, compound, mixture, or preparation which contains any quantity of the following substances having a depressant effect on the central nervous system:

(1) Any substance which contains any quantity of a derivative of barbituric acid, or any salt of a derivative of barbituric acid.
(2) Chorhexadol.
(3) Glutethimide.
(4) Lysergic acid.
(5) Lysergic acid amide.
(6) Methyprylon.
(7) Phencyclidine.
(8) Sulfondiethylmethane.
(9) Sulfonethylmethane.
(10) Sulfonmethane.

(c) Nalorphine.

(d) Unless specifically excepted or unless listed in another schedule, any material, compound, mixture, or preparation containing limited quantities of any of the following narcotic drugs, or any salts thereof:

(1) Not more than 1.8 grams of codeine per 100 milliliters or not more than 90 milligrams per dosage unit, with an equal or greater quantity of an isoquinoline alkaloid of opium.
(2) Not more than 1.8 grams of codeine per 100 milliliters or not more than 90 milligrams per dosage unit, with one or more active, nonnarcotic ingredients in recognized therapeutic amounts.
(3) Not more than 300 milligrams of dihydrocodeinone per 100 milliliters or not more than 15 milligrams per dosage unit, with a fourfold or greater quantity of an isoquinoline alkaloid of opium.
(4) Not more than 300 milligrams of dihydrocodeinone per 100 milliliters or not more than 15 milligrams per dosage unit, with one or more active, nonnarcotic ingredients in recognized therapeutic amounts.
(5) Not more than 1.8 grams of dihydrocodeine per 100 milliliters or not more than 90 milligrams per dosage unit, with one or more active, nonnarcotic ingredients in recognized therapeutic amounts.
(6) Not more than 300 milligrams of ethylmorphine per 100 milliliters or not more than 15 milligrams per dosage unit, with one or more active, nonnarcotic ingredients in recognized therapeutic amounts.
(7) Not more than 500 milligrams of opium per 100 milliliters or per 100 grams, or not more than 25 milligrams per dosage unit, with one or more active, nonnarcotic ingredients in recognized therapeutic amounts.
(8) Not more than 50 milligrams of morphine per 100 milliliters or per 100 grams with one or more active, nonnarcotic ingredients in recognized therapeutic amounts.

(e) Anabolic steroids.

SCHEDULE IV

(1) Barbital.
(2) Chloral betaine.
(3) Chloral hydrate.
(4) Ethchlorvynol.
(5) Ethinamate.
(6) Methohexital.
(7) Meprobamate.
(8) Methylphenobarbital.
(9) Paraldehyde.
(10) Petrichloral.
(11) Phenobarbital.

SCHEDULE V

Any compound, mixture, or preparation containing any of the following limited quantities of narcotic drugs, which shall include one or more nonnarcotic active medicinal ingredients in sufficient proportion to confer upon the compound, mixture, or preparation valuable medicinal qualities other than those possessed by the narcotic drug alone:

(1) Not more than 200 milligrams of codeine per 100 milliliters or per 100 grams.

(2) Not more than 100 milligrams of dihydrocodeine per 100 milliliters or per 100 grams.

(3) Not more than 100 milligrams of ethylmorphine per 100 milliliters or per 100 grams.

(4) Not more than 2.5 milligrams of diphenoxylate and not less than 25 micrograms of atropine sulfate per dosage unit.

(5) Not more than 100 milligrams of opium per 100 milliliters or per 100 grams.

(Pub. L. 91–513, title II, §202, Oct. 27, 1970, 84 Stat. 1247; Pub. L. 95–633, title I, §103, Nov. 10, 1978, 92 Stat. 3772; Pub. L. 98–473, title II, §§507(c), 509(b), Oct. 12, 1984, 98 Stat. 2071, 2072; Pub. L. 99–570, title I, §1867, Oct. 27, 1986, 100 Stat. 3207–55; Pub. L. 99–646, §84, Nov. 10, 1986, 100 Stat. 3619; Pub. L. 101–647, title XIX, §1902(a), Nov. 29, 1990, 104 Stat. 4851.)

AMENDMENTS

1990—Subsec. (c). Pub. L. 101–647 added item (e) at end of schedule III.

1986—Subsec. (c). Pub. L. 99–646 amended schedule II(a)(4) generally. Prior to amendment, schedule II(a)(4) read as follows: "Coca leaves (except coca leaves and extracts of coca leaves from which cocaine, ecgonine, and derivatives of ecgonine or their salts have been removed); cocaine, its salts, optical and geometric isomers, and salts of isomers; and ecgonine, its derivatives, their salts, isomers, and salts of isomers."

Pub. L. 99–570 amended schedule II(a)(4) generally. Prior to amendment, schedule II(a)(4) read as follows: "Coca leaves and any salt, compound, derivative, or preparation of coca leaves (including cocaine and ecgonine and their salts, isomers, derivatives, and salts of isomers and derivatives), and any salt, compound, derivative, or preparation thereof which is chemically equivalent or identical with any of these substances, except that the substances shall not include decocainized coca leaves or extraction of coca leaves, which extractions do not contain cocaine or ecgonine."

1984—Subsec. (c). Pub. L. 98–473, §507(c), in schedule II(a)(4) added applicability to cocaine and ecgonine and their salts, isomers, etc.

Subsec. (d). Pub. L. 98–473, §509(b), struck out subsec. (d) which related to authority of Attorney General to except stimulants or depressants containing active medicinal ingredients.

1978—Subsec. (d)(3). Pub. L. 95–633 added cl. (3).

EFFECTIVE DATE OF 1990 AMENDMENT

Amendment by Pub. L. 101–647 effective 90 days after Nov. 29, 1990, see section 1902(d) of Pub. L. 101–647, set out as a note under section 802 of this title.

EFFECTIVE DATE OF 1978 AMENDMENT

Amendment by Pub. L. 95–633 effective on date the Convention on Psychotropic Substances enters into force in the United States [July 15, 1980], see section 112 of Pub. L. 95–633, set out as an Effective Date note under section 801a of this title.

CONGRESSIONAL FINDING; EMERGENCY SCHEDULING OF GHB IN CONTROLLED SUBSTANCES ACT

Pub. L. 106–172, §§2, 3(a), Feb. 18, 2000, 114 Stat. 7, 8, provided that:

"SEC. 2. FINDINGS.

"Congress finds as follows:

"(1) Gamma hydroxybutyric acid (also called G, Liquid X, Liquid Ecstasy, Grievous Bodily Harm, Georgia Home Boy, Scoop) has become a significant and growing problem in law enforcement. At least 20 States have scheduled such drug in their drug laws and law enforcement officials have been experiencing an increased presence of the drug in driving under the influence, sexual assault, and overdose cases especially at night clubs and parties.

"(2) A behavioral depressant and a hypnotic, gamma hydroxybutyric acid ('GHB') is being used in conjunction with alcohol and other drugs with detrimental effects in an increasing number of cases. It is difficult to isolate the impact of such drug's ingestion since it is so typically taken with an ever-changing array of other drugs and especially alcohol which potentiates its impact.

"(3) GHB takes the same path as alcohol, processes via alcohol dehydrogenase, and its symptoms at high levels of intake and as impact builds are comparable to alcohol ingestion/intoxication. Thus, aggression and violence can be expected in some individuals who use such drug.

"(4) If taken for human consumption, common industrial chemicals such as gamma butyrolactone and 1.4-butanediol are swiftly converted by the body into GHB. Illicit use of these and other GHB analogues and precursor chemicals is a significant and growing law enforcement problem.

"(5) A human pharmaceutical formulation of gamma hydroxybutyric acid is being developed as a treatment for cataplexy, a serious and debilitating disease. Cataplexy, which causes sudden and total loss of muscle control, affects about 65 percent of the estimated 180,000 Americans with narcolepsy, a sleep disorder. People with cataplexy often are unable to work, drive a car, hold their children or live a normal life.

"(6) Abuse of illicit GHB is an imminent hazard to public safety that requires immediate regulatory action under the Controlled Substances Act (21 U.S.C. 801 et seq.).

"SEC. 3. EMERGENCY SCHEDULING OF GAMMA HYDROXYBUTYRIC ACID AND LISTING OF GAMMA BUTYROLACTONE AS LIST I CHEMICAL.

"(a) EMERGENCY SCHEDULING OF GHB.—

"(1) IN GENERAL.—The Congress finds that the abuse of illicit gamma hydroxybutyric acid is an imminent hazard to the public safety. Accordingly, the Attorney General, notwithstanding sections 201(a), 201(b), 201(c), and 202 of the Controlled Substances Act [21 U.S.C. 811(a)–(c), 812], shall issue, not later than 60 days after the date of the enactment of this Act [Feb. 18, 2000], a final order that schedules such drug (together with its salts, isomers, and salts of isomers) in the same schedule under section 202(c) of the Controlled Substances Act as would apply to a scheduling of a substance by the Attorney General under section 201(h)(1) of such Act (relating to imminent hazards to the public safety), except as follows:

"(A) For purposes of any requirements that relate to the physical security of registered manufacturers and registered distributors, the final order shall treat such drug, when the drug is manufactured, distributed, or possessed in accordance with an exemption under section 505(i) of the Federal Food, Drug, and Cosmetic Act [21 U.S.C. 355(i)] (whether the exemption involved is authorized before, on, or after the date of the enactment of this Act [Feb. 18, 2000]), as being in the same schedule as that recommended by the Secretary of Health and Human Services for the drug when the drug is the subject of an authorized investigational new drug application (relating to such section 505(i)). The recommendation referred to in the preceding sentence is contained in the first paragraph of the letter transmitted on May 19, 1999, by such Secretary (acting through the Assistant Secretary for Health) to the Attorney General (acting through the Deputy Administrator of the Drug Enforcement Administration), which letter was in response to the letter transmitted by the Attorney General (acting through such Deputy Administrator) on September

16, 1997. In publishing the final order in the Federal Register, the Attorney General shall publish a copy of the letter that was transmitted by the Secretary of Health and Human Services.

"(B) In the case of gamma hydroxybutyric acid that is contained in a drug product for which an application is approved under section 505 of the Federal Food, Drug, and Cosmetic Act [21 U.S.C. 355] (whether the application involved is approved before, on, or after the date of the enactment of this Act [Feb. 18, 2000]), the final order shall schedule such drug in the same schedule as that recommended by the Secretary of Health and Human Services for authorized formulations of the drug. The recommendation referred to in the preceding sentence is contained in the last sentence of the fourth paragraph of the letter referred to in subparagraph (A) with respect to May 19, 1999.

"(2) FAILURE TO ISSUE ORDER.—If the final order is not issued within the period specified in paragraph (1), gamma hydroxybutyric acid (together with its salts, isomers, and salts of isomers) is deemed to be scheduled under section 202(c) of the Controlled Substances Act [21 U.S.C. 812(c)] in accordance with the policies described in paragraph (1), as if the Attorney General had issued a final order in accordance with such paragraph."

PLACEMENT OF PIPRADROL AND SPA IN SCHEDULE IV TO CARRY OUT OBLIGATION UNDER CONVENTION ON PSYCHOTROPIC SUBSTANCES

Section 102(c) of Pub. L. 95–633 provided that: "For the purpose of carrying out the minimum United States obligations under paragraph 7 of article 2 of the Convention on Psychotropic Substances, signed at Vienna, Austria, on February 21, 1971, with respect to pipradrol and SPA (also known as (-)-1-dimethylamino-1,2-diphenylethane), the Attorney General shall by order, made without regard to sections 201 and 202 of the Controlled Substances Act [this section and section 811 of this title], place such drugs in schedule IV of such Act [see subsec. (c) of this section]."

Provision of section 102(c) of Pub. L. 95–633, set out above, effective on the date the Convention on Psychotropic Substances enters into force in the United States [July 15, 1980], see section 112 of Pub. L. 95–633, set out as an Effective Date note under section 801a of this title.

§ 813. Treatment of controlled substance analogues

A controlled substance analogue shall, to the extent intended for human consumption, be treated, for the purposes of any Federal law as a controlled substance in schedule I.

(Pub. L. 91–513, title II, § 203, as added Pub. L. 99–570, title I, § 1202, Oct. 27, 1986, 100 Stat. 3207–13; amended Pub. L. 100–690, title VI, § 6470(c), Nov. 18, 1988, 102 Stat. 4378.)

REFERENCES IN TEXT

Schedule I, referred to in text, is set out in section 812(c) of this title.

AMENDMENTS

1988—Pub. L. 100–690 substituted "any Federal law" for "this subchapter and subchapter II of this chapter".

§ 814. Removal of exemption of certain drugs

(a) Removal of exemption

The Attorney General shall by regulation remove from exemption under section 802(39)(A)(iv) of this title a drug or group of drugs that the Attorney General finds is being diverted to obtain a listed chemical for use in the illicit production of a controlled substance.

(b) Factors to be considered

In removing a drug or group of drugs from exemption under subsection (a) of this section, the Attorney General shall consider, with respect to a drug or group of drugs that is proposed to be removed from exemption—

(1) the scope, duration, and significance of the diversion;

(2) whether the drug or group of drugs is formulated in such a way that it cannot be easily used in the illicit production of a controlled substance; and

(3) whether the listed chemical can be readily recovered from the drug or group of drugs.

(c) Specificity of designation

The Attorney General shall limit the designation of a drug or a group of drugs removed from exemption under subsection (a) of this section to the most particularly identifiable type of drug or group of drugs for which evidence of diversion exists unless there is evidence, based on the pattern of diversion and other relevant factors, that the diversion will not be limited to that particular drug or group of drugs.

(d) Reinstatement of exemption with respect to particular drug products

(1) Reinstatement

On application by a manufacturer of a particular drug product that has been removed from exemption under subsection (a) of this section, the Attorney General shall by regulation reinstate the exemption with respect to that particular drug product if the Attorney General determines that the particular drug product is manufactured and distributed in a manner that prevents diversion.

(2) Factors to be considered

In deciding whether to reinstate the exemption with respect to a particular drug product under paragraph (1), the Attorney General shall consider—

(A) the package sizes and manner of packaging of the drug product;

(B) the manner of distribution and advertising of the drug product;

(C) evidence of diversion of the drug product;

(D) any actions taken by the manufacturer to prevent diversion of the drug product; and

(E) such other factors as are relevant to and consistent with the public health and safety, including the factors described in subsection (b) of this section as applied to the drug product.

(3) Status pending application for reinstatement

A transaction involving a particular drug product that is the subject of a bona fide pending application for reinstatement of exemption filed with the Attorney General not later than 60 days after a regulation removing the exemption is issued pursuant to subsection (a) of this section shall not be considered to be a regulated transaction if the transaction occurs during the pendency of the application and, if the Attorney General denies the application, during the period of 60 days following the date on which the Attorney General denies the application, unless—

(A) the Attorney General has evidence that, applying the factors described in subsection (b) of this section to the drug product, the drug product is being diverted; and

(B) the Attorney General so notifies the applicant.

(4) Amendment and modification

A regulation reinstating an exemption under paragraph (1) may be modified or revoked with respect to a particular drug product upon a finding that—

(A) applying the factors described in subsection (b) of this section to the drug product, the drug product is being diverted; or

(B) there is a significant change in the data that led to the issuance of the regulation.

(Pub. L. 91–513, title II, §204, as added Pub. L. 103–200, §2(b)(1), Dec. 17, 1993, 107 Stat. 2334; amended Pub. L. 104–237, title IV, §401(c), Oct. 3, 1996, 110 Stat. 3108; Pub. L. 109–177, title VII, §712(a)(2), Mar. 9, 2006, 120 Stat. 263.)

AMENDMENTS

2006—Subsec. (e). Pub. L. 109–177 struck out subsec. (e). Text read as follows: "Pursuant to subsection (d)(1) of this section, the Attorney General shall by regulation reinstate the exemption with respect to a particular ephedrine, pseudoephedrine, or phenylpropanolamine drug product if the Attorney General determines that the drug product is manufactured and distributed in a manner that prevents diversion. In making this determination the Attorney General shall consider the factors listed in subsection (d)(2) of this section. Any regulation issued pursuant to this subsection may be amended or revoked based on the factors listed in subsection (d)(4) of this section."

1996—Subsec. (e). Pub. L. 104–237 added subsec. (e).

EFFECTIVE DATE OF 1996 AMENDMENT

Amendment by Pub. L. 104–237 not applicable to sale of any pseudoephedrine or phenylpropanolamine product prior to 12 months after Oct. 3, 1996, except that, on application of manufacturer of particular drug product, Attorney General may exercise sole and judicially unreviewable discretion to extend such effective date up to additional 6 months, see section 401(g) of Pub. L. 104–237, set out as a note under section 802 of this title.

EFFECTIVE DATE

Section effective on date that is 120 days after Dec. 17, 1993, see section 11 of Pub. L. 103–200, set out as an Effective Date of 1993 Amendment note under section 802 of this title.

PART C—REGISTRATION OF MANUFACTURERS, DISTRIBUTORS, AND DISPENSERS OF CONTROLLED SUBSTANCES

§821. Rules and regulations

The Attorney General is authorized to promulgate rules and regulations and to charge reasonable fees relating to the registration and control of the manufacture, distribution, and dispensing of controlled substances and to listed chemicals.

(Pub. L. 91–513, title II, §301, Oct. 27, 1970, 84 Stat. 1253; Pub. L. 103–200, §3(a), Dec. 17, 1993, 107 Stat. 2336; Pub. L. 108–447, div. B, title VI, §633(b), Dec. 8, 2004, 118 Stat. 2922.)

AMENDMENTS

2004—Pub. L. 108–447 substituted "listed chemicals" for "the registration and control of regulated persons and of regulated transactions".

1993—Pub. L. 103–200 inserted before period at end "and to the registration and control of regulated persons and of regulated transactions".

EFFECTIVE DATE OF 1993 AMENDMENT

Amendment by Pub. L. 103–200 effective on date that is 120 days after Dec. 17, 1993, see section 11 of Pub. L. 103–200, set out as a note under section 802 of this title.

§822. Persons required to register

(a) Period of registration

(1) Every person who manufactures or distributes any controlled substance or list I chemical, or who proposes to engage in the manufacture or distribution of any controlled substance or list I chemical, shall obtain annually a registration issued by the Attorney General in accordance with the rules and regulations promulgated by him.

(2) Every person who dispenses, or who proposes to dispense, any controlled substance, shall obtain from the Attorney General a registration issued in accordance with the rules and regulations promulgated by him. The Attorney General shall, by regulation, determine the period of such registrations. In no event, however, shall such registrations be issued for less than one year nor for more than three years.

(b) Authorized activities

Persons registered by the Attorney General under this subchapter to manufacture, distribute, or dispense controlled substances or list I chemicals are authorized to possess, manufacture, distribute, or dispense such substances or chemicals (including any such activity in the conduct of research) to the extent authorized by their registration and in conformity with the other provisions of this subchapter.

(c) Exceptions

The following persons shall not be required to register and may lawfully possess any controlled substance or list I chemical under this subchapter:

(1) An agent or employee of any registered manufacturer, distributor, or dispenser of any controlled substance or list I chemical if such agent or employee is acting in the usual course of his business or employment.

(2) A common or contract carrier or warehouseman, or an employee thereof, whose possession of the controlled substance or list I chemical is in the usual course of his business or employment.

(3) An ultimate user who possesses such substance for a purpose specified in section 802(25)[1] of this title.

(d) Waiver

The Attorney General may, by regulation, waive the requirement for registration of certain manufacturers, distributors, or dispensers if he finds it consistent with the public health and safety.

(e) Separate registration

A separate registration shall be required at each principal place of business or professional practice where the applicant manufactures, dis-

[1] See References in Text note below.

tributes, or dispenses controlled substances or list I chemicals.

(f) Inspection

The Attorney General is authorized to inspect the establishment of a registrant or applicant for registration in accordance with the rules and regulations promulgated by him.

(Pub. L. 91–513, title II, § 302, Oct. 27, 1970, 84 Stat. 1253; Pub. L. 98–473, title II, § 510, Oct. 12, 1984, 98 Stat. 2072; Pub. L. 103–200, § 3(b), Dec. 17, 1993, 107 Stat. 2336.)

REFERENCES IN TEXT

This subchapter, referred to in subsecs. (b) and (c), was in the original "this title", meaning title II of Pub. L. 91–513, Oct. 27, 1970, 84 Stat. 1242, as amended, and is popularly known as the "Controlled Substances Act". For complete classification of title II to the Code, see second paragraph of Short Title note set out under section 801 of this title and Tables.

Section 802(25) of this title, referred to in subsec. (c)(3), was redesignated section 802(26) of this title by Pub. L. 98–473, title II, § 507(a), Oct. 12, 1984, 98 Stat. 2071, and was further redesignated section 802(27) of this title by Pub. L. 99–570, title I, § 1003(b)(2), Oct. 27, 1986, 100 Stat. 3207–6.

AMENDMENTS

1993—Subsec. (a)(1). Pub. L. 103–200, § 3(b)(1), inserted "or list I chemical" after "controlled substance" in two places.

Subsec. (b). Pub. L. 103–200, § 3(b)(2), inserted "or list I chemicals" after "controlled substances" and "or chemicals" after "such substances".

Subsec. (c). Pub. L. 103–200, § 3(b)(3), inserted "or list I chemical" after "controlled substance" wherever appearing.

Subsec. (e). Pub. L. 103–200, § 3(b)(4), inserted "or list I chemicals" after "controlled substances".

1984—Subsec. (a). Pub. L. 98–473 designated existing provisions as par. (1), struck out provisions relating to dispensing controlled substances, and added par. (2).

EFFECTIVE DATE OF 1993 AMENDMENT

Amendment by Pub. L. 103–200 effective on date that is 120 days after Dec. 17, 1993, see section 11 of Pub. L. 103–200, set out as a note under section 802 of this title.

PROVISIONAL REGISTRATION

Section 703 of Pub. L. 91–513, as amended by Pub. L. 99–514, § 2, Oct. 22, 1986, 100 Stat. 2095, provided that:

"(a)(1) Any person who—

"(A) is engaged in manufacturing, distributing, or dispensing any controlled substance on the day before the effective date of section 302 [this section], and

"(B) is registered on such day under section 510 of the Federal Food, Drug, and Cosmetic Act [section 360 of this title] or under section 4722 of the Internal Revenue Code of 1986 [formerly I.R.C. 1954, section 4722 of Title 26],

shall, with respect to each establishment for which such registration is in effect under any such section, be deemed to have a provisional registration under section 303 [section 823 of this title] for the manufacture, distribution, or dispensing (as the case may be) of controlled substances.

"(2) During the period his provisional registration is in effect under this section, the registration number assigned such person under such section 510 [section 360 of this title] or under such section 4722 [section 4722 of Title 26] (as the case may be) shall be his registration number for purposes of section 303 of this title [section 823 of this title].

"(b) The provisions of section 304 [section 824 of this title], relating to suspension and revocation of registration, shall apply to a provisional registration under this section.

"(c) Unless sooner suspended or revoked under subsection (b), a provisional registration of a person under subsection (a)(1) of this section shall be in effect until—

"(1) the date on which such person has registered with the Attorney General under section 303 [section 823 of this title] or has had his registration denied under such section, or

"(2) such date as may be prescribed by the Attorney General for registration of manufacturers, distributors, or dispensers, as the case may be,

whichever occurs first."

§ 823. Registration requirements

(a) Manufacturers of controlled substances in schedule I or II

The Attorney General shall register an applicant to manufacture controlled substances in schedule I or II if he determines that such registration is consistent with the public interest and with United States obligations under international treaties, conventions, or protocols in effect on May 1, 1971. In determining the public interest, the following factors shall be considered:

(1) maintenance of effective controls against diversion of particular controlled substances and any controlled substance in schedule I or II compounded therefrom into other than legitimate medical, scientific, research, or industrial channels, by limiting the importation and bulk manufacture of such controlled substances to a number of establishments which can produce an adequate and uninterrupted supply of these substances under adequately competitive conditions for legitimate medical, scientific, research, and industrial purposes;

(2) compliance with applicable State and local law;

(3) promotion of technical advances in the art of manufacturing these substances and the development of new substances;

(4) prior conviction record of applicant under Federal and State laws relating to the manufacture, distribution, or dispensing of such substances;

(5) past experience in the manufacture of controlled substances, and the existence in the establishment of effective control against diversion; and

(6) such other factors as may be relevant to and consistent with the public health and safety.

(b) Distributors of controlled substances in schedule I or II

The Attorney General shall register an applicant to distribute a controlled substance in schedule I or II unless he determines that the issuance of such registration is inconsistent with the public interest. In determining the public interest, the following factors shall be considered:

(1) maintenance of effective control against diversion of particular controlled substances into other than legitimate medical, scientific, and industrial channels;

(2) compliance with applicable State and local law;

(3) prior conviction record of applicant under Federal or State laws relating to the manufacture, distribution, or dispensing of such substances;

(4) past experience in the distribution of controlled substances; and

(5) such other factors as may be relevant to and consistent with the public health and safety.

(c) Limits of authorized activities

Registration granted under subsections (a) and (b) of this section shall not entitle a registrant to (1) manufacture or distribute controlled substances in schedule I or II other than those specified in the registration, or (2) manufacture any quantity of those controlled substances in excess of the quota assigned pursuant to section 826 of this title.

(d) Manufacturers of controlled substances in schedule III, IV, or V

The Attorney General shall register an applicant to manufacture controlled substances in schedule III, IV, or V, unless he determines that the issuance of such registration is inconsistent with the public interest. In determining the public interest, the following factors shall be considered:

(1) maintenance of effective controls against diversion of particular controlled substances and any controlled substance in schedule III, IV, or V compounded therefrom into other than legitimate medical, scientific, or industrial channels;

(2) compliance with applicable State and local law;

(3) promotion of technical advances in the art of manufacturing these substances and the development of new substances;

(4) prior conviction record of applicant under Federal or State laws relating to the manufacture, distribution, or dispensing of such substances;

(5) past experience in the manufacture, distribution, and dispensing of controlled substances, and the existence in the establishment of effective controls against diversion; and

(6) such other factors as may be relevant to and consistent with the public health and safety.

(e) Distributors of controlled substances in schedule III, IV, or V

The Attorney General shall register an applicant to distribute controlled substances in schedule III, IV, or V, unless he determines that the issuance of such registration is inconsistent with the public interest. In determining the public interest, the following factors shall be considered:

(1) maintenance of effective controls against diversion of particular controlled substances into other than legitimate medical, scientific, and industrial channels;

(2) compliance with applicable State and local law;

(3) prior conviction record of applicant under Federal or State laws relating to the manufacture, distribution, or dispensing of such substances;

(4) past experience in the distribution of controlled substances; and

(5) such other factors as may be relevant to and consistent with the public health and safety.

(f) Research by practitioners; pharmacies; research applications; construction of Article 7 of the Convention on Psychotropic Substances

The Attorney General shall register practitioners (including pharmacies, as distinguished from pharmacists) to dispense, or conduct research with, controlled substances in schedule II, III, IV, or V and shall modify the registrations of pharmacies so registered to authorize them to dispense controlled substances by means of the Internet, if the applicant is authorized to dispense, or conduct research with respect to, controlled substances under the laws of the State in which he practices. The Attorney General may deny an application for such registration or such modification of registration if the Attorney General determines that the issuance of such registration or modification would be inconsistent with the public interest. In determining the public interest, the following factors shall be considered:

(1) The recommendation of the appropriate State licensing board or professional disciplinary authority.

(2) The applicant's experience in dispensing, or conducting research with respect to controlled substances.

(3) The applicant's conviction record under Federal or State laws relating to the manufacture, distribution, or dispensing of controlled substances.

(4) Compliance with applicable State, Federal, or local laws relating to controlled substances.

(5) Such other conduct which may threaten the public health and safety.

Separate registration under this part for practitioners engaging in research with controlled substances in schedule II, III, IV, or V, who are already registered under this part in another capacity, shall not be required. Registration applications by practitioners wishing to conduct research with controlled substances in schedule I shall be referred to the Secretary, who shall determine the qualifications and competency of each practitioner requesting registration, as well as the merits of the research protocol. The Secretary, in determining the merits of each research protocol, shall consult with the Attorney General as to effective procedures to adequately safeguard against diversion of such controlled substances from legitimate medical or scientific use. Registration for the purpose of bona fide research with controlled substances in schedule I by a practitioner deemed qualified by the Secretary may be denied by the Attorney General only on a ground specified in section 824(a) of this title. Article 7 of the Convention on Psychotropic Substances shall not be construed to prohibit, or impose additional restrictions upon, research involving drugs or other substances scheduled under the convention which is conducted in conformity with this subsection and other applicable provisions of this subchapter.

(g) Practitioners dispensing narcotic drugs for narcotic treatment; annual registration; separate registration; qualifications; waiver

(1) Except as provided in paragraph (2), practitioners who dispense narcotic drugs to individ-

uals for maintenance treatment or detoxification treatment shall obtain annually a separate registration for that purpose. The Attorney General shall register an applicant to dispense narcotic drugs to individuals for maintenance treatment or detoxification treatment (or both)

(A) if the applicant is a practitioner who is determined by the Secretary to be qualified (under standards established by the Secretary) to engage in the treatment with respect to which registration is sought;

(B) if the Attorney General determines that the applicant will comply with standards established by the Attorney General respecting (i) security of stocks of narcotic drugs for such treatment, and (ii) the maintenance of records (in accordance with section 827 of this title) on such drugs; and

(C) if the Secretary determines that the applicant will comply with standards established by the Secretary (after consultation with the Attorney General) respecting the quantities of narcotic drugs which may be provided for unsupervised use by individuals in such treatment.

(2)(A) Subject to subparagraphs (D) and (J), the requirements of paragraph (1) are waived in the case of the dispensing (including the prescribing), by a practitioner, of narcotic drugs in schedule III, IV, or V or combinations of such drugs if the practitioner meets the conditions specified in subparagraph (B) and the narcotic drugs or combinations of such drugs meet the conditions specified in subparagraph (C).

(B) For purposes of subparagraph (A), the conditions specified in this subparagraph with respect to a practitioner are that, before the initial dispensing of narcotic drugs in schedule III, IV, or V or combinations of such drugs to patients for maintenance or detoxification treatment, the practitioner submit to the Secretary a notification of the intent of the practitioner to begin dispensing the drugs or combinations for such purpose, and that the notification contain the following certifications by the practitioner:

(i) The practitioner is a qualifying physician (as defined in subparagraph (G)).

(ii) With respect to patients to whom the practitioner will provide such drugs or combinations of drugs, the practitioner has the capacity to refer the patients for appropriate counseling and other appropriate ancillary services.

(iii) The total number of such patients of the practitioner at any one time will not exceed the applicable number. For purposes of this clause, the applicable number is 30, unless, not sooner than 1 year after the date on which the practitioner submitted the initial notification, the practitioner submits a second notification to the Secretary of the need and intent of the practitioner to treat up to 100 patients. A second notification under this clause shall contain the certifications required by clauses (i) and (ii) of this subparagraph. The Secretary may by regulation change such total number.

(C) For purposes of subparagraph (A), the conditions specified in this subparagraph with respect to narcotic drugs in schedule III, IV, or V or combinations of such drugs are as follows:

(i) The drugs or combinations of drugs have, under the Federal Food, Drug, and Cosmetic Act [21 U.S.C. 301 et seq.] or section 262 of title 42, been approved for use in maintenance or detoxification treatment.

(ii) The drugs or combinations of drugs have not been the subject of an adverse determination. For purposes of this clause, an adverse determination is a determination published in the Federal Register and made by the Secretary, after consultation with the Attorney General, that the use of the drugs or combinations of drugs for maintenance or detoxification treatment requires additional standards respecting the qualifications of practitioners to provide such treatment, or requires standards respecting the quantities of the drugs that may be provided for unsupervised use.

(D)(i) A waiver under subparagraph (A) with respect to a practitioner is not in effect unless (in addition to conditions under subparagraphs (B) and (C)) the following conditions are met:

(I) The notification under subparagraph (B) is in writing and states the name of the practitioner.

(II) The notification identifies the registration issued for the practitioner pursuant to subsection (f) of this section.

(III) If the practitioner is a member of a group practice, the notification states the names of the other practitioners in the practice and identifies the registrations issued for the other practitioners pursuant to subsection (f) of this section.

(ii) Upon receiving a notification under subparagraph (B), the Attorney General shall assign the practitioner involved an identification number under this paragraph for inclusion with the registration issued for the practitioner pursuant to subsection (f) of this section. The identification number so assigned shall be appropriate to preserve the confidentiality of patients for whom the practitioner has dispensed narcotic drugs under a waiver under subparagraph (A).

(iii) Not later than 45 days after the date on which the Secretary receives a notification under subparagraph (B), the Secretary shall make a determination of whether the practitioner involved meets all requirements for a waiver under subparagraph (B). If the Secretary fails to make such determination by the end of the such 45-day period, the Attorney General shall assign the physician an identification number described in clause (ii) at the end of such period.

(E)(i) If a practitioner is not registered under paragraph (1) and, in violation of the conditions specified in subparagraphs (B) through (D), dispenses narcotic drugs in schedule III, IV, or V or combinations of such drugs for maintenance treatment or detoxification treatment, the Attorney General may, for purposes of section 824(a)(4) of this title, consider the practitioner to have committed an act that renders the registration of the practitioner pursuant to subsection (f) of this section to be inconsistent with the public interest.

(ii)(I) Upon the expiration of 45 days from the date on which the Secretary receives a notification under subparagraph (B), a practitioner who in good faith submits a notification under subparagraph (B) and reasonably believes that the conditions specified in subparagraphs (B) through (D) have been met shall, in dispensing narcotic drugs in schedule III, IV, or V or combinations of such drugs for maintenance treatment or detoxification treatment, be considered to have a waiver under subparagraph (A) until notified otherwise by the Secretary, except that such a practitioner may commence to prescribe or dispense such narcotic drugs for such purposes prior to the expiration of such 45-day period if it facilitates the treatment of an individual patient and both the Secretary and the Attorney General are notified by the practitioner of the intent to commence prescribing or dispensing such narcotic drugs.

(II) For purposes of subclause (I), the publication in the Federal Register of an adverse determination by the Secretary pursuant to subparagraph (C)(ii) shall (with respect to the narcotic drug or combination involved) be considered to be a notification provided by the Secretary to practitioners, effective upon the expiration of the 30-day period beginning on the date on which the adverse determination is so published.

(F)(i) With respect to the dispensing of narcotic drugs in schedule III, IV, or V or combinations of such drugs to patients for maintenance or detoxification treatment, a practitioner may, in his or her discretion, dispense such drugs or combinations for such treatment under a registration under paragraph (1) or a waiver under subparagraph (A) (subject to meeting the applicable conditions).

(ii) This paragraph may not be construed as having any legal effect on the conditions for obtaining a registration under paragraph (1), including with respect to the number of patients who may be served under such a registration.

(G) For purposes of this paragraph:

(i) The term "group practice" has the meaning given such term in section 1395nn(h)(4) of title 42.

(ii) The term "qualifying physician" means a physician who is licensed under State law and who meets one or more of the following conditions:

(I) The physician holds a subspecialty board certification in addiction psychiatry from the American Board of Medical Specialties.

(II) The physician holds an addiction certification from the American Society of Addiction Medicine.

(III) The physician holds a subspecialty board certification in addiction medicine from the American Osteopathic Association.

(IV) The physician has, with respect to the treatment and management of opiate-dependent patients, completed not less than eight hours of training (through classroom situations, seminars at professional society meetings, electronic communications, or otherwise) that is provided by the American Society of Addiction Medicine, the American Academy of Addiction Psychiatry, the American Medical Association, the American Osteopathic Association, the American Psychiatric Association, or any other organization that the Secretary determines is appropriate for purposes of this subclause.

(V) The physician has participated as an investigator in one or more clinical trials leading to the approval of a narcotic drug in schedule III, IV, or V for maintenance or detoxification treatment, as demonstrated by a statement submitted to the Secretary by the sponsor of such approved drug.

(VI) The physician has such other training or experience as the State medical licensing board (of the State in which the physician will provide maintenance or detoxification treatment) considers to demonstrate the ability of the physician to treat and manage opiate-dependent patients.

(VII) The physician has such other training or experience as the Secretary considers to demonstrate the ability of the physician to treat and manage opiate-dependent patients. Any criteria of the Secretary under this subclause shall be established by regulation. Any such criteria are effective only for 3 years after the date on which the criteria are promulgated, but may be extended for such additional discrete 3-year periods as the Secretary considers appropriate for purposes of this subclause. Such an extension of criteria may only be effectuated through a statement published in the Federal Register by the Secretary during the 30-day period preceding the end of the 3-year period involved.

(H)(i) In consultation with the Administrator of the Drug Enforcement Administration, the Administrator of the Substance Abuse and Mental Health Services Administration, the Director of the National Institute on Drug Abuse, and the Commissioner of Food and Drugs, the Secretary shall issue regulations (through notice and comment rulemaking) or issue practice guidelines to address the following:

(I) Approval of additional credentialing bodies and the responsibilities of additional credentialing bodies.

(II) Additional exemptions from the requirements of this paragraph and any regulations under this paragraph.

Nothing in such regulations or practice guidelines may authorize any Federal official or employee to exercise supervision or control over the practice of medicine or the manner in which medical services are provided.

(ii) Not later than 120 days after October 17, 2000, the Secretary shall issue a treatment improvement protocol containing best practice guidelines for the treatment and maintenance of opiate-dependent patients. The Secretary shall develop the protocol in consultation with the Director of the National Institute on Drug Abuse, the Administrator of the Drug Enforcement Administration, the Commissioner of Food and Drugs, the Administrator of the Substance Abuse and Mental Health Services Administration and other substance abuse disorder professionals. The protocol shall be guided by science.

(I) During the 3-year period beginning on the date of approval by the Food and Drug Administration of a drug in schedule III, IV, or V, a State may not preclude a practitioner from dispensing or prescribing such drug, or combination of such drugs, to patients for maintenance or detoxification treatment in accordance with this paragraph unless, before the expiration of that 3-year period, the State enacts a law prohibiting a practitioner from dispensing such drugs or combinations of drug.[1]

(J)(i) This paragraph takes effect the date referred to in subparagraph (I), and remains in effect thereafter.

(ii) For purposes relating to clause (iii), the Secretary and the Attorney General may, during the 3-year period beginning on December 29, 2006, make determinations in accordance with the following:

(I) The Secretary may make a determination of whether treatments provided under waivers under subparagraph (A) have been effective forms of maintenance treatment and detoxification treatment in clinical settings; may make a determination of whether such waivers have significantly increased (relative to the beginning of such period) the availability of maintenance treatment and detoxification treatment; and may make a determination of whether such waivers have adverse consequences for the public health.

(II) The Attorney General may make a determination of the extent to which there have been violations of the numerical limitations established under subparagraph (B) for the number of individuals to whom a practitioner may provide treatment; may make a determination of whether waivers under subparagraph (A) have increased (relative to the beginning of such period) the extent to which narcotic drugs in schedule III, IV, or V or combinations of such drugs are being dispensed or possessed in violation of this chapter; and may make a determination of whether such waivers have adverse consequences for the public health.

(iii) If, before the expiration of the period specified in clause (ii), the Secretary or the Attorney General publishes in the Federal Register a decision, made on the basis of determinations under such clause, that subparagraph (B)(iii) should be applied by limiting the total number of patients a practitioner may treat to 30, then the provisions in such subparagraph (B)(iii) permitting more than 30 patients shall not apply, effective 60 days after the date on which the decision is so published. The Secretary shall in making any such decision consult with the Attorney General, and shall in publishing the decision in the Federal Register include any comments received from the Attorney General for inclusion in the publication. The Attorney General shall in making any such decision consult with the Secretary, and shall in publishing the decision in the Federal Register include any comments received from the Secretary for inclusion in the publication.

(h) Applicants for distribution of list I chemicals

The Attorney General shall register an applicant to distribute a list I chemical unless the Attorney General determines that registration of the applicant is inconsistent with the public interest. Registration under this subsection shall not be required for the distribution of a drug product that is exempted under clause (iv) or (v) of section 802(39)(A) of this title. In determining the public interest for the purposes of this subsection, the Attorney General shall consider—

(1) maintenance by the applicant of effective controls against diversion of listed chemicals into other than legitimate channels;

(2) compliance by the applicant with applicable Federal, State, and local law;

(3) any prior conviction record of the applicant under Federal or State laws relating to controlled substances or to chemicals controlled under Federal or State law;

(4) any past experience of the applicant in the manufacture and distribution of chemicals; and

(5) such other factors as are relevant to and consistent with the public health and safety.

(Pub. L. 91–513, title II, § 303, Oct. 27, 1970, 84 Stat. 1253; Pub. L. 93–281, § 3, May 14, 1974, 88 Stat. 124; Pub. L. 95–633, title I, § 109, Nov. 10, 1978, 92 Stat. 3773; Pub. L. 98–473, title II, § 511, Oct. 12, 1984, 98 Stat. 2073; Pub. L. 103–200, § 3(c), Dec. 17, 1993, 107 Stat. 2336; Pub. L. 106–310, div. B, title XXXV, § 3502(a), Oct. 17, 2000, 114 Stat. 1222; Pub. L. 107–273, div. B, title II, § 2501, Nov. 2, 2002, 116 Stat. 1803; Pub. L. 109–56, § 1(a), (b), Aug. 2, 2005, 119 Stat. 591; Pub. L. 109–177, title VII, § 712(a)(3), Mar. 9, 2006, 120 Stat. 263; Pub. L. 109–469, title XI, § 1102, Dec. 29, 2006, 120 Stat. 3540; Pub. L. 110–425, § 3(b), Oct. 15, 2008, 122 Stat. 4824.)

REFERENCES IN TEXT

Schedules I, II, III, IV, and V, referred to in subsecs. (a) to (f) and (g)(2), are set out in section 812(c) of this title.

The Federal Food, Drug, and Cosmetic Act, referred to in subsec. (g)(2)(C)(i), is act June 25, 1938, ch. 675, 52 Stat. 1040, as amended, which is classified generally to chapter 9 (§ 301 et seq.) of this title. For complete classification of this Act to the Code, see section 301 of this title and Tables.

This chapter, referred to in subsec. (g)(2)(J)(ii)(II), was in the original "this Act", meaning Pub. L. 91–513, Oct. 27, 1970, 84 Stat. 1236, as amended. For complete classification of this Act to the Code, see Short Title note set out under section 801 of this title and Tables.

AMENDMENTS

2008—Subsec. (f). Pub. L. 110–425, in introductory provisions, inserted "and shall modify the registrations of pharmacies so registered to authorize them to dispense controlled substances by means of the Internet" after "schedule II, III, IV, or V" and substituted "or such modification of registration if the Attorney General determines that the issuance of such registration or modification" for "if he determines that the issuance of such registration".

2006—Subsec. (g)(2)(B)(iii). Pub. L. 109–469, § 1102(1), substituted "unless, not sooner than 1 year after the date on which the practitioner submitted the initial notification, the practitioner submits a second notification to the Secretary of the need and intent of the practitioner to treat up to 100 patients. A second notification under this clause shall contain the certifications required by clauses (i) and (ii) of this subparagraph. The" for "except that the".

Subsec. (g)(2)(J)(i). Pub. L. 109–469, § 1102(2)(A), substituted "thereafter." for "thereafter except as provided in clause (iii) (relating to a decision by the Secretary or the Attorney General that this paragraph should not remain in effect)."

Subsec. (g)(2)(J)(ii). Pub. L. 109–469, § 1102(2)(B), substituted "December 29, 2006" for "October 17, 2000" in introductory provisions.

[1] So in original. Probably should be "combinations of drugs.".

Subsec. (g)(2)(J)(iii). Pub. L. 109–469, § 1102(2)(C), substituted "subparagraph (B)(iii) should be applied by limiting the total number of patients a practitioner may treat to 30, then the provisions in such subparagraph (B)(iii) permitting more than 30 patients shall not apply, effective" for "this paragraph should not remain in effect, this paragraph ceases to be in effect".

Subsec. (h). Pub. L. 109–177 substituted "clause (iv) or (v) of section 802(39)(A) of this title" for "section 802(39)(A)(iv) of this title" in introductory provisions.

2005—Subsec. (g)(2)(B)(iii). Pub. L. 109–56, § 1(b), substituted "The total" for "In any case in which the practitioner is not in a group practice, the total".

Subsec. (g)(2)(B)(iv). Pub. L. 109–56, § 1(a), struck out cl. (iv) which read as follows: "In any case in which the practitioner is in a group practice, the total number of such patients of the group practice at any one time will not exceed the applicable number. For purposes of this clause, the applicable number is 30, except that the Secretary may by regulation change such total number, and the Secretary for such purposes may by regulation establish different categories on the basis of the number of practitioners in a group practice and establish for the various categories different numerical limitations on the number of such patients that the group practice may have."

2002—Subsec. (g)(2)(I). Pub. L. 107–273, § 2501(1), which directed the substitution of "on the date of approval by the Food and Drug Administration of a drug in schedule III, IV, or V, a State may not preclude a practitioner from dispensing or prescribing such drug, or combination of such drugs," for "on October 17, 2000, a State may not preclude a practitioner from dispensing or prescribing drugs in schedule III, IV, or V, or combinations of such drugs,", was executed by making the substitution for the phrase which in the original began with "on the date of the enactment of the Drug Addiction Treatment Act of 2000," rather than the editorial translation "on October 17, 2000," to reflect the probable intent of Congress.

Subsec. (g)(2)(J)(i). Pub. L. 107–273, § 2501(2), which directed the substitution of "the date referred to in subparagraph (I)," for "October 17, 2000," was executed by making the substitution for text which in the original read "the date of the enactment of the Drug Addiction Treatment Act of 2000," rather than the editorial translation "October 17, 2000," to reflect the probable intent of Congress.

2000—Subsec. (g). Pub. L. 106–310 designated existing provisions as par. (1), substituted "Except as provided in paragraph (2), practitioners who dispense" for "Practitioners who dispense", redesignated former pars. (1) to (3) as subpars. (A) to (C), respectively, of par. (1) and redesignated former subpars. (A) and (B) of former par. (2) as cls. (i) and (ii), respectively, of subpar. (B) of par. (1), and added par. (2).

1993—Subsec. (h). Pub. L. 103–200 added subsec. (h).

1984—Subsec. (f). Pub. L. 98–473 amended subsec. (f) generally, substituting provisions relating to registration authority of Attorney General respecting dispensation or conduct of research with controlled research, and separate authority of Secretary respecting registration, for provisions relating to general registration requirements respecting dispensation or conduct of research with controlled or nonnarcotic controlled substances.

1978—Subsec. (f). Pub. L. 95–633 inserted provision relating to the construction of the Convention on Psychotropic Substances.

1974—Subsec. (g). Pub. L. 93–281 added subsec. (g).

EFFECTIVE DATE OF 2008 AMENDMENT

Amendment by Pub. L. 110–425 effective 180 days after Oct. 15, 2008, except as otherwise provided, see section 3(j) of Pub. L. 110–425, set out as a note under section 802 of this title.

EFFECTIVE DATE OF 2005 AMENDMENT

Pub. L. 109–56, § 1(c), Aug. 2, 2005, 119 Stat. 591, provided that: "This section [amending this section] shall take effect on the date of enactment of this Act [Aug. 2, 2005]."

EFFECTIVE DATE OF 1993 AMENDMENT

Amendment by Pub. L. 103–200 effective on date that is 120 days after Dec. 17, 1993, see section 11 of Pub. L. 103–200, set out as a note under section 802 of this title.

EFFECTIVE DATE OF 1978 AMENDMENT

Amendment by Pub. L. 95–633 effective on date the Convention on Psychotropic Substances enters into force in the United States [July 15, 1980], see section 112 of Pub. L. 95–633, set out as an Effective Date note under section 801a of this title.

PROVISIONAL REGISTRATION

For provisional registration of persons engaged in manufacturing, distributing, or dispensing of controlled substances on the day before the effective date of section 822 of this title who are registered on such date under section 360 of this title or section 4722 of Title 26, Internal Revenue Code, see section 703 of Pub. L. 91–513, set out as a note under section 822 of this title.

§ 824. Denial, revocation, or suspension of registration

(a) Grounds

A registration pursuant to section 823 of this title to manufacture, distribute, or dispense a controlled substance or a list I chemical may be suspended or revoked by the Attorney General upon a finding that the registrant—

(1) has materially falsified any application filed pursuant to or required by this subchapter or subchapter II of this chapter;

(2) has been convicted of a felony under this subchapter or subchapter II of this chapter or any other law of the United States, or of any State, relating to any substance defined in this subchapter as a controlled substance or a list I chemical;

(3) has had his State license or registration suspended, revoked, or denied by competent State authority and is no longer authorized by State law to engage in the manufacturing, distribution, or dispensing of controlled substances or list I chemicals or has had the suspension, revocation, or denial of his registration recommended by competent State authority;

(4) has committed such acts as would render his registration under section 823 of this title inconsistent with the public interest as determined under such section; or

(5) has been excluded (or directed to be excluded) from participation in a program pursuant to section 1320a–7(a) of title 42.

A registration pursuant to section 823(g)(1) of this title to dispense a narcotic drug for maintenance treatment or detoxification treatment may be suspended or revoked by the Attorney General upon a finding that the registrant has failed to comply with any standard referred to in section 823(g)(1) of this title.

(b) Limits of revocation or suspension

The Attorney General may limit revocation or suspension of a registration to the particular controlled substance or list I chemical with respect to which grounds for revocation or suspension exist.

(c) Service of show cause order; proceedings

Before taking action pursuant to this section, or pursuant to a denial of registration under section 823 of this title, the Attorney General shall serve upon the applicant or registrant an order to show cause why registration should not be denied, revoked, or suspended. The order to show cause shall contain a statement of the basis thereof and shall call upon the applicant or registrant to appear before the Attorney General at a time and place stated in the order, but in no event less than thirty days after the date of receipt of the order. Proceedings to deny, revoke, or suspend shall be conducted pursuant to this section in accordance with subchapter II of chapter 5 of title 5. Such proceedings shall be independent of, and not in lieu of, criminal prosecutions or other proceedings under this subchapter or any other law of the United States.

(d) Suspension of registration in cases of imminent danger

The Attorney General may, in his discretion, suspend any registration simultaneously with the institution of proceedings under this section, in cases where he finds that there is an imminent danger to the public health or safety. A failure to comply with a standard referred to in section 823(g)(1) of this title may be treated under this subsection as grounds for immediate suspension of a registration granted under such section. A suspension under this subsection shall continue in effect until the conclusion of such proceedings, including judicial review thereof, unless sooner withdrawn by the Attorney General or dissolved by a court of competent jurisdiction.

(e) Suspension and revocation of quotas

The suspension or revocation of a registration under this section shall operate to suspend or revoke any quota applicable under section 826 of this title.

(f) Disposition of controlled substances or list I chemicals

In the event the Attorney General suspends or revokes a registration granted under section 823 of this title, all controlled substances or list I chemicals owned or possessed by the registrant pursuant to such registration at the time of suspension or the effective date of the revocation order, as the case may be, may, in the discretion of the Attorney General, be placed under seal. No disposition may be made of any controlled substances or list I chemicals under seal until the time for taking an appeal has elapsed or until all appeals have been concluded except that a court, upon application therefor, may at any time order the sale of perishable controlled substances or list I chemicals. Any such order shall require the deposit of the proceeds of the sale with the court. Upon a revocation order becoming final, all such controlled substances or list I chemicals (or proceeds of sale deposited in court) shall be forfeited to the United States; and the Attorney General shall dispose of such controlled substances or list I chemicals in accordance with section 881(e) of this title. All right, title, and interest in such controlled substances or list I chemicals shall vest in the United States upon a revocation order becoming final.

(g) Seizure or placement under seal of controlled substances or list I chemicals

The Attorney General may, in his discretion, seize or place under seal any controlled substances or list I chemicals owned or possessed by a registrant whose registration has expired or who has ceased to practice or do business in the manner contemplated by his registration. Such controlled substances or list I chemicals shall be held for the benefit of the registrant, or his successor in interest. The Attorney General shall notify a registrant, or his successor in interest, who has any controlled substance or list I chemical seized or placed under seal of the procedures to be followed to secure the return of the controlled substance or list I chemical and the conditions under which it will be returned. The Attorney General may not dispose of any controlled substance or list I chemical seized or placed under seal under this subsection until the expiration of one hundred and eighty days from the date such substance or chemical was seized or placed under seal.

(Pub. L. 91–513, title II, § 304, Oct. 27, 1970, 84 Stat. 1255; Pub. L. 93–281, § 4, May 14, 1974, 88 Stat. 125; Pub. L. 98–473, title II, §§ 304, 512, 513, Oct. 12, 1984, 98 Stat. 2050, 2073; Pub. L. 100–93, § 8(j), Aug. 18, 1987, 101 Stat. 695; Pub. L. 103–200, § 3(d), Dec. 17, 1993, 107 Stat. 2337; Pub. L. 103–322, title XXXIII, § 330024(e), Sept. 13, 1994, 108 Stat. 2151; Pub. L. 106–310, div. B, title XXXV, § 3502(b), Oct. 17, 2000, 114 Stat. 1227.)

REFERENCES IN TEXT

This subchapter, referred to in subsec. (a)(1), (2), was in the original "this title", meaning title II of Pub. L. 91–513, Oct. 27, 1970, 84 Stat. 1242, as amended, and is popularly known as the "Controlled Substances Act". For complete classification of title II to the Code, see second paragraph of Short Title note set out under section 801 of this title and Tables.

Subchapter II of this chapter, referred to in subsec. (a)(1), (2), was in the original "title III", meaning title III of Pub. L. 91–513, Oct. 27, 1970, 84 Stat. 1285. Part A of title III comprises subchapter II of this chapter. For classification of Part B, consisting of sections 1101 to 1105 of title III, see Tables.

AMENDMENTS

2000—Subsec. (a). Pub. L. 106–310, § 3502(b)(1), substituted "section 823(g)(1) of this title" for "section 823(g) of this title" in two places in concluding provisions.

Subsec. (d). Pub. L. 106–310, § 3502(b)(2), substituted "section 823(g)(1) of this title" for "section 823(g) of this title".

1994—Subsec. (g). Pub. L. 103–322 inserted "or chemical" after "such substance" in last sentence.

1993—Subsec. (a). Pub. L. 103–200, § 3(d)(1), inserted "or a list I chemical" after "controlled substance" in introductory provisions and par. (2) and inserted "or list I chemicals" after "controlled substances" in par. (3).

Subsec. (b). Pub. L. 103–200, § 3(d)(2), inserted "or list I chemical" after "controlled substance".

Subsec. (f). Pub. L. 103–200, § 3(d)(3), inserted "or list I chemicals" after "controlled substances" wherever appearing.

Subsec. (g). Pub. L. 103–200, § 3(d)(4), inserted "or list I chemicals" after "controlled substances" in two places and "or list I chemical" after "controlled substance" wherever appearing.

1987—Subsec. (a)(5). Pub. L. 100–93 added par. (5).

1984—Subsec. (a)(3). Pub. L. 98–473, § 512(1), inserted provisions relating to suspension, etc., recommended by competent State authority.

Subsec. (a)(4). Pub. L. 98–473, §512(2), added par. (4).

Subsec. (f). Pub. L. 98–473, §304, inserted provisions relating to vesting of right, title, and interest in the United States.

Subsec. (g). Pub. L. 98–473, §513, added subsec. (g).

1974—Subsec. (a). Pub. L. 93–281, §4(a), provided for revocation or suspension of a registration pursuant to section 823(g) of this title for failure of a registrant to comply with standards referred to in such section 823(g).

Subsec. (d). Pub. L. 93–281, §4(b), substituted "A suspension under this subsection" for "Such suspension" in third sentence.

EFFECTIVE DATE OF 1994 AMENDMENT

Amendment by Pub. L. 103–322 effective 120 days after Dec. 17, 1993, see section 330024(f) of Pub. L. 103–322, set out as a note under section 802 of this title.

EFFECTIVE DATE OF 1993 AMENDMENT

Amendment by Pub. L. 103–200 effective on date that is 120 days after Dec. 17, 1993, see section 11 of Pub. L. 103–200, set out as a note under section 802 of this title.

EFFECTIVE DATE OF 1987 AMENDMENT

Amendment by Pub. L. 100–93 effective at end of fourteen-day period beginning Aug. 18, 1987, and inapplicable to administrative proceedings commenced before end of such period, see section 15(a) of Pub. L. 100–93, set out as a note under section 1320a–7 of Title 42, The Public Health and Welfare.

PROVISIONAL REGISTRATION

Applicability of this section to provisional registrations, see section 703 of Pub. L. 91–513, set out as a note under section 822 of this title.

§825. Labeling and packaging

(a) Symbol

It shall be unlawful to distribute a controlled substance in a commercial container unless such container, when and as required by regulations of the Attorney General, bears a label (as defined in section 321(k) of this title) containing an identifying symbol for such substance in accordance with such regulations. A different symbol shall be required for each schedule of controlled substances.

(b) Unlawful distribution without identifying symbol

It shall be unlawful for the manufacturer of any controlled substance to distribute such substance unless the labeling (as defined in section 321(m) of this title) of such substance contains, when and as required by regulations of the Attorney General, the identifying symbol required under subsection (a) of this section.

(c) Warning on label

The Secretary shall prescribe regulations under section 353(b) of this title which shall provide that the label of a drug listed in schedule II, III, or IV shall, when dispensed to or for a patient, contain a clear, concise warning that it is a crime to transfer the drug to any person other than the patient.

(d) Containers to be securely sealed

It shall be unlawful to distribute controlled substances in schedule I or II, and narcotic drugs in schedule III or IV, unless the bottle or other container, stopper, covering, or wrapper thereof is securely sealed as required by regulations of the Attorney General.

(Pub. L. 91–513, title II, §305, Oct. 27, 1970, 84 Stat. 1256.)

REFERENCES IN TEXT

Schedules I, II, III, and IV, referred to in subsecs. (c) and (d), are set out in section 812(c) of this title.

EFFECTIVE DATE

Section effective on first day of seventh calendar month that begins after Oct. 26, 1970, but with Attorney General authorized to postpone such effective date for such period as he might determine to be necessary for the efficient administration of this subchapter, see section 704(c) of Pub. L. 91–513, set out as a note under section 801 of this title.

§826. Production quotas for controlled substances

(a) Establishment of total annual needs

The Attorney General shall determine the total quantity and establish production quotas for each basic class of controlled substance in schedules I and II and for ephedrine, pseudoephedrine, and phenylpropanolamine to be manufactured each calendar year to provide for the estimated medical, scientific, research, and industrial needs of the United States, for lawful export requirements, and for the establishment and maintenance of reserve stocks. Production quotas shall be established in terms of quantities of each basic class of controlled substance and not in terms of individual pharmaceutical dosage forms prepared from or containing such a controlled substance.

(b) Individual production quotas; revised quotas

The Attorney General shall limit or reduce individual production quotas to the extent necessary to prevent the aggregate of individual quotas from exceeding the amount determined necessary each year by the Attorney General under subsection (a) of this section. The quota of each registered manufacturer for each basic class of controlled substance in schedule I or II or for ephedrine, pseudoephedrine, or phenylpropanolamine shall be revised in the same proportion as the limitation or reduction of the aggregate of the quotas. However, if any registrant, before the issuance of a limitation or reduction in quota, has manufactured in excess of his revised quota, the amount of the excess shall be subtracted from his quota for the following year.

(c) Manufacturing quotas for registered manufacturers

On or before October 1 of each year, upon application therefor by a registered manufacturer, the Attorney General shall fix a manufacturing quota for the basic classes of controlled substances in schedules I and II and for ephedrine, pseudoephedrine, and phenylpropanolamine that the manufacturer seeks to produce. The quota shall be subject to the provisions of subsections (a) and (b) of this section. In fixing such quotas, the Attorney General shall determine the manufacturer's estimated disposal, inventory, and other requirements for the calendar year; and, in making his determination, the Attorney General shall consider the manufacturer's current rate of disposal, the trend of the national disposal rate during the preceding calendar year, the manufacturer's production cycle and inventory position, the economic availability of raw materials, yield and stability problems, emergencies such as strikes and fires, and other factors.

(d) Quotas for registrants who have not manufactured controlled substance during one or more preceding years

The Attorney General shall, upon application and subject to the provisions of subsections (a) and (b) of this section, fix a quota for a basic class of controlled substance in schedule I or II for any registrant who has not manufactured that basic class of controlled substance or ephedrine, pseudoephedrine, or phenylpropanolamine during one or more preceding calendar years. In fixing such quota, the Attorney General shall take into account the registrant's reasonably anticipated requirements for the current year; and, in making his determination of such requirements, he shall consider such factors specified in subsection (c) of this section as may be relevant.

(e) Quota increases

At any time during the year any registrant who has applied for or received a manufacturing quota for a basic class of controlled substance in schedule I or II or for ephedrine, pseudoephedrine, or phenylpropanolamine may apply for an increase in that quota to meet his estimated disposal, inventory, and other requirements during the remainder of that year. In passing upon the application the Attorney General shall take into consideration any occurrences since the filing of the registrant's initial quota application that may require an increased manufacturing rate by the registrant during the balance of the year. In passing upon the application the Attorney General may also take into account the amount, if any, by which the determination of the Attorney General under subsection (a) of this section exceeds the aggregate of the quotas of all registrants under this section.

(f) Incidental production exception

Notwithstanding any other provisions of this subchapter, no registration or quota may be required for the manufacture of such quantities of controlled substances in schedules I and II or ephedrine, pseudoephedrine, or phenylpropanolamine as incidentally and necessarily result from the manufacturing process used for the manufacture of a controlled substance or of ephedrine, pseudoephedrine, or phenylpropanolamine with respect to which its manufacturer is duly registered under this subchapter. The Attorney General may, by regulation, prescribe restrictions on the retention and disposal of such incidentally produced substances or chemicals.

(g) Reference to ephedrine, pseudoephedrine, or phenylpropanolamine

Each reference in this section to ephedrine, pseudoephedrine, or phenylpropanolamine includes each of the salts, optical isomers, and salts of optical isomers of such chemical.

(Pub. L. 91–513, title II, § 306, Oct. 27, 1970, 84 Stat. 1257; Pub. L. 94–273, § 3(16), Apr. 21, 1976, 90 Stat. 377; Pub. L. 109–177, title VII, § 713, Mar. 9, 2006, 120 Stat. 264.)

References in Text

Schedules I and II, referred to in text, are set out in section 812(c) of this title.

Amendments

2006—Subsec. (a). Pub. L. 109–177, § 713(1), inserted "and for ephedrine, pseudoephedrine, and phenylpropanolamine" after "for each basic class of controlled substance in schedules I and II".

Subsec. (b). Pub. L. 109–177, § 713(2), inserted "or for ephedrine, pseudoephedrine, or phenylpropanolamine" after "for each basic class of controlled substance in schedule I or II".

Subsec. (c). Pub. L. 109–177, § 713(3), inserted "and for ephedrine, pseudoephedrine, and phenylpropanolamine" after "for the basic classes of controlled substances in schedules I and II".

Subsec. (d). Pub. L. 109–177, § 713(4), inserted "or ephedrine, pseudoephedrine, or phenylpropanolamine" after "that basic class of controlled substance".

Subsec. (e). Pub. L. 109–177, § 713(5), inserted "or for ephedrine, pseudoephedrine, or phenylpropanolamine" after "for a basic class of controlled substance in schedule I or II".

Subsec. (f). Pub. L. 109–177, § 713(6), inserted "or ephedrine, pseudoephedrine, or phenylpropanolamine" after "controlled substances in schedules I and II", "or of ephedrine, pseudoephedrine, or phenylpropanolamine" after "the manufacture of a controlled substance", and "or chemicals" after "such incidentally produced substances".

Subsec. (g). Pub. L. 109–177, § 713(7), added subsec. (g).

1976—Subsec. (c). Pub. L. 94–273 substituted "October" for "July".

Effective Date

Section effective on first day of seventh calendar month that begins after Oct. 26, 1970, but with Attorney General authorized to postpone such effective date for such period as he might determine to be necessary for the efficient administration of this subchapter, see section 704(c) of Pub. L. 91–513, set out as a note under section 801 of this title.

Coordination With United States Trade Representative

Pub. L. 109–177, title VII, § 718, Mar. 9, 2006, 120 Stat. 267, provided that: "In implementing sections 713 through 717 and section 721 of this title [amending this section and sections 830, 842, 952, 960, and 971 of this title], the Attorney General shall consult with the United States Trade Representative to ensure implementation complies with all applicable international treaties and obligations of the United States."

§ 827. Records and reports of registrants

(a) Inventory

Except as provided in subsection (c) of this section—

(1) every registrant under this subchapter shall, on May 1, 1971, or as soon thereafter as such registrant first engages in the manufacture, distribution, or dispensing of controlled substances, and every second year thereafter, make a complete and accurate record of all stocks thereof on hand, except that the regulations prescribed under this section shall permit each such biennial inventory (following the initial inventory required by this paragraph) to be prepared on such registrant's regular general physical inventory date (if any) which is nearest to and does not vary by more than six months from the biennial date that would otherwise apply;

(2) on the effective date of each regulation of the Attorney General controlling a substance

that immediately prior to such date was not a controlled substance, each registrant under this subchapter manufacturing, distributing, or dispensing such substance shall make a complete and accurate record of all stocks thereof on hand; and

(3) on and after May 1, 1971, every registrant under this subchapter manufacturing, distributing, or dispensing a controlled substance or substances shall maintain, on a current basis, a complete and accurate record of each such substance manufactured, received, sold, delivered, or otherwise disposed of by him, except that this paragraph shall not require the maintenance of a perpetual inventory.

(b) Availability of records

Every inventory or other record required under this section (1) shall be in accordance with, and contain such relevant information as may be required by, regulations of the Attorney General, (2) shall (A) be maintained separately from all other records of the registrant, or (B) alternatively, in the case of nonnarcotic controlled substances, be in such form that information required by the Attorney General is readily retrievable from the ordinary business records of the registrant, and (3) shall be kept and be available, for at least two years, for inspection and copying by officers or employees of the United States authorized by the Attorney General.

(c) Nonapplicability

The foregoing provisions of this section shall not apply—

(1)(A) to the prescribing of controlled substances in schedule II, III, IV, or V by practitioners acting in the lawful course of their professional practice unless such substance is prescribed in the course of maintenance or detoxification treatment of an individual; or

(B) to the administering of a controlled substance in schedule II, III, IV, or V unless the practitioner regularly engages in the dispensing or administering of controlled substances and charges his patients, either separately or together with charges for other professional services, for substances so dispensed or administered or unless such substance is administered in the course of maintenance treatment or detoxification treatment of an individual;

(2)(A) to the use of controlled substances, at establishments registered under this subchapter which keep records with respect to such substances, in research conducted in conformity with an exemption granted under section 355(i) or 360b(j) of this title;

(B) to the use of controlled substances, at establishments registered under this subchapter which keep records with respect to such substances, in preclinical research or in teaching; or

(3) to the extent of any exemption granted to any person, with respect to all or part of such provisions, by the Attorney General by or pursuant to regulation on the basis of a finding that the application of such provisions (or part thereof) to such person is not necessary for carrying out the purposes of this subchapter.

Nothing in the Convention on Psychotropic Substances shall be construed as superseding or otherwise affecting the provisions of paragraph (1)(B), (2), or (3) of this subsection.

(d) Periodic reports to Attorney General

(1) Every manufacturer registered under section 823 of this title shall, at such time or times and in such form as the Attorney General may require, make periodic reports to the Attorney General of every sale, delivery or other disposal by him of any controlled substance, and each distributor shall make such reports with respect to narcotic controlled substances, identifying by the registration number assigned under this subchapter the person or establishment (unless exempt from registration under section 822(d) of this title) to whom such sale, delivery, or other disposal was made.

(2) Each pharmacy with a modified registration under section 823(f) of this title that authorizes the dispensing of controlled substances by means of the Internet shall report to the Attorney General the controlled substances it dispenses, in the amount specified, and in such time and manner as the Attorney General by regulation shall require, except that the Attorney General, under this paragraph, may not require any pharmacy to report any information other than the total quantity of each controlled substance that the pharmacy has dispensed each month. For purposes of this paragraph, no reporting shall be required unless the pharmacy has met 1 of the following thresholds in the month for which the reporting is required:

(A) 100 or more prescriptions dispensed.

(B) 5,000 or more dosage units of all controlled substances combined.

(e) Reporting and recordkeeping requirements of drug conventions

In addition to the reporting and recordkeeping requirements under any other provision of this subchapter, each manufacturer registered under section 823 of this title shall, with respect to narcotic and nonnarcotic controlled substances manufactured by it, make such reports to the Attorney General, and maintain such records, as the Attorney General may require to enable the United States to meet its obligations under articles 19 and 20 of the Single Convention on Narcotic Drugs and article 16 of the Convention on Psychotropic Substances. The Attorney General shall administer the requirements of this subsection in such a manner as to avoid the unnecessary imposition of duplicative requirements under this subchapter on manufacturers subject to the requirements of this subsection.

(f) Investigational uses of drugs; procedures

Regulations under sections 355(i) and 360(j) of this title, relating to investigational use of drugs, shall include such procedures as the Secretary, after consultation with the Attorney General, determines are necessary to insure the security and accountability of controlled substances used in research to which such regulations apply.

(g) Change of address

Every registrant under this subchapter shall be required to report any change of professional or business address in such manner as the Attorney General shall by regulation require.

(h) Reporting requirements for GHB

In the case of a drug product containing gamma hydroxybutyric acid for which an application has been approved under section 355 of this title, the Attorney General may, in addition to any other requirements that apply under this section with respect to such a drug product, establish any of the following as reporting requirements:

(1) That every person who is registered as a manufacturer of bulk or dosage form, as a packager, repackager, labeler, relabeler, or distributor shall report acquisition and distribution transactions quarterly, not later than the 15th day of the month succeeding the quarter for which the report is submitted, and annually report end-of-year inventories.

(2) That all annual inventory reports shall be filed no later than January 15 of the year following that for which the report is submitted and include data on the stocks of the drug product, drug substance, bulk drug, and dosage forms on hand as of the close of business December 31, indicating whether materials reported are in storage or in process of manufacturing.

(3) That every person who is registered as a manufacturer of bulk or dosage form shall report all manufacturing transactions both inventory increases, including purchases, transfers, and returns, and reductions from inventory, including sales, transfers, theft, destruction, and seizure, and shall provide data on material manufactured, manufactured from other material, use in manufacturing other material, and use in manufacturing dosage forms.

(4) That all reports under this section must include the registered person's registration number as well as the registration numbers, names, and other identifying information of vendors, suppliers, and customers, sufficient to allow the Attorney General to track the receipt and distribution of the drug.

(5) That each dispensing practitioner shall maintain for each prescription the name of the prescribing practitioner, the prescribing practitioner's Federal and State registration numbers, with the expiration dates of these registrations, verification that the prescribing practitioner possesses the appropriate registration to prescribe this controlled substance, the patient's name and address, the name of the patient's insurance provider and documentation by a medical practitioner licensed and registered to prescribe the drug of the patient's medical need for the drug. Such information shall be available for inspection and copying by the Attorney General.

(6) That section 830(b)(3) of this title (relating to mail order reporting) applies with respect to gamma hydroxybutyric acid to the same extent and in the same manner as such section applies with respect to the chemicals and drug products specified in subparagraph (A)(i) of such section.

(Pub. L. 91–513, title II, § 307, Oct. 27, 1970, 84 Stat. 1258; Pub. L. 93–281, § 5, May 14, 1974, 88 Stat. 125; Pub. L. 95–633, title I, §§ 104, 110, Nov. 10, 1978, 92 Stat. 3772, 3773; Pub. L. 98–473, title II, §§ 514, 515, Oct. 12, 1984, 98 Stat. 2074; Pub. L. 106–172, § 4, Feb. 18, 2000, 114 Stat. 9; Pub. L. 110–425, § 3(c), Oct. 15, 2008, 122 Stat. 4824.)

References in Text

Schedules II, III, IV, and V, referred to in subsec. (c), are set out in section 812(c) of this title.

Amendments

2008—Subsec. (d). Pub. L. 110–425 designated existing provisions as par. (1) and added par. (2).

2000—Subsec. (h). Pub. L. 106–172 added subsec. (h).

1984—Subsec. (c)(1)(A). Pub. L. 98–473, § 514(a), substituted "to the prescribing of controlled substances in schedule II, III, IV, or V by practitioners acting in the lawful course of their professional practice unless such substance is prescribed in the course of maintenance or detoxification treatment of an individual" for "with respect to any narcotic controlled substance in schedule II, III, IV, or V, to the prescribing or administering of such substance by a practitioner in the lawful course of his professional practice unless such substance was prescribed or administered in the course of maintenance treatment or detoxification treatment of an individual".

Subsec. (c)(1)(B). Pub. L. 98–473, § 514(b), substituted "to the administering of a controlled substance in schedule II, III, IV, or V unless the practitioner regularly engages in the dispensing or administering of controlled substances and charges his patients, either separately or together with charges for other professional services, for substances so dispensed or administered or unless such substance is administered in the course of maintenance treatment or detoxification treatment of an individual" for "with respect to nonnarcotic controlled substances in schedule II, III, IV, or V, to any practitioner who dispenses such substances to his patients, unless the practitioner is regularly engaged in charging his patients, either separately or together with charges for other professional services, for substances so dispensed".

Subsec. (g). Pub. L. 98–473, § 515, added subsec. (g).

1978—Subsec. (c). Pub. L. 95–633, § 110, inserted provision following par. (3) relating to the construction of the Convention on Psychotropic Substances.

Subsecs. (e), (f). Pub. L. 95–633 added subsec. (e) and redesignated former subsec. (e) as (f).

1974—Subsec. (c)(1)(A). Pub. L. 93–281 substituted "any narcotic controlled substance" for "narcotic controlled substances" and made section applicable to any narcotic controlled substance prescribed or administered in the course of maintenance treatment or detoxification treatment of an individual.

Effective Date of 2008 Amendment

Amendment by Pub. L. 110–425 effective 180 days after Oct. 15, 2008, except as otherwise provided, see section 3(j) of Pub. L. 110–425, set out as a note under section 802 of this title.

Effective Date of 1978 Amendment

Amendment by Pub. L. 95–633 effective on date the Convention on Psychotropic Substances enters into force in the United States [July 15, 1980], see section 112 of Pub. L. 95–633, set out as an Effective Date note under section 801a of this title.

§ 828. Order forms

(a) Unlawful distribution of controlled substances

It shall be unlawful for any person to distribute a controlled substance in schedule I or II to another except in pursuance of a written order of the person to whom such substance is distributed, made on a form to be issued by the Attorney General in blank in accordance with subsection (d) of this section and regulations prescribed by him pursuant to this section.

(b) Nonapplicability of provisions

Nothing in subsection (a) of this section shall apply to—

(1) the exportation of such substances from the United States in conformity with subchapter II of this chapter;

(2) the delivery of such a substance to or by a common or contract carrier for carriage in the lawful and usual course of its business, or to or by a warehouseman for storage in the lawful and usual course of its business; but where such carriage or storage is in connection with the distribution by the owner of the substance to a third person, this paragraph shall not relieve the distributor from compliance with subsection (a) of this section.

(c) Preservation and availability

(1) Every person who in pursuance of an order required under subsection (a) of this section distributes a controlled substance shall preserve such order for a period of two years, and shall make such order available for inspection and copying by officers and employees of the United States duly authorized for that purpose by the Attorney General, and by officers or employees of States or their political subdivisions who are charged with the enforcement of State or local laws regulating the production, or regulating the distribution or dispensing, of controlled substances and who are authorized under such laws to inspect such orders.

(2) Every person who gives an order required under subsection (a) of this section shall, at or before the time of giving such order, make or cause to be made a duplicate thereof on a form to be issued by the Attorney General in blank in accordance with subsection (d) of this section and regulations prescribed by him pursuant to this section, and shall, if such order is accepted, preserve such duplicate for a period of two years and make it available for inspection and copying by the officers and employees mentioned in paragraph (1) of this subsection.

(d) Issuance

(1) The Attorney General shall issue forms pursuant to subsections (a) and (c)(2) of this section only to persons validly registered under section 823 of this title (or exempted from registration under section 822(d) of this title). Whenever any such form is issued to a person, the Attorney General shall, before delivery thereof, insert therein the name of such person, and it shall be unlawful for any other person (A) to use such form for the purpose of obtaining controlled substances or (B) to furnish such form to any person with intent thereby to procure the distribution of such substances.

(2) The Attorney General may charge reasonable fees for the issuance of such forms in such amounts as he may prescribe for the purpose of covering the cost to the United States of issuing such forms, and other necessary activities in connection therewith.

(e) Unlawful acts

It shall be unlawful for any person to obtain by means of order forms issued under this section controlled substances for any purpose other than their use, distribution, dispensing, or administration in the conduct of a lawful business in such substances or in the course of his professional practice or research.

(Pub. L. 91–513, title II, §308, Oct. 27, 1970, 84 Stat. 1259.)

REFERENCES IN TEXT

Schedules I and II, referred to in subsec. (a), are set out in section 812(c) of this title.

§829. Prescriptions

(a) Schedule II substances

Except when dispensed directly by a practitioner, other than a pharmacist, to an ultimate user, no controlled substance in schedule II, which is a prescription drug as determined under the Federal Food, Drug, and Cosmetic Act [21 U.S.C. 301 et seq.], may be dispensed without the written prescription of a practitioner, except that in emergency situations, as prescribed by the Secretary by regulation after consultation with the Attorney General, such drug may be dispensed upon oral prescription in accordance with section 503(b) of that Act [21 U.S.C. 353(b)]. Prescriptions shall be retained in conformity with the requirements of section 827 of this title. No prescription for a controlled substance in schedule II may be refilled.

(b) Schedule III and IV substances

Except when dispensed directly by a practitioner, other than a pharmacist, to an ultimate user, no controlled substance in schedule III or IV, which is a prescription drug as determined under the Federal Food, Drug, and Cosmetic Act [21 U.S.C. 301 et seq.], may be dispensed without a written or oral prescription in conformity with section 503(b) of that Act [21 U.S.C. 353(b)]. Such prescriptions may not be filled or refilled more than six months after the date thereof or be refilled more than five times after the date of the prescription unless renewed by the practitioner.

(c) Schedule V substances

No controlled substance in schedule V which is a drug may be distributed or dispensed other than for a medical purpose.

(d) Non-prescription drugs with abuse potential

Whenever it appears to the Attorney General that a drug not considered to be a prescription drug under the Federal Food, Drug, and Cosmetic Act [21 U.S.C. 301 et seq.] should be so considered because of its abuse potential, he shall so advise the Secretary and furnish to him all available data relevant thereto.

(e) Controlled substances dispensed by means of the Internet

(1) No controlled substance that is a prescription drug as determined under the Federal Food, Drug, and Cosmetic Act [21 U.S.C. 301 et seq.] may be delivered, distributed, or dispensed by means of the Internet without a valid prescription.

(2) As used in this subsection:

(A) The term "valid prescription" means a prescription that is issued for a legitimate medical purpose in the usual course of professional practice by—

(i) a practitioner who has conducted at least 1 in-person medical evaluation of the patient; or

(ii) a covering practitioner.

(B)(i) The term "in-person medical evaluation" means a medical evaluation that is conducted with the patient in the physical presence of the practitioner, without regard to whether portions of the evaluation are conducted by other health professionals.

(ii) Nothing in clause (i) shall be construed to imply that 1 in-person medical evaluation demonstrates that a prescription has been issued for a legitimate medical purpose within the usual course of professional practice.

(C) The term "covering practitioner" means, with respect to a patient, a practitioner who conducts a medical evaluation (other than an in-person medical evaluation) at the request of a practitioner who—

(i) has conducted at least 1 in-person medical evaluation of the patient or an evaluation of the patient through the practice of telemedicine, within the previous 24 months; and

(ii) is temporarily unavailable to conduct the evaluation of the patient.

(3) Nothing in this subsection shall apply to—

(A) the delivery, distribution, or dispensing of a controlled substance by a practitioner engaged in the practice of telemedicine; or

(B) the dispensing or selling of a controlled substance pursuant to practices as determined by the Attorney General by regulation, which shall be consistent with effective controls against diversion.

(Pub. L. 91–513, title II, §309, Oct. 27, 1970, 84 Stat. 1260; Pub. L. 110–425, §2, Oct. 15, 2008, 122 Stat. 4820.)

REFERENCES IN TEXT

The Federal Food, Drug, and Cosmetic Act, referred to in subsecs. (a), (b), (d), and (e)(1), is act June 25, 1938, ch. 675, 52 Stat. 1040, which is classified generally to chapter 9 (§301 et seq.) of this title. For complete classification of this Act to the Code, see section 301 of this title and Tables.

Schedules II, III, IV, and V, referred to in subsecs. (a) to (c), are set out in section 812(c) of this title.

AMENDMENTS

2008—Subsec. (e). Pub. L. 110–425 added subsec. (e).

EFFECTIVE DATE OF 2008 AMENDMENT

Amendment by Pub. L. 110–425 effective 180 days after Oct. 15, 2008, except as otherwise provided, see section 3(j) of Pub. L. 110–425, set out as a note under section 802 of this title.

EFFECT OF SCHEDULING ON PRESCRIPTIONS

Pub. L. 101–647, title XIX, §1902(c), Nov. 29, 1990, 104 Stat. 4852, provided that: "Any prescription for anabolic steroids subject to refill on or after the date of enactment of the amendments made by this section [Nov. 29, 1990] may be refilled without restriction under section 309(a) of the Controlled Substances Act (21 U.S.C. 829(a))."

§830. Regulation of listed chemicals and certain machines

(a) Record of regulated transactions

(1) Each regulated person who engages in a regulated transaction involving a listed chemical, a tableting machine, or an encapsulating machine shall keep a record of the transaction for two years after the date of the transaction.

(2) A record under this subsection shall be retrievable and shall include the date of the regulated transaction, the identity of each party to the regulated transaction, a statement of the quantity and form of the listed chemical, a description of the tableting machine or encapsulating machine, and a description of the method of transfer. Such record shall be available for inspection and copying by the Attorney General.

(3) It is the duty of each regulated person who engages in a regulated transaction to identify each other party to the transaction. It is the duty of such other party to present proof of identity to the regulated person. The Attorney General shall specify by regulation the types of documents and other evidence that constitute proof of identity for purposes of this paragraph.

(b) Reports to Attorney General

(1) Each regulated person shall report to the Attorney General, in such form and manner as the Attorney General shall prescribe by regulation—

(A) any regulated transaction involving an extraordinary quantity of a listed chemical, an uncommon method of payment or delivery, or any other circumstance that the regulated person believes may indicate that the listed chemical will be used in violation of this subchapter;

(B) any proposed regulated transaction with a person whose description or other identifying characteristic the Attorney General furnishes in advance to the regulated person;

(C) any unusual or excessive loss or disappearance of a listed chemical under the control of the regulated person; and

(D) any regulated transaction in a tableting machine or an encapsulating machine.

Each report under subparagraph (A) shall be made at the earliest practicable opportunity after the regulated person becomes aware of the circumstance involved. A regulated person may not complete a transaction with a person whose description or identifying characteristic is furnished to the regulated person under subparagraph (B) unless the transaction is approved by the Attorney General. The Attorney General shall make available to regulated persons guidance documents describing transactions and circumstances for which reports are required under subparagraph (A) and subparagraph (C).

(2) A regulated person that manufactures a listed chemical shall report annually to the Attorney General, in such form and manner and containing such specific data as the Attorney General shall prescribe by regulation, information concerning listed chemicals manufactured by the person. The requirement of the preceding sentence shall not apply to the manufacture of a drug product that is exempted under section 802(39)(A)(iv) of this title.

(3) MAIL ORDER REPORTING.—(A) As used in this paragraph:

(i) The term "drug product" means an active ingredient in dosage form that has been approved or otherwise may be lawfully marketed under the Food, Drug, and Cosmetic Act[1] [21 U.S.C. 301 et seq.] for distribution in the United States.

(ii) The term "valid prescription" means a prescription which is issued for a legitimate medical purpose by an individual practitioner licensed by law to administer and prescribe the drugs concerned and acting in the usual course of the practitioner's professional practice.

(B) Each regulated person who engages in a transaction with a nonregulated person or who engages in an export transaction which—

(i) involves ephedrine, pseudoephedrine, or phenylpropanolamine (including drug products containing these chemicals); and

(ii) uses or attempts to use the Postal Service or any private or commercial carrier;

shall, on a monthly basis, submit a report of each such transaction conducted during the previous month to the Attorney General in such form, containing such data, and at such times as the Attorney General shall establish by regulation.

(C) The data required for such reports shall include—

(i) the name of the purchaser;

(ii) the quantity and form of the ephedrine, pseudoephedrine, or phenylpropanolamine purchased; and

(iii) the address to which such ephedrine, pseudoephedrine, or phenylpropanolamine was sent.

(D) Except as provided in subparagraph (E), the following distributions to a nonregulated person, and the following export transactions, shall not be subject to the reporting requirement in subparagraph (B):

(i) Distributions of sample packages of drug products when such packages contain not more than two solid dosage units or the equivalent of two dosage units in liquid form, not to exceed 10 milliliters of liquid per package, and not more than one package is distributed to an individual or residential address in any 30-day period.

(ii) Distributions of drug products by retail distributors that may not include face-to-face transactions to the extent that such distributions are consistent with the activities authorized for a retail distributor as specified in section 802(49) of this title, except that this clause does not apply to sales of scheduled listed chemical products at retail.

(iii) Distributions of drug products to a resident of a long term care facility (as that term is defined in regulations prescribed by the Attorney General) or distributions of drug products to a long term care facility for dispensing to or for use by a resident of that facility.

(iv) Distributions of drug products pursuant to a valid prescription.

(v) Exports which have been reported to the Attorney General pursuant to section 954 or 971 of this title or which are subject to a waiver granted under section 971(f)(2) of this title.

(vi) Any quantity, method, or type of distribution or any quantity, method, or type of distribution of a specific listed chemical (including specific formulations or drug products) or of a group of listed chemicals (including specific formulations or drug products) which the Attorney General has excluded by regulation from such reporting requirement on the basis that such reporting is not necessary for the enforcement of this subchapter or subchapter II of this chapter.

(E) The Attorney General may revoke any or all of the exemptions listed in subparagraph (D) for an individual regulated person if he finds that drug products distributed by the regulated person are being used in violation of this subchapter or subchapter II of this chapter. The regulated person shall be notified of the revocation, which will be effective upon receipt by the person of such notice, as provided in section 971(c)(1) of this title, and shall have the right to an expedited hearing as provided in section 971(c)(2) of this title.

(c) Confidentiality of information obtained by Attorney General; non-disclosure; exceptions

(1) Except as provided in paragraph (2), any information obtained by the Attorney General under this section which is exempt from disclosure under section 552(a) of title 5, by reason of section 552(b)(4) of such title, is confidential and may not be disclosed to any person.

(2) Information referred to in paragraph (1) may be disclosed only—

(A) to an officer or employee of the United States engaged in carrying out this subchapter, subchapter II of this chapter, or the customs laws;

(B) when relevant in any investigation or proceeding for the enforcement of this subchapter, subchapter II of this chapter, or the customs laws;

(C) when necessary to comply with an obligation of the United States under a treaty or other international agreement; or

(D) to a State or local official or employee in conjunction with the enforcement of controlled substances laws or chemical control laws.

(3) The Attorney General shall—

(A) take such action as may be necessary to prevent unauthorized disclosure of information by any person to whom such information is disclosed under paragraph (2); and

(B) issue guidelines that limit, to the maximum extent feasible, the disclosure of proprietary business information, including the names or identities of United States exporters of listed chemicals, to any person to whom such information is disclosed under paragraph (2).

(4) Any person who is aggrieved by a disclosure of information in violation of this section may bring a civil action against the violator for appropriate relief.

(5) Notwithstanding paragraph (4), a civil action may not be brought under such paragraph against investigative or law enforcement personnel of the Drug Enforcement Administration.

[1] See References in Text note below.

(d) Scheduled listed chemicals; restrictions on sales quantity; requirements regarding nonliquid forms

With respect to ephedrine base, pseudoephedrine base, or phenylpropanolamine base in a scheduled listed chemical product—

(1) the quantity of such base sold at retail in such a product by a regulated seller, or a distributor required to submit reports by subsection (b)(3) may not, for any purchaser, exceed a daily amount of 3.6 grams, without regard to the number of transactions; and

(2) such a seller or distributor may not sell such a product in nonliquid form (including gel caps) at retail unless the product is packaged in blister packs, each blister containing not more than 2 dosage units, or where the use of blister packs is technically infeasible, the product is packaged in unit dose packets or pouches.

(e) Scheduled listed chemicals; behind-the-counter access; logbook requirement; training of sales personnel; privacy protections

(1) Requirements regarding retail transactions

(A) In general

Each regulated seller shall ensure that, subject to subparagraph (F), sales by such seller of a scheduled listed chemical product at retail are made in accordance with the following:

(i) In offering the product for sale, the seller places the product such that customers do not have direct access to the product before the sale is made (in this paragraph referred to as "behind-the-counter" placement). For purposes of this paragraph, a behind-the-counter placement of a product includes circumstances in which the product is stored in a locked cabinet that is located in an area of the facility involved to which customers do have direct access.

(ii) The seller delivers the product directly into the custody of the purchaser.

(iii) The seller maintains, in accordance with criteria issued by the Attorney General, a written or electronic list of such sales that identifies the products by name, the quantity sold, the names and addresses of purchasers, and the dates and times of the sales (which list is referred to in this subsection as the "logbook"), except that such requirement does not apply to any purchase by an individual of a single sales package if that package contains not more than 60 milligrams of pseudoephedrine.

(iv) In the case of a sale to which the requirement of clause (iii) applies, the seller does not sell such a product unless the sale is made in accordance with the following:

(I) The prospective purchaser—

(aa) presents an identification card that provides a photograph and is issued by a State or the Federal Government, or a document that, with respect to identification, is considered acceptable for purposes of sections 274a.2(b)(1)(v)(A) and 274a.2(b)(1)(v)(B) of title 8, Code of Federal Regulations (as in effect on or after March 9, 2006); and

(bb) signs the written logbook and enters in the logbook his or her name, address, and the date and time of the sale, or for transactions involving an electronic logbook, the purchaser provides a signature using one of the following means:

(AA) Signing a device presented by the seller that captures signatures in an electronic format. Such device shall display the notice described in clause (v). Any device used shall preserve each signature in a manner that clearly links that signature to the other electronically-captured logbook information relating to the prospective purchaser providing that signature.

(BB) Signing a bound paper book. Such bound paper book shall include, for such purchaser, either (aaa) a printed sticker affixed to the bound paper book at the time of sale which either displays the name of each product sold, the quantity sold, the name and address of the purchaser, and the date and time of the sale, or a unique identifier which can be linked to that electronic information, or (bbb) a unique identifier which can be linked to that information and which is written into the book by the seller at the time of sale. The purchaser shall sign adjacent to the printed sticker or written unique identifier related to that sale. Such bound paper book shall display the notice described in clause (v).

(CC) Signing a printed document that includes, for such purchaser, the name of each product sold, the quantity sold, the name and address of the purchaser, and the date and time of the sale. Such document shall be printed by the seller at the time of the sale. Such document shall contain a clearly identified signature line for a purchaser to sign. Such printed document shall display the notice described in clause (v). Each signed document shall be inserted into a binder or other secure means of document storage immediately after the purchaser signs the document.

(II) The seller enters in the logbook the name of the product and the quantity sold. Such information may be captured through electronic means, including through electronic data capture through bar code reader or similar technology.

(III) The logbook maintained by the seller includes the prospective purchaser's name, address, and the date and time of the sale, as follows:

(aa) If the purchaser enters the information, the seller must determine that the name entered in the logbook corresponds to the name provided on such identification and that the date and time entered are correct.

(bb) If the seller enters the information, the prospective purchaser must verify that the information is correct.

(cc) Such information may be captured through electronic means, including through electronic data capture through bar code reader or similar technology.

(v) The written or electronic logbook includes, in accordance with criteria of the Attorney General, a notice to purchasers that entering false statements or misrepresentations in the logbook, or supplying false information or identification that results in the entry of false statements or misrepresentations, may subject the purchasers to criminal penalties under section 1001 of title 18, which notice specifies the maximum fine and term of imprisonment under such section.

(vi) Regardless of whether the logbook entry is written or electronic, the seller maintains each entry in the logbook for not fewer than 2 years after the date on which the entry is made.

(vii) In the case of individuals who are responsible for delivering such products into the custody of purchasers or who deal directly with purchasers by obtaining payments for the products, the seller has submitted to the Attorney General a self-certification that all such individuals have, in accordance with criteria under subparagraph (B)(ii), undergone training provided by the seller to ensure that the individuals understand the requirements that apply under this subsection and subsection (d).

(viii) The seller maintains a copy of such certification and records demonstrating that individuals referred to in clause (vii) have undergone the training.

(ix) If the seller is a mobile retail vendor:

(I) The seller complies with clause (i) by placing the product in a locked cabinet.

(II) The seller does not sell more than 7.5 grams of ephedrine base, pseudoephedrine base, or phenylpropanolamine base in such products per customer during a 30-day period.

(B) Additional provisions regarding certifications and training

(i) In general

A regulated seller may not sell any scheduled listed chemical product at retail unless the seller has submitted to the Attorney General the self-certification referred to in subparagraph (A)(vii). The certification is not effective for purposes of the preceding sentence unless, in addition to provisions regarding the training of individuals referred to in such subparagraph, the certification includes a statement that the seller understands each of the requirements that apply under this paragraph and under subsection (d) and agrees to comply with the requirements.

(ii) Issuance of criteria; self-certification

The Attorney General shall by regulation establish criteria for certifications under this paragraph. The criteria shall—

(I) provide that the certifications are self-certifications provided through the program under clause (iii);

(II) provide that a separate certification is required for each place of business at which a regulated seller sells scheduled listed chemical products at retail; and

(III) include criteria for training under subparagraph (A)(vii).

(iii) Program for regulated sellers

The Attorney General shall establish a program regarding such certifications and training in accordance with the following:

(I) The program shall be carried out through an Internet site of the Department of Justice and such other means as the Attorney General determines to be appropriate.

(II) The program shall inform regulated sellers that section 1001 of title 18 applies to such certifications.

(III) The program shall make available to such sellers an explanation of the criteria under clause (ii).

(IV) The program shall be designed to permit the submission of the certifications through such Internet site.

(V) The program shall be designed to automatically provide the explanation referred to in subclause (III), and an acknowledgement that the Department has received a certification, without requiring direct interactions of regulated sellers with staff of the Department (other than the provision of technical assistance, as appropriate).

(iv) Availability of certification to State and local officials

Promptly after receiving a certification under subparagraph (A)(vii), the Attorney General shall make available a copy of the certification to the appropriate State and local officials.

(C) Privacy protections

In order to protect the privacy of individuals who purchase scheduled listed chemical products, the Attorney General shall by regulation establish restrictions on disclosure of information in logbooks under subparagraph (A)(iii). Such regulations shall—

(i) provide for the disclosure of the information as appropriate to the Attorney General and to State and local law enforcement agencies; and

(ii) prohibit accessing, using, or sharing information in the logbooks for any purpose other than to ensure compliance with this subchapter or to facilitate a product recall to protect public health and safety.

(D) False statements or misrepresentations by purchasers

For purposes of section 1001 of title 18, entering information in the logbook under subparagraph (A)(iii) shall be considered a matter within the jurisdiction of the executive, legislative, or judicial branch of the Government of the United States.

(E) Good faith protection

A regulated seller who in good faith releases information in a logbook under subparagraph (A)(iii) to Federal, State, or local law enforcement authorities is immune from civil liability for such release unless the release constitutes gross negligence or intentional, wanton, or willful misconduct.

(F) Inapplicability of requirements to certain sales

Subparagraph (A) does not apply to the sale at retail of a scheduled listed chemical product if a report on the sales transaction is required to be submitted to the Attorney General under subsection (b)(3).

(G) Certain measures regarding theft and diversion

A regulated seller may take reasonable measures to guard against employing individuals who may present a risk with respect to the theft and diversion of scheduled listed chemical products, which may include, notwithstanding State law, asking applicants for employment whether they have been convicted of any crime involving or related to such products or controlled substances.

(2) Mail-order reporting; verification of identity of purchaser; 30-day restriction on quantities for individual purchasers

Each regulated person who makes a sale at retail of a scheduled listed chemical product and is required under subsection (b)(3) to submit a report of the sales transaction to the Attorney General is subject to the following:

(A) The person shall, prior to shipping the product, confirm the identity of the purchaser in accordance with procedures established by the Attorney General. The Attorney General shall by regulation establish such procedures.

(B) The person may not sell more than 7.5 grams of ephedrine base, pseudoephedrine base, or phenylpropanolamine base in such products per customer during a 30-day period.

(3) Exemptions for certain products

Upon the application of a manufacturer of a scheduled listed chemical product, the Attorney General may by regulation provide that the product is exempt from the provisions of subsection (d) and paragraphs (1) and (2) of this subsection if the Attorney General determines that the product cannot be used in the illicit manufacture of methamphetamine.

(Pub. L. 91–513, title II, § 310, as added Pub. L. 95–633, title II, § 202(a), Nov. 10, 1978, 92 Stat. 3774; amended Pub. L. 100–690, title VI, § 6052(a), Nov. 18, 1988, 102 Stat. 4312; Pub. L. 103–200, §§ 2(c), 10, Dec. 17, 1993, 107 Stat. 2336, 2341; Pub. L. 104–237, title II, § 208, title IV, § 402, Oct. 3, 1996, 110 Stat. 3104, 3111; Pub. L. 106–310, div. B, title XXXVI, § 3652, Oct. 17, 2000, 114 Stat. 1239; Pub. L. 109–177, title VII, §§ 711(a)(2)(B), (b)(1), (c)(1), (2), (d), 716(b)(2), Mar. 9, 2006, 120 Stat. 257, 261, 267; Pub. L. 110–415, § 2, Oct. 14, 2008, 122 Stat. 4349.)

REFERENCES IN TEXT

The Food, Drug, and Cosmetic Act, referred to in subsec. (b)(3)(A)(i), probably means the Federal Food, Drug, and Cosmetic Act, act June 25, 1938, ch. 675, 52 Stat. 1040, as amended, which is classified generally to chapter 9 (§ 301 et seq.) of this title. For complete classification of this Act to the Code, see section 301 of this title and Tables.

This subchapter, referred to in subsecs. (b)(3)(D)(vi), (E) and (e)(1)(C)(ii), was in the original "this title", meaning title II of Pub. L. 91–513, Oct. 27, 1970, 84 Stat. 1242, as amended, and is popularly known as the "Controlled Substances Act". For complete classification of title II to the Code, see second paragraph of Short Title note set out under section 801 of this title and Tables.

Subchapter II of this chapter, referred to in subsecs. (b)(3)(D)(iv), (E) and (c)(2)(A), (B), was in the original "title III", meaning title III of Pub. L. 91–513, Oct. 27, 1970, 84 Stat. 1285, as amended. Part A of title III comprises subchapter II of this chapter. For classification of Part B, consisting of sections 1101 to 1105 of title III, see Tables.

AMENDMENTS

2008—Subsec. (e)(1)(A)(iv) to (vi). Pub. L. 110–415 added cls. (iv) to (vi) and struck out former cls. (iv) to (vi) which related to procedures for sales subject to the logbook requirement.

2006—Subsec. (b)(3)(D)(ii). Pub. L. 109–177, § 711(c)(2), inserted ", except that this clause does not apply to sales of scheduled listed chemical products at retail" before period at end.

Pub. L. 109–177, § 711(a)(2)(B), substituted "section 802(49)" for "section 802(46)".

Subsec. (b)(3)(D)(v). Pub. L. 109–177, § 716(b)(2), substituted "section 971(f)(2)" for "section 971(e)(2)".

Subsec. (d). Pub. L. 109–177, § 711(b)(1), added subsec. (d).

Subsec. (e)(1). Pub. L. 109–177, § 711(b)(1), added subsec. heading and par. (1).

Subsec. (e)(2). Pub. L. 109–177, § 711(c)(1), added par. (2).

Subsec. (e)(3). Pub. L. 109–177, § 711(d), added par. (3).

2000—Subsec. (b)(3). Pub. L. 106–310 added subpars. (A), (D), and (E), redesignated former subpars. (A) and (B) as (B) and (C), respectively, and inserted "or who engages in an export transaction" after "nonregulated person" in introductory provisions of subpar. (B).

1996—Subsec. (a)(1). Pub. L. 104–237, § 208, substituted "for two years after the date of the transaction." for the dash after "record of the transaction" and struck out subpars. (A) and (B) which read as follows:

"(A) for 4 years after the date of the transaction, if the listed chemical is a list I chemical or if the transaction involves a tableting machine or an encapsulating machine; and

"(B) for 2 years after the date of the transaction, if the listed chemical is a list II chemical."

Subsec. (b)(3). Pub. L. 104–237, § 402, added par. (3).

1993—Subsec. (a)(1). Pub. L. 103–200, § 2(c)(1), substituted "list I chemical" for "precursor chemical" in subpar. (A) and "a list II chemical" for "an essential chemical" in subpar. (B).

Subsec. (b). Pub. L. 103–200, § 10, designated existing provisions as par. (1), redesignated former pars. (1) to (4) as subpars. (A) to (D), respectively, in concluding provisions, substituted "subparagraph (A)" for "paragraph (1)" in two places, "subparagraph (B)" for "paragraph (2)", and "subparagraph (C)" for "paragraph (3)", and added par. (2).

Subsec. (c)(2)(D). Pub. L. 103–200, § 2(c)(2), substituted "chemical control laws" for "precursor chemical laws".

1988—Pub. L. 100–690 amended section generally, substituting provisions relating to regulation of listed chemicals and certain machines for provisions relating to reporting by any person who distributes, sells, or imports any piperidine.

EFFECTIVE DATE OF 2006 AMENDMENT

Pub. L. 109–177, title VII, §711(b)(2), Mar. 9, 2006, 120 Stat. 261, provided that: "With respect to subsections (d) and (e)(1) of section 310 of the Controlled Substances Act [21 U.S.C. 830(d), (e)(1)], as added by paragraph (1) of this subsection:

"(A) Such subsection (d) applies on and after the expiration of the 30-day period beginning on the date of the enactment of this Act [Mar. 9, 2006].

"(B) Such subsection (e)(1) applies on and after September 30, 2006."

Pub. L. 109–177, title VII, §711(c)(3), Mar. 9, 2006, 120 Stat. 261, provided that: "The amendments made by paragraphs (1) and (2) [amending this section] apply on and after the expiration of the 30-day period beginning on the date of the enactment of this Act [Mar. 9, 2006]."

EFFECTIVE DATE OF 1993 AMENDMENT

Amendment by Pub. L. 103–200 effective on date that is 120 days after Dec. 17, 1993, see section 11 of Pub. L. 103–200, set out as a note under section 802 of this title.

EFFECTIVE DATE OF 1988 AMENDMENT

Amendment by Pub. L. 100–690 effective 120 days after Nov. 18, 1988, see section 6061 of Pub. L. 100–690, set out as a note under section 802 of this title.

EFFECTIVE DATE; TIME TO SUBMIT PIPERIDINE REPORT; REQUIRED INFORMATION

Section 203(a) of title II of Pub. L. 95–633 provided that:

"(1) Except as provided under paragraph (2), the amendments made by this title [enacting this section and amending sections 841 to 843 of this title] shall take effect on the date of the enactment of this Act [Nov. 10, 1978].

"(2) Any person required to submit a report under section 310(a)(1) of the Controlled Substances Act [subsec. (a)(1) of this section] respecting a distribution, sale, or importation of piperidine during the 90 days after the date of the enactment of this Act [Nov. 10, 1978] may submit such report any time up to 97 days after such date of enactment.

"(3) Until otherwise provided by the Attorney General by regulation, the information required to be reported by a person under section 310(a)(1) of the Controlled Substances Act (as added by section 202(a)(2) of this title) [subsec. (a)(1) of this section] with respect to the person's distribution, sale, or importation of piperidine shall—

"(A) be the information described in subparagraphs (A) and (B) of such section, and

"(B) except as provided in paragraph (2) of this subsection, be reported not later than seven days after the date of such distribution, sale, or importation."

REPEALS

Pub. L. 96–359, §8(b), Sept. 26, 1980, 94 Stat. 1194, repealed section 203(d) of Pub. L. 95–633, which had provided for the repeal of this section effective Jan. 1, 1981.

REGULATIONS FOR PIPERIDINE REPORTING

Section 203(b) of Pub. L. 95–633 required the Attorney General to publish proposed interim regulations for piperidine reporting under section 830(a) of this title not later than 30 days after enactment, and final interim regulations not later than 75 days after enactment, such final interim regulations to be effective on and after the ninety-first day after enactment.

REPORT TO PRESIDENT AND CONGRESS ON EFFECTIVENESS OF TITLE II OF PUB. L. 95–633

Section 203(c) of Pub. L. 95–633 required the Attorney General to analyze and evaluate the impact and effectiveness of the amendments made by title II of Pub. L. 95–633, and report to the President and Congress not later than Mar. 1, 1980.

§831. Additional requirements relating to online pharmacies and telemedicine

(a) In general

An online pharmacy shall display in a visible and clear manner on its homepage a statement that it complies with the requirements of this section with respect to the delivery or sale or offer for sale of controlled substances and shall at all times display on the homepage of its Internet site a declaration of compliance in accordance with this section.

(b) Licensure

Each online pharmacy shall comply with the requirements of State law concerning the licensure of pharmacies in each State from which it, and in each State to which it, delivers, distributes, or dispenses or offers to deliver, distribute, or dispense controlled substances by means of the Internet, pursuant to applicable licensure requirements, as determined by each such State.

(c) Internet pharmacy site disclosure information

Each online pharmacy shall post in a visible and clear manner on the homepage of each Internet site it operates, or on a page directly linked thereto in which the hyperlink is also visible and clear on the homepage, the following information for each pharmacy that delivers, distributes, or dispenses controlled substances pursuant to orders made on, through, or on behalf of, that website:

(1) The name and address of the pharmacy as it appears on the pharmacy's Drug Enforcement Administration certificate of registration.

(2) The pharmacy's telephone number and email address.

(3) The name, professional degree, and States of licensure of the pharmacist-in-charge, and a telephone number at which the pharmacist-in-charge can be contacted.

(4) A list of the States in which the pharmacy is licensed to dispense controlled substances.

(5) A certification that the pharmacy is registered under this part to deliver, distribute, or dispense by means of the Internet controlled substances.

(6) The name, address, telephone number, professional degree, and States of licensure of any practitioner who has a contractual relationship to provide medical evaluations or issue prescriptions for controlled substances, through referrals from the website or at the request of the owner or operator of the website, or any employee or agent thereof.

(7) The following statement, unless revised by the Attorney General by regulation: "This online pharmacy will only dispense a controlled substance to a person who has a valid prescription issued for a legitimate medical purpose based upon a medical relationship with a prescribing practitioner. This includes at least one prior in-person medical evaluation or medical evaluation via telemedicine in accordance with applicable requirements of section 309.".

(d) Notification

(1) In general

Thirty days prior to offering a controlled substance for sale, delivery, distribution, or dispensing, the online pharmacy shall notify the Attorney General, in such form and manner as the Attorney General shall determine, and the State boards of pharmacy in any States in which the online pharmacy offers to sell, deliver, distribute, or dispense controlled substances.

(2) Contents

The notification required under paragraph (1) shall include—

(A) the information required to be posted on the online pharmacy's Internet site under subsection (c) and shall notify the Attorney General and the applicable State boards of pharmacy, under penalty of perjury, that the information disclosed on its Internet site under subsection (c) is true and accurate;

(B) the online pharmacy's Internet site address and a certification that the online pharmacy shall notify the Attorney General of any change in the address at least 30 days in advance; and

(C) the Drug Enforcement Administration registration numbers of any pharmacies and practitioners referred to in subsection (c), as applicable.

(3) Existing online pharmacies

An online pharmacy that is already operational as of the effective date of this section, shall notify the Attorney General and applicable State boards of pharmacy in accordance with this subsection not later than 30 days after such date.

(e) Declaration of compliance

On and after the date on which it makes the notification under subsection (d), each online pharmacy shall display on the homepage of its Internet site, in such form as the Attorney General shall by regulation require, a declaration that it has made such notification to the Attorney General.

(f) Reports

Any statement, declaration, notification, or disclosure required under this section shall be considered a report required to be kept under this part.

(g) Notice and designations concerning Indian tribes

(1) In general

For purposes of sections 802(52) and 882(c)(6)(B) of this title, the Secretary shall notify the Attorney General, at such times and in such manner as the Secretary and the Attorney General determine appropriate, of the Indian tribes or tribal organizations with which the Secretary has contracted or compacted under the Indian Self-Determination and Education Assistance Act [25 U.S.C. 450 et seq.] for the tribes or tribal organizations to provide pharmacy services.

(2) Designations

(A) In general

The Secretary may designate a practitioner described in subparagraph (B) as an Internet Eligible Controlled Substances Provider. Such designations shall be made only in cases where the Secretary has found that there is a legitimate need for the practitioner to be so designated because the population served by the practitioner is in a sufficiently remote location that access to medical services is limited.

(B) Practitioners

A practitioner described in this subparagraph is a practitioner who is an employee or contractor of the Indian Health Service, or is working for an Indian tribe or tribal organization under its contract or compact under the Indian Self-Determination and Education Assistance Act [25 U.S.C. 450 et seq.] with the Indian Health Service.

(h) Special registration for telemedicine

(1) In general

The Attorney General may issue to a practitioner a special registration to engage in the practice of telemedicine for purposes of section 802(54)(E) of this title if the practitioner, upon application for such special registration—

(A) demonstrates a legitimate need for the special registration; and

(B) is registered under section 823(f) of this title in the State in which the patient will be located when receiving the telemedicine treatment, unless the practitioner—

(i) is exempted from such registration in all States under section 822(d) of this title; or

(ii) is an employee or contractor of the Department of Veterans Affairs who is acting in the scope of such employment or contract and is registered under section 823(f) of this title in any State or is utilizing the registration of a hospital or clinic operated by the Department of Veterans Affairs registered under section 823(f) of this title.

(2) Regulations

The Attorney General shall, with the concurrence of the Secretary, promulgate regulations specifying the limited circumstances in which a special registration under this subsection may be issued and the procedures for obtaining such a special registration.

(3) Denials

Proceedings to deny an application for registration under this subsection shall be conducted in accordance with section 824(c) of this title.

(i) Reporting of telemedicine by VHA during medical emergency situations

(1) In general

Any practitioner issuing a prescription for a controlled substance under the authorization to conduct telemedicine during a medical emergency situation described in section 802(54)(F) of this title shall report to the Secretary of Veterans Affairs the authorization of that emergency prescription, in accordance with such requirements as the Secretary of Veterans Affairs shall, by regulation, establish.

(2) To Attorney General

Not later than 30 days after the date that a prescription described in subparagraph (A) is issued, the Secretary of Veterans Affairs shall report to the Attorney General the authorization of that emergency prescription.

(j) Clarification concerning prescription transfers

Any transfer between pharmacies of information relating to a prescription for a controlled substance shall meet the applicable requirements under regulations promulgated by the Attorney General under this chapter.

(Pub. L. 91–513, title II, §311, as added Pub. L. 110–425, §3(d)(1), Oct. 15, 2008, 122 Stat. 4825.)

REFERENCES IN TEXT

Section 309, referred to in subsec. (c)(7), is section 309 of Pub. L. 91–513, which is classified to section 829 of this title.

For effective date of this section, referred to in subsec. (d)(3), see Effective Date note below.

The Indian Self-Determination and Education Assistance Act, referred to in subsec. (g)(1), (2)(B), is Pub. L. 93–638, Jan. 4, 1975, 88 Stat. 2203, which is classified principally to subchapter II (§450 et seq.) of chapter 14 of Title 25, Indians. For complete classification of this Act to the Code, see Short Title note set out under section 450 of Title 25 and Tables.

This chapter, referred to in subsec. (j), was in the original "this Act", meaning Pub. L. 91–513, Oct. 27, 1970, 84 Stat. 1236. For complete classification of this Act to the Code, see Short Title note set out under section 801 of this title and Tables.

EFFECTIVE DATE

Section effective 180 days after Oct. 15, 2008, except as otherwise provided, see section 3(j) of Pub. L. 110–425, set out as an Effective Date of 2008 Amendment note under section 802 of this title.

PART D—OFFENSES AND PENALTIES

§841. Prohibited acts A

(a) Unlawful acts

Except as authorized by this subchapter, it shall be unlawful for any person knowingly or intentionally—

(1) to manufacture, distribute, or dispense, or possess with intent to manufacture, distribute, or dispense, a controlled substance; or

(2) to create, distribute, or dispense, or possess with intent to distribute or dispense, a counterfeit substance.

(b) Penalties

Except as otherwise provided in section 849, 859, 860, or 861 of this title, any person who violates subsection (a) of this section shall be sentenced as follows:

(1)(A) In the case of a violation of subsection (a) of this section involving—

(i) 1 kilogram or more of a mixture or substance containing a detectable amount of heroin;

(ii) 5 kilograms or more of a mixture or substance containing a detectable amount of—

(I) coca leaves, except coca leaves and extracts of coca leaves from which cocaine, ecgonine, and derivatives of ecgonine or their salts have been removed;

(II) cocaine, its salts, optical and geometric isomers, and salts of isomers;

(III) ecgonine, its derivatives, their salts, isomers, and salts of isomers; or

(IV) any compound, mixture, or preparation which contains any quantity of any of the substances referred to in subclauses (I) through (III);

(iii) 50 grams or more of a mixture or substance described in clause (ii) which contains cocaine base;

(iv) 100 grams or more of phencyclidine (PCP) or 1 kilogram or more of a mixture or substance containing a detectable amount of phencyclidine (PCP);

(v) 10 grams or more of a mixture or substance containing a detectable amount of lysergic acid diethylamide (LSD);

(vi) 400 grams or more of a mixture or substance containing a detectable amount of N-phenyl-N-[1-(2-phenylethyl)-4-piperidinyl] propanamide or 100 grams or more of a mixture or substance containing a detectable amount of any analogue of N-phenyl-N-[1-(2-phenylethyl)-4-piperidinyl] propanamide;

(vii) 1000 kilograms or more of a mixture or substance containing a detectable amount of marihuana, or 1,000 or more marihuana plants regardless of weight; or

(viii) 50 grams or more of methamphetamine, its salts, isomers, and salts of its isomers or 500 grams or more of a mixture or substance containing a detectable amount of methamphetamine, its salts, isomers, or salts of its isomers;

such person shall be sentenced to a term of imprisonment which may not be less than 10 years or more than life and if death or serious bodily injury results from the use of such substance shall be not less than 20 years or more than life, a fine not to exceed the greater of that authorized in accordance with the provisions of title 18 or $4,000,000 if the defendant is an individual or $10,000,000 if the defendant is other than an individual, or both. If any person commits such a violation after a prior conviction for a felony drug offense has become final, such person shall be sentenced to a term of imprisonment which may not be less than 20 years and not more than life imprisonment and if death or serious bodily injury results from the use of such substance shall be sentenced to life imprisonment, a fine not to exceed the greater of twice that authorized in accordance with the provisions of title 18 or $8,000,000 if the defendant is an individual or $20,000,000 if the defendant is other than an individual, or both. If any person commits a violation of this subparagraph or of section 849, 859, 860, or 861 of this title after two or more prior convictions for a felony drug offense have become final, such person shall be sentenced to a mandatory term of life imprisonment without release and fined in accordance with the preceding sentence. Notwithstanding section 3583 of title 18, any sentence under this subparagraph shall, in the absence of such a prior conviction, impose a term of supervised release of at least 5 years in addition to such term of imprisonment and shall, if there was such a prior conviction, impose a term of supervised release of at least 10 years in addition to such term of imprisonment. Notwithstanding any other provision of law, the court shall not place on probation or suspend the sentence of any person sentenced under this subparagraph. No person sentenced under this subparagraph shall be eligible for parole during the term of imprisonment imposed therein.

(B) In the case of a violation of subsection (a) of this section involving—

(i) 100 grams or more of a mixture or substance containing a detectable amount of heroin;

(ii) 500 grams or more of a mixture or substance containing a detectable amount of—

(I) coca leaves, except coca leaves and extracts of coca leaves from which cocaine, ecgonine, and derivatives of ecgonine or their salts have been removed;

(II) cocaine, its salts, optical and geometric isomers, and salts of isomers;

(III) ecgonine, its derivatives, their salts, isomers, and salts of isomers; or

(IV) any compound, mixture, or preparation which contains any quantity of any of the substances referred to in subclauses (I) through (III);

(iii) 5 grams or more of a mixture or substance described in clause (ii) which contains cocaine base;

(iv) 10 grams or more of phencyclidine (PCP) or 100 grams or more of a mixture or substance containing a detectable amount of phencyclidine (PCP);

(v) 1 gram or more of a mixture or substance containing a detectable amount of lysergic acid diethylamide (LSD);

(vi) 40 grams or more of a mixture or substance containing a detectable amount of N-phenyl-N-[1-(2-phenylethyl)-4-piperidinyl] propanamide or 10 grams or more of a mixture or substance containing a detectable amount of any analogue of N-phenyl-N-[1-(2-phenylethyl)-4-piperidinyl] propanamide;

(vii) 100 kilograms or more of a mixture or substance containing a detectable amount of marihuana, or 100 or more marihuana plants regardless of weight; or

(viii) 5 grams or more of methamphetamine, its salts, isomers, and salts of its isomers or 50 grams or more of a mixture or substance containing a detectable amount of methamphetamine, its salts, isomers, or salts of its isomers;

such person shall be sentenced to a term of imprisonment which may not be less than 5 years and not more than 40 years and if death or serious bodily injury results from the use of such substance shall be not less than 20 years or more than life, a fine not to exceed the greater of that authorized in accordance with the provisions of title 18 or $2,000,000 if the defendant is an individual or $5,000,000 if the defendant is other than an individual, or both. If any person commits such a violation after a prior conviction for a felony drug offense has become final, such person shall be sentenced to a term of imprisonment which may not be less than 10 years and not more than life imprisonment and if death or serious bodily injury results from the use of such substance shall be sentenced to life imprisonment, a fine not to exceed the greater of twice that authorized in accordance with the provisions of title 18 or $4,000,000 if the defendant is an individual or $10,000,000 if the defendant is other than an individual, or both. Notwithstanding section 3583 of title 18, any sentence imposed under this subparagraph shall, in the absence of such a prior conviction, include a term of supervised release of at least 4 years in addition to such term of imprisonment and shall, if there was such a prior conviction, include a term of supervised release of at least 8 years in addition to such term of imprisonment. Notwithstanding any other provision of law, the court shall not place on probation or suspend the sentence of any person sentenced under this subparagraph. No person sentenced under this subparagraph shall be eligible for parole during the term of imprisonment imposed therein.

(C) In the case of a controlled substance in schedule I or II, gamma hydroxybutyric acid (including when scheduled as an approved drug product for purposes of section 3(a)(1)(B) of the Hillory J. Farias and Samantha Reid Date-Rape Drug Prohibition Act of 2000), or 1 gram of flunitrazepam, except as provided in subparagraphs (A), (B), and (D), such person shall be sentenced to a term of imprisonment of not more than 20 years and if death or serious bodily injury results from the use of such substance shall be sentenced to a term of imprisonment of not less than twenty years or more than life, a fine not to exceed the greater of that authorized in accordance with the provisions of title 18 or $1,000,000 if the defendant is an individual or $5,000,000 if the defendant is other than an individual, or both. If any person commits such a violation after a prior conviction for a felony drug offense has become final, such person shall be sentenced to a term of imprisonment of not more than 30 years and if death or serious bodily injury results from the use of such substance shall be sentenced to life imprisonment, a fine not to exceed the greater of twice that authorized in accordance with the provisions of title 18 or $2,000,000 if the defendant is an individual or $10,000,000 if the defendant is other than an individual, or both. Notwithstanding section 3583 of title 18, any sentence imposing a term of imprisonment under this paragraph shall, in the absence of such a prior conviction, impose a term of supervised release of at least 3 years in addition to such term of imprisonment and shall, if there was such a prior conviction, impose a term of supervised release of at least 6 years in addition to such term of imprisonment. Notwithstanding any other provision of law, the court shall not place on probation or suspend the sentence of any person sentenced under the provisions of this subparagraph which provide for a mandatory term of imprisonment if death or serious bodily injury results, nor shall a person so sentenced be eligible for parole during the term of such a sentence.

(D) In the case of less than 50 kilograms of marihuana, except in the case of 50 or more marihuana plants regardless of weight, 10 kilograms of hashish, or one kilogram of hashish oil, such person shall, except as provided in paragraphs (4) and (5) of this subsection, be sentenced to a term of imprisonment of not more than 5 years, a fine not to exceed the greater of that authorized in accordance with the provisions of title 18 or $250,000 if the defendant is an individual or $1,000,000 if the defendant is other than an individual, or both. If any person commits such a violation after a prior conviction for a felony drug offense has become final, such person shall be sentenced to a term of imprisonment of not more than 10 years, a fine not to exceed the greater of twice that authorized in accordance with the provisions of title 18 or $500,000 if the defendant is an individual or $2,000,000 if the defendant is other than an individual, or both. Notwithstanding section 3583 of title 18, any sentence imposing a term of imprisonment under this paragraph shall, in the absence of such a prior conviction, impose a term of supervised release of at least 2 years in addition to such term of imprisonment and shall, if there was such a prior conviction, impose a term of supervised release of at least 4 years in addition to such term of imprisonment.

(E)(i) Except as provided in subparagraphs (C) and (D), in the case of any controlled substance in schedule III, such person shall be sentenced to a term of imprisonment of not more than 10 years and if death or serious bodily injury results from the use of such substance shall be sentenced to a term of imprisonment of not more than 15 years, a fine not to exceed the greater of that authorized in accordance with the provisions of title 18 or $500,000 if the defendant is an individual or $2,500,000 if the defendant is other than an individual, or both.

(ii) If any person commits such a violation after a prior conviction for a felony drug offense has become final, such person shall be sentenced to a term of imprisonment of not more than 20 years and if death or serious bodily injury results from the use of such substance shall be sentenced to a term of imprisonment of not more than 30 years, a fine not to exceed the greater of twice that authorized in accordance with the provisions of title 18 or $1,000,000 if the defendant is an individual or $5,000,000 if the defendant is other than an individual, or both.

(iii) Any sentence imposing a term of imprisonment under this subparagraph shall, in the absence of such a prior conviction, impose a term of supervised release of at least 2 years in addition to such term of imprisonment and shall, if there was such a prior conviction, impose a term of supervised release of at least 4 years in addition to such term of imprisonment.

(2) In the case of a controlled substance in schedule IV, such person shall be sentenced to a term of imprisonment of not more than 5 years, a fine not to exceed the greater of that authorized in accordance with the provisions of title 18 or $250,000 if the defendant is an individual or $1,000,000 if the defendant is other than an individual, or both. If any person commits such a violation after a prior conviction for a felony drug offense has become final, such person shall be sentenced to a term of imprisonment of not more than 10 years, a fine not to exceed the greater of twice that authorized in accordance with the provisions of title 18 or $500,000 if the defendant is an individual or $2,000,000 if the defendant is other than an individual, or both. Any sentence imposing a term of imprisonment under this paragraph shall, in the absence of such a prior conviction, impose a term of supervised release of at least one year in addition to such term of imprisonment and shall, if there was such a prior conviction, impose a term of supervised release of at least 2 years in addition to such term of imprisonment.

(3) In the case of a controlled substance in schedule V, such person shall be sentenced to a term of imprisonment of not more than one year, a fine not to exceed the greater of that authorized in accordance with the provisions of title 18 or $100,000 if the defendant is an individual or $250,000 if the defendant is other than an individual, or both. If any person commits such a violation after a prior conviction for a felony drug offense has become final, such person shall be sentenced to a term of imprisonment of not more than 4 years, a fine not to exceed the greater of twice that authorized in accordance with the provisions of title 18 or $200,000 if the defendant is an individual or $500,000 if the defendant is other than an individual, or both. Any sentence imposing a term of imprisonment under this paragraph may, if there was a prior conviction, impose a term of supervised release of not more than 1 year, in addition to such term of imprisonment.

(4) Notwithstanding paragraph (1)(D) of this subsection, any person who violates subsection (a) of this section by distributing a small amount of marihuana for no remuneration shall be treated as provided in section 844 of this title and section 3607 of title 18.

(5) Any person who violates subsection (a) of this section by cultivating or manufacturing a controlled substance on Federal property shall be imprisoned as provided in this subsection and shall be fined any amount not to exceed—

(A) the amount authorized in accordance with this section;

(B) the amount authorized in accordance with the provisions of title 18;

(C) $500,000 if the defendant is an individual; or

(D) $1,000,000 if the defendant is other than an individual;

or both.

(6) Any person who violates subsection (a) of this section, or attempts to do so, and knowingly or intentionally uses a poison, chemical, or other hazardous substance on Federal land, and, by such use—

(A) creates a serious hazard to humans, wildlife, or domestic animals,

(B) degrades or harms the environment or natural resources, or

(C) pollutes an aquifer, spring, stream, river, or body of water,

shall be fined in accordance with title 18 or imprisoned not more than five years, or both.

(7) PENALTIES FOR DISTRIBUTION.—

(A) IN GENERAL.—Whoever, with intent to commit a crime of violence, as defined in section 16 of title 18 (including rape), against an individual, violates subsection (a) of this section by distributing a controlled substance or controlled substance analogue to that individual without that individual's knowledge, shall be imprisoned not more than 20 years and fined in accordance with title 18.

(B) DEFINITION.—For purposes of this paragraph, the term "without that individual's knowledge" means that the individual is unaware that a substance with the ability to alter that individual's ability to appraise conduct or to decline participation in or communicate unwillingness to participate in conduct is administered to the individual.

(c) Offenses involving listed chemicals

Any person who knowingly or intentionally—

(1) possesses a listed chemical with intent to manufacture a controlled substance except as authorized by this subchapter;

(2) possesses or distributes a listed chemical knowing, or having reasonable cause to believe, that the listed chemical will be used to manufacture a controlled substance except as authorized by this subchapter; or

(3) with the intent of causing the evasion of the recordkeeping or reporting requirements of section 830 of this title, or the regulations issued under that section, receives or distributes a reportable amount of any listed chemical in units small enough so that the making of records or filing of reports under that section is not required;

shall be fined in accordance with title 18 or imprisoned not more than 20 years in the case of a violation of paragraph (1) or (2) involving a list I chemical or not more than 10 years in the case of a violation of this subsection other than a violation of paragraph (1) or (2) involving a list I chemical, or both.

(d) Boobytraps on Federal property; penalties; "boobytrap" defined

(1) Any person who assembles, maintains, places, or causes to be placed a boobytrap on Federal property where a controlled substance is being manufactured, distributed, or dispensed shall be sentenced to a term of imprisonment for not more than 10 years or fined under title 18, or both.

(2) If any person commits such a violation after 1 or more prior convictions for an offense punishable under this subsection, such person shall be sentenced to a term of imprisonment of not more than 20 years or fined under title 18, or both.

(3) For the purposes of this subsection, the term "boobytrap" means any concealed or camouflaged device designed to cause bodily injury when triggered by any action of any unsuspecting person making contact with the device. Such term includes guns, ammunition, or explosive devices attached to trip wires or other triggering mechanisms, sharpened stakes, and lines or wires with hooks attached.

(e) Ten-year injunction as additional penalty

In addition to any other applicable penalty, any person convicted of a felony violation of this section relating to the receipt, distribution, manufacture, exportation, or importation of a listed chemical may be enjoined from engaging in any transaction involving a listed chemical for not more than ten years.

(f) Wrongful distribution or possession of listed chemicals

(1) Whoever knowingly distributes a listed chemical in violation of this subchapter (other than in violation of a recordkeeping or reporting requirement of section 830 of this title) shall, except to the extent that paragraph (12), (13), or (14) of section 842(a) of this title applies, be fined under title 18 or imprisoned not more than 5 years, or both.

(2) Whoever possesses any listed chemical, with knowledge that the recordkeeping or reporting requirements of section 830 of this title have not been adhered to, if, after such knowledge is acquired, such person does not take immediate steps to remedy the violation shall be fined under title 18 or imprisoned not more than one year, or both.

(g) Internet sales of date rape drugs

(1) Whoever knowingly uses the Internet to distribute a date rape drug to any person, knowing or with reasonable cause to believe that—

(A) the drug would be used in the commission of criminal sexual conduct; or

(B) the person is not an authorized purchaser;

shall be fined under this subchapter or imprisoned not more than 20 years, or both.

(2) As used in this subsection:

(A) The term "date rape drug" means—

(i) gamma hydroxybutyric acid (GHB) or any controlled substance analogue of GHB, including gamma butyrolactone (GBL) or 1,4-butanediol;

(ii) ketamine;

(iii) flunitrazepam; or

(iv) any substance which the Attorney General designates, pursuant to the rulemaking procedures prescribed by section 553 of title 5, to be used in committing rape or sexual assault.

The Attorney General is authorized to remove any substance from the list of date rape drugs pursuant to the same rulemaking authority.

(B) The term "authorized purchaser" means any of the following persons, provided such person has acquired the controlled substance in accordance with this chapter:

(i) A person with a valid prescription that is issued for a legitimate medical purpose in the usual course of professional practice that is based upon a qualifying medical relationship by a practitioner registered by the Attorney General. A "qualifying medical relationship" means a medical relationship that exists when the practitioner has conducted at least 1 medical evaluation with the authorized purchaser in the physical presence of the practitioner, without regard to whether portions of the evaluation are conducted by other heath[1] professionals. The preceding sentence shall not be construed to imply that 1 medical evaluation demonstrates that a prescription has been issued for a legitimate medical purpose within the usual course of professional practice.

(ii) Any practitioner or other registrant who is otherwise authorized by their registration to dispense, procure, purchase, manufacture, transfer, distribute, import, or export the substance under this chapter.

[1] So in original. Probably should be "health".

(iii) A person or entity providing documentation that establishes the name, address, and business of the person or entity and which provides a legitimate purpose for using any "date rape drug" for which a prescription is not required.

(3) The Attorney General is authorized to promulgate regulations for record-keeping and reporting by persons handling 1,4-butanediol in order to implement and enforce the provisions of this section. Any record or report required by such regulations shall be considered a record or report required under this chapter.

(h) Offenses involving dispensing of controlled substances by means of the Internet

(1) In general

It shall be unlawful for any person to knowingly or intentionally—

(A) deliver, distribute, or dispense a controlled substance by means of the Internet, except as authorized by this subchapter; or

(B) aid or abet (as such terms are used in section 2 of title 18) any activity described in subparagraph (A) that is not authorized by this subchapter.

(2) Examples

Examples of activities that violate paragraph (1) include, but are not limited to, knowingly or intentionally—

(A) delivering, distributing, or dispensing a controlled substance by means of the Internet by an online pharmacy that is not validly registered with a modification authorizing such activity as required by section 823(f) of this title (unless exempt from such registration);

(B) writing a prescription for a controlled substance for the purpose of delivery, distribution, or dispensation by means of the Internet in violation of section 829(e) of the title;

(C) serving as an agent, intermediary, or other entity that causes the Internet to be used to bring together a buyer and seller to engage in the dispensing of a controlled substance in a manner not authorized by sections[2] 823(f) or 829(e) of this title;

(D) offering to fill a prescription for a controlled substance based solely on a consumer's completion of an online medical questionnaire; and

(E) making a material false, fictitious, or fraudulent statement or representation in a notification or declaration under subsection (d) or (e), respectively, of section 831 of this title.

(3) Inapplicability

(A) This subsection does not apply to—

(i) the delivery, distribution, or dispensation of controlled substances by nonpractitioners to the extent authorized by their registration under this subchapter;

(ii) the placement on the Internet of material that merely advocates the use of a controlled substance or includes pricing information without attempting to propose or facilitate an actual transaction involving a controlled substance; or

(iii) except as provided in subparagraph (B), any activity that is limited to—

(I) the provision of a telecommunications service, or of an Internet access service or Internet information location tool (as those terms are defined in section 231 of title 47); or

(II) the transmission, storage, retrieval, hosting, formatting, or translation (or any combination thereof) of a communication, without selection or alteration of the content of the communication, except that deletion of a particular communication or material made by another person in a manner consistent with section 230(c) of title 47 shall not constitute such selection or alteration of the content of the communication.

(B) The exceptions under subclauses (I) and (II) of subparagraph (A)(iii) shall not apply to a person acting in concert with a person who violates paragraph (1).

(4) Knowing or intentional violation

Any person who knowingly or intentionally violates this subsection shall be sentenced in accordance with subsection (b).

(Pub. L. 91–513, title II, §401, Oct. 27, 1970, 84 Stat. 1260; Pub. L. 95–633, title II, §201, Nov. 10, 1978, 92 Stat. 3774; Pub. L. 96–359, §8(c), Sept. 26, 1980, 94 Stat. 1194; Pub. L. 98–473, title II, §§224(a), 502, 503(b)(1), (2), Oct. 12, 1984, 98 Stat. 2030, 2068, 2070; Pub. L. 99–570, title I, §§1002, 1003(a), 1004(a), 1005(a), 1103, title XV, §15005, Oct. 27, 1986, 100 Stat. 3207–2, 3207–5, 3207–6, 3207–11, 3702–192; Pub. L. 100–690, title VI, §§6055, 6254(h), 6452(a), 6470(g), (h), 6479, Nov. 18, 1988, 102 Stat. 4318, 4367, 4371, 4378, 4381; Pub. L. 101–647, title X, §1002(e), title XII, §1202, title XXXV, §3599K, Nov. 29, 1990, 104 Stat. 4828, 4830, 4932; Pub. L. 103–322, title IX, §90105(a), (c), title XVIII, §180201(b)(2)(A), Sept. 13, 1994, 108 Stat. 1987, 1988, 2047; Pub. L. 104–237, title II, §206(a), title III, §302(a), Oct. 3, 1996, 110 Stat. 3103, 3105; Pub. L. 104–305, §2(a), (b)(1), Oct. 13, 1996, 110 Stat. 3807; Pub. L. 105–277, div. E, §2(a), Oct. 21, 1998, 112 Stat. 2681–759; Pub. L. 106–172, §§3(b)(1), 5(b), 9, Feb. 18, 2000, 114 Stat. 9, 10, 13; Pub. L. 107–273, div. B, title III, §3005(a), title IV, §4002(d)(2)(A), Nov. 2, 2002, 116 Stat. 1805, 1809; Pub. L. 109–177, title VII, §§711(f)(1)(B), 732, Mar. 9, 2006, 120 Stat. 262, 270; Pub. L. 109–248, title II, §201, July 27, 2006, 120 Stat. 611; Pub. L. 110–425, §3(e), (f), Oct. 15, 2008, 122 Stat. 4828, 4829.)

REFERENCES IN TEXT

This subchapter, referred to in subsecs. (a), (b)(1), (c)(1), (2), (f)(1), (g)(1), and (h)(1), (3)(A)(i), was in the original "this title", meaning title II of Pub. L. 91–513, Oct. 27, 1970, 84 Stat. 1242, and is popularly known as the "Controlled Substances Act". For complete classification of title II to the Code, see second paragraph of Short Title note set out under section 801 of this title and Tables.

Schedules I, II, III, IV, and V, referred to in subsec. (b), are set out in section 812(c) of this title.

Subchapter II of this chapter, referred to in subsec. (b)(1), was in the original "title III", meaning title III of Pub. L. 91–513, Oct. 27, 1970, 84 Stat. 1285. Part A of title III comprises subchapter II of this chapter. For

[2] So in original. Probably should be "section".

classification of Part B, consisting of sections 1101 to 1105 of title III, see Tables.

Section 3(a)(1)(B) of the Hillory J. Farias and Samantha Reid Date-Rape Prohibition Act of 2000, referred to in subsec. (b)(1)(C), is section 3(a)(1)(B) of Pub. L. 106–172, which is set out in a note under section 812 of this title.

This chapter, referred to in subsec. (g)(2)(B), (3), was in the original "this Act", meaning Pub. L. 91–513, Oct. 27, 1970, 84 Stat. 1236. For complete classification of this Act to the Code, see Short Title note set out under section 801 of this title and Tables.

AMENDMENTS

2008—Subsec. (b)(1)(D). Pub. L. 110–425, § 3(e)(1)(A), struck out "or in the case of any controlled substance in schedule III (other than gamma hydroxybutyric acid), or 30 milligrams of flunitrazepam" after "hashish oil".

Subsec. (b)(1)(E). Pub. L. 110–425, § 3(e)(1)(B), added subpar. (E).

Subsec. (b)(2). Pub. L. 110–425, § 3(e)(2), substituted "5 years" for "3 years", "10 years" for "6 years", and "after a prior conviction for a felony drug offense has become final," for "after one or more prior convictions of him for an offense punishable under this paragraph, or for a felony under any other provision of this subchapter or subchapter II of this chapter or other law of a State, the United States, or a foreign country relating to narcotic drugs, marihuana, or depressant or stimulant substances, have become final,".

Subsec. (b)(3). Pub. L. 110–425, § 3(e)(3), substituted "4 years" for "2 years" and "after a prior conviction for a felony drug offense has become final," for "after one or more convictions of him for an offense punishable under this paragraph, or for a crime under any other provision of this subchapter or subchapter II of this chapter or other law of a State, the United States, or a foreign country relating to narcotic drugs, marihuana, or depressant or stimulant substances, have become final," and inserted at end "Any sentence imposing a term of imprisonment under this paragraph may, if there was a prior conviction, impose a term of supervised release of not more than 1 year, in addition to such term of imprisonment."

Subsec. (h). Pub. L. 110–425, § 3(f), added subsec. (h).

2006—Subsec. (b)(5). Pub. L. 109–177, § 732, inserted "or manufacturing" after "cultivating" in introductory provisions.

Subsec. (f)(1). Pub. L. 109–177, § 711(f)(1)(B), inserted ", except to the extent that paragraph (12), (13), or (14) of section 842(a) of this title applies," after "shall".

Subsec. (g). Pub. L. 109–248 added subsec. (g).

2002—Subsec. (b)(1)(A), (B). Pub. L. 107–273, § 3005(a), substituted "Notwithstanding section 3583 of title 18, any sentence" for "Any sentence" in concluding provisions.

Subsec. (b)(1)(C), (D). Pub. L. 107–273, § 3005(a), substituted "Notwithstanding section 3583 of title 18, any sentence" for "Any sentence".

Subsec. (d)(1). Pub. L. 107–273, § 4002(d)(2)(A)(i), substituted "or fined under title 18, or both" for "and shall be fined not more than $10,000".

Subsec. (d)(2). Pub. L. 107–273, § 4002(d)(2)(A)(ii), substituted "or fined under title 18, or both" for "and shall be fined not more than $20,000".

2000—Subsec. (b)(1)(C). Pub. L. 106–172, § 3(b)(1)(A), inserted "gamma hydroxybutyric acid (including when scheduled as an approved drug product for purposes of section 3(a)(1)(B) of the Hillory J. Farias and Samantha Reid Date-Rape Drug Prohibition Act of 2000)," after "schedule I or II," in first sentence.

Subsec. (b)(1)(D). Pub. L. 106–172, § 3(b)(1)(B), substituted "(other than gamma hydroxybutyric acid), or 30" for ", or 30".

Subsec. (b)(7)(A). Pub. L. 106–172, § 5(b), inserted "or controlled substance analogue" after "distributing a controlled substance".

Subsecs. (c) to (g). Pub. L. 106–172, § 9, redesignated subsecs. (d) to (g) as (c) to (f), respectively.

1998—Subsec. (b)(1). Pub. L. 105–277 in subpar. (A)(viii) substituted "50 grams" and "500 grams" for "100 grams" and "1 kilogram", respectively, and in subpar. (B)(viii) substituted "5 grams" and "50 grams" for "10 grams" and "100 grams", respectively.

1996—Subsec. (b)(1)(C). Pub. L. 104–305, § 2(b)(1)(A), inserted ", or 1 gram of flunitrazepam," after "schedule I or II".

Subsec. (b)(1)(D). Pub. L. 104–305, § 2(b)(1)(B), inserted "or 30 milligrams of flunitrazepam," after "schedule III,".

Subsec. (b)(7). Pub. L. 104–305, § 2(a), added par. (7).

Subsec. (d). Pub. L. 104–237, § 302(a), in concluding provisions, substituted "not more than 20 years in the case of a violation of paragraph (1) or (2) involving a list I chemical or not more than 10 years in the case of a violation of this subsection other than a violation of paragraph (1) or (2) involving a list I chemical," for "not more than 10 years,".

Subsec. (f). Pub. L. 104–237, § 206(a), inserted "manufacture, exportation," after "distribution," and struck out "regulated" after "engaging in any".

1994—Subsec. (b). Pub. L. 103–322, § 180201(b)(2)(A), inserted "849," before "859," in introductory provisions.

Subsec. (b)(1)(A). Pub. L. 103–322, §§ 90105(c), 180201(b)(2)(A), in concluding provisions, inserted "849," before "859," and struck out "For purposes of this subparagraph, the term 'felony drug offense' means an offense that is a felony under any provision of this subchapter or any other Federal law that prohibits or restricts conduct relating to narcotic drugs, marihuana, or depressant or stimulant substances or a felony under any law of a State or a foreign country that prohibits or restricts conduct relating to narcotic drugs, marihuana, or depressant or stimulant substances." before "Any sentence under this subparagraph".

Subsec. (b)(1)(B). Pub. L. 103–322, § 90105(a), in sentence in concluding provisions beginning "If any person commits", substituted "a prior conviction for a felony drug offense has become final" for "one or more prior convictions for an offense punishable under this paragraph, or for a felony under any other provision of this subchapter or subchapter II of this chapter or other law of a State, the United States, or a foreign country relating to narcotic drugs, marihuana, or depressant or stimulant substances, have become final".

Subsec. (b)(1)(C). Pub. L. 103–322, § 90105(a), in sentence beginning "If any person commits", substituted "a prior conviction for a felony drug offense has become final" for "one or more prior convictions for an offense punishable under this paragraph, or for a felony under any other provision of this subchapter or subchapter II of this chapter or other law of a State, the United States or a foreign country relating to narcotic drugs, marihuana, or depressant or stimulant substances, have become final".

Subsec. (b)(1)(D). Pub. L. 103–322, § 90105(a), in sentence beginning "If any person commits", substituted "a prior conviction for a felony drug offense has become final" for "one or more prior convictions of him for an offense punishable under this paragraph, or for a felony under any other provision of this subchapter or subchapter II of this chapter or other law of a State, the United States, or a foreign country relating to narcotic drugs, marihuana, or depressant or stimulant substances, have become final".

1990—Subsec. (b). Pub. L. 101–647, § 1002(e)(1), substituted "section 859, 860, or 861" for "section 845, 845a, or 845b" in introductory provisions.

Subsec. (b)(1)(A). Pub. L. 101–647, § 1002(e)(1), substituted "section 859, 860, or 861" for "section 845, 845a, or 845b" in concluding provisions.

Subsec. (b)(1)(A)(ii)(IV). Pub. L. 101–647, § 3599K, substituted "any of the substances" for "any of the substance".

Subsec. (b)(1)(A)(viii). Pub. L. 101–647, § 1202, substituted "or 1 kilogram or more of a mixture or substance containing a detectable amount of methamphetamine" for "or 100 grams or more of a mixture or substance containing a detectable amount of methamphetamine".

Subsec. (b)(1)(B)(ii)(IV). Pub. L. 101–647, §3599K, substituted "any of the substances" for "any of the substance".

Subsec. (c). Pub. L. 101–647, §1002(e)(2), directed amendment of subsec. (c) by substituting "section 859, 860, or 861 of this title" for "section 845, 845a, or 845b of this title". Subsec. (c) was previously repealed by Pub. L. 98–473, §224(a)(2), as renumbered by Pub. L. 99–570, §1005(a), effective Nov. 1, 1987, and applicable only to offenses committed after the taking effect of such amendment. See 1984 Amendment note and Effective Date of 1984 Amendment note below.

1988—Subsec. (b)(1)(A). Pub. L. 100–690, §§6452(a), 6470(g), 6479(1), inserted ", or 1,000 or more marihuana plants regardless of weight" in cl. (vii), added cl. (viii), substituted "a prior conviction for a felony drug offense has become final" for "one or more prior convictions for an offense punishable under this paragraph, or for a felony under any other provision of this subchapter or subchapter II of this chapter or other law of a State, the United States, or a foreign country relating to narcotic drugs, marihuana, or depressant or stimulant substances, have become final" in second sentence, and added provisions relating to sentencing for a person who violates this subpar. or section 485, 485a, or 485b of this title after two or more prior convictions for a felony drug offense have become final and defining "felony drug offense".

Subsec. (b)(1)(B). Pub. L. 100–690, §§6470(h), 6479(2), inserted ", or 100 or more marihuana plants regardless of weight" in cl. (vii) and added cl. (viii).

Subsec. (b)(1)(D). Pub. L. 100–690, §6479(3), substituted "50 or more marihuana plants" for "100 or more marihuana plants".

Subsec. (b)(6). Pub. L. 100–690, §6254(h), added par. (6).

Subsec. (d). Pub. L. 100–690, §6055(a), amended subsec. (d) generally. Prior to amendment, subsec. (d) read as follows: "Any person who knowingly or intentionally—

"(1) possesses any piperidine with intent to manufacture phencyclidine except as authorized by this subchapter, or

"(2) possesses any piperidine knowing, or having reasonable cause to believe, that the piperidine will be used to manufacture phencyclidine except as authorized by this subchapter,

shall be sentenced to a term of imprisonment of not more than 5 years, a fine not to exceed the greater of that authorized in accordance with the provisions of title 18 or $250,000 if the defendant is an individual or $1,000,000 if the defendant is other than an individual, or both."

Subsecs. (f), (g). Pub. L. 100–690, §6055(b), added subsecs. (f) and (g).

1986—Pub. L. 99–570, §1005(a), amended Pub. L. 98–473, §224(a). See 1984 Amendment note below.

Subsec. (b). Pub. L. 99–570, §1103(a), substituted ", 845a, or 845b" for "or 845a" in introductory provisions.

Subsec. (b)(1)(A). Pub. L. 99–570, §1002(2), amended subpar. (A) generally. Prior to amendment, subpar. (A) read as follows: "In the case of a violation of subsection (a) of this section involving—

"(i) 100 grams or more of a controlled substance in schedule I or II which is a mixture or substance containing a detectable amount of a narcotic drug other than a narcotic drug consisting of—

"(I) coca leaves;

"(II) a compound, manufacture, salt, derivative, or preparation of coca leaves; or

"(III) a substance chemically identical thereto;

"(ii) a kilogram or more of any other controlled substance in schedule I or II which is a narcotic drug;

"(iii) 500 grams or more of phencyclidine (PCP); or

"(iv) 5 grams or more of lysergic acid diethylamide (LSD);

such person shall be sentenced to a term of imprisonment of not more than 20 years, a fine of not more than $250,000, or both. If any person commits such a violation after one or more prior convictions of him for an offense punishable under this paragraph, or for a felony under any other provision of this subchapter or subchapter II of this chapter or other law of a State, the United States, or a foreign country relating to narcotic drugs, marihuana, or depressant or stimulant substances, have become final, such person shall be sentenced to a term of imprisonment of not more than 40 years, a fine of not more than $500,000, or both".

Subsec. (b)(1)(B). Pub. L. 99–570, §1002(2), amended subpar. (B) generally. Prior to amendment, subpar. (B) read as follows: "In the case of a controlled substance in schedule I or II except as provided in subparagraphs (A) and (C),, such person shall be sentenced to a term of imprisonment of not more than 15 years, a fine of not more than $125,000, or both. If any person commits such a violation after one or more prior convictions of him for an offense punishable under this paragraph, or for a felony under any other provision of this subchapter or subchapter II of this chapter or other law of a State, the United States, or a foreign country relating to narcotic drugs, marihuana, or depressant or stimulant substances, have become final, such person shall be sentenced to a term of imprisonment of not more than 30 years, a fine of not more than $250,000, or both. Any sentence imposing a term of imprisonment under this paragraph shall, in the absence of such a prior conviction, impose a special parole term of at least 3 years in addition to such term of imprisonment and shall, if there was such a prior conviction, impose a special parole term of at least 6 years in addition to such term of imprisonment."

Subsec. (b)(1)(C). Pub. L. 99–570, §1002(2), added subpar. (C). Former subpar. (C) redesignated (D).

Subsec. (b)(1)(D). Pub. L. 99–570, §1004(a), substituted "term of supervised release" for "special parole term" in two places.

Pub. L. 99–570, §§1002(1), 1003(a)(1), redesignated former subpar. (C) as (D), substituted "a fine not to exceed the greater of that authorized in accordance with the provisions of title 18 or $250,000 if the defendant is an individual or $1,000,000 if the defendant is other than an individual" for "a fine of not more than $50,000" and "a fine not to exceed the greater of twice that authorized in accordance with the provisions of title 18 or $500,000 if the defendant is an individual or $2,000,000 if the defendant is other than an individual" for "a fine of not more than $100,000", and inserted "except in the case of 100 or more marihuana plants regardless of weight,".

Subsec. (b)(2). Pub. L. 99–570, §1004(a), substituted "term of supervised release" for "special parole term" in two places.

Pub. L. 99–570, §1003(a)(2), substituted "a fine not to exceed the greater of that authorized in accordance with the provisions of title 18 or $250,000 if the defendant is an individual or $1,000,000 if the defendant is other than an individual" for "a fine of not more than $25,000" and "a fine not to exceed the greater of twice that authorized in accordance with the provisions of title 18 or $500,000 if the defendant is an individual or $2,000,000 if the defendant is other than an individual" for "a fine of not more than $50,000".

Subsec. (b)(3). Pub. L. 99–570, §1003(a)(3), substituted "a fine not to exceed the greater of that authorized in accordance with the provisions of title 18 or $100,000 if the defendant is an individual or $250,000 if the defendant is other than an individual" for "a fine of not more than $10,000" and "a fine not to exceed the greater of twice that authorized in accordance with the provisions of title 18 or $200,000 if the defendant is an individual or $500,000 if the defendant is other than an individual" for "a fine of not more than $20,000".

Subsec. (b)(4). Pub. L. 99–570, §1003(a)(4), which directed the substitution of "1(D)" for "1(C)" was executed by substituting "(1)(D)" for "(1)(C)" as the probable intent of Congress.

Subsec. (b)(5). Pub. L. 99–570, §1003(a)(5), amended par. (5) generally. Prior to amendment, par. (5) read as follows: "Notwithstanding paragraph (1), any person who violates subsection (a) of this section by cultivating a controlled substance on Federal property shall be fined not more than—

"(A) $500,000 if such person is an individual; and

"(B) $1,000,000 if such person is not an individual."

Subsec. (c). Pub. L. 99–570, §1004(a), substituted "term of supervised release" for "special parole term" wherever appearing, effective Nov. 1, 1987, the effective date of the repeal of subsec. (c) by Pub. L. 98–473, §224(a)(2). See 1984 Amendment note below.

Pub. L. 99–570, §1103(b), substituted ", 845a, or 845b" for "845a" in two places.

Subsec. (d). Pub. L. 99–570, §1003(a)(6), substituted "a fine not to exceed the greater of that authorized in accordance with the provisions of title 18 or $250,000 if the defendant is an individual or $1,000,000 if the defendant is other than an individual" for "a fine of not more than $15,000".

Subsec. (e). Pub. L. 99–570, §15005, added subsec. (e).

1984—Subsec. (b). Pub. L. 98–473, §503(b)(1), inserted reference to section 845a of this title in provisions preceding par. (1)(A).

Pub. L. 98–473, §224(a)(1)–(3), (5), which directed amendment of this subsection effective Nov. 1, 1987 (see section 235(a)(1) of Pub. L. 98–473 set out as an Effective Date note under section 3551 of Title 18, Crimes and Criminal Procedure) was repealed by Pub. L. 99–570, §1005(a), and the remaining pars. (4) and (6) of Pub. L. 98–473, §224(a), were redesignated as pars. (1) and (2), respectively.

Subsec. (b)(1)(A). Pub. L. 98–473, §502(1)(A), added subpar. (A). Former subpar. (A) redesignated (B).

Subsec. (b)(1)(B). Pub. L. 98–473, §502(1)(A), (B), redesignated former subpar. (A) as (B), substituted "except as provided in subparagraphs (A) and (C)," for "which is a narcotic drug", "$125,000" for "$25,000", and "$250,000" for "$50,000", and inserted references to laws of a State and a foreign country. Former subpar. (B) redesignated (C).

Subsec. (b)(1)(C). Pub. L. 98–473, §502(1)(A), (C), redesignated former subpar. (B) as (C), substituted "less than 50 kilograms of marihuana, 10 kilograms of hashish, or one kilogram of hashish oil" for "a controlled substance in schedule I or II which is not a narcotic drug", "and (5)" for ", (5), and (6)", "$50,000" for "$15,000", and "$100,000" for "$30,000", and inserted references to laws of a State and a foreign country.

Subsec. (b)(2). Pub. L. 98–473, §502(2), substituted "$25,000" for "$10,000" and "$50,000" for "$20,000", and inserted references to laws of a State or of a foreign country.

Subsec. (b)(3). Pub. L. 98–473, §502(3), substituted "$10,000" for "$5,000" and "$20,000" for "$10,000", and inserted references to laws of a State or of a foreign country.

Subsec. (b)(4). Pub. L. 98–473, §502(4), substituted "(1)(C)" for "(1)(B)".

Pub. L. 98–473, §224(a)(1), as renumbered by Pub. L. 99–570, §1005(a), substituted "in section 844 of this title and section 3607 of title 18" for "in subsections (a) and (b) of section 844 of this title".

Subsec. (b)(5). Pub. L. 98–473, §502(5), (6), added par. (5) and struck out former par. (5) which related to penalties for manufacturing, etc., phencyclidine.

Subsec. (b)(6). Pub. L. 98–473, §502(5), struck out par. (6) which related to penalties for violations involving a quantity of marihuana exceeding 1,000 pounds.

Subsec. (c). Pub. L. 98–473, §224(a)(2), as renumbered by Pub. L. 99–570, §1005(a), struck out subsec. (c) which read as follows: "A special parole term imposed under this section or section 845, 845a, or 845b of this title may be revoked if its terms and conditions are violated. In such circumstances the original term of imprisonment shall be increased by the period of the special parole term and the resulting new term of imprisonment shall not be diminished by the time which was spent on special parole. A person whose special parole term has been revoked may be required to serve all or part of the remainder of the new term of imprisonment. A special parole term provided for in this section or section 845, 845a, or 845b of this title shall be in addition to, and not in lieu of, any other parole provided for by law."

Pub. L. 98–473, §503(b)(2), inserted reference to section 845a of this title in two places.

1980—Subsec. (b)(1)(B). Pub. L. 96–359, §8(c)(1), inserted reference to par. (6) of this subsection.

Subsec. (b)(6). Pub. L. 96–359, §8(c)(2), added par. (6).

1978—Subsec. (b)(1)(B). Pub. L. 95–633, §201(1), inserted ", except as provided in paragraphs (4) and (5) of this subsection," after "such person shall".

Subsec. (b)(5). Pub. L. 95–633, §201(2), added par. (5).

Subsec. (d). Pub. L. 95–633, §201(3), added subsec. (d).

EFFECTIVE DATE OF 2008 AMENDMENT

Amendment by Pub. L. 110–425 effective 180 days after Oct. 15, 2008, except as otherwise provided, see section 3(j) of Pub. L. 110–425, set out as a note under section 802 of this title.

EFFECTIVE DATE OF 1988 AMENDMENT

Amendment by section 6055 of Pub. L. 100–690 effective 120 days after Nov. 18, 1988, see section 6061 of Pub. L. 100–690, set out as a note under section 802 of this title.

EFFECTIVE DATE OF 1986 AMENDMENT

Section 1004(b) of Pub. L. 99–570 provided that: "The amendments made by this section [amending this section and sections 845, 845a, 960, and 962 of this title] shall take effect on the date of the taking effect of section 3583 of title 18, United States Code [Nov. 1, 1987]."

EFFECTIVE DATE OF 1984 AMENDMENT

Amendment by section 224(a) of Pub. L. 98–473 effective Nov. 1, 1987, and applicable only to offenses committed after the taking effect of such amendment, see section 235(a)(1) of Pub. L. 98–473, set out as an Effective Date note under section 3551 of Title 18, Crimes and Criminal Procedure.

EFFECTIVE DATE OF 1978 AMENDMENT

Amendment by Pub. L. 95–633 effective Nov. 10, 1978, see section 203(a) of Pub. L. 95–633 set out as an Effective Date note under section 830 of this title.

REPEALS

Pub. L. 96–359, §8(b), Sept. 26, 1980, 94 Stat. 1194, repealed section 203(d) of Pub. L. 95–633, which had provided for the repeal of subsec. (d) of this section effective Jan. 1, 1981.

§842. Prohibited acts B

(a) Unlawful acts

It shall be unlawful for any person—

(1) who is subject to the requirements of part C to distribute or dispense a controlled substance in violation of section 829 of this title;

(2) who is a registrant to distribute or dispense a controlled substance not authorized by his registration to another registrant or other authorized person or to manufacture a controlled substance not authorized by his registration;

(3) who is a registrant to distribute a controlled substance in violation of section 825 of this title;

(4) to remove, alter, or obliterate a symbol or label required by section 825 of this title;

(5) to refuse or negligently fail to make, keep, or furnish any record, report, notification, declaration, order or order form, statement, invoice, or information required under this subchapter or subchapter II of this chapter;

(6) to refuse any entry into any premises or inspection authorized by this subchapter or subchapter II of this chapter;

(7) to remove, break, injure, or deface a seal placed upon controlled substances pursuant to section 824(f) or 881 of this title or to remove or dispose of substances so placed under seal;

(8) to use, to his own advantage, or to reveal, other than to duly authorized officers or employees of the United States, or to the courts when relevant in any judicial proceeding under this subchapter or subchapter II of this chapter, any information acquired in the course of an inspection authorized by this subchapter concerning any method or process which as a trade secret is entitled to protection, or to use to his own advantage or reveal (other than as authorized by section 830 of this title) any information that is confidential under such section;

(9) who is a regulated person to engage in a regulated transaction without obtaining the identification required by 830(a)(3) of this title.[1]

(10) negligently to fail to keep a record or make a report under section 830 of this title;

(11) to distribute a laboratory supply to a person who uses, or attempts to use, that laboratory supply to manufacture a controlled substance or a listed chemical, in violation of this subchapter or subchapter II of this chapter, with reckless disregard for the illegal uses to which such a laboratory supply will be put;

(12) who is a regulated seller, or a distributor required to submit reports under subsection (b)(3) of section 830 of this title—

(A) to sell at retail a scheduled listed chemical product in violation of paragraph (1) of subsection (d) of such section, knowing at the time of the transaction involved (independent of consulting the logbook under subsection (e)(1)(A)(iii) of such section) that the transaction is a violation; or

(B) to knowingly or recklessly sell at retail such a product in violation of paragraph (2) of such subsection (d);

(13) who is a regulated seller to knowingly or recklessly sell at retail a scheduled listed chemical product in violation of subsection (e) of such section; or

(14) who is a regulated seller or an employee or agent of such seller to disclose, in violation of regulations under subparagraph (C) of section 830(e)(1) of this title, information in logbooks under subparagraph (A)(iii) of such section, or to refuse to provide such a logbook to Federal, State, or local law enforcement authorities.

As used in paragraph (11), the term "laboratory supply" means a listed chemical or any chemical, substance, or item on a special surveillance list published by the Attorney General, which contains chemicals, products, materials, or equipment used in the manufacture of controlled substances and listed chemicals. For purposes of paragraph (11), there is a rebuttable presumption of reckless disregard at trial if the Attorney General notifies a firm in writing that a laboratory supply sold by the firm, or any other person or firm, has been used by a customer of the notified firm, or distributed further by that customer, for the unlawful production of controlled substances or listed chemicals a firm distributes and 2 weeks or more after the notification the notified firm distributes a laboratory supply to the customer.

(b) Manufacture

It shall be unlawful for any person who is a registrant to manufacture a controlled substance in schedule I or II, or ephedrine, pseudoephedrine, or phenylpropanolamine or any of the salts, optical isomers, or salts of optical isomers of such chemical, which is—

(1) not expressly authorized by his registration and by a quota assigned to him pursuant to section 826 of this title; or

(2) in excess of a quota assigned to him pursuant to section 826 of this title.

(c) Penalties

(1)(A) Except as provided in subparagraph (B) of this paragraph and paragraph (2), any person who violates this section shall, with respect to any such violation, be subject to a civil penalty of not more than $25,000. The district courts of the United States (or, where there is no such court in the case of any territory or possession of the United States, then the court in such territory or possession having the jurisdiction of a district court of the United States in cases arising under the Constitution and laws of the United States) shall have jurisdiction in accordance with section 1355 of title 28 to enforce this paragraph.

(B) In the case of a violation of paragraph (5) or (10) of subsection (a) of this section, the civil penalty shall not exceed $10,000.

(2)(A) If a violation of this section is prosecuted by an information or indictment which alleges that the violation was committed knowingly and the trier of fact specifically finds that the violation was so committed, such person shall, except as otherwise provided in subparagraph (B) of this paragraph, be sentenced to imprisonment of not more than one year or a fine under title 18, or both.

(B) If a violation referred to in subparagraph (A) was committed after one or more prior convictions of the offender for an offense punishable under this paragraph (2), or for a crime under any other provision of this subchapter or subchapter II of this chapter or other law of the United States relating to narcotic drugs, marihuana, or depressant or stimulant substances, have become final, such person shall be sentenced to a term of imprisonment of not more than 2 years, a fine under title 18, or both.

(C) In addition to the penalties set forth elsewhere in this subchapter or subchapter II of this chapter, any business that violates paragraph (11) of subsection (a) of this section shall, with respect to the first such violation, be subject to a civil penalty of not more than $250,000, but shall not be subject to criminal penalties under this section, and shall, for any succeeding violation, be subject to a civil fine of not more than $250,000 or double the last previously imposed penalty, whichever is greater.

(3) Except under the conditions specified in paragraph (2) of this subsection, a violation of this section does not constitute a crime, and a

[1] So in original. Probably should be "section 830(a)(3) of this title;".

judgment for the United States and imposition of a civil penalty pursuant to paragraph (1) shall not give rise to any disability or legal disadvantage based on conviction for a criminal offense.

(4)(A) If a regulated seller, or a distributor required to submit reports under section 830(b)(3) of this title, violates paragraph (12) of subsection (a) of this section, or if a regulated seller violates paragraph (13) of such subsection, the Attorney General may by order prohibit such seller or distributor (as the case may be) from selling any scheduled listed chemical product. Any sale of such a product in violation of such an order is subject to the same penalties as apply under paragraph (2).

(B) An order under subparagraph (A) may be imposed only through the same procedures as apply under section 824(c) of this title for an order to show cause.

(Pub. L. 91–513, title II, § 402, Oct. 27, 1970, 84 Stat. 1262; Pub. L. 95–633, title II, § 202(b)(1), (2), Nov. 10, 1978, 92 Stat. 3776; Pub. L. 100–690, title VI, § 6056, Nov. 18, 1988, 102 Stat. 4318; Pub. L. 104–237, title II, § 205, Oct. 3, 1996, 110 Stat. 3103; Pub. L. 105–277, div. A, § 101(b) [title I, § 117], Oct. 21, 1998, 112 Stat. 2681–50, 2681–68; Pub. L. 107–273, div. B, title IV, § 4002(b)(16), (d)(2)(B), Nov. 2, 2002, 116 Stat. 1808, 1809; Pub. L. 109–177, title VII, §§ 711(f)(1)(A), (2), 714, Mar. 9, 2006, 120 Stat. 262–264.)

REFERENCES IN TEXT

Schedules I and II, referred to in subsec. (b), are set out in section 812(c) of this title.

AMENDMENTS

2006—Subsec. (a)(12) to (14). Pub. L. 109–177, § 711(f)(1)(A), added pars. (12) to (14).

Subsec. (b). Pub. L. 109–177, § 714, inserted ", or ephedrine, pseudoephedrine, or phenylpropanolamine or any of the salts, optical isomers, or salts of optical isomers of such chemical," after "manufacture a controlled substance in schedule I or II" in introductory provisions.

Subsec. (c)(4). Pub. L. 109–177, § 711(f)(2), added par. (4).

2002—Subsec. (c)(2)(A). Pub. L. 107–273, § 4002(d)(2)(B)(i), substituted "under title 18" for "of not more than $25,000".

Subsec. (c)(2)(B). Pub. L. 107–273, § 4002(d)(2)(B)(ii), substituted "under title 18" for "of $50,000".

Subsec. (c)(2)(C). Pub. L. 107–273, § 4002(b)(16), realigned margins.

1998—Subsec. (a)(5). Pub. L. 105–277, § 101(b) [title I, § 117(1)], inserted "negligently" before "fail".

Subsec. (a)(10). Pub. L. 105–277, § 101(b) [title I, § 117(2)], inserted "negligently" before "to fail".

Subsec. (c)(1). Pub. L. 105–277, § 101(b) [title I, § 117(3)], designated existing provisions as subpar. (A), inserted "subparagraph (B) of this paragraph and" before "paragraph (2)", and added subpar. (B).

1996—Subsec. (a). Pub. L. 104–237, § 205(a), added par. (11) and closing provisions.

Subsec. (c)(2)(C). Pub. L. 104–237, § 205(b), added subpar. (C).

1988—Subsec. (a)(8). Pub. L. 100–690, § 6056(a), inserted ", or to use to his own advantage or reveal (other than as authorized by section 830 of this title) any information that is confidential under such section" after "protection".

Subsec. (a)(9). Pub. L. 100–690, § 6056(b), amended par. (9) generally. Prior to amendment, par. (9) read as follows: "to distribute or sell piperidine in violation of regulations established under section 830(a)(2) of this title, respecting presentation of identification."

Subsec. (a)(10). Pub. L. 100–690, § 6056(d), added par. (10).

Subsec. (c)(2)(C). Pub. L. 100–690, § 6056(c), struck out subpar. (C) which read as follows: "Subparagraphs (A) and (B) shall not apply to a violation of subsection (a)(5) of this section with respect to a refusal or failure to make a report required under section 830(a) of this title (relating to piperidine reporting)."

1978—Subsec. (a)(9). Pub. L. 95–633, § 202(b)(1), added par. (9).

Subsec. (c)(2)(C). Pub. L. 95–633, § 202(b)(2), added subpar. (C).

EFFECTIVE DATE OF 1988 AMENDMENT

Amendment by Pub. L. 100–690 effective 120 days after Nov. 18, 1988, see section 6061 of Pub. L. 100–690, set out as a note under section 802 of this title.

EFFECTIVE DATE OF 1978 AMENDMENT

Amendment by Pub. L. 95–633 effective Nov. 10, 1978, see section 203(a) of Pub. L. 95–633 set out as an Effective Date note under section 830 of this title.

REPEALS

Pub. L. 96–359, § 8(b), Sept. 26, 1980, 94 Stat. 1194, repealed section 203(d) of Pub. L. 95–633, which had provided for the repeal of subsecs. (a)(9) and (c)(2)(C) of this section effective Jan. 1, 1981.

§ 843. Prohibited acts C

(a) Unlawful acts

It shall be unlawful for any person knowingly or intentionally—

(1) who is a registrant to distribute a controlled substance classified in schedule I or II, in the course of his legitimate business, except pursuant to an order or an order form as required by section 828 of this title;

(2) to use in the course of the manufacture, distribution, or dispensing of a controlled substance, or to use for the purpose of acquiring or obtaining a controlled substance, a registration number which is fictitious, revoked, suspended, expired, or issued to another person;

(3) to acquire or obtain possession of a controlled substance by misrepresentation, fraud, forgery, deception, or subterfuge;

(4)(A) to furnish false or fraudulent material information in, or omit any material information from, any application, report, record, or other document required to be made, kept, or filed under this subchapter or subchapter II of this chapter, or (B) to present false or fraudulent identification where the person is receiving or purchasing a listed chemical and the person is required to present identification under section 830(a) of this title;

(5) to make, distribute, or possess any punch, die, plate, stone, or other thing designed to print, imprint, or reproduce the trademark, trade name, or other identifying mark, imprint, or device of another or any likeness of any of the foregoing upon any drug or container or labeling thereof so as to render such drug a counterfeit substance;

(6) to possess any three-neck round-bottom flask, tableting machine, encapsulating machine, or gelatin capsule, or any equipment, chemical, product, or material which may be used to manufacture a controlled substance or listed chemical, knowing, intending, or having reasonable cause to believe, that it will be used to manufacture a controlled substance or listed chemical in violation of this subchapter or subchapter II of this chapter;

(7) to manufacture, distribute, export, or import any three-neck round-bottom flask, tableting machine, encapsulating machine, or gelatin capsule, or any equipment, chemical, product, or material which may be used to manufacture a controlled substance or listed chemical, knowing, intending, or having reasonable cause to believe, that it will be used to manufacture a controlled substance or listed chemical in violation of this subchapter or subchapter II of this chapter or, in the case of an exportation, in violation of this subchapter or subchapter II of this chapter or of the laws of the country to which it is exported;

(8) to create a chemical mixture for the purpose of evading a requirement of section 830 of this title or to receive a chemical mixture created for that purpose; or

(9) to distribute, import, or export a list I chemical without the registration required by this subchapter or subchapter II of this chapter.

(b) Communication facility

It shall be unlawful for any person knowingly or intentionally to use any communication facility in committing or in causing or facilitating the commission of any act or acts constituting a felony under any provision of this subchapter or subchapter II of this chapter. Each separate use of a communication facility shall be a separate offense under this subsection. For purposes of this subsection, the term "communication facility" means any and all public and private instrumentalities used or useful in the transmission of writing, signs, signals, pictures, or sounds of all kinds and includes mail, telephone, wire, radio, and all other means of communication.

(c) Advertisement

(1) It shall be unlawful for any person to place in any newspaper, magazine, handbill, or other publications, any written advertisement knowing that it has the purpose of seeking or offering illegally to receive, buy, or distribute a Schedule[1] I controlled substance. As used in this section the term "advertisement" includes, in addition to its ordinary meaning, such advertisements as those for a catalog of Schedule[1] I controlled substances and any similar written advertisement that has the purpose of seeking or offering illegally to receive, buy, or distribute a Schedule[1] I controlled substance. The term "advertisement" does not include material which merely advocates the use of a similar material, which advocates a position or practice, and does not attempt to propose or facilitate an actual transaction in a Schedule[1] I controlled substance.

(2)(A) It shall be unlawful for any person to knowingly or intentionally use the Internet, or cause the Internet to be used, to advertise the sale of, or to offer to sell, distribute, or dispense, a controlled substance where such sale, distribution, or dispensing is not authorized by this subchapter or by the Controlled Substances Import and Export Act [21 U.S.C. 951 et seq.].

(B) Examples of activities that violate subparagraph (A) include, but are not limited to, knowingly or intentionally causing the placement on the Internet of an advertisement that refers to or directs prospective buyers to Internet sellers of controlled substances who are not registered with a modification under section 823(f) of this title.

(C) Subparagraph (A) does not apply to material that either—

(i) merely advertises the distribution of controlled substances by nonpractitioners to the extent authorized by their registration under this subchapter; or

(ii) merely advocates the use of a controlled substance or includes pricing information without attempting to facilitate an actual transaction involving a controlled substance.

(d) Penalties

(1) Except as provided in paragraph (2), any person who violates this section shall be sentenced to a term of imprisonment of not more than 4 years, a fine under title 18, or both; except that if any person commits such a violation after one or more prior convictions of him for violation of this section, or for a felony under any other provision of this subchapter or subchapter II of this chapter or other law of the United States relating to narcotic drugs, marihuana, or depressant or stimulant substances, have become final, such person shall be sentenced to a term of imprisonment of not more than 8 years, a fine under title 18, or both.

(2) Any person who, with the intent to manufacture or to facilitate the manufacture of methamphetamine, violates paragraph (6) or (7) of subsection (a) of this section, shall be sentenced to a term of imprisonment of not more than 10 years, a fine under title 18, or both; except that if any person commits such a violation after one or more prior convictions of that person—

(A) for a violation of paragraph (6) or (7) of subsection (a) of this section;

(B) for a felony under any other provision of this subchapter or subchapter II of this chapter; or

(C) under any other law of the United States or any State relating to controlled substances or listed chemicals,

has become final, such person shall be sentenced to a term of imprisonment of not more than 20 years, a fine under title 18, or both.

(e) Additional penalties

In addition to any other applicable penalty, any person convicted of a felony violation of this section relating to the receipt, distribution, manufacture, exportation, or importation of a listed chemical may be enjoined from engaging in any transaction involving a listed chemical for not more than ten years.

(f) Injunctions

(1) In addition to any penalty provided in this section, the Attorney General is authorized to commence a civil action for appropriate declaratory or injunctive relief relating to violations of this section, section 842 of this title, or 856[2] of this title.

(2) Any action under this subsection may be brought in the district court of the United

[1] So in original. Probably should not be capitalized.

[2] So in original. Probably should be preceded by "section".

States for the district in which the defendant is located or resides or is doing business.

(3) Any order or judgment issued by the court pursuant to this subsection shall be tailored to restrain violations of this section or section 842 of this title.

(4) The court shall proceed as soon as practicable to the hearing and determination of such an action. An action under this subsection is governed by the Federal Rules of Civil Procedure except that, if an indictment has been returned against the respondent, discovery is governed by the Federal Rules of Criminal Procedure.

(Pub. L. 91–513, title II, §403, Oct. 27, 1970, 84 Stat. 1263; Pub. L. 95–633, title II, §202(b)(3), Nov. 10, 1978, 92 Stat. 3776; Pub. L. 98–473, title II, §516, Oct. 12, 1984, 98 Stat. 2074; Pub. L. 99–570, title I, §1866(a), Oct. 27, 1986, 100 Stat. 3207–54; Pub. L. 100–690, title VI, §6057, Nov. 18, 1988, 102 Stat. 4319; Pub. L. 103–200, §3(g), Dec. 17, 1993, 107 Stat. 2337; Pub. L. 103–322, title IX, §90106, Sept. 13, 1994, 108 Stat. 1988; Pub. L. 104–237, title II, §§203(a), 206(b), Oct. 3, 1996, 110 Stat. 3102, 3103; Pub. L. 107–273, div. B, title IV, §4002(d)(2)(C), Nov. 2, 2002, 116 Stat. 1810; Pub. L. 108–21, title VI, §608(d), Apr. 30, 2003, 117 Stat. 691; Pub. L. 110–425, §3(g), Oct. 15, 2008, 122 Stat. 4830.)

References in Text

Schedules I and II, referred to in subsecs. (a)(1) and (c)(1), are set out in section 812(c) of this title.

This subchapter, referred to in subsec. (c)(2)(A), (C)(i), was in the original "this title", meaning title II of Pub. L. 91–513, Oct. 27, 1970, 84 Stat. 1242, and is popularly known as the "Controlled Substances Act". For complete classification of title II to the Code, see second paragraph of Short Title note set out under section 801 of this title and Tables.

The Controlled Substances Import and Export Act, referred to in subsec. (c)(2)(A), is title III of Pub. L. 91–513, Oct. 27, 1970, 84 Stat. 1285, which is classified principally to subchapter II (§951 et seq.) of this chapter. For complete classification of this Act to the Code, see Short Title note set out under section 951 of this title and Tables.

The Federal Rules of Civil Procedure, referred to in subsec. (f)(4), are set out in the Appendix to Title 28, Judiciary and Judicial Procedure.

The Federal Rules of Criminal Procedure, referred to in subsec. (f)(4), are set out in the Appendix to Title 18, Crimes and Criminal Procedure.

Amendments

2008—Subsec. (c). Pub. L. 110–425 designated existing provisions as par. (1) and added par. (2).

2003—Subsec. (f)(1). Pub. L. 108–21 substituted "this section, section 842 of this title, or 856 of this title" for "this section or section 842 of this title".

2002—Subsec. (d). Pub. L. 107–273 substituted "under title 18, or both;" for "of not more than $30,000, or both;" in two places and "under title 18, or both." for "of not more than $60,000, or both." in two places.

1996—Subsec. (d). Pub. L. 104–237, §203(a), inserted par. (1) designation, substituted "Except as provided in paragraph (2), any person" for "Any person", and added par. (2).

Subsec. (e). Pub. L. 104–237, §206(b)(1), inserted "manufacture, exportation," after "distribution," and struck out "regulated" after "engaging in any".

Subsec. (f). Pub. L. 104–237, §206(b)(2), added subsec. (f).

1994—Subsecs. (c) to (e). Pub. L. 103–322 added subsec. (c) and redesignated former subsecs. (c) and (d) as (d) and (e), respectively.

1993—Subsec. (a)(6), (7). Pub. L. 103–200, §3(g)(1), amended pars. (6) and (7) generally. Prior to amendment, pars. (6) and (7) read as follows:

"(6) to possess any three-neck round-bottom flask, tableting machine, encapsulating machine, gelatin capsule, or equipment specially designed or modified to manufacture a controlled substance, with intent to manufacture a controlled substance except as authorized by this subchapter;

"(7) to manufacture, distribute, or import any three-neck round-bottom flask, tableting machine, encapsulating machine, gelatin capsule, or equipment specially designed or modified to manufacture a controlled substance, knowing that it will be used to manufacture a controlled substance except as authorized by this subchapter; or".

Subsec. (a)(9). Pub. L. 103–200, §3(g)(2), (3), added par. (9).

1988—Subsec. (a)(4)(B). Pub. L. 100–690, §6057(a)(1), substituted "a listed chemical" for "piperidine".

Subsec. (a)(6) to (8). Pub. L. 100–690, §6057(a)(2)–(4), added pars. (6) to (8).

Subsec. (d). Pub. L. 100–690, §6057(b), added subsec. (d).

1986—Subsec. (a)(2). Pub. L. 99–570 substituted a semicolon for the period at end.

1984—Subsec. (a)(2). Pub. L. 98–473 added applicability to dispensing, acquiring, or obtaining a controlled substance, and applicability to an expired number.

1978—Subsec. (a)(4). Pub. L. 95–633, §202(b)(3), designated existing provisions as subpar. (A) and added subpar. (B).

Effective Date of 2008 Amendment

Amendment by Pub. L. 110–425 effective 180 days after Oct. 15, 2008, except as otherwise provided, see section 3(j) of Pub. L. 110–425, set out as a note under section 802 of this title.

Effective Date of 1993 Amendment

Amendment by Pub. L. 103–200 effective on date that is 120 days after Dec. 17, 1993, see section 11 of Pub. L. 103–200, set out as a note under section 802 of this title.

Effective Date of 1988 Amendment

Amendment by Pub. L. 100–690 effective 120 days after Nov. 18, 1988, see section 6061 of Pub. L. 100–690, set out as a note under section 802 of this title.

Effective Date of 1978 Amendment

Amendment by Pub. L. 95–633 effective Nov. 10, 1978, except as otherwise provided, see section 203(a) of Pub. L. 95–633, set out as an Effective Date note under section 830 of this title.

Repeals

Pub. L. 96–359, §8(b), Sept. 26, 1980, 94 Stat. 1194, repealed section 203(d) of Pub. L. 95–633, which had provided for the repeal of subsec. (a)(4)(B) of this section effective Jan. 1, 1981.

§844. Penalties for simple possession

(a) Unlawful acts; penalties

It shall be unlawful for any person knowingly or intentionally to possess a controlled substance unless such substance was obtained directly, or pursuant to a valid prescription or order, from a practitioner, while acting in the course of his professional practice, or except as otherwise authorized by this subchapter or subchapter II of this chapter. It shall be unlawful for any person knowingly or intentionally to possess any list I chemical obtained pursuant to or under authority of a registration issued to that person under section 823 of this title or section 958 of this title if that registration has been revoked or suspended, if that registration has expired, or if the registrant has ceased to do business in the manner contemplated by his registration. It shall be unlawful for any person to knowingly or intentionally purchase at retail during a 30 day period more than 9 grams of ephedrine base, pseudoephedrine base, or phenylpropanolamine base in a scheduled listed chemical product, except that, of such 9 grams, not more than 7.5 grams may be imported by means of shipping through any private or commercial carrier or the Postal Service. Any person who violates this subsection may be sentenced to a term of imprisonment of not more than 1 year, and shall be fined a minimum of $1,000, or both, except that if he commits such offense after a prior conviction under this subchapter or subchapter II of this chapter, or a prior conviction for any drug, narcotic, or chemical offense chargeable under the law of any State, has become final, he shall be sentenced to a term of imprisonment for not less than 15 days but not more than 2 years, and shall be fined a minimum of $2,500, except, further, that if he commits such offense after two or more prior convictions under this subchapter or subchapter II of this chapter, or two or more prior convictions for any drug, narcotic, or chemical offense chargeable under the law of any State, or a combination of two or more such offenses have become final, he shall be sentenced to a term of imprisonment for not less than 90 days but not more than 3 years, and shall be fined a minimum of $5,000. Notwithstanding the preceding sentence, a person convicted under this subsection for the possession of a mixture or substance which contains cocaine base shall be imprisoned not less than 5 years and not more than 20 years, and fined a minimum of $1,000, if the conviction is a first conviction under this subsection and the amount of the mixture or substance exceeds 5 grams, if the conviction is after a prior conviction for the possession of such a mixture or substance under this subsection becomes final and the amount of the mixture or substance exceeds 3 grams, or if the conviction is after 2 or more prior convictions for the possession of such a mixture or substance under this subsection become final and the amount of the mixture or substance exceeds 1 gram. Notwithstanding any penalty provided in this subsection, any person convicted under this subsection for the possession of flunitrazepam shall be imprisoned for not more than 3 years, shall be fined as otherwise provided in this section, or both. The imposition or execution of a minimum sentence required to be imposed under this subsection shall not be suspended or deferred. Further, upon conviction, a person who violates this subsection shall be fined the reasonable costs of the investigation and prosecution of the offense, including the costs of prosecution of an offense as defined in sections 1918 and 1920 of title 28, except that this sentence shall not apply and a fine under this section need not be imposed if the court determines under the provision of title 18 that the defendant lacks the ability to pay.

(b) Repealed. Pub. L. 98–473, title II, § 219(a), Oct. 12, 1984, 98 Stat. 2027

(c) "Drug, narcotic, or chemical offense" defined

As used in this section, the term "drug, narcotic, or chemical offense" means any offense which proscribes the possession, distribution, manufacture, cultivation, sale, transfer, or the attempt or conspiracy to possess, distribute, manufacture, cultivate, sell or transfer any substance the possession of which is prohibited under this subchapter.

(Pub. L. 91–513, title II, §404, Oct. 27, 1970, 84 Stat. 1264; Pub. L. 98–473, title II, §219, Oct. 12, 1984, 98 Stat. 2027; Pub. L. 99–570, title I, §1052, Oct. 27, 1986, 100 Stat. 3207–8; Pub. L. 100–690, title VI, §§6371, 6480, Nov. 18, 1988, 102 Stat. 4370, 4382; Pub. L. 101–647, title XII, §1201, title XIX, §1907, Nov. 29, 1990, 104 Stat. 4829, 4854; Pub. L. 104–237, title II, §201(a), Oct. 3, 1996, 110 Stat. 3101; Pub. L. 104–305, §2(c), Oct. 13, 1996, 110 Stat. 3808; Pub. L. 109–177, title VII, §711(e)(1), Mar. 9, 2006, 120 Stat. 262.)

AMENDMENTS

2006—Subsec. (a). Pub. L. 109–177 inserted after second sentence "It shall be unlawful for any person to knowingly or intentionally purchase at retail during a 30 day period more than 9 grams of ephedrine base, pseudoephedrine base, or phenylpropanolamine base in a scheduled listed chemical product, except that, of such 9 grams, not more than 7.5 grams may be imported by means of shipping through any private or commercial carrier or the Postal Service."

1996—Subsec. (a). Pub. L. 104–305 inserted "Notwithstanding any penalty provided in this subsection, any person convicted under this subsection for the possession of flunitrazepam shall be imprisoned for not more than 3 years, shall be fined as otherwise provided in this section, or both." after "mixture or substance exceeds 1 gram."

Pub. L. 104–237, §201(a)(1), inserted after first sentence "It shall be unlawful for any person knowingly or intentionally to possess any list I chemical obtained pursuant to or under authority of a registration issued to that person under section 823 of this title or section 958 of this title if that registration has been revoked or suspended, if that registration has expired, or if the registrant has ceased to do business in the manner contemplated by his registration." and substituted "drug, narcotic, or chemical" for "drug or narcotic" in two places.

Subsec. (c). Pub. L. 104–237, §201(a)(2), substituted "drug, narcotic, or chemical" for "drug or narcotic".

1990—Subsec. (a). Pub. L. 101–647, §1907, inserted subsec. (a) designation.

Pub. L. 101–647, §1201, substituted "shall be imprisoned not less than 5 years and not more than 20 years, and fined a minimum of $1,000" for "shall be fined under title 18 or imprisoned not less than 5 years and not more than 20 years, or both".

1988—Subsec. (a). Pub. L. 100–690, §6480(1)(A)–(C), struck out "but not more than $5,000" after "$1,000", "but not more than $10,000" after "$2,500", and "but not more than $25,000" after "$5,000" in second sentence.

Pub. L. 100–690, §6371, inserted provisions relating to increased penalties in cases of certain serious crack possession offenses, making offenders subject to fines under title 18 or imprisonment to terms not less than 5 years nor more than 20 years, or both.

1986—Subsec. (a). Pub. L. 99–570 amended subsec. (a) generally. Prior to amendment, subsec. (a) read as follows: "It shall be unlawful for any person knowingly or intentionally to possess a controlled substance unless such substance was obtained directly, or pursuant to a valid prescription or order, from a practitioner, while acting in the course of his professional practice, or except as otherwise authorized by this subchapter or subchapter II of this chapter. Any person who violates this subsection shall be sentenced to a term of imprisonment of not more than one year, a fine of not more than $5,000, or both, except that if he commits such offense after a prior conviction or convictions under this subsection have become final, he shall be sentenced to a term of imprisonment of not more than 2 years, a fine of not more than $10,000 or both."

Subsec. (b). Pub. L. 99–570, in amending subsec. (b) generally, substituted "Upon the discharge of such person and dismissal of the proceedings" for "Upon the dismissal of such person and discharge of the proceedings" in par. (2).

Subsec. (c). Pub. L. 99–570, in amending section generally, added subsec. (c).

1984—Pub. L. 98–473 struck out subsec. (a) designation and struck out subsec. (b) which related to probation before judgment and expunging of records for first offense.

EFFECTIVE DATE OF 2006 AMENDMENT

Pub. L. 109–177, title VII, §711(e)(2), Mar. 9, 2006, 120 Stat. 262, provided that: "The amendment made by paragraph (1) [amending this section] applies on and after the expiration of the 30-day period beginning on the date of the enactment of this Act [Mar. 9, 2006]."

EFFECTIVE DATE OF 1984 AMENDMENT

Amendment by Pub. L. 98–473 effective Nov. 1, 1987, and applicable only to offenses committed after the taking effect of such amendment, see section 235(a)(1) of Pub. L. 98–473, set out as an Effective Date note under section 3551 of Title 18, Crimes and Criminal Procedure.

§ 844a. Civil penalty for possession of small amounts of certain controlled substances

(a) In general

Any individual who knowingly possesses a controlled substance that is listed in section 841(b)(1)(A) of this title in violation of section 844 of this title in an amount that, as specified by regulation of the Attorney General, is a personal use amount shall be liable to the United States for a civil penalty in an amount not to exceed $10,000 for each such violation.

(b) Income and net assets

The income and net assets of an individual shall not be relevant to the determination whether to assess a civil penalty under this section or to prosecute the individual criminally. However, in determining the amount of a penalty under this section, the income and net assets of an individual shall be considered.

(c) Prior conviction

A civil penalty may not be assessed under this section if the individual previously was convicted of a Federal or State offense relating to a controlled substance.

(d) Limitation on number of assessments

A civil penalty may not be assessed on an individual under this section on more than two separate occasions.

(e) Assessment

A civil penalty under this section may be assessed by the Attorney General only by an order made on the record after opportunity for a hearing in accordance with section 554 of title 5. The Attorney General shall provide written notice to the individual who is the subject of the proposed order informing the individual of the opportunity to receive such a hearing with respect to the proposed order. The hearing may be held only if the individual makes a request for the hearing before the expiration of the 30-day period beginning on the date such notice is issued.

(f) Compromise

The Attorney General may compromise, modify, or remit, with or without conditions, any civil penalty imposed under this section.

(g) Judicial review

If the Attorney General issues an order pursuant to subsection (e) of this section after a hearing described in such subsection, the individual who is the subject of the order may, before the expiration of the 30-day period beginning on the date the order is issued, bring a civil action in the appropriate district court of the United States. In such action, the law and the facts of the violation and the assessment of the civil penalty shall be determined de novo, and shall include the right of a trial by jury, the right to counsel, and the right to confront witnesses. The facts of the violation shall be proved beyond a reasonable doubt.

(h) Civil action

If an individual does not request a hearing pursuant to subsection (e) of this section and the Attorney General issues an order pursuant to such subsection, or if an individual does not under subsection (g) of this section seek judicial review of such an order, the Attorney General may commence a civil action in any appropriate district court of the United States for the purpose of recovering the amount assessed and an amount representing interest at a rate computed in accordance with section 1961 of title 28. Such interest shall accrue from the expiration of the 30-day period described in subsection (g) of this section. In such an action, the decision of the Attorney General to issue the order, and the amount of the penalty assessed by the Attorney General, shall not be subject to review.

(i) Limitation

The Attorney General may not under this subsection[1] commence proceeding against an individual after the expiration of the 5-year period beginning on the date on which the individual allegedly violated subsection (a) of this section.

(j) Expungement procedures

The Attorney General shall dismiss the proceedings under this section against an individual upon application of such individual at any time after the expiration of 3 years if—

(1) the individual has not previously been assessed a civil penalty under this section;

(2) the individual has paid the assessment;

(3) the individual has complied with any conditions imposed by the Attorney General;

(4) the individual has not been convicted of a Federal or State offense relating to a controlled substance; and

(5) the individual agrees to submit to a drug test, and such test shows the individual to be drug free.

A nonpublic record of a disposition under this subsection shall be retained by the Department of Justice solely for the purpose of determining in any subsequent proceeding whether the person qualified for a civil penalty or expungement under this section. If a record is expunged under

[1] So in original. Probably should be "section".

this subsection, an individual concerning whom such an expungement has been made shall not be held thereafter under any provision of law to be guilty of perjury, false swearing, or making a false statement by reason of his failure to recite or acknowledge a proceeding under this section or the results thereof in response to an inquiry made of him for any purpose.

(Pub. L. 91–513, title II, §405, formerly Pub. L. 100–690, title VI, §6486, Nov. 18, 1988, 102 Stat. 4384, renumbered §405 of Pub. L. 91–513, and amended Pub. L. 101–647, title X, §1002(g)(1), (2), Nov. 29, 1990, 104 Stat. 4828.)

PRIOR PROVISIONS

A prior section 405 of Pub. L. 91–513 was renumbered section 418 and is classified to section 859 of this title.

AMENDMENTS

1990—Subsec. (a). Pub. L. 101–647, §1002(g)(2)(A), made technical amendments to references to sections 841(b)(1)(A) and 844 of this title to correct references to corresponding provisions of original act.

Subsecs. (c), (j)(4). Pub. L. 101–647, §1002(g)(2)(B), (C), struck out "as defined in section 802 of this title" after "controlled substance".

§§845 to 845b. Transferred

CODIFICATION

Section 845, Pub. L. 91–513, title II, §405, Oct. 27, 1970, 84 Stat. 1265, as amended, which related to distribution of controlled substances to persons under age twenty-one, was renumbered §418 of Pub. L. 91–513 by Pub. L. 101–647, title X, §1002(a)(1), Nov. 29, 1990, 104 Stat. 4827, and transferred to section 859 of this title.

Section 845a, Pub. L. 91–513, title II, §405A, as added Pub. L. 98–473, title II, §503(a), Oct. 12, 1984, 98 Stat. 2069, and amended, which related to distribution or manufacturing of controlled substances in or near schools and colleges, was renumbered §419 of Pub. L. 91–513 by Pub. L. 101–647, title X, §1002(b), Nov. 29, 1990, 104 Stat. 4827, and transferred to section 860 of this title.

Section 845b, Pub. L. 91–513, title II, §405B, as added Pub. L. 99–570, title I, §1102, Oct. 27, 1986, 100 Stat. 3207–10, and amended, which related to employment or use of persons under 18 years of age in drug operations, was renumbered §420 of Pub. L. 91–513 by Pub. L. 101–647, title X, §1002(c), Nov. 29, 1990, 104 Stat. 4827, and transferred to section 861 of this title.

§846. Attempt and conspiracy

Any person who attempts or conspires to commit any offense defined in this subchapter shall be subject to the same penalties as those prescribed for the offense, the commission of which was the object of the attempt or conspiracy.

(Pub. L. 91–513, title II, §406, Oct. 27, 1970, 84 Stat. 1265; Pub. L. 100–690, title VI, §6470(a), Nov. 18, 1988, 102 Stat. 4377.)

AMENDMENTS

1988—Pub. L. 100–690 substituted "shall be subject to the same penalties as those prescribed for the offense" for "is punishable by imprisonment or fine or both which may not exceed the maximum punishment prescribed for the offense".

§847. Additional penalties

Any penalty imposed for violation of this subchapter shall be in addition to, and not in lieu of, any civil or administrative penalty or sanction authorized by law.

(Pub. L. 91–513, title II, §407, Oct. 27, 1970, 84 Stat. 1265.)

§848. Continuing criminal enterprise

(a) Penalties; forfeitures

Any person who engages in a continuing criminal enterprise shall be sentenced to a term of imprisonment which may not be less than 20 years and which may be up to life imprisonment, to a fine not to exceed the greater of that authorized in accordance with the provisions of title 18 or $2,000,000 if the defendant is an individual or $5,000,000 if the defendant is other than an individual, and to the forfeiture prescribed in section 853 of this title; except that if any person engages in such activity after one or more prior convictions of him under this section have become final, he shall be sentenced to a term of imprisonment which may not be less than 30 years and which may be up to life imprisonment, to a fine not to exceed the greater of twice the amount authorized in accordance with the provisions of title 18 or $4,000,000 if the defendant is an individual or $10,000,000 if the defendant is other than an individual, and to the forfeiture prescribed in section 853 of this title.

(b) Life imprisonment for engaging in continuing criminal enterprise

Any person who engages in a continuing criminal enterprise shall be imprisoned for life and fined in accordance with subsection (a) of this section, if—

(1) such person is the principal administrator, organizer, or leader of the enterprise or is one of several such principal administrators, organizers, or leaders; and

(2)(A) the violation referred to in subsection (c)(1) of this section involved at least 300 times the quantity of a substance described in subsection 841(b)(1)(B) of this title, or

(B) the enterprise, or any other enterprise in which the defendant was the principal or one of several principal administrators, organizers, or leaders, received $10 million dollars in gross receipts during any twelve-month period of its existence for the manufacture, importation, or distribution of a substance described in section 841(b)(1)(B) of this title.

(c) "Continuing criminal enterprise" defined

For purposes of subsection (a) of this section, a person is engaged in a continuing criminal enterprise if—

(1) he violates any provision of this subchapter or subchapter II of this chapter the punishment for which is a felony, and

(2) such violation is a part of a continuing series of violations of this subchapter or subchapter II of this chapter—

(A) which are undertaken by such person in concert with five or more other persons with respect to whom such person occupies a position of organizer, a supervisory position, or any other position of management, and

(B) from which such person obtains substantial income or resources.

(d) Suspension of sentence and probation prohibited

In the case of any sentence imposed under this section, imposition or execution of such sentence shall not be suspended, probation shall not be granted, and the Act of July 15, 1932 (D.C. Code, secs. 24-203—24-207), shall not apply.

(e) Death penalty

(1) In addition to the other penalties set forth in this section—

(A) any person engaging in or working in furtherance of a continuing criminal enterprise, or any person engaging in an offense punishable under section 841(b)(1)(A) of this title or section 960(b)(1) of this title who intentionally kills or counsels, commands, induces, procures, or causes the intentional killing of an individual and such killing results, shall be sentenced to any term of imprisonment, which shall not be less than 20 years, and which may be up to life imprisonment, or may be sentenced to death; and

(B) any person, during the commission of, in furtherance of, or while attempting to avoid apprehension, prosecution or service of a prison sentence for, a felony violation of this subchapter or subchapter II of this chapter who intentionally kills or counsels, commands, induces, procures, or causes the intentional killing of any Federal, State, or local law enforcement officer engaged in, or on account of, the performance of such officer's official duties and such killing results, shall be sentenced to any term of imprisonment, which shall not be less than 20 years, and which may be up to life imprisonment, or may be sentenced to death.

(2) As used in paragraph (1)(B), the term "law enforcement officer" means a public servant authorized by law or by a Government agency or Congress to conduct or engage in the prevention, investigation, prosecution or adjudication of an offense, and includes those engaged in corrections, probation, or parole functions.

(g)[1] to (p) Repealed. Pub. L. 109-177, title II, § 221(2), Mar. 9, 2006, 120 Stat. 231

(q) Repealed. Pub. L. 109-177, title II, §§ 221(4), 222(c), Mar. 9, 2006, 120 Stat. 231, 232

(r) Repealed. Pub. L. 109-177, title II, § 221(3), Mar. 9, 2006, 120 Stat. 231

(s) Special provision for methamphetamine

For the purposes of subsection (b), in the case of continuing criminal enterprise involving methamphetamine or its salts, isomers, or salts of isomers, paragraph (2)(A) shall be applied by substituting "200" for "300", and paragraph (2)(B) shall be applied by substituting "$5,000,000" for "$10 million dollars".

(Pub. L. 91-513, title II, § 408, Oct. 27, 1970, 84 Stat. 1265; Pub. L. 98-473, title II, §§ 224(b), formerly § 224(c), 305, Oct. 12, 1984, 98 Stat. 2030, 2050; Pub. L. 99-570, title I, §§ 1005(b)(2), 1252, 1253, Oct. 27, 1986, 100 Stat. 3207-6, 3207-14; Pub. L. 100-690, title VI, § 6481, title VII, § 7001, Nov. 18, 1988, 102 Stat. 4382, 4387; Pub. L. 103-322, title XXXIII, §§ 330003(e), 330009(d), 330014, Sept. 13, 1994, 108 Stat. 2141, 2143, 2146; Pub. L. 104-132, title I, § 108, title IX, § 903(b), Apr. 24, 1996, 110 Stat. 1226, 1318; Pub. L. 109-177, title II, §§ 221, 222(c), title VII, § 733, Mar. 9, 2006, 120 Stat. 231, 232, 270.)

[1] So in original. Section does not contain a subsec. (f), see 1988 Amendment note below.

REFERENCES IN TEXT

Act of July 15, 1932 (D.C. Code, secs. 24-203—24-207), referred to in subsec. (d), is act July 15, 1932, ch. 492, 47 Stat. 696, as amended, which is not classified to the Code.

AMENDMENTS

2006—Subsec. (e)(2). Pub. L. 109-177, § 221(1), substituted "(1)(B)" for "(1)(b)".

Subsecs. (g) to (p). Pub. L. 109-177, § 221(2), struck out subsecs. (g) to (p) which related to hearing and sentencing procedures in death penalty cases and sentencing in capital cases in which the death penalty is not sought or imposed.

Subsec. (q). Pub. L. 109-177, §§ 221(4), 222(c), struck out subsec. (q) which related to appeal in capital cases and counsel for financially unable defendants.

Subsec. (r). Pub. L. 109-177, § 221(3), struck out subsec. (r) which provided for refusal by State and Federal correctional employees to participate in executions.

Subsec. (s). Pub. L. 109-177, § 733, added subsec. (s).

1996—Subsec. (q)(9). Pub. L. 104-132, § 108, amended par. (9) generally. Prior to amendment, par. (9) read as follows: "Upon a finding in ex parte proceedings that investigative, expert or other services are reasonably necessary for the representation of the defendant, whether in connection with issues relating to guilt or sentence, the court shall authorize the defendant's attorneys to obtain such services on behalf of the defendant and shall order the payment of fees and expenses therefore, under paragraph (10). Upon a finding that timely procurement of such services could not practicably await prior authorization, the court may authorize the provision of and payment for such services nunc pro tunc."

Subsec. (q)(10). Pub. L. 104-132, § 903(b), amended par. (10) generally. Prior to amendment, par. (10) read as follows: "Notwithstanding the rates and maximum limits generally applicable to criminal cases and any other provision of law to the contrary, the court shall fix the compensation to be paid to attorneys appointed under this subsection and the fees and expenses to be paid for investigative, expert, and other reasonably necessary services authorized under paragraph (9), at such rates or amounts as the court determines to be reasonably necessary to carry out the requirements of paragraphs (4) through (9)."

1994—Subsec. (b)(2)(A). Pub. L. 103-322, § 330003(e), substituted "subsection (c)(1) of this section" for "subsection (d)(1) of this section".

Subsec. (n)(11). Pub. L. 103-322, § 330014, made technical amendment to reference to section 859 of this title to correct reference to corresponding section of original act.

Subsec. (q)(8). Pub. L. 103-322, § 330009(d), substituted "applications for writ" for "applications, for writ".

1988—Subsec. (a). Pub. L. 100-690, § 6481(a), increased minimum term of imprisonment for first violations to 20 from 10 years and for subsequent violations to 30 from 20 years.

Subsecs. (c), (d). Pub. L. 100-690, § 6481(b), redesignated subsecs. (d) and (e) as (c) and (d), respectively.

Subsec. (e). Pub. L. 100-690, § 7001(a)(2), added subsec. (e). Former subsec. (e) redesignated (d).

Pub. L. 100-690, § 7001(a)(1), which directed redesignation of former subsec. (e) as (f), could not be executed because of prior redesignation of former subsec. (e) as (d) by Pub. L. 100-690, § 6481(b), which resulted in there not being a subsec. (f).

Subsecs. (g) to (r). Pub. L. 100-690, § 7001(b), added subsecs. (g) to (r).

1986—Subsec. (a). Pub. L. 99-570, § 1252, substituted "to a fine not to exceed the greater of that authorized in accordance with the provisions of title 18 or $2,000,000 if the defendant is an individual or $5,000,000 if the defendant is other than an individual," for "to a fine of not more than $100,000," and "to a fine not to exceed the greater of twice the amount authorized in accordance with the provisions of title 18 or $4,000,000 if the defendant is an individual or $10,000,000 if the defendant is other than an individual," for "to a fine of not more than $200,000,".

Subsecs. (b) to (e). Pub. L. 99–570, §1253, added subsec. (b) and redesignated former subsecs. (b) and (c) as (d) and (e), respectively, which resulted in there not being a subsec. (c).

1984—Subsec. (a). Pub. L. 98–473, §305, struck out par. (1) designation, substituted references to section 853 of this title for references to paragraph (2) in two places, and struck out par. (2) which related to forfeitures to the United States by any person convicted under par. (1).

Subsec. (d). Pub. L. 98–473, §305(b), struck out subsec. (d) relating to jurisdiction of courts of the United States.

Subsec. (e). Pub. L. 98–473, §224(b), as renumbered by Pub. L. 99–570, §1005(b)(2), which directed the amendment of subsec. (c) of this section by striking out "and section 4202 of title 18 of the United States Code", was executed by striking out that language in subsec. (e) to reflect the probable intent of Congress and the intervening amendment by Pub. L. 99–570, §1253, which redesignated subsec. (c) as (e). See 1986 Amendment note above.

EFFECTIVE DATE OF 1996 AMENDMENT

Amendment by section 903(b) of Pub. L. 104–132 effective as to cases commenced or appeals perfected on or after Apr. 24, 1996, see section 903(c) of Pub. L. 104–132, set out as a note under section 3006A of Title 18, Crimes and Criminal Procedure.

EFFECTIVE DATE OF 1984 AMENDMENT

Amendment by section 224(b) of Pub. L. 98–473 effective Nov. 1, 1987, and applicable only to offenses committed after the taking effect of such amendment, see section 235(a)(1) of Pub. L. 98–473, set out as an Effective Date note under section 3551 of Title 18, Crimes and Criminal Procedure.

GAO STUDY OF COST OF EXECUTIONS

Section 7002 of title VII of Pub. L. 100–690, directed Comptroller General to conduct a study of cost of executions and report to Congress, prior to repeal by Pub. L. 104–66, title I, §1091(d), Dec. 21, 1995, 109 Stat. 722.

§849. Transportation safety offenses

(a) Definitions

In this section—

"safety rest area" means a roadside facility with parking facilities for the rest or other needs of motorists.

"truck stop" means a facility (including any parking lot appurtenant thereto) that—

(A) has the capacity to provide fuel or service, or both, to any commercial motor vehicle (as defined in section 31301 of title 49), operating in commerce (as defined in that section); and

(B) is located within 2,500 feet of the National System of Interstate and Defense Highways or the Federal-Aid Primary System.

(b) First offense

A person who violates section 841(a)(1) of this title or section 856 of this title by distributing or possessing with intent to distribute a controlled substance in or on, or within 1,000 feet of, a truck stop or safety rest area is (except as provided in subsection (b)[1] of this section) subject to—

(1) twice the maximum punishment authorized by section 841(b) of this title; and

(2) twice any term of supervised release authorized by section 841(b) of this title for a first offense.

(c) Subsequent offense

A person who violates section 841(a)(1) of this title or section 856 of this title by distributing or possessing with intent to distribute a controlled substance in or on, or within 1,000 feet of, a truck stop or a safety rest area after a prior conviction or convictions under subsection (a)[2] of this section have become final is subject to—

(1) 3 times the maximum punishment authorized by section 841(b) of this title; and

(2) 3 times any term of supervised release authorized by section 841(b) of this title for a first offense.

(Pub. L. 91–513, title II, §409, as added Pub. L. 103–322, title XVIII, §180201(b)(1), Sept. 13, 1994, 108 Stat. 2046.)

PRIOR PROVISIONS

A prior section 849, Pub. L. 91–513, title II, §409, Oct. 27, 1970, 84 Stat. 1266; Pub. L. 99–514, §2, Oct. 22, 1986, 100 Stat. 2095, related to dangerous special drug offender sentencing, prior to repeal by Pub. L. 98–473, title II, §§219(a), 235(a)(1), Oct. 12, 1984, 98 Stat. 2027, 2031, eff. Nov. 1, 1987, and applicable only to offenses committed after the taking effect of such repeal.

§850. Information for sentencing

Except as otherwise provided in this subchapter or section 242a(a)[1] of title 42, no limitation shall be placed on the information concerning the background, character, and conduct of a person convicted of an offense which a court of the United States may receive and consider for the purpose of imposing an appropriate sentence under this subchapter or subchapter II of this chapter.

(Pub. L. 91–513, title II, §410, Oct. 27, 1970, 84 Stat. 1269.)

REFERENCES IN TEXT

Section 242a of title 42, referred to in text, was repealed by Pub. L. 106–310, div. B, title XXXII, §3201(b)(1), Oct. 17, 2000, 114 Stat. 1190.

§851. Proceedings to establish prior convictions

(a) Information filed by United States Attorney

(1) No person who stands convicted of an offense under this part shall be sentenced to increased punishment by reason of one or more prior convictions, unless before trial, or before entry of a plea of guilty, the United States attorney files an information with the court (and serves a copy of such information on the person or counsel for the person) stating in writing the previous convictions to be relied upon. Upon a showing by the United States attorney that facts regarding prior convictions could not with due diligence be obtained prior to trial or before entry of a plea of guilty, the court may postpone the trial or the taking of the plea of guilty for a reasonable period for the purpose of obtaining such facts. Clerical mistakes in the information

[1] So in original. Probably should be subsection "(c)".

[2] So in original. Probably should be subsection "(b)".

[1] See References in Text note below.

may be amended at any time prior to the pronouncement of sentence.

(2) An information may not be filed under this section if the increased punishment which may be imposed is imprisonment for a term in excess of three years unless the person either waived or was afforded prosecution by indictment for the offense for which such increased punishment may be imposed.

(b) Affirmation or denial of previous conviction

If the United States attorney files an information under this section, the court shall after conviction but before pronouncement of sentence inquire of the person with respect to whom the information was filed whether he affirms or denies that he has been previously convicted as alleged in the information, and shall inform him that any challenge to a prior conviction which is not made before sentence is imposed may not thereafter be raised to attack the sentence.

(c) Denial; written response; hearing

(1) If the person denies any allegation of the information of prior conviction, or claims that any conviction alleged is invalid, he shall file a written response to the information. A copy of the response shall be served upon the United States attorney. The court shall hold a hearing to determine any issues raised by the response which would except the person from increased punishment. The failure of the United States attorney to include in the information the complete criminal record of the person or any facts in addition to the convictions to be relied upon shall not constitute grounds for invalidating the notice given in the information required by subsection (a)(1) of this section. The hearing shall be before the court without a jury and either party may introduce evidence. Except as otherwise provided in paragraph (2) of this subsection, the United States attorney shall have the burden of proof beyond a reasonable doubt on any issue of fact. At the request of either party, the court shall enter findings of fact and conclusions of law.

(2) A person claiming that a conviction alleged in the information was obtained in violation of the Constitution of the United States shall set forth his claim, and the factual basis therefor, with particularity in his response to the information. The person shall have the burden of proof by a preponderance of the evidence on any issue of fact raised by the response. Any challenge to a prior conviction, not raised by response to the information before an increased sentence is imposed in reliance thereon, shall be waived unless good cause be shown for failure to make a timely challenge.

(d) Imposition of sentence

(1) If the person files no response to the information, or if the court determines, after hearing, that the person is subject to increased punishment by reason of prior convictions, the court shall proceed to impose sentence upon him as provided by this part.

(2) If the court determines that the person has not been convicted as alleged in the information, that a conviction alleged in the information is invalid, or that the person is otherwise not subject to an increased sentence as a matter of law, the court shall, at the request of the United States attorney, postpone sentence to allow an appeal from that determination. If no such request is made, the court shall impose sentence as provided by this part. The person may appeal from an order postponing sentence as if sentence had been pronounced and a final judgment of conviction entered.

(e) Statute of limitations

No person who stands convicted of an offense under this part may challenge the validity of any prior conviction alleged under this section which occurred more than five years before the date of the information alleging such prior conviction.

(Pub. L. 91–513, title II, §411, Oct. 27, 1970, 84 Stat. 1269.)

§852. Application of treaties and other international agreements

Nothing in the Single Convention on Narcotic Drugs, the Convention on Psychotropic Substances, or other treaties or international agreements shall be construed to limit the provision of treatment, education, or rehabilitation as alternatives to conviction or criminal penalty for offenses involving any drug or other substance subject to control under any such treaty or agreement.

(Pub. L. 91–513, title II, §412, as added Pub. L. 95–633, title I, §107(a), Nov. 10, 1978, 92 Stat. 3773.)

EFFECTIVE DATE

Section effective on date the Convention on Psychotropic Substances enters into force in the United States [July 15, 1980], see section 112 of Pub. L. 95–633, set out as a note under section 801a of this title.

§853. Criminal forfeitures

(a) Property subject to criminal forfeiture

Any person convicted of a violation of this subchapter or subchapter II of this chapter punishable by imprisonment for more than one year shall forfeit to the United States, irrespective of any provision of State law—

(1) any property constituting, or derived from, any proceeds the person obtained, directly or indirectly, as the result of such violation;

(2) any of the person's property used, or intended to be used, in any manner or part, to commit, or to facilitate the commission of, such violation; and

(3) in the case of a person convicted of engaging in a continuing criminal enterprise in violation of section 848 of this title, the person shall forfeit, in addition to any property described in paragraph (1) or (2), any of his interest in, claims against, and property or contractual rights affording a source of control over, the continuing criminal enterprise.

The court, in imposing sentence on such person, shall order, in addition to any other sentence imposed pursuant to this subchapter or subchapter II of this chapter, that the person forfeit to the United States all property described in this subsection. In lieu of a fine otherwise authorized by this part, a defendant who derives profits or other proceeds from an offense may be fined not more than twice the gross profits or other proceeds.

(b) Meaning of term "property"

Property subject to criminal forfeiture under this section includes—

(1) real property, including things growing on, affixed to, and found in land; and

(2) tangible and intangible personal property, including rights, privileges, interests, claims, and securities.

(c) Third party transfers

All right, title, and interest in property described in subsection (a) of this section vests in the United States upon the commission of the act giving rise to forfeiture under this section. Any such property that is subsequently transferred to a person other than the defendant may be the subject of a special verdict of forfeiture and thereafter shall be ordered forfeited to the United States, unless the transferee establishes in a hearing pursuant to subsection (n) of this section that he is a bona fide purchaser for value of such property who at the time of purchase was reasonably without cause to believe that the property was subject to forfeiture under this section.

(d) Rebuttable presumption

There is a rebuttable presumption at trial that any property of a person convicted of a felony under this subchapter or subchapter II of this chapter is subject to forfeiture under this section if the United States establishes by a preponderance of the evidence that—

(1) such property was acquired by such person during the period of the violation of this subchapter or subchapter II of this chapter or within a reasonable time after such period; and

(2) there was no likely source for such property other than the violation of this subchapter or subchapter II of this chapter.

(e) Protective orders

(1) Upon application of the United States, the court may enter a restraining order or injunction, require the execution of a satisfactory performance bond, or take any other action to preserve the availability of property described in subsection (a) of this section for forfeiture under this section—

(A) upon the filing of an indictment or information charging a violation of this subchapter or subchapter II of this chapter for which criminal forfeiture may be ordered under this section and alleging that the property with respect to which the order is sought would, in the event of conviction, be subject to forfeiture under this section; or

(B) prior to the filing of such an indictment or information, if, after notice to persons appearing to have an interest in the property and opportunity for a hearing, the court determines that—

(i) there is a substantial probability that the United States will prevail on the issue of forfeiture and that failure to enter the order will result in the property being destroyed, removed from the jurisdiction of the court, or otherwise made unavailable for forfeiture; and

(ii) the need to preserve the availability of the property through the entry of the requested order outweighs the hardship on any party against whom the order is to be entered:

Provided, however, That an order entered pursuant to subparagraph (B) shall be effective for not more than ninety days, unless extended by the court for good cause shown or unless an indictment or information described in subparagraph (A) has been filed.

(2) A temporary restraining order under this subsection may be entered upon application of the United States without notice or opportunity for a hearing when an information or indictment has not yet been filed with respect to the property, if the United States demonstrates that there is probable cause to believe that the property with respect to which the order is sought would, in the event of conviction, be subject to forfeiture under this section and that provision of notice will jeopardize the availability of the property for forfeiture. Such a temporary order shall expire not more than ten days after the date on which it is entered, unless extended for good cause shown or unless the party against whom it is entered consents to an extension for a longer period. A hearing requested concerning an order entered under this paragraph shall be held at the earliest possible time and prior to the expiration of the temporary order.

(3) The court may receive and consider, at a hearing held pursuant to this subsection, evidence and information that would be inadmissible under the Federal Rules of Evidence.

(4) ORDER TO REPATRIATE AND DEPOSIT.—

(A) IN GENERAL.—Pursuant to its authority to enter a pretrial restraining order under this section, the court may order a defendant to repatriate any property that may be seized and forfeited, and to deposit that property pending trial in the registry of the court, or with the United States Marshals Service or the Secretary of the Treasury, in an interest-bearing account, if appropriate.

(B) FAILURE TO COMPLY.—Failure to comply with an order under this subsection, or an order to repatriate property under subsection (p) of this section, shall be punishable as a civil or criminal contempt of court, and may also result in an enhancement of the sentence of the defendant under the obstruction of justice provision of the Federal Sentencing Guidelines.

(f) Warrant of seizure

The Government may request the issuance of a warrant authorizing the seizure of property subject to forfeiture under this section in the same manner as provided for a search warrant. If the court determines that there is probable cause to believe that the property to be seized would, in the event of conviction, be subject to forfeiture and that an order under subsection (e) of this section may not be sufficient to assure the availability of the property for forfeiture, the court shall issue a warrant authorizing the seizure of such property.

(g) Execution

Upon entry of an order of forfeiture under this section, the court shall authorize the Attorney General to seize all property ordered forfeited upon such terms and conditions as the court shall deem proper. Following entry of an order declaring the property forfeited, the court may, upon application of the United States, enter such appropriate restraining orders or injunctions, require the execution of satisfactory performance bonds, appoint receivers, conservators, appraisers, accountants, or trustees, or take any other action to protect the interest of the United States in the property ordered forfeited. Any income accruing to or derived from property ordered forfeited under this section may be used to offset ordinary and necessary expenses to the property which are required by law, or which are necessary to protect the interests of the United States or third parties.

(h) Disposition of property

Following the seizure of property ordered forfeited under this section, the Attorney General shall direct the disposition of the property by sale or any other commercially feasible means, making due provision for the rights of any innocent persons. Any property right or interest not exercisable by, or transferable for value to, the United States shall expire and shall not revert to the defendant, nor shall the defendant or any person acting in concert with him or on his behalf be eligible to purchase forfeited property at any sale held by the United States. Upon application of a person, other than the defendant or a person acting in concert with him or on his behalf, the court may restrain or stay the sale or disposition of the property pending the conclusion of any appeal of the criminal case giving rise to the forfeiture, if the applicant demonstrates that proceeding with the sale or disposition of the property will result in irreparable injury, harm, or loss to him.

(i) Authority of the Attorney General

With respect to property ordered forfeited under this section, the Attorney General is authorized to—

(1) grant petitions for mitigation or remission of forfeiture, restore forfeited property to victims of a violation of this subchapter, or take any other action to protect the rights of innocent persons which is in the interest of justice and which is not inconsistent with the provisions of this section;

(2) compromise claims arising under this section;

(3) award compensation to persons providing information resulting in a forfeiture under this section;

(4) direct the disposition by the United States, in accordance with the provisions of section 881(e) of this title, of all property ordered forfeited under this section by public sale or any other commercially feasible means, making due provision for the rights of innocent persons; and

(5) take appropriate measures necessary to safeguard and maintain property ordered forfeited under this section pending its disposition.

(j) Applicability of civil forfeiture provisions

Except to the extent that they are inconsistent with the provisions of this section, the provisions of section 881(d) of this title shall apply to a criminal forfeiture under this section.

(k) Bar on intervention

Except as provided in subsection (n) of this section, no party claiming an interest in property subject to forfeiture under this section may—

(1) intervene in a trial or appeal of a criminal case involving the forfeiture of such property under this section; or

(2) commence an action at law or equity against the United States concerning the validity of his alleged interest in the property subsequent to the filing of an indictment or information alleging that the property is subject to forfeiture under this section.

(*l*) Jurisdiction to enter orders

The district courts of the United States shall have jurisdiction to enter orders as provided in this section without regard to the location of any property which may be subject to forfeiture under this section or which has been ordered forfeited under this section.

(m) Depositions

In order to facilitate the identification and location of property declared forfeited and to facilitate the disposition of petitions for remission or mitigation of forfeiture, after the entry of an order declaring property forfeited to the United States, the court may, upon application of the United States, order that the testimony of any witness relating to the property forfeited be taken by deposition and that any designated book, paper, document, record, recording, or other material not privileged be produced at the same time and place, in the same manner as provided for the taking of depositions under Rule 15 of the Federal Rules of Criminal Procedure.

(n) Third party interests

(1) Following the entry of an order of forfeiture under this section, the United States shall publish notice of the order and of its intent to dispose of the property in such manner as the Attorney General may direct. The Government may also, to the extent practicable, provide direct written notice to any person known to have alleged an interest in the property that is the subject of the order of forfeiture as a substitute for published notice as to those persons so notified.

(2) Any person, other than the defendant, asserting a legal interest in property which has been ordered forfeited to the United States pursuant to this section may, within thirty days of the final publication of notice or his receipt of notice under paragraph (1), whichever is earlier, petition the court for a hearing to adjudicate the validity of his alleged interest in the property. The hearing shall be held before the court alone, without a jury.

(3) The petition shall be signed by the petitioner under penalty of perjury and shall set forth the nature and extent of the petitioner's right, title, or interest in the property, the time and circumstances of the petitioner's acquisi-

tion of the right, title, or interest in the property, any additional facts supporting the petitioner's claim, and the relief sought.

(4) The hearing on the petition shall, to the extent practicable and consistent with the interests of justice, be held within thirty days of the filing of the petition. The court may consolidate the hearing on the petition with a hearing on any other petition filed by a person other than the defendant under this subsection.

(5) At the hearing, the petitioner may testify and present evidence and witnesses on his own behalf, and cross-examine witnesses who appear at the hearing. The United States may present evidence and witnesses in rebuttal and in defense of its claim to the property and cross-examine witnesses who appear at the hearing. In addition to testimony and evidence presented at the hearing, the court shall consider the relevant portions of the record of the criminal case which resulted in the order of forfeiture.

(6) If, after the hearing, the court determines that the petitioner has established by a preponderance of the evidence that—

(A) the petitioner has a legal right, title, or interest in the property, and such right, title, or interest renders the order of forfeiture invalid in whole or in part because the right, title, or interest was vested in the petitioner rather than the defendant or was superior to any right, title, or interest of the defendant at the time of the commission of the acts which gave rise to the forfeiture of the property under this section; or

(B) the petitioner is a bona fide purchaser for value of the right, title, or interest in the property and was at the time of purchase reasonably without cause to believe that the property was subject to forfeiture under this section;

the court shall amend the order of forfeiture in accordance with its determination.

(7) Following the court's disposition of all petitions filed under this subsection, or if no such petitions are filed following the expiration of the period provided in paragraph (2) for the filing of such petitions, the United States shall have clear title to property that is the subject of the order of forfeiture and may warrant good title to any subsequent purchaser or transferee.

(*o*) Construction

The provisions of this section shall be liberally construed to effectuate its remedial purposes.

(p) Forfeiture of substitute property

(1) In general

Paragraph (2) of this subsection shall apply, if any property described in subsection (a) of this section, as a result of any act or omission of the defendant—

(A) cannot be located upon the exercise of due diligence;

(B) has been transferred or sold to, or deposited with, a third party;

(C) has been placed beyond the jurisdiction of the court;

(D) has been substantially diminished in value; or

(E) has been commingled with other property which cannot be divided without difficulty.

(2) Substitute property

In any case described in any of subparagraphs (A) through (E) of paragraph (1), the court shall order the forfeiture of any other property of the defendant, up to the value of any property described in subparagraphs (A) through (E) of paragraph (1), as applicable.

(3) Return of property to jurisdiction

In the case of property described in paragraph (1)(C), the court may, in addition to any other action authorized by this subsection, order the defendant to return the property to the jurisdiction of the court so that the property may be seized and forfeited.

(q) Restitution for cleanup of clandestine laboratory sites

The court, when sentencing a defendant convicted of an offense under this subchapter or subchapter II of this chapter involving the manufacture, the possession, or the possession with intent to distribute, of amphetamine or methamphetamine, shall—

(1) order restitution as provided in sections 3612 and 3664 of title 18;

(2) order the defendant to reimburse the United States, the State or local government concerned, or both the United States and the State or local government concerned for the costs incurred by the United States or the State or local government concerned, as the case may be, for the cleanup associated with the manufacture of amphetamine or methamphetamine by the defendant, or on premises or in property that the defendant owns, resides, or does business in; and

(3) order restitution to any person injured as a result of the offense as provided in section 3663A of title 18.

(Pub. L. 91–513, title II, §413, as added and amended Pub. L. 98–473, title II, §§303, 2301(d)–(f), Oct. 12, 1984, 98 Stat. 2044, 2192, 2193; Pub. L. 99–570, title I, §§1153(b), 1864, Oct. 27, 1986, 100 Stat. 3207–13, 3207–54; Pub. L. 104–237, title II, §207, Oct. 3, 1996, 110 Stat. 3104; Pub. L. 106–310, div. B, title XXXVI, §3613(a), Oct. 17, 2000, 114 Stat. 1229; Pub. L. 107–56, title III, §319(d), Oct. 26, 2001, 115 Stat. 314; Pub. L. 109–177, title VII, §743(a), Mar. 9, 2006, 120 Stat. 272.)

REFERENCES IN TEXT

The Federal Rules of Evidence, referred to in subsec. (e)(3), are set out in the Appendix to Title 28, Judiciary and Judicial Procedure.

The Federal Rules of Criminal Procedure, referred to in subsec. (m), are set out in the Appendix to Title 18, Crimes and Criminal Procedure.

AMENDMENTS

2006—Subsec. (q). Pub. L. 109–177, §743(a)(1), inserted ", the possession, or the possession with intent to distribute," after "manufacture" in introductory provisions.

Subsec. (q)(2). Pub. L. 109–177, §743(a)(2), inserted ", or on premises or in property that the defendant owns, resides, or does business in" after "by the defendant".

2001—Subsec. (e)(4). Pub. L. 107–56, §319(d)(2), added par. (4).

Subsec. (p). Pub. L. 107–56, §319(d)(1), inserted heading and amended text of subsec. (p) generally. Prior to amendment, text read as follows: "If any of the property described in subsection (a) of this section, as a result of any act or omission of the defendant—

"(1) cannot be located upon the exercise of due diligence;

"(2) has been transferred or sold to, or deposited with, a third party;

"(3) has been placed beyond the jurisdiction of the court;

"(4) has been substantially diminished in value; or

"(5) has been commingled with other property which cannot be divided without difficulty;

the court shall order the forfeiture of any other property of the defendant up to the value of any property described in paragraphs (1) through (5)."

2000—Subsec. (q). Pub. L. 106–310, §3613(a)(1), (2), in introductory provisions, inserted "amphetamine or" before "methamphetamine" and substituted "shall" for "may".

Subsec. (q)(2). Pub. L. 106–310, §3613(a)(2), (3), inserted ", the State or local government concerned, or both the United States and the State or local government concerned" after "to reimburse the United States", "or the State or local government concerned, as the case may be," after "costs incurred by the United States", and "amphetamine or" before "methamphetamine".

Subsec. (q)(3). Pub. L. 106–310, §3613(a)(4), substituted "section 3663A of title 18" for "section 3663 of title 18".

1996—Subsec. (q). Pub. L. 104–237 added subsec. (q).

1986—Subsec. (c). Pub. L. 99–570, §1864(1), substituted "subsection (n)" for "subsection (*o*)".

Subsec. (f). Pub. L. 99–570, §1864(2), substituted "subsection (e)" for "subsection (f)".

Subsec. (i)(1). Pub. L. 99–570, §1864(3), substituted "this subchapter" for "this chapter".

Subsec. (k). Pub. L. 99–570, §1864(1), (4), which directed the substitution of "subsection (n)" for "subsection (*o*)" in "the second subsection (h)", and directed the redesignation of "the second subsection (h)" as subsection (k), were executed to this subsection because the "second subsection (h)" had been editorially redesignated subsec. (k) to reflect the probable intent of Congress. See 1984 Amendment note below.

Subsec. (p). Pub. L. 99–570, §1153(b), which directed that "section 413 of title II of the Comprehensive Drug Abuse Prevention and Control Act of 1975" be amended "by redesignating subsection '(p)' as subsection '(q)'" and adding subsec. (p) was executed to this section, which is section 413 of the Comprehensive Drug Abuse Prevention and Control Act of 1970, as the probable intent of Congress, by adding a subsec. (p) in view of the prior redesignation of subsec. (p) as (*o*) by Pub. L. 98–473, §2301(e)(2). See 1984 Amendment note below.

1984—Subsec. (a). Pub. L. 98–473, §2301(d), inserted "In lieu of a fine otherwise authorized by this part, a defendant who derives profits or other proceeds from an offense may be fined not more than twice the gross profits or other proceeds."

Subsec. (d). Pub. L. 98–473, §2301(e), struck out subsec. (d) which related to forfeiture of property other than that described in subsec. (a) and the conditions therefor, and redesignated former subsec. (e) as (d).

Subsecs. (e) to (p). Pub. L. 98–473, §2301(e)(2), which directed that this section be amended by redesignating subsecs. (e), (f), (g), (h), (i), (*l*), (m), (n), (*o*), and (p) as subsecs. (d), (e), (f), (g), (h), (i), (j), (h), (*l*), (m), (n), and (*o*), respectively, was executed by redesignating subsecs. (e) to (p) as (d) to (*o*), respectively, to give effect to the probable intent of Congress.

Subsec. (n)(1). Pub. L. 98–473, §2301(f), struck out "for at least seven successive court days" after "to dispose of the property".

SAVINGS CLAUSE

Pub. L. 109–177, title VII, §743(b), Mar. 9, 2006, 120 Stat. 273, provided that: "Nothing in this section [amending this section] shall be interpreted or construed to amend, alter, or otherwise affect the obligations, liabilities and other responsibilities of any person under any Federal or State environmental laws."

§ 853a. Transferred

CODIFICATION

Section, Pub. L. 100–690, title V, §5301, Nov. 18, 1988, 102 Stat. 4310, which related to denial of Federal benefits to drug traffickers and possessors, was renumbered section 421 of the Controlled Substances Act by Pub. L. 101–647, title X, §1002(d)(1), Nov. 29, 1990, 104 Stat. 4827, and is classified to section 862 of this title.

§ 854. Investment of illicit drug profits

(a) Prohibition

It shall be unlawful for any person who has received any income derived, directly or indirectly, from a violation of this subchapter or subchapter II of this chapter punishable by imprisonment for more than one year in which such person has participated as a principal within the meaning of section 2 of title 18, to use or invest, directly or indirectly, any part of such income, or the proceeds of such income, in acquisition of any interest in, or the establishment or operation of, any enterprise which is engaged in, or the activities of which affect interstate or foreign commerce. A purchase of securities on the open market for purposes of investment, and without the intention of controlling or participating in the control of the issuer, or of assisting another to do so, shall not be unlawful under this section if the securities of the issuer held by the purchaser, the members of his immediate family, and his or their accomplices in any violation of this subchapter or subchapter II of this chapter after such purchase do not amount in the aggregate to 1 per centum of the outstanding securities of any one class, and do not confer, either in law or in fact, the power to elect one or more directors of the issuer.

(b) Penalty

Whoever violates this section shall be fined not more than $50,000 or imprisoned not more than ten years, or both.

(c) "Enterprise" defined

As used in this section, the term "enterprise" includes any individual, partnership, corporation, association, or other legal entity, and any union or group of individuals associated in fact although not a legal entity.

(d) Construction

The provisions of this section shall be liberally construed to effectuate its remedial purposes.

(Pub. L. 91–513, title II, §414, as added Pub. L. 98–473, title II, §303, Oct. 12, 1984, 98 Stat. 2049.)

§ 855. Alternative fine

In lieu of a fine otherwise authorized by this part, a defendant who derives profits or other proceeds from an offense may be fined not more than twice the gross profits or other proceeds.

(Pub. L. 91–513, title II, §415, as added Pub. L. 98–473, title II, §2302, Oct. 12, 1984, 98 Stat. 2193.)

§ 856. Maintaining drug-involved premises

(a) Unlawful acts

Except as authorized by this subchapter, it shall be unlawful to—

(1) knowingly open, lease, rent, use, or maintain any place, whether permanently or temporarily, for the purpose of manufacturing, distributing, or using any controlled substance;

(2) manage or control any place, whether permanently or temporarily, either as an owner, lessee, agent, employee, occupant, or mortgagee, and knowingly and intentionally rent, lease, profit from, or make available for use, with or without compensation, the place for the purpose of unlawfully manufacturing, storing, distributing, or using a controlled substance.

(b) Criminal penalties

Any person who violates subsection (a) of this section shall be sentenced to a term of imprisonment of not more than 20 years or a fine of not more than $500,000, or both, or a fine of $2,000,000 for a person other than an individual.

(c) Violation as offense against property

A violation of subsection (a) of this section shall be considered an offense against property for purposes of section 3663A(c)(1)(A)(ii) of title 18.

(d) Civil penalites

(1) Any person who violates subsection (a) of this section shall be subject to a civil penalty of not more than the greater of—

(A) $250,000; or

(B) 2 times the gross receipts, either known or estimated, that were derived from each violation that is attributable to the person.

(2) If a civil penalty is calculated under paragraph (1)(B), and there is more than 1 defendant, the court may apportion the penalty between multiple violators, but each violator shall be jointly and severally liable for the civil penalty under this subsection.

(e) Declaratory and injunctive remedies

Any person who violates subsection (a) of this section shall be subject to declaratory and injunctive remedies as set forth in section 843(f) of this title.

(Pub. L. 91–513, title II, §416, as added Pub. L. 99–570, title I, §1841(a), Oct. 27, 1986, 100 Stat. 3207–52; amended Pub. L. 106–310, div. B, title XXXVI, §3613(e), Oct. 17, 2000, 114 Stat. 1230; Pub. L. 108–21, title VI, §608(b)(1), (2), (c), Apr. 30, 2003, 117 Stat. 691.)

AMENDMENTS

2003—Pub. L. 108–21, §608(b)(2), substituted "Maintaining drug-involved premises" for "Establishment of manufacturing operations" in section catchline.

Subsec. (a)(1). Pub. L. 108–21, §608(b)(1)(A), substituted "open, lease, rent, use, or maintain any place, whether permanently or temporarily," for "open or maintain any place".

Subsec. (a)(2). Pub. L. 108–21, §608(b)(1)(B), added par. (2) and struck out former par. (2) which read as follows: "manage or control any building, room, or enclosure, either as an owner, lessee, agent, employee, or mortgagee, and knowingly and intentionally rent, lease, or make available for use, with or without compensation, the building, room, or enclosure for the purpose of unlawfully manufacturing, storing, distributing, or using a controlled substance."

Subsecs. (d), (e). Pub. L. 108–21, §608(c), added subsecs. (d) and (e).

2000—Subsec. (c). Pub. L. 106–310 added subsec. (c).

§857. Repealed. Pub. L. 101–647, title XXIV, §2401(d), Nov. 29, 1990, 104 Stat. 4859

Section, Pub. L. 99–570, title I, §1822, Oct. 27, 1986, 100 Stat. 3207–51; Pub. L. 100–690, title VI, §6485, Nov. 18, 1988, 102 Stat. 4384; Pub. L. 101–647, title XXIV, §2401(b), Nov. 29, 1990, 104 Stat. 4859, related to interstate and foreign sale and transportation of drug paraphernalia.

Subsec. (a), which related to unlawful acts, was repealed.

Subsecs. (b) to (f) were redesignated as subsecs. (b) to (f) of section 422 of the Controlled Substances Act by section 2401(b) of Pub. L. 101–647 and transferred to section 863(b) to (f) of this title.

EFFECTIVE DATE

Section 1823 of Pub. L. 99–570 which provided that subtitle O (§§1821–1823) of title I of Pub. L. 99–570, enacting this section and provisions set out as a note under section 801 of this title, was to become effective 90 days after Oct. 27, 1986, was repealed by Pub. L. 101–647, title XXIV, §2401(d), Nov. 29, 1990, 104 Stat. 4859.

§858. Endangering human life while illegally manufacturing controlled substance

Whoever, while manufacturing a controlled substance in violation of this subchapter, or attempting to do so, or transporting or causing to be transported materials, including chemicals, to do so, creates a substantial risk of harm to human life shall be fined in accordance with title 18 or imprisoned not more than 10 years, or both.

(Pub. L. 91–513, title II, §417, as added Pub. L. 100–690, title VI, §6301(a), Nov. 18, 1988, 102 Stat. 4370.)

§859. Distribution to persons under age twenty-one

(a) First offense

Except as provided in section 860 of this title, any person at least eighteen years of age who violates section 841(a)(1) of this title by distributing a controlled substance to a person under twenty-one years of age is (except as provided in subsection (b) of this section) subject to (1) twice the maximum punishment authorized by section 841(b) of this title, and (2) at least twice any term of supervised release authorized by section 841(b) of this title, for a first offense involving the same controlled substance and schedule. Except to the extent a greater minimum sentence is otherwise provided by section 841(b) of this title, a term of imprisonment under this subsection shall be not less than one year. The mandatory minimum sentencing provisions of this subsection shall not apply to offenses involving 5 grams or less of marihuana.

(b) Second offense

Except as provided in section 860 of this title, any person at least eighteen years of age who violates section 841(a)(1) of this title by distributing a controlled substance to a person under twenty-one years of age after a prior conviction under subsection (a) of this section (or under section 333(b) of this title as in effect prior to May 1, 1971) has become final, is subject to (1) three times the maximum punishment authorized by section 841(b) of this title, and (2) at least three times any term of supervised release authorized by section 841(b) of this title, for a second or subsequent offense involving the same controlled substance and schedule. Except to the extent a greater minimum sentence is otherwise provided by section 841(b) of this title, a term of imprisonment under this subsection shall be not less than one year. Penalties for third and subsequent convictions shall be governed by section 841(b)(1)(A) of this title.

(Pub. L. 91–513, title II, § 418, formerly § 405, Oct. 27, 1970, 84 Stat. 1265; Pub. L. 98–473, title II, §§ 224(b), 503(b)(3), Oct. 12, 1984, 98 Stat. 2030, 2070; Pub. L. 99–570, title I, §§ 1004(a), 1005(b)(1), 1105(a), (b), Oct. 27, 1986, 100 Stat. 3207–6, 3207–11; Pub. L. 100–690, title VI, §§ 6452(b), 6455, 6456, Nov. 18, 1988, 102 Stat. 4371, 4372; renumbered § 418 and amended Pub. L. 101–647, title X, §§ 1002(a), 1003(a), title XXXV, § 3599L, Nov. 29, 1990, 104 Stat. 4827, 4828, 4932.)

CODIFICATION

Section was classified to section 845 of this title prior to renumbering by Pub. L. 101–647.

AMENDMENTS

1990—Subsec. (a). Pub. L. 101–647, § 1003(a)(1), substituted "subject to (1) twice the maximum punishment authorized by section 841(b) of this title" for "punishable by (1) a term of imprisonment, or a fine, or both, up to twice that authorized by section 841(b) of this title".

Pub. L. 101–647, § 1002(a)(2)(A), substituted "section 860" for "section 845a".

Subsec. (b). Pub. L. 101–647, § 3599L, substituted "has become final" for "have become final".

Pub. L. 101–647, § 1003(a)(2), substituted "subject to (1) three times the maximum punishment authorized by section 841(b) of this title" for "punishable by (1) a term of imprisonment, or a fine, or both, up to three times that authorized by section 841(b) of this title".

Pub. L. 101–647, § 1002(a)(2)(B), substituted "section 860" for "section 845a".

1988—Subsec. (a). Pub. L. 100–690, § 6455, inserted at end "The mandatory minimum sentencing provisions of this subsection shall not apply to offenses involving 5 grams or less of marihuana."

Subsec. (b). Pub. L. 100–690, § 6452(b), struck out "or subsequent" after "Second" in heading, and in text struck out "or convictions" after "a prior conviction", and inserted at end "Penalties for third and subsequent convictions shall be governed by section 841(b)(1)(A) of this title."

Pub. L. 100–690, § 6456, struck out "The mandatory minimum sentencing provisions of this paragraph shall not apply to offenses involving 5 grams or less of marihuana."

1986—Subsec. (a). Pub. L. 99–570, § 1105(a), inserted "Except to the extent a greater minimum sentence is otherwise provided by section 841(b) of this title, a term of imprisonment under this subsection shall be not less than one year."

Pub. L. 99–570, § 1004(a), substituted "term of supervised release" for "special parole term".

Subsec. (b). Pub. L. 99–570, § 1105(b), inserted "Except to the extent a greater minimum sentence is otherwise provided by section 841(b) of this title, a term of imprisonment under this subsection shall be not less than one year. The mandatory minimum sentencing provisions of this paragraph shall not apply to offenses involving 5 grams or less of marihuana."

Pub. L. 99–570, § 1004(a), substituted "term of supervised release" for "special parole term".

1984—Subsecs. (a), (b). Pub. L. 98–473, § 503(b)(3), substituted "Except as provided in section 845a of this title, any" for "Any".

Pub. L. 98–473, § 224(b), which directed amendment of this section effective Nov. 1, 1987 (see section 235(a)(1) of Pub. L. 98–473 set out as an Effective Date note under section 3551 of Title 18, Crimes and Criminal Procedure) was repealed by Pub. L. 99–570, § 1005(b)(1).

EFFECTIVE DATE OF 1986 AMENDMENT

Amendment by section 1004(a) of Pub. L. 99–570 effective on date of taking effect of section 3583 of Title 18, Crimes and Criminal Procedure (Nov. 1, 1987), see section 1004(b) of Pub. L. 99–570 set out as a note under section 841 of this title.

§ 860. Distribution or manufacturing in or near schools and colleges

(a) Penalty

Any person who violates section 841(a)(1) of this title or section 856 of this title by distributing, possessing with intent to distribute, or manufacturing a controlled substance in or on, or within one thousand feet of, the real property comprising a public or private elementary, vocational, or secondary school or a public or private college, junior college, or university, or a playground, or housing facility owned by a public housing authority, or within 100 feet of a public or private youth center, public swimming pool, or video arcade facility, is (except as provided in subsection (b) of this section) subject to (1) twice the maximum punishment authorized by section 841(b) of this title; and (2) at least twice any term of supervised release authorized by section 841(b) of this title for a first offense. A fine up to twice that authorized by section 841(b) of this title may be imposed in addition to any term of imprisonment authorized by this subsection. Except to the extent a greater minimum sentence is otherwise provided by section 841(b) of this title, a person shall be sentenced under this subsection to a term of imprisonment of not less than one year. The mandatory minimum sentencing provisions of this paragraph shall not apply to offenses involving 5 grams or less of marihuana.

(b) Second offenders

Any person who violates section 841(a)(1) of this title or section 856 of this title by distributing, possessing with intent to distribute, or manufacturing a controlled substance in or on, or within one thousand feet of, the real property comprising a public or private elementary, vocational, or secondary school or a public or private college, junior college, or university, or a playground, or housing facility owned by a public housing authority, or within 100 feet of a public or private youth center, public swimming pool, or video arcade facility, after a prior conviction under subsection (a) of this section has become final is punishable (1) by the greater of (A) a term of imprisonment of not less than three years and not more than life imprisonment or (B) three times the maximum punishment authorized by section 841(b) of this title for a first offense, and (2) at least three times any term of supervised release authorized by section 841(b) of this title for a first offense. A fine up to three times that authorized by section 841(b) of this title may be imposed in addition to any term of imprisonment authorized by this subsection. Except to the extent a greater minimum sentence is otherwise provided by section 841(b) of this title, a person shall be sentenced under this subsection to a term of imprisonment of not less than three years. Penalties for third and subsequent convictions shall be governed by section 841(b)(1)(A) of this title.

(c) Employing children to distribute drugs near schools or playgrounds

Notwithstanding any other law, any person at least 21 years of age who knowingly and intentionally—

(1) employs, hires, uses, persuades, induces, entices, or coerces a person under 18 years of age to violate this section; or

(2) employs, hires, uses, persuades, induces, entices, or coerces a person under 18 years of age to assist in avoiding detection or apprehension for any offense under this section by any Federal, State, or local law enforcement official,

is punishable by a term of imprisonment, a fine, or both, up to triple those authorized by section 841 of this title.

(d) Suspension of sentence; probation; parole

In the case of any mandatory minimum sentence imposed under this section, imposition or execution of such sentence shall not be suspended and probation shall not be granted. An individual convicted under this section shall not be eligible for parole until the individual has served the mandatory minimum term of imprisonment as provided by this section.

(e) Definitions

For the purposes of this section—

(1) The term "playground" means any outdoor facility (including any parking lot appurtenant thereto) intended for recreation, open to the public, and with any portion thereof containing three or more separate apparatus intended for the recreation of children including, but not limited to, sliding boards, swingsets, and teeterboards.

(2) The term "youth center" means any recreational facility and/or gymnasium (including any parking lot appurtenant thereto), intended primarily for use by persons under 18 years of age, which regularly provides athletic, civic, or cultural activities.

(3) The term "video arcade facility" means any facility, legally accessible to persons under 18 years of age, intended primarily for the use of pinball and video machines for amusement containing a minimum of ten pinball and/or video machines.

(4) The term "swimming pool" includes any parking lot appurtenant thereto.

(Pub. L. 91–513, title II, §419, formerly §405A, as added Pub. L. 98–473, title II, §503(a), Oct. 12, 1984, 98 Stat. 2069; amended Pub. L. 99–570, title I, §§1004(a), 1104, 1105(c), 1841(b), 1866(b), (c), Oct. 27, 1986, 100 Stat. 3207–6, 3207–11, 3207–52, 3207–55; Pub. L. 99–646, §28, Nov. 10, 1986, 100 Stat. 3598; Pub. L. 100–690, title VI, §§6452(b)(1), 6457, 6458, Nov. 18, 1988, 102 Stat. 4371, 4373; renumbered §419 and amended Pub. L. 101–647, title X, §§1002(b), 1003(b), title XII, §1214, title XV, §1502, title XXXV, §3599L, Nov. 29, 1990, 104 Stat. 4827, 4829, 4833, 4836, 4932; Pub. L. 103–322, title XIV, §140006, title XXXII, §320107, title XXXIII, §330009(a), Sept. 13, 1994, 108 Stat. 2032, 2111, 2143.)

CODIFICATION

Section was classified to section 845a of this title prior to renumbering by Pub. L. 101–647.

AMENDMENTS

1994—Subsec. (a). Pub. L. 103–322, §320107, substituted "playground, or housing facility owned by a public housing authority, or within" for "playground, or within".

Subsec. (b). Pub. L. 103–322, §§320107, 330009(a), substituted "playground, or housing facility owned by a public housing authority, or within" for "playground, or within" and inserted a period at end of penultimate sentence.

Subsecs. (c) to (e). Pub. L. 103–322, §140006, added subsec. (c) and redesignated former subsecs. (c) and (d) as (d) and (e), respectively.

1990—Subsec. (a). Pub. L. 101–647, §1502(1), inserted "or a playground," after "university," and struck out "playground," after "within 100 feet of a".

Pub. L. 101–647, §1214(1)(C), substituted "a person shall be sentenced under this subsection to a term of imprisonment of not less than one year" for "a term of imprisonment under this subsection shall be not less than one year".

Pub. L. 101–647, §1214(1)(B), inserted "A fine up to twice that authorized by section 841(b) of this title may be imposed in addition to any term of imprisonment authorized by this subsection."

Pub. L. 101–647, §1214(1)(A), which directed the amendment of par. (1) by striking out ", or a fine, or both," could not be executed because those words did not appear. See note below.

Pub. L. 101–647, §1003(b)(1), which directed the substitution of "subject to (1) twice the maximum punishment authorized by section 841(b) of this title" for "punishable (1) by a term of imprisonment, or a fine, or both, up to twice that authorized by section 841(b) of this title", was executed by making the substitution for "punishable (1) by a term of imprisonment, or fine, or both, up to twice that authorized by section 841(b) of this title" to reflect the probable intent of Congress.

Subsec. (b). Pub. L. 101–647, §3599L, substituted "has become final" for "have become final".

Pub. L. 101–647, §1502(2), inserted "or a playground," after "university," and struck out "playground," after "within 100 feet of a".

Pub. L. 101–647, §1214(2)(B), inserted after first sentence "A fine up to three times that authorized by section 841(b) of this title may be imposed in addition to any term of imprisonment authorized by this subsection. Except to the extent a greater minimum sentence is otherwise provided by section 841(b) of this title, a person shall be sentenced under this subsection to a term of imprisonment of not less than three years".

Subsec. (b)(1)(B). Pub. L. 101–647, §1214(2)(A), which directed the amendment of subpar. (B) by striking ", or a fine up to three times that" through "or both", could not be executed because the language did not appear after execution of the intervening amendment by Pub. L. 101–647, §1003(b)(2). See below.

Pub. L. 101–647, §1003(b)(2), substituted "three times the maximum punishment authorized by section 841(b) of this title for a first offense" for "a term of imprisonment of up to three times that authorized by section 841(b) of this title for a first offense, or a fine up to three times that authorized by section 841(b) of this title for a first offense, or both".

Subsec. (c). Pub. L. 101–647, §1214(3), inserted "mandatory minimum" after "In the case of any", struck out "subsection (b) of" after "imposed under", and substituted "An individual convicted under this section shall not be eligible for parole until the individual has served the mandatory minimum term of imprisonment as provided by this section" for "An individual convicted under subsection (b) of this section shall not be eligible for parole under chapter 311 of title 18 until the individual has served the minimum sentence required by such subsection''.

1988—Subsec. (a). Pub. L. 100–690, §§6457, 6458(a), inserted '', possessing with intent to distribute,'' after ''distributing'' and '', or within 100 feet of a playground, public or private youth center, public swimming pool, or video arcade facility,'' after ''university''.

Subsec. (b). Pub. L. 100–690, §§6452(b)(1), 6457, 6458(a), inserted '', possessing with intent to distribute,'' after ''distributing'', and '', or within 100 feet of a playground, public or private youth center, public swimming pool, or video arcade facility,'' after ''university'', substituted ''a prior conviction'' for ''a prior conviction or convictions'', and inserted at end ''Penalties for third and subsequent convictions shall be governed by section 841(b)(1)(A) of this title.''

Subsec. (d). Pub. L. 100–690, §6458(b), added subsec. (d).

1986—Subsec. (a). Pub. L. 99–570, §§1104(a), (b), 1105(c), 1841(b)(1), inserted ''or section 856 of this title'' and ''or manufacturing'', substituted ''a public or private elementary, vocational, or secondary school or a public or private college, junior college, or university'' for ''a public or private elementary or secondary school'', struck out ''involving the same controlled substance and schedule'' after ''for a first offense'', and inserted ''Except to the extent a greater minimum sentence is otherwise provided by section 841(b) of this title, a term of imprisonment under this subsection shall be not less than one year. The mandatory minimum sentencing provisions of this paragraph shall not apply to offenses involving 5 grams or less of marihuana.''

Pub. L. 99–570, §1004(a), substituted ''term of supervised release'' for ''special parole term''.

Subsec. (b). Pub. L. 99–646 which directed that ''parole'' be inserted after ''(2) at least three times any special'' could not be executed in view of prior amendment by Pub. L. 99–570, §1104(c) below.

Pub. L. 99–570, §1166(b), which directed that ''term of supervised release'' be substituted for ''special term'' could not be executed in view of prior amendment by Pub. L. 99–570, §1104(c) below.

Pub. L. 99–570, §§1104(a), 1841(b)(2), inserted reference to section 856 of this title, inserted ''or manufacturing'' after ''distributing'' and substituted ''a public or private elementary, vocational, or secondary school or a public or private college, junior college, or university'' for ''a public or private elementary or secondary school''.

Pub. L. 99–570, §1104(c), amended cls. (1) and (2) generally. Prior to amendment, cls. (1) and (2) read as follows: ''(1) by a term of imprisonment of not less than three years and not more than life imprisonment and (2) at least three times any special term authorized by section 841(b) of this title for a second or subsequent offense involving the same controlled substance and schedule.''

Subsec. (c). Pub. L. 99–570, §1866(c), substituted reference to chapter 311 of title 18 for reference to section 4202 of that title.

EFFECTIVE DATE OF 1986 AMENDMENT

Amendment by section 1004(a) of Pub. L. 99–570 effective on date of taking effect of section 3583 of Title 18, Crimes and Criminal Procedure (Nov. 1, 1987), see section 1004(b) of Pub. L. 99–570 set out as a note under section 841 of this title.

§860a. Consecutive sentence for manufacturing or distributing, or possessing with intent to manufacture or distribute, methamphetamine on premises where children are present or reside

Whoever violates section 841(a)(1) of this title by manufacturing or distributing, or possessing with intent to manufacture or distribute, methamphetamine or its salts, isomers or salts of isomers on premises in which an individual who is under the age of 18 years is present or resides, shall, in addition to any other sentence imposed, be imprisoned for a period of any term of years but not more than 20 years, subject to a fine, or both.

(Pub. L. 91–513, title II, §419a, as added Pub. L. 109–177, title VII, §734(a), Mar. 9, 2006, 120 Stat. 270.)

§861. Employment or use of persons under 18 years of age in drug operations

(a) Unlawful acts

It shall be unlawful for any person at least eighteen years of age to knowingly and intentionally—

(1) employ, hire, use, persuade, induce, entice, or coerce, a person under eighteen years of age to violate any provision of this subchapter or subchapter II of this chapter;

(2) employ, hire, use, persuade, induce, entice, or coerce, a person under eighteen years of age to assist in avoiding detection or apprehension for any offense of this subchapter or subchapter II of this chapter by any Federal, State, or local law enforcement official; or

(3) receive a controlled substance from a person under 18 years of age, other than an immediate family member, in violation of this subchapter or subchapter II of this chapter.

(b) Penalty for first offense

Any person who violates subsection (a) of this section is subject to twice the maximum punishment otherwise authorized and at least twice any term of supervised release otherwise authorized for a first offense. Except to the extent a greater minimum sentence is otherwise provided, a term of imprisonment under this subsection shall not be less than one year.

(c) Penalty for subsequent offenses

Any person who violates subsection (a) of this section after a prior conviction under subsection (a) of this section has become final, is subject to three times the maximum punishment otherwise authorized and at least three times any term of supervised release otherwise authorized for a first offense. Except to the extent a greater minimum sentence is otherwise provided, a term of imprisonment under this subsection shall not be less than one year. Penalties for third and subsequent convictions shall be governed by section 841(b)(1)(A) of this title.

(d) Penalty for providing or distributing controlled substance to underage person

Any person who violates subsection (a)(1) or (2) of this section[1]

(1) by knowingly providing or distributing a controlled substance or a controlled substance analogue to any person under eighteen years of age; or

(2) if the person employed, hired, or used is fourteen years of age or younger,

shall be subject to a term of imprisonment for not more than five years or a fine of not more

[1] So in original. Probably should be followed by a dash.

than $50,000, or both, in addition to any other punishment authorized by this section.

(e) Suspension of sentence; probation; parole

In any case of any sentence imposed under this section, imposition or execution of such sentence shall not be suspended and probation shall not be granted. An individual convicted under this section of an offense for which a mandatory minimum term of imprisonment is applicable shall not be eligible for parole under section 4202 of title 18[2] until the individual has served the mandatory term of imprisonment as enhanced by this section.

(f) Distribution of controlled substance to pregnant individual

Except as authorized by this subchapter, it shall be unlawful for any person to knowingly or intentionally provide or distribute any controlled substance to a pregnant individual in violation of any provision of this subchapter. Any person who violates this subsection shall be subject to the provisions of subsections (b), (c), and (e) of this section.

(Pub. L. 91–513, title II, §420, formerly §405B, as added Pub. L. 99–570, title I, §1102, Oct. 27, 1986, 100 Stat. 3207–10; amended Pub. L. 100–690, title VI, §§6452(b)(1), 6459, 6470(d), Nov. 18, 1988, 102 Stat. 4371, 4373, 4378; renumbered §420 and amended Pub. L. 101–647, title X, §§1002(c), 1003(c), title XXXV, §3599L, Nov. 29, 1990, 104 Stat. 4827, 4829, 4932.)

REFERENCES IN TEXT

Section 4202 of title 18, referred to in subsec. (e), which, as originally enacted in Title 18, Crimes and Criminal Procedure, related to eligibility of prisoners for parole, was repealed and a new section 4202 enacted as part of the repeal and enactment of a new chapter 311 (§4201 et seq.) of Title 18, by Pub. L. 94–233, §2, Mar. 15, 1976, 90 Stat. 219. For provisions relating to the eligibility of prisoners for parole, see section 4205 of Title 18. Pub. L. 98–473, title II, §§218(a)(5), 235(a)(1), (b)(1), Oct. 12, 1984, 98 Stat. 2027, 2031, 2032, as amended, provided that, effective on the first day of the first calendar month beginning 36 months after Oct. 12, 1984 (Nov. 1, 1987), chapter 311 of Title 18 is repealed, subject to remaining effective for five years after Nov. 1, 1987, in certain circumstances. See Effective Date note set out under section 3551 of Title 18.

CODIFICATION

Section was classified to section 845b of this title prior to renumbering by Pub. L. 101–647.

AMENDMENTS

1990—Subsec. (b). Pub. L. 101–647, §1003(c)(1), which directed the substitution of "is subject to twice the maximum punishment otherwise authorized" for "is punishable by a term of imprisonment up to twice that authorized, or up to twice the fine authorized, or both," was executed by making the substitution for "is punishable by a term of imprisonment up to twice that otherwise authorized, or up to twice the fine otherwise authorized, or both," to reflect the probable intent of Congress.

Subsec. (c). Pub. L. 101–647, §3599L, substituted "has become final" for "have become final".

Pub. L. 101–647, §1003(c)(2), which directed the substitution of "is subject to three times the maximum punishment otherwise authorized" for "is punishable by a term of imprisonment up to three times that authorized, or up to three times the fine authorized, or both," was executed by making the substitution for "is punishable by a term of imprisonment up to three times that otherwise authorized, or up to three times the fine otherwise authorized, or both," to reflect the probable intent of Congress.

1988—Subsec. (a)(3). Pub. L. 100–690, §6459, added par. (3).

Subsec. (c). Pub. L. 100–690, §6452(b)(1), struck out "or convictions" after "a prior conviction" and inserted at end "Penalties for third and subsequent convictions shall be governed by section 841(b)(1)(A) of this title."

Subsec. (e). Pub. L. 100–690, §6470(d), struck out "required by section 841(b) of this title" after "mandatory term of imprisonment".

§862. Denial of Federal benefits to drug traffickers and possessors

(a) Drug traffickers

(1) Any individual who is convicted of any Federal or State offense consisting of the distribution of controlled substances shall—

(A) at the discretion of the court, upon the first conviction for such an offense be ineligible for any or all Federal benefits for up to 5 years after such conviction;

(B) at the discretion of the court, upon a second conviction for such an offense be ineligible for any or all Federal benefits for up to 10 years after such conviction; and

(C) upon a third or subsequent conviction for such an offense be permanently ineligible for all Federal benefits.

(2) The benefits which are denied under this subsection shall not include benefits relating to long-term drug treatment programs for addiction for any person who, if there is a reasonable body of evidence to substantiate such declaration, declares himself to be an addict and submits himself to a long-term treatment program for addiction, or is deemed to be rehabilitated pursuant to rules established by the Secretary of Health and Human Services.

(b) Drug possessors

(1) Any individual who is convicted of any Federal or State offense involving the possession of a controlled substance (as such term is defined for purposes of this subchapter) shall—

(A) upon the first conviction for such an offense and at the discretion of the court—

(i) be ineligible for any or all Federal benefits for up to one year;

(ii) be required to successfully complete an approved drug treatment program which includes periodic testing to insure that the individual remains drug free;

(iii) be required to perform appropriate community service; or

(iv) any combination of clause (i), (ii), or (iii); and

(B) upon a second or subsequent conviction for such an offense be ineligible for all Federal benefits for up to 5 years after such conviction as determined by the court. The court shall continue to have the discretion in subparagraph (A) above. In imposing penalties and conditions under subparagraph (A), the court may require that the completion of the conditions imposed by clause (ii) or (iii) be a requirement for the reinstatement of benefits under clause (i).

[2] See References in Text note below.

(2) The penalties and conditions which may be imposed under this subsection shall be waived in the case of a person who, if there is a reasonable body of evidence to substantiate such declaration, declares himself to be an addict and submits himself to a long-term treatment program for addiction, or is deemed to be rehabilitated pursuant to rules established by the Secretary of Health and Human Services.

(c) Suspension of period of ineligibility

The period of ineligibility referred to in subsections (a) and (b) of this section shall be suspended if the individual—

(A) completes a supervised drug rehabilitation program after becoming ineligible under this section;

(B) has otherwise been rehabilitated; or

(C) has made a good faith effort to gain admission to a supervised drug rehabilitation program, but is unable to do so because of inaccessibility or unavailability of such a program, or the inability of the individual to pay for such a program.

(d) Definitions

As used in this section—

(1) the term "Federal benefit"—

(A) means the issuance of any grant, contract, loan, professional license, or commercial license provided by an agency of the United States or by appropriated funds of the United States; and

(B) does not include any retirement, welfare, Social Security, health, disability, veterans benefit, public housing, or other similar benefit, or any other benefit for which payments or services are required for eligibility; and

(2) the term "veterans benefit" means all benefits provided to veterans, their families, or survivors by virtue of the service of a veteran in the Armed Forces of the United States.

(e) Inapplicability of this section to Government witnesses

The penalties provided by this section shall not apply to any individual who cooperates or testifies with the Government in the prosecution of a Federal or State offense or who is in a Government witness protection program.

(f) Indian provision

Nothing in this section shall be construed to affect the obligation of the United States to any Indian or Indian tribe arising out of any treaty, statute, Executive order, or the trust responsibility of the United States owing to such Indian or Indian tribe. Nothing in this subsection shall exempt any individual Indian from the sanctions provided for in this section, provided that no individual Indian shall be denied any benefit under Federal Indian programs comparable to those described in subsection (d)(1)(B) or (d)(2) of this section.

(g) Presidential report

(1) On or before May 1, 1989, the President shall transmit to the Congress a report—

(A) delineating the role of State courts in implementing this section;

(B) describing the manner in which Federal agencies will implement and enforce the requirements of this section;

(C) detailing the means by which Federal and State agencies, courts, and law enforcement agencies will exchange and share the data and information necessary to implement and enforce the withholding of Federal benefits; and

(D) recommending any modifications to improve the administration of this section or otherwise achieve the goal of discouraging the trafficking and possession of controlled substances.

(2) No later than September 1, 1989, the Congress shall consider the report of the President and enact such changes as it deems appropriate to further the goals of this section.

(h) Effective date

The denial of Federal benefits set forth in this section shall take effect for convictions occurring after September 1, 1989.

(Pub. L. 91–513, title II, § 421, formerly Pub. L. 100–690, title V, § 5301, Nov. 18, 1988, 102 Stat. 4310; renumbered § 421 of Pub. L. 91–513 and amended Pub. L. 101–647, title X, § 1002(d), Nov. 29, 1990, 104 Stat. 4827.)

CODIFICATION

Section was classified to section 853a of this title prior to renumbering by Pub. L. 101–647.

AMENDMENTS

1990—Pub. L. 101–647, § 1002(d)(1), renumbered section 853a of this title as this section.

Subsec. (a)(1). Pub. L. 101–647, § 1002(d)(2), struck out "(as such terms are defined for purposes of the Controlled Substances Act)" after "controlled substances" in introductory provisions.

§ 862a. Denial of assistance and benefits for certain drug-related convictions

(a) In general

An individual convicted (under Federal or State law) of any offense which is classified as a felony by the law of the jurisdiction involved and which has as an element the possession, use, or distribution of a controlled substance (as defined in section 802(6) of this title) shall not be eligible for—

(1) assistance under any State program funded under part A of title IV of the Social Security Act [42 U.S.C. 601 et seq.], or

(2) benefits under the food stamp program (as defined in section 3(*l*) of the Food Stamp Act of 1977 [7 U.S.C. 2012(*l*)]) or any State program carried out under the Food Stamp Act of 1977 [7 U.S.C. 2011 et seq.].

(b) Effects on assistance and benefits for others

(1) Program of temporary assistance for needy families

The amount of assistance otherwise required to be provided under a State program funded under part A of title IV of the Social Security Act [42 U.S.C. 601 et seq.] to the family members of an individual to whom subsection (a) of this section applies shall be reduced by the amount which would have otherwise been made available to the individual under such part.

(2) Benefits under the Food Stamp Act of 1977

The amount of benefits otherwise required to be provided to a household under the food stamp program (as defined in section 3(*l*) of the Food Stamp Act of 1977 [7 U.S.C. 2012(*l*)]), or any State program carried out under the Food Stamp Act of 1977 [7 U.S.C. 2011 et seq.], shall be determined by considering the individual to whom subsection (a) of this section applies not to be a member of such household, except that the income and resources of the individual shall be considered to be income and resources of the household.

(c) Enforcement

A State that has not exercised its authority under subsection (d)(1)(A) of this section shall require each individual applying for assistance or benefits referred to in subsection (a) of this section, during the application process, to state, in writing, whether the individual, or any member of the household of the individual, has been convicted of a crime described in subsection (a) of this section.

(d) Limitations

(1) State elections

(A) Opt out

A State may, by specific reference in a law enacted after August 22, 1996, exempt any or all individuals domiciled in the State from the application of subsection (a) of this section.

(B) Limit period of prohibition

A State may, by law enacted after August 22, 1996, limit the period for which subsection (a) of this section shall apply to any or all individuals domiciled in the State.

(2) Inapplicability to convictions occurring on or before August 22, 1996

Subsection (a) of this section shall not apply to a conviction if the conviction is for conduct occurring on or before August 22, 1996.

(e) "State" defined

For purposes of this section, the term "State" has the meaning given it—

(1) in section 419(5) of the Social Security Act [42 U.S.C. 619(5)], when referring to assistance provided under a State program funded under part A of title IV of the Social Security Act [42 U.S.C. 601 et seq.], and

(2) in section 3(s) of the Food Stamp Act of 1977 [7 U.S.C. 2012(s)], when referring to the food stamp program (as defined in section 3(*l*) of the Food Stamp Act of 1977 [7 U.S.C. 2012(*l*)]) or any State program carried out under the Food Stamp Act of 1977 [7 U.S.C. 2011 et seq.].

(f) Rule of interpretation

Nothing in this section shall be construed to deny the following Federal benefits:

(1) Emergency medical services under title XIX of the Social Security Act [42 U.S.C. 1396 et seq.].

(2) Short-term, noncash, in-kind emergency disaster relief.

(3)(A) Public health assistance for immunizations.

(B) Public health assistance for testing and treatment of communicable diseases if the Secretary of Health and Human Services determines that it is necessary to prevent the spread of such disease.

(4) Prenatal care.

(5) Job training programs.

(6) Drug treatment programs.

(Pub. L. 104–193, title I, §115, Aug. 22, 1996, 110 Stat. 2180; Pub. L. 105–33, title V, §5516(a), Aug. 5, 1997, 111 Stat. 620; Pub. L. 110–234, title IV, §4115(c)(2)(C), May 22, 2008, 122 Stat. 1109; Pub. L. 110–246, §4(a), title IV, §4115(c)(2)(C), June 18, 2008, 122 Stat. 1664, 1871.)

REFERENCES IN TEXT

The Social Security Act, referred to in subsecs. (a)(1), (b)(1), (e)(1), and (f)(1), is act Aug. 14, 1935, ch. 531, 49 Stat. 620, as amended. Part A of title IV of the Act is classified generally to part A (§601 et seq.) of subchapter IV of chapter 7 of Title 42, The Public Health and Welfare. Title XIX of the Act is classified generally to subchapter XIX (§1396 et seq.) of chapter 7 of Title 42. For complete classification of this Act to the Code, see section 1305 of Title 42 and Tables.

The Food Stamp Act of 1977, referred to in subsecs. (a)(2), (b)(2), and (e)(2), subsequently renamed the Food and Nutrition Act of 2008, is Pub. L. 88–525, Aug. 31, 1964, 78 Stat. 703, which is classified generally to chapter 51 (§2011 et seq.) of Title 7, Agriculture. For complete classification of this Act to the Code, see Short Title note set out under section 2011 of Title 7 and Tables.

CODIFICATION

Pub. L. 110–234 and Pub. L. 110–246 made identical amendments to this section. The amendments by Pub. L. 110–234 were repealed by section 4(a) of Pub. L. 110–246.

Section was enacted as part of the Personal Responsibility and Work Opportunity Reconciliation Act of 1996, and not as part of the Controlled Substances Act which comprises this subchapter.

AMENDMENTS

2008—Subsecs. (a)(2), (b)(2). Pub. L. 110–246, §4115(c)(2)(C)(i), substituted "section 3(*l*)" for "section 3(h)".

Subsec. (e)(2). Pub. L. 110–246, §4115(c)(2)(C), substituted "section 3(s)" for "section 3(m)" and "section 3(*l*)" for "section 3(h)".

1997—Subsec. (d)(2). Pub. L. 105–33 substituted "a conviction if the conviction is for conduct" for "convictions".

CHANGE OF NAME

References to the food stamp program established under the Food Stamp Act of 1977, now known as the Food and Nutrition Act of 2008, considered to refer to the supplemental nutrition assistance program established under that Act, see section 4002(c) of Pub. L. 110–246, set out as a note under section 2012 of Title 7, Agriculture.

EFFECTIVE DATE OF 2008 AMENDMENT

Amendment of this section and repeal of Pub. L. 110–234 by Pub. L. 110–246 effective May 22, 2008, the date of enactment of Pub. L. 110–234, except as otherwise provided, see section 4 of Pub. L. 110–246, set out as an Effective Date note under section 8701 of Title 7, Agriculture.

Amendment by section 4115(c)(2)(C) of Pub. L. 110–246 effective Oct. 1, 2008, see section 4407 of Pub. L. 110–246, set out as a note under section 1161 of Title 2, The Congress.

EFFECTIVE DATE OF 1997 AMENDMENT

Section 5518(d) of title V of Pub. L. 105–33 provided that: "The amendments made by this chapter to a provision of the Personal Responsibility and Work Opportunity Reconciliation Act of 1996 [Pub. L. 104–193] that have not become part of another statute [chapter 1

(§§5501–5518) of subtitle F of title V of Pub. L. 105–33, amending this section, sections 601 to 603, 604 to 608, 609 to 611, and 612 to 617 of Title 42, The Public Health and Welfare, and provisions set out as notes under section 612c of Title 7, Agriculture, and sections 601 and 613 of Title 42] shall take effect as if the amendments had been included in the provision at the time the provision became law."

EFFECTIVE DATE

Section effective July 1, 1997, with transition rules relating to State options to accelerate such date, rules relating to claims, actions, and proceedings commenced before such date, rules relating to closing out of accounts for terminated or substantially modified programs and continuance in office of Assistant Secretary for Family Support, and provisions relating to termination of entitlement under AFDC program, see section 116 of Pub. L. 104–193, as amended, set out as an Effective Date note under section 601 of Title 42, The Public Health and Welfare.

§862b. Sanctioning for testing positive for controlled substances

Notwithstanding any other provision of law, States shall not be prohibited by the Federal Government from testing welfare recipients for use of controlled substances nor from sanctioning welfare recipients who test positive for use of controlled substances.

(Pub. L. 104–193, title IX, §902, Aug. 22, 1996, 110 Stat. 2347.)

CODIFICATION

Section was enacted as part of the Personal Responsibility and Work Opportunity Reconciliation Act of 1996, and not as part of the Controlled Substances Act which comprises this subchapter.

§863. Drug paraphernalia

(a) In general

It is unlawful for any person—

(1) to sell or offer for sale drug paraphernalia;

(2) to use the mails or any other facility of interstate commerce to transport drug paraphernalia; or

(3) to import or export drug paraphernalia.

(b) Penalties

Anyone convicted of an offense under subsection (a) of this section shall be imprisoned for not more than three years and fined under title 18.

(c) Seizure and forfeiture

Any drug paraphernalia involved in any violation of subsection (a) of this section shall be subject to seizure and forfeiture upon the conviction of a person for such violation. Any such paraphernalia shall be delivered to the Administrator of General Services, General Services Administration, who may order such paraphernalia destroyed or may authorize its use for law enforcement or educational purposes by Federal, State, or local authorities.

(d) "Drug paraphernalia" defined

The term "drug paraphernalia" means any equipment, product, or material of any kind which is primarily intended or designed for use in manufacturing, compounding, converting, concealing, producing, processing, preparing, injecting, ingesting, inhaling, or otherwise introducing into the human body a controlled substance, possession of which is unlawful under this subchapter. It includes items primarily intended or designed for use in ingesting, inhaling, or otherwise introducing marijuana,[1] cocaine, hashish, hashish oil, PCP, methamphetamine, or amphetamines into the human body, such as—

(1) metal, wooden, acrylic, glass, stone, plastic, or ceramic pipes with or without screens, permanent screens, hashish heads, or punctured metal bowls;

(2) water pipes;

(3) carburetion tubes and devices;

(4) smoking and carburetion masks;

(5) roach clips: meaning objects used to hold burning material, such as a marihuana cigarette, that has become too small or too short to be held in the hand;

(6) miniature spoons with level capacities of one-tenth cubic centimeter or less;

(7) chamber pipes;

(8) carburetor pipes;

(9) electric pipes;

(10) air-driven pipes;

(11) chillums;

(12) bongs;

(13) ice pipes or chillers;

(14) wired cigarette papers; or

(15) cocaine freebase kits.

(e) Matters considered in determination of what constitutes drug paraphernalia

In determining whether an item constitutes drug paraphernalia, in addition to all other logically relevant factors, the following may be considered:

(1) instructions, oral or written, provided with the item concerning its use;

(2) descriptive materials accompanying the item which explain or depict its use;

(3) national and local advertising concerning its use;

(4) the manner in which the item is displayed for sale;

(5) whether the owner, or anyone in control of the item, is a legitimate supplier of like or related items to the community, such as a licensed distributor or dealer of tobacco products;

(6) direct or circumstantial evidence of the ratio of sales of the item(s) to the total sales of the business enterprise;

(7) the existence and scope of legitimate uses of the item in the community; and

(8) expert testimony concerning its use.

(f) Exemptions

This section shall not apply to—

(1) any person authorized by local, State, or Federal law to manufacture, possess, or distribute such items; or

(2) any item that, in the normal lawful course of business, is imported, exported, transported, or sold through the mail or by any other means, and traditionally intended for use with tobacco products, including any pipe, paper, or accessory.

(Pub. L. 91–513, title II, §422, as added and amended Pub. L. 101–647, title XXIV, §2401(a)–(c),

[1] So in original. Probably should be "marihuana,".

Nov. 29, 1990, 104 Stat. 4858, 4859; Pub. L. 106–310, div. B, title XXXVI, §3614, Oct. 17, 2000, 114 Stat. 1230.)

CODIFICATION

The text of section 857(b) to (f) of this title, which was transferred to subsecs. (b) to (f) of this section by Pub. L. 101–647, §2401(b), was based on Pub. L. 99–570, title I, §1822(b)–(f), Oct. 27, 1986, 100 Stat. 3207–51; Pub. L. 100–690, title VI, §6485, Nov. 18, 1988, 102 Stat. 4384.

AMENDMENTS

2000—Subsec. (d). Pub. L. 106–310 inserted "methamphetamine," after "PCP," in introductory provisions.

1990—Subsec. (b). Pub. L. 101–647, §2401(c)(1), substituted "fined under title 18" for "fined not more than $100,000".

Pub. L. 101–647, §2401(b), redesignated subsec. (b) of section 857 of this title as subsec. (b) of this section. See Codification note above.

Subsecs. (c) to (e). Pub. L. 101–647, §2401(b), redesignated subsecs. (c) to (e) of section 857 of this title as subsecs. (c) to (e) of this section. See Codification note above.

Subsec. (f). Pub. L. 101–647, §2401(c)(2), made technical amendment to reference to "This section" to correct reference to corresponding provision of original act.

Pub. L. 101–647, §2401(b), redesignated subsec. (f) of section 857 of this title as subsec. (f) of this section. See Codification note above.

§864. Anhydrous ammonia

(a) It is unlawful for any person—

(1) to steal anhydrous ammonia, or

(2) to transport stolen anhydrous ammonia across State lines,

knowing, intending, or having reasonable cause to believe that such anhydrous ammonia will be used to manufacture a controlled substance in violation of this part.

(b) Any person who violates subsection (a) of this section shall be imprisoned or fined, or both, in accordance with section 843(d) of this title as if such violation were a violation of a provision of section 843 of this title.

(Pub. L. 91–513, title II, §423, as added Pub. L. 106–310, div. B, title XXXVI, §3653(a), Oct. 17, 2000, 114 Stat. 1240.)

§864a. Grants to reduce production of methamphetamines from anhydrous ammonia

(a) Definitions

In this section:

(1) Eligible entity

The term "eligible entity" means—

(A) a producer of agricultural commodities;

(B) a cooperative association, a majority of the members of which produce or process agricultural commodities; or

(C) a person in the trade or business of—

(i) selling an agricultural product (including an agricultural chemical) at retail, predominantly to farmers and ranchers; or

(ii) aerial and ground application of an agricultural chemical.

(2) Nurse tank

The term "nurse tank" shall be considered to be a cargo tank (within the meaning of section 173.315(m) of title 49, Code of Federal Regulations, as in effect as of the date of the enactment of this Act).

(b) Grant authority

The Secretary may make a grant to an eligible entity to enable the eligible entity to obtain and add to an anhydrous ammonia fertilizer nurse tank a physical lock or a substance to reduce the amount of methamphetamine that can be produced from any anhydrous ammonia removed from the nurse tank.

(c) Grant amount

The amount of a grant made under this section to an eligible entity shall be the product obtained by multiplying—

(1) an amount not less than $40 and not more than $60, as determined by the Secretary; and

(2) the number of fertilizer nurse tanks of the eligible entity.

(d) Authorization of appropriations

There is authorized to be appropriated to the Secretary to make grants under this section $15,000,000 for the period of fiscal years 2008 through 2012.

(Pub. L. 110–234, title XIV, §14203, May 22, 2008, 122 Stat. 1458; Pub. L. 110–246, §4(a), title XIV, §14203, June 18, 2008, 122 Stat. 1664, 2220.)

REFERENCES IN TEXT

The date of the enactment of this Act, referred to in subsec. (a)(2), is the date of enactment of Pub. L. 110–246, which was approved June 18, 2008.

CODIFICATION

Pub. L. 110–234 and Pub. L. 110–246 enacted identical sections. Pub. L. 110–234 was repealed by section 4(a) of Pub. L. 110–246.

Section was enacted as part of the Food, Conservation, and Energy Act of 2008, and not as part of the Controlled Substances Act which comprises this subchapter.

EFFECTIVE DATE

Enactment of this section and repeal of Pub. L. 110–234 by Pub. L. 110–246 effective May 22, 2008, the date of enactment of Pub. L. 110–234, see section 4 of Pub. L. 110–246, set out as a note under section 8701 of Title 7, Agriculture.

DEFINITION OF "SECRETARY"

"Secretary" as meaning the Secretary of Agriculture, see section 8701 of Title 7, Agriculture.

§865. Smuggling methamphetamine or methamphetamine precursor chemicals into the United States while using facilitated entry programs

(a) Enhanced prison sentence

The sentence of imprisonment imposed on a person convicted of an offense under the Controlled Substances Act (21 U.S.C. 801 et seq.) or the Controlled Substances Import and Export Act (21 U.S.C. 951 et seq.), involving methamphetamine or any listed chemical that is defined in section 102(33) of the Controlled Substances Act (21 U.S.C. 802(33),[1] shall, if the offense is committed under the circumstance de-

[1] So in original. A second closing parenthesis probably should precede the comma.

scribed in subsection (b), be increased by a consecutive term of imprisonment of not more than 15 years.

(b) Circumstances

For purposes of subsection (a), the circumstance described in this subsection is that the offense described in subsection (a) was committed by a person who—

(1) was enrolled in, or who was acting on behalf of any person or entity enrolled in, any dedicated commuter lane, alternative or accelerated inspection system, or other facilitated entry program administered or approved by the Federal Government for use in entering the United States; and

(2) committed the offense while entering the United States, using such lane, system, or program.

(c) Permanent ineligibility

Any person whose term of imprisonment is increased under subsection (a) shall be permanently and irrevocably barred from being eligible for or using any lane, system, or program described in subsection (b)(1).

(Pub. L. 109–177, title VII, §731, Mar. 9, 2006, 120 Stat. 270.)

REFERENCES IN TEXT

The Controlled Substances Act, referred to in subsec. (a), is title II of Pub. L. 91–513, Oct. 27, 1970, 84 Stat. 1242, as amended, which is classified principally to this subchapter. For complete classification of this Act to the Code, see Short Title note set out under section 801 of this title and Tables.

The Controlled Substances Import and Export Act, referred to in subsec. (a), is title III of Pub. L. 91–513, Oct. 27, 1970, 84 Stat. 1285, as amended, which is classified principally to subchapter II (§951 et seq.) of this chapter. For complete classification of this Act to the Code, see Short Title note set out under section 951 of this title and Tables.

CODIFICATION

Section was enacted as part of the USA PATRIOT Improvement and Reauthorization Act of 2005 and also as part of the Combat Methamphetamine Epidemic Act of 2005, and not as part of the Controlled Substances Act which comprises this subchapter.

PART E—ADMINISTRATIVE AND ENFORCEMENT PROVISIONS

§871. Attorney General

(a) Delegation of functions

The Attorney General may delegate any of his functions under this subchapter to any officer or employee of the Department of Justice.

(b) Rules and regulations

The Attorney General may promulgate and enforce any rules, regulations, and procedures which he may deem necessary and appropriate for the efficient execution of his functions under this subchapter.

(c) Acceptance of devises, bequests, gifts, and donations

The Attorney General may accept in the name of the Department of Justice any form of devise, bequest, gift, or donation where the donor intends to donate property for the purpose of preventing or controlling the abuse of controlled substances. He may take all appropriate steps to secure possession of such property and may sell, assign, transfer, or convey any such property other than moneys.

(Pub. L. 91–513, title II, §501, Oct. 27, 1970, 84 Stat. 1270.)

REFERENCES IN TEXT

This subchapter, referred to in subsecs. (a) and (b), was in the original "this title", meaning title II of Pub. L. 91–513, Oct. 27, 1970, 84 Stat. 1242, as amended, and is popularly known as the "Controlled Substances Act". For complete classification of title II to the Code, see second paragraph of Short Title note set out under section 801 of this title and Tables.

§871a. Semiannual reports to Congress

(a) In general

The Attorney General shall, on a semiannual basis, submit to the congressional committees and organizations specified in subsection (b) reports that—

(1) describe the allocation of the resources of the Drug Enforcement Administration and the Federal Bureau of Investigation for the investigation and prosecution of alleged violations of the Controlled Substances Act [21 U.S.C. 801 et seq.] involving methamphetamine; and

(2) the measures being taken to give priority in the allocation of such resources to such violations involving—

(A) persons alleged to have imported into the United States substantial quantities of methamphetamine or scheduled listed chemicals (as defined pursuant to the amendment made by section 711(a)(1));[1]

(B) persons alleged to have manufactured methamphetamine; and

(C) circumstances in which the violations have endangered children.

(b) Congressional committees

The congressional committees and organizations referred to in subsection (a) are—

(1) in the House of Representatives, the Committee on the Judiciary, the Committee on Energy and Commerce, and the Committee on Government Reform; and

(2) in the Senate, the Committee on the Judiciary, the Committee on Commerce, Science, and Transportation, and the Caucus on International Narcotics Control.

(Pub. L. 109–177, title VII, §736, Mar. 9, 2006, 120 Stat. 271.)

REFERENCES IN TEXT

The Controlled Substances Act, referred to in subsec. (a)(1), is title II of Pub. L. 91–513, Oct. 27, 1970, 84 Stat. 1242, as amended, which is classified principally to this subchapter. For complete classification of this Act to the Code, see Short Title note set out under section 801 of this title and Tables.

Section 711(a)(1), referred to in subsec. (a)(2)(A), is section 711(a)(1) of Pub. L. 109–177, which amended section 802 of this title.

CODIFICATION

Section was enacted as part of the USA PATRIOT Improvement and Reauthorization Act of 2005 and also

[1] See References in Text note below.

as part of the Combat Methamphetamine Epidemic Act of 2005, and not as part of the Controlled Substances Act which comprises this subchapter.

CHANGE OF NAME

Committee on Government Reform of House of Representatives changed to Committee on Oversight and Government Reform of House of Representatives by House Resolution No. 6, One Hundred Tenth Congress, Jan. 5, 2007.

§872. Education and research programs of Attorney General

(a) Authorization

The Attorney General is authorized to carry out educational and research programs directly related to enforcement of the laws under his jurisdiction concerning drugs or other substances which are or may be subject to control under this subchapter. Such programs may include—

(1) educational and training programs on drug abuse and controlled substances law enforcement for local, State, and Federal personnel;

(2) studies or special projects designed to compare the deterrent effects of various enforcement strategies on drug use and abuse;

(3) studies or special projects designed to assess and detect accurately the presence in the human body of drugs or other substances which are or may be subject to control under this subchapter, including the development of rapid field identification methods which would enable agents to detect microquantities of such drugs or other substances;

(4) studies or special projects designed to evaluate the nature and sources of the supply of illegal drugs throughout the country;

(5) studies or special projects to develop more effective methods to prevent diversion of controlled substances into illegal channels; and

(6) studies or special projects to develop information necessary to carry out his functions under section 811 of this title.

(b) Contracts

The Attorney General may enter into contracts for such educational and research activities without performance bonds and without regard to section 5 of title 41.

(c) Identification of research populations; authorization to withhold

The Attorney General may authorize persons engaged in research to withhold the names and other identifying characteristics of persons who are the subjects of such research. Persons who obtain this authorization may not be compelled in any Federal, State, or local civil, criminal, administrative, legislative, or other proceeding to identify the subjects of research for which such authorization was obtained.

(d) Affect of treaties and other international agreements on confidentiality

Nothing in the Single Convention on Narcotic Drugs, the Convention on Psychotropic Substances, or other treaties or international agreements shall be construed to limit, modify, or prevent the protection of the confidentiality of patient records or of the names and other identifying characteristics of research subjects as provided by any Federal, State, or local law or regulation.

(e) Use of controlled substances in research

The Attorney General, on his own motion or at the request of the Secretary, may authorize the possession, distribution, and dispensing of controlled substances by persons engaged in research. Persons who obtain this authorization shall be exempt from State or Federal prosecution for possession, distribution, and dispensing of controlled substances to the extent authorized by the Attorney General.

(f) Program to curtail diversion of precursor and essential chemicals

The Attorney General shall maintain an active program, both domestic and international, to curtail the diversion of precursor chemicals and essential chemicals used in the illicit manufacture of controlled substances.

(Pub. L. 91–513, title II, §502, Oct. 27, 1970, 84 Stat. 1271; Pub. L. 95–633, title I, §108(a), Nov. 10, 1978, 92 Stat. 3773; Pub. L. 100–690, title VI, §6060, Nov. 18, 1988, 102 Stat. 4320.)

AMENDMENTS

1988—Subsec. (f). Pub. L. 100–690 added subsec. (f).

1978—Subsecs. (d), (e). Pub. L. 95–633 added subsec. (d) and redesignated former subsec. (d) as (e).

EFFECTIVE DATE OF 1988 AMENDMENT

Amendment by Pub. L. 100–690 effective 120 days after Nov. 18, 1988, see section 6061 of Pub. L. 100–690, set out as a note under section 802 of this title.

EFFECTIVE DATE OF 1978 AMENDMENT

Amendment by Pub. L. 95–633 effective on date the Convention on Psychotropic Substances enters into force in the United States [July 15, 1980], see section 112 of Pub. L. 95–633, set out as an Effective Date note under section 801a of this title.

TRAINING FOR DRUG ENFORCEMENT ADMINISTRATION AND STATE AND LOCAL LAW ENFORCEMENT PERSONNEL RELATING TO CLANDESTINE LABORATORIES

Pub. L. 106–310, div. B, title XXXVI, §3623, Oct. 17, 2000, 114 Stat. 1231, provided that:

"(a) IN GENERAL.—

"(1) REQUIREMENT.—The Administrator of the Drug Enforcement Administration shall carry out the programs described in subsection (b) with respect to the law enforcement personnel of States and localities determined by the Administrator to have significant levels of methamphetamine-related or amphetamine-related crime or projected by the Administrator to have the potential for such levels of crime in the future.

"(2) DURATION.—The duration of any program under that subsection may not exceed 3 years.

"(b) COVERED PROGRAMS.—The programs described in this subsection are as follows:

"(1) ADVANCED MOBILE CLANDESTINE LABORATORY TRAINING TEAMS.—A program of advanced mobile clandestine laboratory training teams, which shall provide information and training to State and local law enforcement personnel in techniques utilized in conducting undercover investigations and conspiracy cases, and other information designed to assist in the investigation of the illegal manufacturing and trafficking of amphetamine and methamphetamine.

"(2) BASIC CLANDESTINE LABORATORY CERTIFICATION TRAINING.—A program of basic clandestine laboratory certification training, which shall provide information and training—

"(A) to Drug Enforcement Administration personnel and State and local law enforcement personnel for purposes of enabling such personnel to meet any certification requirements under law with respect to the handling of wastes created by illegal amphetamine and methamphetamine laboratories; and

"(B) to State and local law enforcement personnel for purposes of enabling such personnel to provide the information and training covered by subparagraph (A) to other State and local law enforcement personnel.

"(3) CLANDESTINE LABORATORY RECERTIFICATION AND AWARENESS TRAINING.—A program of clandestine laboratory recertification and awareness training, which shall provide information and training to State and local law enforcement personnel for purposes of enabling such personnel to provide recertification and awareness training relating to clandestine laboratories to additional State and local law enforcement personnel.

"(c) AUTHORIZATION OF APPROPRIATIONS.—There are authorized to be appropriated for each of fiscal years 2000, 2001, and 2002 amounts as follows:

"(1) $1,500,000 to carry out the program described in subsection (b)(1).

"(2) $3,000,000 to carry out the program described in subsection (b)(2).

"(3) $1,000,000 to carry out the program described in subsection (b)(3)."

EDUCATIONAL PROGRAM FOR POLICE DEPARTMENTS

Pub. L. 104–305, § 4, Oct. 13, 1996, 110 Stat. 3809, provided that: "The Attorney General may—

"(1) create educational materials regarding the use of controlled substances (as that term is defined in section 102 of the Controlled Substances Act [21 U.S.C. 802]) in the furtherance of rapes and sexual assaults; and

"(2) disseminate those materials to police departments throughout the United States."

STUDY AND REPORT ON MEASURES TO PREVENT SALES OF AGENTS USED IN METHAMPHETAMINE PRODUCTION

Pub. L. 104–237, title II, § 202, Oct. 3, 1996, 110 Stat. 3101, provided that:

"(a) STUDY.—The Attorney General of the United States shall conduct a study on possible measures to effectively prevent the diversion of red phosphorous, iodine, hydrochloric gas, and other agents for use in the production of methamphetamine. Nothing in this section shall preclude the Attorney General from taking any action the Attorney General already is authorized to take with regard to the regulation of listed chemicals under current law.

"(b) REPORT.—Not later than January 1, 1998, the Attorney General shall submit a report to the Congress of its findings pursuant to the study conducted under subsection (a) on the need for and advisability of preventive measures.

"(c) CONSIDERATIONS.—In developing recommendations under subsection (b), the Attorney General shall consider—

"(1) the use of red phosphorous, iodine, hydrochloric gas, and other agents in the illegal manufacture of methamphetamine;

"(2) the use of red phosphorous, iodine, hydrochloric gas, and other agents for legitimate, legal purposes, and the impact any regulations may have on these legitimate purposes; and

"(3) comments and recommendations from law enforcement, manufacturers of such chemicals, and the consumers of such chemicals for legitimate, legal purposes."

§ 872a. Public-private education program

(a) Advisory panel

The Attorney General shall establish an advisory panel consisting of an appropriate number of representatives from Federal, State, and local law enforcement and regulatory agencies with experience in investigating and prosecuting illegal transactions of precursor chemicals. The Attorney General shall convene the panel as often as necessary to develop and coordinate educational programs for wholesale and retail distributors of precursor chemicals and supplies.

(b) Continuation of current efforts

The Attorney General shall continue to—

(1) maintain an active program of seminars and training to educate wholesale and retail distributors of precursor chemicals and supplies regarding the identification of suspicious transactions and their responsibility to report such transactions; and

(2) provide assistance to State and local law enforcement and regulatory agencies to facilitate the establishment and maintenance of educational programs for distributors of precursor chemicals and supplies.

(Pub. L. 104–237, title V, § 503, Oct. 3, 1996, 110 Stat. 3112.)

CODIFICATION

Section was enacted as part of the Comprehensive Methamphetamine Control Act of 1996, and not as part of the Controlled Substances Act which comprises this subchapter.

§ 873. Cooperative arrangements

(a) Cooperation of Attorney General with local, State, and Federal agencies

The Attorney General shall cooperate with local, State, and Federal agencies concerning traffic in controlled substances and in suppressing the abuse of controlled substances. To this end, he is authorized to—

(1) arrange for the exchange of information between governmental officials concerning the use and abuse of controlled substances;

(2) cooperate in the institution and prosecution of cases in the courts of the United States and before the licensing boards and courts of the several States;

(3) conduct training programs on controlled substance law enforcement for local, State, and Federal personnel;

(4) maintain in the Department of Justice a unit which will accept, catalog, file, and otherwise utilize all information and statistics, including records of controlled substance abusers and other controlled substance law offenders, which may be received from Federal, State, and local agencies, and make such information available for Federal, State, and local law enforcement purposes;

(5) conduct programs of eradication aimed at destroying wild or illicit growth of plant species from which controlled substances may be extracted;

(6) assist State and local governments in suppressing the diversion of controlled substances from legitimate medical, scientific, and commercial channels by—

(A) making periodic assessments of the capabilities of State and local governments to adequately control the diversion of controlled substances;

(B) providing advice and counsel to State and local governments on the methods by which such governments may strengthen their controls against diversion; and

(C) establishing cooperative investigative efforts to control diversion; and

(7) notwithstanding any other provision of law, enter into contractual agreements with State and local law enforcement agencies to provide for cooperative enforcement and regulatory activities under this chapter.[1]

(b) Requests by Attorney General for assistance from Federal agencies or instrumentalities

When requested by the Attorney General, it shall be the duty of any agency or instrumentality of the Federal Government to furnish assistance, including technical advice, to him for carrying out his functions under this subchapter; except that no such agency or instrumentality shall be required to furnish the name of, or other identifying information about, a patient or research subject whose identity it has undertaken to keep confidential.

(c) Descriptive and analytic reports by Attorney General to State agencies of distribution patterns of schedule II substances having highest rates of abuse

The Attorney General shall annually (1) select the controlled substance (or controlled substances) contained in schedule II which, in the Attorney General's discretion, is determined to have the highest rate of abuse, and (2) prepare and make available to regulatory, licensing, and law enforcement agencies of States descriptive and analytic reports on the actual distribution patterns in such States of each such controlled substance.

(d) Grants by Attorney General

(1) The Attorney General may make grants, in accordance with paragraph (2), to State and local governments to assist in meeting the costs of—

(A) collecting and analyzing data on the diversion of controlled substances,

(B) conducting investigations and prosecutions of such diversions,

(C) improving regulatory controls and other authorities to control such diversions,

(D) programs to prevent such diversions,

(E) preventing and detecting forged prescriptions, and

(F) training law enforcement and regulatory personnel to improve the control of such diversions.

(2) No grant may be made under paragraph (1) unless an application therefor is submitted to the Attorney General in such form and manner as the Attorney General may prescribe. No grant may exceed 80 per centum of the costs for which the grant is made, and no grant may be made unless the recipient of the grant provides assurances satisfactory to the Attorney General that it will obligate funds to meet the remaining 20 per centum of such costs. The Attorney General shall review the activities carried out with grants under paragraph (1) and shall report annually to Congress on such activities.

(3) To carry out this subsection there is authorized to be appropriated $6,000,000 for fiscal year 1985 and $6,000,000 for fiscal year 1986.

(Pub. L. 91–513, title II, §503, Oct. 27, 1970, 84 Stat. 1271; Pub. L. 96–359, §8(a) Sept. 26, 1980, 94 Stat. 1194; Pub. L. 98–473, title II, §517, Oct. 12, 1984, 98 Stat. 2074; Pub. L. 99–570, title I, §1868, Oct. 27, 1986, 100 Stat. 3207–55; Pub. L. 99–646, §85, Nov. 10, 1986, 100 Stat. 3620.)

References in Text

This chapter, referred to in subsec. (a)(7), was in the original as added by Pub. L. 99–646 "this Act", meaning Pub. L. 91–513, Oct. 27, 1970, 84 Stat. 1236, as amended. In the subsec. (a)(7) added by Pub. L. 99–570, the reference was "this title", meaning title II of Pub. L. 91–513 which is popularly known as the "Controlled Substances Act" and is classified principally to this subchapter. For complete classification of this Act and title II to the Code, see Short Title note set out under section 801 of this title and Tables.

Schedule II, referred to in subsec. (c), is set out in section 812(c) of this title.

Amendments

1986—Subsec. (a)(7). Pub. L. 99–570 and Pub. L. 99–646 made substantially identical amendment, adding par. (7).

1984—Subsec. (a)(6). Pub. L. 98–473, §517(a), added par. (6).

Subsec. (d). Pub. L. 98–473, §517(b), added subsec. (d).

1980—Subsec. (c). Pub. L. 96–359 added subsec. (c).

Annual Report on Counterdrug Intelligence Matters

Pub. L. 107–306, title VIII, §826, Nov. 27, 2002, 116 Stat. 2429, provided that:

"(a) Annual Report.—The Counterdrug Intelligence Coordinating Group shall submit to the appropriate committees of Congress each year a report on current counterdrug intelligence matters. The report shall include the recommendations of the Counterdrug Intelligence Coordinating Group on the appropriate number of permanent staff, and of detailed personnel, for the staff of the Counterdrug Intelligence Executive Secretariat.

"(b) Submittal Date.—The date of the submittal each year of the report required by subsection (a) shall be the date provided in section 507 of the National Security Act of 1947 [50 U.S.C. 415b], as added by section 811 of this Act.

"(c) Appropriate Committees of Congress Defined.—In this section, the term 'appropriate committees of Congress' means—

"(1) the Committees on Appropriations of the Senate and House of Representatives; and

"(2) the congressional intelligence committees (as defined in section 3 of the National Security Act of 1947 (50 U.S.C. 401a))."

Combating Amphetamine and Methamphetamine Manufacturing and Trafficking

Pub. L. 106–310, div. B, title XXXVI, §3625, Oct. 17, 2000, 114 Stat. 1233, provided that:

"(a) Activities.—In order to combat the illegal manufacturing and trafficking in amphetamine and methamphetamine, the Administrator of the Drug Enforcement Administration may—

"(1) assist State and local law enforcement in small and mid-sized communities in all phases of investigations related to such manufacturing and trafficking, including assistance with foreign-language interpretation;

"(2) staff additional regional enforcement and mobile enforcement teams related to such manufacturing and trafficking;

"(3) establish additional resident offices and posts of duty to assist State and local law enforcement in rural areas in combating such manufacturing and trafficking;

"(4) provide the Special Operations Division of the Administration with additional agents and staff to

[1] See References in Text note below.

collect, evaluate, interpret, and disseminate critical intelligence targeting the command and control operations of major amphetamine and methamphetamine manufacturing and trafficking organizations;

"(5) enhance the investigative and related functions of the Chemical Control Program of the Administration to implement more fully the provisions of the Comprehensive Methamphetamine Control Act of 1996 (Public Law 104–237) [see Short Title of 1996 Amendments note set out under section 801 of this title];

"(6) design an effective means of requiring an accurate accounting of the import and export of list I chemicals, and coordinate investigations relating to the diversion of such chemicals;

"(7) develop a computer infrastructure sufficient to receive, process, analyze, and redistribute time-sensitive enforcement information from suspicious order reporting to field offices of the Administration and other law enforcement and regulatory agencies, including the continuing development of the Suspicious Order Reporting and Tracking System (SORTS) and the Chemical Transaction Database (CTRANS) of the Administration;

"(8) establish an education, training, and communication process in order to alert the industry to current trends and emerging patterns in the illegal manufacturing of amphetamine and methamphetamine; and

"(9) carry out such other activities as the Administrator considers appropriate.

"(b) ADDITIONAL POSITIONS AND PERSONNEL.—

"(1) IN GENERAL.—In carrying out activities under subsection (a), the Administrator may establish in the Administration not more than 50 full-time positions, including not more than 31 special-agent positions, and may appoint personnel to such positions.

"(2) PARTICULAR POSITIONS.—In carrying out activities under paragraphs (5) through (8) of subsection (a), the Administrator may establish in the Administration not more than 15 full-time positions, including not more than 10 diversion investigator positions, and may appoint personnel to such positions. Any positions established under this paragraph are in addition to any positions established under paragraph (1).

"(c) AUTHORIZATION OF APPROPRIATIONS.—There are authorized to be appropriated for the Drug Enforcement Administration for each fiscal year after fiscal year 1999, $9,500,000 for purposes of carrying out the activities authorized by subsection (a) and employing personnel in positions established under subsection (b), of which $3,000,000 shall be available for activities under paragraphs (5) through (8) of subsection (a) and for employing personnel in positions established under subsection (b)(2)."

NATIONAL DRUG INTELLIGENCE CENTER

Pub. L. 108–487, title I, § 104(e), Dec. 23, 2004, 118 Stat. 3942, provided that:

"(1) IN GENERAL.—Of the amount authorized to be appropriated in subsection (a) [118 Stat. 3941], $42,322,000 shall be available for the National Drug Intelligence Center. Within such amount, funds provided for research, development, testing, and evaluation purposes shall remain available until September 30, 2006, and funds provided for procurement purposes shall remain available until September 30, 2007.

"(2) TRANSFER OF FUNDS.—The Director of National Intelligence shall transfer to the Attorney General funds available for the National Drug Intelligence Center under paragraph (1). The Attorney General shall utilize funds so transferred for the activities of the National Drug Intelligence Center.

"(3) LIMITATION.—Amounts available for the National Drug Intelligence Center may not be used in contravention of the provisions of section 103(d)(1) of the National Security Act of 1947 (50 U.S.C. 403–3(d)(1)).

"(4) AUTHORITY.—Notwithstanding any other provision of law, the Attorney General shall retain full authority over the operations of the National Drug Intelligence Center."

Similar provisions were contained in the following prior authorization acts:

Pub. L. 108–177, title I, § 104(e), Dec. 13, 2003, 117 Stat. 2602.

Pub. L. 107–306, title I, § 104(e), Nov. 27, 2002, 116 Stat. 2387.

Pub. L. 107–108, title I, § 104(e), Dec. 28, 2001, 115 Stat. 1396.

Pub. L. 106–567, title I, § 104(e), Dec. 27, 2000, 114 Stat. 2834.

Pub. L. 106–120, title I, § 104(e), Dec. 3, 1999, 113 Stat. 1609.

Pub. L. 105–272, title I, § 104(e), Oct. 20, 1998, 112 Stat. 2398.

Pub. L. 105–107, title I, § 104(e), Nov. 20, 1997, 111 Stat. 2250.

Pub. L. 104–293, title I, § 104(d), Oct. 11, 1996, 110 Stat. 3464.

Pub. L. 103–139, title VIII, § 8056, Nov. 11, 1993, 107 Stat. 1452, provided that: "During the current fiscal year and thereafter, there is established, under the direction and control of the Attorney General, the National Drug Intelligence Center, whose mission it shall be to coordinate and consolidate drug intelligence from all national security and law enforcement agencies, and produce information regarding the structure, membership, finances, communications, and activities of drug trafficking organizations: *Provided*, That funding for the operation of the National Drug Intelligence Center, including personnel costs associated therewith, shall be provided from the funds appropriated to the Department of Defense."

Similar provisions were contained in the following prior appropriation act:

Pub. L. 102–396, title IX, § 9078, Oct. 6, 1992, 106 Stat. 1919.

§ 874. Advisory committees

The Attorney General may from time to time appoint committees to advise him with respect to preventing and controlling the abuse of controlled substances. Members of the committees may be entitled to receive compensation at the rate of $100 for each day (including traveltime) during which they are engaged in the actual performance of duties. While traveling on official business in the performance of duties for the committees, members of the committees shall be allowed expenses of travel, including per diem instead of subsistence, in accordance with subchapter I of chapter 57 of title 5.

(Pub. L. 91–513, title II, § 504, Oct. 27, 1970, 84 Stat. 1272.)

TERMINATION OF ADVISORY COMMITTEES

Advisory committees in existence on Jan. 5, 1973, to terminate not later than the expiration of the 2-year period following Jan. 5, 1973, and advisory committees established after Jan. 5, 1973, to terminate not later than the expiration of the 2-year period beginning on the date of their establishment, unless in the case of a committee established by the President or an officer of the Federal Government, such committee is renewed by appropriate action prior to the expiration of such 2-year period, or in the case of a committee established by Congress, its duration is otherwise provided by law. See section 14 of Pub. L. 92–463, Oct. 6, 1972, 86 Stat. 776, set out in the Appendix to Title 5, Government Organization and Employees.

§ 875. Administrative hearings

(a) Power of Attorney General

In carrying out his functions under this subchapter, the Attorney General may hold hearings, sign and issue subpenas, administer oaths, examine witnesses, and receive evidence at any place in the United States.

(b) Procedures applicable

Except as otherwise provided in this subchapter, notice shall be given and hearings shall be conducted under appropriate procedures of subchapter II of chapter 5 of title 5.

(Pub. L. 91–513, title II, §505, Oct. 27, 1970, 84 Stat. 1272.)

§876. Subpenas

(a) Authorization of use by Attorney General

In any investigation relating to his functions under this subchapter with respect to controlled substances, listed chemicals, tableting machines, or encapsulating machines, the Attorney General may subpena witnesses, compel the attendance and testimony of witnesses, and require the production of any records (including books, papers, documents, and other tangible things which constitute or contain evidence) which the Attorney General finds relevant or material to the investigation. The attendance of witnesses and the production of records may be required from any place in any State or in any territory or other place subject to the jurisdiction of the United States at any designated place of hearing; except that a witness shall not be required to appear at any hearing more than 500 miles distant from the place where he was served with a subpena. Witnesses summoned under this section shall be paid the same fees and mileage that are paid witnesses in the courts of the United States.

(b) Service

A subpena issued under this section may be served by any person designated in the subpena to serve it. Service upon a natural person may be made by personal delivery of the subpena to him. Service may be made upon a domestic or foreign corporation or upon a partnership or other unincorporated association which is subject to suit under a common name, by delivering the subpena to an officer, to a managing or general agent, or to any other agent authorized by appointment or by law to receive service of process. The affidavit of the person serving the subpena entered on a true copy thereof by the person serving it shall be proof of service.

(c) Enforcement

In the case of contumacy by or refusal to obey a subpena issued to any person, the Attorney General may invoke the aid of any court of the United States within the jurisdiction of which the investigation is carried on or of which the subpenaed person is an inhabitant, or in which he carries on business or may be found, to compel compliance with the subpena. The court may issue an order requiring the subpenaed person to appear before the Attorney General to produce records, if so ordered, or to give testimony touching the matter under investigation. Any failure to obey the order of the court may be punished by the court as a contempt thereof. All process in any such case may be served in any judicial district in which such person may be found.

(Pub. L. 91–513, title II, §506, Oct. 27, 1970, 84 Stat. 1272; Pub. L. 100–690, title VI, §6058, Nov. 18, 1988, 102 Stat. 4319.)

AMENDMENTS

1988—Subsec. (a). Pub. L. 100–690 inserted "listed chemicals, tableting machines, or encapsulating machines," after "with respect to controlled substances,".

EFFECTIVE DATE OF 1988 AMENDMENT

Amendment by Pub. L. 100–690 effective 120 days after Nov. 18, 1988, see section 6061 of Pub. L. 100–690, set out as a note under section 802 of this title.

§877. Judicial review

All final determinations, findings, and conclusions of the Attorney General under this subchapter shall be final and conclusive decisions of the matters involved, except that any person aggrieved by a final decision of the Attorney General may obtain review of the decision in the United States Court of Appeals for the District of Columbia or for the circuit in which his principal place of business is located upon petition filed with the court and delivered to the Attorney General within thirty days after notice of the decision. Findings of fact by the Attorney General, if supported by substantial evidence, shall be conclusive.

(Pub. L. 91–513, title II, §507, Oct. 27, 1970, 84 Stat. 1273.)

§878. Powers of enforcement personnel

(a) Any officer or employee of the Drug Enforcement Administration or any State or local law enforcement officer designated by the Attorney General may—

(1) carry firearms;

(2) execute and serve search warrants, arrest warrants, administrative inspection warrants, subpenas, and summonses issued under the authority of the United States;

(3) make arrests without warrant (A) for any offense against the United States committed in his presence, or (B) for any felony, cognizable under the laws of the United States, if he has probable cause to believe that the person to be arrested has committed or is committing a felony;

(4) make seizures of property pursuant to the provisions of this subchapter; and

(5) perform such other law enforcement duties as the Attorney General may designate.

(b) State and local law enforcement officers performing functions under this section shall not be deemed Federal employees and shall not be subject to provisions of law relating to Federal employees, except that such officers shall be subject to section 3374(c) of title 5.

(Pub. L. 91–513, title II, §508, Oct. 27, 1970, 84 Stat. 1273; Pub. L. 96–132, §16(b), Nov. 30, 1979, 93 Stat. 1049; Pub. L. 99–570, title I, §1869, Oct. 27, 1986, 100 Stat. 3207–55; Pub. L. 99–646, §86, Nov. 10, 1986, 100 Stat. 3620.)

AMENDMENTS

1986—Pub. L. 99–570 and Pub. L. 99–646 amended section substantially identically designating existing provisions as subsec. (a) and adding subsec. (b), with the exception of the amendment of subsec. (a) for which

Pub. L. 99–570 directed the insertion of "or (with respect to offenses under this subchapter or subchapter II of this chapter) any State or local law enforcement officer" and Pub. L. 99–646 directed the insertion of "or any State or local law enforcement officer", the latter of which was executed to reflect the probable intent of Congress.

1979—Pub. L. 96–132 substituted "Drug Enforcement Administration" for "Bureau of Narcotics and Dangerous Drugs".

§879. Search warrants

A search warrant relating to offenses involving controlled substances may be served at any time of the day or night if the judge or United States magistrate judge issuing the warrant is satisfied that there is probable cause to believe that grounds exist for the warrant and for its service at such time.

(Pub. L. 91–513, title II, §509, Oct. 27, 1970, 84 Stat. 1274; Pub. L. 93–481, §3, Oct. 26, 1974, 88 Stat. 1455; Pub. L. 101–650, title III, §321, Dec. 1, 1990, 104 Stat. 5117.)

AMENDMENTS

1974—Pub. L. 93–481 struck out designation "(a)" before "A search warrant", and struck out subsec. (b) which permitted officers authorized to execute search warrants to break open and enter premises under certain circumstances and which required that such officers identify themselves and give reasons and authority for their entry after such entry.

CHANGE OF NAME

"United States magistrate judge" substituted in text for "United States magistrate" pursuant to section 321 of Pub. L. 101–650, set out as a note under section 631 of Title 28, Judiciary and Judicial Procedure.

§880. Administrative inspections and warrants

(a) "Controlled premises" defined

As used in this section, the term "controlled premises" means—

(1) places where original or other records or documents required under this subchapter are kept or required to be kept, and

(2) places, including factories, warehouses, and other establishments, and conveyances, where persons registered under section 823 of this title (or exempt from registration under section 822(d) of this title or by regulation of the Attorney General) or regulated persons may lawfully hold, manufacture, distribute, dispense, administer, or otherwise dispose of controlled substances or listed chemicals or where records relating to those activities are maintained.

(b) Grant of authority; scope of inspections

(1) For the purpose of inspecting, copying, and verifying the correctness of records, reports, or other documents required to be kept or made under this subchapter and otherwise facilitating the carrying out of his functions under this subchapter, the Attorney General is authorized, in accordance with this section, to enter controlled premises and to conduct administrative inspections thereof, and of the things specified in this section, relevant to those functions.

(2) Such entries and inspections shall be carried out through officers or employees (hereinafter referred to as "inspectors") designated by the Attorney General. Any such inspector, upon stating his purpose and presenting to the owner, operator, or agent in charge of such premises (A) appropriate credentials and (B) a written notice of his inspection authority (which notice in the case of an inspection requiring, or in fact supported by, an administrative inspection warrant shall consist of such warrant), shall have the right to enter such premises and conduct such inspection at reasonable times.

(3) Except as may otherwise be indicated in an applicable inspection warrant, the inspector shall have the right—

(A) to inspect and copy records, reports, and other documents required to be kept or made under this subchapter;

(B) to inspect, within reasonable limits and in a reasonable manner, controlled premises and all pertinent equipment, finished and unfinished drugs, listed chemicals, and other substances or materials, containers, and labeling found therein, and, except as provided in paragraph (4) of this subsection, all other things therein (including records, files, papers, processes, controls, and facilities) appropriate for verification of the records, reports, and documents referred to in clause (A) or otherwise bearing on the provisions of this subchapter; and

(C) to inventory any stock of any controlled substance or listed chemical therein and obtain samples of any such substance or chemical.

(4) Except when the owner, operator, or agent in charge of the controlled premises so consents in writing, no inspection authorized by this section shall extend to—

(A) financial data;

(B) sales data other than shipment data; or

(C) pricing data.

(c) Situations not requiring warrants

A warrant under this section shall not be required for the inspection of books and records pursuant to an administrative subpena issued in accordance with section 876 of this title, nor for entries and administrative inspections (including seizures of property)—

(1) with the consent of the owner, operator, or agent in charge of the controlled premises;

(2) in situations presenting imminent danger to health or safety;

(3) in situations involving inspection of conveyances where there is reasonable cause to believe that the mobility of the conveyance makes it impracticable to obtain a warrant;

(4) in any other exceptional or emergency circumstance where time or opportunity to apply for a warrant is lacking; or

(5) in any other situations where a warrant is not constitutionally required.

(d) Administrative inspection warrants; issuance; execution; probable cause

Issuance and execution of administrative inspection warrants shall be as follows:

(1) Any judge of the United States or of a State court of record, or any United States magistrate judge, may, within his territorial jurisdiction, and upon proper oath or affirmation showing probable cause, issue warrants

for the purpose of conducting administrative inspections authorized by this subchapter or regulations thereunder, and seizures of property appropriate to such inspections. For the purposes of this section, the term "probable cause" means a valid public interest in the effective enforcement of this subchapter or regulations thereunder sufficient to justify administrative inspections of the area, premises, building, or conveyance, or contents thereof, in the circumstances specified in the application for the warrant.

(2) A warrant shall issue only upon an affidavit of an officer or employee having knowledge of the facts alleged, sworn to before the judge or magistrate judge and establishing the grounds for issuing the warrant. If the judge or magistrate judge is satisfied that grounds for the application exist or that there is probable cause to believe they exist, he shall issue a warrant identifying the area, premises, building, or conveyance to be inspected, the purpose of such inspection, and, where appropriate, the type of property to be inspected, if any. The warrant shall identify the items or types of property to be seized, if any. The warrant shall be directed to a person authorized under subsection (b)(2) of this section to execute it. The warrant shall state the grounds for its issuance and the name of the person or persons whose affidavit has been taken in support thereof. It shall command the person to whom it is directed to inspect the area, premises, building, or conveyance identified for the purpose specified, and, where appropriate, shall direct the seizure of the property specified. The warrant shall direct that it be served during normal business hours. It shall designate the judge or magistrate judge to whom it shall be returned.

(3) A warrant issued pursuant to this section must be executed and returned within ten days of its date unless, upon a showing by the United States of a need therefor, the judge or magistrate judge allows additional time in the warrant. If property is seized pursuant to a warrant, the person executing the warrant shall give to the person from whom or from whose premises the property was taken a copy of the warrant and a receipt for the property taken or shall leave the copy and receipt at the place from which the property was taken. The return of the warrant shall be made promptly and shall be accompanied by a written inventory of any property taken. The inventory shall be made in the presence of the person executing the warrant and of the person from whose possession or premises the property was taken, if they are present, or in the presence of at least one credible person other than the person making such inventory, and shall be verified by the person executing the warrant. The judge or magistrate judge, upon request, shall deliver a copy of the inventory to the person from whom or from whose premises the property was taken and the applicant for the warrant.

(4) The judge or magistrate judge who has issued a warrant under this section shall attach to the warrant a copy of the return and all papers filed in connection therewith and shall file them with the clerk of the district court of the United States for the judicial district in which the inspection was made.

(Pub. L. 91–513, title II, §510, Oct. 27, 1970, 84 Stat. 1274; Pub. L. 101–647, title XXXV, §3599M, Nov. 29, 1990, 104 Stat. 4932; Pub. L. 101–650, title III, §321, Dec. 1, 1990, 104 Stat. 5117; Pub. L. 103–200, §6, Dec. 17, 1993, 107 Stat. 2339.)

AMENDMENTS

1993—Subsec. (a)(2). Pub. L. 103–200, §6(1), amended par. (2) generally. Prior to amendment, par. (2) read as follows: "places, including factories, warehouses, or other establishments, and conveyances, where persons registered under section 823 of this title (or exempted from registration under section 822(d) of this title) may lawfully hold, manufacture, or distribute, dispense, administer, or otherwise dispose of controlled substances."

Subsec. (b)(3)(B). Pub. L. 103–200, §6(2)(A), inserted ", listed chemicals," after "unfinished drugs".

Subsec. (b)(3)(C). Pub. L. 103–200, §6(2)(B), inserted "or listed chemical" after "controlled substance" and "or chemical" after "such substance".

1990—Subsec. (b)(3)(B). Pub. L. 101–647 substituted "paragraph (4)" for "paragraph (5)".

CHANGE OF NAME

"United States magistrate judge" and "magistrate judge" substituted for "United States magistrate" and "magistrate", respectively, wherever appearing in subsec. (d) pursuant to section 321 of Pub. L. 101–650, set out as a note under section 631 of Title 28, Judiciary and Judicial Procedure.

EFFECTIVE DATE OF 1993 AMENDMENT

Amendment by Pub. L. 103–200 effective on date that is 120 days after Dec. 17, 1993, see section 11 of Pub. L. 103–200, set out as a note under section 802 of this title.

§881. Forfeitures

(a) Subject property

The following shall be subject to forfeiture to the United States and no property right shall exist in them:

(1) All controlled substances which have been manufactured, distributed, dispensed, or acquired in violation of this subchapter.

(2) All raw materials, products, and equipment of any kind which are used, or intended for use, in manufacturing, compounding, processing, delivering, importing, or exporting any controlled substance or listed chemical in violation of this subchapter.

(3) All property which is used, or intended for use, as a container for property described in paragraph (1), (2), or (9).

(4) All conveyances, including aircraft, vehicles, or vessels, which are used, or are intended for use, to transport, or in any manner to facilitate the transportation, sale, receipt, possession, or concealment of property described in paragraph (1), (2), or (9).

(5) All books, records, and research, including formulas, microfilm, tapes, and data which are used, or intended for use, in violation of this subchapter.

(6) All moneys, negotiable instruments, securities, or other things of value furnished or intended to be furnished by any person in exchange for a controlled substance or listed chemical in violation of this subchapter, all proceeds traceable to such an exchange, and

all moneys, negotiable instruments, and securities used or intended to be used to facilitate any violation of this subchapter.

(7) All real property, including any right, title, and interest (including any leasehold interest) in the whole of any lot or tract of land and any appurtenances or improvements, which is used, or intended to be used, in any manner or part, to commit, or to facilitate the commission of, a violation of this subchapter punishable by more than one year's imprisonment.

(8) All controlled substances which have been possessed in violation of this subchapter.

(9) All listed chemicals, all drug manufacturing equipment, all tableting machines, all encapsulating machines, and all gelatin capsules, which have been imported, exported, manufactured, possessed, distributed, dispensed, acquired, or intended to be distributed, dispensed, acquired, imported, or exported, in violation of this subchapter or subchapter II of this chapter.

(10) Any drug paraphernalia (as defined in section 863 of this title).

(11) Any firearm (as defined in section 921 of title 18) used or intended to be used to facilitate the transportation, sale, receipt, possession, or concealment of property described in paragraph (1) or (2) and any proceeds traceable to such property.

(b) Seizure procedures

Any property subject to forfeiture to the United States under this section may be seized by the Attorney General in the manner set forth in section 981(b) of title 18.

(c) Custody of Attorney General

Property taken or detained under this section shall not be repleviable, but shall be deemed to be in the custody of the Attorney General, subject only to the orders and decrees of the court or the official having jurisdiction thereof. Whenever property is seized under any of the provisions of this subchapter, the Attorney General may—

(1) place the property under seal;

(2) remove the property to a place designated by him; or

(3) require that the General Services Administration take custody of the property and remove it, if practicable, to an appropriate location for disposition in accordance with law.

(d) Other laws and proceedings applicable

The provisions of law relating to the seizure, summary and judicial forfeiture, and condemnation of property for violation of the customs laws; the disposition of such property or the proceeds from the sale thereof; the remission or mitigation of such forfeitures; and the compromise of claims shall apply to seizures and forfeitures incurred, or alleged to have been incurred, under any of the provisions of this subchapter, insofar as applicable and not inconsistent with the provisions hereof; except that such duties as are imposed upon the customs officer or any other person with respect to the seizure and forfeiture of property under the customs laws shall be performed with respect to seizures and forfeitures of property under this subchapter by such officers, agents, or other persons as may be authorized or designated for that purpose by the Attorney General, except to the extent that such duties arise from seizures and forfeitures effected by any customs officer.

(e) Disposition of forfeited property

(1) Whenever property is civilly or criminally forfeited under this subchapter the Attorney General may—

(A) retain the property for official use or, in the manner provided with respect to transfers under section 1616a of title 19, transfer the property to any Federal agency or to any State or local law enforcement agency which participated directly in the seizure or forfeiture of the property;

(B) except as provided in paragraph (4), sell, by public sale or any other commercially feasible means, any forfeited property which is not required to be destroyed by law and which is not harmful to the public;

(C) require that the General Services Administration take custody of the property and dispose of it in accordance with law;

(D) forward it to the Bureau of Narcotics and Dangerous Drugs for disposition (including delivery for medical or scientific use to any Federal or State agency under regulations of the Attorney General); or

(E) transfer the forfeited personal property or the proceeds of the sale of any forfeited personal or real property to any foreign country which participated directly or indirectly in the seizure or forfeiture of the property, if such a transfer—

(i) has been agreed to by the Secretary of State;

(ii) is authorized in an international agreement between the United States and the foreign country; and

(iii) is made to a country which, if applicable, has been certified under section 2291j(b) of title 22.

(2)(A) The proceeds from any sale under subparagraph (B) of paragraph (1) and any moneys forfeited under this subchapter shall be used to pay—

(i) all property expenses of the proceedings for forfeiture and sale including expenses of seizure, maintenance of custody, advertising, and court costs; and

(ii) awards of up to $100,000 to any individual who provides original information which leads to the arrest and conviction of a person who kills or kidnaps a Federal drug law enforcement agent.

Any award paid for information concerning the killing or kidnapping of a Federal drug law enforcement agent, as provided in clause (ii), shall be paid at the discretion of the Attorney General.

(B) The Attorney General shall forward to the Treasurer of the United States for deposit in accordance with section 524(c) of title 28, any amounts of such moneys and proceeds remaining after payment of the expenses provided in subparagraph (A), except that, with respect to forfeitures conducted by the Postal Service, the Postal Service shall deposit in the Postal Service Fund, under section 2003(b)(7) of title 39, such moneys and proceeds.

(3) The Attorney General shall assure that any property transferred to a State or local law enforcement agency under paragraph (1)(A)—

(A) has a value that bears a reasonable relationship to the degree of direct participation of the State or local agency in the law enforcement effort resulting in the forfeiture, taking into account the total value of all property forfeited and the total law enforcement effort with respect to the violation of law on which the forfeiture is based; and

(B) will serve to encourage further cooperation between the recipient State or local agency and Federal law enforcement agencies.

(4)(A) With respect to real property described in subparagraph (B), if the chief executive officer of the State involved submits to the Attorney General a request for purposes of such subparagraph, the authority established in such subparagraph is in lieu of the authority established in paragraph (1)(B).

(B) In the case of property described in paragraph (1)(B) that is civilly or criminally forfeited under this subchapter, if the property is real property that is appropriate for use as a public area reserved for recreational or historic purposes or for the preservation of natural conditions, the Attorney General, upon the request of the chief executive officer of the State in which the property is located, may transfer title to the property to the State, either without charge or for a nominal charge, through a legal instrument providing that—

(i) such use will be the principal use of the property; and

(ii) title to the property reverts to the United States in the event that the property is used otherwise.

(f) Forfeiture and destruction of schedule I and II substances

(1) All controlled substances in schedule I or II that are possessed, transferred, sold, or offered for sale in violation of the provisions of this subchapter; all dangerous, toxic, or hazardous raw materials or products subject to forfeiture under subsection (a)(2) of this section; and any equipment or container subject to forfeiture under subsection (a)(2) or (3) of this section which cannot be separated safely from such raw materials or products shall be deemed contraband and seized and summarily forfeited to the United States. Similarly, all substances in schedule I or II, which are seized or come into the possession of the United States, the owners of which are unknown, shall be deemed contraband and summarily forfeited to the United States.

(2) The Attorney General may direct the destruction of all controlled substances in schedule I or II seized for violation of this subchapter; all dangerous, toxic, or hazardous raw materials or products subject to forfeiture under subsection (a)(2) of this section; and any equipment or container subject to forfeiture under subsection (a)(2) or (3) of this section which cannot be separated safely from such raw materials or products under such circumstances as the Attorney General may deem necessary.

(g) Plants

(1) All species of plants from which controlled substances in schedules I and II may be derived which have been planted or cultivated in violation of this subchapter, or of which the owners or cultivators are unknown, or which are wild growths, may be seized and summarily forfeited to the United States.

(2) The failure, upon demand by the Attorney General or his duly authorized agent, of the person in occupancy or in control of land or premises upon which such species of plants are growing or being stored, to produce an appropriate registration, or proof that he is the holder thereof, shall constitute authority for the seizure and forfeiture.

(3) The Attorney General, or his duly authorized agent, shall have authority to enter upon any lands, or into any dwelling pursuant to a search warrant, to cut, harvest, carry off, or destroy such plants.

(h) Vesting of title in United States

All right, title, and interest in property described in subsection (a) of this section shall vest in the United States upon commission of the act giving rise to forfeiture under this section.

(i) Stay of civil forfeiture proceedings

The provisions of section 981(g) of title 18 regarding the stay of a civil forfeiture proceeding shall apply to forfeitures under this section.

(j) Venue

In addition to the venue provided for in section 1395 of title 28 or any other provision of law, in the case of property of a defendant charged with a violation that is the basis for forfeiture of the property under this section, a proceeding for forfeiture under this section may be brought in the judicial district in which the defendant owning such property is found or in the judicial district in which the criminal prosecution is brought.

(*l*)[1] Agreement between Attorney General and Postal Service for performance of functions

The functions of the Attorney General under this section shall be carried out by the Postal Service pursuant to such agreement as may be entered into between the Attorney General and the Postal Service.

(Pub. L. 91–513, title II, §511, Oct. 27, 1970, 84 Stat. 1276; Pub. L. 95–633, title III, §301(a), Nov. 10, 1978, 92 Stat. 3777; Pub. L. 96–132, §14, Nov. 30, 1979, 93 Stat. 1048; Pub. L. 98–473, title II, §§306, 309, 518, Oct. 12, 1984, 98 Stat. 2050, 2051, 2075; Pub. L. 99–570, title I, §§1006(c), 1865, 1992, Oct. 27, 1986, 100 Stat. 3207–7, 3207–54, 3207–59; Pub. L. 99–646, §74, Nov. 10, 1986, 100 Stat. 3618; Pub. L. 100–690, title V, §5105, title VI, §§6059, 6074, 6075, 6077(a), (b), 6253, Nov. 18, 1988, 102 Stat. 4301, 4319, 4323–4325, 4363; Pub. L. 101–189, div. A, title XII, §1215(a), Nov. 29, 1989, 103 Stat. 1569; Pub. L. 101–647, title XX, §§2003, 2004, 2007, 2008, Nov. 29, 1990, 104 Stat. 4855, 4856; Pub. L. 102–239, §2, Dec. 17, 1991, 105 Stat. 1912; Pub. L. 103–447, title I, §102(d), Nov. 2, 1994, 108 Stat. 4693; Pub. L.

[1] So in original. No subsec. (k) has been enacted.

104–237, title II, §201(b), Oct. 3, 1996, 110 Stat. 3101; Pub. L. 106–185, §§2(c)(2), 5(b), 8(b), Apr. 25, 2000, 114 Stat. 210, 214, 216; Pub. L. 107–273, div. B, title IV, §4002(e)(3), Nov. 2, 2002, 116 Stat. 1810.)

REFERENCES IN TEXT

Subchapter II of this chapter, referred to in subsec. (a)(9), was in the original "title III", meaning title III of Pub. L. 91–513, Oct. 27, 1970, 84 Stat. 1285. Part A of title III comprises subchapter II of this chapter. For classification of Part B, consisting of sections 1101 to 1105 of title III, see Tables.

The customs laws, referred to in subsec. (d), are classified generally to Title 19, Customs Duties.

Schedules I and II, referred to in subsecs. (f) and (g), are set out in section 812(c) of this title.

AMENDMENTS

2002—Subsec. (a)(10). Pub. L. 107–273 substituted "section 863 of this title" for "section 1822 of the Mail Order Drug Paraphernalia Control Act".

2000—Subsec. (a)(4). Pub. L. 106–185, §2(c)(2), struck out before period at end ", except that—

"(A) no conveyance used by any person as a common carrier in the transaction of business as a common carrier shall be forfeited under the provisions of this section unless it shall appear that the owner or other person in charge of such conveyance was a consenting party or privy to a violation of this subchapter or subchapter II of this chapter;

"(B) no conveyance shall be forfeited under the provisions of this section by reason of any act or omission established by the owner thereof to have been committed or omitted by any person other than such owner while such conveyance was unlawfully in the possession of a person other than the owner in violation of the criminal laws of the United States, or of any State; and

"(C) no conveyance shall be forfeited under this paragraph to the extent of an interest of an owner, by reason of any act or omission established by that owner to have been committed or omitted without the knowledge, consent, or willful blindness of the owner".

Subsec. (a)(6). Pub. L. 106–185, §2(c)(2), struck out before period at end ", except that no property shall be forfeited under this paragraph, to the extent of the interest of an owner, by reason of any act or omission established by that owner to have been committed or omitted without the knowledge or consent of that owner".

Subsec. (a)(7). Pub. L. 106–185, §2(c)(2), struck out before period at end ", except that no property shall be forfeited under this paragraph, to the extent of an interest of an owner, by reason of any act or omission established by that owner to have been committed or omitted without the knowledge or consent of that owner".

Subsec. (b). Pub. L. 106–185, §5(b), inserted heading and amended text of subsec. (b) generally. Prior to amendment, subsec. (b) authorized the Attorney General to seize property under this subchapter upon process issued pursuant to the Supplemental Rules for Certain Admirality and Maritime claims and to seize it without process in certain described circumstances.

Subsec. (i). Pub. L. 106–185, §8(b), inserted heading and amended text of subsec. (i) generally. Prior to amendment, text read as follows: "The filing of an indictment or information alleging a violation of this subchapter or subchapter II of this chapter, or a violation of State or local law that could have been charged under this subchapter or subchapter II of this chapter, which is also related to a civil forfeiture proceeding under this section shall, upon motion of the United States and for good cause shown, stay the civil forfeiture proceeding."

1996—Subsec. (a)(2), (6). Pub. L. 104–237, §201(b)(1), inserted "or listed chemical" after "controlled substance".

Subsec. (a)(9). Pub. L. 104–237, §201(b)(2), substituted "possessed, distributed, dispensed, acquired, or intended to be distributed, dispensed, acquired," for "possessed, distributed, or intended to be distributed," and struck out "a felony provision of" after "in violation of".

1994—Subsec. (e)(1)(E)(iii). Pub. L. 103–447 substituted "section 2291j(b) of title 22" for "section 2291(h) of title 22".

1991—Subsec. (e)(1)(B). Pub. L. 102–239, §2(1), substituted "except as provided in paragraph (4), sell" for "sell".

Subsec. (e)(4). Pub. L. 102–239, §2(2), added par. (4).

1990—Subsec. (a)(10). Pub. L. 101–647, §2007, added par. (10).

Subsec. (a)(11). Pub. L. 101–647, §2008, added par. (11).

Subsec. (e)(1)(B). Pub. L. 101–647, §2003, inserted ", by public sale or any other commercially feasible means," after "sell".

Subsec. (f). Pub. L. 101–647, §2004, inserted "; all dangerous, toxic, or hazardous raw materials or products subject to forfeiture under subsection (a)(2) of this section; and any equipment or container subject to forfeiture under subsection (a)(2) or (3) of this section which cannot be separated safely from such raw materials or products" after "this subchapter" in pars. (1) and (2).

1989—Subsec. (e)(3)(B). Pub. L. 101–189 amended subpar. (B) generally. Prior to amendment, subpar. (B) read as follows: "is not so transferred to circumvent any requirement of State law that prohibits forfeiture or limits use or disposition of property forfeited to State or local agencies."

1988—Subsec. (a)(3). Pub. L. 100–690, §6059(b), inserted reference to par. (9).

Subsec. (a)(4). Pub. L. 100–690, §§6059(b), 6075, inserted in introductory provisions reference to par. (9) and added subpar. (C).

Subsec. (a)(7). Pub. L. 100–690, §5105, inserted "(including any leasehold interest)" after "interest".

Subsec. (a)(9). Pub. L. 100–690, §6059(a), added par. (9).

Subsec. (e)(1)(A). Pub. L. 100–690, §6077(b), amended subpar. (A) generally. Prior to amendment, subpar. (A) read as follows: "retain the property for official use or transfer the custody or ownership of any forfeited property to any Federal, State, or local agency pursuant to section 1616a of title 19;".

Subsec. (e)(1)(E). Pub. L. 100–690, §6074, added subpar. (E).

Subsec. (e)(2)(B). Pub. L. 100–690, §6253(b), provided for deposit of moneys and proceeds in Postal Service Fund in cases of forfeitures conducted by Postal Service.

Subsec. (e)(3). Pub. L. 100–690, §6077(a), added par. (3).

Subsec. (*l*). Pub. L. 100–690, §6253(a), added subsec. (*l*).

1986—Subsec. (b). Pub. L. 99–570, §1865(1)–(3), and Pub. L. 99–646, §74(1)–(3), in making identical amendments in introductory provision and par. (4), struck out "or criminal" after "subject to civil" and inserted paragraph permitting the Government to request issuance of a warrant authorizing seizure of property subject to forfeiture under this section in the same manner as provided for a search warrant under the Federal Rules of Criminal Procedure.

Subsec. (e). Pub. L. 99–570, §1992, designated existing provisions as par. (1) and former pars. (1) to (4) as subpars. (A) to (D), respectively, and added par. (2) in lieu of former concluding provisions which read as follows: "The Attorney General shall ensure the equitable transfer pursuant to paragraph (1) of any forfeited property to the appropriate State or local law enforcement agency so as to reflect generally the contribution of any such agency participating directly in any of the acts which led to the seizure or forfeiture of such property. A decision by the Attorney General pursuant to paragraph (1) shall not be subject to review. The proceeds from any sale under paragraph (2) and any moneys forfeited under this subchapter shall be used to pay all proper expenses of the proceedings for forfeiture and sale including expenses of seizure, maintenance of custody, advertising, and court costs. The Attorney General shall forward to the Treasurer of the United States for deposit in accordance with section 524(c) of title 28 any amounts of such moneys and proceeds remaining after payment of such expenses."

Subsec. (f). Pub. L. 99–570, §1006(c), which directed the amendment of section 511 of the "Comprehensive Drug Abuse Prevention Act of 1978" was executed to this section which is section 511 of the Comprehensive Drug Abuse Prevention Act of 1970, as the probable intent of Congress, by designating existing provisions as par. (1), inserting "or II" in two places, and adding par. (2).

Subsec. (i). Pub. L. 99–570, §1865(b) and Pub. L. 99–646, §74(b), made identical amendments, inserting ", or a violation of State or local law that could have been charged under this subchapter or subchapter II of this chapter,".

1984—Subsec. (a)(7). Pub. L. 98–473, §306(a), added par. (7).

Subsec. (a)(8). Pub. L. 98–473, §518, added par. (8).

Subsec. (b). Pub. L. 98–473, §306(b)(1), inserted "civil or criminal" after "property subject to".

Subsec. (b)(4). Pub. L. 98–473, §306(b)(2), substituted "is subject to civil or criminal forfeiture under" for "has been used or is intended to be used in violation of".

Subsec. (c). Pub. L. 98–473, §306(c)(1), in provisions preceding par. (1), inserted "any of" after "seized under".

Subsec. (c)(3). Pub. L. 98–473, §306(c)(2), inserted ", if practicable," after "remove it".

Subsec. (d). Pub. L. 98–473, §306(d), inserted "any of" after "incurred, under".

Subsec. (e). Pub. L. 98–473, §§306(e), 309, inserted "civilly or criminally" after "Whenever property is" and in provisions preceding par. (1), inserted provisions relating to transfer of custody or ownership of forfeited property in par. (1), substituted "and dispose of it" for "and remove it for disposition" in par. (3), and, in provisions following par. (4), inserted sentence requiring the Attorney General to ensure equitable transfer of any forfeited property, and substituted "accordance with section 524(c) of title 28" for "the general fund of the United States Treasury".

Subsecs. (h) to (j). Pub. L. 98–473, §306(f), added subsecs. (h) to (j).

1979—Subsec. (d). Pub. L. 96–132 substituted "The provisions" for "All provisions" and struck out "and the award of compensation to informers in respect of such forfeitures" after "compromise of claims".

1978—Subsec. (a)(6). Pub. L. 95–633, §301(1), added par. (6).

Subsec. (e). Pub. L. 95–633, §301(a)(2), (3), struck out of cl. (2) provisions relating to use of proceeds of sale and inserted last sentence relating to the forwarding by the Attorney General of money and proceeds remaining after payment of expenses.

EFFECTIVE DATE OF 2000 AMENDMENT

Amendment by Pub. L. 106–185 applicable to any forfeiture proceeding commenced on or after the date that is 120 days after Apr. 25, 2000, see section 21 of Pub. L. 106–185, set out as a note under section 1324 of Title 8, Aliens and Nationality.

EFFECTIVE DATE OF 1989 AMENDMENT

Section 1215(b) of Pub. L. 101–189 provided that: "The amendment made by subsection (a) [amending this section] shall take effect as of October 1, 1989."

EFFECTIVE DATE OF 1988 AMENDMENT

Amendment by section 6059 of Pub. L. 100–690 effective 120 days after Nov. 18, 1988, see section 6061 of Pub. L. 100–690, set out as a note under section 802 of this title.

Section 6077(c) of Pub. L. 100–690, as amended by Pub. L. 101–162, title II, §208, Nov. 21, 1989, 103 Stat. 1005, provided that: "Section 551(e)(3)(B) of the Controlled Substances Act [probably means section 511(e)(3)(B) of the Controlled Substances Act, 21 U.S.C. 881(e)(3)(B)], as enacted by subsection (a), shall apply with respect to fiscal years beginning after September 30, 1991."

TRANSFER OF FUNCTIONS

Bureau of Narcotics and Dangerous Drugs, including office of Director thereof, in Department of Justice abolished by Reorg. Plan No. 2 of 1973, eff. July 1, 1973, 38 F.R. 15932, 87 Stat. 1091, set out in the Appendix to Title 5, Government Organization and Employees. Reorg. Plan No. 2 of 1973 also created in Department of Justice a single, comprehensive agency for enforcement of drug laws to be known as Drug Enforcement Administration, empowered Attorney General to authorize performance by officers, employees, and agencies of Department of functions transferred to him, and directed Attorney General to coordinate all drug law enforcement functions to assure maximum cooperation between Drug Enforcement Administration, Federal Bureau of Investigation, and other units of Department of Justice involved in drug law enforcement.

CONSTRUCTIVE SEIZURE PROCEDURES

Pub. L. 101–225, title II, §210, Dec. 12, 1989, 103 Stat. 1913, provided that: "Not later than 6 months after the date of enactment of this Act [Dec. 12, 1989], the Secretary of Transportation and the Secretary of the Treasury, in order to avoid the devastating economic effects on innocent owners of seizures of their vessels, shall develop a procedure for constructive seizure of vessels of the United States engaged in commercial service as defined in section 2101 of title 46, United States Code, that are suspected of being used for committing violations of law involving personal use quantities of controlled substances."

REGULATIONS FOR EXPEDITED ADMINISTRATIVE FORFEITURE PROCEDURES

Section 6079 of Pub. L. 100–690 provided that:

"(a) IN GENERAL.—Not later than 90 days after the date of enactment of this Act [Nov. 18, 1988], the Attorney General and the Secretary of the Treasury shall consult, and after providing a 30-day public comment period, shall prescribe regulations for expedited administrative procedures for seizures under section 511(a)(4), (6), and (7) of the Controlled Substances Act (21 U.S.C. 881(a)(4), (6), and (7)); section 596 of the Tariff Act of 1930 (19 U.S.C. 1595a(a)); and section 2 of the Act of August 9, 1939 (53 Stat. 1291; 49 U.S.C. App. 782 [now 49 U.S.C. 80303]) for violations involving the possession of personal use quantities of a controlled substance.

"(b) SPECIFICATIONS.—The regulations prescribed pursuant to subsection (a) shall—

"(1) minimize the adverse impact caused by prolonged detention, and

"(2) provide for a final administrative determination of the case within 21 days of seizure, or provide a procedure by which the defendant can obtain release of the property pending a final determination of the case. Such regulations shall provide that the appropriate agency official rendering a final determination shall immediately return the property if the following conditions are established:

"(A) the owner or interested party did not know of or consent to the violation;

"(B) the owner establishes a valid, good faith interest in the seized property as owner or otherwise; and

"(C)(1) the owner establishes that the owner at no time had any knowledge or reason to believe that the property in which the owner claims an interest was being or would be used in a violation of the law; and

"(2) if the owner at any time had, or should have had, knowledge or reason to believe that the property in which the owner claims an interest was being or would be used in a violation of the law, that the owner did what reasonably could be expected to prevent the violation.

An owner shall not have the seized property returned under this subsection if the owner had not acted in a normal and customary manner to ascertain how the property would be used.

"(c) NOTICE.—At the time of seizure or upon issuance of a summons to appear under subsection (d), the officer making the seizure shall furnish to any person in possession of the conveyance a written notice specifying the procedures under this section. At the earliest practicable opportunity after determining ownership of the seized conveyance, the head of the department or agency that seizes the conveyance shall furnish a written notice to the owner and other interested parties (including lienholders) of the legal and factual basis of the seizure.

"(d) SUMMONS IN LIEU OF SEIZURE OF COMMERCIAL FISHING INDUSTRY VESSELS.—Not later than 90 days after the enactment of this Act [Nov. 18, 1988], the Attorney General, the Secretary of the Treasury, and the Secretary of Transportation shall prescribe joint regulations, after a public comment period of at least 30 days, providing for issuance of a summons to appear in lieu of seizure of a commercial fishing industry vessel as defined in section 2101(11a), (11b), and (11c) of title 46, United States Code, for violations involving the possession of personal use quantities of a controlled substance. These regulations shall apply when the violation is committed on a commercial fishing industry vessel that is proceeding to or from a fishing area or intermediate port of call, or is actively engaged in fishing operations. The authority provided under this section shall not affect existing authority to arrest an individual for drug-related offenses or to release that individual into the custody of the vessel's master. Upon answering a summons to appear, the procedures set forth in subsections (a), (b), and (c) of this section shall apply. The jurisdiction of the district court for any forfeiture incurred shall not be affected by the use of a summons under this section.

"(e) PERSONAL USE QUANTITIES OF A CONTROLLED SUBSTANCE.—For the purposes of this section, personal use quantities of a controlled substance shall not include sweepings or other evidence of non-personal use amounts."

§§ 881–1, 881a. Transferred

CODIFICATION

Section 881–1, Pub. L. 91–513, title II, § 511A, as added Pub. L. 100–690, title VI, § 6080(a), Nov. 18, 1988, 102 Stat. 4326, which related to expedited procedures for seized conveyances, was renumbered § 518 of Pub. L. 91–513 by Pub. L. 101–647, title X, § 1002(h)(1), Nov. 29, 1990, 104 Stat. 4828, transferred to section 888 of this title and subsequently repealed.

Section 881a, Pub. L. 99–198, title XVII, § 1764, Dec. 23, 1985, 99 Stat. 1652, which related to production control of controlled substances, was renumbered section 519 of the Controlled Substances Act by Pub. L. 101–647, title X, § 1002(h)(2), Nov. 29, 1990, 104 Stat. 4828, and is classified to section 889 of this title.

§ 882. Injunctions

(a) Jurisdiction

The district courts of the United States and all courts exercising general jurisdiction in the territories and possessions of the United States shall have jurisdiction in proceedings in accordance with the Federal Rules of Civil Procedure to enjoin violations of this subchapter.

(b) Jury trial

In case of an alleged violation of an injunction or restraining order issued under this section, trial shall, upon demand of the accused, be by a jury in accordance with the Federal Rules of Civil Procedure.

(c) State cause of action pertaining to online pharmacies

(1) In general

In any case in which the State has reason to believe that an interest of the residents of that State has been or is being threatened or adversely affected by the action of a person, entity, or Internet site that violates the provisions of section 823(f), 829(e), or 831 of this title, the State may bring a civil action on behalf of such residents in a district court of the United States with appropriate jurisdiction—

(A) to enjoin the conduct which violates this section;

(B) to enforce compliance with this section;

(C) to obtain damages, restitution, or other compensation, including civil penalties under section 842(b) of this title; and

(D) to obtain such other legal or equitable relief as the court may find appropriate.

(2) Service; intervention

(A) Prior to filing a complaint under paragraph (1), the State shall serve a copy of the complaint upon the Attorney General and upon the United States Attorney for the judicial district in which the complaint is to be filed. In any case where such prior service is not feasible, the State shall serve the complaint on the Attorney General and the appropriate United States Attorney on the same day that the State's complaint is filed in Federal district court of the United States. Such proceedings shall be independent of, and not in lieu of, criminal prosecutions or any other proceedings under this subchapter or any other laws of the United States.

(B) Upon receiving notice respecting a civil action pursuant to this section, the United States shall have the right to intervene in such action and, upon so intervening, to be heard on all matters arising therein, and to file petitions for appeal.

(C) Service of a State's complaint on the United States as required in this paragraph shall be made in accord with the requirements of rule 4(i)(1) of the Federal Rule[1] of Civil Procedure.

(3) Powers conferred by State law

For purposes of bringing any civil action under paragraph (1), nothing in this chapter shall prevent an attorney general of a State from exercising the powers conferred on the attorney general of a State by the laws of such State to conduct investigations or to administer oaths or affirmations or to compel the attendance of witnesses of or the production of documentary or other evidence.

(4) Venue

Any civil action brought under paragraph (1) in a district court of the United States may be brought in the district in which the defendant is found, is an inhabitant, or transacts business or wherever venue is proper under section 1391 of title 28. Process in such action may be served in any district in which the defendant is an inhabitant or in which the defendant may be found.

(5) No private right of action

No private right of action is created under this subsection.

---

[1] So in original. Probably should be "Rules".

(6) Limitation

No civil action may be brought under paragraph (1) against—

(A) the United States;

(B) an Indian Tribe or tribal organization, to the extent such tribe or tribal organization is lawfully carrying out a contract or compact under the Indian Self-Determination and Education Assistance Act [25 U.S.C. 450 et seq.]; or

(C) any employee of the United States or such Indian tribe or tribal organization, provided such agent or employee is acting in the usual course of business or employment, and within the scope of the official duties of such agent or employee therewith.

(Pub. L. 91–513, title II, §512, Oct. 27, 1970, 84 Stat. 1278; Pub. L. 110–425, §3(h), Oct. 15, 2008, 122 Stat. 4830.)

REFERENCES IN TEXT

The Federal Rules of Civil Procedure, referred to in subsecs. (a), (b), and (c)(2)(C), are set out in the Appendix to Title 28, Judiciary and Judicial Procedure.

This subchapter, referred to in subsecs. (a) and (c)(2)(A), was in the original "this title", meaning title II of Pub. L. 91–513, Oct. 27, 1970, 84 Stat. 1242, and is popularly known as the "Controlled Substances Act". For complete classification of title II to the Code, see second paragraph of Short Title note set out under section 801 of this title and Tables.

This chapter, referred to in subsec. (c)(3), was in the original "this Act", meaning Pub. L. 91–513, Oct. 27, 1970, 84 Stat. 1236. For complete classification of this Act to the Code, see Short Title note set out under section 801 of this title and Tables.

The Indian Self-Determination and Education Assistance Act, referred to in subsec. (c)(6)(B), is Pub. L. 93–638, Jan. 4, 1975, 88 Stat. 2203, which is classified principally to subchapter II (§450 et seq.) of chapter 14 of Title 25, Indians. For complete classification of this Act to the Code, see Short Title note set out under section 450 of Title 25 and Tables.

AMENDMENTS

2008—Subsec. (c). Pub. L. 110–425 added subsec. (c).

EFFECTIVE DATE OF 2008 AMENDMENT

Amendment by Pub. L. 110–425 effective 180 days after Oct. 15, 2008, except as otherwise provided, see section 3(j) of Pub. L. 110–425, set out as a note under section 802 of this title.

§883. Enforcement proceedings

Before any violation of this subchapter is reported by the Administrator of the Drug Enforcement Administration to any United States attorney for institution of a criminal proceeding, the Administrator may require that the person against whom such proceeding is contemplated is given appropriate notice and an opportunity to present his views, either orally or in writing, with regard to such contemplated proceeding.

(Pub. L. 91–513, title II, §513, Oct. 27, 1970, 84 Stat. 1278; Pub. L. 96–132, §16(c), Nov. 30, 1979, 93 Stat. 1049.)

AMENDMENTS

1979—Pub. L. 96–132 substituted "Administrator of the Drug Enforcement Administration" for "Director of the Bureau of Narcotics and Dangerous Drugs" and "Administrator may" for "Director may".

§884. Immunity and privilege

(a) Refusal to testify

Whenever a witness refuses, on the basis of his privilege against self-incrimination, to testify or provide other information in a proceeding before a court or grand jury of the United States, involving a violation of this subchapter, and the person presiding over the proceeding communicates to the witness an order issued under this section, the witness may not refuse to comply with the order on the basis of his privilege against self-incrimination. But no testimony or other information compelled under the order issued under subsection (b) of this section or any information obtained by the exploitation of such testimony or other information, may be used against the witness in any criminal case, including any criminal case brought in a court of a State, except a prosecution for perjury, giving a false statement, or otherwise failing to comply with the order.

(b) Order of United States district court

In the case of any individual who has been or may be called to testify or provide other information at any proceeding before a court or grand jury of the United States, the United States district court for the judicial district in which the proceeding is or may be held shall issue, upon the request of the United States attorney for such district, an order requiring such individual to give any testimony or provide any other information which he refuses to give or provide on the basis of his privilege against self-incrimination.

(c) Request by United States attorney

A United States attorney may, with the approval of the Attorney General or the Deputy Attorney General, the Associate Attorney General, or any Assistant Attorney General designated by the Attorney General, request an order under subsection (b) of this section when in his judgment—

(1) the testimony or other information from such individual may be necessary to the public interest; and

(2) such individual has refused or is likely to refuse to testify or provide other information on the basis of his privilege against self-incrimination.

(Pub. L. 91–513, title II, §514, Oct. 27, 1970, 84 Stat. 1278; Pub. L. 100–690, title VII, §7020(f), Nov. 18, 1988, 102 Stat. 4396.)

AMENDMENTS

1988—Subsec. (c). Pub. L. 100–690 inserted reference to Associate Attorney General.

§885. Burden of proof; liabilities

(a) Exemptions and exceptions; presumption in simple possession offenses

(1) It shall not be necessary for the United States to negative any exemption or exception set forth in this subchapter in any complaint, information, indictment, or other pleading or in any trial, hearing, or other proceeding under this subchapter, and the burden of going forward with the evidence with respect to any such exemption or exception shall be upon the person claiming its benefit.

(2) In the case of a person charged under section 844(a) of this title with the possession of a controlled substance, any label identifying such substance for purposes of section 353(b)(2) of this title shall be admissible in evidence and shall be prima facie evidence that such substance was obtained pursuant to a valid prescription from a practitioner while acting in the course of his professional practice.

(b) Registration and order forms

In the absence of proof that a person is the duly authorized holder of an appropriate registration or order form issued under this subchapter, he shall be presumed not to be the holder of such registration or form, and the burden of going forward with the evidence with respect to such registration or form shall be upon him.

(c) Use of vehicles, vessels, and aircraft

The burden of going forward with the evidence to establish that a vehicle, vessel, or aircraft used in connection with controlled substances in schedule I was used in accordance with the provisions of this subchapter shall be on the persons engaged in such use.

(d) Immunity of Federal, State, local and other officials

Except as provided in sections 2234 and 2235 of title 18, no civil or criminal liability shall be imposed by virtue of this subchapter upon any duly authorized Federal officer lawfully engaged in the enforcement of this subchapter, or upon any duly authorized officer of any State, territory, political subdivision thereof, the District of Columbia, or any possession of the United States, who shall be lawfully engaged in the enforcement of any law or municipal ordinance relating to controlled substances.

(Pub. L. 91–513, title II, § 515, Oct. 27, 1970, 84 Stat. 1279.)

REFERENCES IN TEXT

Schedule I, referred to in subsec. (c), is set out in section 812(c) of this title.

§ 886. Payments and advances

(a) Payment to informers

The Attorney General is authorized to pay any person, from funds appropriated for the Drug Enforcement Administration, for information concerning a violation of this subchapter, such sum or sums of money as he may deem appropriate, without reference to any moieties or rewards to which such person may otherwise be entitled by law.

(b) Reimbursement for purchase of controlled substances

Moneys expended from appropriations of the Drug Enforcement Administration for purchase of controlled substances and subsequently recovered shall be reimbursed to the current appropriation for the Administration.[1]

(c) Advance of funds for enforcement purposes

The Attorney General is authorized to direct the advance of funds by the Treasury Department in connection with the enforcement of this subchapter.

[1] See Codification note below.

(d) Drug Pollution Fund

(1) There is established in the Treasury a trust fund to be known as the "Drug Pollution Fund" (hereinafter referred to in this subsection as the "Fund"), consisting of amounts appropriated or credited to such Fund under section 841(b)(6) of this title.

(2) There are hereby appropriated to the Fund amounts equivalent to the fines imposed under section 841(b)(6) of this title.

(3) Amounts in the Fund shall be available, as provided in appropriations Acts, for the purpose of making payments in accordance with paragraph (4) for the clean up of certain pollution resulting from the actions referred to in section 841(b)(6) of this title.

(4)(A) The Secretary of the Treasury, after consultation with the Attorney General, shall make payments under paragraph (3), in such amounts as the Secretary determines appropriate, to the heads of executive agencies or departments that meet the requirements of subparagraph (B).

(B) In order to receive a payment under paragraph (3), the head of an executive agency or department shall submit an application in such form and containing such information as the Secretary of the Treasury shall by regulation require. Such application shall contain a description of the fine imposed under section 841(b)(6) of this title, the circumstances surrounding the imposition of such fine, and the type and severity of pollution that resulted from the actions to which such fine applies.

(5) For purposes of subchapter B of chapter 98 of title 26, the Fund established under this paragraph shall be treated in the same manner as a trust fund established under subchapter A of such chapter.

(Pub. L. 91–513, title II, § 516, Oct. 27, 1970, 84 Stat. 1279; Pub. L. 96–132, § 16(b), Nov. 30, 1979, 93 Stat. 1049; Pub. L. 100–690, title VI, § 6254(i), Nov. 18, 1988, 102 Stat. 4367.)

CODIFICATION

In subsec. (b), "Administration" substituted for "Bureau" as the probable intent of Congress in view of amendment by Pub. L. 96–132, which substituted references to the Drug Enforcement Administration for references to the Bureau of Narcotics and Dangerous Drugs wherever appearing in text.

AMENDMENTS

1988—Subsec. (d). Pub. L. 100–690 added subsec. (d).

1979—Subsecs. (a), (b). Pub. L. 96–132 substituted "Drug Enforcement Administration" for "Bureau of Narcotics and Dangerous Drugs".

REIMBURSEMENT BY DRUG ENFORCEMENT ADMINISTRATION OF EXPENSES INCURRED TO REMEDIATE METHAMPHETAMINE LABORATORIES

Pub. L. 106–310, div. B, title XXXVI, § 3672, Oct. 17, 2000, 114 Stat. 1246, provided that:

"(a) REIMBURSEMENT AUTHORIZED.—The Attorney General, acting through the Administrator of the Drug Enforcement Administration, may reimburse States, units of local government, Indian tribal governments, other public entities, and multi-jurisdictional or regional consortia thereof for expenses incurred to clean up and safely dispose of substances associated with clandestine methamphetamine laboratories which may present a danger to public health or the environment.

"(b) ADDITIONAL DEA PERSONNEL.—From amounts appropriated or otherwise made available to carry out this section, the Attorney General may hire not more than five additional Drug Enforcement Administration personnel to administer this section.

"(c) AUTHORIZATION OF APPROPRIATIONS.—There is authorized to be appropriated to the Attorney General to carry out this section $20,000,000 for fiscal year 2001."

§ 886a. Diversion Control Fee Account

(1) In general

There is established in the general fund of the Treasury a separate account which shall be known as the Diversion Control Fee Account. For fiscal year 1993 and thereafter:

(A) There shall be deposited as offsetting receipts into that account all fees collected by the Drug Enforcement Administration, in excess of $15,000,000, for the operation of its diversion control program.

(B) Such amounts as are deposited into the Diversion Control Fee Account shall remain available until expended and shall be refunded out of that account by the Secretary of the Treasury, at least on a quarterly basis, to reimburse the Drug Enforcement Administration for expenses incurred in the operation of the diversion control program. Such reimbursements shall be made without distinguishing between expenses related to controlled substance activities and expenses related to chemical activities.

(C) Fees charged by the Drug Enforcement Administration under its diversion control program shall be set at a level that ensures the recovery of the full costs of operating the various aspects of that program.

(D) The amount required to be refunded from the Diversion Control Fee Account for fiscal year 1994 and thereafter shall be refunded in accordance with estimates made in the budget request of the Attorney General for those fiscal years. Any proposed changes in the amounts designated in said budget requests shall only be made after notification to the Committees on Appropriations of the House of Representatives and the Senate fifteen days in advance.

(2) Definitions

In this section:

(A) Diversion control program

The term "diversion control program" means the controlled substance and chemical diversion control activities of the Drug Enforcement Administration.

(B) Controlled substance and chemical diversion control activities

The term "controlled substance and chemical diversion control activities" means those activities related to the registration and control of the manufacture, distribution, dispensing, importation, and exportation of controlled substances and listed chemicals.

(Pub. L. 102–395, title I, §111(b), Oct. 6, 1992, 106 Stat. 1843; Pub. L. 105–362, title X, §1001(b), Nov. 10, 1998, 112 Stat. 3291; Pub. L. 108–447, div. B, title VI, §633(a), Dec. 8, 2004, 118 Stat. 2921.)

CODIFICATION

Section was enacted as part of the Departments of Commerce, Justice, and State, the Judiciary, and Related Agencies Appropriations Act, 1993, and not as part of the Controlled Substances Act which comprises this subchapter.

AMENDMENTS

2004—Pub. L. 108–447, §633(a)(2) to (4), designated existing provisions as par. (1) and inserted heading, substituted "program. Such reimbursements shall be made without distinguishing between expenses related to controlled substance activities and expenses related to chemical activities" for "program" in par. (1)(B), and added par. (2).

Pub. L. 108–447, §633(a)(1), which directed redesignation of pars. (1) to (5) as subpars. (A) to (E) and adjustment of margins, was executed by redesignating pars. (1) to (4) as (A) to (D), respectively, to reflect the probable intent of Congress, because Pub. L. 105–362 struck out par. (5). See 1998 Amendment note below.

1998—Par. (5). Pub. L. 105–362 struck out par. (5) which read as follows: "The Attorney General shall prepare and submit annually to the Congress, statements of financial condition of the account, including the beginning balance, receipts, refunds to appropriations, transfers to the general fund, and the ending balance."

§ 887. Coordination and consolidation of post-seizure administration

The Attorney General and the Secretary of the Treasury shall take such action as may be necessary to develop and maintain a joint plan to coordinate and consolidate post-seizure administration of property seized under this subchapter, subchapter II of this chapter, or provisions of the customs laws relating to controlled substances.

(Pub. L. 91–513, title II, §517, as added Pub. L. 100–690, title VI, §6078(a), Nov. 18, 1988, 102 Stat. 4325.)

REFERENCES IN TEXT

The customs laws, referred to in text, are classified generally to Title 19, Customs Duties.

§ 888. Repealed. Pub. L. 106–185, § 2(c)(3), Apr. 25, 2000, 114 Stat. 210

Section, Pub. L. 91–513, title II, §518, formerly §511A, as added Pub. L. 100–690, title VI, §6080(a), Nov. 18, 1988, 102 Stat. 4326; renumbered §518, Pub. L. 101–647, title X, §1002(h)(1), Nov. 29, 1990, 104 Stat. 4828, related to expedited procedures for seized conveyances.

Section was classified to section 881–1 of this title prior to renumbering by Pub. L. 101–647.

EFFECTIVE DATE OF REPEAL

Repeal applicable to any forfeiture proceeding commenced on or after the date that is 120 days after Apr. 25, 2000, see section 21 of Pub. L. 106–185, set out as an Effective Date of 2000 Amendment note under section 1324 of Title 8, Aliens and Nationality.

§ 889. Production control of controlled substances

(a) Definitions

As used in this section:

(1) The term "controlled substance" has the same meaning given such term in section 802(6) of this title.

(2) The term "Secretary" means the Secretary of Agriculture.

(3) The term "State" means each of the fifty States, the District of Columbia, the Commonwealth of Puerto Rico, Guam, the Virgin Islands of the United States, American Samoa,

the Commonwealth of the Northern Mariana Islands, or the Trust Territory of the Pacific Islands.

(b) Persons ineligible for Federal agricultural program benefits

Notwithstanding any other provision of law, following December 23, 1985, any person who is convicted under Federal or State law of planting, cultivation, growing, producing, harvesting, or storing a controlled substance in any crop year shall be ineligible for—

(1) as to any commodity produced during that crop year, and the four succeeding crop years, by such person—

(A) any price support or payment made available under the Agricultural Act of 1949 (7 U.S.C. 1421 et seq.), the Commodity Credit Corporation Charter Act (15 U.S.C. 714 et seq.), or any other Act;

(B) a farm storage facility loan made under section 4(h) of the Commodity Credit Corporation Charter Act (15 U.S.C. 714b(h));

(C) crop insurance under the Federal Crop Insurance Act (7 U.S.C. 1501 et seq.);

(D) a disaster payment made under the Agricultural Act of 1949 (7 U.S.C. 1421 et seq.); or

(E) a loan made, insured or guaranteed under the Consolidated Farm and Rural Development Act (7 U.S.C. 1921 et seq.) or any other provision of law administered by the Farmers Home Administration; or

(2) a payment made under section 4 or 5 of the Commodity Credit Corporation Charter Act (15 U.S.C. 714b or 714c) for the storage of an agricultural commodity that is—

(A) produced during that crop year, or any of the four succeeding crop years, by such person; and

(B) acquired by the Commodity Credit Corporation.

(c) Regulations

Not later than 180 days after December 23, 1985, the Secretary shall issue such regulations as the Secretary determines are necessary to carry out this section, including regulations that—

(1) define the term "person";

(2) govern the determination of persons who shall be ineligible for program benefits under this section; and

(3) protect the interests of tenants and sharecroppers.

(Pub. L. 91–513, title II, § 519, formerly Pub. L. 99–198, title XVII, § 1764, Dec. 23, 1985, 99 Stat. 1652; renumbered § 519 of Pub. L. 91–513, Pub. L. 101–647, title X, § 1002(h)(2), Nov. 29, 1990, 104 Stat. 4828.)

REFERENCES IN TEXT

The Agricultural Act of 1949, referred to in subsec. (b)(1)(A), (D), is act Oct. 31, 1949, ch. 792, 63 Stat. 1051, as amended, which is classified principally to chapter 35A (§ 1421 et seq.) of Title 7, Agriculture. For complete classification of this Act to the Code, see Short Title note set out under section 1421 of Title 7 and Tables.

The Commodity Credit Corporation Charter Act, referred to in subsec. (b)(1)(A), is act June 29, 1948, ch. 704, 62 Stat. 1070, as amended, and is classified generally to subchapter II (§ 714 et seq.) of chapter 15 of Title 15, Commerce and Trade. For complete classification of this Act to the Code, see Short Title note set out under section 714 of Title 15 and Tables.

The Federal Crop Insurance Act, referred to in subsec. (b)(1)(C), is subtitle A of title V of act Feb. 16, 1938, ch. 30, 52 Stat. 72, which is classified generally to subchapter I (§ 1501 et seq.) of chapter 36 of Title 7, Agriculture. For complete classification of this Act to the Code, see section 1501 of Title 7 and Tables.

The Consolidated Farm and Rural Development Act, referred to in subsec. (b)(1)(E), is title III of Pub. L. 87–128, Aug. 8, 1961, 75 Stat. 307, as amended, which is classified principally to chapter 50 (§ 1921 et seq.) of Title 7. For complete classification of this Act to the Code, see Short Title note set out under section 1921 of Title 7 and Tables.

CODIFICATION

Section was classified to section 881a of this title prior to renumbering by Pub. L. 101–647.

AMENDMENTS

1990—Pub. L. 101–647 renumbered section 881a of this title as this section.

TERMINATION OF TRUST TERRITORY OF THE PACIFIC ISLANDS

For termination of Trust Territory of the Pacific Islands, see note set out preceding section 1681 of Title 48, Territories and Insular Possessions.

§ 890. Review of Federal sales of chemicals usable to manufacture controlled substances

A Federal department or agency may not sell from the stocks of the department or agency any chemical which, as determined by the Administrator of the Drug Enforcement Administration, could be used in the manufacture of a controlled substance unless the Administrator certifies in writing to the head of the department or agency that there is no reasonable cause to believe that the sale of the chemical would result in the illegal manufacture of a controlled substance.

(Pub. L. 91–513, title II, § 520, as added Pub. L. 104–201, div. A, title X, § 1034(a), Sept. 23, 1996, 110 Stat. 2640.)

PART F—GENERAL PROVISIONS

CODIFICATION

The letter designation for this Part F was, in the original, Part G. The original Part F of title II of Pub. L. 91–513, consisting of section 601 thereof, is set out as a note under section 801 of this title. The original Part G of title II of Pub. L. 91–513 consisted of sections 701 to 709. Sections 701 to 705 amended and repealed sections in this title and in Title 18, Crimes and Criminal Procedure, and Title 42, The Public Health and Welfare, and enacted provisions set out as notes under sections 321, 801, and 822 of this title. See Tables for classifications of said sections 701 to 705. Sections 706 to 709 of Pub. L. 91–513 are set out as sections 901 to 904 of this title and, for purposes of codification, comprise this Part F.

§ 901. Severability

If a provision of this chapter is held invalid, all valid provisions that are severable shall remain in effect. If a provision of this chapter is held invalid in one or more of its applications, the provision shall remain in effect in all its valid applications that are severable.

(Pub. L. 91–513, title II, § 706, Oct. 27, 1970, 84 Stat. 1284.)

REFERENCES IN TEXT

This chapter, referred to in text, was in the original "this Act", meaning Pub. L. 91–513, Oct. 27, 1970, 84 Stat. 1236, as amended. For complete classification of this Act to the Code, see Short Title note set out under section 801 of this title and Tables.

§902. Savings provisions

Nothing in this chapter, except this part and, to the extent of any inconsistency, sections 827(e) and 829 of this title, shall be construed as in any way affecting, modifying, repealing, or superseding the provisions of the Federal Food, Drug, and Cosmetic Act [21 U.S.C. §301 et seq.].

(Pub. L. 91–513, title II, §707, Oct. 27, 1970, 84 Stat. 1284.)

REFERENCES IN TEXT

The Federal Food, Drug, and Cosmetic Act, referred to in text, is act June 25, 1938, ch. 675, 52 Stat. 1040, as amended, which is classified generally to chapter 9 (§301 et seq.) of this title. For complete classification of this Act to the Code, see section 301 of this title and Tables.

§903. Application of State law

No provision of this subchapter shall be construed as indicating an intent on the part of the Congress to occupy the field in which that provision operates, including criminal penalties, to the exclusion of any State law on the same subject matter which would otherwise be within the authority of the State, unless there is a positive conflict between that provision of this subchapter and that State law so that the two cannot consistently stand together.

(Pub. L. 91–513, title II, §708, Oct. 27, 1970, 84 Stat. 1284.)

REFERENCES IN TEXT

This subchapter, referred to in text, was in the original "this title", meaning title II of Pub. L. 91–513, Oct. 27, 1970, 84 Stat. 1242, as amended, and is popularly known as the "Controlled Substances Act". For complete classification of title II to the Code, see second paragraph of Short Title note set out under section 801 of this title and Tables.

§904. Payment of tort claims

Notwithstanding section 2680(k) of title 28, the Attorney General, in carrying out the functions of the Department of Justice under this subchapter, is authorized to pay tort claims in the manner authorized by section 2672 of title 28, when such claims arise in a foreign country in connection with the operations of the Drug Enforcement Administration abroad.

(Pub. L. 91–513, title II, §709, Oct. 27, 1970, 84 Stat. 1284; Pub. L. 93–481, §1, Oct. 26, 1974, 88 Stat. 1455; Pub. L. 95–137, §1(a), Oct. 18, 1977, 91 Stat. 1169; Pub. L. 96–132, §§13, 15, Nov. 30, 1979, 93 Stat. 1048; Pub. L. 97–414, §9(g)(1), Jan. 4, 1983, 96 Stat. 2064.)

AMENDMENTS

1983—Pub. L. 97–414 struck out subsecs. (a) and (b) which had provided, respectively, that (a) there were authorized to be appropriated $105,000,000 for the fiscal year ending June 30, 1975, $175,000,000 for the fiscal year ending June 30, 1976, $200,000,000 for the fiscal year ending September 30, 1977, $188,000,000 for the fiscal year ending September 30, 1978, $215,000,000 for the fiscal year ending September 30, 1979, and $198,336,000 for the fiscal year ending September 30, 1980, for the expenses of the Department of Justice in carrying out its functions under this subchapter, and that (b) no funds appropriated under any other provision of this chapter could be used for the expenses of the Department of Justice for which funds were authorized to be appropriated by former subsection (a) of this section, and removed the subsection designator (c) before "Notwithstanding".

1979—Subsec. (a). Pub. L. 96–132, §15, inserted provisions authorizing appropriations of $198,336,000 for the fiscal year ending Sept. 30, 1980.

Subsec. (c). Pub. L. 96–132, §13, added subsec. (c).

1977—Subsec. (a). Pub. L. 95–137 substituted "September 30, 1977, $188,000,000 for the fiscal year ending September 30, 1978, and $215,000,000 for the fiscal year ending September 30, 1979," for "June 30, 1977," and struck out "(other than its expenses incurred in connection with carrying out section 803(a) of this title)".

1974—Pub. L. 93–481 designated existing provisions as subsec. (a), substituted authorization of appropriations for fiscal years ending June 30, 1975, June 30, 1976, and June 30, 1977, for authorization of appropriations for fiscal years ending June 30, 1972, June 30, 1973, and June 30, 1974, and added subsec. (b).

SUBCHAPTER II—IMPORT AND EXPORT

CODIFICATION

This subchapter is comprised of Part A of title III of Pub. L. 91–513, Oct. 27, 1970, 84 Stat. 1285. Part B of title III contains amendatory, repealing, and transitional provisions generally classified elsewhere.

§951. Definitions

(a) For purposes of this subchapter—

(1) The term "import" means, with respect to any article, any bringing in or introduction of such article into any area (whether or not such bringing in or introduction constitutes an importation within the meaning of the tariff laws of the United States).

(2) The term "customs territory of the United States" has the meaning assigned to such term by general note 2 of the Harmonized Tariff Schedule of the United States.

(b) Each term defined in section 802 of this title shall have the same meaning for purposes of this subchapter as such term has for purposes of subchapter I of this chapter.

(Pub. L. 91–513, title III, §1001, Oct. 27, 1970, 84 Stat. 1285; Pub. L. 100–418, title I, §1214(m), Aug. 23, 1988, 102 Stat. 1158.)

REFERENCES IN TEXT

The Harmonized Tariff Schedule of the United States, referred to in subsec. (a)(2), is not set out in the Code. See Publication of Harmonized Tariff Schedule note set out under section 1202 of Title 19, Customs Duties.

This subchapter, referred to in subsecs. (a) and (b), was in the original "this title", meaning title III of Pub. L. 91–513, Oct. 27, 1970, 84 Stat. 1285, as amended. Part A of title III comprises this subchapter. For classification of Part B, consisting of sections 1101 to 1105 of title III, see Tables.

AMENDMENTS

1988—Subsec. (a)(2). Pub. L. 100–418 substituted "general note 2 of the Harmonized Tariff Schedule of the United States" for "general headnote 2 to the Tariff Schedules of the United States".

EFFECTIVE DATE OF 1988 AMENDMENT

Amendment by Pub. L. 100–418 effective Jan. 1, 1989, and applicable with respect to articles entered on or after such date, see section 1217(b)(1) of Pub. L. 100–418, set out as an Effective Date note under section 3001 of Title 19, Customs Duties.

EFFECTIVE DATE

Section 1105(a)–(c) of title III of Pub. L. 91–513, as amended by Pub. L. 99–514, §2, Oct. 22, 1986, 100 Stat. 2095, provided that:

"(a) Except as otherwise provided in this section, this title [see Short Title note below] shall become effective on the first day of the seventh calendar month that begins after the day immediately preceding the date of enactment [Oct. 27, 1970].

"(b) Sections 1000, 1001, 1006, 1015, 1016, 1103, 1104 [see Short Title note below and sections 171 note, 951, 956, 957 note, 965, and 966 of this title], and this section shall become effective upon enactment [Oct. 27, 1970].

"(c)(1) If the Attorney General, pursuant to the authority of section 704(c) of title II [set out as a note under section 801 of this title], postpones the effective date of section 306 (relating to manufacturing quotas) [section 826 of this title] for any period beyond the date specified in section 704(a) [set out as a note under section 801 of this title], and such postponement applies to narcotic drugs, the repeal of the Narcotics Manufacturing Act of 1960 [sections 501 to 517 of this title] by paragraph (10) of section 1101(a) of this title is hereby postponed for the same period, except that the postponement made by this paragraph shall not apply to the repeal of sections 4, 5, 13, 15, and 16 of that Act [which were classified to sections 182, 503, 511, and 513 of this title and sections 4702, 4731, and 4731 note of Title 26, Internal Revenue Code].

"(2) Effective for any period of postponement, by paragraph (1) of this subsection, of the repeal of provisions of the Narcotics Manufacturing Act of 1960 [sections 501 to 517 of this title], that Act shall be applied subject to the following modifications:

"(A) The term 'narcotic drug' shall mean a narcotic drug as defined in section 102(16) of title II [section 802(16) of this title], and all references, in the Narcotics Manufacturing Act of 1960 [sections 501 to 517 of this title], to a narcotic drug as defined by section 4731 of the Internal Revenue Code of 1986 [formerly I.R.C. 1954, section 4731 of Title 26] are amended to refer to a narcotic drug as defined by such section 102(16) [section 802(16) of this title].

"(B) On and after the date prescribed by the Attorney General pursuant to clause (2) of section 703(c) of title II, [set out as a note under section 822 of this title], the requirements of a manufacturer's license with respect to a basic class of narcotic drug under the Narcotics Manufacturing Act of 1960 [sections 501 to 517 of this title], and of a registration under section 4722 of the Internal Revenue Code of 1986 [formerly I.R.C. 1954, section 4722 of Title 26] as a prerequisite to issuance of such a license, shall be superseded by a requirement of actual registration (as distinguished from provisional registration) as a manufacturer of that class of drug under section 303(a) of title II [section 823(a) of this title].

"(C) On and after the effective date of the repeal of such section 4722 [section 4722 of title 26] by section 1101(b)(3) of this title, but prior to the date specified in subparagraph (B) of this paragraph, the requirement of registration under such section 4722 [section 4722 of title 26] as a prerequisite of a manufacturer's license under the Narcotics Manufacturing Act of 1960 [sections 501 to 517 of this title] shall be superseded by a requirement of either (i) actual registration as a manufacturer under section 303 of title II [section 823 of this title] or (ii) provisional registration (by virtue of a preexisting registration under such section 4722) under section 703 of title II [set out as a note under section 822 of this title]."

SHORT TITLE

Section 1000 of title III of Pub. L. 91–513 provided that: "This title [enacting this subchapter, amending sections 162 and 967 of this title, section 4251 of Title 18, Crimes and Criminal Procedure, section 1584 of Title 19, Customs Duties, sections 4901, 4905, 6808, 7012, 7103, 7326, 7607, 7609, 7641, 7651, and 7655 of Title 26, Internal Revenue Code, section 2901 of Title 28, Judiciary and Judicial Procedure, sections 529d, 529e, and 529f of former Title 31, Money and Finance, section 304m of former Title 40, Public Buildings, Property, and Works, section 3411 of Title 42, The Public Health and Welfare, section 239a of former Title 46, Shipping, and section 787 of former Title 49, Transportation, repealing sections 171 to 174, 176 to 185, 188 to 188n, 191 to 193, 197, 198, 199, and 501 to 517 of this title, sections 1401 to 1407, and 3616 of Title 18, sections 4701 to 4707, 4711 to 4716, 4721 to 4726, 4731 to 4736, 4741 to 4746, 4751 to 4757, 4761, 4762, 4771 to 4776, 7237, 7238, and 7491 of Title 26, sections 529a and 529g of former Title 31, section 1421m of Title 48, Territories and Insular Possessions, and enacting provisions set out as notes under this section and sections 171 and 957 of this title] may be cited as the 'Controlled Substances Import and Export Act'."

RULES AND REGULATIONS

Section 1105(d) of Pub. L. 91–513 provided: "Any orders, rules and regulations which have been promulgated under any law affected by this title [see Short Title note above] and which are in effect on the day preceding enactment of this title [Oct. 27, 1970] shall continue in effect until modified, superseded, or repealed."

§952. Importation of controlled substances

(a) Controlled substances in schedule I or II and narcotic drugs in schedule III, IV, or V; exceptions

It shall be unlawful to import into the customs territory of the United States from any place outside thereof (but within the United States), or to import into the United States from any place outside thereof, any controlled substance in schedule I or II of subchapter I of this chapter, or any narcotic drug in schedule III, IV, or V of subchapter I of this chapter, or ephedrine, pseudoephedrine, or phenylpropanolamine, except that—

(1) such amounts of crude opium, poppy straw, concentrate of poppy straw, and coca leaves, and of ephedrine, pseudoephedrine, and phenylpropanolamine, as the Attorney General finds to be necessary to provide for medical, scientific, or other legitimate purposes, and

(2) such amounts of any controlled substance in schedule I or II or any narcotic drug in schedule III, IV, or V that the Attorney General finds to be necessary to provide for the medical, scientific, or other legitimate needs of the United States—

(A) during an emergency in which domestic supplies of such substance or drug are found by the Attorney General to be inadequate,

(B) in any case in which the Attorney General finds that competition among domestic manufacturers of the controlled substance is inadequate and will not be rendered adequate by the registration of additional manufacturers under section 823 of this title, or

(C) in any case in which the Attorney General finds that such controlled substance is in limited quantities exclusively for scientific, analytical, or research uses,

may be so imported under such regulations as the Attorney General shall prescribe. No crude opium may be so imported for the purpose of manufacturing heroin or smoking opium.

(b) Nonnarcotic controlled substances in schedule III, IV, or V

It shall be unlawful to import into the customs territory of the United States from any place outside thereof (but within the United States), or to import into the United States from any place outside thereof, any nonnarcotic controlled substance in schedule III, IV, or V, unless such nonnarcotic controlled substance—

(1) is imported for medical, scientific, or other legitimate uses, and

(2) is imported pursuant to such notification, or declaration, or in the case of any nonnarcotic controlled substance in schedule III, such import permit, notification, or declaration, as the Attorney General may by regulation prescribe, except that if a nonnarcotic controlled substance in schedule IV or V is also listed in schedule I or II of the Convention on Psychotropic Substances it shall be imported pursuant to such import permit requirements, prescribed by regulation of the Attorney General, as are required by the Convention.

(c) Coca leaves

In addition to the amount of coca leaves authorized to be imported into the United States under subsection (a) of this section, the Attorney General may permit the importation of additional amounts of coca leaves. All cocaine and ecgonine (and all salts, derivatives, and preparations from which cocaine or ecgonine may be synthesized or made) contained in such additional amounts of coca leaves imported under this subsection shall be destroyed under the supervision of an authorized representative of the Attorney General.

(d) Application for increased importation of ephedrine, pseudoephedrine, or phenylpropanolamine

(1) With respect to a registrant under section 958 of this title who is authorized under subsection (a)(1) to import ephedrine, pseudoephedrine, or phenylpropanolamine, at any time during the year the registrant may apply for an increase in the amount of such chemical that the registrant is authorized to import, and the Attorney General may approve the application if the Attorney General determines that the approval is necessary to provide for medical, scientific, or other legitimate purposes regarding the chemical.

(2) With respect to the application under paragraph (1):

(A) Not later than 60 days after receiving the application, the Attorney General shall approve or deny the application.

(B) In approving the application, the Attorney General shall specify the period of time for which the approval is in effect, or shall provide that the approval is effective until the registrant involved is notified in writing by the Attorney General that the approval is terminated.

(C) If the Attorney General does not approve or deny the application before the expiration of the 60-day period under subparagraph (A), the application is deemed to be approved, and such approval remains in effect until the Attorney General notifies the registrant in writing that the approval is terminated.

(e) Reference to ephedrine, pseudoephedrine, or phenylpropanolamine

Each reference in this section to ephedrine, pseudoephedrine, or phenylpropanolamine includes each of the salts, optical isomers, and salts of optical isomers of such chemical.

(Pub. L. 91–513, title III, §1002, Oct. 27, 1970, 84 Stat. 1285; Pub. L. 95–633, title I, §105, Nov. 10, 1978, 92 Stat. 3772; Pub. L. 98–473, title II, §§519–521, Oct. 12, 1984, 98 Stat. 2075; Pub. L. 109–177, title VII, §715, Mar. 9, 2006, 120 Stat. 264.)

REFERENCES IN TEXT

Schedules I, II, III, IV, and V, referred to in subsecs. (a) and (b), are set out in section 812(c) of this title.

AMENDMENTS

2006—Subsec. (a). Pub. L. 109–177, §715(1)(A), inserted "or ephedrine, pseudoephedrine, or phenylpropanolamine," after "schedule III, IV, or V of subchapter I of this chapter," in introductory provisions.

Subsec. (a)(1). Pub. L. 109–177, §715(1)(B), inserted ", and of ephedrine, pseudoephedrine, and phenylpropanolamine," after "coca leaves".

Subsecs. (d), (e). Pub. L. 109–177, §715(2), added subsecs. (d) and (e).

1984—Subsec. (a)(1). Pub. L. 98–473, §519, amended par. (1) generally, inserting references to poppy straw and concentrate of poppy straw.

Subsec. (a)(2)(C). Pub. L. 98–473, §520, added subpar. (C).

Subsec. (b)(2). Pub. L. 98–473, §521, substituted "is imported pursuant to such notification, or declaration, or in the case of any nonnarcotic controlled substance in schedule III, such import permit, notification, or declaration, as the Attorney General may by regulation prescribe, except that if a nonnarcotic controlled substance in schedule IV or V is also listed in schedule I or II of the Convention on Psychotropic Substances it shall be imported pursuant to such import permit requirements, prescribed by regulation of the Attorney General, as are required by the Convention" for "is imported pursuant to such notification or declaration requirements as the Attorney General may by regulation prescribe, except that if a nonnarcotic controlled substance in schedule III, IV, or V is also listed in schedule I or II of the Convention on Psychotropic Substances it shall be imported pursuant to such import permit requirements, prescribed by regulation of the Attorney General, as are required by the Convention".

1978—Subsec. (b)(2). Pub. L. 95–633 inserted provision relating to exception for nonnarcotic controlled substances listed in schedule I or II of the Convention on Psychotropic Substances.

EFFECTIVE DATE OF 1978 AMENDMENT

Amendment by Pub. L. 95–633 effective on date the Convention on Psychotropic Substances enters into force in the United States [July 15, 1980], see section 112 of Pub. L. 95–633, set out as an Effective Date note under section 801a of this title.

§953. Exportation of controlled substances

(a) Narcotic drugs in schedule I, II, III, or IV

It shall be unlawful to export from the United States any narcotic drug in schedule I, II, III, or IV unless—

(1) it is exported to a country which is a party to—

(A) the International Opium Convention of 1912 for the Suppression of the Abuses of Opium, Morphine, Cocaine, and Derivative Drugs, or to the International Opium Convention signed at Geneva on February 19, 1925; or

(B) the Convention for Limiting the Manufacture and Regulating the Distribution of Narcotic Drugs concluded at Geneva, July 13, 1931, as amended by the protocol signed at Lake Success on December 11, 1946, and the protocol bringing under international control drugs outside the scope of the convention of July 13, 1931, for limiting the manufacture and regulating the distribution of narcotic drugs (as amended by the protocol signed at Lake Success on December 11, 1946), signed at Paris, November 19, 1948; or

(C) the Single Convention on Narcotic Drugs, 1961, signed at New York, March 30, 1961;

(2) such country has instituted and maintains, in conformity with the conventions to which it is a party, a system for the control of imports of narcotic drugs which the Attorney General deems adequate;

(3) the narcotic drug is consigned to a holder of such permits or licenses as may be required under the laws of the country of import, and a permit or license to import such drug has been issued by the country of import;

(4) substantial evidence is furnished to the Attorney General by the exporter that (A) the narcotic drug is to be applied exclusively to medical or scientific uses within the country of import, and (B) there is an actual need for the narcotic drug for medical or scientific uses within such country; and

(5) a permit to export the narcotic drug in each instance has been issued by the Attorney General.

(b) Exception for exportation for special scientific purposes

Notwithstanding subsection (a) of this section, the Attorney General may authorize any narcotic drug (including crude opium and coca leaves) in schedule I, II, III, or IV to be exported from the United States to a country which is a party to any of the international instruments mentioned in subsection (a) of this section if the particular drug is to be applied to a special scientific purpose in the country of destination and the authorities of such country will permit the importation of the particular drug for such purpose.

(c) Nonnarcotic controlled substances in schedule I or II

It shall be unlawful to export from the United States any nonnarcotic controlled substance in schedule I or II unless—

(1) it is exported to a country which has instituted and maintains a system which the Attorney General deems adequate for the control of imports of such substances;

(2) the controlled substance is consigned to a holder of such permits or licenses as may be required under the laws of the country of import;

(3) substantial evidence is furnished to the Attorney General that (A) the controlled substance is to be applied exclusively to medical, scientific, or other legitimate uses within the country to which exported, (B) it will not be exported from such country, and (C) there is an actual need for the controlled substance for medical, scientific, or other legitimate uses within the country; and

(4) a permit to export the controlled substance in each instance has been issued by the Attorney General.

(d) Exception for exportation for special scientific purposes

Notwithstanding subsection (c) of this section, the Attorney General may authorize any nonnarcotic controlled substance in schedule I or II to be exported from the United States if the particular substance is to be applied to a special scientific purpose in the country of destination and the authorities of such country will permit the importation of the particular drug for such purpose.

(e) Nonnarcotic controlled substances in schedule III or IV; controlled substances in schedule V

It shall be unlawful to export from the United States to any other country any nonnarcotic controlled substance in schedule III or IV or any controlled substances in schedule V unless—

(1) there is furnished (before export) to the Attorney General documentary proof that importation is not contrary to the laws or regulations of the country of destination for consumption for medical, scientific, or other legitimate purposes;

(2) it is exported pursuant to such notification or declaration, or in the case of any nonnarcotic controlled substance in schedule III, such export permit, notification, or declaration as the Attorney General may by regulation prescribe; and

(3) in the case of a nonnarcotic controlled substance in schedule IV or V which is also listed in schedule I or II of the Convention on Psychotropic Substances, it is exported pursuant to such export permit requirements, prescribed by regulation of the Attorney General, as are required by the Convention.

(f) Exception for exportation for subsequent export

Notwithstanding subsections (a)(4) and (c)(3) of this section, the Attorney General may authorize any controlled substance that is in schedule I or II, or is a narcotic drug in schedule III or IV, to be exported from the United States to a country for subsequent export from that country to another country, if each of the following conditions is met:

(1) Both the country to which the controlled substance is exported from the United States (referred to in this subsection as the "first country") and the country to which the controlled substance is exported from the first country (referred to in this subsection as the "second country") are parties to the Single Convention on Narcotic Drugs, 1961, and the Convention on Psychotropic Substances, 1971.

(2) The first country and the second country have each instituted and maintain, in conformity with such Conventions, a system of

controls of imports of controlled substances which the Attorney General deems adequate.

(3) With respect to the first country, the controlled substance is consigned to a holder of such permits or licenses as may be required under the laws of such country, and a permit or license to import the controlled substance has been issued by the country.

(4) With respect to the second country, substantial evidence is furnished to the Attorney General by the person who will export the controlled substance from the United States that—

(A) the controlled substance is to be consigned to a holder of such permits or licenses as may be required under the laws of such country, and a permit or license to import the controlled substance is to be issued by the country; and

(B) the controlled substance is to be applied exclusively to medical, scientific, or other legitimate uses within the country.

(5) The controlled substance will not be exported from the second country.

(6) Within 30 days after the controlled substance is exported from the first country to the second country, the person who exported the controlled substance from the United States delivers to the Attorney General documentation certifying that such export from the first country has occurred.

(7) A permit to export the controlled substance from the United States has been issued by the Attorney General.

(Pub. L. 91–513, title III, §1003, Oct. 27, 1970, 84 Stat. 1286; Pub. L. 95–633, title I, §106, Nov. 10, 1978, 92 Stat. 3772; Pub. L. 98–473, title II, §522, Oct. 12, 1984, 98 Stat. 2076; Pub. L. 109–57, §1(b), Aug. 2, 2005, 119 Stat. 592.)

REFERENCES IN TEXT

Schedules I, II, III, IV and V, referred to in text, are set out in section 812(c) of this title.

AMENDMENTS

2005—Subsec. (f). Pub. L. 109–57 added subsec. (f).

1984—Subsec. (e). Pub. L. 98–473 in cl. (1) inserted provisions for consumption for medical, etc., purposes, added cls. (2) and (3), and struck out former cls. (2) to (4), respectively, relating to a special controlled substance invoice, two additional copies of the invoice, and exportation of a nonnarcotic controlled substance in schedule III, IV, or V, also listed in schedule I or II of the Convention.

1978—Subsec. (e)(4). Pub. L. 95–633 added par. (4).

EFFECTIVE DATE OF 1978 AMENDMENT

Amendment by Pub. L. 95–633 effective on date the Convention on Psychotropic Substances enters into force in the United States [July 15, 1980], see section 112 of Pub. L. 95–633, set out as an Effective Date note under section 801a of this title.

§954. Transshipment and in-transit shipment of controlled substances

Notwithstanding sections 952, 953, and 957 of this title—

(1) A controlled substance in schedule I may—

(A) be imported into the United States for transshipment to another country, or

(B) be transferred or transshipped from one vessel, vehicle, or aircraft to another vessel, vehicle, or aircraft within the United States for immediate exportation,

if and only if it is so imported, transferred, or transshipped (i) for scientific, medical, or other legitimate purposes in the country of destination, and (ii) with the prior written approval of the Attorney General (which shall be granted or denied within 21 days of the request).

(2) A controlled substance in schedule II, III, or IV may be so imported, transferred, or transshipped if and only if advance notice is given to the Attorney General in accordance with regulations of the Attorney General.

(Pub. L. 91–513, title III, §1004, Oct. 27, 1970, 84 Stat. 1287.)

REFERENCES IN TEXT

Schedules I, II, III, and IV, referred to in text, are set out in section 812(c) of this title.

§955. Possession on board vessels, etc., arriving in or departing from United States

It shall be unlawful for any person to bring or possess on board any vessel or aircraft, or on board any vehicle of a carrier, arriving in or departing from the United States or the customs territory of the United States, a controlled substance in schedule I or II or a narcotic drug in schedule III or IV, unless such substance or drug is a part of the cargo entered in the manifest or part of the official supplies of the vessel, aircraft, or vehicle.

(Pub. L. 91–513, title III, §1005, Oct. 27, 1970, 84 Stat. 1287.)

REFERENCES IN TEXT

Schedules I, II, III, and IV, referred to in text, are set out in section 812(c) of this title.

§§955a to 955d. Transferred

CODIFICATION

Sections, Pub. L. 96–350, §§1–4, Sept. 15, 1980, 94 Stat. 1159, 1160, relating to maritime drug law enforcement, were transferred to sections 1901 to 1904 of the former Appendix to Title 46, Shipping. Sections 1901 to 1904 of the former Appendix to Title 46 were repealed and restated in chapter 705 of Title 46, Shipping, by Pub. L. 109–304, §§10(2), 19, Oct. 6, 2006, 120 Stat. 1683, 1710. For disposition of sections of the former Appendix to Title 46, see Disposition Table preceding section 101 of Title 46.

§956. Exemption authority

(a) Individual possessing controlled substance

(1) Subject to paragraph (2), the Attorney General may by regulation exempt from sections 952(a) and (b), 953, 954, and 955 of this title any individual who has a controlled substance (except a substance in schedule I) in his possession for his personal medical use, or for administration to an animal accompanying him, if he lawfully obtained such substance and he makes such declaration (or gives such other notification) as the Attorney General may by regulation require.

(2) Notwithstanding any exemption under paragraph (1), a United States resident who enters the United States through an international

land border with a controlled substance (except a substance in schedule I) for which the individual does not possess a valid prescription issued by a practitioner (as defined in section 802 of this title) in accordance with applicable Federal and State law (or documentation that verifies the issuance of such a prescription to that individual) may not import the controlled substance into the United States in an amount that exceeds 50 dosage units of the controlled substance.

(b) Compound, mixture, or preparation

The Attorney General may by regulation except any compound, mixture, or preparation containing any depressant or stimulant substance listed in paragraph (a) or (b) of schedule III or in schedule IV or V from the application of all or any part of this subchapter if (1) the compound, mixture, or preparation contains one or more active medicinal ingredients not having a depressant or stimulant effect on the central nervous system, and (2) such ingredients are included therein in such combinations, quantity, proportion, or concentration as to vitiate the potential for abuse of the substances which do have a depressant or stimulant effect on the central nervous system.

(Pub. L. 91–513, title III, § 1006, Oct. 27, 1970, 84 Stat. 1288; Pub. L. 105–277, div. C, title VIII, § 872(a), Oct. 21, 1998, 112 Stat. 2681–707; Pub. L. 105–357, § 2(a), Nov. 10, 1998, 112 Stat. 3271.)

REFERENCES IN TEXT

Schedules I, III, IV, and V, referred to in text, are set out in section 812(c) of this title.

AMENDMENTS

1998—Subsec. (a). Pub. L. 105–277 and Pub. L. 105–357 amended subsec. (a) identically, designating existing provisions as par. (1), substituting "Subject to paragraph (2), the Attorney General" for "The Attorney General", and adding par. (2).

FEDERAL MINIMUM REQUIREMENT

Pub. L. 105–357, § 2(b), Nov. 10, 1998, 112 Stat. 3271, provided that: "Section 1006(a)(2) of the Controlled Substances Import and Export Act [21 U.S.C. 956(a)(2)], as added by this section, is a minimum Federal requirement and shall not be construed to limit a State from imposing any additional requirement."

Pub. L. 105–277, div. C, title VIII, § 872(b), Oct. 21, 1998, 112 Stat. 2681–707, enacted a provision substantially identical to that enacted by Pub. L. 105–357, § 2(b), set out above.

JURISDICTION OF SECRETARY OF HEALTH AND HUMAN SERVICES

Pub. L. 105–277, div. C, title VIII, § 872(c), Oct. 21, 1998, 112 Stat. 2681–707, and Pub. L. 105–357, § 2(c), Nov. 10, 1998, 112 Stat. 3271, provided that: "The amendment made by subsection (a) [amending this section] shall not be construed to affect the jurisdiction of the Secretary of Health and Human Services under the Federal Food, Drug and Cosmetic Act (21 U.S.C. 301 et seq.)."

§ 957. Persons required to register

(a) Coverage

No person may—

(1) import into the customs territory of the United States from any place outside thereof (but within the United States), or import into the United States from any place outside thereof, any controlled substance or list I chemical, or

(2) export from the United States any controlled substance or list I chemical,

unless there is in effect with respect to such person a registration issued by the Attorney General under section 958 of this title, or unless such person is exempt from registration under subsection (b) of this section.

(b) Exemptions

(1) The following persons shall not be required to register under the provisions of this section and may lawfully possess a controlled substance or list I chemical:

(A) An agent or an employee of any importer or exporter registered under section 958 of this title if such agent or employee is acting in the usual course of his business or employment.

(B) A common or contract carrier or warehouseman, or an employee thereof, whose possession of any controlled substance or list I chemical is in the usual course of his business or employment.

(C) An ultimate user who possesses such substance for a purpose specified in section 802(25)[1] of this title and in conformity with an exemption granted under section 956(a) of this title.

(2) The Attorney General may, by regulation, waive the requirement for registration of certain importers and exporters if he finds it consistent with the public health and safety; and may authorize any such importer or exporter to possess controlled substances or list I chemicals for purposes of importation and exportation.

(Pub. L. 91–513, title III, § 1007, Oct. 27, 1970, 84 Stat. 1288; Pub. L. 98–473, title II, § 523, Oct. 12, 1984, 98 Stat. 2076; Pub. L. 103–200, § 3(e), Dec. 17, 1993, 107 Stat. 2337.)

REFERENCES IN TEXT

Section 802(25) of this title, referred to in subsec. (b)(1)(C), was redesignated section 802(26) of this title by Pub. L. 98–473, title II, § 507(a), Oct. 12, 1984, 98 Stat. 2071, and was further redesignated section 802(27) of this title by Pub. L. 99–570, title I, § 1003(b)(2), Oct. 27, 1986, 100 Stat. 3207–6.

AMENDMENTS

1993—Subsec. (a)(1). Pub. L. 103–200, § 3(e)(1)(A), inserted "or list I chemical" after "controlled substance".

Subsec. (a)(2). Pub. L. 103–200, § 3(e)(1)(B), substituted "or list I chemical," for "in schedule I, II, III, IV, or V,".

Subsec. (b)(1). Pub. L. 103–200, § 3(e)(2)(A), inserted "or list I chemical" after "controlled substance" in introductory provisions and subpar. (B).

Subsec. (b)(2). Pub. L. 103–200, § 3(e)(2)(B), inserted "or list I chemicals" after "controlled substances".

1984—Subsec. (a)(2). Pub. L. 98–473 inserted reference to schedule V.

EFFECTIVE DATE OF 1993 AMENDMENT

Amendment by Pub. L. 103–200 effective on date that is 120 days after Dec. 17, 1993, see section 11 of Pub. L. 103–200, set out as a note under section 802 of this title.

PROVISIONAL REGISTRATION

Section 1104 of Pub. L. 91–513, as amended by Pub. L. 99–514, § 2, Oct. 22, 1986, 100 Stat. 2095, provided that:

[1] See References in Text note below.

"(a)(1) Any person—

"(A) who is engaged in importing or exporting any controlled substance on the day before the effective date of section 1007 [May 1, 1971],

"(B) who notifies the Attorney General that he is so engaged, and

"(C) who is registered on such day under section 510 of the Federal Food, Drug, and Cosmetic Act [section 360 of this title] or under section 4722 of the Internal Revenue Code of 1986 [formerly I.R.C. 1954, section 4722 of title 26],

shall, with respect to each establishment for which such registration is in effect under any such section, be deemed to have a provisional registration under section 1008 [section 958 of this title] for the import or export (as the case may be) of controlled substances.

"(2) During the period his provisional registration is in effect under this section, the registration number assigned such person under such section 510 or under such section 4722 (as the case may be) shall be his registration number for purposes of part A of this title [this subchapter].

"(b) The provisions of section 304 [section 824 of this title], relating to suspension and revocation of registration, shall apply to a provisional registration under this section.

"(c) Unless sooner suspended or revoked under subsection (b), a provisional registration of a person under subsection (a)(1) of this section shall be in effect until—

"(1) the date on which such person has registered with the Attorney General under section 1008 [section 958 of this title] or has had his registration denied under such section, or

"(2) such date as may be prescribed by the Attorney General for registration of importers or exporters, as the case may be,

whichever occurs first."

§958. Registration requirements

(a) Applicants to import or export controlled substances in schedule I or II

The Attorney General shall register an applicant to import or export a controlled substance in schedule I or II if he determines that such registration is consistent with the public interest and with United States obligations under international treaties, conventions, or protocols in effect on May 1, 1971. In determining the public interest, the factors enumerated in paragraph (1) through (6) of section 823(a) of this title shall be considered.

(b) Activity limited to specified substances

Registration granted under this section shall not entitle a registrant to import or export controlled substances other than specified in the registration.

(c) Applicants to import controlled substances in schedule III, IV, or V or to export controlled substances in schedule III or IV; applicants to import or export list I chemicals

(1) The Attorney General shall register an applicant to import a controlled substance in schedule III, IV, or V or to export a controlled substance in schedule III or IV, unless he determines that the issuance of such registration is inconsistent with the public interest. In determining the public interest, the factors enumerated in paragraphs (1) through (6) of section 823(d) of this title shall be considered.

(2)(A) The Attorney General shall register an applicant to import or export a list I chemical unless the Attorney General determines that registration of the applicant is inconsistent with the public interest. Registration under this subsection shall not be required for the import or export of a drug product that is exempted under section 802(39)(A)(iv) of this title.

(B) In determining the public interest for the purposes of subparagraph (A), the Attorney General shall consider the factors specified in section 823(h) of this title.

(d) Denial of application

(1) The Attorney General may deny an application for registration under subsection (a) of this section if he is unable to determine that such registration is consistent with the public interest (as defined in subsection (a) of this section) and with the United States obligations under international treaties, conventions, or protocols in effect on May 1, 1971.

(2) The Attorney General may deny an application for registration under subsection (c) of this section, or revoke or suspend a registration under subsection (a) or (c) of this section, if he determines that such registration is inconsistent with the public interest (as defined in subsection (a) or (c) of this section) or with the United States obligations under international treaties, conventions, or protocols in effect on May 1, 1971.

(3) The Attorney General may limit the revocation or suspension of a registration to the particular controlled substance, or substances, or list I chemical or chemicals, with respect to which grounds for revocation or suspension exist.

(4) Before taking action pursuant to this subsection, the Attorney General shall serve upon the applicant or registrant an order to show cause as to why the registration should not be denied, revoked, or suspended. The order to show cause shall contain a statement of the basis thereof and shall call upon the applicant or registrant to appear before the Attorney General, or his designee, at a time and place stated in the order, but in no event less than thirty days after the date of receipt of the order. Proceedings to deny, revoke, or suspend shall be conducted pursuant to this subsection in accordance with subchapter II of chapter 5 of title 5. Such proceedings shall be independent of, and not in lieu of, criminal prosecutions or other proceedings under this subchapter or any other law of the United States.

(5) The Attorney General may, in his discretion, suspend any registration simultaneously with the institution of proceedings under this subsection, in cases where he finds that there is an imminent danger to the public health and safety. Such suspension shall continue in effect until the conclusion of such proceedings, including judicial review thereof, unless sooner withdrawn by the Attorney General or dissolved by a court of competent jurisdiction.

(6) In the event that the Attorney General suspends or revokes a registration granted under this section, all controlled substances or list I chemicals owned or possessed by the registrant pursuant to such registration at the time of suspension or the effective date of the revocation order, as the case may be, may, in the discretion of the Attorney General, be seized or placed under seal. No disposition may be made of any

controlled substances or list I chemicals under seal until the time for taking an appeal has elapsed or until all appeals have been concluded, except that a court, upon application therefor, may at any time order the sale of perishable controlled substances or list I chemicals. Any such order shall require the deposit of the proceeds of the sale with the court. Upon a revocation order becoming final, all such controlled substances or list I chemicals (or proceeds of the sale thereof which have been deposited with the court) shall be forfeited to the United States; and the Attorney General shall dispose of such controlled substances or list I chemicals in accordance with section 881(e) of this title.

(e) Registration period

No registration shall be issued under this subchapter for a period in excess of one year. Unless the regulations of the Attorney General otherwise provide, sections 822(f), 825, 827, and 830 of this title shall apply to persons registered under this section to the same extent such sections apply to persons registered under section 823 of this title.

(f) Rules and regulations

The Attorney General is authorized to promulgate rules and regulations and to charge reasonable fees relating to the registration and control of importers and exporters of controlled substances or listed chemicals.

(g) Scope of authorized activity

Persons registered by the Attorney General under this section to import or export controlled substances or list I chemicals may import or export (and for the purpose of so importing or exporting, may possess) such substances to the extent authorized by their registration and in conformity with the other provisions of this subchapter and subchapter I of this chapter.

(h) Separate registrations for each principal place of business

A separate registration shall be required at each principal place of business where the applicant imports or exports controlled substances or list I chemicals.

(i) Emergency situations

Except in emergency situations as described in section 952(a)(2)(A) of this title, prior to issuing a registration under this section to a bulk manufacturer of a controlled substance in schedule I or II, and prior to issuing a regulation under section 952(a) of this title authorizing the importation of such a substance, the Attorney General shall give manufacturers holding registrations for the bulk manufacture of the substance an opportunity for a hearing.

(Pub. L. 91–513, title III, §1008, Oct. 27, 1970, 84 Stat. 1289; Pub. L. 98–473, title II, §§524, 525, Oct. 12, 1984, 98 Stat. 2076; Pub. L. 99–570, title I, §1866(d), Oct. 27, 1986, 100 Stat. 3207–55; Pub. L. 103–200, §3(f), Dec. 17, 1993, 107 Stat. 2337; Pub. L. 108–447, div. B, title VI, §633(c), Dec. 8, 2004, 118 Stat. 2922.)

REFERENCES IN TEXT

Schedules I, II, III, IV, and V, referred to in subsecs. (a), (c), and (i), are set out in section 812(c) of this title.

This subchapter, referred to in subsecs. (d)(4) and (g), was in the original "this title", meaning title III of Pub. L. 91–513, Oct. 27, 1970, 84 Stat. 1285, as amended. Part A of title III comprises this subchapter. For classification of Part B, consisting of sections 1101 to 1105 of title III, see Tables.

CODIFICATION

In subsecs. (a) and (d), "May 1, 1971" substituted for "the effective date of this section" and "the effective date of this part", respectively.

AMENDMENTS

2004—Subsec. (f). Pub. L. 108–447, which directed amendment of subsec. (f) of section 1088 of the Controlled Substances Import and Export Act by inserting "and control" after "the registration" and substituting "listed chemicals" for "list I chemicals under this section", was executed to subsec. (f) of this section, which is section 1008 of the Controlled Substances Import and Export Act, to reflect the probable intent of Congress.

1993—Subsec. (c). Pub. L. 103–200, §3(f)(1), designated existing provisions as par. (1) and added par. (2).

Subsec. (d)(3). Pub. L. 103–200, §3(f)(2)(A), inserted "or list I chemical or chemicals," after "substances,".

Subsec. (d)(6). Pub. L. 103–200, §3(f)(2)(B), inserted "or list I chemicals" after "controlled substances" wherever appearing.

Subsec. (e). Pub. L. 103–200, §3(f)(3), inserted reference to section 830 of this title.

Subsecs. (f) to (h). Pub. L. 103–200, §3(f)(4), inserted "or list I chemicals" after "controlled substances".

1986—Subsec. (e). Pub. L. 99–570 substituted "sections" for first reference to "section".

1984—Subsec. (b). Pub. L. 98–473, §524, substituted "Registration granted under this section shall not entitle a registrant to import or export controlled substances other than specified in the registration" for "Registration granted under subsection (a) of this section shall not entitle a registrant to import or export controlled substances in schedule I or II other than those specified in the registration".

Subsecs. (d) to (i). Pub. L. 98–473, §525, added subsec. (d), redesignated former subsec. (d) as (e) and struck out reference to section 824 of this title, and redesignated former subsecs. (e) to (h) as (f) to (i), respectively.

EFFECTIVE DATE OF 1993 AMENDMENT

Amendment by Pub. L. 103–200 effective on date that is 120 days after Dec. 17, 1993, see section 11 of Pub. L. 103–200, set out as a note under section 802 of this title.

§959. Possession, manufacture, or distribution of controlled substance

(a) Manufacture or distribution for purpose of unlawful importation

It shall be unlawful for any person to manufacture or distribute a controlled substance in schedule I or II or flunitrazepam or listed chemical—

(1) intending that such substance or chemical will be unlawfully imported into the United States or into waters within a distance of 12 miles of the coast of the United States; or

(2) knowing that such substance or chemical will be unlawfully imported into the United States or into waters within a distance of 12 miles of the coast of the United States.

(b) Possession, manufacture, or distribution by person on board aircraft

It shall be unlawful for any United States citizen on board any aircraft, or any person on board an aircraft owned by a United States citizen or registered in the United States, to—

(1) manufacture or distribute a controlled substance or listed chemical; or

(2) possess a controlled substance or listed chemical with intent to distribute.

(c) Acts committed outside territorial jurisdiction of United States; venue

This section is intended to reach acts of manufacture or distribution committed outside the territorial jurisdiction of the United States. Any person who violates this section shall be tried in the United States district court at the point of entry where such person enters the United States, or in the United States District Court for the District of Columbia.

(Pub. L. 91–513, title III, §1009, Oct. 27, 1970, 84 Stat. 1289; Pub. L. 99–570, title III, §3161(a), Oct. 27, 1986, 100 Stat. 3207–94; Pub. L. 104–237, title I, §102(a), (b), Oct. 3, 1996, 110 Stat. 3100; Pub. L. 104–305, §2(b)(2)(A), Oct. 13, 1996, 110 Stat. 3807.)

REFERENCES IN TEXT

Schedules I and II, referred to in subsec. (a), are set out in section 812(c) of this title.

AMENDMENTS

1996—Subsec. (a). Pub. L. 104–305 inserted "or flunitrazepam" after "schedule I or II" in introductory provisions.

Pub. L. 104–237, §102(a), inserted "or listed chemical" after "schedule I or II" in introductory provisions and "or chemical" after "substance" in pars. (1) and (2).

Subsec. (b). Pub. L. 104–237, §102(b), inserted "or listed chemical" after "controlled substance" in pars. (1) and (2).

1986—Pub. L. 99–570 designated first sentence as subsec. (a) and inserted "or into waters within a distance of 12 miles of the coast of the United States" in pars. (1) and (2), added subsec. (b), and designated last two sentences as subsec. (c).

§960. Prohibited acts A

(a) Unlawful acts

Any person who—

(1) contrary to section 952, 953, or 957 of this title, knowingly or intentionally imports or exports a controlled substance,

(2) contrary to section 955 of this title, knowingly or intentionally brings or possesses on board a vessel, aircraft, or vehicle a controlled substance, or

(3) contrary to section 959 of this title, manufactures, possesses with intent to distribute, or distributes a controlled substance,

shall be punished as provided in subsection (b) of this section.

(b) Penalties

(1) In the case of a violation of subsection (a) of this section involving—

(A) 1 kilogram or more of a mixture or substance containing a detectable amount of heroin;

(B) 5 kilograms or more of a mixture or substance containing a detectable amount of—

(i) coca leaves, except coca leaves and extracts of coca leaves from which cocaine, ecgonine, and derivatives of ecgonine or their salts have been removed;

(ii) cocaine, its salts, optical and geometric isomers, and salts or isomers;

(iii) ecgonine, its derivatives, their salts, isomers, and salts of isomers; or

(iv) any compound, mixture, or preparation which contains any quantity of any of the substances referred to in clauses (i) through (iii);

(C) 50 grams or more of a mixture or substance described in subparagraph (B) which contains cocaine base;

(D) 100 grams or more of phencyclidine (PCP) or 1 kilogram or more of a mixture or substance containing a detectable amount of phencyclidine (PCP);

(E) 10 grams or more of a mixture or substance containing a detectable amount of lysergic acid diethylamide (LSD);

(F) 400 grams or more of a mixture or substance containing a detectable amount of N-phenyl-N-[1-(2-phenylethyl)-4-piperidinyl] propanamide or 100 grams or more of a mixture or substance containing a detectable amount of any analogue of N-phenyl-N-[1-(2-phenylethyl)-4-piperidinyl] propanamide;

(G) 1000 kilograms or more of a mixture or substance containing a detectable amount of marihuana; or

(H) 50 grams or more of methamphetamine, its salts, isomers, and salts of its isomers or 500 grams or more of a mixture or substance containing a detectable amount of methamphetamine, its salts, isomers, or salts of its isomers.[1]

the person committing such violation shall be sentenced to a term of imprisonment of not less than 10 years and not more than life and if death or serious bodily injury results from the use of such substance shall be sentenced to a term of imprisonment of not less than 20 years and not more than life, a fine not to exceed the greater of that authorized in accordance with the provisions of title 18 or $4,000,000 if the defendant is an individual or $10,000,000 if the defendant is other than an individual, or both. If any person commits such a violation after a prior conviction for a felony drug offense has become final, such person shall be sentenced to a term of imprisonment of not less than 20 years and not more than life imprisonment and if death or serious bodily injury results from the use of such substance shall be sentenced to life imprisonment, a fine not to exceed the greater of twice that authorized in accordance with the provisions of title 18 or $8,000,000 if the defendant is an individual or $20,000,000 if the defendant is other than an individual, or both. Notwithstanding section 3583 of title 18, any sentence under this paragraph shall, in the absence of such a prior conviction, impose a term of supervised release of at least 5 years in addition to such term of imprisonment and shall, if there was such a prior conviction, impose a term of supervised release of at least 10 years in addition to such term of imprisonment. Notwithstanding any other provision of law, the court shall not place on probation or suspend the sentence of any person sentenced under this paragraph. No person sentenced under this paragraph shall be eligible for parole during the term of imprisonment imposed therein.

(2) In the case of a violation of subsection (a) of this section involving—

[1] So in original. The period probably should be a semicolon.

(A) 100 grams or more of a mixture or substance containing a detectable amount of heroin;

(B) 500 grams or more of a mixture or substance containing a detectable amount of—

(i) coca leaves, except coca leaves and extracts of coca leaves from which cocaine, ecgonine, and derivatives of ecgonine or their salts have been removed;

(ii) cocaine, its salts, optical and geometric isomers, and salts or isomers;

(iii) ecgonine, its derivatives, their salts, isomers, and salts of isomers; or

(iv) any compound, mixture, or preparation which contains any quantity of any of the substances referred to in clauses (i) through (iii);

(C) 5 grams or more of a mixture or substance described in subparagraph (B) which contains cocaine base;

(D) 10 grams or more of phencyclidine (PCP) or 100 grams or more of a mixture or substance containing a detectable amount of phencyclidine (PCP);

(E) 1 gram or more of a mixture or substance containing a detectable amount of lysergic acid diethylamide (LSD);

(F) 40 grams or more of a mixture or substance containing a detectable amount of N-phenyl-N-[1-(2-phenylethyl)-4-piperidinyl] propanamide or 10 grams or more of a mixture or substance containing a detectable amount of any analogue of N-phenyl-N-[1-(2-phenylethyl)-4-piperidinyl] propanamide;

(G) 100 kilograms or more of a mixture or substance containing a detectable amount of marihuana; or

(H) 5 grams or more of methamphetamine, its salts, isomers, and salts of its isomers or 50 grams or more of a mixture or substance containing a detectable amount of methamphetamine, its salts, isomers, or salts of its isomers.[1]

the person committing such violat ion shall be sentenced to a term of imprisonment of not less than 5 years and not more than 40 years and if death or serious bodily injury results from the use of such substance shall be sentenced to a term of imprisonment of not less than twenty years and not more than life, a fine not to exceed the greater of that authorized in accordance with the provisions of title 18 or $2,000,000 if the defendant is an individual or $5,000,000 if the defendant is other than an individual, or both. If any person commits such a violation after a prior conviction for a felony drug offense has become final, such person shall be sentenced to a term of imprisonment of not less than 10 years and not more than life imprisonment and if death or serious bodily injury results from the use of such substance shall be sentenced to life imprisonment, a fine not to exceed the greater of twice that authorized in accordance with the provisions of title 18 or $4,000,000 if the defendant is an individual or $10,000,000 if the defendant is other than an individual, or both. Notwithstanding section 3583 of title 18, any sentence imposed under this paragraph shall, in the absence of such a prior conviction, include a term of supervised release of at least 4 years in addition to such term of imprisonment and shall, if there was such a prior conviction, include a term of supervised release of at least 8 years in addition to such term of imprisonment. Notwithstanding any other provision of law, the court shall not place on probation or suspend the sentence of any person sentenced under this paragraph. No person sentenced under this paragraph shall be eligible for parole during the term of imprisonment imposed therein.

(3) In the case of a violation under subsection (a) of this section involving a controlled substance in schedule I or II, gamma hydroxybutyric acid (including when scheduled as an approved drug product for purposes of section 3(a)(1)(B) of the Hillory J. Farias and Samantha Reid Date-Rape Drug Prohibition Act of 2000), or flunitrazepam, the person committing such violation shall, except as provided in paragraphs (1), (2), and (4), be sentenced to a term of imprisonment of not more than 20 years and if death or serious bodily injury results from the use of such substance shall be sentenced to a term of imprisonment of not less than twenty years and not more than life, a fine not to exceed the greater of that authorized in accordance with the provisions of title 18 or $1,000,000 if the defendant is an individual or $5,000,000 if the defendant is other than an individual, or both. If any person commits such a violation after a prior conviction for a felony drug offense has become final, such person shall be sentenced to a term of imprisonment of not more than 30 years and if death or serious bodily injury results from the use of such substance shall be sentenced to life imprisonment, a fine not to exceed the greater of twice that authorized in accordance with the provisions of title 18 or $2,000,000 if the defendant is an individual or $10,000,000 if the defendant is other than an individual, or both. Notwithstanding section 3583 of title 18, any sentence imposing a term of imprisonment under this paragraph shall, in the absence of such a prior conviction, impose a term of supervised release of at least 3 years in addition to such term of imprisonment and shall, if there was such a prior conviction, impose a term of supervised release of at least 6 years in addition to such term of imprisonment. Notwithstanding the prior sentence, and notwithstanding any other provision of law, the court shall not place on probation or suspend the sentence of any person sentenced under the provisions of this paragraph which provide for a mandatory term of imprisonment if death or serious bodily injury results.

(4) In the case of a violation under subsection (a) of this section with respect to less than 50 kilograms of marihuana, except in the case of 100 or more marihuana plants regardless of weight, less than 10 kilograms of hashish, or less than one kilogram of hashish oil, the person committing such violation shall be sentenced in accordance with section 841(b)(1)(D) of this title.

(5) In the case of a violation of subsection (a) involving a controlled substance in schedule III, such person shall be sentenced in accordance with section 841(b)(1) of this title.

(6) In the case of a violation of subsection (a) involving a controlled substance in schedule IV, such person shall be sentenced in accordance with section 841(b)(2) of this title.

(7) In the case of a violation of subsection (a) involving a controlled substance in schedule V, such person shall be sentenced in accordance with section 841(b)(3) of this title.

(c) Repealed. Pub. L. 98–473, title II, § 225, formerly § 225(a), Oct. 12, 1984, 98 Stat. 2030, as amended by Pub. L. 99–570, title I, § 1005(c), Oct. 27, 1986, 100 Stat. 3207–6

(d) Penalty for importation or exportation

A person who knowingly or intentionally—

(1) imports or exports a listed chemical with intent to manufacture a controlled substance in violation of this subchapter or subchapter I of this chapter;

(2) exports a listed chemical in violation of the laws of the country to which the chemical is exported or serves as a broker or trader for an international transaction involving a listed chemical, if the transaction is in violation of the laws of the country to which the chemical is exported;

(3) imports or exports a listed chemical knowing, or having reasonable cause to believe, that the chemical will be used to manufacture a controlled substance in violation of this subchapter or subchapter I of this chapter;

(4) exports a listed chemical, or serves as a broker or trader for an international transaction involving a listed chemical, knowing, or having reasonable cause to believe, that the chemical will be used to manufacture a controlled substance in violation of the laws of the country to which the chemical is exported;

(5) imports or exports a listed chemical, with the intent to evade the reporting or recordkeeping requirements of section 971 of this title applicable to such importation or exportation by falsely representing to the Attorney General that the importation or exportation qualifies for a waiver of the 15-day notification requirement granted pursuant to paragraph (2) or (3) of section 971(f) of this title by misrepresenting the actual country of final destination of the listed chemical or the actual listed chemical being imported or exported;

(6) imports a listed chemical in violation of section 952 of this title, imports or exports such a chemical in violation of section 957 or 971 of this title, or transfers such a chemical in violation of section 971(d) of this title; or

(7) manufactures, possesses with intent to distribute, or distributes a listed chemical in violation of section 959 of this title.[2]

shall be fined in accordance with title 18, imprisoned not more than 20 years in the case of a violation of paragraph (1) or (3) involving a list I chemical or not more than 10 years in the case of a violation of this subsection other than a violation of paragraph (1) or (3) involving a list I chemical, or both.

(Pub. L. 91–513, title III, § 1010, Oct. 27, 1970, 84 Stat. 1290; Pub. L. 98–473, title II, §§ 225, formerly § 225(a), 504, Oct. 12, 1984, 98 Stat. 2030, 2070; Pub. L. 99–570, title I, §§ 1004(a), 1005(c), 1302, 1866(e), Oct. 27, 1986, 100 Stat. 3207–6, 3207–15, 3207–55; Pub. L. 100–690, title VI, §§ 6053(c), 6475, Nov. 18, 1988, 102 Stat. 4315, 4380; Pub. L. 101–647, title XII, § 1204, title XXXV, § 3599J, Nov. 29, 1990, 104 Stat. 4830, 4932; Pub. L. 103–200, §§ 4(b), 5(b), Dec. 17, 1993, 107 Stat. 2338, 2339; Pub. L. 103–322, title IX, § 90105(a), title XXXIII, § 330024(d)(2), Sept. 13, 1994, 108 Stat. 1987, 2151; Pub. L. 104–237, title I, § 102(c), title III, § 302(b), Oct. 3, 1996, 110 Stat. 3100, 3105; Pub. L. 104–305, § 2(b)(2)(B), (C), Oct. 13, 1996, 110 Stat. 3807; Pub. L. 105–277, div. E, § 2(b), Oct. 21, 1998, 112 Stat. 2681–759; Pub. L. 106–172, § 3(b)(2), Feb. 18, 2000, 114 Stat. 9; Pub. L. 107–273, div. B, title III, § 3005(b), Nov. 2, 2002, 116 Stat. 1806; Pub. L. 109–177, title VII, §§ 716(b)(1)(A), 717, Mar. 9, 2006, 120 Stat. 267; Pub. L. 110–425, § 3(i), Oct. 15, 2008, 122 Stat. 4832.)

REFERENCES IN TEXT

Schedules I, II, III, IV, and V, referred to in subsec. (b), are set out in section 812(c) of this title.

Section 3(a)(1)(B) of the Hillory J. Farias and Samantha Reid Date-Rape Prohibition Act of 2000, referred to in subsec. (b)(3), is section 3(a)(1)(B) of Pub. L. 106–172, which is set out in a note under section 812 of this title.

AMENDMENTS

2008—Subsec. (b)(3). Pub. L. 110–425, § 3(i)(3), struck out before period at end ", nor shall a person so sentenced be eligible for parole during the term of such a sentence".

Subsec. (b)(4). Pub. L. 110–425, § 3(i)(1), inserted "or" after "hashish,", struck out "or any quantity of a controlled substance in schedule III, IV, or V, (except a violation involving flunitrazepam and except a violation involving gamma hydroxybutyric acid)" after "hashish oil,", and substituted "sentenced in accordance with section 841(b)(1)(D) of this title" for "imprisoned not more than five years, or be fined not to exceed the greater of that authorized in accordance with the provisions of title 18 or $250,000 if the defendant is an individual or $1,000,000 if the defendant is other than an individual, or both. If a sentence under this paragraph provides for imprisonment, the sentence shall, notwithstanding section 3583 of title 18, in addition to such term of imprisonment, include (A) a term of supervised release of not less than two years if such controlled substance is in schedule I, II, III, or (B) a term of supervised release of not less than one year if such controlled substance is in schedule IV".

Subsec. (b)(5) to (7). Pub. L. 110–425, § 3(i)(2), added pars. (5) to (7).

2006—Subsec. (d)(5). Pub. L. 109–177, § 716(b)(1)(A), substituted "paragraph (2) or (3) of section 971(f) of this title" for "section 971(e)(2) or (3) of this title".

Subsec. (d)(6). Pub. L. 109–177, § 717, amended par. (6) generally. Prior to amendment, par. (6) read as follows: "imports or exports a listed chemical in violation of section 957 or 971 of this title; or".

2002—Subsec. (b)(1), (2). Pub. L. 107–273, § 3005(b)(1), substituted "Notwithstanding section 3583 of title 18, any sentence" for "Any sentence" in concluding provisions.

Subsec. (b)(3). Pub. L. 107–273, § 3005(b)(1), substituted "Notwithstanding section 3583 of title 18, any sentence" for "Any sentence".

Subsec. (b)(4). Pub. L. 107–273, § 3005(b)(2), inserted "notwithstanding section 3583 of title 18," before "in addition to such term of imprisonment".

2000—Subsec. (b)(3). Pub. L. 106–172, § 3(b)(2)(A), inserted "gamma hydroxybutyric acid (including when scheduled as an approved drug product for purposes of section 3(a)(1)(B) of the Hillory J. Farias and Samantha Reid Date-Rape Drug Prohibition Act of 2000)," after "schedule I or II," in first sentence.

Subsec. (b)(4). Pub. L. 106–172, § 3(b)(2)(B), substituted "flunitrazepam and except a violation involving gamma hydroxybutyric acid)" for "flunitrazepam)".

[2] So in original. The period probably should be a comma.

1998—Subsec. (b)(1)(H). Pub. L. 105–277, §2(b)(1), substituted "50 grams" and "500 grams" for "100 grams" and "1 kilogram", respectively.

Subsec. (b)(2)(H). Pub. L. 105–277, §2(b)(2), substituted "5 grams" and "50 grams" for "10 grams" and "100 grams", respectively.

1996—Subsec. (b)(3). Pub. L. 104–305, §2(b)(2)(B), inserted "or flunitrazepam," after "schedule I or II,".

Subsec. (b)(4). Pub. L. 104–305, §2(b)(2)(C), inserted "(except a violation involving flunitrazepam)" after "schedule III, IV, or V,".

Subsec. (d). Pub. L. 104–237, §302(b), in closing provisions, substituted "not more than 20 years in the case of a violation of paragraph (1) or (3) involving a list I chemical or not more than 10 years in the case of a violation of this subsection other than a violation of paragraph (1) or (3) involving a list I chemical," for "not more than 10 years,".

Subsec. (d)(7). Pub. L. 104–237, §102(c), added par. (7).

1994—Subsec. (b)(1), (2). Pub. L. 103–322, §90105(a), in sentence in concluding provisions beginning "If any person commits", substituted "a prior conviction for a felony drug offense has become final" for "one or more prior convictions for an offense punishable under this subsection, or for a felony under any other provision of this subchapter or subchapter I of this chapter or other law of a State, the United States, or a foreign country relating to narcotic drugs, marihuana, or depressant or stimulant substances, have become final".

Subsec. (b)(3). Pub. L. 103–322, §90105(a), in sentence beginning "If any person commits", substituted "a prior conviction for a felony drug offense has become final" for "one or more prior convictions for an offense punishable under this subsection, or for a felony under any other provision of this subchapter or subchapter I of this chapter or other law of a State, the United States or a foreign country relating to narcotic drugs, marihuana, or depressant or stimulant substances, have become final".

Subsec. (d)(5), (6). Pub. L. 103–322, §330024(d)(2), amended directory language of Pub. L. 103–200, §5(b)(3). See 1993 Amendment note below.

1993—Subsec. (d). Pub. L. 103–200, §5(b), as amended by Pub. L. 103–322, §330024(d)(2), added pars. (5) and (6).

Pub. L. 103–200, §4(b), amended subsec. (d) generally. Prior to amendment, subsec. (d) read as follows: "Any person who knowingly or intentionally—

"(1) imports or exports a listed chemical with intent to manufacture a controlled substance in violation of this subchapter or, in the case of an exportation, in violation of the law of the country to which the chemical is exported; or

"(2) imports or exports a listed chemical knowing, or having reasonable cause to believe, that the listed chemical will be used to manufacture a controlled substance in violation of this subchapter or, in the case of an exportation, in violation of the law of the country to which the chemical is exported;

shall be fined in accordance with title 18, or imprisoned not more than 10 years, or both."

1990—Subsec. (b)(1)(H). Pub. L. 101–647, §1204(a), added subpar. (H).

Subsec. (b)(2). Pub. L. 101–647, §3599J, substituted "supervised" for "suspervised" in two places in concluding provisions.

Subsec. (b)(2)(H). Pub. L. 101–647, §1204(b), added subpar. (H).

1988—Subsec. (a)(3). Pub. L. 100–690, §6475, substituted "manufactures, possesses with intent to distribute, or distributes a controlled substance" for "manufactures or distributes a controlled substance".

Subsec. (d). Pub. L. 100–690, §6053(c), added subsec. (d).

1986—Pub. L. 99–570, §1005(c), amended Pub. L. 98–473, §225. See 1984 Amendment note below.

Subsec. (b)(1), (2). Pub. L. 99–570, §1302(a)(2), added pars. (1) and (2) and struck out former pars. (1) and (2) which read as follows:

"(1) In the case of a violation under subsection (a) of this section involving—

"(A) 100 grams or more of a mixture or substance containing a detectable amount of a narcotic drug in schedule I or II other than a narcotic drug consisting of—

"(i) coca leaves;

"(ii) a compound, manufacture, salt, derivative, or preparation of coca leaves; or

"(iii) a substance chemically identical thereto;

"(B) a kilogram or more of any other narcotic drug in schedule I or II;

"(C) 500 grams or more of phencyclidine (PCP);

"(D) 5 grams or more of lysergic acid diethylamide (LSD);

the person committing such violation shall be imprisoned for not more than twenty years, or fined not more than $250,000, or both.

"(2) In the case of a violation under subsection (a) of this section with respect to a controlled substance in schedule I or II, the person committing such violation shall, except as provided in paragraphs (1) and (3), be imprisoned not more than fifteen years, or fined not more than $125,000, or both. If a sentence under this paragraph provides for imprisonment, the sentence shall include a special parole term of not less than three years in addition to such term of imprisonment."

Subsec. (b)(3). Pub. L. 99–570, §1302(a)(2), added par. (3). Former par. (3) redesignated (4).

Subsec. (b)(4). Pub. L. 99–570, §1302(a)(1), (3), (b)(2), (3), redesignated former par. (3) as (4), inserted "except in the case of 100 or more marihuana plants regardless of weight," and substituted "fined not to exceed the greater of that authorized in accordance with the provisions of title 18 or $250,000 if the defendant is an individual or $1,000,000 if the defendant is other than an individual" for "fined not more than $50,000".

Pub. L. 99–570, §§1302(b)(1), 1866(e), made identical amendment striking out ", except as provided in paragraph (4)" after "such violation shall".

Pub. L. 99–570, §1004(a), substituted "term of supervised release" for "special parole term" in two places.

Subsec. (c). Pub. L. 99–570, §1004(a), substituted "term of supervised release" for "special parole term" wherever appearing, effective Nov. 1, 1987, the effective date of the repeal of subsec. (c) by Pub. L. 98–473, §225. See 1984 Amendment note below.

1984—Subsec. (b). Pub. L. 98–473, §225(a), which directed amendment of this subsection effective Nov. 1, 1987 (see section 235(a)(1) of Pub. L. 98–473 set out as an Effective Date note under section 3551 of Title 18, Crimes and Criminal Procedure) was omitted in the general amendment of section 225 of Pub. L. 98–473 by Pub. L. 99–570, §1005(c).

Subsec. (b)(1). Pub. L. 98–473, §504(1), added par. (1). Former par. (1) redesignated (2).

Subsec. (b)(2). Pub. L. 98–473, §504(1), (2), redesignated former par. (1) as (2), inserted provisions excepting pars. (1) and (3), and substituted reference to controlled substance for reference to narcotic drug, and "$125,000" for "$25,000". Former par. (2) redesignated (3).

Subsec. (b)(3). Pub. L. 98–473, §504(1), (3), redesignated former par. (2) as (3) and substituted "less than 50 kilograms of marihuana, less than 10 kilograms of hashish, less than one kilogram of hashish oil, or any quantity of a controlled substance in schedule III, IV, or V, the person committing such violation shall, except as provided in paragraph (4)" for "a controlled substance other than a narcotic drug in schedule I or II, the person committing such violation shall", and "$50,000" for "$15,000".

Subsec. (c). Pub. L. 98–473, §225, as amended by Pub. L. 99–570, §1005(c), struck out subsec. (c) which related to special parole terms imposed under this section or section 962 of this title. Notwithstanding directory language that the amendment be made to "Section 1515 of the Controlled Substances Import and Export Act (21 U.S.C. 960)", the amendment was executed to this section as the probable intent of Congress.

Effective Date of 2008 Amendment

Amendment by Pub. L. 110–425 effective 180 days after Oct. 15, 2008, except as otherwise provided, see section 3(j) of Pub. L. 110–425, set out as a note under section 802 of this title.

EFFECTIVE DATE OF 1994 AMENDMENT

Amendment by section 330024(d)(2) of Pub. L. 103–322 effective 120 days after Dec. 17, 1993, see section 330024(f) of Pub. L. 103–322, set out as a note under section 802 of this title.

EFFECTIVE DATE OF 1993 AMENDMENT

Amendment by Pub. L. 103–200 effective on date that is 120 days after Dec. 17, 1993, see section 11 of Pub. L. 103–200, set out as a note under section 802 of this title.

EFFECTIVE DATE OF 1988 AMENDMENT

Amendment by section 6053(c) of Pub. L. 100–690 effective 120 days after Nov. 18, 1988, see section 6061 of Pub. L. 100–690, set out as a note under section 802 of this title.

EFFECTIVE DATE OF 1986 AMENDMENT

Amendment by section 1004(a) of Pub. L. 99–570 effective on date of taking effect of section 3583 of Title 18, Crimes and Criminal Procedure (Nov. 1, 1987), see section 1004(b) of Pub. L. 99–570 set out as a note under section 841 of this title.

EFFECTIVE DATE OF 1984 AMENDMENT

Amendment by section 225 of Pub. L. 98–473 effective Nov. 1, 1987, and applicable only to offenses committed after the taking effect of such amendment, see section 235(a)(1) of Pub. L. 98–473, set out as an Effective Date note under section 3551 of Title 18, Crimes and Criminal Procedure.

§960a. Foreign terrorist organizations, terrorist persons and groups

(a) Prohibited acts

Whoever engages in conduct that would be punishable under section 841(a)[1] of this title if committed within the jurisdiction of the United States, or attempts or conspires to do so, knowing or intending to provide, directly or indirectly, anything of pecuniary value to any person or organization that has engaged or engages in terrorist activity (as defined in section 1182(a)(3)(B) of title 8) or terrorism (as defined in section 2656f(d)(2) of title 22), shall be sentenced to a term of imprisonment of not less than twice the minimum punishment under section 841(b)(1),[1] and not more than life, a fine in accordance with the provisions of title 18, or both. Notwithstanding section 3583 of title 18, any sentence imposed under this subsection shall include a term of supervised release of at least 5 years in addition to such term of imprisonment.

(b) Jurisdiction

There is jurisdiction over an offense under this section if—

(1) the prohibited drug activity or the terrorist offense is in violation of the criminal laws of the United States;

(2) the offense, the prohibited drug activity, or the terrorist offense occurs in or affects interstate or foreign commerce;

(3) an offender provides anything of pecuniary value for a terrorist offense that causes or is designed to cause death or serious bodily injury to a national of the United States while that national is outside the United States, or substantial damage to the property of a legal entity organized under the laws of the United States (including any of its States, districts, commonwealths, territories, or possessions) while that property is outside of the United States;

(4) the offense or the prohibited drug activity occurs in whole or in part outside of the United States (including on the high seas), and a perpetrator of the offense or the prohibited drug activity is a national of the United States or a legal entity organized under the laws of the United States (including any of its States, districts, commonwealths, territories, or possessions); or

(5) after the conduct required for the offense occurs an offender is brought into or found in the United States, even if the conduct required for the offense occurs outside the United States.

(c) Proof requirements

To violate subsection (a), a person must have knowledge that the person or organization has engaged or engages in terrorist activity (as defined in section 1182(a)(3)(B) of title 8) or terrorism (as defined in section 2656f(d)(2) of title 22).

(d) Definition

As used in this section, the term "anything of pecuniary value" has the meaning given the term in section 1958(b)(1) of title 18.

(Pub. L. 91–513, title III, §1010A, as added Pub. L. 109–177, title I, §122, Mar. 9, 2006, 120 Stat. 225.)

REFERENCES IN TEXT

Section 841, referred to in the original in subsec. (a), probably should have been a reference to section 401 of Pub. L. 91–513, which is classified to section 841 of this title. Pub. L. 91–513 does not contain a section 841.

§961. Prohibited acts B

Any person who violates section 954 of this title or fails to notify the Attorney General of an importation or exportation under section 971 of this title shall be subject to the following penalties:

(1) Except as provided in paragraph (2), any such person shall, with respect to any such violation, be subject to a civil penalty of not more than $25,000. Sections 842(c)(1) and (c)(3) of this title shall apply to any civil penalty assessed under this paragraph.

(2) If such a violation is prosecuted by an information or indictment which alleges that the violation was committed knowingly or intentionally and the trier of fact specifically finds that the violation was so committed, such person shall be sentenced to imprisonment for not more than one year or a fine of not more than $25,000 or both.

(Pub. L. 91–513, title III, §1011, Oct. 27, 1970, 84 Stat. 1290; Pub. L. 100–690, title VI, §6053(d), Nov. 18, 1988, 102 Stat. 4316.)

AMENDMENTS

1988—Pub. L. 100–690 inserted "or fails to notify the Attorney General of an importation or exportation under section 971 of this title".

EFFECTIVE DATE OF 1988 AMENDMENT

Amendment by Pub. L. 100–690 effective 120 days after Nov. 18, 1988, see section 6061 of Pub. L. 100–690, set out as a note under section 802 of this title.

[1] See References in Text note below.

§ 962. Second or subsequent offenses

(a) Term of imprisonment and fine

Any person convicted of any offense under this subchapter is, if the offense is a second or subsequent offense, punishable by a term of imprisonment twice that otherwise authorized, by twice the fine otherwise authorized, or by both. If the conviction is for an offense punishable under section 960(b) of this title, and if it is the offender's second or subsequent offense, the court shall impose, in addition to any term of imprisonment and fine, twice the term of supervised release otherwise authorized.

(b) Determination of status

For purposes of this section, a person shall be considered convicted of a second or subsequent offense if, prior to the commission of such offense, one or more prior convictions of such person for a felony drug offense have become final.

(c) Procedures applicable

Section 851 of this title shall apply with respect to any proceeding to sentence a person under this section.

(Pub. L. 91–513, title III, § 1012, Oct. 27, 1970, 84 Stat. 1290; Pub. L. 98–473, title II, §§ 225(b), 505, Oct. 12, 1984, 98 Stat. 2030, 2070; Pub. L. 99–570, title I, §§ 1004(a), 1005(c), Oct. 27, 1986, 100 Stat. 3207–6; Pub. L. 103–322, title IX, § 90105(b), Sept. 13, 1994, 108 Stat. 1988.)

AMENDMENTS

1994—Subsec. (b). Pub. L. 103–322 substituted "one or more prior convictions of such person for a felony drug offense have become final" for "one or more prior convictions of him for a felony under any provision of this subchapter or subchapter I of this chapter or other law of a State, the United States, or a foreign country relating to narcotic drugs, marihuana, or depressant or stimulant drugs, have become final".

1986—Subsec. (a). Pub. L. 99–570, § 1005(c), amended Pub. L. 98–473, § 225. See 1984 Amendment note below.

Pub. L. 99–570, § 1004(a), substituted "term of supervised release" for "special parole term".

1984—Subsec. (a). Pub. L. 98–473, § 225(b), which directed amendment of this section effective Nov. 1, 1987 (see section 235(a)(1) of Pub. L. 98–473 set out as an Effective Date note under section 3551 of Title 18, Crimes and Criminal Procedure) was omitted in the general amendment of section 225 of Pub. L. 98–473 by Pub. L. 99–570, § 1005(c).

Subsec. (b). Pub. L. 98–473, § 505, inserted references to laws of a State or of a foreign country.

EFFECTIVE DATE OF 1986 AMENDMENT

Amendment by section 1004(a) of Pub. L. 99–570 effective on date of taking effect of section 3583 of Title 18, Crimes and Criminal Procedure (Nov. 1, 1987), see section 1004(b) of Pub. L. 99–570 set out as a note under section 841 of this title.

§ 963. Attempt and conspiracy

Any person who attempts or conspires to commit any offense defined in this subchapter shall be subject to the same penalties as those prescribed for the offense, the commission of which was the object of the attempt or conspiracy.

(Pub. L. 91–513, title III, § 1013, Oct. 27, 1970, 84 Stat. 1291; Pub. L. 100–690, title VI, § 6470(a), Nov. 18, 1988, 102 Stat. 4377.)

AMENDMENTS

1988—Pub. L. 100–690 substituted "shall be subject to the same penalties as those prescribed for the offense" for "is punishable by imprisonment or fine or both which may not exceed the maximum punishment prescribed for the offense".

§ 964. Additional penalties

Any penalty imposed for violation of this subchapter shall be in addition to, and not in lieu of, any civil or administrative penalty or sanction authorized by law.

(Pub. L. 91–513, title III, § 1014, Oct. 27, 1970, 84 Stat. 1291.)

§ 965. Applicability of part E of subchapter I

Part E of subchapter I of this chapter shall apply with respect to functions of the Attorney General (and of officers and employees of the Bureau of Narcotics and Dangerous Drugs) under this subchapter, to administrative and judicial proceedings under this subchapter, and to violations of this subchapter, to the same extent that such part applies to functions of the Attorney General (and such officers and employees) under subchapter I of this chapter, to such proceedings under subchapter I of this chapter, and to violations of subchapter I of this chapter. For purposes of the application of this section to section 880 or 881 of this title, any reference in such section 880 or 881 of this title to "this subchapter" shall be deemed to be a reference to this subchapter, any reference to section 823 of this title shall be deemed to be a reference to section 958 of this title, and any reference to section 822(d) of this title shall be deemed to be a reference to section 957(b)(2) of this title.

(Pub. L. 91–513, title III, § 1015, Oct. 27, 1970, 84 Stat. 1291; Pub. L. 95–633, title III, § 301(b), Nov. 10, 1978, 92 Stat. 3778.)

AMENDMENTS

1978—Pub. L. 95–633 inserted "or 881" after "880" wherever appearing.

TRANSFER OF FUNCTIONS

For abolition of Bureau of Narcotics and Dangerous Drugs, including Office of Director thereof, and creation of a single comprehensive agency for enforcement of drug laws by Reorg. Plan No. 2 of 1973, eff. July 1, 1973, 38 F.R. 15932, 87 Stat. 1091, see note set out under section 881 of this title.

§ 966. Authority of Secretary of the Treasury

Nothing in this chapter shall derogate from the authority of the Secretary of the Treasury under the customs and related laws.

(Pub. L. 91–513, title III, § 1016, Oct. 27, 1970, 84 Stat. 1291.)

REFERENCES IN TEXT

This chapter, referred to in text, was in the original "this Act", meaning Pub. L. 91–513, Oct. 27, 1970, 84 Stat. 1236, as amended. For complete classification of this Act to the Code, see Short Title note set out under section 801 of this title and Tables.

The customs laws, referred to in text, are classified generally to Title 19, Customs Duties.

§ 967. Smuggling of controlled substances; investigations; oaths; subpenas; witnesses; evidence; production of records; territorial limits; fees and mileage of witnesses

For the purpose of any investigation which, in the opinion of the Secretary of the Treasury, is necessary and proper to the enforcement of section 545 of title 18 (relating to smuggling goods into the United States) with respect to any controlled substance (as defined in section 802 of this title), the Secretary of the Treasury may administer oaths and affirmations, subpena witnesses, compel their attendance, take evidence, and require the production of records (including books, papers, documents and tangible things which constitute or contain evidence) relevant or material to the investigation. The attendance of witnesses and the production of records may be required from any place within the customs territory of the United States, except that a witness shall not be required to appear at any hearing distant more than 100 miles from the place where he was served with subpena. Witnesses summoned by the Secretary shall be paid the same fees and mileage that are paid witnesses in the courts of the United States. Oaths and affirmations may be made at any place subject to the jurisdiction of the United States.

(Aug. 11, 1955, ch. 800, §1, 69 Stat. 684; Pub. L. 91–513, title III, §1102(t), Oct. 27, 1970, 84 Stat. 1294.)

CODIFICATION

Section was not enacted as part of the Comprehensive Drug Abuse Prevention and Control Act of 1970 which comprises this chapter.

Section was formerly classified to section 1034 of Title 31 prior to the general revision and enactment of Title 31, Money and Finance, by Pub. L. 97–258, §1, Sept. 13, 1982, 96 Stat. 877.

Section was also formerly classified to section 198a of this title.

AMENDMENTS

1970—Pub. L. 91–513 substituted "section 545 of title 18 (relating to smuggling goods into the United States) with respect to any controlled substance (as defined in section 802 of this title)" for "the laws of the United States relating to narcotic drugs and marihuana" and substituted the customs territory of the United States for any State or any territory or other place subject to the jurisdiction of the United States is the defined area from within which the attendance of witnesses and the production of records may be required, and struck out provisions making the discretion of the Secretary of the Treasury the determinative factor as to what is relevant or material to the investigation.

EFFECTIVE DATE OF 1970 AMENDMENT

Amendment by Pub. L. 91–513 effective on first day of seventh calendar month that begins after Oct. 26, 1970, see 1105(a) of Pub. L. 91–513, set out as an Effective Date note under section 951 of this title.

SAVINGS PROVISION

Prosecutions for any violation of law occurring, and civil seizures or forfeitures and injunctive proceedings commenced, prior to the effective date of amendment of this section by section 1102 of Pub. L. 91–513 not to be affected or abated by reason thereof, see section 1103 of Pub. L. 91–513, set out as a note under sections 171 to 174 of this title.

§968. Service of subpena; proof of service

A subpena of the Secretary of the Treasury may be served by any person designated in the subpena to serve it. Service upon a natural person may be made by personal delivery of the subpena to him. Service may be made upon a domestic or foreign corporation or upon a partnership or other unincorporated association which is subject to suit under a common name, by delivering the subpena to an officer, a managing or general agent, or to any other agent authorized by appointment or by law to receive service of process. The affidavit of the person serving the subpena entered on a true copy thereof by the person serving it shall be proof of service.

(Aug. 11, 1955, ch. 800, §2, 69 Stat. 685.)

CODIFICATION

Section was not enacted as part of the Comprehensive Drug Abuse Prevention and Control Act of 1970 which comprises this chapter.

Section was formerly classified to section 1035 of Title 31 prior to the general revision and enactment of Title 31, Money and Finance, by Pub. L. 97–258, §1, Sept. 13, 1982, 96 Stat. 877.

Section was also formerly classified to section 198b of this title.

§969. Contempt proceedings

In case of contumacy by, or refusal to obey a subpena issued to, any person, the Secretary of the Treasury may invoke the aid of any court of the United States within the jurisdiction of which the investigation is carried on or of which the subpenaed person is an inhabitant, carries on business or may be found, to compel compliance with the subpena of the Secretary of the Treasury. The court may issue an order requiring the subpenaed person to appear before the Secretary of the Treasury there to produce records, if so ordered, or to give testimony touching the matter under investigation. Any failure to obey the order of the court may be punished by the court as a contempt thereof. All process in any such case may be served in the judicial district whereof the subpenaed person is an inhabitant or wherever he may be found.

(Aug. 11, 1955, ch. 800, §3, 69 Stat. 685.)

CODIFICATION

Section was not enacted as part of the Comprehensive Drug Abuse Prevention and Control Act of 1970 which comprises this chapter.

Section was formerly classified to section 1036 of Title 31 prior to the general revision and enactment of Title 31, Money and Finance, by Pub. L. 97–258, §1, Sept. 13, 1982, 96 Stat. 877.

Section was also formerly classified to section 198c of this title.

§970. Criminal forfeitures

Section 853 of this title, relating to criminal forfeitures, shall apply in every respect to a violation of this subchapter punishable by imprisonment for more than one year.

(Pub. L. 91–513, title III, §1017, as added Pub. L. 98–473, title II, §307, Oct. 12, 1984, 98 Stat. 2051.)

§971. Notification, suspension of shipment, and penalties with respect to importation and exportation of listed chemicals

(a) Notification prior to transaction

Each regulated person who imports or exports a listed chemical shall notify the Attorney General of the importation or exportation not later than 15 days before the transaction is to take place.

(b) Regular customers or importers

(1) The Attorney General shall provide by regulation for circumstances in which the requirement of subsection (a) of this section does not apply to a transaction between a regulated person and a regular customer or to a transaction that is an importation by a regular importer. At the time of any importation or exportation constituting a transaction referred to in the preceding sentence, the regulated person shall notify the Attorney General of the transaction.

(2) The regulations under this subsection shall provide that the initial notification under subsection (a) of this section with respect to a customer of a regulated person or to an importer shall, upon the expiration of the 15-day period, qualify the customer as a regular customer or the importer as a regular importer, unless the Attorney General otherwise notifies the regulated person in writing.

(c) Suspension of importation or exportation; disqualification of regular customers or importers; hearing

(1) The Attorney General may order the suspension of any importation or exportation of a listed chemical (other than a regulated transaction to which the requirement of subsection (a) of this section does not apply by reason of subsection (b) of this section) or may disqualify any regular customer or regular importer on the ground that the chemical may be diverted to the clandestine manufacture of a controlled substance (without regard to the form of the chemical that may be diverted, including the diversion of a finished drug product to be manufactured from bulk chemicals to be transferred). From and after the time when the Attorney General provides written notice of the order (including a statement of the legal and factual basis for the order) to the regulated person, the regulated person may not carry out the transaction.

(2) Upon written request to the Attorney General, a regulated person to whom an order applies under paragraph (1) is entitled to an agency hearing on the record in accordance with subchapter II of chapter 5 of title 5. The hearing shall be held on an expedited basis and not later than 45 days after the request is made, except that the hearing may be held at a later time, if so requested by the regulated person.

(d) Information required in notice; updated notice for change in circumstances

(1)(A) Information provided in a notice under subsection (a) or (b) shall include the name of the person to whom the importer or exporter involved intends to transfer the listed chemical involved, and the quantity of such chemical to be transferred.

(B) In the case of a notice under subsection (b) submitted by a regular importer, if the transferee identified in the notice is not a regular customer, such importer may not transfer the listed chemical until after the expiration of the 15-day period beginning on the date on which the notice is submitted to the Attorney General.

(C) After a notice under subsection (a) or (b) is submitted to the Attorney General, if circumstances change and the importer or exporter will not be transferring the listed chemical to the transferee identified in the notice, or will be transferring a greater quantity of the chemical than specified in the notice, the importer or exporter shall update the notice to identify the most recent prospective transferee or the most recent quantity or both (as the case may be) and may not transfer the listed chemical until after the expiration of the 15-day period beginning on the date on which the update is submitted to the Attorney General, except that such 15-day restriction does not apply if the prospective transferee identified in the update is a regular customer. The preceding sentence applies with respect to changing circumstances regarding a transferee or quantity identified in an update to the same extent and in the same manner as such sentence applies with respect to changing circumstances regarding a transferee or quantity identified in the original notice under subsection (a) or (b).

(D) In the case of a transfer of a listed chemical that is subject to a 15-day restriction under subparagraph (B) or (C), the transferee involved shall, upon the expiration of the 15-day period, be considered to qualify as a regular customer, unless the Attorney General otherwise notifies the importer or exporter involved in writing.

(2) With respect to a transfer of a listed chemical with which a notice or update referred to in paragraph (1) is concerned:

(A) The Attorney General, in accordance with the same procedures as apply under subsection (c)(2)—

(i) may order the suspension of the transfer of the listed chemical by the importer or exporter involved, except for a transfer to a regular customer, on the ground that the chemical may be diverted to the clandestine manufacture of a controlled substance (without regard to the form of the chemical that may be diverted, including the diversion of a finished drug product to be manufactured from bulk chemicals to be transferred), subject to the Attorney General ordering such suspension before the expiration of the 15-day period referred to in paragraph (1) with respect to the importation or exportation (in any case in which such a period applies); and

(ii) may, for purposes of clause (i) and paragraph (1), disqualify a regular customer on such ground.

(B) From and after the time when the Attorney General provides written notice of the order under subparagraph (A) (including a statement of the legal and factual basis for the order) to the importer or exporter, the importer or exporter may not carry out the transfer.

(3) For purposes of this subsection:

(A) The terms "importer" and "exporter" mean a regulated person who imports or exports a listed chemical, respectively.

(B) The term "transfer", with respect to a listed chemical, includes the sale of the chemical.

(C) The term "transferee" means a person to whom an importer or exporter transfers a listed chemical.

(e) Broker or trader for international transaction in listed chemical

A person located in the United States who is a broker or trader for an international transaction in a listed chemical that is a regulated transaction solely because of that person's involvement as a broker or trader shall, with respect to that transaction, be subject to all of the notification, reporting, recordkeeping, and other requirements placed upon exporters of listed chemicals by this subchapter and subchapter I of this chapter.

(f) Application of notification requirement to exports of listed chemical; waiver

(1) The Attorney General may by regulation require that the 15-day notification requirement of subsection (a) of this section apply to all exports of a listed chemical to a specified country, regardless of the status of certain customers in such country as regular customers, if the Attorney General finds that such notification is necessary to support effective chemical diversion control programs or is required by treaty or other international agreement to which the United States is a party.

(2) The Attorney General may by regulation waive the 15-day notification requirement for exports of a listed chemical to a specified country if the Attorney General determines that such notification is not required for effective chemical diversion control. If the notification requirement is waived, exporters of the listed chemical shall be required to submit to the Attorney General reports of individual exportations or periodic reports of such exportation of the listed chemical, at such time or times and containing such information as the Attorney General shall establish by regulation.

(3) The Attorney General may by regulation waive the 15-day notification requirement for the importation of a listed chemical if the Attorney General determines that such notification is not necessary for effective chemical diversion control. If the notification requirement is waived, importers of the listed chemical shall be required to submit to the Attorney General reports of individual importations or periodic reports of the importation of the listed chemical, at such time or times and containing such information as the Attorney General shall establish by regulation.

(g) Return declaration

Within 30 days after a transaction covered by this section is completed, the importer or exporter shall send the Attorney General a return declaration containing particulars of the transaction, including the date, quantity, chemical, container, name of transferees, and such other information as the Attorney General may specify in regulations. For importers, a single return declaration may include the particulars of both the importation and distribution. If the importer has not distributed all chemicals imported by the end of the initial 30-day period, the importer shall file supplemental return declarations no later than 30 days from the date of any further distribution, until the distribution or other disposition of all chemicals imported pursuant to the import notification or any update are accounted for.

(h) Importation and distribution of ephedrine, pseudoephedrine, or phenylpropanolamine

(1) With respect to a regulated person importing ephedrine, pseudoephedrine, or phenylpropanolamine (referred to in this section as an "importer"), a notice of importation under subsection (a) or (b) shall include all information known to the importer on the chain of distribution of such chemical from the manufacturer to the importer.

(2) For the purpose of preventing or responding to the diversion of ephedrine, pseudoephedrine, or phenylpropanolamine for use in the illicit production of methamphetamine, the Attorney General may, in the case of any person who is a manufacturer or distributor of such chemical in the chain of distribution referred to in paragraph (1) (which person is referred to in this subsection as a "foreign-chain distributor"), request that such distributor provide to the Attorney General information known to the distributor on the distribution of the chemical, including sales.

(3) If the Attorney General determines that a foreign-chain distributor is refusing to cooperate with the Attorney General in obtaining the information referred to in paragraph (2), the Attorney General may, in accordance with procedures that apply under subsection (c), issue an order prohibiting the importation of ephedrine, pseudoephedrine, or phenylpropanolamine in any case in which such distributor is part of the chain of distribution for such chemical. Not later than 60 days prior to issuing the order, the Attorney General shall publish in the Federal Register a notice of intent to issue the order. During such 60-day period, imports of the chemical with respect to such distributor may not be restricted under this paragraph.

(Pub. L. 91–513, title III, §1018, as added Pub. L. 100–690, title VI, §6053(a), Nov. 18, 1988, 102 Stat. 4314; amended Pub. L. 103–200, §§4(a), 5(a), 9(b), Dec. 17, 1993, 107 Stat. 2338–2340; Pub. L. 103–322, title XXXIII, §330024(c), Sept. 13, 1994, 108 Stat. 2150; Pub. L. 109–177, title VII, §§716(a), (b)(1)(B), 721, Mar. 9, 2006, 120 Stat. 265, 267.)

AMENDMENTS

2006—Subsec. (b)(1). Pub. L. 109–177, §716(a)(1), substituted "or to a transaction that is an importation by a regular importer" for "or to an importation by a regular importer".

Subsec. (c)(1). Pub. L. 109–177, §716(b)(1)(B), inserted "(without regard to the form of the chemical that may be diverted, including the diversion of a finished drug product to be manufactured from bulk chemicals to be transferred)" after "manufacture of a controlled substance".

Subsecs. (d) to (f). Pub. L. 109–177, §716(a)(2), (3), added subsec. (d) and redesignated former subsecs. (d) and (e) as (e) and (f), respectively.

Subsec. (g). Pub. L. 109–177, §716(a)(4), added subsec. (g).

Subsec. (h). Pub. L. 109–177, §721, added subsec. (h).

1994—Subsecs. (b)(1), (2), (c)(1). Pub. L. 103–322, §330024(c)(2), made technical amendment to directory language of Pub. L. 103–200, §9(b). See 1993 Amendment notes below.

Subsec. (e). Pub. L. 103–322, §330024(c)(1), made technical amendment to directory language of Pub. L. 103–200, §5(a). See 1993 Amendment note below.

1993—Subsec. (b)(1). Pub. L. 103–200, §9(b)(1)(A), as amended by Pub. L. 103–322, §330024(c)(2), substituted "to an importation by a regular importer" for "regular supplier of the regulated person".

Subsec. (b)(2). Pub. L. 103–200, § 9(b)(1)(B), as amended by Pub. L. 103–322, § 330024(c)(2), substituted "a customer of a regulated person or to an importer" for "a customer or supplier of a regulated person" and "the importer as a regular importer" for "regular supplier".

Subsec. (c)(1). Pub. L. 103–200, § 9(b)(2), as amended by Pub. L. 103–322, § 330024(c)(2), substituted "regular importer" for "regular supplier".

Subsec. (d). Pub. L. 103–200, § 4(a), added subsec. (d).

Subsec. (e). Pub. L. 103–200, § 5(a), as amended by Pub. L. 103–322, § 330024(c)(1), added subsec. (e).

EFFECTIVE DATE OF 1994 AMENDMENT

Amendment by Pub. L. 103–322 effective 120 days after Dec. 17, 1993, see section 330024(f) of Pub. L. 103–322, set out as a note under section 802 of this title.

EFFECTIVE DATE OF 1993 AMENDMENT

Amendment by Pub. L. 103–200 effective on date that is 120 days after Dec. 17, 1993, see section 11 of Pub. L. 103–200, set out as a note under section 802 of this title.

EFFECTIVE DATE

Section 6053(b) of Pub. L. 100–690 provided that:

"(1) Not later than 45 days after the date of the enactment of this Act [Nov. 18, 1988], the Attorney General shall forward to the Director of the Office of Management and Budget proposed regulations required by the amendment made by subsection (a) [enacting this section].

"(2) Not later than 55 days after the date of the enactment of this Act, the Director of the Office of Management and Budget shall—

"(A) review such proposed regulations of the Attorney General; and

"(B) forward any comments and recommendations for modifications to the Attorney General.

"(3) Not later than 60 days after the date of the enactment of this Act, the Attorney General shall publish the proposed final regulations required by the amendment made by subsection (a).

"(4) Not later than 120 days after the date of the enactment of this Act, the Attorney General shall promulgate final regulations required by the amendment made by subsection (a).

"(5) Subsection (a) of section 1018 of the Controlled Substances Import and Export Act [subsection (a) of this section], as added by subsection (a) of this section, shall take effect 90 days after the promulgation of the final regulations under paragraph (4).

"(6) Each regulated person shall provide to the Attorney General the identity of any regular customer or regular supplier of the regulated person not later than 30 days after the promulgation of the final regulations under paragraph (4). Not later than 60 days after the end of such 30-day period, each regular customer and regular supplier so identified shall be a regular customer or regular supplier for purposes of any applicable exception from the requirement of subsection (a) of such section 1018, unless the the [sic] Attorney General otherwise notifies the regulated person in writing."

Section effective 120 days after Nov. 18, 1988 [except subsec. (a), see above], see section 6061 of Pub. L. 100–690, set out as an Effective Date of 1988 Amendment note under section 802 of this title.

EXCEPTION FOR IODINE TO IMPORTATION AND EXPORTATION REQUIREMENTS FOR LISTED CHEMICALS

Pub. L. 104–237, title II, § 204(b), Oct. 3, 1996, 110 Stat. 3102, provided that:

"(1) Iodine shall not be subject to the requirements for listed chemicals provided in section 1018 of the Controlled Substances Import and Export Act (21 U.S.C. 971).

"(2) EFFECT OF EXCEPTION.—The exception made by paragraph (1) shall not limit the authority of the Attorney General to impose the requirements for listed chemicals provided in section 1018 of the Controlled Substances Import and Export Act (21 U.S.C. 971)."

CHAPTER 14—ALCOHOL AND DRUG ABUSE EDUCATIONAL PROGRAMS AND ACTIVITIES

§§ 1001 to 1007. Repealed. Pub. L. 97–35, title V, § 587(a)(3), Aug. 13, 1981, 95 Stat. 480

Section 1001, Pub. L. 91–527, § 2, Dec. 3, 1970, 84 Stat. 1385; Pub. L. 93–422, § 2(b), Sept. 21, 1974, 88 Stat. 1154; Pub. L. 95–336, § 2, Aug. 4, 1978, 92 Stat. 451, set forth Congressional declaration of purpose for Alcohol and Drug Abuse Education Act.

Section 1002, Pub. L. 91–527, § 3, Dec. 3, 1970, 84 Stat. 1386; Pub. L. 93–422, § 2(c), Sept. 21, 1974, 88 Stat. 1155; Pub. L. 95–336, §§ 3, 4, Aug. 4, 1978, 92 Stat. 451, 452; S. Res. 30, Mar. 7, 1979; Pub. L. 96–88, title III, § 301(a)(1), (2)(Q), (b)(1), title V, § 507, Oct. 17, 1979, 93 Stat. 677, 678, 692, set forth grant and contract authority, etc., for projects and programs.

Section 1003, Pub. L. 91–527, § 4, Dec. 3, 1970, 84 Stat. 1387; Pub. L. 93–422, § 2(d), Sept. 21, 1974, 88 Stat. 1157; Pub. L. 96–88, title III, § 301(a)(1), title V, § 507, Oct. 17, 1979, 93 Stat. 677, 692, related to recordkeeping requirements, and access to and inspection of records.

Section 1004, Pub. L. 91–527, § 5, Dec. 3, 1970, 84 Stat. 1388; Pub. L. 93–422, § 2(e), Sept. 21, 1974, 88 Stat. 1157; Pub. L. 96–88, title V, § 508(i), Oct. 17, 1979, 93 Stat. 693, related to technical assistance to local agencies, etc.

Section 1005, Pub. L. 91–527, § 6, Dec. 3, 1970, 84 Stat. 1388, related to nature of payments.

Section 1006, Pub. L. 91–527, § 7, Dec. 3, 1970, 84 Stat. 1388, related to utilization of services and facilities of Federal agencies and public and private agencies and institutions.

Section 1007, Pub. L. 91–527, § 8, Dec. 3, 1970, 84 Stat. 1388; Pub. L. 93–422, § 2(f), Sept. 21, 1974, 88 Stat. 1157; Pub. L. 95–336, § 5, Aug. 4, 1978, 92 Stat. 453; Pub. L. 96–88, title III, § 301(a)(1), (2)(Q), title V, § 507, Oct. 17, 1979, 93 Stat. 677, 678, 692, defined "Secretary" and "State".

EFFECTIVE DATE OF REPEAL

Repeal effective Oct. 1, 1982, see section 587(a) of Pub. L. 97–35, set out as section 3863(a) of Title 20, Education.

CHAPTER 15—EGG PRODUCTS INSPECTION

§ 1031. Congressional statement of findings

Eggs and egg products are an important source of the Nation's total supply of food, and are used in food in various forms. They are consumed throughout the Nation and the major portion thereof moves in interstate or foreign commerce. It is essential, in the public interest, that the health and welfare of consumers be protected by the adoption of measures prescribed herein for assuring that eggs and egg products distributed to them and used in products consumed by them are wholesome, otherwise not adulterated, and properly labeled and packaged. Lack of effective regulation for the handling or disposition of unwholesome, otherwise adulterated, or improperly labeled or packaged egg products and certain qualities of eggs is injurious to the public welfare and destroys markets for wholesome, not adulterated, and properly labeled and packaged eggs and egg products and results in sundry losses to producers and processors, as well as injury to consumers. Unwholesome, otherwise adulterated, or improperly labeled or packaged products can be sold at lower prices and compete unfairly with the wholesome, not adulterated, and properly labeled and packaged products, to the detriment of consumers and the public generally. It is hereby found that all egg products and the qualities of eggs which are regulated under this chapter are either in interstate or foreign commerce, or substantially affect such commerce, and that regulation by the Secretary of Agriculture and the Secretary of Health and Human Services, and cooperation by the States and other jurisdictions, as contemplated by this chapter, are appropriate to prevent and eliminate burdens upon such commerce, to effectively regulate such commerce, and to protect the health and welfare of consumers.

(Pub. L. 91–597, §2, Dec. 29, 1970, 84 Stat. 1620; Pub. L. 96–88, title V, §509(b), Oct. 17, 1979, 93 Stat. 695.)

References in Text

This chapter, referred to in text, was in the original "this Act", meaning Pub. L. 91–597, Dec. 29, 1970, 84 Stat. 1620, as amended, which enacted this chapter, amended sections 633 and 636 of Title 15, Commerce and Trade, and enacted provisions set out as notes under this section. For complete classification of this Act to the Code, see Short Title note set out below and Tables.

Change of Name

"Secretary of Health and Human Services" substituted for "Secretary of Health, Education, and Welfare" in text pursuant to section 509(b) of Pub. L. 96–88, which is classified to section 3508(b) of Title 20, Education.

Effective Date

Section 29 of Pub. L. 91–597 provided that: "The provisions of this Act [enacting this chapter, amending sections 633 and 636 of Title 15, Commerce and Trade, and enacting provisions set out as notes under this section] with respect to egg products shall take effect six months after enactment [Dec. 29, 1970]. Otherwise, this Act shall take effect eighteen months after enactment."

Short Title

Section 1 of Pub. L. 91–597 provided: "That this Act [enacting this chapter, amending sections 633 and 636 of Title 15, Commerce and Trade, and enacting provisions set out as notes under this section] may be cited as the 'Egg Products Inspection Act'."

Maintenance of Eggs at Proper Temperature

Pub. L. 102–237, title X, §1012(a), Dec. 13, 1991, 105 Stat. 1899, provided that:

"(1) Findings.—Congress finds that—

"(A) food borne illness is a serious health problem;

"(B) its incidence can be reduced through proper handling of food; and

"(C) eggs are perishable and therefore are particularly susceptible to supporting microbial growth if proper temperature controls are not maintained.

"(2) Purposes.—It is the purpose of this section [amending sections 1034, 1037, 1041, 1042, 1046, and 1052 of this title and enacting provisions set out as a note under section 1034 of this title] to prescribe the temperature at which eggs are maintained in order to reduce the potential for harmful microbial growth to protect the health and welfare of consumers."

§ 1032. Congressional declaration of policy

It is hereby declared to be the policy of the Congress to provide for the inspection of certain egg products, restrictions upon the disposition of certain qualities of eggs, and uniformity of standards for eggs, and otherwise regulate the processing and distribution of eggs and egg products as hereinafter prescribed to prevent the movement or sale for human food, of eggs and egg products which are adulterated or misbranded or otherwise in violation of this chapter.

(Pub. L. 91–597, §3, Dec. 29, 1970, 84 Stat. 1621.)

§ 1033. Definitions

For purposes of this chapter—

(a) The term "adulterated" applies to any egg or egg product under one or more of the following circumstances—

(1) if it bears or contains any poisonous or deleterious substance which may render it injurious to health; but in case the substance is not an added substance, such article shall not be considered adulterated under this clause if the quantity of such substance in or on such article does not ordinarily render it injurious to health;

(2)(A) if it bears or contains any added poisonous or added deleterious substance (other than one which is (i) a pesticide chemical in or on a raw agricultural commodity; (ii) a food additive; or (iii) a color additive) which may, in the judgment of the Secretary, make such article unfit for human food;

(B) if it is, in whole or in part, a raw agricultural commodity and such commodity bears or contains a pesticide chemical which is unsafe within the meaning of section 346a of this title;

(C) if it bears or contains any food additive which is unsafe within the meaning of section 348 of this title;

(D) if it bears or contains any color additive which is unsafe within the meaning of section 379e of this title: *Provided*, That an article which is not otherwise deemed adulterated under clause (B), (C), or (D) shall nevertheless be deemed adulterated if use of the pesticide chemical, food additive, or color additive, in or on such article, is prohibited by regulations of the Secretary in official plants;

(3) if it consists in whole or in part of any filthy, putrid, or decomposed substance, or if it is otherwise unfit for human food;

(4) if it has been prepared, packaged, or held under insanitary conditions whereby it may have become contaminated with filth, or whereby it may have been rendered injurious to health;

(5) if it is an egg which has been subjected to incubation or the product of any egg which has been subjected to incubation;

(6) if its container is composed, in whole or in part, of any poisonous or deleterious substance which may render the contents injurious to health;

(7) if it has been intentionally subjected to radiation, unless the use of the radiation was in conformity with a regulation or exemption in effect pursuant to section 348 of this title; or

(8) if any valuable constituent has been in whole or in part omitted or abstracted therefrom; or if any substance has been substituted, wholly or in part therefor; or if damage or inferiority has been concealed in any manner; or if any substance has been added thereto or mixed or packed therewith so as to increase its bulk or weight, or reduce its quality or strength, or make it appear better or of greater value than it is.

(b) The term "capable of use as human food" shall apply to any egg or egg product, unless it is denatured, or otherwise identified, as required by regulations prescribed by the Secretary to deter its use as human food.

(c) The term "commerce" means interstate, foreign, or intrastate commerce.

(d) The term "container" or "package" includes any box, can, tin, plastic, or other receptacle, wrapper, or cover.

(1) The term "immediate container" means any consumer package; or any other container in which egg products, not consumer packaged, are packed.

(2) The term "shipping container" means any container used in packaging a product packed in an immediate container.

(e) The term "egg handler" means any person who engages in any business in commerce which involves buying or selling any eggs (as a poultry producer or otherwise), or processing any egg products, or otherwise using any eggs in the preparation of human food.

(f) The term "egg product" means any dried, frozen, or liquid eggs, with or without added ingredients, excepting products which contain eggs only in a relatively small proportion or historically have not been, in the judgment of the Secretary, considered by consumers as products of the egg food industry, and which may be exempted by the Secretary under such conditions as he may prescribe to assure that the egg ingredients are not adulterated and such products are not represented as egg products.

(g) The term "egg" means the shell egg of the domesticated chicken, turkey, duck, goose, or guinea.

(1) The term "check" means an egg that has a broken shell or crack in the shell but has its shell membranes intact and contents not leaking.

(2) The term "clean and sound shell egg" means any egg whose shell is free of adhering dirt or foreign material and is not cracked or broken.

(3) The term "dirty egg" means an egg that has a shell that is unbroken and has adhering dirt or foreign material.

(4) The term "incubator reject" means an egg that has been subjected to incubation and has been removed from incubation during the hatching operations as infertile or otherwise unhatchable.

(5) The term "inedible" means eggs of the following descriptions: black rots, yellow rots, white rots, mixed rots (addled eggs), sour eggs, eggs with green whites, eggs with stuck yolks, moldy eggs, musty eggs, eggs showing blood rings, and eggs containing embryo chicks (at or beyond the blood ring stage).

(6) The term "leaker" means an egg that has a crack or break in the shell and shell membranes to the extent that the egg contents are exposed or are exuding or free to exude through the shell.

(7) The term "loss" means an egg that is unfit for human food because it is smashed or broken so that its contents are leaking; or overheated, frozen, or contaminated; or an incubator reject; or because it contains a bloody white, large meat spots, a large quantity of blood, or other foreign material.

(8) The term "restricted egg" means any check, dirty egg, incubator reject, inedible, leaker, or loss.

(h) The term "Fair Packaging and Labeling Act" [15 U.S.C. 1451 et seq.] means the Act so entitled, approved November 3, 1966 (80 Stat. 1296), and Acts amendatory thereof or supplementary thereto.

(i) The term "Federal Food, Drug, and Cosmetic Act" [21 U.S.C. 301 et seq.] means the Act so entitled, approved June 25, 1938 (52 Stat. 1040), and Acts amendatory thereof or supplementary thereto.

(j) The term "inspection" means the application of such inspection methods and techniques as are deemed necessary by the responsible Secretary to carry out the provisions of this chapter.

(k) The term "inspector" means:

(1) any employee or official of the United States Government authorized to inspect eggs

or egg products under the authority of this chapter; or

(2) any employee or official of the government of any State or local jurisdiction authorized by the Secretary to inspect eggs or egg products under the authority of this chapter, under an agreement entered into between the Secretary and the appropriate State or other agency.

(*l*) The term "misbranded" shall apply to egg products which are not labeled and packaged in accordance with the requirements prescribed by regulations of the Secretary under section 1036 of this title.

(m) The term "official certificate" means any certificate prescribed by regulations of the Secretary for issuance by an inspector or other person performing official functions under this chapter.

(n) The term "official device" means any device prescribed or authorized by the Secretary for use in applying any official mark.

(*o*) The term "official inspection legend" means any symbol prescribed by regulations of the Secretary showing that egg products were inspected in accordance with this chapter.

(p) The term "official mark" means the official inspection legend or any other symbol prescribed by regulations of the Secretary to identify the status of any article under this chapter.

(q) The term "official plant" means any plant, as determined by the Secretary, at which inspection of the processing of egg products is maintained by the Department of Agriculture under the authority of this chapter.

(r) The term "official standards" means the standards of quality, grades, and weight classes for eggs, in effect upon the effective date of this chapter, or as thereafter amended, under the Agricultural Marketing Act of 1946 (60 Stat. 1087, as amended; 7 U.S.C. 1621 et seq.).

(s) The term "pasteurize" means the subjecting of each particle of egg products to heat or other treatments to destroy harmful viable micro-organisms by such processes as may be prescribed by regulations of the Secretary.

(t) The term "person" means any individual, partnership, corporation, association, or other business unit.

(u) The terms "pesticide chemical," "food additive," "color additive," and "raw agricultural commodity" shall have the same meaning for purposes of this chapter as under the Federal Food, Drug, and Cosmetic Act [21 U.S.C. 301 et seq.].

(v) The term "plant" means any place of business where egg products are processed.

(w) The term "processing" means manufacturing egg products, including breaking eggs or filtering, mixing, blending, pasteurizing, stabilizing, cooling, freezing, drying, or packaging egg products.

(x) The term "Secretary" means the Secretary of Agriculture or his delegate.

(y) The term "State" means any State of the United States, the Commonwealth of Puerto Rico, the Virgin Islands of the United States, and the District of Columbia.

(z) The term "United States" means the States.

(Pub. L. 91–597, §4, Dec. 29, 1970, 84 Stat. 1621; Pub. L. 102–571, title I, §107(15), Oct. 29, 1992, 106 Stat. 4499.)

REFERENCES IN TEXT

The Fair Packaging and Labeling Act, referred to in subsec. (h), is Pub. L. 89–755, Nov. 3, 1966, 80 Stat. 1296, as amended, which is classified generally to chapter 39 (§1451 et seq.) of Title 15, Commerce and Trade. For complete classification of this Act to the Code, see Short Title note set out under section 1451 of Title 15 and Tables.

The Federal Food, Drug, and Cosmetic Act, referred to in subsecs. (i) and (u), is act June 25, 1938, ch. 675, 52 Stat. 1040, as amended, which is classified generally to chapter 9 (§301 et seq.) of this title. For complete classification of this Act to the Code, see section 301 of this title and Tables.

The effective date of this chapter, referred to in subsec. (r), means the effective date of Pub. L. 91–597. For such effective date, see Effective Date note set out under section 1031 of this title.

The Agricultural Marketing Act of 1946, referred to in subsec. (r), is title II of act Aug. 14, 1946, ch. 966, 60 Stat. 1087, as amended, which is classified generally to chapter 38 (§1621 et seq.) of Title 7, Agriculture. For complete classification of this Act to the Code, see Short Title note set out under section 1621 of Title 7 and Tables.

AMENDMENTS

1992—Subsec. (a)(2)(D). Pub. L. 102–571 substituted "379e" for "376".

§ 1034. Inspection of egg products

(a) Processing operations and establishments subject to coverage; rules and regulations

For the purpose of preventing the entry into or flow or movement in commerce of, or the burdening of commerce by, any egg product which is capable of use as human food and is misbranded or adulterated, the Secretary shall, whenever processing operations are being conducted, cause continuous inspection to be made, in accordance with the regulations promulgated under this chapter, of the processing of egg products, in each plant processing egg products for commerce, unless exempted under section 1044 of this title. Without restricting the application of the preceding sentence to other kinds of establishments within its provisions, any food manufacturing establishment, institution, or restaurant which uses any eggs that do not meet the requirements of section 1044(a)(1) of this title in the preparation of any articles for human food shall be deemed to be a plant processing egg products, with respect to such operations.

(b) Authority of Secretary to retain, segregate, and reinspect eggs and egg products

The Secretary, at any time, shall cause such retention, segregation, and reinspection as he deems necessary of eggs and egg products capable of use as human food in each official plant.

(c) Condemnation of adulterated products; destruction or reprocessing; procedure upon appeal from determination of adulteration

Eggs and egg products found to be adulterated at official plants shall be condemned and, if no appeal be taken from such determination of condemnation, such articles shall be destroyed for human food purposes under the supervision of an inspector: *Provided*, That articles which may by reprocessing be made not adulterated need not be condemned and destroyed if so reprocessed under the supervision of an inspector and thereafter found to be not adulterated. If an appeal be taken from such determination, the eggs or egg products shall be appropriately marked and segregated pending completion of an appeal inspection, which appeal shall be at the cost of the appellant if the Secretary determines that the appeal is frivolous. If the determination of condemnation is sustained, the eggs or egg products shall be destroyed for human food purposes under the supervision of an inspector.

(d) Inspection of business premises, facilities, inventory, operations, and records of egg handlers; inspection of records and inventory of others required to keep records; authority of Secretary of Health and Human Services to inspect food manufacturing establishments, institutions, and restaurants; access to places of business

The Secretary shall cause such other inspections to be made of the business premises, facilities, inventory, operations, and records of egg handlers, and the records and inventory of other persons required to keep records under section 1040 of this title, as he deems appropriate (and in the case of shell egg packers, packing eggs for the ultimate consumer, at least once each calendar quarter) to assure that only eggs fit for human food are used for such purpose, and otherwise to assure compliance by egg handlers and other persons with the requirements of section 1037 of this title, except that the Secretary of Health and Human Services shall cause such inspections to be made as he deems appropriate to assure compliance with such requirements at food manufacturing establishments, institutions, and restaurants, other than plants processing egg products. Representatives of said Secretaries shall be afforded access to all such places of business for purposes of making the inspections provided for in this chapter.

(e) Refrigeration and labeling requirements

(1) Subject to paragraphs (2), (3), and (4), the Secretary shall make such inspections as the Secretary considers appropriate of a facility of an egg handler (including a transport vehicle) to determine if shell eggs destined for the ultimate consumer—

(A) are being held under refrigeration at an ambient temperature of no greater than 45 degrees Fahrenheit after packing; and

(B) contain labeling that indicates that refrigeration is required.

(2) In the case of a shell egg packer packing eggs for the ultimate consumer, the Secretary shall make an inspection in accordance with paragraph (1) at least once each calendar quarter.

(3) The Secretary of Health and Human Services shall cause such inspections to be made as the Secretary considers appropriate to ensure compliance with the requirements of paragraph (1) at food manufacturing establishments, institutions, and restaurants, other than plants packing eggs.

(4) The Secretary shall not make an inspection as provided in paragraph (1) on any egg handler with a flock of not more than 3,000 layers.

(5) A representative of the Secretary and the Secretary of Health and Human Services shall be afforded access to a place of business referred to in this subsection, including a transport vehicle, for purposes of making an inspection required under this subsection.

(Pub. L. 91–597, §5, Dec. 29, 1970, 84 Stat. 1624; Pub. L. 96–88, title V, §509(b), Oct. 17, 1979, 93 Stat. 695; Pub. L. 102–237, title X, §1012(b), Dec. 13, 1991, 105 Stat. 1899.)

AMENDMENTS

1991—Subsec. (e). Pub. L. 102–237 added subsec. (e).

CHANGE OF NAME

"Secretary of Health and Human Services" substituted for "Secretary of Health, Education, and Welfare" in subsec. (d) pursuant to section 509(b) of Pub. L. 96–88, which is classified to section 3508(b) of Title 20, Education.

EFFECTIVE DATE OF 1991 AMENDMENT

Section 1012(h) of Pub. L. 102–237 provided that: "This section and the amendments made by this section [amending this section and sections 1037, 1041, 1042, 1046, and 1052 of this title and enacting provisions set out as a note under section 1031 of this title] shall become effective 12 months after the Secretary of Agriculture promulgates final regulations implementing this section and the amendments." [Final regulations were promulgated Aug. 20, 1998, effective Aug. 27, 1999. See 63 F.R. 45663.]

§1035. Sanitary operating practices in official plants

(a) Premises, facilities, and equipment

Each official plant shall be operated in accordance with such sanitary practices and shall have such premises, facilities, and equipment as are required by regulations promulgated by the Secretary to effectuate the purposes of this chapter, including requirements for segregation and disposition of restricted eggs.

(b) Refusal by Secretary to inspect nonconforming plants

The Secretary shall refuse to render inspection to any plant whose premises, facilities, or equipment, or the operation thereof, fail to meet the requirements of this section.

(Pub. L. 91–597, §6, Dec. 29, 1970, 84 Stat. 1625.)

§1036. Pasteurization and labeling of egg products at official plants

(a) Contents of label

Egg products inspected at any official plant under the authority of this chapter and found to be not adulterated shall be pasteurized before they leave the official plant, except as otherwise permitted by regulations of the Secretary, and shall at the time they leave the official plant, bear in distinctly legible form on their shipping containers or immediate containers, or both, when required by regulations of the Secretary, the official inspection legend and official plant number, of the plant where the products were processed, and such other information as the Secretary may require by regulations to describe the products adequately and to assure that they will not have false or misleading labeling.

(b) False or misleading or use of nonapproved labeling or containers; determination by Secretary; procedures applicable; appeal

No labeling or container shall be used for egg products at official plants if it is false or misleading or has not been approved as required by the regulations of the Secretary. If the Secretary has reason to believe that any labeling or the size or form of any container in use or proposed for use with respect to egg products at any official plant is false or misleading in any particular, he may direct that such use be withheld unless the labeling or container is modified in such manner as he may prescribe so that it will not be false or misleading. If the person using or proposing to use the labeling or container does not accept the determination of the Secretary, such person may request a hearing, but the use of the labeling or container shall, if the Secretary so directs, be withheld pending hearing and final determination by the Secretary. Any such determination by the Secretary shall be conclusive unless, within thirty days after receipt of notice of such final determination, the person adversely affected thereby appeals to the United States court of appeals for the circuit in which such person has its principal place of business or to the United States Court of Appeals for the District of Columbia Circuit. The provisions of section 194 of title 7,[1] shall be applicable to appeals taken under this section.

(Pub. L. 91–597, § 7, Dec. 29, 1970, 84 Stat. 1625.)

§ 1037. Prohibited acts

(a)(1) No person shall buy, sell, or transport, or offer to buy or sell, or offer or receive for transportation, in any business in commerce any restricted eggs, capable of use as human food, except as authorized by regulations of the Secretary under such conditions as he may prescribe to assure that only eggs fit for human food are used for such purpose.

(2) No egg handler shall possess with intent to use, or use, any restricted eggs in the preparation of human food for commerce except that such eggs may be so possessed and used when authorized by regulations of the Secretary under such conditions as he may prescribe to assure that only eggs fit for human food are used for such purpose.

(b)(1) No person shall process any egg products for commerce at any plant except in compliance with the requirements of this chapter.

(2) No person shall buy, sell, or transport, or offer to buy or sell, or offer or receive for transportation, in commerce any egg products required to be inspected under this chapter unless they have been so inspected and are labeled and packaged in accordance with the requirements of section 1036 of this title.

(3) No operator of any official plant shall fail to comply with any requirements of section 1035(a) of this title or the regulations thereunder.

(4) No operator of any official plant shall allow any egg products to be moved from such plant if they are adulterated or misbranded and capable of use as human food.

[1] So in original. The comma probably should not appear.

(c) No egg handler shall possess any eggs after the eggs have been packed into a container that is destined for the ultimate consumer unless the eggs are stored and transported under refrigeration at an ambient temperature of no greater than 45 degrees Fahrenheit, as prescribed by rules and regulations promulgated by the Secretary.

(d) No person shall violate any provision of section 1039, 1040 or 1046 of this title.

(e) No person shall—

(1) manufacture, cast, print, lithograph, or otherwise make any device containing any official mark or simulation thereof, or any label bearing any such mark or simulation, or any form of official certificate or simulation thereof, except as authorized by the Secretary;

(2) forge or alter any official device, mark, or certificate;

(3) without authorization from the Secretary, use any official device, mark, or certificate, or simulation thereof, or detach, deface, or destroy any official device or mark; or use any labeling or container ordered to be withheld from use under section 1036 of this title after final judicial affirmance of such order or expiration of the time for appeal if no appeal is taken under said section;

(4) contrary to the regulations prescribed by the Secretary, fail to use, or to detach, deface, or destroy any official device, mark, or certificate;

(5) knowingly possess, without promptly notifying the Secretary or his representative, any official device or any counterfeit, simulated, forged, or improperly altered official certificate or any device or label, or any eggs or egg products bearing any counterfeit, simulated, forged, or improperly altered official mark;

(6) knowingly make any false statement in any shipper's certificate or other nonofficial or official certificate provided for in the regulations prescribed by the Secretary;

(7) knowingly represent that any article has been inspected or exempted, under this chapter, when, in fact, it has, respectively, not been so inspected or exempted; and

(8) refuse access, at any reasonable time, to any representative of the Secretary of Agriculture or the Secretary of Health and Human Services, to any plant or other place of business subject to inspection under any provisions of this chapter.

(f) No person, while an official or employee of the United States Government or any State or local governmental agency, or thereafter, shall use to his own advantage, or reveal other than to the authorized representatives of the United States Government or any State or other government in their official capacity, or as ordered by a court in a judicial proceeding, any information acquired under the authority of this chapter concerning any matter which is entitled to protection as a trade secret.

(Pub. L. 91–597, § 8, Dec. 29, 1970, 84 Stat. 1626; Pub. L. 96–88, title V, § 509(b), Oct. 17, 1979, 93 Stat. 695; Pub. L. 102–237, title X, § 1012(c), Dec. 13, 1991, 105 Stat. 1899.)

AMENDMENTS

1991—Subsecs. (c) to (f). Pub. L. 102–237 added subsec. (c) and redesignated former subsecs. (c) to (e) as (d) to (f), respectively.

CHANGE OF NAME

"Secretary of Health and Human Services" substituted for "Secretary of Health, Education, and Welfare" in subsec. (e)(8) pursuant to section 509(b) of Pub. L. 96–88, which is classified to section 3508(b) of Title 20, Education.

EFFECTIVE DATE OF 1991 AMENDMENT

Amendment by Pub. L. 102–237 effective 12 months after promulgation of final implementing regulations, see section 1012(h) of Pub. L. 102–237, set out as a note under section 1034 of this title.

§ 1038. Cooperation with appropriate State and other governmental agencies; utilization of employees; reimbursement

The Secretary shall, whenever he determines that it would effectuate the purposes of this chapter, cooperate with appropriate State and other governmental agencies, in carrying out any provisions of this chapter. In carrying out the provisions of this chapter, the Secretary may conduct such examinations, investigations, and inspections as he determines practicable through any officer or employee of any such agency commissioned by him for such purpose. The Secretary shall reimburse the States and other agencies for the costs incurred by them in such cooperative programs.

(Pub. L. 91–597, § 9, Dec. 29, 1970, 84 Stat. 1627.)

§ 1039. Eggs and egg products not intended for use as human food; inspection; denaturing or otherwise identifying

Inspection shall not be provided under this chapter at any plant for the processing of any egg products which are not intended for use as human food, but such articles, prior to their offer for sale or transportation in commerce, shall be denatured or otherwise identified as prescribed by regulations of the Secretary to deter their use for human food. No person shall buy, sell, or transport or offer to buy or sell, or offer or receive for transportation, in commerce, any restricted eggs or egg products which are not intended for use as human food unless they are denatured or otherwise identified as required by the regulations of the Secretary.

(Pub. L. 91–597, § 10, Dec. 29, 1970, 84 Stat. 1627.)

§ 1040. Recordkeeping requirements; persons required to maintain records; scope of disclosure; access to records

For the purpose of enforcing the provisions of this chapter and the regulations promulgated thereunder, all persons engaged in the business of transporting, shipping, or receiving any eggs or egg products in commerce or holding such articles so received, and all egg handlers, shall maintain such records showing, for such time and in such form and manner, as the Secretary of Agriculture or the Secretary of Health and Human Services may prescribe, to the extent that they are concerned therewith, the receipt, delivery, sale, movement, and disposition of all eggs and egg products handled by them, and shall, upon the request of a duly authorized representative of either of said Secretaries, permit him at reasonable times to have access to and to copy all such records.

(Pub. L. 91–597, § 11, Dec. 29, 1970, 84 Stat. 1627; Pub. L. 96–88, title V, § 509(b), Oct. 17, 1979, 93 Stat. 695.)

CHANGE OF NAME

"Secretary of Health and Human Services" substituted in text for "Secretary of Health, Education, and Welfare" pursuant to section 509(b) of Pub. L. 96–88, which is classified to section 3508(b) of Title 20, Education.

§ 1041. Enforcement provisions

(a) Violations of section 1037; term of imprisonment and fine

Any person who commits any offense prohibited by section 1037 of this title shall upon conviction be subject to imprisonment for not more than one year, or a fine of not more than $5,000, or both such imprisonment and fine, but if such violation involves intent to defraud, or any distribution or attempted distribution of any article that is known to be adulterated (except as defined in section 1033(a)(8) of this title), such person shall be subject to imprisonment for not more than three years or a fine of not more than $10,000, or both.

(b) Persons preventing enforcement of chapter; term of imprisonment and fine

Any person who forcibly assaults, resists, opposes, impedes, intimidates, or interferes with any person while engaged in or on account of the performance of his official duties under this chapter shall be fined not more than $5,000 or imprisoned not more than three years or both. Whoever, in the commission of any such act, uses a deadly or dangerous weapon, shall be fined not more than $10,000 or imprisoned not more than ten years, or both. Whoever kills any person while engaged in or on account of the performance of his official duties under this chapter shall be punished as provided under sections 1111 and 1112 of title 18.

(c) Civil penalty

(1)(A) Except as otherwise provided in this subsection, any person who violates any provision of this chapter or any regulation issued under this chapter, other than a violation for which a criminal penalty has been imposed under this chapter, may be assessed a civil penalty by the Secretary of not more than $5,000 for each such violation. Each violation to which this subparagraph applies shall be considered a separate offense.

(B) No penalty shall be assessed against any person under this subsection unless the person is given notice and opportunity for a hearing on the record before the Secretary in accordance with sections 554 and 556 of title 5.

(C) The amount of the civil penalty imposed under this subsection—

(i) shall be assessed by the Secretary, by written order, taking into account the gravity of the violation, degree of culpability, and history of prior offenses; and

(ii) may be reviewed only as provided in paragraph (2).

(2)(A) The determination and order of the Secretary under this subsection shall be final and conclusive unless the person against whom such a violation is found under paragraph (1) files an application for judicial review within 30 days after service of the order in the United States court of appeals for the circuit in which the person has its principal place of business or in the United States Court of Appeals for the District of Columbia Circuit.

(B) Judicial review of any such order shall be based on the record on which the determination and order are based.

(C) If the court determines that additional evidence needs to be taken, the court shall order the hearing to be reopened for this purpose in such manner and on such terms and conditions as the court considers proper. The Secretary may modify the findings of the Secretary as to the facts, or make new findings, on the basis of the additional evidence so taken.

(3) If any person fails to pay an assessment of a civil penalty after the penalty has become a final and unappealable order, or after the appropriate court of appeals has entered a final judgment in favor of the Secretary, the Secretary shall refer the matter to the Attorney General. The Attorney General shall institute a civil action to recover the amount assessed in an appropriate district court of the United States. In the collection action, the validity and appropriateness of the Secretary's order imposing the civil penalty shall not be subject to review.

(4) All penalties collected under this subsection shall be paid into the Treasury of the United States.

(5) The Secretary may compromise, modify, or remit, with or without conditions, any civil penalty assessed under this subsection.

(6) Paragraph (1) shall not apply to an official plant.

(d) Scope of liability for violations of section 1037

When construing or enforcing the provisions of section 1037 of this title, the act, omission, or failure of any person acting for or employed by any individual, partnership, corporation, or association within the scope of his employment or office shall in every case be deemed the act, omission, or failure of such individual, partnership, corporation, or association, as well as of such person.

(e) Penalties applicable to carriers or warehousemen

No carrier or warehouseman shall be subject to the penalties of this chapter, other than the penalties for violation of section 1040 of this title or subsection (c) of this section, by reason of his receipt, carriage, holding, or delivery, in the usual course of business, as a carrier or warehouseman of eggs or egg products owned by another person unless the carrier or warehouseman has knowledge, or is in possession of facts which would cause a reasonable person to believe that such eggs or egg products were not eligible for transportation under, or were otherwise in violation of, this chapter, or unless the carrier or warehouseman refuses to furnish on request of a representative of the Secretary the name and address of the person from whom he received such eggs or egg products and copies of all documents, if there be any, pertaining to the delivery of the eggs or egg products to, or by, such carrier or warehouseman.

(Pub. L. 91–597, §12, Dec. 29, 1970, 84 Stat. 1628; Pub. L. 102–237, title X, §1012(d), Dec. 13, 1991, 105 Stat. 1899.)

AMENDMENTS

1991—Subsec. (a). Pub. L. 102–237, §1012(d)(1), (2), substituted "$5,000" for "$1,000" in first sentence, and redesignated last sentence, relating to scope of liability for violations of section 1037 of this title, as subsec. (d).

Subsec. (b). Pub. L. 102–237, §1012(d)(4), redesignated subsec. (c) as (b). Former subsec. (b) redesignated (e).

Subsec. (c). Pub. L. 102–237, §1012(d)(5), added subsec. (c). Former subsec. (c) redesignated (b).

Subsec. (d). Pub. L. 102–237, §1012(d)(2), designated last sentence of subsec. (a), relating to scope of liability for violations of section 1037 of this title, as subsec. (d).

Subsec. (e). Pub. L. 102–237, §1012(d)(3), redesignated subsec. (b) as (e).

EFFECTIVE DATE OF 1991 AMENDMENT

Amendment by Pub. L. 102–237 effective 12 months after promulgation of final implementing regulations, see section 1012(h) of Pub. L. 102–237, set out as a note under section 1034 of this title.

§ 1042. Reporting of violation to United States attorney for institution of criminal proceedings; procedure; presentation of views

Before any violation of this chapter is reported by the Secretary of Agriculture or Secretary of Health and Human Services to any United States attorney for institution of a criminal proceeding, the person against whom such proceeding is contemplated shall be given reasonable notice of the alleged violation and opportunity to present his views orally or in writing with regard to such contemplated proceeding. Nothing in this chapter shall be construed as requiring the Secretary of Agriculture or Secretary of Health and Human Services to report for criminal prosecution violations of this chapter whenever he believes that the public interest will be adequately served and compliance with this chapter obtained by a suitable written notice of warning or an action to assess civil penalties.

(Pub. L. 91–597, §13, Dec. 29, 1970, 84 Stat. 1628; Pub. L. 96–88, title V, §509(b), Oct. 17, 1979, 93 Stat. 695; Pub. L. 102–237, title X, §1012(e), Dec. 13, 1991, 105 Stat. 1900.)

AMENDMENTS

1991—Pub. L. 102–237 inserted "or an action to assess civil penalties" before period at end.

CHANGE OF NAME

"Secretary of Health and Human Services" substituted in text for "Secretary of Health, Education, and Welfare" pursuant to section 509(b) of Pub. L. 96–88, which is classified to section 3508(b) of Title 20, Education.

EFFECTIVE DATE OF 1991 AMENDMENT

Amendment by Pub. L. 102–237 effective 12 months after promulgation of final implementing regulations, see section 1012(h) of Pub. L. 102–237, set out as a note under section 1034 of this title.

§ 1043. Rules and regulations; administration and enforcement

The Secretary shall promulgate such rules and regulations as he deems necessary to carry out the purposes or provisions of this chapter, and shall be responsible for the administration and enforcement of this chapter except as otherwise provided in section 1034(d) of this title.

(Pub. L. 91–597, § 14, Dec. 29, 1970, 84 Stat. 1629.)

§ 1044. Exemption of certain activities

(a) Regulation for exemptions

The Secretary may, by regulation and under such conditions and procedures as he may prescribe, exempt from specific provisions of this chapter—

(1) the sale, transportation, possession, or use of eggs which contain no more restricted eggs than are allowed by the tolerance in the official standards of United States consumer grades for shell eggs;

(2) the processing of egg products at any plant where the facilities and operating procedures meet such sanitary standards as may be prescribed by the Secretary, and where the eggs received or used in the manufacture of egg products contain no more restricted eggs than are allowed by the official standards of United States consumer grades for shell eggs, and the egg products processed at such plant;

(3) the sale of eggs by any poultry producer from his own flocks directly to a household consumer exclusively for use by such consumer and members of his household and his nonpaying guests and employees, and the transportation, possession, and use of such eggs in accordance with this paragraph;

(4) the processing of egg products by any poultry producer from eggs of his own flocks' production for sale of such products directly to a household consumer exclusively for use by such consumer and members of his household and his nonpaying guests and employees, and the egg products so processed when handled in accordance with this paragraph;

(5) the sale of eggs by shell egg packers on his own premises directly to household consumers for use by such consumer and members of his household and his nonpaying guests and employees, and the transportation, possession, and use of such eggs in accordance with this paragraph;

(6) for such period of time (not to exceed two years) during the initiation of operations under this chapter as the Secretary determines that it is impracticable to provide inspection, the processing of egg products at any class of plants and the egg products processed at such plants; and

(7) the sale of eggs by any egg producer with an annual egg production from a flock of three thousand or less hens.

(b) Plants located in noncontiguous areas of United States

The Secretary shall, by regulation and under such procedures as he may prescribe, exempt any plant located within noncontiguous areas of the United States from specific provisions of this chapter, where, despite good faith efforts by the owner of such plant, such owner has not been able to bring his plant into full compliance with this chapter: *Provided*, That in order to provide at least minimum standards for the protection of the public health, whenever processing operations are being conducted at any such plant, continuous inspection shall be maintained to assure that it is operated in a sanitary manner. No exemption under this subsection shall be granted for a period extending beyond December 31, 1971.

(c) Suspension or termination of exemptions

The Secretary may immediately suspend or terminate any exemption under subsection (a)(2) or (6) of this section at any time with respect to any person, if the conditions of exemption prescribed by this section or the regulations of the Secretary are not being met. The Secretary may modify or revoke any regulation granting exemption under this chapter whenever he deems such action appropriate to effectuate the purposes of this chapter.

(Pub. L. 91–597, § 15, Dec. 29, 1970, 84 Stat. 1629; Pub. L. 92–67, Aug. 6, 1971, 85 Stat. 173.)

AMENDMENTS

1971—Subsecs. (b), (c). Pub. L. 92–67 added subsec. (b) and redesignated former subsec. (b) as (c).

§ 1045. Limitation on entry of eggs and egg products and other materials into official plants

The Secretary may limit the entry of eggs and egg products and other materials into official plants under such conditions as he may prescribe to assure that allowing the entry of such articles into such plants will be consistent with the purposes of this chapter.

(Pub. L. 91–597, § 16, Dec. 29, 1970, 84 Stat. 1630.)

§ 1046. Imports

(a) Authorization for importation of restricted eggs; prerequisites for importation of egg products; treatment as domestic articles subject to this chapter; marking and labeling exemption for personal consumption

(1) No restricted eggs capable of use as human food shall be imported into the United States except as authorized by regulations of the Secretary.

(2) No egg products capable of use as human food shall be imported into the United States unless they were processed under an approved continuous inspection system of the government of the foreign country of origin or subdivision thereof and are labeled and packaged in accordance with, and otherwise comply with the standards of this chapter and regulations issued thereunder applicable to such articles within the United States.

(3) No eggs packed into a container that is destined for the ultimate consumer shall be imported into the United States unless the eggs are accompanied by a certification that the eggs have at all times after packaging been stored and transported under refrigeration at an ambient temperature of no greater than 45 degrees

Fahrenheit, as required by sections 1034(e) and 1037(c) of this title.

(4) All such imported articles shall upon entry into the United States be deemed and treated as domestic articles subject to the other provisions of this chapter: *Provided*, That they shall be labeled as required by such regulations for imported articles: *Provided further*, That nothing in this section shall apply to eggs or egg products purchased outside the United States by any individual for consumption by him and members of his household and his nonpaying guests and employees.

(b) Terms and conditions for destruction

The Secretary may prescribe the terms and conditions for the destruction of all such articles which are imported contrary to this section, unless (1) they are exported by the consignee within the time fixed therefor by the Secretary or (2) in the case of articles which are not in compliance solely because of misbranding, such articles are brought into compliance with this chapter under supervision of authorized representatives of the Secretary.

(c) Payment of storage, cartage, and labor charges by owner or consignee; liens

All charges for storage, cartage, and labor with respect to any article which is imported contrary to this section shall be paid by the owner or consignee, and in default of such payment shall constitute a lien against such article and any other article thereafter imported under this chapter by or for such owner or consignee.

(d) Prohibition

The importation of any article contrary to this section is prohibited.

(Pub. L. 91–597, §17, Dec. 29, 1970, 84 Stat. 1630; Pub. L. 102–237, title X, §1012(f), Dec. 13, 1991, 105 Stat. 1901.)

AMENDMENTS

1991—Subsec. (a). Pub. L. 102–237 designated first sentence as par. (1) and second sentence as par. (2), added par. (3), and designated third sentence as par. (4).

EFFECTIVE DATE OF 1991 AMENDMENT

Amendment by Pub. L. 102–237 effective 12 months after promulgation of final implementing regulations, see section 1012(h) of Pub. L. 102–237, set out as a note under section 1034 of this title.

§ 1047. Refusal or withdrawal of inspection services; hearing; grounds; person deemed to have responsible connection with business; finality of order of Secretary; judicial review; other provisions for refusal of services unaffected

The Secretary (for such period, or indefinitely, as he deems necessary to effectuate the purposes of this chapter) may refuse to provide or may withdraw inspection service under this chapter with respect to any plant if he determines, after opportunity for a hearing is accorded to the applicant for, or recipient of, such service, that such applicant or recipient is unfit to engage in any business requiring inspection under this chapter because the applicant or recipient or anyone responsibly connected with the applicant or recipient has been convicted in any Federal or State court, within the previous ten years, of (1) any felony or more than one misdemeanor under any law based upon the acquiring, handling, or distributing of adulterated, mislabeled, or deceptively packaged food or fraud in connection with transactions in food, or (2) any felony, involving fraud, bribery, extortion, or any other act or circumstances indicating a lack of the integrity needed for the conduct of operations affecting the public health.

For the purpose of this section, a person shall be deemed to be responsibly connected with the business if he is a partner, officer, director, holder, or owner of 10 per centum or more of its voting stock, or employee in a managerial or executive capacity.

The determination and order of the Secretary with respect thereto under this section shall be final and conclusive unless the affected applicant for, or recipient of, inspection service files application for judicial review within thirty days after the effective date of such order in the United States court of appeals for the circuit in which such applicant or recipient has its principal place of business or in the United States Court of Appeals for the District of Columbia Circuit. Judicial review of any such order shall be upon the record upon which the determination and order are based. The provisions of section 194 of title 7 shall be applicable to appeals taken under this section.

This section shall not affect in any way other provisions of this chapter for refusal of inspection services.

(Pub. L. 91–597, §18, Dec. 29, 1970, 84 Stat. 1630.)

§ 1048. Administrative detention of violative articles; duration; release; removal of official marks

Whenever any eggs or egg products subject to this chapter, are found by any authorized representative of the Secretary upon any premises and there is reason to believe that they are or have been processed, bought, sold, possessed, used, transported, or offered or received for sale or transportation in violation of this chapter or that they are in any other way in violation of this chapter, or whenever any restricted eggs capable of use as human food are found by such a representative in the possession of any person not authorized to acquire such eggs under the regulations of the Secretary, such articles may be detained by such representative for a reasonable period but not to exceed twenty days, pending action under section 1049 of this title or notification of any Federal, State, or other governmental authorities having jurisdiction over such articles and shall not be moved by any person from the place at which they are located when so detained until released by such representative. All official marks may be required by such representative to be removed from such articles before they are released unless it appears to the satisfaction of the Secretary that the articles are eligible to retain such marks.

(Pub. L. 91–597, §19, Dec. 29, 1970, 84 Stat. 1631.)

§ 1049. Seizure and condemnation proceedings

(a) Jurisdiction; disposal of condemned articles; court costs and fees; conformity to supplemental rules for admiralty and maritime claims; jury trial; United States as plaintiff

Any eggs or egg products that are or have been processed, bought, sold, possessed, used, transported, or offered or received for sale or transportation, in violation of this chapter, or in any other way are in violation of this chapter; and any restricted eggs, capable of use as human food, in the possession of any person not authorized to acquire such eggs under the regulations of the Secretary shall be liable to be proceeded against and seized and condemned, at any time, on a complaint in any United States district court or other proper court as provided in section 1050 of this title within the jurisdiction of which the articles are found. If the articles are condemned they shall, after entry of the decree, be disposed of by destruction or sale as the court may direct and the proceeds, if sold, less the court costs and fees, and storage and other proper expenses, shall be paid into the Treasury of the United States, but the articles shall not be sold contrary to the provision of this chapter, the Federal Food, Drug, and Cosmetic Act [21 U.S.C. 301 et seq.] or the Fair Packaging and Labeling Act [15 U.S.C. 1451 et seq.], or the laws of the jurisdiction in which they are sold: *Provided*, That upon the execution and delivery of a good and sufficient bond conditioned that the articles shall not be sold or otherwise disposed of contrary to the provisions of this chapter, the Federal Food, Drug, and Cosmetic Act, the Fair Packaging and Labeling Act, or the laws of the jurisdiction in which disposal is made, the court may direct that they be delivered to the owner thereof subject to such supervision by authorized representatives of the Secretary as is necessary to insure compliance with the applicable laws. When a decree of condemnation is entered against the articles and they are released under bond, or destroyed, court costs and fees, and storage and other proper expenses shall be awarded against the person, if any, intervening as claimant thereof. The proceedings in such cases shall conform, as nearly as may be, to the supplemental rules for certain admiralty and maritime claims, except that either party may demand trial by jury of any issue of fact joined in any case, and all such proceedings shall be at the suit of and in the name of the United States.

(b) Condemnation or seizure under other provisions unaffected

The provisions of this section shall in no way derogate from authority for condemnation or seizure conferred by other provisions of this chapter, or other laws.

(Pub. L. 91–597, § 20, Dec. 29, 1970, 84 Stat. 1631.)

REFERENCES IN TEXT

The Federal Food, Drug, and Cosmetic Act, referred to in subsec. (a), is act June 25, 1938, ch. 675, 52 Stat. 1040, as amended, which is classified generally to chapter 9 (§ 301 et seq.) of this title. For complete classification of this Act to the Code, see section 301 of this title and Tables.

The Fair Packaging and Labeling Act, referred to in subsec. (a), is Pub. L. 89–755, Nov. 3, 1966, 80 Stat. 1296, as amended, which is classified generally to chapter 39 (§ 1451 et seq.) of Title 15, Commerce and Trade. For complete classification of this Act to the Code, see Short Title note set out under section 1451 of Title 15 and Tables.

§ 1050. Jurisdiction of district courts; United States as plaintiff in enforcement and restraining proceedings; subpenas for witnesses

The United States district courts and the District Court of the Virgin Islands are vested with jurisdiction specifically to enforce, and to prevent and restrain violations of, this chapter, and shall have jurisdiction in all other cases, arising under this chapter, except as provided in section 1047 of this title. All proceedings for the enforcement or to restrain violations of this chapter shall be by and in the name of the United States. Subpenas for witnesses who are required to attend a court of the United States, in any district, may run into any other district in any such proceeding.

(Pub. L. 91–597, § 21, Dec. 29, 1970, 84 Stat. 1632.)

§ 1051. Other Federal laws applicable for administration and enforcement of chapter; prosecution of inquiries; exercise of jurisdiction

For the efficient administration and enforcement of this chapter, the provisions (including penalties) of sections 46, 48, 49, and 50 of title 15 (except paragraphs (c) through (h) of section 46 and the last paragraph of section 49 [1] of title 15), and the provisions of section 409(*l*) [1] of title 47, are made applicable to the jurisdiction, powers, and duties of the Secretary in administering and enforcing the provisions of this chapter and to any person with respect to whom such authority is exercised. The Secretary, in person or by such agents as he may designate, may prosecute any inquiry necessary to his duties under this chapter in any part of the United States, and the powers conferred by said sections 49 and 50 of title 15, on the district courts of the United States may be exercised for the purposes of this chapter by any court designated in section 1050 of this title.

(Pub. L. 91–597, § 22, Dec. 29, 1970, 84 Stat. 1632.)

REFERENCES IN TEXT

The last paragraph of section 49 of title 15, and the provisions of section 409(*l*) of title 47, referred to in text, which related to immunity of witnesses, were repealed by sections 211 and 242, respectively, of Pub. L. 91–452, Oct. 15, 1970, title II, 84 Stat. 929, 930. For provisions relating to immunity of witnesses, see section 6001 et seq. of Title 18, Crimes and Criminal Procedure.

§ 1052. State or local regulation

(a) Prohibition against additional or different requirements than Federal requirements relating to premises, facilities, and operations at official plants; authority to impose recordkeeping and related requirements consistent with Federal requirements

Requirements within the scope of this chapter with respect to premises, facilities, and operations of any official plant which are in addition

[1] See References in Text note below.

to or different than those made under this chapter may not be imposed by any State or local jurisdiction except that any such jurisdiction may impose recordkeeping and other requirements within the scope of section 1040 of this title, if consistent therewith, with respect to any such plant.

(b) Prohibition against additional or different standards than Federal standards of quality, etc., or requiring labeling to show area of production or origin; authority to require name, address, and license number of processor or packer on containers; prohibition against additional or different requirements than Federal requirements relating to labeling, packaging or ingredients; authority to prevent distribution of violative articles; validity of nonconflicting laws

For eggs which have moved or are moving in interstate or foreign commerce, (1) no State or local jurisdiction may require the use of standards of quality, condition, weight, quantity, or grade which are in addition to or different from the official Federal standards, (2) with respect to egg handlers specified in paragraphs (1) and (2) of section 1034(e) of this title, no State or local jurisdiction may impose temperature requirements pertaining to eggs packaged for the ultimate consumer which are in addition to, or different from, Federal requirements, and (3) no State or local jurisdiction other than those in noncontiguous areas of the United States may require labeling to show the State or other geographical area of production or origin: *Provided, however*, That this shall not preclude a State from requiring that the name, address, and license number of the person processing or packaging eggs, be shown on each container. Labeling, packaging, or ingredient requirements, in addition to or different than those made under this chapter, the Federal Food, Drug, and Cosmetic Act [21 U.S.C. 301 et seq.] and the Fair Packaging and Labeling Act [15 U.S.C. 1451 et seq.], may not be imposed by any State or local jurisdiction, with respect to egg products processed at any official plant in accordance with the requirements under this chapter and such Acts. However, any State or local jurisdiction may exercise jurisdiction with respect to eggs and egg products for the purpose of preventing the distribution for human food purposes of any such articles which are outside of such a plant and are in violation of any of said Federal Acts or any State or local law consistent therewith. Otherwise the provisions of this chapter shall not invalidate any law or other provisions of any State or other jurisdiction in the absence of a conflict with this chapter.

(c) Applicability of other Federal laws and authority of other Federal officials relating to eggs, egg products, or other food products unaffected; authority of Secretary of Agriculture to regulate official plants processing egg products

The provisions of this chapter shall not affect the applicability of the Federal Food, Drug, and Cosmetic Act [21 U.S.C. 301 et seq.] or the Fair Packaging and Labeling Act [15 U.S.C. 1451 et seq.] or other Federal laws to eggs, egg products, or other food products or diminish any authority conferred on the Secretary of Health and Human Services or other Federal officials by such other laws, except that the Secretary of Agriculture shall have exclusive jurisdiction to regulate official plants processing egg products and operations thereof as to all matters within the scope of this chapter.

(d) Detainer authority

The detainer authority conferred on representatives of the Secretary of Agriculture by section 1048 of this title shall also apply to any authorized representative of the Secretary of Health and Human Services for the purposes of section 1034(d) of this title, with respect to any eggs or egg products that are outside any plant processing egg products.

(Pub. L. 91–597, § 23, Dec. 29, 1970, 84 Stat. 1632; Pub. L. 96–88, title V, § 509(b), Oct. 17, 1979, 93 Stat. 695; Pub. L. 102–237, title X, § 1012(g), Dec. 13, 1991, 105 Stat. 1901.)

REFERENCES IN TEXT

The Federal Food, Drug, and Cosmetic Act, referred to in subsecs. (b) and (c), is act June 25, 1938, ch. 675, 52 Stat. 1040, as amended, which is classified generally to chapter 9 (§ 301 et seq.) of this title. For complete classification of this Act to the Code, see section 301 of this title and Tables.

The Fair Packaging and Labeling Act, referred to in subsecs. (b) and (c), is Pub. L. 89–755, Nov. 3, 1966, 80 Stat. 1296, as amended, which is classified generally to chapter 39 (§ 1451 et seq.) of Title 15, Commerce and Trade. For complete classification of this Act to the Code, see Short Title note set out under section 1451 of Title 15 and Tables.

AMENDMENTS

1991—Subsec. (b). Pub. L. 102–237 substituted "(2) with respect to egg handlers specified in paragraphs (1) and (2) of section 1034(e) of this title, no State or local jurisdiction may impose temperature requirements pertaining to eggs packaged for the ultimate consumer which are in addition to, or different from, Federal requirements, and (3)" for "and (2)".

CHANGE OF NAME

"Secretary of Health and Human Services" substituted for "Secretary of Health, Education, and Welfare" in subsecs. (c) and (d) pursuant to section 509(b) of Pub. L. 96–88, which is classified to section 3508(b) of Title 20, Education.

EFFECTIVE DATE OF 1991 AMENDMENT

Amendment by Pub. L. 102–237 effective 12 months after promulgation of final implementing regulations, see section 1012(h) of Pub. L. 102–237, set out as a note under section 1034 of this title.

§ 1053. Inspection and administration costs

(a) Overtime and holiday work costs; availability of funds

The cost of inspection rendered under the requirements of this chapter, and other costs of administration of this chapter, shall be borne by the United States, except that the cost of overtime and holiday work performed in official plants subject to the provisions of this chapter at such rates as the Secretary may determine shall be borne by such official plants. Sums received by the Secretary from official plants under this section shall be available without fiscal year limitation to carry out the purposes of this chapter.

(b) "Holiday" defined

The term "holiday" for the purposes of assessment or reimbursement of the cost of inspection performed under this chapter, the Wholesome Poultry Products Act [21 U.S.C. 467a et seq.] and the Wholesome Meat Act [21 U.S.C. 601 et seq.] shall mean the legal public holidays specified by the Congress in section 6103(a) of title 5.

(Pub. L. 91–597, § 24, Dec. 29, 1970, 84 Stat. 1633.)

REFERENCES IN TEXT

The Wholesome Poultry Products Act, referred to in subsec. (b), is Pub. L. 90–492, Aug. 18, 1968, 82 Stat. 791, as amended, which enacted sections 467a to 467f and 470 of this title, amended sections 451 to 461, 463 to 465, and 467 of this title, and enacted provisions set out as notes under section 451 of this title. For complete classification of this Act to the Code, see Short Title of 1968 Amendment note set out under section 451 of this title and Tables.

The Wholesome Meat Act, referred to in subsec. (b), is Pub. L. 90–201, Dec. 15, 1967, 81 Stat. 584, as amended, which enacted sections 601, 602, 624, 641 to 645, 661, 671 to 680, and 691 of this title, amended sections 603 to 623 of this title, repealed section 96 of this title and section 1306(b) of Title 19, Customs Duties, and enacted provisions set out as notes under section 601 of this title. For complete classification of this Act to the Code, see Short Title note set out under section 601 of this title and Tables.

§ 1054. Annual report to Congressional committees

(a)[1] Not later than March 1 of each year following December 29, 1970, the Secretary shall submit to the Committee on Agriculture of the House of Representatives and the Committee on Agriculture, Nutrition, and Forestry of the Senate a comprehensive and detailed written report with respect to—

(1) the processing, storage, handling, and distribution of eggs and egg products subject to the provisions of this chapter; the inspection of establishments operated in connection therewith; the effectiveness of the operation of the inspection, including the effectiveness of the operations of State egg inspection programs; and recommendations for legislation to improve such program; and

(2) the administration of section 1046 of this title (relating to imports) during the immediately preceding calendar year, including but not limited to—

(A) a certification by the Secretary that foreign plants exporting eggs or egg products to the United States have complied with requirements of this chapter and regulations issued thereunder;

(B) the names and locations of plants authorized or permitted to export eggs or egg products to the United States;

(C) the number of inspectors employed by the Department of Agriculture in the calendar year concerned who were assigned to inspect plants referred to in paragraph (B) hereof and the frequency with which each such plant was inspected by such inspectors;

(D) the number of inspectors that were licensed by each country from which any imports were received and that were assigned, during the calendar year concerned, to inspect such imports and the facilities in which such imports were handled; and the frequency and effectiveness of such inspections;

(E) the total volume of eggs and egg products which was imported into the United States during the calendar year concerned from each country, including a separate itemization of the volume of each major category of such imports from each country during such year, and a detailed report of rejections of plants and products because of failure to meet appropriate standards prescribed by this chapter; and

(F) recommendations for legislation to improve such program.

(Pub. L. 91–597, § 26, Dec. 29, 1970, 84 Stat. 1634; Pub. L. 103–437, § 8(4), Nov. 2, 1994, 108 Stat. 4588.)

AMENDMENTS

1994—Pub. L. 103–437 substituted "Agriculture, Nutrition, and Forestry" for "Agriculture and Forestry" in introductory provisions.

§ 1055. Authorization of appropriations

Such sums as are necessary to carry out the provisions of this chapter are hereby authorized to be appropriated.

(Pub. L. 91–597, § 27, Dec. 29, 1970, 84 Stat. 1635.)

§ 1056. Separability

If any provision of this chapter or the application thereof to any person or circumstances is held invalid, the validity of the remainder of the chapter and of the application of such provision to other persons and circumstances shall not be affected thereby.

(Pub. L. 91–597, § 28, Dec. 29, 1970, 84 Stat. 1635.)

REFERENCES IN TEXT

This chapter, referred to in text, was in the original "this Act", meaning Pub. L. 91–597, Dec. 29, 1970, 84 Stat. 1620, as amended, which enacted this chapter, amended sections 633 and 636 of Title 15, Commerce and Trade, and enacted provisions set out as notes under section 1031 of this title. For complete classification of this Act to the Code, see Short Title note set out under section 1031 of this title and Tables.

CHAPTER 16—DRUG ABUSE PREVENTION, TREATMENT, AND REHABILITATION

SUBCHAPTER I—GENERAL PROVISIONS

SUBCHAPTER II—DRUG ABUSE POLICY COORDINATION

SUBCHAPTER III—NATIONAL DRUG ABUSE STRATEGY

SUBCHAPTER IV—OTHER FEDERAL PROGRAMS

[1] So in original. No subsec. (b) has been enacted.

SUBCHAPTER I—GENERAL PROVISIONS

§ 1101. Congressional findings

The Congress makes the following findings:

(1) Drug abuse is rapidly increasing in the United States and now afflicts urban, suburban, and rural areas of the Nation.

(2) Drug abuse seriously impairs individual, as well as societal, health and well-being.

(3) Drug abuse, especially heroin addiction, substantially contributes to crime.

(4) The adverse impact of drug abuse inflicts increasing pain and hardship on individuals, families, and communities and undermines our institutions.

(5) Too little is known about drug abuse, especially the causes, and ways to treat and prevent drug abuse.

(6) The success of Federal drug abuse programs and activities requires a recognition that education, treatment, rehabilitation, research, training, and law enforcement efforts are interrelated.

(7) The effectiveness of efforts by State and local governments and by the Federal Government to control and treat drug abuse in the United States has been hampered by a lack of coordination among the States, between States and localities, among the Federal Government, States and localities, and throughout the Federal establishment.

(8) Control of drug abuse requires the development of a comprehensive, coordinated long-term Federal strategy that encompasses both effective law enforcement against illegal drug traffic and effective health programs to rehabilitate victims of drug abuse.

(9) The increasing rate of drug abuse constitutes a serious and continuing threat to national health and welfare, requiring an immediate and effective response on the part of the Federal Government.

(10) Although the Congress observed a significant apparent reduction in the rate of increase of drug abuse during the three-year period subsequent to March 21, 1972, and in certain areas of the country apparent temporary reductions in its incidence, the increase and spread of heroin consumption since 1974, and the continuing abuse of other dangerous drugs, clearly indicate the need for effective, ongoing, and highly visible Federal leadership in the formation and execution of a comprehensive, coordinated drug abuse policy.

(11) Shifts in the usage of various drugs and in the Nation's demographic composition require a Federal strategy to adjust the focus of drug abuse programs to meet new needs and priorities on a cost-effective basis.

(12) The growing extent of drug abuse indicates an urgent need for prevention and intervention programs designed to reach the general population and members of high risk populations such as youth, women, and the elderly.

(13) Effective control of drug abuse requires high-level coordination of Federal international and domestic activities relating to both supply of, and demand for, commonly abused drugs.

(14) Local governments with high concentrations of drug abuse should be actively involved in the planning and coordination of efforts to combat drug abuse.

(Pub. L. 92–255, title I, §101, Mar. 21, 1972, 86 Stat. 66; Pub. L. 94–237, §1, Mar. 19, 1976, 90 Stat. 241; Pub. L. 96–181, §2, Jan. 2, 1980, 93 Stat. 1309.)

AMENDMENTS

1980—Pars. (11) to (14). Pub. L. 96–181 added pars. (11) to (14).

1976—Par. (10). Pub. L. 94–237 added par. (10).

SHORT TITLE OF 1980 AMENDMENT

Section 1(a) of Pub. L. 96–181 provided that: "This Act [enacting sections 1111 to 1117 and 1181 of this title, amending this section, sections 1102, 1162, 1164, 1176, 1177, 1180, and 1191 to 1193 of this title, and sections 218, 300*l*–2, 300m–3, and 3733 of Title 42, The Public Health and Welfare, omitting sections 1118 to 1120 and 1131 to 1133 of this title, enacting provisions set out as notes under this section and section 1193 of this title, and amending provisions set out as a note below] may be cited as the 'Drug Abuse Prevention, Treatment, and Rehabilitation Amendments of 1979'."

SHORT TITLE OF 1978 AMENDMENT

Pub. L. 95–461, §1, Oct. 14, 1978, 92 Stat. 1268, provided that: "This Act [enacting section 1194 of this title, amending sections 1172, 1176, 1177, 1192, and 1193 of this title, enacting a provision set out as a note under section 1172 of this title and amending a provision set out as a note under section 242 of Title 42, The Public Health and Welfare] may be cited as the 'Drug Abuse Prevention and Treatment Amendments of 1978'."

SHORT TITLE

Section 1 of Pub. L. 92–255, as amended by Pub. L. 96–181, §15(a), Jan. 2, 1980, 93 Stat. 1316, provided that: "This Act [enacting this chapter, and amending sections 5313, 5315, and 5316 of Title 5, Government Organization and Employees, and sections 218, 246, 257, 2684, 2688a, 2688k, 2688n–1, and 2688t of Title 42, The Public Health and Welfare] may be cited as the 'Drug Abuse Prevention, Treatment, and Rehabilitation Act'."

REFERENCES TO DRUG ABUSE OFFICE AND TREATMENT ACT OF 1972

Section 15(b) of Pub. L. 96–181 provided in part that: "Whenever reference is made in any other Federal law, regulation, ruling, or order to the Drug Abuse Office and Treatment Act of 1972, the reference shall be considered to be made to the Drug Abuse Prevention, Treatment, and Rehabilitation Act."

§ 1102. Congressional declaration of national policy

The Congress declares that it is the policy of the United States and the purpose of this chapter to focus the comprehensive resources of the Federal Government and bring them to bear on drug abuse with the objective of significantly reducing the incidence, as well as the social and personal costs, of drug abuse in the United States, and to develop and assure the implementation of a comprehensive, coordinated long-term Federal strategy to combat drug abuse. To reach these goals, the Congress further declares that it is the policy of the United States and the purpose of this chapter to meet the problems of drug abuse through—

(1) comprehensive Federal, State, and local planning for, and effective use of, Federal assistance to States and to community-based programs to meet the urgent needs of special populations, in coordination with all other governmental and nongovernmental sources of assistance;

(2) the development and support of community-based prevention programs;

(3) the development and encouragement of effective occupational prevention and treatment programs within the Government and in cooperation with the private sector; and

(4) increased Federal commitment to research into the behavioral and biomedical etiology of, the treatment of, and the mental and physical health and social and economic consequences of, drug abuse.

(Pub. L. 92–255, title I, §102, Mar. 21, 1972, 86 Stat. 66; Pub. L. 94–237, §2, Mar. 19, 1976, 90 Stat. 241; Pub. L. 96–181, §3, Jan. 2, 1980, 93 Stat. 1309.)

REFERENCES IN TEXT

This chapter, referred to in text, was in the original "this Act", meaning Pub. L. 92–255, Mar. 21, 1972, 86 Stat. 65, as amended, known as the Drug Abuse Prevention, Treatment, and Rehabilitation Act, which comprises this chapter. For complete classification of this Act to the Code, see Short Title note set out under section 1101 of this title and Tables.

AMENDMENTS

1980—Pub. L. 96–181 inserted additional declarations of policy prescribing methods and programs by which the goals are to be reached.

1976—Pub. L. 94–237 substituted "objective of significantly reducing the incidence, as well as the social and personal costs, of drug abuse in the United States, and to develop and assure the implementation of" for "immediate objective of significantly reducing the incidence of drug abuse in the United States within the shortest possible period of time, and to develop".

§1103. Repealed. Pub. L. 100–690, title I, §1007(c)(1), Nov. 18, 1988, 102 Stat. 4187

Section, Pub. L. 92–255, title I, §103, Mar. 21, 1972, 86 Stat. 67; Pub. L. 94–237, §§3, 4(a), Mar. 19, 1976, 90 Stat. 241, defined "drug abuse prevention function", "drug traffic prevention function", and "drug abuse function".

EFFECTIVE DATE OF REPEAL

Repeal effective Jan. 21, 1989, see section 1012 of Pub. L. 100–690.

§1104. Repealed. Pub. L. 94–237, §4(c)(1), Mar. 19, 1976, 90 Stat. 244

Section, Pub. L. 92–255, title I, §104, Mar. 21, 1972, 86 Stat. 67, provided, effective June 30, 1975, that the Special Action Office for Drug Abuse Prevention, each of the positions in the Office of Director, Deputy Director, and Assistant Director, and the National Advisory Council for Drug Abuse Prevention were abolished and former subchapter II of this chapter was repealed.

SUBCHAPTER II—DRUG ABUSE POLICY COORDINATION

§§1111 to 1114. Repealed. Pub. L. 100–690, title I, §1007(c)(1), Nov. 18, 1988, 102 Stat. 4187

Section 1111, Pub. L. 92–255, title II, §201, as added Pub. L. 96–181, §4, Jan. 2, 1980, 93 Stat. 1310; amended Pub. L. 98–473, title II, §1306, Oct. 12, 1984, 98 Stat. 2170, related to concentration of Federal effort in drug abuse prevention.

A prior section 1111, Pub. L. 92–255, title II, §201, as added Pub. L. 94–237, §4(b), Mar. 19, 1976, 90 Stat. 242, which provided for the establishment of the Office of Drug Abuse Policy, was omitted in the general revision of this subchapter by Pub. L. 96–181, §4, Jan. 2, 1980, 93 Stat. 1309. Previously, the Office of Drug Abuse Policy was abolished and the functions of the Office and its Director were transferred to the President by sections 3 and 5 of Reorg. Plan No. 1 of 1977, effective Mar. 27, 1978, as provided by Ex. Ord. No. 12045, Mar. 27, 1978, 43 F.R. 13347, set out as notes preceding section 101 of Title 3, The President.

Another prior section 1111, Pub. L. 92–255, title II, §201, Mar. 21, 1972, 86 Stat. 67, which provided for the establishment of the Special Action Office for Drug Abuse Prevention, was repealed by Pub. L. 92–255, title I, §104, Mar. 21, 1972, 86 Stat. 67, eff. June 30, 1975.

Section 1112, Pub. L. 92–255, title II, §202, as added Pub. L. 96–181, §4, Jan. 2, 1980, 93 Stat. 1310, related to designation of a representative to direct activities required by this subchapter.

A prior section 1112, Pub. L. 92–255, title II, §202, as added Pub. L. 94–237, §4(b), Mar. 19, 1976, 90 Stat. 242; amended Pub. L. 95–83, title III, §311(d), Aug. 1, 1977, 91 Stat. 398, which provided for the appointment of the Director of the Office of Drug Abuse Policy, was omitted in the general revision of this subchapter by Pub. L. 96–181, §4, Jan. 2, 1980, 93 Stat. 1309.

Another prior section 1112, Pub. L. 92–255, title II, §202, Mar. 21, 1972, 86 Stat. 68, which provided for the appointment of a Director of the Special Action Office for Drug Abuse Prevention, was repealed by Pub. L. 92–255, title I, §104, Mar. 21, 1972, 86 Stat. 67, eff. June 30, 1975.

Section 1113, Pub. L. 92–255, title II, §203, as added Pub. L. 96–181, §4, Jan. 2, 1980, 93 Stat. 1310, related to employment of officers and employees.

A prior section 1113, Pub. L. 92–255, title II, §203, as added Pub. L. 94–237, §4(b), Mar. 19, 1976, 90 Stat. 242, which provided for the appointment and functions of Deputy Director of the Office of Drug Abuse Policy, was omitted in the general revision of this subchapter by Pub. L. 96–181, §4, Jan. 2, 1980, 93 Stat. 1309.

Another prior section 1113, Pub. L. 92–255, title II, §203, Mar. 21, 1972, 86 Stat. 68, which provided for the appointment of a Deputy Director of the Special Office for Drug Abuse Prevention, was repealed by Pub. L. 92–255, title I, §104, Mar. 21, 1972, 86 Stat. 67, eff. June 30, 1975.

Section 1114, Pub. L. 92–255, title II, §204, as added Pub. L. 96–181, §4, Jan. 2, 1980, 93 Stat. 1310, related to acceptance of uncompensated services.

A prior section 1114, Pub. L. 92–255, title II, §204, as added Pub. L. 94–237, §4(b), Mar. 19, 1976, 90 Stat. 242, which provided for the delegation of functions by the Director of the Office of Drug Abuse Policy, was omitted in the general revision of this subchapter by Pub. L. 96–181, §4, Jan. 2, 1980, 93 Stat. 1309.

Another prior section 1114, Pub. L. 92–255, title II, §204, Mar. 21, 1972, 86 Stat. 68, which provided for the appointment of six Assistant Directors, was repealed by Pub. L. 92–255, title I, §104, Mar. 21, 1972, 86 Stat. 67, eff. June 30, 1975.

Provisions similar to this section were contained in section 1117 of this title prior to the general revision of this subchapter by Pub. L. 96–181, §4, Jan. 2, 1980, 93 Stat. 1309.

EFFECTIVE DATE OF REPEAL

Repeal effective Jan. 21, 1989, see section 1012 of Pub. L. 100–690.

EXECUTIVE ORDER NO. 12368

Ex. Ord. No. 12368, June 24, 1982, 47 F.R. 27843, as amended by Ex. Ord. No. 12590, Mar. 26, 1987, 52 F.R. 10021, related to assignment of drug abuse policy functions.

§ 1115. Notice relating to the control of dangerous drugs

Whenever the Attorney General determines that there is evidence that—

(1) a drug or other substance, which is not a controlled substance (as defined in section 802(6) of this title), has a potential for abuse, or

(2) a controlled substance should be transferred or removed from a schedule under section 812 of this title,

he shall, prior to initiating any proceeding under section 811(a) of this title, give the President timely notice of such determination. Information forwarded to the Attorney General pursuant to section 811(f) of this title shall also be forwarded by the Secretary of Health and Human Services to the President.

(Pub. L. 92–255, title II, § 201, formerly § 205, as added Pub. L. 96–181, § 4, Jan. 2, 1980, 93 Stat. 1311; amended Pub. L. 97–35, title IX, § 973(a), Aug. 13, 1981, 95 Stat. 598; renumbered § 201, Pub. L. 100–690, title I, § 1007(c)(1), Nov. 18, 1988, 102 Stat. 4187.)

PRIOR PROVISIONS

A prior section 201 of Pub. L. 92–255, title II, as added Pub. L. 96–181, § 4, Jan. 2, 1980, 93 Stat. 1310; amended Pub. L. 98–473, title II, § 1306, Oct. 12, 1984, 98 Stat. 2170, related to concentration of Federal effort in drug abuse prevention, prior to repeal by Pub. L. 100–690, title I, § 1007(c)(1), Nov. 18, 1988, 102 Stat. 4187.

A prior section 1115, Pub. L. 92–255, title II, § 205, as added Pub. L. 94–237, § 4(b), Mar. 19, 1976, 90 Stat. 242, which provided for employment, functions, and travel expenses of employees, was omitted in the general revision of this subchapter by Pub. L. 96–181, § 4, Jan. 2, 1980, 93 Stat. 1309.

Another prior section 1115, Pub. L. 92–255, title II, § 205, Mar. 21, 1972, 86 Stat. 68, provided for the delegation of functions by the Director, prior to repeal by Pub. L. 92–255, title I, § 104, Mar. 21, 1972, 86 Stat. 67, eff. June 30, 1975.

Provisions similar to this section were contained in section 1118 of this title prior to the general revision of this subchapter by Pub. L. 96–181, § 4, Jan. 2, 1980, 93 Stat. 1309.

AMENDMENTS

1981—Pub. L. 97–35 substituted "Health and Human Services" for "Health, Education, and Welfare".

§ 1116. Repealed. Pub. L. 100–690, title I, § 1007(c)(1), Nov. 18, 1988, 102 Stat. 4187

Section, Pub. L. 92–255, title II, § 206, as added Pub. L. 96–181, § 4, Jan. 2, 1980, 93 Stat. 1311, provided that this subchapter not be construed as limiting the statutory authority of the Secretary of Defense or the Administrator of Veterans' Affairs.

EFFECTIVE DATE OF REPEAL

Repeal effective Jan. 21, 1989, see section 1012 of Pub. L. 100–690.

A prior section 1116, Pub. L. 92–255, title II, § 206, as added Pub. L. 94–237, § 4(b), Mar. 19, 1976, 90 Stat. 242, which provided for the employment and compensation of experts and consultants, was omitted in the general revision of this subchapter by Pub. L. 96–181, § 4, Jan. 2, 1980, 93 Stat. 1309.

Another prior section 1116, Pub. L. 92–255, title II, § 206, Mar. 21, 1972, 86 Stat. 68, which provided for the employment and prescription of functions for officers and employees by the Director, was repealed by Pub. L. 92–255, title I, § 104, Mar. 21, 1972, 86 Stat. 67, eff. June 30, 1975.

Provisions similar to this section were contained in section 1119 of this title prior to the general revision of this subchapter by Pub. L. 96–181, § 4, Jan. 2, 1980, 93 Stat. 1309.

§ 1117. Repealed. Pub. L. 98–24, § 4(b), Apr. 26, 1983, 97 Stat. 183

Section, Pub. L. 92–255, title II, § 207, as added Pub. L. 96–181, § 4, Jan. 2, 1980, 93 Stat. 1311, required the President to make annual reports to the Congress on the drug abuse prevention activities under this subchapter. See section 290aa–4 of Title 42, The Public Health and Welfare.

A prior section 1117, Pub. L. 92–255, title II, § 207, as added Pub. L. 94–237, § 4(b), Mar. 19, 1976, 90 Stat. 243, which provided for acceptance of uncompensated services, was omitted in the general revision of this subchapter by Pub. L. 96–181, § 4, Jan. 2, 1980, 93 Stat. 1309.

Another prior section 1117, Pub. L. 92–255, title II, § 207, Mar. 21, 1972, 86 Stat. 68, which provided for the procurement of experts and consultants by the Director, was repealed by Pub. L. 92–255, title I, § 104, Mar. 21, 1972, 86 Stat. 67, eff. June 30, 1975.

§§ 1118 to 1120. Omitted

CODIFICATION

Section 1118, Pub. L. 92–255, title II, § 208, as added Pub. L. 94–237, § 4(b), Mar. 19, 1976, 90 Stat. 243, which related to giving of notice to Director prior to initiation of a section 811(a) proceeding, was omitted in the general revision of title II of Pub. L. 92–255 by Pub. L. 96–181, § 4, Jan. 2, 1980, 93 Stat. 1309. See section 1115 of this title.

A prior section 1118, Pub. L. 92–255, title II, § 208, Mar. 21, 1972, 86 Stat. 68, which provided for acceptance of uncompensated services by Director, was repealed by Pub. L. 92–255, title I, § 104, Mar. 21, 1972, 86 Stat. 67, eff. June 30, 1975.

Section 1119, Pub. L. 92–255, title II, § 210, as added Pub. L. 94–237, § 4(b), Mar. 19, 1976, 90 Stat. 243, which related to effect of this subchapter on statutory requirements and authorities, was omitted in the general revision of title II of Pub. L. 92–255 by Pub. L. 96–181, § 4, Jan. 2, 1980, 93 Stat. 1309. See section 1116 of this title.

A prior section 1119, Pub. L. 92–255, title II, § 209, Mar. 21, 1972, 86 Stat. 68, which provided for notice by Attorney General to Director with respect to control of dangerous drugs, was repealed by Pub. L. 92–255, title I, § 104, Mar. 21, 1972, 86 Stat. 67, eff. June 30, 1975.

A prior section 210 of Pub. L. 92–255, title II, Mar. 21, 1972, 86 Stat. 69, which provided for authority of Director to make grants and enter into contract, was repealed by Pub. L. 92–255, title I, § 104, Mar. 21, 1972, 86 Stat. 67, eff. June 30, 1975.

Section 1120, Pub. L. 92–255, title II, § 211, as added Pub. L. 94–237, § 4(b), Mar. 19, 1976, 90 Stat. 243, which related to authorization of appropriations with regard to this subchapter, was omitted in the general revision of title II of Pub. L. 92–255 by Pub. L. 96–181, § 4, Jan. 2, 1980, 93 Stat. 1309.

A prior section 1120, Pub. L. 92–255, title II, § 210, Mar. 21, 1972, 86 Stat. 69, which provided for authority of Director to make grants and enter into contracts, was repealed by Pub. L. 92–255, title I, § 104, Mar. 21, 1972, 86 Stat. 67, eff. June 30, 1975.

A prior section 211 of Pub. L. 92–255, title II, Mar. 21, 1972, 86 Stat. 69, which provided for appointment of an acting Director until position was initially filled, was repealed by Pub. L. 92–255, title I, § 104, Mar. 21, 1972, 86 Stat. 67, eff. June 30, 1975.

§§ 1121 to 1123. Repealed. Pub. L. 92–255, title I, § 104, Mar. 21, 1972, 86 Stat. 67

Section 1121, Pub. L. 92–255, title II, § 211, Mar. 21, 1972, 86 Stat. 69, provided for appointment of an acting Director until position was initially filled.

Section 1122, Pub. L. 92–255, title II, § 213, Mar. 21, 1972, 86 Stat. 69, prohibited Director or any other Federal officer from waiving or disregarding any limitation or requirement prescribed by law with respect to any Federal program or activity.

Section 1123, Pub. L. 92–255, title II, § 214, Mar. 21, 1972, 86 Stat. 70, provided for authorization of appropriations, and fiscal year availability of such appropriations.

EFFECTIVE DATE OF REPEAL

Section 1104 of this title, prior to repeal by section 4(c)(1) of Pub. L. 94–237, provided for repeal of sections effective June 30, 1975.

§§ 1131 to 1133. Omitted

CODIFICATION

Section 1131, Pub. L. 92–255, title II, § 221, as added Pub. L. 94–237, § 4(b), Mar. 19, 1976, 90 Stat. 243, which related to functions of Director concerning planning and policies, was omitted in the general revision of title II of Pub. L. 92–255 by Pub. L. 96–181, § 4, Jan. 2, 1980, 93 Stat. 1309. See section 1111 of this title.

A prior section 1131, Pub. L. 92–255, title II, § 221, Mar. 21, 1972, 86 Stat. 70, which provided for establishment of overall planning and policy and the criteria to achieve objectives and priorities for all Federal drug abuse prevention functions, was repealed by Pub. L. 92–255, title I, § 104, Mar. 21, 1972, 86 Stat. 67, eff. June 30, 1975.

Section 1132, Pub. L. 92–255, title II, § 222, as added Pub. L. 94–237, § 4(b), Mar. 19, 1976, 90 Stat. 243, which authorized President to designate Director to represent United States in negotiations concerning drug abuse functions, was omitted in the general revision of title II of Pub. L. 92–255 by Pub. L. 96–181, § 4, Jan. 2, 1980, 93 Stat. 1309. See section 1112 of this title.

A prior section 1132, Pub. L. 92–255, title II, § 222, Mar. 21, 1972, 86 Stat. 71, which provided for review and modification of implementation plans and budget requests, was repealed by Pub. L. 92–255, title I, § 104, Mar. 21, 1972, 86 Stat. 67, eff. June 30, 1975.

Section 1133, Pub. L. 92–255, title II, § 223, as added Pub. L. 94–237, § 4(b), Mar. 19, 1976, 90 Stat. 244, which related to an annual report to President and Congress on activities of Office of Drug Abuse Policy, was omitted in the general revision of title II of Pub. L. 92–255 by Pub. L. 96–181, § 4, Jan. 2, 1980, 93 Stat. 1309. See section 1117 of this title.

A prior section 1133, Pub. L. 92–255, title II, § 223, Mar. 21, 1972, 86 Stat. 71, which provided for establishment and the objectives of a Special Fund, was repealed by Pub. L. 92–255, title I, § 104, Mar. 21, 1972, 86 Stat. 67, eff. June 30, 1975.

§§ 1134 to 1143. Repealed. Pub. L. 92–255, title I, § 104, Mar. 21, 1972, 86 Stat. 67

Section 1134, Pub. L. 92–255, title II, § 224, Mar. 21, 1972, 86 Stat. 71, provided for establishment of research and development programs by Director.

Section 1135, Pub. L. 92–255, title II, § 225, Mar. 21, 1972, 86 Stat. 72, provided for establishment of a single non-Federal share requirement.

Section 1136, Pub. L. 92–255, title II, § 226, Mar. 21, 1972, 86 Stat. 72, provided for Director to make drug prevention function recommendations to President and to consult with responsible agencies with respect to drug prevention functions.

Section 1137, Pub. L. 92–255, title II, § 227, Mar. 21, 1972, 86 Stat. 72, provided for resolution of agency conflicts with regard to drug prevention functions.

Section 1138, Pub. L. 92–255, title II, § 228, Mar. 21, 1972, 86 Stat. 72, provided for communications and liaison with respect to drug prevention functions by one of Assistant Directors.

Section 1139, Pub. L. 92–255, title II, § 229, Mar. 21, 1972, 86 Stat. 72, provided, with respect to drug prevention functions, coordination of State and local governments, availability of information and other services and activities.

Section 1140, Pub. L. 92–255, title II, § 230, Mar. 21, 1972, 86 Stat. 73, provided for a management oversight review by a Federal officer.

Section 1141, Pub. L. 92–255, title II, § 231, Mar. 21, 1972, 86 Stat. 73, provided for convening of a council of officials of Federal agencies responsible for drug prevention functions by Director.

Section 1142, Pub. L. 92–255, title II, § 232, Mar. 21, 1972, 86 Stat. 73, provided for designation of the Director to represent Government in international negotiations related to drug prevention functions.

Section 1143, Pub. L. 92–255, title II, § 233, Mar. 21, 1972, 86 Stat. 73, provided for an annual written report to the President by the Director.

EFFECTIVE DATE OF REPEAL

Section 1104 of this title, prior to repeal by section 4(c)(1) of Pub. L. 94–237, provided for repeal of sections effective June 30, 1975.

§§ 1151 to 1155. Repealed. Pub. L. 92–255, title I, § 104, Mar. 21, 1972, 86 Stat. 67

Section 1151, Pub. L. 92–255, title II, § 251, Mar. 21, 1972, 86 Stat. 74, provided for establishment of a National Advisory Council for Drug Abuse Prevention.

Section 1152, Pub. L. 92–255, title II, § 252, Mar. 21, 1972, 86 Stat. 74, provided for membership of National Advisory Council for Drug Abuse Prevention.

Section 1153, Pub. L. 92–255, title II, § 253, Mar. 21, 1972, 86 Stat. 74, provided for designation of chairman of National Advisory Council for Drug Abuse Prevention.

Section 1154, Pub. L. 92–255, title II, § 254, Mar. 21, 1972, 86 Stat. 74, provided for compensation and expenses for members of National Advisory Council for Drug Abuse Prevention.

Section 1155, Pub. L. 92–255, title II, § 255, Mar. 21, 1972, 86 Stat. 74, set forth functions of National Advisory Council for Drug Abuse Prevention.

EFFECTIVE DATE OF REPEAL

Section 1104 of this title, prior to repeal by section 4(c)(1) of Pub. L. 94–237, provided for repeal of sections effective June 30, 1975.

SUBCHAPTER III—NATIONAL DRUG ABUSE STRATEGY

§§ 1161 to 1165. Repealed. Pub. L. 98–509, title III, § 301(d), Oct. 19, 1984, 98 Stat. 2364

Section 1161, Pub. L. 92–255, title III, § 301, Mar. 21, 1972, 86 Stat. 74, related to development, and initial promulgation no later than nine months after Mar. 21, 1972, by the President, of a national drug abuse strategy.

Section 1162, Pub. L. 92–255, title III, § 302, Mar. 21, 1972, 86 Stat. 75; Pub. L. 94–237, § 4(c)(2), (3), (5)(A), Mar. 19, 1976, 90 Stat. 244; Pub. L. 96–181, § 5(a), (b), Jan. 2, 1980, 93 Stat. 1311; Pub. L. 97–35, title IX, § 973(b), Aug. 13, 1981, 95 Stat. 598, related to establishment and membership of a Strategy Council, interim provision of services by the Director, and review and commentary on the national drug abuse strategy by those Federal officials participating in its preparation.

Section 1163, Pub. L. 92–255, title III, § 303, Mar. 21, 1972, 86 Stat. 75, related to contents of the national drug abuse strategy.

Section 1164, Pub. L. 92–255, title III, § 304, Mar. 21, 1972, 86 Stat. 75; Pub. L. 94–237, § 4(c)(4), Mar. 19, 1976, 90 Stat. 244; Pub. L. 96–181, § 5(c), Jan. 2, 1980, 93 Stat. 1311, related to preparation of the national drug abuse strategy.

Section 1165, Pub. L. 92–255, title III, § 305, Mar. 21, 1972, 86 Stat. 75; Pub. L. 94–237, § 5, Mar. 19, 1976, 90 Stat. 244; Pub. L. 98–24, § 4(a), Apr. 26, 1983, 97 Stat. 183, related to submission by the President to the Congress, on or before Aug. 1, 1984, and every two years thereafter, of a written report describing the national drug abuse strategy, and prescribed the contents of the report.

SUBCHAPTER IV—OTHER FEDERAL PROGRAMS

§ 1171. Drug abuse prevention function appropriations

Any request for appropriations by a department or agency of the Government submitted after March 21, 1972, shall specify (1) on a line item basis, that part of the appropriations which the department or agency is requesting to carry out its drug abuse prevention functions, and (2) the authorization of the appropriations requested to carry out each of its drug abuse prevention functions.

(Pub. L. 92–255, title IV, § 404, Mar. 21, 1972, 86 Stat. 77.)

§ 1172. Repealed. Pub. L. 98–24, § 2(c)(2), Apr. 26, 1983, 97 Stat. 182

Section, Pub. L. 92–255, title IV, § 405, Mar. 21, 1972, 86 Stat. 77; Pub. L. 95–461, § 3(b), Oct. 14, 1978, 92 Stat. 1268; Pub. L. 97–35, title IX, § 973(c)(1), Aug. 13, 1981, 95 Stat. 598, required that the Secretary of Health and Human Services make periodic reports to the Congress and to the President on drug abuse in the United States. See section 290aa–4 of Title 42, The Public Health and Welfare.

§ 1173. Transferred and Omitted

CODIFICATION

Section, Pub. L. 92–255, title IV, § 406, Mar. 21, 1972, 86 Stat. 78; Pub. L. 97–35, title IX, § 968(a), Aug. 13, 1981, 95 Stat. 595, established additional drug abuse prevention functions of the Secretary of Health and Human Services.

Subsec. (a) was redesignated as section 503(e) of the Public Health Service Act by Pub. L. 98–24, § 2(b)(5), Apr. 26, 1983, 97 Stat. 177, and was classified to former section 290aa–2(e) of Title 42, The Public Health and Welfare, prior to repeal by Pub. L. 102–321, title I, § 101(b), July 10, 1992, 106 Stat. 331.

Subsec. (b), which directed that the Secretary carry out his functions under subsec. (a) of this section through the National Institute on Drug Abuse, was omitted.

§§ 1174, 1175. Transferred

CODIFICATION

Section 1174, Pub. L. 92–255, title IV, § 407, Mar. 21, 1972, 86 Stat. 78; Pub. L. 94–237, § 6(a), Mar. 19, 1976, 90 Stat. 244; Pub. L. 94–581, title I, § 111(c)(2), Oct. 21, 1976, 90 Stat. 2852, which prohibited discrimination against drug abusers by general hospitals, was redesignated section 526 of the Public Health Service Act by Pub. L. 98–24, § 2(b)(16)(B), Apr. 26, 1983, 97 Stat. 182, and is classified to section 290ee–2 of Title 42, The Public Health and Welfare.

Section 1175, Pub. L. 92–255, title IV, § 408, Mar. 21, 1972, 86 Stat. 79; Pub. L. 93–282, title III, § 303(a), (b), May 14, 1974, 88 Stat. 137, 138; Pub. L. 94–237, § 4(c)(5)(A), (B), Mar. 19, 1976, 90 Stat. 244; Pub. L. 94–581, title I, § 111(c)(3), Oct. 21, 1976, 90 Stat. 2852; Pub. L. 97–35, title IX, § 973(d), Aug. 13, 1981, 95 Stat. 598, which related to confidentiality of patients' records, was redesignated section 527 of the Public Health Service Act by Pub. L. 98–24, § 2(b)(16)(B), Apr. 26, 1983, 97 Stat. 182, and is classified to section 290ee–3 of Title 42.

§ 1176. Repealed. Pub. L. 97–35, title IX, § 969(a), Aug. 13, 1981, 95 Stat. 595

Section, Pub. L. 92–255, title IV, § 409, Mar. 21, 1972, 86 Stat. 80; Pub. L. 94–237, §§ 7, 8(a), 9(a)(1), (b)(1), Mar. 19, 1976, 90 Stat. 245–247; Pub. L. 94–371, § 10(a)(1), (b)(1), July 26, 1976, 90 Stat. 1040; Pub. L. 95–83, title III, § 311(a)(3), Aug. 1, 1977, 91 Stat. 397; Pub. L. 95–461, §§ 2(a), 4, Oct. 14, 1978, 92 Stat. 1268, 1269; Pub. L. 96–79, title I, § 115(j)(2), Oct. 4, 1979, 93 Stat. 610; Pub. L. 96–181, § 6, Jan. 2, 1980, 93 Stat. 1311, provided for creation and funding through the fiscal year ending Sept. 30, 1981, of a program of formula grants to States to operate State plans for the establishment, conduct, and coordination of projects for the development of more effective drug abuse prevention functions in the States and for the evaluation of such programs.

§ 1177. Special project grants and contracts

(a) Scope of programs; priority

The Secretary[1] acting through the National Institute on Drug Abuse, may make grants to and enter into contracts with individuals and public and private nonprofit entities—

(1) to provide training seminars, educational programs, and technical assistance for the development, demonstration, and evaluation of drug abuse prevention, treatment, and rehabilitation programs; and

(2) to conduct demonstration and evaluation projects, with a high priority on prevention and early intervention projects and on identifying new and more effective drug abuse prevention, treatment, and rehabilitation programs.

In the implementation of his authority under this section, the Secretary shall accord a high priority to applications for grants or contracts for primary prevention programs. For purposes of the preceding sentence, primary prevention programs include programs designed to discourage persons from beginning drug abuse. To the extent that appropriations authorized under this section are used to fund treatment services, the Secretary shall not limit such funding to treatment for opiate abuse, but shall also provide support for treatment for non-opiate drug abuse including polydrug abuse. Furthermore, nothing shall prevent the use of funds provided under this section for programs and projects aimed at the prevention, treatment, and rehabilitation of alcohol abuse and alcoholism as well as drug abuse.

(b) Authorization of appropriations

There are authorized to be appropriated $25,000,000 for the fiscal year ending June 30, 1972; $65,000,000 for the fiscal year ending June 30, 1973; $100,000,000 for the fiscal year ending June 30, 1974; $160,000,000 for each of the fiscal years ending June 30, 1975 and June 30, 1976; $40,000,000 for the period July 1, 1976, through September 30, 1976; and $160,000,000 for each of the fiscal years ending September 30, 1977, and September 30, 1978, to carry out this section. For the fiscal year ending September 30, 1979, there is authorized to be appropriated (1) $153,000,000 for grants and contracts under paragraphs (3) and (6) of subsection (a) of this section for drug abuse treatment programs, and (2) $24,000,000 for

[1] So in original. Probably should be followed by a comma.

grants and contracts under such subsection for other programs and activities. For grants and contracts under paragraphs (3) and (6) of subsection (a) of this section for drug abuse treatment programs there is authorized to be appropriated $149,000,000 for the fiscal year ending September 30, 1980, and $155,000,000 for the fiscal year ending September 30, 1981; and for grants and contracts under such subsection for other programs and activities there is authorized to be appropriated $20,000,000 for the fiscal year ending September 30, 1980, and $30,000,000 for the fiscal year ending September 30, 1981. Of the funds appropriated under the preceding sentence for the fiscal year ending September 30, 1980, at least 7 percent of the funds shall be obligated for grants and contracts for primary prevention and intervention programs designed to discourage individuals, particularly those in high risk populations, from abusing drugs; and of the funds appropriated under the preceding sentence for the next fiscal year, at least 10 percent of the funds shall be obligated for such grants and contracts. For carrying out the purposes of this section, there are authorized to be appropriated $15,000,000 for the fiscal year ending September 30, 1982. Of the funds appropriated under the preceding sentence, at least 25 per centum of the funds shall be obligated for grants and contracts for primary prevention and intervention programs designed to discourage individuals, particularly individuals in high risk populations, from abusing drugs.

(c) Coordination of applications for programs in a State; precedence restriction; project evaluation; application approval; criteria; proposed performance standards or research protocol

(1) In carrying out this section, the Secretary shall require coordination of all applications for programs in a State and shall not give precedence to public agencies over private agencies, institutions, and organizations, or to State agencies over local agencies.

(2) Each applicant within a State, upon filing its application with the Secretary for a grant or contract under this section, shall submit a copy of its application for review by the State agency (if any) responsible for the administration of drug abuse prevention activities. Such State agency shall be given not more than thirty days from the date of receipt of the application to submit to the Secretary, in writing, an evaluation of the project set forth in the application. Such evaluation shall include comments on the relationship of the project to other projects pending and approved and to any State comprehensive plan for treatment and prevention of drug abuse. The State shall furnish the applicant a copy of any such evaluation. A State if it so desires may, in writing, waive its rights under this paragraph.

(3) Approval of any application for a grant or contract under this section by the Secretary, including the earmarking of financial assistance for a program or project, may be granted only if the application substantially meets a set of criteria that—

(A) provide that the activities and services for which assistance under this section is sought will be substantially administered by or under the supervision of the applicant;

(B) provide for such methods of administration as are necessary for the proper and efficient operation of such programs or projects; and

(C) provide for such fiscal control and fund accounting procedures as may be necessary to assure proper disbursement of and accounting for Federal funds paid to the applicant.

(4) Each applicant within a State, upon filing its application with the Secretary for a grant or contract to provide treatment or rehabilitation services shall provide a proposed performance standard or standards, to measure, or research protocol to determine, the effectiveness of such treatment or rehabilitation program or project.

(d) Programs and projects aimed at underserved groups; encouragement and special consideration given to applications

The Secretary shall encourage the submission of and give special consideration to applications under this section to programs and projects aimed at underserved populations such as racial and ethnic minorities, Native Americans (including Native Hawaiians and Native American Pacific Islanders), youth, the elderly, women, handicapped individuals, and families of drug abusers.

(e) Payments; advances; reimbursement; installments

Payment under grants or contracts under this section may be made in advance or by way of reimbursement and in such installments as the Secretary may determine.

(f) Prevention and treatment services

Projects and programs for which grants and contracts are made or entered into under this section shall, in the case of prevention and treatment services, seek to (1) be responsive to special requirements of handicapped individuals in receiving such services; (2) whenever possible, be community based, insure care of good quality in general community care facilities and under health insurance plans, and be integrated with, and provide for the active participation of, a wide range of public and nongovernmental agencies, organizations, institutions, and individuals; (3) where a substantial number of the individuals in the population served by the project or program are of limited English-speaking ability (A) utilize the services of outreach workers fluent in the language spoken by a predominant number of such individuals and develop a plan and make arrangements responsive to the needs of such population for providing services to the extent practicable in the language and cultural context most appropriate to such individuals, and (B) identify an individual who is fluent both in that language and English and whose responsibilities shall include providing guidance to the individuals of limited English-speaking ability and to appropriate staff members with respect to cultural sensitivities and bridging linguistic and cultural differences; and (4) where appropriate, utilize existing community resources (including community mental health centers).

(g) Authorization by chief executive officer of State required; maximum amount and duration of grants

(1) No grant may be made under this section to a State or to any entity within the government of a State unless the grant application has been duly authorized by the chief executive officer of such State.

(2) No grant or contract may be made under this section for a period in excess of five years.

(3)(A) The amount of any grant or contract under this section may not exceed 100 per centum of the cost of carrying out the grant or contract in the first fiscal year for which the grant or contract is made under this section, 80 per centum of such cost in the second fiscal year for which the grant or contract is made under this section, 70 per centum of such cost in the third fiscal year for which the grant or contract is made under this section, and 60 per centum of such cost in each of the fourth and fifth fiscal years for which the grant or contract is made under this section.

(B) For purposes of this paragraph, no grant or contract shall be considered to have been made under this section for a fiscal year ending before September 30, 1981.

(Pub. L. 92–255, title IV, §410, Mar. 21, 1972, 86 Stat. 82; Pub. L. 94–237, §§10, 11, Mar. 19, 1976, 90 Stat. 247; Pub. L. 94–371, §10(c)(1), July 26, 1976, 90 Stat. 1040; Pub. L. 95–461, §§2(b), 6(a), Oct. 14, 1978, 92 Stat. 1268, 1270; Pub. L. 96–181, §7, Jan. 2, 1980, 93 Stat. 1312; Pub. L. 97–35, title IX, §970(b)–(f), Aug. 13, 1981, 95 Stat. 596, 597; Pub. L. 98–24, §5(a)(3), Apr. 26, 1983, 97 Stat. 183.)

AMENDMENTS

1983—Subsec. (d). Pub. L. 98–24 substituted "Native Americans (including Native Hawaiians and Native American Pacific Islanders)" for "native Americans".

1981—Subsec. (a). Pub. L. 97–35, §970(b), substituted "The Secretary acting through the National Institute on Drug Abuse, may make grants to and enter into contracts with individuals, and public and private nonprofit entities" for "The Secretary shall" in introductory provision preceding par. (1), reduced the enumeration of authorized activities of the Secretary from six paragraphs to two paragraphs thereby eliminating provisions relating to the recruitment, training, and employment of participants in treatment programs, the establishment, conduct, and evaluation of drug abuse prevention, treatment, and rehabilitation programs, the development of methods to deal with drug abuse in particular areas, the improvement of drug maintenance techniques or programs, and the establishment, conduct, and evaluation of drug abuse prevention and treatment programs, and inserted provision that nothing shall prevent the use of funds provided under this section for programs and projects aimed at the prevention, treatment, and rehabilitation of alcohol abuse and alcoholism as well as drug abuse.

Subsec. (b). Pub. L. 97–35, §970(c), inserted provisions relating to fiscal year ending Sept. 30, 1982.

Subsec. (c)(2). Pub. L. 97–35, §970(d)(1), substituted "responsible for the administration of drug abuse prevention activities" for "designated or established under section 1176 of this title" and "any State" for "the State" and struck out reference to drug abuse under section 1176 of this title.

Subsec. (c)(3)(D). Pub. L. 97–35, §970(d)(2), struck out subpar. (D) which had provided that approval of a grant or contract could be granted only if the application provided for reasonable assurances that Federal funds made available under this section would be used to supplement and increase the level of State, local, and other non-Federal funds that would in the absence of such Federal funds be made available for the programs described in this section and would not supplant State or local funds.

Subsec. (d). Pub. L. 97–35, §970(e), inserted applicability to racial and ethnic minorities, handicapped, native Americans, and families of drug abusers.

Subsec. (g). Pub. L. 97–35, §970(f), added subsec. (g).

1980—Subsec. (a)(1). Pub. L. 96–181, §7(a)(1), substituted "development, demonstration and evaluation of drug abuse" for "development of drug abuse".

Subsec. (a)(5). Pub. L. 96–181, §7(a)(2), substituted "drug maintenance and detoxification techniques" for "drug maintenance techniques".

Subsec. (a)(6). Pub. L. 96–181, §7(a)(3), in provisions relating to evaluation of drug abuse prevention and treatment programs, inserted provision that such evaluation be with particular emphasis on replicating effective prevention and treatment programs.

Subsec. (b). Pub. L. 96–181, §7(b), inserted authorization of appropriations for grants and contracts under pars. (3) and (6) of subsec. (a) and for other programs and activities for fiscal years ending Sept. 30, 1980, and Sept. 30, 1981, and required certain percentage of appropriated funds to be obligated for grants and contracts for primary prevention and intervention programs designed to discourage individuals from abusing drugs.

Subsec. (d). Pub. L. 96–181, §7(c), inserted provisions for special consideration to applications for programs and projects for prevention and treatment of drug abuse and drug dependence by elderly.

Subsec. (f). Pub. L. 96–181, §7(d), added subsec. (f).

1978—Subsec. (a). Pub. L. 95–461, §6(a), inserted provision requiring Secretary to act through National Institute on Drug Abuse in making special project grants.

Subsec. (b). Pub. L. 95–461, §2(b), inserted provisions authorizing appropriations for fiscal year ending Sept. 30, 1979.

1976—Subsec. (a). Pub. L. 94–237, §10(a), inserted provisions which authorized Secretary to give a high priority to applications for grants and contracts for primary prevention programs, and set forth programs included within primary prevention programs and scope of Secretary's funding authority.

Subsec. (b). Pub. L. 94–237, §11, substituted "$160,000,000 for each of the fiscal years ending June 30, 1975 and June 30, 1976; $40,000,000 for the period July 1, 1976, through September 30, 1976; and $160,000,000 for each of the fiscal years ending September 30, 1977, and September 30, 1978," for "and $160,000,000 for the fiscal year ending June 30, 1975,".

Subsec. (c)(4). Pub. L. 94–237, §10(b), added par. (4).

Subsecs. (d), (e). Pub. L. 94–371 added subsec. (d) and redesignated former subsec. (d) as (e).

EFFECTIVE DATE OF 1976 AMENDMENT

Section 10(c)(2) of Pub. L. 94–371 provided that: "The amendment made by paragraph (1) [amending this section] shall apply with respect to applications submitted for grants or contracts under section 410 of the Drug Abuse Office and Treatment Act of 1972 [this section] after June 30, 1976."

§ 1178. Records and audit

(a) Assistance records; contents

Each recipient of assistance under section 1177 of this title pursuant to grants or contracts entered into under other than competitive bidding procedures shall keep such records as the Secretary shall prescribe, including records which fully disclose the amount and disposition by such recipient of the proceeds of such grant or contract, the total cost of the project or undertaking in connection with which such grant or contract is given or used, and the amount of that portion of the cost of the project or undertaking supplied by other sources, and such other records as will facilitate an effective audit.

(b) Access to pertinent information for audit and examination

The Secretary and Comptroller General of the United States, or any of their duly authorized representatives, shall have access for the purpose of audit and examination to any books, documents, papers, and records of such recipients that are pertinent to such grants or contracts.

(Pub. L. 92–255, title IV, §411, Mar. 21, 1972, 86 Stat. 83; Pub. L. 97–35, title IX, §971, Aug. 13, 1981, 95 Stat. 597.)

AMENDMENTS

1981—Subsec. (a). Pub. L. 97–35 struck out reference to section 1176 of this title.

§1179. National Drug Abuse Training Center

(a) Establishment; functions; general policies; transfer of supervision

The Director shall establish a National Drug Abuse Training Center (hereinafter in this section referred to as the "Center") to develop, conduct, and support a full range of training programs relating to drug abuse prevention functions. The Director shall consult with the National Advisory Council for Drug Abuse Prevention regarding the general policies of the Center. The Director may supervise the operation of the Center initially, but shall transfer the supervision of the operation of the Center to the National Institute on Drug Abuse not later than December 31, 1974.

(b) Activities and material

The Center shall conduct or arrange for training programs, seminars, meetings, conferences, and other related activities, including the furnishing of training and educational materials for use by others.

(c) Persons eligible for services and facilities

The services and facilities of the Center shall, in accordance with regulations prescribed by the Director, be available to (1) Federal, State, and local governmental officials, and their respective staffs, (2) medical and paramedical personnel, and educators, and (3) other persons, including drug dependent persons, requiring training or education in drug abuse prevention.

(d) Authorization of appropriations; fiscal year availability

(1) For the purpose of carrying out this section, there are authorized to be appropriated $1,000,000 for the fiscal year ending June 30, 1972, $3,000,000 for the fiscal year ending June 30, 1973, $5,000,000 for the fiscal year ending June 30, 1974, and $6,000,000 for the fiscal year ending June 30, 1975.

(2) Sums appropriated under this subsection shall remain available for obligation or expenditure in the fiscal year for which appropriated and in the fiscal year next following.

(Pub. L. 92–255, title IV, §412, Mar. 21, 1972, 86 Stat. 84.)

NATIONAL ADVISORY COUNCIL FOR DRUG ABUSE PREVENTION

Section 1151 of this title, which established the National Advisory Council for Drug Abuse Prevention, was repealed by Pub. L. 92–255, title I, §104, Mar. 21, 1972, 86 Stat. 67, eff. June 30, 1975.

§1180. Transferred

CODIFICATION

Section, Pub. L. 92–255, title IV, §413, Mar. 21, 1972, 86 Stat. 84; Pub. L. 96–181, §8(a), (b)(1), Jan. 2, 1980, 93 Stat. 1313, 1314; Pub. L. 97–35, title IX, §973(e), Aug. 13, 1981, 95 Stat. 598, which related to drug abuse among government and other employees, was redesignated section 525 of the Public Health Service Act by Pub. L. 98–24, §2(b)(16)(A), Apr. 26, 1983, 97 Stat. 182, and is classified to section 290ee–1 of Title 42, The Public Health and Welfare.

§1181. Contract authority

The authority of the Secretary to enter into contracts under this subchapter and subchapter V of this chapter shall be effective for any fiscal year only to such extent or in such amounts as are provided in advance by appropriation Acts.

(Pub. L. 92–255, title IV, §414, as added Pub. L. 96–181, §9(a), Jan. 2, 1980, 93 Stat. 1314.)

REFERENCES IN TEXT

Subchapter V of this chapter, referred to in text, consisted of sections 501 to 504 of title V of Pub. L. 92–255, Mar. 21, 1972, 86 Stat. 85, which were classified to sections 1191 to 1194 of this title, respectively. Sections 501 to 503 were made part of the Public Health Service Act by Pub. L. 98–24, §2(b)(4), (11), (15), Apr. 26, 1983, 97 Stat. 177, 180, 181, and were transferred to former sections 290aa–2, 290ee, and 290cc, respectively, of Title 42, The Public Health and Welfare. Section 290aa–2 of Title 42 was repealed by Pub. L. 102–321, §101(b). Section 290cc of Title 42 was repealed by Pub. L. 102–321, §123(c). Section 290ee of Title 42 was omitted in the general revision of part D of subchapter III–A of chapter 6A of Title 42 by Pub. L. 102–321. Section 1194 of this title was repealed by Pub. L. 98–24, §2(c)(2).

SUBCHAPTER V—NATIONAL INSTITUTE ON DRUG ABUSE

§§1191 to 1193. Transferred

CODIFICATION

Section 1191, Pub. L. 92–255, title V, §501, Mar. 21, 1972, 86 Stat. 85; Pub. L. 93–282, title II, §204, May 14, 1974, 88 Stat. 136; Pub. L. 94–237, §12(a), Mar. 19, 1976, 90 Stat. 247; Pub. L. 96–181, §10, Jan. 2, 1980, 93 Stat. 1314; Pub. L. 97–35, title IX, §973(f), Aug. 13, 1981, 95 Stat. 598, which established the National Institute on Drug Abuse, was redesignated section 503(a)–(d) of the Public Health Service Act by Pub. L. 98–24, §2(b)(4), Apr. 26, 1983, 97 Stat. 177, transferred to section 290aa–2(a)–(d) of Title 42, The Public Health and Welfare, and subsequently repealed.

Section 1192, Pub. L. 92–255, title V, §502, as added Pub. L. 94–237, §12(b)(1), Mar. 19, 1976, 90 Stat. 247; amended Pub. L. 95–461, §5, Oct. 14, 1978, 92 Stat. 1269; Pub. L. 96–181, §11, Jan. 2, 1980, 93 Stat. 1315, which related to the coordination, information, assistance, and assignment activities and services, was redesignated section 524 of the Public Health Service Act by Pub. L. 98–24, §2(b)(15), Apr. 26, 1983, 97 Stat. 181, transferred to section 290ee of Title 42, and subsequently omitted.

Section 1193, Pub. L. 92–255, title V, §503, as added Pub. L. 94–237, §13(a), Mar. 19, 1976, 90 Stat. 248; amended Pub. L. 95–461, §2(c), Oct. 14, 1978, 92 Stat. 1268; Pub. L. 96–181, §12, Jan. 2, 1980, 93 Stat. 1315; Pub. L. 97–35, title IX, §972(a), (b), Aug. 13, 1981, 95 Stat. 597, which related to research and development functions, was redesignated section 515 of the Public Health Service Act by Pub. L. 98–24, §2(b)(11), Apr. 26, 1983, 97 Stat. 180, transferred to section 290cc of Title 42, and subsequently repealed.

PRIOR PROVISIONS

A prior section 502 of Pub. L. 92–255, Mar. 21, 1972, 86 Stat. 85, amended section 217 of the Public Health Service Act by adding subsec. (e) [section 218(e) of Title 42, The Public Health and Welfare], and amended section 266 of the Community Mental Health Centers Act [former section 2688t of Title 42].

§1194. Repealed. Pub. L. 98–24, §2(c)(2), Apr. 26, 1983, 97 Stat. 182

Section, Pub. L. 92–255, title V, §504, as added Pub. L. 95–461, §6(b)(1), Oct. 14, 1978, 92 Stat. 1270, related to review by the Secretary of programs and activities. See section 290aa–5 of Title 42, The Public Health and Welfare.

CHAPTER 17—NATIONAL DRUG ENFORCEMENT POLICY

§§1201 to 1204. Repealed. Pub. L. 100–690, title I, §1007(a)(3), Nov. 18, 1988, 102 Stat. 4187

Section 1201, Pub. L. 98–473, title II, §1302, Oct. 12, 1984, 98 Stat. 2168, set forth Congressional findings and declaration of purpose relating to illegal flow of narcotics into United States.

Section 1202, Pub. L. 98–473, title II, §1303, Oct. 12, 1984, 98 Stat. 2168, established National Drug Enforcement Policy Board.

Section 1203, Pub. L. 98–473, title II, §1304, Oct. 12, 1984, 98 Stat. 2169, delineated responsibilities and functions of National Drug Enforcement Policy Board.

Section 1204, Pub. L. 98–473, title II, §1305, Oct. 12, 1984, 98 Stat. 2170, related to reports to Congress.

EFFECTIVE DATE OF REPEAL

Section 1007(a)(3) of Pub. L. 100–690 provided that the repeal of this chapter is effective on 30th day after first Director of National Drug Control Policy is confirmed by the Senate.

SHORT TITLE

Pub. L. 98–473, title II, §1301, Oct. 12, 1984, 98 Stat. 2168, which provided that chapter XIII (§§1301 to 1307) of title II of Pub. L. 98–473 was to be cited as the National Narcotics Act of 1984, was repealed by Pub. L. 100–690, title I, §1007(a)(3), Nov. 18, 1988, 102 Stat. 4187.

EXECUTIVE ORDER NO. 12590

Ex. Ord. No. 12590, Mar. 26, 1987, 52 F.R. 10021, as amended by Ex. Ord. No. 13284, §11, Jan. 23, 2003, 68 F.R. 4076, provided for the establishment of a National Drug Policy Board, designated its membership and functions, and authorized coordinating groups.

CHAPTER 18—PRESIDENT'S MEDIA COMMISSION ON ALCOHOL AND DRUG ABUSE PREVENTION

§§1301 to 1308. Omitted

CODIFICATION

Section 1301, Pub. L. 99–570, title VIII, §8002, Oct. 27, 1986, 100 Stat. 3207–161 related to the establishment of the President's Media Commission on Alcohol and Drug Abuse Prevention.

Section 1302, Pub. L. 99–570, title VIII, §8003, Oct. 27, 1986, 100 Stat. 3207–161, related to duties of the Commission.

Section 1303, Pub. L. 99–570, title VIII, §8004, Oct. 27, 1986, 100 Stat. 3207–162, required appointment of members of the Commission within 30 days after Oct. 27, 1986.

Section 1304, Pub. L. 99–570, title VIII, §8005, Oct. 27, 1986, 100 Stat. 3207–162, related to meetings.

Section 1305, Pub. L. 99–570, title VIII, §8006, Oct. 27, 1986, 100 Stat. 3207–163, related to employment of Director and staff and the procurement of the services of experts and consultants.

Section 1306, Pub. L. 99–570, title VIII, §8007, Oct. 27, 1986, 100 Stat. 3207–163, related to the powers of the Commission.

Section 1307, Pub. L. 99–570, title VIII, §8008, Oct. 27, 1986, 100 Stat. 3207–163, related to an annual report to Congress.

Section 1308, Pub. L. 99–570, title VIII, §8009, Oct. 27, 1986, 100 Stat. 3207–163, related to termination of Commission three years after the date on which members of the Commission were first appointed unless the President extended the authority of the Commission by Executive order.

SHORT TITLE

Pub. L. 99–570, title VIII, §8001, Oct. 27, 1986, 100 Stat. 3207–161, provided that title VIII of Pub. L. 99–570, which enacted this chapter, was to be cited as the "President's Media Commission on Alcohol and Drug Abuse Prevention Act".

CHAPTER 19—PESTICIDE MONITORING IMPROVEMENTS

§1401. Pesticide monitoring and enforcement information

(a) Data management systems

(1) Not later than 480 days after August 23, 1988, the Secretary of Health and Human Services shall place in effect computerized data management systems for the Food and Drug Administration under which the Administration will—

(A) record, summarize, and evaluate the results of its program for monitoring food products for pesticide residues,

(B) identify gaps in its pesticide monitoring program in the monitoring of (i) pesticides, (ii) food products, and (iii) food from specific countries and from domestic sources,

(C) detect trends in the presence of pesticide residues in food products and identify public health problems emerging from the occurrence of pesticide residues in food products,

(D) focus its testing resources for monitoring pesticide residues in food on detecting those residues which pose a public health concern,

(E) prepare summaries of the information listed in subsection (b) of this section, and

(F) provide information to assist the Environmental Protection Agency in carrying out its responsibilities under the Federal Insecticide, Fungicide, and Rodenticide Act [7 U.S.C. 136 et seq.] and the Federal Food, Drug, and Cosmetic Act [21 U.S.C. 301 et seq.].

(2) As soon as practicable, the Secretary of Health and Human Services shall develop a means to enable the computerized data management systems placed into effect under paragraph (1) to make the summary described in subsection (c) of this section.

(3)(A) Paragraph (1) does not limit the authority of the Food and Drug Administration to—

(i) use the computerized data management systems placed in effect under paragraph (1), or

(ii) develop additional data management systems,

to facilitate the regulation of any substance or product covered under the requirements of the Federal Food, Drug, and Cosmetic Act [21 U.S.C. 301 et seq.].

(B) In placing into effect the computerized data management systems under paragraph (1) and in carrying out paragraph (2), the Secretary shall comply with applicable regulations governing computer system design and procurement.

(b) Information

The Food and Drug Administration shall use the computerized data management systems placed into effect under subsection (a)(1) of this section to prepare a summary of—

(1) information on—

(A) the types of imported and domestically produced food products analyzed for compliance with the requirements of the Federal Food, Drug, and Cosmetic Act [21 U.S.C. 301 et seq.] regarding the presence of pesticide residues,

(B) the number of samples of each such food product analyzed for such compliance by country of origin,

(C) the pesticide residues which may be detected using the testing methods employed,

(D) the pesticide residues in such food detected and the levels detected,

(E) the compliance status of each sample of such food tested and the violation rate for each country-product combination, and

(F) the action taken with respect to each sample of such food found to be in violation of the Federal Food, Drug, and Cosmetic Act [21 U.S.C. 301 et seq.] and its ultimate disposition, and

(2) information on—

(A) the country of origin of each imported food product referred to in paragraph (1)(A), and

(B) the United States district of entry for each such imported food product.

(c) Volume data

The Food and Drug Administration shall use the computerized data management systems placed into effect under subsection (a)(1) of this section to summarize the volume of each type of food product subject to the requirements of the Federal Food, Drug, and Cosmetic Act [21 U.S.C. 301 et seq.] which is imported into the United States and which has an entry value which exceeds an amount established by the Secretary of Health and Human Services. The summary shall be made by country of origin and district of entry. Information with respect to volumes of food products to be included in the summary shall, to the extent feasible, be obtained from data bases of other Federal agencies.

(d) Compilation

Not later than 90 days after the expiration of 1 year after the data management systems are placed into effect under subsection (a) of this section and annually thereafter, the Secretary of Health and Human Services shall compile a summary of the information described in subsection (b) of this section with respect to the previous year. When the Food and Drug Administration is able to make summaries under subsection (c) of this section, the Secretary shall include in the compilation under the preceding sentence a compilation of the information described in subsection (c) of this section. Compilations under this subsection shall be made available to Federal and State agencies and other interested persons.

(Pub. L. 100–418, title IV, § 4702, Aug. 23, 1988, 102 Stat. 1412.)

REFERENCES IN TEXT

The Federal Insecticide, Fungicide, and Rodenticide Act, referred to in subsec. (a)(1)(F), is act June 25, 1947, ch. 125, as amended generally by Pub. L. 92–516, Oct. 21, 1972, 86 Stat. 973, which is classified generally to subchapter II (§ 136 et seq.) of chapter 6 of Title 7, Agriculture. For complete classification of this Act to the Code, see Short Title note set out under section 136 of Title 7 and Tables.

The Federal Food, Drug, and Cosmetic Act, referred to in subsecs. (a) to (c), is act June 25, 1938, ch. 675, 52 Stat. 1040, as amended, which is classified generally to chapter 9 (§ 301 et seq.) of this title. For complete classification of this Act to the Code, see section 301 of this title and Tables.

SHORT TITLE

Section 4701 of Pub. L. 100–418 provided that: "This subtitle [subtitle G (§§ 4701–4704) of title IV of Pub. L. 100–418, enacting this chapter] may be cited as the 'Pesticide Monitoring Improvements Act of 1988'."

IMPORTED MEAT, POULTRY PRODUCTS, EGGS, AND EGG PRODUCTS

Section 4506 of Pub. L. 100–418 provided that:

"(a) REPORT.—Not later than 90 days after the date of the enactment of this Act [Aug. 23, 1988], the Secretary of Agriculture shall submit a report to Congress—

"(1) specifying the planned distribution, in fiscal years 1988 and 1989, of the resources of the Department of Agriculture available for sampling imported covered products to ensure compliance with the requirements of the Federal Meat Inspection Act (21 U.S.C. 601 et seq.), the Poultry Products Inspection Act (21 U.S.C. 451 et seq.), and the Egg Products Inspection Act (21 U.S.C. 1031 et seq.) that govern the level of residues of pesticides, drugs, and other products permitted in or on such products;

"(2) describing current methods used by the Secretary to enforce the requirements of such Acts with respect to the level of residues of pesticides, drugs, and other products permitted in or on such products;

"(3) responding to the audit report of the Inspector General of the Department of Agriculture, Number 38002—2—hy, dated January 14, 1987;

"(4) providing a summary with respect to the importation of covered products during fiscal years 1987 and 1988 that specifies—

"(A) the number of samples of each such product taken during each such fiscal year in carrying out the requirements described in paragraph (1); and

"(B) for each violation of such requirements during each such fiscal year—

"(i) the covered products with respect to which such violation occurred;

"(ii) the residue in or on such product in violation of such requirements;

"(iii) the country exporting such product;

"(iv) the actions taken in response to such violation and the reasons for such actions; and

"(v) the level of testing conducted by the countries exporting such products;

"(5) describing any research conducted by the Secretary to develop improved methods to detect residues subject to such requirements in or on covered products; and

"(6) providing any recommendations the Secretary considers appropriate for legislation to add or modify penalties for violations of laws, regulations, and other enforcement requirements governing the level of residues that are permitted in or on imported covered products.

"(b) REVISION.—Not later than November 15, 1989, the Secretary of Agriculture shall revise, as necessary, the report prepared under subsection (a) and submit the revision to Congress.

"(c) DEFINITION.—As used in this section, the term 'covered products' means meat, poultry products, eggs, and egg products."

§ 1402. Foreign pesticide information

(a) Cooperative agreements

The Secretary of Health and Human Services shall enter into cooperative agreements with the governments of the countries which are the major sources of food imports into the United States subject to pesticide residue monitoring by the Food and Drug Administration for the purpose of improving the ability of the Food and Drug Administration to assure compliance with the pesticide tolerance requirements of the Federal Food, Drug, and Cosmetic Act [21 U.S.C. 301 et seq.] with regard to imported food.

(b) Information activities

(1) The cooperative agreements entered into under subsection (a) of this section with governments of foreign countries shall specify the action to be taken by the parties to the agreements to accomplish the purpose described in subsection (a) of this section, including the means by which the governments of the foreign countries will provide to the Secretary of Health and Human Services current information identifying each of the pesticides used in the production, transportation, and storage of food products imported from production regions of such countries into the United States.

(2) In the case of a foreign country with which the Secretary is unable to enter into an agreement under subsection (a) of this section or for which the information provided under paragraph (1) is insufficient to assure an effective pesticide monitoring program, the Secretary shall, to the extent practicable, obtain the information described in paragraph (1) with respect to such country from other Federal or international agencies or private sources.

(3) The Secretary of Health and Human Services shall assure that appropriate offices of the Food and Drug Administration which are engaged in the monitoring of imported food for pesticide residues receive the information obtained under paragraph (1) or (2).

(4) The Secretary of Health and Human Services shall make available any information obtained under paragraph (1) or (2) to State agencies engaged in the monitoring of imported food for pesticide residues other than information obtained from private sources the disclosure of which to such agencies is restricted.

(c) Coordination with other agencies

The Secretary of Health and Human Services shall—

(1) notify in writing the Department of Agriculture, the Environmental Protection Agency, and the Department of State at the initiation of negotiations with a foreign country to develop a cooperative agreement under subsection (a) of this section; and

(2) coordinate the activities of the Department of Health and Human Services with the activities of those departments and agencies, as appropriate, during the course of such negotiations.

(d) Report

Not later than one year after August 23, 1988, the Secretary of Health and Human Services shall report to the Committee on Agriculture, Nutrition, and Forestry and the Committee on Labor and Human Resources of the Senate and the House of Representatives on the activities undertaken by the Secretary to implement this section. The report shall be made available to appropriate Federal and State agencies and to interested persons.

(Pub. L. 100–418, title IV, § 4703, Aug. 23, 1988, 102 Stat. 1413.)

REFERENCES IN TEXT

The Federal Food, Drug, and Cosmetic Act, referred to in subsec. (a), is act June 25, 1938, ch. 675, 52 Stat. 1040, as amended, which is classified generally to chapter 9 (§ 301 et seq.) of this title. For complete classification of this Act to the Code, see section 301 of this title and Tables.

CHANGE OF NAME

Committee on Labor and Human Resources of Senate changed to Committee on Health, Education, Labor, and Pensions of Senate by Senate Resolution No. 20, One Hundred Sixth Congress, Jan. 19, 1999.

§ 1403. Pesticide analytical methods

The Secretary of Health and Human Services shall, in consultation with the Administrator of the Environmental Protection Agency—

(1) develop a detailed long-range plan and timetable for research that is necessary for the development of and validation of—

(A) new and improved analytical methods capable of detecting at one time the presence of multiple pesticide residues in food, and

(B) rapid pesticide analytical methods, and

(2) conduct a review to determine whether the use of rapid pesticide analytical methods by the Secretary would enable the Secretary to improve the cost-effectiveness of monitoring and enforcement activities under the Federal Food, Drug, and Cosmetic Act [21 U.S.C. 301 et seq.], including increasing the number of pesticide residues which can be detected and the number of tests for pesticide residues which can be conducted in a cost-effective manner.

The Secretary shall report the plan developed under paragraph (1), the resources necessary to carry out the research described in such paragraph, recommendations for the implementation of such research, and the result of the review conducted under paragraph (2) not later than the expiration of 240 days after August 23, 1988, to the Committee on Agriculture, Nutrition, and Forestry and the Committee on Labor and Human Resources of the Senate and the House of Representatives.

(Pub. L. 100–418, title IV, § 4704, Aug. 23, 1988, 102 Stat. 1414.)

REFERENCES IN TEXT

The Federal Food, Drug, and Cosmetic Act, referred to in text, is act June 25, 1938, ch. 675, 52 Stat. 1040, as amended, which is classified generally to chapter 9 (§ 301 et seq.) of this title. For complete classification of this Act to the Code, see section 301 of this title and Tables.

CHANGE OF NAME

Committee on Labor and Human Resources of Senate changed to Committee on Health, Education, Labor, and Pensions of Senate by Senate Resolution No. 20, One Hundred Sixth Congress, Jan. 19, 1999.

CHAPTER 20—NATIONAL DRUG CONTROL PROGRAM

SUBCHAPTER I—OFFICE OF NATIONAL DRUG CONTROL POLICY

SUBCHAPTER I—OFFICE OF NATIONAL DRUG CONTROL POLICY

§§ 1501, 1502. Repealed. Pub. L. 100–690, title I, § 1009, Nov. 18, 1988, 102 Stat. 4188, as amended by Pub. L. 105–20, § 2(b), June 27, 1997, 111 Stat. 234

Section 1501, Pub. L. 100–690, title I, § 1002, Nov. 18, 1988, 102 Stat. 4181, established Office of National Drug Control Policy in Executive Office of President. See section 1702 of this title.

Section 1502, Pub. L. 100–690, title I, § 1003, Nov. 18, 1988, 102 Stat. 4182; Pub. L. 103–322, title IX, §§ 90201, 90202, 90207, Sept. 13, 1994, 108 Stat. 1990, 1991, 1995, related to appointment and duties of Director, Deputy Directors, and Associate Director of Office of National Drug Control Policy. See section 1703 of this title.

EFFECTIVE DATE OF REPEAL

Repeal effective Sept. 30, 1997, see section 1009 of Pub. L. 100–690, as amended, which was formerly classified to section 1506 of this title.

SHORT TITLE OF 1997 AMENDMENT

Pub. L. 105–20, § 1, June 27, 1997, 111 Stat. 224, provided that: "This Act [enacting subchapter II of this chapter and amending former sections 1504, 1506 to 1508 of this title, section 2291 of Title 22, Foreign Relations and Intercourse, and provisions set out as notes under this section] may be cited as the 'Drug-Free Communities Act of 1997'."

SHORT TITLE

Section 1 of Pub. L. 100–690 provided that: "This Act [see Tables for classification] may be cited as the 'Anti-Drug Abuse Act of 1988'."

Section 1001 of Pub. L. 100–690 provided that: "This subtitle [subtitle A (§§ 1001–1048) of title I of Pub. L. 100–690, enacting this chapter, amending section 1115 of this title, sections 5312, 5314, and 5315 of Title 5, Government Organization and Employees, section 1105 of Title 31, Money and Finance, and section 402 of Title 50, War and National Defense, repealing sections 1103, 1111 to 1114, 1116, and 1201 to 1204 of this title, enacting provisions set out as notes under sections 1201 and 1501 of this title, and repealing provisions set out as notes under section 1201 of this title may be cited as the 'National Narcotics Leadership Act of 1988'."

REFERENCES TO SUBTITLE A OF PUB. L. 100–690

Pub. L. 105–20, § 2(b), June 27, 1997, 111 Stat. 234, provided that: "Each reference in Federal law to subtitle A of the Anti-Drug Abuse Act of 1988 [see section 1001 of Pub. L. 100–690, set out above], with the exception of section 1001 of such subtitle, in any provision of law that is in effect on the day before the date of enactment of this Act [June 27, 1997] shall be deemed to be a reference to chapter 1 of the National Narcotics Leadership Act of 1988 [chapter 1 of subtitle A (§§ 1002–1012) of title I of Pub. L. 100–690, see Tables for classification] (as so designated by this section)."

§ 1502a. Transferred

CODIFICATION

Section, Pub. L. 100–690, title I, § 1003A, as added Pub. L. 101–510, div. A, title X, § 1011, Nov. 5, 1990, 104 Stat. 1633, and amended, which related to the Counter-Drug Technology Assessment Center, was renumbered section 1008 of Pub. L. 100–690 by Pub. L. 103–322, title IX, § 90204(c)(2), (3), Sept. 13, 1994, 108 Stat. 1994, and transferred to former section 1505 of this title.

§§ 1503 to 1505. Repealed. Pub. L. 100–690, title I, § 1009, Nov. 18, 1988, 102 Stat. 4188, as amended by Pub. L. 105–20, § 2(b), June 27, 1997, 111 Stat. 234

Section 1503, Pub. L. 100–690, title I, § 1004, Nov. 18, 1988, 102 Stat. 4184, related to coordination between Office of National Drug Control Policy and executive branch departments and agencies. See section 1704 of this title.

Section 1504, Pub. L. 100–690, title I, § 1005, Nov. 18, 1988, 102 Stat. 4185; Pub. L. 103–322, title IX, § 90203, Sept. 13, 1994, 108 Stat. 1991; Pub. L. 105–20, § 2(b), June 27, 1997, 111 Stat. 234, related to annual development and submission of National Drug Control Strategy by President to Congress. See section 1705 of this title.

Section 1505, Pub. L. 100–690, title I, § 1008, formerly § 1003A, as added Pub. L. 101–510, div. A, title X, § 1011, Nov. 5, 1990, 104 Stat. 1633; renumbered § 1008 and amended Pub. L. 103–322, title IX, § 90204(a), (b), (c)(2), (3), Sept. 13, 1994, 108 Stat. 1993, 1994, established Counter-Drug Technology Assessment Center within Office of National Drug Control Policy. See section 1707 of this title.

A prior section 1505, Pub. L. 100–690, title I, § 1008, Nov. 18, 1988, 102 Stat. 4188, provided for an executive reorganization study and report to Congress and the President no later than Jan. 15, 1990, prior to repeal by Pub. L. 103–322, § 90204(c)(1).

EFFECTIVE DATE OF REPEAL

Repeal effective Sept. 30, 1997, see section 1009 of Pub. L. 100–690, as amended, which was formerly classified to section 1506 of this title.

§ 1505a. Annual report on development and deployment of narcotics detection technologies

(a) Report requirement

Not later than December 1st of each year, the Director of the Office of National Drug Control Policy shall submit to Congress and the President a report on the development and deployment of narcotics detection technologies by Federal agencies. Each such report shall be prepared in consultation with the Secretary of Defense, the Secretary of State, the Secretary of Homeland Security, and the Secretary of the Treasury.

(b) Matters to be included

Each report under subsection (a) of this section shall include—

(1) a description of each project implemented by a Federal agency relating to the development or deployment of narcotics detection technology;

(2) the agency responsible for each project described in paragraph (1);

(3) the amount of funds obligated or expended to carry out each project described in paragraph (1) during the fiscal year in which the report is submitted or during any fiscal year preceding the fiscal year in which the report is submitted;

(4) the amount of funds estimated to be obligated or expended for each project described in paragraph (1) during any fiscal year after the fiscal year in which the report is submitted to Congress; and

(5) a detailed timeline for implementation of each project described in paragraph (1).

(Pub. L. 105–85, div. A, title X, § 1034, Nov. 18, 1997, 111 Stat. 1884; Pub. L. 107–296, title XVII, § 1704(e)(10), Nov. 25, 2002, 116 Stat. 2315.)

CODIFICATION

Section was enacted as part of the National Defense Authorization Act for Fiscal Year 1998, and not as part of the National Narcotics Leadership Act of 1988 which comprises this chapter.

AMENDMENTS

2002—Subsec. (a). Pub. L. 107–296 substituted "of Homeland Security" for "of Transportation".

EFFECTIVE DATE OF 2002 AMENDMENT

Amendment by Pub. L. 107–296 effective on the date of transfer of the Coast Guard to the Department of Homeland Security, see section 1704(g) of Pub. L. 107–296, set out as a note under section 101 of Title 10, Armed Forces.

§§ 1506 to 1508. Repealed. Pub. L. 100–690, title I, § 1009, Nov. 18, 1988, 102 Stat. 4188, as amended by Pub. L. 105–20, § 2(b), June 27, 1997, 111 Stat. 234

Section 1506, Pub. L. 100–690, title I, § 1009, Nov. 18, 1988, 102 Stat. 4188; Pub. L. 103–322, title IX, § 90208(a), Sept. 13, 1994, 108 Stat. 1995; Pub. L. 105–20, § 2(b), June 27, 1997, 111 Stat. 234, repealed this subchapter, and the amendments made by this subchapter, except for section 1007, effective Sept. 30, 1997.

Section 1507, Pub. L. 100–690, title I, § 1010, Nov. 18, 1988, 102 Stat. 4188; Pub. L. 105–20, § 2(b), June 27, 1997, 111 Stat. 234, defined terms for purposes of this subchapter. See section 1701 of this title.

Section 1508, Pub. L. 100–690, title I, § 1011, Nov. 18, 1988, 102 Stat. 4189; Pub. L. 103–322, title IX, § 90206, Sept. 13, 1994, 108 Stat. 1995; Pub. L. 105–20, § 2(b), June 27, 1997, 111 Stat. 234, authorized appropriations to carry out this subchapter. See section 1711 of this title.

EFFECTIVE DATE OF REPEAL

Repeal effective Sept. 30, 1997, see section 1009 of Pub. L. 100–690, as amended, which was formerly classified to section 1506 of this title.

§ 1509. Repealed. Pub. L. 109–469, title XI, § 1101(b), Dec. 29, 2006, 120 Stat. 3539

Section, Pub. L. 100–690, title VI, § 6073, Nov. 18, 1988, 102 Stat. 4323; Pub. L. 101–647, title XX, § 2001(b), Nov. 29, 1990, 104 Stat. 4854; Pub. L. 102–393, title VI, § 638(c), Oct. 6, 1992, 106 Stat. 1788; Pub. L. 103–322, title IX, § 90205(a), (d), Sept. 13, 1994, 108 Stat. 1994, 1995; Pub. L. 105–277, div. C, title VII, § 712, Oct. 21, 1998, 112 Stat. 2681–692, related to establishment of Special Forfeiture Fund.

SUBCHAPTER II—DRUG-FREE COMMUNITIES

§ 1521. Findings

Congress finds the following:

(1) Substance abuse among youth has more than doubled in the 5-year period preceding 1996, with substantial increases in the use of marijuana, inhalants, cocaine, methamphetamine, LSD, and heroin.

(2) The most dramatic increases in substance abuse has occurred among 13- and 14-year-olds.

(3) Casual or periodic substance abuse by youth today will contribute to hard core or chronic substance abuse by the next generation of adults.

(4) Substance abuse is at the core of other problems, such as rising violent teenage and violent gang crime, increasing health care costs, HIV infections, teenage pregnancy, high school dropouts, and lower economic productivity.

(5) Increases in substance abuse among youth are due in large part to an erosion of understanding by youth of the high risks associated with substance abuse, and to the softening of peer norms against use.

(6)(A) Substance abuse is a preventable behavior and a treatable disease; and

(B)(i) during the 13-year period beginning with 1979, monthly use of illegal drugs among youth 12 to 17 years of age declined by over 70 percent; and

(ii) data suggests that if parents would simply talk to their children regularly about the dangers of substance abuse, use among youth could be expected to decline by as much as 30 percent.

(7) Community anti-drug coalitions throughout the United States are successfully developing and implementing comprehensive, long-term strategies to reduce substance abuse among youth on a sustained basis.

(8) Intergovernmental cooperation and coordination through national, State, and local or tribal leadership and partnerships are critical to facilitate the reduction of substance abuse among youth in communities throughout the United States.

(Pub. L. 100–690, title I, § 1021, as added Pub. L. 105–20, § 2(a)(2), June 27, 1997, 111 Stat. 224.)

FIVE-YEAR EXTENSION OF DRUG-FREE COMMUNITIES SUPPORT PROGRAM

Pub. L. 107–82, § 1(a), Dec. 14, 2001, 115 Stat. 814, provided that: "Congress makes the following findings:

"(1) In the next 15 years, the youth population in the United States will grow by 21 percent, adding 6,500,000 youth to the population of the United States. Even if drug use rates remain constant, there will be a huge surge in drug-related problems, such as academic failure, drug-related violence, and HIV incidence, simply due to this population increase.

"(2) According to the 1994–1996 National Household Survey, 60 percent of students age 12 to 17 who frequently cut classes and who reported delinquent behavior in the past 6 months used marijuana 52 days or more in the previous year.

"(3) The 2000 Washington Kids Count survey conducted by the University of Washington reported that students whose peers have little or no involvement with drinking and drugs have higher math and reading scores than students whose peers had low level drinking or drug use.

"(4) Substance abuse prevention works. In 1999, only 10 percent of teens saw marijuana users as popular, compared to 17 percent in 1998 and 19 percent in 1997. The rate of past-month use of any drug among 12- to 17-year-olds declined 26 percent between 1997 and 1999. Marijuana use for sixth through eighth graders is at the lowest point in 5 years, as is use of cocaine, inhalants, and hallucinogens.

"(5) Community Anti-Drug Coalitions throughout the United States are successfully developing and implementing comprehensive, long-term strategies to reduce substance abuse among youth on a sustained basis. For example:

"(A) The Boston Coalition brought college and university presidents together to create the Cooperative Agreement on Underage Drinking. This agreement represents the first coordinated effort of Boston's many institutions of higher education to address issues such as binge drinking, underage drinking, and changing the norms surrounding alcohol abuse that exist on college and university campuses.

"(B) In 2000, the Coalition for a Drug-Free Greater Cincinnati surveyed more than 47,000 local students in grades 7 through 12. The results provided evidence that the Coalition's initiatives are working. For the first time in a decade, teen drug use in Greater Cincinnati appears to be leveling off. The data collected from the survey has served as a tool to strengthen relationships between schools and communities, as well as facilitate the growth of anti-drug coalitions in communities where such coalitions had not existed.

"(C) The Miami Coalition used a three-part strategy to decrease the percentage of high school seniors who reported using marijuana at least once during the most recent 30-day period. The development of a media strategy, the creation of a network of prevention agencies, and discussions with high school students about the dangers of marijuana all contributed to a decrease in the percentage of seniors who reported using marijuana from over 22 percent in 1995 to 9 percent in 1997. The Miami Coalition was able to achieve these results while national rates of marijuana use were increasing.

"(D) The Nashville Prevention Partnership worked with elementary and middle school children in an attempt to influence them toward positive life goals and discourage them from using substances. The Partnership targeted an area in East Nashville and created after school programs, mentoring opportunities, attendance initiatives, and safe passages to and from school. Attendance and test scores increased as a result of the program.

"(E) At a youth-led town meeting sponsored by the Bering Strait Community Partnership in Nome, Alaska, youth identified a need for a safe, substance-free space. With help from a variety of community partners, the Partnership staff and youth members created the Java Hut, a substance-free coffeehouse designed for youth. The Java Hut is helping to change norms in the community by providing a fun, youth-friendly atmosphere and activities that are not centered around alcohol or marijuana.

"(F) Portland's Regional Drug Initiative (RDI) has promoted the establishment of drug-free workplaces among the city's large and small employers. Over 3,000 employers have attended an RDI training session, and of those, 92 percent have instituted drug-free workplace policies. As a result, there has been a 5.5 percent decrease in positive workplace drug tests.

"(G) San Antonio Fighting Back worked to increase the age at which youth first used illegal substances. Research suggests that the later the age of first use, the lower the risk that a young person will become a regular substance abuser. As a result, the age of first illegal drug use increased from 9.4 years in 1992 to 13.5 years in 1997.

"(H) In 1990, multiple data sources confirmed a trend of increased alcohol use by teenagers in the Troy community. Using its 'multiple strategies over multiple sectors' approach, the Troy Coalition worked with parents, physicians, students, coaches, and others to address this problem from several angles. As a result, the rate of twelfth grade students who had consumed alcohol in the past month decreased from 62.1 percent to 53.3 percent between 1991 and 1998, and the rate of eighth grade students decreased from 26.3 percent to 17.4 percent. The Troy Coalition believes that this decline represents not only a change in behavior on the part of students, but also a change in the norms of the community.

"(6) Despite these successes, drug use continues to be a serious problem facing communities across the United States. For example:

"(A) According to the Pulse Check: Trends in Drug Abuse Mid-Year 2000 report—

"(i) crack and powder cocaine remains the most serious drug problem;

"(ii) marijuana remains the most widely available illicit drug, and its potency is on the rise;

"(iii) treatment sources report an increase in admissions with marijuana as the primary drug of abuse—and adolescents outnumber other age groups entering treatment for marijuana;

"(iv) 80 percent of Pulse Check sources reported increased availability of club drugs, with ecstasy (MDMA) and ketamine the most widely cited club drugs and seven sources reporting that powder cocaine is being used as a club drug by young adults;

"(v) ecstasy abuse and trafficking is expanding, no longer confined to the 'rave' scene;

"(vi) the sale and use of club drugs has grown from nightclubs and raves to high schools, the streets, neighborhoods, open venues, and younger ages;

"(vii) ecstasy users often are unknowingly purchasing adulterated tablets or some other substance sold as MDMA; and

"(viii) along with reports of increased heroin snorting as a route of administration for initiates, there is also an increase in injecting initiates and the negative health consequences associated with injection (for example, increases in HIV/AIDS and Hepatitis C) suggesting that there is a generational forgetting of the dangers of injection of the drug.

"(B) The 2000 Parent's Resource Institute for Drug Education study reported that 23.6 percent of children in the sixth through twelfth grades used illicit drugs in the past year. The same study found that monthly usage among this group was 15.3 percent.

"(C) According to the 2000 Monitoring the Future study, the use of ecstasy among eighth graders increased from 1.7 percent in 1999 to 3.1 percent in 2000, among tenth graders from 4.4 percent to 5.4 percent, and from 5.6 percent to 8.2 percent among twelfth graders.

"(D) A 1999 Mellman Group study found that—

"(i) 56 percent of the population in the United States believed that drug use was increasing in 1999;

"(ii) 92 percent of the population viewed illegal drug use as a serious problem in the United States; and

"(iii) 73 percent of the population viewed illegal drug use as a serious problem in their communities.

"(7) According to the 2001 report of the National Center on Addiction and Substance Abuse at Columbia University entitled 'Shoveling Up: The Impact of Substance Abuse on State Budgets', using the most conservative assumption, in 1998 States spent $77,900,000,000 to shovel up the wreckage of substance abuse, only $3,000,000,000 to prevent and treat the problem and $433,000,000 for alcohol and tobacco regulation and compliance. This $77,900,000,000 burden was distributed as follows:

"(A) $30,700,000,000 in the justice system (77 percent of justice spending).

"(B) $16,500,000,000 in education costs (10 percent of education spending).

"(C) $15,200,000,000 in health costs (25 percent of health spending).

"(D) $7,700,000,000 in child and family assistance (32 percent of child and family assistance spending).

"(E) $5,900,000,000 in mental health and developmental disabilities (31 percent of mental health spending).

"(F) $1,500,000,000 in public safety (26 percent of public safety spending) and $400,000,000 for the state workforce.

"(8) Intergovernmental cooperation and coordination through national, State, and local or tribal leadership and partnerships are critical to facilitate the reduction of substance abuse among youth in communities across the United States.

"(9) Substance abuse is perceived as a much greater problem nationally than at the community level. According to a 2001 study sponsored by The Pew Charitable Trusts, between 1994 and 2000—

"(A) there was a 43 percent increase in the percentage of Americans who felt progress was being made in the war on drugs at the community level;

"(B) only 9 percent of Americans say drug abuse is a 'crisis' in their neighborhood, compared to 27 percent who say this about the nation; and

"(C) the percentage of those who felt we lost ground in the war on drugs on a community level fell by more than a quarter, from 51 percent in 1994 to 37 percent in 2000."

AUTHORIZATION FOR NATIONAL COMMUNITY ANTIDRUG COALITION INSTITUTE

Pub. L. 107–82, §4, Dec. 14, 2001, 115 Stat. 821, as amended by Pub. L. 109–469, title VIII, §805, Dec. 29, 2006, 120 Stat. 3535, provided that:

"(a) IN GENERAL.—The Director of the Office of National Drug Control Policy shall, using amounts authorized to be appropriated by subsection (d), make a directed grant to Community Anti-Drug Coalitions of America to provide for the continuation of the National Community Anti-drug Coalition Institute.

"(b) USE OF GRANT AMOUNT.—The organization receiving the grant under subsection (a) shall establish a National Community Antidrug Coalition Institute to—

"(1) provide education, training, and technical assistance for coalition leaders and community teams, with emphasis on the development of coalitions serving economically disadvantaged areas;

"(2) develop and disseminate evaluation tools, mechanisms, and measures to better assess and document coalition performance measures and outcomes; and

"(3) bridge the gap between research and practice by translating knowledge from research into practical information.

"(c) AUTHORIZATION OF APPROPRIATIONS.—There is authorized to be appropriated for purposes of activities under this section, including the grant under subsection (a), amounts as follows:

"(1) For each of fiscal years 2002 and 2003, $2,000,000.

"(2) For each of fiscal years 2004 and 2005, $1,000,000.

"(3) For each of fiscal years 2006 and 2007, $750,000.

"(4) For each of the fiscal years 2008 through 2012, $2,000,000."

PROHIBITION AGAINST DUPLICATION OF EFFORT

Pub. L. 107–82, §5, Dec. 14, 2001, 115 Stat. 821, provided that: "The Director of the Office of National Drug Control Policy shall ensure that the same or similar activities are not carried out, through the use of funds for administrative costs provided under subchapter II [probably means chapter 2] of the National Narcotics Leadership Act of 1988 (21 U.S.C. 1521 et seq.) or funds provided under section 4 of this Act [set out as a note above], by more than one recipient of such funds."

§ 1522. Purposes

The purposes of this subchapter are—

(1) to reduce substance abuse among youth in communities throughout the United States, and over time, to reduce substance abuse among adults;

(2) to strengthen collaboration among communities, the Federal Government, and State, local, and tribal governments;

(3) to enhance intergovernmental cooperation and coordination on the issue of substance abuse among youth;

(4) to serve as a catalyst for increased citizen participation and greater collaboration among all sectors and organizations of a community that first demonstrates a long-term commitment to reducing substance abuse among youth;

(5) to rechannel resources from the fiscal year 1998 Federal drug control budget to provide technical assistance, guidance, and financial support to communities that demonstrate a long-term commitment in reducing substance abuse among youth;

(6) to disseminate to communities timely information regarding the state-of-the-art practices and initiatives that have proven to be effective in reducing substance abuse among youth;

(7) to enhance, not supplant, local community initiatives for reducing substance abuse among youth; and

(8) to encourage the creation of and support for community anti-drug coalitions throughout the United States.

(Pub. L. 100–690, title I, §1022, as added Pub. L. 105–20, §2(a)(2), June 27, 1997, 111 Stat. 225.)

§ 1523. Definitions

In this subchapter:

(1) Administrator

The term "Administrator" means the Administrator appointed by the Director under section 1531(c) of this title.

(2) Advisory Commission

The term "Advisory Commission" means the Advisory Commission established under section 1541 of this title.

(3) Community

The term "community" shall have the meaning provided that term by the Administrator, in consultation with the Advisory Commission.

(4) Director

The term "Director" means the Director of the Office of National Drug Control Policy.

(5) Eligible coalition

The term "eligible coalition" means a coalition that meets the applicable criteria under section 1532(a) of this title.

(6) Grant recipient

The term "grant recipient" means the recipient of a grant award under section 1532 of this title.

(7) Nonprofit organization

The term "nonprofit organization" means an organization described under section 501(c)(3) of title 26 that is exempt from taxation under section 501(a) of title 26.

(8) Program

The term "Program" means the program established under section 1531(a) of this title.

(9) Substance abuse

The term "substance abuse" means—

(A) the illegal use or abuse of drugs, including substances listed in schedules I through V of section 812 of this title;

(B) the abuse of inhalants; or

(C) the use of alcohol, tobacco, or other related product as such use is prohibited by State or local law.

(10) Youth

The term "youth" shall have the meaning provided that term by the Administrator, in consultation with the Advisory Commission.

(Pub. L. 100–690, title I, § 1023, as added Pub. L. 105–20, § 2(a)(2), June 27, 1997, 111 Stat. 225.)

REFERENCES IN TEXT

Section 812 of this title, referred to in par. (9)(A), was in the original "section 112 of the Controlled Substances Act (21 U.S.C. 812)", and was translated as reading "section 202", meaning section 202 of Pub. L. 91–513, to reflect the probable intent of Congress, because Pub. L. 91–513 does not contain a section 112.

§ 1524. Authorization of appropriations

(a) In general

There are authorized to be appropriated to the Office of National Drug Control Policy to carry out this subchapter—

(1) $10,000,000 for fiscal year 1998;
(2) $20,000,000 for fiscal year 1999;
(3) $30,000,000 for fiscal year 2000;
(4) $40,000,000 for fiscal year 2001;
(5) $50,600,000 for fiscal year 2002;
(6) $60,000,000 for fiscal year 2003;
(7) $70,000,000 for fiscal year 2004;
(8) $80,000,000 for fiscal year 2005;
(9) $90,000,000 for fiscal year 2006;
(10) $99,000,000 for fiscal year 2007;
(11) $109,000,000 for fiscal year 2008;
(12) $114,000,000 for fiscal year 2009;
(13) $119,000,000 for fiscal year 2010;
(14) $124,000,000 for fiscal year 2011; and
(15) $129,000,000 for fiscal year 2012.

(b) Administrative costs

(1) Limitation

Not more than 3 percent of the funds appropriated for this subchapter may be used by the Office of National Drug Control Policy to pay for administrative costs associated with their responsibilities under the subchapter.

(2) Designated agency

The agency delegated to carry out this program under section 1531(d) of this title may use up to 5 percent of the funds allocated for grants under this subchapter for administrative costs associated with carrying out the program.

(Pub. L. 100–690, title I, § 1024, as added Pub. L. 105–20, § 2(a)(2), June 27, 1997, 111 Stat. 226; amended Pub. L. 107–82, § 1(b), (c), Dec. 14, 2001, 115 Stat. 817; Pub. L. 109–469, title VIII, § 801, Dec. 29, 2006, 120 Stat. 3535.)

CODIFICATION

Pub. L. 109–469, § 801, which directed amendment of section 1024 of the "Drug-Free Communities Act of 1997", was executed to this section, which is section 1024 of the National Narcotics Leadership Act of 1988, to reflect the probable intent of Congress. See 2006 Amendment notes below.

AMENDMENTS

2006—Subsec. (a)(11) to (15). Pub. L. 109–469, § 801(a), added pars. (11) to (15). See Codification note above.

Subsec. (b). Pub. L. 109–469, § 801(b), amended subsec. (b) generally. See Codification note above. Prior to amendment, text read as follows: "Not more than the following percentages of the amounts authorized under subsection (a) of this section may be used to pay administrative costs:

"(1) 10 percent for fiscal year 1998.
"(2) 6 percent for fiscal year 1999.
"(3) 4 percent for fiscal year 2000.
"(4) 3 percent for fiscal year 2001.
"(5) 6 percent for each of fiscal years 2002 through 2007."

2001—Subsec. (a)(5) to (10). Pub. L. 107–82, § 1(b), added pars. (5) to (10) and struck out former par. (5) which read as follows: "$43,500,000 for fiscal year 2002."

Subsec. (b)(5). Pub. L. 107–82, § 1(c), added par. (5) and struck out former par. (5) which read as follows: "3 percent for fiscal year 2002."

PART A—DRUG-FREE COMMUNITIES SUPPORT PROGRAM

§ 1531. Establishment of drug-free communities support program

(a) Establishment

The Director shall establish a program to support communities in the development and implementation of comprehensive, long-term plans and programs to prevent and treat substance abuse among youth.

(b) Program

In carrying out the Program, the Director shall—

(1) make and track grants to grant recipients;

(2) provide for technical assistance and training, data collection, and dissemination of information on state-of-the-art practices that the Director determines to be effective in reducing substance abuse; and

(3) provide for the general administration of the Program.

(c) Administration

Not later than 30 days after receiving recommendations from the Advisory Commission under section 1542(a)(1) of this title, the Director shall appoint an Administrator to carry out the Program.

(d) Contracting

The Director may employ any necessary staff and may enter into contracts or agreements with national drug control agencies, including interagency agreements to delegate authority for the execution of grants and for such other activities necessary to carry out this subchapter.

(Pub. L. 100–690, title I, § 1031, as added Pub. L. 105–20, § 2(a)(2), June 27, 1997, 111 Stat. 226.)

§ 1532. Program authorization

(a) Grant eligibility

To be eligible to receive an initial grant or a renewal grant under this part, a coalition shall meet each of the following criteria:

(1) Application

The coalition shall submit an application to the Administrator in accordance with section 1533(a)(2) of this title.

(2) Major sector involvement

(A) In general

The coalition shall consist of 1 or more representatives of each of the following categories:

(i) Youth.

(ii) Parents.

(iii) Businesses.

(iv) The media.

(v) Schools.

(vi) Organizations serving youth.

(vii) Law enforcement.

(viii) Religious or fraternal organizations.

(ix) Civic and volunteer groups.

(x) Health care professionals.

(xi) State, local, or tribal governmental agencies with expertise in the field of substance abuse (including, if applicable, the State authority with primary authority for substance abuse).

(xii) Other organizations involved in reducing substance abuse.

(B) Elected officials

If feasible, in addition to representatives from the categories listed in subparagraph (A), the coalition shall have an elected official (or a representative of an elected official) from—

(i) the Federal Government; and

(ii) the government of the appropriate State and political subdivision thereof or the governing body or an Indian tribe (as that term is defined in section 450b(e) of title 25).

(C) Representation

An individual who is a member of the coalition may serve on the coalition as a representative of not more than 1 category listed under subparagraph (A).

(3) Commitment

The coalition shall demonstrate, to the satisfaction of the Administrator—

(A) that the representatives of the coalition have worked together on substance abuse reduction initiatives, which, at a minimum, includes initiatives that target drugs referenced in section 1523(9)(A) of this title, for a period of not less than 6 months, acting through entities such as task forces, subcommittees, or community boards; and

(B) substantial participation from volunteer leaders in the community involved (especially in cooperation with individuals involved with youth such as parents, teachers, coaches, youth workers, and members of the clergy).

(4) Mission and strategies

The coalition shall, with respect to the community involved—

(A) have as its principal mission the reduction of substance abuse, which, at a minimum, includes the use and abuse of drugs referenced in section 1523(9)(A) of this title, in a comprehensive and long-term manner, with a primary focus on youth in the community;

(B) describe and document the nature and extent of the substance abuse problem, which, at a minimum, includes the use and abuse of drugs referenced in section 1523(9)(A) of this title, in the community;

(C)(i) provide a description of substance abuse prevention and treatment programs and activities, which, at a minimum, includes programs and activities relating to the use and abuse of drugs referenced in section 1523(9)(A) of this title, in existence at the time of the grant application; and

(ii) identify substance abuse programs and service gaps, which, at a minimum, includes programs and gaps relating to the use and abuse of drugs referenced in section 1523(9)(A) of this title, in the community;

(D) develop a strategic plan to reduce substance abuse among youth, which, at a minimum, includes the use and abuse of drugs referenced in section 1523(9)(A) of this title, in a comprehensive and long-term fashion; and

(E) work to develop a consensus regarding the priorities of the community to combat substance abuse among youth, which, at a minimum, includes the use and abuse of drugs referenced in section 1523(9)(A) of this title.

(5) Sustainability

The coalition shall demonstrate that the coalition is an ongoing concern by demonstrating that the coalition—

(A) is—

(i)(I) a nonprofit organization; or

(II) an entity that the Administrator determines to be appropriate; or

(ii) part of, or is associated with, an established legal entity;

(B) receives financial support (including, in the discretion of the Administrator, in-kind contributions) from non-Federal sources; and

(C) has a strategy to solicit substantial financial support from non-Federal sources to ensure that the coalition and the programs operated by the coalition are self-sustaining.

(6) Accountability

The coalition shall—

(A) establish a system to measure and report outcomes—

(i) consistent with common indicators and evaluation protocols established by the Administrator; and

(ii) approved by the Administrator;

(B) conduct—

(i) for an initial grant under this part, an initial benchmark survey of drug use among youth (or use local surveys or performance measures available or accessible in the community at the time of the grant application); and

(ii) biennial surveys (or incorporate local surveys in existence at the time of the evaluation) to measure the progress and effectiveness of the coalition; and

(C) provide assurances that the entity conducting an evaluation under this paragraph, or from which the coalition receives information, has experience—

(i) in gathering data related to substance abuse among youth; or

(ii) in evaluating the effectiveness of community anti-drug coalitions.

(7) Additional criteria

The Director shall not impose any eligibility criteria on new applicants or renewal grantees not provided in this subchapter.

(b) Grant amounts

(1) In general

(A) Grants

(i) In general

Subject to clause (iv), for a fiscal year, the Administrator may grant to an eligible coalition under this paragraph, an amount not to exceed the amount of non-Federal funds raised by the coalition, including in-kind contributions, for that fiscal year.

(ii) Suspension of grants

If such grant recipient fails to continue to meet the criteria specified in subsection (a) of this section, the Administrator may suspend the grant, after providing written notice to the grant recipient and an opportunity to appeal.

(iii) Renewal grants

Subject to clause (iv), the Administrator may award a renewal grant to a grant recipient under this subparagraph for each fiscal year following the fiscal year for which an initial grant is awarded, in an amount not to exceed the amount of non-Federal funds raised by the coalition, including in-kind contributions, for that fiscal year, during the 4-year period following the period of the initial grant.

(iv) Limitation

The amount of a grant award under this subparagraph may not exceed $125,000 for a fiscal year.

(B) Coalition awards

(i) In general

Except as provided in clause (ii), the Administrator may, with respect to a community, make a grant to 1 eligible coalition that represents that community.

(ii) Exception

The Administrator may make a grant to more than 1 eligible coalition that represents a community if—

(I) the eligible coalitions demonstrate that the coalitions are collaborating with one another; and

(II) each of the coalitions has independently met the requirements set forth in subsection (a) of this section.

(2) Rural coalition grants

(A) In general

(i) In general

In addition to awarding grants under paragraph (1), to stimulate the development of coalitions in sparsely populated and rural areas, the Administrator, in consultation with the Advisory Commission, may award a grant in accordance with this section to a coalition that represents a county with a population that does not exceed 30,000 individuals. In awarding a grant under this paragraph, the Administrator may waive any requirement under subsection (a) of this section if the Administrator considers that waiver to be appropriate.

(ii) Matching requirement

Subject to subparagraph (C), for a fiscal year, the Administrator may grant to an eligible coalition under this paragraph, an amount not to exceed the amount of non-Federal funds raised by the coalition, including in-kind contributions, for that fiscal year.

(iii) Suspension of grants

If such grant recipient fails to continue to meet any criteria specified in subsection (a) of this section that has not been waived by the Administrator pursuant to clause (i), the Administrator may suspend the grant, after providing written notice to the grant recipient and an opportunity to appeal.

(B) Renewal grants

The Administrator may award a renewal grant to an eligible coalition that is a grant recipient under this paragraph for each fiscal year following the fiscal year for which an initial grant is awarded, in an amount not to exceed the amount of non-Federal funds raised by the coalition, including in-kind contributions, during the 4-year period following the period of the initial grant.

(C) Limitations

(i) Amount

The amount of a grant award under this paragraph shall not exceed $125,000 for a fiscal year.

(ii) Awards

With respect to a county referred to in subparagraph (A), the Administrator may award a grant under this section to not more than 1 eligible coalition that represents the county.

(3) Additional grants

(A) In general

Subject to subparagraph (F), the Administrator may award an additional grant under this paragraph to an eligible coalition awarded a grant under paragraph (1) or (2) for any first fiscal year after the end of the 4-year period following the period of the initial grant under paragraph (1) or (2), as the case may be.

(B) Scope of grants

A coalition awarded a grant under paragraph (1) or (2), including a renewal grant under such paragraph, may not be awarded another grant under such paragraph, and is eligible for an additional grant under this section only under this paragraph.

(C) No priority for applications

The Administrator may not afford a higher priority in the award of an additional grant under this paragraph than the Administrator would afford the applicant for the grant if the applicant were submitting an application for an initial grant under paragraph (1) or (2) rather than an application for a grant under this paragraph.

(D) Renewal grants

Subject to subparagraph (F), the Administrator may award a renewal grant to a grant recipient under this paragraph for each of the fiscal years of the 4-fiscal-year period following the fiscal year for which the initial additional grant under subparagraph (A) is awarded in an amount not to exceed amounts as follows:

(i) For the first and second fiscal years of that 4-fiscal-year period, the amount equal to 80 percent of the non-Federal funds, including in-kind contributions, raised by the coalition for the applicable fiscal year.

(ii) For the third and fourth fiscal years of that 4-fiscal-year period, the amount equal to 67 percent of the non-Federal funds, including in-kind contributions, raised by the coalition for the applicable fiscal year.

(E) Suspension

If a grant recipient under this paragraph fails to continue to meet the criteria specified in subsection (a) of this section, the Administrator may suspend the grant, after providing written notice to the grant recipient and an opportunity to appeal.

(F) Limitation

The amount of a grant award under this paragraph may not exceed $125,000 for a fiscal year.

(4) Process for suspension

A grantee shall not be suspended or terminated under paragraph (1)(A)(ii), (2)(A)(iii), or (3)(E) unless that grantee is afforded a fair, timely, and independent appeal prior to such suspension or termination.

(c) Treatment of funds for coalitions representing certain organizations

Funds appropriated for the substance abuse activities of a coalition that includes a representative of the Bureau of Indian Affairs, the Indian Health Service, or a tribal government agency with expertise in the field of substance abuse may be counted as non-Federal funds raised by the coalition for purposes of this section.

(d) Priority in awarding grants

In awarding grants under subsection (b)(1)(A)(i) of this section, priority shall be given to a coalition serving economically disadvantaged areas.

(Pub. L. 100–690, title I, § 1032, as added Pub. L. 105–20, § 2(a)(2), June 27, 1997, 111 Stat. 227; amended Pub. L. 107–82, § 1(d), (g), (h), Dec. 14, 2001, 115 Stat. 818, 819; Pub. L. 109–469, title VIII, §§ 802(a), 803, 804, Dec. 29, 2006, 120 Stat. 3535.)

CODIFICATION

Pub. L. 109–469, §§ 802(a), 803, 804, which directed amendment of section 1032 of the "Drug-Free Communities Act of 1997", were executed to this section, which is section 1032 of the National Narcotics Leadership Act of 1988, to reflect the probable intent of Congress. See 2006 Amendment notes below.

AMENDMENTS

2006—Subsec. (a)(7). Pub. L. 109–469, § 804, added par. (7). See Codification note above.

Subsec. (b)(1)(A)(iv), (2)(C)(i), (3)(F). Pub. L. 109–469, § 803, substituted "$125,000" for "$100,000". See Codification note above.

Subsec. (b)(4). Pub. L. 109–469, § 802(a), added par. (4). See Codification note above.

2001—Subsec. (b)(3). Pub. L. 107–82, § 1(d), added par. (3).

Subsec. (c). Pub. L. 107–82, § 1(g), added subsec. (c).

Subsec. (d). Pub. L. 107–82, § 1(h), added subsec. (d).

REPORT TO CONGRESS

Pub. L. 109–469, title VIII, § 802(b), Dec. 29, 2006, 120 Stat. 3535, provided that: "Not later than 60 days after the date of enactment of this Act [Dec. 29, 2006], the Director of the Office of National Drug Control Policy shall submit to Congress a report detailing the appeals process required by section 1032(b)(4) of the Drug-Free Communities Act of 1997 [probably means 21 U.S.C. 1532(b)(4)], as added by subsection (a) [see 2006 Amendments note above]."

§ 1533. Information collection and dissemination with respect to grant recipients

(a) Coalition information

(1) General auditing authority

For the purpose of audit and examination, the Administrator—

(A) shall have access to any books, documents, papers, and records that are pertinent to any grant or grant renewal request under this subchapter; and

(B) may periodically request information from a grant recipient to ensure that the grant recipient meets the applicable criteria under section 1532(a) of this title.

(2) Application process

The Administrator shall issue a request for proposal regarding, with respect to the grants awarded under section 1532 of this title, the application process, grant renewal, and suspension or withholding of renewal grants. Each application under this paragraph shall be in writing and shall be subject to review by the Administrator.

(3) Reporting

The Administrator shall, to the maximum extent practicable and in a manner consistent with applicable law, minimize reporting requirements by a grant recipient and expedite any application for a renewal grant made under this part.

(b) Data collection and dissemination

(1) In general

The Administrator may collect data from—

(A) national substance abuse organizations that work with eligible coalitions, community anti-drug coalitions, departments or agencies of the Federal Government, or State or local governments and the governing bodies of Indian tribes; and

(B) any other entity or organization that carries out activities that relate to the purposes of the Program.

(2) Activities of Administrator

The Administrator may—

(A) evaluate the utility of specific initiatives relating to the purposes of the Program;

(B) conduct an evaluation of the Program; and

(C) disseminate information described in this subsection to—

(i) eligible coalitions and other substance abuse organizations; and

(ii) the general public.

(3) Consultation

The Administrator shall carry out activities under this subsection in consultation with the Advisory Commission and the National Community Antidrug Coalition Institute.

(4) Limitation on use of certain funds for evaluation of Program

Amounts for activities under paragraph (2)(B) may not be derived from amounts under section 1524(a) of this title except for amounts that are available under section 1524(b) of this title for administrative costs.

(Pub. L. 100–690, title I, §1033, as added Pub. L. 105–20, §2(a)(2), June 27, 1997, 111 Stat. 230; amended Pub. L. 107–82, §1(e), (f), Dec. 14, 2001, 115 Stat. 818.)

AMENDMENTS

2001—Subsec. (b)(3). Pub. L. 107–82, §1(e), added par. (3).

Subsec. (b)(4). Pub. L. 107–82, §1(f), added par. (4).

§1534. Technical assistance and training

(a) In general

(1) Technical assistance and agreements

With respect to any grant recipient or other organization, the Administrator may—

(A) offer technical assistance and training; and

(B) enter into contracts and cooperative agreements.

(2) Coordination of programs

The Administrator may facilitate the coordination of programs between a grant recipient and other organizations and entities.

(b) Training

The Administrator may provide training to any representative designated by a grant recipient in—

(1) coalition building;

(2) task force development;

(3) mediation and facilitation, direct service, assessment and evaluation; or

(4) any other activity related to the purposes of the Program.

(Pub. L. 100–690, title I, §1034, as added Pub. L. 105–20, §2(a)(2), June 27, 1997, 111 Stat. 231.)

§1535. Supplemental grants for coalition mentoring activities

(a) Authority to make grants

As part of the program established under section 1531 of this title, the Director may award an initial grant under this subsection, and renewal grants under subsection (f) of this section, to any coalition awarded a grant under section 1532 of this title that meets the criteria specified in subsection (d) of this section in order to fund coalition mentoring activities by such coalition in support of the program.

(b) Treatment with other grants

(1) Supplement

A grant awarded to a coalition under this section is in addition to any grant awarded to the coalition under section 1532 of this title.

(2) Requirement for basic grant

A coalition may not be awarded a grant under this section for a fiscal year unless the coalition was awarded a grant or renewal grant under section 1532(b) of this title for that fiscal year.

(c) Application

A coalition seeking a grant under this section shall submit to the Administrator an application for the grant in such form and manner as the Administrator may require.

(d) Criteria

A coalition meets the criteria specified in this subsection if the coalition—

(1) has been in existence for at least 5 years;

(2) has achieved, by or through its own efforts, measurable results in the prevention and treatment of substance abuse among youth;

(3) has staff or members willing to serve as mentors for persons seeking to start or expand

the activities of other coalitions in the prevention and treatment of substance abuse;

(4) has demonstrable support from some members of the community in which the coalition mentoring activities to be supported by the grant under this section are to be carried out; and

(5) submits to the Administrator a detailed plan for the coalition mentoring activities to be supported by the grant under this section.

(e) Use of grant funds

A coalition awarded a grant under this section shall use the grant amount for mentoring activities to support and encourage the development of new, self-supporting community coalitions that are focused on the prevention and treatment of substance abuse in such new coalitions' communities. The mentoring coalition shall encourage such development in accordance with the plan submitted by the mentoring coalition under subsection (d)(5) of this section.

(f) Renewal grants

The Administrator may make a renewal grant to any coalition awarded a grant under subsection (a) of this section, or a previous renewal grant under this subsection, if the coalition, at the time of application for such renewal grant—

(1) continues to meet the criteria specified in subsection (d) of this section; and

(2) has made demonstrable progress in the development of one or more new, self-supporting community coalitions that are focused on the prevention and treatment of substance abuse.

(g) Grant amounts

(1) In general

Subject to paragraphs (2) and (3), the total amount of grants awarded to a coalition under this section for a fiscal year may not exceed the amount of non-Federal funds raised by the coalition, including in-kind contributions, for that fiscal year. Funds appropriated for the substance abuse activities of a coalition that includes a representative of the Bureau of Indian Affairs, the Indian Health Service, or a tribal government agency with expertise in the field of substance abuse may be counted as non-Federal funds raised by the coalition.

(2) Initial grants

The amount of the initial grant awarded to a coalition under subsection (a) of this section may not exceed $75,000.

(3) Renewal grants

The total amount of renewal grants awarded to a coalition under subsection (f) of this section for any fiscal year may not exceed $75,000.

(h) Fiscal year limitation on amount available for grants

The total amount available for grants under this section, including renewal grants under subsection (f) of this section, in any fiscal year may not exceed the amount equal to five percent of the amount authorized to be appropriated by section 1524(a) of this title for that fiscal year.

(i) Priority in awarding initial grants

In awarding initial grants under this section, priority shall be given to a coalition that expressly proposes to provide mentorship to a coalition or aspiring coalition serving economically disadvantaged areas.

(Pub. L. 100–690, title I, § 1035, as added Pub. L. 107–82, § 2, Dec. 14, 2001, 115 Stat. 819.)

PART B—ADVISORY COMMISSION

§ 1541. Establishment of Advisory Commission

(a) Establishment

There is established a commission to be known as the "Advisory Commission on Drug-Free Communities".

(b) Purpose

The Advisory Commission shall advise, consult with, and make recommendations to the Director concerning matters related to the activities carried out under the Program.

(Pub. L. 100–690, title I, § 1041, as added Pub. L. 105–20, § 2(a)(2), June 27, 1997, 111 Stat. 231.)

§ 1542. Duties

(a) In general

The Advisory Commission—

(1) shall, not later than 30 days after its first meeting, make recommendations to the Director regarding the selection of an Administrator;

(2) may make recommendations to the Director regarding any grant, contract, or cooperative agreement made by the Program;

(3) may make recommendations to the Director regarding the activities of the Program;

(4) may make recommendations to the Director regarding any policy or criteria established by the Director to carry out the Program;

(5) may—

(A) collect, by correspondence or by personal investigation, information concerning initiatives, studies, services, programs, or other activities of coalitions or organizations working in the field of substance abuse in the United States or any other country; and

(B) with the approval of the Director, make the information referred to in subparagraph (A) available through appropriate publications or other methods for the benefit of eligible coalitions and the general public; and

(6) may appoint subcommittees and convene workshops and conferences.

(b) Recommendations

If the Director rejects any recommendation of the Advisory Commission under subsection (a)(1) of this section, the Director shall notify the Advisory Commission in writing of the reasons for the rejection not later than 15 days after receiving the recommendation.

(c) Conflict of interest

A member of the Advisory Commission shall recuse himself or herself from any decision that would constitute a conflict of interest.

(Pub. L. 100–690, title I, § 1042, as added Pub. L. 105–20, § 2(a)(2), June 27, 1997, 111 Stat. 231.)

§ 1543. Membership

(a) In general

The President shall appoint 11 members to the Advisory Commission as follows:

(1) four members shall be appointed from the general public and shall include leaders—

(A) in fields of youth development, public policy, law, or business; or

(B) of nonprofit organizations or private foundations that fund substance abuse programs.

(2) four members shall be appointed from the leading representatives of national substance abuse reduction organizations, of which no fewer than three members shall have extensive training or experience in drug prevention.

(3) three members shall be appointed from the leading representatives of State substance abuse reduction organizations.

(b) Chairperson

The Advisory Commission shall elect a chairperson or co-chairpersons from among its members.

(c) Ex officio members

The ex officio membership of the Advisory Commission shall consist of any two officers or employees of the United States that the Director determines to be necessary for the Advisory Commission to effectively carry out its functions.

(Pub. L. 100–690, title I, § 1043, as added Pub. L. 105–20, § 2(a)(2), June 27, 1997, 111 Stat. 232.)

§ 1544. Compensation

(a) In general

Members of the Advisory Commission who are officers or employees of the United States shall not receive any additional compensation for service on the Advisory Commission. The remaining members of the Advisory Commission shall receive, for each day (including travel time) that they are engaged in the performance of the functions of the Advisory Commission, compensation at rates not to exceed the daily equivalent to the annual rate of basic pay payable for grade GS–10 of the General Schedule.

(b) Travel expenses

Each member of the Advisory Commission shall receive travel expenses, including per diem in lieu of subsistence, in accordance with sections 5702 and 5703 of title 5.

(Pub. L. 100–690, title I, § 1044, as added Pub. L. 105–20, § 2(a)(2), June 27, 1997, 111 Stat. 232.)

REFERENCES IN TEXT

Grade GS–10 of the General Schedule, referred to in subsec. (a), is set out under section 5332 of Title 5, Government Organization and Employees.

§ 1545. Terms of office

(a) In general

Subject to subsection (b) of this section, the term of office of a member of the Advisory Commission shall be 3 years, except that, as designated at the time of appointment—

(1) of the initial members appointed under section 1543(a)(1) of this title, two shall be appointed for a term of 2 years;

(2) of the initial members appointed under section 1543(a)(2) of this title, two shall be appointed for a term of 2 years; and

(3) of the initial members appointed under section 1543(a)(3) of this title, one shall be appointed for a term of 1 year.

(b) Vacancies

Any member appointed to fill a vacancy for an unexpired term of a member shall serve for the remainder of the unexpired term. A member of the Advisory Commission may serve after the expiration of such member's term until a successor has been appointed and taken office.

(Pub. L. 100–690, title I, § 1045, as added Pub. L. 105–20, § 2(a)(2), June 27, 1997, 111 Stat. 233.)

§ 1546. Meetings

(a) In general

After its initial meeting, the Advisory Commission shall meet, with the advanced approval of the Administrator, at the call of the Chairperson (or Co-chairpersons) of the Advisory Commission or a majority of its members or upon the request of the Director or Administrator of the Program.

(b) Quorum

Six members of the Advisory Commission shall constitute a quorum.

(Pub. L. 100–690, title I, § 1046, as added Pub. L. 105–20, § 2(a)(2), June 27, 1997, 111 Stat. 233.)

§ 1547. Staff

The Administrator shall make available to the Advisory Commission adequate staff, information, and other assistance.

(Pub. L. 100–690, title I, § 1047, as added Pub. L. 105–20, § 2(a)(2), June 27, 1997, 111 Stat. 233.)

§ 1548. Termination

The Advisory Commission shall terminate at the end of fiscal year 2007.

(Pub. L. 100–690, title I, § 1048, as added Pub. L. 105–20, § 2(a)(2), June 27, 1997, 111 Stat. 234; amended Pub. L. 107–82, § 3, Dec. 14, 2001, 115 Stat. 820.)

AMENDMENTS

2001—Pub. L. 107–82 substituted "2007" for "2002".

CHAPTER 21—BIOMATERIALS ACCESS ASSURANCE

§ 1601. Findings

The Congress finds that—

(1) each year millions of citizens of the United States depend on the availability of lifesaving or life-enhancing medical devices,

many of which are permanently implantable within the human body;

(2) a continued supply of raw materials and component parts is necessary for the invention, development, improvement, and maintenance of the supply of the devices;

(3) most of the medical devices are made with raw materials and component parts that—

(A) move in interstate commerce;

(B) are not designed or manufactured specifically for use in medical devices; and

(C) come in contact with internal human tissue;

(4) the raw materials and component parts also are used in a variety of nonmedical products;

(5) because small quantities of the raw materials and component parts are used for medical devices, sales of raw materials and component parts for medical devices constitute an extremely small portion of the overall market for the raw materials and component parts;

(6) under the Federal Food, Drug, and Cosmetic Act (21 U.S.C. 301 et seq.) manufacturers of medical devices are required to demonstrate that the medical devices are safe and effective, including demonstrating that the products are properly designed and have adequate warnings or instructions;

(7) notwithstanding the fact that raw materials and component parts suppliers do not design, produce, or test a final medical device, the suppliers have been the subject of actions alleging inadequate—

(A) design and testing of medical devices manufactured with materials or parts supplied by the suppliers; or

(B) warnings related to the use of such medical devices;

(8) even though suppliers of raw materials and component parts have very rarely been held liable in such actions, such suppliers have ceased supplying certain raw materials and component parts for use in medical devices for a number of reasons, including concerns about the costs of such litigation;

(9) unless alternate sources of supply can be found, the unavailability of raw materials and component parts for medical devices will lead to unavailability of lifesaving and life-enhancing medical devices;

(10) because other suppliers of the raw materials and component parts in foreign nations are refusing to sell raw materials or component parts for use in manufacturing certain medical devices in the United States, the prospects for development of new sources of supply for the full range of threatened raw materials and component parts for medical devices are remote;

(11) it is unlikely that the small market for such raw materials and component parts in the United States could support the large investment needed to develop new suppliers of such raw materials and component parts;

(12) attempts to develop such new suppliers would raise the cost of medical devices;

(13) courts that have considered the duties of the suppliers of the raw materials and component parts have generally found that the suppliers do not have a duty—

(A) to evaluate the safety and efficacy of the use of a raw material or component part in a medical device; or

(B) to warn consumers concerning the safety and effectiveness of a medical device;

(14) because medical devices and the raw materials and component parts used in their manufacture move in interstate commerce, a shortage of such raw materials and component parts affects interstate commerce;

(15) in order to safeguard the availability of a wide variety of lifesaving and life-enhancing medical devices, immediate action is needed—

(A) to clarify the permissible bases of liability for suppliers of raw materials and component parts for medical devices; and

(B) to provide expeditious procedures to dispose of unwarranted suits against the suppliers in such manner as to minimize litigation costs;

(16) the several States and their courts are the primary architects and regulators of our tort system; Congress, however, must, in certain circumstances involving the national interest, address tort issues, and a threatened shortage of raw materials and component parts for lifesaving medical devices is one such circumstance; and

(17) the protections set forth in this chapter are needed to assure the continued supply of materials for lifesaving medical devices, although such protections do not protect negligent suppliers.

(Pub. L. 105–230, §2, Aug. 13, 1998, 112 Stat. 1519.)

REFERENCES IN TEXT

The Federal Food, Drug, and Cosmetic Act, referred to in par. (6), is act June 25, 1938, ch. 675, 52 Stat. 1040, as amended, which is classified generally to chapter 9 (§301 et seq.) of this title. For complete classification of this Act to the Code, see section 301 of this title and Tables.

EFFECTIVE DATE

Pub. L. 105–230, §8, Aug. 13, 1998, 112 Stat. 1529, provided that: "This Act [enacting this chapter] shall apply to all civil actions covered under this Act that are commenced on or after the date of enactment of this Act [Aug. 13, 1998], including any such action with respect to which the harm asserted in the action or the conduct that caused the harm occurred before the date of enactment of this Act."

SHORT TITLE

Pub. L. 105–230, §1, Aug. 13, 1998, 112 Stat. 1519, provided that: "This Act [enacting this chapter] may be cited as the 'Biomaterials Access Assurance Act of 1998'."

§ 1602. Definitions

As used in this chapter:

(1) Biomaterials supplier

(A) In general

The term "biomaterials supplier" means an entity that directly or indirectly supplies a component part or raw material for use in the manufacture of an implant.

(B) Persons included

Such term includes any person who—

(i) has submitted master files to the Secretary for purposes of premarket approval of a medical device; or

(ii) licenses a biomaterials supplier to produce component parts or raw materials.

(2) Claimant

(A) In general

The term "claimant" means any person who brings a civil action, or on whose behalf a civil action is brought, arising from harm allegedly caused directly or indirectly by an implant, including a person other than the individual into whose body, or in contact with whose blood or tissue, the implant is placed, who claims to have suffered harm as a result of the implant.

(B) Action brought on behalf of an estate

With respect to an action brought on behalf of or through the estate of a deceased individual into whose body, or in contact with whose blood or tissue the implant was placed, such term includes the decedent that is the subject of the action.

(C) Action brought on behalf of a minor or incompetent

With respect to an action brought on behalf of or through a minor or incompetent, such term includes the parent or guardian of the minor or incompetent.

(D) Exclusions

Such term does not include—

(i) a provider of professional health care services in any case in which—

(I) the sale or use of an implant is incidental to such services; and

(II) the essence of the professional health care services provided is the furnishing of judgment, skill, or services;

(ii) a person acting in the capacity of a manufacturer, seller, or biomaterials supplier; or

(iii) a person alleging harm caused by either the silicone gel or the silicone envelope utilized in a breast implant containing silicone gel, except that—

(I) neither the exclusion provided by this clause nor any other provision of this chapter may be construed as a finding that silicone gel (or any other form of silicone) may or may not cause harm; and

(II) the existence of the exclusion under this clause may not—

(aa) be disclosed to a jury in any civil action or other proceeding; and

(bb) except as necessary to establish the applicability of this chapter, otherwise be presented in any civil action or other proceeding.

(3) Component part

(A) In general

The term "component part" means a manufactured piece of an implant.

(B) Certain components

Such term includes a manufactured piece of an implant that—

(i) has significant non-implant applications; and

(ii) alone, has no implant value or purpose, but when combined with other component parts and materials, constitutes an implant.

(4) Harm

(A) In general

The term "harm" means—

(i) any injury to or damage suffered by an individual;

(ii) any illness, disease, or death of that individual resulting from that injury or damage; and

(iii) any loss to that individual or any other individual resulting from that injury or damage.

(B) Exclusion

The term does not include any commercial loss or loss of or damage to an implant.

(5) Implant

The term "implant" means—

(A) a medical device that is intended by the manufacturer of the device—

(i) to be placed into a surgically or naturally formed or existing cavity of the body for a period of at least 30 days; or

(ii) to remain in contact with bodily fluids or internal human tissue through a surgically produced opening for a period of less than 30 days; and

(B) suture materials used in implant procedures.

(6) Manufacturer

The term "manufacturer" means any person who, with respect to an implant—

(A) is engaged in the manufacture, preparation, propagation, compounding, or processing (as defined in section 360(a)(1) of this title) of the implant; and

(B) is required—

(i) to register with the Secretary pursuant to section 360 of this title and the regulations issued under such section; and

(ii) to include the implant on a list of devices filed with the Secretary pursuant to section 360(j) of this title and the regulations issued under such section.

(7) Medical device

The term "medical device" means a device, as defined in section 321(h) of this title, and includes any device component of any combination product as that term is used in section 353(g) of this title.

(8) Raw material

The term "raw material" means a substance or product that—

(A) has a generic use; and

(B) may be used in an application other than an implant.

(9) Secretary

The term "Secretary" means the Secretary of Health and Human Services.

(10) Seller

(A) In general

The term "seller" means a person who, in the course of a business conducted for that purpose, sells, distributes, leases, packages, labels, or otherwise places an implant in the stream of commerce.

(B) Exclusions

The term does not include—

(i) a seller or lessor of real property;

(ii) a provider of professional health care services in any case in which—

(I) the sale or use of the implant is incidental to such services; and

(II) the essence of the professional health care services provided is the furnishing of judgment, skill, or services; or

(iii) any person who acts in only a financial capacity with respect to the sale of an implant.

(Pub. L. 105–230, § 3, Aug. 13, 1998, 112 Stat. 1520.)

§ 1603. General requirements; applicability; preemption

(a) General requirements

(1) In general

In any civil action covered by this chapter, a biomaterials supplier may—

(A) raise any exclusion from liability set forth in section 1604 of this title; and

(B) make a motion for dismissal or for summary judgment as set forth in section 1605 of this title.

(2) Procedures

Notwithstanding any other provision of law, a Federal or State court in which an action covered by this chapter is pending shall, in connection with a motion under section 1605 or 1606 of this title, use the procedures set forth in this chapter.

(b) Applicability

(1) In general

Except as provided in paragraph (2), this chapter applies to any civil action brought by a claimant, whether in a Federal or State court, on the basis of any legal theory, for harm allegedly caused, directly or indirectly, by an implant.

(2) Exclusion

A civil action brought by a purchaser of a medical device, purchased for use in providing professional health care services, for loss or damage to an implant or for commercial loss to the purchaser—

(A) shall not be considered an action that is subject to this chapter; and

(B) shall be governed by applicable commercial or contract law.

(c) Scope of preemption

(1) In general

This chapter supersedes any State law regarding recovery for harm caused by an implant and any rule of procedure applicable to a civil action to recover damages for such harm only to the extent that this chapter establishes a rule of law applicable to the recovery of such damages.

(2) Applicability of other laws

Any issue that arises under this chapter and that is not governed by a rule of law applicable to the recovery of damages described in paragraph (1) shall be governed by applicable Federal or State law.

(d) Statutory construction

Nothing in this chapter may be construed—

(1) to affect any defense available to a defendant under any other provisions of Federal or State law in an action alleging harm caused by an implant; or

(2) to create a cause of action or Federal court jurisdiction pursuant to section 1331 or 1337 of title 28 that otherwise would not exist under applicable Federal or State law.

(Pub. L. 105–230, § 4, Aug. 13, 1998, 112 Stat. 1523.)

§ 1604. Liability of biomaterials suppliers

(a) In general

Except as provided in section 1606 of this title, a biomaterials supplier shall not be liable for harm to a claimant caused by an implant unless such supplier is liable—

(1) as a manufacturer of the implant, as provided in subsection (b) of this section;

(2) as a seller of the implant, as provided in subsection (c) of this section; or

(3) for furnishing raw materials or component parts for the implant that failed to meet applicable contractual requirements or specifications, as provided in subsection (d) of this section.

(b) Liability as manufacturer

(1) In general

A biomaterials supplier may, to the extent required and permitted by any other applicable law, be liable for harm to a claimant caused by an implant if the biomaterials supplier is the manufacturer of the implant.

(2) Grounds for liability

The biomaterials supplier may be considered the manufacturer of the implant that allegedly caused harm to a claimant only if the biomaterials supplier—

(A)(i) registered or was required to register with the Secretary pursuant to section 360 of this title and the regulations issued under such section; and

(ii) included or was required to include the implant on a list of devices filed with the Secretary pursuant to section 360(j) of this title and the regulations issued under such section;

(B) is the subject of a declaration issued by the Secretary pursuant to paragraph (3) that states that the supplier, with respect to the implant that allegedly caused harm to the claimant, was required to—

(i) register with the Secretary under section 360 of this title, and the regulations issued under such section, but failed to do so; or

(ii) include the implant on a list of devices filed with the Secretary pursuant to section 360(j) of this title and the regulations issued under such section, but failed to do so; or

(C) is related by common ownership or control to a person meeting all the requirements described in subparagraph (A) or (B), if the court deciding a motion to dismiss in accordance with section 1605(c)(3)(B)(i) of this title finds, on the basis of affidavits submitted in accordance with section 1605 of this title, that it is necessary to impose liability on the biomaterials supplier as a manufacturer because the related manufacturer meeting the requirements of subparagraph (A) or (B) lacks sufficient financial resources to satisfy any judgment that the court feels it is likely to enter should the claimant prevail.

(3) Administrative procedures

(A) In general

The Secretary may issue a declaration described in paragraph (2)(B) on the motion of the Secretary or on petition by any person, after providing—

(i) notice to the affected persons; and

(ii) an opportunity for an informal hearing.

(B) Docketing and final decision

Immediately upon receipt of a petition filed pursuant to this paragraph, the Secretary shall docket the petition. Not later than 120 days after the petition is filed, the Secretary shall issue a final decision on the petition.

(C) Applicability of statute of limitations

Any applicable statute of limitations shall toll during the period from the time a claimant files a petition with the Secretary under this paragraph until such time as either (i) the Secretary issues a final decision on the petition, or (ii) the petition is withdrawn.

(D) Stay pending petition for declaration

If a claimant has filed a petition for a declaration with respect to a defendant, and the Secretary has not issued a final decision on the petition, the court shall stay all proceedings with respect to that defendant until such time as the Secretary has issued a final decision on the petition.

(c) Liability as seller

A biomaterials supplier may, to the extent required and permitted by any other applicable law, be liable as a seller for harm to a claimant caused by an implant only if—

(1) the biomaterials supplier—

(A) held title to the implant and then acted as a seller of the implant after its initial sale by the manufacturer; or

(B) acted under contract as a seller to arrange for the transfer of the implant directly to the claimant after the initial sale by the manufacturer of the implant; or

(2) the biomaterials supplier is related by common ownership or control to a person meeting all the requirements described in paragraph (1), if a court deciding a motion to dismiss in accordance with section 1605(c)(3)(B)(ii) of this title finds, on the basis of affidavits submitted in accordance with section 1605 of this title, that it is necessary to impose liability on the biomaterials supplier as a seller because the related seller meeting the requirements of paragraph (1) lacks sufficient financial resources to satisfy any judgment that the court feels it is likely to enter should the claimant prevail.

(d) Liability for failure to meet applicable contractual requirements or specifications

A biomaterials supplier may, to the extent required and permitted by any other applicable law, be liable for harm to a claimant caused by an implant if the claimant in an action shows, by a preponderance of the evidence, that—

(1) the biomaterials supplier supplied raw materials or component parts for use in the implant that either—

(A) did not constitute the product described in the contract between the biomaterials supplier and the person who contracted for the supplying of the product; or

(B) failed to meet any specifications that were—

(i) accepted, pursuant to applicable law, by the biomaterials supplier;

(ii) published by the biomaterials supplier;

(iii) provided by the biomaterials supplier to the person who contracted for such product;

(iv) contained in a master file that was submitted by the biomaterials supplier to the Secretary and that is currently maintained by the biomaterials supplier for purposes of premarket approval of medical devices; or

(v) included in the submissions for purposes of premarket approval or review by the Secretary under section 360, 360c, 360e, or 360j of this title, and received clearance from the Secretary if such specifications were accepted, pursuant to applicable law, by the biomaterials supplier; and

(2) such failure to meet applicable contractual requirements or specifications was an actual and proximate cause of the harm to the claimant.

(Pub. L. 105–230, § 5, Aug. 13, 1998, 112 Stat. 1524.)

§ 1605. Procedures for dismissal of civil actions against biomaterials suppliers

(a) Motion to dismiss

A defendant may, at any time during which a motion to dismiss may be filed under applicable law, move to dismiss an action against it on the grounds that the defendant is a biomaterials supplier and one or more of the following:

(1) The defendant is not liable as a manufacturer, as provided in section 1604(b) of this title.

(2) The defendant is not liable as a seller, as provided in section 1604(c) of this title.

(3) The defendant is not liable for furnishing raw materials or component parts for the implant that failed to meet applicable contractual requirements or specifications, as provided in section 1604(d) of this title.

(4) The claimant did not name the manufacturer as a party to the action, as provided in subsection (b) of this section.

(b) Manufacturer of implant shall be named a party

In any civil action covered by this chapter, the claimant shall be required to name the manufacturer of the implant as a party to the action, unless—

(1) the manufacturer is subject to service of process solely in a jurisdiction in which the biomaterials supplier is not domiciled or subject to a service of process; or

(2) a claim against the manufacturer is barred by applicable law or rule of practice.

(c) Proceeding on motion to dismiss

The following rules shall apply to any proceeding on a motion to dismiss filed by a defendant under this section:

(1) Effect of motion to dismiss on discovery

(A) In general

Except as provided in subparagraph (B), if a defendant files a motion to dismiss under subsection (a) of this section, no discovery shall be permitted in connection with the action that is the subject of the motion, other than discovery necessary to determine a motion to dismiss for lack of jurisdiction, until such time as the court rules on the motion to dismiss.

(B) Discovery

If a defendant files a motion to dismiss under subsection (a)(3) of this section on the grounds that it did not furnish raw materials or component parts for the implant that failed to meet applicable contractual requirements or specifications, the court may permit discovery limited to issues that are directly relevant to—

(i) the pending motion to dismiss; or

(ii) the jurisdiction of the court.

(2) Affidavits

(A) Defendant

A defendant may submit affidavits supporting the grounds for dismissal contained in its motion to dismiss under subsection (a) of this section. If the motion is made under subsection (a)(1) of this section, the defendant may submit an affidavit demonstrating that the defendant has not included the implant on a list, if any, filed with the Secretary pursuant to section 360(j) of this title.

(B) Claimant

In response to a motion to dismiss, the claimant may submit affidavits demonstrating that—

(i) the Secretary has, with respect to the defendant and the implant that allegedly caused harm to the claimant, issued a declaration pursuant to section 1604(b)(2)(B) of this title; or

(ii) the defendant is a seller of the implant who is liable under section 1604(c) of this title.

(3) Basis of ruling on motion to dismiss

The court shall rule on a motion to dismiss filed under subsection (a) of this section solely on the basis of the pleadings and affidavits of the parties made pursuant to this subsection. The court shall grant a motion to dismiss filed under subsection (a) of this section—

(A) unless the claimant submits a valid affidavit that demonstrates that the defendant is not a biomaterials supplier;

(B) unless the court determines, to the extent raised in the pleadings and affidavits, that one or more of the following apply:

(i) the defendant may be liable as a manufacturer, as provided in section 1604(b) of this title;

(ii) the defendant may be liable as a seller, as provided in section 1604(c) of this title; or

(iii) the defendant may be liable for furnishing raw materials or component parts for the implant that failed to meet applicable contractual requirements or specifications, as provided in section 1604(d) of this title; or

(C) if the claimant did not name the manufacturer as a party to the action, as provided in subsection (b) of this section.

(4) Treatment of motion as motion for summary judgment

The court may treat a motion to dismiss as a motion for summary judgment subject to subsection (d) of this section in order to determine whether the pleadings and affidavits, in connection with such action, raise genuine issues of material fact concerning whether the defendant furnished raw materials or component parts of the implant that failed to meet applicable contractual requirements or specifications as provided in section 1604(d) of this title.

(d) Summary judgment

(1) In general

(A) Basis for entry of judgment

If a motion to dismiss of a biomaterials supplier is to be treated as a motion for summary judgment under subsection (c)(4) of this section or if a biomaterials supplier moves for summary judgment, the biomaterials supplier shall be entitled to entry of judgment without trial if the court finds there is no genuine issue of material fact for each applicable element set forth in paragraphs (1) and (2) of section 1604(d) of this title.

(B) Issues of material fact

With respect to a finding made under subparagraph (A), the court shall consider a genuine issue of material fact to exist only if the evidence submitted by the claimant would be sufficient to allow a reasonable jury to reach a verdict for the claimant if the jury found the evidence to be credible.

(2) Discovery made prior to a ruling on a motion for summary judgment

If, under applicable rules, the court permits discovery prior to a ruling on a motion for summary judgment governed by section 1604(d) of this title, such discovery shall be limited solely to establishing whether a genuine issue of material fact exists as to the applicable elements set forth in paragraphs (1) and (2) of section 1604(d) of this title.

(3) Discovery with respect to a biomaterials supplier

A biomaterials supplier shall be subject to discovery in connection with a motion seeking dismissal or summary judgment on the basis of the inapplicability of section 1604(d) of this title or the failure to establish the applicable elements of section 1604(d) of this title solely to the extent permitted by the applicable Federal or State rules for discovery against nonparties.

(e) Dismissal with prejudice

An order granting a motion to dismiss or for summary judgment pursuant to this section shall be entered with prejudice, except insofar as the moving defendant may be rejoined to the action as provided in section 1606 of this title.

(f) Manufacturer conduct of litigation

The manufacturer of an implant that is the subject of an action covered under this chapter shall be permitted to conduct litigation on any motion for summary judgment or dismissal filed by a biomaterials supplier who is a defendant under this section on behalf of such supplier if the manufacturer and any other defendant in such action enter into a valid and applicable contractual agreement under which the manufacturer agrees to bear the cost of such litigation or to conduct such litigation.

(Pub. L. 105–230, §6, Aug. 13, 1998, 112 Stat. 1526.)

§1606. Subsequent impleader of dismissed biomaterials supplier

(a) Impleading of dismissed defendant

A court, upon motion by a manufacturer or a claimant within 90 days after entry of a final judgment in an action by the claimant against a manufacturer, and notwithstanding any otherwise applicable statute of limitations, may implead a biomaterials supplier who has been dismissed from the action pursuant to this chapter if—

(1) the manufacturer has made an assertion, either in a motion or other pleading filed with the court or in an opening or closing statement at trial, or as part of a claim for contribution or indemnification, and the court finds based on the court's independent review of the evidence contained in the record of the action, that under applicable law—

(A) the negligence or intentionally tortious conduct of the dismissed supplier was an actual and proximate cause of the harm to the claimant; and

(B) the manufacturer's liability for damages should be reduced in whole or in part because of such negligence or intentionally tortious conduct; or

(2) the claimant has moved to implead the supplier and the court finds, based on the court's independent review of the evidence contained in the record of the action, that under applicable law—

(A) the negligence or intentionally tortious conduct of the dismissed supplier was an actual and proximate cause of the harm to the claimant; and

(B) the claimant is unlikely to be able to recover the full amount of its damages from the remaining defendants.

(b) Standard of liability

Notwithstanding any preliminary finding under subsection (a) of this section, a biomaterials supplier who has been impleaded into an action covered by this chapter, as provided for in this section—

(1) may, prior to entry of judgment on the claim against it, supplement the record of the proceeding that was developed prior to the grant of the motion for impleader under subsection (a) of this section; and

(2) may be found liable to a manufacturer or a claimant only to the extent required and permitted by any applicable State or Federal law other than this chapter.

(c) Discovery

Nothing in this section shall give a claimant or any other party the right to obtain discovery from a biomaterials supplier at any time prior to grant of a motion for impleader beyond that allowed under section 1605 of this title.

(Pub. L. 105–230, §7, Aug. 13, 1998, 112 Stat. 1528.)

CHAPTER 22—NATIONAL DRUG CONTROL POLICY

§1701. Definitions

In this chapter:

(1) Demand reduction

The term "demand reduction" means any activity conducted by a National Drug Control Program agency, other than an enforcement activity, that is intended to reduce the use of drugs, including—

(A) drug abuse education;

(B) drug abuse prevention;

(C) drug abuse treatment;

(D) drug abuse research;

(E) drug abuse rehabilitation;

(F) drug-free workplace programs;

(G) drug testing, including the testing of employees;

(H) interventions for drug abuse and dependence;

(I) international drug control coordination and cooperation with respect to activities described in this paragraph; and

(J) international drug abuse education, prevention, treatment, research, rehabilitation activities, and interventions for drug abuse and dependence.

(2) Director

The term "Director" means the Director of National Drug Control Policy.

(3) Drug

The term "drug" has the meaning given the term "controlled substance" in section 802(6) of this title.

(4) Drug control

The term "drug control" means any activity conducted by a National Drug Control Program agency involving supply reduction or demand reduction.

(5) Fund

The term "Fund" means the fund established under section 1702(d) of this title.

(6) National Drug Control Program

The term "National Drug Control Program" means programs, policies, and activities undertaken by National Drug Control Program agencies pursuant to the responsibilities of such agencies under the National Drug Control Strategy, including any activities involving supply reduction, demand reduction, or State, local, and tribal affairs.

(7) National Drug Control Program agency

The term "National Drug Control Program agency" means any agency that is responsible for implementing any aspect of the National Drug Control Strategy, including any agency that receives Federal funds to implement any aspect of the National Drug Control Strategy, but does not include any agency that receives funds for drug control activity solely under the National Intelligence Program, the Joint Military Intelligence Program or Tactical Intelligence and Related Activities, or (for purposes of section 1703(d) of this title) an agency that is described in section 530C(a) of title 28, unless such agency has been designated—

(A) by the President; or

(B) jointly by the Director and the head of the agency.

(8) National Drug Control Strategy

The term "National Drug Control Strategy" means the strategy developed and submitted to Congress under section 1705 of this title.

(9) Office

Unless the context clearly indicates otherwise, the term "Office" means the Office of National Drug Control Policy established under section 1702(a) of this title.

(10) State, local, and tribal affairs

The term "State, local, and tribal affairs" means domestic activities conducted by a National Drug Control Program agency that are intended to reduce the availability and use of illegal drugs, including—

(A) coordination and enhancement of Federal, State, local, and tribal law enforcement drug control efforts;

(B) coordination and enhancement of efforts among National Drug Control Program agencies and State, local, and tribal demand reduction and supply reduction agencies;

(C) coordination and enhancement of Federal, State, local, and tribal law enforcement initiatives to gather, analyze, and disseminate information and law enforcement intelligence relating to drug control among domestic law enforcement agencies; and

(D) other coordinated and joint initiatives among Federal, State, local, and tribal agencies to promote comprehensive drug control strategies designed to reduce the demand for, and the availability of, illegal drugs.

(11) Supply reduction

The term "supply reduction" means any activity or program conducted by a National Drug Control Program agency that is intended to reduce the availability or use of illegal drugs in the United States or abroad, including—

(A) law enforcement outside the United States;

(B) source country programs, including economic development programs primarily intended to reduce the production or trafficking of illicit drugs;

(C) activities to control international trafficking in, and availability of, illegal drugs, including—

(i) accurate assessment and monitoring of international drug production and interdiction programs and policies; and

(ii) coordination and promotion of compliance with international treaties relating to the production, transportation, or interdiction of illegal drugs;

(D) activities to conduct and promote international law enforcement programs and policies to reduce the supply of drugs; and

(E) activities to facilitate and enhance the sharing of domestic and foreign intelligence information among National Drug Control Program agencies, relating to the production and trafficking of drugs in the United States and in foreign countries.

(12) Appropriate congressional committees

Except where otherwise provided, the term "appropriate congressional committees" means the Committee on the Judiciary, the Committee on Appropriations, and the Caucus on International Narcotics Control of the Senate and the Committee on Government Reform, the Committee on the Judiciary, and the Committee on Appropriations of the House of Representatives.

(13) Law enforcement

The term "law enforcement" or "drug law enforcement" means all efforts by a Federal, State, local, or tribal government agency to enforce the drug laws of the United States or any State, including investigation, arrest, prosecution, and incarceration or other punishments or penalties.

(Pub. L. 105–277, div. C, title VII, §702, Oct. 21, 1998, 112 Stat. 2681–670; Pub. L. 109–469, title I, §101, Dec. 29, 2006, 120 Stat. 3503.)

REPEAL OF SECTION

For repeal of section on Sept. 30, 2010, see section 1712 of this title.

REFERENCES IN TEXT

This chapter, referred to in text, was in the original "this title", meaning title VII of div. C of Pub. L. 105–277, Oct. 21, 1998, 112 Stat. 2681–670, which is classified principally to this chapter. For complete classification of title VII to the Code, see Short Title note set out below and Tables.

CODIFICATION

The repeal of this chapter and of the amendments made by this chapter, effective Sept. 30, 2003, by section 1712 of this title, as in effect on Sept. 30, 2003, has not been given effect in the Code, to reflect the probable intent of Congress, because of the amendment to section 1712 of this title by Pub. L. 109–469 which substituted "September 30, 2010" for "September 30, 2003" as the effective date of the repeal.

AMENDMENTS

2006—(1)(G). Pub. L. 109–469, §101(a)(2), substituted ", including the testing of employees;" for period at end.

Par. (1)(H) to (J). Pub. L. 109–469, §101(a)(1), (3), added subpars. (H) to (J).

Par. (6). Pub. L. 109–469, §101(b), inserted ", including any activities involving supply reduction, demand reduction, or State, local, and tribal affairs" before period at end.

Par. (7). Pub. L. 109–469, §101(c), in introductory provisions, substituted "National Intelligence Program," for "National Foreign Intelligence Program," and inserted "or (for purposes of section 1703(d) of this title) an agency that is described in section 530C(a) of title 28," after "Related Activities,".

Par. (9). Pub. L. 109–469, §101(d), substituted "indicates" for "implicates".

Par. (10). Pub. L. 109–469, §101(e), amended par. (10) generally. Prior to amendment, text defined the term "State and local affairs".

Par. (11). Pub. L. 109–469, §101(f), amended par. (11) generally. Prior to amendment, text defined the term "supply reduction".

Pars. (12), (13). Pub. L. 109–469, §101(g), added pars. (12) and (13).

CHANGE OF NAME

Committee on Government Reform of House of Representatives changed to Committee on Oversight and Government Reform of House of Representatives by House Resolution No. 6, One Hundred Tenth Congress, Jan. 5, 2007.

SHORT TITLE OF 2006 AMENDMENT

Pub. L. 109–469, §1(a), Dec. 29, 2006, 120 Stat. 3502, provided that: "This Act [enacting sections 1708a, 1714, 2001 to 2003, and 2011 to 2014 of this title, amending this section, sections 823, 1524, 1532, 1702 to 1708, 1710 to 1712 of this title, and section 458 of Title 6, Domestic Security, repealing sections 1509, 1709, and 1801 to 1804 of this title, enacting provisions set out as notes under this section, sections 1532, 1705, 1706, and 2001 of this title, and section 112 of Title 32, National Guard, amending provisions set out as a note under section 1521 of this title, and repealing provisions set out as a note under section 1801 of this title] may be cited as the 'Office of National Drug Control Policy Reauthorization Act of 2006'."

Pub. L. 109–469, title III, §302(a), Dec. 29, 2006, 120 Stat. 3524, provided that: "This section [amending section 1706 of this title and enacting provisions set out as a note under section 1706 of this title] may be cited as the 'Dawson Family Community Protection Act'."

SHORT TITLE

Pub. L. 105–277, div. C, title VII, §701, Oct. 21, 1998, 112 Stat. 2681–670, provided that: "This title [enacting this chapter, amending section 1509 of this title, sections 5312 to 5314 of Title 5, Government Organization and Employees, section 1105 of Title 31, Money and Finance, and section 402 of Title 50, War and National Defense] may be cited as the 'Office of National Drug Control Policy Reauthorization Act of 1998'."

MODEL ACTS

Pub. L. 109–469, title XI, §1105, Dec. 29, 2006, 120 Stat. 3541, provided that:

"(a) IN GENERAL.—The Director of the Office of National Drug Control Policy shall provide for or shall enter into an agreement with a non-profit corporation that is described in section 501(c)(3) of the Internal Revenue Code of 1986 [26 U.S.C. 501(c)(3)] and exempt from tax under section 501(a) of such Code to—

"(1) advise States on establishing laws and policies to address alcohol and other drug issues, based on the model State drug laws developed by the President's Commission on Model State Drug Laws in 1993; and

"(2) revise such model State drug laws and draft supplementary model State laws to take into consideration changes in the alcohol and drug abuse problems in the State involved.

"(b) AUTHORIZATION OF APPROPRIATIONS.—There is authorized to be appropriated to carry out this subsection [probably should be "section"] $1,500,000 for each of fiscal years 2007 through 2011."

EX. ORD. NO. 13165. WHITE HOUSE TASK FORCE ON DRUG USE IN SPORTS AND UNITED STATES REPRESENTATIVE ON THE BOARD OF THE WORLD ANTI-DOPING AGENCY

Ex. Ord. No. 13165, Aug. 9, 2000, 65 F.R. 49469, as amended by Ex. Ord. No. 13286, §11, Feb. 28, 2003, 68 F.R. 10622, provided:

By the authority vested in me as President by the Constitution and the laws of the United States of America, including the Office of National Drug Control [Policy] Reauthorization Act of 1998, (21 U.S.C. 1701 *et seq.*), and in order to develop recommendations for Federal agency actions to address the use of drugs in sports, in particular among young people, it is hereby ordered as follows:

SECTION 1. *Policy*. The use of drugs in sports has reached a level that endangers not just the legitimacy of athletic competition but also the lives and health of athletes—from the elite ranks to youth leagues. The National Household Survey on Drug Abuse issued in 1999 found that in just 1 year's time the rate of steroid use among young people rose roughly 50 percent among both sexes and across all age groups. It is the policy of my Administration to take the steps needed to help eliminate illicit or otherwise banned drug use and doping in sports at the State, national, and international level.

SEC. 2. *Establishment of a White House Task Force on Drug Use in Sports*. (a) There is established a White House Task Force on Drug Use in Sports (Task Force). The Task Force shall comprise the co-vice chairs of the White House Olympic Task Force (the "Olympic Task Force Vice Chairs"), and representatives designated by the Office of National Drug Control Policy, the Department of Health and Human Services, the Department of Labor, the President's Council on Physical Fitness and Sports, the Office of Management and Budget, the National Security Council, the Department of State, the Department of the Treasury, the Department of Education, the Department of Justice, the Department of Transportation, the Department of Homeland Security, the National Institute on Drug Abuse, and the Substance Abuse and Mental Health Services Administration.

(b) The Task Force shall develop recommendations for the President on further executive and legislative actions that can be undertaken to address the problem of doping and drug use in sports. In developing the recommendations, the Task Force shall consider, among other things: (i) the health and safety of America's athletes, in particular our Nation's young people; (ii) the integrity of honest athletic competition; and (iii) the views and recommendations of State and local governments, the private sector, citizens, community groups, and nonprofit organizations, on actions to address this threat. The Task Force, through its Chairs, shall submit its recommendations to the President.

(c) The Director of the Office of National Drug Control Policy (the Director), the Secretary of the Department of Health and Human Services, and the Olympic Task Force Vice Chairs or their designees shall serve as the Task Force Chairs.

(d) To the extent permitted by law and at the request of the Chairs, agencies shall cooperate with and provide information to the Task Force.

SEC. 3. *Participation in the World Anti-Doping Agency.* (a) As part of my Administration's efforts to address the problem of drug use in sports, the United States has played a leading role in the formation of a World Anti-Doping Agency (WADA) by the Olympic and sports community and the nations of the world. Through these efforts, the United States has been selected to serve as a governmental representative on the board of the WADA. This order will authorize the Director to serve as the United States Government's representative on the WADA board.

(b) Pursuant to 21 U.S.C. 1701 *et seq.*, the Director, or in his absence his designee, is hereby authorized to take all necessary and proper actions to execute his responsibilities as United States representative to the WADA.

(c) To assist the Director in carrying out these responsibilities as the United States Government representative to the WADA and to the extent permitted by law, Federal employees may serve in their official capacity, *inter alia*, on WADA Committees or WADA advisory committees, serving as experts to the WADA.

§ 1702. Office of National Drug Control Policy

(a) Establishment of Office

There is established in the Executive Office of the President an Office of National Drug Control Policy, which shall—

(1) develop national drug control policy;

(2) coordinate and oversee the implementation of the national drug control policy;

(3) assess and certify the adequacy of National Drug Control Programs and the budget for those programs; and

(4) evaluate the effectiveness of the national drug control policy and the National Drug Control Program agencies' programs, by developing and applying specific goals and performance measurements.

When developing the national drug control policy, any policy of the Director relating to syringe exchange programs for intravenous drug users shall be based on the best available medical and scientific evidence regarding their effectiveness in promoting individual health and preventing the spread of infectious disease, and their impact on drug addiction and use. In making any policy relating to syringe exchange programs, the Director shall consult with the National Institutes of Health and the National Academy of Sciences.

(b) Director of National Drug Control Policy and Deputy Directors

(1) Director

There shall be a Director of National Drug Control Policy who shall head the Office (referred to in this chapter as the "Director") and shall hold the same rank and status as the head of an executive department listed in section 101 of title 5.

(2) Deputy Director

There shall be a Deputy Director of National Drug Control Policy who shall report directly to the Director (referred to in this chapter as the "Deputy Director").

(3) Other Deputy Directors

(A) In general

There shall be a Deputy Director for Demand Reduction, a Deputy Director for Supply Reduction, and a Deputy Director for State, Local, and Tribal Affairs.

(B) Reporting

The Deputy Director for Demand Reduction, the Deputy Director for Supply Reduction, and the Deputy Director for State, Local, and Tribal Affairs shall report directly to the Deputy Director of the Office of National Drug Control Policy.

(C) Deputy Director for Demand Reduction

The Deputy Director for Demand Reduction shall be responsible for the activities in subparagraphs (A) through (H) of section 1701(1)[1] of this title.

(D) Deputy Director for Supply Reduction

The Deputy Director for Supply Reduction shall—

(i) have substantial experience and expertise in drug interdiction and other supply reduction activities; and

(ii) be responsible for the activities in subparagraphs (A) through (C) in section 1701(11) of this title.

(E) Deputy Director for State, Local, and Tribal Affairs

The Deputy Director for State, Local, and Tribal Affairs shall be responsible for the activities—

(i) in subparagraphs (A) through (D) of section 1701(10) of this title;

(ii) in section 1706 of this title, the High Intensity Drug Trafficking Areas Program; and

(iii) in section 1707 of this title, the Counterdrug Technology Assessment Center.

(c) Access by Congress

The location of the Office in the Executive Office of the President shall not be construed as affecting access by Congress, or any committee of the House of Representatives or the Senate, to any—

(1) information, document, or study in the possession of, or conducted by or at the direction of the Director; or

---

[1] See References in Text note below.

(2) personnel of the Office.

(d) Office of National Drug Control Policy Gift Fund

(1) Establishment

There is established in the Treasury of the United States a fund for the receipt of gifts, both real and personal, for the purpose of aiding or facilitating the work of the Office under section 1703(c) of this title.

(2) Contributions

The Office may accept, hold, and administer contributions to the Fund.

(3) Use of amounts deposited

Amounts deposited in the Fund are authorized to be appropriated, to remain available until expended for authorized purposes at the discretion of the Director.

(Pub. L. 105–277, div. C, title VII, §703, Oct. 21, 1998, 112 Stat. 2681–672; Pub. L. 109–469, title I, §102, title XI, §1120, Dec. 29, 2006, 120 Stat. 3505, 3548.)

REPEAL OF SECTION

For repeal of section on Sept. 30, 2010, see section 1712 of this title.

REFERENCES IN TEXT

This chapter, referred to in subsec. (b)(1), (2), was in the original "this Act" and was translated as reading "this title", meaning title VII of Pub. L. 105–277, div. C, Oct. 21, 1998, 112 Stat. 2681–670, which is classified principally to this chapter, to reflect the probable intent of Congress. For complete classification of title VII to the Code, see Short Title note set out under section 1701 of this title and Tables.

Section 1701(1) of this title, referred to in subsec. (b)(3)(C), was in the original "section 702(1)", and was translated as reading "section 702(1)", meaning section 702(1) of Pub. L. 105–277, to reflect the probable intent of Congress, because section 702 of Pub. L. 105–277 does not contain a subsec. (l).

AMENDMENTS

2006—Subsec. (a). Pub. L. 109–469, §1120, inserted concluding provisions.

Pub. L. 109–469, §102(a), amended subsec. (a) generally. Prior to amendment, subsec. (a) related to establishment of Office of National Drug Control Policy.

Subsec. (b). Pub. L. 109–469, §102(b), amended subsec. (b) generally. Prior to amendment, subsec. (b) related to Director and Deputy Directors of National Drug Control Policy.

GIFTS TO OFFICE OF NATIONAL DRUG CONTROL POLICY

Pub. L. 110–161, div. D, title II, Dec. 26, 2007, 121 Stat. 1983, provided in part: "That the Office [of National Drug Control Policy] is authorized to accept, hold, administer, and utilize gifts, both real and personal, public and private, without fiscal year limitation, for the purpose of aiding or facilitating the work of the Office."

Similar provisions were contained in the following prior appropriation acts:

Pub. L. 109–115, div. A, title V, Nov. 30, 2005, 119 Stat. 2475.

Pub. L. 108–447, div. H, title III, Dec. 8, 2004, 118 Stat. 3249.

Pub. L. 108–199, div. F, title III, Jan. 23, 2004, 118 Stat. 324.

Pub. L. 108–7, div. J, title III, Feb. 20, 2003, 117 Stat. 446.

Pub. L. 107–67, title III, Nov. 12, 2001, 115 Stat. 530.

Pub. L. 106–554, §1(a)(3) [title III], Dec. 21, 2000, 114 Stat. 2763, 2763A–139.

Pub. L. 106–58, title III, Sept. 29, 1999, 113 Stat. 447.

Pub. L. 105–277, div. A, §101(h) [title III], Oct. 21, 1998, 112 Stat. 2681–480, 2681–496.

Pub. L. 105–61, title III, Oct. 10, 1997, 111 Stat. 1293.

Pub. L. 104–208, div. A, title I, §101(f) [title III], Sept. 30, 1996, 110 Stat. 3009–314, 3009–329.

Pub. L. 104–52, title III, Nov. 19, 1995, 109 Stat. 479.

Pub. L. 103–329, title III, Sept. 30, 1994, 108 Stat. 2394.

Pub. L. 103–123, title III, Oct. 28, 1993, 107 Stat. 1237.

Pub. L. 102–393, title III, Oct. 6, 1992, 106 Stat. 1741.

Pub. L. 102–141, title III, Oct. 28, 1991, 105 Stat. 847.

Pub. L. 101–509, title III, Nov. 5, 1990, 104 Stat. 1402.

Pub. L. 101–136, title III, Nov. 3, 1989, 103 Stat. 793.

EX. ORD. NO. 12911. SEAL FOR OFFICE OF NATIONAL DRUG CONTROL POLICY

Ex. Ord. No. 12911, Apr. 25, 1994, 59 F.R. 21121 [22121], provided:

By the authority vested in me as President by the Constitution and the laws of the United States of America, it is hereby ordered as follows:

SECTION 1. There is approved for the Office of National Drug Control Policy in the Executive Office of the President an official seal described as follows:

On a blue disc the Arms of the United States proper above a curved gold scroll inscribed "OFFICE OF NATIONAL DRUG CONTROL POLICY" in blue letters, all within a white border edged in gold and inscribed "EXECUTIVE OFFICE OF THE PRESIDENT OF THE UNITED STATES" in blue letters.

This design is appropriate for the Office of National Drug Control Policy. The dark blue in this seal is suggested by the Seal of the President and denotes the direct organizational link of the Office of National Drug Control Policy with the Presidential office. The Arms of the United States refer to the entire Nation and represent the involvement in drug control policies that are necessary to assist the President in his role as Chief Executive of the United States.

SEC. 2. The seal shall be of the design that is attached hereto and made a part of this order.

WILLIAM J. CLINTON.

§1703. Appointment and duties of Director and Deputy Directors

(a) Appointment

(1) In general

The Director, the Deputy Director of National Drug Control Policy, the Deputy Director for Demand Reduction, the Deputy Director for Supply Reduction, and the Deputy Director for State and Local Affairs, shall each be appointed by the President, by and with the advice and consent of the Senate, and shall serve at the pleasure of the President. In appointing the Deputy Director for Demand Reduction under this paragraph, the President shall take into consideration the scientific, educational or professional background of the individual, and whether the individual has experience in the fields of substance abuse prevention, education, or treatment.

(2) Duties of Deputy Director of National Drug Control Policy

The Deputy Director of National Drug Control Policy shall—

(A) carry out the duties and powers prescribed by the Director; and

(B) serve as the Director in the absence of the Director or during any period in which the office of the Director is vacant.

(3) Acting Director

If the Director dies, resigns, or is otherwise unable to perform the functions and duties of the office, the Deputy Director shall perform the functions and duties of the Director temporarily in an acting capacity pursuant to subchapter III of chapter 33 of title 5.

(4) Prohibition

No person shall serve as Director or a Deputy Director while serving in any other position in the Federal Government.

(5) Prohibition on political campaigning

Any officer or employee of the Office who is appointed to that position by the President, by and with the advice and consent of the Senate, may not participate in Federal election campaign activities, except that such official is not prohibited by this paragraph from making contributions to individual candidates.

(b) Responsibilities

The Director—

(1) shall assist the President in the establishment of policies, goals, objectives, and priorities for the National Drug Control Program;

(2) shall promulgate the National Drug Control Strategy under section 1705(a) of this title and each report under section 1705(b) of this title in accordance with section 1705 of this title;

(3) shall coordinate and oversee the implementation by the National Drug Control Program agencies of the policies, goals, objectives, and priorities established under paragraph (1) and the fulfillment of the responsibilities of such agencies under the National Drug Control Strategy and make recommendations to National Drug Control Program agency heads with respect to implementation of Federal counter-drug programs;

(4) shall make such recommendations to the President as the Director determines are appropriate regarding changes in the organization, management, and budgets of National Drug Control Program agencies, and changes in the allocation of personnel to and within those departments and agencies, to implement the policies, goals, priorities, and objectives established under paragraph (1) and the National Drug Control Strategy;

(5) shall consult with and assist State and local governments with respect to the formulation and implementation of National Drug Control Policy and their relations with the National Drug Control Program agencies;

(6) shall appear before duly constituted committees and subcommittees of the House of Representatives and of the Senate to represent the drug policies of the executive branch;

(7) shall notify any National Drug Control Program agency if its policies are not in compliance with the responsibilities of the agency under the National Drug Control Strategy, transmit a copy of each such notification to the President and the appropriate congressional committees, and maintain a copy of each such notification;

(8) shall provide, by July 1 of each year, budget recommendations, including requests for specific initiatives that are consistent with the priorities of the President under the National Drug Control Strategy, to the heads of departments and agencies with responsibilities under the National Drug Control Program, which recommendations shall—

(A) apply to the next budget year scheduled for formulation under chapter 11 of title 31, and each of the 4 subsequent fiscal years; and

(B) address funding priorities developed in the National Drug Control Strategy;

(9) may serve as representative of the President in appearing before Congress on all issues relating to the National Drug Control Program;

(10) shall, in any matter affecting national security interests, work in conjunction with the Assistant to the President for National Security Affairs;

(11) may serve as spokesperson of the Administration on drug issues;

(12) shall ensure that no Federal funds appropriated to the Office of National Drug Control Policy shall be expended for any study or contract relating to the legalization (for a medical use or any other use) of a substance listed in schedule I of section 812 of this title and take such actions as necessary to oppose any attempt to legalize the use of a substance (in any form) that—

(A) is listed in schedule I of section 812 of this title; and

(B) has not been approved for use for medical purposes by the Food and Drug Administration;

(13) shall require each National Drug Control Program agency to submit to the Director on an annual basis an evaluation of progress by the agency with respect to drug control program goals using the performance measures for the agency developed under section 1705(c) of this title, including progress with respect to—

(A) success in reducing domestic and foreign sources of illegal drugs;

(B) success in protecting the borders of the United States (and in particular the Southwestern border of the United States) from penetration by illegal narcotics;

(C) success in reducing violent crime associated with drug use in the United States;

(D) success in reducing the negative health and social consequences of drug use in the United States; and

(E) implementation of drug treatment and prevention programs in the United States and improvements in the adequacy and effectiveness of such programs;

(14) shall submit to the appropriate congressional committees on an annual basis, not later than 60 days after the date of the last day of the applicable period, a summary of—

(A) each of the evaluations received by the Director under paragraph (13); and

(B) the progress of each National Drug Control Program agency toward the drug control program goals of the agency using the performance measures for the agency developed under section 1705(c) of this title;

(15) shall ensure that drug prevention and drug treatment research and information is effectively disseminated by National Drug Control Program agencies to State and local governments and nongovernmental entities involved in demand reduction by—

(A) encouraging formal consultation between any such agency that conducts or sponsors research, and any such agency that disseminates information in developing research and information product development agendas;

(B) encouraging such agencies (as appropriate) to develop and implement dissemination plans that specifically target State and local governments and nongovernmental entities involved in demand reduction; and

(C) supporting the substance abuse information clearinghouse administered by the Administrator of the Substance Abuse and Mental Health Services Administration and established in section 290aa(d)(16) of title 42 by—

(i) encouraging all National Drug Control Program agencies to provide all appropriate and relevant information; and

(ii) supporting the dissemination of information to all interested entities;

(16) shall coordinate with the private sector to promote private research and development of medications to treat addiction;

(17) shall seek the support and commitment of State, local, and tribal officials in the formulation and implementation of the National Drug Control Strategy;

(18) shall monitor and evaluate the allocation of resources among Federal law enforcement agencies in response to significant local and regional drug trafficking and production threats;

(19) shall submit an annual report to Congress detailing how the Office of National Drug Control Policy has consulted with and assisted State, local, and tribal governments with respect to the formulation and implementation of the National Drug Control Strategy and other relevant issues; and

(20) shall, within 1 year after December 29, 2006, report to Congress on the impact of each Federal drug reduction strategy upon the availability, addiction rate, use rate, and other harms of illegal drugs.

(c) National Drug Control Program budget

(1) Responsibilities of National Drug Control Program agencies

(A) In general

For each fiscal year, the head of each department, agency, or program of the Federal Government with responsibilities under the National Drug Control Program Strategy shall transmit to the Director a copy of the proposed drug control budget request of the department, agency, or program at the same time as that budget request is submitted to their superiors (and before submission to the Office of Management and Budget) in the preparation of the budget of the President submitted to Congress under section 1105(a) of title 31.

(B) Submission of drug control budget requests

The head of each National Drug Control Program agency shall ensure timely development and submission to the Director of each proposed drug control budget request transmitted pursuant to this paragraph, in such format as may be designated by the Director with the concurrence of the Director of the Office of Management and Budget.

(C) Content of drug control budget requests

A drug control budget request submitted by a department, agency, or program under this paragraph shall include all requests for funds for any drug control activity undertaken by that department, agency, or program, including demand reduction, supply reduction, and State, local, and tribal affairs, including any drug law enforcement activities. If an activity has both drug control and nondrug control purposes or applications, the department, agency, or program shall estimate by a documented calculation the total funds requested for that activity that would be used for drug control, and shall set forth in its request the basis and method for making the estimate.

(2) National Drug Control Program budget proposal

For each fiscal year, following the transmission of proposed drug control budget requests to the Director under paragraph (1), the Director shall, in consultation with the head of each National Drug Control Program agency and the head of each major national organization that represents law enforcement officers, agencies, or associations—

(A) develop a consolidated National Drug Control Program budget proposal designed to implement the National Drug Control Strategy and to inform Congress and the public about the total amount proposed to be spent on all supply reduction, demand reduction, State, local, and tribal affairs, including any drug law enforcement, and other drug control activities by the Federal Government, which shall conform to the content requirements set forth in paragraph (1)(C);

(B) submit the consolidated budget proposal to the President; and

(C) after submission under subparagraph (B), submit the consolidated budget proposal to Congress.

(3) Review and certification of budget requests and budget submissions of National Drug Control Program agencies

(A) In general

The Director shall review each drug control budget request submitted to the Director under paragraph (1).

(B) Review of budget requests

(i) Inadequate requests

If the Director concludes that a budget request submitted under paragraph (1) is inadequate, in whole or in part, to implement the objectives of the National Drug Control Strategy with respect to the department, agency, or program at issue for the year for which the request is submitted, the Director shall submit to the head of the applicable National Drug Control Program agency a written description of funding levels and specific initiatives that would, in the determination of the Director, make the request adequate to implement those objectives.

(ii) Adequate requests

If the Director concludes that a budget request submitted under paragraph (1) is adequate to implement the objectives of the National Drug Control Strategy with respect to the department, agency, or program at issue for the year for which the request is submitted, the Director shall submit to the head of the applicable National Drug Control Program agency a written statement confirming the adequacy of the request.

(iii) Record

The Director shall maintain a record of each description submitted under clause (i) and each statement submitted under clause (ii).

(C) Specific requests

The Director shall not confirm the adequacy of any budget request that—

(i) requests funding for Federal law enforcement activities that do not adequately compensate for transfers of drug enforcement resources and personnel to law enforcement and investigation activities;

(ii) requests funding for law enforcement activities on the borders of the United States that do not adequately direct resources to drug interdiction and enforcement;

(iii) requests funding for drug treatment activities that do not provide adequate results and accountability measures;

(iv) requests funding for any activities of the Safe and Drug-Free Schools Program that do not include a clear anti-drug message or purpose intended to reduce drug use;

(v) requests funding for drug treatment activities that do not adequately support and enhance Federal drug treatment programs and capacity;

(vi) requests funding for fiscal year 2007 for activities of the Department of Education, unless it is accompanied by a report setting forth a plan for providing expedited consideration of student loan applications for all individuals who submitted an application for any Federal grant, loan, or work assistance that was rejected or denied pursuant to 1091(r)(1)[1] of title 20 by reason of a conviction for a drug-related offense not occurring during a period of enrollment for which the individual was receiving any Federal grant, loan, or work assistance; and

(vii) requests funding for the operations and management of the Department of Homeland Security that does not include a specific request for funds for the Office of Counternarcotics Enforcement to carry out its responsibilities under section 458 of title 6.

(D) Agency response

(i) In general

The head of a National Drug Control Program agency that receives a description under subparagraph (B)(i) shall include the funding levels and initiatives described by the Director in the budget submission for that agency to the Office of Management and Budget.

(ii) Impact statement

The head of a National Drug Control Program agency that has altered its budget submission under this subparagraph shall include as an appendix to the budget submission for that agency to the Office of Management and Budget an impact statement that summarizes—

(I) the changes made to the budget under this subparagraph; and

(II) the impact of those changes on the ability of that agency to perform its other responsibilities, including any impact on specific missions or programs of the agency.

(iii) Congressional notification

The head of a National Drug Control Program agency shall submit a copy of any impact statement under clause (ii) to the Senate and the House of Representatives and the appropriate congressional committees, at the time the budget for that agency is submitted to Congress under section 1105(a) of title 31.

(E) Certification of budget submissions

(i) In general

At the time a National Drug Control Program agency submits its budget request to the Office of Management and Budget, the head of the National Drug Control Program agency shall submit a copy of the budget request to the Director.

(ii) Certification

The Director—

[1] So in original. Probably should be preceded by "section".

(I) shall review each budget submission submitted under clause (i); and

(II) based on the review under subclause (I), if the Director concludes that the budget submission of a National Drug Control Program agency does not include the funding levels and initiatives described under subparagraph (B)—

(aa) may issue a written decertification of that agency's budget; and

(bb) in the case of a decertification issued under item (aa), shall submit to the Senate and the House of Representatives and the appropriate congressional committees, a copy of—

(aaa) the decertification issued under item (aa);

(bbb) the description made under subparagraph (B); and

(ccc) the budget recommendations made under subsection (b)(8) of this section.

(4) Reprogramming and transfer requests

(A) In general

No National Drug Control Program agency shall submit to Congress a reprogramming or transfer request with respect to any amount of appropriated funds in an amount exceeding $1,000,000 that is included in the National Drug Control Program budget unless the request has been approved by the Director. If the Director has not responded to a request for reprogramming subject to this subparagraph within 30 days after receiving notice of the request having been made, the request shall be deemed approved by the Director under this subparagraph and forwarded to Congress.

(B) Appeal

The head of any National Drug Control Program agency may appeal to the President any disapproval by the Director of a reprogramming or transfer request under this paragraph.

(d) Powers of the Director

In carrying out subsection (b) of this section, the Director may—

(1) select, appoint, employ, and fix compensation of such officers and employees of the Office as may be necessary to carry out the functions of the Office under this chapter;

(2) subject to subsection (e)(3) of this section, request the head of a department or agency, or program of the Federal Government to place department, agency, or program personnel who are engaged in drug control activities on temporary detail to another department, agency, or program in order to implement the National Drug Control Strategy, and the head of the department or agency shall comply with such a request;

(3) use for administrative purposes, on a reimbursable basis, the available services, equipment, personnel, and facilities of Federal, State, and local agencies;

(4) procure the services of experts and consultants in accordance with section 3109 of title 5, relating to appointments in the Federal Service, at rates of compensation for individuals not to exceed the daily equivalent of the rate of pay payable under level IV of the Executive Schedule under section 5311 of title 5;

(5) accept and use gifts and donations of property from Federal, State, and local government agencies, and from the private sector, as authorized in section 1702(d) of this title;

(6) use the mails in the same manner as any other department or agency of the executive branch;

(7) monitor implementation of the National Drug Control Program, including—

(A) conducting program and performance audits and evaluations; and

(B) requesting assistance from the Inspector General of the relevant agency in such audits and evaluations;

(8) transfer funds made available to a National Drug Control Program agency for National Drug Control Strategy programs and activities to another account within such agency or to another National Drug Control Program agency for National Drug Control Strategy programs and activities, except that—

(A) the authority under this paragraph may be limited in an annual appropriations Act or other provision of Federal law;

(B) the Director may exercise the authority under this paragraph only with the concurrence of the head of each affected agency;

(C) in the case of an interagency transfer, the total amount of transfers under this paragraph may not exceed 3 percent of the total amount of funds made available for National Drug Control Strategy programs and activities to the agency from which those funds are to be transferred;

(D) funds transferred to an agency under this paragraph may only be used to increase the funding for programs or activities authorized by law; and

(E) the Director shall—

(i) submit to Congress, including to the Committees on Appropriations of the Senate and the House of Representatives, the authorizing committees for the Office, and any other applicable committees of jurisdiction, a reprogramming or transfer request in advance of any transfer under this paragraph in accordance with the regulations of the affected agency or agencies; and

(ii) annually submit to Congress a report describing the effect of all transfers of funds made pursuant to this paragraph or subsection (c)(4) of this section during the 12-month period preceding the date on which the report is submitted;

(9) issue to the head of a National Drug Control Program agency a fund control notice described in subsection (f) of this section to ensure compliance with the National Drug Control Program Strategy and notify the appropriate congressional committees of any fund control notice issued in accordance with subsection (f)(5);

(10) participate in the drug certification process pursuant to section 2291j of title 22 and section 2291j–1 of title 22.

(e) Personnel detailed to Office

(1) Evaluations

Notwithstanding any provision of chapter 43 of title 5, the Director shall perform the evaluation of the performance of any employee detailed to the Office for purposes of the applicable performance appraisal system established under such chapter for any rating period, or part thereof, that such employee is detailed to such office.

(2) Compensation

(A) Bonus payments

Notwithstanding any other provision of law, the Director may provide periodic bonus payments to any employee detailed to the Office.

(B) Restrictions

An amount paid under this paragraph to an employee for any period—

(i) shall not be greater than 20 percent of the basic pay paid or payable to such employee for such period; and

(ii) shall be in addition to the basic pay of such employee.

(C) Aggregate amount

The aggregate amount paid during any fiscal year to an employee detailed to the Office as basic pay, awards, bonuses, and other compensation shall not exceed the annual rate payable at the end of such fiscal year for positions at level III of the Executive Schedule.

(3) Maximum number of detailees

The maximum number of personnel who may be detailed to another department or agency (including the Office) under subsection (d)(2) of this section during any fiscal year is—

(A) for the Department of Defense, 50; and

(B) for any other department or agency, 10.

(f) Fund control notices

(1) In general

A fund control notice may direct that all or part of an amount appropriated to the National Drug Control Program agency account be obligated by—

(A) months, fiscal year quarters, or other time periods; and

(B) activities, functions, projects, or object classes.

(2) Unauthorized obligation or expenditure prohibited

An officer or employee of a National Drug Control Program agency shall not make or authorize an expenditure or obligation contrary to a fund control notice issued by the Director.

(3) Disciplinary action for violation

In the case of a violation of paragraph (2) by an officer or employee of a National Drug Control Program agency, the head of the agency, upon the request of and in consultation with the Director, may subject the officer or employee to appropriate administrative discipline, including, when circumstances warrant, suspension from duty without pay or removal from office.

(4)[2] Congressional notice

A copy of each fund control notice shall be transmitted to the appropriate congressional committees.

(5)[3] Restrictions

The Director shall not issue a fund control notice to direct that all or part of an amount appropriated to the National Drug Control Program agency account be obligated, modified, or altered in any manner—

(A) contrary, in whole or in part, to a specific appropriation; or

(B) contrary, in whole or in part, to the expressed intent of Congress.

(4)[2] Congressional notice.—

A copy of each fund control notice shall be transmitted to the appropriate congressional committees.

(5)[3] Restrictions

The Director shall not issue a fund control notice to direct that all or part of an amount appropriated to the National Drug Control Program agency account be obligated, modified, or altered in any manner contrary, in whole or in part, to a specific appropriation or statute.

(g) Inapplicability to certain programs

The provisions of this section shall not apply to the National Intelligence Program, the Joint Military Intelligence Program, and Tactical and Related Activities, unless such program or an element of such program is designated as a National Drug Control Program—

(1) by the President; or

(2) jointly by—

(A) in the case of the National Intelligence Program, the Director and the Director of National Intelligence; or

(B) in the case of the Joint Military Intelligence Program and Tactical and Related Activities, the Director, the Director of National Intelligence, and the Secretary of Defense.

(h) Construction

Nothing in this chapter shall be construed as derogating the authorities and responsibilities of the Director of National Intelligence or the Director of the Central Intelligence Agency contained in the National Security Act of 1947 (50 U.S.C. 401 et seq.), the Central Intelligence Agency Act of 1949 (50 U.S.C. 403a et seq.), or any other law.

(Pub. L. 105–277, div. C, title VII, §704, Oct. 21, 1998, 112 Stat. 2681–672; Pub. L. 109–469, title I, §§103(a)–(e), (f)(3), 105, Dec. 29, 2006, 120 Stat. 3506, 3507, 3510, 3511.)

REPEAL OF SECTION

For repeal of section on Sept. 30, 2010, see section 1712 of this title.

REFERENCES IN TEXT

Levels III and IV of the Executive Schedule, referred to in subsecs. (d)(4) and (e)(2)(C), are set out in sections

[2] So in original. Two pars. (4) have been enacted.

[3] So in original. Two pars. (5) have been enacted.

5314 and 5315, respectively, of Title 5, Government Organization and Employees.

This chapter, referred to in subsec. (h), was in the original "this Act" and was translated as reading "this title", meaning title VII of Pub. L. 105–277, div. C, Oct. 21, 1998, 112 Stat. 2681–670, which is classified principally to this chapter, to reflect the probable intent of Congress. For complete classification of title VII to the Code, see Short Title note set out under section 1701 of this title and Tables.

The National Security Act of 1947, referred to in subsec. (h), is act July 26, 1947, ch. 343, 61 Stat. 495, as amended. For complete classification of this Act to the Code, see Short Title note set out under section 401 of Title 50, War and National Defense, and Tables.

The Central Intelligence Agency Act of 1949, referred to in subsec. (h), is act June 20, 1949, ch. 227, 63 Stat. 208, as amended, which is classified generally to section 403a et seq. of Title 50, War and National Defense. For complete classification of this Act to the Code, see Short Title note set out under section 403a of Title 50 and Tables.

CODIFICATION

In subsec. (b)(8)(A), "chapter 11 of title 31" substituted for "the Budget and Accounting Act of 1921" on authority of Pub. L. 97–258, §4(b), Sept. 13, 1982, 96 Stat. 1067, the first section of which enacted Title 31, Money and Finance.

AMENDMENTS

2006—Subsec. (a)(3). Pub. L. 109–469, §103(a), amended par. (3) generally. Prior to amendment, text read as follows: "In the absence of the Deputy Director, or if the Office of the Deputy Director is vacant, the Director shall designate such other permanent employee of the Office to serve as the Director, if the Director is absent or unable to serve."

Subsec. (b)(4). Pub. L. 109–469, §103(b)(1), substituted "National Drug Control Program agencies" for "Federal departments and agencies engaged in drug enforcement".

Subsec. (b)(7). Pub. L. 109–469, §103(b)(2), inserted "and the appropriate congressional committees" after "President".

Subsec. (b)(13). Pub. L. 109–469, §103(b)(3), struck out "(beginning in 1999)" after "basis" in introductory provisions.

Subsec. (b)(14). Pub. L. 109–469, §103(b)(4), added par. (14) and struck out former par. (14) which read as follows: "shall submit to the Appropriations committees and the authorizing committees of jurisdiction of the House of Representatives and the Senate on an annual basis, not later than 60 days after the date of the last day of the applicable period, a summary of—

"(A) each of the evaluations received by the Director under paragraph (13); and

"(B) the progress of each National Drug Control Program agency toward the drug control program goals of the agency using the performance measures for the agency developed under section 1705(c) of this title; and".

Subsec. (b)(15)(C). Pub. L. 109–469, §103(b)(5), added subpar. (C) and struck out former subpar. (C) which read as follows: "developing a single interagency clearinghouse for the dissemination of research and information by such agencies to State and local governments and nongovernmental agencies involved in demand reduction."

Subsec. (b)(16) to (20). Pub. L. 109–469, §103(b)(6), added pars. (16) to (20).

Subsec. (c)(1)(C). Pub. L. 109–469, §105(a), added subpar. (C).

Subsec. (c)(2). Pub. L. 109–469, §105(b)(1), inserted "and the head of each major national organization that represents law enforcement officers, agencies, or associations" after "agency" in introductory provisions.

Subsec. (c)(2)(A). Pub. L. 109–469, §105(b)(2), inserted "and to inform Congress and the public about the total amount proposed to be spent on all supply reduction, demand reduction, State, local, and tribal affairs, including any drug law enforcement, and other drug control activities by the Federal Government, which shall conform to the content requirements set forth in paragraph (1)(C)" before semicolon at end.

Subsec. (c)(3)(C). Pub. L. 109–469, §105(c)(2), added subpar. (C). Former subpar. (C) redesignated (D).

Subsec. (c)(3)(C)(iii). Pub. L. 109–469, §103(c)(1), inserted "and the appropriate congressional committees," after "House of Representatives".

Subsec. (c)(3)(D). Pub. L. 109–469, §105(c)(1), redesignated subpar. (C) as (D). Former subpar. (D) redesignated (E).

Subsec. (c)(3)(D)(ii)(II)(bb). Pub. L. 109–469, §103(c)(2), inserted "and the appropriate congressional committees," after "House of Representatives".

Subsec. (c)(3)(D)(iii). Pub. L. 109–469, §105(c)(3), which directed amendment of cl. (iii) by inserting "and the appropriate congressional committees," after "House of Representatives", was not executed in view of the identical amendment made by Pub. L. 109–469, §103(c)(1) to subpar. (C)(iii) prior to its redesignation as (D)(iii). See above.

Subsec. (c)(3)(E). Pub. L. 109–469, §105(c)(1), redesignated subpar. (D) as (E).

Subsec. (c)(3)(E)(ii)(II)(bb). Pub. L. 109–469, §105(c)(4), which directed amendment of item (bb) by inserting "and the appropriate congressional committees," after "House of Representatives", was not executed in view of the identical amendment made by Pub. L. 109–469, §103(c)(2) to subpar. (D)(ii)(II)(bb) prior to its redesignation as (E)(ii)(II)(bb). See above.

Subsec. (c)(4)(A). Pub. L. 109–469, §105(d), substituted "$1,000,000" for "$5,000,000" and inserted at end "If the Director has not responded to a request for reprogramming subject to this subparagraph within 30 days after receiving notice of the request having been made, the request shall be deemed approved by the Director under this subparagraph and forwarded to Congress."

Subsec. (d)(8)(D). Pub. L. 109–469, §105(e)(1), substituted "authorized by law;" for "have been authorized by Congress;".

Subsec. (d)(9). Pub. L. 109–469, §105(e)(2), which directed the substitution of "Strategy and notify the appropriate congressional committees of any fund control notice issued; and" for "Strategy; and", could not be executed because the words "Strategy; and" did not appear subsequent to amendment by Pub. L. 109–469, §103(d)(1). See below.

Pub. L. 109–469, §103(d)(1), substituted "Strategy and notify the appropriate congressional committees of any fund control notice issued in accordance with subsection (f)(5);" for "Strategy; and".

Subsec. (d)(10). Pub. L. 109–469, §§103(d)(2) and 105(e)(3), made identical amendments, inserting "and section 2291j–1 of title 22" before period at end.

Subsec. (f)(4), (5). Pub. L. 109–469, §105(f), added pars. (4) and (5) set out second.

Pub. L. 109–469, §103(e), added pars. (4) and (5) set out first.

Subsec. (g). Pub. L. 109–469, §103(f)(3)(A), amended subsec. (g) generally. Prior to amendment, text read as follows: "The provisions of this section shall not apply to the National Foreign Intelligence Program, the Joint Military Intelligence Program and Tactical Intelligence and Related Activities unless the agency that carries out such program is designated as a National Drug Control Program agency by the President or jointly by the Director and the head of the agency."

Subsec. (h). Pub. L. 109–469, §103(f)(3)(B), amended subsec. (h) generally. Prior to amendment, text read as follows: "Nothing in this chapter shall be construed as derogating the authorities and responsibilities of the Director of Central Intelligence contained in sections 403–4 and 414 of title 50 or any other law."

REPORT ON STREAMLINING FEDERAL PREVENTION AND TREATMENT EFFORTS

Pub. L. 105–277, div. D, title II, §221, Oct. 21, 1998, 112 Stat. 2681–758, expressed sense of Congress that efforts of the Federal Government to reduce demand for illegal drugs in United States are frustrated by fragmentation of those efforts across multiple departments and agencies, and improvement of those efforts can best be achieved through consolidation and coordination, and further provided that not later than 18 months after Oct. 21, 1998, Director of the Office of National Drug Control Policy was to prepare and submit to Congress a report evaluating options for increasing efficacy of drug prevention and treatment programs, including a thorough review of activities and potential consolidation of existing Federal drug information clearinghouses.

EX. ORD. NO. 12880. NATIONAL DRUG CONTROL PROGRAM

Ex. Ord. No. 12880, Nov. 16, 1993, 58 F.R. 60989, as amended by Ex. Ord. No. 13008, June 3, 1996, 61 F.R. 28721, provided:

The Office of National Drug Control Policy has the lead responsibility within the Executive Office of the President to establish policies, priorities, and objectives for the Nation's drug control program, with the goal of reducing the production, availability, and use of illegal drugs. All lawful and reasonable means must be used to ensure that the United States has a comprehensive and effective National Drug Control Strategy.

Therefore, by the authority vested in me as President by the Constitution and the laws of the United States of America, including the National Narcotics Leadership Act of 1988, as amended (former 21 U.S.C. 1501 *et seq.*), and in order to provide for the effective management of the drug abuse policies of the United States, it is hereby ordered as follows:

SECTION 1. GENERAL PROVISIONS. (a) Because the United States considers the operations of international criminal narcotics syndicates as a national security threat requiring an extraordinary and coordinated response by civilian and military agencies involved in national security, the Director of the Office of National Drug Control Policy (Director), in his role as the principal adviser to the National Security Council on national drug control policy (50 U.S.C. 402(f)), shall provide drug policy guidance and direction in the development of related national security programs.

(b) The Director shall provide oversight and direction for all international counternarcotics policy development and implementation, in coordination with other concerned Cabinet members, as appropriate.

(c) An Interagency Working Group (IWG) on international counternarcotics policy, chaired by the Office of National Drug Control Policy, shall develop and ensure coordinated implementation of an international counternarcotics policy. The IWG shall report its activities and differences of views among agencies to the Director for review, mediation, and resolution with concerned Cabinet members, and if necessary, by the President.

(d) A coordinator for drug interdiction shall be designated by the Director to ensure that assets dedicated by Federal drug program agencies for interdiction are sufficient and that their use is properly integrated and optimized. The coordinator shall ensure that interdiction efforts and priorities are consistent with overall U.S. international counternarcotics policy.

(e) The Director shall examine the number and structure of command/control and drug intelligence centers operated by drug control program agencies involved in international counter-narcotics and suggest improvements to the current structure for consideration by the President and concerned members of the Cabinet.

(f) The Director, utilizing the services of the Drugs and Crime Data Center and Department of Justice Clearinghouse, shall assist in coordinating and enhancing the dissemination of statistics and studies relating to anti-drug abuse policy.

(g) The Director shall provide advice to agencies regarding ways to achieve efficiencies in spending and improvements to interagency cooperation that could enhance the delivery of drug control treatment and prevention services to the public. The Director may request agencies to provide studies, information, and analyses in support of this order.

SEC. 2. GOALS, DIRECTION, DUTIES AND RESPONSIBILITIES WITH RESPECT TO THE NATIONAL DRUG CONTROL PROGRAM. (a) *Budget Matters.* (1) In addition to the budgetary authorities and responsibilities provided to the Director by statute, [former] 21 U.S.C. 1502, for those agency budget requests that are not certified as adequate to implement the objectives of the National Drug Control Strategy, the Director shall include in such certifications initiatives or funding levels that would make such requests adequate.

(2) The Director shall provide, by July 1 of each year, budget recommendations to the heads of departments and agencies with responsibilities under the National Drug Control Program. The recommendations shall apply to the second following fiscal year and address funding priorities developed in the annual National Drug Control Strategy.

(b) *Measurement of National Drug Control Strategy Outcomes.* (1) The National Drug Control Strategy shall include long-range goals for reducing drug use and the consequences of drug use in the United States, including burdens on hospital emergency rooms, drug use among arrestees, the extent of drug-related crime, high school dropout rates, the number of infants exposed annually to illicit drugs in utero, national drug abuse treatment capacity, and the annual national health care costs of drug use.

(2) The National Drug Control Strategy shall also include an assessment of the quality of techniques and instruments to measure current drug use and supply and demand reduction activities, and the adequacy of the coverage of existing national drug use instruments and techniques to measure the total illicit drug user population and groups at-risk for drug use.

(3) The Director shall coordinate an effort among the relevant drug control program agencies to assess the quality, access, management, effectiveness, and standards of accountability of drug abuse treatment, prevention, education, and other demand reduction activities.

(c) *Provision of Reports.* To the extent permitted by law, heads of departments and agencies with responsibilities under the National Drug Control Program shall make available to the Office of National Drug Control Policy, appropriate statistics, studies, and reports, pertaining to Federal drug abuse control.

WILLIAM J. CLINTON.

§1704. Coordination with National Drug Control Program agencies in demand reduction, supply reduction, and State and local affairs

(a) Access to information

(1) In general

Upon the request of the Director, the head of any National Drug Control Program agency shall cooperate with and provide to the Director any statistics, studies, reports, and other information prepared or collected by the agency concerning the responsibilities of the agency under the National Drug Control Strategy that relate to—

(A) drug control; or

(B) the manner in which amounts made available to that agency for drug control are being used by that agency.

(2) Protection of intelligence information

(A) In general

The authorities conferred on the Office and the Director by this chapter shall be exercised in a manner consistent with provisions of the National Security Act of 1947 (50 U.S.C. 401 et seq.). The Director of National Intelligence shall prescribe such regulations as may be necessary to protect information provided pursuant to this chapter regarding intelligence sources and methods.

(B) Duties of Director

The Director of National Intelligence and the Director of the Central Intelligence Agency shall, to the maximum extent practicable in accordance with subparagraph (A), render full assistance and support to the Office and the Director.

(3) Required reports

(A) Secretaries of the Interior and Agriculture

Not later than July 1 of each year, the Secretaries of Agriculture and the Interior shall jointly submit to the Director and the appropriate congressional committees an assessment of the quantity of illegal drug cultivation and manufacturing in the United States on lands owned or under the jurisdiction of the Federal Government for the preceding year.

(B) Secretary of Homeland Security

Not later than July 1 of each year, the Secretary of Homeland Security shall submit to the Director and the appropriate congressional committees information for the preceding year regarding—

(i) the number and type of seizures of drugs by each component of the Department of Homeland Security seizing drugs, as well as statistical information on the geographic areas of such seizures; and

(ii) the number of air and maritime patrol hours primarily dedicated to drug supply reduction missions undertaken by each component of the Department of Homeland Security.

(C) Secretary of Defense

The Secretary of Defense shall, by July 1 of each year, submit to the Director and the appropriate congressional committees information for the preceding year regarding the number of air and maritime patrol hours primarily dedicated to drug supply reduction missions undertaken by each component of the Department of Defense.

(D) Attorney General

The Attorney General shall, by July 1 of each year, submit to the Director and the appropriate congressional committees information for the preceding year regarding the number and type of—

(i) arrests for drug violations;

(ii) prosecutions for drug violations by United States Attorneys; and

(iii) seizures of drugs by each component of the Department of Justice seizing drugs, as well as statistical information on the geographic areas of such seizures.

(b) Certification of policy changes to Director

(1) In general

Subject to paragraph (2), the head of a National Drug Control Program agency shall, unless exigent circumstances require otherwise, notify the Director in writing regarding any proposed change in policies relating to the activities of that agency under the National Drug Control Program prior to implementation of such change. The Director shall promptly review such proposed change and certify to the head of that agency in writing whether such change is consistent with the National Drug Control Strategy.

(2) Exception

If prior notice of a proposed change under paragraph (1) is not practicable—

(A) the head of the National Drug Control Program agency shall notify the Director of the proposed change as soon as practicable; and

(B) upon such notification, the Director shall review the change and certify to the head of that agency in writing whether the change is consistent with the National Drug Control Strategy.

(c) General Services Administration

The Administrator of General Services shall provide to the Director, on a reimbursable basis, such administrative support services as the Director may request.

(d) Accounting of funds expended

The Director shall—

(A) require the National Drug Control Program agencies to submit to the Director not later than February 1 of each year a detailed accounting of all funds expended by the agencies for National Drug Control Program activities during the previous fiscal year, and require such accounting to be authenticated by the Inspector General for each agency prior to submission to the Director; and

(B) submit to Congress not later than April 1 of each year the information submitted to the Director under subparagraph (A).

(Pub. L. 105–277, div. C, title VII, § 705, Oct. 21, 1998, 112 Stat. 2681–680; Pub. L. 109–469, title I, § 104, Dec. 29, 2006, 120 Stat. 3510.)

REPEAL OF SECTION

For repeal of section on Sept. 30, 2010, see section 1712 of this title.

REFERENCES IN TEXT

The National Security Act of 1947, referred to in subsec. (a)(2)(A), is act July 26, 1947, ch. 343, 61 Stat. 495, as amended. For complete classification of this Act to the Code, see Short Title note set out under section 401 of Title 50, War and National Defense, and Tables.

AMENDMENTS

2006—Subsec. (a)(1)(A). Pub. L. 109–469, § 104(1), struck out "abuse" after "drug".

Subsec. (a)(2)(A). Pub. L. 109–469, § 104(2), substituted "Director of National Intelligence" for "Director of Central Intelligence".

Subsec. (a)(2)(B). Pub. L. 109–469, § 104(3), substituted "Director of National Intelligence and the Director of the Central Intelligence Agency" for "Director of Central Intelligence".

Subsec. (a)(3). Pub. L. 109–469, § 104(4), amended par. (3) generally. Prior to amendment, text read as follows: "The Secretary of Agriculture shall annually submit to the Director an assessment of the acreage of illegal drug cultivation in the United States."

Subsec. (b)(2)(B). Pub. L. 109–469, § 104(5), substituted "Strategy" for "Program".

Subsec. (c). Pub. L. 109–469, §104(6), substituted "on" for "in".

§1705. Development, submission, implementation, and assessment of National Drug Control Strategy

(a) Timing, contents, and process for development and submission of National Drug Control Strategy

(1) Timing

Not later than February 1 of each year, the President shall submit to Congress a National Drug Control Strategy, which shall set forth a comprehensive plan for the year to reduce illicit drug use and the consequences of such illicit drug use in the United States by limiting the availability of, and reducing the demand for, illegal drugs.

(2) Contents

(A) In general

The National Drug Control Strategy submitted under paragraph (1) shall include the following:

(i) Comprehensive, research-based, long-range, quantifiable goals for reducing illicit drug use and the consequences of illicit drug use in the United States.

(ii) Annual quantifiable and measurable objectives and specific targets to accomplish long-term quantifiable goals that the Director determines may be achieved during each year beginning on the date on which the National Drug Control Strategy is submitted.

(iii) A 5-year projection for program and budget priorities.

(iv) A review of international, State, local, and private sector drug control activities to ensure that the United States pursues coordinated and effective drug control at all levels of government.

(v) An assessment of current illicit drug use (including inhalants and steroids) and availability, impact of illicit drug use, and treatment availability, which assessment shall include—

(I) estimates of drug prevalence and frequency of use as measured by national, State, and local surveys of illicit drug use and by other special studies of nondependent and dependent illicit drug use;

(II) illicit drug use in the workplace and the productivity lost by such use; and

(III) illicit drug use by arrestees, probationers, and parolees.

(vi) An assessment of the reduction of illicit drug availability, as measured by—

(I) the quantities of cocaine, heroin, marijuana, methamphetamine, ecstasy, and other drugs available for consumption in the United States;

(II) the amount of marijuana, cocaine, heroin, methamphetamine, ecstasy, and precursor chemicals and other drugs entering the United States;

(III) the number of illicit drug manufacturing laboratories seized and destroyed and the number of hectares of marijuana, poppy, and coca cultivated and destroyed domestically and in other countries;

(IV) the number of metric tons of marijuana, heroin, cocaine, and methamphetamine seized and other drugs; and

(V) changes in the price and purity of heroin, methamphetamine, and cocaine, changes in the price of ecstasy, and changes in tetrahydrocannabinol level of marijuana and other drugs.

(vii) An assessment of the reduction of the consequences of illicit drug use and availability, which shall include—

(I) the burden illicit drug users placed on hospital emergency departments in the United States, such as the quantity of illicit drug-related services provided;

(II) the annual national health care cost of illicit drug use; and

(III) the extent of illicit drug-related crime and criminal activity.

(viii) A determination of the status of drug treatment in the United States, by assessing—

(I) public and private treatment utilization; and

(II) the number of illicit drug users the Director estimates meet diagnostic criteria for treatment.

(ix) A review of the research agenda of the Counterdrug Technology Assessment Center to reduce the availability and abuse of drugs.

(x) A summary of the efforts made to coordinate with private sector entities to conduct private research and development of medications to treat addiction by—

(I) screening chemicals for potential therapeutic value;

(II) developing promising compounds;

(III) conducting clinical trials;

(IV) seeking Food and Drug Administration approval for drugs to treat addiction;

(V) marketing the drug for the treatment of addiction;

(VI) urging physicians to use the drug in the treatment of addiction; and

(VII) encouraging insurance companies to reimburse the cost of the drug for the treatment of addiction.

(xi) An assessment of Federal effectiveness in achieving the National Drug Control Strategy for the previous year, including a specific evaluation of whether the objectives and targets for reducing illicit drug use for the previous year were met and reasons for the success or failure of the previous year's Strategy.

(xii) A general review of the status of, and trends in, demand reduction activities by private sector entities and community-based organizations, including faith-based organizations, to determine their effectiveness and the extent of cooperation, coordination, and mutual support between such entities and organizations and Federal, State, local, and tribal government agencies.

(xiii) Such additional statistical data and information as the Director considers appropriate to demonstrate and assess trends relating to illicit drug use, the effects and consequences of illicit drug use (including the effects on children of substance abusers), supply reduction, demand reduction, drug-related law enforcement, and the implementation of the National Drug Control Strategy.

(xiv) A supplement reviewing the activities of each individual National Drug Control Program agency during the previous year with respect to the National Drug Control Strategy and the Director's assessment of the progress of each National Drug Control Program agency in meeting its responsibilities under the National Drug Control Strategy.

(B) Classified information

Any contents of the National Drug Control Strategy that involve information properly classified under criteria established by an Executive order shall be presented to Congress separately from the rest of the National Drug Control Strategy.

(C) Selection of data and information

In selecting data and information for inclusion under subparagraph (A), the Director shall ensure—

(i) the inclusion of data and information that will permit analysis of current trends against previously compiled data and information where the Director believes such analysis enhances long-term assessment of the National Drug Control Strategy; and

(ii) the inclusion of data and information to permit a standardized and uniform assessment of the effectiveness of drug treatment programs in the United States.

(3) Process for development and submission

In developing and effectively implementing the National Drug Control Strategy, the Director—

(A) shall consult with—

(i) the heads of the National Drug Control Program agencies;

(ii) Congress;

(iii) State, local, and tribal officials;

(iv) private citizens and organizations, including community and faith-based organizations with experience and expertise in demand reduction;

(v) private citizens and organizations with experience and expertise in supply reduction; and

(vi) appropriate representatives of foreign governments;

(B) in satisfying the requirements of subparagraph (A), shall ensure, to the maximum extent possible, that State, local, and tribal officials and relevant private organizations commit to support and take steps to achieve the goals and objectives of the National Drug Control Strategy;

(C) with the concurrence of the Attorney General, may require the El Paso Intelligence Center to undertake specific tasks or projects to support or implement the National Drug Control Strategy; and

(D) with the concurrence of the Director of National Intelligence and the Attorney General, may request that the National Drug Intelligence Center undertake specific tasks or projects to support or implement the National Drug Control Strategy.

(b) Submission of revised strategy

The President may submit to Congress a revised National Drug Control Strategy that meets the requirements of this section—

(1) at any time, upon a determination of the President, in consultation with the Director, that the National Drug Control Strategy in effect is not sufficiently effective; or

(2) if a new President or Director takes office.

(c) Performance measurement system

Not later than February 1 of each year, the Director shall submit to Congress as part of the National Drug Control Strategy, a description of a national drug control performance measurement system, that—

(1) develops 2-year and 5-year performance measures and targets for each National Drug Control Strategy goal and objective established for reducing drug use, availability, and the consequences of drug use;

(2) describes the sources of information and data that will be used for each performance measure incorporated into the performance measurement system;

(3) identifies major programs and activities of the National Drug Control Program agencies that support the goals and annual objectives of the National Drug Control Strategy;

(4) evaluates the contribution of demand reduction and supply reduction activities as defined in section 1701 of this title implemented by each National Drug Control Program agency in support of the National Drug Control Strategy;

(5) monitors consistency between the drug-related goals and objectives of the National Drug Control Program agencies and ensures that each agency's goals and budgets support and are fully consistent with the National Drug Control Strategy; and

(6) coordinates the development and implementation of national drug control data collection and reporting systems to support policy formulation and performance measurement, including an assessment of—

(A) the quality of current drug use measurement instruments and techniques to measure supply reduction and demand reduction activities;

(B) the adequacy of the coverage of existing national drug use measurement instruments and techniques to measure the illicit drug user population, and groups that are at risk for illicit drug use;

(C) the adequacy of the coverage of existing national treatment outcome monitoring systems to measure the effectiveness of drug abuse treatment in reducing illicit drug use and criminal behavior during and after the completion of substance abuse treatment; and

(D) the actions the Director shall take to correct any deficiencies and limitations identified pursuant to subparagraphs (A) and (B) of this subsection.

(d) Modifications

A description of any modifications made during the preceding year to the national drug performance measurement system described in subsection (c) shall be included in each report submitted under subsection (b).

(Pub. L. 105–277, div. C, title VII, §706, Oct. 21, 1998, 112 Stat. 2681–681; Pub. L. 109–469, title II, §§201, 202, Dec. 29, 2006, 120 Stat. 3513, 3517.)

REPEAL OF SECTION

For repeal of section on Sept. 30, 2010, see section 1712 of this title.

AMENDMENTS

2006—Pub. L. 109–469, §201, amended section generally. Prior to amendment, section related to development, submission, implementation, and assessment of National Drug Control Strategy.

Subsecs. (c), (d). Pub. L. 109–469, §202, added subsecs. (c) and (d).

REQUIREMENT FOR SOUTHWEST BORDER COUNTERNARCOTICS STRATEGY

Pub. L. 109–469, title XI, §1110, Dec. 29, 2006, 120 Stat. 3543, provided that:

"(a) IN GENERAL.—Not later than 120 days after the date of enactment of this Act [Dec. 29, 2006], and every 2 years thereafter, the Director of National Drug Control Policy shall submit to the Congress a Southwest Border Counternarcotics Strategy.

"(b) PURPOSES.—The Southwest Border Counternarcotics Strategy shall—

"(1) set forth the Government's strategy for preventing the illegal trafficking of drugs across the international border between the United States and Mexico, including through ports of entry and between ports of entry on that border;

"(2) state the specific roles and responsibilities of the relevant National Drug Control Program agencies (as defined in section 702 of the Office of National Drug Control Policy Reauthorization Act of 1998 (21 U.S.C. 1701)) for implementing that strategy; and

"(3) identify the specific resources required to enable the relevant National Drug Control Program agencies to implement that strategy.

"(c) SPECIFIC CONTENT RELATED TO DRUG TUNNELS BETWEEN THE UNITED STATES AND MEXICO.—The Southwest Border Counternarcotics Strategy shall include—

"(1) a strategy to end the construction and use of tunnels and subterranean passages that cross the international border between the United States and Mexico for the purpose of illegal trafficking of drugs across such border; and

"(2) recommendations for criminal penalties for persons who construct or use such a tunnel or subterranean passage for such a purpose.

"(d) CONSULTATION WITH OTHER AGENCIES.—The Director shall issue the Southwest Border Counternarcotics Strategy in consultation with the heads of the relevant National Drug Control Program agencies.

"(e) LIMITATION.—The Southwest Border Counternarcotics Strategy shall not change existing agency authorities or the laws governing interagency relationships, but may include recommendations about changes to such authorities or laws.

"(f) REPORT TO CONGRESS.—The Director shall provide a copy of the Southwest Border Counternarcotics Strategy to the appropriate congressional committees (as defined in section 702 of the Office of National Drug Control Policy Reauthorization Act of 1998 (21 U.S.C. 1701)), and to the Committee on Armed Services and the Committee on Homeland Security of the House of Representatives, and the Committee on Homeland Security and Governmental Affairs and the Committee on Armed Services of the Senate.

"(g) TREATMENT OF CLASSIFIED OR LAW ENFORCEMENT SENSITIVE INFORMATION.—Any content of the Southwest Border Counternarcotics Strategy that involves information classified under criteria established by an Executive order, or whose public disclosure, as determined by the Director or the head of any relevant National Drug Control Program agency, would be detrimental to the law enforcement or national security activities of any Federal, State, local, or tribal agency, shall be presented to Congress separately from the rest of the strategy."

§1706. High Intensity Drug Trafficking Areas Program

(a) Establishment

(1) In general

There is established in the Office a program to be known as the High Intensity Drug Trafficking Areas Program (in this section referred to as the "Program").

(2) Purpose

The purpose of the Program is to reduce drug trafficking and drug production in the United States by—

(A) facilitating cooperation among Federal, State, local, and tribal law enforcement agencies to share information and implement coordinated enforcement activities;

(B) enhancing law enforcement intelligence sharing among Federal, State, local, and tribal law enforcement agencies;

(C) providing reliable law enforcement intelligence to law enforcement agencies needed to design effective enforcement strategies and operations; and

(D) supporting coordinated law enforcement strategies which maximize use of available resources to reduce the supply of illegal drugs in designated areas and in the United States as a whole.

(b) Designation

(1) In general

The Director, in consultation with the Attorney General, the Secretary of the Treasury, the Secretary of Homeland Security, heads of the National Drug Control Program agencies, and the Governor of each applicable State, may designate any specified area of the United States as a high intensity drug trafficking area.

(2) Activities

After making a designation under paragraph (1) and in order to provide Federal assistance to the area so designated, the Director may—

(A) obligate such sums as are appropriated for the Program;

(B) direct the temporary reassignment of Federal personnel to such area, subject to the approval of the head of the department or agency that employs such personnel;

(C) take any other action authorized under section 1703 of this title to provide increased Federal assistance to those areas; and

(D) coordinate activities under this section (specifically administrative, recordkeeping, and funds management activities) with State, local, and tribal officials.

(c) Petitions for designation

The Director shall establish regulations under which a coalition of interested law enforcement agencies from an area may petition for designation as a high intensity drug trafficking area. Such regulations shall provide for a regular review by the Director of the petition, including a recommendation regarding the merit of the petition to the Director by a panel of qualified, independent experts.

(d) Factors for consideration

In considering whether to designate an area under this section as a high intensity drug trafficking area, the Director shall consider, in addition to such other criteria as the Director considers to be appropriate, the extent to which—

(1) the area is a significant center of illegal drug production, manufacturing, importation, or distribution;

(2) State, local, and tribal law enforcement agencies have committed resources to respond to the drug trafficking problem in the area, thereby indicating a determination to respond aggressively to the problem;

(3) drug-related activities in the area are having a significant harmful impact in the area, and in other areas of the country; and

(4) a significant increase in allocation of Federal resources is necessary to respond adequately to drug-related activities in the area.

(e) Organization of high intensity drug trafficking areas

(1) Executive Board and officers

To be eligible for funds appropriated under this section, each high intensity drug trafficking area shall be governed by an Executive Board. The Executive Board shall designate a chairman, vice chairman, and any other officers to the Executive Board that it determines are necessary.

(2) Responsibilities

The Executive Board of a high intensity drug trafficking area shall be responsible for—

(A) providing direction and oversight in establishing and achieving the goals of the high intensity drug trafficking area;

(B) managing the funds of the high intensity drug trafficking area;

(C) reviewing and approving all funding proposals consistent with the overall objective of the high intensity drug trafficking area; and

(D) reviewing and approving all reports to the Director on the activities of the high intensity drug trafficking area.

(3) Board representation

None of the funds appropriated under this section may be expended for any high intensity drug trafficking area, or for a partnership or region of a high intensity drug trafficking area, if the Executive Board for such area, region, or partnership, does not apportion an equal number of votes between representatives of participating Federal agencies and representatives of participating State, local, and tribal agencies. Where it is impractical for an equal number of representatives of Federal agencies and State, local, and tribal agencies to attend a meeting of an Executive Board in person, the Executive Board may use a system of proxy votes or weighted votes to achieve the voting balance required by this paragraph.

(4) No agency relationship

The eligibility requirements of this section are intended to ensure the responsible use of Federal funds. Nothing in this section is intended to create an agency relationship between individual high intensity drug trafficking areas and the Federal Government.

(f) Use of funds

The Director shall ensure that no Federal funds appropriated for the Program are expended for the establishment or expansion of drug treatment programs, and shall ensure that not more than 5 percent of the Federal funds appropriated for the Program are expended for the establishment of drug prevention programs.

(g) Counterterrorism activities

(1) Assistance authorized

The Director may authorize use of resources available for the Program to assist Federal, State, local, and tribal law enforcement agencies in investigations and activities related to terrorism and prevention of terrorism, especially but not exclusively with respect to such investigations and activities that are also related to drug trafficking.

(2) Limitation

The Director shall ensure—

(A) that assistance provided under paragraph (1) remains incidental to the purpose of the Program to reduce drug availability and carry out drug-related law enforcement activities; and

(B) that significant resources of the Program are not redirected to activities exclusively related to terrorism, except on a temporary basis under extraordinary circumstances, as determined by the Director.

(h) Role of Drug Enforcement Administration

The Director, in consultation with the Attorney General, shall ensure that a representative of the Drug Enforcement Administration is included in the Intelligence Support Center for each high intensity drug trafficking area.

(i) Annual HIDTA Program budget submissions

As part of the documentation that supports the President's annual budget request for the Office, the Director shall submit to Congress a budget justification that includes—

(1) the amount proposed for each high intensity drug trafficking area, conditional upon a review by the Office of the request submitted by the HIDTA and the performance of the HIDTA, with supporting narrative descriptions and rationale for each request;

(2) a detailed justification that explains—

(A) the reasons for the proposed funding level; how such funding level was determined based on a current assessment of the drug trafficking threat in each high intensity drug trafficking area;

(B) how such funding will ensure that the goals and objectives of each such area will be achieved; and

(C) how such funding supports the National Drug Control Strategy; and

(3) the amount of HIDTA funds used to investigate and prosecute organizations and individuals trafficking in methamphetamine in the prior calendar year, and a description of how those funds were used.

(j) Emerging threat response fund

(1) In general

Subject to the availability of appropriations, the Director may expend up to 10 percent of the amounts appropriated under this section on a discretionary basis, to respond to any emerging drug trafficking threat in an existing high intensity drug trafficking area, or to establish a new high intensity drug trafficking area or expand an existing high intensity drug trafficking area, in accordance with the criteria established under paragraph (2).

(2) Consideration of impact

In allocating funds under this subsection, the Director shall consider—

(A) the impact of activities funded on reducing overall drug traffic in the United States, or minimizing the probability that an emerging drug trafficking threat will spread to other areas of the United States; and

(B) such other criteria as the Director considers appropriate.

(k) Evaluation

(1) Initial report

Not later than 90 days after December 29, 2006, the Director shall, after consulting with the Executive Boards of each designated high intensity drug trafficking area, submit a report to Congress that describes, for each designated high intensity drug trafficking area—

(A) the specific purposes for the high intensity drug trafficking area;

(B) the specific long-term and short-term goals and objectives for the high intensity drug trafficking area;

(C) the measurements that will be used to evaluate the performance of the high intensity drug trafficking area in achieving the long-term and short-term goals; and

(D) the reporting requirements needed to evaluate the performance of the high intensity drug trafficking area in achieving the long-term and short-term goals.

(2) Evaluation of HIDTA Program as part of National Drug Control Strategy

For each designated high intensity drug trafficking area, the Director shall submit, as part of the annual National Drug Control Strategy report, a report that—

(A) describes—

(i) the specific purposes for the high intensity drug trafficking area; and

(ii) the specific long-term and short-term goals and objectives for the high intensity drug trafficking area; and

(B) includes an evaluation of the performance of the high intensity drug trafficking area in accomplishing the specific long-term and short-term goals and objectives identified under paragraph (1)(B).

(*l*) Assessment of drug enforcement task forces in high intensity drug trafficking areas

Not later than 1 year after December 29, 2006, and as part of each subsequent annual National Drug Control Strategy report, the Director shall submit to Congress a report—

(1) assessing the number and operation of all federally funded drug enforcement task forces within each high intensity drug trafficking area; and

(2) describing—

(A) each Federal, State, local, and tribal drug enforcement task force operating in the high intensity drug trafficking area;

(B) how such task forces coordinate with each other, with any high intensity drug trafficking area task force, and with investigations receiving funds from the Organized Crime and Drug Enforcement Task Force;

(C) what steps, if any, each such task force takes to share information regarding drug trafficking and drug production with other federally funded drug enforcement task forces in the high intensity drug trafficking area;

(D) the role of the high intensity drug trafficking area in coordinating the sharing of such information among task forces;

(E) the nature and extent of cooperation by each Federal, State, local, and tribal participant in ensuring that such information is shared among law enforcement agencies and with the high intensity drug trafficking area;

(F) the nature and extent to which information sharing and enforcement activities are coordinated with joint terrorism task forces in the high intensity drug trafficking area; and

(G) any recommendations for measures needed to ensure that task force resources are utilized efficiently and effectively to reduce the availability of illegal drugs in the high intensity drug trafficking areas.

(m) Assessment of law enforcement intelligence sharing in High Intensity Drug Trafficking Areas Program

Not later than 180 days after December 29, 2006, and as part of each subsequent annual National Drug Control Strategy report, the Director, in consultation with the Director of National Intelligence, shall submit to Congress a report—

(1) evaluating existing and planned law enforcement intelligence systems supported by each high intensity drug trafficking area, or utilized by task forces receiving any funding under the Program, including the extent to which such systems ensure access and availability of law enforcement intelligence to Federal, State, local, and tribal law enforcement agencies within the high intensity drug trafficking area and outside of it;

(2) the extent to which Federal, State, local, and tribal law enforcement agencies participating in each high intensity drug trafficking area are sharing law enforcement intelligence

information to assess current drug trafficking threats and design appropriate enforcement strategies; and

(3) the measures needed to improve effective sharing of information and law enforcement intelligence regarding drug trafficking and drug production among Federal, State, local, and tribal law enforcement participating in a high intensity drug trafficking area, and between such agencies and similar agencies outside the high intensity drug trafficking area.

(n) Coordination of Law enforcement intelligence sharing with Organized Crime Drug Enforcement Task Force program

The Director, in consultation with the Attorney General, shall ensure that any drug enforcement intelligence obtained by the Intelligence Support Center for each high intensity drug trafficking area is shared, on a timely basis, with the drug intelligence fusion center operated by the Organized Crime Drug Enforcement Task Force of the Department of Justice.

(*o*) Use of funds to combat methamphetamine trafficking

(1) Requirement

As part of the documentation that supports the President's annual budget request for the Office, the Director shall submit to Congress a report describing the use of HIDTA funds to investigate and prosecute organizations and individuals trafficking in methamphetamine in the prior calendar year.

(2) Contents

The report shall include—

(A) the number of methamphetamine manufacturing facilities discovered through HIDTA-funded initiatives in the previous fiscal year;

(B) the amounts of methamphetamine or listed chemicals (as that term is defined in section 802(33) of this title[1] seized by HIDTA-funded initiatives in the area during the previous year; and

(C) law enforcement intelligence and predictive data from the Drug Enforcement Administration showing patterns and trends in abuse, trafficking, and transportation in methamphetamine and listed chemicals.

(3) Certification

Before the Director awards any funds to a high intensity drug trafficking area, the Director shall certify that the law enforcement entities participating in that HIDTA are providing laboratory seizure data to the national clandestine laboratory database at the El Paso Intelligence Center.

(p) Authorization of appropriations

There is authorized to be appropriated to the Office of National Drug Control Policy to carry out this section—

(1) $240,000,000 for fiscal year 2007;

(2) $250,000,000 for fiscal year 2008;

(3) $260,000,000 for fiscal year 2009;

(4) $270,000,000 for fiscal year 2010; and

(5) $280,000,000 for each of[2] fiscal year 2011.

(q) Specific purposes

(1) In general

The Director shall ensure that, of the amounts appropriated for a fiscal year for the Program, at least $7,000,000 is used in high intensity drug trafficking areas with severe neighborhood safety and illegal drug distribution problems.

(2) Required uses

The funds used under paragraph (1) shall be used—

(A) to ensure the safety of neighborhoods and the protection of communities, including the prevention of the intimidation of potential witnesses of illegal drug distribution and related activities; and

(B) to combat illegal drug trafficking through such methods as the Director considers appropriate, such as establishing or operating (or both) a toll-free telephone hotline for use by the public to provide information about illegal drug-related activities.

(Pub. L. 105–277, div. C, title VII, § 707, Oct. 21, 1998, 112 Stat. 2681–686; Pub. L. 109–469, title III, §§ 301, § 302(c), Dec. 29, 2006, 120 Stat. 3518, 3525.)

REPEAL OF SECTION

For repeal of section on Sept. 30, 2010, see section 1712 of this title.

REFERENCES IN TEXT

December 29, 2006, referred to in subsecs. (k)(1), (*l*), and (m) was in the original "the date of the enactment of this section", which was translated as meaning the date of enactment of Pub. L. 109–469, which amended this section generally, to reflect the probable intent of Congress.

AMENDMENTS

2006—Pub. L. 109–469, § 301, amended section generally. Prior to amendment, section related to the High Intensity Drug Trafficking Areas Program.

Subsec. (q). Pub. L. 109–469, § 302(c), added subsec. (q).

FINDINGS

Pub. L. 109–469, title III, § 302(b), Dec. 29, 2006, 120 Stat. 3524, provided that: "Congress finds the following:

"(1) In the early morning hours of October 16, 2002, the home of Carnell and Angela Dawson was firebombed in apparent retaliation for Mrs. Dawson's notification to police about persistent drug distribution activity in their East Baltimore City neighborhood.

"(2) The arson claimed the lives of Mr. and Mrs. Dawson and their 5 young children, aged 9 to 14.

"(3) The horrific murder of the Dawson family is a stark example of domestic narco-terrorism.

"(4) In all phases of counternarcotics law enforcement—from prevention to investigation to prosecution to reentry—the voluntary cooperation of ordinary citizens is a critical component.

"(5) Voluntary cooperation is difficult for law enforcement officials to obtain when citizens feel that cooperation carries the risk of violent retaliation by illegal drug trafficking organizations and their affiliates.

"(6) Public confidence that law enforcement is doing all it can to make communities safe is a prerequisite for voluntary cooperation among people who may be subject to intimidation or reprisal (or both).

[1] So in original. There probably should be a closing parenthesis.

[2] So in original.

"(7) Witness protection programs are insufficient on their own to provide security because many individuals and families who strive every day to make distressed neighborhoods livable for their children, other relatives, and neighbors will resist or refuse offers of relocation by local, State, and Federal prosecutorial agencies and because, moreover, the continued presence of strong individuals and families is critical to preserving and strengthening the social fabric in such communities.

"(8) Where (as in certain sections of Baltimore City) interstate trafficking of illegal drugs has severe ancillary local consequences within areas designated as high intensity drug trafficking areas, it is important that supplementary High Intensity Drug Trafficking Areas Program funds be committed to support initiatives aimed at making the affected communities safe for the residents of those communities and encouraging their cooperation with tribal, local, State, and Federal law enforcement efforts to combat illegal drug trafficking."

COMBATING METHAMPHETAMINE AND AMPHETAMINE IN HIGH INTENSITY DRUG TRAFFICKING AREAS

Pub. L. 106–310, div. B, title XXXVI, §3624, Oct. 17, 2000, 114 Stat. 1232, provided that:

"(a) IN GENERAL.—

"(1) IN GENERAL.—The Director of National Drug Control Policy shall use amounts available under this section to combat the trafficking of methamphetamine and amphetamine in areas designated by the Director as high intensity drug trafficking areas.

"(2) ACTIVITIES.—In meeting the requirement in paragraph (1), the Director shall transfer funds to appropriate Federal, State, and local governmental agencies for employing additional Federal law enforcement personnel, or facilitating the employment of additional State and local law enforcement personnel, including agents, investigators, prosecutors, laboratory technicians, chemists, investigative assistants, and drug-prevention specialists.

"(b) AUTHORIZATION OF APPROPRIATIONS.—There is authorized to be appropriated to carry out this section—

"(1) $15,000,000 for fiscal year 2000; and

"(2) such sums as may be necessary for each of fiscal years 2001 through 2004.

"(c) APPORTIONMENT OF FUNDS.—

"(1) FACTORS IN APPORTIONMENT.—The Director shall apportion amounts appropriated for a fiscal year pursuant to the authorization of appropriations in subsection (b) for activities under subsection (a) among and within areas designated by the Director as high intensity drug trafficking areas based on the following factors:

"(A) The number of methamphetamine manufacturing facilities and amphetamine manufacturing facilities discovered by Federal, State, or local law enforcement officials in the previous fiscal year.

"(B) The number of methamphetamine prosecutions and amphetamine prosecutions in Federal, State, or local courts in the previous fiscal year.

"(C) The number of methamphetamine arrests and amphetamine arrests by Federal, State, or local law enforcement officials in the previous fiscal year.

"(D) The amounts of methamphetamine, amphetamine, or listed chemicals (as that term is defined in section 102(33) of the Controlled Substances Act (21 U.S.C. 802(33)) seized by Federal, State, or local law enforcement officials in the previous fiscal year.

"(E) Intelligence and predictive data from the Drug Enforcement Administration and the Department of Health and Human Services showing patterns and trends in abuse, trafficking, and transportation in methamphetamine, amphetamine, and listed chemicals (as that term is so defined).

"(2) CERTIFICATION.—Before the Director apportions any funds under this subsection to a high intensity drug trafficking area, the Director shall certify that the law enforcement entities responsible for clandestine methamphetamine and amphetamine laboratory seizures in that area are providing laboratory seizure data to the national clandestine laboratory database at the El Paso Intelligence Center.

"(d) LIMITATION ON ADMINISTRATIVE COSTS.—Not more than 5 percent of the amount appropriated in a fiscal year pursuant to the authorization of appropriations for that fiscal year in subsection (b) may be available in that fiscal year for administrative costs associated with activities under subsection (a)."

FUNDING FOR HIGH INTENSITY DRUG TRAFFICKING AREAS PROGRAM

Pub. L. 106–58, title III, Sept. 29, 1999, 113 Stat. 448, provided in part: "That, hereafter, of the amount appropriated for fiscal year 2000 or any succeeding fiscal year for the High Intensity Drug Trafficking Areas Program, the funds to be obligated or expended during such fiscal year for programs addressing the treatment or prevention of drug use as part of the approved strategy for a designated High Intensity Drug Trafficking Area (HIDTA) shall not be less than the funds obligated or expended for such programs during fiscal year 1999 for each designated HIDTA without the prior approval of the Committees on Appropriations".

§1707. Counter-Drug Technology Assessment Center

(a) Establishment

There is established within the Office the Counter-Drug Technology Assessment Center (referred to in this section as the "Center"). The Center shall operate under the authority of the Director of National Drug Control Policy and shall serve as the central counter-drug technology research and development organization of the United States Government.

(b) Chief Scientist

There shall be at the head of the Center the Chief Scientist, who shall be appointed by the Director from among individuals qualified and distinguished in the area of science, medicine, engineering, or technology.

(c) Research and development responsibilities

The Director, acting through the Chief Scientist, shall—

(1) identify and define the short-, medium-, and long-term scientific and technological needs of Federal, State, local, and tribal drug supply reduction agencies, including—

(A) advanced surveillance, tracking, and radar imaging;

(B) electronic support measures;

(C) communications;

(D) data fusion, advanced computer systems, and artificial intelligence; and

(E) chemical, biological, radiological (including neutron and electron), and other means of detection;

(2) identify demand reduction basic and applied research needs and initiatives, in consultation with affected National Drug Control Program agencies, including—

(A) improving treatment through neuroscientific advances;

(B) improving the transfer of biomedical research to the clinical setting; and

(C) in consultation with the National Institute of Drug Abuse and the Substance Abuse and Mental Health Services Administration, and through interagency agreements or grants, examining addiction and rehabilitation research and the application of technology to expanding the effectiveness and availability of drug treatment;

(3) make a priority ranking of such needs identified in paragraphs (1) and (2) according to fiscal and technological feasibility, as part of a National Counterdrug Research and Development Program;

(4) oversee and coordinate counterdrug technology initiatives with related activities of other Federal civilian and military departments;

(5) provide support to the development and implementation of the national drug control performance measurement system established under subsection (c) of section 1705 of this title; and

(6) pursuant to the authority of the Director of National Drug Control Policy under section 1703 of this title, submit requests to Congress for the reprogramming or transfer of funds appropriated for counterdrug technology research and development.

(d) Limitation on authority

The authority granted to the Director under this section shall not extend to the awarding of contracts, management of individual projects, or other operational activities.

(e) Assistance and support to the Office of National Drug Control Policy

The Secretary of Defense, the Secretary of Homeland Security, and the Secretary of Health and Human Services shall, to the maximum extent practicable, render assistance and support to the Office and to the Director in the conduct of counterdrug technology assessment.

(f) Technology transfer program

(1) Program

The Chief Scientist, with the advice and counsel of experts from State, local, and tribal law enforcement agencies, shall be responsible to the Director for coordination and implementation of a counterdrug technology transfer program.

(2) Purpose

The purpose of the Technology Transfer Program shall be for the Counterdrug Technology Assessment Center to transfer technology and associated training directly to State, local, and tribal law enforcement agencies.

(3) Priority of receipts

Transfers shall be made in priority order based on—

(A) the need of potential recipients for such technology;

(B) the effectiveness of the technology to enhance current counterdrug activities of potential recipients; and

(C) the ability and willingness of potential recipients to evaluate transferred technology.

(4) Agreement authority

The Director may enter into an agreement with the Secretary of Homeland Security to transfer technology with both counterdrug and homeland security applications to State, local, and tribal law enforcement agencies on a reimbursable basis.

(5) Report

On or before July 1 of each year, the Director shall submit a report to the appropriate congressional committees that addresses the following:

(A) The number of requests received during the previous 12 months, including the identity of each requesting agency and the type of technology requested.

(B) The number of requests fulfilled during the previous 12 months, including the identity of each recipient agency and the type of technology transferred.

(C) A summary of the criteria used in making the determination on what requests were funded and what requests were not funded, except that such summary shall not include specific information on any individual requests.

(D) A general assessment of the future needs of the program, based on expected changes in threats, expected technologies, and likely need from potential recipients.

(E) An assessment of the effectiveness of the technologies transferred, based in part on the evaluations provided by the recipients, with a recommendation whether the technology should continue to be offered through the program.

(Pub. L. 105–277, div. C, title VII, §708, Oct. 21, 1998, 112 Stat. 2681–687; Pub. L. 109–469, title IV, §401, Dec. 29, 2006, 120 Stat. 3525.)

REPEAL OF SECTION

For repeal of section on Sept. 30, 2010, see section 1712 of this title.

AMENDMENTS

2006—Subsec. (b). Pub. L. 109–469, §401(a), amended subsec. (b) generally. Prior to amendment, text read as follows: "There shall be at the head of the Center the Director of Technology, who shall be appointed by the Director of National Drug Control Policy from among individuals qualified and distinguished in the area of science, medicine, engineering, or technology."

Subsec. (c). Pub. L. 109–469, §401(b)(1)(B), added subsec. (c) and struck out former subsec. (c) which related to additional responsibilities of the Director of National Drug Control Policy.

Subsec. (d). Pub. L. 109–469, §401(c), which directed insertion of ", the Secretary of Homeland Security," after "The Secretary of Defense", could not be executed because the words "The Secretary of Defense" did not appear subsequent to amendment by Pub. L. 109–469, §401(b)(1). See below.

Pub. L. 109–469, §401(b)(1)(B), added subsec. (d). Former subsec. (d) redesignated (e).

Subsec. (e). Pub. L. 109–469, §401(b)(2), amended subsec. (e) generally. Prior to amendment, text read as follows: "The Secretary of Defense and the Secretary of Health and Human Services shall, to the maximum extent practicable, render assistance and support to the Office and to the Director in the conduct of counterdrug technology assessment."

Pub. L. 109–469, §401(b)(1)(A), redesignated subsec. (d) as (e).

Subsec. (f). Pub. L. 109–469, §401(b)(3), added subsec. (f).

§1708. National youth anti-drug media campaign

(a) In general

The Director shall conduct a national youth anti-drug media campaign (referred to in this chapter[1] as the "national media campaign") in accordance with this section for the purposes of—

(1) preventing drug abuse among young people in the United States;

(2) increasing awareness of adults of the impact of drug abuse on young people; and

(3) encouraging parents and other interested adults to discuss with young people the dangers of illegal drug use.

(b) Use of funds

(1) In general

Amounts made available to carry out this section for the national media campaign may only be used for the following:

(A) The purchase of media time and space, including the strategic planning for, and accounting of, such purchases.

(B) Creative and talent costs, consistent with paragraph (2)(A).

(C) Advertising production costs.

(D) Testing and evaluation of advertising.

(E) Evaluation of the effectiveness of the national media campaign.

(F) The negotiated fees for the winning bidder on requests for proposals issued either by the Office or its designee to enter into contracts to carry out activities authorized by this section.

(G) Partnerships with professional and civic groups, community-based organizations, including faith-based organizations, and government organizations related to the national media campaign.

(H) Entertainment industry outreach, interactive outreach, media projects and activities, public information, news media outreach, and corporate sponsorship and participation.

(I) Operational and management expenses.

(2) Specific requirements

(A) Creative services

(i) In using amounts for creative and talent costs under paragraph (1)(B), the Director shall use creative services donated at no cost to the Government (including creative services provided by the Partnership for a Drug-Free America) wherever feasible and may only procure creative services for advertising—

(I) responding to high-priority or emergent campaign needs that cannot timely be obtained at no cost; or

(II) intended to reach a minority, ethnic, or other special audience that cannot reasonably be obtained at no cost; or

(III) the Director determines that the Partnership for a Drug-Free America is unable to provide, pursuant to subsection (d)(2)(B).

(ii) Subject to the availability of appropriations, no more than $1,500,000 may be expended under this section each fiscal year on creative services, except that the Director may expend up to $2,000,000 in a fiscal year on creative services to meet urgent needs of the national media campaign with advance approval from the Committee on Appropriations of the Senate and of the House of Representatives upon a showing of the circumstances causing such urgent needs of the national media campaign.

(B) Testing and evaluation of advertising

In using amounts for testing and evaluation of advertising under paragraph (1)(D), the Director shall test all advertisements prior to use in the national media campaign to ensure that the advertisements are effective and meet industry-accepted standards. The Director may waive this requirement for advertisements using no more than 10 percent of the purchase of advertising time purchased under this section in a fiscal year and no more than 10 percent of the advertising space purchased under this section in a fiscal year, if the advertisements respond to emergent and time-sensitive campaign needs or the advertisements will not be widely utilized in the national media campaign.

(C) Evaluation of effectiveness of media campaign

In using amounts for the evaluation of the effectiveness of the national media campaign under paragraph (1)(E), the Director shall—

(i) designate an independent entity to evaluate by April 20 of each year the effectiveness of the national media campaign based on data from—

(I) the Monitoring the Future Study published by the Department of Health and Human Services;

(II) the Attitude Tracking Study published by the Partnership for a Drug-Free America;

(III) the National Household Survey on Drug Abuse; and

(IV) other relevant studies or publications, as determined by the Director, including tracking and evaluation data collected according to marketing and advertising industry standards; and

(ii) ensure that the effectiveness of the national media campaign is evaluated in a manner that enables consideration of whether the national media campaign has contributed to reduction of illicit drug use among youth and such other measures of evaluation as the Director determines are appropriate.

(3) Purchase of advertising time and space

Subject to the availability of appropriations, for each fiscal year, not less than 77 percent of the amounts appropriated under this section shall be used for the purchase of advertising time and space for the national media campaign, subject to the following exceptions:

(A) In any fiscal year for which less than $125,000,000 is appropriated for the national media campaign, not less than 72 percent of the amounts appropriated under this section

[1] See References in Text note below.

shall be used for the purchase of advertising time and space for the national media campaign.

(B) In any fiscal year for which more than $195,000,000 is appropriated under this section, not less than 82 percent shall be used for advertising production costs and the purchase of advertising time and space for the national media campaign.

(c) Advertising

In carrying out this section, the Director shall ensure that sufficient funds are allocated to meet the stated goals of the national media campaign.

(d) Division of responsibilities and functions under the program

(1) In general

The Director, in consultation with the Partnership for a Drug-Free America, shall determine the overall purposes and strategy of the national media campaign.

(2) Responsibilities

(A) Director

The Director shall be responsible for implementing a focused national media campaign to meet the purposes set forth in subsection (a), and shall approve—

(i) the strategy of the national media campaign;

(ii) all advertising and promotional material used in the national media campaign; and

(iii) the plan for the purchase of advertising time and space for the national media campaign.

(B) The Partnership for a Drug-Free America

The Director shall request that the Partnership for a Drug-Free America—

(i) develop and recommend strategies to achieve the goals of the national media campaign, including addressing national and local drug threats in specific regions or States, such as methamphetamine and ecstasy;

(ii) create all advertising to be used in the national media campaign, except advertisements that are—

(I) provided by other nonprofit entities pursuant to subsection (f);

(II) intended to respond to high-priority or emergent campaign needs that cannot timely be obtained at no cost (not including production costs and talent reuse payments), provided that any such advertising material is reviewed by the Partnership for a Drug-Free America;

(III) intended to reach a minority, ethnic, or other special audience that cannot be obtained at no cost (not including production costs and talent reuse payments), provided that any such advertising material is reviewed by the Partnership for a Drug-Free America; or

(IV) any other advertisements that the Director determines that the Partnership for a Drug-Free America is unable to provide or if the Director determines that another entity is more appropriate, subject to the requirements of subsection (b)(2)(A).

If the Director determines that another entity is more appropriate under clause (ii)(IV), the Director shall notify Congress, through the committees of jurisdiction in the House and Senate, in writing, not less than 30 days prior to contracting with a party other than the Partnership for a Drug-Free America.

(C) Media buying contractor

The Director shall enter into a contract with a media buying contractor to plan and purchase advertising time and space for the national media campaign. The media buying contractor shall not provide any other service or material, or conduct any other function or activity which the Director determines should be provided by the Partnership for a Drug-Free America.

(e) Prohibitions

None of the amounts made available under subsection (b) may be obligated or expended for any of the following:

(1) To supplant current anti-drug community-based coalitions.

(2) To supplant pro bono public service time donated by national and local broadcasting networks for other public service campaigns.

(3) For partisan political purposes, or express advocacy in support of or to defeat any clearly identified candidate, clearly identified ballot initiative, or clearly identified legislative or regulatory proposal.

(4) To fund advertising that features any elected officials, persons seeking elected office, cabinet level officials, or other Federal officials employed pursuant to section 213 of Schedule C of title 5, Code of Federal Regulations.

(5) To fund advertising that does not contain a primary message intended to reduce or prevent illicit drug use.

(6) To fund advertising containing a primary message intended to promote support for the media campaign or private sector contributions to the media campaign.

(f) Matching requirement

(1) In general

Amounts made available under subsection (b) for media time and space shall be matched by an equal amount of non-Federal funds for the national media campaign, or be matched with in-kind contributions of the same value.

(2) No-cost match advertising direct relationship requirement

The Director shall ensure that at least 70 percent of no-cost match advertising provided directly relates to substance abuse prevention consistent with the specific purposes of the national media campaign, except that in any fiscal year in which less than $125,000,000 is appropriated to the national media campaign, the Director shall ensure that at least 85 percent of no-cost match advertising directly relates to substance abuse prevention consistent with the specific purposes of the national media campaign.

(3) No-cost match advertising not directly related

The Director shall ensure that no-cost match advertising that does not directly relate to substance abuse prevention consistent with the purposes of the national media campaign includes a clear anti-drug message. Such message is not required to be the primary message of the match advertising.

(g) Financial and performance accountability

The Director shall cause to be performed—

(1) audits and reviews of costs of the national media campaign pursuant to section 254d of title 41; and

(2) an audit to determine whether the costs of the national media campaign are allowable under section 256 of title 41.

(h) Report to Congress

The Director shall submit on an annual basis a report to Congress that describes—

(1) the strategy of the national media campaign and whether specific objectives of the media campaign were accomplished;

(2) steps taken to ensure that the national media campaign operates in an effective and efficient manner consistent with the overall strategy and focus of the national media campaign;

(3) plans to purchase advertising time and space;

(4) policies and practices implemented to ensure that Federal funds are used responsibly to purchase advertising time and space and eliminate the potential for waste, fraud, and abuse; and

(5) all contracts entered into with a corporation, partnership, or individual working on behalf of the national media campaign.

(i) Local target requirement

The Director shall, to the maximum extent feasible, use amounts made available under this section for media that focuses on, or includes specific information on, prevention or treatment resources for consumers within specific local areas.

(j) Prevention of marijuana use

(1) Findings

The Congress finds the following:

(A) 60 percent of adolescent admissions for drug treatment are based on marijuana use.

(B) Potency levels of contemporary marijuana, particularly hydroponically grown marijuana, are significantly higher than in the past, rising from under 1 percent of THC in the mid-1970s to as high as 30 percent today.

(C) Contemporary research has demonstrated that youths smoking marijuana early in life may be up to 5 times more likely to use hard drugs.

(D) Contemporary research has demonstrated clear detrimental effects in adolescent educational achievement resulting from marijuana use.

(E) Contemporary research has demonstrated clear detrimental effects in adolescent brain development resulting from marijuana use.

(F) An estimated 9,000,000 Americans a year drive while under the influence of illegal drugs, including marijuana.

(G) Marijuana smoke contains 50 to 70 percent more of certain cancer causing chemicals than tobacco smoke.

(H) Teens who use marijuana are up to 4 times more likely to have a teen pregnancy than teens who have not.

(I) Federal law enforcement agencies have identified clear links suggesting that trade in hydroponic marijuana facilitates trade by criminal organizations in hard drugs, including heroin.

(J) Federal law enforcement agencies have identified possible links between trade in cannabis products and financing for terrorist organizations.

(2) Emphasis on prevention of youth marijuana use

In conducting advertising and activities otherwise authorized under this section, the Director may emphasize prevention of youth marijuana use.

(k) Prevention of methamphetamine abuse and other emerging drug abuse threats

(1) Requirement to use 10 percent of funds for methamphetamine abuse prevention

The Director shall ensure that, of the amounts appropriated under this section for the national media campaign for a fiscal year, not less than 10 percent shall be expended solely for the activities described in subsection (b)(1) with respect to advertisements specifically intended to reduce the use of methamphetamine.

(2) Authority to use funds for other drug abuse upon certification that methamphetamine abuse fell during fiscal year 2007

With respect to fiscal year 2008 and any fiscal year thereafter, if the Director certifies in writing to Congress that domestic methamphetamine laboratory seizures (as reported to the El Paso Intelligence Center of the Drug Enforcement Administration) decreased to at least 75 percent of the 2006 level, or the Director has documented a highly, statistically significant increase in a specific drug, from a baseline determined by locally collected data, that can be defined as a local drug crisis, the Director may apply paragraph (1)(A) for that fiscal year with respect to advertisements specifically intended to reduce the use of such other drugs.

(*l*) Authorization of appropriations

There is authorized to be appropriated to the Office to carry out this section, $195,000,000 for each of fiscal years 2007 and 2008 and $210,000,000 for each of fiscal years 2009 through 2011.

(Pub. L. 105–277, div. C, title VII, §709, Oct. 21, 1998, 112 Stat. 2681–688; Pub. L. 109–469, title V, §501(a), Dec. 29, 2006, 120 Stat. 3527.)

REPEAL OF SECTION

For repeal of section on Sept. 30, 2010, see section 1712 of this title.

REFERENCES IN TEXT

This chapter, referred to in subsec. (a), was in the original "this subtitle" and was translated as reading "this title", meaning title VII of Pub. L. 105–277, div. C, Oct. 21, 1998, 112 Stat. 2681–670, which is classified principally to this chapter, to reflect the probable intent of Congress. Title VII does not contain subtitles. For complete classification of title VII to the Code, see Short Title note set out under section 1701 of this title and Tables.

AMENDMENTS

2006—Pub. L. 109–469 amended section catchline and text generally. Prior to amendment, section related to the President's Council on Counter-Narcotics.

EX. ORD. NO. 12992. PRESIDENT'S COUNCIL ON COUNTER-NARCOTICS

Ex. Ord. No. 12992, Mar. 15, 1996, 61 F.R. 11287, as amended by Ex. Ord. No. 13023, §§ 2, 3, Nov. 6, 1996, 61 F.R. 57767; Ex. Ord. No. 13284, § 8, Jan. 23, 2003, 68 F.R. 4076, provided:

By the authority vested in me as President by the Constitution and the laws of the United States of America, including section 301 of title 3, United States Code, it is hereby ordered as follows:

SECTION 1. *Establishment.* There is established the President's Drug Policy Council ("Council").

SEC. 2. *Membership.* The Council shall comprise the:

(a) President, who shall serve as Chairman of the Council;

(b) Vice President;

(c) Secretary of State;

(d) Secretary of the Treasury;

(e) Secretary of Defense;

(f) Attorney General;

(g) Secretary of the Interior;

(h) Secretary of Agriculture;

(i) Secretary of Health and Human Services;

(j) Secretary of Housing and Urban Development;

(k) Secretary of Transportation;

(*l*) Secretary of Education;

(m) Secretary of Veterans Affairs;

(n) Secretary of Homeland Security;

(*o*) Representative of the United States of America to the United Nations;

(p) Director of the Office of Management and Budget;

(q) Chief of Staff to the President;

(r) Director of National Drug Control Policy;

(s) Director of Central Intelligence;

(t) Assistant to the President for National Security Affairs;

(u) Counsel to the President;

(v) Chairman, Joint Chiefs of Staff;

(w) National Security Advisor to the Vice President; and

(x) Assistant to the President for Domestic Policy.

As applicable, the Council shall also comprise such other officials of the departments and agencies as the President may, from time to time, designate.

SEC. 3. *Meetings of the Council.* The President, or upon his direction, the Vice President, may convene meetings of the Council. The President shall preside over meetings of the Council, provided that in his absence, the Vice President will preside. The Council will meet at least quarterly.

SEC. 4. *Functions.* (a) The functions of the Council are to advise and assist the President in: (1) providing direction and oversight for the national drug control strategy, including relating drug control policy to other national security interests and establishing priorities; and (2) ensuring coordination among departments and agencies concerning implementation of the President's national drug control strategy.

(b) The Director of National Drug Control Policy will continue to be the senior drug control policy official in the executive branch and the President's chief drug control policy spokesman.

(c) In matters affecting national security interests, the Director of National Drug Control Policy shall work in conjunction with the Assistant to the President for National Security Affairs.

SEC. 5. *Administration.* (a) The Council may utilize established or ad hoc committees, task forces, or interagency groups chaired by the Director of National Drug Control Policy or his representative, in carrying out its functions under this order.

(b) The staff of the Office of National Drug Control Policy, in coordination with the staffs of the Vice President and the Assistant to the President for National Security Affairs, shall act as staff for the Council.

(c) All executive departments and agencies shall cooperate with the Council and provide such assistance, information, and advice as the Council may request, to the extent permitted by law.

EX. ORD. NO. 13023. EXPANDING AND CHANGING NAME OF PRESIDENT'S COUNCIL ON COUNTER-NARCOTICS

Ex. Ord. No. 13023, Nov. 6, 1996, 61 F.R. 57767, provided:

By the authority vested in me as President by the Constitution and the laws of the United States of America, including section 301 of title 3, United States Code, and in order to change the name of the "President's Council on Counter-Narcotics" to the "President's Drug Policy Council" and to make the Secretaries of the Interior, Agriculture, Health and Human Services, Housing and Urban Development, Education, Veterans Affairs, and the Assistant to the President for Domestic Policy, permanent members of the Council, it is hereby ordered as follows:

SECTION 1. The Council established by Executive Order 12992 [set out above] shall henceforth be called the "President's Drug Policy Council."

[SECS. 2, 3. Amended Ex. Ord. No. 12992, set out above.]

WILLIAM J. CLINTON.

§ 1708a. Annual report requirement

(a) In general

On or before February 1 of each year, the Director shall submit a report to Congress that describes—

(1) the strategy of the national media campaign and whether specific objectives of the campaign were accomplished;

(2) steps taken to ensure that the national media campaign operates in an effective and efficient manner consistent with the overall strategy and focus of the campaign;

(3) plans to purchase advertising time and space;

(4) policies and practices implemented to ensure that Federal funds are used responsibly to purchase advertising time and space and eliminate the potential for waste, fraud, and abuse;

(5) all contracts entered into with a corporation, partnership, or individual working on behalf of the national media campaign;

(6) specific policies and steps implemented to ensure compliance with title IV of this Act;

(7) steps taken to ensure that the national media campaign will secure, to the maximum extent possible, no cost matches of advertising time and space or in-kind contributions that are directly related to the campaign in accordance with title IV of this Act; and

(8) a review and evaluation of the effectiveness of the national media campaign strategy for the past year.

(b) Audit

The Government Accountability Office shall, at a frequency of not less than once per year—

(1) conduct and supervise an audit and investigation relating to the programs and operations of the—

(A) Office; or

(B) certain programs within the Office, including—

(i) the High Intensity Drug Trafficking Areas Program;

(ii) the Counterdrug Technology Assessment Center; or

(iii) the National Youth Anti-drug Media Campaign; and

(2) provide the Director and the appropriate congressional committees with a report containing an evaluation of and recommendations on the—

(A) policies and activities of the programs and operations subject to the audit and investigation;

(B) economy, efficiency, and effectiveness in the administration of the reviewed programs and operations; and

(C) policy or management changes needed to prevent and detect fraud and abuse in such programs and operations.

(Pub. L. 109–469, title II, §203, Dec. 29, 2006, 120 Stat. 3517.)

REFERENCES IN TEXT

Title IV of this Act, referred to in subsec. (a)(6), (7), is title IV of Pub. L. 109–469, Dec. 29, 2006, 120 Stat. 3525, which amended section 1707 of this title.

CODIFICATION

Section was enacted as part of the Office of National Drug Control Policy Reauthorization Act of 2006, and not as part of the Office of National Drug Control Policy Reauthorization Act of 1998 which comprises this chapter.

§1709. Repealed. Pub. L. 109–469, title XI, §1101(a), Dec. 29, 2006, 120 Stat. 3539

Section, Pub. L. 105–277, div. C, title VII, §710, Oct. 21, 1998, 112 Stat. 2681–689, related to Parents Advisory Council on Youth Drug Abuse.

§1710. Drug Interdiction Coordinator and Committee

(a) United States Interdiction Coordinator

(1) In general

The United States Interdiction Coordinator shall perform the duties of that position described in paragraph (2) and such other duties as may be determined by the Director with respect to coordination of efforts to interdict illicit drugs from entering the United States.

(2) Responsibilities

The United States Interdiction Coordinator shall be responsible to the Director for—

(A) coordinating the interdiction activities of the National Drug Control Program agencies to ensure consistency with the National Drug Control Strategy;

(B) on behalf of the Director, developing and issuing, on or before March 1 of each year and in accordance with paragraph (3), a National Interdiction Command and Control Plan to ensure the coordination and consistency described in subparagraph (A);

(C) assessing the sufficiency of assets committed to illicit drug interdiction by the relevant National Drug Control Program agencies; and

(D) advising the Director on the efforts of each National Drug Control Program agency to implement the National Interdiction Command and Control Plan.

(3) Staff

The Director shall assign such permanent staff of the Office as he considers appropriate to assist the United States Interdiction Coordinator to carry out the responsibilities described in paragraph (2), and may also, at his discretion, request that appropriate National Drug Control Program agencies detail or assign staff to the Office of Supply Reduction for that purpose.

(4) National Interdiction Command and Control Plan

(A) Purposes

The National Interdiction Command and Control Plan shall—

(i) set forth the Government's strategy for drug interdiction;

(ii) state the specific roles and responsibilities of the relevant National Drug Control Program agencies for implementing that strategy; and

(iii) identify the specific resources required to enable the relevant National Drug Control Program agencies to implement that strategy.

(B) Consultation with other agencies

The United States Interdiction Coordinator shall issue the National Interdiction Command and Control Plan in consultation with the other members of the Interdiction Committee described in subsection (b).

(C) Limitation

The National Interdiction Command and Control Plan shall not change existing agency authorities or the laws governing interagency relationships, but may include recommendations about changes to such authorities or laws.

(D) Report to Congress

On or before March 1 of each year, the United States Interdiction Coordinator shall provide a report on behalf of the Director to the appropriate congressional committees, to the Committee on Armed Services and the Committee on Homeland Security of the House of Representatives, and to the Committee on Homeland Security and Governmental Affairs and the Committee on Armed Services of the Senate, which shall include—

(i) a copy of that year's National Interdiction Command and Control Plan;

(ii) information for the previous 10 years regarding the number and type of seizures of drugs by each National Drug Control Program agency conducting drug interdiction activities, as well as statistical information on the geographic areas of such seizures; and

(iii) information for the previous 10 years regarding the number of air and maritime patrol hours undertaken by each National Drug Control Program agency conducting drug interdiction activities, as well as statistical information on the geographic areas in which such patrol hours took place.

(E) Treatment of classified or law enforcement sensitive information

Any content of the report described in subparagraph (D) that involves information classified under criteria established by an Executive order, or the public disclosure of which, as determined by the Director, the Director of National Intelligence, or the head of any Federal Government agency the activities of which are described in the plan, would be detrimental to the law enforcement or national security activities of any Federal, State, or local agency, shall be presented to Congress separately from the rest of the report.

(b) Interdiction Committee

(1) In general

The Interdiction Committee shall meet to—

(A) discuss and resolve issues related to the coordination, oversight and integration of international, border, and domestic drug interdiction efforts in support of the National Drug Control Strategy;

(B) review the annual National Interdiction Command and Control Plan, and provide advice to the Director and the United States Interdiction Coordinator concerning that plan; and

(C) provide such other advice to the Director concerning drug interdiction strategy and policies as the committee determines is appropriate.

(2) Chairman

The Director shall designate one of the members of the Interdiction Committee to serve as chairman.

(3) Meetings

The members of the Interdiction Committee shall meet, in person and not through any delegate or representative, at least once per calendar year, prior to March 1. At the call of either the Director or the current chairman, the Interdiction Committee may hold additional meetings, which shall be attended by the members either in person, or through such delegates or representatives as they may choose.

(4) Report

Not later than September 30 of each year, the chairman of the Interdiction Committee shall submit a report to the Director and to the appropriate congressional committees describing the results of the meetings and any significant findings of the Committee during the previous 12 months. Any content of such a report that involves information classified under criteria established by an Executive order, or whose public disclosure, as determined by the Director, the chairman, or any member, would be detrimental to the law enforcement or national security activities of any Federal, State, local, or tribal agency, shall be presented to Congress separately from the rest of the report.

(Pub. L. 105–277, div. C, title VII, § 711, Oct. 21, 1998, 112 Stat. 2681–691; Pub. L. 109–469, title I, § 103(f)(1), Dec. 29, 2006, 120 Stat. 3507.)

REPEAL OF SECTION

For repeal of section on Sept. 30, 2010, see section 1712 of this title.

AMENDMENTS

2006—Pub. L. 109–469, which directed that section 711 of Office of National Drug Control Policy Reauthorization Act of 1998 (Pub. L. 105–277, div. C, title VII) be amended by "adding at the end" a new section 711, was executed by substituting the new section 711 for this section which was the existing section 711 of the Act, to reflect the probable intent of Congress. Prior to amendment, this section related to drug interdiction.

§ 1710a. Requirement for disclosure of Federal sponsorship of all Federal advertising or other communication materials

(a) Requirement

Each advertisement or other communication paid for by the Office, either directly or through a contract awarded by the Office, shall include a prominent notice informing the target audience that the advertisement or other communication is paid for by the Office.

(b) Advertisement or other communication

In this section, the term "advertisement or other communication" includes—

(1) an advertisement disseminated in any form, including print or by any electronic means; and

(2) a communication by an individual in any form, including speech, print, or by any electronic means.

(Pub. L. 105–277, div. C, title VII, § 712, as added Pub. L. 109–469, title XI, § 1118, Dec. 29, 2006, 120 Stat. 3546.)

REPEAL OF SECTION

For repeal of section on Sept. 30, 2010, see section 1712 of this title.

CODIFICATION

Another section 712 of title VII of div. C of Pub. L. 105–277 amended former section 1509 of this title.

§ 1711. Authorization of appropriations

There are authorized to be appropriated to carry out this chapter except activities otherwise specified, to remain available until expended, such sums as may be necessary for each of fiscal years 2006 through 2010.

(Pub. L. 105–277, div. C, title VII, § 714, Oct. 21, 1998, 112 Stat. 2681–693; Pub. L. 109–469, title VI, § 601, Dec. 29, 2006, 120 Stat. 3533.)

REPEAL OF SECTION

For repeal of section on Sept. 30, 2010, see section 1712 of this title.

REFERENCES IN TEXT

This chapter, referred to in text, was in the original "this title", meaning title VII of Pub. L. 105–277, div. C, Oct. 21, 1998, 112 Stat. 2681–670, which is classified principally to this chapter. For complete classification of title VII to the Code, see Short Title note set out under section 1701 of this title and Tables.

AMENDMENTS

2006—Pub. L. 109–469 substituted "chapter except activities otherwise specified," for "chapter," and "2006 through 2010" for "1999 through 2003".

APPROPRIATIONS

Provisions appropriating funds to carry out activities authorized by the Office of National Drug Control Policy Reauthorization Act of 1998, which enacted this chapter, notwithstanding section 1712 of this title, were contained in the following appropriation acts:

Pub. L. 109–115, div. A, title V, Nov. 30, 2005, 119 Stat. 2475.

Pub. L. 108–447, div. H, title III, Dec. 8, 2004, 118 Stat. 3249, 3250.

Pub. L. 108–199, div. F, title III, Jan. 23, 2004, 118 Stat. 324.

§1712. Termination of Office of National Drug Control Policy

(a) In general

Except as provided in subsection (b) of this section, effective on September 30, 2010, this chapter and the amendments made to this chapter are repealed.

(b) Exception

Subsection (a) of this section does not apply to section 713 or the amendments made by that section.

(Pub. L. 105–277, div. C, title VII, §715, Oct. 21, 1998, 112 Stat. 2681–693; Pub. L. 109–469, title VI, §602, Dec. 29, 2006, 120 Stat. 3533.)

REFERENCES IN TEXT

This chapter, referred to in subsec. (a), was in the original "this title", meaning title VII of Pub. L. 105–277, div. C, Oct. 21, 1998, 112 Stat. 2681–670, which is classified principally to this chapter. For complete classification of title VII to the Code, see Short Title note set out under section 1701 of this title and Tables.

Section 713, referred to in subsec. (b), is section 713 of Pub. L. 105–277, div. C, title VII, Oct. 21, 1998, 112 Stat. 2681–693, which amended sections 5312 to 5314 of Title 5, Government Organization and Employees, section 1105 of Title 31, Money and Finance, and section 402 of Title 50, War and National Defense.

CODIFICATION

The repeal of this chapter and of the amendments made by this chapter, effective Sept. 30, 2003, by this section, as in effect on Sept. 30, 2003, has not been given effect in the Code, to reflect the probable intent of Congress, because of the amendment to this section by Pub. L. 109–469 which substituted "September 30, 2010" for "September 30, 2003" as the effective date of the repeal. See 2006 Amendment note below.

AMENDMENTS

2006—Pub. L. 109–469 substituted "September 30, 2010, this chapter and the amendments made to this chapter" for "September 30, 2003, this chapter and the amendments made by this chapter".

§1713. Authorization of use of environmentally-approved herbicides to eliminate illicit narcotics crops

The Secretary of State, the Attorney General, the Secretary of Agriculture, the Secretary of Defense, the Director of the Office of National Drug Control Policy, and the Administrator of the Environmental Protection Agency are authorized to support the development and use of environmentally-approved herbicides to eliminate illicit narcotics crops, including coca, cannabis, and opium poppy, both in the United States and in foreign countries.

(Pub. L. 105–277, div. C, title VIII, §834, Oct. 21, 1998, 112 Stat. 2681–702.)

CODIFICATION

Section was enacted as part of the Western Hemisphere Drug Elimination Act, and not as part of the Office of National Drug Control Policy Reauthorization Act of 1998 which comprises this chapter.

§1714. Awards for demonstration programs by local partnerships to coerce abstinence in chronic hard-drug users under community supervision through the use of drug testing and sanctions

(a) Awards required

The Director shall make competitive awards to fund demonstration programs by eligible partnerships for the purpose of reducing the use of illicit drugs by chronic hard-drug users living in the community while under the supervision of the criminal justice system.

(b) Use of award amounts

Award amounts received under this section shall be used—

(1) to support the efforts of the agencies, organizations, and researchers included in the eligible partnership;

(2) to develop and field a drug testing and graduated sanctions program for chronic hard-drug users living in the community under criminal justice supervision; and

(3) to assist individuals described in subsection (a) by strengthening rehabilitation efforts through such means as job training, drug treatment, or other services.

(c) Eligible partnership defined

In this section, the term "eligible partnership" means a working group whose application to the Director—

(1) identifies the roles played, and certifies the involvement of, two or more agencies or organizations, which may include—

(A) State, local, or tribal agencies (such as those carrying out police, probation, prosecution, courts, corrections, parole, or treatment functions);

(B) Federal agencies (such as the Drug Enforcement Agency, the Bureau of Alcohol, Tobacco, Firearms, and Explosives, and United States Attorney offices); and

(C) community-based organizations;

(2) includes a qualified researcher;

(3) includes a plan for using judicial or other criminal justice authority to administer drug tests to individuals described in subsection (a) at least twice a week, and to swiftly and certainly impose a known set of graduated sanctions for non-compliance with community-release provisions relating to drug abstinence (whether imposed as a pre-trial, probation, or parole condition or otherwise);

(4) includes a strategy for responding to a range of substance use and abuse problems and a range of criminal histories;

(5) includes a plan for integrating data infrastructure among the agencies and organiza-

tions included in the eligible partnership to enable seamless, real-time tracking of individuals described in subsection (a);

(6) includes a plan to monitor and measure the progress toward reducing the percentage of the population of individuals described in subsection (a) who, upon being summoned for a drug test, either fail to show up or who test positive for drugs.

(d) Reports to Congress

(1) Interim report

Not later than June 1, 2009, the Director shall submit to Congress a report that identifies the best practices in reducing the use of illicit drugs by chronic hard-drug users, including the best practices identified through the activities funded under this section.

(2) Final report

Not later than June 1, 2010, the Director shall submit to Congress a report on the demonstration programs funded under this section, including on the matters specified in paragraph (1).

(e) Authorization of appropriations

There is authorized to be appropriated to carry out this section $4,900,000 for each of fiscal years 2007 through 2009.

(Pub. L. 105–277, div. C, title VII, § 716, as added Pub. L. 109–469, title XI, § 1119, Dec. 29, 2006, 120 Stat. 3547.)

REPEAL OF SECTION

For repeal of section on Sept. 30, 2010, see section 1712 of this title.

CHAPTER 23—NATIONAL YOUTH ANTI-DRUG MEDIA CAMPAIGN

§§ 1801 to 1804. Repealed. Pub. L. 109–469, title V, § 501(b), Dec. 29, 2006, 120 Stat. 3533

Section 1801, Pub. L. 105–277, div. D, title I, § 102, Oct. 21, 1998, 112 Stat. 2681–752, related to requirement to conduct national media campaign.

Section 1802, Pub. L. 105–277, div. D, title I, § 103, Oct. 21, 1998, 112 Stat. 2681–752, related to use of funds.

Section 1803, Pub. L. 105–277, div. D, title I, § 104, Oct. 21, 1998, 112 Stat. 2681–753, related to reports to Congress.

Section 1804, Pub. L. 105–277, div. D, title I, § 105, Oct. 21, 1998, 112 Stat. 2681–753, related to authorization of appropriations.

SHORT TITLE

Pub. L. 105–277, div. D, § 1(a), Oct. 21, 1998, 112 Stat. 2681–751, provided that: "This division [enacting this chapter and section 7144 of Title 20, Education, and enacting provisions set out as notes under this section, section 1703 of this title, section 6301 of Title 20, and section 3751 of Title 42, The Public Health and Welfare] may be cited as the 'Drug Demand Reduction Act'."

Pub. L. 105–277, div. D, title I, § 101, Oct. 21, 1998, 112 Stat. 2681–752, which provided that subtitle A (§§ 101–105) of title I of div. D of Pub. L. 105–277, enacting this chapter, was to be cited as the "Drug-Free Media Campaign Act of 1998", was repealed by Pub. L. 109–469, title V, § 501(b), Dec. 29, 2006, 120 Stat. 3533.

CHAPTER 24—INTERNATIONAL NARCOTICS TRAFFICKING

§ 1901. Findings and policy

(a) Findings

Congress makes the following findings:

(1) Presidential Decision Directive 42, issued on October 21, 1995, ordered agencies of the executive branch of the United States Government to, inter alia, increase the priority and resources devoted to the direct and immediate threat international crime presents to national security, work more closely with other governments to develop a global response to this threat, and use aggressively and creatively all legal means available to combat international crime.

(2) Executive Order No. 12978 of October 21, 1995, provides for the use of the authorities in the International Emergency Economic Powers Act (IEEPA) (50 U.S.C. 1701 et seq.) to target and apply sanctions to four international narcotics traffickers and their organizations that operate from Colombia.

(3) IEEPA was successfully applied to international narcotics traffickers in Colombia and based on that successful case study, Congress believes similar authorities should be applied worldwide.

(4) There is a national emergency resulting from the activities of international narcotics traffickers and their organizations that threatens the national security, foreign policy, and economy of the United States.

(b) Policy

It shall be the policy of the United States to apply economic and other financial sanctions to significant foreign narcotics traffickers and their organizations worldwide to protect the national security, foreign policy, and economy of the United States from the threat described in subsection (a)(4) of this section.

(Pub. L. 106–120, title VIII, § 802, Dec. 3, 1999, 113 Stat. 1626.)

REFERENCES IN TEXT

Executive Order No. 12978, referred to in subsec. (a)(2), is Ex. Ord. No. 12978, Oct. 21, 1995, 60 F.R. 54579, which is listed in a table under section 1701 of Title 50, War and National Defense.

The International Emergency Economic Powers Act, referred to in subsec. (a)(2), is title II of Pub. L. 95–223, Dec. 28, 1977, 91 Stat. 1626, as amended, which is classified generally to chapter 35 (§ 1701 et seq.) of Title 50, War and National Defense. For complete classification of this Act to the Code, see Short Title note set out under section 1701 of Title 50 and Tables.

EFFECTIVE DATE

Pub. L. 106–120, title VIII, § 811, Dec. 3, 1999, 113 Stat. 1636, provided that: "This title [see Short Title note set out below] shall take effect on the date of the enactment of this Act [Dec. 3, 1999]."

SHORT TITLE

Pub. L. 106–120, title VIII, § 801, Dec. 3, 1999, 113 Stat. 1626, provided that: "This title [enacting this chapter and amending section 1182 of Title 8, Aliens and Nationality] may be cited as the 'Foreign Narcotics Kingpin Designation Act'."

§ 1902. Purpose

The purpose of this chapter is to provide authority for the identification of, and application of sanctions on a worldwide basis to, significant foreign narcotics traffickers, their organizations, and the foreign persons who provide support to those significant foreign narcotics traffickers and their organizations, whose activities threaten the national security, foreign policy, and economy of the United States.

(Pub. L. 106–120, title VIII, § 803, Dec. 3, 1999, 113 Stat. 1626.)

REFERENCES IN TEXT

This chapter, referred to in text, was in the original "this title", meaning title VIII of Pub. L. 106–120, Dec. 3, 1999, 113 Stat. 1626, which is classified generally to this chapter. For complete classification of this Act to the Code, see Short Title note set out under section 1901 of this title and Tables.

§ 1903. Public identification of significant foreign narcotics traffickers and required reports

(a) Provision of information to the President

The Secretary of the Treasury, the Attorney General, the Secretary of Defense, the Secretary of State, and the Director of Central Intelligence shall consult among themselves and provide the appropriate and necessary information to enable the President to submit the report under subsection (b) of this section. This information shall also be provided to the Director of the Office of National Drug Control Policy.

(b) Public identification and sanctioning of significant foreign narcotics traffickers

Not later than June 1, 2000, and not later than June 1 of each year thereafter, the President shall submit a report to the Permanent Select Committee on Intelligence, and the Committees on the Judiciary, International Relations, Armed Services, and Ways and Means of the House of Representatives; and to the Select Committee on Intelligence, and the Committees on the Judiciary, Foreign Relations, Armed Services, and Finance of the Senate—

(1) identifying publicly the foreign persons that the President determines are appropriate for sanctions pursuant to this chapter; and

(2) detailing publicly the President's intent to impose sanctions upon these significant foreign narcotics traffickers pursuant to this chapter.

The report required in this subsection shall not include information on persons upon which United States sanctions imposed under this chapter, or otherwise on account of narcotics trafficking, are already in effect.

(c) Unclassified report required

The report required by subsection (b) of this section shall be submitted in unclassified form and made available to the public.

(d) Classified report

(1) Not later than July 1, 2000, and not later than July 1 of each year thereafter, the President shall provide the Permanent Select Committee on Intelligence of the House of Representatives and the Select Committee on Intelligence of the Senate with a report in classified form describing in detail the status of the sanctions imposed under this chapter, including the personnel and resources directed towards the imposition of such sanctions during the preceding fiscal year, and providing background information with respect to newly-identified significant foreign narcotics traffickers and their activities.

(2) Such classified report shall describe actions the President intends to undertake or has undertaken with respect to such significant foreign narcotics traffickers.

(3) The report required under this subsection is in addition to the President's obligations to keep the intelligence committees of Congress fully and currently informed pursuant to the provisions of the National Security Act of 1947.

(e) Exclusion of certain information

(1) Intelligence

Notwithstanding any other provision of this section, the reports described in subsections (b) and (d) of this section shall not disclose the identity of any person, if the Director of Central Intelligence determines that such disclosure could compromise an intelligence operation, activity, source, or method of the United States.

(2) Law enforcement

Notwithstanding any other provision of this section, the reports described in subsections (b) and (d) of this section shall not disclose the name of any person if the Attorney General, in coordination as appropriate with the Director of the Federal Bureau of Investigation, the Administrator of the Drug Enforcement Administration, and the Secretary of the Treasury, determines that such disclosure could reasonably be expected to—

(A) compromise the identity of a confidential source, including a State, local, or foreign agency or authority or any private institution that furnished information on a confidential basis;

(B) jeopardize the integrity or success of an ongoing criminal investigation or prosecution;

(C) endanger the life or physical safety of any person; or

(D) cause substantial harm to physical property.

(f) Notification required

(1) Whenever either the Director of Central Intelligence or the Attorney General makes a determination under subsection (e) of this section, the Director of Central Intelligence or the Attorney General shall notify the Permanent Select Committee on Intelligence of the House of Representatives and the Select Committee on Intelligence of the Senate, and explain the reasons for such determination.

(2) The notification required under this subsection shall be submitted to the Permanent Select Committee on Intelligence of the House of Representatives and the Select Committee on Intelligence of the Senate not later than July 1, 2000, and on an annual basis thereafter.

(g) Determinations not to apply sanctions

(1) The President may waive the application to a significant foreign narcotics trafficker of any sanction authorized by this chapter if the President determines that the application of sanctions under this chapter would significantly harm the national security of the United States.

(2) When the President determines not to apply sanctions that are authorized by this chapter to any significant foreign narcotics trafficker, the President shall notify the Permanent Select Committee on Intelligence, and the Committees on the Judiciary, International Relations, Armed Services, and Ways and Means of the House of Representatives, and the Select Committee on Intelligence, and the Committees on the Judiciary, Foreign Relations, Armed Services, and Finance of the Senate not later than 21 days after making such determination.

(h) Changes in determinations to impose sanctions

(1) Additional determinations

(A) If at any time after the report required under subsection (b) of this section the President finds that a foreign person is a significant foreign narcotics trafficker and such foreign person has not been publicly identified in a report required under subsection (b) of this section, the President shall submit an additional public report containing the information described in subsection (b) of this section with respect to such foreign person to the Permanent Select Committee on Intelligence, and the Committees on the Judiciary, International Relations, Armed Services, and Ways and Means of the House of Representatives, and the Select Committee on Intelligence, and the Committees on the Judiciary, Foreign Relations, Armed Services, and Finance of the Senate.

(B) The President may apply sanctions authorized under this chapter to the significant foreign narcotics trafficker identified in the report submitted under subparagraph (A) as if the trafficker were originally included in the report submitted pursuant to subsection (b) of this section.

(C) The President shall notify the Secretary of the Treasury of any determination made under this paragraph.

(2) Revocation of determination

(A) Whenever the President finds that a foreign person that has been publicly identified as a significant foreign narcotics trafficker in the report required under subsection (b) of this section or this subsection no longer engages in those activities for which sanctions under this chapter may be applied, the President shall issue public notice of such a finding.

(B) Not later than the date of the public notice issued pursuant to subparagraph (A), the President shall notify, in writing and in classified or unclassified form, the Permanent Select Committee on Intelligence, and the Committees on the Judiciary, International Relations, Armed Services, and Ways and Means of the House of Representatives, and the Select Committee on Intelligence, and the Committees on the Judiciary, Foreign Relations, Armed Services, and Finance of the Senate of actions taken under this paragraph and a description of the basis for such actions.

(Pub. L. 106–120, title VIII, § 804, Dec. 3, 1999, 113 Stat. 1626.)

REFERENCES IN TEXT

The National Security Act of 1947, referred to in subsec. (d)(3), is act July 26, 1947, ch. 343, 61 Stat. 495, as amended. For complete classification of this Act to the Code, see Short Title note set out under section 401 of Title 50, War and National Defense, and Tables.

CHANGE OF NAME

Committee on International Relations of House of Representatives changed to Committee on Foreign Affairs of House of Representatives by House Resolution No. 6, One Hundred Tenth Congress, Jan. 5, 2007.

Reference to the Director of Central Intelligence or the Director of the Central Intelligence Agency in the Director's capacity as the head of the intelligence community deemed to be a reference to the Director of National Intelligence. Reference to the Director of Central Intelligence or the Director of the Central Intelligence Agency in the Director's capacity as the head of the Central Intelligence Agency deemed to be a reference to the Director of the Central Intelligence Agency. See section 1081(a), (b) of Pub. L. 108–458, set out as a note under section 401 of Title 50, War and National Defense.

DELEGATION OF FUNCTIONS

For delegation of Congressional reporting functions of President under subsec. (d) of this section, see section 1 of Ex. Ord. No. 13313, July 31, 2003, 68 F.R. 46075, set out as a note under section 301 of Title 3, The President.

§ 1904. Blocking assets and prohibiting transactions

(a) Applicability of sanctions

A significant foreign narcotics trafficker publicly identified in the report required under subsection (b) or (h)(1) of section 1903 of this title and foreign persons designated by the Secretary of the Treasury pursuant to subsection (b) of this section shall be subject to any and all sanctions as authorized by this chapter. The application of sanctions on any foreign person pursuant to subsection (b) or (h)(1) of section 1903 of this title or subsection (b) of this section shall remain in effect until revoked pursuant to section 1903(h)(2) of this title or subsection (e)(1)(A) of this section or waived pursuant to section 1903(g)(1) of this title.

(b) Blocking of assets

Except to the extent provided in regulations, orders, instructions, licenses, or directives issued pursuant to this chapter, and notwithstanding any contract entered into or any license or permit granted prior to the date on which the President submits the report required under subsection (b) or (h)(1) of section 1903 of this title, there are blocked as of such date, and any date thereafter, all such property and interests in property within the United States, or within the possession or control of any United States person, which are owned or controlled by—

(1) any significant foreign narcotics trafficker publicly identified by the President in the report required under subsection (b) or (h)(1) of section 1903 of this title;

(2) any foreign person that the Secretary of the Treasury, in consultation with the Attorney General, the Director of Central Intelligence, the Director of the Federal Bureau of Investigation, the Administrator of the Drug Enforcement Administration, the Secretary of Defense, and the Secretary of State, designates as materially assisting in, or providing financial or technological support for or to, or providing goods or services in support of, the international narcotics trafficking activities of a significant foreign narcotics trafficker so identified in the report required under subsection (b) or (h)(1) of section 1903 of this title, or foreign persons designated by the Secretary of the Treasury pursuant to this subsection;

(3) any foreign person that the Secretary of the Treasury, in consultation with the Attorney General, the Director of Central Intelligence, the Director of the Federal Bureau of Investigation, the Administrator of the Drug Enforcement Administration, the Secretary of Defense, and the Secretary of State, designates as owned, controlled, or directed by, or acting for or on behalf of, a significant foreign narcotics trafficker so identified in the report required under subsection (b) or (h)(1) of section 1903 of this title, or foreign persons designated by the Secretary of the Treasury pursuant to this subsection; and

(4) any foreign person that the Secretary of the Treasury, in consultation with the Attorney General, the Director of Central Intelligence, the Director of the Federal Bureau of Investigation, the Administrator of the Drug Enforcement Administration, the Secretary of Defense, and the Secretary of State, designates as playing a significant role in international narcotics trafficking.

(c) Prohibited transactions

Except to the extent provided in regulations, orders, instructions, licenses, or directives issued pursuant to this chapter, and notwithstanding any contract entered into or any license or permit granted prior to the date on which the President submits the report required under subsection (b) or (h)(1) of section 1903 of this title, the following transactions are prohibited:

(1) Any transaction or dealing by a United States person, or within the United States, in property or interests in property of any significant foreign narcotics trafficker so identified in the report required pursuant to subsection (b) or (h)(1) of section 1903 of this title, and foreign persons designated by the Secretary of the Treasury pursuant to subsection (b) of this section.

(2) Any transaction or dealing by a United States person, or within the United States, that evades or avoids, or has the effect of evading or avoiding, and any endeavor, attempt, or conspiracy to violate, any of the prohibitions contained in this chapter.

(d) Law enforcement and intelligence activities not affected

Nothing in this chapter prohibits or otherwise limits the authorized law enforcement or intelligence activities of the United States, or the law enforcement activities of any State or subdivision thereof.

(e) Implementation

(1) The Secretary of the Treasury, in consultation with the Attorney General, the Director of Central Intelligence, the Director of the Federal Bureau of Investigation, the Administrator of the Drug Enforcement Administration, the Secretary of Defense, and the Secretary of State, is authorized to take such actions as may be necessary to carry out this chapter, including—

(A) making those designations authorized by paragraphs (2), (3), and (4) of subsection (b) of this section and revocation thereof;

(B) promulgating rules and regulations permitted under this chapter; and

(C) employing all powers conferred on the Secretary of the Treasury under this chapter.

(2) Each agency of the United States shall take all appropriate measures within its authority to carry out the provisions of this chapter.

(3) Section 552(a)(3) of title 5 shall not apply to any record or information obtained or created in the implementation of this chapter.

(Pub. L. 106–120, title VIII, § 805, Dec. 3, 1999, 113 Stat. 1629; Pub. L. 107–108, title III, § 307, Dec. 28, 2001, 115 Stat. 1399.)

AMENDMENTS

2001—Subsec. (f). Pub. L. 107–108 struck out heading and text of subsec. (f). Text read as follows: "The determinations, identifications, findings, and designations made pursuant to section 1903 of this title and subsection (b) of this section shall not be subject to judicial review."

CHANGE OF NAME

Reference to the Director of Central Intelligence or the Director of the Central Intelligence Agency in the Director's capacity as the head of the intelligence community deemed to be a reference to the Director of National Intelligence. Reference to the Director of Central Intelligence or the Director of the Central Intelligence Agency in the Director's capacity as the head of the Central Intelligence Agency deemed to be a reference to the Director of the Central Intelligence Agency. See section 1081(a), (b) of Pub. L. 108–458, set out as a note under section 401 of Title 50, War and National Defense.

§ 1905. Authorities

(a) In general

To carry out the purposes of this chapter, the Secretary of the Treasury may, under such regulations as he may prescribe, by means of instructions, licenses, or otherwise—

(1) investigate, regulate, or prohibit—

(A) any transactions in foreign exchange, currency, or securities; and

(B) transfers of credit or payments between, by, through, or to any banking institution, to the extent that such transfers or payments involve any interests of any foreign country or a national thereof; and

(2) investigate, block during the pendency of an investigation, regulate, direct and compel, nullify, void, prevent, or prohibit any acquisition, holding, withholding, use, transfer, withdrawal, transportation, placement into foreign or domestic commerce of, or dealing in, or exercising any right, power, or privilege with respect to, or transactions involving, any property in which any foreign country or a national thereof has any interest,

by any person, or with respect to any property, subject to the jurisdiction of the United States.

(b) Recordkeeping

Pursuant to subsection (a) of this section, the Secretary of the Treasury may require recordkeeping, reporting, and production of documents to carry out the purposes of this chapter.

(c) Defenses

(1) Full and actual compliance with any regulation, order, license, instruction, or direction issued under this chapter shall be a defense in any proceeding alleging a violation of any of the provisions of this chapter.

(2) No person shall be held liable in any court for or with respect to anything done or omitted in good faith in connection with the administration of, or pursuant to, and in reliance on this chapter, or any regulation, instruction, or direction issued under this chapter.

(d) Rulemaking

The Secretary of the Treasury may issue such other regulations or orders, including regulations prescribing recordkeeping, reporting, and production of documents, definitions, licenses, instructions, or directions, as may be necessary for the exercise of the authorities granted by this chapter.

(Pub. L. 106–120, title VIII, §806, Dec. 3, 1999, 113 Stat. 1631.)

§1906. Enforcement

(a) Criminal penalties

(1) Whoever willfully violates the provisions of this chapter, or any license rule, or regulation issued pursuant to this chapter, or willfully neglects or refuses to comply with any order of the President issued under this chapter shall be—

(A) imprisoned for not more than 10 years,

(B) fined in the amount provided in title 18 or, in the case of an entity, fined not more than $10,000,000,

or both.

(2) Any officer, director, or agent of any entity who knowingly participates in a violation of the provisions of this chapter shall be imprisoned for not more than 30 years, fined not more than $5,000,000, or both.

(b) Civil penalties

A civil penalty not to exceed $1,000,000 may be imposed by the Secretary of the Treasury on any person who violates any license, order, rule, or regulation issued in compliance with the provisions of this chapter.

(c) Judicial review of civil penalty

Any penalty imposed under subsection (b) of this section shall be subject to judicial review only to the extent provided in section 702 of title 5.

(Pub. L. 106–120, title VIII, §807, Dec. 3, 1999, 113 Stat. 1631.)

§1907. Definitions

As used in this chapter:

(1) Entity

The term "entity" means a partnership, joint venture, association, corporation, organization, network, group, or subgroup, or any form of business collaboration.

(2) Foreign person

The term "foreign person" means any citizen or national of a foreign state or any entity not organized under the laws of the United States, but does not include a foreign state.

(3) Narcotics trafficking

The term "narcotics trafficking" means any illicit activity to cultivate, produce, manufacture, distribute, sell, finance, or transport narcotic drugs, controlled substances, or listed chemicals, or otherwise endeavor or attempt to do so, or to assist, abet, conspire, or collude with others to do so.

(4) Narcotic drug; controlled substance; listed chemical

The terms "narcotic drug", "controlled substance", and "listed chemical" have the meanings given those terms in section 802 of this title.

(5) Person

The term "person" means an individual or entity.

(6) United States person

The term "United States person" means any United States citizen or national, permanent resident alien, an entity organized under the laws of the United States (including its foreign branches), or any person within the United States.

(7) Significant foreign narcotics trafficker

The term "significant foreign narcotics trafficker" means any foreign person that plays a significant role in international narcotics trafficking, that the President has determined to be appropriate for sanctions pursuant to this chapter, and that the President has publicly identified in the report required under subsection (b) or (h)(1) of section 1903 of this title.

(Pub. L. 106–120, title VIII, §808, Dec. 3, 1999, 113 Stat. 1632.)

§1908. Judicial Review Commission on Foreign Asset Control

(a) Establishment

There is established a commission to be known as the "Judicial Review Commission on Foreign Asset Control" (in this section referred to as the "Commission").

(b) Membership and procedural matters

(1) The Commission shall be composed of five members, as follows:

(A) One member shall be appointed by the Chairman of the Select Committee on Intelligence of the Senate.

(B) One member shall be appointed by the Vice Chairman of the Select Committee on Intelligence of the Senate.

(C) One member shall be appointed by the Chairman of the Permanent Select Committee on Intelligence of the House of Representatives.

(D) One member shall be appointed by the Ranking Minority Member of the Permanent

Select Committee on Intelligence of the House of Representatives.

(E) One member shall be appointed jointly by the members appointed under subparagraphs (A) through (D).

(2) Each member of the Commission shall, for purposes of the activities of the Commission under this section, possess or obtain an appropriate security clearance in accordance with applicable laws and regulations regarding the handling of classified information.

(3) The members of the Commission shall choose the chairman of the Commission from among the members of the Commission.

(4) The members of the Commission shall establish rules governing the procedures and proceedings of the Commission.

(c) Duties

The Commission shall have as its duties the following:

(1) To conduct a review of the current judicial, regulatory, and administrative authorities relating to the blocking of assets of foreign persons by the United States Government.

(2) To conduct a detailed examination and evaluation of the remedies available to United States persons affected by the blocking of assets of foreign persons by the United States Government.

(d) Powers

(1) The Commission may hold such hearings, sit and act at such times and places, take such testimony, and receive such evidence as the Commission considers advisable to carry out the purposes of this section.

(2) The Commission may secure directly from any executive department, agency, bureau, board, commission, office, independent establishment, or instrumentality of the Government information, suggestions, estimates, and statistics for the purposes of this section. Each such department, agency, bureau, board, commission, office, establishment, or instrumentality shall, to the extent authorized by law, furnish such information, suggestions, estimates, and statistics directly to the Commission, upon request of the chairman of the Commission. The Commission shall handle and protect all classified information provided to it under this section in accordance with applicable statutes and regulations.

(3) The Attorney General and the Secretary of the Treasury shall provide to the Commission, on a nonreimbursable basis, such administrative services, funds, facilities, and other support services as are necessary for the performance of the Commission's duties under this section.

(4) The Commission shall receive the full and timely cooperation of any official, department, or agency of the United States Government whose assistance is necessary for the fulfillment of the duties of the Commission under this section, including the provision of full and current briefings and analyses.

(5) No department or agency of the Government may withhold information from the Commission on the grounds that providing the information to the Commission would constitute the unauthorized disclosure of classified information or information relating to intelligence sources or methods.

(6) The Commission may use the United States mails in the same manner and under the same conditions as the departments and agencies of the United States.

(e) Staff

(1) Subject to paragraph (2), the chairman of the Commission, in accordance with rules agreed upon by the Commission, shall appoint and fix the compensation of a staff director and such other personnel as may be necessary to enable the Commission to carry out its duties, without regard to the provisions of title 5 governing appointments in the competitive service, and without regard to the provisions of chapter 51 and subchapter III or[1] chapter 53 of such title relating to classification and General Schedule pay rates, except that no rate of pay fixed under this subsection may exceed the equivalent of that payable to a person occupying a position at level V of the Executive Schedule under section 5316 of such title.

(2)(A) Any employee of a department or agency referred to in subparagraph (B) may be detailed to the Commission without reimbursement from the Commission, and such detailee shall retain the rights, status, and privileges of his or her regular employment without interruption.

(B) The departments and agencies referred to in this subparagraph are as follows:

(i) The Department of Justice.

(ii) The Department of the Treasury.

(iii) The Central Intelligence Agency.

(3) All staff of the Commission shall possess a security clearance in accordance with applicable laws and regulations concerning the handling of classified information.

(f) Compensation and travel expenses

(1)(A) Except as provided in subparagraph (B), each member of the Commission may be compensated at not to exceed the daily equivalent of the annual rate of basic pay in effect for a position at level IV of the Executive Schedule under section 5315 of title 5 for each day during which that member is engaged in the actual performance of the duties of the Commission under this section.

(B) Members of the Commission who are officers or employees of the United States shall receive no additional pay by reason of their service on the Commission.

(2) While away from their homes or regular places of business in the performance of services for the Commission, members of the Commission may be allowed travel expenses, including per diem in lieu of subsistence, in the same manner as persons employed intermittently in the Government service are allowed expenses under section 5703(b)[2] of title 5.

(g) Report

(1) Not later than 1 year after December 3, 1999, the Commissions[3] shall submit to the com-

[1] So in original. Probably should be "of".

[2] So in original. Section 5703 of title 5 does not contain a subsec. (b).

[3] So in original. Probably should be "Commission".

mittees of Congress referred to in paragraph (4) a report on the activities of the Commission under this section, including the findings, conclusions, and recommendations, if any, of the Commission as a result of the review under subsection (c)(1) of this section and the examination and evaluation under subsection (c)(2) of this section.

(2) The report under paragraph (1) shall include any additional or dissenting views of a member of the Commission upon the request of the member.

(3) The report under paragraph (1) shall be submitted in unclassified form, but may include a classified annex.

(4) The committees of Congress referred to in this paragraph are the following:

(A) The Select Committee on Intelligence and the Committees on Foreign Relations and the Judiciary of the Senate.

(B) The Permanent Select Committee on Intelligence and the Committees on International Relations and the Judiciary of the House of Representatives.

(h) Termination

The Commission shall terminate at the end of the 60-day period beginning on the date on which the report required by subsection (g) of this section is submitted to the committees of Congress referred to in that subsection.

(i) Inapplicability of certain administrative provisions

(1) The provisions of the Federal Advisory Committee Act (5 U.S.C. App.) shall not apply to the activities of the Commission under this section.

(2) The provisions of section 552 of title 5 (commonly referred to as the Freedom of Information Act) shall not apply to the activities, records, and proceedings of the Commission under this chapter.

(j) Funding

The Attorney General shall, from amounts authorized to be appropriated to the Attorney General by this Act, make available to the Commission $1,000,000 for purposes of the activities of the Commission under this section. Amounts made available to the Commission under the preceding sentence shall remain available until expended.

(Pub. L. 106–120, title VIII, § 810, Dec. 3, 1999, 113 Stat. 1633.)

REFERENCES IN TEXT

The provisions of title 5 governing appointments in the competitive service, referred to in subsec. (e)(1), are classified generally to section 3301 et seq. of Title 5, Government Organization and Employees.

The Federal Advisory Committee Act, referred to in subsec. (i), is Pub. L. 92–463, Oct. 6, 1972, 86 Stat. 770, as amended, which is set out in the Appendix to Title 5, Government Organization and Employees.

This Act, referred to in subsec. (j), is Pub. L. 106–120, Dec. 3, 1999, 113 Stat. 1606, known as the Intelligence Authorization Act for Fiscal Year 2000. For complete classification of this Act to the Code, see Tables.

CHANGE OF NAME

Committee on International Relations of House of Representatives changed to Committee on Foreign Affairs of House of Representatives by House Resolution No. 6, One Hundred Tenth Congress, Jan. 5, 2007.

CHAPTER 25—MISCELLANEOUS ANTI-DRUG ABUSE PROVISIONS

SUBCHAPTER I—ANTI-DOPING AGENCY

SUBCHAPTER I—ANTI-DOPING AGENCY

§ 2001. Designation of United States Anti-Doping Agency

(a) Definitions

In this subchapter:

(1) United States Olympic Committee

The term "United States Olympic Committee" means the organization established by the "Ted Stevens Olympic and Amateur Sports Act" (36 U.S.C. 220501 et seq.).

(2) Amateur athletic competition

The term "amateur athletic competition" means a contest, game, meet, match, tournament, regatta, or other event in which amateur athletes compete (36 U.S.C. 220501(b)(2)).

(3) Amateur athlete

The term "amateur athlete" means an athlete who meets the eligibility standards established by the national governing body or paralympic sports organization for the sport in which the athlete competes (36 U.S.C. 22501(b)(1)).[1]

(4) Gene doping

The term "gene doping" means the nontherapeutic use of cells, genes, genetic elements, or of the modulation of gene expression, having the capacity to enhance athletic performance.

(b) In general

The United States Anti-Doping Agency shall—

(1) serve as the independent anti-doping organization for the amateur athletic competitions recognized by the United States Olympic Committee;

(2) ensure that athletes participating in amateur athletic activities recognized by the United States Olympic Committee are prevented from using performance-enhancing drugs, or performance-enhancing genetic modifications accomplished through gene-doping;

(3) implement anti-doping education, research, testing, and adjudication programs to prevent United States Amateur Athletes participating in any activity recognized by the

[1] So in original. Probably should be "220501(b)(1))."

United States Olympic Committee from using performance-enhancing drugs, or performance-enhancing genetic modifications accomplished through gene-doping;

(4) serve as the United States representative responsible for coordination with other anti-doping organizations coordinating amateur athletic competitions recognized by the United States Olympic Committee to ensure the integrity of athletic competition, the health of the athletes and the prevention of use of performance-enhancing drugs, or performance-enhancing genetic modifications accomplished through gene-doping by United States amateur athletes; and

(5) permanently include "gene doping" among any list of prohibited substances adopted by the Agency.

(Pub. L. 109–469, title VII, §701, Dec. 29, 2006, 120 Stat. 3533.)

REFERENCES IN TEXT

The Ted Stevens Olympic and Amateur Sports Act, referred to in subsec. (a)(1), is chapter 2205 of Title 36, Patriotic and National Observances, Ceremonies, and Organizations.

SHORT TITLE

Pub. L. 109–469, title X, §1001, Dec. 29, 2006, 120 Stat. 3537, provided that: "This title [enacting subchapter II of this chapter] may be cited as the 'National Methamphetamine Information Clearinghouse Act of 2006'."

§2002. Records, audit, and report

(a) Records

The United States Anti-Doping Agency shall keep correct and complete records of account.

(b) Report

The United States Anti-Doping Agency shall submit an annual report to Congress which shall include—

(1) an audit conducted and submitted in accordance with section 10101 of title 36; and

(2) a description of the activities of the agency.

(Pub. L. 109–469, title VII, §702, Dec. 29, 2006, 120 Stat. 3534.)

§2003. Authorization of appropriations

There are authorized to be appropriated to the United States Anti-Doping Agency—

(1) for fiscal year 2007, $9,700,000;

(2) for fiscal year 2008, $10,300,000;

(3) for fiscal year 2009, $10,600,000;

(4) for fiscal year 2010, $11,000,000; and

(5) for fiscal year 2011, $11,500,000.

(Pub. L. 109–469, title VII, §703, Dec. 29, 2006, 120 Stat. 3534.)

SUBCHAPTER II—NATIONAL METHAMPHETAMINE INFORMATION CLEARINGHOUSE

§2011. Definitions

In this subchapter—

(1) the term "Council" means the National Methamphetamine Advisory Council established under section 2012(b)(1) of this title;

(2) the term "drug endangered children" means children whose physical, mental, or emotional health are at risk because of the production, use, or other effects of methamphetamine production or use by another person;

(3) the term "National Methamphetamine Information Clearinghouse" or "NMIC" means the information clearinghouse established under section 2012(a) of this title; and

(4) the term "qualified entity" means a State, local, or tribal government, school board, or public health, law enforcement, nonprofit, community anti-drug coalition, or other nongovernmental organization providing services related to methamphetamines.

(Pub. L. 109–469, title X, §1002, Dec. 29, 2006, 120 Stat. 3537.)

§2012. Establishment of clearinghouse and advisory council

(a) Clearinghouse

There is established, under the supervision of the Attorney General of the United States, an information clearinghouse to be known as the National Methamphetamine Information Clearinghouse.

(b) Advisory council

(1) In general

There is established an advisory council to be known as the National Methamphetamine Advisory Council.

(2) Membership

The Council shall consist of 10 members appointed by the Attorney General—

(A) not fewer than 3 of whom shall be representatives of law enforcement agencies;

(B) not fewer than 4 of whom shall be representatives of nongovernmental and nonprofit organizations providing services or training and implementing programs or strategies related to methamphetamines; and

(C) 1 of whom shall be a representative of the Department of Health and Human Services.

(3) Period of appointment; vacancies

Members shall be appointed for 3 years. Any vacancy in the Council shall not affect its powers, but shall be filled in the same manner as the original appointment.

(4) Personnel matters

(A) Travel expenses

The members of the Council shall be allowed travel expenses, including per diem in lieu of subsistence, at rates authorized for employees of agencies under subchapter I of chapter 57 of title 5, while away from their homes or regular places of business in the performance of services for the Council.

(B) No compensation

The members of the Council shall not receive compensation for the performance of the duties of a member of the Council.

(Pub. L. 109–469, title X, §1003, Dec. 29, 2006, 120 Stat. 3538.)

§ 2013. NMIC requirements and review

(a) In general

The NMIC shall promote sharing information regarding successful law enforcement, treatment, environmental, prevention, social services, and other programs related to the production, use, or effects of methamphetamine and grants available for such programs.

(b) Components

The NMIC shall include—

(1) a toll-free number; and

(2) a website that provides a searchable database, which—

(A) provides information on the short-term and long-term effects of methamphetamine use;

(B) provides information regarding methamphetamine treatment and prevention programs and strategies and programs for drug endangered children, including descriptions of successful programs and strategies and contact information for such programs and strategies;

(C) provides information regarding grants for methamphetamine-related programs, including contact information and links to websites;

(D) allows a qualified entity to submit items to be posted on the website regarding successful public or private programs or other useful information related to the production, use, or effects of methamphetamine;

(E) includes a restricted section that may only be accessed by a law enforcement organization that contains successful strategies, training techniques, and other information that the Council determines helpful to law enforcement agency efforts to identify or combat the production, use, or effects of methamphetamine;

(F) allows public access to all information not in a restricted section; and

(G) contains any additional information the Council determines may be useful in identifying or combating the production, use, or effects of methamphetamine.

Thirty days after the website in paragraph (2) is operational, no funds shall be expended to continue the website methresources.gov.

(c) Review of posted information

(1) In general

Not later than 30 days after the date of submission of an item by a qualified entity, the Council shall review an item submitted for posting on the website described in subsection (b)(2)—

(A) to evaluate and determine whether the item, as submitted or as modified, meets the requirements for posting; and

(B) in consultation with the Attorney General, to determine whether the item should be posted in a restricted section of the website.

(2) Determination

Not later than 45 days after the date of submission of an item, the Council shall—

(A) post the item on the website described in subsection (b)(2); or

(B) notify the qualified entity that submitted the item regarding the reason such item shall not be posted and modifications, if any, that the qualified entity may make to allow the item to be posted.

(Pub. L. 109–469, title X, § 1004, Dec. 29, 2006, 120 Stat. 3538.)

§ 2014. Authorization of appropriations

There are authorized to be appropriated—

(1) for fiscal year 2007—

(A) $500,000 to establish the NMIC and Council; and

(B) such sums as are necessary for the operation of the NMIC and Council; and

(2) for each of fiscal years 2008 and 2009, such sums as are necessary for the operation of the NMIC and Council.

(Pub. L. 109–469, title X, § 1005, Dec. 29, 2006, 120 Stat. 3539.)

CHAPTER 26—FOOD SAFETY

§ 2101. Findings

Congress finds that—

(1) the safety and integrity of the United States food supply are vital to public health, to public confidence in the food supply, and to the success of the food sector of the Nation's economy;

(2) illnesses and deaths of individuals and companion animals caused by contaminated food—

(A) have contributed to a loss of public confidence in food safety; and

(B) have caused significant economic losses to manufacturers and producers not responsible for contaminated food items;

(3) the task of preserving the safety of the food supply of the United States faces tremendous pressures with regard to—

(A) emerging pathogens and other contaminants and the ability to detect all forms of contamination;

(B) an increasing volume of imported food from a wide variety of countries; and

(C) a shortage of adequate resources for monitoring and inspection;

(4) according to the Economic Research Service of the Department of Agriculture, the United States is increasing the amount of food that it imports such that—

(A) from 2003 to 2007, the value of food imports has increased from $45,600,000,000 to $64,000,000,000; and

(B) imported food accounts for 13 percent of the average American diet including 31 percent of fruits, juices, and nuts, 9.5 percent of red meat, and 78.6 percent of fish and shellfish; and

(5) the number of full-time equivalent Food and Drug Administration employees conducting inspections has decreased from 2003 to 2007.

(Pub. L. 110–85, title X, §1001, Sept. 27, 2007, 121 Stat. 962.)

§2102. Ensuring the safety of pet food

(a) Processing and ingredient standards

Not later than 2 years after September 27, 2007, the Secretary of Health and Human Services (referred to in this chapter as the "Secretary"), in consultation with the Association of American Feed Control Officials and other relevant stakeholder groups, including veterinary medical associations, animal health organizations, and pet food manufacturers, shall by regulation establish—

(1) ingredient standards and definitions with respect to pet food;

(2) processing standards for pet food; and

(3) updated standards for the labeling of pet food that include nutritional and ingredient information.

(b) Early warning surveillance systems and notification during pet food recalls

Not later than 1 year after September 27, 2007, the Secretary shall establish an early warning and surveillance system to identify adulteration of the pet food supply and outbreaks of illness associated with pet food. In establishing such system, the Secretary shall—

(1) consider using surveillance and monitoring mechanisms similar to, or in coordination with, those used to monitor human or animal health, such as the Foodborne Diseases Active Surveillance Network (FoodNet) and PulseNet of the Centers for Disease Control and Prevention, the Food Emergency Response Network of the Food and Drug Administration and the Department of Agriculture, and the National Animal Health Laboratory Network of the Department of Agriculture;

(2) consult with relevant professional associations and private sector veterinary hospitals;

(3) work with the National Companion Animal Surveillance Program, the Health Alert Network, or other notification networks as appropriate to inform veterinarians and relevant stakeholders during any recall of pet food; and

(4) use such information and conduct such other activities as the Secretary deems appropriate.

(Pub. L. 110–85, title X, §1002, Sept. 27, 2007, 121 Stat. 963.)

References in Text

This chapter, referred to in subsec. (a), was in the original "this title", meaning title X of Pub. L. 110–85, Sept. 27, 2007, 121 Stat. 962, which enacted this chapter and section 350f of this title, amended sections 321 and 331 of this title, and enacted provisions set out as notes under sections 350f and 2110 of this title. For complete classification of title X to the Code, see Tables.

§2103. Ensuring efficient and effective communications during a recall

The Secretary shall, during an ongoing recall of human or pet food regulated by the Secretary—

(1) work with companies, relevant professional associations, and other organizations to collect and aggregate information pertaining to the recall;

(2) use existing networks of communication, including electronic forms of information dissemination, to enhance the quality and speed of communication with the public; and

(3) post information regarding recalled human and pet foods on the Internet Web site of the Food and Drug Administration in a single location, which shall include a searchable database of recalled human foods and a searchable database of recalled pet foods, that is easily accessed and understood by the public.

(Pub. L. 110–85, title X, §1003, Sept. 27, 2007, 121 Stat. 963.)

§2104. State and Federal cooperation

(a) In general

The Secretary shall work with the States in undertaking activities and programs that assist in improving the safety of food, including fresh and processed produce, so that State food safety programs and activities conducted by the Secretary function in a coordinated and cost-effective manner. With the assistance provided under subsection (b), the Secretary shall encourage States to—

(1) establish, continue, or strengthen State food safety programs, especially with respect to the regulation of retail commercial food establishments; and

(2) establish procedures and requirements for ensuring that processed produce under the jurisdiction of State food safety programs is not unsafe for human consumption.

(b) Assistance

The Secretary may provide to a State, for planning, developing, and implementing such a food safety program—

(1) advisory assistance;

(2) technical assistance, training, and laboratory assistance (including necessary materials and equipment); and

(3) financial and other assistance.

(c) Service agreements

The Secretary may, under an agreement entered into with a Federal, State, or local agency, use, on a reimbursable basis or otherwise, the personnel, services, and facilities of the agency to carry out the responsibilities of the agency under this section. An agreement entered into with a State agency under this subsection may provide for training of State employees.

(Pub. L. 110–85, title X, §1004, Sept. 27, 2007, 121 Stat. 964.)

§2105. Enhanced aquaculture and seafood inspection

(a) Findings

Congress finds the following:

(1) In 2007, there has been an overwhelming increase in the volume of aquaculture and seafood that has been found to contain substances that are not approved for use in food in the United States.

(2) As of May 2007, inspection programs are not able to satisfactorily accomplish the goals of ensuring the food safety of the United States.

(3) To protect the health and safety of consumers in the United States, the ability of the Secretary to perform inspection functions must be enhanced.

(b) Heightened inspections

The Secretary is authorized to enhance, as necessary, the inspection regime of the Food and Drug Administration for aquaculture and seafood, consistent with obligations of the United States under international agreements and United States law.

(c) Report to Congress

Not later than 180 days after September 27, 2007, the Secretary shall submit to Congress a report that—

(1) describes the specifics of the aquaculture and seafood inspection program;

(2) describes the feasibility of developing a traceability system for all catfish and seafood products, both domestic and imported, for the purpose of identifying the processing plant of origin of such products; and

(3) provides for an assessment of the risks associated with particular contaminants and banned substances.

(d) Partnerships with States

Upon the request by any State, the Secretary may enter into partnership agreements, as soon as practicable after the request is made, to implement inspection programs to Federal standards regarding the importation of aquaculture and seafood.

(Pub. L. 110–85, title X, § 1006, Sept. 27, 2007, 121 Stat. 969.)

§ 2106. Consultation regarding genetically engineered seafood products

The Commissioner of Food and Drugs shall consult with the Assistant Administrator of the National Marine Fisheries Service of the National Oceanic and Atmospheric Administration to produce a report on any environmental risks associated with genetically engineered seafood products, including the impact on wild fish stocks.

(Pub. L. 110–85, title X, § 1007, Sept. 27, 2007, 121 Stat. 969.)

§ 2107. Sense of Congress

It is the sense of Congress that—

(1) it is vital for Congress to provide the Food and Drug Administration with additional resources, authorities, and direction with respect to ensuring the safety of the food supply of the United States;

(2) additional inspectors are required to improve the Food and Drug Administration's ability to safeguard the food supply of the United States;

(3) because of the increasing volume of international trade in food products the Secretary should make it a priority to enter into agreements with the trading partners of the United States with respect to food safety; and

(4) Congress should work to develop a comprehensive response to the issue of food safety.

(Pub. L. 110–85, title X, § 1008, Sept. 27, 2007, 121 Stat. 970.)

§ 2108. Annual report to Congress

The Secretary shall, on an annual basis, submit to the Committee on Health, Education, Labor, and Pensions and the Committee on Appropriations of the Senate and the Committee on Energy and Commerce and the Committee on Appropriations of the House of Representatives a report that includes, with respect to the preceding 1-year period—

(1) the number and amount of food products regulated by the Food and Drug Administration imported into the United States, aggregated by country and type of food;

(2) a listing of the number of Food and Drug Administration inspectors of imported food products referenced in paragraph (1) and the number of Food and Drug Administration inspections performed on such products; and

(3) aggregated data on the findings of such inspections, including data related to violations of the Federal Food, Drug, and Cosmetic Act [21 U.S.C. 301 et seq.], and enforcement actions used to follow-up on such findings and violations.

(Pub. L. 110–85, title X, § 1009, Sept. 27, 2007, 121 Stat. 970.)

References in Text

The Federal Food, Drug, and Cosmetic Act, referred to in par. (3), is act June 25, 1938, ch. 675, 52 Stat. 1040, which is classified generally to chapter 9 (§ 301 et seq.) of this title. For complete classification of this Act to the Code, see section 301 of this title and Tables.

§ 2109. Publication of annual reports

(a) In general

The Commissioner of Food and Drugs shall annually submit to Congress and publish on the Internet Web site of the Food and Drug Administration, a report concerning the results of the Administration's pesticide residue monitoring program, that includes—

(1) information and analysis similar to that contained in the report entitled "Food and Drug Administration Pesticide Program Residue Monitoring 2003" as released in June of 2005;

(2) based on an analysis of previous samples, an identification of products or countries (for imports) that require special attention and additional study based on a comparison with equivalent products manufactured, distributed, or sold in the United States (including details on the plans for such additional studies), including in the initial report (and subsequent reports as determined necessary) the results and analysis of the Ginseng Dietary Supplements Special Survey as described on page 13 of the report entitled "Food and Drug Administration Pesticide Program Residue Monitoring 2003";

(3) information on the relative number of interstate and imported shipments of each tested commodity that were sampled, including recommendations on whether sampling is statistically significant, provides confidence intervals or other related statistical information, and whether the number of samples should be increased and the details of any plans to provide for such increase; and

(4) a description of whether certain commodities are being improperly imported as another commodity, including a description of additional steps that are being planned to prevent such smuggling.

(b) Initial reports

Annual reports under subsection (a) for fiscal years 2004 through 2006 may be combined into a single report, by not later than June 1, 2008, for purposes of publication under subsection (a). Thereafter such reports shall be completed by June 1 of each year for the data collected for the year that was 2-years prior to the year in which the report is published.

(c) Memorandum of understanding

The Commissioner of Food and Drugs, the Administrator of the Food Safety and Inspection Service, the Department of Commerce, and the head of the Agricultural Marketing Service shall enter into a memorandum of understanding to permit inclusion of data in the reports under subsection (a) relating to testing carried out by the Food Safety and Inspection Service and the Agricultural Marketing Service on meat, poultry, eggs, and certain raw agricultural products, respectively.

(Pub. L. 110–85, title X, §1010, Sept. 27, 2007, 121 Stat. 970.)

§2110. Rule of construction

Nothing in this chapter (or an amendment made by this chapter) shall be construed to affect—

(1) the regulation of dietary supplements under the Dietary Supplement Health and Education Act of 1994 (Public Law 103–417); or

(2) the adverse event reporting system for dietary supplements created under the Dietary Supplement and Nonprescription Drug Consumer Protection Act (Public Law 109–462).

(Pub. L. 110–85, title X, §1011, Sept. 27, 2007, 121 Stat. 971.)

References in Text

This chapter, referred to in text, was in the original "this title", meaning title X of Pub. L. 110–85, Sept. 27, 2007, 121 Stat. 962, which enacted this chapter and section 350f of this title, amended sections 321 and 331 of this title, and enacted provisions set out as notes under this section and section 350f of this title. For complete classification of title X to the Code, see Tables.

The Dietary Supplement Health and Education Act of 1994, referred to in par. (1), is Pub. L. 103–417, Oct. 25, 1994, 108 Stat. 4325, which enacted sections 343–2 and 350b of this title and section 287c–11 of Title 42, The Public Health and Welfare, amended sections 321, 331, 342, 343, and 350 of this title and section 281 of Title 42, and enacted provisions set out as notes under sections 321 and 343 of this title. For complete classification of this Act to the Code, see Short Title of 1994 Amendments note set out under section 301 of this title and Tables.

The Dietary Supplement and Nonprescription Drug Consumer Protection Act, referred to in par. (2), is Pub. L. 109–462, Dec. 22, 2006, 120 Stat. 3469, which enacted sections 379aa and 379aa–1 of this title, amended sections 331, 343, 352, and 381 of this title, and enacted provisions set out as notes under sections 331, 343, 352, 379aa, and 381 of this title. For complete classification of this Act to the Code, see Short Title of 2006 Amendment note set out under section 301 of this title and Tables.

Construction

Pub. L. 110–85, title X, §1005(g), Sept. 27, 2007, 121 Stat. 969, provided that: "Nothing in this title [enacting this chapter and section 350f of this title, amending sections 321 and 331 of this title, and enacting provisions set out as notes under section 350f of this title], or an amendment made by this title, shall be construed to alter the jurisdiction between the Secretaries of Agriculture and of Health and Human Services, under applicable statutes and regulations."

Made in the USA
Coppell, TX
05 November 2026

11299175R00341